SAND
& STEEL

PETER CADDICK-ADAMS

SAND
& STEEL

THE D-DAY INVASION
AND THE LIBERATION
OF FRANCE

OXFORD
UNIVERSITY PRESS

OXFORD
UNIVERSITY PRESS

Oxford University Press is a department of the University of Oxford.
It furthers the University's objective of excellence in research, scholarship,
and education by publishing worldwide. Oxford is a registered trade mark of
Oxford University Press in the UK and certain other countries.

Published in the United States of America by Oxford University Press
198 Madison Avenue, New York, NY 10016, United States of America.

© Peter Caddick-Adams 2019

All rights reserved. No part of this publication may be reproduced,
stored in a retrieval system, or transmitted, in any form or by any means,
without the prior permission in writing of Oxford University Press,
or as expressly permitted by law, by license, or under terms agreed with
the appropriate reproduction rights organization. Inquiries concerning
reproduction outside the scope of the above should be sent to the
Rights Department, Oxford University Press, at the address above.

You must not circulate this work in any other form
and you must impose this same condition on any acquirer.

Library of Congress Cataloging-in-Publication Data

Names: Caddick-Adams, Peter, 1960– author.
Title: Sand and steel : the D-Day invasions and the liberation of France /
Peter Caddick-Adams.
Description: New York : Oxford University Press, 2019.
Identifiers: LCCN 2018055471 | ISBN 9780190601898 (hardback)
Subjects: LCSH: World War, 1939–1945—Campaigns—France—Normandy. | World
War, 1939–1945—Campaigns—France. | Operation Overlord. | Normandy
(France)—History, Military. | BISAC: HISTORY / Military / World War II. |
HISTORY / Modern / 20th Century.
Classification: LCC D756.5.N6 C33 2019 | DDC 940.54/21421—dc23
LC record available at https://lccn.loc.gov/2018055471

This book is dedicated to Professor John Buckley and Professor Gary Sheffield,
two men who, at different times in my career as a military historian, have
mentored and encouraged me and provided me with outstanding guidance,
help and advice. They are, by the happy chance of fate, both now professors in
the War Studies Department of the University of Wolverhampton, UK. I am
proud to call them my friends as well as professional colleagues.

1 3 5 7 9 8 6 4 2
Printed by Sheridan Books, Inc.
United States of America

Contents

Glossary

Ia	German chief of staff/chief operations officer
Ib	German chief quartermaster/supply staff officer
Ic	German chief intelligence staff officer
I Corps (British)	Lieutenant General Sir John Crocker's 1st Corps (British Second Army)
III Flak-Corps	General der Flakartillerie Wolfgang Pickert's 3rd Anti-Aircraft Corps (Luftwaffe)
4th/7th Royal Dragoon Guards	British tank battalion
V Corps (US)	Major General Leonard T. Gerow's 5th Corps (US First Army)
6×6	US six-wheeled truck, usually a two-and-a-half ton 'Jimmy'
VII Corps (US)	Major General J. Lawton Collins' 7th Corps (US First Army)
13th/18th Royal Hussars	British tank battalion
LXXXIV Corps	General Erich Marcks' 84th Armeekorps, HQ in Saint-Lô

88mm	German anti-tank/anti-aircraft gun; term widely used to mean hostile artillery
105mm	US field howitzer, towed or mounted in the M7 'Priest'. It had a max range of twelve thousand yards
A-20	Douglas 'Havoc' twin-engined light bomber and fighter (the *Boston* in RAF service)
A-26	Douglas 'Invader' twin-engined light bomber and ground attack aircraft
AAA	Anti-Aircraft Artillery
Abwehr	German military intelligence service
Achilles	British M10 tank destroyer equipped with 17-pounder anti-tank gun
Albany	D-Day paratroop drop of US 101st Airborne Division into Normandy
'All American'	Major General Matthew B. Ridgeway's 82nd Airborne Division
APA	Attack Transport – US Navy ship fitted with large davits to handle landing craft
ARC	American Red Cross, which manned Clubmobiles and the Rainbow Corner
Arcadia	Washington Conference of 22 December 1941–14 January 1942, which established the CCS
Argonaut	Washington Conference of 20–25 June 1942, which postponed Channel invasion
Army Group 'B'	German forces north of the River Loire, led by Erwin Rommel
Army Group 'G'	German forces south of the River Loire, led by Johannes Blaskowitz
Argument	(aka 'Big Week') Allied air operations to destroy the Luftwaffe, 20–25 February 1944
AS	*Armée Secrète* (Gaullist Resistance)

ATS	Auxiliary Territorial Service (1938–49), British all-female land force of WW2
Avalanche	Anglo-American amphibious assault at Salerno, 9–16 September 1943
AVRE	Armoured Vehicle Royal Engineers; specialist engineer tank based on the Churchill
AWOL	Absent without Leave, a severe military offence
B-17	US four-engined Boeing 'Flying Fortress' heavy bomber
B-24	US four-engined Consolidated 'Liberator' heavy bomber
B-25	US twin-engined North American 'Mitchell' medium bomber
B-26	US twin-engined Martin 'Marauder' medium bomber
Bagration	Huge Soviet land operation, launched on 22 June 1944 in Belorussia, to complement Overlord
Bailey bridge	British-designed combat bridge made of man-portable, pre-fabricated parts
Band	Code name for Normandy invasion beaches east of the River Orne (not used)
Bangalore torpedo	Lengths of explosive-filled pipe, used to destroy barbed-wire entanglements
Battalion	Single-arm unit of 500 to a thousand men, commanded by a lieutenant colonel or major
battery	Artillery unit of company size, usually of between four and eight guns
BCRA	*Bureau Central de Renseignements et d'Action*; Gaullist intelligence service
'Beetle'	Nickname for Walter Bedell Smith, SHAEF chief of staff

Big Drum	D-Day radar jamming deception operation on the West flank of Overlord, off Utah
'Big Week'	*see* Argument
BIGOT	Highest level of secrecy for Overlord
'Big Red One'	Major General Clarence R. Huebner's US 1st Infantry Division
Black Watch	Kilted Highland battalions of infantry, Scottish in origin
Bletchley Park	Allied code-breaking centre in Buckinghamshire, UK
'Blue and Gray'	US 29th Division, nicknamed because it recruited from both former Union (blue) and Confederate (grey) states
bocage	High earth banks and thick hedgerows that lined many Normandy fields
Bodyguard	Series of deception operations to distract German attention from Normandy
Bolero	Code name for build-up of US ground and air forces in UK, 1942–3
Boston	D-Day paratroop drop of US 82nd Airborne Division into Normandy
'Brad'	Nickname for General Omar Nelson Bradley
Brigade	Anglo-Canadian equivalent of a combat regiment, made up of around two to three thousand men
Brigade Major	First staff officer in a brigade headquarters, chief of staff or XO
Bronze Star	US award for valour below Silver Star, established 1944
C-47	Twin-engined Douglas 'Skytrain' or 'Dakota' (RAF designation) transport aircraft

Canloan	673 Canadian junior officers who volunteered to serve in British infantry battalions
CCS	Combined Chiefs of Staff, Anglo-US body established in 1942 to help determine the strategic direction of the war
Centaur	Cromwell tank fitted with 95mm howitzer; used by Royal Marines
Chemical Battalion	Operated 4.2-inch (107mm) mortars, which fired high explosive, white phosphorus (incendiary) and smoke marker shells up to 4,400 yards (US Army)
Chicago	D-Day glider landings with support weapons of 101st Airborne Division
Churchill	40-ton British tank with 75mm gun, and basis for AVREs
CIC	US Counter-Intelligence Corps, founded 1 January 1942
CIGS	Chief of the Imperial General Staff (FM Sir Alan Brooke)
CO	Commanding Officer
Combined arms	A combination of infantry, artillery, armour (and sometimes air) assets
Combined Chiefs	*See* CCS
Copperhead	Deception operation in Gibraltar and Algiers involving an actor impersonating Sir Bernard Montgomery
COPP	Combined Operations Pilotage Parties: Special Forces' teams who covertly surveyed landing beaches for invasions
Corncob	Blockship, sunk in rows to form Gooseberry breakwaters, protecting D-Day beaches

COSSAC	Chief of Staff to the Supreme Allied Commander, pre-D-Day planning
CSM/RSM	Company (Regimental) Sergeant Major
Crab	Sherman mine-clearing Flail tank
DD	Duplex Drive, swimming Sherman tank
Deadstick	D-Day airborne operation to seize the Caen Canal and Orne river bridges
Detroit	D-Day glider landings with support weapons of 82nd Airborne Division
DFC, DFM	Distinguished Flying Cross, Distinguished Flying Medal: RAF decorations
Distinguished Service Cross	America's second highest decoration for valour, established in 1918
Division	All-arms formation of ten to twenty thousand men, usually commanded by a major general
DSO	Distinguished Service Order, the British military decoration below the VC
DUKW	The 'Duck', a US six-wheeled amphibious truck; 2,000 were used in Overlord
E-boat	Allied term for German Motor Torpedo Boat, known in German as the *Schnellboot* (*S-Boote*)
Eighth Air Force	US strategic bomber command, led by Lieutenant Generals Ira C. Eaker (until January 1944) and Jimmy Doolittle; operated heavy bombers from UK against North European targets
Elmira	Glider landings supporting 82nd Airborne Division on the evening of D-Day
Enigma	German enciphering machine whose secrets were unlocked at Bletchley Park
Eureka (1)	Code name for the Tehran Conference of 28 November–1 December 1943, which confirmed Overlord

Eureka (2)	Ground-based radio transmitter to guide Allied aircraft to drop zones
FA	Field Artillery (US Army)
Fallschirmjäger	German paratrooper (individual or unit)
Fascine	Bundle of logs used to fill craters and gaps by Royal Engineers
Feldwebel	German Army/Luftwaffe Sergeant; *see also Oberfeldwebel*
Field Regiment RA	British artillery battalion, usually of twenty-four 25-pounder field guns
Field Company RE	Tactical unit of British Royal Engineers
Fifteenth Army (German)	HQ at Tourcoing, led by General Hans von Salmuth
Firefly	Sherman tank with British 17-pounder gun, capable of penetrating all panzer armour
First Army (US)	Led by Omar Bradley (until 1 August 1944); thereafter Courtney H. Hodges
Flak	*Fliegerabwehrkanone*, German anti-aircraft gun or unit
flail	Mine-clearing Sherman tank with chains fixed to a forward-mounted rotating drum
FOB	(UK) Forward Officer, Bombardment, for Royal Navy
Focke-Wulf	The FW 190 was principal Luftwaffe single-seat fighter alongside the Me-109
FOO	(UK) Forward Observation Officer (for artillery)
Fortitude, North and South	Deception operations to distract German attention away from Normandy towards Norway (Fortitude North) and the Pas de Calais (Fortitude South)
Freiherr	German term of nobility, equivalent to Baron

FTP	*Francs-Tireurs et Partisans* (Communist French Resistance Movement)
Führerbefehl	Order emanating directly from Hitler
Führerhauptquartier	Hitler's personal headquarters
'Funnies'	Specialised armoured vehicles of Major General Percy Hobart's 79th Armoured Division
FUSAG	First US Army Group, a fictional command in South-East England, led by George S. Patton before D-Day
Gefreiter	German Lance Corporal; *see also Obergefreiter*
Generalleutnant	German Major General (two-star rank)
Generalmajor	German Brigadier General (one-star rank)
Generaloberst	German General (four-star rank)
Gestapo	Abbreviation of *Geheime Staatspolizei*, Secret State Police
Glimmer	D-Day deception operation involving boats and air-dropped 'window' (thin metal strips) off the Pas de Calais
Gold	Normandy invasion beach for British XXX Corps
Gooseberry	Row of sunken ships (Corncobs) off each D-Day beach
Graf	German term of nobility, equivalent to Count
Green Howards	British infantry battalions from Yorkshire, UK
Grenadier	German infantryman
GSO1	British lieutenant colonel Staff Officer; GSO2 was a major, GSO3 a captain
Hadrian	US glider made by Waco; could carry thirteen men, one jeep or six stretchers (litters)
Halcyon	Alternative code word for D-Day

Halifax	RAF Bomber Command four-engined bomber, manufactured by Handley Page
Hamilcar	British-built vehicle-carrying heavy glider, used in Overlord
Hauptmann	German Army/Luftwaffe Captain
Heer	German Army, which with the Kriegsmarine and Luftwaffe comprised the Wehrmacht
Higgins Boat	US mass-produced LCVP, designed by Andrew Higgins of New Orleans
Hitlerjugend	Hitler Youth, modelled on the Boy Scouts; also the name of the 12th SS Panzer Division
Hornpipe	Alternative code name for Overlord
Horsa (1)	Wooden glider made by Airspeed, capable of carrying thirty fully-equipped troops
Horsa (2)	Code name for Ranville Bridge over the River Orne, captured on 5–6 June 1944
Husky	Allied invasion of Sicily, 10 July–17 August 1943
'Ike'	Universal nickname for General Dwight D. Eisenhower
'Indianhead'	Walter M. Robertson's US 2nd Infantry Division
IPW	Interrogation of Prisoner of War team, attached to each US division
'Ivy'	Raymond O. 'Tubby' Barton's US 4th Infantry Division
Jabo	German abbreviation for *Jagdbomber* (Allied fighter-bomber)
Jedburgh	Three-man Allied Special Forces team liaising with Maquis in occupied France
Jeep	US GP (General Purpose, hence jeep) 4×4 vehicle (aka Peep in US armour units)

Jerry	Allied slang for a German (also Heinie, Boche, Kraut, Hun)
Jerrycan	Military twenty-litre/five-gallon fuel can, modelled on the German invention
Jimmy	US 6×6 cargo truck, mostly manufactured by General Motors (abbreviated to GM, hence 'Jimmy')
Joint Chiefs	US committee of service chiefs advising the President on military matters
Jubilee	Dieppe Raid of 19 August 1942, mounted by UK Combined Operations
Junkers	German aircraft manufacturer of the Ju-87 Stuka and twin-engined Ju-88 bomber
Juno	Normandy invasion beach for Canadian 3rd Division
Kampfgruppe	German combat group of variable size, typically named after its leader
Kanonier	German artillery private
KBE, CBE, OBE, MBE	Knight, Commander, Order and Member of the British Empire
Keokuk	Glider reinforcement operation to 101st Airborne Division on D-Day evening
K-rations	US individual packaged meal units for breakfast, lunch and supper
Kriegsmarine	German war navy, commanded by Grand Admiral Karl Dönitz
Kriegstagebuch	German daily war diary
KRRC	King's Royal Rifle Corps (battalion of British infantry)
KSLI	King's Shropshire Light Infantry (battalion of British infantry)
Lancaster	RAF four-engined bomber, manufactured by Avro; mainstay of Bomber Command

Landser	German slang for German soldier
LCA	Landing Craft Assault; British equivalent of LCVP, carried thirty troops, four crew
LCG	Landing Craft Gun; carried two turreted 17- or 25-pounder guns, thirty crew
LCI	Landing Craft Infantry, larger assault vessels which carried around two hundred troops, twenty-four crew
LCM	Landing Craft Mechanised, carrying one tank or sixty to a hundred troops, four to six crew
LCOCU	Landing Craft Obstacle Clearance Units (on British/Canadian beaches)
LCT	Landing Craft Tank, many designs but all capable of carrying four to ten tanks, twelve crew
LCVP	Landing Craft Vehicle, Personnel; the US Higgins Boat; carried thirty-six troops, four crew
Leutnant	German Second Lieutenant
LST	Landing Ship Tank; amphibious landing vessel that carried around twenty tanks and a hundred crew
Luftlande	The German Army's 91st *Luftlande-Division* was stationed in the Cotentin Peninsula
Luftwaffe	German Air Force, established 26 February 1935; often GAF to the Allies
M7	US Priest; 105mm SP gun (Sexton when armed with British 25-pounder gun)
M10	US Wolverine tank destroyer, with 3-inch (76.2 mm) gun; (Achilles with 17-pounder)
Mallard	Glider operation supporting 6th Airborne Division on evening of D-Day

Maquis, maquisard	Generic term for French Resistance, or member
MC, MM	Military Cross, Military Medal; British decorations for junior officers and other ranks
Medal of Honor	America's highest award for valour, established 1861
Messerschmitt	Usually the Me-109, a single-seat German fighter
MG-34 or 42	Belt-fed 7.92mm machine-gun, aka Spandau or 'Hitler's band-saw'
MI5	British domestic counter-intelligence and security agency, established 1909
MI6	British overseas intelligence agency, the SIS (Secret Intelligence Service)
'Monty'	Nickname for FM Sir Bernard Montgomery (1887–1976)
MTB	Motor Torpedo Boat (RN); similar to PT-Boat (USN) or E-Boat (Kriegsmarine)
Mulberry	Temporary portable harbours anchored off Gold and Omaha beaches after D-Day
NCDU	Naval Combat Demolition Unit (on US beaches)
Nebelwerfer	German six-barrelled mortar on two-wheeled trailer
Neptune	All naval aspects of Overlord, commanded by Admiral Sir Bertram Ramsay
Ninth Air Force	US medium bomber, troop carrier and fighter command operating from the UK
Northumbria	North-East England, from where the 50th (Northumbrian) Division recruited
OB West	*Oberbefehlshaber West*; High Command of Western Forces – Gerd von Rundstedt or his HQ
Oberfeldwebel	German Army/Luftwaffe Master Sergeant/WO2; *see also Feldwebel*

Obergefreiter	German Army/Luftwaffe Corporal; *see also Gefreiter*
Oberleutnant	German Army/Luftwaffe 1st Lieutenant
Oberst	German Army/Luftwaffe Colonel; *Oberstleutnant* – Lieutenant Colonel
OKW	*Oberkommando der Wehrmacht* (German Armed Forces High Command, established 1938)
Omaha	Normandy invasion beach for US V Corps
Organisation Todt, OT	Nazi Civil Engineering Service, headed by Albert Speer
OSS	Office of Strategic Service (US); modelled on the British SOE, established June 1942: the future CIA
Ost battalions	German units of pro-Axis volunteers (Russians, Czechs, Poles, Ukrainians)
Ostfront	Eastern Front (Russia), as opposed to *Westfront* (the war in Normandy and beyond)
Overlord	Allied operation to invade North-West Europe, beginning 6 June 1944
Ox and Bucks LI	Light Infantry battalions recruited in Oxfordshire and Buckinghamshire, UK
P-38	US twin-engined Lockheed 'Lightning' multi-role fighter
P-47	US single-engined Republic 'Thunderbolt' fighter, usually used in ground attack role
P-51	US single-engined North American 'Mustang' fighter, used to escort and intercept
Panther	German 45-ton Mark V tank with distinctive frontal sloping armour, 75mm main gun
Panzer, Pz	German for armour or tank

Panzer (Mark) IV	Most numerous German tank of 1943–4; thirty tons with 75mm main gun
Panzerfaust	Single shot, hand-held German anti-armour weapon
PanzerGrenadier	Mechanised infantry soldier or unit, often using armoured half-tracks
PanzerGruppe West	Training formation for armoured units in West; later called Fifth Panzer Army
Pegasus	Code name for bridge over the Caen Canal, captured on 5–6 June 1944
Phoenix	Concrete caissons which formed the breakwaters of the Mulberry harbours
PIAT	Projector, Infantry, Anti-Tank; standard British 'stovepipe' anti-armour weapon
PIR	(US) Parachute Infantry Regiment (of three battalions)
Platoon	Infantry unit of thirty to fifty troops or US armour unit of four tanks
Pluto	Pipe Line Under The Ocean (to Normandy), operational from 22 September 1944
Pointblank	Allied air offensive June 1943–April 1944 to draw the Luftwaffe into defending German airspace, thus destroying its offensive capability before D-Day
Priest	M7 self-propelled 105mm artillery piece on tracked Sherman hull
Purple Heart	US medal awarded to wounded or killed, established 1932 but backdated to 1917
QM	Quartermaster
Quadrant	Quebec Conference of 17–24 August 1943, which fixed Overlord for May 1944
Quicksilver	Deception operations by FUSAG of fake air, ground and radio activity

RA	Royal Regiment of Artillery (or numbered battalions of British artillery)
RAC	Royal Armoured Corps, battalion of armour
RAF	Royal Air Force; also RAFVR – RAF Volunteer Reserve
RAMC	Royal Army Medical Corps
Rangers	US Army commandos, first raised on 19 June 1942 and deployed at Dieppe and Anzio
Rankin	Allied plans to occupy Germany in event of sudden Nazi collapse
RASC	Royal Army Service Corps (British Army transport and supply units)
RCAF	Royal Canadian Air Force
RCN	Royal Canadian Navy
RE	Royal Engineers
REME	Royal Electrical and Mechanical Engineers
Rhino	Barge for tanks and vehicles, constructed from pontoons with outboard motors
Ripcord	Allied code word to delay D-Day by 24 hours
Ritter	German title of nobility, equivalent to that of a knight in the UK ('Sir')
Ritterkreuz	German Knight's Cross of the Iron Cross; worn at the neck
RM	Royal Marines
RN/RNR/RNVR	Royal Navy/Naval Reserve/Naval Volunteer Reserve
Roundhammer	Plan for 1943 invasion of France, merger of Roundup and Sledgehammer
Roundup	Plan for major Anglo-US–Canadian cross-Channel attack in 1943
RTR	Royal Tank Regiment (battalion of British armour)

S-	S-1: Personnel officer at Regimental HQ; S-2: Intelligence; S-3: Operations; S-4: Supply
SAS	Special Air Service, British Special Forces regiment; operated behind German lines
'Screaming Eagles'	Major General Maxwell D. Taylor's US 101st Airborne Division
SD	*Sicherheitsdienst*, the intelligence and internal security service of the SS
Second Army (British)	Formation commanded by General Sir Miles Dempsey
Second Tactical Air Force (2nd TAF)	RAF formation, supporting British and Canadians from D-Day and throughout the North-West Europe campaign, commanded by Air Marshal Sir Arthur Coningham
Seventh Army (German)	Formation led by General Friedrich Dollmann
Sextant	Code name for the Cairo Conferences (22–26 November and 3–7 December 1943)
Sexton	British tracked, self-propelled 25-pounder field gun, very similar to the US M7 Priest
SHAEF	Supreme Headquarters Allied Expeditionary Force, code name 'Shellburst'
Sherman	The M4 standard Allied tank of 1943–5
Sherwood Rangers Yeomanry	British tank battalion
Shingle	Anglo-US amphibious landing at Anzio–Nettuno, Italy, on 22 January 1944
Sickle	Build-up in the UK of the US Eighth Air Force from 1942 onwards
Siegfried Line	Germany's fortified west frontier, with dragon's teeth, bunkers and minefields

Silver Star	US award for valour above the Bronze Star and below the Distinguished Service Cross, established 1918
Skyscraper	1943 Invasion study by 21st Army Group under General Bernard Paget
Sledgehammer	Plan for a limited Anglo-US–Canadian cross-Channel attack in 1942
SOE	Special Operations Executive (UK); aided partisans and resistance units, established July 1940
Spitfire	The iconic RAF single-seat, Merlin-engined fighter, made by Supermarine
Squad	Smallest military unit of eight to twelve soldiers (corresponds to British army section)
SS	*Schutzstaffel* (Protection Squad); Hitler's original 'blackshirt' bodyguards
Stalag	German *Stammlager*, prisoner of war camp for all ranks
Stars and Stripes	US daily military newspaper, founded 1861
Sten gun	British 9mm sub machine-gun, used by army NCOs and Resistance movements
Stirling	RAF heavy bomber and glider tug, manufactured by Short Brothers
Sword	Normandy invasion beach for I British Corps
Symbol	Casablanca Conference of 14–24 January 1943
Taxable	D-Day deception operation, using boats and air-dropped 'window' off Le Havre
Tiger	D-Day exercise of 27–28 April 1944 for US VII Corps; resulted in mass casualties
Titanic	D-Day airborne deception operation which dropped five hundred dummy parachutists

Tonga	Initial D-Day glider and parachute landings by British 6th Airborne Division
Torch	Anglo-US invasion of Morocco and Algeria, 8–16 November 1942; originally Gymnast
Trident	Anglo-US Washington Conference of 12–25 May 1943
Twenty-First Army Group	Anglo-Canadian formation, led by General Sir Bernard Montgomery
Typhoon	RAF single-seat, ground-attack fighter, manufactured by Hawker
U-boat	*Unterseeboot*, a German submarine; mostly Type VIIs, a spent force by 1944
Ultra	Radio traffic deciphered at Bletchley Park
USAAF	United States Army Air Force, succeeded in 1947 by the USAF
USN	US Navy; also USNR – US Navy Reserve
Utah	Normandy invasion beach for US VII Corps
VC	Victoria Cross, the British Empire's premier decoration for bravery
Volksdeutsche	Citizens of a non-German country considered to be ethnically German
WAAF	Women's Auxiliary Air Force (UK), established June 1939
WAC	Women's Army Corps (US), established July 1943
Waffen-SS	The 'Fighting SS' (as opposed to other branches)
Wehrmacht	All the German Armed Forces, but excluding the SS
Werfer	*Nebelwerfer* (mortar) units
'window'	aka *chaff*: small strips of aluminium foil designed to create false radar pictures

Wolfsschanze	Hitler's headquarters, near Rastenburg in East Prussia
WN	*Widerstandsnest* (literally Resistance nest); Wehrmacht strongpoint defending invasion beach
WRNS	Women's Royal Naval Service (UK); hence 'Wren'
XO	Executive Officer, US term for second in command
X-Craft	27-ton British miniature submarine, fifty feet long, with crew of four
Yeomanry	British reserve cavalry founded in 1794, which by 1944 manned artillery and armour

Operation Overlord
Orders of Battle

Showing principal units only

ALLIED FORCES

Prime Minister Winston S. Churchill
President Franklin D. Roosevelt

Combined Chiefs of Staff

BRITISH CHIEFS OF STAFF
Chief of the Imperial General Staff (CIGS):
Sir Alan Brooke
Chief of Air Staff: Sir Charles Portal
First Sea Lord & Chief of Naval Staff:
Sir Andrew Cunningham
Secretary: Major General L. C. Hollis

US JOINT CHIEFS OF STAFF
Chairman, Joint Chiefs of Staff: Admiral William D. Leahy
Chief of Staff, US Army: General George C. Marshall
Commander-in-Chief, US Fleet: Admiral Ernest J. King
Secretary: Brigadier General A. J. McFarland

SHAEF (Supreme Headquarters Allied Expeditionary Force)
Supreme Commander: General Dwight D. Eisenhower (USA)
Deputy Supreme Commander: Air Chief Marshal Sir Arthur W. Tedder (RAF)
Naval Forces Commander: Admiral Sir Bertram Ramsay (RN)
Air Forces Commander: Air Marshal Sir Trafford Leigh-Mallory (RAF)
Land Forces Commander: General Sir Bernard L. Montgomery (UK)
Chief of Staff: Lieutenant General Walter Bedell Smith (USA)
Deputy Chief of Staff (Operations): Lieutenant General Sir Frederick E. Morgan (UK)
Deputy Chief of Staff (Administrative): Lieutenant General Sir Humfrey M. Gale (UK)
Deputy Chief of Staff (Air): Air Vice-Marshal James M. Robb (RAF)
Secretary, General Staff: Colonel Ford Trimble (USA)
G-1: Major General Ray W. Barker (USA)
G-2: Major General Kenneth W. D. Strong (UK)
G-3: Major General Harold R. Bull (USA)
G-4: Major General Robert W. Crawford (USA)
G-5: Lieutenant General A. E. Grasett (Canada)
Services of Supply/Communications Zone: Lieutenant General John C. H. Lee (USA)

NAVAL COMPONENT
WESTERN TASK FORCE
Rear Admiral Alan G. Kirk, USN (USS *Augusta*)
Force 'U': Rear Admiral Don P. Moon, USN (USS *Bayfield*)
Force 'O': Rear Admiral John L. Hall Jr, USN (USS *Ancon*)

EASTERN TASK FORCE
Rear Admiral Sir Philip Vian (HMS *Scylla*)
Force 'G': Rear Admiral Arthur G. Talbot (HMS *Largs*)
Force 'J': Commodore Geoffrey N. Oliver (HMS *Hilary*)
Force 'S': Commodore Cyril E. Douglas-Pennant (HMS *Bulolo*)

AIR COMPONENT
US EIGHTH AIR FORCE
Lieutenant General James H. Doolittle (1,908 aircraft)

US NINTH AIR FORCE
Lieutenant General Lewis H Brereton (1,746 aircraft)

SECOND TACTICAL AIR FORCE
Air Marshal Sir Arthur Coningham (1,044 aircraft)

RAF BOMBER COMMAND
Air Marshall Sir Arthur Harris (1,280 aircraft)

ADGB (prev. RAF FIGHTER COMMAND)
Air Marshal Sir Roderick Hill (796 aircraft)

Note all figures are for operational aircraft with available crews

LAND COMPONENT
21st ARMY GROUP
General Sir Bernard L. Montgomery
(Chief of Staff: Major General Sir Francis W. de Guingand)

US FIRST ARMY
Lieutenant General Omar N. Bradley

V Corps (Omaha Beach)
Major General Leonard T. Gerow
<u>1st Infantry Division</u> Major General Clarence R. Huebner
(Assistant Commander: Brigadier General Willard G. Wyman)
16th, 18th and 26th Infantry Regiments
5th, 7th, 32nd and 33rd Field Artillery (FA) Battalions
Attached: 741st and 745th Tank Battalions; 20th Engineer Combat
Battalion; 81st Chemical Weapons Battalion; 62nd Armored FA
Battalion; 635th TD Battalion
<u>5th Engineer Special Brigade</u> Colonel Doswell Gullatt
147th, 149th and 203rd Engineer Combat Battalions; 6th Naval Beach
Battalion, plus other units
<u>29th Infantry Division</u> Major General Charles H. Gerhardt
(Assistant Commander: Brigadier General Norman D. Cota)

115th, 116th and 175th Infantry Regiments
110th, 111th, 224th and 227th FA Battalions
Attached: 743rd and 747th Tank Bns; 112th Engr Combat Bn; 58th
Armored FA Bn;
467th AAA (Anti-Aircraft Artillery) Battalion
6th Engineer Special Brigade Colonel Paul W. Thompson
37th, 336th, 348th Engineer Combat Battalions, 7th Naval Beach
Battalion, plus other units
Provisional Ranger Group Lieutenant Colonel James E. Rudder
2nd and 5th Ranger Battalions

VII Corps (Utah Beach)
Major General J. Lawton Collins
4th Infantry Division Major General Raymond O. Barton
(Assistant Commander: Brigadier General Theodore Roosevelt, Jr.)
8th, 12th and 22nd Infantry Regiments
29th, 42th, 44th and 20th Field Artillery Battalions
359th Infantry Regiment and 915th FA Battalion
(from 90th Infantry Division)
4th Cavalry Group Colonel Joseph M. Tully
4th and 24th Cavalry Squadrons
6th Armored Group Colonel Francis F. Fainter
70th and 746th Tank Battalions, 899th Tank Destroyer Battalion
Attached: 65th and 87th Armored FA Battalions; 801st Tank Destroyer
Battalion; 87th Chem Mortar Battalion; 474th AAA Battalion (SP half-
tracks); Battery 'C', 320th AA Barrage Balloon Battalion
1st Engineer Special Brigade Colonel Eugene M. Caffey
4th, 49th and 237th Combat Engineer Battalions; 2nd Naval Beach
Battalion, plus other units
82nd Airborne Division Major General Matthew B. Ridgway
(Assistant Commander: Brigadier General James M. Gavin)
505th, 507th and 508th Parachute Infantry Regiments, 325th Glider
Infantry Regiment
319th and 320th Glider FA Bns; 376th and 456th Parachute FA
Battalions
101st Airborne Division Brigadier General Maxwell D. Taylor
(Assistant Commander: Brigadier General Don F. Pratt)
501st, 502nd and 506th Parachute Infantry Regiments, 327 Glider
Infantry Regiment

321st and 907th Glider FA Battalions; 377th Parachute FA
Battalion

BRITISH SECOND ARMY
General Sir Miles C. 'Bimbo' Dempse
79th Armoured Division ('Funnies'; specialist armour, Major General
Percy Hobart)
5th and 6th Assault Regiments (AVREs) and 30th Assault
Brigade ('Flails')

I British Corps (Sword/Juno Beaches)
Lieutenant General Sir John T. Crocker
6th Airborne Division Major General Richard N. Gale
3rd and 5th Parachute Brigades, 6th Air Landing Brigade
53rd (Worcestershire Yeomanry) Airlanding Light Regiment, RA
3rd British Division Major General Tom G. Rennie
8th, 9th and 185th Infantry Brigades
7th, 33rd and 76th Field Regiments; 20th Anti-Tank Regiment; 92nd
LAA Regiment, Royal Artillery
Attached for D-Day: 77th and 79th Assault Squadrons & 'A' Squadron,
22nd Dragoons (all 5th Assault Regiment, Royal Engineers); 2nd RM
Armoured Support Regiment (Centaur tanks), 41 RM Commando
5th Beach Group 5th King's Regiment, plus other units (1st wave)
6th Beach Group 1st Buckinghamshire, plus other units (2nd wave)
1st Special Service Brigade Brigadier The Lord Lovat
Nos 3, 4 and 6 Commandos, 45 RM Commando (1st and 8th Troops
of 4 Commandos comprised 177 men of Commandant Philippe
Keiffer's French *Fusiliers-Marins Commandos*)
27th Armoured Brigade Brigadier Erroll Prior-Palmer
13th/18th Hussars, East Riding and Staffordshire Yeomanry
3rd Canadian Division Major General Rodney F. L. Keller
7th, 8th and 9th Canadian Infantry Brigades
12th, 13th, 14th and 19th Canadian Field Regts, RCA
Attached for D-Day: 26th and 80th Assault Squadrons & 'B' Squadron,
22nd Dragoons (all 5th Assault Regiment, Royal Engineers); Inns of
Court Regiment (armoured cars);
62nd Anti-Tank Regiment, RA; 102nd LAA Regiment, RA and 48 RM
Commando

7th Beach Group
8th King's Regiment, plus other units (Mike – Courseulles)
8th Beach Group
5th Royal Berkshire, plus other units
(Nan – Bernières/Saint-Aubin)
2nd Canadian Armoured Brigade Brigadier R. A. Wyman
1st Hussars, Fort Garry Horse and Sherbrooke Fusiliers

XXX British Corps (Gold Beach)
Lieutenant General Gerard (Gerry) C. Bucknall
50th (Northumbrian) Division Major General Douglas A. H. Graham
69th, 151st and 231st Brigades (attached for D-Day: 56th Brigade)
74th, 90th and 124th Field Regiments; 102nd Anti-Tank Regt; 25th
LAA Regt, RA
Attached for D-Day: 86th and 147th Field Regts, RA; 81st and 82nd
Assault Sqns & 'B' and 'C' Sqns, Westminster Dragoons (all 6th
Assault Regiment, Royal Engineers); 1st RM Armoured Support
Regiment (Centaur tanks)
9th Beach Group
2nd Hertfordshire Regiment, plus other units (King – Ver-sur-Mer)
10th Beach Group
6th Border Regiment, plus other units (Jig – Asnelles)
4th Special Service Brigade Brigadier Bernard W. 'Jumbo' Leicester
41, 46, 47 and 48 RM Commandos
8th Armoured Brigade Brigadier H. J. Bernard Cracroft
4/7th Dragoon Guards, Sherwood Rangers Yeomanry, 24th Lancers;
12th KRRC

GERMAN CHAIN OF COMMAND

Führer und Kanzler Adolf Hitler

All Police, ⚡⚡ and Gestapo (Including Waffen-⚡⚡) Forces
Reichsführer-⚡⚡ Heinrich Himmler – Berlin

Air Forces
OBERKOMMANDO DER LUFTWAFFE (OKL) – Berlin
Reichsmarschall Hermann Göring

Luftflotte 3
Generalfeldmarschall Hugo Sperrle; HQ: Paris
497 aircraft available on 30 May

III Flak Corps
General Wolfgang Pickert

Maritime Forces
OBERKOMMANDO DER KRIEGSMARINE (OKM) – Berlin
Grand-Admiral Karl Donitz

MarineGruppenKommando West
Commander-in-Chief: Admiral Theodor Kranke – Paris
Channel Fleet: 163 minesweepers, 57 patrol boats, 42 Flak ships, 34
S-Boats, 49 U-boats

Land Forces
OBERKOMMANDO DER WEHRMACHT (OKW) – Berlin
Chief of Staff: *Generalfeldmarschall* Wilhelm Keitel
Chief of *Wehrmachtführungsstab* (Operations/Plans Department):
Generaloberst Alfred Jodl
Deputy to Jodl: *General der Artillerie* Walter Warlimont

Militärbefehlshaber Frankreich (Military Governor of France)
*Subordinate to OKW; responsible for internal security, away from
combat zone. No control over SS, Gestapo, police, intelligence services*
General der Infanterie Carl Heinrich von Stülpnagel

OBERBEFEHLSHABER WEST (SUPREME COMMANDER, WEST)
*Responsible for combat operations; no control over SS, Kriegsmarine or
Luftwaffe forces*
Generalfeldmarschall Gerd von Rundstedt; HQ: St Germaine-en-Laye,
Paris – 58 divisions
Chief of Staff: *Generalleutnant* Günther Blumentritt; Deputy: *Oberst*
Bodo Zimmermann

ARMY GROUP 'B'

Generalfeldmarschall Erwin Rommel

All units north of River Loire – HQ: Château La Roche-Guyon – 35 divisions

Naval Advisor: *Vizeadmiral* Friedrich Ruge; Chief Engineer: *Generalleutnant* Dr Wilhelm Meise; Chief of Staff: *Generalleutnant* Hans Speidel

FIFTEENTH ARMY

Generaloberst Hans von Salmuth

NE France/Belgium, W of River Scheldt, E of River Dives; HQ: Tourcoing – 18 divisions

711th Infantry Division Generalleutnant Josef Reichert – Vauville 731st and 744th Grenadier Regiments; 781st Ost Battalion

SEVENTH ARMY

Generaloberst Friedrich Dollmann

(Chief of Staff: *Generalmajor* Max Pemsel)

North-West France, all units west of the River Orne – HQ: Le Mans – 14 divisions

LXXXIV Corps

General der Artillerie Erich Marcks, Saint-Lô – 4 divisions:

716th Infantry Division *Generalleutnant* Wilhelm Richter – Caen 726th and 736th Grenadier Regiments; 439th, 441st and 642nd Ost battalions

(726th Regiment under command of 352nd Division, behind Gold and Omaha Beaches)

352nd Infantry Division *Generalleutnant* Dietrich Kraiss – Château de Molay, Bayeux 914th, 915th and 916th Grenadier Regiments

709th Infantry Division *Generalleutnant* Karl-Wilhelm von Schlieben – Valognes 729th and 739th Grenadier Regiments; 635th, 649th, 795th and 797th Ost battalions

319th Infantry Division *Generalleutnant* Rudolf, *Graf* von Schmettow – Channel Islands

LXXIV Corps
Guingamp, Brittany – 3 divisions
77th Infantry Division (Saint-Malo)
266th Infantry Division (Belle Isle, Brittany)
353rd Infantry Division (Brest)

XXV Corps
Pontivy – 3 divisions
343rd Infantry Division (Brest)
265th Infantry Division (Quimper/L'Orient)
275th Infantry Division (Vannes/Redon)

SEVENTH ARMY RESERVE
91st Luftlande Division *Generalmajor* Wilhelm Falley – Picauville, Cotentin, 1057th and 1058th Grenadier Regiments
6th Fallschirmjäger Regiment Major Friedrich-August, *Freiherr* von der Heydte – Cotentin
100th Panzer-Battalion Major Bardtenschlager, 32 ex-French tanks – Cotentin
243rd Infantry Division *Generalleutnant* Heinz Hellmich – Barneville/Cotentin
206th Panzer-Battalion Major Ernst Went, 46 ex-French tanks – Auderville
30th Schnelle-Brigade *Oberstleutnant* Hugo, *Freiherr* von Aufsess, 505th, 507th, 513th, 517th and 518th Bicycle Battalions
7th Army Storm-Battalion Major Hugo Messerschmidt – Le Vicel

ARMY GROUP 'G'
Generaloberst Johannes Blaskowitz
All units South of River Loire – HQ: Rouffiac-Toulouse; 13 divisions

FIRST ARMY
General der Infanterie Kurt von der Chevallerie
Southwest France – HQ: Bordeaux; 4 divisions

NINETEENTH ARMY
General der Infanterie Georg von Sodenstern
Southeast France – HQ: Avignon; 9 divisions

Panzergruppe West (later renamed Fifth Panzer Army)
Training command for all panzer formations in the West
General der Panzertruppe Leo, *Freiherr* Geyr von Schweppenburg
HQs: Paris and Château La Caine, Normandy; 10 panzer divisions

I ⚡⚡ Panzer Korps
Obergruppenführer Josef 'Sepp' Dietrich
OKW Reserve: 4 divisions; HQ: Septeuil, West of Paris
1st ⚡⚡-Pz Division *Leibstandarte Adolf Hitler* Theodor Wisch –
Beverloo, Belgium
12th ⚡⚡ -Pz Division *HitlerJugend* Fritz Witt – Livarot/Vimoutiers area
Panzer Lehr Division Fritz Bayerlein – Paris
17th ⚡⚡ -PzGr Division *Götz von Berlichingen* Werner Ostendorff –
Thouars
101st ⚡⚡ Heavy Panzer Battalion Beauvais – Tiger tanks

LVIII Panzer Korps
General der Panzertruppe Walter Krueger
Army Group 'G' Reserve: 3 divisions; HQ: Toulouse
2nd ⚡⚡ -Panzer Division *Das Reich* Heinz Lammerding – Montauban
9th Panzer Division Erwin Jolasse – Nîmes
11th Panzer Division Wend von Wietersheim – Libourne

XLVII Panzer Korps
General der Panzertruppe Hans, *Freiherr* von Funck
Army Group 'B' Reserve: 3 divisions
2nd Panzer Division Heinrich, *Freiherr* von Lüttwitz – Amiens
21st Panzer Division Edgar Feuchtinger – Caen area
125th and 192nd *PanzerGrenadier* Regiments, 22nd Panzer Regiment
116th (*Windhund*) Panzer Division Gerhard, *Graf* von Schwerin – Les
Andelys/Rouen

SUPREME HEADQUARTERS
ALLIED EXPEDITIONARY FORCE

Soldiers, Sailors and Airmen of the Allied Expeditionary Force!

You are about to embark upon the Great Crusade, toward which we have striven these many months. The eyes of the world are upon you. The hopes and prayers of liberty-loving people everywhere march with you. In company with our brave Allies and brothers-in-arms on other Fronts, you will bring about the destruction of the German war machine, the elimination of Nazi tyranny over the oppressed peoples of Europe, and security for ourselves in a free world.

Your task will not be an easy one. Your enemy is well trained, well equipped and battle-hardened. He will fight savagely.

But this is the year 1944! Much has happened since the Nazi triumphs of 1940-41. The United Nations have inflicted upon the Germans great defeats, in open battle, man-to-man. Our air offensive has seriously reduced their strength in the air and their capacity to wage war on the ground. Our Home Fronts have given us an overwhelming superiority in weapons and munitions of war, and placed at our disposal great reserves of trained fighting men. The tide has turned! The free men of the world are marching together to Victory!

I have full confidence in your courage, devotion to duty and skill in battle. We will accept nothing less than full Victory!

Good Luck! And let us all beseech the blessing of Almighty God upon this great and noble undertaking.

Dwight D. Eisenhower

Introduction

Tuesday 6 June 1944 was a day like no other. Although every military operation has a D-day, in the popular mind there is only one D-Day.[1] As Robert Capa, the acclaimed war photographer who found himself on Omaha Beach that morning, observed, 'from North Africa to the Rhine there were too many D-days, and for every one of them we had to get up in the middle of the night'. It was massively over-insured against every conceivable setback or adversity, making the twenty-four hours of the 'Longest Day' one of the best-prepared military endeavours of history.[2]

Sand and Steel charts the lifting of the German yoke from a small corner of Normandy during one day, but it was an enterprise that involved millions of people. Hence this is also the story of a generation, the majority of whom were born across the world in the decade 1916–26, and who are no longer with us. We know them as heroes, but for them, the Second World War sucked in all their contemporaries: they were all involved, it was something everyone participated in and if fortunate survived. They did not see themselves as heroes and many were reluctant to discuss their wartime years. However, I was lucky enough to meet a dozen D-Day veterans, including Lord Lovat's piper Bill Millin, willing to talk, on the sands of Normandy as far back as July 1975. That was the genesis of *Sand and Steel*. Since then, I have spoken to over one thousand Second World War veterans, whenever I have found them.

It was in 1991, in the aftermath of the First Gulf War, that I first interviewed Kingston Adams, a platoon commander on D-Day, about his wartime experiences. Before I could ask my first question, he began, 'Let's start at the beginning, because by far the most important part was rehearsing for it, getting it right.'

The regular army officer, commissioned into General Sir (as he was in June 1944) Bernard Montgomery's regiment – the Royal Warwicks – and who retired as a lieutenant colonel, was quite correct. From him and many other interviewees came the dawning realisation that D-Day had a vitally important hinterland. For those associated with that iconic day, 6 June 1944 was simply the culmination of months – sometimes years – of dedicated training. The first day of the landings in Normandy and subsequent campaign was only half the story.

When compared with the Germans, most servicemen who assaulted northern France had experienced an incredible degree of rugged and realistic training that put them at the peak of physical fitness, acclimatised them to battle, and equipped them, mentally and physically, well enough to win. Overlooked until now is the incredible statistic that more lives were lost preparing for D-Day than in its twenty-four hours. It is an uncomfortable aspect of Overlord entirely airbrushed from history. Most accounts plunge straight into the combat, with no more than a cursory nod to what went before. The reader will find that *Sand and Steel* spends an equal amount of time examining the plans and training that made success on D-Day possible. Without this – previously unexplored and sometimes necessarily dangerous – preparation, the airborne troops would not have prevailed and the seaborne warriors – wet, miserable with seasickness, cold and under intense fire – would not have known how to drag themselves through the obstacles and off the shingle.

Some of this hinterland also included the largely forgotten American 'occupation' of Britain during the war years. For North Americans, the journey to Normandy emphatically did *not* start on a plane or in a landing craft off the French coast, as suggested by some movies and documentaries. That would be to ignore the presence of Canadian troops in Britain from 1940, and the incredible build-up and training of American forces in the United Kingdom which began in January 1942 and peaked at 1.6 million GIs stationed in Britain by the end of May 1944 – including 385,000 personnel operating the bombers and fighters of the Eighth and Ninth Army Air Forces, seventeen thousand female staff with the Army Nurse Corps, eight thousand Women's Army Corps personnel serving across the US Army. To these we ought to add 122,000 sailors of the US Navy, plus seven thousand from the US Coast Guard and over a thousand American Red Cross civilian volunteers.[3]

The impact on the resident population, numbering forty-seven million, of the three million Americans who passed through Britain during 1942–5 was both profound and lasting. Canadian and other Allied service personnel – principally the Free French and Polish forces – stationed in Britain in 1944 amounted to another quarter of a million. The effect was further exaggerated because several million Britons were away serving in their armed forces and merchant navy overseas. The transatlantic arrivals meant that well over ten per cent of the adult male population in Britain aged between eighteen and forty in 1944 were Americans, including 130,000 black troops, an ethnic group then almost unknown. The legacy lingers to this day in NATO; with Anglo-American intelligence sharing; it has lasted politically with the so-called 'special relationship'; the nine thousand children born out of wedlock to GI fathers; and the offspring of the tens of thousands of wartime brides the departing servicemen took home.

Very many voices speak from these pages about their experiences – Americans, Canadians, Britons and French – from generals and politicians to the private in his foxhole. To balance the narrative of *Sand and Steel*, there are numerous Germans, who provoke the conclusion that the Wehrmacht waiting in Normandy was extraordinarily poorly led, abysmally trained and shoddily equipped. While it is true that the reinforcements rushed to Normandy after D-Day contained a leavening of steely-eyed, Nazi-motivated killers, those facing the assault troops on 6 June – apart from a few *Fallschirmjäger* (paratroops) and panzermen – were generally past their prime, recovering from wounds received in Russia and often not even German. Jack Heath, serving aboard *LCT-522* at Juno beach, recalled his first sight of captured Germans at Courseulles. Loaded onto his craft to take to England were 'about 200 prisoners of war. We were shocked by the ages of some of them; they looked like children and old age pensioners, though some were tough looking guys.'[4] If the reader is seeking confirmation of the view that 'in terms of kit, training, tactical ability, tenacity and sheer guts, fighting without air cover or naval gunfire support and hampered by interference from Adolf Hitler, the German Army was undoubtedly the best army in the field', they will not find it here.[5]

Normandy has become a second home for me, to the extent that I have been guiding tours over its terrain for service personnel, business leaders, politicians, veterans, their families, history classes and the curious for over thirty years. When walking the ground, the majority of questions I am asked still reference either Cornelius Ryan's epic account, *The Longest Day*, first published in 1959, the subsequent film released three years later, or Steven Spielberg's *Saving Private Ryan* of 1998. This is because the interpretations of Ryan and Spielberg still dominate the D-Day story. Thus, *Sand and Steel* is also an examination of how our understanding of D-Day has changed over the intervening decades.

A good reason for this fresh look at the campaign to liberate France on its seventy-fifth anniversary is the ease with which the battlegrounds can now be visited and experienced. I have watched the fields of France morph from anonymous beaches, meadows and towns into tourist sites adorned with plaques, statues and memorials of almost Gettysburg proportions. The narrow, tree-flanked lanes have widened into highways shorn of their foliage; overwhelming hedgerows – the famous bocage that loom large in everyone's recollections – are now trimmed to insignificance or ripped out altogether.

Farmhouses that hosted headquarters and aid posts, still evidently bomb-damaged to the visitor of the 1970s, have been demolished to make way for the new. Industrial estates and modern housing, particularly around Caen, Carentan and Saint-Lô, adorn the once-contested landscape. Graffiti today decorates the coastal bunkers that are left – most have been demolished over the years – where in 1975 ammunition from the war years was still to be found, and as much of it as possible transported back to England in my schoolboy pockets. What is left these days is well signposted, even if the acres of car parking seem overdone. The process has been gradual as other generations beyond the veterans have taken an interest, but need assistance to understand what took place. This is why you will find the occasional modern impression of the 1944 terrain in these pages.

In writing *Sand and Steel*, I was struck by how much the sea dominates the story of the liberation of France. The bulk of the invasion forces arrived by sea. It was naval gunfire support onto the German defenders that enabled the Allies to land. And without the massive maritime sustainment of Admiral Sir Bertram Ramsay's Operation Neptune, the Allied coalition would not have broken out into France.

To beat the Germans, across the water came an inventory of 700,000 separate items, from 137,000 jeeps, trucks and half-tracks, 4,217 tanks and fully tracked vehicles, and 3,500 artillery pieces, to a replacement rail network with 1,800 steam locomotives; 240 million pounds of potatoes; fifty-four million gallons of beer; twenty-six million jerrycans; sixteen million tons of fuel, food and ammunition; fifteen million condoms; ten million 'bags, vomit'; 2.4 million tent pegs; a million gallons of fresh drinking water (for the first three days alone); 800,000 pints of blood plasma (segregated carefully by black and white donors); 300,000 telegraph poles; 260,000 grave markers; cigarettes; toothbrushes – and 210 million maps.

If warriors striding through the surf on D-Day can be assessed as 'beginning the end' of the European war, then for the United States, Canada and Britain their respective wars also began with water. In America's case, literally with Pearl Harbor; for Canadian troops, it was the long trip across the Atlantic; whilst British soldiers equated their rescue from the waves at Dunkirk four years earlier as the beginning of their fightback against Nazi Germany. In June 1944, sometimes it was the same British soldiers who were to wade from the same English Channel onto French sand, and turn the tables on their former oppressors. Occasionally some of the ships that had rescued troops from Dunkirk would make the return journey, too.

One of the takeaway impressions offered by *Saving Private Ryan* was the primacy of US forces on D-Day. Whilst this would be true later on during the campaign to liberate France, 6 June 1944 perhaps represented Britain's last hurrah. A significant proportion of the maritime and land forces deployed on the day of invasion were British. Even in the US sector, for example, of the fifteen major troop transports and landing ships which lay off Omaha Beach feeding troops ashore, eight were British, and seven American.[6] Additionally, the navies of Canada, France, Poland, Norway, the Netherlands and Greece amounted to a substantial presence.

However, this is *not* a flag-waving exercise: American-, British- and Canadian-manned landing vessels operated equally off all five landing beaches, for on D-Day, in the words of the Supreme Commander, General Dwight David Eisenhower, 'there was only one nation – Allied'. Apart from Ike's battle-cry, for students of modern military history, D-Day is the epitome of a tri-service operation: one where the maritime, air and land components were of equal importance, and totally reliant on each other for victory. These pages, therefore, explain the build-up and invasion from the viewpoint of those flying gliders, transports, fighters and bombers and their ground crew, of the sailors manning warships, troop transports and landing craft, as well as those on both sides of the beach. It is a timely reminder that at a time when alliances – and budgets – are under strain on both sides of the Atlantic, no one country – or arm of service – could have succeeded alone. It was a time when every nation needed not just partners, but extraordinarily close friends, who were prepared to put their own young men in harm's way in pursuit of a greater cause – freedom.

PART ONE: PREPARATION

'I thank God you are here. And from the bottom of my heart I wish you good fortune and success.'

Winston Churchill, inspecting US troops in Britain,
23 March 1944

1

France and America

'I speak to you knowingly and tell you that nothing is lost for France. The same means that overcame us, can one day bring victory. Because France is not alone! She has a vast empire behind her. This war is not limited to the unfortunate territory of our country. This war is not decided by the Battle of France. This war is a World War. Whatever happens, the flame of French resistance must not be extinguished and will not be extinguished.'[1]

Extract from Charles de Gaulle's Appeal of 18 June 1940

FOR BRITONS, 18 June is the anniversary of the Battle of Waterloo. At a pinch, some might associate the date with Churchill's 'This was their finest hour' speech, delivered that afternoon in 1940 to the House of Commons.[2] The Prime Minister was responding to the French request for an armistice with Hitler, announced earlier. However, another far more important speech was made that day, well known to the French, but largely overlooked by the Anglo-Saxon community. It would ultimately prove to be more significant than Churchill's call to arms.

Colonel Charles de Gaulle, an officer of the French Army, had twice stalled the Wehrmacht with his 4th Armoured Division, virtually the only offensive actions of the May 1940 campaign. For this he received his promotion to *général de brigade* – the rank he would adopt for the rest of his life.[3] At the same time, Prime Minister Paul Reynaud appointed him Junior Minister for National Defence and War, with responsibility for coordination with the British.

Surrounded by defeatist figures like Maxime Weygand, Charles Huntziger, Pierre Laval and Philippe Pétain, de Gaulle twice flew to London, on 9 and 16 June (reciprocating Churchill's four visits to France made at the same time), planning to carry on the fight from French North Africa. After the latter meeting, de Gaulle returned to France to find he was no longer a minister and in danger of arrest: Reynaud had been replaced by the ageing Pétain, who was seeking an armistice.[4] The break with Pétain was a significant moment in de Gaulle's life, for the *maréchal de France* had been de Gaulle's first superior, who had mentored and commanded his protégé throughout the 1920s and 1930s; the younger man had even named his son Philippe in Pétain's honour.

On 17 June 1940, de Gaulle – unhappy at deserting his beloved French Army and conscious he would be considered by some a traitor – had escaped to London with 100,000 gold francs given him by Reynaud, arriving at Heston aerodrome with no possessions, no legit-imacy, few prospects, but extraordinary self-belief. The following day over the BBC, and repeated on 22 June, he appealed to France not to be demoralised, and to resist the German occupation. 'Honour, common sense, and the interests of the country require that all free Frenchmen, wherever they be, should continue the fight as best they may. I, Général de Gaulle, am undertaking this national task here in England,' he proclaimed.

He concluded, 'I call upon all French servicemen of the land, sea, and air forces; I call upon French engineers and skilled armaments workers who are on British soil, or have the means of getting here, to come and join me. I call upon the leaders, together with all soldiers, sailors, and airmen of the French land, sea, and air forces, wherever they may now be, to get in touch with me. I call upon all Frenchmen who want to remain free to listen to my voice and follow me.'

Jean-Louis Crémieux-Brilhac later observed that de Gaulle's Appeal 'brought a light and expressed a French will that nothing had broken down. It maintained, with a single voice, a national tradition, making the link with our entire history. It aroused an indelible recognition, even though listeners did not then associate the "idea of France" with Général de Gaulle.' Although the Anglo-American world to this day continues to regard de Gaulle with the suspicion first adopted by Churchill, in French eyes, he was nothing less than the saviour of their country. As Crémieux-Brilhac observed,

The Appeal of 18 June was like tossing a stone onto the snowy surface of a mountain. Barely a shudder, and then, very slowly, a movement starts which spreads and leads to a slide, which provokes an avalanche, and becomes a deafening noise. Thanks to the miracle of radio, because the brutality of the defeat had paralysed the masses and Pétain's government had silenced the few potential protesters, the date is now part of the national heritage. It is in all history textbooks, the benchmark of honour, courage and hope. It is inscribed in French memories as one of the greatest dates of a great past.[5]

One of the many who recalled the broadcast was former French President Valéry Giscard d'Estaing. 'My mother was a patriot and her father had been at Oxford; she listened to the BBC every day. We heard that a French general would speak and listened to him, but with no idea who he was. Only the day before Pétain had broadcast his belief that France had been defeated and he was seeking an armistice with Germany. De Gaulle's speech had a huge effect on us. For the first time we understood the war was not lost, after all.'[6]

Capitaine de Corvette Philippe Kieffer joined de Gaulle the very next day, though at the time few joined his Free French Forces in London. Born to an Alsatian family, Kieffer had been a New York bank director, volunteered for the French Navy aged forty at the outbreak of war, and the following year heeded de Gaulle's call to arms, joining him in England on 19 June 1940. Described as 'a torrent of energy', within a year Kieffer had raised the *Fusiliers-Marins Commandos* which by 1944 would comprise three troops of 177 hand-picked and extremely well-trained, hardy men.

Churchill was less worried about numbers; in June 1940, it was de Gaulle's profile that was of more use to the British premier, lining up a series of governments-in-exile to oppose Nazi-dominated Europe. At the height of the Battle of Britain in July 1940 at RAF Odiham, de Gaulle recruited three hundred Free French pilots to his cause. It was while inspecting their four aircraft that he first saw the Cross of Lorraine – associated with Joan of Arc's resistance to the English – painted on their airframes. Initially angered and embarrassed by its anti-British connotations, he nevertheless realised the emblem's potential as a symbol of resistance. However, by late 1940 de Gaulle commanded only 260 army and naval officers, 2,109 soldiers and 1,746 ratings.[7]

Yet over time, when they could escape, many Frenchmen and -women responded to de Gaulle's vision of an alternative to Pétain's France.

Stéphane Hessel made his way to London because 'de Gaulle inspired me to continue the fight as a Frenchman'.[8] Daniel Cordier, a teenager living in Pau in the south, remembered of the armistice, 'It was unbearable – it made me cry. I went to my room to cry for rather a long time. I told myself this is not possible. Not possible.' When Cordier reached London, he found 'Communists, socialists and Jews, all kinds of Frenchmen. We were all young. London was blacked out. We lay down to try to sleep in the dark all crammed together. We didn't know each other. Then someone started to sing the "Marseillaise" and we all joined in.' Seventy years on, Cordier broke down during the interview at the recollection of what de Gaulle meant to his generation: 'Even now, it was the most extraordinary moment of my life.'[9] To a much younger generation of *résistants*, such as schoolboy Jean Jammes with the Maquis in Épernon, he was a hero, the conscience of France. 'This one man inspired me: for us, there was no other figure to lead our generation.

The Cross of Lorraine, symbol of the Free French, proudly displayed by former maquisard Jean Jammes. Wearing this brassard, aged sixteen, in the summer of 1944 Jammes captured three German officers and was awarded the *Croix de Guerre*. Many of his generation saw beyond Pétain and the Occupation. Belief in the values espoused by Charles de Gaulle and his broadcasts from London inspired him to join the Épernon Resistance Group. (Author's photograph)

He *was* France. No sacrifice would be too great for his vision of our country.'[10]

All of Kieffer's future commandos were adventurers who had chosen to escape occupied France by various means. Initially there were just sixteen; by 1942, their numbers had grown to twenty-three; a year later, eighty-one. They would train hard at Achnacarry Commando School in the Scottish Highlands with other Britons, US Army Rangers, Dutch, Belgians, Norwegians, Poles and Czechs – learning to climb mountains, wading fast-flowing rivers, running for miles with a heavy pack, and engaging in hand-to-hand combat – to earn their *bérets verts* and Fairbairn–Sykes fighting knives. Kieffer's second in command was Guy Hattu, a militant anti-Fascist who had sailed to London from Brazil and had been broadcasting to France on Radio Gaulle, an anti-Pétain radio station.[11]

Also in their headquarters was Maurice Chauvet, born when the Battle of Belleau Wood was raging near Paris, and later sentenced to ten years' hard labour by the Vichy government for attempting to join the Free French Navy. He had arrived in England after eighteen months' incarceration, on 6 June 1943. Their medical officer, Robert Lion, and chaplain, Father René du Naurois, were also escapees from Vichy. Naurois, 'a French Friar Tuck, not so rotund but with strong, mischievous eyes', had acted deaf and dumb to cross into Spain and arrived in Liverpool via Barcelona and Gibraltar.[12] Lieutenant Pierre Marc Azoulay-Amaury commanded Kieffer's Gun Troop, with Francis Guezennec, an eighteen-year-old Breton, and François Andriot, a twenty-year-old French printing apprentice who had cycled from his home in eastern France to reach England via Fascist Spain.

Guy Vourch, a future pioneer of anaesthesia, who had been picked up floating in the Channel in a near-disastrous attempt to cross in an old boat, led One Troop (his brother Francis was second in command of Gun Troop) with Guy, Comte de Montlaur – scion of a family who had served in the Crusades, and originated from the tenth-century castle of Montlaur in the Languedoc – as his sergeant. With Hattu, they would be known as the 'three Guys'. They were accompanied by Hubert Faure, a cavalry officer of the *22ème régiment de Dragons* who fought under de Gaulle in 1940; Jean Masson, an apprentice blacksmith; sailor Louis Bégot; and Parisian Jean Morel, who had escaped by fishing smack to Plymouth in 1940. Lieutenant Alexandre Lofi led Eight Troop, whose men included Léon Gautier, a former bodybuilder from Rennes and gunner on the battleship *Courbet*; sailor Paul Chouteau, who escaped occupied France by kayak; and orphan Yves Meudal.[13] Chauvet designed their badge – a sailing brig crossed by a commando dagger – still worn by their successors today. On 6 June 1944, these men would be some of the very first to return to France.

De Gaulle based himself at 4 Carlton Gardens in central London, waging war through the medium of broadcasts to France via the BBC, rallying right-wing *résistants* still within France and unifying them uneasily with the Communists, the latter fast becoming a major political influence in the underground. 'To this day,' observed the veteran BBC broadcaster Ed Stourton in 2018, 'the initials BBC still open doors in Parisian government circles because of the wartime association.'[14] Churchill, no mean wordsmith himself, observed, 'He might be Stalin, with two hundred divisions behind his words. France without an army is not France. De Gaulle is the spirit of that Army. Perhaps the last survivor of a warrior race.'[15]

In May 1943, de Gaulle moved his headquarters to Algiers after the success of Operation Torch. There, he managed to outmanoeuvre America's preferred head of the Free French armed forces, Général Henri Giraud, a more experienced military figure, but political naïf. The switch of allegiance of the pro-Vichy troops to the Allies in Tunisia and Algeria gave de Gaulle a secure power base and a significant army to control. Yet Churchill and he were always at loggerheads – de Gaulle incorrectly believing the British wanted to seize French colonial possessions (Syria and Lebanon, for example) and trump French interests around the world.

His view was that France 'did not have friends, but interests', and he often seemed to antagonise Churchill for the sake of it, if only to prove he was not a British puppet – ironically, speaking German better than English. He was not consulted beforehand over a range of military issues, from the British invasion of Vichy-controlled Madagascar in 1942, to Operation Torch, to which de Gaulle reacted, 'I hope the Vichy people will fling them into the sea! You don't get France by burglary!' Although de Gaulle and Churchill would go on to forge a curious and mercurial love–hate relationship, the former had sown the seeds for the eventual liberation of his country.

In the summer of 1940, as France and much of Western Europe fell under totalitarian domination, many Americans were wondering whether the word 'conscription' might again return to blight their lives. France may have brought notions of liberty to the United States in 1776, but after the French Republic raised an army of 300,000 men through compulsion in 1793 – allegedly to defend the country against counter-revolutionary invasion – the concept that every able citizen 'owed themselves the defence of their nation' became another French import. The federal government duly resorted to it on 3 March 1863 in the Civil War, and on 18 May 1917 during the First World War. The third incarnation of the draft – such an easier word to swallow – came into being on 16 September 1940 through the Burke–Wadsworth Act passed by wide margins in both Houses of Congress. It was the nation's first peacetime resort to the forcible arming of its youth.

The new law required all men between the ages of twenty-one and thirty-five to register with their local draft boards on 16 October 1940. On that day, in 6,175 offices across the country, slightly over sixteen million registered, each receiving a number. Two weeks later, Secretary of War Henry L. Stimson, symbolically blindfolded with a swatch of material taken from a chair used by the signatories of the 1776 Declaration of Independence, was led to the glass bowl used for the same purpose in 1917. It was filled with nine thousand capsules each containing a number; Stimson drew one and handed it to President Roosevelt, who called out 'one-five-eight'. Incredibly, among the 6,175 registrants of that number was Alden C. Flagg, Jr of Boston, Massachusetts, whose father had held the first number drawn from the same bowl in 1917. Flagg and his buddies of the 137th Infantry (35th Division) would cross the Atlantic in May 1944, train in Devon and Cornwall, arriving in Normandy shortly after the 168th anniversary of the Declaration of Independence.[16]

Steps had been taken earlier in the year to create the framework for a wartime army through the Selective Training and Service Act. Men voluntarily enlisting into the US Army prior to the spring of 1940 could choose to join the Regular Army, National Guard or Organized Reserve, thus allowing many to 'beat the draft'. After 14 May 1940, all voluntary enlistments were to be into the 'Army of the United States', a wartime-only national force which actually came into being the following February. By July 1941, 600,000 had been inducted into this army, and in September it absorbed the National Guard. After Pearl Harbor, the Act was amended to require the registration of all men between eighteen and sixty-four. Of the millions who complied, ten million – aged eighteen to forty-four – were inducted into uniform, whether army (the air force then being part of the army), navy or Marine Corps; service was for the duration of the war, plus six months.

In June 1933, the US Army had numbered 136,000, including sixteen thousand officers; by 1940 it had increased to 270,000 scattered across 130 posts, camps and stations. At the outbreak of the Second World War, it amounted to the seventeenth largest army in the world – just behind Portugal's. It comprised four paper armies with token staffs of a few thousand each, one cavalry and three infantry divisions, a mechanised brigade, three hundred primitive tanks in two skeleton armoured divisions and 1,800 aircraft, few of which could be regarded as modern. Even after the First World War, some officers regarded the Air Corps as 'an adjunct to the cavalry', which led to a much celebrated regulation of 1920 stating 'pilots will not wear spurs while flying'. The Army Air Corps would only become the US Army Air Force (USAAF) on 20 June 1941 – the name by which it was known throughout the Second World War.[17]

In 1939, there was no military-industrial manufacturing base to speak of. In any case, Congress and the population were generally hostile to any increased military spending. This was not anti-militarism per se, rather a sense of 'America *first*': cure the Depression, create jobs and restore the country's wealth; then worry about the rest of the world. American industry was simply unable to equip a huge army quickly, supplying rifles, clothing, helmets, tanks, ammunition, bombers, landing ships and all the rest. The chief factor influencing any American involvement in Europe – should that happen – was shipping capacity. Assuming the Atlantic was clear, which it was not from mid-1941, projections utilising America's entire merchant fleet still limited the total number of GIs that could be deployed overseas to around four million, and only by the end of 1944.[18]

American mobilisation was well under way before the outbreak of war in December 1941, with over 1.4 million in the US Army spread between thirty-six divisions and a substantial air component. The earliest troops deployed to the United Kingdom as soon as the following month.

Let us join some of them as they set foot on European soil for the first time since 1918:

Britain may look a little shop-worn and grimy to you. The British are anxious to have you know that you are not seeing their country at its best. There's been a war on since 1939. For many months the people of Britain have been doing without things which Americans take for granted. But you will find that shortages, discomforts, blackouts, and bombings have not made the British depressed … You are coming to Britain from a country where your home is still safe, food is still plentiful, and lights are still burning. So it is doubly important for you to remember that the British soldiers and civilians have been living under a tremendous strain. It is always impolite to criticize your hosts. It is militarily stupid to insult your allies. So stop and think before you sound off about lukewarm beer, or cold boiled potatoes, or the way English cigarettes taste.[19]

Thus read a small seven-page foolscap document *Instructions for American Servicemen in Britain*, issued from 1942 to all GIs arriving in what was called the ETO (European Theater of Operations). In fewer than six thousand words it offered advice on the peculiarities of the British, their country, and their ways, and amongst its first recipients was Private First Class Milburn H. Henke from Hutchinson, Minnesota. He was captured by the world's cameras as the first GI in Britain, disembarking from the troopship USS *Chateau Thierry* to a welcoming committee of civic worthies and reporters in Belfast docks.

The date was 26 January 1942, as Henke – a twenty-two-year-old who used to work in his father's diner and had joined the National Guard to 'beat the draft' – recalled: 'I was sitting on some barracks bags, there were about fifteen of us, and this colonel came up the gangplank, and demanded, "I want a man from Company 'B', 133rd Infantry." I followed thinking I'd be unloading cargo, until asked if I could talk to reporters … I had to walk down the plank six times so photographers could get the perfect shot. With all the attention I got, it looked as though the US Army's plan was for me to win the war single-handed.'[20] The public relations colonel striding *up* the gangplank indicated there was already a sizeable American contingent in the British Isles before the *Chateau Thierry* (a purpose-built troop transport named after an American First World War battlefield) arrived, in company with the *Strathaird*, the pair transporting the entire 34th 'Red Bull' Division.[21]

You will find that all Britain is a war zone and has been since September 1939. Every light in England is blacked out every night and all night. The British have been bombed, night after night and month after month. Thousands of them have lost their houses, their possessions, their families. Soap is now so scarce that girls working in the factories often cannot get the grease off their hands or out of their hair. And food is more strictly rationed than anything else.[22]

The Red Bulls were the first of four US divisions to arrive in 1942; the 1st Armored soon followed, also to Northern Ireland, whilst the 1st and 29th Infantry Divisions crossed later to Scotland and were immediately sent by train to Dorset and Wiltshire. However, they were *not* the first, for uniformed Americans had been active across the Atlantic for nearly a year, and long *before* Pearl Harbor.

In accordance with Lend-Lease deal protocols agreed the preceding month, in April 1941 construction had begun of four extensive US naval bases, with ammunition stores, repair facilities, offices, hospitals and barracks, at Londonderry and Lough Erne in Northern Ireland and at Rosneath and Loch Ryan in Scotland. The labour comprised American and local contractors, supervised by US officers, with the projects being funded jointly by both governments. At the same time an 'observer group' of staff officers was activated in London to reconnoitre potential sites for ground and air force installations.

Preceding them were civilian pilots from the United States who had joined the three Eagle Squadrons operating in RAF colours between September 1940 and 29 September 1942, when they were absorbed into the US Eighth Air Force. Of the many thousands who volunteered, 244 were selected to serve, initially under British squadron and flight commanders, achieving seventy-three victories. The casualty rate was horrendous, with ninety-four lost or captured in combat or training, including several US pilots who had served in the Battle of Britain, even before the Eagle Squadrons (Nos. 71, 121 and 130) were raised. Other American citizens had elected to join the ranks of the Royal Canadian Air Force (RCAF), rather than sit out the war in splendid isolation. To them Britain seemed a natural partner, whilst the plight of France – her ally throughout the Revolutionary War and donor of the Statue of Liberty in 1885 – was a deep wound.

One Eagle who later transferred to the USAAF was Californian LeRoy Gover, who crossed the Atlantic to his war from Halifax, Nova Scotia. Preceding the later torrent of GIs, he sailed aboard the SS *Emma Alexander* in November 1941 with 115 other trained pilots – Americans, Australians, New Zealanders and Canadians. They joined a convoy of forty-three other ships ominously at the height of the Battle of the

Atlantic, with U-boats attacking on a nightly basis. 'We are ordered to carry our life belts at all times – even when sleeping – and to sleep in our clothes,' he wrote on 22 November. Two days later his diary recorded, 'There are now just thirty-seven of us [ships] – one tanker went down last night and three others just disappeared.' Gover arrived in Liverpool on 7 December after an uncomfortable and nerve-wracking sixteen-day passage. The following afternoon at the Air Ministry in London, he was confirmed as an officer in the RAF – against the direction of his own United States.

As his train pulled out of Waterloo station on the morning of Monday, 8 December 1941, Gover read the headline 'Japan Declares War on United States', and was suddenly aware that the European war had become global, with the likelihood that millions of his fellow countrymen would be following him after all.[23] Churchill wrote later that it was then he 'knew that the United States was in the war, up to its neck and in to the death – after seventeen months of lonely fighting, England would live. Once again in our long history, we should emerge, however mauled or mutilated, safe and victorious.'[24]

Charles 'Chuck' Hurlbut, who grew up in Auburn, New York State, recollected: 'Ever since high school I had heard about Hitler and all this stuff in Europe, but I never realised how deeply it was going to affect me. Hitler and Europe, that was their war, don't get involved. I played the clarinet and joined the Auburn community band. I was on a bowling team and a softball team. I met a few girls. Everything was going great. Pearl Harbor turned everyone around. I don't think there'll ever be a time again when this country is so unified. I never wanted to be a soldier; that was the farthest thing from my mind. But when something like Pearl Harbor happens, you get a feeling, "I'm supposed to do something." I couldn't wait to become eighteen so I could be drafted. I wanted to do my part. So when I hit eighteen, within days I was down at the draft board, and registered.'[25]

Such martial endeavour was despite widespread Middle America's antipathy to intervention, influenced by the Great Depression and memory of losses in the First World War. The much respected anti-war stance of the Quakers and other religious groups, and fears that much of the USA's Germanic heritage would be put at risk, additionally played their part. Besides, America was not necessarily pro-British. In addition to the powerful east coast anti-monarchist and Irish-American lobby, many also remembered being taught at school that the *Brits* were the enemy in the Revolutionary War and had sided with the Confederacy during the Civil War. The America First Committee, too, helped fan the flames of isolationism. With the aviator and influential orator Charles Lindbergh at its helm, at one stage it boasted 800,000 paying members in 450 chapters, though profoundly pro-Fascist and anti-Semitic in character.

Other advocates of isolationism drew upon history, quoting George Washington's farewell address in which he had advocated non-involvement in European wars and politics. Indeed, for much of the nineteenth century, the buffers of the Atlantic and Pacific had allowed the United States to remain detached from Old World tensions. Found wanting by naked military aggression in Abyssinia, Spain and Manchuria in the late 1930s, US neutrality made increasingly little sense after the defeat of France. As a pro-interventionist, Franklin D. Roosevelt – who assumed leadership of his country in the same month as Adolf Hitler took the helm in Germany – was obliged to negotiate with the isolationist-dominated Congress in order to push through aspects of his New Deal and other programmes. He was thus powerless to nudge America in his preferred direction, and that of his good friend, the British Prime Minister.

The events of Pearl Harbor and Hitler's (in retrospect bizarre and totally unnecessary) declaration of war on the United States, made four days after the Japanese attack on 11 December 1941, and reciprocated the same afternoon, changed everything. Until then, US military missions had to be discreet and possessed only limited briefs to observe, scope, but not participate.

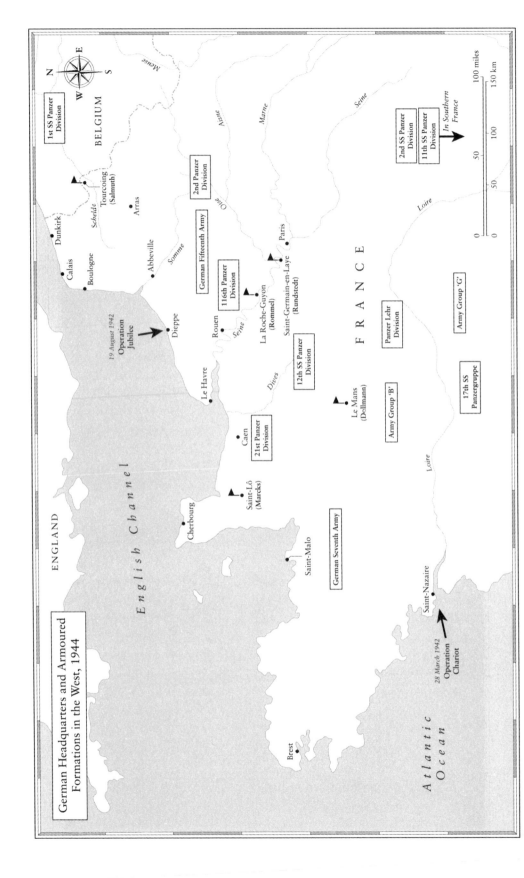

German Headquarters and Armoured Formations in the West, 1944

ENGLAND

English Channel

Atlantic Ocean

FRANCE

BELGIUM

1st SS Panzer Division

Tourcoing (Salmuth)

Dunkirk

Calais

Boulogne

Abbeville

Arras

2nd Panzer Division

German Fifteenth Army

116th Panzer Division

La Roche-Guyon (Rommel)

Saint-Germain-en-Laye (Rundstedt)

Paris

Rouen

Dieppe

19 August 1942 Operation Jubilee

Le Havre

12th SS Panzer Division

21st Panzer Division

Caen

Saint-Lô (Marcks)

Cherbourg

Saint-Malo

German Seventh Army

Brest

Saint-Nazaire

28 March 1942 Operation Chariot

Le Mans (Dollmann)

Army Group 'B'

Panzer Lehr Division

Army Group 'G'

17th SS Panzergruppe

2nd SS Panzer Division

11th SS Panzer Division

In Southern France

Meuse

Aisne

Marne

Seine

Oise

Somme

Schelde

Dives

Seine

Loire

Loire

0   50   100 miles

0   50   100   150 km

2

Atlantikwall

'In the east, west and south are to be found the last resting places of those German soldiers who, for home and Fatherland, followed the path of duty to the bitter end. They are a constant reminder to us, who remain behind, and to our future generations, that we must not fail them, when it becomes a question of making sacrifices for Germany.'

Oberst Erwin Rommel, *Infantry Attacks* (1937)

S EATED IN THE front passenger seat next to his driver, Oberfeldwebel Karl Daniel, who had been with him since Africa days, pennant fluttering from the front mudguard, Generalfeldmarschall Johannes Erwin Eugen Rommel spent the first five months of 1944 criss-crossing northern France.[1] We know much about these days because he was accompanied everywhere by his *Ordonnanzoffizier* (aide-de-camp), Hauptmann Helmuth Lang, and his naval advisor, Vice-Admiral Friedrich Ruge. The pair sat in the back, often keeping company with war correspondents, who were always keen to trail the former *Wüstenfuchs* (Desert Fox), or followed the field marshal's powerful Horch 951 cabriolet staff car. Lang and Ruge would record everything, both surviving the war.[2]

The Horch took him everywhere. Rommel particularly liked to drop in on his infantrymen – often referred to as grenadiers or *Landser*, and the branch with whom he had started his own career in 1910. He frequently carried a pile of accordions in the car, which he enjoyed distributing to the troops – not dissimilar to his nemesis, Montgomery,

Despite the propaganda surrounding the *Atlantikwall* – as in this Dutch language poster claiming that German strength in 1943 was far superior to that of 1918 – Generalfeldmarschall Erwin Rommel (1891–1944) was aware that the project was 'a figment of the Führer's *Wolkenkuckucksheim* [cloud cuckoo land] … an enormous bluff'. Rommel nevertheless made many snap visits to raise the morale of his men and inspire belief in their defences. One of his proven methods was to distribute accordions to encourage bonding through community singing. (Author's collection)

handing out cigarettes and newspapers to his men. Much of the Reich's military tradition was perpetuated by marching songs – there was one for every army and most regions – so all units, however small, boasted an accordion player. Rommel recognised that efficiency in battle came not from bravery but comradeship, the fear of letting down one's mates. He understood that a song around a camp fire, accompanied by the wistful notes of an accordion, was a good way of binding his men together for the coming storm.

Rommel – as de Gaulle – was another man whose reputation had been forged in 1940. During the invasion of France, it was his 7th Panzer Division that advanced faster, travelled further, took more prisoners and destroyed more armoured vehicles than any other. Hitler had a special interest in following Rommel's progress, for the young general had previously commanded the *Führerbegleitbatallion*, guarding his leader's field headquarters during the invasion of Poland. In the bizarre, contradictory and competitive world that was the Third Reich, advancement often came because of recognition, rather than solid achievement. Rommel was a face and a name to Hitler, which then won him his next job – that of commanding a few German troops in

North Africa at the beginning of 1941 – which turned into something else entirely.

In June 1944 the German commander in France was not Rommel, but Generalfeldmarschall Gerd von Rundstedt, who rejoiced in the title of Supreme Commander or *Oberbefehlshaber West* (both the person and the office abbreviated to OB West). Assisted by his chief of staff, Gunther Blumentritt, Rundstedt controlled fifty-eight divisions, besides numerous other formations and detachments, totalling around 800,000 troops; these comprised the army's ground combat forces in the west, including France, Belgium and the Netherlands. Two formations comprised paratroops, ten were formed from panzers and armoured infantrymen, while thirteen were infantry divisions. All these, due to their relative mobility and high-grade personnel, were graded as 'fit for duty in the East'.

However, OB West's remaining twenty-three *Bodenständige* (static position) divisions were either immobile or reserve infantry formations, with low *Kampfwert* (combat effectiveness) ratings. They were assessed as incapable of taking on offensive missions, and suitable only for limited defence. For the latter's transportation needs, in Rundstedt's domain there were 115,000 military horses on strength, a stark reminder of how reliant on these creatures the German armed forces were in 1944 – by contrast, the Allies would bring with them not a single equine.[3] A year earlier, roughly twenty-five per cent of officers stationed in France had fought in Russia; by 1944, this figure had almost doubled to sixty per cent. This did not necessarily reflect a reinforcement of the west, but a higher proportion of wounded and convalescing leaders.

The ability to order even tactical panzer deployments had been removed from OB West, and sometimes the *Generalfeldmarschall* felt he only commanded the sentries outside his gate – which reflected the fact that Rundstedt's was a superfluous level of command. Hitler and the *Oberkommando der Wehrmacht* (OKW, the High Command of the German Armed Forces, based in bunkers at Zossen-Wünsdorf, twenty miles south of Berlin) could, and did, bypass him when it suited them. Long past his prime, the aged field marshal by 1944 was merely a trusted rubber stamp for the regime.[4] Rundstedt in turn answered to OKW. It is worth noting here that the Wehrmacht comprised the three German armed forces of the *Heer* (army), Luftwaffe (air force) and Kriegsmarine (navy), each with their own command chain, but theoretically subordinate to the OKW. The Waffen-SS units, fighting alongside those of the army, were not even answerable to OKW, but to the Reichsführer-SS, Heinrich Himmler, and through him to Hitler. OKW served as the Reich's general staff, but in practice acted as Hitler's personal military advisors, translating his whims into orders and asserting direct control over army units in the west.

This complicated and lengthened military decision-making, resulting in orders issued in Berlin for the deployment of quite small tactical forces, irrespective of local needs and conditions. The head of OKW, Generalfeldmarschall Wilhelm Keitel, was usually to be found at Hitler's side – at the *Führerhauptquartiere*, the military headquarters code-named *Wolfsschanze* (Wolf's Lair) at Rastenburg in East Prussia; sometimes at his mountain retreat at Berchtesgaden; and infrequently in Berlin, for Hitler loathed the German capital. The day-to-day running of OKW was left to Keitel's cleverer deputy, Generaloberst Alfred Jodl, technically Chief of Operations Staff.

German generals referred to these arrangements privately as *Befehlschaos* (command by confusion), though it has been observed that the reason for the chaos probably originated in Hitler's very Roman obsession – common with dictators – of keeping significant military and political power away from the hands of potential rivals.[5] By this stage of the war, whatever magic Hitler may once have possessed in the eyes of his senior generals had disappeared. Shakespeare's *Macbeth* springs to mind: 'Those he commands move only in command / Nothing in love.' As Blumentritt, Rundstedt's chief of staff, observed, 'a dictator does not favour putting too much power in the hands of one man'.[6]

A month after the 23 March 1942 British raid on the French port of Saint-Nazaire, *Führerbefehl* (Führer Directive) No. 40 ordered the construction of coastal defences along the fringes of North-West Europe. With the additional distractions of making the Channel Islands impregnable – Hitler assumed their recapture would be a top British priority – constructing bombproof facilities for U-boats, and building V-weapons sites, the *Atlantikwall* programme was not only chaotic but soon behind schedule. It was born from the military assessments of the Wehrmacht, but it also mirrored Hitler's personal obsession with grand architectural programmes – the pre-war construction of the first autobahn and *Westwall* (Siegfried Line) being two prime examples.

The aim in 1942 was to defend Europe with modest forces in order to send the majority to Russia: as Hitler stated on 13 August 1942, 'There is only one battle front. The others can be held with modest units.' He conjured up a figure of fifteen thousand bunkers to be erected between Norway and Spain, manned by 300,000 troops, with priority given to ports, but only 12,247 would be completed by June 1944. The standard of workmanship varied enormously, with some of the earliest designs already viewed as obsolete by D-Day. This was partly due to a lack of central direction, but in France most of the work was done by local labourers working for subcontractors, often French-owned companies, and many not having the best interests of the Reich in their building efforts.

When Hitler discovered the programme was nowhere near his planned completion date of 1 May 1943 for the *Atlantikwall*, Rundstedt was ordered to investigate. The head of OB West examined the physical defences, the personnel allocated to man them, and the wider doctrine of defence. He immediately outlined the concerns he had been expressing since 1942: that the troops were few in number, generally of poor quality and reserves were sparse – because the Russian Front took the lion's share of available resources. Rundstedt cited the fact that Berlin had just ordered twenty of his best battalions to pack their bags and redeploy to the Eastern Front, but in exchange gave him sixty, recruited from Russian volunteers and prisoners. Led by a smattering of German officers, they may have been capable of internal security and policing, but OB West expected none of them to last more than a few hours in hard combat. 'Things look black,' he stated. 'It doesn't suffice to build a few pillboxes – one needs defence in depth,' he warned on 28 October 1943.[7]

The damning report immediately prompted Hitler's Führer Directive No. 51 of 3 November 1943, which outlined, in near panic, his concerns about the western defences and the means of strengthening them. It began: 'For the last two and one-half years the bitter and costly struggle against Bolshevism has made the utmost demands upon the bulk of our military resources and energies. This commitment was in keeping with the seriousness of the danger, and the over-all situation. The situation has since changed. The threat from the East remains, but an even greater danger looms in the West: the Anglo-American landing!'[8]

The Führer realised that 'If the enemy here succeeds in penetrating our defences on a wide front, consequences of staggering proportions will follow within a short time. All signs point to an offensive against the Western Front of Europe no later than spring, and perhaps earlier.' He went on to state, 'I can no longer justify the further weakening of the West in favour of other theatres of war. I have therefore decided to strengthen the defences in the West, particularly at places from which we shall launch our long-range war against England' – he was referring here to the future V-weapons programme. 'For those are the very points at which the enemy must, and will attack; there – unless all indications are misleading – will be fought the decisive invasion battle.'[9] This was the first time Hitler had put serious strategic thought into the implications of the operation the Allies knew as Overlord, prompted by Rundstedt's frightening submission of the previous month.

In this document, Hitler set out his thinking and doctrine, which was to dominate the forthcoming campaign until its conclusion:

> Holding attacks and diversions on other fronts are to be expected. During the opening phase of the battle, the entire striking power of the enemy will of necessity be directed against our forces manning the coast. Only an all-out effort in the construction of fortifications, an unsurpassed effort that will enlist all available manpower and physical resources of Germany and the occupied areas, will be able to strengthen our defences along the coasts, within the short time that still appears to be left to us. Should the enemy nevertheless force a landing by concentrating his armed might, he must be hit by the full fury of our counter-attack.[10]

The immediate consequence of Rundstedt's report and *Führerbefehl* No. 51 was an increase in OB West's strength from forty-six to fifty-eight divisions, but, as Blumentritt observed, Hitler had a 'predilection for steel, concrete and iron', preferring 'illusory situation maps, six hundred miles from reality', which had a 'calming effect on those with a flair for fantasy'.[11]

At the end of 1943, with the Afrika Korps vanquished, Rommel was kicking his heels in Italy. Not exactly unemployed – he was assessing possible ways of defending northern Italy from Allied attack – he was certainly underemployed, his talent for leading and inspiring men on the battlefield ignored. He had been expecting to command the German Tenth and Fourteenth Armies in Italy against his old adversary Montgomery, and was already based with a skeleton Army Group headquarters in a pleasant villa on the shores of Lake Garda in northern Italy.

However, he had been outmanoeuvred for the job by a rival, Field Marshal Albert Kesselring. Not wishing to waste Rommel's talents, Hitler ordered him instead to assess the strength of the *Atlantikwall*, in response to Rundstedt's memorandum that it was 'a Propaganda Wall'. It was to give his Führer Directive some teeth that he sent his best-known marshal – Rommel, as the newly appointed Inspector-General of the Western Coast, along with his Army Group headquarters staff – to review the areas most threatened, and report back.

The former Afrika Korps commander started straight away, visiting Denmark on 1 December. Relations were cordial with OB West; long past retirement at sixty-nine, Rundstedt had been at the helm since March 1942, and although equal in rank to Rommel, there was a difference of sixteen years between the pair – pretty much a generation. The *Wüstenfuchs* had last served under Rundstedt in the French campaign of 1940 when he was a lowly major general. Initially he shared the collective wisdom that the invasion would fall within the Fifteenth Army's sector, and on 20 December lunched with its commander, Hans von Salmuth, in Tourcoing. This view was also shared by the navy's *Marinegruppenkommando West*, which discounted the likelihood of an assault in the Seine Bay, because of the complete lack of harbours (apart from the heavily defended Le Havre and Cherbourg), the shallow coastal shelf, tidal variations and openness to Atlantic storms. Two principal areas in Salmuth's sector concerned Rommel: around Calais, and the Scheldt estuary leading to the port of Antwerp, which he considered ripe for an airborne assault.

In his report to Hitler of 31 December 1943, Rommel reflected the great disparity between the much-photographed 406mm guns of the *Batterie-Lindemann* at Sangatte near Calais, or the impressive bunkers housing four 380mm Krupp weapons of the *Batterie-Todt* at Cap Gris-Nez, with the non-existent beach defences elsewhere.[12] Rommel further bemoaned the fact that the Seventh Army 'possessed over thirty-two different weapon systems with 252 different types of ammunition, of which forty-seven types were no longer produced.[13] The entire Seventh Army had only sixty-eight 88mm and one hundred and seventy 75mm anti-tank guns.'[14] The concept of a wall was a complete misnomer: many so-called strongpoints consisted only of trenches and sandbags protected by a few strands of barbed wire; more dummy minefields existed than real ones; there were no measures in place against aerial assault; countless open sandy beaches lay unguarded, in some cases relying on a pre-existing sea wall or anti-tank ditch as their only form of linear defence. The only significant fortifications clustered around ports. In any case, none of the positions possessed any depth: one determined penetration and the whole network would be overwhelmed.

Much of the subsequent debate about Rommel's defensive assets would revolve around tanks. Yet, at the turn of 1943, he was the first to acknowledge what was needed were anti-tank guns, which could debilitate an Allied breakout, firing from camouflaged, fixed positions. His well-sited eighty-eights had massacred British armour at long ranges in the Western Desert. Tanks, on the other hand, attracted hostile aircraft like flies, and required costly fuel and highly trained crews. Rommel noted, too, the average ages of the defending formations: in Kurt von Schlieben's 709th Division, guarding the Cotentin, it was thirty-six; in the naval batteries encased in thick concrete along the coast, it was forty-five; he had even encountered gunners aged fifty-six.[15]

The true state of the *Atlantikwall* was worse than Rundstedt's October report had suggested: if an invasion were to arrive within the next few months, Germany was essentially defenceless. Rommel also observed that building programmes had actually *slowed* during the second half of 1943, due to the removal of labourers to other projects – including repairs to bombed dams in the Ruhr.[16] By early 1944 the supply of labour would almost completely dry up as personnel were diverted to repair bomb damage to factories and homes within the Reich, leaving little for the west – which would cause Rommel to direct his troops to build their defences instead of train for battle.

The Desert Fox also noted:

> The centre of gravity of the enemy landings will probably be the sector held by the Fifteenth Army. It is quite likely that the enemy's main effort will be directed against the sector between Boulogne and the mouth of the Somme, and on either side of Calais, where he will derive maximum advantage from the support of his long range guns, from the shortest crossing for the assault and later supply operations, and from the best utilisation of his air power. His chief objective will almost certainly be to obtain possession as quickly as possible of ports capable of accommodating large numbers of ships.[17]

After the war, Heinz Guderian would observe with some glee of the Desert Fox's incorrect predictions, 'Rommel assured me several times that the English and American landings would take place in the coastal areas north of the mouth of the Somme. Rommel's views coincided with those of Hitler.'[18] In fact, Guderian was playing with history: every German headquarters had a slightly different view of where the Allies might strike, which altered on an almost monthly basis. General Walter Warlimont at OKW recalled his assessment that the Allies would definitely attack in 1944 to assuage Soviet demands, and that an assault on Calais might lead them quickly to Germany's war economy, fixed on the Rhine and Ruhr, without which the Reich would collapse militarily – but they were by no means certain this was what the Allies planned to do.[19]

However, Vice-Admiral Ruge recalled that later – once Rommel had studied the terrain in more detail – he expected the invasion might arrive in one of three possible areas:

> the Scheldt, the Somme and the western part of the Bay of the Seine, where the assault actually took place. At first Rommel thought that the coast on both sides of the mouth of the Somme the most probable location because our defences there were especially weak. Later the Calvados and Cotentin seemed to him most likely, because of allied air activity in May 1944. He thought, besides the main invasion, there possibly would be minor operations such as cutting off the northwest part of Brittany by taking Brest, or cutting off the Cotentin or Le Havre.[20]

Günther Blumentritt, OB West's chief of staff, nevertheless observed, 'armies under the orders of Rundstedt did not know who was now in charge, Rundstedt or Special Inspector Rommel', which led to friction.[21]

The aged Rundstedt had to be reassured by Keitel that he was not being put out to grass and that the erstwhile *Wüstenfuchs*, a fellow field marshal, would be subordinated to him. After that, things went well and Rommel – at Rundstedt's suggestion – was offered and accepted leadership of the areas threatened with invasion, effective 15 January 1944. Both Rundstedt and Hitler were aware of the enhanced status within Germany of the former Afrika Korps commander.[22] The *Sicherheitsdienst* (SD), who monitored dissent within the Third Reich, noted that enormous faith was placed in Rommel's ability to turn the tide of the war in the west, both amongst servicemen and civilians – though until then, Rommel's brief in the West had been to observe, not command.[23]

His future subordinates included Generals Friedrich Dollmann's Seventh Army and Salmuth's Fifteenth Army, deployed north of the Loire and between Brittany and the Netherlands, and the resultant army group became an intermediate tier of authority under Rundstedt – whose

Rommel's Army Group 'B' was really run by Generalleutnant Hans Speidel (1897–1984), its diligent – and anti-Nazi – chief of staff. The Desert Fox was a brilliant front-man and tactician and a great inspiration to his men, but disdained the minutiae of running large military formations. For example, he made no attempt to establish forward or tactical command posts, necessitating long drives to and from his HQ at La Roche-Guyon. (Author's collection)

authority was in fact undermined. The Seventh Army comprised 198,000 men; the Fifteenth was rather better off with 313,000 men in eighteen divisions, garrisons and fortress detachments. Initially, Rommel and his staff were quartered at Fontainebleau, but moved on 9 March to La Roche-Guyon – ancestral home of the Dukes of Rochefoucauld – a thousand-year-old château on the Seine, and equidistant between his two formations, whose inter-army boundary was the Dives river.[24]

On 1 April 1944 his new chief of staff, Generalleutnant Hans Speidel, arrived, and very soon the Desert Fox came to rely on the bright, bespectacled and crafty soldier-scholar (he had gained a PhD before the war), who ran his headquarters like clockwork. The two chiefs of staff, Blumentritt (at OB West) and Speidel (at Army Group 'B'), had 'known one another since 1920 and worked harmoniously together', according to the former, who also described Speidel as 'very shrewd, who had a natural understanding of how to gloss over friction'.[25] Rommel was remarkably ignorant of the logistics required to run his campaigns: in April 1941, the army had been obliged to send its quartermaster general (the then little-known Friedrich Paulus) to the Western Desert, to remind the errant Afrika Korps commander of some fundamental principles of logistics for sustained operations. Speidel would have to do the same in the coming months. Rommel, for example, had never led formations equipped with large numbers of horses, of which the Seventh Army had 43,000 and the Fifteenth 33,000.[26]

Rundstedt's own command, OB West, was eventually subdivided into two army groups: Rommel's *Heeresgruppe* 'B', and Army Group 'G', created on 26 April, under Generaloberst Johannes Blaskowitz, covering terrain south of the Loire. The First and Nineteenth Armies of Army Group 'G' covered the Biscay coast and the Riviera with seventeen divisions.

Yet German doctrine and experience of the Eastern Front (the Desert Fox had uniquely never served in Russia) would provoke a tactical rift between Rommel and Rundstedt. The former wished to repel the Allies as they landed – when they were most vulnerable: disorganised, wet, cold, seasick and disorientated. North Africa had taught him the damage Allied air interdiction could do to reinforcements moving into the combat zone – therefore the closer his reserves were to the main effort, the better. As Rommel correctly predicted to Helmuth Lang in April, 'The war will be won or lost here on the beach. We have only one possibility – to bring the enemy to a stop. We must get him as long as he is in the water and is fighting to get to land. Reinforcement troops will never be able to get to the battle; it is foolish to even count on this.'[27]

Rundstedt, who had not witnessed Allied close air support at work in 1942–3, believed that it would be impossible to defend the coast for long, if at all, and that any positions should act merely as a tripwire while mobile reserves were husbanded, concentrated and unleashed. The older man knew the *Atlantikwall* could never be a physical, continuous obstruction. The most it could do would be to canalise opponents onto ground of the Germans' choosing, or buy time – as the obstacle belt was demolished and crossed – for reinforcements to be rushed to the correct spot. Then, as many panzer divisions as could be assembled should counter-attack. This was precisely the response to the Sicilian landings of July 1943, when a counter-attack by a battlegroup from the Hermann Göring Panzer Division nearly threw the US landings at Gela back into the sea. Two months later at Salerno, and in January 1944 at Anzio, the scenario repeated itself, where powerful *Kampfgruppen*, including panzers, struck at the invaders. In each case the attackers prevailed, due to naval gunfire support, but to Rundstedt's mind the concept seemed proven, especially if the Allies could be enticed a little inland, beyond the range of their warships' guns.

Yet in Berlin, Rundstedt was aware the very name *Atlantikwall* conjured up images of solid castle walls, with the same sort of mythical, impregnable status the Maginot Line had represented for the French in 1940. Some commanders, like Generalleutnant Josef Reichert of the 711th Infantry Division, in Salmuth's Fifteenth Army, refused to believe the Allies were planning an invasion at all: in his mind it was all a huge bluff to help the Soviets by fixing all the Wehrmacht's reserves in the West – that is until two British paratroopers arrived literally on his front lawn in the early hours of 6 June.[28]

To oversee the collective training and deployment of OB West's ten armoured divisions, and direct them in battle, Hitler created *Panzergruppe West* (later renamed the Fifth Panzer Army) under Freiherr (Baron) Geyr von Schweppenburg, which was placed under Rundstedt on 24 January, and was arguably the only organisation with the ability to destroy an Allied beachhead.[29] Its headquarters was stationed near Paris, partly because of anxieties about an Allied airborne desant onto the city, and because the capital was the 'handle of the fan' – equidistant from any threatened area. However, the existence of *Panzergruppe West* made no sense: no other nation's forces put their armoured formations under separate control – usual practice across the world was for tank formations to operate to the same command chain as infantry units.

The panzer divisions were the Wehrmacht's elite and there were frequent squabbles within the German hierarchy as to who should control them. Heinz Guderian, architect of the panzer arm, and Inspector-General of Armoured Troops, was adamant they remain under army control: Geyr, therefore, was Guderian's watchman in the West, keeping the tanks out of the clutches of Himmler and Göring (though there was a Luftwaffe panzer division fighting in Italy). Geyr utilised many of the staff from *Panzergruppe Afrika*, dissolved the previous year, and was charged with training and deploying all panzer units in the West, including those of the Waffen-SS.

As one of the architects of the May 1940 victory over the French and virtual guru of tank soldiers, Guderian exerted much influence in Berlin, but was a meddler. Forthright, he frequently fell out with colleagues – and Hitler. He acknowledged Rommel 'was not only an open, upright man and a brave soldier; he was also a highly gifted commander, possessed energy and subtlety of appreciation; he always found an answer to the most difficult of problems, and had a great understanding of his men'.[30]

Yet Guderian backed Geyr and disagreed with Rommel over the positioning of panzers in the West, and continued to defend his views long
after the war. Specifically, the Guderian–Geyr lobby were anxious 'that
the panzer divisions were to be committed as units and not piecemeal
by companies and regiments ... In the event, however, the exact reverse
took place.' Geyr noted that 'the arm-chair strategy of Berchtesgaden,
and Rommel's lack of strategic training, resulted in the panzer divisions
being frittered away in piecemeal operations of a minor and defensive
nature'.[31]

Guderian felt 'all the Panzer and PanzerGrenadier divisions should
be concentrated ready in two groups, one north and the other south of
Paris'.[32] The mention of the French capital is significant, for all the
German hierarchy believed part of the Allied plan would involve
marching on Paris (which was not the case), enabled by a mass airborne
assault, as noted earlier. This explains the positioning of many German
mobile formations, which were to meet two threats: they were stationed
along main roads that would lead them either to the invasion front,
wherever it might be, or to defend Paris, for lightly armed paratroops
would have little defence against tanks. Other units, too, lingered in
northern Belgium, reflecting concerns that the Allies might try to seize
the vital port of Antwerp from the air – a concept also encouraged by
the Canadian Army as part of the Allied deception.[33]

Based near Paris, Geyr seemingly trained his command well. His ideas
have a very modern ring to them: there were night exercises three times
a week and extensive studies and experiments in hedgerow fighting, with
demonstration battalions schooled in British doctrine engaging in simulated combat against German units. Once a week was *Fliegertag* (aviation
day), set aside for training against air attack. Yet both Geyr and Rundstedt
were demonstrably out of date: neither had appreciated the extent of
Allied air superiority by 1944 or the ability of close air support to interdict troops and tanks moving forward to the combat zone; the Soviets
had not yet developed this capability when either had last served in the
east. As Günther Blumentritt recalled of a conversation with Rommel
in February 1944, 'He had got to know the *modus operandi* of the British
Air Force in North Africa and was convinced that in this situation panzer
divisions could not in any case be moved, either by day or by night,
because they would immediately be attacked from the air.'[34]

Fritz Bayerlein, former chief of staff to Rommel in Africa, recollected
a similar conversation from this time: 'It's not a matter of fanatical hordes

to be driven forward in masses against our line, with no regard for casualties, and little recourse to tactical craft; here we are facing an enemy who applies all his native intelligence to the use of his many technical resources, who spares no expenditure of material and whose every operation goes its course, as though it had been the subject of repeated rehearsal. Dash and doggedness alone no longer make a soldier.'[35] Although Rommel and Rundstedt disagreed over the placement of the panzers, the two field marshals appear to have got on quite well. The acrimony over tanks was centred on Rommel and Geyr – the pair were talented trainers and leaders of men who understood their enemy, but were headstrong, and worked against one another.

Eventually, Rundstedt and Hitler grew tired of the endless *Panzer-Kontroverse* bickering between Rommel, Guderian and Geyr, and when

Although both held the same rank of *Generalfeldmarschall*, Rommel's superior was Gerd von Rundstedt (1875–1953). He was sixteen years older than the Desert Fox – pretty much a generation. Reassured by Berlin that Rommel (right) would not replace him as OB West, the senior marshal formed a good relationship with the commander of Army Group 'B', though they differed on how best to use their panzers. All were aware that Rommel's principal value in 1944 was as a propaganda icon, his name alone being worthy many bayonets. (Author's collection)

on 26 April Hitler announced the formation of Army Group 'G' to oversee the First and Nineteenth Armies in southern France (effective on 12 May), he attached to Army Group 'G' three of Geyr's panzer divisions, the 9th, 11th and 2nd SS. At the same time, three were put under Rommel's tactical control (2nd, 21st and 116th Panzer Divisions), leaving the remaining four in the West (three SS: the 1st, 12th and 17th, and Fritz Bayerlein's Panzer Lehr) under Geyr as a strategic reserve. The 17th SS possessed no tanks at all – just a battalion of assault guns – and was, in fact, designated a panzer grenadier division; this was a point of detail missed by Allied intelligence prior to Overlord.

The crucial rider was that any deployment of the panzers was to be cleared with Berlin first – which overrode all German military doctrine, and logic. This assignment of panzer divisions in France was as much a compromise by Hitler to assuage the demands of Rommel, Geyr and Rundstedt, as it was an attempt to anticipate where the Allies would land. Apart from suiting no one, the sad reality was that *Panzergruppe West* was an extra layer to an already overcomplicated command structure and ensured that any response to an invasion was bound to be slow and interrupted by petty jealousies.

In combat, the normal groupings of all panzer divisions disappeared, for instead they had learned to form all-arms *Kampfgruppen* (battlegroups) at battalion and regimental level. These comprised a variable blend of tanks, armoured infantry, artillery, anti-tank gunners, engineers and logistic support. Battlegroups took the name of the senior commander present, and were very much a hallmark of the successful German defensive battles throughout the campaign.

Another key ingredient of German success on the battlefield was the concept of giving a local commander freedom to act as he thought best. The idea was to give a leader his mission or goal, but leave him to decide how best to carry it out; it encouraged momentum. Known as *Auftragstaktik*, it has been translated in modern military terminology as 'mission command'. The opposite, which often seemed to characterise much British activity, entailed lengthy orders which included every aspect of a mission, from its aim, to how many hand grenades each man was to carry, and in which pocket a field dressing was to be found.

Auftragstaktik appears to have been drummed into every senior and junior commander, for it is assumed to be behind the early German triumphs of 1939–42. Even the defensive achievements in Sicily, Salerno, Monte Cassino and Anzio of 1943–4 have been put down to these broad principles. But we must be wary of attributing too much to doctrinal success. By 1944, Hitler was micromanaging his forces more and more, and commanders at every level were nervous of appearing to contradict the wishes of OKW, the Nazi Party – or *der Führer* himself. In a postwar memoir, Geyr von Schweppenburg called the previous era of freedom of initiative 'the pre-corporal days – that is, before Hitler and his cronies began to conduct the war with complete disregard of the trained military experts'.[36]

Geyr went on to note, 'We would not have been unduly worried by the situation in the front line becoming apparently critical. We should have waited unperturbed until all the reserve divisions involved had assembled and should then have launched them in a counter-blow against the enemy. Under the regime now in vogue, however, this method was not possible. Neither Hitler, nor Supreme Command West understood – nor had the courage – to let "panzer situations" ripen.'[37] Thus, the very initiative that had created success in the early years began to ebb, partly through fear, partly because the National Socialist regime encouraged it to wane. *Auftragstaktik* was out – at least in name. In a telling 2014 interview with the *Fallschirmjäger* trooper Johannes Börner, who fought in Normandy, when asked what he knew of *Auftragstaktik*, replied, 'That doesn't tell me anything; I don't know it.'[38]

In the summer of 1944, there were three factors that Wehrmacht doctrine had not taken into account. Two were linked: the crushing might of Allied air power to which the Germans had no answer, and the *Materialschlacht* (battle of equipment) that flowed out of American factories, dwarfing the quantities, and eventually the quality, of anything the Third Reich could produce.[39] The third factor was home-grown: the illogical, bullying interference of Adolf Hitler.

One of the Führer's many diktats from Russia followed his troops to Normandy: that each position should be held to the last round, the last man; retreat was *verboten* (forbidden). The Seventh Army very sensibly asked Rommel, if men from one coastal strongpoint came to the aid of another, would they be in violation of Hitler's order? Such a conundrum would have stymied most commanders, but not Rommel. A few days later, a '*Rommelbefehl*' decreed 'within divisional areas, the tactical movement of subordinate units would be at the discretion of field commanders'. Furthermore, the movement of divisions would require Rommel's authority, not Hitler's. The Desert Fox, used to being his own boss, also had to overcome the mind-set of the occupation forces in France. One of his subordinate commanders, General von Schlieben, arrived in December 1943 to find that 'for someone who had served only in the East, the flood of orders, directives, and regulations which continually showered the troops was a novelty for me. This paper flood impressed me more than the tide along the Atlantic coast. Higher headquarters concerned themselves with trivial affairs of subordinate commanders. For example, it became a problem whether a machine-gun was to be placed twenty metres more to the right or the left' – which neatly illustrated how the spirit of *Auftragstaktik* had mostly been abandoned by the Wehrmacht by 1944.[40]

The defenders of Normandy used a wide range of captured small arms, much of it Czech, Polish and Russian, as well as French and Belgian, all of which became a procurement nightmare for the Wehrmacht's quartermasters – who were routinely expected to furnish ammunition and spare parts for at least a dozen different rifles and machine-guns. While the German arsenal in France ensured that everyone had a weapon, this was achieved at the expense of uniformity, but there was never enough of anything to turn the tide of the campaign. As Leutnant Hans Heinz with the 916th *Grenadier-Regiment* of the 352nd Division reported, 'A large percentage of machine-guns in our bunkers were captured weapons that did not fit our standard ammunition.'[41]

It was a similar story with the panzer arm. By 1944, the Germans were fielding at least four kinds of main battle tank, plus the tracked turretless *Sturmgeschütz* (StuG) assault gun, an endless variety of tank destroyers and self-propelled guns, usually of 75mm calibre, based on outmoded German tank hulls, and those from captured nations; eight-wheeled armoured cars; and anti-tank weapons mounted in half-tracks.[42] To the tired, nervous Allied soldier in his foxhole, these were all 'panzers', or in the terminology of the day, 'hornets'.

British, American and Canadian planners in 1944 made comparisons with their own armoured units (mostly based on Shermans, though a few on Churchills or Cromwells), where everything was standardised, there was commonality of spare parts and uniformity of replacement: like for like, supplied immediately. Yet what the Allies failed to appreciate was that there was no such thing as a standard panzer division. The Germans had a theoretical template, long since disregarded: the June 1944 reality was that no two panzer formations were the same. To state, that 'weapon for weapon, tank for tank, even in 1944, its equipment decisively outclassed that of the Allies in every category save artillery and transport' as some historians have claimed, is to skate over the truth of the Wehrmacht in 1944.[43] Although the Allies (wrongly) assumed the Germans were awash with Tiger tanks and MG-42 machine-guns, the truth was more mundane. Most of its soldiers had lost any commitment to the war they might have possessed in 1940, and very few believed in final victory: they just wanted to go home. The Germans had some excellent designs but a bomb-ravaged manufacturing base; they often had an adequate (but never generous) supply of ammunition, but little means of moving it quickly to where it needed to be, while Allied airpower endangered every daylight move they made.

'A cross-Channel invasion would be not unlike a First World War battle,' thought Rommel: the Channel was a wide obstacle, an equivalent of No Man's Land, to be traversed before an assault on his trenches. He placed a premium on laying minefields and beach obstacles – from his experience of trying to penetrate the British Gazala Line in Libya. From 1941 to October 1943 OB West had overseen the laying of 1,992,895 anti-tank and anti-personnel mines. By May 1944, with Rommel's energy, this figure had increased to 6,508,330, with 517,000 foreshore obstacles strewn in three rows between the high- and low-water marks. Some 31,000 of them were fitted with mines, but Rommel wanted double this, in six rows along every threatened beach. Inland, two-metre-high stakes, sharpened at the end, were placed on likely glider and parachute drop zones, to destroy aircraft and impale paratroopers.[44] These all amounted to a re-creation of the barbed-wire entanglements of the Western Front, so well-known to the 1914–18 generation – yet these figures fell woefully short of Rommel's estimated need of *fifty million* mines.

Blumentritt, Rundstedt's chief of staff, remembered, 'Rommel did not smoke, and ate and drank but little. No landscape, no historic building, interested him; he was just a soldier. During a meal he would often take his pencil and a sheet of paper and sketch some new technical idea. Then he would hand it to his engineer general with the request that he would give his views on it the next morning before starting out.'[45] If he relaxed at all, he read Wild West novels by Karl May and detective stories, recommended to him by Hitler.[46] Rommel was an excellent illustrator and once stated if he had not been a soldier he would like to have been an artist. Blumentritt continued, 'Engineers, artillerymen and sailors were for the most part pressed into service as attendants, and Rommel was always requiring new proposals from them'. Not unlike Montgomery, he 'went to bed very early in order to be able to start off fresh again in the morning. As a rule he had one or two keepers of war records with him who took photographs on every possible occasion.'[47]

Rommel's technical solutions included steel girders welded together – 'hedgehogs' – and simple wooden stakes embedded in the sand with mines attached to detonate on contact with seaborne assault craft. Collectively these were known as the 'Rommelbelt', or Rommelspargel (Rommel's asparagus) – his sketches of obstacles made the beaches look like vegetable gardens. The Desert Fox also arrived at some of the same concepts of deception as the Allies to mask his true strength, as Vice-Admiral Ruge recorded on 11 May: 'Subordinated units received orders to quickly construct mock tanks in order to simulate fast mobile units and, as with dummy batteries, divert the enemy.'[48] This order arrived too late to affect the invasion, but might have had an impact had the Allies attacked later.

Beyond the various obstacles were reinforced-concrete structures which served many purposes: housing munitions, air defences, communications, headquarters staff, artillery observation and fire-direction, searchlights, power generators and personnel. Even unfinished, it was an enormous construction effort, with around five thousand bunkers completed by December 1942 and eight thousand by the following June. Between 1942 and 1944 they consumed 1.3 million tons of steel – for reinforcing rods, doors and cupolas – around five per cent of the Reich's total output in those two years, in addition to 17.3 million cubic yards of concrete.[49] By comparison, the six-year project to tunnel under the English Channel, completed in 1994, used 1.7 million cubic yards – exactly one tenth of the concrete poured into the Atlantikwall.[50]

The hard core of these defences was its coastal gun batteries, with 343 built along the French coast, housing 1,348 guns of 150mm calibre or greater. Each site comprised multiple bunkers housing the guns, ammunition, personnel quarters and local defences – all were surrounded by minefields. The larger gun sites incorporated small rail networks to convey ammunition from storage bunkers to the main cannon. Their assembled weaponry comprised Czech, French, British and Russian cannon captured during the victory years. In Salmuth's Fifteenth Army sector, some 495 separate artillery casemates and other emplacements had been constructed by June 1944, while Dollmann's Seventh Army area contained around two hundred, with a further sixty-five erected in the First Army's area, overlooking the Bay of Biscay.

In 1942 Rundstedt had rationalised the hierarchy of his coastal defences, ranging from *Festungen* (fortresses), accommodating large guns placed in reinforced concrete structures, via *Verteidigungsbereiche* (defence sectors), down to *Stützpunktgruppen* (strongpoint groups), comprising an individual *Stützpunkt* (strongpoint) or *Widerstandsnest* (resistance nest). All were designed to be self-sufficient enough to hold out for up to a week – though in the event, none would manage more than a day. There were some 250 basic types of bunker, of which the most common was the 'Tobruk', named after a pattern first employed in Libya. Essentially, a small concrete box with a circular hole from which a two-man machine-gun crew could emerge, hundreds of these Tobruks still litter the beaches of Normandy and Brittany which seventy-five years' worth of winter storms have generally filled with sand.

Other Tobruks housed light mortars or incorporated small tank turrets, taken from obsolete French or German panzers, whose guns added to the firepower – these are not evident today as post-war scrap metal dealers quickly stripped the *Atlantikwall* of all its steel fittings. Yet the time, resources and manpower required to build even one small Tobruk were in short supply. For example, a standard six-man bunker with room for ammunition required 650 cubic yards of concrete, twenty-five tons of steel reinforcing rods and another six tons of steel for protective doors, embrasures and ventilation shafts.[51]

The defences of the *Atlantikwall* included massive artillery gun emplacements set at intervals along the coast, like this one at Longues-sur-Mer. Now a museum, the site still houses its 155mm naval guns (left) which menaced the fleet off Omaha. More numerous were the humble, two-man Tobruk bunkers (right), housing a machine-gun or mortar. Dozens would be encountered off each invasion beach. Both examples used huge quantities of concrete, in short supply throughout the Reich. (Author's photographs)

In preparation, just as the Allies would do in southern England, Rommel had some of the coastal regions of Army Group 'B' evacuated, along with villages along the Caen Canal. At Bénouville, a café where Grenadiers Wilhelm Furtner, Erwin Sauer and Helmut Römer relaxed while guarding an important bridge, was one of the few properties left inhabited for the service it provided to his soldiers. The Allies were aware that from June 1943, the Germans had encouraged the removal of the population from the Channel coast and nearby inland towns, to allow the defenders to prepare their positions, though essential civilians such as doctors, teachers, farmers, local officials, priests and policemen – and anyone who served the Wehrmacht, such as restaurateurs and shop-keepers – were allowed to remain.

Ouistreham and Arromanches were partly emptied by order, and in May 1944 – clearly anticipating trouble – the local prefect of the *département* appealed for all children to be removed from the coast between Grandcamp and Ouistreham. By June, thousands had left Caen, Cabourg, Bayeux and Deauville and moved inland. All this suited Rommel, for the combined population of the Caen–Bayeux arrondissements (admin-istrative districts) alone was around 250,000, for whom he had no wish to be responsible should the fighting come to Normandy.[52]

It was Rommel's idea, too, to flood low-lying areas behind the Seventh Army's coast, turning them into inaccessible marsh – which would see the demise of hundreds of paratroopers on D-Day. Blumentritt recalled that Rommel also 'intended to flood wide stretches of land behind the Fifteenth Army, but out of consideration for the French population, Rundstedt rejected the idea' – which doesn't accord with the usual, sympathetic portrayal of the Desert Fox.[53] Building the fixed defensive positions was challenging – a never-ending series of missives from Berlin ordered that all bunkers had to be capable of self-defence; possess their own independent water supply, a kitchen, latrines, an electricity dynamo; be gas-proof; and be able to communicate with other bunkers by armoured field telephone wire. Much was robbed from the Maginot Line and other inland fortress systems, even the Siegfried Line, but as we have observed, the *Atlantikwall* project was still well short of Hitler's aspira-tions for it by June 1944.

As Oberstleutnant Fritz Ziegelmann, chief of staff of the 352nd Division, noted, 'Almost half of the battle installations were outmoded. In our division's sector alone, analysis showed that only fifteen percent of the cement fortifications were bomb-resistant and forty-five percent were shrapnel-proof. The availability of cement and dealing with four independent construction authorities were decisive issues.' He observed of the inter-service rivalry: 'Rommel's authority was not enough. Luftwaffe workers, Kriegsmarine, *Organisation-Todt* (the prime construction contractor), and our own fortress engineers worked side by side, often duplicating work. The Air Force built concrete positions while our infantry with their heavy weapons were in poor earth emplacements prone to flooding.'[54]

Slave labourers of the Third Reich's *Organisation Todt* (OT), named after its founder, Fritz Todt, an engineer and senior Nazi figure, were responsible for contract construction.[55] Some French workers measured what they built and trickled the information back to London. Others surreptitiously added tiny amounts of sugar to the wet concrete mix, which would fatally weaken its ability to withstand bombardment.[56] Blumentritt recorded that Rommel 'determined to requisition the [French] male population' to build the *Atlantikwall* and 'let it be known he would provide meals and wages if volunteers reported for this work. They did so and thus presented the remarkable picture of German troops and French civilians working together with great zeal' – a bizarre notion, as far removed from popular French memory as it is possible to be.[57]

Many labourers were also drafted in from the Netherlands, Belgium, Russia and Italy (which had changed sides in 1943); they received poor rations, minimal healthcare and their lives were considered cheap. In the rush to get the defences built, eventually Wehrmacht troops, too, were obliged to roll up their sleeves. At the beginning of 1944, on Rommel's orders, most military training ground to a halt, as all troops became involved in erecting beach defences, siting mines and uncoiling miles of barbed wire. After the war, Geyr thought 'the time and numerical strength of the troops was wasted on the construction of fortifications, at the expense of training'.[58]

It still comes as a surprise to many that the German Army in Normandy was predominantly horse-drawn. When Second Lieutenant Bob Sheehan of the US 60th Chemical Company (an outfit responsible for smoke weapons) breasted a rise over the dunes of Omaha on 7 June, he saw 'a mind-shattering sight that convinced me the war was as good as won. It was a dead horse. The poor animal was still attached to the wagon it had been pulling. The wagon was a German army one and covered with military symbols. Scattered around it lay the artillery shells it had been carrying. The mighty Wehrmacht, the inventors of the blitzkrieg, had been reduced to using ancient, slow fragile horses and carts to exist.'[59] We have already noted that 115,000 of them were assigned to OB West, with exactly 33,739 on the books of the Seventh Army on 1 March 1944, and another ten thousand arriving by 1 June.[60] These numbers came as a shock to Rommel, who, of course, had commanded the 7th Panzer Division in 1940 and the Afrika Korps in 1941–3, neither of which used horses.

Wehrmacht reductions in the number of artillery pieces and soldiers assigned to infantry divisions in France saw further cutbacks in their transport; by 1944 such formations averaged 3,100 horses and 370 trucks each, though even these figures were rarely achieved.[61] Of note is that the supposedly modern, mechanised Wehrmacht received 158,900 horse wagons in 1943 and 190,700 in 1944; generally of wooden construction with four spoked wheels and a canvas tarpaulin supported on beech or ash hoops, they perpetuated the Wehrmacht's reliance on nineteenth-century wagon trains – and would not have looked out of place in a Wild West movie. Unterveterinär Dr Reinhardt Schwartz was one of the Seventh Army's veterinary surgeons in Normandy. He was drafted into the German veterinary corps in 1941, being posted to Normandy in the autumn of 1943. He had to keep an eye on the horses of Richter's 716th, Kraiss's 352nd and Schlieben's 709th Divisions along the invasion coast. Once in Calvados, Schwartz recalled, he was summoned to the aid of some Wehrmacht artillerymen who were struggling to pull their guns along a rutted, muddy country lane with commandeered *cattle*, and was struck by the similarity of the scene to an image of the Thirty Years War.[62]

For its needs in Poland, France and Russia, the Wehrmacht had impounded many civilian trucks from within Germany and conquered lands, but they foresaw they would not be able to sustain them – and indeed most vehicle attrition in those campaigns was due to wear and tear, not combat.[63] A close look at photographs and newsreels of Wehrmacht vehicles in Normandy reveals a huge variety of manufacturers – Fiats from Italy, French Peugeots, Renaults and Citroëns, captured Fords and Bedfords from Britain, alongside Czech Tatras and Skodas, plus German VWs, Mercedes and Opels. Here was the nub of the Wehrmacht's motor transport problem: lack of spare parts meant it simply could not maintain such a varied vehicle fleet.

Hitler's economists similarly foresaw that shortages of oil, imported from Mexico and Russia before the war and Romania during it, or synthesised from domestic coal supplies, would not be easily overcome.[64] The Wehrmacht tried to adapt its vehicles to run on wood gas – but on 29 May 1944 Army Group 'B''s quartermaster observed that only 3,552 out of the truck fleet of 14,578 had been converted.[65] Rubber for tyres and other components was also in great shortage, a commodity Britain, via the empire, and the US had in relative abundance. Thus, the conscious German Army decision – even in pre-war plans dating back to 1936 – to shy away from the internal combustion engine and rely more on horses.[66]

Franco-German relations were a sore point during the occupation and have understandably remained a touchy issue since; as Obergefreiter Josef Brass, with the 352nd Division, observed: 'For the most part, the French people were amiable towards us. Some hated us and were probably in the Maquis, others supported us – the collaborators – but most were just concerned with getting on with everyday life.'[67] Oberleutnant Gustav Pflocksch, with the 716th Infantry Division and second in command of strongpoint WN.28 on Juno Beach, had only fond memories of his time in the area: 'Saint-Aubin was a happy place for us. The soldiers were young people. They had their girlfriends, and made music in private houses, they danced and they drank.'[68] Feldwebel Karl Schieck agreed; he had been posted from Paris – with some reluctance – to the Second Battalion of the 736th *Grenadier-Regiment* at Tailleville, a mile inland from Saint-Aubin. His job as a master tailor brought him into frequent contact with the local population: 'I was responsible for shopping and went to our neighbours, the Cassigneuls, and asked if they would be able to help us out in any way, with various kinds of foodstuffs. I bought milk at their farm, for example, and out of this there developed a friendly relationship.'[69] Rémy Cassigneul, then nineteen, who had been 'requisitioned' to plant anti-landing obstacles in the fields between Saint-Aubin and Tailleville, remembered the relationship and thought, '*Our* Germans were fine. We had no problems at all. Many of them were farmers and we were all the same age and traded information about farming methods.' His wife Marguerite recollected, 'There were two soldiers staying with us. They left in the morning, returned in the late afternoon, but my father told us that we should not say anything to them.'[70]

However, there was the ugly side of collaboration, as Feldwebel Eugen Griesser, with No. 5 Company of Major Friedrich von der Heydte's 6th *Fallschirmjäger-Regiment* – highly trained paratroopers all – recalled when going to visit a friendly farmer who had given them some freshly slaughtered rabbits: 'We went to pay him a visit and offer our collective tobacco rations in thanks. We found him lying in his living room with a crushed-in skull; his wife and children had disappeared. Someone, probably his murderers, had drawn the sign for the Resistance in charcoal on the wall.'[71]

The Wehrmacht's older female hosts soon became surrogate mothers, cooking and mending the clothes of the lonely young men, who promptly fell in love with their daughters. Sometimes the relationships were of a more commercial nature – *collaboration horizontale*, as it was called, whether paid or unpaid. Yet many young Germans chose not to see France in terms of available young women, as the youthful Grenadier Heinrich Böll wrote home to his parents: 'France is beautiful, full of humanity and sweetness, full of beautiful towns and villages and pleasant people, who are truly human – that's why it's all the harder to be a soldier here, totally excluded from this life.'[72]

The invasion caught the Seventh Army's Generaloberst Friedrich Dollmann by surprise. He was out of his depth, but those in the know understood he was a figurehead, and that the Seventh was really run by its chief of staff, the very able Generalmajor Max Pemsel. Based in Le Mans, Dollmann had taken over the Seventh Army in 1939 and with them had served on occupation duties in northern France since 1940. He was happy with his lot, fluent in French, not overanxious to serve in Russia, but had little experience of modern war and no understanding of armour – and made no effort to understand new techniques and weapon systems. The avuncular, pipe-smoking, almost casual Dollmann, renowned for slapping his subordinates on the back to put them at ease, was noticeably older than most of his fellows – sixty-two at the time of the invasion. He happened to be stationed in Munich (the cradle of Nazism) continuously from 1923–33 and thus saw the way the political wind was blowing. He had kept in private contact with the rising National Socialist movement, and joined the Nazis – illegally, as officers were supposed to be non-political – which advanced his career after Hitler came to power. Dollmann typified the old guard, with little or no combat experience, a love of the bottle, and an aversion to discomfort.

When Leutnant Raimund Steiner, a newly commissioned officer recovering from wounds in Russia, reported for duty in Caen on Christmas Day 1943 he immediately found himself 'ill at ease with the overtly-relaxed lifestyle of the German occupation there'. Posted to a gun battery behind Sword Beach, on arrival he found some of his fellow officers drunk, and French civilians seemingly doing all the administration: 'I was bewildered and unhappy about this. For me, such a reception after my Eastern front experiences was unbelievable – so much so, that I contemplated going back to my old mountain artillery unit.' As Oberleutnant Heyde of the 716th Division's artillery observed, 'There was always a certain discord between the original veterans of the 1940 France campaign and the in-coming recently-wounded from the Russian front hospitals. Many of us suffered withdrawal symptoms, which we did not or could not communicate.'[73]

As we have seen, over 1942–3 the Seventh Army lost its best troops to the Eastern Front, who were replaced by less fit, older conscripts, *Volksdeutsche* (ethnic Germans from the occupied east) and *Osttruppen* (Eastern European volunteers), the latter comprising twenty-three battalions or about seventeen per cent of Dollmann's infantry.[74] Given his lamentable lack of combat experience, Dollmann was the worst possible choice anyone could have made for senior command on a potential invasion coast. He shoulders the blame for the Seventh Army's lack of training, poor defences and hopeless reaction to D-Day. A Seventh Army with almost anyone else at its helm would have given the Allies a much harder fight on 6 June.

On 9 May 1944, Rommel 'drove to the Cotentin Peninsula, which seems to become the focal point of the invasion'. He visited the local corps commander, General Erich Marcks, in his headquarters at Saint-Lô, where he received briefings from him and Generalleutnant Edgar Feuchtinger of the 21st Panzer Division, and 'requested from him a precise reconnaissance of all roads suitable for troop transport and of all readiness areas for a combat group on the Cotentin. Feuchtinger figured four hours from Caen to Cherbourg for wheeled units and twenty-four hours for tracked units.' Using his military antennae, Rommel had thus anticipated some of the precise Allied plans, and planned to move extra forces closer to the Cherbourg area.

Erich Marcks, leading the 84th Corps, would have been a different proposition commanding the Seventh Army. In fact, he had been suggested as a possible commander of it by Rommel, replacing the indolent Dollmann, but as Marcks was of independent mind and antipathetic to the Nazi Party, Hitler preferred to keep Dollmann – a proven Nazi – in place, to the Seventh Army's detriment. As it was, Marcks' 84th

Corps was responsible for what would become the invasion coast; he also happened to agree with Rommel's forward defence proposals. Acknowledged to possess one of the finest minds in the German army, the austere, bespectacled and energetic Marcks had helped plan Operation Barbarossa, the invasion of Russia in 1941, but had lost a leg subsequently leading troops there. On recovery, he posted to command the 84th Corps, housed in a bunker complex located in the centre of Saint-Lô. Russia may have robbed him of a limb, but combat in Normandy would cost him his life – and a similar, terminal fate awaited four of his seven divisional commanders.[75]

Marcks' other formations included Generalleutnant Heinz Hellmich's 243rd Division, headquartered at Barneville on the Cotentin's west coast. Originally a static unit, it had been gradually upgrading its weaponry and mobility, and included eighteen-year-old Jürgen Horst, who served in No. 3 Company of Oberstleutnant Franz Müller's 922nd *Grenadier-Regiment*. He wrote home, 'our Russian shoe-mender is excellent and has expertly repaired my marching boots; however, we all have bicycles to get about the countryside. Parents! Do not concern yourselves about me, for we have good rations here, from the local farmers. We eat better than in the Reich!'[76]

After 6 June, Erich Marcks would also command the 77th Division around the old port of Saint-Malo, and a final unit – Rudolf, Graf (Count) von Schmettow's 319th Division in the Channel Islands. The latter would take no part in the battle for Normandy, and its three hundred bunkers housing long-range cannon of up to 305mm (twelve-inch) calibre, several miles of concrete anti-tank walls, and vast arsenal of equipment and impressive manpower would be left to fester until the islands' liberation on 9 May 1945. Some *Landser* had been stationed there so long that they joked they would soon receive cuff titles embroidered with the text the *König Eigene deutsche Grenadiere* ('King's Own German Grenadiers'). Major Hübner, Schmettow's chief of staff, noted his division was the largest in the German Army on 6 June 1944, with over twenty-six thousand very well-armed men under command – which might have tipped the balance in repelling the Allied assault.[77]

Erich Marcks had arranged to drive to Rennes at 0500 hours on Tuesday, 6 June. He was hosting war games in the city, three hours distant – the old Prussian concept of the *kriegsspiel* (war game) being a proven method of trying out tactics and military ideas, and still used today.

These followed on from an earlier *kriegsspiel* held in Rundstedt's head-quarters at Saint-Germain-en-Laye, in the western suburbs of Paris. This was in February, and Marcks had assumed the role of attacker. Back then, following landings on the north coast of the Cotentin, Marcks had occupied Normandy and Brittany, annihilating the Seventh Army. He had immediately warned Rundstedt and Rommel, 'without mincing matters', that he 'could carry out neither defence nor even a delaying action on the coast' with his meagre forces. Marcks stated he had 'emplacements without guns, ammunition depots without ammunition, minefields without mines, and a large number of men in uniform with hardly a soldier among them'.[78]

In Rennes on 6 June, he again anticipated playing the role of Eisenhower invading Normandy, and hoped the defenders would do better. This time the theme would be different: Marcks had asked one of his fellow corps commanders, *Fallschirmjäger* Eugen Meindl, a veteran of Norway, Crete and Russia, who led the two parachute divisions stationed in Brittany, to frame the exercise around airborne landings in northern France. A nightmare scenario, although they couldn't know the Allies had vastly insufficient capacity to transport all their para-troopers. But where might they land? We have seen that Antwerp, Paris and the Cotentin peninsula were the obvious worries, and the latter two would be the objects of Marcks' *kriegsspiel*. But alas, Erich Marcks' zeal worked against him, for the Rennes war games would ensure that many key division commanders and staff officers would be absent from their headquarters during the initial hours of 6 June.[79]

On 4 May Rommel had requested from OKW the transfer of the Panzer Lehr Division from Le Mans to Bayeux, the move of the 12th SS Panzer from Lisieux to Carentan, with Generalmajor Paul Tzschöckell's 7th *Werfer-Brigade* (one hundred – or six battalions – of multi-barrelled *Nebelwerfer* mortars, towed or mounted on half-tracks) moved from Beauvais to the southern Cotentin. With the 21st Panzer Division close to Caen, he would have three armoured formations ranged along the Calvados coast, and the area bristling with guns. However, the Inspector-General of Armour, Guderian, managed to stymie any movement of armour – and the mortar formation – closer to the Normandy coast, but on 26 May, General Wolfgang Pickert himself arrived at La Roche-Guyon with the welcome news that he was now under Rommel's command.

The Desert Fox had first noticed Pickert's powerful *III Flak-Korps* of anti-aircraft artillery on his arrival in France. With twelve thousand personnel, it was fully mobile and comprised around one hundred 88mm dual-purpose anti-aircraft/anti-tank cannon, and three hundred smaller-calibre weapons, scattered throughout France defending airfields and V-weapon sites. Once familiar with the terrain, and searching for troops and weapons with which to defend it, Rommel started to lobby Göring and OKW to release the *Flak-Korps* to him, for he wanted it to accompany his panzer divisions as they charged for the coast. Its high mobility could open a corridor, and keep it open under attack from the dreaded *Jabos* (*Jagdbomber* – Allied fighter-bombers) as his tanks thundered through. Rommel, alone of most commanders in the West, knew what it was like to be under aerial assault from the Allies.

Three of Pickert's *Flak* regiments would be committed to both sides of the Somme, whilst the fourth was assigned to the Bayeux–Isigny area.[80] As soon as the invasion was announced, Pickert assured Rommel, the entire *Flak-Korps* would be on the road to the threatened area with all haste. No sanction from Berlin would be required. Yet, as Pickert observed, 'the men were inexperienced in combat and had grown soft in the West'. As a veteran commander from the Eastern Front, Pickert immediately started to train and harden them in the arts of 'reconnaissance, camouflage, digging in, and gunnery against an aerial enemy, under ever-changing conditions'. As Pickert remembered immediately after the war, 'The officers were young, fresh and select, but had only little combat experience and no knowledge of cooperation with ground forces.'[81] In less than two weeks, his arrangements would be put to the test.

All these troops, however – the panzermen, anti-aircraft gunners, *Fallschirmjäger* and infantrymen – were not supermen. Most campaign histories of Normandy have gone out of their way to stress the Germans' expertise and how, man for man, they were superior to their Allied opponents in experience, equipment, doctrine and resolute loyalty to their Führer. Nothing could be further from the truth. Their average age was much higher than that of their opponents; they had moved away from the war-winning formulae of their earlier doctrine; many were inexperienced, or medically downgraded after service in Russia; a strikingly high proportion had been previously wounded in action; all were ill-equipped and unfit; some were not even German; and few had conducted much meaningful military training in 1944, in favour of strengthening their defences. As General Blumentritt observed of the divisions garrisoning the coastal areas, they possessed only 'two organic infantry regiments, weak artillery, and very limited mobility; most of the officers and men had been wounded and were of limited medical status.'[82] They were not so much 'chosen men' as 'broken men'.

While infantry formations were entirely reliant on horses – or bicycles – for mobility, even the much vaunted panzer units had a great disparity of truck and tank types that militated against their effectiveness, instead of adding to their performance. In 1946, Blumentritt concluded that most of the SS and army panzer outfits which fought in Normandy had 'been employed both in the East and in the West. They had been reorganised several times and were not the divisions of 1939–40.'[83] All German units soon shrunk with combat casualties, which were not replaced. Blumentritt noted of tank formations, 'the East swallowed those newly-manufactured panzers. Hence there were some panzer divisions without panzers, and others with thirty, fifty or sixty panzers. Eighty serviceable panzers were regarded as good.'[84] Just as the Allies exaggerated their achievements after the war, so the Germans tended to overstate their losses – attempting to demonstrate their ability to soldier on in extreme adversity; Blumentritt's observations of the panzer divisions may not be strictly accurate, but the gist of his comments was certainly true.

The German war machine was nothing like as dangerous as supposed by the Allies in 1944. Yet, during and after the Normandy campaign, Hitler's armies gained almost superhuman status. Today they continue to enjoy a surprisingly undiminished reputation. The June–August 1944 battles were shockingly violent and viciously fought, and from some of the more laudatory reports of German manoeuvres, the reader might be forgiven for thinking the Allies were the vanquished and the Wehrmacht and Waffen-SS the victors. So where does the idea of Nazi military superiority come from?

The effect of terrain worked a good deal in the Germans' favour and against the Allies, particularly the narrow roads winding through old villages, bocage hedgerows and stone-built Norman farmhouses – some medieval in origin with fortress-like architecture designed to keep out English pirates. All were tailor-made for ambushing opponents with automatic weapons and *Panzerfausts* (hand-held anti-tank weapons) of which the Reich's forces had a preponderance. The very many forests, woods and copses, all in full leaf, assisted the Germans in concealing much from Allied eyes. Hitler's armies also started with an awesome reputation, despite being outmatched by superior Allied staff work, logistics, firepower and air supremacy.

The stature of the Nazi war machine, forged in North Africa, Italy and on the Eastern Front, was still feared in 1944, though demonstrably hollowed out. It also helped Berlin that the Western Allies, particularly the 21st Army Group, were also excessively cautious, which played to the German inclination – despite their convoluted command – of tactical speed of reaction. Finally, it also suited many Allied commanders after the war to talk up the prowess of their opponents, making the achievement of subduing them all the greater. The same had occurred in Italy, where Field Marshal Sir Harold Alexander observed of the *Fallschirmjäger* defending Monte Cassino, 'the tenacity of these German paratroops is quite remarkable … I doubt if there are any other troops in the world who could have gone on fighting with the ferocity they have.'

It is also easy to forget that the German main effort was still on the Eastern Front: Normandy was a 'secondary show' for the Third Reich, but not so the Western Allies. The statistics confirm this: on 1 June 1944, Rundstedt had fifty-eight divisions in the West; elsewhere, however, lurked 228 divisions, mostly facing the Red Army.

In the midst of invasion fever, Rommel was making arrangements to leave his headquarters for Germany during the first week in June. He had some important business to attend to. First, a visit to his wife and son Manfred at their home in Herrlingen, midway between Stuttgart and Munich – Frau Lucie Rommel's birthday was on 6 June. Then the field marshal intended to drive on to Berchtesgaden and insist that Hitler release more reserves to Army Group 'B'. Rommel could have cited many reports highlighting the shortcomings within his command: a Seventh Army briefing note of 13 May had revealed the shocking statistic that it fielded an average of two anti-tank weapons per mile of front, while the Fifteenth Army possessed double that; neither were remotely sufficient for modern war.[85]

Whatever the motive, Rommel's departure amounted to a major lapse of judgement at such a crucial time. His journey – a full day to Herrlingen, a second day with his family, another day's motoring to Berchtesgaden, at least a day with Hitler before the two-day return leg to France, via the road networks of the day – promised to take him away from his duties for a minimum of six days and possibly longer.

In retrospect, it seems strange that such an important commander should waste several valuable days in his car – but with flying out of the question, and the Allies attacking every train, what else could he do? The weather worsened as he left La Roche-Guyon at 0700 hours on Sunday, 4 June, two staff officers riding with him. The conditions reassured him somewhat, forgetting his own maxim that the enemy would attack in poor weather. Nevertheless, Rommel felt it a perfect time to attend to important matters before the skies cleared and an invasion might again threaten. With Daniel at the wheel, his Horch sped down the gravel drive and took the road to Paris. The French capital also beckoned to General Edgar Feuchtinger of the 21st Panzer Division; with the inclement weather, he had decided to spend the night there, wooing his mistress.

As the cathedral bell of Notre-Dame de Saint-Lô tolled midnight on 5 June, a band of headquarters officers, led by the 84th Corps chief of staff, Oberstleutnant Friedrich von Criegern, and intelligence chief, Major Friedrich Hayn, knocked and entered Erich Marcks' room for a surprise celebration. They bore with them 'a cake and on a silver tray some excellent bottles of Chablis'. Their austere commander preferred soldier's rations and usually refused such luxuries, with the admonition 'I do not wish to see these again as long as our country is starving', but on this occasion relented, as Tuesday, 6 June 1944 was his fifty-third birthday.[86]

Meanwhile, many of Marcks' senior officers had already driven to Rennes for their war game, each ordered to bring two regimental commanders with them. Starting at 1000 hours sharp on 6 June, they would test the scenario of an Allied airborne assault on Normandy.[87]

3

Heading Over There

'Prime Minister King arrived today in a banker's suit to shake hands with a few of the men. He tried very hard to be pleasant but wound up instead being political. It is hard to imagine him leading anybody anywhere. Even more strange that anyone would want to follow.'

Brigadier Harry Foster, 7th Canadian Infantry Brigade,
18 May 1944

YANKS WERE NOT the only North Americans crossing the Atlantic to war in 1939–40. In contrast to the USA's studied isolationism, the Dominion of Canada chose to declare war on Germany a week after Britain, in September 1939. As Canada's Prime Minister, Mackenzie King, boldly announced, 'It is now left to the British peoples and those of British stock to save the world.' Partly to silence the strident French-Canadian opposition to the war, King promised there would be no conscription for overseas service. However, his country's pre-war militia was tiny: combined, the full-time army and reserves numbered fewer than fifty-five thousand, though in time this would grow thirteen-fold to 730,000. As soon as it was mobilised, the 1st Canadian Division was sent to England in December 1939 and based at Aldershot – the huge British garrison complex built in the Crimean and Boer Wars, with parade-ground discipline to match – which became Little Canada. Most of the 330,000 Canuck (the affectionate term for Canadians adopted during 1914–18) troops who at some stage deployed to Britain would pass through the old military town.[1]

Meanwhile, spurred by a sense of adventure and the opportunity to travel – the sort of motivations which through history have appealed to young men and women – Canada's youth flooded into the ranks of the part-time Militia, some fifty-eight thousand before the dawn of 1940. The government also introduced conscription for home service, without the obligation to serve overseas – and the army which fought in Europe would remain *almost* until the end a resolutely all-volunteer force.[2] Just before D-Day, on 18 May 1944 the Canadian premier inspected his troops in southern England, making a poor impression on the 7th Infantry Brigade's commander, Harry Foster, and his officers. However, Foster recorded, 'after everybody left I reprimanded two officers for giving him a horse laugh during his talk. He may not look or sound like much, but he is our Prime Minister and I will not tolerate disrespect.'[3]

The Royal Canadian Navy was born in the Second World War; from six ocean-going vessels and 3,500 men, it would expand to become the third-largest navy in the world with 115,000 men and women in uniform and 434 RCN warships. Vital in winning the Battle of the Atlantic, 1944 would see 121 vessels – over a quarter of its fleet, crewed by 6,676 personnel – supporting the invasion of Normandy.[4] The Royal Canadian Air Force had become an independent force only in 1938, when it numbered 150 officers, fewer than a thousand other ranks, and operated thirty-one obsolete aircraft; it was effectively an auxiliary arm for land and naval units. By the war's end, the RCAF had trained 260,000 personnel; Canuck volunteer pilots fought in the Battle of Britain and would supply seventeen squadrons for the RAF's Second Tactical Air Force (2nd TAF) in France. Meanwhile, their country supplied Britain, principally by sea, with much-needed food, while making ammunition, fourteen thousand aircraft, 3,500 tanks and 800,000 military vehicles using American mass production methods and tooling.[5]

New Brunswicker Raymond Hickey grew up in a religious family and to no one's surprise was ordained a Roman Catholic priest in 1933. In June 1940, he was asked to become chaplain of the North Shore Regiment. He agreed, though at thirty-five felt he was rather old for the post. He sailed with the battalion from Halifax to Liverpool in 1941 and trained with them in England for the next three years in readiness for Normandy; Hickey saw his job as keeping morale high and coached the regimental team to become baseball champions of the Canadian forces in 1942.

An astute observer of the war, he recorded the impression an air raid made on the Canadian arrivals to Britain.

Night after night, just as darkness was falling, up would go the awful wail of the sirens ... In all directions people would run to cold cement air raid shelters; on would go the searchlights that swept the sky like giant northern lights; from a distance would come the unmistakable *ou, ou, ou* of German planes; with a deafening roar our anti-aircraft guns would open up – you huddled as small as you could, covered your head, held your breath and waited for bombs that came with a terrifying whistle, and shook the earth with an awful blast and covered the place with death and destruction.[6]

Vancouver-born James Montgomery Doohan was one of those who volunteered for the Canadian militia early in 1940, aged twenty. He was surprised that he had to supply his own black boots and dismayed to find First World War equipment in widespread use. Almost immediately he found himself in a field battery of Canada's 2nd Infantry Division and volunteered for overseas service. Soon commissioned, he spent much of his first year training before his unit arrived in England with the 3rd Division. He spent three uneventful years based at Aldershot, progressing by 1944 to the role of gun position officer with the 13th Field Regiment, while their wheeled 25-pounders had been replaced with American-made 105mm guns on a Sherman tank chassis. For aerial defence, their armoured vehicle mounted a Browning machine-gun in a circular structure on the right-hand side that resembled a church pulpit, so for ease, Lieutenant Doohan and the rest of the Canadian gunners dubbed their M7 105mm Howitzer Motor Carriages, simply 'Priests'.

Doohan's 3rd Canadian Division was experiencing a frustrating war, for their comrades of the 2nd Division had already fought at Dieppe in response to governmental pressure to see their men in action at the earliest opportunity. Two Victoria Crosses were won by Canadians during their 19 August 1942 raid on the French port (Operation Jubilee), the only major land assault on occupied France prior to Normandy. However, it sustained huge casualties, and of the mostly Canadian 6,086 who landed, 3,367 – fifty-five per cent – were killed, wounded or captured. (Fifty US Rangers had also landed, three of whom were killed, including Louisiana native Lieutenant Edward Loustalot, the first American to be killed in ground combat by German forces.) The Allies put a brave face on Dieppe. Louis Mountbatten's official line, then and subsequently, was that 'important lessons about amphibious operations and likely German reactions to them were learnt, and for every soldier who died at Dieppe, ten were saved on D-Day'.

Institutions will always seek to put a positive gloss on a major tragedy, and to suggest that Dieppe was in any way successful as a vital stepping stone to Normandy is akin to alleging that the *Titanic* disaster was an important milestone in passenger ship design. Notwithstanding the bravery of those present, Mountbatten's observations were in self-justi-fication of a bungled and deeply flawed plan mounted by his Combined Operations. Most of the lessons learned about attacking a strong-defended port were self-evident. When Canada's other division based in England – the 1st, accompanied by the 1st Armoured Brigade, and later the 5th Armoured Division – set sail from England to fight in Sicily and Italy from July 1943, Doohan and his mates must have felt the war was passing them by. They were unaware that their formation had already been selected for the assault wave in France, whenever that was to take place.

Born to Jewish parents in Toronto, Barnett 'Barney' Danson was acutely aware of the threat Hitler's Germany posed to democracy. It was after the 1938 Munich crisis that he decided to join his local militia unit, the Queen's Own Rifles of Canada – the nation's oldest regiment – but had to wait until his eighteenth birthday in February 1939 before he could be officially sworn in. Danson enjoyed the training and lectures every Monday and Wednesday, and weeks away at the military camp in Niagara. May 1939 saw him as part of the guard of honour to greet King George VI and Queen Elizabeth in Toronto. He remembered 'a mounted escort of the Royal Canadian Dragoons and the Governor General's Horse Guards had placed itself in front (backsides facing us). Loyally and obediently we presented arms and the horses proceeded to respond rudely to the excitement of the moment'. Mobilised in June 1940 with the 8th Brigade of the 3rd Division, Danson and the Queen's Own sailed overseas in July 1941 escorted by 'a horizon full of First World War American four-stacker destroyers [these were fifty ex-US Navy warships being transferred to Britain under Lend-Lease].[7] With us were many American civilians bound for [Northern] Ireland to build airbases, and together we became players in truly the largest floating crap game ever assembled.'[8]

Later on, the Canucks would depart for pre-invasion training in Scotland before returning to Hampshire in September 1943. Canadian officers censoring their troops' mail noted how 'relations between British civilians and Canadian troops continue to be very cordial, with not one adverse comment [from our men about the British] seen'.[9] This was in contrast to the Canadians' view of GIs, who seemed to them to be 'brasher, rowdier and wealthier', which inevitably drew the British and Canadian troops closer together. Stephen Dyson, a British Churchill tank crewman, recalled: 'Other than isolated bits of friction caused by Canucks up to their eyeballs in booze, we generally got on very well with them; although their vernacular on some things had a different connotation to ours, which led to misunderstandings at times.'[10] Such cooperation would prove vital on the battlefield, where both armies in any case were completely interchangeable, wearing the same scratchy woollen battle-dress and distinctive 'soup bowl' Tommy helmets pioneered in the First World War, and operating with the same ranks, doctrine, equipment, weapons, artillery, calibres of ammunition, vehicles and staff systems. Indeed at a glance, until an accent was heard or the distinctive 'Canada' shoulder flash was seen, they appeared *exactly* the same.

Until their arrival on Britain's shores, Americans only knew of their future wartime ally through the broadcasts of Ed Murrow, CBS's star reporter based in London from 1937. He had pioneered live broadcasting during Hitler's occupation of Austria in 1938 and electrified American radio audiences with his reports at the height of the Blitz in his programme *London After Dark*. With nightly bombing raids, Murrow echoed the tension of the era – that Londoners might not necessarily see each other the next morning – with his enduring sign-off catch-phrase, 'Good night, and good luck'.[11] From 2 January 1942 this general ignorance of Britain began to change with the signing of orders acti-vating the US Eighth Air Force, overseen by the red-headed Major General Carl Spaatz, then in his fiftieth year. A native of Boyertown, Pennsylvania, and formerly named Spatz, he had a paternal grandparent who still spoke German, which induced Mrs Spatz to add another 'a' in 1937 to make their surname look less Germanic and more Dutch – and made sure it was pronounced 'Spotz'. However, everyone knew him as 'Tooey', because of his similarity to another red-headed West Point cadet named Toohey. Spaatz was already familiar with England, having been a military attaché posted to London in 1940. He had even been arrested 'dressed in crumpled tweeds, having wandered into a restricted area whilst witnessing an aerial dogfight near Dover'. Thereafter he signed himself into British military establishments as 'Colonel Carl Spaatz, German spy'.[12]

Within days the US Air Forces in the British Isles (USAFBI) had come into being, and staff officers began arriving in London and at RAF Bomber Command's headquarters at High Wycombe. Under Spaatz, Brigadier General Ira C. Eaker, another German-American of Alsatian ancestry, headed up VIII Bomber Command. At the same time, fighter, Air Support (for reconnaissance, transport and tactical bombing) and Service Commands were established. Spaatz himself arrived on 15 June, creating the Eighth's headquarters at Bushy Park, west of London. Their work would soon trigger the flow of hundreds of thousands of US airmen and their aircraft into Britain to take the fight to the Third Reich.

Spaatz's personnel also received their copies of *Instructions for American Servicemen*:

> Don't be misled by the British tendency to be soft-spoken and polite. If they need to be, they can be plenty tough. Sixty thousand British civilians – men, women, and children – have died under bombs, and yet the morale of the British is unbreakable and high. A nation doesn't come through that, if it doesn't have plain, common guts. The British are tough, strong people, and good allies. The British have theaters and movies (which they call cinemas), as we do. But the great place of recreation is the pub. You will be welcome in the British pubs as long as you remember one thing. The pub is 'the poor man's club', the neighbourhood or village gathering place, where the men have come to see their friends, not strangers.[13]

That summer, one of Spaatz's men, Lieutenant Will Seaton Arnett, flew with his squadron of B-17 Flying Fortress bombers across the North Atlantic in a seven-day staged flight. They had rest stops in Maine, Labrador, Greenland, Reykjavik and Stornoway on the Isle of Lewis, before landing at Prestwick – about thirty miles south-west of Glasgow. Pretty much hugging the Arctic Circle, this was one of two routes taken by all larger American aircraft, the smaller ones being shipped across with other air force personnel. Arnett's initial impressions, however, were not rosy, as his first letter home from Scotland observed:

> I thought I'd seen everything but this place takes the cake. The people are so backward it is pitiful. This seems to have been a wealthy place at one time. The homes and buildings are just like the pictures. The streets are narrow and very crooked, bicycles are the main means of transpor-

tation. There are very few cars and traffic is left-handed; the buses are two-deckers and very old. Scotland is almost as far north as Greenland, so it is pretty cold. The people of Scotland are very friendly but their language is unusually strange and hard to understand.[14]

In Norfolk the accent was equally hard to comprehend, as Captain Philip Pendleton Ardery, with the 389th 'Sky Scorpions' Bomb Group based at RAF Hethel, Norwich, recalled: 'all in all, I liked England. My first contact with a real Englishman was when this old man come ridin' along on his bicycle. He stopped and said: "Hey, ere mite" – we could hardly understand him. He wanted to know if we'd like him to do our laundry. We were tickled to death to let him do it for just a few shillings.'[15] Also flying the northern route in a twin-engined B-26 Marauder medium bomber was Baltimore-born Staff Sergeant Clarence Elmer 'Cy' Cyford. He had enlisted in the Army Air Corps in 1940, aware the US might be going to war, and 'wanted to be a part of it'. Initially training as a spotter on anti-submarine planes, Cyford transferred to the 555th Squadron of the 386th Medium Bomb Group. 'The Group was nicknamed "the Crusaders" and we were "the Red Devil Squadron". We crossed the Atlantic in a brand-new B-26 along the northern route via Greenland and Iceland to Scotland. I flew as mechanic and top-turret gunner, whilst our group's entire ground crew crossed on *Queen Elizabeth*. When we heard of their sailing conditions, I'm sure we had the better deal,' recalled Cyford, who would fly seventy-two combat missions in B-26s.[16]

Lieutenant Russell Chandler, Jr also flew across the Atlantic in his twin-engined C-47 'Gooney Bird' transport. Flying had been a childhood dream, and he had qualified as a pilot in 1943. 'The Brits called them *Dakotas* – I liked that better than the *Skytrain* designation we used.' Chandler and his squadron followed the southern route, 'from Miami, to Puerto Rico, Trinidad, British Guiana, and on to Recife, Brazil. Then we took the long hop to Wideawake Airbase on Ascension Island in the middle of the Atlantic, and on to Freetown, Sierra Leone; next to Marrakesh, Morocco; before heading north to England, more than twelve thousand miles and about seventy hours of flying time'. On arrival Chandler was assigned to the 44th Squadron, 316th Troop Carrier Group (Ninth Air Force), flying out of RAF Cottesmore near Nottingham.[17]

Also taking his four-engined B-24 on the southern route was Missouri-born Lieutenant Curt M. Vogel. He had married and started a law degree before Pearl Harbor intervened to disrupt his life plan. Vogel enlisted before the draft and qualified as a pilot in 1942, but remembered the deaths of two colleagues in training. On returning to their barracks room, 'all of the belongings of these two cadets were gone and the beds were realigned so that it appeared that they had never been there. This same procedure was also followed while flying combat.'

Known as 'Old Man Vogel' – he was twenty-seven – in January 1944 the pilot flew his heavy bomber from Florida, where 'We were handed an envelope just prior to take off, marked "Secret Orders" and we were not to open it until one hour into the flight to Waller Field, Trinidad ... it told us we headed for: "Eighth Air Force, England". It could have been China–Burma, Africa or Italy. Since I announced this on the intercom, I do not know how the other nine crew members reacted, but each of them knew the 8th Air Force was suffering very heavy losses in the air over Europe.'

From Trinidad they flew to Natal, Brazil. Whilst there, they named their B-24 'Rough Riders', after President Theodore Roosevelt's regiment: 'the name was arrived at after a lot of discussion by the crew; some of them probably would have liked something more current, but I had emphatically stated, *no nude or semi-nude girls*'. Their next stop was Dakar, French West Africa, where they were guarded by 'Senegalese native troops carrying long-bayoneted rifles, wearing red fez caps, blue pants and khaki shirts'; then it was on to Marrakesh, and finally Valley airbase on Anglesey, north Wales. Soon they made their way to RAF Horsham St Faith, near Norwich, home of the 458th Bomb Group.[18]

Some of their B-24 colleagues ran out of fuel over the Bay of Biscay and were obliged to land on the first flat field they found near Land's End. 'Immediately they were surrounded by curious farmers bearing pitchforks and asking questions. This terrified the crew, who – unable to identify the broad Cornish accent – assumed they had landed in German-occupied France, and drew their .45-inch Colt pistols to defend themselves.' Fortunately for all, the large stars on the wings and fuselage proclaimed them as Allies and they were soon ensconced in the local pub.[19]

Lieutenant Malcolm Brannen of the 82nd Airborne Division wrote home to his sister of Nottinghamshire,

The country here is very much like USA, especially New England – green lawns and lots of trees and pretty brick houses ... There are loads of stores (called shops, I think) of all kinds and types – but we can't buy anything because all is rationed. Food is scarce – and so is beer and liquor, sweets and smokes. I see more buses – double-deckers and singles, trolleys than I ever saw in the USA. There are very few taxis and very, very few private cars. The blackouts are *real* ones – not just practice – and have been going on for five years. According to the Sheriff [i.e. Nottingham – his way of getting round the censor] that is one reason that he hasn't caught Robin Hood.[20]

England's wartime travails were evidenced to newly arrived GIs by the 'British queue'; but it irked their hosts that most Americans had no idea what a queue was or how to behave in one – although both sides soon found queuing was an ideal way to strike up a friendship, and if necessary sever it at the end. Americans, on the other hand, arrived with equally preconceived notions, courtesy of Hollywood, of the British as complete automatons to class and privilege; that they rarely thought for themselves, possessed no initiative, and would stop every ten minutes for a tea break. 'The power of the old school tie in this great stronghold of democracy is a dangerous matter,' thought Lieutenant Robert S. Raymond, an American volunteer in the RAF (like LeRoy Gover) who would complete thirty missions with Bomber Command, before switching to his own USAAF. He was convinced 'General Rommel would never have risen above the rank of NCO in the British Army'.[21] Both governments therefore put huge effort into improving relations between their respective armies and the civilian population. Two publications were astutely distributed to all secondary schools by the Ministry of Information. One was a twenty-four-page paperback written by BBC playwright Louis MacNeice, *Meet the US Army*; the other, a specially commissioned edition of *A Brief History of the United States*, containing an introduction by John Winant, US ambassador.[22]

Winifred Pine was a Royal Navy Wren stationed at Kingswear, near the Britannia Naval College, Dartmouth, then occupied by a US naval unit. 'Our Wrennery was on a hill overlooking the River Dart, and each morning we would wake up to the sound of Glenn Miller or the Andrews Sisters coming through their loudhailer system,' she recalled. 'They were always curious about us, as we were probably the first Englishwomen they had met. We found them to be courteous and well mannered. I mainly remember the Americans for being extremely kind and generous to the children of Dartmouth, as they would often hire a hall in town to entertain them. The children would always leave with Hershey chocolate bars and other goodies. They also put on parties for us, and were

Americans and their habits were remote to most Britons until the 'friendly invasion' of GIs – mostly the US Eighth Army Force until late 1943. The British only knew the USA through Hollywood, while the GIs had to revise their view that the average Britisher lacked initiative and were part of a class-ridden society. Helped along by the stereotypical view that the islanders stopped every ten minutes for tea, both sides – especially a whole generation of children – found that tea breaks were the quickest way of breaking down their mutual suspicions. (Getty Images)

horrified at the size of our rations. They of course had all of their rations brought over from the United States, and it was at their parties that I first encountered Spam and hot dogs.'[23]

Hospitality invariably included dances in town and village halls; near the ports, there was an endless stream of welcome-to-Britain 'disembarkation dances'. If run by the local community, these tended to be heavily stage-managed at first, where the invited females were assessed by the local vicar and his middle-class colleagues, to ensure they were the 'right class of girl', ones who would not lead the GIs astray and were known *not* to sleep around. One nineteen-year-old remembered attending many camp dances, for which she was vetted by the Red Cross, and found them 'highly decorous and strictly chaperoned'.[24] At GI army and air bases, such pettifogging restrictions lapsed, but US venues also witnessed lavish parties held for neighbourhood youngsters, overflowing with candy and presents. For example, the 392nd Bomb Group at RAF Wendling in Norfolk hosted Christmas festivities for 160 orphans, refugees and local schoolchildren; they were conveyed to the base in US Army transport, shown the inside of a B-24, serenaded by the base orchestra, played movie cartoons of Popeye and Mickey Mouse, and served tea, cakes and fruit jelly. Santa Claus then awarded each child a wrapped festive present and candy, bought with money donated by GIs; 'with full stomachs and full of Christmas spirit the children were piled back into the trucks and taken home', remembered one of the organisers.[25]

Britons were quickly besotted with the idea of the USA and its inhabitants, but their only knowledge was furnished by Hollywood. A BBC poll of early 1942 observed that its respondents 'are simply without opinions of any kind, or even prejudices, about anything *so remote as America*'. Such ignorance led *The Times* to report on 4 August 1942 that the new visitors were 'Friendly and simple, rather than Hollywood stars or two-gun Texans with five-gallon hats. Their manners were good, though a little different from those in Britain. Americans were perhaps a little quicker on the uptake, but they made friends more easily.'[26] For Britons, this was their first sight of pinball machines, jukeboxes (both adjusted to operate with British coins) and jeeps, whilst most 1940s children were introduced to the dubious delights of peanut butter, candy, chewing gum and Coca-Cola by these exotic visitors.

'Got any gum, chum?' became a common street call to any American, who must have wished the stuff had never been invented. To this, the invariable GI reply was 'Got any sisters, mister?' Sergeant Forrest Pogue recalled being 'engulfed by a mob of urchins' yelling the irksome phrase and being rescued by an old man 'who ordered them away, asked my pardon for the begging and expressed shame because English children "didn't used to be like that". Although he himself was ragged and poor, he had his pride for London and England.'[27] Pogue, later a distinguished official US historian of the war, remembered being accosted by a little lad near London's Tower Bridge. 'First he wanted candy, then in order, gum, shoulder patches, and uniform buttons ... he showed his knowledge of history by asking if I were a Rebel or Yankee ... Our conversation was brought to an abrupt halt when a girl of about twenty approached, bade him on his way, and asked for a cigarette for herself. She was not interested in history.'[28]

4

The Commandos

'We won't do much talking until we've done more fighting. After we've gone, we hope you'll be glad we came.'
Brigadier General Ira C. Eaker on taking command of the
Eighth Air Force in England, December 1942

F OR AMERICANS SERVING far away from home, Christmas 1942 was a difficult time, and as many as possible were given leave. Posters around their camps suggested they spend the day with their civilian hosts: 'Fill the chairs left empty by British fighting men – GIs, spend your Christmas at home with a British family.' Those who took up invitations that first 'Yank Christmas' were given special ration packs to share, containing rare or unknown commodities such as Spam (US spiced ham, invented in 1937), fruit juice, evaporated milk, canned peaches, bacon, sugar, rice and peas. Coffee, too, arrived with the visitors, and not just in tins of the usual beans, but in the form of freeze-dried granules from K-ration packs – the nation's first introduction to Nescafé instant coffee.

Some more advice from the *Instructions for American Servicemen*:

One thing to be careful about – if you are invited into a British home and the host exhorts you to 'eat up, there's plenty on the table', go easy. It may be the family's rations for a whole week spread out to show their hospitality. The British know that gasoline and food represent the lives of merchant sailors. And when you burn gasoline needlessly, it will seem to them as if you are wasting the blood of those seamen – when you destroy or waste food you have wasted the life of another sailor.[1]

GIs only realised how fortunate they were when faced with British home front rations of tea tablets with National Dried Milk; grated carrots to replace fruit in cakes; 'a gray, glutinous, fishy meat that might once have been a whale; powdered eggs which yielded a dull yellow, rubbery-like apology for the real thing; meat containing cereal that tasted like sawdust, and milk heavily diluted with water', as one disgusted GI noted.[2] Staff Sergeant William B. Dowling was a crew chief with the 578th Bomb Squadron based near Norwich who remembered, 'At the end of the war,

Although a carefully managed publicity shot, this image echoed the truth that most Britons volunteered to welcome American servicemen into their homes. The three million visitors brought coffee, candies and canned goods not seen on British tables, and – far from their native land – received the warmth of family friendship in return. Many households stayed in touch with their temporary guests long after the war. (Getty Images)

I rode back to Massachusetts on a B-24. The first thing I did when I hit the ground was to give it a kiss; it was good to be back after two years away – the Red Cross greeted us with donuts and fresh cold milk: I'd forgotten it existed, because the only milk we saw in England was powdered and I got so tired of it.'[3]

Once word spread of the extra GI Christmas food on offer, so many invitations were extended to Americans that one base commander recorded receiving at least fifty invitations for every one available man. With the food, GIs introduced their own festive traditions, including Christmas crackers, while in return the Americans were offered Advent calendars and candles. Despite the Nescafé, the *Instructions for American Servicemen* warned, 'the British don't know how to make a good cup of coffee – but you don't know how to make a good cup of tea. It's an even swap.'[4]

Another way into an English home was through getting their laundry done in exchange for rations. As Nottingham resident Harry Blankly recalled, 'Those American boys were a godsend. With the shortages of food we had, just imagine getting those chocolates and cigarettes; they brought their washing powder, soap and clothes to be done and came round later to pick it up.'[5]

By the end of 1942, around sixty thousand of Carl Spaatz's USAAF personnel were building airbases in Britain, the majority situated within the old Saxon kingdom of East Anglia. Bulging out into the North Sea, with its flat, open fields, the region proved the perfect springboard for endless streams of heavy bombers to attack German-held Europe and inevitably became the cannon's mouth for the US Eighth Air Force. Within two years, with seventy-one thousand GIs stationed in Suffolk (population 400,000 and another of East Anglia's five counties), one in six residents was American. When the Yanks occupied Wiltshire in May–June 1944, the ratio would be one in three. Bill Ong, an American arriving to build one of East Anglia's many airfields, was shocked 'at the sight of all the bomb damage and the whole atmosphere of dirt and dinginess around the docks. Maybe it was the wintry weather, the cold gray days, no leaves on the trees, no sun. I wondered why the Germans wanted England at all.'[6] Yet Ong was left wondering whether 'Americans at home could have taken the punishment that the British had'.

Staff Sergeant Robert S. Arbib, Jr, of the 820th Engineer Aviation Battalion, was also in the airfield-building business. He observed that his unit had been trained to build temporary airstrips for fighter aircraft near the front line, not concrete airbases for heavy bombers in England. They were surprised to find that they had first to live under canvas before constructing their own wooden barracks. Arbib recalled: 'my first taste of austerity travel on the railways of Britain came the day following our arrival in Scotland. The date was 18 August 1942 and the newspapers were full of the first American air raid on France. As the train pulled out of the station the sky was growing dark. We could see nothing, not even a single light. This was our first experience with the blackout. We marvelled at its completeness. We slept on the floor. I was stiff and bruised when we arrived.'[7]

The greatest concentration of GIs in the UK was initially within a thirty-mile radius of Norwich, county town of Norfolk, where around fifty thousand air and ground crew alone were stationed at eighteen airfields. One of them was RAF Wendling, where Sergeant Bernard Sender worked as a turret mechanic on the B-24s of the 392nd Bomb Group. He remembered of his English home for two years, 'Wendling was just a stop in the middle of the Norwich-to-Kings Lynn road, twenty miles from either end. The airfield itself had been a quiet little farm: what we found when we got there was an undertaker, a church, a general store and a pub. We lived in Quonset huts almost two miles away from the aircraft; sometimes we walked, sometimes rode to work on bicycles. As winter drew near, the sun went down earlier; let me tell you, it could be bitter cold at night over there, and we did all our work outside. You couldn't put spotlights up either, because we never knew when Jerry was coming around.'[8]

In total, of the more than 140 UK airfields constructed or improved by the USAAF, Air Transport Command operated seven, while over 385,000 personnel of the Eighth and Ninth Air Forces occupied the others, mostly in eastern England.[9] They would fly a third of a million sorties from these bases during their thousand days of being stationed in Britain. Each base tended to house a bomb or fighter group of three squadrons, initially amounting to thirty-six aircraft, plus a few spare. These establishments were huge, with up to three thousand flying and ground personnel – ranging from cooks, bakers, welders and drivers to medics, mechanics, armourers, ordnance and instrument repair technicians, plus aircrew – working on an average airbase of five hundred acres. They exaggerated the impact of Americans by swamping nearby towns. Besides them, the personnel roster of the 493rd Bombardment Group, stationed at RAF Debach in Suffolk, included Bobbie the headquarters cat; Boop, a ring-tailed monkey; and Dick, Esther and Nick, all dogs and mascots of the 860th, 861st and 863rd Bomb Squadrons. The US Twelfth and Fifteenth Air Forces also stationed units in the UK, but in 1943 moved their operations to the North African and Mediterranean theatres.

The airmen were followed from 1942 by over ten thousand men of the US Navy's Construction Battalions (USNCBs – known as 'Seabees', after their initials), who erected coastal bases throughout south Wales and all along Britain's south coast. Later they would prepare and man the invasion's floating harbours.[10] US sailors manning warships also trickled into the UK and by 1944 they would number 122,000, serving in a wide variety of shore bases, naval aircraft, landing craft and warships. The US Coast Guard, too, made an important contribution, crewing troopships, twelve LSTs and twenty-four LCIs, as well as a flotilla of sixty small, wooden cutters, which would cruise off all five invasion beaches as search-and-rescue craft, and were known as the 'Matchbox fleet'. The attack transports USS *Samuel Chase* and *Joseph T. Dickman* and the Utah headquarters ship USS *Bayfield* would be amongst the many Coast Guard-manned vessels off Normandy on D-Day.

The New Year of 1943 brought hundreds of thousands more Yanks, mostly ground forces. Forty of the eighty-nine US divisions deployed in combat passed through Britain; four in 1942, nine in 1943, and the remaining twenty-seven in 1944. Including air force and service troops (principally the Quartermasters Corps of supply personnel), by May 1945 this had totalled 2,914,843 American servicemen and -women arriving in the UK by sea, plus over 100,000 more by air.

They appeared with their jitterbug dances and the unmissable tones of Glenn Miller's trombone. Volunteering for Air Force duty whilst at the height of his fame in America and Britain, Miller himself was credited with raising forty-nine US Army bands and toured the USA with his own for a year before arriving in England with his musicians. Although for most, Glenn Miller *was* wartime Britain, he only started entertaining with his sixty-two-strong troupe including support staff on 14 July 1944, but reached audiences in the millions.

Whilst transatlantic musical influences were slowly infiltrating the UK, notably jazz and blues, the regular dances held at American bases spread the popularity of swing, boogie-woogie and bebop, genres generally disdained by the BBC, thus giving them a popular edge. Many GIs could play an instrument and units quickly formed bands, playing the latest jives from the US, which speedily bridged the military–civilian divide in England. The 508th Parachute Infantry, billeted in Nottingham, for example, boasted a twelve-piece dance band which played all over town. Others formed vocal groups, which sang at concerts but also in local churches. One facet of American life that surprised many Brits was the high proportion of churchgoing GIs.

Bill Coughlan, a young evacuee living in Camborne in Cornwall, recalled,

> I had the opportunity to hear all the black choirs from their segregated units. The Cornishmen sang in a stately, serious, hymn-like way but, in complete contrast, the black Americans had all the rhythms of Scott Joplin, George Gershwin and the Jazz age. The movements of their bodies in time with their voices turned the Methodist chapels where they performed from sedate places of nonconformity into palaces of Swing. Cornwall being a musical place, the black GIs were not only praised for their performances but were offered the food special to Cornwall. We noticed their good manners and I know now that the surprise on their faces confirmed that they did not expect white people to treat them as equals and brothers.[11]

British civilian women on the whole welcomed Americans – especially if they traded on access to Glenn Miller's orchestra – and benefited from their largesse, soon learning that with the candy and Coca-Cola came cigarettes and nylon stockings. Nylons (introduced by DuPont in 1939) were a welcome replacement for silk stockings, then unobtainable since Britain's imports of silk were diverted entirely into making parachutes.[12] Metal zip fasteners for clothing and Ray-Ban aviator sunglasses (sold to the American public since 1937) arrived at the same time.

Uniformed British females were not immune from Yankee charms either, as a US Army doctor noted from his jeep: 'we passed some ATS [Auxiliary Territorial Service, Britain's uniformed women's army] girls, and they whistled and yelled at us, just as much as the males had flirted with passing girls back in the States'.[13] Wren Margaret Seeley, based at the 'stone frigate' of HMS *Squid*, was often on the receiving end of friendly whistles and cheers as truckloads of GIs passed her bicycle. 'They threw us Mars bars and chocolate. It was a question of maintaining your dignity and pedalling on, or dismounting and grovelling about to pick up the candy – which of course we did because we were on rations.'[14]

Mavis Boswell was a Wren stationed in Cornwall who observed that because of the blackout, most servicemen carried small flashlights: 'Soldiers often kept a torch in their hip pockets and I remember when dancing ballroom style with a nice officer, getting quite embarrassed not realising it was a torch in his pocket! This gave rise to our joke of the moment: a Wren asked a GI, "Do you mind taking that torch out of your pocket?" He replied, "Lady, that ain't no torch." Being buttoned-up before, we shrieked with laughter at such humour, and became suddenly very liberated. I had never before encountered a condom, but at my first Christmas party in uniform, my fellow Wrens inflated them and let them fly around the room. I thought they were strange-looking balloons until it was explained to me that they were "Frenchies".'[15]

An American officer noted of a Home Guard dance, 'Some of the Land Army girls were in their uniform pants. The soldiers said all it took to get the pants down was *one strong yank*.' Another claimed: 'the Women's Land Army motto was "Back to the Land", which became "Backs on the Land" when we arrived'.[16] Later on, when troops were sealed into their D-Day camps in May 1944, remembered Hampshire resident Brian Selman, 'Southampton Common was a huge transit camp packed with American soldiers; their military police patrolled the perimeter with guns. The surrounding barbed wire was hung with "No Fraternisation" notices. Yet, through a hole in the wire, I saw numbers of young ladies entering and leaving with impunity.'[17] British men were unimpressed, and saw their overseas visitors – invariably met in their leisure time at dances and in pubs, when brash and bois-terous if not drunk – as competition. However, one British soldier, when questioned, was forced to admit that 'in 1939 in France, British soldiers had pressed their advantage when they found they were paid more than the French'.[18]

The *Instructions for American Servicemen* warned:

British money is in pounds, shillings and pence. They won't be pleased to hear you call it 'funny money'. They sweat hard to get it ... and won't think any better of you for throwing money around. The British 'Tommy' is apt to be specially touchy about the difference between his wages and yours ... the English language didn't spread across the oceans and over the mountains and jungles and swamps of the world because these people were panty-waists ... You won't be able to tell the British much about 'taking it'. They are not particularly interested in taking it any more. They are far more interested in getting together in solid friendship with us, so that we can all start dishing it out to Hitler.[19]

Most resented by British males was the average American's huge spending power; true, the money was injected into the UK economy, and brought some relief from the misery of the time – what else could they do with their earnings? GIs had no families of their own to go home to; most had never left their own town or state, never mind their home country before. Clad in smart walking-out uniforms with shirts, ties and shoes (their counterparts had no off-duty attire, just battledress suits, collarless shirts and boots, as collars and ties were reserved for British officers), GIs were accused by their jealous rivals of being 'oversexed, overpaid and over here'. The standard American riposte was that the British 'were underpaid, undersexed and under Eisenhower', while an office worker recalled that every time 'There'll Always Be an England' came over the wireless, the instant GI retort was 'as long as we're here to defend you'.[20] Many young boys learned to smoke at this time due to the generosity of GIs; but there was usually an ulterior motive – in exchange for a carton of Camels, Cuban cigars or large bars of unsweetened chocolate, a photograph of a sister or aunt was expected, with the promise to arrange a date.

The *Instructions for American Servicemen* explained that 'You will naturally be interested in getting to know your opposite number, the British soldier, the "Tommy" you have heard and read about. You can understand that two actions on your part will slow up the friendship – swiping his girl, and not appreciating what his army has been up against. Yes, and rubbing it in that you are better paid than he is.'[21] Frequently encountered were GI privates, young and very well paid, earning five times a British soldier's wage. US privates started on $50 a month, with a sergeant earning $85, a second lieutenant pulling in $150, and a captain $200, all tax-free. By comparison, British privates started on less than £3 per month, and sergeants at under £9, second lieutenants £15, and captains £25. (The average British civilian earned up to £25 a month, all taxed at fifty per cent.)[22] For both nations these rates increased with overseas service – a standard twenty per cent for the Yanks; specialist qualifications; time spent in the forces; and 'proficiency' pay – for example, US and RAF airmen received far more, and US paratroopers an extra $50 per month.[23]

However, with an exchange rate of $4 to a British pound, a Tommy private was earning the equivalent of just $12 a month, less stoppages for clothing, food and sometimes accommodation, compared to a GI's $50. Isaac A. Coleman, a black master sergeant stationed in England with the 377th Engineer General Service Regiment, recalled, 'I got about $140 per month. You could send home part of your salary; I sent the maximum, seventeen dollars, and the government sent sixteen, so thirty-three dollars actually went home. It was a volunteer thing: the folks at home needed it, as my father farmed.'[24] In an acknowledgement that British troops were underpaid, in August 1942 they received a twenty per cent pay rise.

Whereas the British serviceman still attended a tedious weekly pay parade at which he received his wage in cash, Americans were paid monthly, so received a much larger sum of disposable income to spend, often blown in the course of a few days. It was a truism that even the lowliest GI private – on the equivalent of a British captain's net pay – could dine out in the best London establishments (unlike his British counterpart), but only if he could negotiate his way past the imperious doorman; however, with his cap, smart uniform and tie, the American often looked the part.

All of this has to be seen in the context of the GI generation who grew up in the Great Depression. In little more than a decade they had gone from chronic unemployment and near starvation to being able to outspend the old money of Old England in the finest of hotels, rubbing shoulders with the likes of Glenn Miller, and doing so as servants of Uncle Sam. Wonders indeed. Far from being resentful at being drafted, for many GIs military service gave them not just a full wallet, but decent clothing and the best food they'd ever eaten.[25] The consequent status of *all* Americans as big spenders – in their own eyes and those of the average Briton – has lasted ever since.

Tommies were advised, through pamphlets issued by the Army Bureau of Current Affairs, 'Americans are not Englishmen who are different, but foreigners who are rather like us.'[26] Dunkirk and Sicily veteran Bill Cheall (6th Green Howards of 69th Brigade) remembered meeting his first GIs in April 1944: 'they appeared to be from a different planet. The smell from their kitchens was fantastic; they even had donuts for afters. We had rice pudding most times. They were well equipped and I was sure they would give a good account of themselves when the time for action came. They were our allies and it was hoped we would learn from one another. They were very good natured and treated us like friends.'[27]

On the other hand, two soldiers in the 50th Northumbrian Division, Corporal George Richardson and Sergeant George Self, remembered that troops from their brigade of ex-miners from the grim landscape of north-east England gained a fierce reputation for picking fights with the GIs. On returning home from the Mediterranean, 'British women wouldn't look at us. Nobody wanted to know. The Americans were going around with lots of money and half a dozen medals and had never seen action.' This went on for weeks until Eisenhower himself paid them a visit: 'No way can you cooperate with the US Army if you're fighting with them in the streets of England. I want you to be friends and find out you can be friends,' the Supreme Commander reasoned with them.[28]

British girls, like the rest of the population, obtained their view of America from the cinema, which suggested that the USA was entirely Chicago with its gangsters, the Wild West and cowboys, or California and Manhattan – immaculate clothes, penthouses with cocktails, Martinis at six; there was no concept of Minnesota and Montana in between. A UK Home Office survey in 1945 reported that British girls saw the USA as a 'magic country' and American 'proneness to spoil a girl' made them attractive to suitors.[29]

One nineteen-year-old Nottingham girl with stars in her eyes remembered the 82nd Airborne Division invading her city: 'I mean, just take the uniform the American paratroopers wore, it was fantastic and we were attracted to them straight away. You must imagine what it was like back then. Before the war, all we could do for entertainment was to go to the pictures, and most of the films we saw were made in Hollywood. So for us to actually meet and hear these young men talk like our screen idols was to us, like something out of this world,' she recalled. 'We had been at war for nearly five years, suffering daily hardships through rationing, so the arrival of the Americans to our city brought a welcome change, and offered a ray of light to our otherwise drab and boring lives.'[30]

Airmen of any nationality with 'wings' were much sought after by young women, and not just because of their pay and uniforms. There was a genuine romance attached to the concept of flight, which has still not eroded with time. Not only that, but in 1943–4 Hollywood came to England in the form of several glamorous figures associated with the US Army Air Force. Not least amongst them, as we have seen, was Major Glenn Miller with his Air Force band, but also Major James Stewart, who had already wooed cinema-goers in 1939 and 1940 with *Mr Smith Goes to Washington*, *Destry Rides Again* and *The Philadelphia Story*. He was now commander of the 703rd Bombardment Squadron, flying B-24 Liberators out of RAF Tibenham in Norfolk.

Then there was Captain Clark Gable – reputed to have exchanged the second-highest salary in Hollywood for a lowly USAAF captain's pay – who throughout 1943 flew B-17 combat missions with the 351st Bomb Group based at RAF Polebrook, whilst making a film about air gunners.[31] His air war documentary was released in 1945 as *Combat America*, which Gable, by then a major, also narrated. When he left the military his release papers were signed by another Hollywood actor-turned-soldier and future president, Captain Ronald Reagan. Technically they were part of the USAAF's Motion Picture Unit, whose ranks were exclusively film industry professionals who had donned uniform – their best-known contribution to America's war effort was the 1944 movie *Memphis Belle: A Story of a Flying Fortress*. The documentary was the story of one of the first B-17s and her crew to complete twenty-five combat missions, flying out of RAF Bassingbourn between November 1942 and May 1943.[32]

Leave passes to the big English towns were popular, but underlined differences between 'us' – the American invaders – and 'them', the occupied Britons. Every major town had a range of servicemens' clubs, where enlisted ranks – both GIs and their foreign counterparts – could relax, of which the American Red Cross-run Rainbow Corner at the junction of Piccadilly Circus and Shaftesbury Avenue in London was the best known. As dance band leader Corporal Jim McDowell of the 44th Bomb Group, based at RAF Shipdham, Norfolk, recalled: 'The Rainbow was a magnet for off-duty GIs; in the heart of London, it was where the homesick servicemen would go. You could shoot pool, play jukeboxes and have your hair cut in a home-town barber shop. There were doughnuts served by great gals, you could drink, sleep, shower, anything you needed – it was a lifesaver for the guys.' Generally, London was an extraordinarily cosmopolitan experience for most Americans brought up outside of New York City. McDowell remembered, 'At times, it was so foggy in London, that you literally could not see your hand in front of your face. Then we had the blackout; you had blankets over each door that you went through, and all windows. No light was allowed, period, nothing that could be seen from the sky.'[33]

GIs also discovered that wartime London had lost its colour, 'the Beefeaters were gorgeous no longer as they had shed their medieval costumes for modern battledress', and strict blackout regulations stymied much late-night activity, for 'plays and movies opened in late afternoon so that the streets might be well emptied by the time darkness fell'. The

The American Red Cross-run Rainbow Corner, off central London's Piccadilly Circus, provided a respite for US servicemen from duty, with a taste of home. 'You could shoot pool, play jukeboxes and have your hair cut in a home town barber shop', remembered one. 'It was a lifesaver for the guys'. The ARC also ran other clubs across England, providing meals and cheap hotel accommodation for off-duty US service personnel. (Getty Images)

cosmopolitan nature of the 'representatives of empire, troops of governments-in-exile, different accents of British soldiers, and shoulder patches of foreign forces, most of whom wore British battledress' in London's streets, brought home to GIs the full extent of the Allied alliance of which they were now a part. When speaking of the Anglo-American coalition that invaded the Continent, we must not overlook the thirty-five thousand Free French, twenty-five thousand Poles, 3,200 Czechs, two thousand Belgians, a similar number of Dutch, and 1,750 Norwegian service personnel, as well as 170,000 Canadians, who roamed England by the end of 1943 and likewise were preparing to cross the Channel.

All were prey for the 'Piccadilly Commandos'. The contemporary novelist Anthony Powell in his twelve-volume epic *A Dance to the Music of Time* refers to London's painted ladies plying their trade in the blackout by flickering small electric torches on their legs. There were, as Powell's anti-hero Lieutenant Colonel Kenneth Widmerpool observed, 'Plenty of pretty little bits in the blackout.'³⁴ The observant US Army historian Forrest Pogue explained:

> Piccadilly, I take it, has always had its quota of streetwalkers, but the prices offered – from five to twenty-five pounds, or twenty to a hundred dollars, the latter for an evening of excess, steak dinner and bed included – as the troops came up to London for that last furlough before they shoved off for the Continent, brought girls from all over the United Kingdom. Looking all the more glamourous with a fur coat bought from the proceeds of one month's activities, the former four-shilling girls of the London slums suddenly found themselves squired by sergeants and colonels.³⁵

Such prices were astronomical by the standards of the day, even to Americans: 'Honey, I want to rent it, not buy it' became the GI response to some of the extortionate sums demanded.

These 'Piccadilly Commandos', and the 'Hyde Park Rangers', were eulogised by US airmen in the nose art on their aircraft: one B-17 was christened *Piccadilly Commando* – she was shot down over Guernsey on New Year's Eve 1943. Paul Wagner, a B-17 pilot with 600 Squadron, based in Hertfordshire, remembered being 'curious to see what the action was at Piccadilly Circus. Sure enough, right across from the sandbagged statue of Eros at the center of the Circus were the famous Piccadilly Commandos, who strolled openly along the street.' They brazenly offered 'good times' to servicemen wearing the uniforms of a dozen countries. To Wagner, 'an American raised in the puritanical culture of the Great Depression, this open discussion of sex for sale, carried out in broad daylight by girls who looked exactly like their wholesome American counterparts, was most astounding'. He recalled that the price for 'an evening's entertainment ran about sixteen dollars. Many of the girls were young, eighteen was not an unusual age, and were often quite pretty.'³⁶

They also included the likes of Marthe Watts, a somewhat older but enterprising French prostitute who had arrived in London before the war, and was a prolific offender with over four hundred court appearances for soliciting. She had earned her living 'on her back in Spain, Italy, France and North Africa', but not until she came to Mayfair's Stafford Street did she have to cater for clients who 'wanted to be tied up and beaten'; her wartime record was apparently forty-nine clients on VE Day.³⁷ Wallace Patterson, of the 448th Bomb Group which flew B-24

Liberators from RAF Seething, an airbase near Norwich, remembered a weekend pass spent in London: 'after a wild cab ride from Liverpool Street Station, we put up at the Red Crown in Clifford Street. Immediately we washed, had supper, and went to the Regent Palace for a drink and to watch the Piccadilly Commandos at work. There were more of them inside the hotel and on the streets. They'll back the boys up in an alley for eight dollars; take them home for from twelve to eighty dollars. They're a pretty sorry lot, most of them, but a few people said some of them had to do what they do or starve, while others are financing future businesses.'[38] Stephen Dyson, a British tank crewman with the 107th Regiment Royal Armoured Corps, recalled thinking the invasion of France would be 'a devastating blow for the prostitutes, who now had to vie with one another amid intense competition to attract customers. After being accosted several times as we walked from Piccadilly Circus to Soho, I commented, I wouldn't be surprised if they put up "sale notices", and paraded with sandwich boards advertising their prices.'[39] An Eighth Air Force GI remembered: 'One gal had a fur coat on, and underneath that she didn't have any clothes on! True story! Well, the guys got in line to hug her!'[40]

Far more upmarket were the haunts of British officers who introduced their comrades-in-arms to the likes of Mrs Featherstonhaugh's (pronounced 'Fanshawe') high-class 'Private Hotel' in Knightsbridge, or Rosa Lewis, proprietor of the Cavendish Hotel in St James, who was well known for finding suitable companions for the well-bred in need of such entertainment. In the former, a Guards officer was rumoured to have been shown a room, only to encounter his own sister.

Senior American staff based in the UK eventually complained about the more overt forms of prostitution, with the resultant venereal disease infection rates; Brigadier General Paul Hawley, senior US surgeon in Britain, concluded that thirty per cent of all VD cases among GIs were contracted in London, whilst Liverpool, Bristol and Bedford – the latter a hub of several Eighth Air Force bases – accounted for a further twenty-seven per cent. The Home Office was obliged to pursue the matter when a Foreign Office minister, Richard Law, suggested that 'if American soldiers contract VD in this country, they and their relatives in the United States will not think kindly of us after the war'. As a result, London's police force investigated.

Recently declassified is the August 1942 report by Superintendent E. Cole of the West End Central Division of the Metropolitan Police. In it he noted that alongside the regulars of the oldest profession, many quite young female munitions workers were drawn to the West End by the promise of easy money from the new visitors. He surveyed the range of ladies on offer: those in Burlington Gardens were 'rather expensive'; Maddox Street's were 'overwhelmingly French, a colony amongst themselves, clean and businesslike, who rarely cause any trouble'; the Piccadilly Commandos were of the 'lower type, quite indiscriminate in their choice of client, and persistent thieves'; Glasshouse Street was 'similar to Piccadilly – perhaps a slightly better class'; whilst Old Compton Street in Soho supplied 'the lowest type of all drabs'.

Cole also surveyed various venues, noting The Woolly Lamb, Chappie's and Eve's were notorious for their resident ladies, but GIs visiting the aforementioned Rainbow Corner, or staying at the Washington Club and 100 Piccadilly, all US establishments, were also at risk on account of 'the modern version of the camp follower – the "good-time girl" – some in their *early teens*, who swarm and pester American soldiers, clinging to their arms, refusing to be shaken off, telling stories of poverty'. Another report from September 1943 claimed that 'Leicester Square at night is the resort of the worst type of women and girls consorting with men of the British and American forces. Of course the American soldiers are encouraged by these young sluts, many of whom should be serving in the forces. At night the square is apparently given over to vicious debauchery.'[41]

Understandably, US servicemen were reticent in memoirs and letters about their physical encounters with the opposite sex, but the ex-Eagle pilot LeRoy Gover, in the USAAF from late 1942, reminisced in the 1980s about his encounters with Rose, married to a British army officer stationed in the Middle East:

> I met her one night when I was at a pub having beer. She got up, came over and opened my greatcoat to see if I had wings. When she saw them, she dumped the guy she was with. That first night we went to her apartment, and wow, did I learn some things. Anyway, the last train left the station near her apartment at 2200 hours, so I often missed it. It was fine to stay with her all night, but I always had to sneak out in the morning, because she didn't want her neighbours to know she was 'entertaining' a male friend.[42]

On the other hand, WAAF servicewoman Joan Wyndham recalled, 'we only went out with our own kind. The pilots were heroes: if we could, we'd only go out with an RAF boy who'd got his wings. The others we called *wingless wonders*.'[43]

The Piccadilly Commandos and other enthusiastic amateurs also invaded that ultimate male preserve, the English public house. These were considered generally a 'men-only' and often working-class environment before the war. Newspapers still referred to 'pubs' in inverted commas, as if accepting the abbreviation somehow lowered journalism in the eyes of their middle-class readership. In wartime, these drinking venues became classless as everyone sought refreshment, and young women started appearing in them, invariably on the arm of a GI.[44]

Civilian Dougie Alford recalled of his local tavern near St Just, Cornwall, 'every night a truckload of fifteen or twenty Yanks would arrive at the Queen's Arms. Ladies didn't go to pubs in those days but when the GIs arrived, some of the older girls started – that was the beginning of women going to the pub in our village.'[45] One American visitor commented that the pub was so much a part of 'the Yank in England' that it would have to 'be remembered by the scriptwriter who does the European war movie'. Troops were amused when pub landlords, at the end of licensing hours – another novelty for Americans – would call out, 'Time, gentlemen, please – and you bloody Yanks, too', which they took in the spirit with which it was given.

In cities, pubs tended to be 'always crowded, the air foul, with barmaids who looked as if they were hired more for their ability as bouncers than dispensers of brew'. However, the same serviceman observed that in the quieter country pubs, GIs learned not only 'the game of darts, the rules of Shove Ha'penny, but also words of a dozen naughty songs'.[46] An airman with the 493rd Bomb Group, stationed at Debach in Suffolk (pronounced 'Dee-bark' by the Americans, but not by the locals, who insisted on 'Deb-bidge'), reflected, 'Odd these British pubs. The Yanks seemed to think that a pub wasn't worth walking into unless it was at least a century old, and nearly every Britisher would boast that his father, grandfather or great grandfather had drunk ale in the same chair. All the British smoke, from little brother and sister to grandpa and grandma, so that after an hour, many of the fellows claimed they needed a radar set to find their way through the fog to the bar.'[47]

Yet this was a very different culture to the saloons in the United States, and the novelty of 'loafing around a piano singing old-time music hall greats whilst quaffing the warm ale' quickly waned. GIs missed their music and the baseball league results from back home. If British music was different and behind the times, then their sport was a complete mystery – cricket, football and rugby left all GIs nonplussed.

To them, also, the BBC's radio offerings were stale. America had already before the war spawned a massive network of commercial radio stations which offered a wide selection of music, drama and comedy. On the outbreak of war Auntie (as the BBC was affectionately known) replaced all its regional programmes with the single Home Service. From it grew comedy and popular music programmes, including Vera Lynn's *Sincerely Yours*, and it was forced to adopt a more informal style, including a Forces Programme and a European Service, broadcasting news in French, German and Italian.

Little of this appealed to the visiting Yanks, hence Eisenhower's personal initiative which resulted in the launch, on Independence Day 1943, of the American Forces Network (AFN), still in business today. The first day's wireless programming included five hours of Bing Crosby, Dinah Shore and Charlie McCarthy, pre-recorded in the USA; by June 1944, its popularity had resulted in the five hours stretching to nineteen. On D-Day the top ten US radio requests included four by Bing Crosby and others by Dinah Shore, Jimmy Dorsey and Judy Garland.[48]

Officers and enlisted men tended to drink separately, an 82nd Airborne GI remembering, 'there was an unwritten agreement that we didn't frequent their pubs and they didn't ours … We also learned that darts was an Englishman's game and that the Americans' function was to lose and buy the drinks.'[49] However, Lieutenant Jack Bryant of the B-24 Liberator-equipped 486th Bomb Group, stationed at Sudbury, recollected, 'after partaking of various beverages over the course of the evening it was necessary to make use of a facility called a water closet. It was close to pitch black. I waited my turn. Then one of the Englishmen spoke to another beside him, and showing forbearance impossible for an American, said: "Pardon me old chap, but you're urinating on my leg."'[50]

This fervent wartime drinking culture and potential American gift to the British birth-rate was not necessarily due to glamour, money or loose morals but, in the case of airmen, a reflection of the fact that each beer or fumbling kiss in the blackout might be their last. Red Komarek, of the 93rd Bomb Group, was a tail gunner on a B-24 Liberator named *Yardbird*. As one of the earliest arrivals in England, flying out of RAF Alconbury in Cambridgeshire, he recalled that near his base, was a billet for twenty-three bonnie Land Army girls, all of whom were spoken for. We met them the second night at the Nissen hut next to the road. I began a romantic interlude with Jeannie with the light blonde hair. The girls worked in the surrounding fields and used to wave as we taxied out to the runways. They confided that they knew when we were going on a mission by either the early take-off or the length of runway it took to get off the ground. What a war ... mission in the morning ... dating in the evening ... bed and blankets at night, that was our theme song.[51]

Major Harry H. Crosby, lead navigator with the 100th Bomb Group, flying B-17s out of RAF Thorpe Abbotts in Norfolk, completed his full tour of twenty-five missions, and when the odds were against even surviving a tour, signed on for several more. A gentle soul, he once when over the target suddenly diverted his squadron from bombing Bonn on a recollection that Beethoven had been born and gone to school in that city. Crosby spoke for many in the Eighth Air Force when he observed that 'at nine o'clock in the morning we might be bombing Berlin and by midnight be at a fancy dance in London'.[52] Alternating between the two was disorientating to say the least, if not downright nerve-wracking. This was the purpose of Glenn Miller's concerts, the dances at airbases and leave passes to London – to unwind. As Forrest Pogue observed, and as generations of servicemen will attest, the taut nerves and inner tension that accompany the stress of combat were best relieved by partying, alcohol or sex – or all three.

5

Warm Hearts

'Here you are on this little island surrounded by Northern mists.
I cannot give you any guarantees on the weather, but can guarantee
that you will be welcomed by warm hearts.
Winston Churchill welcoming US troops to Britain

MOST OF THE great tidal wave of GIs who arrived in the United Kingdom in 1943–4 came by sea. American service personnel were generally assembled at Camp Kilmer, New Jersey, and taken to their ship, waiting in New York harbour. Herded like cattle – there was no other way – they struggled under the weight of hundred-pound kit bags, webbing, packs with bed rolls, rifles and steel helmets. Often a band played whilst they climbed the gangway onto, most usually, a converted peacetime passenger liner. Accommodation was spartan and the holds crowded with makeshift canvas-and-steel hammocks, built three high; ventilation was poor. GIs were rarely told their destination before they set sail.

The crossing was not without extreme risk: in February 1943 the 6,000-ton troopship *Dorchester* was torpedoed off Newfoundland with the loss of 672 out of 902 on board. Unless men found space in a lifeboat their chances of survival in the unforgiving North Atlantic were zero. Nurse Mildred A. MacGregor aboard the 81,000-ton Cunard luxury liner RMS *Queen Mary* remembered their orders:

There will be absolutely no smoking on deck at blackout. Positively no flashlights are to be used outside of enclosed areas. If anyone has a radio in his possession it will be confiscated for the duration of this voyage.

You should also be aware that Hitler has offered a $250,000 reward to any of his seagoing vessels for sinking *Queen Mary*. I remind you again that you must have your life preserver, your canteen full of water and your survivor rations on you at all times. Should any of you fall overboard, this ship will not turn back for any reason.[1]

Her sister ship, RMS *Queen Elizabeth* hosted Fighter pilot Lieutenant Norman J. 'Bud' Fortier from New Hampshire as he crossed the Atlantic. 'Built to accommodate three thousand passengers in luxury, on this trip she carried two fighter groups and an entire infantry division – close to sixteen thousand men – but *not* in luxury. Three GIs took turns sleeping on the same bed, each for eight hours over a twenty-four hour period.'[2] The feat was only replicated on the *Queen Mary*, known as the 'Grey Ghost', from the grey camouflage job both ships received.

Virginian Sergeant Robert 'Bob' Slaughter, with the 116th Infantry of 29th Division, was one of those who had watched the Statue of Liberty fade into the distance when aboard the *Queen Mary* in September 1942. 'The British food was, in a word, terrible. This was my introduction to wartime rations, and I never did get used to them.' On his voyage the liner collided with her escorting cruiser, HMS *Curacoa*, slicing her in two: 'In minutes, 332 British sailors died before our horrified eyes. The stern of the cruiser bumped the port side, and quickly sank in *Queen Mary*'s wake. The much larger bow – black smoke pouring from its funnel – stayed afloat for about six minutes before it too was swept into our wake. The broken *Curacoa* slowly raised its nose until almost vertical, then slid backward into a sea of bubbling foam.'[3]

Fitted with 40mm anti-aircraft guns, the two *Queens*' greatest defence was speed; sailing at twenty-eight knots, too fast for German submarines or surface vessels, the pair travelled unaccompanied by escorting warships, their security increased by zig-zagging at regular intervals. At such speeds, passage from New York to Greenock in Scotland took five days. As the thirty-seven officers, including Bud Fortier, and 252 enlisted men of the 354th Fighter Squadron disembarked from the *Queen Elizabeth*, they were advised to wear their steel helmets. 'Because of enemy activity?' Fortier asked. 'No, sir,' came the reply, 'it's the seagulls.' He recalled, 'The steel helmets protected our heads, but most of us wore messy badges of passage on our uniforms when we reached the dock.'[4]

The *Queen Mary* experienced more bad luck that December on another New York–Scotland run when laden with 950 crew and 10,389

GIs, including Nurse MacGregor of the 3rd Auxiliary Surgical Group. Her unit comprised very valuable medical personnel, including '216 officer surgeons, anaesthetists, dentists, 227 enlisted men and 122 nurses from every state of the Union'. This was the *Queen Mary*'s first voyage since the *Curacoa* collision, which had kept her in dry dock for two months. On the third day out she hit a squall, which developed into a storm on the fourth, and by the fifth day at sea a full-blown hurricane. The waves grew more intense until one broke windows on the bridge – ninety feet above the ocean – while others blew open portholes, flooded cabins and took lifeboats and bolted-down deck furniture as though they were made of paper.

'The *Queen* battled the fierce storm for three days,' MacGregor wrote. 'At times the ship lifted so high on a wave that her huge propeller blades were exposed. Several British seamen manning the crow's nest high over the deck were swept away.' At its peak, on 11 December, the ship rolled to an astonishing fifty-two degrees and the crew thought she was going to capsize; maritime experts later concluded she was only three degrees from the roll becoming fatal, with catastrophic results for all on board, but, spaniel-like, the rugged ship brushed off the wave and continued her voyage.

'Many people fell. The ship's hospital began to fill with the injured as well as the seasick. Time dragged endlessly for those lying in their bunks retching each time the ship hesitated on the crest of a ten story wave then plunged forward into the void. To top it off, Captain Ralph Coffey had to operate on a fellow traveller with acute appendicitis,' MacGregor recounted. Of their arrival she observed, 'We were two days off-schedule and the convoy that had been sent to escort the *Queen* into harbour had had difficulty in locating us. They guided her through the submarine net into the estuary where we were greeted by blasting horns and raised flags. The *Queen* raised her Union Jack as the guns roared. She had survived the worst storm of her career.'[5] By the war's end *Queen Mary* would have carried 765,429 (mostly US) military personnel, including the still unbroken record of 16,683 on a single vessel, during a July 1943 trans-atlantic crossing. MacGregor's horrific voyage later came to the attention of a writer named Paul Gallico who collected accounts from several terrified GIs on board, and twenty-five years later used them to pen *The Poseidon Adventure*, about a huge luxury liner which rolled all the way.

Lynchburg-native Lieutenant Harry P. Carroll of the 356th Fighter Group was travelling with Bud Fortier in calmer seas on the *Queen*

Elizabeth: 'It was thrilling when we saw British Spitfires come off the coast of Ireland to greet us.'[6] New Yorker Hal Baumgarten was another GI from the 116th Infantry who, like Bob Slaughter, crossed in the luxury of five days, in his case aboard a requisitioned French liner, the 44,300-ton SS *Île de France*, the world's third-largest passenger vessel at that time. When he caught up with the rest of the 116th – known as the 'Stonewall Brigade', because of its Southern composition and Civil War heritage – in Plymouth, they were warned, 'two out of three of you are not going to make it back, because you are going to be the spearhead for the second front'.[7]

On the same ship as Baumgarten was the Irish-American Mike Joseph Daly, a private bound for the 18th Regiment of America's oldest division, the 1st, known affectionately as the 'Big Red One'. On his last night in New York, Daly had enjoyed a live performance by Nat King Cole off Broadway, but unable to produce a leave pass when challenged by a roving MP, had been arrested. Consequently, he spent his transatlantic crossing cleaning pots and pans in the officers' mess galley. Once in England he found himself in the Somerset coastal town of Minehead preparing for D-Day.[8] The 1st Infantry Division had already seen action in Tunisia and Sicily before returning to England in November 1943, and the greenhorn Daly – albeit the son of a professional soldier who had commanded doughboys (the affectionate term for 1917–18 American soldiers) during the First World War – therefore had the hard task of integrating himself into a unit of already battle-hardened GIs.

Also attached to the 1st Division was Chaplain John G. Burkhalter, a Southern Baptist minister and, before that, a professional boxer for eight years. In 1942 he had heeded a call to preach the Gospel in the US Army, and after negotiating the Atlantic, joined the division training in Wales. He was soon well known, holding field services under the trees, heralded by jeep and trailer, which carried his portable organ, desk, typewriter and song books.[9]

The US Army newspaper *Stars and Stripes* described him as 'one who looks and lives like a combat chaplain. In appearance Chaplain John G. Burkhalter is more than a match for the toughest combat soldier. He stands before his congregation in a faded fatigue uniform, feet braced, chest thrown out, jaw thrust forward. His strong-looking hands hold firmly to the hymn book.' Clearly the ex-boxer cut an impressive figure: 'He stands there, a powerful figure, his eyes meeting every man's glance like a boxer looking for an opening. When he talks, he speaks like a coach addressing a group of athletes in training. He doesn't harangue or plead or scold. His words carry his own conviction and confidence in what he is saying.'[10]

At the other end of the scale to the two *Queens* was the boat conveying a Wisconsin signals sergeant, Don R. Marsh – a 10,000-ton Liberty ship named *George Sharswood*, which he soon nicknamed 'the ship from hell'. Marsh recollected: 'its speed was a maximum eleven knots, if the screws of the single propeller remained in the water long enough, but they seldom did.' He remembered her armament included a four-inch cannon on the stern. 'This ancient piece still bore the brass plaque on its side that said it was on loan, reclaimed from a public park in the City of Philadelphia and manufactured in 1903. The Navy sailors on board refused to test fire it for fear it might burst the barrel.' Marsh's fears rose further when he learned that 'On the bridge were four 25-man lifeboats, two per side. The lifeboats were designated for the civilian crew only and *Off limits to all soldiers.*' Marsh and his buddies were expected to use life rafts.[11]

A Signal Corps German-speaking linguist, Sergeant Carl Dannemann of Houston, Texas, wrote home of the difference of British troopships over American: 'first, they used hammocks for sleeping and second, Britain's wartime food shortages were evident. The average lunch consisted of two pieces of bread with two slices of baloney [Bologna sausage], coffee, and one apple per person. On the other hand, the evening meal was quite adequate: boiled beef or roast mutton, with potatoes, Brussels sprouts, tea and Jello for dessert. Breakfast would be porridge; on Sunday, powdered eggs and a bit of bacon' – he was unaware that in austerity Britain this would be a feast.[12] Michigan-born Donald R. Burgett of the 101st Airborne enjoyed an eleven-day Atlantic crossing in September 1943 aboard HMS *Empire Anvil*, an American ship transferred to Britain under Lend-Lease that would later land troops on Omaha Beach. Landing at Belfast, Burgett recalled some of the troopers 'were throwing packs of cigarettes onto the dock and the Irish laborers were scooping them up as fast as they hit, but we soon found out that everything was rationed here – *everything*'.

Within days Burgett and his colleagues had absconded from their base for a dance in the local village. Reflecting the general social confidence of the average American, he remembered the scene: 'There were civilians and GIs all drinking and having a ball. At the moment they were singing "Roll Me Over in the Clover" to the accompaniment of an old piano in the corner … we put our caps on, minded our manners and soon each of us had a girl sitting on our laps.'[13] Others in the 101st were not so lucky; the 502nd Parachute Infantry had much earlier embarked on SS *Strathnaver*, which en route sprung a leak and was obliged to put into Saint John's, Newfoundland, for lengthy repairs. Abandoning the *Strathnaver*, the paratroopers completed their voyage aboard a former Swedish liner, USS *John Ericsson*, but their transatlantic journey had taken forty-four days.

In the same convoy and also aboard the *John Ericsson* was Alabaman Lieutenant Belton Youngblood Cooper of the 3rd Armored Division. With a total of nine troopships carrying his entire division and men of the 101st Airborne, they joined nine tankers loaded with fuel and supplies, and were escorted by the battleship *Nevada* and nine destroyers. Cooper shared a cabin with five other officers but noted the enlisted men 'slept in the holds in bunks stacked five-high'. When not 'hot-bunking', each soldier had to carry his duffle bag holding all his personal gear with him everywhere on board. Cooper witnessed one exasperated GI, on finding nowhere to rest with his burden, throw his bag overboard into the waves.[14] On arrival, the 3rd Armored were sent to Bruton in Somerset.

Making the transatlantic hop on another of the twenty-seven wartime passages made by the *John Ericsson* was Montanan Hobert Winebrenner with the 358th Infantry of the 90th Division. His voyage was in April 1944, when the Atlantic threw him around. Of his own admission, 'I numbered among the sorriest of land lovers [*sic*] and suffered seasickness almost immediately. To this day, bad memories of pea soup and chocolate bars haunt me.' When ordered to explain his absence from boat drill and other activities, he explained to his battalion CO, 'Sir, in this state, I'm going down with the ship.' He spent his voyage below decks until gratefully setting foot on Liverpool's docks; the troops were immediately scattered around Birmingham and Warwickshire by train.[15]

Ultimately destined for Omaha Beach, New Yorker Chuck Hurlbut, of the 299th Engineer Combat Battalion, had left New York City in April 1944 aboard the 7,000-ton transport SS *Exchequer*. He particularly remembered the U-boat threat: 'about halfway over, we get a submarine alert. That's scary. You're out in the middle of the Atlantic. Everybody put on a life jacket. You all get up on deck, and it's dark as hell; there was no moon that night. And you just wait, because you don't know what the hell's happening. But we hear pretty soon that some of our destroyers found the sub, they depth bombed and they got it. That felt pretty good.'[16]

Don Marsh in his 'ship from hell' remembered of his slow, plodding voyage that 'some read their Bibles or said their Rosaries, while others gambled in the non-stop crap games and poker tables'. His vessel 'took on the appearance of a floating asylum being run by the inmates. When the second week rolled by, the tempers became shorter and petty quarrels burst into brief fistfights that were quickly broken up by cooler heads.' Eventually, Scotland with its lush green hills came into sight, 'giving many of us a touch of homesickness after almost three weeks at sea'. Marsh was then sent by train and truck to the 10th US Army Replacement Depot at Lichfield, formerly Whittington Barracks. This had been the home of the North Staffordshire Regiment (and coincidentally was where this author started his military career).[17]

Perhaps a passage aboard a former Caribbean cruise ship, the 12,500-ton *Santa Paula*, best evokes the collective GI experience. Designed for 250 passengers, the transport was converted to take 2,200 troops and armed with three-inch guns and 20mm anti-aircraft cannon. The records show that in her four years of war service the *Santa Paula* made twenty-eight troop-carrying voyages from the United States. Amongst others on this voyage, she was carrying the 756th Railway Shop Battalion 'to join the nightmare life created by blackouts, ration restrictions, robot bombs, rockets and other uncertainties in "Buzz-Bomb Alley"', as the battalion history put it.

Their job was to maintain the US Army's rolling stock in England and eventually France, but first they had to endure the Atlantic. The *Santa Paula* was 'turned GI from stem to stern, except the engine room which was off-limits. Only a few of us escaped an attack of seasickness at some stage.' Their historian described the typical crowded voyage: 'you make a mental calculation of how overloaded the ship is. After three days on the promenade deck, you finally get a bunk – and the next night wander around like a lost soul trying to find a corner where it's fairly warm and dry and hope nobody will step or stumble on you.'

Illness and boredom were the two chief characteristics for the millions of GIs who made the voyage:

the tankers to port wallow as sickeningly as yesterday, rain squalls occur regularly and you're being washed down the scuppers with every wave that breaks ... half-hearted attempts are made to write letters; some try and find oblivion in sleep. Everybody hopes the days will pass quickly and that soon we may stretch our legs again on a base that doesn't roll, pitch, or wobble ... An occasional dry run with the AA guns causes momentary excitement, while the jangling bells, signifying lifeboat drill, at first demanding and peremptory in tone, are rapidly losing their effectiveness and became signals for just another chore.

All these discomforts vanished when the ship 'was electrified into action as finally land was seen – gray, rocky, cold and forbidding, but, brother, it is *land*'. Eventually the inhabitants were sighted: 'The crowds on board *Daffodil II* seem cheery enough and the girls lining its rails are left in no doubt that more Yanks are invading their land ... and they rather give the impression of welcome.'[18]

For Chuck Hurlbut aboard the SS *Exchequer* it was Easter Sunday afloat that he most recalled: 'the chaplains got together and they put on an interfaith service up on deck. The Navy guys, the Army guys, they all were together. It was a simple service, just straightforward. But the setting: The ocean. The ships. A beautiful day. It's the most memorable, meaningful religious service I've ever attended. I'm not that big a religious guy, but that really got me.'[19]

In March 1944 Guy Charland, with Company 'G' of the 375th Infantry – with the 90th 'Tough Ombres' Division – had boarded a British troopship, the *Dominion Monarch*, in New York harbour. A quadruple-screw luxury liner built for the London–Australia run and designed for 525 first-class passengers, according to the manifest when Charland encountered her, she accommodated 3,556 GIs. 'We were destined for God knows where – the Mediterranean area, Italy maybe? Or else the United Kingdom? Bets were made. All of us who picked England won; I made fifty dollars on that deal.'

Their voyage was uneventful until 'a few miles off the Irish coast we were visited by a pair of four-engined Focke-Wulf Condor bombers. We were on deck when the sirens sounded and the gun crews started shooting; the planes came in between the ships a few feet from the waves, and close enough for me to see the pilots and crewmen in the gun turrets. This was my first view of enemy aircraft; instead of being scared, I was really excited and amazed to see my first action,' enthused Charland. 'Some of the guns hit one of the aircraft in the wing, tearing it off. The other got a blast in the engine which started to smoke. The one with the torn-off wing crashed into the sea. We cheered. The other decided this was enough and headed back to its base in France.'[20]

Daniel Folsom of New Carlisle, Indiana, then nineteen, had been drafted into the Seabees, emerging after boot camp as seaman second class in the 111th Naval Construction Battalion. Destined to offload LSTs during the forthcoming invasion, he arrived in England on the brand-new 36,000-ton Cunarder RMS *Mauretania*. He thought his crossing 'terrible. It was a British ship, and of course, it was wartime. The food was lousy, we got fed twice a day, and on the way over they gave us some shots. We were down in D-Deck, where they transported the automobiles in those days, bunked in hammocks, five high. The guy on the top hammock would get sick, and the four guys down suffered from it; so, it was horrendous. Jimmy Cagney went over with us; he came down to entertain us and our battalion booed him out of the place; I've always been a little ashamed of that, but he was very gracious about it.'[21]

Finally, let us not forget Alden C. Flagg, Jr, the first draftee, whose GI experience speaks for millions. As a conscript he had been thrust into the bosom of a National Guard division which recruited in Kansas; the Bostonian had to get to know his fellow guardsmen of Company 'A', who mostly hailed from Atchison, Kansas. After four years' hard training in Alabama and Tennessee they had moved for final exercises to Camp Butner, North Carolina, and learned to carry ninety-pound packs in the mountains of West Virginia. Here they were observed by Secretary of War Robert P. Patterson and Senator Harry S. Truman. The morning of 11 May 1944 found Flagg and the rest of the heavily laden 137th Infantry sailing with the ebb tide past the Statue of Liberty, aboard the *Thomas H. Barry*, an 11,500-ton former liner once known as SS *Oriente*, which used to ply between New York and Cuba. Docking at Avonmouth thirteen days later, the 137th were whisked by train to south-west England.

Georgian Captain Bedford Davis, a combat surgeon with the 28th Division, had also crossed the Atlantic aboard the *Santa Paula*. On arrival in Swansea, he remembered, 'a band greeted us, along with doughnuts and coffee, served by American Red Cross girls from their Clubmobile'.[22] The all-female members of the American Red Cross (ARC) played an important role in making their fellow countrymen feel at home in England and feature often in memoirs and letters. Volunteers were required to be 'single, between the ages of twenty-five and thirty-five,

Whether fresh from their harrowing trans-Atlantic voyages or on duty at one of the Eighth's air bases – as here – GIs looked forward to the arrival of the American Red Cross Clubmobile. Their pretty female staff dispensed coffee, donuts and sympathy in equal measure to homesick GIs 'with proper, Red Cross decorum, of course', as one recounted in her letters home. (Getty Images)

possess college education and work experience'; they also had to be 'healthy, physically hardy, sociable and attractive'.

Lipsticked and clad in boots and military-style uniforms, their job was to raise morale, dispensing cookies and hot drinks with a constant smile. They worked out of hundreds of 'Clubmobiles' – single-decker buses (later, 6×6 trucks as well), fitted with doughnut- and coffee-making facilities – which were also equipped with a lounge at the back where GIs could relax with music, books and magazines, candy, gum and cigarettes. Male drivers navigated the large, camouflaged vehicles as they trundled down narrow, muddy lanes to US Army camps and airbases throughout England, and later in France, but the face of each Clubmobile was an all-female team of three – the ARC insisted they be called 'girls'.

'For many GIs in England, the sight of an American woman was so unusual,' explained ARC girl Liz Richardson in a letter home, following six weeks' training and a transatlantic passage aboard the *Queen Elizabeth*. 'You feel sort of like a museum piece – Hey, look, fellows! A real, live American girl!' But selection was tough for the ARC: as well as being able to act as a mother hen to homesick GIs, they had to deflect sexual advances and cope with the inevitable wolf whistles. As

Richardson wrote to her brother, 'How the men refrain from "whoopsing" when they see us, I don't know... I certainly have improved my stock of evasive tactics. And you should see me jitterbug, with proper, Red Cross decorum, of course.'[23] Later, the ARC would operate mobile cinemas and a chain of cheap hotels across England, where servicemen could stay and eat for a few cents.

Whereas the majority of American visitors from 1942 had been airmen who were concentrated in East Anglia, and supply troops based in the north Midlands, the new wave of GIs in 1943–4 were the infantry and armoured divisions, who invaded the south-west counties of Wiltshire, Dorset, Devon, Somerset and Cornwall. The locals, who had rarely seen a US serviceman until this moment, found overnight that ports like Weymouth, Plymouth, Brixham, Falmouth and Dartmouth were suddenly 'annexed to become New, New England'. Ruth Haskins, married to an RAF officer, recalled that 'from the autumn of 1943 Bath became crowded as most of the troops made their way here when they had a few hours' leave, especially in the evenings. Buses and trucks ferried them in, coming back about 11 p.m. to collect them. Cinema queues were longer. Local girls who were keen on dancing complained bitterly next day at work about being danced off their feet. It was standing room only in the pubs – civilian men grumbled it wasn't their local anymore.'[24]

The Americans' arrival irreversibly changed south-west England. One Cornish resident suggested, 'With the GIs, the county woke up. Prior to the 1940s, we were probably fifty years behind the times – no cinemas opened on a Sunday, pubs had limited hours ("time" was called at ten o'clock); the only thing to do on a Sunday was Sunday School. Toilet paper was the *West Briton* newspaper; many homes only had earth closets and were without electricity or running water. These were still, for some, the days of oil lamps and fetching water from the well. Then in 1943 the "New World" arrived with its jazz and jitterbugs, cigars and chewing gum, and Cornwall came out of the Edwardian world.'[25]

In fact, for those who cared to ponder, Devon and Cornwall were redolent with memories of the 200-ton *Mayflower*, the ship that transported the first English Puritans to the New World. The vessel had set sail from London in mid-July 1620, then anchored in Southampton Water to rendezvous with the *Speedwell*, carrying pilgrims from the Netherlands; later they were obliged to put into Dartmouth for repairs to the *Speedwell*, and subsequently Plymouth for the same reason. Eventually the *Mayflower* alone set sail into the history books with her hundred passengers on 6 September. From all four ports in June 1944, some of the Allied invasion flotilla would set forth, bearing their own pilgrims to the Third Reich.

The US Army's *Instructions for American Servicemen* was supplemented in 1943 by a British Ministry of Information film, *A Welcome to Britain*, which tried to explain Blighty's unique culture and character to the newly arrived GI. This British initiative is still considered a remarkably progressive film and was far removed from the clunky propaganda offerings of the era. It started with the inevitable pub visit – 'If you like beer, you'd better like it warm. This particular pub was founded about the time our country was founded'; moved on to how to behave when invited to a rationed meal in an English home; home front food; and – set in an English village school-room, complete with Mr Chips the schoolmaster – geography.

Geography was important because the visitors would find themselves spread unevenly throughout the country, and were completely mystified as to how the component parts of England, Scotland, Wales and Northern Ireland – each with their incomprehensible accents and customs – managed to constitute Britain, the British Isles or the United Kingdom. In the same way, Britons were just as guilty of regarding all their visitors as 'Americans', when most GIs identified only with their state or home town, and had no knowledge of their wider country. The northern states still regarded the South with suspicion; small-town America had little in common with the big cities; income and parentage often dictated education and friendships. In the days before mass travel, the social and geographical jumble that became the US Army was instrumental in teaching GIs themselves how to be Americans.

Far from their own homes in the United States, the experience of meeting such alien English-speakers, Brits and Canucks alike, probably confirmed for many GIs – perhaps for the first time – a sense of their own difference, a sense of *nationality*. This was as true for Canadians, and would be for the Brits once they hit French soil – exactly as it had been in 1914–18. Few young men destined to become the warriors of 1944–5 had even stepped outside their own class or region, let alone been exposed to foreign cultures, prior to the Second World War. There is nothing like a dose of isolation in somewhere foreign to confirm in one's own mind a sense of national identity.

Though produced in London, *A Welcome to Britain* nevertheless relied on the standard Hollywood device of defining class and profession by dress and accent, where all the labourers spoke cockney (a specifically working-class London dialect), whilst their 'betters' conversed in 'BBC English'. The countryside was depicted as exclusively thatched cottages and horse-powered – and, naturally, 'the English drink tea like we drink Coke'.[26] It suffered from two awkwardly scripted cameos from Bob Hope (failing to explain pounds, shillings and pence) and Major General John C. H. Lee, head of US Army Services and Supplies, discussing racial segregation and equality (more of which later).

To additionally prepare GIs for life in their host nation, *A Welcome to Britain* was complemented in 1944 by its US-made counterpart, *Know Your Ally: Britain*. A more stilted contribution, it might just as well have had 'official US propaganda' stamped all over it. Servicemen learned through archival news footage about the recent military history of the country that Americans 'knew just enough about to confuse us. The little island is no larger than the state of Idaho. Half a million people live in Idaho, but ninety-six times that number live in Britain, which makes it as congested as a sardine can. They have so little crime in Britain that, believe it or not, even in wartime the British cop does not carry a gun!' In Britain, the audience was reminded, 'no place is more than one hundred miles from the sea. It is only twenty miles from German guns and planes; where every man and woman, young or old, is on the front line.' Culturally, the film observed, 'we go for baseball: they have a little number called cricket. The dukes and earls don't run the country any more. So when you read of Lord Louis Mountbatten or Lord Beaverbrook, don't think they got their jobs because of their titles, they got them because they were the best men for the jobs.'[27]

By 1944 the southern counties of Cornwall and Devon, Wiltshire and Dorset, Gloucestershire and Somerset were overwhelmed with Americans preparing to invade France. Wiltshire boy Stan Jones remembered: 'Trowbridge was one of those towns completely taken over by the US Army during the war and where I lived was one huge tank park: they lined Union Street and from our bedroom windows we could almost look down the turrets and watch as the soldiers prepared their equipment for battle. Up Middle Lane half-tracked vehicles were parked on the wide grass verges. Just over the hedge old Farmer Hancock was still keeping his cows, driving them down to market through the lines of tanks and supplying us with milk.'[28]

Patricia Barnard lived in Wimborne: 'in April 1944 we began to see the arrival and build-up of American soldiers on our roads. Their trucks suddenly appeared, parked up everywhere throughout the countryside and back inland for twenty miles. Thousands and thousands of them. Each truck home to six or eight soldiers; they played cards or dice on the pavements, and baseball with children. They talked to local people as we went by, and made friends with families in whose gateways they were parked. One young GI of nineteen became a friend of our family; we were so pleased when we heard that he had returned safely to Georgia in 1945.'[29]

Seemingly, every magnificent old country house, hotel or institution in southern England became headquarters to some US Army organisation or other. Apart from occupying several adjoining houses in London's Bryanston Square, Lieutenant General Omar Bradley's First Army (radio call sign and code name 'Master') was lodged at Clifton College, Bristol, 'whose beautiful halls and lawns seemed ill at ease in the presence of so many soldiers', and where 'cricket had been replaced on the playing fields by baseball', observed one GI, seemingly unaware of Clifton's military heritage.[30] Its old boys included no less than eight winners of the Victoria Cross and Britain's commander in the First World War, Field Marshal Earl Haig, 'whose statue', recalled Bradley in his memoirs, 'overlooked the rugby field'. Clifton had been suggested to the American general – who made himself at home in School House using the housemaster's drawing room as his office – by General Frederick Morgan, responsible for devising the original Overlord plan, and himself an Old Cliftonian.[31]

Bradley's arrival pushed out Major General 'Gee' Gerow's V Corps (radio call sign 'Victor') to Norton Fitzwarren Manor, near Taunton. J. Lawton Collins' VII Corps ('Jayhawk') was based in the Elizabethan splendour of Breamore House, just north of Fordingbridge in Hampshire, which later housed Lieutenant General George S. Patton's Third Army HQ ('Lucky'). Patton was quite at home using for his office the panelled and tapestried 84-foot-long Great Hall, which dated from 1583 and where maps of France replaced the Van Dycks and ancestral portraits.[32]

Such accommodation played up to the Hollywood image of Britain, very much encouraged by novels and plays then in vogue by P. G. Wodehouse, Agatha Christie, Daphne du Maurier, Dorothy L. Sayers and Ben Travers, all anchored firmly in the English country house. Choosing such elegant residences wasn't snobbery – despite the towers, ivy-clad battlements, armour-adorned walls and ancient pedigree, many were past their former glory and expensive for their owners to maintain. Evelyn Waugh's portrayal of 1940s soldiery in *Brideshead Revisited* springs to mind.[33]

Guy Charland, who had witnessed the downing of a Focke-Wulf Condor unwise enough to attack his Atlantic convoy, had meanwhile ended up at Kinlet Hall in Shropshire, a grand Palladian house dating from the 1720s which he described as 'a large baronial estate turned over to the US Army for a camp'. Charland remembered his preparation 'to do mortal battle with the dirty satanic Kraut was really hard and took a lot out of us, but it really toughened us up. I'll swear Wales is full of hills, just right for forced marches, or a twenty-five-mile hike with a sixty-pound backpack and all the rest of the gear ... You talk about feeling bushed and beat! Running up and down those mounds would tax the strongest man, I'd wager. The US Army really knew where to establish a training camp ... They taught us how to neutralise mines. This, together with hand-to-hand fighting, bayonet, rifle range, and mock battles was our schedule – we were sometimes too fagged out to go out on pass.' Charland recollected, 'That's how severe the training was ... Those Welsh hills are not little ones; they are *huge*, and it rained just about every day.'[34]

Yet, there was a relevance to this latter-day 'château generalship' of commandeering big houses. Flanked by gate lodges, at the end of long drives, with extensive fenced-in grounds of their own, these secluded, multi-roomed mansions, which usually included extensive servants' quarters and stable blocks, were easy to police and could accommodate numerous offices and personnel, whilst the lawns were used for tent cities, airstrips and vehicle parks, away from prying eyes. Of the airborne divisions, Matthew Ridgway's 82nd ('Champion') resided in the Midlands at Braunstone Park, Leicester, whilst Maxwell Taylor's 101st ('Kangaroo') were ensconced at Greenham Lodge, outside Newbury. Of the assault wave, Clarence Huebner's 1st Infantry Division ('Danger') were to be found headquartered at Langton House, near Blandford, and Tubby Barton's 4th ('Ivy') lodged at Collipriest House, Tiverton in Devon. Charlie Gerhardt's 29th ('Latitude') moved frequently, having arrived in October 1942, but spent a year at Tidworth House, before moving to Abbotsfield House, Tavistock in Devon, in May 1943.

The relative luxury of the headquarters units wasn't always shared by the line battalions, who were often parcelled out to freezing British Army hutted or tented camps. Dale E. Gillespie was an aid-man with the 307th

Airborne Medical Company of the 82nd Airborne Division who wound up in Northern Ireland in December 1943. 'The toilet facilities were open air and there was little heat. One pot belly stove and not enough coal ration to last the night. We had already experienced the piercing, bone-chilling cold in England before North Africa, but this was something extra, having just come back from Italy.'[35] Sergeant Bob Slaughter with the 29th Division likewise remembered of Tidworth (still a British Army base today) that 'the interior looked more like a penitentiary than a barracks, and the English winter made it worse. We slept in our uniforms and socks, and when the 0530 hours wake-up bugle blew, we were almost dressed. The training was seven days a week, and once a month we were given forty-eight-hour leave passes, if we kept our noses clean. We saw such landmarks as Stonehenge and Salisbury Cathedral, but I'm not sure we adequately appreciated them under the circumstances.'[36]

By contrast, when Don Burgett of the 506th Parachute Infantry – with the 101st 'Screaming Eagles' Airborne Division – arrived by truck in the small Wiltshire village of Aldbourne (about one hour's drive north of Bob Slaughter in Tidworth), he was 'led up a small hill and through a gate in a brick wall': 'This used to be the stables for a mansion,' his sergeant told him. 'They were built of wood and ran the full length of the courtyard and were the best barracks I had ever been in, small, neat, comfortable and yet large enough for four men to live in and have a certain amount of privacy – something almost unknown in the service.'[37]

Some US servicemen were billeted on local families, where their treatment varied from motherly to sullen resentment; some hosts shared their precious rations, invited GIs to sit before warm fires and listen to the family wireless sets, whereas others stubbornly offered none of their home comforts.

Billets in larger towns and cities were less popular, because rationing bit deeper. In the countryside, fresh produce from a garden or local farm was always on hand, and the warmth of a wood fire was not dictated by the amount of rationed coal available. Forrest Pogue was lucky: when visiting his brother in the 703rd Tank Destroyer Battalion of the 3rd Armored Division, in Mere, Wiltshire, he was caught in a downpour. On reaching his brother's civilian hosts,

Mr Gray built up a roaring fire and hung our wet things in front of it while we warmed ourselves. Despite the severity of rationing, he and his wife soon set out cakes and tea, not only for us, but for the dozen chaps who came in during the four hours that we stayed there ... They played symphonies for us on their phonograph. These people, not because we were Yanks to be welcomed, but because they were friendly folk, wrote our parents back home not to worry, and did for us the wonderfully thoughtful things that make up true hospitality.[38]

Daniel Folsom with the Seabees, whom we met crossing the Atlantic aboard the *Mauretania*, was billeted in a private house just before D-Day: 'they were very, very nice to us in that part of England. We had been instructed to eat only our K-rations, and not to eat anything the English had because that was their only food. In my billet this woman had a cat; next morning she invited us for breakfast and I saw this dark meat on the table. And – until I heard the cat *meow* – I wouldn't eat that meat,' Folsom reminisced with a smile.[39]

Bob Slaughter recalled the unappetising imported 'Australian mutton – we called it goat meat – and as the odor of goat meat permeated the chow lines, we hungry GIs bleated *baa, baa!*'[40] Generally, the Yanks stuck to their own imported and prepared food, disdaining British rations, as Sergeant Arthur J. Whalen, who flew B-17s out of RAF Bury St Edmunds with 410th Bomb Squadron, remembered: 'we ate pretty good, but one time we were at a British air force station, we had to eat their food which was too greasy, horrible, so we didn't eat much, even though we had to stay there a day or two, to get our plane going again. About the best thing you could get was fish and chips; I mean like potato chips [French fries] and fried fish wrapped in old newspaper, which was a great thing over there.'[41]

The country house formula was repeated for all the various US regiments. Colonel George Taylor's 16th Infantry, of the 1st Division, occupied one of Dorset's oldest stately homes, Parnham House near Beaminster; Colonel Robert F. Sink's 506th Parachute Infantry, with the 101st Airborne, lodged at Littlecote Park, which dated from 1592.[42] Canadian forces and their British counterparts were similarly housed along the south coast, from Hampshire to Kent: the Earl of Wilton's sixteenth-century home, Wilton House outside Salisbury, accommodated Southern Command, where Overlord planning conferences frequently took place. King George VI would stay there when inspecting the assembled Neptune flotillas on 24 May, as he wrote in his personal journal, now preserved in the Royal Archives at Windsor: 'From Wilton, I motored to Exbury, which is now a naval shore base, HMS *Mastodon*, where landing craft crews are trained. I spent the day with the Eastern Task Force to see the officers and men of the British Naval Assault Forces in *Overlord*. I must have seen over 300 landing crafts and other ships attached in the command. I spent a most interesting day. I got back to Wilton at 1800 hours.'[43]

Basildon Park, a fine 1770s Palladian mansion near Reading built from the proceeds of East India Company trading, had housed convalescent soldiers from Berkshire during the First World War. In September 1943, it witnessed the arrival of the 81st Anti-Aircraft and the 326th Engineer Battalions, both 101st Airborne Division outfits, whose officers were quartered in rooms on the top floor whilst the enlisted men lived in Quonset huts in the extensive grounds, where they set up rifle ranges and practised glider training.[44]

The grounds of Lord Leconfield's seventeenth-century Petworth Park, originally landscaped by Capability Brown and painted by Turner, were chewed up by the Sherman tanks of the British 27th Armoured Brigade and vehicles of No. 6 Beach Unit. In 2015, classified documents relating to Normandy were found at the stately Balmer Lawn Hotel in Brockenhurst, Hampshire, somehow overlooked since 1944 when it served as HQ of the 3rd Canadian Division.[45] The pattern of using big houses and châteaux for headquarters would be replicated when the Allies moved to France, in many cases hard on the heels of the recently departed local German *Kommandant*.

The temporary owners were not always careful with the properties entrusted to their care: a major portion of the Georgian Shillinglee Park, in West Sussex, was gutted by Canadian troops during a party in 1943; Piercefield Park, a late-eighteenth-century masterpiece by Sir John Soane outside Chepstow, was used by US forces practising urban warfare techniques with live ammunition, and remains a sad ruin to this day; whilst Arundel Castle's herd of red deer was shot and eaten. Other grand residences became prisoner-of-war camps, or housed service units, such as the nineteenth-century Malpas Court near Newport, south Wales, which hosted the 756th Railway Shop Battalion, whom we have already met crossing the Atlantic. Their job was to reassemble and re-steam locomotives imported from the USA and then despatch them as needed throughout Britain and France to replace damaged ones. The battalion's senior officers enjoyed rooming at the nearby Tredegar Arms Hotel. Junior officers occupied Malpas Court itself, while the other ranks were relegated to wooden huts in the grounds.[46]

Other houses, as in the First World War, became auxiliary hospitals. The US Army's 74th General Hospital took over Tyntesfield, a forty-seven-bedroomed Gothic mansion in north Somerset. Lydiard Park outside Swindon in Wiltshire, home to the St John family since 1420, housed 302nd Station Hospital. Lilford Hall, a Tudor house dating to 1495 in Northamptonshire hosted 303rd Station Hospital, while Shugborough Park, Staffordshire, home of the Anson family for over three centuries, witnessed the arrival of 312th Station Hospital. These were amongst a legion of other houses to have been used as medical facilities. They were vast establishments: on 3 April 1944, the 28th General Hospital opened, comprising seven hundred medical staff in one hundred temporary buildings, including cinema, library and hospital radio station, sprawled over seventy-two acres of the Kingston Lacey estate, Dorset, home to the wealthy Bankes family since the seventeenth century. When the 28th moved to France in July, they were replaced by the 106th General Hospital, both establishments treating a total of twenty thousand patients before the war's end. Once the hospitals had relocated to Continental Europe, Kingston Lacey and most other sites became POW camps.[47] On the Sherborne Castle estate in Dorset, the huts of the 228th Field Hospital were erected in 1943; it had to deal with tragedy on its own doorstep in March 1944 when twenty-nine GIs of the 294th Engineer Combat Battalion preparing for D-Day were killed when a truckload of anti-tank mines exploded in their midst. Later on, it would receive the dead and injured from Exercise Tiger.[48]

Posted to these great old estates, some GIs really felt they had stepped into an old novel, or onto a movie set. Californian Hank LeFebvre of the 82nd Airborne Division was one of two officers asked to dinner with the 2nd Lord Trent (whose father, Jesse Boot, had founded a well-known chain of British pharmacies):

It was a beautiful home. Lord Trent looked just like Churchill. After dinner the ladies adjourned to the parlour, and Lord Trent, my friend and I were in a formal room having port, brandy and cigars. Lord Trent led the conversation, '*Have you seen Jim lately?*' We looked at one other and I said '*Jim, Lord Trent?*' and he replied, '*Yes, Jim Gavin*'. He was talking about our assistant divisional commander, way beyond our lowly level. After some more small talk, his lordship slowly stood up, and talking as though the room was full of people said, '*Shall we join the ladies?*' It was like we'd been transported back in time to a 1930s movie.[49]

6

A Question of Colour

'Here we are together defending all that to free men is dear. Twice in a single generation the catastrophe of world war has fallen upon us. Do we not owe it to ourselves, to our children, to mankind tormented, to make sure that these catastrophes shall not engulf us for a third time?'

Winston Churchill, addressing the US Congress,
26 December 1941

FIFTY AMERICAN HOSPITALS were dotted around south-west England before D-Day. The huge number was not just to service the ordinary illnesses and accidents of GIs (including the substantial VD infection rate), but to cope with the vast numbers of anticipated combat casualties.[1] Wounded were to be conveyed to them by fleets of ambulances or hospital trains, the latter being converted in the Great Western Railway workshops at Swindon from old rolling stock to specific US Army patterns. New Englander Lieutenant Helen Pavlovsky of the US Naval Reserve worked in one of them, Naval Base Hospital No. 12 (or Netley Hospital to the British): 'Southampton became an American town; it took at least a week for all the ships to gather just outside our hospital in Southampton Water; we could go outside and sit on the waterfront and watch.' Of 6 June she would recall that 'one day it seemed like the whole area was full of ships and the next morning there was not a single one, so we knew *it* was beginning, but it took three or four days before we started receiving casualties.'[2]

Those US troops Dorset-bound also received a small booklet about the county, in which the Lord Lieutenant – the King's representative for the county – had written, 'We rejoice to think that American forces might feel at home in our County, and would have them know that the hand of comradeship is at all times held out to our gallant allies and kinsmen. Anything we in Dorset can do to strengthen the bonds of friendship and ties that bind us, will always be our first aim and endeavour.'[3]

One of those arriving in Dorset was Valentine M. Miele with the 1st Infantry Division; he had joined Colonel George Taylor's 16th Infantry in North Africa, fought through Sicily and sailed to Liverpool with them in November 1943: 'We went straight off the ship to Dorchester, didn't do much training until January, but it was cold. Luckily they fed you twenty-four hours a day and we had the little stoves we used to make hot coffee. And we were issued a pack of cigarettes each day. That kept us warm, too … We did some sixteen-mile forced marches, and a lot of guys dropped out, but I made it. I was a machine-gunner and carried the tripod, which was twelve pounds, and ammunition boxes, rifle, belt and pack. The assistant gunner carried the thirty-two-pound air-cooled gun.'

In addition, Miele carried his raincoat. 'You used it to cover yourself up at night. Also a field jacket; mess kit; the stove. We carried a lot of weight, maybe fifty pounds: the only other thing I carried was the new gas mask, I always carried that. Not that I was afraid of gas, but because it was a good pillow. And it was waterproof, too, you could put your cigarettes in there; and that's it: no blankets, we couldn't carry nothing else.'[4]

The Canadians and British, too, carried gas masks, though not for cigarettes. There remained a fear in all the combatant armies that poison gas would return to Europe's battlefields, from where it had emerged as a major weapon in the First World War. Chemical warfare is particularly effective where there are high concentrations of troops and their equipment – such as the invading force the Allies would soon concentrate in Normandy. General Omar Bradley would record, 'while planning the Normandy invasion, we had weighed the possibility of enemy gas attack and for the first time during the war speculated on the probability of his resorting to it. For perhaps only then could persistent gas have forced a decision in one of history's climactic battles.' Bradley noted, 'Since Africa we had lugged our masks through each succeeding invasion, always rejecting the likelihood of gas, but equally reluctant to chance an assault without defences against it.'

Just before the invasion, as a precaution every assaulting soldier and sailor would be issued with a set of clothing impregnated with anti-gas chemicals. Universally unpopular for inducing sweating, the material stank of rotten eggs, and many memoirs recall the unpleasant odour of the clothing, mixed with the nauseating smell of vomit and the scent of fear on board the invasion fleet. 'Even though gas warfare on the Normandy beaches would have brought deadly retaliation against German cities,' Bradley recounted, 'I reasoned that Hitler in his determination to resist to the end, might risk gas in a gamble for survival. When D-Day ended without a whiff of mustard, I was vastly relieved. For even a light sprinkling of persistent gas on Omaha beach could have cost us our footing there.'[5]

There was inevitably a coterie of well-connected and cultured Americans caught up in the 'friendly invasion', best epitomised by Evelyn Waugh's character Loot ('Lieutenant' abbreviated) who appears in the *Sword of Honour* trilogy. He was cast as a positive influence in Waugh's make-believe world, the opposite of the stereotypical GI whom the acutely snobbish Waugh loathed. Loot loved literature and architecture, was charming and erudite, had elegant manners, enjoyed the nuances of English society and moved easily within it.

There was a real Loot of Waugh's acquaintance: 'Sarge' as he was known to all (actually Technical Sergeant – he turned down a commission) Stuart Duncan Preston, who worked in London on Eisenhower's staff from 1942 and seemed, almost overnight, to be on intimate terms with London's intellectual aristocracy and its prominent hostesses. A New York bon viveur of wealthy parentage, Harold Nicolson, Nancy Mitford, Harold Acton, Anthony Powell and Osbert Sitwell all wrote fondly of him; Cecil Beaton photographed him. When once hospitalised for jaundice, it was said that King George VI brushed off a late visitor, saying, 'Never mind, I expect you've been to St George's hospital to see *the Sergeant.*' When asked what he did in June 1944 (his real job was to save works of art with the 'Monuments Men'), Sarge Preston replied, 'Oh, I would just drive ahead to the French next town and ask the mayor if he had parking for twenty Jeeps' – for which the aforesaid French were moved enough to award the modest Preston a *Croix de Guerre.*[6]

USAAF airmen were the most popular tribe of Yanks, as they were seen to be fighting and suffering from the moment of their arrival. Less popular were the ground troops; first arriving in 1942, some units would spend two years or more in the UK before departing for war. This was more than enough time to make themselves despised in some eyes.

Middle-aged men (like the peppery novelist-soldier Evelyn Waugh, forty-one in 1944) and older ladies tended to be less under the spell of all things American than younger women. They thought GIs sloppy in appearance and accomplished at bragging, drinking and fornicating, but not at beating the Germans.

The early American setback at Kasserine in Tunisia seemed to justify the initial, prejudiced views of US military abilities – though such opinions would be rapidly reversed after their successes in Normandy – and in popular memory these views didn't dominate and haven't lingered. British resident Vera Anderson neatly summarised the national view of the 'friendly invasion': 'I am so glad I did not miss those years. Everyone helped and shared what little we had and it left me with so many memories. When the Americans came to Britain, it was a huge boost for us all and I am so proud to have known them.'[7]

Mutual Anglo-American fondness was expressed in many forms. Estimates suggest around nine thousand war babies were born out of wedlock as a result of transatlantic liaisons. Though white American soldiers were permitted to marry at their commanding officers' discretion only after July 1942, tens of thousands of young women became GI brides, emigrating at the end of the war. Unrecorded at the time, the oft-quoted totals range from 60,000 to 70,000, although historian David Reynolds has demonstrated that the still significant total of 40,000–45,000 war brides is more likely.[8]

Canadians feel aggrieved at all the fuss made about GIs far away from home and their British girlfriends, for they too were as much distanced from their homes and kin. As a result, the Canadian Army exercised a more relaxed policy towards international liaisons and put fewer obstacles in the way of wartime unions. Some forty-eight thousand Canadians married overseas during the six years of war, the much smaller Canadian force eventually bringing home 41,251 war brides.[9]

Another measure of the love affair between the two nations was the extent that Americanisms had started to penetrate British English. As this was the era of the jeep and the jerrycan, civilians quickly came to recognise and use the slang of their guests, and a wide range of US words and phrases entered British daily speech. Some had obvious military connotations ('on a wing and a prayer'); many related to females ('birds', 'broads', 'dames' or 'dishes') and their anatomy ('pegs' for legs being the most polite and printable); but amongst scores of others traceable to the Second World War, there remain in common use: 'above my pay grade' (don't ask me), 'bail out' (quit or rescue), 'chicken' (coward), 'cooking on gas' (doing something right), 'eager beaver' (enthusiastic helper), 'fat-head' (stupid person), 'fuddy-duddy' (old-fashioned), 'geezer' (old person), 'gobbledygook' (complicated speech), 'humdinger' (outstanding), 'in cahoots with' (conspiring with), 'jiffy' (quick), 'lay off' (leave alone), 'mitts' (hands), 'pass the buck' (avoid responsibility), 'R and R' (rest and relaxation), 'scrubbed' (cancelled) and 'swell' (great). Some idioms – selected because still familiar to the author – had themselves crept into GI usage from the cinema before arriving in Britain; perhaps surprising is how long they have lasted.

Away from the moist-eyed, rose-tinted world of Glenn Miller and swooning British gals – and simply glossed over until relatively recently – the GI influx also imported racial divisions for the 130,000 black Americans who arrived as part of the United States military machine. In the 1940s the US Army was as segregated as the Southern states, from whence, ironically, came a disproportionate share of its peacetime officer class and wartime military heroes. Overall, the 694,818 African Americans who made up 7.4 per cent of the US Army were assigned to service units, performing manual tasks such as handling cargo, driving trucks, building roads, constructing huts, felling trees, digging holes, cooking or serving food – the majority of these jobs being performed by the Quartermaster Corps.[10]

One QM Corps GI was twenty-four-year-old Leon Hutchinson, who had arrived aboard the *Queen Elizabeth*: 'We wound up in London. Didn't have no trucks, didn't have nothing, so they made chauffeurs out of us and we drove British cars hauling officers around. We lived in Chelsea Barracks with the Scottish Troopers [Scots Guards] who guarded Buckingham Palace, and our first night we had an air raid. We didn't know nothing about what to do and ran down some stairs and waited for the All Clear. In the daylight we found it wasn't an air raid shelter at all, we were stood in a greenhouse.'[11]

Most Second World War photographs support this servile image, frequently picturing black troops in fatigues without weapons or combat gear, driving trucks, unloading ships, stacking supplies or filling jerrycans. In all cases these units were officered by white Americans, often from the South, there being fewer than a thousand black officers in the entire US forces. A few would volunteer for – and be permitted to join – combat units, notably the 99th Fighter Squadron (later expanded to 332nd

Reflecting both the official and unofficial discrimination of the era, a striking number of official US photographs portrayed black GIs performing menial tasks. The British public were puzzled by American attitudes to colour, though Churchill's government acceded to all requests to extend the segregation policies commonplace in the United States. (Getty Images)

Fighter Group) of the Air Corps, known as the 'Tuskegees', after the Alabama airbase where they trained, the 92nd Infantry Division, which fought in Italy, and the 761st Tank Battalion, the 'Black Panthers', who fought under Patton, but these were rare exceptions.

The US Navy was equally reticent; although 150,000 African Americans served in their ranks, only two ships, the destroyer escort *Mason* and submarine chaser *PC-1264*, were exclusively crewed with black sailors – the latter having an all-black crew, including her captain. The *Mason*, however, was commanded by six white officers, although all her 150 enlisted men, including all the chief petty officers, were black, but was routinely denied letters of commendation for her war service, although her record was excellent.[12]

Churchill's government did not conduct itself at all well over this issue, believing the alliance with America should take priority over its social conscience. Thus no concessions on US military racial regulations were sought, and none offered. Aside from the voices of a few highly placed advocates for black rights – notably Eleanor Roosevelt – the official Allied policy was that maintenance of the social status quo was an essential prerequisite for the more pressing issue of beating the Germans. Recently discovered notes of a UK Cabinet meeting where the issue was discussed, kept by Deputy Cabinet Secretary Sir Norman Brook, concluded, 'If any segregation, US must do it, not us ... we will not adopt such practices in [our] own barracks & canteens. Morrison [Herbert Morrison, the Home Secretary] refuses to have British police enforce segregation for US troops.'

In a remarkably craven contribution to the debate, Sir James Grigg, Churchill's Secretary of State for War, stated the official British view in September 1942 that 'coloured troops themselves probably expect to be treated in this country as in the United States, and a markedly different treatment might well cause political difficulties at the end of the war'. This was a policy subsequently described as a 'marriage of prejudice and expediency'.[13]

The US Army welcomed such endorsement of their collective pre-war practices. The prevailing view of the time was that the range of liberties enjoyed by black servicemen in Britain, including the freedom to associate with white women, constituted a threat to civil well-being back in America. In other words, British hospitality towards black soldiers during wartime would make re-segregation after the war challenging, if not impossible. Unthinkable today, importing such controversial mores was feasible because the black community in the UK at that time was tiny – numbering no more than about eight thousand, and concentrated in a few urban areas and ports. Thus, with no pre-existing racial tensions, most Britons viewed the arrival of black GIs with an open and favourable mind.

Patricia Barnard, who lived with her family in the Dorset town of Wimborne, remembered the 'very young men from all parts of America. As the GIs moved slowly forward from the outer areas, imperceptibly it seemed, nearer and nearer to the coast, so came a new company to replace them. The black troops were well received in our town by local people. They seemed quieter, more kindly, and we noticed they were so very homesick and always cold in England.'[14] One black GI observed astutely, 'I'd say England is a grand country, mainly because the Englishman does not look at a colored person in the way an American does, you know what I mean? You are not looked on as a dumb native, or something worse, as you are in the States.'[15]

This was in stark contrast to the First World War, when US forces sailed directly to the west coast of France and were culturally obliged to cope with huge numbers of battle-hardened black troops wearing French uniform. A handy accommodation was reached whereby most black doughboys served alongside black French colonial forces, allowing America to temporarily shoulder-slope the management of its social prejudices to a coalition partner. However, in 1940s Britain, the sight of an Allied partner visibly separating army units, mess halls, accommodation and off-duty entertainment on grounds of colour caused unanticipated reaction in domestic newspaper editorials and throughout the nation at grass-roots level. Whilst the US forces continued their social policies with renewed determination, it was in the face of increasing resentment of the host population, if not their government.

Local antipathy to the US Army's race policies expressed itself in clever reverse discrimination. One West Country farmer spoke for many when he said, 'I love the Americans but I don't like these white ones they've brought with them.' With the connivance of chief constables, towns and bars instituted 'white days' and 'black days' to avoid confrontations, but occasionally wayward GIs overstepped the mark in assaulting black and Asian Britons out of uniform, assuming they hailed from the USA. June 1943 saw a public outcry when four black GIs were refused service in a US military 'whites only' drinking den in Bath. One resident complained to the *Bath Chronicle and Weekly Gazette*, 'these men have been sent to this country to help in its defence, and whatever their race or creed they should be entitled to the same treatment as our own soldiers'.

It moved George Orwell to observe, 'The general consensus of opinion seems to be that the only American soldiers with decent manners are the Negroes.' In a letter to *The Times*, a café owner in Oxford outlined the shame he felt when a black GI presented him with a letter from his CO asking to be served. 'Had there been the slightest objection from other customers', wrote the proprietor, 'I should not have had any hesitation in asking them all to leave.'

The recollection of this prompted GI Willie Howard, of the all-black 320th Barrage Balloon Battalion (whose task was to raise a protective curtain of inflated balloons on Utah and Omaha beaches shielding GIs from German aircraft), to claim in 2015, 'Our biggest enemy was our own troops.' In February 1944 his unit had arrived in Pontypool, South Wales, to find itself billeted with a population that had never seen a black face before. They were met with nothing but kindness; a local family wrote home to the parents of one of Howard's GI buddies, 'You have a son to treasure and feel very proud of. We have told him he can look upon our home as his home while in our country. We shall take every care of him... we will look upon him now as our own.'[16]

A unique voice was Ralph Ellison, a black seaman and author with the US Merchant Marine, based in Swansea, Cardiff and Barry (all in South Wales), during the war. In 1944 he fictionalised some of his experiences in the short story 'In a Strange Country', portraying a GI in Wales, brutalised by racists in his own unit but given calm by the patriotic singing of his Welsh hosts; Ellison wrote of the 'warm hospitality of a few private homes' and a Red Cross club in Swansea where the ladies prepared 'amazing things with powdered eggs and a delicious salad from the flesh of hares'. His time there was rounded off by a 'memorable evening drinking in a private men's club where the communal singing was excellent'.[17]

Equally unusual was the voice of a black American engineer officer, Lieutenant Joseph O. Curtiss, who wrote in the spring of 1944, 'the more I see of the English, the more disgusted I become with Americans. After the war, with the eager and enthusiastic support of every negro who will have served in Europe, I shall start a movement to send white Americans back to England and bring the English to America.'[18]

A view from the other side of the fence was offered by Chicagoan George Maruschak, serving with the 320th Glider Field Artillery Battalion of the 82nd Airborne Division. On arrival in Leicestershire in February 1944 he was stationed on a farm near Husbands Bosworth, a stone's throw from the ancient battlefield that had resulted in the death of an English king. As Maruschak recalled, 'we had already seen action at Salerno under Colonel Paul E. Wright with our 105mm howitzers and felt kinda cocky when we arrived in England; our discipline was bad and our focus was not on our guns, but daily visiting Stratford upon Avon, birthplace of William Shakespeare, or Leicester, with two main objectives – finding pubs that were open, and meeting young females'.

Enjoying these pleasures apparently took a setback for the 82nd when a unit of black soldiers were quartered nearby: 'we soon learned that they were buying the girls fur stoles and other garments, throwing money and gifts at them; and quite probably were more charming than us combat grunts, though we didn't see it that way. And of course, the girls responded by openly preferring them to the paratroopers. Anyway, there were fights and knifings. We were warned officially, and all passes for the 82nd into Leicester were revoked.'[19]

How were they viewed by their admirers? Elsie Ross, a middle-class Bournemouth schoolgirl of fifteen, unashamedly recollected being over-whelmed by a call:

> 'Hey girl! Over here!' A voice straight out of the movies stopped me in my tracks. Never mind remembering not to speak to strange men – they didn't come much stranger than this. Six-foot-four, black and shining as ebony, and a whiter-than-white smile like a crocodile, the sergeant's deep-coffee-cream voice reverberated through the trees. I expected pine cones to fall in a shower around us. His tank looked like a great beast, covered in camouflage nets. Draped around it, like extras in a cheap Western, the crew chewed amiably as they beckoned to me. 'Here girl', I found myself holding a collection of chocolate bars, candy sticks and chewing gum, offered with an old-fashioned bow. When news of the invasion finally broke, I bit my lip, remembering a pair of pale blue eyes in a sunburnt, heartbreakingly young face.[20]

The absurdities of the colour bar back home were highlighted when a GI wrote to *Yank* magazine in April 1944 describing an incident with a small group of uniformed black soldiers travelling from Louisiana to an Arizona military hospital. After being refused entry at all the local cafés, the rail station lunchroom agreed to serve the GIs but only if they ate in the kitchen. Then a couple of dozen German prisoners of war, escorted by two white MPs, entered the restaurant and were served. The writer mused, 'I could not help but ask myself these questions: are we not American soldiers, sworn to fight for and die if need be for this our country? Why are we pushed around like cattle? Why are they [the German POWs] treated better than we are? If we are fighting for the same thing, if we are to die for our country, then why does the Government allow such things to go on? Some of the boys are saying that you will not print this letter. I'm saying that you will.'[21] Alas, the typical readers of that edition of *Yank* were probably more distracted by the accompanying pin-up of Ingrid Bergman than by the searching letter.

Official attitudes hardened on both sides, reflected in several violent and bloody dramas. Between November 1943 and February 1944 there were fifty-six clashes between black and white US troops in the UK, an average of nearly four a week. Neville Paddy recalled Christmas 1943 when Truro 'was literally crawling with Yanks and about forty to fifty white and coloured GIs started a fight using broken bottles, glasses and knives on each other outside the Globe public house'. There were 'several bodies lying about in the road covered with blood. Sirens filled the air as trucks arrived filled with military police who waded into the melee, swinging their staves and knocking to the ground many of the fighters. Others picked up unconscious GIs and threw them into the backs of waiting lorries and ambulances.' After that, Truro was segregated on alternate evenings, 'black on one night, white the next'. By way of recompense, their senior officer apologised to the public, 'hosted a children's New Year's Day variety show, and issued candy, chocolate, tinned fruit and doughnuts to the children of Truro'.[22]

A GI of the 508th Parachute Infantry with the 82nd Airborne recalled driving through Nottingham seeing

> something that we had never seen before in our lives – there on the sidewalk were Negro troops arm-in-arm with white girls, walking along as though they owned the place. The guys in the trucks stared in disbelief – this just couldn't be happening; it wasn't allowed in the States and they were going to make damn sure it wouldn't happen again here. It got pretty bad in Nottingham, troopers were fighting the Negros everywhere they could find them, in pubs, on the streets, and cinemas. I know for sure that quite a few were even thrown into the River Trent, and at the end of the day, at least three Negros had been killed.[23]

Sergeant Bob Slaughter of the 29th Division remembered another incident at Ivybridge, the small village in Devon where his company of the 116th Infantry were billeted, after a battalion of black GIs moved in nearby. 'Our battle-fit First Battalion was itching for a fight. The fuse was lit when one of the prettiest girls in town was seen with one of the newcomers. Fights broke out and a few men were severely wounded. It was a very serious problem and it soon became apparent that the soldiers had to be separated.'[24] Tim Parr, a civilian living in Launceston, Cornwall, remembered the 'rather nasty affair one night when some coloured Americans were turned out of a pub by their military police, which they took a dim view of. They went back to camp, got their guns, came back and shot up the town square in Launceston. I can remember bullet holes in some of the windows.'[25]

In June 1943, an armed confrontation between the white 234th US Military Police Company and black soldiers of the 1511th Quartermaster

Truck Regiment in Lancashire left one soldier dead and several injured. The incident took place against a backdrop of race riots in Detroit earlier that week which had led to thirty-four deaths, including twenty-five black casualties. Fearful of such disorder riding the Atlantic, American commanders throughout Britain demanded a colour bar on drinking houses. In many towns, including Bamber Bridge, where the gunfight took place, local pubs responded with 'black troops only' signs.

Significantly, when MPs – widely known as 'snowdrops' on account of their white helmets and webbing – arrived to arrest black soldiers who were drinking after hours in Ye Olde Hob Inn, local people and British servicewomen of the Auxiliary Territorial Service sided with their black guests. Guns were drawn, both then and later, when several jeeps full of MPs arrived at the truck regiment's camp, bent on what can only be called revenge. The armoury was raided, and a large group of black GIs left in pursuit of the MPs. The soldiers warned the towns-people to stay inside, and began shooting at the military policemen, who returned fire.

An almost identical incident took place after D-Day in the leafy Hampshire village of Kingsclere, when black soldiers from the 3247th Quartermaster Service Company were confronted by US military policemen in the Bolton Arms pub. Told to return to base for being improperly dressed and without passes, as at Bamber Bridge, the GIs complied, but later returned with weapons and opened fire on the MPs, who were by then drinking in another pub, the Crown. In the resulting fusillade, two black soldiers and the pub landlord's wife lay dead. Ann Rowan, who was nine at the time, remembered the thrill of something so dramatic happening to her small wartime village: 'Going to school the next day, a more knowing friend showed us where bullets had chipped the bricks on another friend's house and an impression in the grass where they had laid one of the bodies.'[26]

Perhaps a rare voice from the wartime African American community is needed here. Sergeant James Hudson drove GMC 6×6s ('Jimmies') with the 3rd Platoon, 3683th Quartermaster Truck Company, and was stationed in Kingsclere in February–June 1944, before the killings in the Crown.[27] He had nothing but pleasant memories of the locale: 'We took over from some other QM guys. Our executive officer, Major George C. Blackwell, organised everything with the town mayor so we could drink that warm English beer in the saloon opposite the church [the Crown]. We was lonely, far from home, and the currency with all those coins was real confusing, but the local folks, specially the English gals, made us feel at home, unlike some of our own officers. We were no trouble to anyone, but there sure was a lot of us GIs in that small area, hundreds, thousands, maybe. We must have swamped the area with our trucks. Our job was to keep the combat guys in bacon, beans and bullets. When we left, we handed over to another QM outfit and moved to France.'[28]

A court martial later convicted thirty-two soldiers of mutiny at Bamber Bridge, but also blamed bad man management in the truck battalion and inherent racism in the military police company. The US Army was forced to recognise flaws in its own units: all but one of the truck regiment's officers were white, whereas all their soldiers were black. Moreover, it was realised that quartermaster units were riddled with incompetent officers (at that time the QM Corps was something of a 'dumping ground' for less able officers), and their leadership was abysmal.

Morale among black troops stationed in Britain improved when the sentences were all reduced on appeal, the Quartermaster Corps purged of poor officers, likewise the military police, who then began racially integrated patrols. Work rates were found to improve and instances of going absent without (official) leave (AWOL) declined when senior officers took the trouble to visit quartermaster units and explain 'how their tedious work played an important part of the larger war effort'.[29] Ten black GIs were convicted of murder at Kingsclere, being sentenced to hard labour for life, but there was no doubt that in both these and many other cases, official US Army racial segregation was the cause of much unhappiness in 1940s Britain.

Immediately after Pearl Harbor an editorial in the *Pittsburgh Courier* demanded, 'We call upon the President and Congress to declare war on Japan and racial prejudice in our country. Certainly we should be strong enough to whip them both.' The same paper later published a letter to its editor in January 1942: 'Being an American of dark complexion and some twenty-six years, should I sacrifice my life to live as a half-American? Is the kind of America I know worth defending? Will colored Americans suffer still the indignities that have been heaped upon them in the past? These and other questions need answering.'[30]

In Britain, the best policy eventually was found to be all-out avoidance of black–white GI confrontation. The 19th US Army General Hospital based in Malvern, Worcestershire, had an African American unit attached to it, the 701st Medical Sanitary Company. According to the 19th's archives, white medical staff were warned 'to in no way interfere with the British custom of allowing white girls to entertain colored men'.[31]

The British attitude to colour within the US Army during the war was a major theme of Nevil Shute's novel *The Chequer Board*, written in 1945 and published two years later. Shute wanted to reflect the 'wartime popularity of American Negroes in England' and built part of his story around a black GI wronged by the inherent racism of the white US Army, and against whom charges of rape were laid and eventually dropped. Shute was concerned about the impact the subject matter might have on his American readers, but his sympathetic writing ensured it sold as well in the USA as it did in post-war Britain.[32]

The novel closely follows the facts of a real case which played out in British newspaper headlines in the weeks before D-Day. Leroy Henry, a thirty-year-old black GI truck driver, was accused of rape near Bath in May 1944. Poorly defended by a junior officer and pressured into signing a confession, he was found guilty by a US military court and sentenced to death. British journalists discovered that the accused and his alleged victim had met on two previous occasions for consensual sex when money had changed hands; furthermore, the 'victim' had a reputation for 'loose morals' in the neighbourhood.

Two days after the Normandy landings, Eisenhower received a petition from the mayor of Bath and thirty-three thousand locals pleading clemency for the GI, whilst the UK press suggested the evidence against the accused was so biased it would have resulted in acquittal under English law. Eisenhower had the Henry case reviewed and in a colour-blind re-examination of the facts the guilty decision was reversed and the GI returned to his unit. Although the story was swamped by the positive news coming out of Normandy, for those who remembered and cared, it confirmed suspicions of white American bias against black GIs and had threatened to damage Anglo-US relations at a sensitive time.[33]

This, then, was the context of Lieutenant General John C. H. Lee's clunky cameo in the information film *A Welcome to Britain*. Eisenhower remembered Lee as an 'engineer officer of long experience with a reputation for getting things done. Because of his mannerisms and stern insistence upon the outward forms of discipline, which he himself meticulously observed, he was considered a martinet by most of his contemporaries.' Ike thought him 'a man of the highest character and religious fervour. I sometimes felt he was a modern Cromwell.'[34] This

There was little colour prejudice in the pre-war United Kingdom. Thus the 130,000 black GIs who arrived were welcomed with the same respect given to their white brethren. This put great strain on official US–UK government relations. Generally, black GIs were regarded as unfailingly polite, prompting one Briton to observe, 'I love the Americans but I don't like the white ones they've brought with them.' (NARA)

led those under his command to interpret the initials of his three Christian names as 'Jesus Christ Himself'.

Lee commanded all the service troops in the UK, and his homily in the film – clearly scripted by a British pen – was an attempt to placate black ill feeling towards the mostly white US military. 'Everyone is treated the same when it comes to dying,' Lee stated,[35] but it remains historical fact that in the British public memory at least, black troops were generally felt to have behaved more courteously and with more dignity than some of their brasher white counterparts, who were inclined to mock Britain's old-fashioned cars, left-hand driving and – with good reason – abominably bad food.

The much-attested lingering fondness the majority of Americans had for the United Kingdom was demonstrated on the big screen five years after D-Day. This was the acclaimed 20th Century Fox movie *Twelve O'Clock High*, released in 1949. It starred Gregory Peck in a leadership study of the fictional 918th Bomb Group, operating B-17s out of 'RAF Archbury' in England, and portrayed many aspects of the love affair with England that countless wartime airmen genuinely felt. Winning two Oscars, it was warmly praised by Eighth Air Force veterans who considered it depicted aspects of their service lives with great accuracy and understanding.[36]

The interaction of locals and Americans around another USAAF base ('RAF Halfpenny Field') also featured in the latter part of the 1945 British-made film *The Way to the Stars* (aka *Johnny in the Clouds* in the USA), which was as popular with its British audiences as *Twelve O'Clock High* was with Americans. The movies are related, for both revolve partly around a local pub, and begin with exactly the same device of a camera tracking around the lonely, deserted post-war airfield, before going back in time to portray the wartime dramas they witnessed.

Second Lieutenant Bob Sheehan, stationed in Shepton Mallet, Somerset, recalled falling 'in love with the British cinema. Apart from showing excellent motion pictures, they became a trysting place and a refuge for many of our GIs and their girls ... Before the war in my native Indianapolis, we never saw a "foreign" film. For the first time, I realised just how good a well-made British movie could be. My new-found love lasted, and even today', Sheehan wrote in the 1980s, 'I will travel miles to see a British film.'[37]

A real airman – as opposed to an actor – recorded life with the 379th Fighter Squadron, one of the original outfits of the Ninth Air Force operating out of Wormingford, near Colchester in Essex. Later killed in action, George Rarey flew P-47 Thunderbolts, but was also an artist who designed the squadron's 'Rarey Bird' motif – 'a scraggly parrot with a cigar in its mouth, revolver in its claw, perched on a skull' – that was applied to all the squadron's fighters. He recorded: 'Painted some aircraft cowlings this afternoon. It is a colourful thing to see the old 379th lined up for take-off – looks like a menagerie. It sort of gives personality to an otherwise pretty cold collection of machinery.'[38]

Lieutenant Rarey's letters home to his wife Betty-Lou captured the affection his fellow airmen shared for England: 'It's just dusk and we've finished chow and put another day behind us. Through the open tent flap I can see the pleasant English countryside stretching away into the gray, misty horizon. The smoke from the many tents hangs low in this little cup of land. Some guy is playing a harmonica and a little old bird is singing his wonderful fool heart out. I've come to the part of the day I like most.'[39]

On the other side of the fence, Margaret Meen was a nine-year-old living in Wendling, Norfolk, when the 392nd Bomb Group arrived to take over the local airbase in the late summer of 1943. Operating B-24s, it was the most northerly of the Eighth's heavy bomber fields, built by contractors Taylor-Woodrow in 1942. Her schoolgirl memories – which speak for tens of thousands of her generation – were of 'watching the stragglers, badly-damaged solitary planes, at first appearing as tiny specks above the distant horizon, limping back to land safely in the late afternoons, long after the main group of Liberators had returned'. Her mother did the laundry for flyers and ground crews alike, and she recalled 'scrubbing dungarees and washing other clothes for the GIs'. Then there were the 'long convoys of trucks hauling bombs for the B-24s from Wendling Railway Station to the airfield's bomb dump in Honeypot Wood, and the frustration of the drivers as they occasionally failed to negotiate the sharp bends on narrow country roads, resulting in long delays while trucks and bombs were recovered from roadside ditches'.[40]

Children and soldiers are indivisible, and like all kids living close to US airbases, for whom the friendly occupation formed their earliest childhood memories, the MPs on the gate 'allowed us to enter the base and talk with the ground crews. Occasionally we saw the airmen before they left for a mission. I also have vague memories of watching one of the ground crewmen painting the nose art on a B-24 Liberator named *War Horse* and I took a special interest in the plane, cycling up to see it every evening. Then one day it failed to return from a raid, and I was too upset to go to school the following morning.'[41] Like many schoolchildren born in the 1930s, Margaret grew up very quickly, finally recollecting 'the trains slowly pulling out of Wendling railway station taking deceased American airmen on the first stage of their long journey back home to their families. I stood on the school perimeter wall as the trains left, with tears streaming down my face.'[42]

7

Committees and Code Words

'At what we and our American Allies judge to be the right time, this front will be thrown open and the mass invasion of the Continent from the west, in combination with the invasion from the south, will begin.'

Winston Churchill, speech to House of Commons,
21 September 1943

THE TIMING OF *when* to invade France had vexed the Allied leaders ever since America's entry into the European war. Immediately, Roosevelt and Churchill had held a series of meetings in Washington DC beginning on 22 December, code-named 'Arcadia', which agreed to invade Axis-held North Africa and unify the war effort of their two countries – in the direction of the virtuous, harmonious future its code name suggested. When the required resources became available they would launch an assault on Nazi-occupied Europe, using England as a springboard. It was agreed the most likely point of entry would be somewhere along the French coast. The US Army chief of staff, George C. Marshall, was assisted at the 'Arcadia' Conference by his newly appointed Assistant Chief of the War Plans Division, Brigadier General Eisenhower. The latter lobbied hard for a combined command system; as a result, the Combined Chiefs of Staff was established in January 1942, unifying the British Chiefs of Staff Committee with their American opposite numbers, the Joint Chiefs.[1]

Subsequently, partly in response to huge Russian pressure for a Second Front – the Soviet Union was bleeding heavily and Stalingrad had yet to happen – and partly through ignorance of the vast logistics required, the Combined Chiefs agreed to immediately build up all available Anglo-American forces in England – Operation Bolero; aficionados of Ravel's classical piece might have divined a reference to the slow-tempo beginning, gradually rising to a crescendo. Also planned was a massive cross-Channel assault in the spring of 1943, utilising perhaps forty divisions, christened 'Roundup' (suggesting its American conception). Optimistically, there were also initial plans for an 'exploratory' landing in France in 1942 – either at Calais, Le Havre or the Cotentin peninsula – named 'Sledgehammer', employing six to ten divisions, should Germany by some miracle suddenly weaken or the Eastern Front suddenly become critical. The author of all these plans was Eisenhower.[2]

Admiral Bertram Ramsay – who as Flag Officer Dover had rescued the British Expeditionary Force (BEF) from Dunkirk in 1940 – was naval advisor to the Roundup/Sledgehammer strategy. He soon discovered it was being undermined by none other than his own prime minister, the Chief of the Imperial General Staff (CIGS) – General Sir Alan Brooke, appointed in December 1941 – and the head of Combined Operations, Lord Louis Mountbatten. They were backing an alternative strategy to keep Britain's war in the Mediterranean predominant, in the expectation that they would make more headway against the Italians, against whom they were making some progress in the summer of 1942.

Marshall – Brooke's opposite number in America and Roosevelt's chief military confidant – and the US Navy's brilliant but overly Anglophobic commander in chief, Admiral Ernest J. King, were bullish about implementing the Roundup/Sledgehammer concepts. Yet, the British argued (with good reason in 1942), the alliance was not ready to tackle the complexities of a cross-Channel invasion. However, with the Germans running riot all over the Soviet Union, the British and Americans had to be seen to take the offensive. As Roosevelt was personally keen on his forces – in concert with the British – taking the field against the Germans in 1942, the Churchill–Brooke option to land Anglo-US troops in French North Africa in November 1942, Operation Torch (clearly an American reference to Lady Liberty returning across the Atlantic), was agreed in place of bouncing across the Channel to France.

Roosevelt personally backed Torch against the advice of Marshall and King – indeed, they had to be ordered to implement it by their president.

Largely to prevent the pair from 'sabotaging' Torch in any way, Churchill asked that it have an American commander. Marshall thereupon nominated Eisenhower, his most trusted protégé, then serving as commander of US forces in Britain. He was a face already peripherally known to Churchill, and at the time, Ike himself was leaning heavily on the organising genius of his deputy, Mark W. Clark. When he arrived in England on 26 June 1942 the *Daily Express* carried Major General Eisenhower's photograph with the caption 'US Second Front General is Here'.[3] They could not have known how prophetic the headline would become.

In this instance, the *Express* was only trying its best in the face of atrocious war news from Malta, the Atlantic convoys, Russia and North Africa, and Eisenhower's UK arrival did not herald what the *Express* assumed. The new front with which Ike would be concerned was far away from France. Reciprocating the gesture that led to Eisenhower's appointment for Torch, the American Joint Chiefs of Staff Committee agreed that his chief subordinates for maritime, land and air operations should all be British.

Operation Torch witnessed three sets of landings against Casablanca, Oran and Algiers in Vichy-held Morocco and Algeria on 8 November 1942, deep in Rommel's rear.[4] Most GIs staged through Britain and Gibraltar, but Major General George S. Patton's Western Task Force sailed directly from the United States. Here, Ramsay's genius at coordinating huge shipping movements showed, working as deputy to the Allied naval commander, Andrew Cunningham. This was America's first seaborne attack outside the Pacific, and fortunately for them it was only briefly and ineffectively opposed.

The landings were complemented by America's first airborne assault, made by the 2nd Battalion of the 509th Parachute Infantry. Torch was a vital milestone in Anglo-US military relations, but historically has not received the attention it deserves. Partly this is because the eventual land force commander, General Sir Kenneth Anderson of the British First Army, was not thought to have performed well and was demoted into obscurity after the campaign. There was little initial bloodshed, the Vichy French soon siding with the Allies. An undoubted logistic and planning triumph, the real reason for the dim memory of Torch lies in the fact that it was the *French* – albeit Vichy-controlled forces – who were the foe on this occasion.

By 13 May 1943 the Anglo-US Torch land forces – Anderson's First Army – had linked up with Montgomery's Eighth Army advancing from

El Alamein and forced the surrender of the Afrika Korps in Tunis. As its talismanic leader, Rommel, had been ordered home earlier, it was Generaloberst Hans-Jürgen von Arnim who was captured, not the Desert Fox, along with 240,000 of his German and Italian soldiers – enough for Churchill to speak of his own 'Tunisgrad'. Yet Hitler's militarily illogical behaviour in reinforcing the failing front, contesting every mile, had surprised and perplexed the Allies, who had expected to be 'the new masters of ancient Carthage' (as Churchill pleasingly put it) before the New Year.

Churchill himself had wintered in the region, earlier hosting a series of Anglo-American talks at the turn of the year in Casablanca over 14–23 January 1943, code-named 'Symbol'. This important summit directed the establishment of an Anglo-American tri-service headquarters under General Frederick Morgan to coordinate planning for future landings in France, code-named 'Overlord' (the first appearance of the name), albeit with no firm date. The same conference agreed to an invasion of Sicily – Operation Husky – later in the year, continuing with the same formula of Eisenhower as Supreme Commander, with British service chiefs working under him.[5]

Later that year, over 12–25 May, Churchill conferred with Roosevelt and Marshall in Washington DC, code name 'Trident', and took the opportunity to address a joint session of Congress for a second time. Many of the basic Overlord details were thrashed out at 'Trident', the name chosen by Churchill in reference to the tool of the sea god Neptune/ Poseidon, on whose goodwill the whole endeavour would rely. Apparently, during lifeboat drill on the transatlantic trip the Prime Minister insisted on having a machine-gun mounted in the boat to which he was allotted – indicative of the mood with which he approached everything during his wartime life: both pugnacious and perverse.

With Churchill safely arrived in Washington, American dominance of the wartime alliance began to be asserted. Not unreasonably, Churchill and Brooke wanted the main military effort to continue in Italy after Sicily – only two months away – with Churchill persisting in his view that a front in the Balkans might also be opened. The Prime Minister also argued (correctly) that because Tunis had fallen much later than expected, it was already too late to switch their forces in North Africa to France for Operation Roundup in the summer of 1943. Roosevelt, Marshall and the US Joint Chiefs grew alarmed that lingering in the Mediterranean would delay their strategic plans for invading France until the following year.

Thus, on 19 May 1943 and somewhat against their wishes, Churchill and Brooke were forced to accept a French invasion date of 1 May 1944. The postponement from 1943 was also due to the logistics of landing craft; most available had been deployed to the Mediterranean for Operation Husky – though the Americans had quietly diverted some to the Pacific – whilst only one US division was ready in Britain, due to the massive build-up of the US Eighth Air Force, Operation Sickle, which had taken much of the available shipping space. Further Overlord details were fleshed out at the subsequent UK–US–Canadian summit in Quebec, code-named 'Quadrant', held over 17–24 August 1943.[6]

Twice, at Churchill's behest, the British had lobbied to postpone the invasion of France and instead pursue operations in the Mediterranean, initially in favour of Operation Torch, then for the invasion of Sicily. Although there were sound military reasons behind both deferrals, American suspicions had grown by the time of the 'Trident' Conference that the Prime Minister was opposed to a cross-Channel invasion, period. His personal history of having instigated the unsuccessful and costly Gallipoli campaign of 1915 might also have been seen as antipathetic to large-scale amphibious activity.

Certainly the lessons from the Anglo-Canadian raid on Dieppe in August 1942, the American reversal at Kasserine in February 1943, and the unexpectedly long German defence of Tunisia must have contributed to Churchill's scepticism, but the consistency of his own utterances – in favour of operations in the Balkans, bringing Turkey into the war, and a projected assault on Norway, Operation Jupiter – were instrumental in Marshall and Roosevelt concluding that the British had lost faith in the cross-Channel option. This was also the view of the Soviets, for whom the only worthwhile second front was a major invasion of German-held France.

The British capitulation at 'Trident' may have been influenced by concerns that – even though for good military logic – if the UK didn't facilitate cross-Channel landings in 1944, America would renege on its Germany-first policy. Certainly, whatever Roosevelt's public position, 'fifteen air groups originally designated for Britain, as well as troops and landing craft', had been redeployed to the Pacific in 1942, to shore up the Guadalcanal campaign.[7] Brooke and Churchill were also aware that the US build-up in Britain – Bolero – had only delivered four US divisions in 1942, perhaps indicative that America was also hedging its strategic bets.

Irrespective of the enthusiasm, or lack of it, of the Prime Minister and his Chief of the Imperial General Staff, the Allied planning organisation for a French invasion came into being on 12 March 1943 with the pugnacious acronym of COSSAC. This stood for Chief of Staff to the Supreme Allied Commander (Designate) – as the commander had yet to be appointed, 'amounting to a body without a head', and with only limited authority. However, in military terms a Cossack had an altogether different association, and one not lost on the Soviets. Its chief planner, Lieutenant General Frederick Morgan, and his US deputy, Brigadier General Ray W. Barker, were to prepare for an invasion on 1 May 1944, and incorporate all of the lessons learned from previous seaborne assaults. Morgan, a descendant of the notorious pirate Henry Morgan, remains one of the unsung heroes of the invasion of France, for it was he and his Anglo-American staff who devised the plan – with some later tinkering by Eisenhower, Montgomery and the SHAEF (Supreme Headquarters Allied Expeditionary Force) team – that remains the Western Allies' predominant military operation of the Second World War. Ike rated Morgan as 'an extraordinarily fine officer who had, long before my arrival, won the high admiration and respect of General Marshall. I soon came to place an equal value upon his qualifications.'[8]

COSSAC emerged, as directed by the Casablanca 'Symbol' Conference, guided by Brooke's challenging observation, 'It won't work, but you must bloody well make it!' Morgan's task at Norfolk House, 31 St James's Square, site of the birthplace of George III, was clouded by a few tiny obstacles. He had nothing to direct – initially just an aide, two batmen and a car with driver – nor did his commander yet exist. Indeed in his view, COSSAC was 'not highly regarded by the War Office' at all.[9] 'Morgan was a workaholic, often sleeping in his office,' recalled a member of his staff; 'he was very energetic and inspired a team who worked very long hours, often well into the evening. There was certainly no official leave in the twelve months I worked on the invasion plans.'[10]

Starting the process on 17 April, by the time he submitted an outline on 15 July (although the planning work would carry on until COSSAC merged with SHAEF the following February), his Anglo-American staff numbered 320 officers and six hundred other ranks in five departments – land, air, maritime, intelligence and administration – each headed by a two-star commander.[11] Later these departments took the American designations for staff branches, intelligence becoming G-2, operations

G-3 and so on. Morgan's first and most comprehensive draft was submitted to the British War Cabinet and Chiefs of Staff Committee as a 143-page document on 15 July 1943 entitled 'Operation Overlord: Report and Appreciation' and included thirteen maps referencing the planned outline of the invasion – in reality a feasibility study, rather than a firm plan.

Morgan's personal staff included his chief of operations staff, Major General C. R. West, and Wren Ginger Thomas. She was a shorthand typist when she joined the WRNS in March 1943, aged twenty-two. After basic training she was posted to Morgan's staff in Norfolk House. 'The first time I met him was in a huge room with maps covering the walls. I was the only Wren working on his staff, and in those days a shorthand typist was a very important person; I went everywhere with him, note-book in hand. I took dictation, notes at staff meetings and typed letters. We all realised that it was very hush-hush, very important. Norfolk House was buzzing with activity; I usually had to attend the chief of staff's conferences in the morning and evening, and the rest of the time I dealt with anything the general wanted answered or typed. The atmosphere was *very* focused; there was always a feeling of confidence among the staff – there had to be, with an operation of that magnitude.'[12]

COSSAC had to develop two plans for two scenarios: Operation Rankin, an Allied occupation of Germany if the Nazi regime suddenly collapsed, and Overlord – the name already chosen and pre-dating COSSAC – 'a full scale assault against the Continent in 1944'.[13] Morgan's staff solved the primary challenge of where to land by ruling out the Pas-de-Calais – so close to England that no surprise was possible – and favouring the Calvados coast. This was a conclusion also arrived at by General Sir Bernard Paget, then commanding 21st Army Group, who in late 1942 had – unbidden – initiated his own investigation into a possible invasion of Northern France. His plan, code-named 'Skyscraper', presented to the British Chiefs of Staff in March 1943, bore remarkable similarity to the final version of Overlord, adopted by SHAEF in June 1944. The 'Skyscraper' files were passed to Morgan, which greatly simplified COSSAC's work, though have been completely ignored by historians.[14]

To prepare those troops for their invasion, Wren Thomas also remembered 'a BBC appeal had gone out to the public to send in postcards of the coast of France, maps, Michelin guidebooks or any other information that might help with the planning of the operation – I still remember rooms with postcards of Normandy stuck on the wall'.[15] The appeal had actually been broadcast in March 1942 when Commander Rodney Slessor, a Royal Naval Volunteer Reserve (RNVR) officer, explained on air how a commando raid had achieved success with the help of 'thousands of guidebooks, photographs, postcards and holiday snaps'. Would listeners care to peruse their photo albums and cabinets for any images of the French coast and send them in – with helpful annotations – to the BBC? Within thirty-six hours 30,000 letters had arrived by post; by 1944 the tally was ten million.[16] Many were, of course, irrelevant and discarded but those retained – particularly some of the postcards reproduced in this book – were incorporated into briefing materials and recognition booklets issued to the assault wave troops.

A further challenge emerged with COSSAC's choice of beaches: none of them was near a decent harbour, vital for the sustainment of any invasion. It was one of Morgan's naval planners, Captain John Hughes-Hallett, who brought with him a throwaway comment made in the aftermath of Dieppe in 1942: 'If we can't capture ports, we'll have to take them with us' – there was general laughter until a voice muttered, 'Well, why not?' This would translate into the Mulberry harbours.[17] COSSAC's work was not only vital, but successful, in that it became the basis for Neptune, but as Morgan noted of their efforts, 'Never were so few asked to do so much in so short a time.' Ginger Thomas kept in touch with her boss after the war. 'We used to send letters and Christmas cards to each other. I still have a wonderful letter from him, which I cherish very much, in which he says, "Do you remember that it's eighteen years now since you and I put Ike on the road to victory?"'[18]

In selecting Normandy, COSSAC also concluded that a massive investment in deception would be needed to fool their opponents, which would become Operation Fortitude. The drawback of Normandy was its hinterland. Tactically, the bocage of thick hedgerows and sunken lanes, which limited visibility and manoeuvre, could restrict the Allies to their beachhead, enabling the Germans to counter-attack and push them into the sea. Operationally, the terrain and road network – running east–west, rather than the required north–south – did not lead the Allies towards Germany. The roads out of Calais did – which would help the deception campaign, but it meant that Anglo-American forces landing in Normandy would be fighting against the grain of the land and infrastructure. The hedgerow country would also inhibit the Allies from constructing temporary airstrips for their fighters.[19]

The fiasco of the August 1942 Dieppe raid had proved that the Allies needed air supremacy, German coastal defences needed softening up beforehand, and tanks and assault engineering equipment had to be landed in the first wave – all twenty-nine tanks landed at Dieppe proved incapable of even getting off the shingle beach.[20] The future invasion would have to be an overwhelming concentration of force at a given point, backed up by a massive logistics chain, while German reinforcements would have to be prevented from reaching the battle zone. The tenacity with which they held Dieppe, and the extent of its defences – later much strengthened – suggested that it was extremely unlikely that the Allies would be able to capture a working port intact, capable of handling the invading army's needs.

The solution, as Hughes-Hallett had concluded, was for the Allies to build their own ports and float them to the invasion area – hence the two artificial Mulberry harbours, thrashed out in a development conference at the amphibious Combined Training Centre, near Largs, Scotland. This was the 'Rattle' Conference of 28 June–2 July, held on the eve of the invasion of Sicily, 'a combination of intensive study and a 1920s house party'. Hosted by Lord Louis Mountbatten and Generals Frederick Morgan and Harold Alexander, who chaired seminars dealing with COSSAC's various challenges, the conference was nicknamed the 'Field of the Cloth of Gold' because of the number of high-ranking officers taking part. Both Churchill and Eisenhower attended, amongst eight admirals, twenty generals, eleven air marshals, with brigadiers and air commodores galore. Under the shadow of the monument commemorating the 1263 defeat of the Norsemen, the military staff were entertained with pipe bands and champagne suppers.

Besides finalising Mulberry, the delegates, who also numbered fifteen Americans and five Canadians, identified the need for the various Fortitude deceptions, special aircraft recognition measures, modified landing craft, the establishment of beach groups, also concluding that Normandy rather than Calais offered their best hope of success. Away from the distractions of London, more progress was made during 'Rattle' towards the eventual success of Overlord than on any other single occasion.[21]

The Mulberries were only conceived as temporary expedients until a fixed harbour could be captured and operated, which all the staff hoped would be Cherbourg. To ensure a flow of fuel to the armies in France, the concept of shore-to-shore submarine pipelines was already under way, known as PLUTO (Pipe-Line Under The Ocean). This idea did not originate with COSSAC and was under active experimentation in the

Bristol Channel before Morgan's command was established.[22] Morgan's team anticipated delivering five thousand tons per day of petroleum, oil and lubricants from D+20, and ten thousand tons per day by D+90. Some would arrive by tanker as well as by PLUTO, but these figures would later prove grossly inadequate.

The floating harbour idea can be traced to Churchill's famous memo of 30 May 1942 to Mountbatten at Combined Operations HQ: 'Piers for use on beaches. They must float up and down with the tide. The anchor problem must be mastered. Let me have the best solution worked out. Don't argue the matter. The difficulties will argue for themselves.' Progress at first was slow as discussions on competing ideas by the many interested parties were considered. Prototypes were built in remote areas of north Wales and tested in the even more unpopulated region of Wigtown Bay, south-west Scotland.

Churchill was irritated by the apparent lack of progress and penned a number of increasingly irate messages culminating on 10 May 1943: 'This matter is being much neglected. Dilatory experiments with varying types and patterns have resulted in us having nothing. It is now nearly six months since I urged the construction of several miles of pier.'[23] In fact as early as 1917, Churchill had drafted detailed plans for the capture of two islands, Borkum and Sylt, which lay off the Dutch and Danish coasts. He envisaged using a number of flat-bottomed barges or caissons which would form the basis of an artificial harbour when lowered to the seabed and filled with sand. Events moved on and Churchill's proposal was filed away and never published. The very fact that the strongest German defences were concentrated around ports suggested that an attack elsewhere, where defences were somewhat weaker, would stand a greater chance of success. Harbours apart, landing craft design also had to be improved – something else Churchill had taken periodic interest in – and British shipyards had no spare capacity.

To appease his Russian allies and prove that plans for the Second Front were under way, Churchill nailed his colours to the mast with his 7 June 1943 communication to Stalin: 'Most Especially Secret. We are planning to construct very quickly two large synthetic harbours on the beaches of this wide sandy bay of the Seine estuary. Great ocean liners will be able to discharge and run by numerous piers supplies to the fighting troops. This must be quite unexpected by the enemy, and will enable the build-up to proceed with very great independence of weather conditions.'[24]

The Quebec conference, 'Quadrant', had confirmed the need for two artificial harbours, code-named 'Mulberries', one each for the American and British-Canadian forces, and both designed to handle twelve thousand tons of cargo per day. The sites chosen incorporated two of the landing beaches, Omaha and Gold. The principal element of each Mulberry would be a fixed breakwater, made from seven thousand-ton hollow concrete caissons, code-named 'Phoenixes', which were to be towed across the Channel, flooded and sunk in position, resting on the seabed. Of the 210 eventually constructed in England, thirty-nine were deployed to the American Mulberry but not all the remainder arrived in Normandy – several were lost in transit and lie at the bottom of the Channel, whilst a few remain around England's south coast, manufactured as 'spares' and never used.

Each Phoenix was to be equipped with an anti-aircraft gun, ranged five storeys high, two hundred feet long and sixty-nine feet in beam. More than 330,000 cubic yards of concrete and thirty-one thousand tons of steel would go into their construction under conditions of the highest secrecy – workers had no idea what they were making; some guessed it might be 'a causeway across the Channel'. Mick Crossley was with 416 Battery of the 127th Light Anti-Aircraft Regiment manning a 40mm Bofors anti-aircraft gun on a Phoenix caisson with seventeen others, as it was towed across the Channel. Despite the slow tow by a tug, the rough seas eventually overwhelmed their concrete box, and while Crossley and four of his mates survived, the others drowned.[25]

Floating piers with seven miles of flexible roadway stretching into the Channel from the shore would complete each port, making them capable of quickly unloading ocean-going vessels and LSTs. Manufacturing of all the various steel and concrete Mulberry harbour elements took place at over five hundred sites in the United Kingdom, and at one time 45,000 men were employed on these tasks. Whether this was a worthwhile diversion of such a huge proportion of the nation's scarce resources and manpower remains to be seen. The basic concept was hinted at by the popular *Picture Post* magazine in May 1944, when in all innocence it observed: 'Something comparable to the city of Birmingham hasn't merely got to be shifted, it's got to be kept moving when it's on the other side. We must take everything with us – and take it in the teeth of the fiercest opposition.'[26]

In addition, fifty-nine old merchantmen and warships – the vessels were code-named 'Corncobs' – would be scuttled bow-to-stern in three fathoms (eighteen feet), along the five landing beaches. The resultant

The two Mulberry harbours, based around these concrete Phoenix caissons sunk onto the seabed off Omaha and Gold beaches, would make a huge difference to Allied logistics. The Germans knew that ports were vital to any Allied success, but never conceived their opponents might bring their own with them. (Getty Images)

breakwaters, code-named 'Gooseberries', would form barriers against the waves and create in effect five miniature harbours.[27] The two Gooseberry breakwaters at Omaha and Gold would eventually form part of the American and British Mulberry harbours. A huge fleet of 150 ocean-going tugs – most of those working in British and American east coast waters – would be required to tow the Phoenixes and Corncobs across the Channel, as well as the many component parts of the piers. Whereas much of the vast arsenal used in France was of American manufacture, all of the Mulberry components were inspired by Churchill, and British-designed and -made – which is why they receive so much attention in British war literature.[28]

The various memos and records of the Prime Minister's interest in landing craft design and the artificial harbours, and of his observations from as early as 1940 that sooner or later Britain and her allies would have to mount an amphibious assault against Nazi-occupied Europe, are included in the six volumes of his *The Second World War*, which appeared during 1948–53. Whilst they demonstrate his undoubted strategic fore-sight, the wealth of documents Churchill directed to be published as appendices in each volume are there for another purpose altogether. As we have seen, for several reasons the Prime Minister had gained a repu-tation in American wartime eyes of being 'against Overlord until the last minute'. Several American post-war memoirs from the credible circles of Roosevelt, Eisenhower and Bradley cited the British premier's oppo-sition as fact.

In order to refute such allegations of disloyalty – particularly impor-tant during his second 1951–5 premiership, when standing firm against Communism with his wartime ally – Churchill 'seeded' each volume of his history with selected documentation to demonstrate he had been committed to a cross-Channel assault from the very start, that he was the visionary, the torch-bearer from as far back as 1940. Indeed, in Volume 5 he explicitly observed there were those who thought '(a) that I wanted to abandon "Overlord", (b) that I wanted to deprive "Overlord" of vital resources, or (c) that I contemplated a campaign by armies operating in the Balkan peninsula. These are legends. Never had such a wish entered my mind.' As the historian David Reynolds has ably demon-strated, the documents Churchill included were the subject of much debate and scrutiny by the writing team who helped him on *The Second World War*, with some even doctored (to the extent of paragraphs and sentences omitted) to enhance the premier's post-war reputation, making Churchill's 'truth' about his support for Overlord, and other matters, much less objective.[29]

Lieutenant General Frederick Morgan's ideas that evolved into Overlord dated from the time when he had commanded a corps-sized defensive sector of Britain in 1941 and war-gamed a projected *German* cross-Channel invasion to test his troops. The scale of planning and mounting a successful amphibious operation became apparent to him and he was under no illusions as to the complexity of his task. The original COSSAC plan (incorporating, as we have seen, much of Paget's earlier 'Skyscraper' study) involved dropping two airborne divisions, and landing three infantry divisions on long stretches of sand – the future Omaha, Gold and Juno beaches – amounting to a thirty-mile front, followed by two tank brigades, two infantry divisions in reserve and twenty-one others committed to the ensuing campaign – all these numbers being governed by the amount of assault shipping and air transportation available. Importantly, Morgan also laid down three prerequisites for a successful assault: 'a substantial reduction in German fighter strength over northwest Europe; not more than twelve mobile German divisions in Northern France, of which no more than three should oppose the invasion on D-Day, and at least two effective "synthetic harbours"'.[30]

Notwithstanding the reasons for lobbying against invasions of France in 1942 and 1943, Operations Sledgehammer and Roundup, Churchill and Brooke may indeed have stayed – or become – lukewarm after perusing Morgan's draft COSSAC plan, submitted on 15 July 1943. True, Morgan had limited staff at his disposal, few resources and little authority; but he also understood he had restricted amounts of shipping and landing craft at his disposal. If the timidity of the first COSSAC plan alarmed Churchill – quite possibly putting him off the cross-Channel concept – it might have been because of the parameters he himself helped set at the 'Quadrant' Conference. Four days after Morgan submitted his draft, Churchill responded with a minute to the Chiefs of Staff, 'I do not believe that twenty-seven Anglo-American divisions are sufficient for Overlord', pleading 'the extraordinary fighting efficiency of the German Army and the much larger forces they could so readily bring to bear against our troops, even if the landings were successfully accomplished'.[31]

In addition to Morgan's three prerequisites for a successful invasion, Churchill instigated one of his own: that Stalin must initiate a Russian attack in support of the second front for which he had been lobbying so hard. Whether this was in expectation of a Russian refusal, which might cast doubt on Overlord, remains to be seen. In the event, the Soviets complied with their own spectacular Operation Bagration, launched on the third anniversary of the German invasion of Russia, Operation Barbarossa, 22 June. What is significant, though, is that when Eisenhower and Montgomery separately inspected Morgan's plans, neither was disheartened, and both expanded the original plan into what became Overlord, using the authority and resources denied to Morgan and COSSAC.[32]

Churchill finally revealed to Roosevelt what was probably his true hand in a cable of 23 October 1943. In it he observed that he was less concerned about the Alliance achieving a contested *landing*, but his anxiety lay in holding out against the substantial German reserves that might be sent by road and rail 'between the thirtieth and sixtieth day'.[33] Roosevelt and his Joint Chiefs remained unmoved, and despite Churchill's efforts to argue for continued priority in the Mediterranean, the British premier was finally overwhelmed at the Tehran Conference, code-named 'Eureka', of 28 November–1 December 1943. It was there – the first meeting of the wartime 'Big Three' – on 29 November that Stalin demanded to know who would command Overlord, the Russian leader not unreasonably surmising that an operation without a leader was not rooted in fact. This decision was really Roosevelt's, for America would be supplying the lion's share of the resources. It was assumed the Overlord job was Marshall's; that Eisenhower would replace him as US Army chief of staff in Washington DC; and General Sir Harold Alexander would succeed Ike in the Mediterranean.

In the event, the President decided he preferred to lean on Marshall at home, and the latter recommended Eisenhower for Overlord. Churchill's public explanation was that in view of America's contribution, the overall commander for the French invasion should be a US officer. In private, as far back as the 'Quadrant' Conference in Quebec of 17–24 August, there is documentary evidence the Prime Minister had offered to 'trade' American domination of Overlord for British supremacy in the Mediterranean theatre. There may also have been a frisson of *Schadenfreude* at work. If for any reason Overlord failed, a British commander – if not Churchill himself – would be under severe criticism from the American public. Having Overlord led by an American was a good insurance policy, were anything to go wrong.[34]

Here is the nub of Churchill's gut instinct towards the cross-Channel invasion. He may not have been as warm to it as the Americans, but he was not *against* it. However, the Prime Minister was far more enthralled by the Mediterranean theatre, which he felt held more promise, and was a known quantity. The Anglo-US forces fighting there already had a measure of their opponents and the ground, and in September 1943 the Italians would crack, forcing Mussolini's resignation. True, the Germans subsequently flooded into the country and, as in Tunisia, would contest every yard of Italian terrain, but progress was being made. Of course, the prize was not Italy itself, but access to the German–Austrian southern flank, which was being brought into range of Allied heavy bombers stationed on Italian airfields around Foggia.

Why risk all of this, reasoned Churchill and Brooke, in favour of the uncertainties of a cross-Channel attack? Ugly geopolitics also lay at the root of this strategic thinking. The Mediterranean was a British-dominated theatre, and the 'trade' in handing Overlord to the Americans had ensured that it would remain so. In Winston Churchill's heart of hearts, he still hoped the attritional slogging match of the Western European war would be decided in the boxing ring of the Mediterranean, under British leadership, even if Overlord were to deliver the final knockout blow. Churchill's nominee for the French invasion until 'Quadrant' had been his own CIGS, Sir Alan Brooke, who was also a passionate supporter of the Mediterranean-first policy. However, the long-overdue publication of Brooke's own diaries in 2001 reveal that he was privately sceptical of the American military machine and its various personalities. As Supreme Commander, most probably, he would have tried to pursue the North West European campaign as a British-dominated one. If his private thoughts are anything to go by, he was nothing like as committed to the idea of Allied unity as Eisenhower.

The principal beneficiary of Churchill's 'trade', which also continued the winning formula from the Mediterranean, was the Kansan Dwight David Eisenhower, then aged fifty-three, who emerged on 4 December 1943 as Supreme Commander of the Allied Expeditionary Force.[35] Controversially, 'Ike' was a desk soldier, and easily the best staff officer of his generation, but who had 'missed' the First World War and whose first operational command was as the guiding hand for Operation Torch, though he had briefly commanded small units in peacetime. In short, he was not the sort of bemedalled, moustachioed figurehead the British would have chosen; rather, he owed his fortuitous appointment entirely to his mentor, Marshall, under whom he had gained experience of planning, and dealing with Washington DC. Culturally, the British and US armies were and have remained quite different: the former insisting that officers alternated between staff and command appointments all the way through their careers; in the latter, officers might be streamed early on into branches that best reflected their abilities, and could thus progress far up the staff chain without constantly switching to command appointments.

Britain's CIGS, Sir Alan Brooke, watched Eisenhower at a conference in May 1944. There was perhaps just a hint of sour grapes – through not having the Supreme Command, which Churchill had implied earlier might be his – in his observation of the SHAEF commander: 'The main impression I gathered was that Eisenhower was a swinger and no real director of thought, plans, energy or direction! Just a coordinator – a good mixer, a champion of inter-Allied cooperation, and in those respects few can hold a candle to him. But is that enough? Or can we not find all the qualities of a commander in one man? Maybe I am getting too hard to please, but I doubt it.'[36] In retrospect, Brooke's bias seems shocking and indefensible. However, what were the prerequisites for Eisenhower's post? There was no job description. No one would dispute that Ike's core belief was the sanctity of the Anglo-US relationship, which for him assumed the status of a religion when he took up his new post in England on 14 January 1944. Incidentally, this also marked the last day of COSSAC – although it effectively continued to function as the genesis of SHAEF.

At the other end of the scale, Group Captain Desmond Scott, a New Zealander in charge of the Typhoon-equipped No. 123 Wing, based at RAF Thorney Island, West Sussex, remembered a visit from Ike before

General Dwight David Eisenhower (1890–1969) with his principal wartime aide Commander Harry C. Butcher, USNR (1901–85). 'Ike' was well-regarded and blessed with a naturally sunny countenance. More than anyone he held the wartime alliance together. The British field marshal Brooke thought him 'a good mixer, a champion of inter-Allied cooperation, and in those respects few can hold a candle to him'. (US Army Signal Corps)

D-Day. 'The impression he made on me was a revelation. Some people you take to immediately – Eisenhower was one of them. Most of the British generals I met during my time in England were as stiff and unbending as the silly little sticks they carried. Eisenhower's authority, humility and broad friendly smile made you feel when meeting him that you had made his day.'[37] The American was a 'natural' with soldiers, as Major George P. Chambers of the 8th Durham Light Infantry, in the 50th Northumbrian Division, recalled when the Supreme Commander addressed his battalion. 'At this stage the troops were bored stiff, bolshie, and had had all this so many times before. But, you know, at the end of his speech, the troops burst into spontaneous applause, which was tremendous praise of the man. His personality carried across to the troops.' William Brown, Chambers' company sergeant major (CSM), echoed this: 'He was great. There was no bullshit about him. You'd have thought he was cut out of chocolate.'[38]

As we shall see, there was an inclination amongst some British commanders – not all, but notably Brooke and his protégé Montgomery – to look down their noses at American colleagues, whom they regarded as inexperienced newcomers, though they had to be careful of their Prime Minister's own outlook, for Winston was himself half American. Harold Macmillan, Churchill's resident minister in the Mediterranean, inadvertently revealed the British attitude: 'You will always permit your American colleague not only to have superior rank to yourself and much higher pay, but also the feeling that he is running the show. This will enable you to run it yourself.'[39]

Eisenhower's undisputed qualities lay in being an outstanding organiser and planner, the pick of the US Army after Marshall – and in his ability to lead a multinational coalition of forces, each with their own national jealousies, characteristics and sensitivities. Indeed, Ike was – as he became – a politician in uniform, as Montgomery noted in a letter to Brooke of 4 April 1943: 'Eisenhower came and stayed a night with me on 31 March. He is a very nice chap, I should say probably quite good on the political side. But I can also say, quite definitely, that he knows nothing whatever about how to make war or to fight battles; he should be kept away from all that business if we want to win this war. The American Army will never be any good until we can teach the generals their stuff.'[40]

Here is the nub of Anglo-US wartime tensions, for Alexander had also handwritten to Brooke in similar terms (marked 'Most Secret'), by coincidence the day before Monty, observing that the Americans were 'very nice, very matey, but they simply do not know their job as soldiers, and this is the case from the highest to the lowest, from the General to the private soldier'.[41] These may have been fair criticisms in April 1943 when the US Army was fresh to combat and command, but what their British colleagues failed to appreciate was that the Yanks were *very* quick learners.

Major Tom Bigland was one of the first British officers to attend the US Command and Staff College, Fort Leavenworth, in 1943–4, and went on to become a liaison officer between Montgomery and Bradley. 'It began to dawn on me that the Americans were at the same stage of war in 1944 at which we had been in 1941–2, but that, while we [the British] were then fighting a superior German, better prepared for war and with superior equipment, they [the Americans] were now superior in men and equipment, and in the air.'[42] The superbly trained and equipped GIs who landed in Normandy were quite different in combat wisdom, equipment, organisation, doctrine and tactics to their alter egos who had landed in North Africa, then Sicily and Italy. Even while battling in France the US Army matured, adapted and learned – and far quicker than their British counterparts.

Most were won over by Eisenhower's natural charm and humility. Sergeant Norman Kirby, in charge of Montgomery's personal security detail, recalled that while de Gaulle refused to show his identity card, expecting to be recognised, Eisenhower had no such pretensions when challenged. He wrote later of 'Eisenhower putting his hand on my shoulder, handing me his wallet and saying "Help yourself, son"'.[43] Montgomery, too, was occasionally won over. The two dined quietly together on 2 June 1944 in Monty's headquarters on the eve of the invasion, after which the Briton uncharacteristically wrote of his boss, 'Eisenhower is just the man for the job; he is a really "big" man and is, in every way, an Allied commander – holding the balance between the Allied contingents. I like him immensely; he is a generous and lovable character and I would trust him to the last gasp.'[44]

Yet they were fundamentally different. Eisenhower's busy life was fuelled by caffeine, chain-smoking Camel cigarettes, and, of an evening, the odd glass of Johnnie Walker Black Label Scotch – a taste he acquired during SHAEF days – while he was never far from his British driver and companion, Captain Kay Summersby. Many commanders acquired pets as another form of stress release: Montgomery was famous for his various dogs including a spaniel named Rommel, and a wire-haired fox terrier that answered to Hitler – presented to him by BBC reporters attached to his HQ; Eisenhower also relaxed with his headquarters cat, called *Shaef*.[45] Montgomery was more solitary; he neither smoked nor drank and retired each night at 9 p.m. One of his staff officers, Goronwy Rees, observed:

> What was impressive was the air he had of extraordinary quietness and calm, as if nothing in the world could disturb his peace of mind ... And as one talked to him, one was aware all the time of the stillness and quietness that reigned all around him, in the study itself, in the entire household, in the garden outside, as if even the birds were under a spell of silence; it was a kind of stillness one would associate more easily with an interview with a priest than a general.[46]

Perhaps of equal importance to Eisenhower's appointment, it was at Tehran on 30 November – Churchill's sixty-ninth birthday – that Brooke recorded, 'We had a difficult time trying to arrive at some agreement which we could put before our Russian friends in the afternoon. After much agreement we decided that the cross-Channel operation could be put off to 1 June. This did not meet all our requirements, but was arranged to fit in with supporting the Russian spring offensive.'[47] If necessary – and the decision was in the balance for a while – this would give Eisenhower and his planners more time to firm up Overlord, and Ramsay and his naval logisticians an extra month to assemble the shipping they would need. In fact, it was only on 31 January 1944 that the Combined Chiefs agreed to postpone Overlord for the required month.

Sir Bernard Montgomery, flushed with the triumphs of his Eighth Army, had been agitating for the post of commanding the 21st Army Group, formed in England on 31 July 1943 to oversee the training of those Anglo-Canadian forces allocated to it. He was contending against his slightly senior contemporary Sir Harold Alexander. Brooke's private diary for 11 December 1943 is revealing in this respect and gives the lie that he was Monty's uncritical fan. 'Ike's suggested solution [for leadership in the Mediterranean] was to put [Field Marshal Sir Henry Maitland] Wilson in Supreme Command, replace Alex by Monty, and take Alex home to command the land forces for *Overlord*,' wrote Brooke. 'This almost fits with my idea except I would invert Alex and Monty, *but I don't mind much.*[48] Thus Monty's position in history was a lot less assured than one might assume.

In fact, the 21st Army Group *already* had a chief, the former Commander in Chief of Home Forces, whom we have already met – Sir Bernard Paget, appointed on 23 July 1943. He was exactly Montgomery's age, and someone of whom Sir Alan Brooke was inordinately fond, yet had a reputation for being 'difficult' and a dislike of Eisenhower. Brooke noted:

> I wish it had been possible to leave him in command for D-Day. I had a great personal admiration and affection for him which made it all the more difficult to have to replace him at the last moment. He had, however, no experience in this war of commanding a large formation in action. I felt it essential to select some general who had already proved his worth and in whom all had confidence. I had selected Monty for this job in my own mind, but thought I might well have trouble with Winston and Ike (or Marshall) who might prefer Alexander.[49]

The prospect of an Alexander-led 21st Army Group is intriguing; it would have been an entirely different formation. Although perhaps not as lively in the planning stages – Montgomery's forte was certainly that of an excellent trainer – there would have been little of the Anglo-American rancour that Monty consistently generated in the subsequent campaign. The multilingual Alexander in Italy had already proved as adept as Eisenhower at managing a multinational coalition that included the Free French and Poles, as well as Canadians. Crucially, he also saw eye to eye with Bradley, Patton and Clark. Perhaps the fighting would still have continued until May 1945, but the roll-out of Eisenhower's war would have been different: it is difficult to see Alexander backing Operation Market Garden (the September airborne drop on the Netherlands) as Montgomery did, and undoubtedly, the North-West European campaign would have been a more harmonious, less fractious affair for Eisenhower and his colleagues.

However, Monty was agitating for the 21st Army Group role, whereas Alexander was not, already with his hands full leading the 15th Army Group in Italy (and under whom Montgomery was serving as commander of the Eighth Army). Besides, whatever Churchill's own wishes, the ardent socialists in Churchill's War Cabinet felt that elevating General the Honourable Sir Harold Rupert Leofric George Alexander, Irish

Guardsman, son of the 4th Earl of Caledon, to lead Britain's premier force in Europe was beyond the pale, and instead they backed the less polished Montgomery, the 'Citizen's General'.

Just as Montgomery never revised his views of Eisenhower, Ike's initial impressions of Monty would colour their future working relationship. The American confided to Marshall in March 1943,

> Montgomery is of different calibre from some of the outstanding British leaders you have met. He is unquestioningly able, but very conceited. For your most secret and confidential information, I will give you my opinion, which is that he is so proud of his successes to date that he will never willingly make a single move until he is absolutely certain of success – in other words, until he had concentrated enough resources so that anybody could practically guarantee the outcome.

However, Eisenhower conceded, referring to the Mediterranean theatre, 'This may be somewhat unfair to him, but it is the definite impression I received. Unquestionably he is an able tactician and organiser and, provided only that Alexander will never let him forget for one second who is the boss, he should deliver in good style.'[50]

As it was, the cards for command of the 21st Army Group fell Monty's way through Churchill's urging on 18 December, with Brooke cabling him privately on the 23rd. Within the week he had relinquished Eighth Army command in Italy to his protégé Sir Oliver Leese, and flown to Marrakesh, where the Prime Minister was recovering from pneumonia, arriving on the evening of 31 December. There, Montgomery was shown a copy of the outline invasion plans drawn up by COSSAC. He immediately drew up a paper arguing that the plan was too modest and the front too narrow, and that more troops should be employed in attacking on a wider front, with a far greater number of follow-on units and reserves available. Even Bernard Paget in 'Skyscraper' had foreseen this, so Monty's insight was hardly unique. Eisenhower had meanwhile come to the same conclusion.

In fact, back in October 1943, Ike had been shown the original COSSAC plans for his opinion. This was when he was still Supreme Allied Commander in the Mediterranean, and Marshall, not Eisenhower, was expected to command Overlord. Back then, the American had observed that the proposed three-division assault was too weak, suggesting an increase to five divisions, with two in reserve. Prior to the

Monty–Churchill meeting, Eisenhower and his chief of staff, Walter Bedell Smith, conferred with Monty in Algiers to discuss Overlord on 27 December, again agreeing the COSSAC plan was too modest.

When Monty was shown the plans on 31 December by Churchill, he claimed never to have seen them before, writing in his *Memoirs* that he 'had not seen the plan, and had not discussed the subject with any responsible naval or air authority'. Monty then wrote a memo for the Prime Minister overnight, hand-delivered on 1 January 1944, which began: 'Today, 1 January 1944, is the first time I have seen the appreciation and proposed plan or considered the problem in any way.'[51] Churchill recorded that Montgomery said at once, 'This will not do. I must have more in the initial punch.'[52] Yet this is 'Montyfied' history and utter nonsense, for it overlooks the Monty–Eisenhower meeting of 27 December, and the fact that Montgomery's appreciation was simply a summary of the earlier meeting. Montgomery's falsification of the historical record was in order to create the impression that he was the true architect of Overlord, and he alone had identified the flaws of the COSSAC plan.

He would go on to denigrate COSSAC's work – though Frederick Morgan himself was on record as saying his invasion proposals were framed on too narrow a front, deploying too few troops in the first waves, but they reflected what he had been given: enough naval lift only for a three-division attack. Bernard Paget had observed the same even earlier in his semi-official Skyscraper study. Eisenhower would observe that Morgan 'had been compelled to develop his plan on the basis of a fixed number of ships, landing craft and other resources. Consequently he had no recourse except to work out an attack along a three-division front.'[53] In fact, Morgan's work was invaluable, for it had identified where and when to attack and solved many of the complex logistical conundrums, including the artificial harbours, and need for a deception campaign. He also bequeathed SHAEF a fully functioning staff.

The eventual three British/Canadian beaches had been coded 'Gold', 'Jelly' and 'Sword' – all types of fish. However, Churchill disapproved of the word 'Jelly' for a strip of sand on which many men could die, so he had it changed to 'Juno', after the Roman goddess, often portrayed clutching a weapon. The origins of 'Omaha' and 'Utah' are less clear – originally they were designated 'X-Ray' and 'Yoke', from the phonetic alphabet of the day. There was, additionally, provision for a *sixth*, spare beach, code-named 'Band'. Situated to the east of the Orne river estuary, between Merville and Cabourg, it has disappeared from history because it was not used – though given the subsequent struggle for Caen, perhaps it ought to have been.

Code names for operations were a relatively new practice, pioneered by the Germans during the First World War. Although the words listed in the US and British code indices were chosen randomly, Churchill was fascinated by them and personally selected ones for major operations. Borrowing the practice from the Germans – whose names he knew well from writing his First World War history ('Winston has written another book about himself and called it *The World Crisis*,' quipped his critics) – Churchill saw the names of culturally significant figures as useful sources. He had clear ideas about what constituted appropriate code names, and after coming across several he considered unsuitable, demanded that all future names be submitted to him for approval. He dropped this requirement when he learned the magnitude of the task. Only Winston Churchill, at the height of a world war but ever the wordsmith, could have devoted himself to writing this sparkling memo, to Major General Hastings Ismay, his chief military assistant, on 8 August 1943:

1. I have crossed out on the attached paper many unsuitable names. Operations in which large numbers of men may lose their lives ought not to be described by code words which imply a boastful and overconfident sentiment, such as 'Triumphant', or, conversely, which are calculated to invest the plan with an air of despondency, such as 'Woebetide', 'Massacre', 'Jumble', 'Trouble', 'Fidget', 'Flimsy', 'Pathetic', and 'Jaundice'. They ought not to be names of a frivolous character, such as 'Bunnyhug', 'Billingsgate', 'Aperitif', and 'Ballyhoo'. They should not be ordinary words often used in other connections, such as 'Flood', 'Smooth', 'Sudden', 'Supreme', 'Full Force', and 'Full Speed'. Names of living people, ministers, or commanders should be avoided, e.g. 'Bracken'.

2. After all, the world is wide, and intelligent thought will readily supply an unlimited number of well-sounding names which do not suggest the character of the operation or disparage it in any way, and do not enable some widow or mother to say that her son was killed in an operation called 'Bunnyhug' or 'Ballyhoo'.

3. Proper names are good in this field. The heroes of antiquity, figures from Greek and Roman mythology, the constellations and stars, famous racehorses, names of British and American war heroes, could be used, provided they fall within the rules above.[54]

Churchill's hand was without doubt evident in the names for the forthcoming invasion. The Normandy landings, dominated as they were by the sea, became 'Neptune'. The plan for the overall invasion of Europe was originally 'Roundhammer', a combination of the code names for assaults planned in previous years, Roundup and Sledgehammer; while Churchill's personal response to 'Roundhammer' is not recorded (the Official British History thought it a 'revolting neologism'), with remarkable inspiration at the Casablanca Conference he substituted 'Overlord'. Undoubtedly the best-known code name of the war, it does suggest the majesty and irresistible power that he no doubt intended. Certainly one can see the backs of military officers straightening up, even before they read the contents, when presented with a document named 'Overlord': clearly not another raid on a ball-bearing factory.[55]

Many historians have erroneously claimed that the two American beach names – 'Omaha' and 'Utah' – were associated with the V and VII Corps commanders, but this cannot be right, for Leonard T. Gerow was born and brought up in Virginia, while J. Lawton Collins hailed from Louisiana. In fact, the historical record has been curiously silent on the origins of these names. However, in 2008 an explanation was offered in a US newspaper, whose attention had been drawn to an old notebook belonging to a former soldier stationed in Bradley's London headquarters.

The jottings revealed how PFC Gayle Eyler, from Omaha, Nebraska, had been assigned in 1943 to the Headquarters Company supporting the staff of General Omar Bradley at 20 Bryanston Square. (The general described his offices as 'a row of fashionable West End flats with fireplaces of Italian marble, ornate rococo ceilings. Now the windows were curtained. An assortment of GI tables and field desks crowded the drawing room. Its walls were papered with Top Secret maps.')[56] Eyler and a fellow carpenter from Provo, Utah, were the security-cleared GIs who demolished interior walls and set up plywood screens onto which Bradley's maps were hung.

According to Eyler's notebook, they often queued for doughnuts and coffee with senior commanders and, once, Bradley – known as the GI's general – asked where the two soldiers hard at work in his office were from. Later on, they were invited to rest their coffee cups on a table with Eisenhower and Bradley, who were discussing the naming of landing areas; apparently it was then that Bradley suggested '*Omaha* and *Utah* – for your hard work getting the place ready in a hurry'. It is an intriguing addendum to history, but impossible to verify. Certainly, Amendment No. 1 dated 3 March 1944 changed all references of 'beaches *X-Ray* and *Yoke* to *Utah* and *Omaha*' – which would have been about the time Churchill was admonishing those preparing to send Canadians to die on a beach called 'Jelly'.[57]

8

Soapsuds and Tidal Waves

'Air Power is, above all, a psychological weapon – and only short-sighted soldiers, too battle-minded, underrate the importance of psychological factors in war.'

Captain B. H. Liddell Hart

T HE APPEARANCE OF Allied aircraft over the Netherlands was gradually becoming commonplace to both the Dutch citizenry and their German overlords. On Saturday, 4 July 1942, a drone in the skies and the wail of air raid sirens signified more raiders on their way in from the North Sea. Those on the ground may have recognised them as Douglas A-20 twin-engined medium bombers, operating close to the edge of their range from bases in England. In between the ugly black bursts of anti-aircraft fire, observers might have counted twelve aircraft, but their formation soon split up to bomb separate Luftwaffe aerodromes.

The raid on De Kooy airfield by a pair of A-20s – the British called them Bostons – met with particularly heavy fire, as the base, near Den Helder, the northernmost point of the North Holland peninsula, was an important German naval anchorage, and on the direct flight path to the Reich.[1] In the First World War, the Anglo-Saxon community had referred to anti-aircraft fire as 'Archie', on account of the way tracer ammunition arced through the skies. By 1940, Britons were calling it 'ack-ack', from the noise heavier guns made thudding against German planes and the phonetic alphabet of the day. By 1942 all were calling it 'flak', a German abbreviation of *Fliegerabwehrkanone* (literally, air defence cannon), and it was flak that brought down one of the Bostons over De Kooy, severely damaging the other. When the Dutch and Germans reached the flaming wreckage of the downed A-20, they were surprised to find the remains of the crew wearing US uniforms. It was Independence Day, and the flyers were operating a borrowed RAF aircraft to participate in one of America's first raids over German-held territory.

Its four-man crew – Second Lieutenants William G. Lynn and Boyd S. Grant, Staff Sergeant William A. Murphy and Corporal Charles P. Kramarewicz – became the first US Air Force personnel killed in action in Europe and lie buried in the Netherlands. The second Boston was badly mauled, but Captain Charles C. Kegelman managed to coax it back home, with the crew later awarded Distinguished Flying Crosses for their skill. Another American-crewed A-20 bombing Bergen airbase was also shot down by ground fire, crashing on Texel Island. While three of its crew were also killed (Frederick A. Loehrl, James W. Wright and Robert L. Whitham), the navigator, Second Lieutenant Marshall D. Draper, became the first American airman to be captured.

The raid had been launched from RAF Swanton Morley, Norfolk, by the Royal Air Force's No. 226 Squadron, which operated Boston IIIs. The USAAF's 15th Bomb Squadron had been invited to contribute six crews – half the attacking force – on their national day. One crew had already flown on a mission with 226 Squadron over France on 29 June, but with no loss or damage. The 15th Bomb Squadron flew out of Grafton Underwood, Northamptonshire, purpose-built for the Eighth Air Force. The USAAF squadron was led by Texan Hal A. Radetsky, who had entered the Air Corps as a flying cadet barely a year earlier, and would retire in the Vietnam era, commanding B-52 bomber wings.

'The squadron had spent a few months fighting the Japs before we arrived at Swanton Morley in May. It was very primitive with few facilities, so we soon moved to another base. We flew that mission because both we and the neighbouring Limey squadron operated the same aircraft, and to begin with, we borrowed their planes while we prepared our own,' Radetsky subsequently reminisced. 'Those first losses over Holland were a shock, as we reckoned it would be a while before we took any casualties; we flew another raid against the "yellow-nosed boys" at Abbeville fighter base, then repainted our A-20s in USA colours to fly our own missions under Eighth Air Force control. But we didn't stay in England for long. We were soon sent to Algeria to bomb Rommel's Afrika Korps. I returned to England in early 1944 for the run-up to D-Day, attacking railway yards and other targets in France.'[2] Radetsky's activities and those of the 15th Bomb Squadron were only the first hint of what would become a vast undertaking by close to half a million US Air Corps personnel.

As we have seen, American airmen were in England within days of finding themselves at war with Germany, and four elements were quickly set up. VIII Bomber Command was established on 19 January 1942 to undertake strategic bombardment. It used four-engined bombers, including B-24 Liberators piloted by the likes of Curt Vogel, the Missouri lawyer-turned-airman, and B-17 Flying Fortresses flown by Will Seaton Arnett, whom we met earlier ferrying his plane around the Arctic Circle. VIII Fighter Command was formed on the same date to escort them; it initially comprised singled-engined Spitfires, soon replaced by P-47 Thunderbolts and, later, P-51 Mustangs, operated by men like LeRoy Gover (once his Eagle squadron had left the RAF and joined the Eighth), and Bud Fortier, whom we witnessed crossing the Atlantic aboard RMS *Queen Elizabeth*. VIII Air Support Command was responsible for troop transports – such as the C-47 'Gooney Bird' Russell Chandler flew to England via Ascension Island. It also undertook tactical bombardment using twin-engine medium bombers, including the B-26 Marauders flown by Cy Cyford, and Hal Radetsky's A-20 Bostons. Finally, VIII Air Service Command came into being, overseeing all service and logistical support, comprising large numbers of black GIs, whose discriminatory fate we have also examined.

Meanwhile, RAF Bomber Command had been attacking Germany relentlessly since the first day of the war, when eighteen Hampdens and nine Wellingtons raided the Wilhelmshaven naval base. They continued to bomb the Reich, under pressure from Churchill, and later the Russians, to do their utmost to inconvenience the Germans. However, the Butt Report, circulated in August 1941, found few attacking aircraft were even getting within five miles of their targets. In response, on 14 February 1942 the bombing force received an Air Ministry Directive listing targets, including cities to be raided, clarified the following day by the Chief of the Air Staff, Sir Charles Portal. 'With reference to the new bombing directive: I suppose it is clear the aiming points will be the built up areas, and not, for instance, the dockyards or aircraft factories. This must be made quite clear if it is not already understood.' In other words, German civilians, not just their war industries, were to be targeted.

This was coupled with the appointment of Arthur Harris as commander-in-chief of Bomber Command on 23 February 1942.[3] A daylight raid against Augsburg, deep in Germany, in April 1942 – where seven out of twelve brand-new Lancasters were shot down and forty-nine valuable crew lost for no appreciable result – proved the vulnerability of RAF bombers in daylight attacks, and led to Harris's decision to abandon such missions and concentrate on night bombing.[4] Bomber Command thus attacked the Baltic ports of Lübeck and Rostock in March and April with success (if success can be measured in terms of the destruction of a city), which led to Operation Millennium, the first 'thousand-bomber raid', launched against Cologne on 30 May. It yielded tangible damage to the target, a low loss rate and excellent propaganda for Harris and his Bomber Command, then struggling to prove their worth.

The US Eighth Air Force's heavy bombing missions began on 17 August 1942, when twelve B-17s, including one with its commander, Ira Eaker, on board, of the 97th Bomb Group flew out of RAF Polebrook against Rouen's marshalling yards. Throughout the year the number of missions gradually increased as more aircraft became available, ferried across the Atlantic, while Robert Arbib and his colleagues built airbases in East Anglia, and all the resources and personnel needed to run them arrived by sea. Eaker had arrived with Major General Carl Spaatz at the beginning of 1942, and first led the Eighth's Bomber Command. In December 1942 he stepped up to command the whole of the Eighth Air Force, on Spaatz's moving to command forces in the Mediterranean.

For the rest of 1942, the two forces played to their own strengths, with Harris's RAF aircraft carrying heavier bomb loads deep into the Reich by night, and Eaker's US Eighth Air Force undertaking 'precision attacks' on specific targets they could see, by day. Whilst the latter's attacks were not necessarily any more precise, their solution was to persist, up-gunning their bombers and providing some limited fighter escort. Both air forces had to contend with competing theatres elsewhere. For political reasons, Allied aero-industries were manufacturing a steady trickle of bombers for Russia. Long-range aircraft, inevitably four-engined bombers, were needed to bridge the air gap in the North Atlantic – where 1,664 vessels, representing nearly eight million tons of shipping capacity, were sunk during 1942 by U-boats. Other bombers were diverted to Coastal Command. The growing bands of partisans across Europe needed equipment dropped from the air. More bombers were needed, too, in Burma, elsewhere in the Pacific, and in the Mediterranean theatre, which had opened with Operation Torch in November 1942.

That winter, Harris and Eaker were given more focus by the January 1943 'Symbol' Conference, held at Casablanca – which also established COSSAC to plan for the invasion of France. 'Symbol' laid down the strategy for the destruction of the Axis powers by aiming to knock Italy out of the war in 1943, and – to keep Stalin happy, since there would be no second front that year – increasing the bomber offensive against Germany. It was at Casablanca that Churchill observed critically that the USAAF 'had yet to drop a single bomb on Germany'. As a result, a new directive was issued on 21 January to the Allied air forces: 'Your primary objective will be the progressive destruction and dislocation of the German military, industrial and economic system, and the undermining of the morale of the German people to a point where their capacity for armed resistance is fatally weakened.' The first part was implicitly addressed to the US Eighth Air Force, the second part to RAF Bomber Command.

It effectively endorsed what they had already been doing, if in rather vague terms, but required both to increase the intensity of their activities. Stung by Churchill's remark, Eaker immediately ordered his bombers over Germany. On 27 January 1943 sixty-four B-17s and B-24s were launched against Vegesack-Bremen, which was found to be obscured by cloud. Mindful of the propaganda and politics of a successful mission, the port of Wilhelmshaven was instead attacked by the fifty-three bombers who reached their secondary target. Led by the 306th Bomb Group (subsequently known as 'The Reich Wreckers'), they and others from the 91st, 303rd and 305th Bomb Groups claimed twenty-two German fighters destroyed, for the loss of three of their own.

The Anglo-American alliance realised that to gain and maintain a foothold in France they would need complete mastery of the air, with the Luftwaffe dispersed, harried and destroyed. Accordingly, on 3 June 1943, the Combined Chiefs of Staff refined their instructions to include attacks on Luftwaffe 'airframe, engine and component factories and the ball-bearing industry on which the strength of the German fighter force depends'; aircraft repair depots; and the 'destruction of enemy fighters in the air and on the ground' – to pave the way for the invasion of France the following year; the wording of this directive, code-named 'Pointblank', was confirmed at the August 1943 Quebec 'Quadrant' Conference.[5]

At this stage, the US Eighth Air Force was still small, but growing rapidly. In April 1943, it still only possessed 264 heavy bombers and 172 escort fighters, but felt confident enough to strike at cities on the German frontier. Such missions, however, enabled the Luftwaffe to get a feel for American tactics, by logging the Eighth's bomber-formation speeds, strengths and destinations. Thus the Germans perfected their defences and started to station aircraft at interception points along likely bomber routes. These tactics soon wore down the US bomber crews. In August, recalled the lead bombardier of the 384th Bomb Group, Lieutenant Joseph W. Baggs, flying out of RAF Grafton Underwood, near Kettering, only eight of the group's forty-plus original crews were left. 'Who's Afraid of Focke-Wulf?' was the title of a magazine article pinned up in one bombardment group mess hall – to which every flying officer, led by the group commander, signed his name below.

Spaatz's staff officers noted that every ten thousand tons of bombs dropped cost the Eighth thirteen planes and sixty-seven men. The Luftwaffe weren't the only challenge. 'It was always cold up there,' one pilot remembered of temperatures that could plunge below −50°F. In such conditions, thick ice formed on windows and unprotected hands froze to equipment and guns. Even on the first, 27 January, mission the 303rd Bomb Group had recorded two men hospitalised with frostbite. Thus, US aircrew wore leather fleece-lined flying helmets, mitts and jackets, often with their aircraft's name painted on the back. Electrically heated suits and oxygen were essential at heights above ten thousand feet. However, the suits, oxygen bottles and tubing frequently froze or malfunctioned, and the resultant hypoxia killed as frequently as German shells. The medical officer of the 381st Bomb Group, based at RAF Ridgewell, Essex, wrote of this period that 'morale is the lowest that has yet been observed'.[6]

The fighter crews, too, quickly tired, and the stress piled up on squadron commanders, as Captain LeRoy Gover of the 336th Fighter Squadron, based at RAF Debden, also in Essex, remembered:

> It was the duty of the squadron commander to write to the parents or wife of those shot down and tell them what happened and offer sympathy. I just wasn't any good at that, so I had the adjutant write the letters. Then a friend would go through the lost pilot's belongings and screen them for anything that would make the situation worse back home, before we packed them up and sent them to his family. Most of

the kids that were lost were shot down over the Continent and so we didn't know their fate for several days or even weeks. If they were captured, the Red Cross would know.[7]

If they deteriorated in performance, aircrew could be rested temporarily or grounded permanently. US flyers were entitled to be sent home after a certain number of missions. Initially it was twenty-five, later thirty, for bomber crews. For fighter pilots it was hours – typically three hundred hours of combat flying.

The Pointblank directive translated within weeks into attacks on German ball-bearing plants at Schweinfurt on 17 August, and the Messerschmitt plant at nearby Regensburg, a year to the day after the first B-17 mission to Rouen. The anniversary was not pleasant: American losses totalled sixty of the 367 planes deployed over occupied Europe, with five more ditched near or over England, and seventeen aircraft damaged beyond repair. A second mission on 14 October fared no better, with another sixty out of 291 aircraft lost, but 121 suffering irreparable damage.[8] The Schweinfurt missions started to undermine the Eighth's confidence in its bombers to self-defend.

They flew in tight combat boxes of around twenty aircraft to maximise their array of ten to thirteen 0.50-inch machine guns – and began to experiment by adding wing and belly drop-tanks to their fleets of P-38s, P-47s and P-51s to develop long-range fighters. The RAF never made much effort to fit extra fuel tanks to its Spitfires, because their long-range bombers flew by night and had less need of escorts. However, to support the second Schweinfurt raid on 14 October, Pierre Clostermann, a Free French Spitfire pilot with 602 Squadron, RAF, recorded that 'in three days, not an hour over, a Watford factory undertook to manufacture eight hundred 90-gallon tanks. Close on one thousand workmen worked day and night, and on 13 October at dawn, RAF fitters were fixing them to the bellies of our Spitfires.'[9]

On the second Schweinfurt mission Clostermann's squadron escorted the raiders out as far as their fuel allowed, returned for lunch, then flew out again to shepherd them home. He described the aerial combat on the return leg as 'a scene of frightful panic. It was the first time that under the concerted efforts of the flak and avalanches of Junkers 88s and Messerschmitt 410s armed with rockets, boxes of Fortresses had been broken up, dislocated, reduced to shreds'. The Frenchman recollected, 'The big bombers were scattered all over the sky, vainly trying to bunch in threes or fours to cross their fire. The Focke-Wulfs were rushing in for the kill. I had the impression I was diving into an aquarium full of demented fish! Nothing but radial engines, yellow bellies, black crosses and clipped wings beating the air like fins. The air was criss-crossed with multi-coloured tracer bullets.' Returning back across the North Sea, Clostermann remembered, 'on my right was a Fortress holed like a sieve, but flying all the same, and on my left a red-nosed P-47 limped along'.[10]

There had also been a growing American presence in the air throughout the Middle East – at El Alamein, P-40s of the 57th Fighter Group fought alongside Sir Arthur Tedder's Desert Air Force. Just before Torch, the USAAF in the region was regularised with the creation on 12 November 1942 of the Ninth Air Force under Major General Lewis H. Brereton. They participated in the Tunisian and Sicilian campaigns, and bombed the Romanian oil refineries at Ploeşti (the superbly titled Operation 'Tidal Wave' – another of Churchill's inspirational code names), vital for Hitler's tanks, planes and ships. Flown on 1 August 1943 through 2,600 miles of difficult skies, the attack was made alongside three groups from the Eighth Air Force based in Britain, and demonstrated what could be achieved if the strategic air forces pooled their resources. The mission, however, came at a cost the USAAF couldn't afford. Of 177 aircraft, fifty-three with 660 crewmen failed to return. 'Tidal Wave' also triggered Churchill's 8 August 1943 missive about code words, for it was originally titled Operation 'Soapsuds' – until the great man intervened.

Ploeşti preceded the 17–24 August Quebec 'Quadrant' Conference, where – aside from Pointblank – the Allies confirmed the need for separate air forces dedicated to ground support. While the RAF raised the Second Tactical Air Force, which grew partly out of Exercise Spartan, the US chose to transfer the headquarters staff of the Ninth, led by Brereton – though not its aircraft – to England to support future US ground operations in Western Europe. It would be entirely separate from, but equal in authority to, the Eighth Air Force. In parallel, on 1 May 1943 the British Chiefs of Staff had approved Air Marshal Sir Arthur Coningham's conceptual Air Expeditionary Force (AEF), headquartered in Hillingdon House, RAF Uxbridge, and later at Bracknell. It was to provide composite groups – containing fighter, bomber and reconnaissance aircraft – for the British and Canadian armies operating in France, where commanders would be free to move aircraft from one group to another as needed.

'Mary' Coningham (the nickname was a corruption of 'Maori', an indication of his New Zealander roots) had emerged from the Western Desert and Sicilian campaigns as the leading exponent of tactical air warfare. More than anyone else, he directed the development of early fighter-bombers, supported by efficient ground crews who could keep their aircraft operational even in a rapid advance. Linking the two, he devised a command and control system to allow ground observers to call down air attacks. It was Coningham who took the initiative to co-locate his command caravan with Montgomery's (not the other way about, as the latter alleged in his *Memoirs*) to better coordinate air–land operations. Coningham's air power concepts, evolved at and after El Alamein in November 1942, are the basis of modern joint operations doctrine. He and Montgomery both agreed that tactical air power had to be closely coordinated with land forces, but the air element had to command it. In essence, Coningham's philosophy was first to gain air superiority; then to use that superiority to interdict enemy reinforcements and isolate the battlefield; and finally to combine air and land assaults to overwhelm their opponents.

Renamed the Second Tactical Air Force (2nd TAF) on 1 June, it eventually included Basil Embry's No. 2 Group (transferred from Bomber Command), Harry Broadhurst's No. 83 and Leslie Brown's No. 84 Composite Groups, and comprised British, Polish, Czech, Norwegian, French, South African, Australian and New Zealand aircrew, as well as seventeen Canadian squadrons.[11] They immediately began experimenting with forward air controllers equipped with VHF radios calling down loitering aircraft onto army-indicated targets. This would evolve into the 'cab-rank' system used in Normandy. RAF Servicing Commando Units and mobile operations rooms units emerged at the same time, as a direct result of the lessons learned in Exercise Spartan.[12]

Such innovations filtered down to New Zealander Group Captain Desmond Scott, who on being appointed to command the brand-new No. 123 Wing of three Typhoon squadrons initiated 'mobile air warfare' exercises. He taught his entire wing, including all the ground support elements, to divide into two equal elements, 'each capable of catering for and servicing the squadrons, and be independent of the other'. They moved frequently under canvas, at the same time being 'attacked' by the wing's own aircraft, providing 'excellent training for both pilot and ground staff'. Scott was 'agreeably surprised at how quickly the personnel left their vehicles and dispersed' when he swooped down on them one morning near Shoreham. He had 'a large semi-collapsible three-roomed caravan built on a six-wheeled Austin truck', which was always parked adjacent to his 'mobile briefing complex, staffed by both Army and Air Force intelligence officers'.[13]

Once the Allies set foot in Italy in September 1943, an additional distraction to the strategic bombing offensive in Europe arose in terms of the need to divert substantial air resources to the interdiction of German lines of supply in that country – Operation Strangle. It produced immediate dividends in terms of slowing German military movements, and requiring them to divert their own efforts into repairing bridges, roads and railways, then defending them. The success of Strangle suggested the opportunity for a similar operation prior to the invasion of France in 1944. The experience of the Mediterranean was to prove crucial, for from that theatre, Eisenhower brought two esteemed airmen colleagues whom he trusted – Arthur Tedder and James Harold Doolittle.

On 15 October 1943, four medium bomber groups, equipped with B-26s, and two C-47 troop carrier groups were transferred from Eaker's Eighth Air Force to Brereton's Ninth, to become the latter's first operational units in England. Baltimore-born Staff Sergeant Clarence Elmer 'Cy' Cyford's 555th Squadron of the 386th Medium Bomb Group, operating B-26s, was one of these. Initially assigned to the Eighth Air Force, 'We were a little disillusioned when we first got to England because our base was still under construction, so we moved within a week to Boxted, Essex, and became part of the Ninth Air Force, though it made no difference to us – same missions, different brass giving the orders.' Cyford, who manned the dorsal (top) turret, remembered his first mission 'was against some German base in Holland at the end of July, when we were escorted by RAF Spitfires. Flak was being fired at the formation ahead of us. We went on taking evasive action and a few miles from the target airfield, they put their sights on us and let go with everything they had. I felt sure I was going to get it. I honestly believe no other plane could have come through such a barrage of fire with such a low loss. We owed our lives to the ability of the B-26 to take such terrific punishment and still keep flying back to our base over the sea.'[14]

Another Bomb Group which transferred to the Ninth was the 323rd (whose motto was *Vincamus sine timoris* – 'Without fear we conquer'), flying out of RAF Earl's Colne in Essex. They had already flown thirty-three missions for the Eighth with their B-26s, as Texan Carlos B. Pegues remembered: 'For about a year-and-a-half we conducted bombing missions on airfields, railyards, gun emplacements and bridges. Sometimes it was one mission a day, some days two,' he recorded. 'Then came D-Day. We returned to low-level flying, bombing gun installations on the coast of Normandy. For several days after D-Day we conducted at least two missions a day. By the time I returned home, I had flown sixty-seven separate missions.' Pegues, also a dorsal turret gunner and flight engineer, mused: 'To say I was lucky is an understatement. When we initially landed in England, the 323rd Bomb Group had thirty-six crews which would total 216 men. We flew so many missions that when you lost a plane, a replacement plane and crew would take their place; it didn't take us long to forget the loss. It was fairly recently I determined that of those original 216, only thirty-six of us returned home.'[15]

Prior to the Ninth's arrival, eleven advanced landing grounds had to be built – with twelve also for 2nd TAF – each capable of supporting fifty aircraft. Spread across Kent, Hampshire and Sussex, within easy range of France, their facilities were basic compared to the airfields of the Eighth, infrastructure being limited to hangars and concrete runways, and many nearby buildings were requisitioned.[16] At the same time, several fighter outfits arrived from America in England – they included Lieutenants Bud Fortier and Harry P. Carroll of the 355th and 356th Fighter Groups, whom we met earlier travelling on the *Queen Elizabeth*. Under Brereton, the Ninth was formally reactivated in England on 16 October, with its headquarters in the old VIII Air Support Command building, an ivy-clad mansion called Sunninghill Park, in Berkshire. Initially its fighters and bombers functioned under the control of the Eighth, until the Ninth's first mission was flown on 1 December 1943, a fighter sweep over north-eastern France.

Many of the fighter squadrons in the Eighth – soon to be transferred to the Ninth – flew P-47 Thunderbolts, known from their appearance as 'Jugs'. Captain LeRoy Gover, the RAF Eagle pilot now transferred to the 4th Fighter Group of the USAAF, described how his squadron operated. 'The man running the whole shebang is a major,' he wrote home to his folks. 'The squadron is divided into two flights, each has twelve pilots and is led by a captain. We have eighteen aircraft but fly with twelve, six from each flight in three lines of four. I have been flying in the major's place and leading the squadron.' Later the size of US fighter squadrons would be increased from eighteen to twenty-five aircraft and eventually thirty-six.[17]

As most memoirs of the European air war were written by flying personnel, the extensive ground crews – without whom none of the planes would function – are frequently overlooked. The majority of those serving with the Allied air forces were non-flyers, who rarely have a voice in the historiography of this aspect of the war. Of them, Gover recorded, 'The squadron's ground crew consists of 250 enlisted men. Each P-47 has an assigned Crew Chief and an assistant. They are responsible for everything about the plane, from keeping the engine in perfect tune, to ensuring that the canopy is clean. If they have a special problem, like something wrong with the radios, they call in a specialist. They are really the key to the success of a mission, because they keep the planes flying.'[18]

Bombers were likewise maintained by teams of enlisted ground crew, led by crew chiefs like Staff Sergeant William B. Dowling. He had been drafted in 1942 and trained as an aircraft mechanic on B-24s, crossing to Scotland aboard the *Queen Mary* in mid-1943. 'We docked to the sound of bagpipes playing and were given a very nice welcome. From there we boarded the train to join the 392nd Bomb Group at Wendling airfield near Norwich for what ended up as a two-year tour of duty,' he reminisced. 'The planes flew every day when there was decent weather. When I first arrived at the 578th Bomb Squadron, I was a member of the crew but was soon promoted to crew chief, maintaining four or five planes. Our duties included gassing the plane up, checking plugs and oil, defrosting the windows and checking the control instruments to make sure they were working.' Dowling remembered the first planes he worked on 'were *Gypsy Queen, Niagara Special* and *Cannon Ball*. We would go out to spot the planes as they returned and it hurt when the *Cannon Ball* did not return because you couldn't help but get attached to the crew flying the aircraft. When the crew of *Gypsy Queen* returned to the States after twenty-five combat missions, they gave me a silver cigarette case engraved with her name, one of my most valued possessions.'[19]

Sergeant Bernard Sender was also at Wendling, working as a turret mechanic with the 579th Bomb Squadron. 'By the time we reached full steam, there were several hundred of us ground crew. Each squadron had their own cooks, mechanics, orderlies, and so on. There were about twenty planes to a squadron, but they didn't all fly: we always had a few spares. You started working as soon as the planes came back – air mechanics, armorers, and radio-men all headed out about the same time, and assembled on the line to wait,' he recalled. 'When the crews and planes touched down, we'd go over and talk to the gunners to see what problems they'd had: were the guns jamming? Did the turret motors behave properly? If it was three o'clock in the afternoon, you'd start immediately and work right through the night; you'd get some sleep only when we finished, but that might not be until eight o'clock the next morning,' Sender reminisced – 'there were no working hours, and we didn't belong to a union!'[20]

September 1943 saw the arrival of the first US P-51 Mustang squadrons, which became operational in December. The type had already entered service with the RAF in early 1942, but was found to be underpowered at higher altitudes. This changed radically with the substitution of a Rolls-Royce Merlin engine and by using four-bladed propellers. The result was what Ernest Hemingway called 'a bad, tough, husky, angry plane'. The P-51B already had an impressive combat radius of 475 miles, and in the hands of a skilled pilot performed exceptionally well against the Luftwaffe's front-line Focke-Wulf 190s and Messerschmitt Bf 109s – it was 70mph faster than a Focke-Wulf and could out-dive it. By adding two seventy-five-gallon wing tanks the later P-51D – the definitive escort fighter of the Second World War – could reach Berlin, and a pair of 108-gallon tanks allowed it to escort bombers as far as Vienna. Eventually, more than fifteen thousand P-51s would be built, mostly at Inglewood, California, and Dallas, Texas, which more than helped turn the tide of aerial combat in the Allies' favour.

The machinery of the air war was all very well, but the quality of the manpower was often the measure between success and failure in 1943–4. As the conflict ground on, Luftwaffe pilots received less training because of fuel shortages and the need to generate numbers. From an average of 240 hours of flying training before combat in 1942, a Luftwaffe pilot was receiving only 170 hours in 1943 and this had often shrunk to around 110 hours by 1944. Conversely, US pilots received on average 320 hours in 1943 before becoming operational, and in 1944 this had risen to 360. The comparable RAF figures were two hundred hours in 1942, and 340 by 1944. Choosing quantity over quality meant that the attrition of young German pilots actually rose, while even the most experienced fell prey to the onslaught of American numbers. Ten Knight's Cross aces with combined tallies of over one thousand Allied aircraft were killed in the 1943 air war over Germany. The inexperience the Luftwaffe brought to the air battle was reflected in its ground crew also, where more personnel took longer to service, maintain and repair their Messerschmitts and Focke-Wulfs than ever before.[21] Not only was the Luftwaffe having to face superior numbers of US aircraft by 1944 – but better-trained aircrew and longer-range fighter escorts, powered by unlimited supplies of fuel, as well.

The appointment of Air Chief Marshal Sir Trafford Leigh-Mallory as commander of the Allied Expeditionary Air Forces (AEAF) on 15 November 1943 would prove unhappy because his experience was anchored exclusively in the narrow realms of RAF fighters. Since 1937 he had been Air Officer Commanding Nos. 12 then 11 Groups, subsequently of Fighter Command itself. As such, he possessed limited knowledge of expeditionary war-making or the subtleties of coalition operations. He was partly appointed on the strength of his input to the Sledgehammer invasion planning back in 1942.

Leigh-Mallory's relative lack of experience need not have been an impediment of itself, but his personality tended towards confrontation rather than collaboration, and in his new position he was to make few friends and generate many opponents. Based at Stanmore Park, north-west London, his role was to direct the Allied aerial armadas – with 2nd TAF and the Ninth Air Force under his personal control – in implementing four phases of SHAEF's air strategy. These were the continued strategic bombing of Germany as directed by 'Symbol' and 'Quadrant'; the targeting of communications nodes, coastal defence batteries and airfields; and the direct support of the invasion itself. Finally, they would have to prevent the arrival of hostile reinforcements and generally hinder German movement by road and rail.

There was another dimension to the tensions Leigh-Mallory generated, for he had no direct control over the two Allied bomber organisations, which would be loaned to him as necessary. Montgomery had presciently noted in his diary at the beginning of March 1944, 'I can see trouble ahead. Harris and Spaatz will not take orders from Leigh-Mallory.'[22] Spaatz, commander of US Strategic Air Forces in Europe from January 1944, and Harris at RAF Bomber Command saw any diversion of aircraft from their strategic role of bombing Germany to pieces as detrimental to the war effort. Harris, too, had a bullish personality which saw him as particularly obstructive to Leigh-Mallory ('L-M' to his colleagues), necessitating the frequent intervention of Air Chief Marshal Sir Arthur Tedder, deputising for the Supreme Commander. Leigh-Mallory was initially beset with calls from Spaatz to deploy Spitfires from 2nd TAF as escorts for the Eighth Air Force's heavy bombers, and bitter internal disputes among the Allies over the best use of their precious air resources would mar the workings of SHAEF for the rest of the war. Indeed, it was only on 1 April 1944 that Eisenhower directed that Brereton's Ninth Air Force be released 'from its overriding commitment of assisting Eighth Air Force Pointblank operations', to support the run-up to the invasion.

The resources – including strategic bombing forces – Leigh-Mallory would have at his disposal for these tasks were awesome: according to a staff study of 26 March 1944, the USAAF then had 6,935 aircraft available, including 2,187 B-24s and B-17s; 3,266 fighters, P-38s, P-47s and P-51s, plus 844 troop carriers, mostly C-47s. On the same day, the RAF mustered 4,387 planes, of which 1,450 were heavy bombers, 1,828 fighters and 210 troop carriers. This made a grand total of 11,322 aeroplanes – a force unequalled in military history.[23] Of note, his own RAF – then spread across the world at that stage – totalled 1,170,000 personnel, comprising 8,300 aircraft in 487 squadrons.[24]

Yet the physical aspect of numbers and statistics does not tell the whole story of the air war; more important by far was the moral component – the men behind the machines. Birdie Schmidt was American Red Cross director at the Aeroclub serving the 392nd Bomb Group near Norwich. She remembered, 'In serving a returning mission we always covered the tables with white sheets for table cloths because we thought it added a homely touch, making it nicer to come back to. We could always tell what kind of a day it had been by the way the boys came in. If they were kidding around and talking, it had been an easy mission. If they looked like ghosts and said "Just give me something hot", we knew it had been a rough one.' Schmidt observed at such moments the airmen 'moved limply. Their hair was dishevelled; faces were sweaty and streaked with dirt. Maybe they were still wearing their heated flying suits and orange Mae Wests. Perhaps they'd been on oxygen for hours. They clomped around in their heavy sheepskin boots to find a chair and collapse.'[25]

The whole base would share the trauma that 'after some missions, familiar faces were missed. However, if the ships weren't seen to actually blow up, there was always hope that somehow they managed to get out. Later the engineers, radio men and gunners of the crews would come to the club and talk: not so much about flak and fighters, but about the empty barracks in which they'd have to sleep. Sometimes I think that bothered them more than being shot at. What could we or I do? Just listen,' Schmidt thought. The crews were certainly grateful and even named one of their B-24s after her. 'Then they felt able to carry out promises made to each other, that if one went down, the other would write his wife. And their faith in flying came back.'[26]

9

COSSACs, Spartans and Chiefs

'In preparing for battle I have always found that plans are useless, but planning is indispensable.'

General Dwight D. Eisenhower

A IR CHIEF MARSHAL Sir Arthur Tedder was announced on 17 January 1944 as Eisenhower's deputy, on the same day as the SHAEF chief of staff, the American Major General Walter 'Beetle' Bedell Smith. The command team then assembled on 1 February for the famous series of photographs, reproduced in every Overlord history, of the group around a table at Norfolk House with large maps of the British Isles and Europe in the background. Admiral Bertram Ramsay recorded, 'Had ¾ hour of frightful photographing in the big conference room. There must have been seventy press & the snapping and flashing was continuous.'[1] We can see from the date of their appointments that the SHAEF command team was the subject of much Anglo-American wrangling, coming together gradually, rather than as a complete whole.

Although he had previously worked with much of this group, Eisenhower's challenge was that he had not chosen his senior leadership: for a land commander, Ike would have undoubtedly picked Alexander, with whom he had worked harmoniously in the Mediterranean, in preference to Montgomery. Ramsay was the first in post (25 October) as an original COSSAC appointee, sitting alongside Bernard Paget, then 21st Army Group commander. He was followed by Air Chief Marshal

Bradley, Ramsay, Tedder, Eisenhower, Montgomery, Leigh-Mallory and Bedell Smith at their London HQ, Norfolk House, in St James's Square on 1 February 1944. Ramsay disliked the occasion, recording, 'Had 3/4 hour of frightful photographing in the big conference room. There must have been seventy press & the snapping and flashing was continuous'. Both Ramsay and Leigh-Mallory were appointed before Ike himself and, as such, few around the table were the Supreme Commander's own appointees. (NARA)

Sir Trafford Leigh-Mallory (15 November), both identified before the Supreme Commander himself. Eisenhower's appointment was made on 4 December (made public on the sixth), then Monty (23 December, announced on the thirty-first), and finally Tedder and the 'Beetle'. Acquiring their huge staffs was far more difficult, as keeping continuity in other theatres was important, never mind the fact that some officers fiercely resisted being drawn into headquarters planning teams when they preferred to be forging their reputations in combat.

Bedell Smith had risen rapidly through the US Army staff chain as Marshall's other favoured protégé. He was the first secretary to the US Joint Chiefs of Staff on their inception in January 1942, performing the same task, for the Combined Chiefs of Staff meetings. When Eisenhower was posted to the Mediterranean in June 1942 he requested Smith as chief of staff at Allied Forces Headquarters (AFHQ). On moving to London, Ike insisted that the 'Beetle' accompany him – in the face of opposition from Churchill, who wanted Smith to remain at AFHQ as Deputy Supreme Commander in the Mediterranean. Promoted to lieutenant general, Bedell Smith arrived in London on 18 January.[2]

The announcement of Eisenhower's deputy worried the Wehrmacht, as German intelligence observed:

Tedder is on good terms with Eisenhower to whom he is superior in both intelligence and energy. The coming operations will be conducted by him to a great extent. He regards the air force as a 'spearhead artillery' rendering the enemy vulnerable to an attack. His tactics in North Africa, Sicily and Italy, based on this theory, provided for air support for the advance of even the smallest Army units. Under Tedder's influence the cooperation between the Air Force and Army has become excellent. Tedder does not take unnecessary risks. Unless other factors play a part, he will undertake the invasion only after achieving complete air supremacy and after large-scale bombing of the Reich.[3]

How prophetic these predictions were to prove.

Tedder's appointment made sense: he had been air commander in the Mediterranean, and as air power was expected to be dominant in the forthcoming campaign, it was logical to put an airman in as Eisenhower's deputy. Tedder had also learned, unlike most of his contemporaries, the necessity of treating Americans as equals, rather than the traditional British habit of looking down on them as unqualified newcomers. In this respect, Ramsay was also a known quantity, having planned most of the maritime aspects of Torch and Husky, as well as Dunkirk in 1940. However, Leigh-Mallory was a bizarre choice: known to be prickly even with his fellow nationals, he had no experience of multinational command, or of even working outside the realm of fighters – a grave oversight if the 'bomber barons' and troop-carrying air fleets were to be involved, which they surely would – and we shall explore the tensions among the various air commanders in due course.

Bernard Law Montgomery, aged fifty-six, was assigned as temporary commander-in-chief of all land forces for the first assault, initially directing two vast formations – Omar Nelson Bradley's First US and Miles 'Bimbo' Dempsey's Second British Armies. They were to be followed once the bridgehead was secure by George Smith Patton's Third US and Harry Crerar's First Canadian Armies, which would tip the balance in favour of American numbers. On 1 September 1944, Eisenhower was scheduled to assume personal control of all land forces, when Montgomery would step down to command the 21st Army Group which would then comprise the First Canadian and British Second Armies.

From 14 July, Bradley would step up to command the newly created US 12th Army Group (the US First and Third Armies), making him Monty's equal, rather than a subordinate. With his signature precision, Bedell Smith would later observe, 'We would have saved a lot of trouble if we had started off with Montgomery and Bradley as equals.'[4] Bradley was a natural choice to lead the US First Army and later the 12th Army Group, for he had been a contemporary of Eisenhower's at West Point and had succeeded Patton as commander of II Corps, commanding it very creditably in Tunisia and Sicily. In the latter campaign he had worked with Ramsay, Montgomery, Dempsey of XIII Corps, Harry Crerar, then leading I Canadian Corps, Coningham (air commander over Sicily), and his boss, Tedder. Bradley's deputy, Courtney Hicks Hodges – 'a soft-voiced Georgian', commissioned from the ranks and 'without temper, drama, or visible emotion' – would take over the US First Army on Bradley's elevation to the army group.[5]

Miles Dempsey (the source of his 'Bimbo' nickname is, alas, lost to history) was as obscure to the British as Montgomery was well known. This was deliberate, as he avoided the limelight whenever he could – which was precisely why the publicity-hungry Montgomery selected him: there would be no clash of egos. An outstanding tactician, Dempsey was legendary among war correspondents for his ability to 'read terrain and make a map come alive' and had spent the interwar years visiting the battlefields of France and Belgium that he felt would witness further conflict.[6] Major Johnny Langdon of the 3rd Royal Tank Regiment noted that 'to a man everyone knew of Montgomery, but few had ever heard of their army commander, Dempsey'.[7] With his legendary insensitivity, Monty initially suggested that Dempsey command the First Canadian Army on the grounds that he had been chief of staff to the Canadian Corps in 1940, but as we have seen, Harry Crerar quite properly took over the national force on his return from Italy. The latter never quite commanded Monty's respect in the way his eventual successor, Guy Simonds, did. The latter had worked in Monty's HQ in Tunisia, commanded the 1st Canadian Division in Sicily, and would lead II Canadian Corps in Normandy.

Many of Monty's senior staff officers and divisional and brigade commanders had been students of his when instructing at the Camberley Staff College between 1926 and 1929 – a pivotal time, as it would turn out, for the British Army – when lieutenant colonels Montgomery, O'Connor, Paget and Pownall lectured under the director of studies,

Colonel Alan Brooke. This was the era when bonds were formed: Brooke would become Monty's patron, while the latter's protégés would include many of his future generals.

By January 1944 Montgomery was established in the requisitioned headmaster's study of his old school, St Paul's, on the Thames at Hammersmith in south-west London. On the twenty-first Eisenhower called the first initial meeting of his staff at Norfolk House to reaffirm the choice of Normandy and confirm expansion of the old COSSAC plan from three to five beaches. Once these amendments were accepted, SHAEF absorbed Morgan's staff, including Wren Ginger Thomas, on 13 February, taking over Norfolk House. By this time the luckless Morgan found his efforts were being denigrated by Montgomery, who was now touting the revised plan as his own, with no reference to COSSAC.

Morgan's star had waned somewhat. In July 1943 he had led a delegation to Washington DC, meeting President Roosevelt and George C. Marshall, US Army chief of staff. He was told to plan on the basis that Marshall would be the Supreme Allied Commander, with Morgan his chief of staff. Now Montgomery was spitefully shredding his reputation. Therefore Morgan declined to join Monty's 21st Army Group headquarters, staying with SHAEF. He became one of Bedell Smith's three deputy chiefs of staff, responsible for intelligence and operations and would be knighted for his contribution to Overlord's success in August 1944. Although superior in rank, Montgomery would still be obliged to take direction from Morgan at SHAEF: it mirrored their pre-war relationship, when Morgan had been a divisional chief of staff and Monty one of his brigade commanders.

Eisenhower's own headquarters at this stage was in Grosvenor Square, central London, but on 5 March he relocated SHAEF to the relative seclusion of Camp Griffiss, Bushy Park, in west London. Known by its call sign 'Widewing', this was a sixty-acre military camp established in 1942 to house the headquarters of the US Eighth Air Force.[8] The Eighth thereupon moved to Camp Lynn, code name 'Pinetree', in the Gothic splendour of the former girls' school at Wycombe Abbey, from where VIII Bomber Command had been directing its missions since 1942.

WAAF Edna Hodgson especially recollected at Bushy Park 'the American drummer, with the SHAEF badge emblazoned on his drum, who knew how to make a lot of noise. Every evening at six o'clock both the American and British flags were lowered from their masts; the Stars and Stripes by three MPs, complete with white gloves and spats, and the

Union Jack by three guardsmen.' Her boss, Sir Arthur Tedder, had 'his office in one of the huts and it was quite a common occurrence to see him driving his own little blue and cream sports car around the camp, with four prominent stars on the front signifying his rank'.[9]

The revised 'Montyfied' Overlord plan called for eight full divisions, three airborne and five infantry, attacking five beaches on an eighty-mile front. Each would be supported by a massive aerial and sea bombardment. Its hallmarks were a surprise amphibious assault with a lightning armoured advance to Caen and beyond, where the flat, open terrain would best suit Allied armour and facilitate the building of many temporary airstrips. The major change was the landing at Utah and the insertion of two airborne divisions behind it, an attempt to seal off the Cotentin peninsula and quickly seize the port of Cherbourg – necessary to take the strain off the untested Mulberry harbours.

From his first viewing of the COSSAC plan, Monty identified 'it was evident that airborne forces could play an extremely important role in the assault, and it seemed unfortunate that such a small lift should be at our disposal when there would be three or four airborne divisions available for operations on D-Day'.[10] The challenge here was the amount of transport aircraft and gliders available, and the number of qualified pilots who would be trained in time. Air lift resources, as with sea lift, would prove an effective brake on the aspirations of the Allied commanders. Notwithstanding this, Leigh-Mallory, who understood little of the potential of air assault forces, was not inclined to cooperate and resisted the deployment of two extra airborne divisions, citing – untruthfully – little extra capacity, and his expectations of *sixty per cent* casualties amongst the glider troops. In April, Eisenhower had to insist that the airborne operation was essential to Overlord, and the notoriously prickly Leigh-Mallory afterwards conceded he had been wrong.[11]

The original COSSAC concept outlined an assault by a division from each of the invading nations – the British 3rd was given the left flank, with the Canadian 3rd in the centre and the American 29th to the west, on a strip of sand initially known as 'Beach 313' – Bradley later observing that the 29th 'had staked out squatter's rights on *Omaha* beach since their arrival in England in October 1942'.[12] Substantial reserves were to follow on, each beach becoming the focus for a whole army corps. However, none of the three divisions earmarked had seen combat since Monty had commanded the British 3rd in 1940. The alteration and expansion of the COSSAC proposals were to be the subject of considerable wrangling between Monty, Ramsay and Eisenhower for most of January 1944, juggling the dream plan with the art of the possible.

The effect of these changes of plan, which necessitated a vastly increased number of landing craft, reduced the number of vehicles for each division by five hundred in order to economise shipping space. Here, too, Churchill was inclined to interfere. In the Anzio landings the Prime Minister happened to note that by 10 February there were some eighteen thousand vehicles for seventy thousand troops; 'We must have a great superiority of chauffeurs' was his angry comment, but Brooke realised his boss, whose soldiering dated back to the North-West Frontier of India and Afghanistan, was both blind to logistics and dreadfully out of date – that in modern war, mobility was essential.[13] Brooke would record that even after D-Day, Churchill was still pursuing this particular issue, complaining on 14 June that the army was sending '"dental chairs and YMCA institutions instead of bayonets" into France …We argued with him that fighting men without food, ammunition and petrol were useless, but he was in one of his foolish moods and not open to conviction. It is appalling the false conception of modern war that he has.'[14]

Ramsay was nearly in despair as he foresaw the need to double the Royal Navy's commitment from very limited resources – Eisenhower requested thirty-six more destroyers, five cruisers, two battleships and 271 extra landing craft, including forty-seven scarce LSTs. His revised invasion fleet would total nearly seven thousand vessels – including 1,200 warships, four thousand landing craft and 1,500 other vessels, rescue craft, salvage vessels, tugs, launches and tenders. Ramsay also had to contend with serviceability issues, losses to U-boats and accidents.

He remedied the problem by requesting three things: the switch of US naval resources to Overlord, as maritime support for the French invasion had originally been envisaged as an all-British affair; recommending that the invasion be put back a month to maximise the number of newly manufactured landing craft available – hence Brooke's recommendation for postponement on 30 November at Tehran; and advising the landings in southern France be delayed.[15] Originally the strategic plan had been to launch a simultaneous landing along the French Riviera – Operation Anvil – but this would become contentious because there were too few craft to mount both.

The provision of assault shipping was the main factor that drove Allied strategic planning, for the Pacific campaign needed them too, the bulk being made in the United States, where a wartime total of four thousand ocean-going landing ships and 79,000 landing craft were eventually manufactured. An officer in the 15th Scottish Division noted that his Landing Ship, Infantry (LSI), built in the USA in 1942, had already 'sailed the world. She had carried GIs across the Pacific, and taken part in the Sicily landings. Her crew were now Royal Navy Volunteer Reservists.'[16] The southern France operation, the next appointment for many of the Neptune landing fleet, was originally named 'Anvil' in conjunction with the northern landings, then called 'Sledgehammer', with the obvious connotations of how the Germans would be caught between the two. Churchill would remain hostile to Anvil, even when it was launched on 15 August 1944, and at the last moment demanded its code name to be changed to Dragoon – allegedly because he was 'dragooned' into it by his American partners. Ramsay was relieved to be granted each of his three wishes – which still only provided, in his mind, the bare minimum necessary with which to launch the assault.

To prepare GIs, Tommies and Canucks for the eventual second front, huge areas of the United Kingdom were taken over as training areas using the catch-all Compensation (Defence) Act of 1939. Some five hundred civilians were evicted from several Norfolk farms and villages near Thetford, amounting to real estate of 118,000 acres, in July 1942. Residents were led to believe they would return at the war's end. Instead, Sturston Hall, an Elizabethan moated manor house, Buckenham Tofts Hall, one of the great houses of Norfolk, and six villages were emptied and left to the mercy of wartime soldiery. Buckenham Tofts dated to the reign of Charles II; it possessed a stable block, orangery, extensive gardens, a large ornamental lake and a cricket pitch which had attracted the first-class sportsmen of the day. By 1944 their former owners were unaware that these buildings and ancient settlements had already been shelled to pieces. They had survived the Black Death and the seventeenth-century plague; each had sent men to battle in 1914–18 who failed to return to their meadows. Today only a few overgrown bricks and four lonely churches hint at the thriving communities which had to make way for war.[17]

Reg Warner of the 1st/7th Middlesex was one of those who remembered training at Thetford; a pre-war Territorial and Dunkirk veteran who would land on D-Day, his battalion had been attached to the 51st Highland Division in November 1941, and accompanied them to North Africa in August 1942. Warner fought from El Alamein via Tunis to Sicily before returning home to prepare for D-Day with the Highlanders. 'I could never understand a word they said, and never got used to their [expletive] bagpipes – everywhere we went, on training, in battle. And kilts, too. They weren't meant to [wear them], in case of a gas attack, but they took them; there was always one, usually a piper or an RSM in a kilt, even in Normandy. We had training at Thetford in March–April 1944, doing lots of exercises and simulated attacks, street fighting in bombed-out villages and the like. We destroyed some quite nice houses, the sort I'd want to live in. Just wrecked them.'[18]

A similar fate befell Imber village on Salisbury Plain, a settlement with Roman origins of which mention was first made in 967 and later on, in the Domesday Book. A classic English village, it included the thirteenth-century church of St Giles, a Baptist chapel, post office, the Bell Inn, the manor house of Imber Court, as well as a scattering of ancient cottages. In November 1943 the community's 150 residents were called to a meeting in the village schoolroom and given a month's notice to leave their homes. Most complied, though the occupants of one farm had to be forcibly evicted. Albert Nash, Imber's blacksmith for over forty years, was said to have been found sobbing over his anvil; none would ever return, for the village remains in military hands to this day and is a reminder of the drastic measures deemed necessary to defeat the Third Reich.[19]

Exercises in preparation for France can be traced back to the first half of March 1943. Politically and militarily Canadian forces were always destined to be part of the invasion force. In this respect their French-speaking population were important, with some families actually hailing from Normandy. Their commander, Andrew McNaughton, had refused to let his men join Australian and New Zealander troops in what he regarded as the 'side-show' of the Western Desert. In his view they had journeyed to fight Hitler in Europe. Most Canadian troops consequently spent much of 1940–3 bored, restless and resentful, with the French-Canadian contingent particularly isolated and lonely. Thus GHQ's Exercise Spartan, the largest exercise in Britain to that date, was held to test the mettle of McNaughton's First Canadian Army and its commanders.

Operating over 4–12 March 1943 and in the field for the first time as 'Southland', McNaughton's enemy was 'Eastland', whose forces had overrun an area from Cambridge and Coventry to Gloucester. Southland's task was to regain the occupied terrain, from a start line stretching from Swindon to Maidenhead and pushing north.[20] Spartan included friendly ('Z' Group) and opposing ('X' Group) air forces as well as all the Canadian ground forces in England and seven divisions' worth of Britons – several hundred thousand fully-mechanised troops. As such, it was impossible to conceal and significant enough to provoke positive comment in *The Times* on 23 March, where it was seen as 'welcome progress towards the Second Front'.[21]

Lieutenant General Harry Crerar's well-trained I Corps (2nd and 3rd Canadian Infantry Divisions and 1st Tank Brigade) shone with a well-planned counter-attack near Reading, but II Corps (5th Canadian and Guards Armoured Divisions) suffered traffic jams, fuel shortages and a breakdown of communications during night moves. Spartan also tested Canadian engineers, who had to build sixty Bailey bridges to replace those notionally destroyed by Eastland. New concepts were assessed, including the use of deception with dummy tanks, guns, and vehicles to draw enemy fire.[22]

Harry Crerar was judged to have performed well in Spartan, paving his way as McNaughton's eventual successor, but the latter was heavily criticised by generals Bernard Paget, Commander of Home Forces, and Alan Brooke (the CIGS and a lifelong opponent of McNaughton's – the two were artillerymen who had clashed consistently since 1917). Brooke damned McNaughton – having already blamed him, unfairly, for the poor showing of his troops at Dieppe in August 1942. He assessed him during Spartan as 'proving my worst fears that he is quite incompetent to command an army! He does not know how to begin the job and was tying up his forces in the most awful muddle. Then went to Newbury to see Crerar and his Corps HQ, a real good show.'[23] As it turned out, Crerar would take his corps overseas to fight in Italy, and return in March 1944 to take over the First Canadian Army just in time for Normandy.[24]

Although emphatically a Canadian exercise, Spartan was to have ramifications for the British and American ways of war in France a year hence. In terms of air–land cooperation, it aspired to reflect the experience of North Africa, where tactical air support could be called down rapidly to support ground forces. It also tested the RAF's airfield construction, servicing and defence units, which enabled fighter aircraft to be based closely behind their own front-line troops. Despite the poor weather that afflicted periods of Spartan, the 'Z' Air Group supported Southland's tactical air requirements.

Its airfield construction, servicing and defence units soon evolved into RAF Servicing Commando units (SCUs). During Spartan, they built advanced landing grounds (temporary airstrips) in recently 'liberated' territory, from which three flying squadrons were designed to operate. Pilots and ground crew had to be mobile and flexible, operating under canvas with minimal facilities, often in bad weather, and be on call to carry out missions at short notice – exactly as they would in the summer of 1944.

In fact, so successful was Spartan in this respect that the 'Z' Air Group formed the basis of No. 83 Group of the Second Tactical Air Force, which would support Dempsey's Second Army in France. This was always the intention, for in January 1943, Leigh-Mallory had led a team of the future 'Z' Air Group's personnel to North Africa to study the Desert Air Force's methodology and air–land liaison. This was one factor which would lead to his appointment as commander of the Allied Expeditionary Air Force (AEAF).[25] Meanwhile, No. 83 Group was established on 1 April 1943, quickly followed by No. 84 Group, inaugurated in July, which would be the flying arm of Crerar's First Canadian Army. Commanders of the future US Ninth Air Force – the counterpart to the RAF's Second Tactical Air Force – took close notice and incorporated much of this doctrine and wisdom into their own preparations for invading France.[26]

The BBC, too, trialled its procedures for the future invasion during Spartan, providing simulated commentaries, interviews and recordings which were sent back to Broadcasting House, censored, made into dummy programmes, and treated as if live. On listening to the final products, both the Secretary of State for War and Commander of Home Forces recommended the BBC should be a participant in the real invasion and not just confined to a press pool. The BBC thereupon formed its own War Reporting Unit to select and deploy correspondents, engineers and equipment; its staff trained with army units, studied censorship and were instructed in the use of all its broadcasting equipment, so each could perform any task, from reporter to sound engineer.

Shortly after Spartan, the Canadian Parachute Battalion arrived from their native shores to join the British 6th Airborne Division. In their ranks was Lance Corporal John Ross. During the Depression his father had dragged the family across Canada and North America in search of work. Later, Ross and his family sailed to England but 'when the war broke out I was eighteen, and because we had been more than three years in England I was liable for conscription,' he recalled. 'So I decided I might as well return and join the Canadian Army. I came to St John and enlisted in the New Brunswick Rangers.' In 1943 when the opportunity arose, he volunteered for the 1st Canadian Parachute Battalion, joining 'C' Company. Ross started training at Camp Shilo, Manitoba, jumping from a 250-foot tower, then crossed to England with the battalion aboard the *Queen Elizabeth*.

'There we joined 3 Parachute Brigade under Brigadier James Hill. He taught us four battle principles: speed of action and decision making; simplicity; control; and fire-effect. We had to be proficient with a wide range of weapons, including those of the enemy.' Something of a legend in the British Army, James Hill had won the Sword of Honour at Sandhurst in 1931, served as a captain at Dunkirk, led a battalion in Tunisia and was an airborne brigade commander by 1943.[27] He was especially noted for training his paratroopers to the peak of physical fitness. 'In August and September 1943, we ran five miles every morning and completed a fifty-mile march with full gear in eighteen hours,' Ross remembered. 'We dropped from Albemarles, old twin-engined converted bombers, each holding ten men, and fought a never-ending series of combat exercises, simulating landings on the French shores. Normandy was our first time in battle; we were as green as could be. Later, when a German officer told us how his men feared the "battle-hardened Canadian paratroops", we laughed – before we jumped, we'd never heard a shot fired in anger.'[28]

Meanwhile, many of the commando units that would accompany the assault waves had long been training in the Scottish Highlands and causing mayhem throughout occupied Europe. After a few independent companies of volunteers had demonstrated the possibilities of inconveniencing the Germans in Norway in 1940, Churchill had decided he wanted a more formalised 'Corps of shock troops'. Lieutenant Colonel Dudley Clarke (Military Assistant to the Chiefs of the Imperial General Staff) devised the initial organisation. Churchill, inevitably, chose the name from the Boer commandos he had soldiered against and been captured by in 1899. Twelve army commandos were formed from early 1940, and two Royal Marine commandos, Nos. 40 and 41, raised from volunteers in 1942, followed by a further seven from disbanded RM battalions.

Each commando unit trained separately until the Commando Basic Training Centre at Achnacarry House was established in 1942. Called 'the castle', it was in fact a large estate near Ben Nevis that dated back to 1655. Also the seat of Clan Cameron, its owner vacated his home while 25,000 men passed through it until 1945. Some inadvertently set fire to the mansion, while fifty-five deaths were recorded in training. Completing the course gave a soldier the right to wear the coveted green beret. A commando resembled a small battalion, numbering around 450 men, divided into six 75-man troops and a headquarters troop.

What was the secret of their success? Peter Young, commanding officer of No. 3 Commando and already the possessor of a Military Cross with two bars, felt the real difference was 'the quality of our NCOs, who were in general incomparably better than those of the field army. I am deeply conscious that No. 3 Commando was well served by its officers and men, but owed its successes more than any single factor to its peerless NCOs.'[29] The wearers of the green beret are commemorated today by the Commando Memorial at Spean Bridge, which overlooks the area where they trained. One of Scotland's best-known monuments and cast in bronze, the sculpture depicts three commandos in wartime dress, with webbing and equipment, standing atop a stone plinth. It was unveiled in 1952 by the Queen Mother, and sits aside the busy A82, one of the main roads through the Highlands.

The Royal Navy, too, raised their own commando units, of which eight would train at Achnacarry and deploy to France. These were very different organisations to those of the Royal Marines. Signaller Alan Whiting was one who undertook a three-week commando course at Spean Bridge. 'I was instructed how to kill swiftly and silently in different ways,' he recalled. 'To use anything as a weapon, swing on ropes in full kit over water and pits full of barbed wire, how to fall across a barricade of barbed wire and make a bridge so that others could run over your back, cross an obstacle course and still be able to bayonet somebody at the end of it.' Whiting and his mates labelled the landing craft crews at Achnacarry 'saltwater cowboys', observing that 'in any swell, the LCAs behaved like bucking broncos and you had to be some kind of cowboy to ride-em and stay on'.[30]

Royal Naval Commandos were khaki-clad, 100-strong units, designed to help establish and defend landing beaches against counter-attacks, whilst ensuring the steady and efficient flow of men and materiel to the front. They formed part of a beach group, and trained at HMS *Armadillo*, a 'stone frigate' which operated exclusively for the RN Commandos at Glenfinart, also attending the Beach Training Centre in Gullane. Lieutenant Commander Edward 'Teddy' Gueritz, destined to land on Sword Beach, trained with them. 'We had distinguishing marks on our helmets for easy identification; as a Principal Beach Master, my helmet was painted blue. My own contribution was a red scarf and a walking stick.'[31]

The right to wear the green beret – still highly coveted today – can be traced to a letter from the head of Combined Operations, Lord Louis Mountbatten, to the Secretary of State for War, requesting that commandos be permitted to wear the distinctive headgear 'similar in design to the maroon beret worn by the Airborne division', onto which they would fix the badge of their own regiment.[32]

Whilst berets have since become common military headdress the world over, the only other organisation wearing them at that time, apart from the airborne mafia, was the Royal Tank Regiment, who wore black.[33] In due course an order, 'Berets, Green – Introduction of', appeared. The headgear was issued to other ranks, whilst officers were instructed 'to make their own arrangements'.[34] Though usually wearing their hard-won berets or home-knitted cap comforters in battle, for D-Day the commandos 'had been advised to wear steel helmets, an indication there would be a lot of jagged metal flying about', remembered one. 'However most of us had a *geise* – a sort of spell or taboo – about our headgear and stuck faithfully to our berets.'[35]

By 1944 there was a Commando Group, the equivalent of more than a division, comprising four commando brigades, two of whom would land in France. In emulation, from 1942 the US Army raised five of its own equivalent battalions, called Rangers. Virginian Staff Sergeant Robert L. Sales, with Company 'B' of the 116th Infantry, with the US 29th Division, had volunteered for ranger training and was sent to Achnacarry, 'the toughest battle school in the world', he remembered. 'The discipline was unbelievable and we were on British rations up there. If you didn't ever think you'd starve to death, you should try that! We started speed marches at seven miles and went on up and up, and if you fell out, you washed out. But I was young and fit and when I passed out I got a week's leave in London.'[36]

One of Peter Young's men in No. 3 Commando, Tom Duncan, observed of their training, 'Our main objective was to keep one hundred per cent fit. We had two weeks in bombed-out areas of London practising street fighting, and two weeks training with landing craft and stalking deer in north-west Scotland. On 21 February 1944 Monty paid us a visit at Hove, stood on top of his jeep and called us his *corps d'élite*, inspiring no end of enthusiasm and confidence, then we went up to Scotland for more training before moving down to the south coast to get ready for France; everybody knew invasion was soon, but not the date.'[37]

Due to land on Sword Beach was the 1st Special Service Brigade (the name being soon altered on account of the unfortunate 'SS' initials, and 'Commando' substituted) of 45 Royal Marine and Nos. 3, 4 and 6 Army Commandos, led by Brigadier the Lord Lovat. As the 24th Chieftain of Clan Fraser, Shimi (from the Gaelic *MacShimidh*) had leadership in his genes: David Stirling, who founded the SAS, was his cousin. Six foot tall, tough and charismatic, Churchill called him 'the handsomest man to ever cut a throat'.[38] A true clan chief, Lovat was often accompanied by his personal piper, Bill Millin. Aged twenty-one, he was aware of a War Office ruling that banned pipers from the front line due to their high casualties during 1914–18. Thus when Lovat asked Millin to pipe his commandos ashore on D-Day, the young private in the Queen's Own Cameron Highlanders, who had trained alongside Lovat at Achnacarry, declined. Lovat replied, 'Ah, but that's the English War Office. You and I are both Scottish, and it doesn't apply.'

In the event as they left England on 5 June 1944, Bill Millin aboard *LCI-519* 'stood at the bow of our landing craft piping "The Road to the Isles". Just off the Isle of Wight we met thousands of other boats and ships carrying troops. Our skipper put it on the public address system; the other vessels heard me, threw their hats in the air and cheered,' Millin recalled. 'I shall never forget hearing the skirl of Bill Millin's pipes,' remembered Tom Duncan of No. 3 Commando; 'it is seared into my psyche; it's hard to describe the impact it had. It gave us a great lift and increased our determination. As well as the pride we felt, it reminded us of home, and why we were there fighting for our lives and those of our loved ones.'[39]

We will meet Bill Millin later on Sword Beach. This is where I first met him in 1975 playing 'Hielan' Laddie' – as he did then – armed only with a dirk sheathed in his right sock. He was right to be worried about his safety. His D-Day pipes were silenced four days later by shrapnel. Undeterred, Millin immediately procured another set. Later a captured German sniper told him that 'although I was in his sights, I was discounted as a target because *you are obviously mad – why waste bullets on a madman?*'[40]

10

Rhinos, Camels and Roundabouts

'Combat makes extremely heavy demands on the soldier's strength and nerves. For this reason, make heavy demands on your men in training exercises.'

Generalfeldmarschall Erwin Rommel

FOR THE ALLIED formations landing in France, four aspects of preparation were put into motion. In the late summer of 1943 the corps, division, regimental and brigade staffs studied the principles governing combined (land–air–sea) operations and formulated the first drafts of their eventual plans for Omaha, Gold, Juno and Sword. The incorporation of the fifth beach, Utah, lay in the future. In the meantime, mock landing craft were constructed from concrete and timber in the coastal dunes of southern England, East Anglia and Scotland – some are still there today – from which companies and platoons practised boat drills, attacking pillboxes, scaling obstacles, and minefield clearance.

The autumn of 1943 saw the second phase of amphibious training, carried out by groups from each division at the Combined Training Centres in Inveraray and Castle Toward (the latter rhyming counter-intuitively with 'coward'), in western Scotland. At both, troops practised disembarking from landing ships into smaller craft, which were carried on the larger vessels instead of lifeboats. From the rocking mother ships, infantrymen learned to climb down scramble nets into the waiting barges, which would then race for the shore to deposit their human cargo. The men subsequently studied how to make beach assaults, eventually under live fire. These courses were usually a soldier's first introduction to seaborne operations.

By 1944 the Allies possessed nearly fifty thousand landing vessels of all types, though almost none had featured in any of the world's navies in 1939. At Gallipoli in 1915, troops had initially disembarked under fire from adapted merchant ships and were rowed ashore in lifeboats, though powered lighters and barges with frontal ramps were in use by the end of that campaign. Little progress was made in assault boat design due to the financial austerity of the interwar period, but by 1939 a US boat builder, Andrew Higgins of New Orleans, had developed a series of shallow-draught landing vessels. These drew less than a foot and possessed a front ramp copied from Japanese amphibious craft. Higgins' boats were bought by the US Marine Corps as the Landing Craft Vehicle, Personnel (LCVP). In parallel the British had developed their own Landing Craft, Assault (LCA) with armoured sides, a silenced engine, hinged bow doors and ramp. Both designs were made of wood, could carry a platoon of around thirty men with their equipment, and amounted to the 'jeeps of the naval war'. One observer described them as 'low in the water, olive drab in colour and shaped like open shoe-boxes with ramps at the bows'.[1] The Royal Marines, who frequently manned them, referred to them as 'floating coffins'.

The British journalist Alistair Cooke was touring the United States in the autumn of 1942 and recorded 'that citizens by and large, have been content to let New Orleans be known as a town of historic squares, graceful houses by the levee, fine indigenous food, the whole giving off a mellow odor of magnolia blossom and chicory'. Apart from the blues, which many locals 'loudly resented', being 'raffish and thoroughly uncul-tural', Cooke observed, 'these days the old and leisurely citizens have another indignity to swallow. It is Mr Higgins. Nowadays the first thing the visitor is likely to ask to see is one of the shipyards of Higgins Industries. He is big business in person. Aggressive, appallingly successful, he has a vocabulary richer than a Marine, and makes a point of hiring Negroes. Higgins has taken over the manufacture of practically all the landing barges, PT [patrol torpedo] boats and tank lighters that are being used, and will be used, by the United Nations forces.'[2]

Cooke's visit was before Higgins had got into his stride; by 1944, whilst the British maritime workshops of Bolson's of Poole, Dorset, were turning out one LCA a day, their US counterparts, Higgins Industries, were mass-producing LCVPs in New Orleans, where eighty-five thousand workers built twenty thousand landing craft. Eisenhower would dub Higgins 'the man who won the war for us; if he had not designed and built those LCVPs, the whole strategy of the war would have been different'.[3] These tiny craft – of which some 1,991 examples were deployed on 6 June alone – were not ocean-going, but designed to be carried on larger ships, from which they would be lowered, then run onto a beach at six to ten knots.[4]

The larger landing ships came in a variety of sizes, most being converted from merchantmen, which could carry a flotilla of twelve or more LCAs or LCVPs. Lieutenant Peter Prior of the 5th Royal Berkshires, destined to land on Juno with No. 8 Beach Group, would cross the Channel on HMS *Monowai*, a former 10,000-ton P&O trans-Pacific steamer requisitioned and converted by the Ministry of War Transport. For D-Day, she would convey 1,800 fully equipped troops to France, and ferry them ashore in her twenty LCAs – all but six of which would succumb to mines or obstacles off Gold Beach. Prior remembered the unique way he entered his assault boat: 'we slid down canvas chutes into the waiting craft'.[5]

While the British operated converted merchantmen, US forces deployed 'attack transports', purpose-built ships of around ten thousand tons which carried 1,500–2,000 GIs plus their landing craft. USS *Barnett* was one of these, on which New Jersey resident William Tomko served. Tomko joined the 10,000-ton *Barnett* after navy boot camp in Norfolk, Virginia. The ship had already seen extensive service in the battles of the Coral Sea and Midway and at Guadalcanal. 'The day after I reported for duty, we departed for Oran in Algeria to prepare for the invasion of Sicily.' In Operation Husky, Tomko was wounded by shrapnel when the *Barnett* was hit in the bows. He recovered in time to see action at Salerno, before sailing back with the ship to the United States, where she was overhauled.

'We sailed from Norfolk, Virginia, to Scotland and joined our troops training, but never knew where we were going or why until we got there,' said Tomko. 'It turned out we were preparing for D-Day; we took 1,500 first-wave troops from the 8th Infantry of 4th US Division to *Utah* beach out of Plymouth, Devon, and collected some wounded from *Omaha*.' Critically injured men were transferred to USS *Barnett* from landing craft that lacked medical facilities. 'The injured men were swung across by wire in a cradle, because we couldn't drop anchor – we'd have been a sitting target for the Germans,' Tomko recounted. After Normandy, Tomko and USS *Barnett* transported troops to southern France for Operation Dragoon, and later participated in the invasion of Okinawa.[6]

Some 208 smaller Landing Craft, Infantry (LCI) would be used on D-Day. They resulted from analysis of the Dieppe landings, which identified the need for a craft capable of landing a company-sized force. Philadelphian Pete Fantacone had graduated from high school on 6 June 1943. 'Exactly one year later', he recalled, 'I was in the US Navy aboard *LCI-492*, carrying two hundred troops to Omaha beach. We were 150 feet long, with a twenty-five-foot beam; the men were housed below decks, crammed into three-tier bunks. With a flat bottom, so we could beach, they were not designed for comfort. We had two ramps that could be lowered either side of the bow, like gangplanks; soldiers ran down them onto the beach,' he remembered. 'LCIs were the smallest ocean-going ships in the US Navy, but when we beached on an enemy shore, we became the biggest target among the landing craft – we were part of Coast Guard Flotilla 4–10 which lost four out of twelve ships, some to mines, other to shellfire.'

Fantacone recalled, 'I was a radioman; there were twenty-four crew of us with four officers, and we all had to contribute to the success of the ship – the guy in the engine room, the cook: our mission was to land those troops on Omaha Beach, no matter what.'[7] Tanks and vehicles were too large for LCIs, and carried instead in Landing Craft, Mechanised (LCM, for a single Sherman tank), of which 486 operated off Normandy on D-Day. However the backbone of the tank-carrying fleet were the Landing Craft, Tank (LCT, whose tank load varied with design), which arrived on 6 June in sixty-four flotillas, numbering 768 craft. The largest vessels in the vehicle-bearing armada were the Landing Ship, Tank (LST). The latter – more than a thousand of which were prefabricated at inland locations in the USA and shipped to the coast for assembly – had logistically underpinned Torch, Husky, Avalanche and Shingle, as well as operations throughout the Pacific, and would do for Overlord and the Southern France landings.

Some 233 LSTs would be deployed on 6 June, and they are the predecessors of today's ro-ro ferries: 3,000-ton ocean-going vessels, crewed by over one hundred, with hinged bow doors. Sub Lieutenant John Sharples remembered that his, *LST-405*, 'had room for thirty Sherman tanks on the lower deck and a lift to enable lighter vehicles such as lorries and jeeps to park on the upper deck. There was also accommodation for two to three hundred soldiers.'[8] With a speed of only twelve knots, they were dubbed by their crews 'Large, Slow Targets', but robust enough to cope with both of their two major opponents: the weather and the enemy.

Drawing just eight feet, they were able to be beached, but, as Sharples recalled, 'we were not supposed to beach because, once we did, we would be stranded there for eleven to twelve hours until the next high tide lifted us off'.[9] LSTs were designed to loiter offshore – out of range of enemy guns – discharging their vehicles onto smaller craft, or Rhino ferries, as piloted by Seabee Daniel Folsom. These were self-propelled rafts that provided the ship-to-shore service for many Allied vehicles landing in France. Most LSTs chugging across the Channel towed their own Rhino ferries behind them on the journey to France – with varying degrees of success in the foul weather they encountered.

The Allies would use 233 LSTs on D-Day. These 3,000-ton vessels were designed to sit offshore and discharge their cargo onto a flat-decked ferry known as a Rhino. The latter, powered by outboard engines, would convey everything ashore. When it was found on 8 June that LSTs could beach and unload directly onto the sand without breaking their backs, the Rhinos were abandoned. The common images of rows of LSTs discharging cargo onto D-Day beaches therefore all date from 9 June onwards. (US Army Signal Corps)

A tank commander recalled with alarm the Rhino's 'glistening flat plate, about as big as four tennis courts, a small island in the sea, and large enough for twenty tanks. A flat platform of pontoons bolted together, swimming just above the water's surface, with large outboard engines.' Driving a 40-ton tank from the ramp of a wallowing LST onto the pitching deck of a Rhino several miles out to sea required both skill and courage. 'The tank commander had to give his signals to a driver who was shut away below, using periscopes, in a sea spray, as they emerged from the fuming belly of the LST.'[10]

Travelling in the hold of an LST was claustrophobic and not for the faint-hearted. Private Wally MacKenzie was taken to Arromanches in one, and recalled the moment he was 'ushered through a hatch-like door,

The backbone of Neptune comprised 768 LCTs, deployed in sixty-four assault flotillas. Most numerous was the LCT Mark V, a 200-foot-long craft with a beam of thirty feet that could carry a variety of tanks, half-tracks, other vehicles, or 150 tons of cargo. Pictured here is part of Omaha Flotilla-18 rehearsing at Slapton. On D-Day, *LCT-199* (left) landed on Easy Red, *LCT-195* (centre) and *LCT-20* (right) on Fox Green, all at H+120. (US Army Signal Corps)

and had to find a place to sit amongst numerous tanks, before the door was sealed in a submarine-like fashion. I was absolutely terrified with the horrible feeling of not being able to get out. That was the most worrying moment of my life, but when we got to Normandy they opened the door and let us down. I was like a pigeon being let out of a cage – a breeze of fresh air.'[11] Sailing in the opposite direction, German POW Arno Christiansen remembered 'an enormous, square, iron box, with floors, walls and ceilings of steel. It had no windows, only very small round portholes high up, so that no one was able to see out of them, and they only let in minimal fresh air. Slowly the boarding ramp was winched up and every vestige of daylight, and every sound, faded from eye and ear. As the last crack of daylight disappeared from the top of the ramp, a little rustle of panic rippled fitfully among the POWs.'[12]

Landing vessels proved very adaptable for Overlord, with some LSTs designated as floating hospitals. Several LCIs were converted to become Landing Craft, Support (LCS), bristling with an array of rocket launchers, three-inch and 40mm guns. Other LCIs were fitted out to accommodate flotilla commanders, becoming Landing Craft, Headquarters (LCH). When a pair of revolving gun turrets were added to LCTs, they were designated Landing Craft, Gun (LCG). Yet more were equipped with anti-aircraft artillery to become Landing Craft, Flak (LCF), and we will encounter Landing Craft, Rocket, in due course. A few craft served as Fighter Direction Tenders, or on salvage or maintenance duties. Most of these were sold off after the war for use as houseboats or barges and almost none are left today. Of the many landing ships built, just one – *LST-325*, a veteran of Torch, Husky and Omaha Beach – has survived as a floating museum to the type, preserved in Evansville, Indiana.

A single tank landing craft from D-Day remains in the UK. Initially landing nine armoured vehicles on Gold Beach, *LCT-7074* of the 17th LCT Flotilla made thirty-two subsequent cross-Channel trips during Operation Neptune and now sits in Portsmouth's D-Day museum. Possibly the last Overlord vessel afloat in British waters is the former *LBK-6* (Landing Barge, Kitchen), which produced hot meals for small ships' crews off Sword and Gold beaches, and still does good service today as the clubhouse of the Harwich and Dovercourt Sailing Club.[13]

To understand the scale of resources put into the two Scottish Combined Training Centres (CTCs), where military personnel from all three services and of many nationalities were trained to work with landing craft, it is worth lingering with them for a moment. The No. 1 CTC at Inveraray – the site chosen because it was beyond the range of all German reconnaissance aircraft – was set up in October 1940 as part of Churchill's programme to 'hit back at the enemy'. He was a regular and enthusiastic visitor, as were the King, Mountbatten and Eisenhower. On the upper reaches of Loch Fyne, Argyllshire, and named HMS *Quebec* (the Royal Navy's shore-based establishments being traditionally known as 'stone frigates'), it possessed a substantial fleet of landing ships and dozens of smaller landing craft.

It had its own air force on call – No. 516 (Combined Operations) Squadron, based at nearby RAF Dundonald. Inveraray was huge, catering for up to fifteen thousand instructors, maintenance staff and students on a variety of courses in seven Nissen-hutted sub-camps and two accommodation ships. In the nearby seaplane base of Largs, the Vanduara Hotel was requisitioned as Combined Operations HQ, becoming HMS *Monk*, while Combined Operations staff officers' courses were held in the adjacent Hollywood Hotel (aka HMS *Warren*), which was where the basics of the Mulberry harbour project were thrashed out at the 'Rattle' Conference in the summer of 1943.

Troops visiting the Inverary CTC – including every D-Day assault formation – were pushed through on two-week courses, catering to the specific needs of infantry, armour, artillery, engineer, signals, ordnance, medical and commando units, at regiment or brigade, battalion and company levels. Gunners were trained to fire their weapons from craft under way at sea; drivers were shown how to waterproof their vehicles, manoeuvre them onto wet decks and drive them ashore through several feet of water; medical staff rehearsed lowering stretcher cases into and out of boats. For all, there were endless beach assaults onto the many islands and inlets in the vicinity, under simulated and eventually live fire, from machine guns, mortars, artillery and aircraft, with equal emphasis on day and night operations.

Destined for Sword Beach, Major Hugh Gillies, company commander with the 1st King's Own Scottish Borderers, with the 9th Brigade of the 3rd Division, recalled of his course in January 1944, 'I threw myself into the uninviting Scottish swell and struggled ashore, followed by my company. During the next three days of the exercise my clothes froze on me, but such was my high state of physical fitness, that I did not catch so much as a cold.'[14] Another company commander, Major Francis Goode, who would land on Gold with 'D' Company, 2nd Glosters (56th

Independent Brigade, supporting 50th Division), took his men through an Inverary course in March 1944. 'We practised getting in and out of the landing craft, which were manned by enthusiastic marines. One of them, we were told, had been too enthusiastic and steering his assault craft across the loch in semi-darkness, hit a buoy. Thinking it was the beach, he ordered *Down Ramp!* and some ten fully equipped infantrymen dashed into the loch – and vanished for ever.'[15]

The Royal Air Force, too, sent personnel from their Servicing Commando Units (SCUs) for amphibious training at Inveraray – these were the men we encountered in Exercise Spartan. RAF commandos were designed to disembark from landing craft, with their own transport and equipment, to help maintain temporary airstrips for incoming fighters, or take over airbases recently abandoned by the enemy. Peter Brown had volunteered in March 1943 for a 'special unit', and found himself in one. 'Simply explained, our task was to follow the army as close to the front line as possible. A temporary airstrip would be laid down and we would refuel, rearm and service the aircraft attacking the Germans. This enabled our aircraft to continue operations without having to return to their bases – we also had, if needed, to help defend the base.'[16]

At Inveraray, Brown remembered, 'we were taught to swim, drive trucks, complete assault courses, undertake gas drills and work with landing craft. Instead of RAF blue we were kitted out with khaki battle-dress onto which we sewed red and black Combined Operations badges, blue RAF Eagles, trade insignia and our stripes. When asked what mob we belonged to, we replied we were NAAFI managers,' he chuckled. 'We also had to be familiar with a wide variety of aircraft – Hurricanes, Spitfires, Mustangs and Mosquitos – and to understand our many tasks, we visited thirty-one different aerodromes and airstrips in the fourteen months before landing in France.'[17] Their capability had been developed from experience in North Africa, where the availability of tactical air support to ground forces was governed by how close the fighter squadrons were to the front, and RAF ground crews were constantly leapfrogging from strip to strip to keep up with the Allied advance. The six SCUs (each of 150 men) sent to Normandy would make a vital contribution to air support in France.[18]

Altogether, an estimated quarter of a million Allied personnel were processed through Inveraray CTC during the war; Canadian reservist Sub Lieutenant Kendall Kidder was one of them. He wrote to his wife:

some of us had tea with the Duke of Argyle [*sic*] who seems to own everything in these parts, even the roads. He is very interested in Canada because his uncle, Lord Tweedsmuir was Governor-General. Others climbed his mountains, used Mills bombs to fish his salmon streams, explored his deer park and inflicted 'light casualties' on his sheep. I am so glad you are sending a parcel. The one thing we miss more than anything else is good Canadian chocolate. English cigarettes are horrible and it is virtually impossible to get woollen clothing. We would all enjoy the occasional magazine, just to look at the food ads.

Later Kidder's landing craft ran aground in front of the WRNS training establishment. Without thinking, he ordered his men to strip off, jump into the waters below and free the craft. The Wrens enjoyed the show but Kidder was reprimanded for his 'display'.[19]

No. 2 CTC was Castle Toward, a twenty-five-bedroomed nineteenth-century castle overlooking the Clyde estuary. It was requisitioned by the Admiralty in 1942. A huge village of huts was built in its grounds and the establishment renamed HMS *Brontosaurus*. Its training programme was similar to that of Inveraray's, with PT every morning in all weathers at 0600 hours; swimming in full kit – in preparation for the wade ashore from landing craft; firing every conceivable weapon, including German, on ranges; and demanding hikes up nearby hills. These activities progressed from company-size exercises up to full-scale brigade rehearsals with artillery, engineer and all-arms support.

Each course (Churchill and Mountbatten watched one) culminated in a live-firing amphibious exercise where troops arrived in landing craft off the shores of the castle's estates, under fire from fixed-height machine-guns. Soldiers returned fire as they advanced up the beach with the aid of live ammunition, smokescreens and attacks by low-level aircraft, fighting their way inland. Today's coastguards note that 'as the sands continue to move around, they regularly reveal evidence of all this activity. Spent and live rifle and pistol bullets are found in abundance, whilst high explosive, smoke and phosphorus mortar bombs and hand grenades cause quite a stir when they are placed on the bar of the local hotel or handed in at the local police station.'[20]

The landing craft crews themselves were also learning their trade. The young sub lieutenants in charge of these craft were usually from the Royal Naval Volunteer Reserve, and had been processed through six-week courses at HMS *Lochailort*, another 'stone frigate' in western Scotland, which was in reality Inverailort Castle, near Fort William. There, they were taught how to communicate by light and flag, maintain position, turn in formation, and – rather like Napoleonic troops – be able to deploy from column into line abreast.

They also learned the rudiments of small boat handling, seamanship and – vitally important – tides and coastal navigation. For, as an admiral pointed out, 'If you were in a landing craft looking toward the coast of France, from ten miles away – with a freeboard of six or seven feet, you just don't see the shore.'[21] The flotillas approaching Sword, Juno, Gold and Omaha had little difficulty navigating because of the many landmarks (chiefly prominent houses and church spires) behind the beaches, but Force 'U', having nothing equivalent, would end up nearly a mile south of their intended beaches at Utah.

Such skills were needed equally by crews on the smaller LCAs, LCVPs, LCMs and slightly larger LCTs, but Lochailort struggled to keep pace with the huge number of landing craft skippers required, and the US Navy encountered the same challenge. As Admiral Ramsay discovered, building huge numbers of craft was all very well, but training their crews and commanders proved infinitely more difficult, for there also had to be plenty of fully qualified spare personnel to replace casualties, as well as meeting the needs of the Mediterranean and Pacific campaigns. This manpower crisis was exacerbated when Overlord's shipping requirements suddenly escalated in early 1944 with the addition of extra beaches, and the increased personnel and equipment required.

If the landing craft crews were generally inexperienced, those on board the larger landing ships were far more conversant with amphibious operations. The Australian war correspondent Alan Moorhead recounted of the vessel that took him to Normandy, '*LST-816* had already made three assault landings: North Africa, Sicily and Salerno. On this, their fourth major landing, the sailors showed no excitement or emotion. The Captain himself had trained his officers on the voyage to Europe, and during the actual assaults.'[22]

Freddie Robertson served on HMS *Royal Ulsterman* – a 3,000-ton Royal Navy Reserve ex-passenger ship which had sailed the Glasgow–Belfast ferry route before the war. He recalled how she first landed troops in Norway and evacuated the BEF from Saint-Nazaire (both in 1940); disembarked soldiers in Madagascar and Algeria (1942), Pantelleria, Sicily and Salerno in 1943, and Anzio in January 1944 – where US Ranger Jud 'Lucky' Luckhurst remembered, 'Some of the crew saved up their RN grog ration for their Ranger friends; the crew were a good bunch of men and were highly respected by the Rangers.' Normandy was therefore the *Royal Ulsterman*'s ninth major operation. Robertson recorded in his log, 'On our return from the Med., we took on new LCAs at Southampton, then at Berth 37 embarked men from Highland Light Infantry of Canada; Stormont, Dundas & Glengarry Highlanders; and North Nova Scotia Highlanders, all troops with 9 Brigade of the 3rd Canadian Division, whom we conveyed to Juno beach at Bernières and St Aubin-sur-Mer.'[23]

Likewise the headquarters ship HMS *Largs*, which features often in the British D-Day story. She was one of several Royal Navy HQ vessels – an important legacy which Lord Louis Mountbatten had bestowed on his Combined Operations command. Whilst it is widely understood today that such complex maritime operations need to be controlled *in situ* from a dedicated vessel fitted for communications, this was not the case until 1942. *Largs* was a 5,000-ton former 'banana boat' seized from Vichy France whilst at anchor in Gibraltar and – converted to accommodate an extensive communications suite, as well as the ability to carry troops and landing craft – would accompany the *Royal Ulsterman* in most of the major landings before Normandy.

John Emery served on board the *Largs* as a signaller, like many on board, and recalled being under fire at Pantelleria (where he spent a day plugging holes made by machine-gun fire from hostile aircraft), Sicily and Salerno before 'returning to England for a refit; whilst ashore I remember taking part in the land-based deception in Scotland [Operation Fortitude], driving up and down the coast in company with other vehicles sending dummy messages purporting to be a fleet of destroyers exercising off the coast near Inverness.' He confided, 'We were looking forward to the Big One; it was what we'd all been waiting for. I'd say we were confident, but, honestly, anxious too, for we knew the price of failure if this landing failed – it would undo all the work of the previous five years.'[24]

There were five such headquarters vessels, converted merchantmen all, one for each beach – *Bayfield* and *Ancon* for Utah and Omaha; while *Bulolo, Hilary* and *Largs* operated off Gold, Juno and Sword. Each carried the relevant maritime force admirals, corps and divisional commanders of the assaulting troops, providing them with a real-time picture of everything happening at sea and on land.

Admiral Ramsay also discovered a gap between the expectations of the land force commanders and the terminology of their maritime colleagues. Along the Calvados coast were ten major coastal artillery four-gun batteries of 155mm or 105mm calibre; thirty-one lesser four-gun batteries, supported by thirty-four observation posts and twenty-eight command bunkers; on the five invasion beaches lay fifty-five individual positions mounting 88mm or 75mm guns; and further forty-five infantry *Widerstandsnester* (strongpoints) of multiple bunkers housing smaller weapons, mortars and machine-guns. In nearly every case, these were enveloped in reinforced concrete up to two metres thick.[25] Patton may have called them 'bulwarks of human stupidity', but all of the naval losses at Dieppe – amounting to a destroyer and thirty-three smaller craft – had been caused by shore-based artillery firing from such positions.[26] These needed suppressing, though frequently only a direct hit through an embrasure would do the job.

They could only be systematically attacked on the day of invasion, lest attention be drawn to the future invasion area. Some batteries were bombed beforehand, but it was known the strategic air forces could be a blunt weapon. For example, of one thousand bombs released over the Merville battery, fewer than fifty fell within the four-gun battery site, of which two struck concrete casemates, in neither case damaging the weapons inside.[27] Apart from infantry or airborne assault, only the extensive battleship, cruiser and destroyer bombardment forces had the firepower to eliminate these as a threat.

Ramsay would later report that many of these defences 'were active until overcome by the infantry'. Captain J. W. Josselyn, of the British cruiser *Hawkins*, explained why: 'A salvo which straddles the target at sea is regarded as a hit in naval terms, for the double pressure will buckle ships' plates and superstructures. On land, the earth absorbed the shock waves of our near misses, hence many positions had to be rolled up the old-fashioned way, with boots on the ground.'[28]

In south-west England the US Army opened its own version of Inveraray – the Assault Training Centre (ATC) – at Woolacombe, on the north Devon coast in September 1943. It had been many months in the planning and a high-level conference was held there for a month over 24 May–23 June, just before the Sicilian invasion, to discuss assault landings and how to execute them. Operation Torch had been largely unopposed, so there was almost no institutional experience of how to manage them.[29] Within sixteen square miles of real estate, including beaches, cliffs, headlands, sand dunes and ten miles of Atlantic coastline, the ATC trained commanders and machine-gun, mortar, rocket launcher, demolition and flamethrower teams in the assault techniques they would need to over-whelm the defenders of Hitler's *Atlantikwall*.

Each course was tough, taking no account of the weather: on 18 December 1943 three landing craft foundered in the surf, swamping the tanks on board and drowning fourteen; DUKWs turned turtle in other incidents. On 25 October 1943 five GIs were killed and fourteen wounded by machine-gun fire intended to pass over their heads on the ATC's Exmoor firing range. Altogether ninety-eight troops died at Woolacombe preparing for D-Day, mostly Americans.[30] Roy Burton was a British guardsman sent for weapons training at Woolacombe. On the three-inch mortar course, 'our mortars were firing over our heads when a few dropped short with the excuse that the tails of the bombs had come off – a little closer and our tails would have come off. Then a mortar bomb exploded in one of the barrels, killing three and the instructor. Firing was postponed whilst the remaining batch of bombs were sent for inves-tigation, but we carried on, as there was no alternative.'[31]

Gordon Golding, in the Weapons Platoon of Company 'E', 175th Infantry, with the US 29th Infantry Division, trained in the area in September 1943. His delightful letters home sum up the general experi-ence of most GIs going through their tough preparation for D-Day. Naturally, he was not allowed to mention his location: 'I wish I could go into detail and tell you exactly where we are, and what is happening, but I'm afraid our friend the censor would start snapping his ole' scis-sors. It looks as if my letters from now on will have to be strictly *billets d'amour* without much mention of the army.'[32] He nevertheless hinted he was near the coast, 'if we can get a few of the mines out of the way, I will get in some swimming. The beach is heavily mined and I don't particularly relish the idea of ending up in little pieces.'

Living in tents, the 175th Regiment soon hardened to their environ-ment: 'I even have hot water to shave and wash with tonight, so feel pretty good. A Red Cross Clubmobile cruised around a couple of nights ago with coffee, donuts and [Glenn] Miller's latest recordings.' Importantly, he and his buddies got to know the British landing craft crews who would eventually take them to France: 'My ole' machine-gun is really clicking these days and if the damn thing wasn't so heavy I wouldn't mind so much. A lot of our operations are with the Royal Navy and those boys are swell to work with. One of our landing craft went down yesterday morning but we got all the boys out. I'm glad I know how to swim, 'cause I don't think much of these life preservers.'[33]

Golding alarmed his wife in one letter with the admission, 'day before yesterday, I failed to put enough *oomph* behind a hand grenade and mother earth kissed me firmly on the cheek'. For their final exercise, with artillery afloat firing live ammunition onto bunkers lining the cliffs, as Golding splashed ashore he was bucked to see 'those Spitfires raking hell out of those pillboxes with machine-gun fire. This tremendous air support we have really means a lot.' He also referred to the realism which resulted in two GI friends becoming casualties; they were hit by 'some nasty shrapnel – one in the stomach and the other through the arm. The one who got his arm mangled used to sit up and play the trumpet at night for the boys ... Luckily the [other] kid's cartridge belt saved his stomach from being torn to hell.'[34]

Other visitors to the ATC included Chuck Hurlbut and the 299th Engineer Combat Battalion, whom we last met in mid-Atlantic. They had arrived in south Wales, where he remembered marching through Cardiff. 'All along the way people were waving little flags shouting "Hi, Americans", which felt good as we'd never had our own parade. A train took us straight to Camp Braunton, Ilfracombe; we took a day to rest up, and then started assault landings in our rubber boats. Just practice, practice, practice.'

Later, Hurlbut and the 299th drove south to Dorchester, where they were told of the invasion plans. 'We knew there was going to be an invasion but we didn't know where or when. Some big brass told us: "The 299th has been selected to be part of this great crusade. In fact, you're gonna be right in the front row." There, we were shown models of the [Omaha] beach area, saw aerial photographs that were only hours old; our battalion had eight assault teams, and our mission as engineers was to cut pathways through the obstacles – the tetrahydra, hedgehogs, Belgian gates and wooden poles, most with mines attached – that were all along the beach. That's when all the practice suddenly made sense.'[35]

Captain Charles 'Hank' Hangsterfer, commanding Company 'H' of the 16th Infantry, with the US 1st Division, was another GI who passed through the ATC with his men. He recalled a Russian general observing the training: 'One of our staff officers asked him how they did it in the Red Army. He replied they kept rushing the area until the enemy ran out of ammo. I was happy I was in the US Army when I heard this.'[36] The ATC provided other units with strenuous physical training programmes and refresher courses to prepare the GIs for combat. It was maintained by the 146th Engineer Combat Battalion, who soon found rebuilding the bunkers destroyed by each course too arduous. They substituted solid concrete squares of pillbox dimensions that were easily repairable – which explains the curious lumps of battered cement still studding the local landscape.

Amongst the weapons the Allies would take to Normandy were three which they literally consumed. Candy was an easy way to pep up the troops, providing a quick burst of energy with sugar, and was soon found to be an excellent method of barter. Thus the Hershey 'D' bar proved a useful addition to the Allied armoury. The company had been approached back in 1937 to create an energy bar for US Army emergency rations. The requirements were very specific: it had to weigh four ounces, be rich in energy and withstand high temperatures. The result incorporated chocolate, sugar, cocoa butter, skim milk powder and oat flour, but was almost impossible to chew: troops had to shave slices off with a bayonet before eating it, but by the war's end Hershey's had produced more than three billion ration bars, huge numbers ending up in the sticky hands of grateful French children.

If candy was a natural way to energise tired soldiers, their commanders also introduced an artificial method. From the earliest hours of the blitzkrieg in Poland, modern warfare was seen to test human endurance to unprecedented limits. The War Office discovered that the Germans had 'consumed thirty-five million 3mg tablets of benzedrine sulphate in 1940, marketed under the name Pervitin' – panzer crews knew them as *Panzerschokolade*; to Luftwaffe pilots they were *Stuka-Tabletten* or *Hermann-Göring-Pillen*. Allied attention thus turned to the interwar advances made in pharmacology which had resulted in the development of synthetic adrenaline, patented as Benzedrine in 1932 by a US company, Smith, Kline & French. Assuming this was the secret to the runaway success of blitzkrieg, the Allies responded with field tests on military performance and medical officers began issuing packets of six Benzedrine 'pep pills' per soldier before combat. After tests, RAF scientists also recommended 'Benzedrine for every RAF mission, for the "determination and aggression" that it offered'.

Ohioan D. Zane Schlemmer was a nineteen-year-old sergeant belonging to Headquarters Company of the 508th Parachute Infantry (82nd Airborne Division), who recalled being loaded up with all the paraphernalia he would need for his jump on D-Day: 'rifle and binoculars, mortar ammunition, grenades, mortar bombs, an anti-tank mine.

Thereafter we were given a series of additional objects like a small silk escape map, a tiny compass, two hundred francs of invasion currency, and Benzedrine to help us remain awake, as well as two morphine syringes if wounded.'[37] By June 1944, Allied aircrew, airborne forces, commandos and some infantrymen were equipped with their 'Bennies' – some of the estimated 200 million tablets supplied to the US and British armed forces in the war.

Sub Lieutenant Peter Miles, RNVR, was in charge of a flight of three small landing craft, training with the Gold assault force on the south coast before the invasion. 'It was stressed to us that our job was to keep the men under our command alive and afloat; expect exhaustion as you have not known before; sleep in short snatches and order a rating to shake you periodically every fifteen minutes' – but as it turned out, 'we were also given Benzedrine to keep us awake'.[38] British instructions on its use recommended that 'soldiers should ingest 5mg–10mg of Benzedrine sulphate every five to six hours, not exceeding 20mg per day, issued at the discretion of the unit medical officer when sleep was severely limited for several days'.[39]

Benzedrine apart, soldiers had a third method of staying alert and dulling their appetite: tobacco. Cigarettes had been introduced to British and French soldiers by their Turkish compatriots in the trenches of the 1853–6 Crimean War and their popularity grew rapidly in the late nineteenth century, replacing snuff and peaking in the First World War. There was something indivisible about the soldier and his cigarette or pipe: it brought warmth; lighting cigarettes was a physically intimate act when the rigours of military life were bleak; and smoking was a welcome distraction from forthcoming combat, settling the nerves and appetite. They were an ever-present feature of 1944; Eisenhower smoked his way through the war on four packs a day of his favourite Camels (their campaign slogans featured pictures of GIs relaxing with the strapline 'Camels – a taste of home'), whilst his GIs could claim a packet of twenty per day and received little packets of four in their daily C-rations.

When Lucky Strike launched an advertising campaign at the time of Operation Torch in 1942, 'Lucky Strike has Gone to War', sales rocketed by thirty-eight per cent. The following year, Phillip Morris and its competitors sold a record 290 billion cigarettes, thirty per cent of which ended up in the hands of young GIs. British and Canadian soldiers were also entitled to twenty-five free cigarettes a day, which came in round cans of fifty, enabling almost everyone to build up a reserve for barter, particularly with French civilians. Not only that – as one Tommy observed – 'The cigarette was regarded as a form of medicine. The first thing they'd give a wounded chap was a cigarette. They just stuck it in his mouth whether he wanted it or not. It took the stress away.'[40]

The third phase of Allied training was the marrying up of troops with the naval assault force that would convey them to Normandy. In May 1943, I Canadian Corps had handed over their responsibility for guarding Sussex against invasion to incoming British troops in order 'to free the Corps from all static responsibilities and to allow it to concentrate on training for offensive operations'.[41] The summer and autumn of 1943 saw Major General Rod Keller's 3rd Canadian Division, headquartered at the Balmer Lawn Hotel, Brockenhurst, rehearse with their escorting warships, under Commodore John Hughes-Hallett, based at Cowes. He had overseen the maritime forces at Dieppe, been maritime advisor to COSSAC, led part of the landings in Sicily, and on returning to the Isle of Wight had built up his flotilla's capacity to lift a division.

'H-H' – invariably known as Hughes-Hitler – was a stickler for discipline who devised the 3rd Canadian Division's searching and realistic training which culminated in Exercise Pirate of 16–19 October 1943, where the 7th Canadian Brigade assaulted Studland Bay, Dorset, followed by a build-up ashore of the rest of the division. Air support was rained off, but indicated the scale of resources allocated to these undertakings. Aspects were filmed and it featured in *Canadian Army Newsreel 19*, released within weeks of the exercise.[42] When the capable Hughes-Hallett was promoted away to command the cruiser HMS *Jamaica* in November 1943, he was succeeded by Rear Admiral Philip Vian. In the year preceding Overlord, between them, the pair directed twelve assault and three maritime transportation exercises for Keller's Canadians.

The British 3rd Division, destined for Sword Beach a year hence, had undertaken similar amphibious rehearsals in July 1943 on the Pembrokeshire coast of south Wales. One day of the fortnight-long Exercise Jantzen, mounted in Saundersfoot Bay, was viewed by the Prime Minister and Mountbatten from the Wiseman's Bridge Inn – where Churchill's letter of thanks for the landlord's hospitality is displayed on the wall. Jantzen demonstrated many flaws in inter-service cooperation and the mechanics of moving vast numbers of men by sea in challenging weather.

As plans for Overlord began to develop, more attention was paid to the command teams. Montgomery's old command, the British 3rd

Division, was at this stage led by Major General William Ramsden, who had led a division and corps in North Africa, but – not being one of Montgomery's chosen men – was demoted and sent home to the 3rd Division.[43] When Montgomery was confirmed as the land commander for the invasion, Ramsden was immediately replaced by Tom Rennie, who had led the 5th Black Watch at El Alamein, and was therefore an officer far more to Monty's liking.

The US Army, too, had shuffled its pack of tactical leaders prior to the summer of 1944, most prominently when the popular leader of the 1st Infantry Division (the 'Big Red One'), was removed. Major General Terry de la Mesa Allen had commanded them since May 1942, and under Bradley had taken them through tough combat in North Africa and Sicily. However, as the latter observed, 'although Terry had become a hero to his troops, he was known as a maverick among the senior commanders'. Ill-disciplined to the point of insubordination, yet one of the army's rising stars, he was both a 'superbly competent trainer and inspirational battle captain', wrote Bradley, 'but fiercely antagonistic to any echelon above that of division. As a result he was inclined to be stubborn and independent. Skillful, adept and aggressive, he frequently ignored orders, and fought in his own way.'[44] His assistant divisional commander, the likeable and well-connected Brigadier General Theodore 'Ted' Roosevelt, Jr (son of the 26th President), was cast in a similar mould. Both were lionised by their troops and when Bradley relieved both of their positions on 7 August 1943, during the Sicilian campaign, the 1st Division's mood turned ugly and morale slumped.

Bradley devoted three pages of his memoirs to the sacking episode, observing that it was 'one of my most unpleasant duties of the entire war'.[45] Thus, when he led the division back to England from Sicily in November 1943, Allen's successor, Clarence R. Huebner – who would take them to Omaha Beach – was hugely resented, being as unpopular as Allen had been popular. Although military command is never about winning the popularity stakes, in an ideal world, Huebner and his division might not have been deployed on such a risky venture as the assault wave on D-Day, when they were still ill at ease with one another; however, the Big Red One was Bradley's only complete, battle-trained infantry formation to hand in England.

The other two assault divisions, Raymond 'Tubby' Barton's 4th, and the 29th – a National Guard formation that originated in Virginia and Maryland and commanded by Charlie Gerhardt – would be new to combat. As an aside, it is worthwhile remembering the destinies of Eisenhower, Gerhardt and Huebner had been shaped by the English Channel they were about to cross. Their ancestors, Darmstadt-born Hans Nicholas Eisenhauer, had sailed through it in 1741 on his way to Pennsylvania; four years later he was followed by Friedrich Gerhardt on his way from Bohemia; whilst over a century later, in 1857, it was the turn of Gottfried Huebner, making his way from Stuttgart down the Channel towards Kansas.

His descendant, Major General Clarence Ralph Huebner, had worked his way up from private to colonel within the 1st Division, leading a company, battalion and its 28th Infantry Regiment during the First World War. A stickler for drill and fieldcraft, during the pre-Overlord training he won grudging respect by accompanying his men on every exercise, firing every weapon on the ranges, and being first into a foxhole to let a demonstration tank roll over him. The transition between the two contrasting Allen–Huebner leadership styles has been the basis for several modern change-management studies.[46]

It is to Huebner's enormous credit that by 6 June 1944, his division had begun to give him the benefit of the doubt, and his effectiveness was proven by his men on D-Day – though, Bradley noted, 'by this time the 1st Infantry Division had swallowed a bellyful of heroics and wanted to go home. When they learned they were to make a third assault, the troops grumbled bitterly over the injustices of war. Although I disliked subjecting them to still another landing, I felt that as a commander, I had no other choice, and felt compelled to use the best troops I had.'[47] This exactly mirrored the complaints against Montgomery, aired for precisely the same reasons, by his Eighth Army divisions when they learned they were slated for D-Day.

Both Allen and Roosevelt made good, the former taking another division into combat, whilst the latter accompanied the 4th Infantry Division onto Utah Beach as its assistant divisional commander – more of whom later. Allen's chief of staff, Norman 'Dutch' Cota, moved on to become an Overlord planner, and landed on Omaha as assistant divisional commander of the 29th, later winning a division of his own. Like Montgomery, Bradley had concerns that his senior commanders were not experienced enough. He kept Leonard T. Gerow, a West Point class contemporary of his and Eisenhower's, on at V Corps, on the basis that he had been immersed in Overlord planning for two years. Gerow was a former commander of the 29th Division, which would be part of his

The First US Army's Omar Bradley (1893–1981) (left), poses with the commander of V Corps, Leonard 'Gee' Gerow (1888–1972) (second left), Eisenhower, and J. Lawton Collins (1896–1987) of VII Corps (right). All these generals had previously worked together at various stages in their careers; Gerow had been planning Overlord for over a year and Collins was one of the few with combat experience from the Pacific. (NARA)

corps in France, and had given up his division in July 1943 to lead V Corps.

Highly regarded and liked by Bradley and Eisenhower, 'according to his men, Gerow's chief fault was a tendency in combat to move his headquarters too close to the front', thought historian Forrest C. Pogue; he was 'noted for his desire to be where the action was. I can recall in Normandy actually going *back* a little way from corps to reach a division CP [command post]'.[48] Happy as he was with his V Corps commander, Bradley felt obliged to replace Major General Willis D. Crittenberger at XIX Corps, which would follow Gerow onto Omaha, and Major General Roscoe B. Woodruff, the commander of VII Corps assaulting Utah. He had no criticisms of them, but was offered two more experienced officers with battle experience from the Pacific. J. Lawton Collins relinquished his 25th Division at Guadalcanal to take on VII Corps, whilst Charles

H. Corlett also left his 7th Division in the Pacific theatre to assume the reins of XIX Corps in France.[49]

Back at the British 3rd Division, the newly appointed Tom Rennie joined his formation and its supporting arms in Scotland for the next phase of their training. This was on the Tarbat peninsula, in Easter Ross, which bears a passing resemblance to the Normandy coastline. In a story identical to that of Imber village on Salisbury Plain, nearly a thousand civilians, including the entire community of Inver near Tarbat, had their homes and farms requisitioned in November 1943. All were obliged to leave, move or sell their livestock, equipment and crops within a month in order to create the 3rd Division's live-firing training area. Local children, brought up in remote communities which lacked modern facilities, recalled the mixed emotions of relocating to bigger towns. Twelve-year-old Marion Fleming remembered moving to somewhere 'dreadful. There was traffic and pavements, no beaches to play on. We didn't have any road sense, we didn't need it – there were only two cars in Inver. But there were pluses: electricity, running water, a flushing loo: we nearly drove my granny bananas, flushing it over and over.' They were allowed to return after the war, and on 6 June 2004 inscribed boulders were unveiled to commemorate the contribution the area made to D-Day.[50]

Once the civilians had departed, over thirty thousand troops destined for Sword Beach – 3rd Division, 27th Armoured Brigade, the mine-clearing flail tanks of the 22nd Dragoons, and Nos. 5 and 6 Beach Groups – moved in. They formed a vast concentration centred on Inverness, with Tom Rennie's HQ in Cameron Barracks, and began relentlessly attacking Tarbat and the surrounding area. The two commando brigades – Shimi Lovat's 1st and Jumbo Leicester's 4th, also assigned to Sword – were already training hard elsewhere in Scotland, in between other military duties – some in Italy – and planning their own aspects of Overlord.

Conducted under the highest secrecy – not even the residents were told why they were being moved, other than for 'military purposes' – the 3rd Division's exercises began 'dry shod', where the troops 'disembarked' onto an imaginary beach start line and then assaulted a series of concrete and other obstacles under fire. Their training package began in Galloway, progressed to the divisional battle school in Moffat, then moved to the Combined Training Centre at Inveraray, which we have visited. For the 'wet' phases, units embarked in LCTs at Fort George, were taken by sea to an area off Wick before turning south for the Tarbat peninsula, the length of the journey simulating the cross-Channel passage. Endless beach assaults followed, using live ammunition, with naval support firing them in.

Marine Eddie Williams supported all of the 3rd Division's amphibious exercises as part of the three-man crew on *LCA-602*. They were part of the 539th LCA Flotilla carried by the 12,000-ton *Empire Halberd*. She had joined them straight from America; crewed by 250, she could carry a thousand troops and eighteen LCAs. Of the *Halberd* Williams recalled, 'We had a good merchant crew but they were a bit militant; when we went on an exercise, if we could not get back to the ship before 1700 hours due to bad weather, they would not pick our craft out of the water because they were not paid overtime. Consequently we spent a few miserable nights ashore in schoolrooms or village halls with no food laid on.' He and the 539th Flotilla were destined for Gold Beach on D-Day.[51] Edwin 'Nobby' Clark with the 74th Field Regiment, Royal Artillery, of the 50th Division, would encounter something not dissimilar, also off Gold. Two merchant seamen operating winches that were lowering his regiment's 25-pounder guns and vehicles into landing craft 'were halfway through unloading when one of the men looked at his watch and remarked "five o'clock", and both disappeared below deck'.[52]

With the three tank regiments of the 27th Armoured Brigade was Major Derrick Wormald, a regular officer commissioned into the 13th/18th Royal Hussars in 1936, joining them on the North-West Frontier of India in the days of spurs and saddles. They had converted to armour in 1938 and saw action in France two years later. By 1944 he was commanding 'A' Squadron, equipped with swimming tanks. In Scotland, Wormald operated with the 14th LCT Flotilla that would land him in Normandy:

we trained together in the Moray Firth out of Fort George during the spring of 1944 in some very bad weather conditions. From the tank crews' point of view, life in the LCTs were extremely unpleasant; the five tanks and their crews in each LCT were confined to the well-decks from which they could only see the sky… When their diesel engines were running the exhaust fumes produced an unhealthy atmosphere which, when added to the wallowing motion of the crafts in rough seas, produced a horrible vomiting sickness among us.[53]

Captain Julius Neave, in the same regiment as Derrick Wormald, recalled that 'forty-eight hours on virtually open landing craft followed by forty-eight hours on open and windswept moorland' was hardly comfortable, but 'by dint of wearing every garment possible, and keeping a full flask, we managed to survive. The chaos on the beach itself was on each occasion quite unbelievable, but this strangely was an asset, for on 6 June itself chaos reigned, and our experience had taught us it was the normal thing.'[54] Brigadier Erroll Prior-Palmer's 27th Armoured Brigade (whose badge was a yellow seahorse – a witty reference to its cavalry regiments), equipped with swimming tanks, lost eight armoured vehicles in these exercises; the 13th/18th Hussars recorded one casualty through drowning. Their tanks still lie on the seabed of the Moray Firth, watched over by the occasional recreational diver. Later, the 3rd Division left a fitting stone memorial facing the sea at Nairn beach: 'Silent we came. Silent we left, to strike a blow for Freedom.'

For planning purposes during these exercises all of 3rd Division's staff, brigade personnel and commanding officers decamped to the relative peace and security of Aberlour House, a large pedimented mansion on the River Spey and once home to generations of Jacobite Gordons. There they drew up planning and landing schedules for every man, weapon and vehicle that would go to France. These would apply to all interme-diate exercises, as well as Overlord. Everything had to be stowed and landed to a precise timetable without wasting shipping space, with the frustrating result that every unit and headquarters were spread between different ships and landing craft, a story repeated across the five beaches.[55]

Captain Douglas Aitken, medical officer of the 24th Lancers of the 8th Armoured Brigade, recorded his frustration in spending 'hectic hours working out which vehicle will have to be landed first and therefore which order they will go in the boat', and his 'struggle with innumerable forms in duplicate trying to discover whom we have brought, who ought to be here and what and which vehicle has arrived or ought to be here'.[56] With full war scales of ammunition, personnel and equipment, an Allied infantry division, like Rennie's 3rd, required 270,000 'ship tons' – the equivalent of twenty-eight Liberty shiploads – to move across the Channel; for an armoured division, with more vehicles, the figure was forty ships.[57] In May 1944 the logistics challenge would arise not of a shortage of any equipment, personnel or ammunition, but the lack of port space to handle the incessant flow of materiel from the United States: Britain had simply run out of capacity.

Lieutenant Commander Teddy Gueritz, a future admiral and beach-master at Sword whom we have already met training, noted that 'it was a harsh winter, we had a lot of poor weather so we got accustomed to fairly bad conditions. That was an important factor, as it turned out, because 6 June was not a typical June day, it was absolutely vile.'[58] Gueritz reported to Captain Eric Bush, RN, who was already a veteran of one amphibious assault landing – at Gallipoli in 1915. Major Robin Dunn with the 7th Field Regiment, Royal Artillery, underlined the importance of the training for their leaders: 'British 3rd Division had a new divisional commander, Tom Rennie, who had led a brigade of 51st Highland Division with distinction in Eighth Army and had a high reputation, whereas the brigadier of 185 Brigade was K. P. Smith, who had been with them for some time and had so far seen no action. He was a good trainer of troops and worked us hard during our time in Scotland.'[59]

Rennie's 3rd Division actually trained all over Scotland; Albert Walker was a Bren gunner with 'B' Company, 2nd Royal Warwicks, who had joined his battalion at a camp near Lockerbie. 'We drove to Glasgow for street fighting in the slums of the Gorbals which had been evacuated, then did assault landings from the sea,' he recalled. 'I enlisted at seventeen, and my parents had died earlier, so I wrote to my brother serving in Tunisia telling him that he was my next-of-kin, but the letter was returned marked "Killed in Action".'[60]

Admiral Ramsay aboard the headquarters ship HMS *Largs* witnessed their final rehearsal – Exercise Leapyear, held between 26 March and 1 April – before they moved south. One participant of this recalled, 'In theory a quick trip across the Channel in June sounds very agreeable; in the event, on 5–6 June it was cold, rough and most unpleasant', but at least the Scottish weather had prepared him:

At midday on 28 March we went on board our LCT near Inverness and put to sea, but had no means of combating the extreme cold; at 1615 hours we approached the coast. There had been some kind of real bombardment earlier and this had set fire to some pine woods and marram grass on the sandhills. By the time we landed there were squads of Land Army girls beating out the fires, which tended to spoil the realism. The ramp went down amid yelling from the bridge above, and the troops pitched themselves off the end of the ramp into some five feet of freezing cold sea. Just ahead of me I saw a very short man disappear completely for a few seconds before he emerged and struggled up the sand.[61]

There were also the ten Roundabout exercises in Scotland, which practised different beach groups in the rapid unloading of stores, day and night, in all weathers. Corporal William Smith, with 261 Company, Pioneer Corps, suddenly found himself on one of these. With no warning, his unit deployed by train to the specially created Beach Training Centre (BTC) at Gullane, north-east of Edinburgh. He spent three weeks unloading ammunition from coasters, which was then driven onto the beach by DUKW and loaded onto trucks. The lorries thereupon drove to the port of Leith, where their cargo was put on board waiting vessels, which sailed back to Gullane – hence Exercise Roundabout.[62] Living on the beach under canvas, Smith recalled, 'This went on for about three weeks and there was always a ship waiting to be unloaded. During this period I think we only lost one DUKW, which got swamped in a rough sea.' Later on in Normandy, Smith was struck by the similarity of Asnelles – part of Gold Beach – where he landed, to Gullane – 'which, no doubt, was why it was chosen for our spell of training'.[63]

This was the first time most troops had met the DUKW, dubbed 'Duck'. The revolutionary two-and-a-half-ton amphibious truck had made its combat debut in the Sicily invasion of 10 July 1943 with huge success. Its ability to unload vital supplies from ships lying offshore and swim them to supply dumps onshore eased the Allied logistic burden in the absence of a functioning port, and some two thousand were earmarked for Overlord, operated by eleven Royal Army Service Corps (RASC) companies.[64]

One of the first UK-based units to receive their DUKWs was 536 General Transport Company, who trained with them on Annick Water in Ayrshire, Scotland, in the winter of 1943–44. Subsequently, they were issued with one hundred of their own DUKWs in January at the Amphibious School, Towyn in north Wales, where Lieutenant Douglas Day commanding 'A' Platoon had to quell a small uprising. His men were complaining they had chosen to join the army, not the navy. He addressed them: 'You're lucky to be driving these wonderful vehicles, which can go everywhere ordinary lorries and ships can't. Now, if any of you wish to complain, take one pace forward, but remember if you do, that might be mutiny and you all know what that could mean!' No one moved, and he would later take his platoon of thirty-three DUKWs and ninety-nine men ashore on Sword Beach during 6 June. As he later observed, 'To my surprise and the delight of my men, they named the whole event after me – D. Day!'[65]

Three aspects of the invasion: a DUKW backs out of the hold of an LST, protected from aerial attack by a barrage balloon. Some two thousand DUKWs were allocated to the Overlord assault. The six-wheeled swimming truck vehicle had first proved its versatility in the Sicily landings of July 1943, at Salerno and at Anzio. It was a game-changer in Normandy. (US Army Signal Corps)

The 1st Buckinghamshire Battalion also found themselves on a Roundabout exercise. After Exercise Spartan with the Canadians, they had been converted into No. 6 Beach Group, a new concept intended to supervise the landing of men, vehicles and equipment under fire on a hostile shore. A beach group was designated for each assault area, with another in reserve, which included an infantry battalion, in this case the Bucks, with various engineer and transport companies, military police, field dressing stations, an RN commando and RAF detachments; altogether it comprised over three thousand men.[66]

Bill Adams, then eighteen and with the 1st Bucks, got fed up of the hard work and living under canvas in midwinter. One night he crept under the barbed wire and made his way into Gullane. 'Imagine my surprise: the Marine Hotel was full of Polish women soldiers. Hundreds of them. Several of us went back a few nights later to have a drink with them. But they weren't interested in us; they were homesick and serious. All they wanted to do was kill Germans on account of what had happened to their homeland.'[67]

All the Allied follow-on units were equally hard at work. Norman Smith had been motivated to join the Territorials as a medic after Munich, enlisting in November 1938. He enjoyed an annual training camp in 1939 before the war pulled him over to France with a field ambulance, later escaping aboard the destroyer HMS *Vivacious* on her third run to Dunkirk; she was hit by shore fire from German howitzers and Smith helped to treat the casualties on board – both the *Vivacious* and Smith were destined to re-cross the Channel exactly four years later. By 1943 the newly promoted Sergeant Smith had joined the 22nd Field Dressing Station with the 15th Scottish Division, 'changing hats for tam-o'-shanters – I was now a Jock'.

He remembered the kind of training the entire British Army had to undergo to make them fighting fit for the second front: 'We marched thirty miles a day, once a week; cross-country runs added to the tough routine; and stretcher-bearing mock casualties over difficult ground. Every man in our unit had to be Class A fit.' That the army had become highly professional was reflected by the courses Smith attended in 1943: one for senior NCOs, another to bring him up to date with the latest blood transfusion techniques; a Royal Engineers mines awareness programme; plus two weeks of medical training at Newcastle Royal Infirmary. Much of his time was taken up, he remembered, in treating soldiers' feet after the long marches. 'Some troops had blisters as big as barrage balloons; they could have walked across the Channel on them.'[68]

11

Ducks and Eagles

'There was a strange, unreal quality about those April days of waiting. I have never seen so much blossom as there seemed to be on the trees as we sped through those quiet Sussex lanes on our way to and from our Portsmouth conferences during that lovely spring.'

Lieutenant Commander Maxwell O. W. Miller, RN[1]

Phase Four training began in January 1944 with divisional assaults and exercises for brigade groups and US regimental combat teams. For the American forces assigned to Omaha, these included Exercises Duck and Fox; each was larger than the last, and progressed from blank to live ammunition. Overseen by Rear Admiral John P. Hall in the latter's headquarters ship USS *Ancon*, the first Duck exercise involved over two hundred landing craft, which deposited an assault group at Slapton Sands on the south Devon coast. This amounted to ten thousand men and a thousand vehicles from the US 1st and 29th Divisions. In support, four British destroyers bombarded the coast, underlining the combined nature of this and all future exercises.[2]

Of all the Neptune rehearsal areas, Slapton Sands features most consistently in the story of pre-Overlord training, and it is worth exploring why. It was a few miles west of the Royal Naval College at Dartmouth – itself a small harbour for many landing craft – and within easy reach of Brixham and Plymouth, where more of the invasion fleet rode at anchor. The exercise area was a seven-mile-long beach composed of coarse sand and shingle, and overlooked by cliffs. In many ways akin to the similarly long Omaha Beach, directly behind it is Slapton Ley, 'an armpit-deep salt marsh', in the words of Sergeant Bob Slaughter of the 29th Division – and through which GIs had to wade after assaulting the beach.[3] The silted, salt lake offered parallels to the flooded areas behind Utah Beach; while the rolling terrain beyond, with its small fields and sunken lanes, was not unlike corners of Normandy. The lengthy beach allowed many troops to be landed, whilst the area had the advantage of being sparsely populated – in any case, the residents of the seven nearby villages of Blackawton, Chillington, East Allington, Slapton, Stokenham, Strete and Torcross had been forcibly evicted, to enable live firing to take place. A US Assault Training School was established at Torcross, and sections of the coast strewn with exact replicas of Rommel's beach obstacles, barbed wire, sea walls, bunkers and minefields. Thus, most of the GIs due to land at Omaha or Utah were thrown again and again onto the uncompromising shingle of Slapton, as we shall see.

Mediterranean veteran Sergeant Valentine M. Miele, with the 16th Infantry of the US 1st Division, endured the misery of these early exercises. 'We'd had to retrain as an amphibious assault regiment, so started

Slapton Sands, where countless pre-invasion exercises were held for US forces. The village of Torcross in the foreground was forcibly evacuated. Duplicates of Rommel's anti-invasion obstacles were strewn along the beaches, and facsimiles of his bunkers littered the coastline. The inland lake of Slapton Ley replicated the inundated marshes behind Omaha and Utah beaches. The exhaustive rehearsals cost many lives. (Author's collection)

doing invasion manoeuvres off the coast. They would walk us out to their Higgins boats waiting off the beaches. Often they had Brits driving them, other times, US Coast Guards,' remembered Miele. 'We'd climb aboard with all our gear, with a rubber life preserver round our waists. I was always throwing my guts up in those damn square-bottomed boats. We'd pull out into the bay, circle around, and we'd invade England; then we'd go out again. Boy, it was cold; in those flat-bottomed boats the spray would come over; your field jacket would get icy; that was a rough few weeks. We used to call them "dry runs" but there was nothing dry about them.'[4]

The Post Exercise Report for Duck noted, 'craft commanders, particularly of LSTs, did not appreciate the necessity of beaching at the proper points, and coordination between army and navy was generally lacking. Security was very bad. Camouflage of assembly areas was very poor. Radio silence was consistently violated. A radio intelligence section, without previous knowledge of the situation, obtained a complete battle order of the participating units.' Duck was repeated twice more in February and early March to iron out these problems and many more, followed by Exercise Fox on 10 March.

This practice was observed by General Gerow of V Corps, and admirals Ramsay, Kirk – the Western Task Force commander – and Hall aboard USS *Ancon*, after which it was observed, 'fifteen DUKWs were brought ashore preloaded with balanced loads of ammunition for emergency issue, and this proved so satisfactory that it was incorporated in Plan *Neptune*'.[5] Indeed, Bradley later admitted, 'Had it not been for the ninety preloaded DUKWs that waded ashore on D-day, we might have been hard put for ammunition on *Omaha*.'[6] Many Rhino ferries were trialled during Fox, with 'very impressive results', whilst two Sherman DD swimming tanks were lost.[7] This time, the warship support had increased to a pair of cruisers and eight destroyers, all providing live ship-to-shore fire.

However, Fox also witnessed the 110th Field Artillery of the 29th Division being ordered to experiment by putting some of their 105mm howitzers aboard DUKWs, each with fourteen men and fifty rounds of ammunition, the whole protected by filled sandbags. The idea was not to fire while afloat, but create an amphibious self-propelled gun that could get ashore quickly to support the troops. The 110th's officers saw how the now-overloaded DUKWs quickly became unmanoeuvrable in the waters off Slapton, the problem 'further intensified by the fact that few of the DUKW coxswains knew how to handle their craft in high sea conditions and the green hands frequently got their DUKWs broadside to the wind'. Their worst fears would be realised in due course off Omaha, when most of their deployed DUKWs would founder in the tougher sea state, or be sunk by shelling.[8]

Meanwhile, acceptance of Montgomery's proposed revisions had resulted in late changes to the Overlord plan. Major General Douglas Graham's 50th Northumbrian Division, newly returned from the Mediterranean, were obliged to start training as an assault wave formation for Gold Beach – in place of the 49th West Riding Division, who, despite having no battle experience, had trained for the first wave since July. The switch was made by Montgomery on assuming command of the 21st Army Group, who preferred to use a tried and tested formation. This did not sit well with either of the divisions concerned: the 49th were furious at losing their assault role, while the 50th felt they had already done their bit. In February, Montgomery not unreasonably insisted the tank formations that had fought in North Africa also share their experience: for example, the 8th Armoured Brigade shed two of their three battle-hardened tank units – the 3rd Royal Tank Regiment and the Staffordshire Yeomanry – to beef up less combat-savvy brigades that were also destined for France.

At the same time, US forces saw the addition of Utah Beach on the Cotentin peninsula. This was in order to expand the beachhead westwards; give the Allies an opportunity to seize Cherbourg early; and also to offset the potential logistical burden on the untried Mulberry harbours. The 4th Division, then training at Fort Jackson in South Carolina, was alerted for overseas duty in December 1943 and its three infantry regiments – some of the oldest in the US Army, the 8th, 12th and 22nd – hurriedly left New York on 18 January 1944. They were spread between USS *George Washington* and the requisitioned liners *Britannic, Franconia* and *Capetown Castle*, and formed part of convoy UT 7, in which twenty out of twenty-four vessels were troopships rushing 50,500 GIs to England; they arrived in Liverpool eleven days later.[9] 'The military bearing of Major John Dowdy', records the history of the 22nd Infantry, 'was no match for the rough Atlantic. Suffering from *mal-de-mer*, Dowdy took to his bunk, making the crossing for the most part horizontally. A day or so out of Liverpool, he managed to make it to breakfast, but on encountering the head and tail of a very British kippered herring protruding from a bowl of warm milk, he turned green and left the presence of his fellow officers hurriedly', an experience presumably not only afflicting the good major. Dowdy would soon prove a much better soldier than he was a sailor.[10]

Richard M. Good was with Company 'I' of the 12th Infantry in the same rough convoy: 'I had never been on anything bigger than a rowboat. It didn't take long to discover that I got seasick. We were nine days getting to England and I was sick the whole way. Many of the guys going over worried about getting hit by German torpedoes. Me, I was so sick I was afraid they *weren't* going to hit us!'[11] Arriving only four months shy of the proposed invasion date, the 4th Division had to catch up on their assault training and were scattered in billets and camps around the divisional HQ in South Brent, Devon. It was only whilst training in Devon and Cornwall that some GIs got to know their weapons; 'that's where my mortar platoon became more expert – most of the men had never fired it', recalled one.[12]

Immediately, its commander, Major General Raymond 'Tubby' Barton, was alerted to SHAEF's concerns about Utah Beach. The Germans had flooded the ground beyond so that three of four exits were effectively causeways across a water obstacle. Being separated from the other beaches by rivers, it was feared that a German counter-attack would swiftly overwhelm the beachhead. Thus the reasoning behind the insertion of two airborne divisions behind, who were to capture and protect the causeways, and hasten the move towards Cherbourg. This part of the Overlord plan did not originate from SHAEF, but was in fact borrowed from a Sledgehammer study of 1942. Then the concept was to seal off the Cotentin, capture Cherbourg, and use the occupied territory as a springboard for further offensive operations in France. While unlikely to have worked in 1942, it succeeded spectacularly in 1944.[13]

In late March, Rear Admiral Don P. Moon and Major General 'Lightning Joe' Collins tested the Utah assault group with Exercise Muskrat, when the newly arrived 4th Division mounted their transports in the Clyde (Scotland), then sailed down to Devon for an assault landing. On board one of these ships was New Yorker Harry Cooper, who joined the 16,000-ton attack transport USS *Henrico* on her maiden voyage to Scotland in February 1944. 'For six weeks before D-day, we'd load up GIs and take them out for training at night. We'd teach them how to get into landing craft, head for shore, and return to us. At times, we carried as many as 5,500 soldiers and twenty landing craft, although our official capacity was something like 1,500.' He remembered, 'We'd get them in the landing boats which would rendezvous in a circle with a flag boat. After the red flag went up, they would head toward the beach. When they got close enough, a green flag would go up and that meant form a line and hit the shingle.'[14]

Muskrat was followed immediately by Exercise Beaver, which saw the 8th Regimental Combat Team – essentially the 8th Infantry with all its supporting arms – loaded in landing ships and deployed from Plymouth, Dartmouth and Brixham, as they would in June. Two minesweeping flotillas swept ahead of them before they hit Slapton Sands; a bombardment force of two cruisers and four destroyers provided live naval gunfire support. Beaver involved not just the 4th Infantry Division but the 1st Engineer Special Brigade that would support them on D-Day, and paratroopers from the 502nd Parachute Infantry of the 101st Airborne Division, who were to land ahead and seize the exits from Utah. The engineers cleared paths through the specially constructed obstacle belt that mimicked those spread along the Normandy coastline, and service units brought ashore 1,800 tons of supplies and ammunition. Lesser Force 'U' rehearsals included exercises Otter and Mink, with a final, all-encompassing rehearsal, Tiger, scheduled for mid-April.

Like the 4th Infantry Division, Major General Matthew Ridgway's 82nd 'All American' Airborne Division – formerly an infantry outfit commanded by Omar Bradley and whose title dated to 1917, when it was found to contain draftees from every state – was affected by the late revision to Overlord requiring an airborne drop in the Cotentin. They had already fought a distinguished war in Sicily and Salerno, and arrived in Northern Ireland on 9 December 1943. They were incomplete, being obliged to leave the 504th Parachute Infantry to assault Anzio; it would catch up with them in England in March. From Ireland the 82nd were ferried to the Midlands counties of Leicestershire and Nottinghamshire to prepare for their foray into France. With them was Ohioan Sergeant Milton E. Chadwick, who served in its 319th Glider Field Artillery Battalion, and had already landed at Salerno by sea and liberated Naples. 'Parachute soldiers carried a certain status, so at first we weren't at all pleased being in a damn glider outfit. But once in it, after a couple of campaigns we were pretty well satisfied,' Chadwick enthused.

'We were headquartered at Papillon Hall outside Market Harborough, an ancient house with a moat that dated from the 1600s, I believe. It was rumoured to be cursed – if it was, it didn't work on us!' Whilst training, his battalion studied aerial photos of their landing zones in Normandy: 'the pictures showed small fields surrounded by what appeared to be hedges, but the photos were taken at noon, when the shadows of the tall trees made them look like shrubs. That's what ripped our gliders apart, those trees, tearing them all to pieces.' More than anything else, Chadwick recalled that he 'loved my time in England. Maybe the common language helped. The people treated us as their very own, and gave us a big welcome at the railroad station upon our return from Normandy. If I could not have returned to the USA after the war, I would have chosen England as my place to live.'[15]

In March 1944, another unit of the 82nd, Colonel Roy E. Lindquist's 508th Parachute Infantry of 2,056 GIs, moved into a tent city at Wollaton Park – a 'large, fairy-tale estate guarded by stone walls and iron gates' in the centre of Nottingham. The location excited the unit, who were very much alive to the legends of Robin Hood and the Sheriff of Nottingham. Wollaton was an Elizabethan country house of the 1580s, home to fourteen generations of the Willoughby family, and would become the 508th's base and rear detachment HQ until the war's end. It was there that Jack Schlegel 'noticed the estate boasted its own royal herd of deer'. The paratrooper was born in Bremerhaven and had emigrated to the USA with his parents in 1930.

Schlegel remembered 'some of us in the Third Battalion decided deer steak would be nice, and since many of us were deer hunters in the USA, we felt His Majesty would not miss a few. Immediately a few of us went out with our M-1s and several "disappeared", but the local constabulary got word of our deed – I don't know how, perhaps one of their jobs was to count them. Anyway, a few days later, this signal came from General Ridgway's headquarters putting the entire 508th under base arrest, warning that "All deer in England were owned by the King and protected by law. Did we know it was still a hanging offence to kill the King's deer without permission?" After that, deer hunting was off limits in Nottingham – but those steaks were great, though!'[16]

Sergeant Fred Patheiger, a 'Screaming Eagle' in the 502nd Parachute Infantry, had left Germany later than Schlegel, in 1938. Removed from the Hitler Youth on the discovery that his great-grandfather had been Jewish, he had emigrated to relatives in Chicago. Refused permission to enlist in 1940 on the grounds that he was an 'enemy alien', Patheiger pestered the US authorities until they relented, and served in the 502nd's Interrogation of Prisoners of War (IPW) team. Amongst many other

GIs of recent Germanic origin, the 506th Parachute Infantry, of the 101st Airborne, contained Corporal Bobbie Jack Rommel from California, third cousin to the better known Desert Fox and defender of Normandy. Storming ashore on Omaha with the 26th Infantry of the Big Red One Division would be another distant relative, PFC Aaron L. Rommel.[17]

Another character in the 101st Airborne was one of its chaplains, Francis L. Sampson, who had completed his month-long army chaplain's course at Harvard University in January 1943 before volunteering for airborne duty. Assigned to the 501st Parachute Infantry, he later admitted, 'Frankly, I did not know when I signed up for the airborne that chaplains would be expected to jump from an airplane in flight. Had I known this beforehand, and particularly had I known the tortures of mind and body prepared at Fort Benning for those who sought the coveted parachute wings, I am positive that I should have turned a deaf ear to the plea for airborne chaplains. However, once having signed up, I was too proud to back out.'[18]

Schlegel, Patheiger, Rommel, Sampson and their colleagues of the 82nd and 101st would have been alarmed to read a slim, hardbound book, published by Messrs Faber & Faber of London in the previous year. The title would have appealed: *Paratroops: The History, Organization, and Tactical Use of Airborne Formations*. Its author was Captain Ferdinand Otto Miksche, a Czech officer attached to Free French forces in England. Something of a military theorist, the multilingual Miksche had fought in the Spanish Civil War and in France in 1940, and had already produced two volumes, *Blitzkrieg* in 1941 and, two years later, *Is Bombing Decisive?* In *Paratroops*, Miksche summarised airborne actions in the war to date, then speculated about future airborne missions. What set the hares running was Miksche's hypothetical plan for an airborne assault by three divisions onto an unspecified stretch of hostile coast. The author had no access to SHAEF planning – none of the French did – but the unidentified map that accompanied his ideas was clearly of Normandy.[19] In a stroke, Miksche had accurately predicted many of the airborne elements of the Overlord plan, and the area of Utah Beach for an accompanying seaborne assault.

There was nothing anyone could do; recalling the volume would only draw attention to it, but generals Richard Gale of the British 6th, Matthew Ridgway of the 82nd and Maxwell Taylor of the 101st Airborne Divisions had to proceed with the niggling feeling that if Miksche by theorising had stumbled on their plans by accident, then so could the Wehrmacht.

In any case, it was felt German defence attachés had probably picked up copies of *Paratroops* in neutral countries, though whether they had read or ignored the contents was open to question.[20]

Major General Richard 'Windy' Gale at the 6th Airborne Division had been briefed on his proposed tasks in mid-February. They were modest: one of his parachute brigades and an air-landed anti-tank battery were to be attached to the British 3rd Division to seize a pair of bridges over the Caen Canal and the River Orne near the towns of Bénouville and Ranville, dubbed Operation Deadstick. In retrospect this was a puzzling under-use of an elite formation, and probably driven by Leigh-Mallory's antipathy to airborne assaults. Worried about a relatively small force cut off behind enemy lines, Gale suggested his entire division be deployed, and was eventually given the go-ahead to devise ways of protecting the eastern flank of the landings, destroying the heavily fortified Merville artillery battery and cutting several bridges over the River Dives before the seaborne troops arrived.

The new, wider mission was christened Operation Tonga, and planning began the same month, which led to several exercises: in early February, the 3rd Parachute Brigade was dropped by ninety-eight RAF transports in Exercise Cooperation; during March, nearly three hundred US aircraft deployed the entire division – including gliders – on exercises Bizz One and Two around Faringdon and Lechlade, Oxfordshire, where the river networks resembled the Orne and Dives. These were not without cost: on 4 April a Stirling towing a Horsa glider hit a tree during Exercise Dreme, a tug-and-glider night navigation practice involving 140 gliders being towed out of RAF Keevil. Both aircraft crashed, with the loss of all six of the Stirling's aircrew, both Horsa pilots and the glider's twenty-four passengers – an entire platoon of the 7th King's Own Scottish Borderers. During Dreme, seventeen other gliders crashed, but this was the only mishap that proved fatal.

It was at the debriefing for Bizz on 15 April 1944 that thirty-two-year-old John Howard was alerted by his commanding officer that he and his men were to take the Bénouville and Ranville bridges by glider assault. Howard's background well illustrated the stale pre-war British Army that was inclined to ignore talent. He had enlisted in 1932 for six years as a regular into the 1st King's Shropshire Light Infantry. Refused officer training, he left as a corporal in 1938 to join the Oxford City Police. Returning to the KSLI at the outbreak of war, within five months he was regimental sergeant major of his old battalion and then accepted for officer training. By 1942 he had become a major, commanding 'D' Company of the 2nd Oxfordshire and Buckinghamshire Light Infantry. What was impossible in peacetime – Howard's elevation beyond corporal and selection for officer training – proved immediately possible in war.[21]

The battalion trained hard, Lieutenant David Wood recalling that soldiers had buckets of entrails and blood splashed on them as they tackled assault courses to 'make them more aggressive'.[22] Howard's company was deemed to have easily outperformed all the others in the 'Ox and Bucks' and within Brigadier Hugh Kindersley's 6th Airlanding Brigade, and was immediately married up with the twelve glider pilots who would waft them into battle, those of Howard's glider being Staff Sergeants Jim Wallwork and John Ainsworth.

Both belonged to the Glider Pilot Regiment. Wallwork had joined the Territorial Army in early 1939 because 'You could smell a war coming. I joined to cover myself with glory, medals and free beer for the duration, surrounded by adoring females.' He followed his father – a Somme veteran – into the Royal Artillery but experienced none of what he'd expected. Bored, he several times applied for a transfer to the RAF, but was always blocked by his CO, reluctant to lose a handy NCO. On 24 February 1942 the Army Air Corps had been formed, comprising the 1st Glider Pilot Regiment, later joined by the Parachute battalions and Special Air Service. Wallwork responded to one of the former's requests for pilot volunteers in 1942.[23]

'We had six weeks' aircrew selection at Tilshead, overseen by the RAF. Twelve weeks on Tiger Moths and Maggies [Miles Magisters] followed; to qualify as a pilot we had to have one hundred hours before going solo. Then another twelve weeks of glider training on Hotspurs towed by the Maggies – they flew so slowly I remember being overtaken by a cyclist on a road below. When I passed this course, I was awarded my wings and red beret with AAC badge and was officially a sergeant in the GPR. Six weeks conversion to the Horsa followed – it was endless flying training to get in our hours. I mostly flew behind Stirlings; the Whitley was much slower, which made the Horsa drift all over the place, like a kite on the end of a string.'[24]

The RAF oversaw his flying, while the army supervised his field training, and by 1944, Staff Sergeant Jim Wallwork was already a veteran of the July 1943 combat glider assault into Sicily – Operation Husky. Their preparation for D-Day was so thorough that by 6 June the pilots and Howard's men had notched up fifty-four training sorties with their gliders, in all weathers, day and night.[25] One of Howard's men, Raymond 'Tich' Rayner, recalled their preparations: 'first of all we were sent to Ilfracombe in Devon for three weeks of intensive field exercises, which included cliff climbing. We did street fighting in a bombed-out area, and unarmed combat. At the end we had to march back to Bulford, one hundred and thirty-one miles, carrying full packs weighing eighty pounds. This took us four days. We thought we were fit before, but by then we were at the peak of physical condition.'[26]

Fed up with life in a Young Soldiers' unit of the Royal Norfolks, Corporal Edwin Booth had volunteered for the 9th Parachute Battalion in 1943. Until he was old enough to join the army, he had worked with construction gangs building airfields for the Eighth Air Force, so was pretty fit. 'The big attraction in volunteering was the extra two shillings a day, which doubled what we were getting. We were posted to Hardwick Hall, near Chesterfield – the training was very tough, and quite a number were returned to their former units as unsuitable,' he remembered. 'We first practised exiting aircraft from dummy fuselages, about twelve feet off the ground. To qualify as a parachutist you had to do seven descents, two from a static balloon at Tatton Park, near the city of Manchester – including one at night – and five from aircraft. Then we continued with day and night practice jumps from our home base at Larkhill on Salisbury Plain.'[27]

The downside of becoming a trained jumper, however, was that 'after the ceremony of receiving the coveted wings you became a qualified parachutist, and any refusal to jump was a Court Martial offence with imprisonment. Later we started to get American Dakotas where we exited out of a door instead of a hole in the floor – it was far more comfortable to sit on seats, than sliding along on your back side and swinging your legs into a hole.' He took part in the 3rd Parachute Brigade's mass drop in February over Winterbourne Stoke: 'so many planes, there was only about fifteen feet between wingtips. We threw out two folding cycles on parachutes, but never saw them again.'

The intensive training of spring of 1944 alerted him to the fact 'that something was coming up, but we did not know when or where: we practised storming a mock gun battery at Inkpen, West Berkshire, and divided into different parties, some to clear minefields, others to blow surrounding wire, and more to storm the four gun emplacements.'[28] When Montgomery, wearing a maroon beret with a Parachute Regiment badge, addressed them on 8 March 1944 and instructed the assembled men to break ranks and gather round him, 'No one moved' – to them, he had never made a parachute jump, and had no right to wear their badge next to his general's insignia on his beret. They found him 'distant and not one of their own'.[29]

The battalion had been led very ably from April 1943 by the debonair former polar explorer Lieutenant Colonel Martin Lindsay, who had expanded a gaggle of fewer than two hundred misfits and adventurers into one of the fittest, most efficient battalions in the British Army. At the end of March 1944, he had discussed the high number of breaks and sprains – not unexpected in a parachute outfit – with a local orthopaedic surgeon, during the course of which the subject of 'jumping into France' came up. This was, perhaps, a minor indiscretion, but was seized upon by Lindsay's second in command, Terrence Otway, who disliked his superior and had been scheming to replace him.

Lindsay's slip of the tongue seems to have been the opportunity he needed, for after a discussion at 3rd Parachute Brigade HQ, the battalion war diary states simply that at 1130 hours on 1 April 1944, Major T. B. Otway assumed command of the battalion Vice Lieutenant Colonel M. A. Lindsay. Whereas Lindsay's men worshipped him, Otway was considered 'a very hard man, very stand-offish; you daren't make a mistake with the Colonel'.[30] Otway tore up Lindsay's plan for attacking the objective – the Merville battery – and substituted a more complex scheme of his own, which, as we will see, very nearly came to grief.

Mystery surrounds the whole Lindsay–Otway episode. Files were lost or burned after the war, but some of those in the know felt that Lindsay should have continued to lead his battalion, and might have gone further – as both men's respective post-war careers suggested. Otway would be wounded and evacuated from Normandy in mid-July and later awarded a DSO. Probably miscast for his role of usurper, Otway left the army in 1948 and was thereafter renowned for being forthright, if not downright obstreperous, until his dying day. The demoted Lindsay would eventually arrive in Normandy as second in command of the 1st Gordons in the 51st Highland Division, regain his lieutenant colonelcy, win a DSO, then enter Parliament, and was knighted in 1962.[31] One of the battalion's senior officers always felt that their eventual success was entirely due to Lindsay's year of hard training, not Otway's three and a half months of suffocating leadership.[32]

However, the security of Overlord was paramount: there could be no room for any verbal mishaps. Lindsay disappeared as the battalion departed on leave; they returned to find Otway in command and, as a good battalion does, simply picked up where they had left off, and continued their preparations for D-Day. These culminated on 21–26 April, when Browning's entire I Airborne Corps – the British 1st and 6th Divisions and the Polish 1st Parachute Brigade – deployed throughout Gloucestershire, Oxfordshire and Wiltshire on the exquisitely termed Exercise Mush. While the 6th had a task in Overlord, the 1st was an operational reserve, so it made sense for them all to participate.

Major Napier Crookenden, brigade major (chief of staff) of the glider-equipped 6th Airlanding Brigade, recalled with horror the moment on 17 April when 'an air photo arrived at 6th Airborne Division HQ showing a mass of white dots all over our landing zones; these were holes for the erection of anti-air-landing poles. For a moment we thought the gaff was blown, but subsequent photos showed similar holes all along the French coast. In consequence, General Gale relegated us to the second lift in the evening of D-Day, in order for the first to remove the obstacles.' They were instead rescheduled to land at 9 p.m. on D-Day in 258 Horsa and Hamilcar gliders.[33]

When war had been declared in September 1939, the National Service (Armed Forces) Act required all males aged between eighteen and forty-one to register for service, exempting the medically unfit and those in key industries. Conscientious objectors had to appear before a tribunal to explain their refusal to join up; many were given non-combatant jobs. In the run-up to D-Day, Brigadier James Hill was asked to accept conscientious objectors into his 3rd Parachute Brigade. 'I would be delighted to have them,' he responded. 'I knew these would be good men because they were ready to face danger. They were prepared to give up their lives, but not to shoot or kill anybody else. They acted as stretcher bearers, looking after Brits, Germans or anybody else.' Eventually, forty-six 'conshies' joined the 224th Parachute Field Ambulance. 'They were splendid chaps,' thought Hill.[34]

Lieutenant Russell Chandler, Jr – whom we met taking his C-47 across the Southern Atlantic via Ascension Island – and his fellow transport pilots were training hard with the airborne troops they would take to France. Flying with the 44th Squadron, 316th Troop Carrier Group of the Ninth Air Force, out of RAF Cottesmore near Nottingham, Chandler also had some night missions over France, dropping intelligence personnel and supplies to the Resistance forces. His troop carrier

The Allied airborne commanders were very experienced. Richard Gale of the British 6th (top left) had already led parachute troops in the Mediterranean. So too had Max Taylor (bottom left), former chief of staff of the 82nd, who took over the 101st when its commander suffered a stroke in February 1944. Matthew Ridgway (centre) inherited the 82nd from its previous commander, Omar Bradley, converting it to its airborne role. Jim Gavin (right) was his talented subordinate who led the 505th PIR in Sicily and was assistant divisional commander on D-Day. (Author's photograph of Gale; other images US Signal Corps)

rehearsals included flying wing tip to wing tip, in tight formations at night, for miles on end. 'We started on daytime jumps, moving on to night-time work, dropping those guys at six hundred feet. Once the shroud line was pulled, they were on the ground in seconds, with as little time as possible as a target. Our biggest fear in training was friendly fire as we had lost many aircraft that way in Sicily, but the one thing we couldn't replicate was the German flak we would receive over Normandy.'[35]

The two US airborne divisions were endlessly rehearsed, culminating on 11–14 May with Exercise Eagle, where paratroopers of the 82nd and 101st dropped by night in the Hungerford–Newbury area, followed by their glider troops the following day; they encountered stiff resistance from their 'enemy' (in reality the US 28th Infantry Division). The paratroops flew out of the eleven airfields they would use for the invasion,[36] while the 82nd's gliders took off from Ramsbury, and those of the 101st departed Aldermaston. During the exercise, one formation ran into a German bombing raid over London and dispersed to avoid the unfriendly flak.

Two other C-47s of the 316th Troop Carrier Group collided mid-air, killing all fourteen on board, including the commander of the 36th Squadron and two officers of the 505th Parachute Infantry. Chandler was flying his C-47 just behind, and remembered, 'the lead aircraft suddenly climbed up out of formation, for what reason we will never know, and collided with another plane crossing overhead. That aircraft was carrying the commander, the chaplain and other high-ranking officers. We flew directly through the flames and debris, which gave us a horrible foretaste of what the Big Day might be like.'[37] Ominously during Eagle, eight of the nine C-47s carrying men of 'H' Company, 502nd Parachute Infantry, dropped their jumpers nine miles from the intended drop zone. This anticipated what would happen a month hence in Normandy, but Eagle ensured that everyone dropping into Normandy had rehearsed with the aircraft and aircrew they would accompany in June.

Bracklesham Bay in West Sussex witnessed several British amphibious rehearsals in March, including Exercises Cropper and Goldbraid. The US Ninth Air Force, activated in October 1943 (more of which later) also prepared its ground crews, who simulated setting up dumps and airbases in a hostile country, whilst American and British artillery, anti-aircraft and tank destroyer units also held their own exercises concurrently on British ranges. In fact, everything and everyone was put through their paces: landing craft practised unloading at sea into DUKWs; hospitals tested their ability to accept tidal waves of casualties; ports rehearsed the mass embarkation and disembarkation of men and materiel; one logistics unit manhandled two thousand tons of supplies over a beach in one day to assess its methodology and efficiency.

At the beginning of April 1944, a ten-mile-deep strip along Britain's southern and eastern coastlines became a restricted zone in lock-down; visitors living outside could not enter without a pass, whilst those dwelling inside were forbidden from leaving without good reason – and travellers who arrived without a permit were escorted onto trains by the police. Much of the south-west coast, if not housing troops, became range areas, where armour and artillery shot out to sea. Stephen Dyson, a Churchill tank crewman with the 107th Royal Armoured Corps of the 34th Armoured Brigade, recorded, 'The new regulations brought home to people that the long-awaited Second Front was now imminent. Wherever one went in London the air was full of speculation about the Second Front. Everyone had their own ideas of date and venue, and some were even putting money on it in local pub or workplace sweepstakes.' Dyson recalled, 'It was Second Front fever, and everybody was caught up in it. But they all shared one belief: the Channel would run red with blood. Not very comforting for those of us who would be taking part!'[38]

In a series of measures impossible today – initially contested by Churchill, until insisted upon by Eisenhower – Britain was isolated from the outside world as much as possible: foreign travel was suspended for non-military reasons; outgoing diplomatic bags were halted on 17 April, which caused howls of outrage from those countries affected – all, excluding the British Empire, USA and Soviet Russia. Of course, this overt move came to the Germans' attention, provoking Hitler to observe this combat indicator that could be sustained for 'only six to eight weeks'. More south coast villages, such as Tyneham in Dorset, were emptied to create additional live-firing areas. Their residents each received an official letter from a faceless bureaucrat, Mr K. G. Harper at the Ministry of Home Security: 'It is regretted that, in the National Interest, it is necessary to move you from your homes; everything possible will be done to help you, both by payment of compensation, and by finding other accommodation for you if you are unable to do so yourself.'[39]

Not all farm animals could be moved as local cattle markets were saturated; beloved family pets had to be put down because there was no room for them in temporary housing. Known as the 'village that died for England', Tyneham remains part of the Royal Armoured Corps' live-firing range complex to this day. When civilians returned to the Devon settlement of Slapton – another Domesday village – after the D-Day training was over, they would find the roof of St James' Church, dating to 1318, pitted with shell holes, its medieval stained glass shattered beyond repair, and at the very minimum every single window in their homes shattered by explosions, missing roof tiles and, frequently, treasured possessions looted. Ironically, it was German and Italian POWs who cleared up the mess, whilst the Canadian and American Red Cross donated replacement crockery, pans and bed linen. The villagers of nearby Blackawton proudly insisted their tavern be renamed the Normandy Arms.

This additional layer of security was necessary because the final invasion rehearsals differed in that they used actual Overlord plans. For example, on 12 April 1944 in Exercise Trousers held at Slapton Sands, one hundred landing craft and over thirty thousand men bound for Juno Beach rehearsed their marshalling, embarkation, maritime passage, approach and assault landing in detail, with live firing by artillery, while the 3rd Canadian Division HQ practised signal communications and fire support. The Canadians had 'plenty of scope for fun with such code signals as "Trousers Down," "Trousers Up," "Trousers Wet," and "Trousers Dry" – meaning respectively, start or stop loading, postponement or cancellation of the exercise'.[40] Royal Marine Arthur Hill with the 801st LCVP Flotilla remembered of it, 'The exercise was to give the Canadians a preview of what they might expect later. The weather was atrocious; we had duffle coats, oilskins, sea boots and our grog rations, but those poor Canucks in their normal khaki kit, cold, wet, and most of them seasick, we did the best we could for them, but it was never enough.'[41]

Lieutenant Peter Hinton aboard *LCI-262* recalled recognising Montgomery himself watching the landings. 'To our delight, Monty detached himself and strode down the beach and I thought he was going to give us some inspiring message, but all he did was stop, unbutton his fly and solemnly urinate.' Hinton was left thinking this 'might have been editorial comment on our performance'.[42] Poor weather cancelled the later phases of Trousers, including the air support, but the exercise was hailed a success by Ramsay, Montgomery and Dempsey, who watched the proceedings keenly. 'Exercise went well', noted Ramsay, 'but fire of self-propelled artillery was bad, with ninety percent of shells falling in sea. Spent morning on the beaches discussing technique and very pleasant it was as a change from the office.'[43] Also observing was the popular novelist Nevil Shute, and a portrait of the rehearsal appears as a backdrop to his 1955 work about the build-up to D-Day, *Requiem for a Wren*.[44]

Separate from the sequence of landing rehearsals were the four Smash exercises held in April to test the concept of swimming tanks wading ashore. Extensively waterproofed, with all-round canvas skirts to keep the water out and propellers at the rear, they were 'thirty tons of steel in a canvas bucket', as one tanker put it. These armoured vehicles were designed to be launched two to three miles offshore and swim under their own power to the shallows, preceding the first-wave assault on each of the five landing beaches. With their ability to manoeuvre on water and land they were known as Duplex Drive tanks (DDs), and dated back to June 1941 when successful trials were held in Brent Reservoir and Portsmouth harbour.

Specialised armour used in all five beach landings included the top secret Sherman Duplex Drive (DD) tank. Once its eleven-foot-high canvas screen had been raised by rubberised columns full of compressed air, it swam ashore powered by twin propellers. Though successfully tested at Orford on the Suffolk coast, and deployed by British, Canadian and US tank battalions, large numbers sank in the rough conditions encountered on 6 June and DDs were rarely used again. (NARA)

Although armour battalions had trained and experimented with them – at this stage on British-made Valentine tanks in East Anglia, Wales and Scotland – the limits of their seaworthiness were not known. Different units would participate with their swimming tanks on each Smash exercise. However, it was understood from experiments that DD tanks with their canvas screens were so heavy that an LCT running at full power struggled to tow them. Their attraction was that they presented a small target in the water, with the 'psychological shock of transforming from what appeared to be a row-boat at sea into a tank on the beach'.[45]

Crewing such tanks was nerve-wracking in the extreme. Laurie Burn operated one belonging to the 13th/18th Hussars, whom we have already met exercising in Scotland. 'My brother Pete and I were members of the same Sherman tank crew: Pete was the co-driver and I was the gunner. I had nicknamed our tank *Icanhopit*, and by the end of the war we were in *Icanhopit Four*.' To test their underwater escape drill they were issued with special breathing apparatus, and Burn 'underwent weeks of practice at the submarine station in Gosport, sitting in an improvised tank turret in a twenty-foot-deep concrete bath and having two thousand gallons of water poured in, which was a strain on the nervous system to say the least!'[46] Even in action, few wanted to be inside their tank if a mishap at sea occurred, as Lance Corporal Patrick Hennessey, also of the 13th/18th, remembered: 'the crew were all on deck apart from Harry Bone who was crouched in the driving compartment intent on keeping the engine running'.[47]

On 4 April, from Fort Henry, a ninety-foot-long concrete observation post on Redend Point at Studland, Dorset, the King, Churchill, Eisenhower, Monty, Ramsay, Leigh-Mallory and Major General Hobart of the British 79th Armoured Division (of whom more shortly) watched the live-firing exercise Smash One. It culminated with the 50th Division's troops emerging from landing craft, accompanied by tanks of the 8th Armoured Brigade swimming ashore. Ramsay recorded meeting the VIPs and it being 'a lovely morning for craft, but cloud prevented air coop-eration. Large assembly of admirals, generals, etc. The exercise proceeded according to plan, but DD tanks were twenty minutes late, arriving at beach after the LCTs with AVREs, and the LCAs. It was not possible to see them launched, which was sad, but they lost direction and were wrongly piloted on their way in. This may well happen in action,' Ramsay warned.[48] Yet, unknown to the admiral and his fellow VIPs, of the thirty-two Valentine DDs launched by the 4th/7th Royal Dragoon Guards that morning, six sank when the sea state suddenly worsened and a seventh was abandoned, later sinking.

Ramsay continued, 'The fire support was good, though a large proportion of the shells fell into the sea to start with. After it was over, the general impression was that fire support must be increased.' Out on the waves, one of the DD tank commanders, Lieutenant Robert Ford, recalled the moment: 'We were on the surface of the water after coming off the landing craft and increasingly apprehensive. The water was coming in very fast and although we had small pumps, they were just not effective,' said Ford. 'We were still floating with all four of us standing on top of the tank; then a great wave crashed over the top and we sank to the bottom. I was in an air pocket, formed when the canvas screen fell over and trapped us. I had air to breathe and with my lifejacket I managed to rise to the surface; it seemed a long way up. Unfortunately my colleagues did not make it.'[49]

In April 2004, a small memorial to the six 4th/7th Dragoon Guards who perished in Smash One was unveiled alongside Fort Henry.[50] Accompanying the Studland Bay exercises with the 8th Armoured Brigade were the 147th (Essex Yeomanry) Regiment, Royal Horse Artillery, equipped with self-propelled 25-pounder guns. Lieutenant Peter Mitchell, gun position officer of 'A' Troop, 413th Battery, recalled leaving Poole harbour 'in line ahead – a fleet of long, low craft, bristling with guns, in a colour mixture of battleship grey, and army black and brown camouflage – a purposeful, menacing air about them all'. Each exercise entailed sailing towards the Needles, turning and mounting an exact replica of their invasion assault. 'Under our barrage, the 1st Dorsets of 231 Brigade were going to land on Studland Beach, but for the purpose of the exercise our guns did not actually land, but turned for home.'[51]

His fellow officer Lieutenant Tony Gregson, who had been a prisoner of the Germans in the Italian campaign and escaped after several efforts, witnessed another tragedy: 'One of the Sapper (Royal Engineers) LCTs struck a sandbank one hundred yards off the beach and the first of their tanks trundled off into deeper water and just disappeared in a welter of oily foam.' This was despite being 'issued with "Kits, Waterproofing", one per vehicle, consisting of boards, tubes, sticky tape and a new sealing compound called Bostick. With these we built up our vehicles and proofed them against seawater so they could wade ashore through water several feet deep.'[52]

As a direct result the army took responsibility for deciding when to launch the swimming armour, the navy traditionally having primacy until the high-water mark. This would have ramifications on the assault day itself – when all the units concerned were re-equipped with Sherman tanks. On the British and Canadian beaches the DD tanks of the 13th/18th Hussars, 1st Canadian Hussars, Fort Garry Horse, 4th/7th Dragoon Guards and Sherwood Rangers Yeomanry would be taken much closer inshore, but on Omaha this change in doctrine was not instigated – with fatal results for the crews, as we shall see.

Corporal Harvey 'Willie' Williamson commanded one of the Fort Garry Horse's Sherman DDs and remembered 'they were one of the best-kept secrets of the war. We were stationed on the south coast at Calshot, near Portsmouth, but could only practise under cover of darkness. We used to swim the tanks to the Isle of Wight one night, hide them in the grounds of the Royal Palace of Osborne House, then swim them back the next night.'[53] Three US independent tank battalions – the 741st and 743rd bound for Omaha and the 70th for Utah – had also been transferred to the UK in November 1943 to prepare for the invasion and learn the mysteries of swimming tanks. An American tank school – Camp MacDevon – was set up under the guidance of the British 79th Division, at Torcross near Slapton Sands, and began training their crews in great secrecy on 15 March. In the event, each US battalion would only deploy two companies of swimming tanks, the rest landing 'dry-shod'; it conducted over five hundred DD tank launches from shore and over 1,200 from LCTs at sea, losing three tanks with three crewmen drowned on exercises.[54]

Training Allied units equipped with swimming tanks was just one responsibility of the British 79th Armoured Division. Although the formation HQ never deployed in combat, it oversaw the training of regiments that did. Its origins lay in the 1st Assault Brigade, Royal Engineers, which had been raised in December 1942 following the Dieppe raid, later expanded into a division. Churchill's attention was drawn to the enthusiastic Percy Hobart, a pre-war armour expert since retired and languishing as a lance corporal in the Home Guard. Supported also by Brooke, Hobart was plucked out of obscurity and promoted first to train the 11th, and subsequently to command the 79th Armoured Divisions.[55] This act reveals as much about Winston Churchill's ever-inventive mind as it does about Bernard Montgomery's conventionality, for Hobart was the latter's brother-in-law – but there is no record of Monty ever attempting to help his relative or utilise his undoubted skills. Before being forced into retirement in 1940, Hobart had commanded the Mobile Force in Egypt, forerunner of the 'Desert Rats' 7th Armoured Division, and thus was perfectly suited to his new role.

An innovative genius and counter-intuitive, but inclined to be obsessive and cranky (qualities which had led to him being side-lined and retired), Hobart was aware of his reputation as a 'bull in a china shop'. Thus the insignia of his new division – the black face of a charging bull with flared nostrils and red-tipped horns – reflected both his temperament and his expectations that with energy, focus and zeal, any problems connected with Allied armour entrusted to his care would be overcome. Hobart endorsed his prime minister's view that 'it is only by devising new weapons and above all by scientific leadership that we shall best cope with the enemy's superior strength'.

Taking command of the 79th in April 1944, Hobart analysed the armoured lessons learned at Dieppe and in the Mediterranean and studied the *Atlantikwall*, overseeing the design of armoured vehicles meant to overcome the specific challenges presented by modern war. He ordered that 'suggestions from all ranks for improvements in equipment are to be encouraged. All ranks are to have direct access to their CO for putting forward their ideas' – considered a dangerous innovation in the intensely hierarchical British Army of 1944.[56] Known as the 'Funnies' and crewed by Armoured Corps and Royal Engineers, Hobart's creations were adaptions of standard Sherman or Churchill tanks which hurled explosives, spat flame, crossed rivers and trenches, lumbered over sea walls, or crawled through barbed wire and soft terrain. Apart from signature swimming Shermans, it was the AVREs (Armoured Vehicles Royal Engineers) – Churchill tanks equipped with a powerful *Petard* 'bunker-busting' 290mm-calibre main gun – that were the most numerous.[57]

The AVREs were robust enough to also carry a variety of obstacle-crossing devices on their superstructure, including a temporary steel bridge, or bundle of logs, known as a fascine, to span narrow gaps; it was one of these that Tony Gregson saw vanish into Studland Bay. In early 1944 Captain Tony Younger – then with the 26th Squadron of 5 Assault Regiment, and equipped with Churchill AVREs – was ordered to carry out a practice landing just below Osborne House on the Isle of Wight. 'The novelty of this occasion was that we were ordered to fire our Petards against the sea wall, to see if we could knock it down and drive over the rubble towards an imaginary enemy,' remembered Younger. 'The exercise went well; we landed at the correct place but the Petard was inaccurate, obliging us to fire more rounds than expected, though by the end we had renewed confidence in the weapon. Several years later when I was serving in Burma, I received a huge bill, addressed to me personally, for repairs to the sea wall at Osborne; some civil servant must have spent months in tracking me down.'[58]

The 79th also developed armour-plated earth movers; Shermans equipped with a revolving drum of chains which pulverised the ground ahead, thus exploding anti-tank mines (these were called flails or Crabs); and Churchill tanks mounting a flamethrower (known as Crocodiles). Other specialised armour carried various kinds of bridges, whilst the Bobbin unrolled canvas matting from a giant drum to enable passage

Other specialised armour included mine-clearing Sherman tanks, mounting a revolving drum of chain-link flails (the Crab, top left); a hydraulic dozer blade to shift obstacles (top right); and a British Churchill tank with a 290mm-calibre bunker-buster mortar known as the AVRE (Armoured Vehicle Royal Engineers). The Churchill could also carry a variety of assault bridges, a drum of flexible roadway or a fascine (a bundle of logs to fill an anti-tank ditch). The British Centaur tank (bottom right) carried a 95mm gun, was manned by Royal Marines and used at Gold, Juno and Sword. (Upper pictures, US Army Signal Corps; lower images, Author's photographs)

over soft ground. The 79th were able to design a wide range of equipment in a short space of time because they utilised international off-the-shelf technology; its armoured bulldozers were based on the pre-war earth movers designed by Caterpillar, an American company; the DD had been largely devised by the Hungarian inventor Nicholas Straussler in 1941; and a predecessor of the Sherman flail (the Matilda Scorpion), designed by a South African, had driven through German minefields at El Alamein with considerable success in 1942.

Most land forces in the world today still utilise modern equivalents of Hobart's 'Funnies' – surely a tribute to his visionary genius. The spirit of armoured innovation had already spread beyond the 79th Division in 1944 with the employment of the Sherman BARV – a Beach Armoured Recovery Vehicle (its title tells all), and Sherman tanks fitted with hydraulic dozer blades, with which all armoured units were equipped.

The traditional D-Day narrative is that Eisenhower and Bradley observed displays of Hobart's inventions on 27 January and 11 February 1944, but Bradley declined all for his US forces – save the DD tanks. This is incorrect. In fact, Bradley *approved* the use of the 79th's vehicles for Normandy in a letter of 16 February to the British War Office, requesting the support of British-manned AVREs in addition to ordering twenty-five Sherman flails and one hundred Churchill Crocodile flame-throwers for the use of his GIs. The War Office agreed and responded, 'In the event of the US Army being equipped with similar equipment ['Funnies'] from its own sources … the equipment will be returned to the British.'[59]

Bradley's initial ideas for V Corps at Omaha suggested 'they [DD tanks] go in first, followed by engineers, then Churchill tanks with their [British] engineers, and then our infantry comes in at H+25'.[60] The truth is that US forces used both armoured bulldozers and 105 dozer-bladed Shermans, but there was simply no time – despite every intention – to supply more specialised armour to the Americans, and train their crews, before the invasion.[61] Of Hobart's units that made up the 1st Assault Brigade, the British assault on Sword would be supported by 5 Assault Regiment; the British and Canadians at Gold and Juno were accompanied by 6 Assault Regiment; it was the third element of the brigade, 42 Assault Regiment, who were earmarked to support the Americans at Omaha and Utah – in the event, they would arrive later, as a reserve formation.

Although its invention predated Hobart and his 79th Division, of all the Funnies it is the swimming Shermans that have received a disproportionate amount of attention. Praised by writers and historians as a tribute to Allied innovation and considered a tactical success, the truth is that this tank was a waste of valuable lives, time and resources. Hopelessly over-engineered, they fell woefully short of fulfilling their promise. Let's look at the evidence. Of 240 employed on D-Day, only ninety swimming Shermans were launched into the waves as planned, mainly due to the sea state. Of these, sixty-six sank during the run in to the five beaches; at Utah nine would be lost at sea, twenty-seven at Omaha, thirteen on Gold, eight at Juno and nine at Sword. Due to the extreme sea conditions on D-Day, the remaining 150 were landed on or near the beaches – where conventional tanks with standard waterproofing could have operated – or were stranded on landing craft unable to offload them. Thus only twenty-four out of 240, exactly ten per cent, functioned as planned; at Omaha it was just two out of sixty-four, swimming several miles successfully and reaching the shoreline to give support – and many of these were knocked out immediately.

The United States already had their own solution to the problem the Sherman DD was meant to address – that of intimate armoured support to infantry landing on a beach. In the Pacific, the US Marine Corps had developed the LVT (Landing Vehicle, Tracked), originally used for logistic support at Guadalcanal in 1942 and in combat at Tarawa in November 1943. The LVT was an armoured, tracked amphibious assault vehicle with a loading ramp – often called an Amtrac – and tank-like versions were available which incorporated a revolving gun turret. When later deployed to Europe, the British called them 'Buffalos' or 'Alligators', but for 6 June 1944 none were made available due to inter-service rivalries between the Marine Corps and US Army, although over ten thousand were produced.

When, during April 1944, Major General Charles H. Corlett arrived in England to take over XIX Corps, he came with more experience of amphibious operations than any other US Army officer. His extensive Pacific service was unrivalled – as recently as February 1944 his men had captured Kwajalein, the world's largest atoll defended by five thousand Japanese troops determined to die for their emperor. George C. Marshall acknowledged this as 'the most perfect of all US amphibious operations due to Corlett's flawless execution of a well-thought-out plan, and miniscule casualties'.

Having an interest in Omaha – his corps would land there on 10 June – Corlett looked over the assault plans and questioned why vulnerable wooden landing craft were being used instead of LVTs. The response from the Mediterranean 'amphibious experts' was far from enthusiastic: Corlett wrote later that he was 'squelched for his trouble and made to feel the Pacific was a bush league campaign'.[62] Thus there were no cross-theatre comparisons of doctrine or tactics, which would have revealed immediately the utility of LVTs and pointlessness of Sherman DDs. After the war, LVTs continued in USMC service and a descendant vehicle is used in combat to this day, whereas – apart from Rhine crossings of March 1945 – no Sherman DD tanks, or equivalent successor, were ever used again.

One of the lessons from Operation Jubilee of August 1942 was the need to accurately survey landing beaches in advance. The fist-sized shingle on the main beach at Dieppe proved to be of exactly the right size and consistency to clog the suspension and break the tracks of nearly every Churchill tank landed; consequently none of the Calgary Regiment's armour even made it off the beach. As a result, Combined Operations HQ in London directed that detailed beach reconnaissances, including the taking of rock and sand samples, should be undertaken by members of the Special Boat Service (SBS) prior to the invasion of North Africa. These led directly to the formation of Combined Operations Pilotage Parties (COPPs) in September 1942, whose value was more than justified on Operations Torch and Husky. By June 1944, they numbered 174 men, divided into ten COPPs, averaging a dozen personnel each, all volunteers from the Royal Navy, commandos, SBS and Royal Engineers.

Cloaked in secrecy, armed, and kitted out with special wetsuits, they deployed from small, collapsible two-man canoes called folboats, crept ashore in the night hours, assessed enemy defences, took depth soundings and retrieved sand and soil samples. A mission on 18 January 1944 found Captain Logan Scott-Bowden of the Royal Engineers and Sergeant Bruce Ogden-Smith of the SBS surveying the future Omaha Beach by X-Craft, a British-designed miniature submarine. The Americans wanted to be sure the beach was capable of taking substantial quantities of wheeled transport. On first looking through his periscope, Scott-Bowden had found himself staring into the face of a pipe-smoking Wehrmacht soldier on the stern of a French trawler. Later, having swum ashore, he and Ogden-Smith had to freeze, face down, as suspicious sentries aimed powerful torches in their direction. They returned after three exhausting nights on the chilling Calvados sands and four days on the seabed, whereupon Scott-Bowden was whisked up to an address in central London: 'This turned out to be COSSAC headquarters in Norfolk House and the very senior American general to whom I had to report, I later realised, was Omar Bradley.'

Bradley referenced Scott-Bowden's activities in his own 1951 memoirs, relating how at Norfolk House the Briton had waved a test-tube of sand, whilst explaining 'the night before last we visited Omaha beach to drill this core in the shingle, which is firmly bedded upon rock. There is little danger of your trucks bogging down.' With barely concealed admiration, Bradley noted that Scott-Bowden had 'taken a submarine through the minefields off the coast of France. There he paddled ashore one evening in a rubber boat directly under the muzzles of the Germans' big, casemated guns.'[63] Later, when Bradley privately asked him about the prospects for a successful assault on that stretch of shore, Scott-Bowden felt bound to answer, 'Sir, I hope you don't mind my saying it, but it is a very formidable proposition indeed. There are bound to be tremendous casualties.' The commander of the US First Army, knowing this was the best, longest, most usable beach along the whole Calvados coast, shook his head mournfully and put his hand on Scott-Bowden's shoulder, 'I know, my boy, I know.'[64]

12

Bigots and Tigers

'The Second Front, the thing one wants and fears so terribly, that's at the back of one's thoughts all the time, like a tidal wave coming in from the horizon blotting out everything.'

Naomi Mitchison, 14 May 1944[1]

O N 1 APRIL 1944, Admiral Bertram Ramsay established his head-quarters outside Portsmouth in the RN's former School of Navigation. This was Southwick House, a colonnaded Georgian mansion dating to 1800, and home to the Thistlethwaite family, proud owners of two local villages and the surrounding 8,000 acres since 1539.[2] Colonel Evelyn Thistlethwaite had innocently offered accommodation at Southwick to a few Royal Naval officers bombed out of Portsmouth in 1940; alas for him, this soon led to the mansion being requisitioned and renamed HMS *Dryad*. Hunting for his future needs, Ramsay had stayed there on 23 January 1944, confiding to his diary, 'This place most suit-able from the point of view of accommodation and proximity to Combined HQ in Fort Southwick', whereupon he earmarked the house with its several large reception rooms – ideal for the needs of a staff – as his planning headquarters.[3]

Fort Southwick, a mile south of the Thistlethwaite mansion, was a series of bombproof underground tunnels under Southwick Hill containing a plotting room, cypher office, teleprinters, wireless office, telephone exchange and staff rooms. The all-female staff even designed their own coat of arms, with WRNS and WAAF ratings supporting a shield depicting six sailing ships, surmounted by a WRNS officer's hat and underscored by the motto 'This Blessed Plot'. It acted as the head-quarters of the Commander-in-Chief, Portsmouth and overlooked the harbour. Wren Kay Martin remembered the run-up to D-Day, 'which is printed deep in my memory after all these years. All around the area, inland, the troops were camped in woods and anywhere where there was space for them. Each in turn was moved on towards the embarkation area, and another took its place, like a game of draughts.'[4]

In the drawing room of Southwick House a large plywood map of Southern England, the Channel and Normandy, specially made by the Chad Valley Toy Company, was installed, taking up one entire wall. It remains there to this day. From it any visitor could instantly assess the progress of cross-Channel naval operations. Temporary military buildings sprawled throughout the once-leafy parkland, and Southwick village was 'locked down' – the Golden Lion pub became the officers' mess, where a plaque today reminds the visitor that Eisenhower was known to quaff a pint of beer, while Montgomery kept to his grapefruit juice.[5]

Admiral Sir Bertram Ramsay (1883–1945) moved his headquarters into Southwick House on 1 April 1944. The ancestral home of the ancient Thistlethwaite family, it was located twenty minutes' drive outside the naval base of Portsmouth. Loaned to the Admiralty in 1941, the grounds were filled with Nissen huts housing staff, while Montgomery commandeered Broomfield House in Southwick village. In nearby woods, Eisenhower established SHAEF's forward headquarters, code-named Sharpener. (Author's collection)

The last draft of the Overlord plan was formally distributed on 10 March, addressed personally to Ramsay, Montgomery and Leigh-Mallory. It began, 'The object of Operation Overlord is to secure a lodgement area on the Continent from which further offensive operations can be developed. The lodgement area must contain sufficient port facilities to maintain a force of some twenty-six to thirty divisions, and enable that force to be augmented by follow-up shipments from the United States, and elsewhere, of additional divisions and supporting units, at the rate of three to five divisions per month.' It identified 'Y-Day', the date by which all preparations would be complete, as 31 May 1944. The simple, outline document amounted to five pages of directives and eight of appendices – the countdown had begun.[6]

From this, the component commanders developed their own detailed orders, of which Ramsay's Operation Neptune was the most important, as it identified how the lodgement would be made and supported. At this stage, the maritime planning had been conducted in the minutest detail at Norfolk House in London. Once complete, the Neptune Operation Order was issued on 10 April – although an initial version had been in circulation since 12 February. From the Neptune plan, detailed orders for the Eastern and Western Task Forces had to be final-ised, the latter being issued after two revisions, on 21 April 1944. Ramsay's orders for Neptune were four inches thick and ran to 1,100 pages.

The earliest drafts of Leigh-Mallory's Allied Expeditionary Air Forces (AEAF) directive had been circulating since 6 December 1943. Of the land component plans, the US First Army had already distributed 324 numbered copies of their initial plan on 25 February, Bradley noting that 'it had more words than *Gone with the Wind*'.[7] The two hundred numbered Administrative Orders for Overlord issued on 10 April, of nineteen pages followed by ten maps, twenty annexes, and twenty-two appendices, included instructions for the issue of 'one briefing tent per thousand men with blackboard, seats and lighting; one accommodation tent per ten men in marshalling areas; US cots for all troops with three blankets per man; gratuitous PX supplies; ten motion sickness tablets per individual; three prophylactics; one lifebelt; and two bags, vomit'.[8]

Official US Army historian Forrest Pogue, on being shown the US V Corps orders, was amazed at the detail, which included 'the amounts of cocoa, wheat, meat and vegetables to be distributed in French towns where food shortages were acute'. There were estimates of 'uniforms, bandages, Purple Hearts, and even Bronze Stars' for quartermasters; he was equally staggered by the 'lists of prostitutes who might be able to supply information concerning the Germans'.[9] Each formation extracted the relevant details and issued their own set of orders. Those of the 175th Infantry, part of the US 29th Division of V Corps, 'were thicker than the biggest telephone book you've ever seen'. After briefing his men, the 175th's commander, Colonel Paul Good, 'stood up and tried to tear it in half, but it was so thick that this strong man couldn't do it. So he simply threw it over his shoulder and said, "Forget this goddamned thing. You get your ass on the beach. I'll be there waiting for you and I'll tell you what to do."'[10]

Security concerns abounded, so these and all other plans were stamped 'BIGOT' in large red letters, a classification beyond 'Top Secret'. The code name was *not* (as some historians have claimed) a cover name or precursor to Overlord, rather the process of being admitted to its secrets. To qualify for access to these plans, officers had to be 'Bigoted' – vetted – which qualified them as 'Bigots'. The term dated from the Torch plans of 1942, when the cover story for convoys bound for North Africa was that they were sailing 'To Gib[raltar]'. 'Bigot' was simply 'To Gib' reversed. Omar Bradley recorded that 'our commands were carefully seeded with CIC [Counter Intelligence Corps] agents who rifled desks nightly and rattled safes in search of security violations.'[11]

The classification was taken so seriously that – according to Commander George M. Elsey, one of Roosevelt's naval advisors assigned to the head-quarters ship USS *Ancon* for D-Day – when King George VI visited the ship on 25 May 1944, and asked what was beyond a curtained-off compartment, a junior officer answered, 'Very secret information, sir,' and remained motionless before the curtains. 'His Majesty took the hint and moved on. An angry Captain demanded why he had been so rude to the King. He received the entirely correct answer, "Sir, nobody told me he was a Bigot."'[12]

With the planning over, Ramsay and his staff moved to Southwick; Wren Ginger Thomas, who had worked at COSSAC with Lieutenant General Morgan, joined them. 'Southwick House was set in a vast area of parkland in those days. We slept in Nissen huts in the grounds, but worked in the main house. We were more or less sealed off and never left the premises. I had a wonderful time working for Admiral Ramsay, because morale amongst the staff was excellent. Wrens, officers and ratings mixed remarkably well. We even had mixed hockey and cricket teams. I wasn't a very good shot with the ball, and during one game I

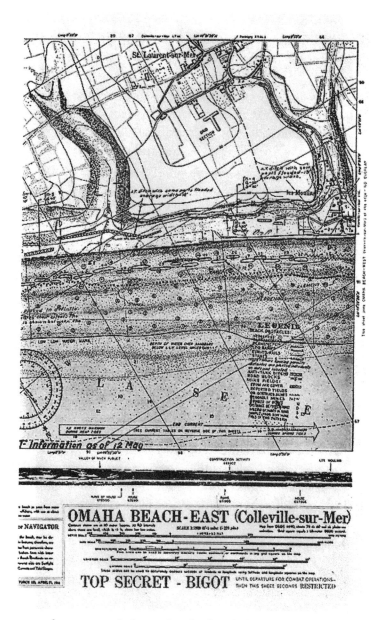

All top secret documents relating to Overlord, including every map, were stamped 'BIGOT'. An abbreviation usually said to stand for 'British Invasion of German Occupied Territory', it in fact originated from deception measures employed for the 1942 Torch landings. On that occasion, documents were stamped 'TOGIB' (To Gibraltar, the cover story for the flow of forces). BIGOT was simply TOGIB reversed – reflecting the move of forces away from the Mediterranean to the Channel. (Author's collection)

threw the ball and broke an officer's nose! There was blood everywhere, and I thought I would be court-martialled, but nothing happened.'[13]

This was the Whitsun bank holiday, which turned out to be the hottest day of the year at 94°F in the sun – a far cry from the following week. Sport was an excellent way of easing the tension, and the sixty-one-year-old Ramsay himself recorded of the match: 'played cricket for our Mess vs. Wrens and beat them by four wickets. Scored 67 vs. 70 for five. Made sixteen [runs]. Very stiff; very hot playing and *very* hot evening.'[14] Wren Jean Irvine noted, 'Once I arrived at Southwick House, I was sealed in until after D-Day. We worked eighty hours a week for more than four months with secret documents. On the night before the invasion, I was up all night but on 6 June I fell asleep at my desk, such was the release of tension.'[15] Despite his time-consuming responsibilities, Ramsay never forgot he was a leader as well as a commander, and the next day he 'took the occasion to address the Wrens of the secretariat, amounting to about sixty, and thank them for their hard work. Only a few days to go now [until D-Day], and everyone is thankful for that.'[16]

Montgomery took over Broomfield House, a stuccoed late Georgian house on the edge of Southwick, and joining him, Eisenhower formally established his advance headquarters on 2 June in woods nearby. He occupied a series of camouflaged office trucks and trailers linked by cinder paths code-named 'Sharpener'. The Supreme Commander copied Montgomery's sensible notion of having a fully mobile headquarters. The latter had acquired in the course of his campaigns a travelling circus of three pantechnicons, comprising sleeping quarters, a map trailer and an office truck. Eisenhower's equivalents were three sixty-foot, air-conditioned caravans, custom-built by Lockheed and designed by a company which built mobile homes for Hollywood stars.[17]

Montgomery, true to form, did not live indoors, but – attended by twenty officers and two hundred other ranks – camped gypsy-style in the grounds of Broomfield House. With his three caravans, a dining marquee, and other tents and trailers, this formed the 21st Army Group's first TAC (tactical) Headquarters.[18] In his office vehicle, he had hung a large portrait of Rommel, 'to try and decide what sort of person he was, and how he was likely to react to any moves I might make against him'. However, this was more Montgomery nonsense, because his moves against Rommel were influenced by Ultra from Bletchley Park – which he could not reveal in his lifetime – not from looking into Rommel's eyes. Montgomery also used a train, called *Rapier*, to visit troops around the country. Eisenhower had one too, known as *Bayonet*, inherited from Bernard Paget. Not to be outdone, Churchill – who was somewhat inevitably wont to drop in on them – used the King's royal train, housed in a cutting outside nearby Droxford station.

The naval assault had mushroomed on the expansion of the COSSAC plan to 6 battleships, 2 monitors, 23 cruisers, 3 major headquarters ships, 101 destroyers, 17 frigates, 21 corvettes, 6 sloops and 97 minesweepers – a total of 1,213 warships of all sizes from eight navies, plus 864 merchant ships, 4,126 landing craft of all descriptions and 736 ancillary craft such as tugs, tenders, barges and lighters, making a grand total of 6,939 vessels. As Sicily and Salerno had shown how valuable naval gunfire support to the land component could be, Bradley was keen to enlist as many US warships in the bombardment force as possible.

He wrote later in *A Soldier's Story* that, 'because an American destroyer [with five-inch guns, as opposed to the RN's four-inch weapons] packed almost the fire-power of a British cruiser [sporting six-inch cannon], while the American cruiser [with eight-inchers] outgunned her British rival, I was anxious that our allotment in naval support be tallied in US ships. Although the preponderance of US naval strength had been concentrated in the Pacific, the fleet was enlarged from twelve destroyers to twenty-six, with another six destroyer escorts.'[19]

This was in addition to three USN battleships, the fourteen-inch-gunned *Texas* and *Nevada; Arkansas*, armed with twelve inchers; three eight-inch cruisers, *Augusta, Quincy* and *Tuscaloosa*; two headquarters ships, *Ancon* and *Bayfield*; and nine minesweepers. In addition to ninety-seven destroyers, frigates, corvettes and sloops, the Royal Navy contributed the battleships *Nelson, Warspite* and *Ramillies*, with *Rodney* in reserve (all armed with fifteen- or sixteen-inch guns); two monitors with fifteen-inch guns, *Roberts* and *Erebus*; and seventeen cruisers. Shells from these battleships and monitors could reach between fifteen and twenty miles inland. To help manage this fleet of Nelsonian equivalence, Ramsay asked his close friend the dashing former destroyer commander Admiral Sir Philip Vian to be his deputy.[20] They divided their responsibilities into a Western Task Force responsible for the two American beaches, under Rear Admiral Alan G. Kirk, and an Eastern Task Force for the three Anglo-Canadian landing areas under Vian.

These were further subdivided into the groupings of land and maritime forces heading for each beach; Forces 'U', based in Plymouth, and

'O', located in Portland, would head for Utah and Omaha. Forces 'G' (in Southampton), 'J' (on the Isle of Wight) and 'S' (headquartered in Portsmouth) were bound for Gold, Juno and Sword. To aid recognition, just before D-Day all vessels in Force 'S' would have their funnels and hulls painted with a green stripe; craft going to Juno Beach with Force 'J' were to be similarly painted red, while those headed to Gold would boast a blue stripe. These individual forces were commanded by a rear admiral or commodore, and each was far larger than the size of today's Royal Navy.

Commanding Force 'S' was Rear Admiral Arthur 'Noisy' Talbot aboard HMS *Largs*. Under him, in charge of the naval assault group landing the first wave, the 8th Infantry Brigade, on Sword was Captain Eric Bush, who could be forgiven for thinking he'd seen it all before. As a midshipman aboard HMS *Bacchante*, he had served at Gallipoli in 1915. Some 255 wooden-hulled minesweepers, including many converted trawlers and launches, would clear channels to the five beaches; bombardment fleets of battleships, cruisers and destroyer squadrons were to provide ship-to-shore fire support – all with reserves on hand.

With Force 'G' was the 606th Landing Craft, Mechanised (LCM) Flotilla, consisting of sixteen small craft, and based at the 'stone frigate' of HMS *Cricket* – the Landing Craft Crew Training Base on the River Hamble. Sub Lieutenant Peter Miles, RNVR, recalled that 'each LCM had a crew of six, a coxswain who stood aft with a stoker/driver in an armoured wheelhouse, and four deckhands; every third craft carried a boat officer, which was me. I was nineteen; it was a big responsibility, my flight of three craft and eighteen men. Ours were Mark IIIs, made in America, larger and more powerful than British LCMs. We were powered by two marine diesels and were the smallest craft to cross the Channel on our own. We carried either sixty soldiers, a lorry or a Sherman tank. However, our LCMs were old and knackered, having served in Sicily and all had engine problems – the repair teams swarmed over them for weeks and it was touch and go whether they'd be ready for D-Day.'[21]

Bertram Ramsay's deft organising hand was vital, for his vast fleet would depart 171 different anchorages around the United Kingdom, each with their own tidal restrictions, but had to come together as a seamless whole at precise times off the Normandy coast. Over four hundred component parts for the two Mulberry harbours had to be towed by tugs over the waves at three or four knots towards Normandy

– each of the Phoenix concrete caissons required a separate tug – a distance of just over ninety nautical miles, together with the fifty-nine Corncob merchantmen and warships who would be making their last journey before being sunk in place off each beach to provide the 'Gooseberry' artificial breakwaters. All these convoys would need shepherding and protecting from mines, submarines, E-boats, the Luftwaffe and the weather.

Thereafter the process had to be repeated and sustained as follow-on troops and supplies succeeded the assault wave, for endless weeks. There could be no delays, so every vessel had to be preloaded with its precise complement of troops, vehicles and war materiel, to be landed in the sequence desired by the land commanders. Surge capacity for the 'unknowns', such as replacing sunk vessels, lost Mulberry components, and the supply of extra ammunition, fuel or medical supplies, had to be catered for, as well as returning casualties and prisoners of war to England. Ramsay instituted a useful checkpoint, code-named 'Area Z', but colloquially known as 'Piccadilly Circus', twenty miles south-east of the Isle of Wight, through which all ocean-going traffic had to pass.

Though a wonderful plan that worked superbly well, with hindsight we can say that Overlord and Neptune suffered from a lack of clear doctrine, and were an unhappy fusion of British and US traditions of amphibious warfare. No framework had been developed for amphibious operations in the interwar period by any of the Allies, or the Germans for that matter. Many interwar theorists assumed that the Gallipoli landings of 1915 represented the future of amphibious warfare, and its failure was 'fought all over again in printer's ink and at Staff Colleges in Britain, the US and Australia; daylight assaults against a defended shore were considered a folly. Money was tight and what there was had to be spent on more obviously urgent experiments than amphibious operations.'[22] Typically, a pushy US lieutenant colonel named George S. Patton argued the opposite in his 1936 study of Gallipoli, and other professional officers might have embraced the positive aspects of the Zeebrugge raid of 23 April 1918. Nonetheless, showing any interest in such matters was considered a kiss of death to a military career in the 1930s.[23]

Operations Chariot at Saint-Nazaire, on 28 March 1942, and Jubilee at Dieppe on 19 August of the same year, both represented the British tradition of using amphibious operations for limited raids, nothing more, where inter-service cooperation was limited and temporary. The US Marine Corps, by contrast, evolved a different doctrine from its experience in the Pacific. In that theatre, the USMC owned its own air, naval and ground assets, removing inter-service rivalry as a factor. The Marines believed that firepower was more important than surprise and their island-hopping experiences in the Pacific confirmed this: massive pre-invasion naval and aerial bombardments lasting days could destroy over fifty per cent of enemy fixed defences before the troops arrived in daylight.

At Tarawa in November 1943 the pre-invasion bombardment lasted three hours; at Iwo Jima – February 1945 – it was three days; and at Okinawa in April 1945, it lasted seven days. On 6 June 1944 Utah and Omaha were to receive just thirty minutes each, from a smaller naval fleet, whilst most aerial bombs missed altogether. In contrast, British planners determined that tactical surprise was absolutely essential for a successful amphibious assault, which usually meant a night-time or pre-dawn operation and sacrificing the naval gunfire and aerial bombing support that would destroy or suppress enemy positions. Such timings and tactics had been adopted for Dieppe (Operation Jubilee), North Africa (Torch), Sicily (Husky), Salerno (Avalanche) and Anzio (Shingle).

The original COSSAC plan had called for a silent assault, a night landing against what was then the relatively lightly defended Calvados coast. From the New Year, Rommel had begun to thicken his strongpoints and obstacle belts, with the result that both Ramsay and Montgomery favoured altering their plan to one of obliterating the defences by satu-ration air and sea bombardment. Ramsay's diary for 10 February 1944 reflects the debate: 'After dinner sat with Monty in his room and discussed the technique of the beach assault. He liked my ideas, which differ from the silent assault now in vogue and decided then and there to issue directions to the armies. This is not what I wanted at all, as they must be allowed to give *their* views on what *they* want.'[24]

On the other hand, Brigadier General Norman 'Dutch' Cota, an Overlord planner and destined to land on Omaha Beach with the 29th Division on D-Day, was a leading advocate of the night-time or pre-dawn assault; his view was that 'tactical surprise is one of the most powerful factors in determining success. I therefore favor the night landing. I do not believe the daylight assault can succeed.'[25] He was supported by the V Corps commander, Leonard T. Gerow, and Admiral Hall, in charge of Force 'O'. They lost the argument, largely to Montgomery's bulldozing through his own views. The eventual Neptune plan was a compromise, combining a daylight assault (the Pacific doctrine) with minimal fire support (the British solution). Captain Hank Hangsterfer, due to land on Omaha Beach with the 16th Infantry, certainly found it 'very disturbing to finally learn the landing was to take place in daylight. The landings in Africa and Sicily were at night. I recall how naked I felt in Sicily when a searchlight picked up our landing craft.'[26]

Early in 1944 it was assessed that Douglas Graham's 50th Northumbrian Division, destined for Gold Beach, which had the task of linking up with the Canadians on Juno in the east and Bradley's US forces at Omaha to the west – a twenty-mile gap – had too little combat power. For the assault phase he was loaned the 56th Infantry Independent Brigade, bringing the collective strength of Force 'G', which also included the 50th Division; 8th Armoured Brigade; 47 Royal Marine Commando; an American battalion of 105mm self-propelled guns; three British artillery regiments; two anti-tank batteries; and Nos. 9 and 10 Beach Groups, to an impressive 38,000 men. Whilst at sea it came under the command of Commodore Cyril Douglas-Pennant, who shared his flagship, HMS *Bulolo*, with the 50th Division's commander.[27]

Brigadier Sir Alexander 'Sammy' Stanier of the 231st Brigade, an assault formation of the 50th Division, outlined the planning sequence as far as he was concerned:

> In January 1944, I went to London for intensive planning. I was given a flat, just by Westminster Cathedral, and the divisional commander, General Graham, described his plan and told me to make my brigade plan ... The next thing was a big corps conference at Cambridge. We met in the Cambridge Union building and each commander described his plan in turn, starting with Lieutenant General Bucknall of XXX Corps, then the divisional commanders and finally brigade commanders. Artillery and sapper officers were also present, but I, as a brigadier, was about the most junior officer there. I had an opportunity to meet the commanders flanking me; Brigadier Knox had 69th Brigade on our left. On our right was the American 16th Regimental Combat Team, under Colonel George Taylor. I then had to write my orders for my battalion COs.[28]

The other four Forces, 'U', 'O', 'J' and 'S', were not dissimilar in size or structure, and for each there was a dedicated headquarters vessel. Force 'G', which included twenty assorted flotillas of landing craft, had been late in assembling and forming, partly because its 50th Division were still trickling back from the Mediterranean. It had initially concentrated in Weymouth, but in April was obliged to shift east, to the inlets of the

Solent and Southampton Water. Their place in Weymouth and Portland was taken by Force 'O', which eventually comprised 865 vessels of all sizes, who themselves had been obliged to make way for the men bound for Utah. The latter, as we have seen, were included in Overlord far later than everybody else. At this stage, Huebner's 1st Infantry Division, with the supporting elements of Gerhardt's 29th Division, amounted to 34,142 men, billeted throughout Dorset, with 3,306 vehicles; their fleet under Rear Admiral John L. Hall, Jr comprised two dozen LSTs and thirty-seven LCIs besides 170 LCTs.

April 1944 would see the Utah assault force – over thirty thousand GIs, including the 4th Infantry Division and other supporting arms – hold their last preparatory exercise, called Tiger, at Slapton Sands. This was marred by tragedy and a degree of lasting controversy. Like the Tarbat peninsula in Scotland, the Slapton coastal area of eight villages, 180 farms and 750 families – a total of three thousand civilians – had been cleared in November–December 1943. The Royal Sands Hotel was declared off-limits and slowly shelled to bits over a succeeding series of exercises, which began in January with Duck and Fox, and concluded with Tiger, which lasted nine days, with six given over to mounting and embarkation. Tiger began on the morning of 27 April and included a live naval bombardment to acclimatise the troops. At the last minute, H-hour was delayed for sixty minutes, but some landing craft did not receive word of the change. Arriving at their original scheduled time, they were then hit by live 'friendly' fire, allegedly suffering a never-specified number of 'casualties' – rumours circulated at the time that these amounted to hundreds.

But these were unsubstantiated rumours. Admiral Bertram Ramsay's diary is an important primary source in this respect, because his private journal was never revised for publication, Ramsay being killed in an air crash on 2 February 1945. Thus he never joined the post-war 'Battle of the Memoirs' – of which Montgomery's was probably the most brazen attempt to rewrite history. Ramsay's unexpurgated – and therefore more reliable – testimony was published by an academic imprint only in 1994.

In it, he noted of the Tiger rehearsal:

A perfect morning for a landing. Spent about four hours waiting for the assault, which was timed for 0730 hours, and didn't take place until 0830. Moon [Don P. Moon, commanding Force 'U'] put it off at about

0600 hours, but the signal only partially got round, with the result that while ships carried out their bombardment & two companies landed, nothing else happened. It was a flop & putting it off was a fatal error. We spent the day on the beaches watching the troops & MT [motor transport] coming ashore. There was much to criticise but the main thing was the lack of senior naval or army officers on the beach to take charge & to supervise.[29]

There is no mention here of any casualties, which, one assumes, he would have seen, being physically present on the beach, and might have featured in a private diary. However, what happened next was beyond dispute. The following morning, in the early hours of 28 April, with the bulk of the infantry already ashore, a convoy of eight LSTs made their way through Lyme Bay towards Slapton, bringing in the next wave of supporting engineers, quartermaster staff, signallers, medics and their vehicles.

Lieutenant Eugene E. Eckstam was medical officer aboard *LST-507*, one of the eight LSTs assigned to Tiger. He had crossed the Atlantic in March 1944, and the following month they loaded DUKW amphibious trucks and jeeps, all fully fuelled and chained to the deck, and GIs, in preparation for Tiger. His and two other LSTs sailed from Brixham on the afternoon of 27 April to join five LSTs coming from Plymouth. Without warning, early on the 28th they were attacked by a flotilla of nine Kriegsmarine E-boats which had been alerted by heavy radio traffic in Lyme Bay. Theirs was a hit-and-run mission, which stumbled across the three-mile-long procession, launching torpedoes at what they assumed was an ordinary coastal convoy escorted by destroyers, before hightailing it away. Many Allied soldiers initially thought the attack was part of the exercise.

Eckstam remembered:

General Quarters rudely aroused us about 0130 hours. I remember hearing gunfire and saying they had better watch where they were shooting or someone would get hurt. I was stupidly trying to go topside to see what was going on and suddenly *Boom!* There was a horrendous noise accompanied by the sound of crunching metal and dust everywhere. The lights went out and I was thrust violently in the air to land on the steel deck on my knees, which became very sore immediately. Now I knew how getting torpedoed felt.[30]

Eckstam's LST was one of three hit by torpedoes; it lost all power and was dead in the water. He opened a hatch to descend to the deck where the DUKWs were: 'I found myself looking into a raging inferno which pushed me back. It was impossible to enter. The screams and cries of those army troops in there still haunt me.' The fire forced those still able to abandon ship at 0230 hours, when he 'watched the most spectacular fireworks ever. Gas cans and ammunition exploding and the enormous fire blazing only a few yards away are sights forever etched in my memory.'[31]

Another LST disobeyed orders and returned to rescue survivors, saving 134 lives, including Eckstam. Ten US officers with knowledge of the wider invasion plans (Bigots all) were reported missing, potentially compromising the whole of Neptune; a vast search of Lyme Bay was undertaken and, incredibly, all ten bodies were recovered. Signalman Jack 'Buster' Brown aboard the fleet minesweeper HMS *Kellett* remembered the 'dozens of corpses covered in fuel oil floating in the sea, and our ship's boats being lowered to recover them. We had about seventy brought aboard, but only one was still alive and he died shortly afterwards.'[32]

Often overlooked was the – albeit belated – Allied response which saw two British Motor Gun Boats (*MGB-77* and *MGB-81*) engage the E-boats. The Germans escaped, but *MGB-81* sustained damage, though not enough to prevent her from being at the forefront of the invasion fleet on 6 June. Unaware of the E-boat incursion, David Kenyon Webster and 'E' Company of the 506th Parachute Infantry, with the 101st Airborne Division, had been trucked to the area from Torquay, then marched through the morning mists to guard a bridge overlooking Slapton Sands in simulation of the airborne drop they would make for real behind Utah Beach. He recalled, 'We could see a vast fleet of amphibious craft moving solely in to land. I've never seen so many ships together at one time; an invasion fleet is the most impressive sight in the world.'[33]

With at least 749 Americans killed and missing, the tragedy was kept a closely guarded secret. Medical staff of the 228th Station Hospital at Sherborne Castle were suddenly warned by their CO, 'In less than an hour we will receive hundreds of emergency cases of shock due to immersion, compounded by explosion wounds,' remembered Captain Ralph C. Greene. 'You will ask no questions and take no histories. There will be no discussion. Follow standard procedures. Anyone who talks about these casualties, regardless of their severity, will be subject to court martial. No one will be allowed to leave our perimeter until further orders.'

Within minutes the hospital was ringed by a cordon of Counter Intelligence Corps GIs and soon 'a stream of ambulances and trucks were pouring through the gate, filled with wet, shivering, blue-skinned, blanketed and bandaged young Army and Navy men, many in great pain', recalled Greene.[34] The security blanket around the incident was extensive: nineteen-year-old Daniel Folsom was at Slapton Sands with the 111th Naval Construction Battalion ('Seabees') as a coxswain on a Rhino barge. He had arrived in England on RMS *Mauretania* and was training to offload LSTs. He recollected that 'they put the lid on us the night after some German E-boats had gotten into the flotilla. They put a clamp on us – so nobody could tell anybody about it.'[35] Pete Nevill, an RAF Beaufighter pilot who happened to be flying in the vicinity, later reported that his logbook was confiscated and destroyed, while the crew of the destroyer HMS *Onslow*, who retrieved many of the dead, were instructed 'never to speak of this event again'.[36]

The impact could have been much worse, for also at sea that morning in a pitching LCI were Generals Omar Bradley and Lewis H. Brereton, observing the second day of landings. The latter commanded the US Ninth Air Force, which would support the former's First Army in Normandy, and to the chagrin of both, Brereton's air support for the exercise failed to materialise due to the low cloud – an ill omen if ever there was one.[37]

Much later, conflicting casualty totals from the US Army and Navy led some to speculate that the alleged friendly fire losses from the beach attack were massaged into the LST losses, giving a truer total of 946 killed and missing. The Americans were furious about the whole incident and held the British to blame for inadequately guarding the LST convoy. Kirk wanted to send the battleship USS *Nevada* to destroy the E-boat 'nest of vipers' in their reinforced concrete pens at Cherbourg – an idea which Ramsay went to great lengths to stymie on the grounds that it might alert the Kriegsmarine as to the significance of their actions.

Whatever the final tally of casualties, Eisenhower immediately instituted a cover-up for perfectly valid security reasons. News of the German ambush would have been inevitably associated with invasion rehearsals, and knowledge of the tragedy would hardly increase morale among the assault forces. It would be obvious, too, that anyone exercising off the south Devon coast was likely to be invading the not-dissimilar enemy shore opposite, in this case Normandy, rather than the Pas-de-Calais. Less commendable were the efforts of successive US administrations to keep quiet about the drama for decades, initially denying any losses in the area, despite beachcombers finding evidence of the Tiger assault and local fishermen snagging their nets on large seabed objects.

A granite obelisk was presented by the United States in 1954, paying tribute to the locals who 'generously left their homes and their lands to provide a battle practice area for the successful assault in Normandy in June 1944; their action resulted in the saving of many hundreds of lives and contributed in no small measure to the success of the operation'. Yet it was only after the passing of the US Freedom of Information Act in 1974 – and the persistence of a local man, Ken Small, in uncovering the true events – that a Sherman tank lost on an earlier 1944 exercise was salvaged from the bay, and inaugurated in 1984 as a memorial to the killed and missing.[38] All is now out in the open, and though much nonsense is still claimed about secret mass graves of GIs along the Devon coast in the run-up to each D-Day anniversary, it is just that – humbug.

However, with two LSTs sunk and a third severely damaged six weeks before Overlord, Ramsay warned that he had just lost his strategic reserve of major landing ships: any more losses would compromise the invasion. Additionally, in Ramsay's warship and requisitioned merchant flotillas, there was no spare margin of craft to cope with issues of serviceability, engine overhaul or accidents – never mind losses inflicted by the enemy – and it is to the credit of the combined fleet that the Royal Navy reported 97.6 per cent operational capability, only eclipsed by the astounding 99.3 per cent reported by the US Navy, on the eve of D-Day.[39]

If there was a positive side to Exercise Tiger, the lessons learned – better warship escorts, all units on the same wireless frequencies, improved designs of life jackets and overall stricter adherence to time-tables – meant that for J. Lawton Collins and his VII Corps, Utah losses on 6 June would be minimal. As for Eugene Eckstam, assigned to another LST: 'D-Day was a piece of cake'.[40]

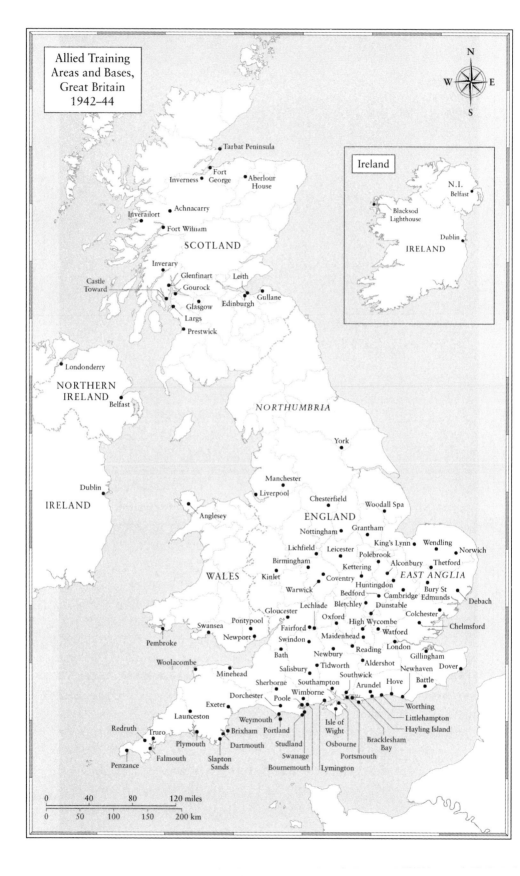

Allied Training
Areas and Bases,
Great Britain
1942–44

N
W E
S

Ireland

N.I.
Belfast

Blacksod
Lighthouse

Dublin

IRELAND

Tarbat Peninsula

Fort
Inverness George
Aberlour
House

Achnacarry

Inverailort

Fort William

SCOTLAND

Inverary

Glenfinart Leith

Castle Gourock
Toward Gullane
Glasgow Edinburgh
Largs
Prestwick

Londonderry

NORTHERN
IRELAND
Belfast

NORTHUMBRIA

York

Dublin

Manchester
Liverpool Chesterfield
Woodall Spa

IRELAND

ENGLAND

Anglesey

Nottingham Grantham

King's Lynn Wendling
Lichfield Leicester Norwich
Polebrook
Birmingham Kettering Alconbury Thetford
WALES Kinlet Coventry EAST ANGLIA
Huntingdon
Warwick Bedford Bury St
Cambridge Edmunds
Gloucester Lechlade Bletchley Dunstable Debach
Pontypool Oxford Colchester
Swansea Fairford High Wycombe Chelmsford
Newport Watford
Pembroke Swindon Maidenhead
London
Bath Reading
Newbury Gillingham
Woolacombe Salisbury Tidworth Aldershot Dover
Minehead Newhaven
Sherborne Southampton Southwick Battle
Dorchester Wimborne Arundel Hove
Exeter Poole Worthing
Launceston Weymouth Littlehampton
Redruth Portland Isle of Hayling Island
Truro Brixham Wight Bracklesham
Plymouth Dartmouth Studland Osbourne Bay
Falmouth Swanage Portsmouth
Penzance Slapton Bournemouth Lymington
Sands

0   40   80   120 miles
0   50   100   150   200 km

13

Thunderclaps and Fabius

'I do not think you could have chosen any man more capable than General Eisenhower of keeping his very large heterogeneous force together through bad times as well as good, and of creating the conditions of harmony and energy which were the indispensable elements of victory.'

Winston Churchill, speech to the Joint Houses of Congress,
19 May 1943[1]

THE OVERLORD PLAN was finalised in two major briefings on 7–8 April and 15 May 1944 at Montgomery's headquarters, St Paul's School in west London, coincidentally where he had once been a pupil. At the first – both were code-named 'Thunderclap' – the British general in the presence of Eisenhower set forth the detailed plan for the ground assault against the beaches. As Eisenhower recalled: 'an entire day was spent in presentation, examination and co-ordination of detail'. According to Bradley, 'A relief map of Normandy the width of a city street had been spread on the floor of a large room in Saint Paul's School. With rare skill, Monty traced his 21st Army Group plan of maneuver as he tramped about like a giant through Lilliputian France.'[2]

It was a long session, with Monty introducing the day and speaking for ninety minutes; Ramsay's and Leigh-Mallory's presentations concluded the morning. Sergeant John Green was part of the detail responsible for the plan's safety, with his comrades of the 50th Field Security Section attached to GHQ. He remembered the map 'laid out on the floor of the lecture room for the high-ups. Two of us slept there every night and one of us was always on duty at the door. It was a very big model. The shores of Normandy all laid out with the phase lines, D+1, D+2, and so on, that Monty expected to reach. It was rather frightening knowledge to have.'[3]

Later, Green's task was to mix with the thousands of waiting troops and listen for any loose talk. Monty liked his phase lines, but the Americans were furious that they had been included, as they felt a failure to adhere to what, at best, were guidelines to the forthcoming fighting might be used as evidence in the future, were there to be political squabbling about the conduct of the campaign (how prophetic).

However, his putting a D+90 phase line next to Paris was felt to be unnecessarily optimistic. Monty's stated view, however, was that 'it was not of any importance where he would be ground-wise between D+1 and D+90, because he felt sure he could capture the line D+90 by the end of three months'. Besides, he saw his task as *not* to capture ground – he was out to destroy German forces. His ideas were not appreciated by French and Allied politicians, who thought of the campaign in terms of winning back territory.[4]

The afternoon saw Bradley, Gerow and Collins, the V and VII Corps commanders, present the American forecast of their battle, followed by the Second Army's Dempsey with Lieutenant Generals John Crocker and Gerard Bucknall (of British I and XXX Corps). Sir Alan Brooke, the CIGS, noted: 'A long day with Monty! I paraded at Saint Paul's School to attend a wonderful day which Monty ran to run over all the plans for the coming offensive. Bucknall was very weak, and I am certain quite unfit to command a Corps. The PM turned up and addressed a few remarks to the meeting. He was in a very weepy condition, looking old and lacking a great deal of his usual vitality.'[5] General Sir John Kennedy, Director of Military Operations at the War Office, observed, 'when the conference started in the morning, Montgomery has asked us not to smoke. Later on he announced that he had had a message from Winston to say that he would join us after tea. Monty [an obsessive non-smoker] added that, as the Prime Minister would undoubtedly arrive with a large cigar, smoking would be allowed after tea. He made the announcement in such a puckish way that there was a great roar of laughter.'[6]

The accounts of Brooke and Kennedy leave it in no doubt that it was Montgomery who was in charge of the 'Thunderclap' Conference, not his American counterparts. Perhaps he sensed that command would soon slip from British hands. Ramsay recorded, 'First day of Ex. *Thunderclap* at Saint Paul's. Monty gave 1½ hours of the army plan layout. I gave one hour of the naval problems which affect the army & L.M. gave an hour of the air plan. I was congratulated by many people on my talk which I think was good & it certainly it went much better than I anticipated.'[7]

Bradley's recall of the eventual strategy is important because the conduct of the Normandy invasion would provoke huge debate, with allegations that the British were slow and had been 'fixed' by the Germans at Caen, when they intended to break out. The American general continued:

> The American forces would then pivot on the British position like a windlass in the direction of Paris. Third Army would then advance into Brittany to clean up that peninsula. In the meantime we were to complete our turning movement until the Allied line faced east toward the Seine on a 140-mile north–south front. Its left flank would be anchored on the British beaches, its open right flank on the Loire. From there we would advance to the Seine, where it was anticipated the enemy would hold behind that river bank.
>
> During our battle for Normandy the British and Canadian armies were to decoy the enemy reserves and draw them to their front on the extreme eastern edge of the Allied beachhead. Thus while Monty taunted the enemy at Caen, we were to make our break on the long roundabout road toward Paris … [W]hen reckoned in terms of national pride, this British decoy mission became a sacrificial one, for while we tramped around the outside flank, the British were to sit in place and pin down Germans. Yet strategically it fitted into a logical division of labors, for it was toward Caen that the enemy reserves would race once the alarm was sounded … As Monty discussed this plan for Caen, he became increasingly optimistic. Pointing towards Falaise, he talked on breaking his tanks free on D-Day 'to knock a bit down there'. Falaise lay thirty-two miles inland by road from the beach; it was to take Monty sixty-eight days to get there.[8]

Much of Montgomery's plan for I Corps, including his old 3rd Infantry Division, was based on the premise of not only capturing Caen, eight miles inland, on D-Day itself, but reaching to the billiard-table-flat, open landscape further south, near Falaise – suitable both for his tanks and temporary airstrips. He and Bradley agreed that all the panzer units, even those heading towards the American beaches, would likely pass through the great road and rail centre of Caen to counter-attack the invasion – thus capturing it at the earliest opportunity made sense. However, having handed the task to Crocker's I Corps, Monty then did little to ensure they had enough resources to achieve the task.

Initially the 3rd Division were to land on a two-brigade front (as at Juno, Gold and Omaha), but due to shipping resources this was trimmed back to a couple of infantry battalions from the 8th Brigade with a battalion of tanks (the 13th/18th Hussars) assaulting at H-Hour. They were to be followed by successive waves, each of a brigade plus armour, at roughly two-hour intervals. The deployment of the 6th Airborne Division to the north-east of Caen was meant to offset some of the 3rd Division's tasks. Nevertheless, the Sword Beach assault had been fatally compromised. An official Russian military delegation visiting the area during a British-hosted staff ride in 1994 noted that according to their doctrine, 'the 6 June attack at Sword and advance to the city of Caen required at least a two-division corps landing during the day to be sure of success – nothing less would do the job. They couldn't understand Montgomery's "incorrect" allocation of insufficient forces.'[9]

Indeed. This lack of combat power arriving early meant that the 3rd Division, whose three brigades trickled into Normandy sequentially, thus failing to achieve a basic principle of war – concentration of force, or mass – had no hope of taking Caen on D-Day, as Bradley observed. Writing in 1951, the American's observation seemed pretty level-headed and objective criticism, but Montgomery took great offence, which eventually bubbled to the surface in his retaliatory *Memoirs* of 1958.

There is no doubt that Monty was bullish and over-optimistic on 7 April (in retrospect absurdly so), but with good reason. The Anzio landings had recently taken place on 22 January, which saw John P. Lucas's Anglo-US VI Corps capture the small Italian port; but instead of striking out, Lucas had lingered at the beachhead to consolidate his position, allowing the Germans to rush in substantial reserves by road and rail and surround his forces. The Allied troops would stay bottled up until 23 May, incurring casualties of forty-three thousand killed and wounded. Lucas was roundly criticised for his inaction and sacked on 22 February. Thus, Monty's plan to reach out from the invasion beaches towards Caen and Falaise immediately was also a demonstration to Brooke and Churchill that there would be no second Anzio in Normandy.

Certainly Anzio, Salerno and Sicily – all of which had seen violent German reactions nearly pushing the invaders back into the sea – played on the minds of those connected with Overlord, never mind the debacle of Dieppe. This was an unquestionably anxious time, with Alliance tensions beginning to affect even the mild-mannered Ramsay, who despite noting that the second day's conference at St Paul's of 8 April 'went off quite well & was of value', then recorded: 'The US were tiresome, demanding flotillas of minesweepers which they know I cannot provide. It is a curse that we should have undertaken to provide all naval forces for *Overlord* and given the US a blank cheque to demand what they want from us.'

In the event, the naval split was roughly twenty per cent USN (with forty-nine major warships) to eighty per cent Royal Navy and other Allied nations (258 major vessels).[10] Emphasising the wide-ranging nature of the Western Alliance that comprised Neptune, this included contributions from the free navies of France (nine vessels), Poland (three), Norway (three destroyers), Greece (two corvettes) and the Netherlands (two sloops).[11]

The final conference at St Paul's on Monday 15 May was a far different affair. Exactly 146 formal gilt-edged invitations and passes were issued. Attendees included the King, Prime Minister, the War Cabinet and scores of Allied generals. Eisenhower began with engaging humility: 'Here we are on the eve of a great battle, to deliver to you the various plans made by the different force commanders. I would emphasise but one thing – that I consider it to be the duty of anyone who sees a flaw in the plan not to hesitate to say so.' The conference was barely under way when there was a furious hammering at the door that would not cease. Eventually the doors were opened and George Patton strode in, unabashed, 'fashionably late' – in all probability, deliberately so.[12]

Eisenhower recalled in *Crusade in Europe*:

During the whole war I attended no other conference so packed with rank as this one. This meeting gave us an opportunity to hear a word from both the King and the Prime Minister. The latter made one of his typical fighting speeches, in the course of which he used an expression that struck many of us, particularly the Americans, with peculiar force. He said 'Gentlemen, I am hardening toward this enterprise', meaning to us that, though he had long doubted its feasibility and had previously advocated its further postponement in favor of operations elsewhere, he had finally, at this late date, come to believe with the rest of us that this was the true course of action in order to achieve the victory.[13]

Churchill's undisputed 'hardening' quote was published in Eisenhower's book in 1948, when the former Prime Minister was out of office, and illustrated the depth of American scepticism of the British commitment to invading Normandy. It was in part the beginning of the 'Churchill against Overlord' American narrative, though the Prime Minister was to blame for lighting the fuse in the first place. It mattered enough to Churchill that he tried – unconvincingly – three years later to qualify his 'hardening' comment in Volume 5 of his *The Second World War*.

Eisenhower was writing partly in response to the first post-war tide of sensationalist books – one by his own personal aide, Commander Harry C. Butcher, which magnified some of the Anglo-US disagreements.[14] However, as we can see, if Churchill might have been lukewarm towards the cross-Channel enterprise, then Montgomery was positively bubbling with excitement for Overlord. In fact, Churchill had used the 'hardening' term in speeches, conversation and memos elsewhere, as an antonym of his true meaning. He often used understatement as a linguistic device, when meaning the opposite; but its use here caused the Americans – and subsequent historians – great confusion.

At the second Saint Paul's Conference, wartime austerity abounded, General Sir John Kennedy remembering, 'It was very cold. Winston and [Field Marshal] Smuts came in overcoats, and kept them on for luncheon. I got hold of a blanket and shared it with an admiral and an air marshal; we were glad to have it on our knees.' The King's biographer noted that the hall was a big panelled room:

> The King and Mr. Churchill accorded the privilege of armchairs, but the rest of the company sat on school forms facing a large map of the invasion area which hung above a low dais. After a brief introduction by General Eisenhower, each commander demonstrated his own particular role and task in the invasion. When the last had concluded his statement on this portentous blue-print of the shape of things to come, the King rose and, to the surprise of all, stepped on to the platform. He had not been expected to speak and he did so without notes.[15]

King George VI was by nature rather shy and not a natural public speaker – a situation aggravated by a pronounced stammer, which had been tentatively cured by an Australian speech therapist, of which many in his audience were aware – the 2010 movie *The King's Speech* depicted this very well. Consequently it took personal courage on his part to mount the dais and make his short speech, which Kennedy observed 'was perfect for the occasion, and created an excellent impression on the Americans, as well as on us. I met Alan Lascelles [the King's private secretary] at dinner and he told me he had no idea the King would speak until he got onto the platform.'[16]

Although the Allied armies had grown in expertise and confidence, their lacklustre performance at Anzio that January had provoked unease among the most senior generals and politicians about the forthcoming Normandy operation. This was such a vast undertaking that it could not be allowed to fail. Overlord utilised the best of commanders, their staff and equipment. Any setback which resulted in the landings being rebuffed would prolong the war, give the Germans new hope and disillusion the Russians. The futures of Eisenhower, Churchill and Roosevelt and their retinues were on the line. The two 'Thunderclap' Conferences were probably Montgomery's finest moments. He more than any other Allied commander was associated with battlefield victories over the Germans. His stage management and egotistical self-belief – no matter how much historians would pick over his words in the future – brought much needed confidence; every memoir suggests this. They were performances, rather than briefings. After 'Thunderclap', the leading commanders went into battle convinced they would win – which had not been the case beforehand.

However, removing some of the positive gloss, General Hastings 'Pug' Ismay, Churchill's chief military assistant during the war, noted of this conference,

The administrative arrangements were explained in considerable detail by Humfrey Gale, 21st Army Group's Chief Administrative Officer. In his desire to give an idea of the magnitude of the undertaking, he revealed that the number of vehicles to be landed within the first twenty days was not far off two hundred thousand. The Prime Minister winced. He had been much amused, but shocked, by the tale – probably apocryphal – that in the *Torch* operation, twenty dental chairs had been landed with the first landing craft flight. The first instruction he gave me as we drove away from Saint Paul's was to write to Montgomery and tell him that the Prime Minister was concerned about the large number of non-combatants and non-fighting vehicles which were to be shipped across the Channel in the early stages of *Overlord*.[17]

Churchill – embarrassingly ignorant, as we have seen, of modern military logistics – certainly had an obsession about the administrative tail of the 21st Army Group and was prepared to push the point sufficiently to want to quiz Monty's staff over what equipment was absolutely necessary. Alanbrooke noted on 17 May that his PM 'was very disturbed at statements connected with the thousand clerks of the third echelon and the fact that the invasion catered for one lorry for every five men. It took me ¾ hour to pacify him.'[18] Not enough, for on 19 May, the Prime Minister visited his general's temporary headquarters at Broomfield House in Southwick village.

Montgomery took the 'long screwdriver' of Churchill's interference personally and led the Prime Minister into his study, and behind closed doors the two strong personalities came head to head. No one else was present but it was clearly a spirited debate. Monty – according to his not-quite-reliable *Memoirs* – bade the Prime Minister sit, then said: 'I understand, Sir, that you want to discuss with my staff the proportion of soldiers to vehicles landing on the beaches in the first flights. I cannot allow you to do so. My staff advise me and I give the final decision; they then do what I tell them. I consider what we have done is right; that will be proved on D-Day. If you think it is wrong, that can only mean you have lost confidence in me.'[19]

Monty's alleged response was clever, for he knew he could not be replaced at such short notice. It was a charged atmosphere and both parties clearly became very emotional. Again, Churchill devoted some paragraphs in Volume 5 of his *The Second World War* (1951) to refuting allegations of an emotional encounter, but admitted, 'I do not remember the actual course of the conversation. All of our proceedings were of a most friendly character' – which hardly rings true, and goes a long way to illustrating how the premier was selective with the history he reproduced for his readership.

In later life, Churchill apparently threatened to sue Monty's first biographer, Alan Moorhead, if he revealed that 'he had broken down and wept', and the wartime diary of his CIGS, Sir Alan Brooke, is highly illustrative of how mercurial and ill-tempered Churchill was at times. Eventually the doors opened and Churchill was introduced to Monty's waiting staff officers, and said 'with a twinkle in his eye', 'I wasn't allowed to have any discussion with you gentlemen.'[20]

Exercise Tiger had been the final preparation for Force 'U'. The last major practices for the other four Normandy task forces were the Fabius exercises of May 1944. These witnessed the assault-wave forces bound for Omaha, Gold, Juno and Sword – each of more than thirty thousand personnel – mount dress rehearsals of everything learned, amounting to the largest ever simultaneous amphibious exercise.[21] Troops were herded into marshalling areas from 27 April, embarking on their landing craft between 29 April and 1 May. The 'invasion' was originally scheduled for 2 May, but was postponed by poor weather for twenty-four hours – fortuitously, just as the real D-Day would be. Thus, on 3–4 May 1944, Exercise Fabius I put the Omaha assault troops (Force 'O') through their paces at Slapton Sands. As Sergeant Bob Slaughter observed, 'some of the men remarked that the code name, *Fabius I*, stood for *Final Assault Before Invasion, US Infantry*. Even a blind man could see that something big was about to happen.'[22]

Lieutenant George 'Jimmy' Green with the 551st Landing Craft Assault Flotilla recalled, 'Live ammunition was used in this exercise and our first wave had little time after the ceasefire to make for the shore. At the scheduled time, the bombardment ceased and we left the safety of our mother ship, HMS *Empire Javelin*, making full speed for the beach. As we neared the shore, about ten minutes after ceasefire, we were straddled by a salvo of fourteen-inch shells from USS *Texas* [in fact, the 7.5-inch shells of the British heavy cruiser HMS *Hawkins*], which missed our craft but soaked most of the occupants.'[23] Two cruisers and nine destroyers were part of the bombarding force, but the weather was not good, and after twenty-four hours Fabius I was cut short, most of the vital issues having been exercised.[24]

Landing at Slapton on Fabius I was Brooklyn-born-and-bred Sergeant Mike McKinney with the Omaha-bound 16th Infantry of the 1st Division. One of ten kids whose father had died when he was young, he had signed on for a three-year stint in the regular US Army in 1940, without a thought of war coming. McKinney had already taken part in two amphibious landings, Torch and Husky, before June 1944; after the Sicilian campaign, 'Somebody said Eisenhower needed a good outfit to lead the invasion into Normandy, so he tagged the Big Red One. We felt pretty cocky and pretty good about that, and went back to England to

The 5th Special Engineer Brigade lands in Exercise Duck, January 1944, during one of many rehearsals held at Slapton Sands, Devon. *LST-325* would take the same engineers to Omaha on D-Day and today lies at anchor at Evansville, Indiana, as a floating museum. Nearer the camera, LCTs 27 and 153 were part of Omaha Flotilla-18. On D-Day *LCT-27* turned turtle 1,500 yards offshore, scattering her vehicles on the ocean floor. In the foreground M10 tank destroyers climb ashore. (US Army Signal Corps)

a place called Weymouth. They told us we were going to go up against pillboxes.'

McKinney recalled, 'We broke the platoon down into four sections and headquarters section; each section had riflemen; a couple of guys who were gonna handle Bangalore torpedoes [tubes bearing explosives that could be connected together]; a few who were gonna have satchel charges. We'd blow the barbed wire up, to make a path for the guys with the flamethrower and the satchel charge to get through.' He mused, 'I knew it was gonna be tough, but I also knew it was gonna be the last fight of the war, the last big fight addressing all of the drudgery of ground fighting, dig a hole, get up, walk ten miles, dig another hole and get up, walk another ten miles, dig another hole, but I knew it was the beginning of the end. That's what I was hoping for.'[25]

Brigadier 'Sammy' Stanier of the 231st Brigade with Force 'G' on Fabius II, observed: 'the plan was exactly the same as the real thing, but nobody below the rank of lieutenant colonel knew that. These exercises gave us the opportunity to meet the Royal Navy personnel who would be transporting us over and providing additional gunfire from offshore and our relations were excellent throughout.'[26] Private Stan Hodge, a newly arrived soldier with the 2nd Essex of the 56th Brigade, was nervous he had never learned to swim: 'My biggest fear was that my landing craft would be sunk and I'd drown. I wanted to be part of it; I wouldn't have minded taking a bullet later on, but I did not want to die on the first day.' In the event, the immature eighteen-year-old would win a Military Medal on 6 June – his first day in action.[27]

Ken Watts of the 2nd Devons, in Stanier's 231st Brigade, remembered of Fabius II, 'Our rurally recruited battalion of farm boys was known in the brigade as "the Swedebashers" and camped in the New Forest near Beaulieu. We lived in bell tents, but the weather was wet and everywhere got muddy, so we were glad to get away for our dress rehearsal. We embarked onto HMS *Glenroy*, our landing ship and anchored off the Isle of Wight. We spent about a week on board, sleeping in hammocks; the food was good and we had a rum ration; if you were a smoker there was cigarette issue too. On the run-in, waves picked up our flat-bottomed LCA and pitched it about, and it wasn't long before the crew and a lot of the troops were seasick. Being unaffected, my job was to throw the sick bags over the side. We eventually staggered ashore on Hayling Island, and were later taken back by amphibian DUKWs.'[28]

Accompanying Fabius II was Lieutenant Ian Hammerton of the 22nd Dragoons, leading a troop of Sherman mine-clearing flail tanks. He recalled 'loading on to LCTs at Lymington and making a full-scale landing on the beaches of Hayling Island, where it seemed incongruous to find all this military hardware among the deserted holiday chalets'.[29] A Sherman tank commander with the Sherwood Rangers Yeomanry (8th Armoured Brigade), Corporal John Lanes, also recollected the holiday atmosphere of Hayling Island, to the extent that his crew 'brought a football and we had a bit of a kick-about on the beach'. Unfortunately their commander, Brigadier Bernard Cracroft, chose this moment to drop by and was less than impressed, shouting, 'What do you think you're doing? Don't you know there's a war on?'[30] Their 'invasion', but not the football, was captured by the British Army Film and Photographic Unit, deploying to test their own equipment.[31]

Fabius III at Bracklesham Bay witnessed the landing on East Wittering beach of those Canadian troops soon to head for Juno, and was observed by Churchill.[32] Lieutenant Peter Hinton with the 262nd LCI Flotilla recalled watching several of the heavily laden troops drown after a vicious undertow sucked them away during the disembarkation. He thought this 'a bitter lesson in how not to do things', but it emphasised that casualties were inevitable with realistic training.[33] Exercise Fabius IV, held at Littlehampton, confirmed the readiness of the Sword forces, based on Rennie's British 3rd Division. Wren Doris Hayball remembered these preparations: 'Shoreham harbour became so full of ships you could walk across it on the landing craft. For the month before 6 June, I couldn't get home from Hove to Worthing without a special military permit.'[34] Ramsay watched with Vian as the LCTs of Force 'S' passed out to sea. 'They looked remarkably workmanlike,' he thought; the naval and land commanders, Rear Admiral Talbot and Major General Rennie, observed from the bridge of the landing ship HMS *Glenearn* as their troops scrambled into smaller landing craft to be deposited ashore.[35]

Eighteen-year-old Private Richard Harris of the 1st Suffolks was one of those splashing ashore during Fabius IV. He recalled embarking on *Empire Broadsword* on 3 May 1944 for what he thought was 'The Day'. 'After sailing all night somewhere in the direction of France, we were lowered in assault craft at dawn and found we were storming the beaches of Angleterre, between Littlehampton and Bognor Regis.'[36] Captain Peter R. Cruden, a Cambridge graduate with No. 6 Commando, who would be wounded on 6 June, also recollected disembarking 'at about 0900 hours, more or less the same timing as on D-Day. I seem to remember it was a rather nice spring morning and the weather was calm: quite different from the real thing. There were background effects in the form of smoke and explosions to make the whole thing more warlike.'[37]

Cruden was part of Lovat's 1st Special Service Brigade. Lovat himself remembered of Fabius IV that his commandos 'seized all the cars of the spectators. They reckoned they were getting rather far behind the sweeping inland movement, took the cars, much to the rage of the drivers and people who owned them, and formed a mobile column that followed the main advance towards Arundel Castle.'[38] The infantry and commandos were followed by Sherman tanks of the 27th Armoured Brigade who had to advance on the town of Arundel, standing in for Caen.

Everything possible was rehearsed and umpired: minesweepers cleared the sea; aircraft dropped ordnance; the coast was bombarded with live ammunition; command ships issued orders and monitored frequencies. Alongside swimming tanks, LCTs landed armour onto beaches; obstacles and real minefields were removed by engineers; troops waded through the surf covered by smoke screens; the three Ranger companies attached to Force 'O' landed away from the main body to destroy artillery positions, as they would on 6 June at La Pointe du Hoc. Bridge-laying tanks spanned anti-tank ditches, whilst engineers and infantry attacked pillboxes. Later on, supplies were landed, simulated casualties treated and prisoners processed. In theory, everyone landing on D-Day was present on a Fabius exercise. At Littlehampton beach the 'invasion' was watched keenly by the Second Army's commander, Miles Dempsey.

Simultaneously, two further Fabius exercises took place, which rehearsed the embarkation of personnel and equipment in the Thames estuary and east coast ports that would head for Sword (Fabius V), and those in the Southampton–Portsmouth area, destined for Juno, Gold and Omaha (Fabius VI). Touring the exercise areas with Vian aboard his flagship, HMS *Scylla*, Ramsay was 'very favourably impressed by all that I saw', and by the afternoon of 4 May, with the weather deteriorating rapidly, the order was given for the landings to cease and maritime forces to return to harbour.[39] In retrospect, it is remarkable how much attention has been paid by journalists and historians to Exercise Tiger, because of its unexpected casualties, while the series of Fabius exercises, far larger and ultimately more important, have lapsed into complete obscurity.

The armies were spiritually prepared also, and we have met some of their chaplains already. Once the air was full of hot metal it was the padres of the Royal Army Chaplains' Department who took the lead in maintaining British morale, and who get only the slightest of mentions in the narratives of D-Day. The majority of 21st Army Group soldiers were Church of England, in addition to 300,000 Roman Catholics and 160,000 Methodists. Amongst the other religions registered in personal documents and on identity discs were Jews, fourteen thousand Christian Scientists, five hundred allegedly pacifist Quakers, Salvationists, Orthodox, Baptists, Mormons, Plymouth Brethren, Muslims, Hindus and ten Druids.

Montgomery, whose father was a bishop, and Dempsey, the Second Army commander, were of a boarding school generation associated with strong religious observance, brought up to attend church every Sunday. Dempsey took his headquarters to Christ Church Portsdown, near Portsmouth, on the eve of D-Day for a special service 'to dedicate to Almighty God the task which lay before them'.[40] Amongst the lesser-known vehicles being readied for the invasion, Dempsey encouraged the adaption of two mobile churches, converted by Royal Electrical and Mechanical Engineers (REME) fitters from three-ton trucks. As recalled by the staff chaplain at the 21st Army Group, 'It fell to me to take the first, dedicated to Saint Paul, by Archbishop Temple, "somewhere in England", in a tank landing craft to the beaches of Normandy. After an apocalyptic crossing we crashed ashore in pouring rain and darkness, to see the spire of Bayeux Cathedral early next day.'[41]

The 21st Army Group commander understood that his D-Day army was a force of citizen soldiers who were less deferential and more curious than their predecessors of 1914–18. His generals were part of the First World War generation that remained under 'the shadow of the Somme', who appreciated that their men – never mind Churchill's government and the public at large – would not tolerate the scale of casualties sustained in the earlier world war. However, there was also a general anxiety that 'our lads are not killers by nature'. Commanders who had experienced the extremes of the trenches expressed concern that the generation who went to war in 1939 were 'too soft'. Monty's superior and patron, Field Marshal Sir Alan Brooke, mused in his memoirs whether it would have been wiser to reintroduce the death penalty for cowardice or desertion. One brigadier addressed his men shortly before D-Day, as remembered by his signaller, 'Some of you will be blown to pieces; that does not matter. But if anyone deserts, he will be court-martialled and shot' – although he knew full well that military courts could no longer apply the death sentence.[42]

To avoid losing another generation of young men, British methodology evolved to use 'metal, not flesh' to fight the nation's battles; thus the army of 1944 played to these strengths, excelling in firepower, engineering, intelligence, logistics and staff planning – while acknowledging the Germans' superiority at close-combat tactics and manoeuvre. The reluctance to deploy infantry until the battlefield had been prepared by artillery – and, where possible, air support – was practised from the morning of 6 June onwards, the guidance coming from the strategically wise Brooke – a gunner by trade. Thus, while bayonet-wielding infantrymen made up fifteen per cent of Montgomery's 21st Army Group, it was His Majesty's Royal Artillery which comprised eighteen per cent, or 700,000 men – roughly the size of the wartime Royal Navy. The actual figures were Royal Artillery, 699,993; Infantry, 551,742; Royal Engineers, 231,985; Royal Signals, 133,920; and Royal Armoured Corps, 120,433.[43]

The Royal Artillery serviced unrivalled firepower – by reputation more deadly than any of their equivalents in the German, Russian or American armies. In addition to the three field regiments totalling seventy-two 25-pounders of each British division, heavier guns were assigned at corps and army levels. By 1944 these were grouped into Army Groups Royal Artillery (AGRAs), often allocated to a corps for a specific battle. Their fire was directed by forward observation officers (FOOs) of three-man teams in Bren carriers, or air observation posts, flying light aircraft. If the other arms providing logistical support to the gunners – particularly the drivers of the Royal Army Service Corps, armourers of the Ordnance Corps and REME fitters – are included, then fully one-third of British soldiers were involved in the business of supplying and lobbing shells at the Germans.[44]

Amongst the millions now preparing to enter France was the Dunkirk veteran and medic Norman Smith. Now promoted to sergeant major with the 22nd Field Dressing Station of the 15th Scottish Division, he sensed a change in everybody's pattern of life: 'Practically all the forces in Britain were moving to the south in huge convoys.' His medical unit reached Brighton, where they started 'marching around carrying all our kit on our backs, plus about thirty pounds of medical kit. We poured with sweat in the sun. It was annoying to see Italian prisoners of war travelling in trucks.' Soon, he knew, he would be 'back to finish the job. A nostalgic moment for us Dunkirk wallahs.'[45]

A GI sergeant noted how 'the hedges along the way had suffered badly from vehicles too outsized for such a tiny countryside. And in the little towns,' he observed, 'tanks, not built for manoeuvring in such cramped space, had knocked pieces of corner buildings as they attempted to make sharp turns on a little street that had never been expected to cope with anything worse than a coach-and-four.'[46] Scotsmen with the Territorial 5th Black Watch of the 51st Highland Division, who had returned from Sicily the previous November, were training in 'street fighting techniques and practising in a bomb-torn area off Whitechapel in London. This brought close contact with many of the Cockney dockers and their families, many of whom had remained in that area right through the worst of the blitz. They were a wonderful community and it was hard to reconcile that side of their character', recorded the battalion's war diarist acidly, 'with the fact that they were threatening strike action, unless they were paid danger money for loading ships with ammunition – which had been mostly manufactured by women.'[47]

The unions soon pulled their men out on strike, which affected troops of the 49th West Riding Division, and Rifleman Eric Patience of the 8th Rifle Brigade, the latter an infantry battalion. 'We arrived just outside Tilbury and stayed in a transit camp for the night while our vehicles were loaded onto the ships. As we went to board the ships the people lined the streets to bid us farewell – they did all right because we threw all our spare change to the children. We were really annoyed that the dockyard crews were on strike and refused to load our transport. Our own engineers and the ship's cranes had to do the job. The names we called those dockers – well, they were unrepeatable.'[48]

There was, sadly, a wide differentiation in the pay and conditions of British servicemen and their highly unionised colleagues. We have seen how those in uniform were remarkably poorly rewarded compared to American troops, but they were badly paid even in comparison with *British* industrial workers, some of whom started work as young as fourteen. Those in industry on average received £25 a month, but the most skilled four times that. In the militant shipbuilding and engineering sectors, some 526,000 working days were lost to labour disputes in 1942, which had doubled to a million by 1944. In the nation's vital aero industries, the figure was 3.7 million days lost in 1944.

The fiercely misogynistic and pro-Communist trades unions instituted stoppages over issues like the use of women workers, or the refusal to allow collections for the Red Army during factory hours. There was also discontent, as we have seen, in the nation's ports, where there appeared to be – to the servicemen at least – 'a less than wholehearted commitment to the war effort'. This was evidenced by vehicles and equipment being shamelessly damaged by slapdash handling – bewildering onlooking US Navy personnel, who were equally astonished at the theft of life-sustaining lifeboat rations from their vessels.

If the servicemen felt disharmony with the workforce, the same was true with some civilians. An impatient Lieutenant Tony Gregson with his Essex Yeomanry gunners found themselves billeted in Bournemouth's Carlton Hotel, on the East Cliff, which had hosted Eisenhower and Montgomery when touring south coast units in February. In May 1944, Gregson recalled, 'the hotel had suffered from the soldiers, with long dingy corridors bereft of all furnishings. Our guns and half-tracks were lined up on the cliff-top gardens in front of the hotel and they soon made a fearful mess of the tarmac drives to the obvious displeasure of the aged ladies who still seemed to occasionally motor by in their chauf-feur-driven Daimlers.'[49]

Though suffering none of the setbacks of Tiger, the Fabius exercises had still resulted in killed and wounded, as recollected by local civilian policemen, news of which the War Office was obliged to suppress until after the real invasion. When the details of the last pre-invasion fatalities were sent to next of kin, it was implied that they had died during the actual landings in France. Brigadier 'Shimi' Lovat recalled asking a new padre to hold a pre-battle service. The chaplain 'preached a rotten sermon about death and destruction which caused surprise. There were a number of complaints; the cleric was suspended and told to return from whence he came. The incident was forgotten but the dismissal was taken badly. On the last day in camp the unfortunate man took his own life. He was put down as a battle casualty.'[50] Likewise, Major Francis Goode with the 2nd Glosters of the 56th Brigade recorded how 'one unfortunate who was playing in his tent with a loaded rifle accidentally shot himself in the heart. I arrived a minute after to find blood spurting literally six feet and no hope. We notified his next of kin after the landing [on Gold Beach] that he had been killed in action. It seemed kinder.'[51]

14

My Headmaster Was a Spy

'As we were to learn later, the road to Victory was badly signposted, full of potholes, and with more than one river to cross.'
Group Captain Desmond Scott, 123 Wing, RAF

Fresh from their Fabius exercises, all the assault troops and those who would follow them were moved into assembly areas nearer the Channel. There they waterproofed their vehicles, were issued with full scales of specialist equipment and shed any unwanted kit and administrative staff – thus, technically, the end of Fabius marked the beginning of Neptune. General Omar Bradley took up the story: 'From those assembly areas, the troops were shifted to forward areas called "sausages" because of their peculiar oval designations on our maps. These were nearer the "hards" – or concrete ramps – where troops were to mount their craft; the sausages had been sealed inside a barbed wire cordon, for it was here that many of the troops were to be briefed on their missions. Once briefed, they were to be cut off from the rest of England.'[1]

Nationwide, all military and civilian mail was impounded on 25 May and only delivered two weeks later. For security purposes, there was no leave or contact with the outside world. Y-Day, by which all preparations would be complete, was now only days away. Gunner Arthur Berry, a signaller with the 127th Field Regiment, Royal Artillery, recalled of these final days, 'We lived under canvas in Leytonstone Park, London, where we were "sealed in" – the atmosphere was unusual, to say the least: there was almost a bank holiday atmosphere; we watched the latest American films, were fed incredibly well and given free beer and cigarettes.' Just as Admiral Ramsay played cricket with his staff in the warm weather to work off the tension of the moment, so Berry and his entire regiment, 'surrounded by barbed wire and tents, played endless games in the park of football, cricket, quoits, with boxing, running and other athletics competitions to kill the time, for we didn't know how long'.[2]

Lieutenant Jack Swaab was an officer in the same regiment, who had fought in Tunisia and Sicily. He wrote in his diary:

> we have been paid in francs today, which removes any lingering doubts about our destination; my own guess is that we shall try and bite off the Cherbourg peninsula. They have been community singing in the big marquee just near this tent – the strains of Suvla Bay[3] and Tipperary are mingling with the setting sun. I wonder how many of them will come back. The hot camp, more like a *Stalag*, daily presents a veritable picture of resigned boredom.[4] Men are lying about nearly naked, sunbathing, or gambling. The barbed wire is lined with half-naked men commenting vociferously on the passers-by. Girls on bicycles get rousing cheers.[5]

Captain Douglas Aitken also noticed the girls. The medical officer of the 24th Lancers with the 8th Armoured Brigade wrote: 'the girls look more attractive when we know we won't see any for a long time to come. Three attractive ones pass on bicycles on their way to tennis – they look very cool and very English. I occasionally find myself thinking foolish thoughts about not coming back.'[6]

Some of these camps in the London area, where troops were concentrated for Tilbury docks, were pretty unpleasant, as Royal Engineer Staff Sergeant Ralph Cheshire wrote home: 'The place is a derelict area of slums, smashed by bombing. Tents have been placed where there were once houses. Hundreds of troops are here, caged in behind barbed wire; a loud speaker announces when certain units should be ready to depart. Dust is flying about all over the place: our boots are covered with it two minutes after cleaning: we can taste it in our mouths.' There was no hint of sport, films or good eating in Cheshire's despatch; the depressing tone in his last letter before heading overseas continued, 'Over the barbed wire we can see slum cottages and dirty faced, ragged kiddies continually asking, "Got any badges or buttons?" In the south-west corner is the charred shell of a church, the steeple still remaining, towering over the ruins.'[7]

All in all, hardly an auspicious start for the invasion, and seemingly *not* repeated in most of the other assembly areas. His spirits might have been lifted by the recollections of Jim Sullivan, a merchant seaman aboard the *Empire Duke*, full of Canadian troops, who saw 'the River Thames lined and crowded with women blowing kisses, cheering and waving flags and banners. I remember one which read "God Bless Our Troops and Keep Them Safe".'[8]

Cheshire's bomb site may have been the same assembly area occupied by Charles Hanaway and the 6th Royal Scots Fusiliers, who recounted, 'we drove through the East End of London, where the pavements were thick with people cheering us on. It was very emotional, but also uplifting to know the people who had suffered so much in those parts were with us in spirit. We finished up in a barbed-wired encampment on Wanstead Flats to stay in tents; civilians still had to walk on the other side of the road, which was more than a little bizarre.'[9] Australian war correspondent Alan Moorhead in another camp echoed this, ruminating, 'More and more the feeling grew that one was cut off, that all the normal things would go on, the tramcars and the shops, but they were, for you, of no consequence any longer. In some strange way you had been committed to the landing, to the blank space ahead. But how had it happened, at what point had it been decided that you should be separated from the other people on earth?'[10]

It was to ease this tension that the Scots Fusilier Hanaway and a pal crept under the fence and soon the pair were celebrating in a pub, 'giving away our French francs as souvenirs to the locals who were buying us beers. We staggered back at 2200 hours that night to discover that everyone else had departed for Normandy, and were put under close arrest.'[11] Lieutenant Robert Woollcombe and the 6th King's Own Scottish Borderers were conveyed south in a special train. 'Everywhere through London it was the same greeting; on walls and the backs of great high tenements overlooking the railway, painted in large, bold white lettering: *Good Luck Boys!* – while people waved from crowded back windows and in groups along the embankment.'[12]

Departing paratroopers of the US 101st Airborne Division left their billets in the small towns and villages of Wiltshire in fleets of buses, bound for the same airfields they had used in Exercise Eagle. Once assembled under canvas near their planes and gliders, they were then locked in behind barbed-wire fences, patrolled by armed guards. Despite the prevailing 'Careless Talk Costs Lives' atmosphere, tearful locals had lined the streets and wished the departing airborne units goodbye and good luck, sensing this time the troops would not be returning for a long while – if at all. Lieutenant Richard Winters of 'E' Company, 506th Parachute Infantry, later told of quitting their Wiltshire billets, 'the English knew we were pushing off. When I went to say goodbye, as if I was off for another maneuver, it got me to see them cry.' He felt 'leaving Aldbourne was a tough job. A fellow couldn't say a thing to anybody due to security.'[13]

George Rosie in the Mortar Platoon of the 3rd Battalion, 506th Parachute Infantry, travelled by train and truck to Exeter airfield, where he was sealed in and issued with 'a ten-cent metal toy cricket for identification purposes – a single squeeze – *click, clack* – was to be answered by two – *click clack, click clack*. Ten dollars in French money followed, together with a five-by-three-inch American flag to be sewn on the right sleeve of my jump jacket, ammunition, two hand grenades, and K-rations.' As he tucked into steak, green peas and mashed potatoes, served with white bread and the first ice cream he had tasted since arriving in England, Rosie remarked to a comrade, 'They're fattening us up for the kill.'[14]

Eric Broadhead with the 9th Durham Light Infantry, 151th Brigade in the 50th Division, recalled life in his tented camp about five miles from Southampton: 'We discussed our ideas of where it would be, but the real question was when? Sometimes the question got on our nerves. We all had our own theories as to when it would be. Around 10 May, the camps were sealed, our training over. The days that followed were strange to be sure. Barbed wire skirted the camp area, armed guards too. We received no mail, but were still allowed to write home, subject to strict censorship.' Shortly afterwards his battalion, destined for Gold Beach, were briefed in a guarded Nissen hut on the forthcoming invasion, but much detail was still withheld. Broadhead observed there was 'a huge map on an equally huge blackboard. On the map we could see a small strip of coastline, the names of towns and villages were false, New York, Istanbul, etc. So we learned little as to the exact whereabouts of the assault. All we knew was that our objective was to capture the beachhead and press on to high ground and above all, hold our ground until armoured divisions were ashore.'[15]

Bound for Omaha, Mediterranean veteran Sergeant Valentine Miele, with the 16th Infantry, recalled thinking he was 'going on another exercise, but instead they drove us to the staging area. Then all of a sudden, we were taken to tents where they had sand tables and maps of the whole beach set out; and postcards, each one with a different picture of our beach, and aerial photos and stuff. After we'd seen those, we were told to stay in the camp, no leaving, no talking to the civilians. There were sentries, armed guards with orders to shoot. All we did there was eat – they fed you twenty-four hours a day, we ate good. We were there about a week; from there they took us to Weymouth, where we got aboard *Samuel Chase*, which also carried our Higgins boats.'[16]

Also bound for Omaha, New Yorker Hal Baumgarten with the 116th Infantry took time out to draw an elaborate Star of David on the back of his field jacket, as an act of defiance against his Nazi opponents.[17] In Hampshire, Hambone Junior, mascot of the US 47th Infantry Regiment, was mourned. A 'brown and white scruffy little terrier' who lived in their camp in The Dene, Alresford, he was accidentally run over by a 'deuce and a half' truck in the last few frantic days before 6 June, and buried beside the River Arle which runs nearby. At first his grave was marked by a wooden memorial, but when that rotted away in 1962 the parish council replaced it with a proper headstone; on the fiftieth anniversary of D-Day in 1994, one returning GI left flowers on Hambone Junior's grave with the note 'I still remember you'.[18]

The Oxford- and Sorbonne-educated Major Jo Gullet had already experienced combat in Libya, Greece and New Guinea. Awarded a Military Cross, he was attached to Australian Headquarters in London, from where he got himself seconded to the 7th Green Howards of the 50th Northumbrian Division a few days before D-Day. As one of the very few Australian officers to serve in Normandy, he would be heading for Gold Beach and likewise noted his briefing 'was tremendously thorough. There were maps, sand tables, photographs, and film of the area where we were to land. We went over it day after day until we could picture exactly the country that would lie ahead of us, and what we would have to do when we got there. The only thing we did not know was exactly where we would land,' Gullet remembered. 'The villages and towns through which we would pass were given code names so that neither we, nor anyone else, could identify them.'[19]

The wealth of detail for Overlord both overwhelmed and reassured the waiting troops: 'The intelligence people had drawn from old road maps, hotel guides, tourist information, postcards, recollections of visitors, French Resistance information, and the like to depict for the soldier the area he was to invade.' They were shown 'silhouette photographs of the coast, showing the beach as it looked at one-half mile, two miles, and five miles out. In other cases the men gathered around sand tables or maps spread on the ground.'[20] Sergeant Pat Lindsay with 'A' Company, 501st Parachute Infantry, noted that from the sand tables, 'each man knew which job he was to do, even down to the direction in which foxholes would be dug'.[21] The glider pilot Staff Sergeant Jim Wallwork, who was to fly in John Howard's men to capture the bridges at Ranville and Bénouville, observed that 'the quality of the models and photographs of our target area was remarkable. Someone had even made a film of our simulated flight path with which we could practise. The detail was incredible; I remember some wag saying, "Someone's taking an awful lot of trouble over this operation, so we'd better not cock it up or the King will be rather cross!"'[22]

Making one of the detailed models was the job of Lieutenant Peter Prior, intelligence officer of the 5th Royal Berkshires with No. 8 Beach Group. Using plaster of Paris, clay and wood, working from 'intelligence photographs and pre-war postcards', even taking a flight along the invasion coast in an RAF Mosquito, he responded to his CO's direction 'to build a model of the actual beach [Juno], about thirty feet long, for the whole division to be paraded in front of. There was an armed guard day and night round this building which had formerly been a barn.'[23]

WAAF Mary E. Harrison had trained at art college prior to enlisting in the air force. Until 1943, she was based at RAF Watnall, Nottinghamshire, headquarters of No. 12 Group, where she made models of targets for Bomber Command. In 1944 she was transferred to Overlord model-making duties. 'The work was carried out by three teams of American and British model-makers, each working eight-hour shifts for twenty-four hours a day, with twenty members to each team. We had to make ninety-seven panels of the objectives, each five feet by three feet in size.' They studied aerial photographs through stereoscopes and made buildings 'out of linoleum, cut to shape with razor blades and inserted in place with eyebrows tweezers'. Roads, rivers and railways were painted on, with coloured sawdust representing woods and scrublands. Harrison recalled, 'Secrecy was such that for some considerable time we had no idea what these particular models were for, but on the morning of 6 June 1944, as I sat with several colleagues at breakfast, the announcement was made over our crackly old radio about the invasion. There was complete silence in the mess as we looked at one another in comprehension – *so that's what it's all been about*.'[24]

Working adjacent to Admiral Ramsay's HQ was Wren Elsie Horton in the underground complex of Fort Southwick, who observed of those heady days, 'All leave was cancelled. On buses, within a few miles of the coast, paybooks had to be shown, or identity cards for civilians – only those who lived on the Isle of Wight were allowed home. Portsmouth harbour was a solid mass of ships and landing craft of every description. Every little river along the south coast had its share of moored LCTs and LCAs. When we were free of an evening, we liked to take a walk, in any direction, and have a chat with these boys, who would often make us a cup of tea.'[25]

Ramsay was constantly on the prowl, making sure his well-oiled machine was working. On 2 June he noticed a jeep backing onto an LCT, as its driver, Les 'Titch' Holden, remembered: 'Admiral Ramsay touched me on the collar with his baton, then pointed to the name I had painted on the fascia of my Jeep. I had previously noted that most vehicles in our convoy were named after famous lords, such as Haig, Kitchener or Roberts. I had christened my Jeep *Lord Elphus*. Giving me a smile, the Admiral said, "I'm sure he will, driver."'[26]

Tim Parr, a civilian living in Launceston, Cornwall, noted that 'in all the lanes at about every twenty-five yards the hedges had been cut away, and beyond lay endless metal boxes of what I presumed was ammunition, row after row of shells, tins of petrol, wooden crates, all under netting and guarded, of course. Jerry only had to drop one bomb, for the whole of Cornwall was a vast monumental magazine, crawling with left-hand-drive vehicles, and these supplies distributed in every field and wood.'[27] *New Yorker* columnist Mollie Panter-Downes told her readers:

Living on this little island just now, uncomfortably resembles living on the combination of a vast aircraft carrier and a warehouse stacked to the ceiling with materiel labelled 'Europe.' It's not at all difficult for one to imagine that England's coastline can actually be seen bulging. The fight everybody is waiting for hasn't started yet, but all over England, from the big cities to the tiniest hamlet, people, at least in spirit, seem already to have begun it. It's evident in the faces of women looking up thoughtfully at gliders passing overhead. The troops look unfailingly cheerful and light-hearted, and it is obvious that they are in wonderful physical shape.[28]

Hampshire resident Brian Selman recalled that 'Poole Park was packed with British Army vehicles parked side by side under the trees. I remember their surprise when they were handed buckets of white paint and big stencils and told to paint large white stars on the tops of their vehicles for all to see. We wondered what this portended.' This was, in fact, the Allied air recognition symbol, applied to every Allied vehicle at this time.[29] Wren Joan Dale was based ashore managing the paperwork for the 33rd LCG (Landing Craft, Gun) Flotilla, part of Force 'G' preparing for Gold Beach. She remembered, 'Every day more and more troops, tanks and guns poured into Southampton. The town was packed, it didn't seem possible to get any more in, but still they came … Then suddenly everything disappeared. We woke up and troops, tanks, guns had gone. They were all now crammed into those little ships and nothing of war was visible on the streets anymore.'[30] On 28 May, to enable all his shipping to position themselves correctly, Ramsay's headquarters at Southwick House had issued their historic two-word signal: 'Commence Neptune!' The long wait was over.[31]

'We came on parade every morning in full battle order, down to the last grenade,' wrote the Australian Major Jo Gullett, 'and at least once during the day or night, transport drove up and without warning we piled into it in our fighting order. One afternoon when we had done this, the trucks, instead of going a few hundred yards and unloading us, drove down to Southampton, and we knew it was on.'[32] Tommy Platt, with the 1st South Lancashires, 8th Brigade of the 3rd Division, recalled leaving camp for Portsmouth docks and embarkation: 'There were security troops – who wore green armbands to distinguish them from assault troops – lining the roads and streets to make sure we couldn't talk to civilians, but very often trays of beer were brought out from pubs for the convoys, which the security *wallahs* couldn't do much about.'[33]

Gerald Reybold was struck that Dorchester was 'a total one-way town for that period. Every household opposite the tanks made it their business to supply the troops with tea, coffee and hot water. They gave us candies in return. By night the soldiers huddled around large fires they had lit in the middle of the road and we were serenaded throughout the evening with Jazz, Blues and old Country and Western songs. In the morning, they were gone.'[34] 'The streets of Southampton were packed with columns of American and British troops,' resident Brian Selman noted. 'Each night, at 3 a.m., a column would pull out and drive to the docks for loading. At 4 a.m., the next unit would arrive for its twenty-three-hour stop. One day, it was heavy artillery; then infantry; the next tanks, vibrating the bomb-damaged houses and bringing down the loose plaster and the odd brick. The petrol bowsers parked nose-to-tail outside our house were the most worrying even though each house was provided with a couple of large fire extinguishers.'[35]

When it was allowed to cover the great military assembly, the *Southern Evening Echo* reported:

> Miles and miles of suburban streets became parking places for the biggest and most fantastic motor show on earth. What made the people of Southampton gasp were the American tank transporters, each as long as a cricket pitch. Their driving cabins were as big as a bungalow, and every vehicle had eighteen wheels. When departing, many of the GIs decided it was pointless taking English money with them, and local schoolchildren scrambled for the thousands of coins they threw from their turrets.

This reflected similar scenes at other embarkation ports. It continued: 'Many a Southampton housewife played foster-mother to the Americans in their roadside camps. Cakes, jam tarts, sandwiches and biscuits were passed over garden gates. Much appreciated also were the many offers to darn socks and sew on buttons.' The *Echo* failed to inform its readers that immediately afterwards Southampton Council's workmen were quickly on the scene repairing the foot-deep potholes left behind in every road and pavement.[36]

Chuck Hurlbut with the US 299th Engineer Combat Battalion remembered of his drive down to Weymouth, 'in the trees along the roadside was mile after mile after mile of every piece of military equipment you could think of, tanks, guns, jeeps, in their thousands. It was incredible – acres and acres of, well, stuff under netting; and we realised that ninety-eight percent of it was American, had come across the Atlantic.' Hurlbut recalled that 'Weymouth was a madhouse. MPs all over the place; you've heard of traffic jams, this was the mother of them all. It was total confusion – but organised confusion. The port was full of boats going this way and that; we ended up on an old converted channel steamer, *Princess Maude*. We laughed at the name; but she was only small and by the time we got on board her with all of our gear, there was no room to move.'[37] Another GI with the 29th Division remarked what they must all have felt: 'Jesus, now we can get started on the road home.'[38]

Lionel Thomas was labouring on a farm near Penzance and recollected, 'One day in May our local bobby [policeman] came round to tell us that all farm activities had to stop. We discovered why the next day: all the narrow Cornish lanes for miles around were jam-packed with American vehicles – nose to tail – big half-track troop carriers, trucks, jeeps and motorbikes, with thousands of troops. They were with us for several days, living and sleeping in their vehicles and in our hayricks, playing baseball or cards, taking weapons apart and cleaning them, listening to music over their wirelesses.

'GIs would come into the farm to buy milk and eggs; we'd smell their breakfast fry-ups of bacon and eggs. I recall we worked out prices in cans of peaches, chocolate bars, tobacco and, best of all, petrol – which was very welcome as it was so scarce, being strictly rationed – some even used it to wash down their vehicles; now that amazed us. Some of the black Americans felt the cold, even in summer, and I can still picture them stamping around in Thrupenny Field, wrapped in their greatcoats. A few mornings later we came out and everything was completely empty; they'd all crept away in the night and we hadn't heard a thing.'[39]

On 23 May an American sergeant, heading towards the US 175th Infantry's marshalling area near Redruth, paused on a hilltop and saw 'below us thousands of trucks, jammed with men and equipment, all moving to the south. There were half-concealed airfields, meadows that hid tanks and Jeeps, and hedgerows harbouring piles of shells. The little towns, still filled with centuries-old quaintness, looked out of place, as troops streamed through in a floodtide towards the sea.'[40] Basildon resident Nellie Nowlan never forgot East Ham High Street, in south-east London, reverberating to the sound of 'thousands upon thousands of lorries loaded with soldiers, towed guns and tanks making their way to Woolwich. They were laughing and waving. The older people, knowing what was happening, were standing by the kerb with tears in their eyes, saying "Good luck, boys, God bless you." When I walked across the road to get my bus they all gave me a wolf-whistle. I smiled and waved my hand, but found I was crying too.'[41]

Had all the high-level secrecy worked? One RAF officer flying P-51 Mustangs with 168 Squadron, who knew much of the secret, was stunned when he met a very junior New Zealander pilot at RAF Odiham. The latter calmly stated he knew

> where it will be and when. 'Do you?' I asked with a painfully superior smile. 'Yes. Caen or thereabouts, on 5 or 6 of June.' I was aghast. Here

was the most closely guarded piece of information in the world, and a junior officer in an RAF squadron knew all about it. 'You are, in fact, absolutely wrong' – said I, lying as convincingly as I could. 'But what gave you that silly idea?' – 'Well, anybody who has been flying over the north coast of France for two years can see the only beaches, within range of air support, on which an army could possibly land are between the Cherbourg Peninsula and River Orne. And obviously it has got to be full moon. With all the preparations in all the ports which you can see from the air, it can't be as far ahead as July. *So it must be 5 or 6 of June.*'[42]

As with Ferdinand Miksche's volume *Paratroops*, if an innocent airmen could stumble on the secret using a pilot's logic, then why not the Germans? However ignorant of Allied plans the Germans were, they knew something was going on. In the weeks preceding D-Day, the Luftwaffe was still strong enough to mount two largely unreported heavy raids at Portsmouth, on 25–26 April, with eighty bombers; Plymouth on 28 April; with further raids by eighty and one hundred aircraft on Southampton and Weymouth in May. A mystery bomber was shot down by Typhoons on 18 April, Flight Lieutenant James Kyle of No. 197 Squadron remembering it 'flying straight and level, slogging slowly and earnestly towards the shores of the south coast. Within a short space of time that medium bomber, a Junkers 188, very unlucky to find a Typhoon squadron airborne, was lying in a horrible wreck in a field on the edge of the Exbury estate [Edmund de Rothschild's home, requisitioned and renamed HMS *Mastodon*]. The only thing alive and ticking was the watch of the Junkers pilot.' Normally crewed by four, the doomed aircraft had contained seven and it was thought they were either spying or defecting.[43]

Then came the great crossword crisis. On 3 May 1944, a four-letter word appeared in a solution to that morning's *Daily Telegraph* crossword: 'Utah', a word then pregnant with meaning. Later, on 22 May, came the clue for 3 Down: 'Red Indian on the Missouri (five letters)'. The solution, 'Omaha', caused panic in secret service circles, but more was to come. On 27 May the solution to another clue was 'Overlord', and three days later, the word 'Mulberry' appeared as an answer to 11 Across – 'This bush is the centre of nursery revolutions'. Finally on 1 June, the crossword solution to 15 Down – 'Britannia and he hold to the same thing' – which was of course the trident held by Neptune. Five code words, five clues – was this a way of communicating with the Axis? More than enough reason for two MI5 agents to pay a visit to Leonard Dawe, the paper's crossword compiler and headmaster of a school in Surrey. His head boy at the time recalled how 'an official-looking car turned up. I was interested, so I kept watching. After a time, I saw Mr Dawe go off in the car with whoever it was. We were astonished at the thought that Dawe was a traitor. He was a member of the local golf club!'

Dawe himself recalled, 'They turned me inside out, then they went to my fellow crossword compiler and put him through the works. But they eventually decided not to shoot us.' It turned out that Dawe got his senior boys to supply him with words, for which he would concoct the crossword clues. Only in 1984 did some of his former pupils admit that some terms they had heard from Canadian soldiers camped nearby. 'Everyone knew the outline invasion plan and the various codewords, but no one knew the time until the last moment. I was not a German spy; hundreds of kids must have known what I knew,' said one of Leonard Dawe's fourteen-year-old students.[44]

There were at least two serious breaches of security. Most notorious was the indiscretion of Major General Henry J. F. Miller, chief supply officer of the US Ninth Air Force, who – drink having been taken – talked freely about the difficulties he was having in obtaining supplies. This was during a cocktail party on 18 April in the public dining room of London's Claridge's Hotel.[45] He added that his problems would ease after D-Day, declaring that would be before 15 June. Bradley referred to this incident in his memoirs without mentioning his name: 'I had known this major general since cadet days at West Point. I respected him and cherished his friendship. But I had no choice. I telephoned Ike. A speedy investigation proved the officer guilty of indiscretion. He was banished from the Theater within twenty-four hours and sent home as a colonel.'[46]

Bradley continued, 'His friends from Claridge's were visited by Counter Intelligence Corps agents and cautioned to forget the conversation. The prompting was probably unnecessary; by that time all of them had been badly frightened. Had I been in Eisenhower's shoes, I would have been no less severe. Rank has no privileges when the safety of men's lives is at stake.' Bradley, Miller and Eisenhower had been members of the West Point Military Academy graduating class of 1915, of which an astonishing fifty-nine officers out of 164, thirty-six per cent, reached the rank of brigadier general or above. In exactly the same way that Montgomery knew most of his subordinates personally through staff training and prior military service, it would aid Eisenhower greatly that he likewise had already worked alongside most of his generals, even if he had to sack one of them. This certainly puts Lieutenant Colonel Martin Lindsay's verbal indiscretion, when discussing paratroopers' injuries with his local surgeon, into a little more context.

Miller's dangerous banter had been preceded on 23 February 1944 by Technical Sergeant Richard Tymm, tired and overworked, sending home to Chicago a wrapped bundle of papers, to which he accidentally attached a sheaf of 'BIGOT' documents. They 'included the codewords Overlord, Anvil, the date of Y-Day, and US Order of Battle'. By chance the package broke open in a Chicago postal sorting office, and on seeing 'Top Secret' stamped on documents – 'BIGOT' was a mystery to them – the FBI were summoned. A flurry of eleven 'Eyes Only' signals between Eisenhower and Marshall followed, so worried were they that Overlord had been betrayed to the Reich. However, an in-depth investigation of the sergeant, his family – who were of German descent – their neighbours and assorted British and US postal workers by the FBI, MI5 and Scotland Yard concluded that it was all a dreadful mistake. No one was accused of espionage, but twelve individuals were placed under surveillance and isolated until after D-Day.[47]

Similar quarantine was applied to the British civilian carpenters who had erected the Chad Valley Toy Company's plywood map of the Normandy coast at Southwick House: the company had supplied the whole European coast, but only their workmen knew that all but the Normandy section had been discarded and burned – an innocent after-noon's work for the Admiralty translated into enforced detention of several weeks 'in the National Interest'. Other historians have observed of the unfortunate Southwick workers that 'in another age and another civilisation they would probably have been strangled'.[48]

Disaster nearly struck Major Goronwy Rees, of the 21st Army Group's planning staff, who absent-mindedly left a folder containing Overlord orders on a London bus: 'Only by running back faster than I've ever run in my life did I catch the bus up and find it on the seat where I'd left it.'[49] Sometimes the elements seemed to be pro-German: in May a gust of wind blew a dozen sets of an Overlord resumé out of a Whitehall office window into the street. Desperate officers charged outside, recov-ering eleven. After a heart-thumping two hours the twelfth copy was handed in to a London police station by an unknown civilian.[50]

In December 2014, evidence surfaced of fears that Overlord and some of the other code names had been compromised. Major Sam Wheeler was a logistician on the staff of the 21st Army Group who left his son a bundle of Second World War memorabilia, which included Top Secret documents issued to him in 1944 detailing changes to several code words, almost certainly in reaction to the Tymm and Miller episodes. They stated that 'Overlord' was to be replaced with 'Hornpipe' and 'D-Day' by 'Halcyon'; there was also a new code word for 'postponement', which was 'Ripcord'. The documents were issued on 19 May 1944, and the changes came into play for the postponement of D-Day by twenty-four hours due to the weather.[51]

Apart from Exercise Tiger, which in popular memory completely over-shadows the run-up to D-Day (and is often confused in memoirs and narratives with the many other practices at Slapton Sands), most of the other rehearsals have been forgotten. Military historians gloss over the extensive preparations in a couple of lines. Yet they underline the exten-sive and thorough groundwork every Allied serviceman had for the 'Great Undertaking'. Some British and Canadian formations had trained for the invasion for as much as four years.

One soldier painted this picture of the rather tedious life endured by one of those battalions stuck on the home front since 1940:

> For four-and-a-half years it had led its own placid life, moving from one village to another, guarding bridges that no one ever crossed and defending dumps that even the War Office appeared to have forgotten. Men joined the battalion, went on their leaves, got girls into trouble, punched their sergeants' noses and went to jail, did legendary deeds in public houses and left the battalion. Only from time to time, when fighters thundered overhead; when they heard the guns of Alamein, as recorded by the BBC, reverberating in their huts; when they waited each morning at the sentry-box for the newspaper boy on his bicycle to bring the latest news from Stalingrad, did they stir with excitement.[52]

The 1st Norfolks, 185th Brigade in the 3rd British Division, fell into this category, having fired their last shots in anger at Dunkirk. Norman Brooks had joined his battalion as a cornet player, aged fifteen, and was the regimental sergeant major by 1944. He recalled, 'Our training in Scotland was in about the hardest conditions you could have had. It was a weeding-out process – if a man couldn't do his ten miles in two hours with full field order on, then he was out. I've never seen a battalion so fit. Each man landed carrying eighty-eight pounds of kit: greatcoat, blanket, groundsheet, enough rations for forty-eight hours, fifty rounds for the Bren, several hand grenades, a mortar bomb and two bandoliers of rifle ammunition. We were also given water purification tablets, a French phrasebook and for some reason the last thing foisted upon us was a tin of foot powder. After our final rehearsal off the south coast we just waited for The Day. We were briefed on Whit Monday [29 May, the day after Pentecost in the Christian calendar and a national holiday]; it was a glorious hot day and we went through a town full of holiday-makers enjoying themselves. You can imagine how we felt knowing we were on our way to be briefed for The Big Job. I found myself wondering where I would be next Whit Monday.'[53]

A few units had been in the UK for only months, but their training was just as intense as those who had been there longer. The 1st Engineer Special Brigade, due on Utah at H-Hour, had arrived in England from the Mediterranean in December 1943 yet managed to complete no less than *fifteen* major amphibious exercises before the real thing. As the troops waited, they were visited by their commanders. Amongst them strode King George, who had been trained at Dartmouth before the First World War and, being a younger son (then known as Prince Albert), had been allowed to see action at Jutland in 1916 aboard HMS *Collingwood*. Hence His Majesty's incognito code name of 'Colonel Collingwood'. Churchill, bearing among his many honours the medieval title of Lord Warden of the Cinq Ports, was 'Colonel Warden'.

At Portsmouth the royal personage mounted the ramp of a landing vessel being loaded, to be confronted by a stony-faced, clipboard-wielding USN quartermaster. 'Rank?' he was asked. 'Admiral of the Fleet.' Undeterred, the questioner continued, 'Name?' The reply was unhesitating: 'Windsor.' A final query: 'First name?' He wasn't often asked that one. 'George.' Which is why the visitor's log of a US Navy LST recorded the visit of an Admiral George Windsor on 24 May 1944.[54]

15

Big Week, Berlin and Nuremberg

'Once the command of the air is obtained by one of the contending armies, the war becomes a conflict between a seeing host and one that is blind.'

H. G. Wells, *The War in the Air* (1907)

W E HAVE SEEN how the 17 January 1944 announcement of Tedder as deputy to Eisenhower concerned the Germans. When he arrived in England, it was after thirty-eight months of Middle East and Mediterranean service, broken only by two very brief visits to London. For eighteen of those months he had worked closely with Eisenhower and, with varying degrees of mateyness, Montgomery. His time abroad had taught him how much Britain relied on partner nations to wage her war: the support of all the empire forces on land, sea and in the air was vital, but so, too, was a growing list of other coalition colleagues, headed by the United States, but also including France and Poland.[1]

Tedder realised this to a greater extent than most of his contemporaries, and certainly more than anyone who had spent their war in the British Isles. When it came to the Allied command chain, this experience of 'sand in his shoes' gave him little in common with his fellow RAF airmen Harris and Leigh-Mallory, or Carl 'Tooey' Spaatz. On the other hand, Tedder's knowledge of the Mediterranean brought him fellow feeling with Admiral Ramsay, US airmen like Doolittle and Brereton, and American generals like Bradley, Patton and Bedell Smith. Tedder also appreciated – *unlike* Montgomery – that the United States had become the senior partner in the wartime alliance and its representatives needed to be respected as such. This was why he functioned so well as Eisenhower's deputy, and managed to bring consensus to many a confrontation between his Anglo-American colleagues.

Part of the 1943 Pointblank directive had always included an intense, all-out phase of operations against the Luftwaffe, Operation Argument. The idea was to exhaust the German Air Force by launching near-continuous day and night missions against aircraft factories, whilst trying to destroy as many Luftwaffe fighters as possible in aerial combat. Its implementation was much delayed by the diversion of resources to the Mediterranean theatre and poor flying conditions: Spaatz and Doolittle were briefed by the British Meteorological Office at Dunstable that for 240 days of a typical English year, weather fronts originating in the Atlantic and moving from west to east across the British Isles produced lousy flying weather of rain and fog, and that 'a forecast for more than a day or two ahead in this country can be nothing more than speculation'.[2] Consequently, even when weather stations in the USA and ships taking readings in the Atlantic suggested a spell of cold and clear weather for the end of February 1944, the decision to launch Argument was in doubt until the last minute.

As late as the morning of Sunday, 19 February 1944 there were cloud bases of up to 5,000 feet over East Anglia, preventing the assembly of the great bomber formations needed to pound Germany – aircraft frequently collided in such 'clag' as they circled to gain height and join formations, while the cold also induced icing, which affected the fighter escorts as well as the bombers. However, these delays cumulatively worked in the USAAF's favour as the number of American aircraft had dramatically increased from twenty-two heavy bomb groups (each of forty aircraft) and twelve fighter groups in November 1943 to double that by the time Argument – known to aircrew as 'Big Week' – was launched.[3] Later on 19 February, Spaatz instructed Doolittle to 'Let 'em go' and the unprecedented aerial assault was under way.

RAF Bomber Command opened the assault during the night of 19–20 February with a costly raid on Leipzig; on the following day the Eighth Air Force put up over one thousand B-17s and B-24s, escorted by their entire fighter force, to which the RAF added sixteen squadrons of Mustangs and Spitfires. They attacked twelve aircraft factories, the RAF following with a night raid on Stuttgart. Thereafter the Eighth launched more daytime attacks on aero plants on the twenty-first. On the third day, 22 February, weather hindered some of the Eighth's effort, but bombers from the Fifteenth Air Force in Italy joined in the assault. The story was the same on the twenty-third, but on the twenty-fourth, nearly one thousand bombers took to the skies to raid Schweinfurt, with RAF Bomber Command attacking the same target that night. Another thousand bombers from the Eighth and Fifteenth attacked more aircraft production and assembly centres on the twenty-fifth, after which poor weather brought Big Week to a close.

The commander of all US Air Forces, General Henry H. Arnold, was an airman who had been taught to fly by the Wright Brothers in 1911; he was nicknamed 'Hap' because of his sunny countenance. Like Carl Spaatz, he had a grandparent who still spoke German, and assessed that Big Week was 'a battle as decisive as Gettysburg. Those five days changed the history of the air war.'[4] Five huge daytime raids over the course of the week cost the Eighth, Ninth and Fifteenth Air Forces 226 bombers and twenty-eight fighters, about six per cent of those committed. This was far less than the prevailing rate amongst Harris's night-time bombing force, while 355 Luftwaffe aircraft were brought down – ten per cent of those sent into battle. More significantly, this cost the Luftwaffe the irreplaceable loss of 150 pilots – though there were wild Allied claims made at the time of far higher figures.

While US bomber casualties were kept tolerably low, their escorts caused most of the German fighter casualties, and it was realised the Luftwaffe could be tempted into the skies and overwhelmed, using the B-17s and B-24s – plodding on to German cities and factories – as live bait. Big Week cost the Germans an estimated 750 fighters in lost production, but forced the Reich to disperse its manufacturing industry: twenty-seven major plants were immediately broken up and reconstituted in 729 smaller centres, camouflaged in tunnels, disused mines and natural caves. It was a policy the British had implemented as far back as 1940. Although output rose – the true figures are difficult to ascertain as German bureaucrats were inclined to inflate their own figures to impress the Nazi Party machinery – quality declined as the size of their unskilled, enslaved workforce rose.

The activities of the Reich's slave labourers came to light when the B-17 of navigator Lieutenant Elmer Bendiner was hit by flak over Kassel. Flying out of RAF Kimbolton with the 527th Squadron of the 379th Bombardment Group, Bendiner recorded how his aircraft, named the

Tondelayo, was repeatedly hit in her wing tanks. The crew were amazed that none of the rounds had ignited the gasoline. All of the eleven warheads later retrieved appeared to be inert. Sent for defusing, Bendiner noted, 'when the armorers opened each of those shells, they found no explosive charge. They were clean as a whistle and just as harmless [but] one contained a carefully rolled piece of paper. On it was a scrawl in Czech. Translated, the note read: *This is all we can do for you now.*'[5]

On 22 February, during Big Week, American air power in Europe was reorganised on an impressive scale. The Fifteenth (based in Italy) and Eighth Air Forces, both operating heavy bombers, were placed under a single headquarters, the United States Strategic Air Forces (USSTAF), under Spaatz. This enabled the coordination of simultaneous attacks by both air forces, and for the Eighth's bombers to range further, flying on to the Fifteenth's bases in Italy rather than having to return to East Anglia, and vice versa. At the same time, Major General Jimmy Doolittle relinquished command of his Fifteenth Air Force in the Mediterranean and took over the Eighth from Ira C. Eaker. The uncompromising Eaker was reassigned as commander in chief of the Mediterranean Allied Air Forces (MAAF), the post previously held by Tedder. Doolittle was best known for leading the first raid against Tokyo in April 1942, flying sixteen B-25s off a carrier to reach the Japanese capital. For this he had won a Medal of Honor and was one of the few American names with which the British public were familiar when he arrived on 6 January 1944 to take up his new appointment.

While Eisenhower may have brought from the Mediterranean to the Eighth Air Force the affable Doolittle, Leigh-Mallory's appointment – the choice was British-made – was often disruptive. His post was not infrequently rendered superfluous, by Tedder intervening to fulfil the role that L-M had been appointed to undertake. While Tedder's collaborative character helped turn the wheels of Allied cooperation, the air component commander's prickly nature definitely hindered the progress of the AEAF. However, there was one important contribution to success that did emerge from his office, which was the adoption of the Transportation Plan.

Leigh-Mallory, Tedder and Dr Solly Zuckerman, L-M's scientific advisor, were convinced of the necessity to implement an interdiction campaign using the available tactical and strategic air power, along the lines of Strangle in Italy. An AEAF Bombing Committee study had shown that two-thirds of French and Belgian rail capacity was being used for military traffic and observed that its disruption – effectively creating a 'railway desert' within 150 miles of Caen – would be the most efficient way of slowing German reactions to the invasion.

Its findings suggested that marshalling yards could be destroyed by employing four 500-pound bombs per acre; with sixty railway yards occupying an average of five hundred acres each, the Bombing Committee recommended dropping 45,000 tons of bombs.[6] Zuckerman and Tedder concurred with the wider idea of systematically attacking not just the railway system, but roads, bridges, rivers and canals, having witnessed the MAAF's recent aerial campaign in Italy. Railways and waterways were the arteries of the German military system and played to the Reich's strengths. The German war economy was dominated by one word: '*benzin*'. Having no oil-based economic resources of their own, Germany relied on what she possessed in abundance – coal, wood and iron – which resulted in an unrivalled railway network, none of which required *benzin* to function.

With the addition of all the foreign railway networks absorbed during occupation, *Deutsches Reichsbahn*, the German state railway, could call on around fifty thousand locomotives and three million pieces of rolling stock to shunt its war materiel and troops around Europe. The Germans understood trains in a way no other European nation could. They even had rail-borne mobile teams that could repair bomb damage to lines and infrastructure within hours, being fully equipped with personnel, lifting gear and replacement items. Therefore, Leigh-Mallory, Zuckerman and Tedder argued, it was vital this network be not merely raided, but overwhelmed to the point of obliteration.

They faced violent dissention from Harris and Spaatz, who remained opposed to any diversion of their bombing force away from the strategic Pointblank campaign, centred on the destruction of the wider German war economy and generally undermining morale through hitting cities. Frederick Morgan, the former chief of COSSAC, then with SHAEF, referred to the 'problem of persuading the Bomber Barons to play with us in spite of the overriding demands of their private war over the Reich, at this time getting into its thunderous stride'.[7] Spaatz was extremely antipathetic to *any* calls on his strategic bombing forces – back on 20 November 1943 he had claimed to Roosevelt's advisor Harry Hopkins that he could end the war against Germany with three months of clear flying weather, without the need for *any land campaign at all*.[8]

As late as April 1944, according to conference minutes, Spaatz had exclaimed in a mixture of metaphors:

the Allied air forces might be batting their heads against a stone wall in the *Overlord* operation. If the purpose of *Overlord* is to seize and hold advanced air bases, this purpose is no longer necessary since the strategic air forces can already reach all vital targets in Germany with fighter cover. It is of paramount importance the combined bomber offensive continue without interruption and the proposed diversion of the Eighth Air Force to support *Overlord* is highly dangerous. Much more effective would be the combined operation on strategic missions under one command of the Eighth, Ninth and Fifteenth air forces. If this were done, the highly dangerous *Overlord* operation could be eliminated.[9]

Harris agreed with Spaatz, additionally objecting that the degree of precision required to hit railway facilities without killing French civilians would be beyond his force. Behind Spaatz's bullish attitude – shared by Arnold and Eaker but not Doolittle, who was more subtle – was the institutional mentality that the United States Army Air Force was 'young, aggressive and conscious of its growing power, and guided by the sense of a special mission to perform. It sought for itself both as free a hand as possible to execute the air war in accordance with its own ideas, and the maximum credit for its performance.'[10]

Spaatz also sowed the seeds of discontent by submitting absurdly high estimates of French civilian deaths were the Transportation Plan to be implemented: these ranged from 40,000 to 100,000 killed, plus more injured. This set Churchill against the plan, though Tedder – by now its champion – refused to back down, and had to endure the odium of the Prime Minister, as on 3 May, when the latter challenged, 'You will smear the good name of the Royal Air Force across the world.'[11] During February and March, Spaatz repeated his misgivings to Eisenhower, bypassing Leigh-Mallory and Tedder, in an attempt to stymie the Transportation Plan, writing that the use of a strategic force against tactical targets would be 'a misdirection of effort'. He may also have harboured a private belief that the invasion would fail. Harris likewise felt that the Transportation Plan would 'divert Bomber Command from its true function.'[12] On 25 March the Chief of the Air Staff, Sir Charles Portal, summoned all concerned to thrash out their differences in the presence of Eisenhower, where Leigh-Mallory and his staff presented the benefits of the Transportation Plan.

Spaatz and his team suggested a radically different target set for attacks by the strategic air forces, and a deviation from Pointblank:

Our plan is to attack the German petroleum industry, along with the aircraft industry as a secondary objective. We would be hitting at a weak link in the enemy war economy. We are quite certain that such attacks would produce constant air battles, resulting in the progressive destruction of enemy front-line fighters and force him to retain his remaining fighters for the defence of his industry. The shortage of fuel that would result from successful attacks would, we estimate, be felt on the battlefield, and so reduce his mobility, and his chances of staging a counter attack against our bridgehead.[13]

All of which contained an inescapable logic, but Spaatz eventually had to concede that the benefits of his 'oil plan' were longer term, whereas Eisenhower needed *immediate* results that would stymie his opponents before and during the invasion, less than three months distant.

Spaatz, meanwhile, defiantly ordered his men to continue their strategic assault against Germany, and on 6 March the Eighth reached a milestone with its first daylight raid on Berlin, escorted by 730 fighters. The propaganda rewards alone were considered worth the investment, although eleven fighters and sixty-one of the 748 bombers despatched failed to return, with the loss of 427 aircrew killed, wounded and missing. A quarter of the casualties came from the 100th Bomb Group, who had already acquired the moniker of the 'Bloody Hundredth'. Lieutenant Vern L. Moncur of the 359th 'Hell's Angels' Squadron with the 303rd Bomb Group flew the mission out of RAF Molesworth, Cambridgeshire. He remembered:

our fighter support was splendid, and even though the Krauts kept ripping through other wings, our combat wing was rather lucky in not getting too many direct fighter attacks that seriously threatened us. Over the target it looked like the Fourth of July – flak bursting in red flashes and billowing out black smoke all around us. It seemed almost thick enough to drop your wheels and taxi around on it. The Krauts were practically able to name the engine they were shooting at.[14]

Of the return to England, Moncur witnessed

a few passes made at our group, but the P-51 fighter escorts very quickly took care of those Me-109s. Our fighter escort was really swell on this mission. We put up twenty-seven ships, and every one of them went across the target, and every one of them came back. Our ship, the *Thunderbird*, received the heaviest damage of any of the planes in our squadron. I had a close call. A piece of flak came through the cockpit and cut the left sleeve of my leather flying jacket, but didn't touch me.[15]

Luftwaffe pilots claimed 108 bombers and twenty fighters, with Nazi media suggesting 140 B-24s and B-17s brought down, more than double the true total.

Lieutenant Bud Fortier, with the 354th Fighter Squadron, flying P-47s out of RAF Steeple Morden, Hertfordshire, was one of the many protecting the hundred-mile-long bomber train that day. He surprised a Messerschmitt attacking a crippled B-17:

The 109 was just a few feet above the ground, and I wasn't much higher, so as I tried to get it in my gunsight, I had to be careful not to fly into the ground. I closed to within about three hundred yards, firing whenever I could get him in my gunsight for more than a split second. I saw hits on the wings and tail section, but every time those eight 0.50s fired, the recoil slowed my P-47 down by twenty to forty miles per hour, allowing the 109 to stay ahead of me. By this time he had led us on a long, merry chase over towns, farms and airfields.

Moments later, Fortier's quarry crash-landed in a field, bringing him his first 'kill' since arriving in England the previous July.[16] Three other raids of similar magnitude followed in quick succession, on 8, 9 and 22 March, aimed at industrial plants in the suburbs, and proved the USAAF could range over Germany at will. In the longer term, these raids caused the Luftwaffe to pull back more fighters from France to defend the Reich's airspace, meaning there would be fewer to oppose Overlord.

The Luftwaffe's ability to combat operations in all theatres demonstrably declined as hoped for after Big Week. From a peak strength directed against Russia of sixty-seven per cent of Luftwaffe aircraft on 22 June 1941, the numbers had fallen to fifty per cent by 10 December 1942 and forty per cent by 10 February 1944 – most of the remainder were not over France or the Mediterranean, but defending Germany. Altogether, Berlin would be bombed 363 times by Allied aircraft; one of the millions on the receiving end was seventeen-year-old Gerda Drews, working in a sewing factory making uniforms for the Luftwaffe. 'When the first night raids took place on Berlin, my mother said, "We must keep our faith in Herr Hitler. He will protect us!" My father, who was a First World War veteran and had refused to join the Nazi Party, never said a word.'

Drews remembered the 6 March daylight raid, when Vern Moncur and the 303rd Bomb Group were overhead. 'When the alarm sounded we ran to shelter in the Humboldthain bunker, with swarms of others from all directions.'[17] This was the biggest shelter in Berlin, seven storeys tall, with room for thousands of people. 'There were anti-aircraft guns on the roof and when they fired the whole building shook – very nerve-wracking. Because I was working, I obtained a ticket that allowed me to sleep there every night, starting from March 1944 until the end of the war.'

Drews recalled, 'I had to be inside by 10 p.m., and home for breakfast at 6 a.m., to show my parents that I was fine. One day there was a daylight raid and we ran to the bunker; when we returned our factory was a pile of rubble. After that, we only thought one day ahead.'[18] Also under the bombs was Ursula von Kardorff, a liberal-minded journalist with the *Deutsche Allgemeine Zeitung*; her family moved among Berlin's middle-class intelligentsia and her father had had to resign from the Academy of Art for his refusal to support anti-Semitism. Yet she was moved to note in early 1944: 'A mine fell on our house during the last raid, and now nothing is left of it. This disaster, which hits Nazis and anti-Nazis alike, is welding the people together. After every raid special rations are issued – cigarettes, coffee, meat. If the British think that they are going to undermine our morale, they are barking up the wrong tree.'[19]

The spirit of resistance was echoed by another German writer, Christabel Bielenberg. Born in London and the well-connected niece of two peers, Lords Rothermere and Northcliffe, she had married a handsome young Berlin lawyer in 1934, exchanging her British passport for a German one. She was deeply involved with the Stauffenberg Plot; although the bombs raining down were delivered by her fellow countrymen, Bielenberg wrote, 'I learned when I was in Berlin that those wanton, quite impersonal killings, that barrage from the air which mutilated, suffocated, burned and destroyed, did not so much breed fear and a desire to bow before the storm, but rather a certain fatalistic cussedness, a dogged determination to survive and, if possible, help others to survive, whatever their politics, whatever their creed.'[20]

Although Harris had witnessed at first hand the fortitude of Londoners in the Blitz, both he and Spaatz seemed unaware that they were actually increasing the resolve of the Third Reich, not diminishing it. Harris's

Bomber Command had been plugging away at Berlin for months: for example, the war diary of the Lancaster-equipped 100 Squadron, flying out of RAF Waltham, noted six major night-time raids against the German capital in January 1944 alone.[21] Yet these attacks were accomplishing a military objective by imposing an attritional battle on the German Air Force they knew it could not win. US losses during the 6 March raid over Berlin stood at less than ten per cent of the force committed, but Spaatz's bombers claimed ninety-seven kills and the escorts eighty-one, a total of 178. Though actual German losses (caused mostly by the escorts) amounted to sixty-six, this was still *twenty per cent* of Luftwaffe aircraft deployed, a crippling loss rate the Third Reich could not sustain – and from Eisenhower's point of view, these were sixty-six aircraft that would not intervene with their aircrew against Overlord.

Overall, Pointblank triggered a crisis in the Luftwaffe: in the west, its fighter force lost 1,052 aircraft in the last quarter of 1943, 2,180 in the first quarter of 1944 and 3,057 in the second quarter, the majority inflicted by USAAF escorts (though bomber crews and flak played their part also). This was more in nine months than had been lost during two years on the Eastern Front. The drain of skilled Luftwaffe flyers was, in more ways, even worse, with 264 day-fighter aircrew lost in January, 366 in February, 322 in March, 395 in April and 462 trained airmen lost in May. These statistics, plus the effects of Spaatz's oil plan, which had begun to eat into the Luftwaffe's stocks of fuel, effectively neutered the Luftwaffe's ability to intervene when Overlord began.[22]

Harris's Bomber Command, too, kept plugging away at its targets by night. He wanted to strike at one last major target before Pointblank formally ended on 1 April. Perhaps in competition with the Eighth's mission to Berlin, he sent 795 bombers to attack the cradle of Nazism, Nuremberg, during the night of 30–31 March. The raid, flying for eight hours deep into Germany, proved catastrophic. 'They started to go down just after we crossed the coast, and after that it never seemed to stop; I weaved all over the shop like a madman, trying to make it as hard for the buggers as I could,' recalled Australian pilot Squadron Leader Arthur Doubleday of 61 Squadron, flying out of RAF Coningsby.[23] Flight Sergeant Bob Gill, a 'tail-end Charlie' rear gunner from 35 Squadron from RAF Graveley, Huntingdon, described the burning wreckage of nine aircraft shot down on their bombing runs as 'funeral pyres stretching sixty miles into the distance'.[24]

Flight Lieutenant Neville Sparks of 83 Squadron from RAF Wyton, Cambridgeshire, recollected, 'Contrary to the forecasts, there was no layer cloud in which they could hide from German fighters. They were clearly visible, glinting in the moon light.'[25] These three crewmen flew on Lancasters, of which sixty-four failed to return that night. In all, sixty RAF bombers were downed on the way out, another thirty-five on the return leg, while fourteen more would crash on British soil, and many others having to be scrapped on return. Bomber Command lost 545 aircrew that night – more than had perished in the Battle of Britain, and a rate Harris could ill afford. The damage done to the Germans, including the destruction of ten night fighters, was minimal.[26] These casualties came on top of seventy-eight RAF bombers lost over Leipzig on 19–20 February, the opening night of Big Week, and another seventy-two which failed to return from a raid on Berlin on 24–25 March. Together, such losses forced a temporary suspension of Harris's night bombing offensive.

At SHAEF, the depressing results of Operation Grayling – the Nuremberg raid – only served to underline the need to shift the bomber fleets towards more positive support for Overlord. After the 25 March Portal conference, Eisenhower found himself having to adjudicate between the two rival schemes: bombing German oil refineries or blowing the French and Belgian railroad system to pieces. As it had become apparent that the French civilian casualty estimates presented by Spaatz and company were likely to be incorrect, and in some cases were found to be deliberately exaggerated, Eisenhower backed Portal, Tedder and Leigh-Mallory and formally opted for the Transportation Plan. He was also prompted to do so by the results of several trial raids. On 6–7 March the French railway centre at Trappes, in the western suburbs of Paris, was hit by 261 Halifaxes, led by six Mosquito pathfinders, where 1,258 tons of bombs yielded instant and conclusive results – it was out of action for a month with no loss to the RAF. Strikes against the railway hubs of Le Mans soon followed, then Aulnoye, Amiens, Laon and Courtrai (Kortrijk).

The Transportation Plan was implemented with Harris's support – it being seen as a way of showcasing Bomber Command's expertise. Spaatz was never truly won over, and acquiesced only grudgingly. Thereafter seventy-nine transportation targets were attacked before D-Day. In 21,949 sorties, RAF and USAAF strategic bombers released 66,517 tons of bombs, all finely nuanced so that operations against Calais, rather

The aerial preparation for Overlord was vital to its success. Despite much hostility from the 'bomber barons', the Transportation Plan gradually saw Normandy isolated from the rest of France, with the destruction of roads, railways and bridges. Saint-Sever-Calvados is about twenty miles south of Saint-Lô, but such attacks had to be cleverly nuanced so that Calais, rather than further west, seemed the object of the Allies' attention. (US Army Signal Corps)

than Normandy, seemed to be its intent.[27] Of these missions, RAF Bomber Command flew 13,349 sorties against rail targets in and beyond France, dropping 52,347 tons of bombs with a low casualty rate of 2.6 per cent during April–July 1944; the equivalent loss rate against Nuremberg had been twelve per cent.[28]

Harris would later write, graciously, in his memoirs:

Bomber Command's attacks in the three months before D-Day were so effective, and the new means and tactics of precision bombing were so rapidly mastered (I myself did not anticipate that we should be able to bomb the French railways with anything like the precision that was achieved) that the invasion proved an infinitely easier task than had been expected. Not even the most hopeful of the Allied leaders had thought the casualties would be so light or the setbacks so few.[29]

Even Harris had been shocked by his losses over Nuremberg and he may have privately welcomed the opportunity to switch targets.

For his crews, the switch meant fewer hours in the air, much lighter casualties, and more of a sense of direct military contribution to the war effort – attacking towns and cities was never an easy 'sell' to bomber crews, many of whom had been brought up in such environs themselves. Wireless operator Bertie 'Butch' Lewis of 102 Squadron, flying out of RAF Pocklington, recalled the good fortune that his Halifax was grounded during 'the terrible night Bomber Command lost almost a hundred aircraft against Nuremberg. It seemed impossible to carry on with night bombing of Germany. Good luck cropped up, however – preparing for the second front. French railway marshalling yards were to be reduced to impotence. There were very few enemy fighters that could be spared, so our losses over France were greatly reduced, to about two per cent. Bomber Command was saved from a massacre.'[30]

There was a flaw with the Transportation Plan, however. Successfully hindering the arrival of German reinforcements by destroying the French road and rail networks would equally put the brakes on a rapid Allied breakout. Therefore, a staggering 1,548,000 man-days were allocated for French road, railroad and bridge reconstruction. Illustrative of the forethought and thoroughness that defined COSSAC and SHAEF preparations, besides locomotives, rolling stock, rail lines and sleepers, 11,700 tons of construction plant – everything from graders, tipper trucks and cranes, to rock-crushing equipment to operate quarries and make roadstone – 15,800 tons of asphalt and 112,000 tons of bridging (including 975 standard and heavy Bailey bridging sets and 365 standard and heavy pontoon Bailey sets) were included in the Neptune shipping plans, in phased arrivals.

Thus the amount of damage inflicted on French infrastructure from the air had to be finely balanced against the time it would take to repair everything in time to still be of military value to the Allies. Likewise, in letting loose the heavy bomber forces to destroy everything of value to the Germans in fifteen major French ports, a similar number of man-days had to be set aside towards the reconstruction of those same installations once their occupiers had been subdued.

In the three months preceding D-Day, two-thirds of sorties mounted by Harris and Spaatz were still against the Third Reich's aero industrial complexes and German cities, but the remaining third was, as directed, against transportation targets, mostly railways. This was further refined in May when restrictions on bombing rail marshalling yards in cities were lifted, as were caveats on attacking moving trains – which hitherto had been considered to be carrying some civilian traffic. Meanwhile, a raid on 24 April by fighter-bombers of 438 (Canadian) Squadron had demonstrated that individual bridges could be successfully struck, in this case by Typhoons carrying two 1,000-pound bombs – which in itself was an illustration of how far aircraft design had progressed since 1939, when a typical RAF bomber carried a maximum load of four thousand pounds.[31] Thereafter, 'bridge-busting' strikes were ordered against many crossings with spectacular results: all thirty-six significant bridges over the Seine between Paris and Rouen had been destroyed by 6 June.

However, even when the Transportation Plan was *under way* and delivering results, Churchill perversely tried to get Roosevelt to cancel it. He first cabled the President on 14 April claiming the results 'failed to justify the *massacre* of French civilians. I beg you to put pressure on LeMay [Colonel Curtis E. LeMay, commander of the US 3rd Air Division of heavy bombers], Eaker and Spaatz about this.' Met with stony silence, he repeated his entreaties on 29 April, then on 7 May, disregarding the advice of Eisenhower and Tedder. The President refused to overrule the Allied policy, responding after over a week's deliberation with a cold, fifteen-word missive to his opposite number on the fifteenth: 'Whatever is necessary for the safety of our boys is at the discretion of Ike.'[32]

This was probably *not* a last-ditch attempt to put the brakes on Overlord – Churchill's hardening-to-Overlord comment was made on 15 May – but Brooke's diaries make frequent mention of his prime minister looking and sounding very frail at this time. 'The [War] Cabinet finished with another long discussion on the bombing strategy of attack on French railways and killing of Frenchmen. More waffling about vacillating politicians unable to accept the consequences of war,' he noted on 2 May. The following day it was the same: 'at 2230 hours another meeting with PM on bombing French railways which lasted until 0115 hours!! Winston gradually coming round to the policy.'[33]

The cause may have been the final battle for Monte Cassino, which was being fought in Italy at this time. Its name may have resonated for the damage done to the historic abbey and town in the strategic bombing raids of 15 February and 15 March. However, we can now say that fewer than six thousand French civilians perished as a result of the Transportation Plan, which ensured the success of the invasion in a way no other single initiative could.

After the war, an Allied staff study dated 11 May 1945 summarised the value of the plan: 'The measure of the success of these attacks on the enemy lines of communication in delaying the movement of troops into the battle area exceeded the highest hopes of the Allies. It had been estimated that in spite of air attack, the enemy forces on D+7 would have increased from nine to twenty-four divisions, and by D+17 would total thirty-one divisions. Actually the strength on D+7 was only fifteen divisions, and by D+17 only eighteen divisions,' read the report. It continued,

> Moreover, some enemy formations suffered heavily *en route*. Long detours were forced on troops who had to move by truck, horse-drawn vehicles, bicycles and even on foot from the Paris area. Heavy equipment, especially tanks, entered the battle with greatly reduced efficiency – and the fighting value of troops, who walked a hundred miles from Paris under constant air attack, must also be considered in assessing the results of the air attacks on communication.[34]

Nevertheless, Free French Spitfire pilot Pierre Clostermann with 602 Squadron later reflected on the stress of escorting B-17s to bomb his native land. He found himself over Rouen watching a raid which left 'the rail yards undamaged, but hundreds of wrecked houses were blazing right up to the foot of the cathedral. Its graceful spire, through some divine providence, appeared intact. How many of my fellow Frenchmen – all civilians – had died or would die for nothing, before our eyes? A murderous rage exploded inside me. I started yelling over the radio, so everyone could hear: "You American sons of bitches! You immoral bastards, you've got no feelings at all."'[35]

The whole Transportation Plan debate, bringing together many headstrong characters, brought to the surface one of Eisenhower's other concerns, that the strategic air forces were responsible to the Combined Chiefs and not to SHAEF. With Pointblank completed, and after much kicking and screaming (as we have seen), they were brought under his formal command from 1 April. On the seventeenth of the month, the Supreme Commander issued a directive to Spaatz and Harris which concluded, 'The particular mission of the Strategical air forces prior to the "Overlord" assault is: (a) to deplete the German air force and particularly the German fighter forces and to destroy and disorganise the facilities supporting them; (b) to destroy and disrupt the enemy's rail

The Transportation Plan also acknowledged the growing capabilities of the Allied air forces to pinpoint and attack quite small targets, such as bridges and moving trains. The requirement to destroy the German transport infrastructure had to be balanced against the Allies' need to use it in the future. The Plan would cost nearly six thousand French lives, but not nearly as many as Churchill feared. (US Army Signal Corps)

communications, particularly those affecting the enemy's movement towards the "Overlord" lodgement area.'[36] Like the January 1943 directive, it was a compromise, in that it allowed Spaatz to keep plugging away at oil refineries, ball bearing plants and other targets deep in Germany on the grounds that they were supporting the German fighter forces, but left both bomber barons in no doubt that they were now subordinate to Eisenhower.

In addition to the transport targets, factories and Luftwaffe airfields, SHAEF also directed the 2nd TAF and the Ninth to concentrate on V-weapon sites (known as 'Noball' or 'Crossbow' targets). These had earlier been targeted by the strategic forces, but in May the tactical air forces intensified this campaign, and before D-Day some 103 out of 140 launch sites had been destroyed. Although the subsequent campaign by V-1 flying bombs and V-2 rockets would prove to be imprecise and of limited military value, there was pre-invasion anxiety that they would be used against waiting troops, concentrated in their ports of embarkation, or against the Overlord lodgement areas, possibly conveying poison gas. All military logic pointed to this application, which could potentially defeat the invasion, and their use as an area weapon against London seemed a waste of a valuable asset.[37]

German airfields, too, came within the cross hairs of the tactical air forces before D-Day. They were divided into those 150 miles from the beaches, and others beyond. These had to be cleverly nuanced so as not to indicate Normandy as the future invasion area. By 5 June, forty Luftwaffe fighter and fifty-nine bomber airfields had received ninety-one major attacks which delivered seven thousand tons of high explosives: runways were cratered, hangars and maintenance and repair facilities were shattered, the aim being to keep the Luftwaffe away from the arrival of the Overlord forces. Coastal gun emplacements clearly needed to be struck, but this was done in a ratio of two in the Pas-de-Calais and Dieppe areas for each one in Normandy; by 5 June, sixteen thousand tons of bombs have been released over twenty-one batteries threatening the Neptune area alone. At the same time, the German Signals Intelligence Centre in France and forty-two major radar and communications sites between Ostend and the Channel Islands were hit in a campaign to blind the defenders of Fortress Europe. Some of these controlled night fighters, others coastal defence batteries; all tended to be heavily defended and needed to be eliminated.[38]

Group Captain Desmond Scott, leading No. 123 Wing of rocket-firing Typhoons, recalled, 'getting at them was like fighting your way into a hornet's nest. Most were near the coast and all held a commanding view; no matter from which direction you approached you could never surprise them, and the amount of light *flak* surrounding them was a true indication of their value.'[39] Some were blinded electronically by the jamming of No. 100 Group of RAF Bomber Command, formed in November 1943 – who had an equal ability to 'manufacture' air fleets and naval flotillas where none existed, through the use of aluminium strips called 'window' scattered in the clouds, which dazzled and distracted operators. Likewise, the Atlantic sea lanes – vital for the sustainment of Overlord – were cleansed of submarines by Liberators, Catalinas, Beaufighters and Mosquitos of RAF Coastal Command, by then well experienced in their maritime protection role after winning the Battle of the Atlantic. In northern waters, the 1944 monthly losses of U-boats to aircraft and surface vessels speak for themselves: fourteen in January; fifteen in

February; seventeen in March; sixteen in April; and fifteen in May, totalling seventy-seven – in the same period, twenty-five Allied vessels of small tonnage and ten warships were sunk.[40]

All the while, RAF and USAAF Mustangs, Spitfires, Mosquitos and F-5 Lightnings (a twin-engined P-38 fighter with nose cameras replacing machine guns) were daily conducting photo reconnaissance (PR) sorties, with the eight British and four American PR squadrons at the AEAF's disposal. Other 'Special Duties' squadrons dropped supplies to the French and Belgian underground. Four thousand containers of weapons, explosives and other supplies were released between January and April – but six thousand in May. Staff Sergeant Wilbur R. Richardson, a B-17 ball turret gunner with the USAAF 331st Squadron, with the 94th Bomb Group flying out of RAF Rougham, Suffolk, recalled that 'Invasion fever was rife. In May all us aircrew were ordered to carry their .45s at all times, while ground crews were issued carbines in case German paratroops dropped on the airfield to disrupt our invasion plans.'[41]

Lieutenant Bud Fortier of the USAAF 354th Fighter Squadron remembered a comment made by a fellow P-51 pilot at the beginning of June: 'That whole French coastline is one huge gun emplacement. The Germans know the invasion's coming. They just don't know when or where.' Neither did he, then – but within hours he observed 'all afternoon and into the night ground crews were busily painting large black and white stripes around the fuselage and wings of the fighters. It didn't take the rumour mill long to put all the pieces together, but the biggest piece came when the bars at the officers' and NCO club were closed at 1900 hours. Pilots were advised to go to bed and get some sleep.'[42]

B-17 navigator Lieutenant Franklin L. Betz flew thirty-five missions with the 524th Squadron of the 379th Bomb Group out of RAF Kimbolton, but most remembered 'to be awakened at about 0400 hours for a mission was pretty much routine, but to be hauled out of the sack at 0130 hours was something unusual. We waited sleepily on benches, smoking to wake up. "Tenshun!" someone bawled up front in the briefing room when the CO strode in. "At ease," Colonel Preston said. "This is it, men – this is D-Day!" Cheers and whoops shattered the quiet of a moment before.'[43]

Bud Fortier recalled being woken: 'Briefing at midnight':

The briefing room door was locked, and the large reading room next to it was jammed with pilots. High-spirited chatter filled the room. As the pilots filed in, they were greeted by "This is it!" Major Rosenblatt arrived and called the roll – a most unusual procedure that somehow injected a note of gravity into the proceedings. Then the briefing room door was unlocked and the pilots swarmed in laughing and jostling each other, exclaiming about the display on the large mission map.

It showed more than the usual information. Bold black and red arrows pointed to the landing areas. At nine minutes after midnight, we were called to attention as Colonel Cummings strode to the stage. 'The general told me this afternoon that the biggest show in history has started – the invasion of France. We're going to do our part, and we're going to do it well!' After the weather and intelligence briefings, Cummings came back onstage. *On the way out this morning you'll see the largest fleet in history in the channel. If you have to bail out over that fleet, try to land on a ship that's headed back to England.*[44]

16

Fortitude, FUSAG and France

'The enemy must not know where I intend to give battle. For if he does not know where I intend to give battle, he must prepare in a great many places. And when he prepares in a great many places, those I have to fight in any one place will be few.'

Sun Tzu, *The Art of War*[1]

Miss Jane Hughes described it as 'one of the ugliest country houses ever to have been constructed in England', but Bletchley Park was always affectionately 'B.P.' to those who worked there. Officially, they laboured at the Government Code and Cipher School (GC&CS), but informally, the curious blend of debs (high society debutantes) – of which Hughes was one – and boffins (scientists) called themselves the 'Golf, Cheese and Chess Society'. She recalled fondly of the war years, 'We were a mix of beautiful girls and very desirable young men, all in our twenties; class barriers didn't exist at all. Working for the same goal, we women were treated as equals. They were great days.'[2]

Established in 1938, by the time Hughes arrived Bletchley had evolved into a production-line factory analysing the signals sent between German military units using their Polish-designed Enigma enciphering machine. She had been recruited by an old school friend in 1940 who wrote to her complaining of the 'frightful' workload: 'We're so overworked, so desperately busy. You must come and join us.' Aged eighteen, Hughes passed her interview with the chess-playing Stuart Milner-Barry, one of

Bletchley Park, Bucks, Seat of Sir George Edward Leon, Bt

It was only in 1974 that the secret of Bletchley Park was disclosed to the world. This was where nearly nine thousand worked, decoding and analysing signals traffic sent by the supposedly secure German Enigma enciphering machine. 'B.P.' – as it was known to those who worked there – witnessed the birth of US–UK intelligence sharing. After much prevarication the government eventually surrendered the house and it has become a world-class museum devoted to this aspect of the war. (Author's archives)

the senior codebreakers, who was 'desperately shy. He couldn't think of a single thing to say and I couldn't think of anything to say to him because I wasn't supposed to say anything.' She signed documents promising never to reveal her work and the 'loose lips sink ships' wartime secrecy stayed with her for fifty years. It was only in the 1990s that she came clean to her family: 'It felt quite overwhelming. I'd never told a soul, not even my husband. My grandchildren were very surprised.'[3]

Milner-Barry was one of the many cryptographers, linguists and mathematicians seconded from Oxford and Cambridge as well as the armed forces who gravitated to Bletchley. By 1944, almost nine thousand personnel worked there in three daily shifts. Their contribution to the war – against Italy and Japan as well as Germany – cannot be understated. All Wehrmacht and SS headquarters, even the German police and railway services, used improved versions of Enigma, which was considered impregnable – when they felt security was compromised, the Reich looked for human traitors, rather than mechanical ones. Enigma transmissions were monitored and transcribed by around forty 'Y' (listening) stations around Britain, who pinpointed their source and sent the copied signals by despatch rider or teleprinter for processing at Bletchley, known as Station 'X'. Leading Aircraftman Peter Read worked for the 'Y' service aboard *Fighter Direction Tender-216*, 'the most ungainly vessel I had ever seen', which sprouted a variety of radar aerials and antennae, and lay 'off Dunoon, at the mouth of the Clyde. It was staffed by German-speaking RAF and WAAF personnel of all ranks who listened to Luftwaffe traffic.'[4]

Bletchley's methodology of signals interception and analysis was assessed as being so sensitive as to be rated 'Ultra Secret', or code-named simply 'Ultra'. Hughes, who had learned German at St Moritz before the war, embraced the station's social life, joining the choral and Highland dancing societies. However, she recalled, 'We were always working against time, there was always a crisis, a lot of stress and a lot of excitement.' In May 1941, Hughes decoded messages during the hunt for the battleship *Bismarck*. When the BBC announced it had been located and sunk, she recalled 'a great cheer went up in the dining room', for this was the first time the codebreaking teams had seen tangible evidence of the importance of their work. In 1942 naval Enigma signals traffic between weather stations, submarines and Kriegsmarine HQ was first deciphered in Hut 8 and translated in Hut 4, where their significance was assessed, allowing U-boats to be pinpointed and destroyed, so turning the Battle of the Atlantic.

Prior to and during the Normandy campaign, German Army and Luftwaffe Enigma traffic was deciphered in Hut 6, where Hughes worked, then translated and assessed in Hut 3. The latter hut then distributed published extracts – with appropriate safeguards to protect the source (usually said to be the well-placed agent 'Boniface') – to field commands who needed to know their contents and could use them. Only Allied army group and army headquarters were generally permitted to access Ultra material, which amounted to 'about twenty-five thousand signals sent out from Hut 3 to western commands between the opening of Eisenhower's HQ in January 1944 and the end of hostilities'.[5] While photo reconnaissance missions flown by the RAF and USAAF acted as the Allies' eyes, Ultra performed the task of their ears, delivering accurate German orders of battle. For example, on 20 April 1944 Guderian's HQ transmitted the itinerary of a tour of inspection of panzer formations in the West, offering 'a splendid insight into the German distribution of armour a month before the landings'.[6]

Such was the sensitivity of the project that its very existence was only uncovered when Group Captain F. W. Winterbotham, who trained personnel to distribute Ultra material to senior officers, was allowed to publish his memoirs in 1974 as *The Ultra Secret*. He wrote from memory and without reference to archives, which the UK Public Record Office in Kew began to declassify soon after. They revealed how crucial Ultra was to the success of Normandy, something earlier memoirs – for example those of Eisenhower, Bradley, Churchill or Montgomery – and all other narrative histories were forbidden from mentioning. It is no understatement to claim that subsequent historians have had to completely revise their understanding of the way the Second World War was fought.

After its finest moments, Bletchley Park was much neglected following the war, partly because of the secrecy under which Ultra operated, and seemed ripe for demolition in 1991.[7] Hughes, by then Mrs Fawcett, had forged a second career in the Victorian Society, founded to prevent the destruction of old buildings, and knew a thing or two about obstructing such processes. She was almost as proud of rescuing London's St Pancras railway station – now the departure point for the *Eurostar* to Paris and Lille – as of helping to save Bletchley: frustrated officials knew her as 'the Furious Mrs Fawcett'. Today the site, including the main house and the huts where penetrations of Enigma's secrets occurred, through the lobbying of Hughes and many others who worked there, has been restored and given international recognition for the war-winning dramas that occurred there – various sources claim the Second World War was shortened by anything between six months and two years by the work done at B.P.

In the forthcoming intelligence war, Ultra would not only pry into the Reich's confidences, but also confirm the success of the Allied strategic-level misinformation campaign, labelled Operation Fortitude, guarding the secret of when and where the invasion of France would take place. When Morgan's COSSAC had been set up in April 1943, a group of officers within the G-3 staff, known as Ops (B), was given the twin tasks of overseeing physical deception and espionage missions implemented by the 'controlled leakage of information'. These evolved into Fortitude, which was formally agreed by the Combined Chiefs of Staff on 20 January 1944 and sketched out in a secret directive of 3 February, addressed to Bedell Smith, SHAEF chief of staff.[8] The deception was designed 'to induce the enemy to make faulty strategic dispositions in relation to operations by the United Nations [as they were then known] against Germany'.[9]

It had many subsidiary aspects, six of which were known as Operations Quicksilver I–VI. Quicksilver I was the basic distraction of a First US Army Group (FUSAG) based in south-east England ready to invade Calais. For the benefit of the German Army's signals intelligence units, Quicksilver II consisted of FUSAG's entirely bogus signal traffic. Quicksilver III was the display of dummy landing craft and other military equipment that would allegedly launch FUSAG. The air plan supporting a FUSAG assault was the central theme of Quicksilver IV, with much bombing of the Pas-de-Calais beach defences prior to D-Day. Increased activity around Dover to suggest embarkation preparations formed the logic behind Quicksilver V, while Quicksilver VI would simulate activity at night where the imitation landing fleet was anchored.

In fact, there were two Fortitudes: the main effort was Fortitude South, which acknowledged that the Allies couldn't conceal the presence of Montgomery's real 21st Army Group, but set out to persuade the Germans that a second, fictitious, First US Army Group (FUSAG) – comprising the equally notional Fourteenth US and Fourth British Armies – was waiting in England to invade German-held Europe. It was made more convincing by having a real commander – the most able Allied tactician, in German eyes – George S. Patton. The Germans swallowed FUSAG whole: in late 1943, Ultra picked up a German Foreign Armies West intelligence assessment (more of them later) that there were thirty-four divisions in southern England. However, of the itemised formations, the Allies knew eleven were fake FUSAG units.[10]

Fortitude North also came into play, similarly equipped with the ruse of non-existent formations waiting in Scotland, Northern Ireland and northern England to make a smaller landing in Norway. By January 1944, the Germans estimated a total of fifty-five divisions in the British Isles – when in reality there were thirty-seven – rising on 27 May to fifty-seven British, Canadian, Free French and Polish divisions, twenty-two US formations, plus a further ten of armoured and airborne troops – totalling eighty-nine divisions, plus twenty-two other brigades – poised to attack.[11] The actual Allied strength at that moment in 1944 was precisely half that, at forty-five divisions.[12]

The Quicksilver I detail was incredible: headquartered in Edinburgh Castle, the fake Fourth British Army was overseen by the personable General Andrew Thorne, who had once been military attaché in Berlin.

14th Army   XXXI Corps   XXXIII Corps

6th Airborne Division

9th Airborne Division

14th Division   17th Division

18th Airborne Division

21st Airborne Division   22nd Division

46th Division (variation)   48th Division

50th Division   55th Division   59th Division

119th Division   119th Division (variation)   130th Division   135th Airborne Division   141st Division

Time and resources were invested on a huge scale in the strategic deception surrounding the Patton Army Group (FUSAG) to make it convincing. As far back as a year before D-Day, details of the notional Fourteenth US Army were published. None of these units existed, but magazine features in the international press, available in neutral Sweden, Switzerland, Spain and Portugal – and double agents – persuaded the Germans otherwise. (US Army National Archives)

Its phoney VII Corps in Dundee contained the equally false 5th British Armoured Division, comprised of the bogus 37th Armoured and 43rd Infantry Brigades. Based in Lincolnshire, the British 2nd Airborne

Division included the 11th and 12th Parachute and 13th Air-Landing Brigades – not a word of it true. The notional Fourteenth US Army, led by real John P. Lucas, who had recently commanded an army corps at Anzio, was comprised of the mythical XXXIII and XXXVII Corps, based in Bury St Edmunds and Chelmsford, respectively. The US Army's heraldry department even devised unit shoulder patches for their phantom army, its corps and divisions – some were featured in US magazines available in neutral Spain, Portugal, Sweden and Switzerland – which Quicksilver operatives wore conspicuously in London and elsewhere.[13]

Quicksilver I's success was confirmed when 'a German map of the British order of battle as on 15 May 1944, which was later captured in Italy, showed how completely our imaginary order of battle had been accepted'. It clearly showed the FUSAG formations in south-east England. Later, 'a recognition booklet captured in France, which would have been issued to field commanders, included coloured drawings of our notional divisional signs'.[14] Allegedly, the Fourteenth Army's ranks were filled with bloodthirsty convicts who were released from prisons to serve in the military – information which reappeared in interrogation of nervous German POWs by the British Combined Services Detailed Interrogation Centre. This organisation collected and assessed material from prisoners, and was, in fact, nine 'cages' established across the United Kingdom where captured soldiers were questioned by the Prisoner of War Interrogation Section of the Intelligence Corps' Field Security Police, and agencies such as MI5 and MI9, before being sent to POW camps. One Russian-speaking interrogator consistently produced interesting nuggets of intelligence by wearing Soviet uniform, which frightened those who'd served on the Eastern Front into revealing all they knew. These organisations formed an important, and often overlooked, adjunct to Ultra in checking the effectiveness of the Fortitude ruses.

The convict legend was widely circulated throughout the German Army, surfacing, for example, in the memoirs of Gunner Hein Severloh, with the artillery regiment of the 352nd Infantry Division behind Omaha Beach. On being taken prisoner, he noted one of his captors was 'an unattractive, tough-looking type with a fearsome Iroquois haircut, and I could see conspicuous prison numbers tattooed on the left side of his skull – the Americans having deployed many hardened criminals in front of the attacking troops'.[15] The tattoos and haircut would have been a voluntary indulgence by a unit before combat, for no federal penitentiary since the nineteenth century has tattooed their convicts, let alone released them for suicidal combat duty – though this was, tellingly, a German tradition, hence being widely believed. Waiting impatiently to cross the Channel, a British soldier remembered his North American neighbours shaving 'their heads, leaving tufts of hair as diamonds or squares, or sometimes they'd give themselves a Mohican cut'.[16]

In addition to the Quicksilver units, several real formations waiting to cross the Channel in follow-on waves were also nominally part of FUSAG, making it a mixture of truth and falsehood. In reality, no more than a few hundred signals troops were actually assigned to FUSAG, who began transmitting wireless details of their fantasy activities on 26 April.[17] Corporal Les Phillips was one of them. 'You would be given a map reference, take the truck to that spot, and at a certain time broadcast according to a script you were given. It might be asking for reinforcements, ammunition supplies, all sorts of things. You'd pretend to be a whole corps. The timing was very important because it had to seem as if one tank was answering another. You had the audio sound of the tanks, to hear them, too. It was all very secret.'[18] Phillips worked alongside the US Army's 3103rd Signals Service Battalion.

Most of the details were worked out by Frederick Morgan's staff at COSSAC, prior to their absorption into SHAEF, who foresaw the need for a large investment of time and resources to craft a convincing and foolproof deception. For Quicksilver III, due to the acute shortage of real landing craft, fake stand-ins, code-named 'Bigbobs', were placed in likely south-east England anchorages. Lieutenant Colonel White of the Royal Engineers recalled driving past some at anchor in Hampshire one day: 'They looked very realistic and at half a mile away I certainly couldn't tell them from the real thing. We'd leave them for two or three days then move them elsewhere, so it looked as if the troops were moving around.'[19] They were made of canvas stretched over a steel frame, floating on an array of 45-gallon oil drums; building them was very labour intensive, as each kit filled six or seven three-ton trucks, and took twenty men six hours to assemble. Ray Marshall, Normandy bound with the 5th Royal Horse Artillery, recalled embarking with his 25-pounder Sexton self-propelled guns in LCTs and finding 'the Thames Estuary was full of dummy boats'.[20]

Meanwhile, inflatable tank and truck kits made of rubber were assembled by Montgomery's 1,200-strong 'R' Force, responsible for tactical deception, and five hundred men of the US 603rd Camouflage Engineers, many of them artists drafted from schools in New York.[21] Made by the US Rubber Company of Rhode Island, Goodyear and others, the tanks weighed in at ninety-three pounds, and were lifted easily by four men. 'R' Force soldier Arthur Merchant remembered being confronted with several mysterious cases of different sizes at an ordnance depot in Essex. 'One was a machine with two handles that was a sort of pump. We plugged it in and started blowing this rubber thing up. It looked like a giant sausage at first, but it suddenly turned into a 75mm gun barrel. Then we got some more mysterious boxes and had a go at them, and a Sherman tank gradually flipped out and took shape.'[22]

Hundreds of other vehicles, artillery pieces and even planes were made by movie prop men at Shepperton Film Studios in west London. Together with the 406th Engineer Combat Company, who handled security and construction, they made the fakes look realistic, providing 'poor' camouflage netting, and tent cities around them, with vehicle and tank tracks, using special rolling tools. The camoufleurs remember the plan was nearly unhinged by an irate bull, which suddenly lunged at a column of Sherman tanks parked in 'his field'. Instead of the thud of horns against armour, the puzzled bovine was confronted by the hiss of air as a tank deflated into a puddle of olive-drab rubber: bull 1, tank 0.

The Quicksilver deceptions were designed to delay the move west to Normandy of Salmuth's Fifteenth Army for up to seven weeks after D-Day. Once the invasion was under way, the Allies would feed a battle plan piecemeal to the Germans that Normandy was only a feint, and a further assault would take place later on the Pas-de-Calais, with a smaller operation against Norway – Fortitude North. We met John Emery earlier, the signaller on HMS *Largs*; he spent a while driving up and down the British east coast sending his dummy messages to reinforce this northern ruse.[23]

Also part of the Fortitude plan was Operation Copperhead, initiated when British intelligence discovered a lieutenant in the Royal Army Pay Corps who bore an uncanny resemblance to Montgomery. Fortunately, Lieutenant Meyrick Clifton James had been an actor before the war and, duly briefed by MI5 and having studied his subject's mannerisms and voice, was deployed to Gibraltar and Algiers – at Montgomery's insistence on a full general's pay for the duration of his impersonation – in an attempt to distract German attention away from the obvious target of northern France.[24] The real George S. Patton, itching to invade the

Continent, reciprocated in the world's newsreels and newspapers, by inspecting troops in south-east England.

The traditional narrative is that Fortitude put the Germans off their guard in Normandy, as confirmed by Ultra. However, as more documents come to light from the war years it becomes apparent that the Germans knew far more about the Allies' preparations than the traditional Overlord historiography would have us believe.

Headquarters, Signals Intelligence Regiment No. 5 (*Kommandeur der Nachrichtenaufklärung.5*; KONA 5) does not usually rate an appearance in the accounts of 1944, yet it was the eyes and ears of Rommel's Army Group 'B'. It consisted of long- and close-range mobile intelligence-gathering companies which intercepted and decoded Allied transmissions, passing that material back to their regimental signal intelligence evaluation centre. Under its commander, Oberst Walter Kopp, KONA 5's headquarters then undertook evaluation and traffic analysis, crypt-analysis, collation and dissemination of all intelligence passed to them. Kopp had two jobs, being also attached to Rundstedt's HQ at OB West, with responsibility for all signal intelligence matters, also copying his findings to OKW in Berlin.[25]

Kopp's unit was not intended to solve complex Allied cryptography, along the lines of the Allied effort associated with Bletchley Park, but concentrated on exploiting lower-level ciphers, which yielded plenty to keep them busy. For example, much appears to have come via the M-209-A cipher machine, manufactured by Corona typewriters. Used extensively by US air and ground forces throughout 1943–5, the portable, rotor-based device was not as strong as its Enigma counterpart, and could be read in as little as four hours by the Germans. Between February and May, intercepts of nearly two thousand administrative signals sent by M-209 revealed details of the Allied order of battle. KONA 5 also managed to break some of the Royal Navy's 'small ship's basic code' used by landing vessels, which confirmed general movement patterns of craft from the Mediterranean and Scotland to southern and eastern England.[26]

They also listened to British railway signals – just as Bletchley was monitoring *Deutsche Reichsbahn* Enigma traffic – and claimed 'a ninety-eight percent success rate in reading over four thousand signals from late November 1943 to February 1944', which pointed to a general build-up in the south of troops and supplies.[27] Another indicator was the

absence of test radio transmissions and practice wireless traffic, which
ceased altogether from March 1944 – suggesting that offensive operations, rather than exercises, were imminent. However, in the second half
of May exercise radio traffic between aircraft control stations aboard
warships and personnel was intercepted for the first time; their locations
were confirmed by direction finding as Plymouth and Southampton.

As a result, on 1 June 1944, the head of intelligence for Army Group
'B', Oberst Anton Staubwasser, noted that the German High Command
became convinced that Normandy would be the site of Allied landings.[28]
KONA 5 also worked out the tactical field code book of the US 29th
Infantry Division, stationed primarily in Devon and Cornwall, and were
decoding much of their training and administrative traffic in May and
June.[29] One routine message assessed as highly significant noted the
receipt of shipments of whole blood, which was known to have a shelf
life of a month.

On another level, General Walter Schellenberg of the *Sicherheitsdienst*
(SD, or security service of the SS) claimed in his memoirs, 'Early in 1944
we hit a bull's eye by tapping a telephone conversation between Roosevelt
and Churchill which was overheard and deciphered by the giant German
listening post in Holland. Though the conversation was scrambled, we
unscrambled it by means of a highly complicated apparatus. It lasted
almost five minutes, and disclosed a crescendo of military activity in
Britain, thereby corroborating the many reports of impending invasion.'[30]
He was referring to the Allies' use of the Bell A-3 speech scrambler, used
on the Washington–London telephone link during the war. Although
the two leaders talked person-to-person, their speech was meant to be
'guarded', and monitored in Washington and Whitehall by operators
who had, on occasion, to intervene and remind the great men not to
divulge specific military details or dates, even over this 'secure' line. At
most, intercepting scrambled calls would merely have confirmed general
Allied intentions.

Further breaches of supposedly secure Allied communications were
revealed during a post-war debriefing at Berchtesgaden on 18 May 1945,
when Oberstleutnant Friedrich, a senior German signals intelligence
officer, claimed that his cryptographers in Paris 'had intercepted and
broken US non-Morse teleprinter traffic between Washington and
Europe. This success was maintained throughout 'owing to the lamentable insecurity of the operators'. The Germans therefore had always
known all the details of ferry flights, strength of the US air forces in

Europe, and a good deal about training and replacements.' Pencilled in the margin of the report, an Allied interrogator wrote: 'I don't believe this came from M-228 traffic' – a reference to the SIGCUM, a rotor cipher machine used to encrypt US teleprinter traffic from April 1943. Whatever the source, although Overlord was not directly threatened, the Allied aerial preparations for the invasion would have been clear to German signals analysts.[31]

Schellenberg, head of the SD foreign intelligence department from 1941, confirmed in his memoirs that the SS were running their own signals intelligence service, which had been founded by Reinhard Heydrich in 1931 – in parallel to that of other agencies.[32] The German chief air historian observed in 1990 that 'about twelve major intelligence services existed in Germany. They were run by the army, navy and air force, by the Nazi Party and some ministries, but there was no real evaluation centre or clearing office for all.'[33] Within the Luftwaffe, for example, there were no less than eight intelligence collecting agencies, who rarely cooperated and thus never compared their findings. This was the nub of the German problem: sometimes the quality of their intelligence products was excellent – but they competed Darwinian-style against one another, at the expense of the regime. Schellenberg's retrospective view, for example, was that their failures were 'not due to a lack of ability but rather to a lack of historical integration of intelligence into the command structure'.[34]

The SD had long loathed the *Abwehr*, the principal German military intelligence service founded in 1929, which they wanted to control. Eventually they were able to prove the anti-Nazi credentials of its director, Admiral Wilhelm Canaris, and his deputy, General Hans Oster, and on 18 February 1944, they were sacked; however, it took until May for the *Abwehr* to be formally abolished, and for Schellenberg to persuade the regime to let him take over all its functions.[35] Many of Canaris's staff were inherited by Schellenberg, including Oberst Georg Hansen, who became his new second in command. However, embarrassingly for Schellenberg, Hansen was arrested and executed in the aftermath of the 20 July 1944 Stauffenberg Plot, along with Canaris and Oster.

The *Abwehr*–SD clash was partly a political one, the former playing a long, professional intelligence game against their opponents, the latter being driven by short-term demands for results from Berlin. They additionally trod on each other's toes, duplicating effort and wasting manpower and resources. Each agency also attracted different kinds of people: the *Abwehr* being a military organisation, it was led by career soldiers with codes of conduct, who tended to avoid physical violence, preferring psychological ploys, making deals and recruiting double agents – although fewer, and with less success than the British. The *Sicherheitsdienst*, on the other hand, were less scrupulous, recruiting criminals and freely employing extortion, bribes – and torture.

The *Abwehr* occasionally used this to their advantage by frightening suspects into talking merely by threatening to send them to the SD. Yet historians have not been kind to Canaris or his *Abwehr*, noting that it failed to predict the massive mobilisation capabilities of the Soviet Union, the United Kingdom or America. Neither did it anticipate Torch or Husky, or (prior to the *Abwehr*'s abolition) warn of Overlord looming.[36] The Admiral himself is often assessed as being more interested in anti-Nazi intrigue than in his official duties. However, much German intelligence traffic remained opaque to their Allied opposite numbers, as the Enigma key of the SD, though not that of the *Abwehr*, remained unbroken during the war. This was compounded by the one weakness of Bletchley Park: it was only able to intercept messages sent by *radio* – in Western Europe the *Abwehr*, SD and German police forces tended to rely on landlines.

The February 1944 abolition of the *Abwehr* was also to the general detriment of the Wehrmacht, who had to rely more than ever on their own signals intelligence service, run by the German Army's chief signals officer. This was Generaloberst Erich Fellgiebel, another anti-Nazi executed after the 20 July Stauffenberg Plot. This had the effect of discrediting his command, whose professional advice was subsequently ignored at the expense of agencies like the SD, who knew how to present to Hitler's circle a picture they liked to hear, whatever the truth on the ground.[37]

A senior NATO officer observed of German wartime intelligence,

In NATO the J-3 (Operations) and J-2 (Intelligence) staff organisations are on a superior level, set apart from all other functions, and working as co-equals. However, during the Third Reich, the commander and his chief of staff prepared the situation assessment, with minimal input from the intelligence officer – if he was asked at all. Amidst the rivalry and friction of various headquarters, information was sometimes deliberately withheld, because to know more than others gave one more influence. Intelligence officers were also called 'defeatists' if their estimates were too unfavourable, and their products considered as 'lies'. Self-delusion became the counter to intelligence.[38]

In Hitler's mind, because of ideology and the euphoria of the early victories gained in 1939–41, there was a 'conviction of the superiority of the German warrior over the Anglo-American tradesman', which eschewed the contribution of intelligence.[39]

Confusion was increased by the reporting activities of Oberst Alexis, Freiherr von Roenne, the head of the army's *Fremde Heere West* (Foreign Armies West), the intelligence department responsible for evaluating intelligence relating to the British Isles – and therefore Overlord. He noticed when his Allied troop estimates were submitted to OKW and Hitler's headquarters, they were reduced by half to make them more palatable to Hitler. Roenne and his deputy then started doubling their numbers before submitting them, thus playing into the hands of the Operation Fortitude deceivers.[40] After the war, surviving German officers would make claims about what they, or their departments, knew about the Allied build-up. Such assertions were also used to illustrate the gladiatorial nature of the Third Reich command systems, where chaos and confrontation was the order of the day, rather than collaboration. The implication was usually 'if they had listened to me and not those other bastards', the outcome would have been different.[41]

The French department of the SD, based at 82–84 avenue Foch in Paris, and directed from 1 June 1942 by the SS and police leader for France, General Karl Oberg, had also penetrated several Resistance movements.[42] French memoirs and Hollywood often refer to the Gestapo's sinister activities in France and elsewhere. The moniker was a postal clerk's unofficial abbreviation of *Geheime Staatspolizei* (Secret State Police), which had begun life as part of the Prussian police under Hermann Göring, and was expanded to a national agency in 1936 with the task of investigating treason, espionage, sabotage and criminal attacks within the Reich. In 1944 the Gestapo's D-4 department dealt with such matters in France, whilst its *Amt* (Department) E-3 was responsible for counter-intelligence in the west.

Throughout the war, the Gestapo mostly comprised German policemen, relatively few of whom were Nazi Party members; they wore plain clothes (unlike Hollywood's insistence of a fetching two-piece black uniform), possessed police detective ranks, and were charged with making investigations – in France into the Resistance. They usually worked on the same cases as the SD, though the latter were creatures from a different stable. The SD were not policemen, known in Gestapo circles as 'bad detectives but good Nazis', and wore grey SS uniform and bore membership of the Nazi Party. The SD and Gestapo were separate agencies but both came under direct command of Himmler, chief of all SS and police in the Reich; as the war ground on, SD and Gestapo personnel were loaned and seconded to each other, the SD effectively becoming the intelligence agency for local Gestapo detachments – and it became often difficult to distinguish between the two – although their combined numbers in France totalled no more than three thousand.[43]

In Paris, the Gestapo logically took over the headquarters of the French secret police, the *Sûreté Nationale*, at 11 rue des Saussaies, which was bursting with files on communists, refugees and foreign agents.[44] However 'Gestapo headquarters' is historical shorthand, for both it and avenue Foch housed offices of every branch of the German intelligence services and police. By 1944, the SD and Gestapo wielded the real power in occupied France, cooperating with frightening efficiency – in contrast to the previous SD–*Abwehr* antipathy – and were represented by the armed sentries outside their many buildings, fleets of black Citroëns at their disposal that flashed through the streets and lanes, spreading terror, and thirty-two thousand informers at all levels of French society. In the eyes of the Resistance and associated Allied saboteurs and agents, the SD and Gestapo were one and the same, and since the war the term Gestapo has been used widely – and incorrectly – to signify both.

All German personnel were instructed to recognise the Resistance as terrorists, rather than legitimate warriors, and termed anti-partisan operations as *Bandenbekämpfung* – combating banditry.[45] Thus, with an invasion looming, German reaction to Maquis activity was to be swift and brutal. As General Carl-Heinrich von Stülpnagel, Military Commander of France (destined to be another victim of the post-Stauffenberg hunt for conspirators), ordered on 12 February 1944, 'The main task in the coming weeks and months is fully to re-pacify the areas which are contaminated by bandits and to break up the secret resistance organisations and to seize their weapons. In areas where gangs form, these must be combated with a concentrated use of all available forces. The objective must be to break up all terrorist and resistance groups before the enemy landing.'[46]

More harsh still was the angry directive issued at the same time by Rundstedt's deputy, Luftwaffe Field Marshal Hugo Sperrle: 'We are not in the occupied Western territories to allow our troops to be shot at and abducted by saboteurs who go unpunished. If troops are attacked, all civilians in the locality, regardless of rank or person, are to be taken into custody. Houses from which shots have been fired are to be burnt down. Measures regarded subsequently as too severe cannot, in view of the present situation, provide reason for punishment.'[47] This encouraged all those in German uniform, not just the SD/Gestapo and wider SS, to employ extreme measures against the Maquis, often in contravention of Hague and Geneva conventions which recognised the laws and customs of war, and to which Germany was a signatory. The immediate conse- quence was several large-scale punitive operations undertaken by Wehrmacht units before the invasion. These were Operations *Corporal, Haute-Savoie, Brehmer* and *Spring* of February–April 1944, which had the dual aim of destroying the Maquis and terrifying civilians from cooperating with partisans in the future.[48]

As the Resistance knew they could expect no quarter from their oppressors, it merely made them more determined. An SD report dated 20 March 1944 observed, 'continuing observation of enemy air attacks, agent's activities, and agent's wireless networks in the occupied areas of the West unanimously and clearly show [partisan] concentrations in the areas Pas-de-Calais, Paris, Tours, Loire estuary and the South coast of France.'[49] On 1 June, the last Foreign Armies West intelligence summary issued before D-Day – intercepted, but not decoded by Bletchley for ten days – noted, 'Considerable increase in parachuting of weapons since the full moon of 28 May. Officers in uniform have been dropped in small groups. Since they can hardly stay underground for long, there is reason to regard the period beginning 12 June – the moon's last quarter – as dangerous.'[50]

The SD were also aware that Resistance members would be alerted to the imminence of invasion in order to enact several missions. *Tortue* (Tortoise), as its name implied, required the slowing down of German reinforcements with the sabotage of roads, bridges and viaducts. *Plan Vert* (Green) would see railway stations, switches and lines simultane- ously damaged en masse. *Plan Bleu* (Blue) was concerned with destroying electrical facilities and power lines, whilst *Violet* involved the cutting of underground long-distance telephone cables.[51]

From his office on the second floor of avenue Foch, Dr Josef Götz, head of the SD's Section IV (Signals Intelligence), and Oberstleutnant Oscar

Reile, head of *Abwehr* Section IIIF (Counterintelligence in France), operating out of the elegant Hôtel Lutétia at 43 boulevard Raspail, had discovered that some Maquis partisans had been instructed to listen to the BBC French language service on the 1st, 2nd, 15th and 16th of each month for coded messages relating to the invasion. They understood that on hearing the first three lines of Paul Verlaine's 1886 poem '*Chanson d'automne*' (Autumn Song), partisans should ready themselves for landings within the next two weeks, and monitor the BBC continuously for a second trio of Verlaine's lines. When this was also received, it meant simply that the assault would take place within forty-eight hours.[52] However, these much-quoted lines of poetry were not the only indications to prepare. The first coded message of Thursday, 1 June 1944 preceding the Verlaine, warned quite explicitly '*L'heure des combats viendra*' (The hour of combat is at hand), though other signals that night were more in keeping with the spring: '*Les fleurs sont très rouges*' (The flowers are very red).

Since September 1941, it was an open secret that the BBC had been broadcasting coded messages to the French Resistance at the behest of Colonel Maurice Buckmaster, the spymaster running the French section of the Special Operations Executive (SOE). Götz and Reile reported on 2 June 1944 that the BBC in London had broadcast the previous evening some '125 phrases of which twenty-eight were recognised as advance-warning codes', indicating their level of penetration of the Resistance.[53] In fact they miscounted, for preceded by the four opening notes of Beethoven's Fifth Symphony (which also spelt out the Morse code letter 'V' for victory) and fifteen minutes of war news, the BBC's French service, *Ici Londres! Les Français parlent aux Français*, put out 162 *messages d'alerte* that night.[54]

Hubert Verneret, a nineteen-year-old maquisard in Burgundy, committed the offence of listening to the BBC French service. 'Although banned by the occupying enemy, the magic of wireless is such that all we have to do is turn a small black Bakelite knob to the long wave frequency of two hundred kilohertz (fifteen hundred metres) to be reunited as brothers, in perfect communion. There is the usual jamming and the words are practically inaudible at times, but we cling to this unclear noise, as if to a friend's heartbeat, for it brings us every day, from London, a little hope.'[55]

Every evening at 2015 hours (2115 hours in France), after the news in French, Franck Bauer was one of those who took his position for fifteen minutes behind the microphone in one of Bush House's airless cubbyhole studios to read out and repeat coded phrases that had an air of Alice in Wonderland about them. The twenty-one-year-old had fled his home town of Troyes by bicycle in 1940, and was elated to be waging his war against Germany and Vichy with a *Radio Londres* microphone. Bauer recalled, 'The BBC was trusted throughout France for its broadcasts; we helped create Général de Gaulle and the notion of Free France. We had a slogan: *Radio Paris ment, Radio Paris est allemand* (Radio Paris is lying, Radio Paris is German).'[56] Bauer and his better-known colleague Pierre Holmes (son of a French mother and English father) did not always read poetry.

After the news on 5 June – which announced the fall of Rome to Mark Clark's Fifth Army – the local Resistance leader in Bayeux, Guillaume Mercader, was overcome with emotion on hearing '*Il fait chaud à Suez*' (It is hot in Suez), which he knew meant to begin *Plan Tortue* (Tortoise), the sabotage of road networks.[57] Jean Château, an electricity board inspector who organised agents in the Caen area, and his wife were sitting down to an omelette supper when they heard '*Les dés sont sur le table*' (The dice are on the table). 'Why – I think this is it,' Château exclaimed to his wife, knowing he had just been ordered to initiate *Plan Vert* (Green) – the destruction of railway lines.[58]

Other seemingly random phrases also portended the invasion – in Caen a young teacher with the *Organisation Civil et Militaire* (OCM) Resistance group, André Heintz, anxiously listened for '*Ne faites pas de plaisanteries*' (Don't make jokes). His eyes still well up at the recollection of that prelude to his own liberation, whilst having to evade the attention of local SD chief, Hauptscharführer Harald Heyns headquartered at 44 rue des Jacobins.[59] Following the BBC broadcast, another maquisard recorded outside his home, 'Suddenly the village exploded into unusual activity. Despite the black-out, lights suddenly burst on in the windows of apartments and houses. Someone knocked on the door. The order for mobilisation had been given. We were to report immediately to HQ. Right under the noses of the Germans, everyone was alerted. In the darkened streets, silhouettes flitted from door to door, and shadows moved silently down walls and streets.'[60]

Elsewhere on 5 June, '*Le chapeau de Napoléon est dans l'arène*' (Napoléon's hat is in the ring), '*La Guerre de Troie n'aura pas lieu*' (The Trojan War will not take place), '*La flèche ne percera pas*' (The arrow does not pierce), '*Messieurs, faites vos jeux*' (Gentlemen, place your bets),

'*Méfie toi du toréador*' (Beware of the toreador) or '*Les carottes sont cuites*' (The carrots are cooked) each told different Resistance circuits (or *réseaux* to their French membership) that now was the moment to pull on their boots, grab a weapon or some explosives, slip through the darkness, quietly wake their neighbours to tell them 'The Hour' had come, and go about their respective missions.[61]

Jean Dacier, a *résistant* in southern France, recollected, 'On the evening of 5 June we were all gathered round our little radio, which we had christened "Biscuit" because of the tin in which it was hidden. The Captain had the headphones on and I was almost lying on top of him trying to hear what was being said. Suddenly London announced D-Day was happening. We all jumped around delirious with joy.'[62] The final message of 5 June, '*Les enfants s'ennuient sur dimanche*' (The children get bored on Sunday), was addressed to all; it meant get ready, distribute arms, contact your leader and report every move the Germans make: it was a general call to arms.[63]

However, as the Maquis maintained their own security and discipline, not all their followers were immediately aware of the wider picture, as Jacques Lazare Julius – a young Jewish lad who had joined a Resistance group near Lyon – recalled. He remembered what he did on 6 June, then aged twenty-two – though he had no idea that this was supporting the invasion. 'One day we were ordered to cause as much disruption as possible – to cut telephone lines, destroy bridges, railway tunnels and railway lines, as well as blocking roads by blowing them up. Up until then we operated under cover of darkness; this was unusual because we were ordered to act in broad daylight – it was only that night the BBC told us that the Allies landed in Normandy.'[64]

Their chiefs had been trained in England. The numerous requisitioned country houses used by SOE for the purpose give rise to the joke that its initials stood for 'Stately Omes of England', after Noël Coward's popular divertissement of the time. Founded by Churchill on 22 July 1940 with instructions to 'go and set Europe ablaze', the French sections of SOE (there were two – Gaullist and Communist) supported the many Resistance *réseaux* to the tune of depositing nearly three hundred agents and four thousand tons of war materiel into wartime France between the springs of 1941 and 1944, but were not the only Allied players in the field.

De Gaulle's own intelligence services – the *2ème Bureau*, subsequently the *Bureau Central de Renseignements et d'Action* (BCRA), run by Colonel

Passy, the undercover name for André Dewavrin, based in London – had an interest. So, too, did those of the Polish government-in-exile; Britain's MI6 (also known as the Secret Intelligence Service, SIS), controlled by the Foreign Office; MI9 (the wartime service that helped POWs and airmen behind enemy lines), administered by the War Office; uniformed SAS units; Jedburgh, Sussex and Proust teams (which comprised multi-national US, British and French two- or three-person intelligence-gathering teams); as well as the American Office of Strategic Services (OSS – which became the post-war CIA): all operated personnel in France and not infrequently trod on each other's toes.

Despite this assistance some maquisards remained a law unto themselves – and working not just for the good of France. Such duplication of effort in any case led to poor security, which occasionally allowed the Germans to penetrate groups. In the end – despite the protests of an incandescent de Gaulle – Churchill decreed in January 1944 that all *réseaux* must use British or American radio equipment and recognised codes.

With the Resistance given their specific marching orders, what to do about the rest of the people? Jean-Louis Crémieux-Brilhac with the Free French Forces in London recalled the heated debate about how far to incite the population into immediate acts against the Germans on D-Day. 'The Communist party – whose *Francs-Tireurs et Partisans* (FTP) were extremely influential – wanted an immediate general insurrection on D-Day, with workers going on strike and calls to arms across the country. It would have been a very stupid mistake. The Germans would have taken massive reprisals – as indeed they did. The policy we decided on was of a gradual, phased insurrection, developing in accordance with the advance of Allied forces. Nevertheless, we advised that all French men and women should consider themselves engaged in the total war against the invader in order to liberate their homeland. We told the people of Normandy that every minute lost to the Germans was a minute gained by the Allies. A car stuck on the road could delay traffic for ten minutes – and blocking an enemy transport for ten minutes might ensure the success of an Allied operation.'[65]

The 1962 movie *The Longest Day* made much of Oberstleutnant Helmuth Meyer in the Fifteenth Army's signals bunker at Tourcoing excitedly noting the lines of Verlaine on 1 June: '*Les sanglots longs / Des violons / De l'automne*' (The long sighs of the violins of autumn). On 5 June, Meyer heard: '*Bercent mon coeur / D'une langueur / Monotone*' (Lull my heart with a monotonous languor).[66] He understood its significance, though not for whom. In fact it was a specific message to Pierre de Vomécourt's *Ventriloque* (Ventriloquist) Resistance circuit to commence attacking railways around Tours, rather than all *résistants*. The Fifteenth Army's war diary recorded that Meyer immediately alerted Salmuth's chief of staff, Rommel's Army Group 'B' headquarters, Rundstedt at OB West and Generaloberst Jodl at OKW in Berlin.

This is where the popular understanding of London's signals to the Resistance is in error; according to the BBC archives at Caversham, the Verlaine lines were merely one of 187 coded messages transmitted on 5 June warning of the invasion within forty-eight hours – more than on any previous evening – and something which Walter Schellenberg in Berlin, Helmuth Mayer in Tourcoing, Josef Götz at avenue Foch and others listening in immediately spotted. If the quantity was not enough of a concern, the Germans recognised that at least fifteen of these confirmed the imminence of invasion.

The Fifteenth Army was placed at readiness; Generalleutnant Hans Speidel, deputising for the absent Rommel, did not immediately issue an alert – although he later relented – and thus had not warned his other formation, Dollmann's Seventh Army. Rundstedt did nothing, assuming Speidel had the matter in hand. Jodl did not issue an alert, assuming Rundstedt had done so – which highlighted the individualistic approach of different commanders to their intelligence services.[67]

Schellenberg also sent a warning up through the SS chain of command – but why did Army Group 'B' not react? Because OKW had already issued an invasion alert on 18 May: 'Main effort in Normandy, with secondary attack in Brittany. It is thought that the enemy will attack land targets with very heavy bombs, concentrating on small areas, and will try to silence coastal defences in the same way, combined with heavy naval bombardment and attacks from the sea. The use of new weapons cannot be excluded. Large-scale paratroop drops may be made after nightfall.'[68]

The earlier alert, made on the Kriegsmarine's advice, came to nothing, and infuriated the Desert Fox, who vowed that no more false alarms would waste his time. May had also seen the SD intercept BBC coded phrases addressed to the *Armée Secrète* in Le Havre, and other groups in Brittany and the Lille–Amiens area, ordering them on full alert in readiness for the invasion – again illustrating the SD's success in penetrating the Maquis – though these later proved to be an error made by the BBC.[69]

Meanwhile, Buckmaster had a final trick up his sleeve: not all the *messages personnels* transmitted by the BBC to France were real. His French operatives had been encouraged to let slip that any broadcasts containing references to soup indicated an Allied interest in the Calais region. As Buckmaster recorded in his autobiography, 'we broadcast endless sentences of the order of *Monsieur Gerald aime le potage* (Mr Gerald loves his soup), *Caroline demande bouillon* (Caroline asks for broth), and so forth'. It left the Germans scratching their heads and wondering whether to shuffle more troops towards Calais.[70]

Militarily, Cherbourg seemed to beckon to the Germans as a likely option for invasion, because of its transatlantic port facilities, and by May 1944 some attention had shifted away from Calais towards the Normandy–Brittany area. Assuming the construction of their extensive fortifications in the Calais area – with substantial military reinforcements behind them – would act as a deterrent, Wehrmacht staff work had shifted by early 1944 to scoping alternative landing sites. Attention focused on ports like Le Havre, Cherbourg, Saint-Malo and Brest, capable of handling the logistics needs of an invading army – though the idea of an artificial, towable harbour was never seriously entertained. By June 1944, all likely anchorages were heavily defended by fortress troops, and a spider's web of artillery housed in concrete bunkers, which were daily being increased – for by 6 June, the *Atlantikwall* was merely 'work in progress'.

At his debriefing in July 1945, General Walter Warlimont, deputy chief of the Armed Forces Operations Staff under Jodl, claimed the late transfer of German units to Normandy and Brittany was a response to intelligence reports showing the concentration of Allied forces in south-east and south-west Britain.[71] He was referring to the move in mid-May of Falley's 91st *Luftlande* Division, with Heydte's 6th *Fallschirmjäger* Regiment and 100th Panzer Battalion (armed with captured French light tanks) and other units, which caused huge upset to Allied planners when they discovered it.

However, as we have seen, this was in fact a response to Generalleutnant von Schlieben's request for reinforcements and Rommel's own appreciation of his defences, and not due to intelligence reports. In another post-war interrogation, Generaloberst Alfred Jodl observed that 'signals intelligence provided very little definite information regarding the invasion before D-Day. They had not much idea where the *Schwerpunkt* [main target] was going to be, but thought it would probably be at

Cherbourg, with a second attack in the Pas-de-Calais'[72] – which appeared to reflect Rommel's own anxieties.

Meanwhile, in early 1943 the very efficient Luftwaffe signals intelligence service at Asnières-sur-Seine (north-west of Paris)[73] monitored the pre-invasion Exercise Spartan and, in 1944, Tiger, both compromised by clear-speech conversations. Later in 1943, they worked out that call signs used by Brereton's US Ninth Air Force had been altered to correspond to those used by Coningham's British Second Tactical Air Force, suggesting the two organisations had merged (which they had, as the Allied Expeditionary Air Forces, under Leigh-Mallory).

By the middle of May 1944, Luftwaffe signals monitors had concluded that both Elwood 'Pete' Quesada's IX (comprising the P-47s and P-51s that would support Bradley's US First Army in Normandy) and Otto P. Weyland's XIX (similarly assisting Patton's Third Army) Air Support Commands had been redesignated Tactical Air Commands and changed their frequencies to those used by the Ninth Air Force. Traffic analysis showed a large concentration of squadrons in the Middle Wallop area of southern England, and a smaller one in south-east England. Similarly, Luftwaffe traffic analysis and direction finding indicated in April and May 1944 that most units of the British 2nd TAF were transferring to the Portsmouth–Tangmere and Reading–Odiham areas of southern England.[74]

Statistical analysis, codebreaking and direction finding by Asnières also contributed to breaking the simple codes used by the US IX Troop Carrier Command's C-47 fleet, which revealed the formation of three subcommands (the 50th, 52nd and 53rd Troop Carrier Wings), bunching in the three locations of Grantham–Cottesmore (in fact, the concentration area of the US 82nd Airborne Division), Aldermaston (British 6th Airborne) and Exeter (where the 101st Airborne were gathering). They also concluded that the C-47 fleet was over one thousand aircraft strong, which could enable a mass airborne drop of eighteen thousand fully-kitted paratroops in a single lift up to six hundred miles distant. This was an accurate assessment, for the Allies had available 1,200 C-47s and 1,400 gliders. Based on the known range – 1,200 miles – of a fully-loaded C-47, which was capable of carrying eighteen fully laden men, and using maps and dividers, Luftwaffe analysts began to triangulate likely areas for paratroop operations, of which the Cotentin peninsula was the most obvious, with Caen, Dieppe, Calais, Antwerp and Paris assessed as also at risk.[75]

Some RAF codes had been compromised, too. Through cryptanalysis of the codes belonging to Air Vice-Marshal Leslie Norman Hollinghurst's No. 38 Group (which operated troop-carrying aircraft and gliders), traffic analysis and direction finding, the Luftwaffe's signal intelligence service was further able to surmise that group's known activities – taking agents and SAS operatives into occupied Europe and airdropping weapons and equipment to Resistance movements – had increased markedly from February 1944, and that they were additionally training in glider operations (also revealed by clear speech transmissions such as 'Have you the glider in tow?') and the dropping of paratroops.

They were traced as having moved to the rough area of West Oxfordshire, West Berkshire and South Gloucestershire (the locations of their bases at RAFs Brize Norton, Fairford, Harwell, Keevil and Tarrant Rushton).[76] The conclusion of all these indicators was that the Luftwaffe SIGINT (Signals Intelligence) headquarters at Asnières issued an invasion warning at the end of May: 'All preparations by the British and American Air Forces are complete. Two British and two American close support corps for the support of four armies are available. The beginning of a large scale landing must now be reckoned with any day.'[77]

However, while they clearly identified the allied assembly locales, did the Germans manage in any way to identify the invasion target area? Both Rundstedt and Rommel felt the key 'combat indicator' of where and when would be found in England's south coast harbours. Luftwaffe aerial photo reconnaissance was rarely able to penetrate the thorough defences around Britain. During the months of April and May the Luftwaffe had managed to fly only 120 reconnaissance missions over Britain, recording little of interest except on 24 April 1944, when a successful sortie by *Aufklärungsgruppen* (Long-Range Reconnaissance Groups) 121 and 122 equipped with Me 410s flying from bases near Paris, detected '234 LCTs, 254 small and 170 auxiliary landing boats and fifteen transports in Portsmouth, Southampton and Selsey Bill', judged 'capable of transporting seventy thousand men'.[78] Frustratingly, a subsequent Messerschmitt Bf 109 sortie managed to take pictures of Portsmouth harbour shortly before D-Day but the aircraft was damaged beyond repair on landing in France.

However, a further mission was able to photograph the south coast, using one of three captured P-47 Thunderbolts of the Luftwaffe's élite *Kampfgeschwader* (Bomber Wing) KG-200, who also operated a pair of captured B-17s. Collectively the imagery seemed to suggest a coming offensive against Cherbourg rather than Calais.[79] Luftwaffe reconnaissance flights made at *night*, however, told a different story. Pilots reported 'a great deal of road traffic in south west England, apparent because some drivers were careless about lights', though confirmatory daytime flights were impossible. 'Air reconnaissance has provided *no* information,' complained the Army Group 'B' weekly summary dated 21 May 1944, and one of 5 June pleaded, 'Survey urgently needed of harbour moorings on the entire English south coast by air reconnaissance' – but on the key date, bad weather confined the Luftwaffe to its airfields.[80]

On 2 May 1944, Rundstedt had received a message from Hitler which concluded: 'The Führer thinks the attack will first be on Normandy, and then on Brittany.'[81] However, Rundstedt knew that Hitler was mercurial and disdained intelligence. In his view, the Führer's conclusions were based on nothing more concrete than a gut instinct. Personally convinced the Allies would attack Calais, the OB West decided to overlook this latest whim of his boss. Less easy to ignore were two Luftwaffe signals intelligence appreciations of 8 May (both intercepted by Ultra with the first decoded immediately, the second a week later), which were based on solid military detective work. 'Based on Allied air attacks on railroads and waterways,' read the first with deadly accuracy, 'our assessment that the landing is planned in the area Le Havre–Cherbourg, is confirmed once more.'[82]

The second document of the same date was more pithy and summarised the recent 2–4 May 'Anglo-American landing exercise *Fabius* in the area of the Isle of Wight' [probably Fabius II, and clearly the subject of careful monitoring by English-speaking linguists], where 'the enemy, in view of the outer beach obstacles known to him, is attempting to achieve a modified landing and battle technique for his foremost landing wave'. Despite the best efforts of SHAEF, the Germans knew of Fabius in detail, though, curiously, reaction to the 28 April E-boat attack during Exercise Tiger never surfaced in their signals traffic, and its significance as a major pre-invasion practice seems to have completely escaped the Wehrmacht. Yet security surrounding the Allied plan was far from watertight – in fact, it had been all but compromised.

In depth, the 8 May report continued,

Invasion preparations by the Anglo-Americans in the English Motherland are completed. The observed concentrations of landing shipping space, especially in the area north of the Isle of Wight, Portsmouth–

Southampton, give a clear picture of a main concentration defining itself in that area. Tonnage of shipping space for landings which has so far been observed can be assumed to be sufficient for twelve to thirteen divisions. The point of main effort appears to be roughly from Boulogne as far as Normandy inclusive. In this connection, the enemy's chief concern must be to gain possession of large harbours. Of primary importance would be Le Havre and Cherbourg, and of secondary importance Boulogne and Brest. The enemy landing exercise which took place most recently indicates that the enemy attaches special importance to recognising and clearing the outer-beach obstacles at low water, with attacks coming not only on the incoming tide before dawn, but also later.[83]

In fact, the shipping space was wildly overestimated, as fewer than half this number of divisions were preparing to land, and the follow-on troops were anchored elsewhere.

Thus, from many trusted intelligence sources, it was obvious that a major landing operation would come soon in the west. Hein Severloh, behind the future Omaha Beach, wrote to his sister on 28 April 1944, 'All leaves are suspended as of yesterday. Something is going to happen here.' He later recorded seeing two top secret signals addressed to his battery commander on 30 May and 1 June. The first read, 'Ship concentrations in southern English harbours', the second, 'The ships in the English harbours are being loaded.'[84] Subsidiary operations were anticipated in Norway and southern France, but the main effort was expected along the northern coast of France, from Le Havre to Cherbourg. However, the real question would turn out to be whether the Germans trusted what all their intelligence agencies were clearly telling them – that it would be Normandy.

17

The Giants

Actors waiting in the wings of Europe,
We already watch the lights on the stage,
And listen to the colossal overture begin.
For us entering at the height of the din,
It will be hard to hear our thoughts,
Hard to gauge how much our conduct owes to fear or fury.
Captain Keith Douglas, Nottinghamshire (Sherwood Rangers)
Yeomanry, unfinished poem written while waiting to
cross the Channel

IN THE RUN-UP to the invasion, Montgomery, inevitably, was making his presence felt. 'Thousands of us, from various units, were assembled in a large field before his arrival,' remembered Stephen Dyson, a Churchill crewman of the 107th Regiment, Royal Armoured Corps. 'When he ascended the platform, a deathly hush came over the waiting throng – you could sense the air of expectancy on all sides to hear the great man speak. One awed voice behind me spoke for us all as he murmured, "It's like the coming of the Messiah."'[1] When he visited Lieutenant Robert Woollcombe's unit, the general was preceded by a procession of motorcycle outriders and staff cars. He thought Montgomery's slow walk through the midst of the assembled throng was 'hardly an inspection. It was a one-man progress.'[2]

However, when Brigadier 'Shimi' Lovat was called to a final briefing at Southwick House, he noted: 'Monty missed an opportunity of remaining modest and to the point, and his lengthy address largely concerned himself. I left feeling that I had been listening to a headmaster taking a backward class. Concise in his approach, but egotistical to a fault and, on this occasion, something of a *poseur* into the bargain.'[3] Monty later claimed to have visited 'well over a million men' prior to Overlord, dashing about the country in his train, *Rapier*, assorted jeeps, his Rolls-Royce, and aircraft – he had a C-47 presented by Eisenhower and a more modest four-seater Miles Messenger at his personal disposal. Proof of the value of his exhaustive inspection programme came after D-Day, in a letter from Lieutenant General Walter Bedell Smith at SHAEF, which demonstrated how popular the British commander was at this stage with his American colleagues – alas never to be repeated. Typically, Montgomery quoted Bedell Smith's missive in his 1958 *Memoirs*:

> Dear General,
>
> I have just received from a most reliable and intelligent source a report on attitude and state of mind of American troops in action. The writer is completely unbiased, and his report contains the following paragraph, which I hope will give you as much pleasure as it has given me:
>
> 'Confidence in the high command is absolutely without parallel. Literally dozens of embarking troops talked about General Montgomery with actual hero-worship in every inflection. And unanimously what appealed to them – beyond his friendliness, and genuineness, and lack of pomp – was the story (or, for all I know, the myth) that the General "visited every one of us outfits going over and told us he was more anxious than any of us to get this thing over and get home". This left a warm and indelible impression.'
>
> The above is an exact quotation. Having spent my life with American soldiers, and knowing only too well their innate distrust of everything foreign, I can appreciate far better than you can what a triumph of leadership you accomplished in inspiring such feeling and confidence.[4]

This was Bedell Smith laying on the flattery with a trowel. Colonel Red Reeder, hand-picked by George C. Marshall to command an assault regiment in Barton's US 4th Infantry Division, recorded how on a visit

> Montgomery seized the microphone in a confident manner. It had rained hard the night before and the grass was saturated. "Sit down," said Monty. Not a man moved. A few looked at the ground and shifted their positions so they might stand in a drier place. The little general barked

"Sit down, I say!" About six of the 3,220 men carried out his order. General Sir Bernard Law Montgomery was angry. He shouted as hard as he could, "I Said: Sit Down!" The regiment sat down, but I think few heard his speech. I knew of his reputation but I began to doubt if Monty was the type who could lead Americans successfully in a prolonged operation.[5]

However a completely opposite impression was left with the Australian war correspondent Alan Moorhead, who remembered the formula: 'The speech was followed by three cheers for the general. I listened to it four and sometimes five times a day for nearly a week. We went from camp to camp over Southern England, sometimes standing on wet hilltops, sometimes surrounded by civilians in city parks, sometimes on a football field or under the shelter of a wood. Always the same rush to the Jeep, the same tense attention.' Moorhead reckoned he knew the words by heart but each time was 'swept into the contagious and breathless interest of the audience'.

He concluded, 'I must have heard fifty generals addressing their soldiers, most of them with much better speeches than his. But spoken by Montgomery to the soldiers who were about to run into the *Atlantikwall* this speech had magic.'[6] Eisenhower was just as busy, often using his train, *Bayonet*, to drop in on thousands of all nationalities, for he saw himself as an *Allied* commander, not an American one. Between February and June he addressed twenty-six divisions, twenty-four airfields, five warships and an unrecorded number of hospitals, depots, bases – and the Royal Military Academy, Sandhurst, where on 11 March he took the salute of the graduating Royal Armoured Corps officer cadets.[7]

News footage of the event shows that he was a remarkably erudite public speaker, using no notes, and eclipsed many other figures of his era – including Montgomery. Listening to recordings of both men, Eisenhower still conveys gravitas decades later, whereas Montgomery's words and manner definitely belong to another era. The Supreme Commander was no doubt aware that his own son, John D. Eisenhower, would be graduating from the US equivalent at West Point on 6 June – a day when he already knew he would be preoccupied with other matters.[8]

The younger Eisenhower later admitted, 'I always felt a secret discomfort that West Point's Class of 1944 was savoring its graduation at the same time that boys younger than us were clinging desperately to the cliffs of Normandy or sinking in the English Channel.'[9] First Lieutenant Harold Akridge, bound for Utah with the 8th Infantry, recalled the moment when Eisenhower appeared to borrow Monty's technique. He arrived by jeep to inspect the regiment, drawn up on the edge of Dartmoor; 'driving up to the center of our group, Ike got out, climbed on the hood, yelled, "Break ranks and gather round." He gave a short and peppy speech. As he drove off, he yelled, "Remember, when we get to Berlin, I'm buying the champagne!"'[10] The North Africa and Sicily veteran Captain Hank Hangsterfer with the 16th Infantry recollected the visit of General Omar Bradley 'to give us a pep talk on the importance of our mission. I remember him saying he would give anything to be going in the assault waves with us. I was tempted when I shook hands with him to tell him I would sell him my place for twenty bucks.'[11]

For Signaller Lewis Goodwin with Combined Operations aboard HMS *Largs* – the ex-Vichy French 'banana boat' we met earlier and now flagship and headquarters vessel of Force 'S' controlling the landings on Sword – it was the visit of the Prime Minister on 25 May that he distinctly remembered. 'As Mr Churchill disembarked, he raised his hat several times in salute to the ship's company, and called out, "I would far rather be with you gentlemen aboard this fine man-o'-war, than waiting here for news of your endeavours. Good luck to you all." He twirled his hat on his cane, waved his cigar and flashed us his "V for Victory" sign with his fingers. Now *that*, I can tell you, made us feel special: we wanted him to come with us.'[12]

In fact, Churchill, ever the old warhorse, *was* planning to accompany the fleet to Normandy on D-Day on the cruiser HMS *Belfast* – but kept the fact to himself, as he knew there would be violent opposition to his presence midst shot and shell. It was during their lunchtime audience on Tuesday, 30 May 1944 that Churchill mentioned it to the King – for technically, as a minister of the Crown, he could not travel abroad without the King's consent. George VI was not only enthusiastic, but felt he should be there too, at the head of his navy. Churchill was happy in the knowledge that it would strengthen his own case. It was only when Sir Alan Lascelles, the King's private secretary, issued all sorts of warnings about grave constitutional crises should the pair perish that the King was dissuaded – but not his prime minister.

Poor Admiral Ramsay was caught in the middle, recording on 1 June, 'we settled down to discuss features of *Overlord*. Then I was told to leave

H.M. & the P.M. together. After five minutes I was recalled and the P.M. explained that H.M. wished to embark on the same venture, namely to go over with the assault forces. To cut a long story short I said that I considered the risk was unacceptable in view of the fact that it was only for him a "joy ride". But the P.M. said this ban didn't extend to him.'[13] Eventually news of the plan reached Eisenhower, who immediately vetoed it. The seventy-year-old Churchill absurdly responded that he would make himself a bona fide member of the *Belfast*'s complement.

With the Prime Minister deaf to the pleas of the War Cabinet, service chiefs and the Supreme Commander, King George realised he was probably the only one able to change Churchill's mind, and penned an astute missive urging him to delay his cross-Channel visit. The latter grudgingly assented and the pair soon visited the front: Churchill on D+6, followed four days later by the King.[14]

The King's two-day visit to his pre-invasion fleet from Wilton House on 24–25 May was a highly choreographed affair code-named Operation Aerolite. From the 'stone frigate' HMS *Mastodon*, he boarded a naval launch which slowly proceeded down the Beaulieu River, where most landing craft flotillas had been assembled. 'All the COs saluted in turn. It was a very quiet and sombre occasion.'[15]

During the King's inspection,

one CO was entertaining a Wren (Women's Royal Navy Service) and insisted she take her place. The King's launch passed miles of LCTs and thousands of men in one single line, officers at the salute, and so close did he pass that many of the men discovered for the first time – and with a slight shock – that he was wearing make-up. His Majesty remained at the salute, his face expressionless – except once, when his eyes alighted on the little figure of the solitary Wren amongst this host of men. For a second his face registered astonishment and the royal eyebrows rose – then the mask descended again. As the launch passed, there was a bit of a swell and I saw one of the Royal Marine officers suddenly topple straight into the drink – and I swear he was still at the salute as he entered the water.[16]

In the Solent he also visited Admiral Vian's flagship, the cruiser HMS *Scylla*. As he followed His Majesty, Vian stopped in front of one of his ratings and pointed to a medal ribbon he didn't recognise: 'What on earth is that?' The embarrassed sailor stuttered, 'Metropolitan Police,

Long Service and Good Conduct Medal, sir!' Vian thought this hilarious and observed, 'Well, that's one bugger I'll never get!'[17] The King himself was sped around Portland harbour reviewing the assembled fleets in a US patrol boat, *PT-507*. 'The cook provided His Majesty with coffee,' recalled its skipper, Lieutenant Harold B. Sherwood, USNR. 'On leaving, the King complimented our cook on a most excellent cup of coffee. After that, any complaints about his chow were silenced by "If it's good enough for the King of England, it's good enough for youse guys".'[18]

It was on the gorgeous summer evening of Thursday, 1 June that the 21st Army Group's leader entertained his four army commanders – Bradley, Patton, Dempsey and Crerar – at an eve-of-invasion dinner in the grounds of Broomfield House. For once, Montgomery forewent his usual habit of turning in at 9 p.m. sharp. By all accounts it was a most convivial and optimistic evening, and epitomised the peak of Allied friendship. Patton bet Monty the astronomical sum of £100 that 'the armed forces of Great Britain will be involved in another war in Europe within ten years of the cessation of the present hostilities'; Dempsey bet Bradley £5 that 'the war with Germany will have ended by 1 November'. Monty toasted his subordinates. Patton, as the most senior, replied on their behalf, exclaiming their 'satisfaction in serving under him'.[19] The following evening Montgomery dined with Eisenhower, and revelled in more Anglo-American bonhomie.

These chapters have indicated that a substantial number of lives were lost in the months of realistic training that preceded Normandy. Looking back, Lieutenant Colonel Trevor Hart-Dyke, commanding the Hallamshire Battalion of the British 49th Division, wrote: 'like other units we had our toll of accidents, but to make the training more realistic, normal safety procedures had to be relaxed. This policy was well rewarded when we went into battle, as we were not then unduly perturbed by the noise and danger of war.'[20] Many men would echo the observation of Corporal Chris Portway, with the 4th Dorsets of the 43rd Wessex Division, that 'all those ghastly exercises which preceded Normandy were far more painful than the real thing'.[21] Due to the insistence of the first commander of the 21st Army Group, Bernard Paget, and his successor, Montgomery, that training be as realistic as possible, the casualty bill was high, but less noticed as it was spread evenly through every unit.

As civilian Roy Nethercott was watching 'the American Rangers and our Commandos practising beach landings and cliff climbing around

Burton Bradstock and Swanage in the weeks prior to D-Day, one of them fell to his death just as he reached the top,' he recalled.[22] Lieutenant Colonel Robert Dawson's No. 4 Commando also held several cliff-climbing pre-invasion exercises on the Cornish coast. On one, 'in the rough conditions at the base of the cliff, one of the boats foundered in the heavy swell and two men were lost'.[23]

Three fatal incidents which befell one well-honed and by no means careless battalion training in Scotland will serve to illustrate the experience of every Allied unit training for Normandy. George Burnham of the 2nd East Yorks explained one incident where 'we were introduced to live ammunition and being fired at, and the Bren gun was on a fixed line. It couldn't move, and was firing about three feet above the ground, and you came to this place and there was a big sign and it said *Crawl or else*. Of course, these three lads went straight out, straight into the machine-gun fire and were cut to pieces.' Later the same battalion lost a Bren Carrier (small tracked vehicle) during one of the Scottish exercises after another unit had mistakenly laid live mines along the track it was using. Its passengers were all fatally wounded. Alf Harrison, also of the 2nd East Yorks, watched a soldier trip as he left a landing craft during amphibious rehearsals: 'As he tripped he knocked the safety catch off and his rifle went off, and he shot the bloke in front. It went right through the collar of his shirt and that killed him instantly. The chap who had done it was an ex-Glasgow policeman and knew all about first aid, runs over to try to stop him bleeding, but couldn't.'[24] This battalion was not slap-dash or inefficient; rather, it served to emphasise just how dangerous was their preparation for the coming campaign.

Thomas G. Finigan, a sapper with the 85th Field Company, Royal Engineers (No. 7 Beach Group), remembered several men killed from the nearby 8th King's Liverpool Regiment when using a Bangalore torpedo. 'It went off a matter of a hundred yards away and was quite gruesome. I think there were seventeen that died.'[25] Tank commander Captain William Douglas Home, with the 141st Regiment, Royal Armoured Corps (formerly the 7th Royal East Kents, who insisted on wearing their former cap badge, and were equipped with Churchill flame-throwing tanks), observed an exercise in Kent where 'shells from the supporting artillery started exploding all around us and in the wood ahead, killing a few infantry soldiers who had already reached it. We hurriedly took cover in some bushes and wirelessed back to stop the barrage. After what seemed hours, but was probably only a few minutes, the gunfire stopped.'[26] During Exercise Fabius, eight men from the 2nd Battalion, Essex Regiment of the 56th Infantry Brigade attached by rope to an LCI were pulled out of their depth when a wave suddenly wrenched the craft away from the beach. One man was saved, but one officer and six men drowned.[27]

Lieutenant David Holbrook of the East Yorkshire Yeomanry (27th Armoured Brigade) likewise recorded two soldiers drowned in rehearsals, whilst Donald S. Vaughan of the 5th Assault Regiment, Royal Engineers in the 79th Armoured Division, recalled 'in the holding camp we had four or five chaps blown up dismantling a Bowes torpedo full of gelignite. Something went wrong and they were killed.'[28] Sergeant Edward Wallace of the 86th (Hertfordshire Yeomanry) Field Regiment, Royal Artillery, in the 50th Northumbrian Division, recalled his men being briefed by a specialist on how to defuse a German Teller mine, when 'the blasted thing blew up on him, left him in bits, and two or three of those with him. Those bits were paraded about the camp so that everybody knew what a Teller mine did to you. Many men went back into their tents and were violently sick.'[29]

Vernon Church, with the 68th Anti-Tank Regiment of the British 49th Division, noted that just before the invasion, his unit 'went on exercise that involved crossing the river. One of the men let go of his rope and was swept away. Our troop officer, Lieutenant Burton, went in to save the man but both were drowned.'[30] In March 1944, Major John Cramphorn of the 13th Parachute Battalion recalled a jump where 'one man's chute became caught in the tail wheel and for over an hour the plane flew round and round with the poor unfortunate man spinning in the slipstream. Eventually, with a motor launch close at hand, the aircraft flew at wave-top height over Studland Bay, and the man's static line was severed. There was no happy ending to the story: but we had volunteered knowing full well the risks, and our morale was not affected in any way.'[31]

Being so unusual and public, this tragic incident imprinted itself on the memory of Marine William Cockburn and at least two other interviewees. Cockburn was aboard *LCG-764*, a converted LCT that carried nineteen sailors and thirty-three Marines manning 4.7-inch guns in two armoured turrets. He never forgot the hot Saturday afternoon in Poole, thronged by civilians and servicemen, all enjoying the sunshine: 'this pleasant scene was shattered by the sudden appearance overhead of an RAF Dakota with its side door open and hanging there by his parachute cords was a paratrooper ... The plane cruised around until a number of small craft had positioned themselves; the plane made a run over the bay, very low and as slow as possible, cutting him free at a height of maybe fifty feet – sadly he fell into shallow water and did not survive.'[32]

Captain Charles R. Cawthon of the 116th Infantry (US 1st Division), based at Tidworth Barracks in Wiltshire recalled that 'a British glider troop's training camp nearby appeared wasteful of human life to the point of disregard; few days passed, it seemed, that a caisson bearing a flag-draped coffin, escorted by troopers in red berets, did not rumble by on the way to the British army cemetery'. Among the several accidental deaths and injuries Cawthon noted was the final moment of a member of his Ammunition and Pioneer Platoon, who triggered a mine laid in the dunes at Slapton. 'There was a blinding flash and a clap of sound, and he disappeared as if by a magician's sleight of hand. The illusion terminated in pieces of anatomy plopping into the sand around us.'[33] Another American officer, Second Lieutenant Wesley R. Ross, with Company 'B' of the US 146th Engineers, recalled four fatalities at various stages of their training:

> I saw two wounded infantrymen, both of whom later died, caused by a faulty 81mm mortar round that exploded in the tube. Later, an infantryman was killed by flying steel fragments while taking a nap in the sand dunes a hundred yards above our demolition area. The day before we left for the marshalling area, we lost Melvin Vest, who was killed when a quarter-pound block of TNT exploded in his hand. I bundled up Vest and hustled him by truck to a nearby hospital, but he died of shock four hours later from extensive damage to his hands, legs, and groin. This was a gut-wrenching disaster and the fact that he was such a neat guitar-playing soldier and so well liked by everyone, made it even more of a tragedy.[34]

Communications Corporal Ernest P. Leh in Company 'E' of the 18th Infantry was waiting with his buddies in Dorchester. Already a combat veteran of Oran and Sicily, his regiment of the 29th Division was the third echelon, due to arrive on Omaha after the 16th and 26th Infantry. The security was so tight, he recollected, that on 1 June 'we were restricted to the camp area and wired in. The place was heavily guarded, with British troops posted along with our own. Evidently, the commanding officers were determined that no one should get out. One man who tried it was shot.'[35]

Airborne forces were particularly prone to accidents, and the final Eagle exercise of the 82nd and 101st Airborne Divisions resulted in a reported five hundred breaks and sprains due to high winds. The regimental surgeon of the 508th Parachute Infantry – whose regiment we met trying deer steaks at Wollaton Park – noted that it took three days to find the remains of a trooper whose parachute was seen to malfunction. 'When we found him, I took his gloves and laundered them carefully three or four times to get the sweet odor of death out of them.' Major David Thomas then wore them himself on D-Day, commenting, 'I'm not superstitious, but I figured that those gloves couldn't be unlucky twice.'[36]

It was the same elsewhere on the waves. Admiral Ramsay noted on 4 May 1944 during the Fabius exercises that 'Our MTBs were shot up on Thursday morning by our *Beaufighters* & many casualties inflicted.'[37] This was the result of the E-boat scare caused by Exercise Tiger, and another craft, *MTB-732*, was later sunk in error by an Allied warship on 28 May. Every war diary and log reveals the same: each unit or organisation preparing for France had suffered fatalities and violent injuries in their preparations over the preceding year. Excluding Exercise Tiger, more were killed in training mishaps around the United Kingdom than were killed on 6 June.

Nevertheless, by the end of May 1944 the great gathering of Allied service personnel were as ready as their commanders could make them. All there was left to do was wait for the weather and the signal to go. Marcus Cunliffe, an intelligence officer with the Royal Tank Regiment in Normandy and later a distinguished professor of American history, observed that his colleagues 'faced a very capable enemy, but in courage, stamina and battle-craft, the British soldier could challenge any in the world. Months and years of training and preparation at every level had preceded the landings. The campaign that ensued would prove how profitably the time had been spent.'[38] This applied equally to the waiting Americans and Canadians, but the essential point was that every one of the 2,876,600 soldiers camped in southern England – the joke of the moment was that Britain was being kept afloat only by the number of barrage balloons attached to her – just before D-Day had experienced far longer and more meaningful combat preparation than their opponents, waiting across the Channel.

As Lieutenant Colonel James Moulton of 48 Royal Marine Commando neatly summarised, 'we could certainly do with more training but there is a limit to the time you can train the way we had been doing, and the tension would now be snapped – better to go and have it over'.[39] Another lieutenant colonel told his second in command, 'You know, there's such a thing as over-training a battalion. That's what I'm afraid of now. I told the brigadier it was hard to keep a training programme going in these circumstances.'[40] Sergeant Mike McKinney with the 16th Infantry, due to land on Omaha, remembered waiting for battle: 'It's your job. You're young. You're invincible.' He thought, '"Other guys are gonna get killed but not me … If a bullet's got my name on it I'm gonna get it; there's nothing I can do about it. Don't worry about it." You develop that kind of attitude. Youth plus fatalism plus faith or trust in a higher power, whatever it is. That kept me in good stead for a long time. I knew my mother was praying hard for me. I knew my fiancée was praying hard. So I figured I was going to be taken care of. A couple of near misses convinced me that I was lucky, so that helped too – I'm Irish.'[41]

The USS *Henrico*, carrying twenty-seven landing craft, embarked the 2nd Battalion of McKinney's 16th Infantry, on 26 May at Weymouth. On board, Harry Cooper recalled: 'us Navy guys knew we were going to hit a beachhead in France for a good week in advance of D-Day, but we didn't know where until we left for Normandy the night of 5 June. We didn't care where the invasion was going to be, or what was going to happen. We just wanted to go out and do it.'[42] Roaming around the *Henrico* in Weymouth was the acclaimed war photographer Robert Capa, with his signature Contax camera slung around his neck. For *Life* magazine, he captured GIs playing craps in an aerial shot; on the top deck, Capa snapped Corporal Samuel M. Fuller, head on an ammunition box, trying to rest. Fuller was a thirty-two-year-old former newspaper reporter, novelist and Hollywood screenwriter who chose to serve in a rifle company. Both he and Capa would bequeath something of D-Day to posterity. In 1978, Sam Fuller, destined to win a Silver Star on D-Day, would direct the film *The Big Red One* in tribute to his old division, whilst Capa would be responsible for the most famous, graphic, grainy images of combat on Omaha Beach.[43]

Taking the 3rd Battalion of the 16th Infantry from Weymouth to Omaha was the 7,000-ton *Empire Anvil*, crewed by a mixture of Royal Navy and merchant navy Britons. New Yorker Joseph L. Argenzio had lied about his age to enlist, and found himself, as a late replacement and two days shy of his seventeenth birthday, walking up the gangplank of the *Anvil* to the jeers and catcalls of the 16th's veterans from North Africa and Sicily: 'Hey, baby face, go home, this is for men, not boy scouts.' 'I kept my exact age a secret,' Argenzio recounted. 'I had not trained with the outfit, in fact had only twelve weeks of basic infantry training.'

There was a debate among the officers as to whether to keep him, partly solved by the ship sailing. 'Okay, we'll keep you, we can't throw you overboard,' they said. 'I mentioned my dad served with the First Division in World War One; I think that helped. So we started having briefings, and they had a layout of Omaha beach and were explaining how we were gonna go in – which company would go here, which there. In the wee hours of the morning we had a non-denominational Mass.'[44]

The presence of British crews and Royal Navy craft at the two US beaches perfectly illustrated the multinationality of every aspect of Overlord. The compliment was returned on Sword Beach, where a flotilla of ten American LCIs landed some of the second wave of the British 3rd Division. Aboard one of them, *LCI-35*, was Ohioan Stanley Galik, the seventh of ten children born to immigrant parents; his father hailed from Poland, his mother from Slovakia. After schooling he joined the Civilian Conservation Corps, enlisting in the US Navy in September 1942. He joined *LCI-35* in North Africa, saw action at Salerno and Anzio before sailing to England in April 1944, when he wrote home: 'Overjoyed above all to be here, cause I sure believe I'm going to like this place a lot. Just think: one doesn't have to learn the language. Had one liberty [shore leave] already and though it was short, had a better time in those few hours than in all the time I had in Africa.' Berthed at Newhaven with Force 'S' on 2 June, Galik recorded, 'entire crew mustered for pre-invasion lectures. All liberties cancelled until further notice.' By three that afternoon, *LCI-35* had 'been stripped of unnecessary gear, finished camouflage painting, now ready and waiting to take on troops'.[45]

Major Kenneth Baxter, with the 2nd Middlesex of the British 3rd Division, recalled that 'we were driven under security escort to the docks at Portsmouth. Once in the docks we were rapidly embarked on *Empire Battleaxe*, carrying the craft of the 537th LCA Flotilla suspended in davits on both port and starboard sides. This vessel was one of a small group carrying the assaulting companies of infantry together with specialised units making up breaching teams and beach signal communications.' At this stage, Baxter and those aboard *Battleaxe* were actually heading for

Sword Beach, though they were not told this until 'well into the Channel when we were issued with further maps, photographs and the last briefing instructions, this time with full place names instead of code references, and any doubts amongst the many guesses as to the true landing areas were finally dispelled'.[46]

Fresh out of Dartmouth Naval College, nineteen-year-old Sub Lieutenant Michael Hutton had served his apprenticeship on the cruiser HMS *Jamaica* as a midshipman, being posted to the battleship HMS *Warspite* just before D-Day. He remembered stopping at Plymouth, 'where we took on a boatload of photographers and war correspondents, two Russians – an admiral and a general – and a rather portly Chinese naval officer; all had been invited to observe the invasion. They were rather unfairly given over to my care – I remember this clearly, because it was the first independent responsibility the Royal Navy ever gave me.'[47] Artillery officer Jack Swaab, due to land in France during D+1, found himself sailing down the Thames on 3 June, having 'passed an enormous gathering of all the different vessels required for an invasion of an enemy coastline. I saw LSIs – the ex-passenger ships whose lifeboats are now assault boats, and from whom the Commandos steal forth in the darkness; and then like one of those old-time ballroom dances, a huge line of LSTs, each with its barrage balloon floating above it. And in between, the grey little ships slid about the grey river – MTBs, corvettes, destroyers and gunboats.'[48]

Anxiety peaked as all waited for the order to depart; Lieutenant Peter Mitchell with the Essex Yeomanry, an artillery unit, remembered 'one particularly aggressive Royal Marine lieutenant sharpening a foot-long commando knife with serrated edges and finding how many hand grenades he could festoon about his body. I only hope he survived.'[49] The Australian Alan Moorhead was killing time in one of the marshalling camps, alongside the troops. 'At the paymaster's tent I asked how much money I could change. "Ten pounds if you like."' The journalist probed, 'Into what currency?' The reply was prompt: 'Francs.' He mused, 'So it was going to be France, then. That was definite. My driver showed that he was feeling the strain of waiting. Everybody felt it. The invasion was already like an over-rehearsed play.'[50] Or, as a veteran of the US 508th Parachute Infantry, kicking his heels in Nottingham, observed: 'You can only do so many practice jumps, only clean your weapons so many times, only run in formation so much, and only dig so many practice foxholes; we wanted to go fight the war for which we were trained.'[51]

Captain Alistair Bannerman, commanding the Anti-Tank Platoon of the 2nd Royal Warwicks in the 3rd Division bound for Sword, began a letter to his wife on 28 May, 'I have tried explaining to my own platoon that we're about to make history and that one day their children will read of our deeds in the history books.' Before the war, Bannerman (a descendant of the 1905–8 Prime Minister) had been a professional actor, sharing the stage with Michael Redgrave, Alec Guinness, Peggy Ashcroft and Anthony Quayle. He observed in a surprisingly downbeat tone that 'to soldiers, Churchill's radio rhetoric sounds a bit embarrassing. They have no great faith in the new world, or any belief in any great liberating mission. They know it's going to be a charnel house. All they want is to put an end to it all, and get back to "Civvy Street", to their homes, their private lives, their wives and loved ones. Yet, we're all here, we're all going, as ordered, willingly into battle.' Later, Bannerman would be captured along with his unfinished letter, which was translated and forwarded to Rommel.[52]

Some were euphoric, others resigned, but the waiting got men down, and Alan Moorhead remembered the 'dead, heavy mood' that had settled over the country, 'an emptiness and a mental weariness' as soldiers and civilians waited, observing 'a sense of implacable helplessness. You were without identity, a number projected in unrelated space among a million other numbers. All around in the mess, one could read the same ideas in the faces of soldiers going by. No wonder another twenty men had deserted that night.'[53]

Telegraphist George Downing was aboard HMS *Glenearn*, an assault ship which was carrying two flotillas (the 535th and 543rd, of twelve craft each) of Royal Marine-manned LCAs bound for Sword Beach. His most poignant memory of the invasion was of an incident before they even sailed – the suicide of a nervous American soldier who took his own life on the quayside, while waiting to embark.[54]

Having set sail, the mishaps continued. Several of the 2nd East Yorks on their way to Sword recollected a Sten gun, loaded with a fresh magazine by its owner and put on a mess table. The pitching and rolling of their landing craft caused the sub-machine gun to fall onto the deck. 'It went off with several rounds ricocheting round the steel bulkheads. A lad got hit in the heel. Another, Sergeant Eric Ibbetson, bled to death when a bullet cut his femoral artery.'[55]

Lieutenant Jimmy Green, aboard another landing ship, the *Empire Javelin*, recalled arriving at Weymouth harbour to take on his GIs. 'They were a friendly, but shy, bunch of fresh-faced country lads who must have felt at home in Ivybridge, the small town in Devon where they had trained for the invasion. We had a series of briefings in the Weymouth Pavilion, for I was to be leader of the first wave, and it was my task to land Company "A" of the 116th Infantry at Vierville-sur-Mer at 0630 hours.' Green remembered, 'We were referred to in the Flotilla as the "Suicide Wave", something we felt with pride represented the danger we faced, rather than the prospect of casualties. We had trained day and night, including fog. Many of the men in 551st Flotilla had taken part in earlier landings in the Mediterranean. Like so many on D-Day, we felt we simply had a job to do and that we were ready for it.'[56]

Seaman Charles 'Buster' Shaeff was a confident youth from Norristown, Pennsylvania, who had volunteered for the US Navy at seventeen after seeking his parents' permission, because he didn't want to be drafted into the army. 'When we got to England, we knew there was going to be an invasion and we would be involved, but we didn't know dates or

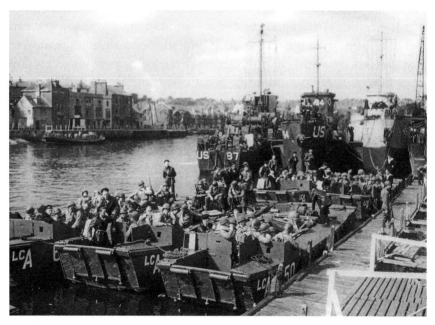

Late May 1944, in the southern English port of Weymouth, US Coast Guard LCI Flotilla 4, including *LCIs-87, 84* and *497*, is preparing to cross the Channel. Within days they will land men from V Corps on Omaha, where *497* will be wrecked. In the foreground are little Royal Navy LCAs, which will be taken aboard their transports for the voyage. (NARA)

anything,' he recounted. Trained as a machinist's mate to operate some of the six smaller LCVPs carried by *LST-291*, his initial task was to ferry part of the 2nd Ranger Battalion to climb the Pointe du Hoc, west of Omaha. As they left Weymouth he 'wasn't apprehensive about going in; I was an eighteen-year-old kid who figured nothing would happen to me. You think – if it happens, it'll happen to someone else.'[57]

Also leaving Weymouth for Omaha, and equally confident, was Major John F. Dulligan. A native of Worcester, Massachusetts, and commissioned in 1933, he had invaded North Africa with the 1st Division in 1942, fought in Tunisia, then Sicily, and was now a battalion executive officer with the 26th Infantry. Watching his 2nd Battalion, he penned a letter home: 'I love these men. They sleep all over the ship, on the decks, in, on top and underneath the vehicles. They smoke, play cards, wrestle and indulge in general horseplay. They gather round in groups and talk mostly about girls, home and experiences, with and without girls. They are good soldiers, the best in the world.'[58]

Omaha-bound Sergeant Hyam Haas, a draftee from Brooklyn, remembered the religious services before they left their billets in Devon. 'We Jewish men were led by a rabbi in a long beard completely covered with his prayer shawl and phylacteries; alongside was a Catholic Mass led by a priest with full religious dress and nearby a Protestant service led by a minister in Navy uniform.' Then Haas and his 467th Anti-Aircraft Artillery Battalion moved towards their marshalling areas. 'When we left Exmouth on 30 May, the townsfolk lined the streets and cheered us on – we noticed many of them in tears. It seemed as if the entire nation was in motion … This was the biggest parade ever; the only thing missing were the marching bands. There was constant cheering as we went through towns – everyone knew what was happening.'

Haas was aware they were on the move on US Memorial Day, then fixed for 30 May every year (though now the last Monday of May), the unofficial start of the summer vacation season. (It was initiated in 1868 as Decoration Day, when the graves of the Civil War dead were decorated with flowers and wreaths.) Haas thought his 'the biggest Decoration Day parade of them all.'[59]

Later, British Lieutenant Peter Mitchell experienced the incredible organisation of Neptune, right down to a hot drink before departure. 'At midnight on 2 June our convoy began a carefully timed journey to the embarkation point. Halfway into our slow progress a soldier stepped out of the hedge with his arm raised to halt us. "Are you 'A' Troop, Essex

Yeomanry, sir?" he asked. "Yes," I said. Out of the darkness appeared six soldiers bearing enormous enamel jugs full of steaming tea. After this illustration of efficient planning, I really began to feel that our invasion was bound to succeed.'[60]

First to leave were the minesweepers. Alan Johnson was aboard HMS *Onyx*, which bore the pennant number J-221. Only when he read the signal flashed at them, 'Good luck, minesweeping flotilla; hope to see you all return', did he realise the danger of the task ahead. Mustered on the quarterdeck with the rest of the ship's company, Johnson remembered their skipper's address that evening: "'Right, lads, I suppose you've all guessed where we're going. It's the Big One. I know you'll do your duty. If the ship ahead hits a mine, we will not stop to pick up survivors. We're going to Action Stations shortly. Good luck and God bless us all." We then received leaflets bearing a message from Eisenhower on the importance of the invasion in freeing Europe.'[61] Many signals were exchanged by semaphore and Aldis lamp, but among the more memorable was that sent by Commodore Cyril Douglas-Pennant, commanding Force 'G', from his flagship, HMS *Bulolo*. A keen cricketer, his message read: 'Best of luck to you all. Keep a good length, and your eye on the middle stump, and we shall soon have the enemy all out.'

Sergeant Hyam Haas on his LCT recalled leaving Portland harbour: 'amidst much whistle blowing, it seemed as if every ship was blowing its fog horn. There were ships and boats of every description everywhere. I couldn't help reflecting that we had, since leaving Exmouth, seen and were part of one of the greatest spectacular events ever. Fast cutters pulled up nearby and men with megaphones were shouting "Good luck" at us. They were cheering at us and we were cheering back. We took our place in a long line of LCTs and made our way into the English Channel.'[62]

The security was so tight and effective that at least one medical detachment thought they were bound for the West African Gold Coast (the nation of Ghana in pre-independence days), rather than Gold Beach, and even at this stage, many troops and sailors had yet to be told of their precise destination, place names and timings being withheld from all but commanding officers and ships' captains until they were at sea. Alan Wellington, a junior merchant navy officer, had just returned from Egypt when he was assigned to the 8,000-ton troopship *City of Canterbury*, bound for an 'unknown destination'. As troop movements and convoys were generally shrouded in mystery until the last possible moment, he was not unduly surprised when they were ordered to drop anchor 'somewhere along the south coast'. They were then 'surrounded by landing craft carrying GIs. The assault boats and troops were loaded onto our ship – we had derricks, handy for bringing craft aboard and lowering them back on the water', and only when under way did his skipper reveal that they were bound for Normandy and 'somewhere called Omaha Beach'.[63]

Dennis Chaffer found himself sailing from Southampton on board Landing Craft, Flak *LCF-34*, an LCT converted into an anti-aircraft barge. He recollected that 'our captain organised a competition to see who could find our landing beach. He produced a map which covered the coastline for Holland, Belgium, France (north and south), Norway and Denmark. At sixpence a go per person, the prize was a heady two pounds seven shillings, which I won.'[64] Mancunian Harold Addie was itching to escape the boredom of a job that he disliked and remembered the moment he received his call-up papers in June 1943 as 'the happiest day of my life'. A year later found him in Southampton aboard *LCT-501* as one of its fourteen-man crew. 'We were not allowed ashore, nor to use a phone. We set off on the evening of 5 June, but it was at sea that our skipper opened a sealed package and found we were to cross the Channel and deliver our Canadians, with their six tanks, to a place called Juno.'[65]

As *LCT-884*, leading the 24th LCT Flotilla bound for Gold, pulled out of port, its skipper asked Sub Lieutenant Dick Boustred to fetch him his sealed orders. 'I asked him for the key to the secure cupboard, but search as he might in his pockets, it could not be found.' With a flash of inspiration, Boustred turned to their passengers, armoured crewmen of the Hertfordshire Yeomanry, and asked loudly, 'Are there any professional burglars on board?' As he recalled: 'Very soon a burly soldier with a figure not unlike that of a circus strongman came up and said, "Whadya wont dun?" I told him, and in about twenty seconds he had picked the lock, and the sealed orders were on the bridge.'[66]

Leading Aircraftman James Douglas was a member of the advance party of No. 126 Wing of the RCAF; given a Diamond T wrecker truck with two other fitters, his task was also to land at Juno and help establish the first airstrip for Canadian Spitfires in Normandy. Surrounded by tugs towing concrete blocks for the Mulberry harbour and other craft, he had little idea of the gravity of what lay ahead until the church service aboard his LST as they left the Solent. 'In the Canadian padre's prayer were words I will always remember: "Some of you may die for others to live", followed by the hymn "Take my life and let it be/Consecrated, Lord, to Thee" – now, didn't that tell us something?'[67]

Canadian vehicles were aboard another tank landing craft, *LCT-941*, which was towing a barrage balloon for protection from air attack, noted Signaller Harry Farrar. He and his mates of the 37th LCT Flotilla were based on the 'stone frigate' of HMS *Shrapnel* (in reality the South Western Hotel in Southampton). He recalled their departure for Juno Beach: 'All the ships and other shore establishments gave us a grand send-off with hooters sounding and cranes dipping in salute. It really was quite moving and this carried on until we were out of the Solent.'[68]

Perhaps it was Shimi Lovat, the thirty-two-year-old brigadier leading many of the commandos, who best caught the eve-of-invasion mood. He had kept his men busy with swimming and athletics competitions. In the brigade football final, the navy beat the army – 45 Royal Marine Commando triumphing over No. 3 Commando. Then followed a service in a sodden Hampshire field. 'I wish you all the best of luck in what lies ahead,' he told his men. 'This will be the greatest military venture of all time. The Commando Brigade has an important role to play, and one hundred years from now your children's children will say, "They must have been giants in those days."'[69]

18

Weathermen

'On 20 January 1961, during their ride to the Capitol for his inauguration, President-elect John F. Kennedy asked his predecessor why the Normandy invasion had been so successful. Eisenhower's answer was simple – "'Because we had better meteorologists than the Germans.'"
Charles C. Bates, former chief scientist for the US Coast Guard

STRAINING AT THE leash as they were, the Allied fleet could not depart without one final piece of the jigsaw puzzle: the right weather. Here, too, the great disparity between the intelligence services of the Allies and of the Germans showed up in their meteorological forecasting. As weather was considered a matter of national security, neither side issued public weather forecasts for the duration of the war. The 29 May 1944 edition of *Life* magazine portentously carried a front-cover photograph of the air general 'Tooey' Spaatz – but even his huge bomber fleets were at the mercy of the elements. At the end of the day, mankind was still unable to precisely anticipate or control the vagaries of the weather gods.

Thursday 1 June had been the date finally agreed six months earlier at the Tehran Conference for initiating Overlord; it subsequently slipped to Monday 5 June, just before the full moon of the sixth. Yet the actual decision to launch – incorporating a perilous sea journey across over one hundred miles of English Channel, with air cover deemed vital, paratroopers to be dropped and gliders to be landed on target – was subject to fair weather.

Admiral Ramsay may have been playing cricket the previous week, but according to the forecasters, the fine weather would deteriorate. After

Whitsun, the Wehrmacht lining the Calvados shores breathed a sigh of disbelief that the Allies had not taken advantage of the excellent conditions, while war correspondent Alan Moorhead recalled, 'May turned into June. Surely it could not be much longer now? Standing on the South Downs, one could see the Channel, bright and clear and calm. It was a hot, midsummer sun. The country never looked more calm and beautiful.'[1]

In 1939, over two years before America came into the war, General MacArthur had tasked one of his staff officers to write a paper on amphibious operations. The obscure major, then stationed in the Philippines, concluded that a landing from the sea across a defended beach was the most difficult operation in war. By 1944, Major Eisenhower, now himself a general, had to deliver on the very difficulties he had foreseen. Furthermore, he would have to base his decision to go on the advice of his meteorologists.

From its publication in 1959, Cornelius Ryan's *The Longest Day* (and the subsequent movie version of 1962) has dominated the weather story of Overlord – where Group Captain James Stagg of the Royal Air Force, SHAEF's senior weatherman, advised postponement of the invasion early on 4 June, for twenty-four hours; then later offered Eisenhower a window of barely adequate conditions to launch the invasion on the 6th.[2] What popular memory has glossed over was that Stagg and his US deputy, Colonel Donald N. Yates, director of weather for the Eighth Air Force, were merely reporting to the Supreme Commander the conclusions of three two-man teams of forecasters who also attended the SHAEF weather conferences. They were from the UK Meteorological Office (the 'Met Office') at Dunstable, the USAAF at the Eighth Air Force headquarters in High Wycombe, and the Royal Navy at Portsmouth.[3]

Lieutenant Commander Lawrence Hogben of the Royal New Zealand Navy and Commander Geoffrey Wolfe, RN, comprised the latter team. Hogben recollected, 'We six never agreed about anything except that Stagg was not a good meteorologist and that he was a bit of a glory hound.'[4] Contrary to his Hollywood alter ego, Stagg was a dour forty-three-year-old Scot of humble origins who had led an Arctic polar expedition in 1932–3, and was at heart a geophysicist; his only forecasting experience stemmed from two years in the Iraqi desert. The war found him superintendent of the Kew Gardens Observatory before being tasked to coordinate army and RAF forecasting. It was his administrative skills that led to his appointment as SHAEF's weatherman, which created distance between the temporary RAF group captain and the career meteorologists working under him.[5]

Among the hundreds of thousands impatiently waiting the forecasters' verdict was Captain Charles R. Cawthon of the 116th Infantry. A pre-war journalist and editor of the Charlottesville *Daily Progress*, he had joined the Virginia National Guard in 1940 to soldier with friends, rather than be drafted to an unfamiliar unit. Commanding HQ Company of the Second Battalion he, like the rest of the Stonewall Brigade, was kicking his heels aboard the attack transport *Thomas Jefferson* in Portland harbour. He noted, 'The weather was of that "un-rare" English June, that threatens both fair and foul, ready to go either way'.[6]

In the midst of the excellent conditions of 29 May, Stagg had given an optimistic long-range forecast for the first week of June, and Bertram Ramsay noted on Tuesday 30 May, 'another boiling hot day', though 'slightly cooler' the day afterwards. By Thursday 1 June, the admiral recorded, 'A dull morning, overcast with slight rain. Cooler. No doubt the general lull is but a precursor of the storm to follow.' On 2 June, '1000 hours: Commander's meeting at which main topic was the change for the worse in the weather, affecting air [operations] generally & the carriage of airborne troops in particular.'[7] Nevertheless, at midnight on the 2nd, the first elements of the invasion armada – two 27-ton midget submarines, *X-20* and *X-23*, which were to mark the paths to Sword and Juno beaches in Operation Gambit – left their berths for Normandy. Sub Lieutenant Jim Booth, aboard *X-23*, recollected, 'Basically, they were thirty-foot-long smelly tin cans, manned by four of us. On the surface they pitched, rolled and shipped water. We went across under tow by a big submarine on 3 June, and lay on the bottom that night and the next day, ready to surface and put light up our beacon for the assault fleet.'[8]

Outside Portsmouth, a tense meeting was held at 1615 on 3 June at Southwick House, to where all the senior commanders had relocated, to give the go-ahead for the invasion. Ramsay had moved into the building, while Montgomery was ensconced at Broomfield House in Southwick village. Eisenhower's personal office tent, sleeping trailer, a mobile office and telephone switchboard, trailers with maps and teletype machines, and tents for senior aides, weather maps, guards and cooks were in woods a mile distant, code-named 'Sharpener'. From there, the Supreme Commander maintained contact with Washington and 10 Downing Street, though the Prime Minister, unhelpfully breathing down

A pair of Royal Navy X-Craft miniature submarines. Originally designed to approach and sink the battleship *Tirpitz* in Norway, X-Craft were used initially to survey the Normandy coast. In Operation Gambit, *X-20* and *X-23* lurked off Juno and Sword beaches, surfacing before dawn on 6 June and, using lights and flags, directed the fleet to their positions. (NARA)

everyone's necks, lurked nearby at Droxford station, occupying the royal train commandeered from the King over the weekend of 2–4 June.[9]

Churchill had, in his own words, 'busied myself with the many technical matters of *Overlord* preparations'. His *Second World War* itemises his interest in everything from setting up a weekly Overlord committee to review progress, to conferences and memos about the Mulberry harbours, the airborne assault, waterproofing of DD tanks, tallies of aircraft manufacture, the naval bombardment, amongst a whole host of other subjects not usually found in the job description for a British prime minister.[10] It irritated his CIGS Sir Alan Brooke no end, who recorded his exasperation: 'My God, how tired I am of working for him! He can never grasp a whole plan. His method is entirely opportunistic, gathering one flower here, another there!'[11]

After the settled period which had produced the Whitsun weather, the three SHAEF teams produced forecasts that contradicted one another. Both British groups predicted a sudden and serious decline, with storms that would rule out air support of the invasion and make a landing potentially treacherous. Yet the USAAF forecasters, Irving P. Krick and Ben Holtzman, thought better weather was in the offing, which would enable the 5 June invasion. 'The Americans had previously been providing forecasts for daylight bombing runs over Germany and relied on analogue forecasting, comparing forty years of daily weather maps, and from these they figured the weather would improve. We felt that this was pure bunk,' remembered Hogben. A former Rhodes Scholar at Oxford, who knew a thing or two about storms on the high seas having taken part in the hunts for the *Bismarck* and *Scharnhorst*, Hogben continued, 'We used data garnered from special weather recce [reconnaissance] flights, ship observations, UK weather sites and pinched what we could from the Germans – once we broke their weather codes – and redrew our charts every few hours ... None of us were operating with any of the technology and equipment that our successors today take for granted, such as satellites, weather radar, computer modelling and instant communications, and predicting conditions more than a day or two in advance was hazardous. All we knew was there were several storms blowing across the Atlantic towards us, any one of which would have whipped up the waters where the fleet was gathering, and provided unwelcome cloud over Normandy.'[12] There is evidence the US team even telephoned the civilian forecasters at the Met Office, C. K. M. Douglas and Sverre Petterssen, to pressure them to change their unfavourable forecast. This was the same C. K. M. Douglas who had briefed Spaatz and Doolittle in 1942 that 'a forecast for more than a day or two ahead in this country can be nothing more than speculation'.[13]

When the Met Office team demurred, the US meteorologists pressed their case with Spaatz, but Stagg, the mediator who had failed to find a consensus, was forced to tell Eisenhower on 3 June that the weather two days hence was unlikely to meet the criteria laid down by the Overlord planners.[14] Aboard the cruiser USS *Augusta* in Plymouth, Bradley was preparing for the Channel crossing; he recalled the forecast on Saturday 3 June: 'Mist from Sunday to Wednesday, with low clouds and reduced visibility in the mornings. Winds not to exceed seventeen to twenty-two knots. Choppy water in the Channel with five-foot breakers. A four-foot surf on the beaches.'[15]

A go/no-go decision was postponed until dawn on Sunday 4 June. Sverre Petterssen was a respected but temperamental Norwegian Air Service forecaster who felt the USAAF officers, Krick in particular, were

The Normandy situation map erected in the former drawing room of Southwick House. In 1964 Eisenhower and veteran broadcaster Walter Cronkite (left) returned to the scene of the historic decision to launch D-Day in the face of appalling weather reports. The map – custom built by the Chad Valley Toy Company – remains in situ to this day. (Getty Images)

talking nonsense and at a 'hairy 0415 hours briefing' on 4 June at Southwick, presented his own weather map showing a violent storm brewing.[16] Ramsay recorded the report was 'bad. The low cloud predicted would prohibit the use of airborne troops, the majority of air action, including air spotting [for naval gunfire]. The sea conditions were unpromising but not prohibitive.'[17]

There is no doubt the moment weighed very heavily on Eisenhower's shoulders; going round the room, he found Ramsay neutral, Montgomery in favour, Tedder against. 'Weighing all the factors, I decided that the attack would have to be postponed,' Eisenhower wrote in his 1948 memoir *Crusade in Europe*.[18] He didn't add that Montgomery didn't merely advise they 'go', but insisted upon it, 'regardless of casualties or air support – if we didn't have it, the other fellow wouldn't have it either'. This stirred up great antipathy with the two airmen, Tedder and Leigh-Mallory, as well as Ramsay.

Pending further reviews of the weather that day, everything would be delayed by twenty-four hours and the code word 'Bowsprit' was sent to those ships at sea, recalling them. Having furthest to go, convoy U 2 was already on its way to Utah Beach and failed to heed the summons. Captain Richard Courage in the Southwick war room had to despatch a Walrus seaplane and Admiral Moon a destroyer, USS *Forrest*, before it was eventually turned around, enduring several nerve-wracking hours lest this flotilla attempt to assault the Continent alone. The signal 'Ripcord plus 24' was likewise transmitted to the waiting airborne forces, warning them to stand down temporarily.[19]

Meanwhile, off Normandy, the *X-23* had surfaced, Jim Booth noted, only to be told, 'the invasion has gone back twenty-four hours. So down we went again.'[20] 'From midday on the 4th', Ramsay observed, 'the weather got progressively worse. Force "U" had a bad time in regaining shelter and will have suffered great discomfort.'[21] Commander Denis Glover, in charge of *LCI-516*, recollected, 'What a night – dark and wet, with just the sort of sea that makes the old tub wallow like a lovesick hippopotamus. All right for sailors, but I'm thinking about the troops.'[22] Sub Lieutenant Leslie Hasker, aboard the minesweeper HMS *Chamois*, had sailed from the River Clyde on 2 June and out into the Irish Sea, accompanied by the cruiser HMS *Belfast*. 'We went around Land's End, and along the south coast. We kept close to land and could see the holiday crowds on the beach. About noon on 4 June off Falmouth we received the Admiralty signal, "Regatta postponed 24 hours".'[23] In the intervening time Admiral Ramsay managed to get those vessels in need refuelled, and noted: 'No enemy reactions' – this was where the absence of Luftwaffe and Kriegsmarine patrols told against the Germans.

At Southwick, there were two more weather conferences on 4 June, at 1715 and 2100 hours. Outside, the trees were buffeted by a hard wind and raindrops beat against the windows of the Georgian house. On the basis of a single weather ship, stationed six hundred miles west of Northern Ireland, reporting a rising barometer, and a neutral Irish light-house keeper, Stagg advised that the weather could improve to winds of Force 3–4 (up to 18mph) – one of the basic requirements for landing craft – by Monday evening, 5 June, along the French coast. At the nine o'clock meeting, noted Ramsay, 'we decided to continue with the oper-ation as ordered. The grounds were not good and we were obviously taking a big chance, but it seemed to be Tuesday or not this week at all.'

Eisenhower recalled, 'The conference on the evening of 4 June presented little, if any, added brightness to the picture of the morning, and tension mounted even higher because the inescapable consequences of postponement were almost too bitter to contemplate.'[24] At 2145 hours, Eisenhower announced his decision: 'I'm quite positive we must give the order. I don't like it, but there it is. I don't see how we can possibly do anything else.' His decision, however, would be confirmed by a last, early-morning weather conference at Southwick: the final result would be right up to the wire.

The Irishman was Ted Sweeney, keeper of the Blacksod lighthouse, County Mayo, in a remote stretch of north-west Ireland, who phoned weather observations through to the Met Office at Dunstable under a secret agreement concluded between London and neutral Dublin in 1939. Sweeney recalled sending his 4 June report: 'heavy rain and drizzle cleared, cloud at nine hundred feet and visibility on land and sea very clear', and was immediately challenged: '"Please check and repeat the whole report." I was wondering what was wrong. I thought I had made some error or something like that. They sent a second message to me about an hour later to please check and repeat again. I thought this was a bit strange so I checked and repeated again. It never dawned on me that this was the weather for invading or anything like that.'[25]

Given the specific moon and tidal requirements for the landing, Hogben recalled they had just six possible days to invade in June: 5th–7th and 19th–21st. 'We worked out the odds on the weather on any one of those four days conforming to our needs as being 13–1 against. So meteorologically, D-Day was bound to be a gamble against the odds.'[26] Admiral Alan G. Kirk, commanding the Western Task Force, recorded the factors that needed to come together for the invasion: 'The night before D-Day had to be reasonably light so that convoys could keep station with ships darkened,' he wrote. 'Airborne operations also required this, necessitating a night with a full moon, or nearly so.' Next, Kirk identified that 'H-Hour needed one hour of daylight before the initial landings to enable bombarding ships to neutralise German batteries and drench the landing beaches', but it needed to be 'sufficiently before high water for the demolition parties to remove beach obstacles while still dry'.

However, it also had to be 'sufficiently after low water in order to permit the landing on certain British beaches where sand bars prevented an assault until two or three hours later'. Ideally, the day would be fixed to ensure 'a second high water in daylight to permit maximum unloading'. In conclusion, wrote Kirk, 'the only dates on which all these factors were available were 21–23 May; 5–7 and 19–21 June, or 3–5 July', though Stagg later observed that if they waited for the perfect set 'it would take 140 years'.[27]

A myth has grown up that the Allies spotted the break in the storm, whereas the Germans did not – but this is playing fast and loose with history. In fact, the Reich had excellent meteorologists, and an adequate number of weather reports, gathered from all parts of occupied Europe by weather reconnaissance flights, U-boats – though most of their weather ships had been captured – automatic stations on remote islands, as well as data harvested from intercepted Russian meteorology. However, as the charts in the National Meteorological Archive in Exeter show, Allied weather mapping was better, being drawn from more sources, and – as with their intelligence agencies – the Luftwaffe, Kriegsmarine and *Heer* (Army) failed to coordinate their forecasting.

The German Meteorological Library has recently rediscovered the maps of the Luftwaffe's *Zentrale-Wetterdienst-Gruppe* (ZWG – Main Meteorological Centre). Created in Potsdam in 1938 to provide meteorology to OKW – founded at the same time – its chief, Professor Werner Schwerdtfeger, oversaw the hand-drawing of weather maps and forecasts for all combat areas four times a day. They, too, unquestionably forecast the poor weather front of 4–5 June, and anticipated conditions moderating on 6 June.[28] Schwerdtfeger's forecast issued at noon on 4 June was actually similar to Stagg's for D-Day: 'prevailing winds of Beaufort Force five, varying between four and six, equivalent to 15–23 knots'.[29]

In Paris, Oberst Professor Walter Stöbe, chief Luftwaffe meteorologist for France, concurred, as did Dr Müller, chief meteorologist at OB West. However, the Germans, with no experience of amphibious assaults, had applied *different criteria* for a successful invasion. The Allies would choose to land after low tide, with the beach obstacles exposed, one hour after dawn to enable accurate naval bombardment and aerial bombing. A full moon was preferred to enable the airborne assault to identify their drop zones. The Germans expected the seaborne assault at or near high tide, covering the beach obstacles, in order to minimise the killing zone from landing craft to shore cover, at or before dawn, and under cover of darkness. Therefore a full moon featured less in their calculations. Furthermore, they refused to believe the Allies would risk their landing fleet in conditions worse than Force three (8–12mph), whereas Ramsay was content with Force four (13–18mph), and had on 4 June labelled worse sea conditions 'unpromising but not prohibitive'.

A final twist to the mismatch of expectations was that OB West and the Luftwaffe used the tidal measurements for the Pas-de-Calais – perhaps in response to Fortitude – in their calculations of danger periods for an invasion, whereas those of Normandy were different.[30] Thus when Rommel consulted Major Heinz Lettau, his meteorologist at Army Group 'B', the advice he received was there could be no invasion during the next fortnight on account of the weather, and on that basis the field marshal drove home to Germany early on 4 June.[31] His English-speaking Ia (chief of operations staff), Oberst Hans-Georg von Tempelhof, went on leave at the same time.[32] In the western suburbs of Paris, Rundstedt dined at his favourite restaurant, *Le Coq Hardi* in Bougival, as usual; his Ic (intelligence chief), Oberst Wilhelm Meyer-Detring, had scuttled back to the Fatherland for a long-overdue break, and Admiral Theodor Krancke, commanding *Marinegruppenkommando West*, likewise departed to visit his fleet in Bordeaux – and cancelled maritime patrols out of Cherbourg because of the weather.

This wisdom was repeated down the chain of command in the Seventh Army. In his office overlooking Saint-Lô's cathedral, the intelligence officer of Marcks' 84th Corps, Major Friedrich Hayn, noted the forecast was 'such heavy sea states that a landing would appear practically impossible'.[33] Hauptmann Eberhard Wagemann, the duty officer at the 21st Panzer Division in Saint-Pierre-sur-Dives, south-west of Caen, was deeply troubled that both his commander, Generalleutnant Feuchtinger, and the chief of staff, Oberstleutnant Wolf-Götz, Freiherr von Berlichingen, were loafing in Paris: he thought their actions disloyal to their men.[34] His comrade, Major Hans von Luck, leading the 125th Panzer Grenadier Regiment, recorded, 'the evening of 5 June 1944 was unpleasant. Normandy was showing its bad side; during the day there had been rain and high winds. We did not anticipate any landings.'[35]

Eisenhower held his final go/no-go weather conference at four in the morning on 5 June, writing of the 'wind of almost hurricane proportions shaking and shuddering' his 'Sharpener' camp; that the 'mile-long trip through muddy roads to the naval headquarters [Southwick] was anything but a cheerful one, since it seemed impossible that in such conditions there was any reason for even discussing the situation'. A fire had been lit in the grate to take the chill from the midsummer early morning; Southwick's chef served fresh coffee in porcelain cups and saucers; heavy blackout curtains hid the wind and rain lashing the tall windows; the dozen or so senior officers sat around the conference table; tension and cigarette smoke filled the air.

Stagg began, confirming the newly predicted high pressure was holding and building. Ramsay noted, 'this time the prophets came in smiling'.[36] Hogben mused, 'I was scared – I think we all were – of getting it wrong; we knew we were making history.'[37] Eisenhower looked around the room: his principal three commanders, Ramsay, Leigh-Mallory and Montgomery, all advised 'go!' There was a long pause while Eisenhower wrestled in silence, weighing the evidence. He sat, he paced, he smoked, brow furrowed. The seconds recorded by the ticking carriage clock on the marble mantelpiece multiplied into minutes. 'The time was then 4:15 a.m.,' remembered Eisenhower. 'I quickly announced the decision to go ahead with the attack on 6 June.' By most accounts, he looked up and said: 'OK. We'll go on 6 June.' No one present disagreed.[38]

The British CIGS, Field Marshal Brooke, who wasn't present, was full of foreboding: 'I am very uneasy about the whole operation. At best, it will fall so far short of the expectation of the bulk of the people, namely all those who know nothing of its difficulties. At worst, it may well be the most ghastly disaster of the whole war. I wish to God it were safely over' – which demonstrated just how out of touch a career soldier could get.[39] A more positive Ramsay vouchsafed to his journal, 'we must trust in our invisible assets to tip the balance in our favour [his only reference to Ultra in the journal] – and shall require all the help that God can give us and I cannot believe that this will not be forthcoming'.[40] Deep underground in the map room of his secret headquarters in London's government district of Whitehall, Clementine Churchill had joined her husband as he looked over the final dispositions and plan of attack. 'Do you realise', the Prime Minister turned to her, 'that by the time you wake up in the morning, twenty thousand men may have been killed?'[41]

Captain Charles Cawthon of the 116th Infantry recalled the moment word came that the invasion was on. 'Signal lamps set up a frenzy of blinking; that afternoon the anti-submarine net across the harbor curved open, and the *Thomas Jefferson* churned out into the wind-roughened waters of the Channel. Vessels of all shapes and sizes, towing barrage balloons as if in some gigantic, colorless carnival procession, were before, behind and to either side'.[42] Having unleashed his subordinates like a pack of greyhounds, Eisenhower was about to head back to Sharpener. But then he paused, drew out a pen and sat at the conference table, scrawling a quick note. It was a memo to himself, the tension evident in his handwriting: 'Our landings in the Cherbourg–Havre area have failed to gain a satisfactory foothold and I have withdrawn the troops', it began. 'My decision to attack at this time and place was based upon the best information available. The troops, the air and the navy did all that bravery and devotion to duty could do. If any blame or fault attaches to the attempt it is mine alone.' Sixty-six words – it contained several insertions and crossings out; distractedly, he dated it 5 July, rather than June, and folded it untidily into his wallet. Commander Harry C. Butcher, his naval aide, found it months later and kept it.

Those sixty-six words explain why the modest Kansan became Supreme Commander and, later, a two-term president. He had no pretensions; was prepared to shoulder the blame if things went wrong. As *The Longest Day* author Cornelius Ryan observed, 'apart from the four stars of his rank, a single ribbon of decorations above his breast pocket and the flaming shoulder patch of SHAEF, Eisenhower shunned all distinguishing marks'.[43] It was his self-effacing humility of character that those around him recalled, rather than his bearing or the trappings of his office: he had no need for flags, framed directives or signed photographs of the great to remind him of his job.

Eisenhower's tortuous decision was the correct call – by the afternoon of 6 June, the conditions had moderated on the Normandy beaches to 'mainly sunny skies, northwest winds around fifteen mph and a temperature of 59°F (fifteen degrees Celsius)'.[44]

In speculating what would have happened if the poor weather had persisted on 6 June, leading to postponement until the nineteenth, the New Zealander Hogben stated, 'As it happened, on 17 June, all six of us produced a forecast for the nineteenth for almost perfect conditions – the invasion would definitely have gone ahead, and would have been an utter catastrophe. Complete failure – for on 19 June the biggest storm of the twentieth century lashed the Channel and I doubt many landing craft would have even made it to the beaches. They would all have been swamped with the high winds. It does not bear thinking about.'[45]

Recent statistical analysis supports this. The storm was a 'once in forty years' event, a tempest of slightly less ferocity having lashed the Calvados coast in February 1905, emphasising how lucky Eisenhower was to have opted to go on 6 June. Furthermore, the builders of Mulberry 'A' off Omaha – completely wrecked in the squall – were extremely unfortunate. At the height of the gale, which hit two weeks after D-Day, the waves

The Overlord meteorologists were aware that violent storms often blew in from the Atlantic to batter the Normandy coast. Much documented was the hurricane of February 1905, which threw huge columns of water at the future invasion beaches and sites for the two artificial harbours. In June 1944, the Allied weathermen spotted a lull in the bad weather, but the tempest that began on 19 June replicated the violence of 1905. Postponing the invasion from 6 June to the nineteenth would thus have been disastrous for D-Day and the landings would have failed. (Author's collection)

crashing against the American harbour were often ten feet above the norm, whereas those hitting Mulberry 'B' were less, at an average of five feet; in either case that represented a huge extra volume of water being hurled at excessive speeds, for which the Phoenix caissons simply had not been designed. Ramsay's Neptune had incorporated so many variables, and included excessive redundancy, but no one had – or could have – anticipated the hurricane of the century.[46]

In the late afternoon of 5 June, another senior commander held his usual weekly conference with his subordinates. They discussed training programmes and the work of their soldiers. Turning to intelligence matters, and looking at the wintry weather outside, he quipped that he had heard on good authority that the invasion 'would come between 3–10 June, during the period of the full moon'. Pleased with his little joke, at about 7 p.m. Generalleutnant Wilhelm Richter of the 716th Infantry Division brought his command conference in Caen to a close. Had his sentries been able to see that far through the murk of the angry weather, within the hour they might have glimpsed the first British minesweepers that hove into sight of the French coast.[47]

Hogben and the other forecasters afterwards received Bronze Stars for their professionalism, but if one accepts Patton's dictum that 'if everybody's thinking alike, then somebody's not thinking', the fact that they disagreed might actually have been reassuring to some minds. The conference room at Southwick House, where Eisenhower underwent his mental torture and the free world held its breath, remains preserved to this day, adjacent to the restored maps on the walls of the old war room. Jim Booth surfaced on time to direct the armada towards the Germans, enjoying a grandstand view of the invasion: 'A really tremendous sight, with hundreds of ships all around us and the skies black with planes.'[48] A sister boat to his, the *X-24*, sits open to claustrophobic inspection at the Royal Navy's Submarine Museum, Gosport.

19

The Great Armada

'The long coil of hollow little oblong boats – the long winding queue of the Armada – it was all here, crowded in a thick huddle offshore, like a packed boating lake! At first he noticed a ship here and a ship there, but then he saw they were just a confused mass – it was too much to take in the hugeness of the fleet. Destroyers, cruisers, battle-ships, minesweepers, dark turrets and grey hulls galore, were scattered over the bright choppy sea, hulking over the crammed small assault craft. There was too much for any one pair of eyes to see.'
David Holbrook, *Flesh Wounds* (1966)[1]

THE B-24J LIBERATOR stood on the concrete, bristling with ten 0.50-inch-calibre machine-guns. Its high-wing design and four Pratt & Whitney R-1830 engines enabled it to fly higher and farther than the B-17s – there was always rivalry between B-17 and B-24 crews as to which was better. Along the roomy fuselage, twenty-four 250-pound general purpose bombs hung ready in the bomb bay. On her nose, her name was painted proudly: *Call Me Later*. As Staff Sergeant James Kirk Varner recalled, 'We could never think of a name and kept telling the squadron artist to "call us later", so we named her *Call Me Later*.'

In December 1943 he and his nine fellow crew members had assembled for training in Salt Lake City, Utah, then flown their ship to England, stopping off at Palm Beach; overflying Jamaica and Cuba to reach Trinidad; with further stopovers at Belém and Natal in Brazil. Crossing the Atlantic, *Call Me Later* and her crew made Dakar in Senegal; Marrakesh, Morocco, and finally St Mawgans in Cornwall: they had landed in England on 6 May, exactly a month before Overlord. The two-week flight had settled them as a crew and soon they were integrated into the 704th Squadron of the USAAF's 446th Bomb Group at Bungay, south-east of Norwich.[2]

Call Me Later's sorties provide a good narrative of the air picture for D-Day. Her initial combat missions, on 24, 25 and 27 May, were in preparation. First they hit the Luftwaffe aerodrome at Orly, then railway marshalling yards at Mulhouse and Trier; on the 31st of the month, they attacked a rail bridge at Longwy, before turning their attention to German positions along the French coast. On 3 June, Varner wrote in his mission log: 'Today we went after gun emplacements on the Pas-de-Calais. We really bombed them good. We were getting much *flak* until the bomb hits – after that, no more *flak*.' The next day, 'went after anti-invasion gun emplacements on the coast of France. We saw no *flak* today. Our bomb hits on the target were good. *Der Führer* won't have any use for those guns after this.' On the eve of D-Day, *Call Me Later* and her crew again attacked 'gun emplacements on the coast of France. We're expecting something big to happen soon – the way we've been bombing the coast of France. Bomb hits on the target were good.'[3]

Of his tenth combat mission, Varner, the B-24's engineer and top turret gunner, wrote, 'Today is D-Day. We bombed road bridges at Caen, France. Bomb hits were good. When we crossed the Channel, I never saw so many boats in my life. It made me very proud of myself to be there and doing my part in the invasion of Europe. I later found out that the 704th Squadron led the 446th Bomb Group that morning, and the 446th led the whole Eighth AAF. We were the very first Americans over the invasion coast.'[4]

Call Me Later would have met some of Lieutenant Russell Chandler's fellow C-47 pilots haring in the opposite direction. Aware he had two more missions to fly on 6 June after dropping his paratroopers, Chandler noted, 'After exiting the drop zone, we broke formation; it was basically a race home, with every man for himself. The safest location was down low, so we were screaming back across the Channel just above the deck, and suddenly this large shape appears through my windscreen and starts firing its entire portside armament toward us. I never identified the cruiser that we encountered.'[5]

Among other C-47 pathfinder crews hurrying home, Staff Sergeant Arthur Een noted, 'We yelled to Captain Greer to kick the plane in the ass and get us the hell out of there, hedgehopping to the coast – an effective way to escape *flak*. Over the Channel, we spotted several planes that had ditched. The crews appeared to be all right and we waved to them, noticing launches of the British Air Sea Rescue racing to the scene. On every occasion as we approached the English coast, I was reminded of a bunch of little chicks scampering back to the mother hen after straying a little too far away and being frightened by some unknown terror in the barnyard.'[6]

Typhoon pilot Flying Officer Douglas Gordon, with No. 440 (City of Ottawa) Squadron, Royal Canadian Air Force, flying out of Hurn, Bournemouth, observed 'They had us up at 0400 hours and served a great big platter of fried eggs sitting in white grease. The goddamn things were cold. Not the best thing to have. The Channel was wall-to-wall boats of every sort. We were over the beach [Sword] about seven.' This was, according to his logbook, the first of his two missions that day, the first lasting ninety minutes, the second slightly longer.[7]

The invasion was massively over-insured in terms of air cover. With so many aircraft in the skies, the issue of 'friendly fire' would be the bane of D-Day, as Spitfire pilot Flight Lieutenant Tony Cooper with No. 64 Squadron noted of the first of his two D-Day sorties: '0430 hours: Airborne. 0520 hours: Low cover for *Utah* beach. Patrolling. 0620 hours: Nearly shot down by Thunderbolt. Spitfire in front actually *was*. Another Spit hit by naval shell & blew up. Naval barrage so intense that not safe to be over the coast.'[8] Pierre Clostermann and his Free French Spitfire pilots, whose No. 602 Squadron flew *five* sequential missions on D-Day, noted that 'the Channel was congested with an inextricable jumble of warships, merchant vessels of every tonnage, tankers, tank landing craft, minesweepers, all dragging their little silvery barrage balloons at the end of a string. We passed half a dozen tugs sweating and puffing away, dragging a kind of enormous concrete tower sitting on a frame as big as a floating dock – one of the sections of the "Mulberry" prefabricated harbour.'[9]

The 357th Fighter Group, flying P-51s out of Leiston, Suffolk, logged *eight* missions on D-Day, but lost three pilots: on the third, 'Lieutenant Irving Smith flew into heavy overcast and was never seen again.'[10] These P-51s and Spitfires were among the total of *171 squadrons* of Allied fighters supporting the invasion: fifteen provided shipping cover; fifty-four overflew the beaches; thirty-three were engaged in bomber escort and offensive fighter sweeps; thirty-three hit targets inland; while the remaining thirty-six squadrons provided direct air support to the troops.[11]

Other airmen were at the end of their allotted missions. Curt Vogel, who had brought his B-24 'Rough Riders' over to RAF Horsham St Faith, Norwich, home of the 458th Bomb Group, completed his twenty-ninth mission – to bomb the rail hub of Bourges in central France – on 4 June. His thirtieth and final was on 5 June, which 'turned out to be very easy, because we dropped our bombs on the coast of France and returned to the base. The next day a fellow pilot woke me and told me that it was D-Day. All I remember saying was "Good luck" and went back to sleep. We had flown our last combat mission, and to me and the crew this was "Right to Life-Day" as our percentage of making it home alive suddenly went up about eighty percent.'[12]

Flying Officer James Hudson, DFC, flew his last and thirtieth combat mission on D-Day itself; he was a Lancaster navigator who had earlier been interned by the Vichy French overflying Tunisia; later repatriated, he joined No. 100 Squadron at RAF Waltham, Lincolnshire. From there he bombed German bunkers at Dieppe and Dunkirk on 10 and 24 May, attacked the Merville battery on the 27th, and hit more coastal defences on 3, 4 and 5 June. On the evening of 6 June at 2215 hours 'we took-off for Vire. From the relative safety of our Lancaster we saw the armada below; thousands of brave men, who within the next few hours, would be facing grave perils – for many, certain death. For them, it was the beginning. For us it was the end. At 0310 hours on the morning of 7 June our operational tour was over.'[13]

Overall, the contribution of both these latter crews mattered: Vogel, Hudson and other aircrew like them were as responsible for the success of D-Day as those who fought through the campaign, but are in danger of becoming overlooked. For others, 6 June 1944 was their first mission: Ohioan First Lieutenant James E. 'Jim' Frolking remembered flying his P-38 out of Wattisham, Suffolk, on an offensive sweep over France with his colleagues of the 479th Fighter Group: 'it was a day of saying my prayers and trying to stay alive'.[14]

The airmens' efforts were much admired by those on the ground, for whom the sheer quantity of aeroplanes in the southern English skies seared an indelible memory. Fourteen-year-old Richard Payne recollected being shaken awake by his parents to watch as the aerial armada passed by: 'the sky was black with planes; hardly a space between the bombers, many towing gliders as large as themselves. They reminded me of nothing so much as a swarm of wasps, in perfect formation, each ringed with their invasion stripes. Even their wasp-like drone – a steady hum at first, slowly rising to an ear-splitting crescendo as they passed overhead – was deafening, and we clapped our hands over our ears, open-mouthed at the sight. It seemed to last for ages, as wave after wave of them passed, then faded into the early morning haze.'[15]

No. 75 General Hospital, on the Sussex coast at Littlehampton – itself fully involved in the war effort, with LCAs, motor-torpedo boats and air–sea rescue launches built at Hillyard's and Osborne's yards across the way – was holding a dance on 5 June. Sister Brenda McBryde left briefly to cool off outside and was immediately distracted by the hundreds of tiny specks in the distance that multiplied into formations of planes. Soon the dance music was drowned out by the waves of bombers, then troop carriers, some towing gliders, that processed above. 'The noise grew deafening, the party was abandoned, as our moon faces were upturned to the great V-shaped arrowheads, made up of smaller arrow-

Once news of the invasion spread, churches throughout the United Kingdom and United States opened for prayers. President Roosevelt and King George VI led their people in special prayers, broadcast over the airwaves. 'For these men are lately drawn from the ways of peace,' the President intoned. 'They fight not for the lust of conquest. They fight to end conquest. They fight to liberate. They fight to let justice arise, and tolerance and good will among all Thy people'. King George called for 'a worldwide vigil of prayer as the great crusade sets forth', firmly believing his 'Nation and Empire to be fulfilling God's purpose'. (NARA)

heads, that stretched purposefully towards France. We all knew what it meant: most of us would soon be following. As the planes faded, a great drawn-out sigh went up, like the *Ahhhhh* that follows a particularly good firework display.'[16]

Vicars opened up churches, understanding that many would need the comfort of prayer at such a moment. Windows rattled and shook; tiles slipped off roofs. Johnnie Grant, too young to be at the dance, felt the departure of the Allied soldiers acutely. His exciting childhood was one of air raids, the seafront barricaded with rolls of barbed wire, his class-room windows covered with criss-crossed tape to prevent flying glass, and watching aerial dogfights. 'Most of us had at least a couple of empty 0.303 cartridge cases, usually ejected from British fighters,' he recalled. He made friends easily with all the Brits, Canucks and Yanks in Littlehampton, scrounging their rations and chewing gum. 'What I liked most were the cigarette cards they gave me; my favourites were Canadian *Sweet Caporals*, with their aircraft recognition silhouettes: each card had three views: from head-on, side and a perspective. We swapped them at school, and were soon expert plane spotters'; but for young Johnnie Grant, 'D-Day robbed me of my uniformed pals.'[17]

Long before the seaborne invasion craft touched down, in a carefully sequenced pattern of events, thousands of aircraft pounded the bunkers that studded the Calvados coast and laced their way up the Cherbourg peninsula. Initially it had been 1,136 four-engined 'heavies' from RAF Bomber Command unloading 5,853 tons of munitions from just before midnight to 0545 hours. Richard Stout, a war correspondent for the *Observer*, watched them. 'We were under heavy cumulus clouds, through which the moon occasionally peeked. All that time, out-of-sight overhead bombers rumbled past like an endless freight train going over a viaduct. Streams of incendiaries went up like fountains from France and clusters of flares were dropped, twisting long smoke trails behind them. I saw two airplanes go down like falling stars, and flare up suddenly when they hit.'[18]

Beginning at precisely sixty minutes before H-Hour, a further 1,083 US bombers hit the beach defences with 7,348 tons of missiles. Ironically, in their anxiety not to hit the landing craft already en route, bomb aimers peering through the 'clag' – and the drifting clouds of dirt and debris thrown up by previous explosions – waited an extra five to twenty-five seconds before releasing their ordnance; thus not a single aerial bomb was recorded as falling actually on the five landing beaches.[19]

The B-26 Marauders, four of which had collided over England, were part of this effort, too, striking the Cotentin behind Utah. Besides the hundreds of American and British squadrons, in the skies over Normandy on D-Day ranged twenty-eight Canadian squadrons, fourteen Polish, seven Australian, six Free French, five New Zealander, three Czech, one Rhodesian, and two each from Belgium, the Netherlands and Norway. May and June 1944 were maximum-effort months for RAF Bomber Command, mounting 11,353 and 13,592 sorties respectively and another 11,500 in July – the majority in support of the invasion, despite 'Bert' Harris's claims he could win the war without Overlord.[20]

Call Me Later's mission on 7 June would be just as important, striking 'the railyards at Alençon. The idea was to keep the Germans from bringing up replacements and equipment. We did a very good job of it. Bomb hits were good. No flak – no fighters.'[21] The B-17-equipped 457th Bomb Group, who had arrived at RAF Glatton, Cambridgeshire, in time for 'Big Week', flew twenty-three missions in the thirty days of June 1944 alone, mostly against fixed defences, airfields and rail yards in northern France. This involved eight hundred individual sorties, with only nine B-17s lost. By contrast, for the last five months of 1944, the 457th flew a total of eighty-seven missions – about 2,700 sorties – losing sixty-six Fortresses, and far below the Eighth Air Force's unsustainable loss rates of 1943.[22]

Droning steadily towards the Continent, Lieutenant Franklin L. Betz in a 379th Bomb Group B-17, out of Kimbolton, Cambridgeshire, watched D-Day through holes in the clouds. He had left his cramped navigator's table to get a better look at the spectacle below from the right waist gunner's position.

> Stretching back to England was a highway of shipping; vessels in neat rows towing their balloons, which swayed lazily above, attached by stout cables. I started to count them, but gave up as there were too many. I realise now that none of us were looking out for enemy aircraft – they could have easily bounced us at this moment – as we all had our eyes trained downwards. Fascinated, I saw silent puffs of white smoke fired from the miniature warships beneath us, and soon afterwards a short distance inland I could make out detonations of their shells, equally silent.[23]

New Yorker Frank Skrzynski, on a B-24 with the newly arrived 489th Bomb Group, flying out of Halesworth, Suffolk, noted he was 'awakened at 0030 hours for briefing at 0130; that's when we found out the invasion was starting, and were to play a part in it. Passed over the Channel about 0900 hours, and through breaks in the under-cast was able to see part of the invasion fleet.'[24] Lowell J. Davidson, a B-24 turret gunner, reflected, 'D-Day will also always be in my memory because that was the only day we flew two missions, both at low levels. We were low enough that day to see them shooting at us. I will also always remember the sight of all those ships and the wakes they made going across the channel: even from the height of our plane, there were ships as far as you could see.'

Ball turret gunner Henry A. Tarcza, flying in *El's Bells*, a B-17 with the 95th Bomb Group out of Horham in Suffolk, remembered the moment when all forty aircraft in their group dropped their bombs simultaneously over the French coast defences. Their D-Day strike was 'the only mission over Europe when I actually felt the concussion of our own bombs. The explosion caused our aircraft to bounce and vibrate. Afterwards my pilot, Matthew J. McEntee, thanked us for our fine cooperation as a combat crew, observing, "It is doubtful in our lifetime if any of us will ever participate in a historic undertaking of such magnitude."'[25]

To help them wake up for their early-morning briefings, all were served breakfast by the likes of Birdie Schmidt – looking after the 392nd Bomb Group at Wendling, Norfolk – and her colleagues of the American Red Cross:

> I've never had in my life a greater thrill and privilege as when I saw our boys off in the very early hours of D-Day. We took them coffee, cocoa, lemonade, cookies and sandwiches; they all had an air of suppressed excitement, of expectancy about them … One of the boys saw some of the hard candy we had for them on the serving table and he said, 'Gee, it's like Christmas.' In a way it was like Christmas Eve, because here at last was something for which you'd been waiting ages. In another way, it was just before curtain time on opening night of the big show: the cast had the spirit to work together and make it a success. In the energy of the moment, Walter Joachim, a bombardier, gave me an enthusiastic hug and kiss over the coffee urn saying, 'Honey, this is it!'[26]

Other B-24s protected Ramsay's armada from the air, covering the south-western approaches and determined to destroy U-boats. These maritime Liberators, equipped with extra fuel tanks, depth charges and long-range radar, flew with No. 19 Group of RAF Coastal Command, the formation a microcosm of the nations assembled for Overlord. Along with Czech, Polish and New Zealander squadrons, there were two from Australia and three from Canada. The Czech squadron, No. 311, included many who had fled their homeland in 1938, others who had fought alongside the French in 1940. František Pospíchal recalled their motto, '*Na množství nehled'te*' (Disregard their numbers). He reminisced, 'I was in the air on D-Day, flying a Costal Command Liberator hunting for U-boats near Brest. It's hard to say now what you felt: fear, excitement?' A fellow airman from the 311th, Charles Marlich, summed up what they all felt: 'I don't think there was nervousness. It was more an elated feeling that something was happening – *finally*.'[27] A further unit in the group, No. 224 Squadron, based at St Eval in north Cornwall, comprised 137 Britons, forty-four Canadians, thirty-three Anzacs, two Americans, a Swiss, a Chilean, a South African and a Brazilian. It was eventually credited with sinking ten U-boats, including *U-626* and *U-373* on 8 June, with the result that not a single U-boat penetrated the English Channel.

Below the airmen, a vast fleet was ploughing through the angry waves towards France: the unfolding of Admiral Ramsay's Operation Neptune. Crewing his ships were 285,000 men. Feeling the breath of history on his neck, his chief of staff had already addressed his captains: 'Gentlemen, what Philip of Spain failed to do, what Napoleon tried and failed to do, and what Hitler never had the courage to try, we are about to do – and with God's grace, we shall.'

This was an occasion when history mattered; some of the Royal Navy's vessels had been specially selected. From the flotilla of warships and launches that had scooped, amongst others, Bernard Montgomery's 3rd Division off the sands of Dunkirk four years previously, at least thirty-one – the destroyers *Impulsive* and *Vivacious*, ten minesweepers, gunboat *Locust*, *MTB-102*, launch *Devon Belle*, tug *Challenge*, ferry *Isle of Thanet*, cargo ship *Haslemere*, and eleven requisitioned steamers, including the *Princess Maude* and *Ben-my-Chree* – would be present on the opening day of Operation Neptune, the latter two conveying GIs to Omaha Beach.[28] HMS *St Helier*, a Channel Islands ferry which had rescued over 10,000 troops in 1940, for which her captain, first and second officers and quartermaster were awarded bravery medals, and HMS *Isle of Guernsey*, another former ferry and Dunkirk veteran, would both transport British troops to Gold on 6 June 1944.[29]

'From Dunkirk to D-Day' was a journey undertaken by many of the chiefs, not least Admiral Bertram Ramsay, who had planned and executed both operations: Dynamo and Neptune, and been knighted for his achievement after each.[30] Perhaps as much as fifteen per cent of the 1944 British West European Force (as it was initially called) that landed on Continental Europe had served in the 1940 British Expeditionary Force which had left it four years earlier.[31]

Eisenhower and Montgomery had both penned short messages which were mass-printed for the widest possible distribution, or read out over public address systems; Ike told his 'Soldiers, sailors and airmen of the Allied Expeditionary Force' they were 'about to embark upon the Great Crusade, towards which we have striven these many months'. Less well known, the formula was repeated further down the line by other commanders. Emphasising the combined nature of the maritime–land operation, Rear Admiral A. G. Talbot, commanding Force 'S' from HMS *Largs*, published a brief exhortation to his men, overlaid with a Trafalgaresque gloom:

> The great day for which we have all been training is at hand. The task allotted to us is a formidable one, and calls for all that is best in every one of us. The 3rd British Infantry Division has been entrusted to our care. They are old friends of ours; we have grown up together; we have come to look on them as our own. Let every officer and man in the Force feel a personal responsibility for the comfort, safety and maintenance of his opposite number in the 3rd Division. And above all, fight: fight to help the Army; fight to help yourselves; fight to save your ship; fight to the very end.[32]

Sub Lieutenant Ludovic Kennedy – a future television broadcaster who had lost his father aboard the SS *Rawalpindi* when it had attacked the battlecruiser *Scharnhorst* in 1939, and had redressed the balance by taking part in the hunt for the *Bismarck* two years later – felt he had earned a place aboard Talbot's ship, HMS *Largs*. Aware of its traditions, Kennedy was unprepared for the wardroom standards the Royal Navy maintained, even on this day of battle. As he sat down to breakfast, a white tablecloth was laid, followed by the steward's polite enquiry: 'Porridge or cereal this morning, sir?'[33] Rather more unconventional was the breakfast aboard *LCT-354*, a veteran craft of the Sicily and Italy campaigns. Her cook had made a huge stew from tinned steak and tomatoes, serving it to their passengers of the Sherman-equipped Fort Garry Horse – with no other receptacle to hand – from an unissued portable toilet. The tank crews wolfed it down and two weeks later their CO sent Midshipman John Lund, the craft's first lieutenant, a note saying they had all made it through D-Day 'thanks to the stew'.[34]

In another printed exhortation, Major General Douglas Graham instructed his veteran Eighth Army formation heading for Gold,

> The time is at hand to strike. To break through the Western Wall and into the heart of Europe. To you, officers and men of the 50th Northumbrian Division, has been given the great honour of being in the vanguard of this mighty blow for freedom. It is my unshakeable belief that we, together with Force 'G' of the Royal Navy, the special regiments of the Royal Armoured Corps, the Royal Artillery and the Royal Engineers attached to us, and with the help of the RAF, and American Air Force, will deliver such an overpowering punch that the enemy will be unable to recover.[35]

Significantly, Graham barely mentioned air power, and Talbot not at all, which reflected army concerns particularly that the RAF and USAAF were fighting their own war, with little reference to the land component. Looking back, Brigadier 'Sammy' Stanier, the one-eyed former Welsh Guardsman commanding the 231st Brigade in Graham's 50th Division, felt liaison before Overlord with the RAF was poor, and their officers at times arrogant and aloof.[36]

The invasion armada was preceded by 255 wooden-hulled minesweepers, all but thirty-two crewed by the Royal Navy or Royal Canadian Navy, assisted by trawlers, launches and converted landing vessels – a total of 350 craft. In the lead, the 1,000-ton HMS *Pelorus*, heading the 7th Minesweeper Flotilla at the point of a vast arrow. They assembled thirteen miles south-east of the Isle of Wight and cleared a rough circle, ten nautical miles across. That became 'Piccadilly Circus', where the invasion traffic would shake out into their five separate convoys, one for each beach. At 2000 hours, the Royal Navy minesweepers were called to 'action stations', those of the USN to 'general quarters', and started clearing ten parallel channels towards France, two per beach – one for fast traffic, the other for slow, including all the small landing craft. On charts it resembled a giant spout, with shipping poured in at the broad end, from

'Piccadilly Circus'. Major Tom Bigland, British liaison officer to Bradley's headquarters, remembered 'the thousands of ships moving in lanes, and then turning right and left to their landing beaches at dawn on the sixth'.[37]

The eighty-five-strong company of HMS *Pelorus* was told through the ship's tannoy that they 'had the honour and privilege to lead the invasion fleet across the Channel', to which a petty officer was heard to mutter, 'Did the Captain just say "honour" or "horror"?' Some of their escort force – to avoid a repeat of Exercise Tiger – included squadrons of American PT boats, built by Andrew Higgins and commanded by Medal of Honor-winner Lieutenant Commander John Bulkeley. His superior, Rear Admiral Alan Kirk, later reported the sweeping 'was the keystone in the arch of this operation. All of the waters were suitable for mining, and plans of unprecedented complexity were required. The performance of the minesweepers can only be described as magnificent.'[38]

The arithmetic proved their value: seventy-eight moored mines were disabled before H-Hour and 335 of all kinds would be swept by 3 July. Other vessels accounted for an additional seventy-four. In return, German mines would account for forty-three Allied vessels of all kinds by D+27. Without the sweeping fleet, this total of losses would have been hundreds more.[39] Less glamourous than the destroyers and cruisers, the sweepers played an often forgotten vital role, as Ramsay had written in his journal earlier: 'the mine is our greatest obstacle to success and if we manage to reach the enemy coast without becoming disorganised & suffering serious losses we shall be fortunate'.[40] Fortune did smile, although not without cost: the value of the sweep was soon confirmed when one of the American sweepers, USS *Osprey*, hit a mine and went down with six killed, the first USN personnel to die in Neptune. Having run a signal up the halliards – 'Nelson in the van' – at exactly midnight, HMS *Pelorus* and the rest of His Majesty's ships at sea 'spliced the mainbrace' – that is, the ship's company received an issue of rum. Such seafaring traditions caused tensions with the US Navy, who are traditionally 'dry'.

Lurking under camouflaged netting, *LCT-1171* rode at anchor amid the assault flotillas tied up in Plymouth harbour. Two hundred feet long, armed with a pair of 20mm Oerlikon anti-aircraft guns, her twin engines capable of ten knots and a complement of twelve, her first officer, Sub Lieutenant Austin Prosser, was enormously proud of her. She had just taken on board six Shermans, six half-track carriers, two half-track ambulances and all their crews. However, there was a fly in the ointment: Prosser had just learned that they were under US Navy command, which meant a ban on alcohol. 'There was nearly a mutiny throughout His Majesty's 57th LCT Flotilla. This caused more debate than our plans to kick the Hun out of France. After a lot of heated discussion, it was decided to keep us "wet": a popular decision for all concerned, as on the way over our guests helped us drain our supply, fearing it would be a one-way trip,' Prosser related in 2004. 'The Yanks added to the party a jar of neat surgical spirit from one of their ambulances, topped up with fruit juice – "invasion hooch"; it was revolting, but calmed the nerves: I'm quite sure they must have landed at Omaha with severe hangovers.'[41]

In Portland, another craft, *LCT-637*, skippered by American Lieutenant Charles Lilly, was being loaded with bridging equipment, jeeps, ammunition and steel matting. Watching the large crane at work, and as his craft sank lower into the harbour, Lilly went to the officer in charge and asked how much he was listed to carry. 'I was told I was down for 250 tons. At which point I exploded. "This LCT can take a maximum of 180 tons, so hold it right there." This caused another flap, since majors don't like to be told "no" by junior naval officers, but I refused to back down and finally won out – though we got to Normandy by sailing through the Channel, rather than over it.'[42]

Able Seaman Stan Hough was aboard the troopship HMS *Prinses Astrid*, a 3,000-ton former Belgian cross-Channel ferry carrying eight LCAs; his meticulous log shows that whilst at anchor off the Isle of Wight, his captain addressed the crew at 1630 hours on 5 June. They were told for the first time that 'We are going to land on the French Coast. Our LCAs will leave the ship at 0610 hours tomorrow and touch down on the beach at 0750,' he recorded. 'It is the job of No. 4 Commando, on board, to take the beach and destroy the shore batteries.'

The orders that were transmitted to every warship, launch, craft, cutter and merchant vessel of the Neptune fleet continued: 'As long as we get the troops ashore nothing else matters; on no account is any ship or landing craft to stop and pick up survivors on the way in. Loss of life does not count as long as we get the troops to the beach. There will be US Coast Guard cutters there specially to pick up survivors.' The *Prinses Astrid* weighed anchor at 2100 hours on 5 June and headed for Sword Beach in their own special convoy – 'just one small part of the gigantic landing, with five other landing ships, each carrying their own flotilla of LCAs – HMS *Glenearn, Empire Broadsword, Empire Cutlass, Empire Battleaxe* and *Maid of Orleans* – escorted by a cruiser and five destroyers'.[43]

With so many craft manoeuvring, there had already been accidents. Late on Monday evening, *LCT-2428* had broken down in the Solent en route to Normandy. Taken under tow she had subsequently capsized, spilling her cargo of Royal Marine Centaur tanks and armoured bulldozers into the Channel; she had to be deliberately sunk with gunfire by her tug.[44] Later, *LCT-427* would collide with the battleship HMS *Rodney* south-east of the Isle of Wight, sinking immediately and taking her crew of thirteen with her. Each LST towed a Rhino ferry with a crew aboard; several were lost with their passengers during the long, rough night, as war correspondent Alan Moorhead aboard *LST-816* recollected. 'A German mine, shaped like a top, came floating by. We turned and let it pass astern. Our tow-rope broke, and the Rhino ferry was washed astern with its stranded crew on board. No ship was allowed to delay in that danger area, and we sailed on.'[45]

Emotions were mixed as they departed. Surrounded by the headquarters of 'Shimi' Lovat's brigade of commandos aboard their various craft, Captain Tony Smith aboard *LCI-519* thought the atmosphere was 'more like a regatta than a page of history'. On hearing that an admiral had thrown his hat in the air, Smith confided, 'I have never loved England so truly as at that moment.' It was on the bows of this craft, bearing two hundred men, that the (illegally) kilted Bill Millin stood, playing 'The Road to the Isles', to Lovat's instructions.[46]

Even RN Captain Eric Bush, the Gallipoli veteran, was moved, recalling he had 'never seen so many ships together at one time: thousands and thousands of ships of all classes stretched from horizon to horizon'.[47] Aboard USS *Ancon*, First Lieutenant William G. Pepe, with the 5th Engineer Special Brigade, recorded the mood as one of 'nervous apprehension with the close confinement beginning to take its toll. Tempers were short and everyone was somewhat edgy. No one slept that night and it was reassuring when we finally dropped anchor off Omaha Beach at 0230 hours.'[48]

The nine Free French warships played the 'Marseillaise' over their loudspeakers as their crews alternately 'wept and leapt' on deck, emotional and excited at the prospect of returning to France after four long years. Aboard his craft with men of the 2nd King's Royal Rifle Corps, a British infantry battalion in the 4th Armoured Brigade, Lieutenant Edwin 'Dwin' Bramall – a future field marshal – recalled the 'mixture of excitement at being part of such a great enterprise, and apprehension of somehow not coming up to expectations and doing what was expected of us'. Sensing the young officer's anxiety, one of his old sweats reassured him, 'Don't worry, sir, we'll look after you.'[49]

The weather that had taxed Group Captain Stagg, Colonel Yates, Lieutenant Commander Hogben and the rest of the meteorological teams made for an uncomfortable crossing. Michigan-born Arvo Lohela, in a B-24, remembered the conditions were 'stinko'.[50] Captain Gervase Middleton, commanding the battleship HMS *Ramillies*, noted 'strong winds and lumpy seas', and that dodging the slow landing craft convoys was 'an exciting sport, especially at night'.[51] For smaller boats and launches, this translated into four- to six-foot waves, which tossed flat-bottomed landing craft around mercilessly. US Marine Corporal Bill O'Neill aboard the American *LCT-544* out of Weymouth observed, 'With three engines and rudders, LCTs were very manoeuvrable in calm water, but difficult to control in bad weather. Sometimes speeding up or slowing down to avoid collisions, sailing sideways at the whim of the wind, sitting high on the top of a wave then sliding down to a bone-shaking crash at the bottom, with decks deep in water, the LCTs wallowed along in their wavy lines towards the far shore.'[52]

Soldiers and sailors aboard the troopships got the best views and most comfortable crossings. Closer to the briny blue, those in landing craft saw less. Even so, Private John Bain (later the poet Vernon Scannell) wrote of looking out 'at the surrounding seas that, close to the LCI, rolled and subsided and swelled like a collapsed silken tent continuously agitated by undercurrents of wind. Farther away the waves seemed smaller except that the other landing-craft could be observed sinking and reappearing in their troughs. The sky and the sea and the ships were all the colour of pewter or the dull blades of bayonets.'[53] Below decks on another LCI, Sapper Bob Heath recalled the 'continuous programme of rearing and plunging' which his craft kept up for fourteen hours, and the three-tier bunks 'from which hung discarded assault equipment soiled with cascades of vomit'.[54] Anchor cables and halyards whistled, flags and pennants flapped loudly, creating a strange environment for soldiers, who – wrapped in ponchos, huddled on steel decks in spume and spitting rain – were wishing themselves back in the warmth of Georgia, Mississippi or the Carolinas. Lieutenant Joseph Alexander of Indianapolis led a flotilla of craft from his vessel, *LCT-856*. He recalled 'the distance from Portland to Omaha Beach was exactly 110 nautical miles. Because I could only make five knots fully loaded, with the sea running as it was, I needed twenty-six hours before my scheduled time to hit the beach. You see, all the shipping had to leave at slightly different times, according to their loads, speed and the tides, to reach the rendez-vous point in time.'[55]

Some LCTs with added two-inch armour plates – LCT(A)s – suffered tremendously from the unforgiving waves. Weighed down by the extra protection and impeded by the LCMs each one towed, they shipped much of the Channel into their open vehicle decks. *LCT(A)-2229* started to flood at about 0400 hours; a PT boat managed to take off most personnel on board, but an hour later she sank, taking down both officers, four members of the crew, three soldiers and three tanks: perhaps the first US landing craft lost on D-Day.[56] A similar fate befell the British *LCT(A)-2039*, making her way to Gold Beach. Loaded with Centaur and Sherman tanks of the 1st Royal Marine Armoured Support Group, she was turned turtle in the heavy seas, which drowned two.[57]

When *LCT-2273*, towing an LCM, started foundering shortly after midnight, their passengers from 146th Engineer Combat Battalion, due on Omaha at H-Hour, transferred to the LCM and continued their journey.[58] Royal Marine Stan Blacker remembered, 'All the LCM flotillas began to lose formation and we were ordered to make our way inde-pendently, following the bigger ships to France. One of our number broke down and drifted into Le Havre where they were taken prisoner.'[59] Signaller Eric Brown in *LCT-1170* recalled the crossing. 'There were twelve craft in our flotilla, each carrying nine American Shermans, a total of 108 tanks along with their crews. Our designated speed was five knots and as we headed for Omaha Beach, we must have carried half the English Channel with us. We gave up navigation, barely chugged along, dodged the capital ships by inches – who appeared not to spot us – and tried to follow the craft in front, when we could see it. I don't know how we got there, much less in formation, but we did, arriving – as scheduled – off the beach at dawn. I am proud we did our bit – to have been part of getting the Yanks ashore on Omaha.'[60]

Lieutenant Tony Lowndes with the 802nd (LCVP) Flotilla, piloting his tiny Higgins boat across the Channel loaded with stores, recalled, 'We started engines at 0300 hours on the 5th, leaving in line astern like chicks following a mother duck; we proceeded after our trawler in two lines, side by side, in a calm sea and moderate wind. Everything was fine until we left the lee of the Isle of Wight when we were hit by a strong gale blowing up the Channel from the west. This was accompanied by a deep swell from starboard to port. This meant that when we were in the trough of a wave, the craft beside us on the crest of the next wave was between thirty to forty feet above us. Fortunately none of the crew was seasick and it was just a case of holding on for dear life. We took it in turns to do an hour as coxswain.'[61]

Arthur McNeil on *LCT-2440* had loaded at Brixham with US Assault Engineers, their vehicles and explosives, and was part of Force 'U'. They had suffered a hellish time at sea, having set sail on Saturday 3 June, and although they returned when the invasion was postponed, had remained off the English south coast. After forty hours on the aggravated ocean, 'one of the GIs, a youngster of about my own age,' recalled McNeil, 'lifted himself off the quarterdeck guard rail where he was trying to be sick. "Hey, Limey," he said. "Have you ever been in combat before? ... I don't care how bad it is, it can't be any worse than this ..."'[62] Yet the thorough training through the previous year had prepared most for the awfulness of riding small craft in challenging waters – while the SHAEF planners, as we have seen, had the foresight to include ten million of the frankly named 'bags, vomit, two per man' in the Overlord inventory. Ninety MTBs with Vian's Eastern Task Force and 113 American PT boats with Kirk's Western Task Force roamed the flanks at high speed, looking for adversaries, though none had put to sea.

Royal Navy chaplain Mike Crooks, on *LST-529* heading for Juno Beach, witnessed 'the relief when the engines came alive, and the rumble of the anchor chain. The sense of brooding suddenly evaporated and gave way to smiling faces, jokes, light-heartedness and rudery. Men were sitting on top of their wagons, one playing a banjo, another having a haircut, gunners swivelling their weapons – a spirit of nonchalance,' he thought. 'But this was short-lived as we approached a large curious-looking object in the water and passed close by it – it was the hull of an upturned landing craft – which had an instant, a sobering effect. My Holy Communion service was a momentous occasion, the communicants all aware that in a short while they might be dead – as some of them were. I knew the Holy Mysteries of Christian Communion probably meant more to them that day than at any other time in their lives: I shall never forget the look in the eyes of some; we were all trimmed down to size at that moment.'[63]

With Force 'G', Captain John Archibald Ford – a Royal Artillery forward observation officer with the 50th Division, devout Anglican and future

High Commissioner for Canada – remembered the multi-denominational service aboard his landing ship as it ploughed across the Channel. 'Despite the weather, every man on board appeared for church parade. In the bows where we could all see him, our padre stood wiping the spray out of his eyes behind a makeshift altar bearing a silver cross. With the spindrift and wind, I remember the moment a sudden gust tore at the cloth, at the same instant the ship lurched, the table fell over, and the crucifix fell to the deck and shattered. Such a little thing really, but the men took this as the judgement of God! Complete pandemonium, fear and confusion reigned, as the padre tried, vainly, to restore order.'[64]

A simpler formula was that adopted by Lieutenant Commander Balfour of the destroyer HMS *Scourge*, who recited over the tannoy the Breton Fisherman's Prayer: 'Dear God be with us. Thy sea is so great and our ship is so small. Amen.'[65] French commando officer Philippe

On every ship and at each airbase, priests led those of all faiths and none in religious services. Here Major Edward J. Waters, from Owego, New York, who had served as Chaplain with the US 1st Infantry Division in North Africa and Sicily, celebrates Mass at Custom House Quay, Weymouth, prior to departure. At the same time, printed messages from Eisenhower or Montgomery, various admirals and generals were read out or distributed. (NARA)

Kieffer remembered Sir Jacob Astley's prayer before Edgehill in 1642, 'Oh Lord, Thou knowest how busy I must be this day. If I forget Thee, do not Thou forget me.'[66] Ahead, navigation buoys had been set out by launches, red for port, green for starboard, which resembled to some 'a highway leading us to our own section of beach'. To others, the vast convoys, lit only by single blue lights on the stern of each vessel, seemed like 'a gigantic, twisting dragon'.[67]

Undeterred by this nautical melee, the minesweepers ploughed on with their dangerous task, finding that mines off the Normandy coast were not as numerous as they had feared. They knew they were up against the traditional 'floaters', magnetic and acoustic sea mines, but, unknown to them, there had been a heated debate in Kriegsmarine circles about where and whether to lay their new pressure 'oyster' mines – that rested on the bottom and only detonated when a substantial ship passed overhead. The German conclusion had been to delay releasing the oysters until it was clear where amphibious operations would suffer most. Not all of these mines were swept successfully: as late as August 2018, one was found in the nets of a French trawler off Grandcamp. The eight-foot parachute *Luftmine-B*, containing 1,900 pounds of explosive, was one of hundreds dropped by the Luftwaffe in the immediate aftermath of the invasion.

'Our ship was sealed at 2400 hours last night which means *IT* is very close now. Padres on board today, another sign. No one can leave the ship under any circumstances,' Winnipegger Frank Curry scribbled in his daily journal. His ship, HMCS *Caraquet*, was just one of the 126 RCN vessels that supported the invasion fleet, manned by eleven thousand Canadian sailors.[68] An ex-Royal Navy sweeper transferred to Canada in 1942, the *Caraquet* had escorted convoys across the Atlantic before joining the all-Canadian 31st Minesweeping Flotilla. Now, under the watchful eye of Commander Anthony Storrs, and with six officers and seventy-seven ratings aboard, the *Caraquet* and her seven sister ships had slipped out of Portland naval base at 2200 hours on the 5th, the moon playing 'hide and seek with the clouds'. Curry wrote, 'we expect any moment to be the target for shore batteries. RAF blasting away all along the coast, so close that we could feel the jar of the bombs continuously.'[69] Stoically, the little 700-ton *Caraquet* and the rest of the 31st Flotilla tried to ignore the cannonade and get on with their task of clearing safe channels to the American beaches.

A few miles eastwards, sweeping towards Gold Beach with Force 'G', was Alan Johnson, a gunner's mate aboard HMS *Onyx*, one of eight vessels with the 18th Minesweeping Flotilla. He recollected the excitement of the moment, the masses of ships, exchanges of inspiring signals, battle ensigns hoisted, but enjoyed the exercise they'd supported in May, Fabius II, far more, 'on account of its perfect calm weather. On D-Day, I remember it was just after 0500 hours when the mist suddenly began to clear, and looking astern I could see from that horizon to that horizon nothing but ships and landing craft coming straight towards me.'[70] Sub Lieutenant Leslie Hasker aboard the sweeper HMS *Chamois* remembered first seeing the smudge of French coastline on the horizon: 'We had the special job of closing in to a point three miles off Arromanches and putting down a special radar buoy. This was to be used by incoming vessels if mist developed or if the enemy managed to put down a smoke-screen. As we moved in it was a nice clear morning. Once we reached the right spot, over went the radar buoy and we turned to come away. We could see the town quite clearly, and the low hills of Normandy in the background with little church spires. There was no movement at all; everything was absolutely still.'[71]

The minesweepers turned back, job done, their places to be taken by the five naval bombardment forces, every one as powerful as the fleets that had clashed at Jutland in 1916. 'It was like a fox hunt,' thought one witness. 'There sat a battleship, like the Master of the Hunt, surveying the proceedings, dominating both in size and firepower. Closer inshore lurked cruisers – the whippers-in, bringing dignified order, and finally packs of destroyers, milling around like several unruly, adolescent packs of hounds.'[72] Aboard the landing ship *Prinses Astrid* bound for Sword, members of No. 4 Commando remembered the 'eerie silence' on their arrival.

Captain Marcel Kelsey, commanding the battleship HMS *Warspite*, thoughtfully told his ship's company, 'All personnel not on full "Action Stations" can come up on deck to witness a sight you will never see again in your lifetime.' Able Seaman Ronald Martin, also on the *Warspite*, noted they had been led by their minesweepers 'slowly towards Gold Beach. We arrived just as dawn was breaking and at 0550 hours opened up against our first shore battery with our fifteen-inch main guns – so we fired the first naval shots of the invasion [many were to subsequently claim this honour]. Each shell weighed nearly one ton; we were helped by Fleet Air Arm spotters, and later others onshore, who were very accurate.'[73] *Warspite* would run out of ammunition after nearly four hundred rounds of fifteen-inch and had to return to Portsmouth to load more through the night.

John Dennett, aboard *LST-322*, and already a veteran of the Sicily, Salerno and Anzio landings, remembered HMS *Warspite* as she opened up: 'We hadn't seen her since Salerno and knew her affectionately as the "Old Lady". She was such a fantastic sight: the whole ship rocked backwards in recoil, with a great belch of flame before being covered in smoke.'[74] This was the first of *LST-322*'s fifteen crossings, each time returning with injured troops and prisoners. Captain Donald Gilchrist with No. 4 Commando recounted that 'as dawn rose – a pink and grey light – a hellish cacophony of sound, a storming barrage of death and destruction erupted. So effective was it that instantly, those puking into their greaseproof bags stopped being sick. Their queasiness departed as rapidly as the noise had begun.'[75] Midshipman John Lund, whose cook had served stew from a portable toilet, noted that HMS *Warspite* made 'a magnificent sight firing her broadsides, the snag was that every time she let go, *LCT-354* nearly leapt out of the water'.[76] R. G. Watts aboard *LCT-2455*, which with the rest of the 103rd Flotilla was taking Centaur tanks to the Nan Red sector of Juno Beach, remembered the cramped living conditions for the two officers and fifteen crew. Ninety per cent of their Canadian soldiers 'were extremely sea sick, just holding on to anything to hand, and the crew was unable to help them. I remember looking down from the poop deck and thinking what a healthy lot they were, all that training for fitness, but now old Mother Nature was laughing at us.' As the sky lightened off France, one member of his crew shouted, *Right, where are you? You Nazi bastards, we're ready.* The exhaustion of their passage evaporated when 'Suddenly we were reminded that this was no holiday trip, as the *Warspite* opened a broadside. The shells were screeching over the top of us. The blast knocked my tin helmet over my eyes.'[77]

On another battleship, HMS *Ramillies*, Seaman Gunner Edward Wightman noted in his journal, 'we went to Action Stations at 2130 hours on Monday June the 5th, all wondering for how long. Once in position off the French coast we opened fire with fifteen-inch at a German battery on a high ridge. It had six guns in armoured casemates, so was no walkover.' The *Ramillies* (the Prime Minister's favourite, being named after the 1706 victory of his ancestor John Churchill, later Duke of Marlborough) carried out several bombardments, fired 220 fifteen-inch shells, 'but not one AA gun ever opened fire'.[78]

Those in the smaller craft felt the shock waves of battleships and cruisers firing over their heads, the heavy shells creating a vacuum in their wake. Signaller Jack 'Buster' Brown, who had encountered oil-covered corpses after Exercise Tiger, was with HMS *Kellett* of the 4th Minesweeping Flotilla off Omaha, and recollected: 'every ship that had a gun opened up with such a barrage, that the whole of the French coast, as far as the eye could see, appeared to be bathed in one, long, continuous concussive wave'.[79] 'The big guns', thought Lieutenant Ludovic Kennedy on HMS *Largs*, 'made your chest feel that somebody had put their arms around you and given you a good squeeze.'[80]

Unlike the Royal Navy, which fired their turrets sequentially, the USN battleships *Nevada*, *Texas* and *Arkansas* of the Western Task Force – the former supporting Utah, the latter pair, Omaha – fired broadsides with all their main guns at once, causing the ships to 'lean back' as they fired. Even at a distance the turbulence could be felt. 'We were fascinated by the 'water rising up to follow the shells, then dropping back into the sea,' recalled one matelot.[81] The largest battery along the invasion coast – the six 155mm guns on the Pointe-du-Hoc – was struck by USS *Texas*, who fired 255 fourteen-inch shells (costed at $10,000 apiece) in thirty-four minutes, a rate of one every eight seconds. Each left a freight-car-sized hole on the gun site – still visible today – but this was merely a softening-up exercise, for the position was also to be assaulted by 225 men of the 2nd Rangers, scaling the cliffs to reach them. Simultaneously, *Texas*'s five-inch guns were engaging the western fringes of Omaha, and from 0626 hours, bringing her main guns to bear, as the Rangers started on the Pointe-du-Hoc.

With the *Texas* and *Arkansas* was the monitor HMS *Erebus* – a curious shallow-draft vessel that carried a pair of fifteen-inch guns in a single, outsized turret, four cruisers and twelve destroyers. (Her sister, HMS *Roberts*, was operating in the British sector.) Petty Officer Peter Walker was on the cruiser HMS *Bellona*, 'named after the goddess of war; her motto was "Battle is our business". D-Day was exhausting,' he recalled. 'We were at action stations for sixty hours firing at targets well inland; the nauseating stench of burnt cordite permeated the whole ship. Even now I can't stand fireworks displays for the same reason: not the noise, but the smell. At the end, the captain played Frank Sinatra singing "I Didn't Sleep a Wink Last Night" over the tannoy.'[82] Two of the cruisers off Omaha flew the 'largest *tricolore* battle flags we had ever seen, sixty by one hundred feet in size, that could be seen from the shore' – they were the Free French *Montcalm* and *Georges Leygues*, whose crews found the idea of shelling their own homeland repugnant – rather in the way that Spitfire pilot Pierre Clostermann had reacted to USAAF aircraft bombing Rouen – but understood it to be a necessary evil in order to drive the Germans out.

Vice Admiral Robert Jaujard had earlier told the French fleet, 'Soon we shall engage in combat. In order to defeat the enemy, we must fire on our homeland. This is the price of liberty. *Vive la France!*' Appropriately, it was his boss, Admiral André Lemonnier aboard the *Montcalm*, anchored about 7,500 yards off the beach, who fired the first salvo. Her nine 152mm guns let rip at 0536 hours, watched by other Free French vessels nearby – the frigates *L'Escarmouche* and *Aventure*, corvette *Roselys* and six French-crewed MTBs of the 23rd Motor Torpedo Boat Flotilla. As René Cérisoles, a sailor aboard the *Montcalm*, remembered, 'Around 0530 hours, the curtain of protective smoke has dissipated. A poignant moment to see France again, even if it's through binoculars. Soon the Longues battery opens a duel. Despite our formal instructions not to open fire before H−40 (0550 hours), we are given permission to fire the first salvo on our country.'[83]

The French were by no means the only forces with scores to settle. The Polish Navy, too, smelt blood and fielded a cruiser and two destroyers. Lieutenant Commander Tadeusz Lesisz was second gunnery officer aboard the six-inch cruiser *Dragon*, a First World War-vintage cruiser given to the Poles by the Royal Navy, anchored off Sword. Born sixty miles south of Warsaw in 1918, he might have been forgiven for wondering who his real enemy was. Two of his three brothers were murdered by the Soviets at Katyn, the other by the Nazis at Dachau. 'Normandy was my second amphibious landing; I had already supported Operation Torch in 1942. On destroyers, I escorted several convoys in the Atlantic, including Americans coming to Britain,' he recollected. 'On D-Day, our task was to wipe out German positions around Ouistreham and Colleville-sur-Orne, which we did.'[84]

Able Seaman Franciszek Rumiński was on the destroyer *Ślązak*, which had likewise supported an earlier coastal landing – at Dieppe: 'We are now closed up for action. Troops are going in to the beaches. As the battle intensifies we become aware of bodies floating in the water.' His crewmate Jan Stępek remembered escorting the landing fleet, carrying smaller landing craft on their decks, across the Channel, and the message of thanks received from the CO of the commandos: 'I think you saved our bacon. Thank you. Stand by to do it again', and in the afternoon, another one: '*Ślązak* – fine work!'[85]

20

Shells, Rockets and Flies

'We must have seemed to ooze, the thousands of us, like a stream of dark oil.'
Sub Lieutenant Bill Golding, RNVR, on the Neptune fleet

KORVETTENKAPITÄN HEINRICH HOFFMANN had wearily answered the call in his command bunker at Le Havre. He had been kept up all night by Allied aircraft passing overhead, and his own flak, receiving endless reports of RAF bombers shot down, of aircrew parachuting to safety, and radar stations being jammed. At 0332 hours the teletype machine had clattered out an urgent message from his superior, Konteradmiral von Tresckow, the *Seekommandant Seine-Somme*, reporting Allied parachute assaults in the Ouistreham–Cabourg area. It was still dark, and his coastal positions could not confirm what was happening out to sea. Now the telephone call ordered a combat reconnaissance to the Orne estuary with all available units.

In Cherbourg, Admiral Hennecke had been holding an after-dinner soiree in the drawing room of the former French naval headquarters. The wife of Korvettenkapitän Wist was playing Schumann's *Papillons* when her piano solo was interrupted at 2330 hours by reports of heavy bombing all along the coast. Hennecke felt uneasy enough to cancel the rest of the evening.[1] On his way to Bordeaux the commander of Naval Group West, Admiral Theodor Kranke, had been alerted to the BBC French Service *messages personnels* at 0100 hours. His gruff response was: 'it is hardly likely that the invasion would be announced in advance over the radio', and given his understanding of the weather conditions, took no further action. At 0150 hours, the telephone rang in the Hôtel de la Marine on the place de la Concorde. The building where Marie Antoinette's death certificate was signed, and from whose balcony her execution by guillotine was witnessed, had been the French Navy's headquarters from 1789 until taken over by the Kriegsmarine in 1940. Breathlessly, the duty officer at the Seventh Army announced British paratroop landings over the Orne, and identification of others in the Cotentin, belonging to the 101st Airborne Division. Two separate locations, two different formations.

Still wearing his silk dressing gown, but in quiet, measured tones, remembered one officer present, 'the Navy Chief of Staff, *Konteradmiral* Karl Hoffmann [no relation to the officer in Le Havre] summoned us all into the Operations Room. "There are *Fallschirmjäger* landings here and here," his hands stretched over the maps. "Coastal radar stations report very many signals on their cathode ray tubes. Technicians assure me this isn't jamming." He paused and looked each of us in the eyes. "Gentlemen, I believe the invasion has begun."'[2] Elsewhere in the suburbs of Paris, grumpy at being woken by his own naval liaison officer, Fregattenkapitän Richard Konig, Field Marshal von Rundstedt of OB West was dismissive. 'Perhaps you've picked up seagulls' was his only response.[3] The next message to naval headquarters clinched it. At 0209 hours, the telephone log recorded, 'large vessels reported to the seaward of Port-en-Bessin' – the minesweepers of Force 'G'. Paris immediately ordered Admirals Hennecke in Cherbourg and Treskow in Le Havre to find out what was going on. The former ordered his 5th and 9th E-boat Flotillas out of Cherbourg at 0445, but bad weather compelled their return, after which Allied aircraft ensured they stayed bottled up until nightfall. It was up to Le Havre to unravel the mystery of what was out there.

The Kriegsmarine weather report of 'wind: west 6–7, sea: 3–4, heavy clouds, low clouds, good visibility' confirmed the Germans' awareness that the poor weather was already moderating. Hoffmann immediately alerted the three available vessels in his 5th *Torpedoboot-Flottille* – the *Möwe, Jaguar* and *T-28*. Two weeks earlier he had boasted six torpedo boats in his flotilla, but their plans to transit the Seine Bay on a minelaying expedition had been unravelled by Bletchley Park, and an RAF reception committee arranged. During the early hours of 24 May, aircraft hit the *Greif* with two bombs, and *S-100* (an E-boat) was sunk. Whilst she was being towed, the *Greif* accidentally collided with the *Falke*, later sinking. The disaster continued with the *Kondor* striking a mine, and having to be towed into Le Havre. This was a good illustration of the many tentacles of Bletchley's work affecting Overlord.

Thus, with the *Greif* at the bottom of the Channel, the *Kondor* and the *Falke* in dock, Hoffmann was down to three boats. Of 1,250 tons displacement each, with crews of 120 and three 105mm guns, they resembled small destroyers and had a mean turn of speed – around thirty-three knots. At the same time, Hoffmann ordered seven vessels from the 15th *Vorpostenboot-Flottille* of smaller patrol boats, mostly ex-whalers of 300–400 tons, to be made ready. With his old command, the *Falke*, out of commission, Hoffmann placed himself on the bridge of *T-28*, and exited Le Havre's outer mole at 0445.

Just over half an hour later, according to Hoffmann's After Action Report, at 0522 hours, his little flotilla encountered 'artificial fog' – smokescreens laid by the Allies – sighting in between 'the silhouettes of enemy units'. Charging through the smoke, Hoffmann opened fire. Three minutes later his three larger boats released a spread of seventeen torpedoes. Heinrich Frömke aboard the *Jaguar* had never seen so many ships; his ship fired six, which narrowly missed Admiral Talbot's flagship, HMS *Largs*, and the Polish destroyer *Ślązak*.[4] However, at 0537 hours the Norwegian destroyer *Svenner* was struck amidships, remembered Lieutenant Stephen Brown, on HMS *Scourge*: 'we saw her torpedoed; as she went down, her bow and stern stuck up like a defiant "V" for victory. She was a sister ship of ours, and in the same 23rd Destroyer Flotilla. We had no time to grieve, but afterwards it hit us: with only eleven officers, a fleet destroyer is like a family,' he reflected.[5]

The *Svenner* and her companion, the *Stord*, were two S-class destroyers made over to the Royal Norwegian Navy, the former captained by thirty-year-old Lieutenant Commander Tore Holthe from Trondheim, and was straight from the builders' yard. She had no chance to outmanoeuvre the torpedo, being stationary at the time. Stan Hough, aboard the landing ship *Prinses Astrid*, also saw the hit: 'Norwegian destroyer *Svenner*, about fifty yards from us, has been torpedoed amidships. One great column of smoke goes up and she breaks in two. Starting to go under amidships within thirty seconds, forming a "V" with her fore and after ends. In five minutes she has touched the seabed, and the two halves are sticking up out of the sea about twenty feet. Rafts have been dropped and survivors are on them, cannot see many. A US Coast Guard cutter is racing to pick men up. I could see men jumping into the sea from the upturned bows.'[6]

Korvettenkapitän Heinrich Hoffmann leading three warships of the 5th *Torpedoboot-Flotille* struck the first blows against the invasion armada. At 0537 hours, *Jaguar* unleashed a spread of torpedoes which passed through the densely packed Allied shipping, narrowly missing the headquarters ship HMS *Largs* and battleship HMS *Ramillies*. Two weeks earlier, an air attack had disabled three of Hoffmann's other ships. With six vessels, he might have inflicted untold carnage on the assembled vessels. (Author's collection)

Coming up on deck in readiness to land on Sword, Lieutenant Philip Webber, with the 1st South Lancashires on the landing ship *Empire Cutlass*, noticed in the half-light 'a great flash in the distance on our port quarter. I could just distinguish the bow and stern of a destroyer lifting out of the sea after being torpedoed amidships. Soon twinkling lights appeared from the life jackets of the crew as they dived overboard.' Standing by his side was his batman, Private John Welsh, whose twenty-second birthday had just begun. 'He looked at the dying ship and told me then and there he knew he would soon be killed. Unfortunately he was right and died of wounds on 29 June.'[7]

Seaman Edward Wightman aboard the battleship HMS *Ramillies* also recorded,

two enemy destroyers attacked with torpedoes, three came perilously close, no more than fifty yards away; one of the tin fish [torpedoes] fired at us hit the destroyer *Svenner*, a Norwegian escort of ours. She sank almost immediately and I don't think any survivors were picked up. Bodies and wreckage, rafts, and timber floated past and we observed the bow and stern of the wreck showing above water. Must be pretty shallow here. Apparently she broke her back. Poor chaps; leaves a nasty taste in the mouth.[8]

Many remembered the *Svenner*'s demise because it was the first and the most unexpected incident they witnessed on D-Day. Royal Marine Corporal William R. 'Bill' Jones, a landing craft coxswain aboard another landing ship, the *Empire Battleaxe*, recorded: 'coming up on deck in the grey dawn of D-Day we saw the destroyer *Svenner* just to the east of us. It was breaking in two amidships and sinking. A shocking sight so early in the day.' Playing cards with his newly issued French currency – everyone had been given 200 French francs in specially printed five-franc notes – aboard HMS *Glenearn*, Private Harold Isherwood of the 2nd East Yorkshires vividly observed the destroyer 'folding in two, like a penknife'.[9] Sapper Alfred Lane, with 263 Field Company, Royal Engineers, recollected with distress, 'I saw over the side pieces of wreckage floating, some with figures clinging to it. Our ship appeared to me to sail over the drifting wreckage. I was horrified to see some of the wreckage and figures disappeared directly under our ship; and furious that nothing was being done to save the poor devils in the sea.'[10]

H.M.No.5. 'Svenner' 2,530 tons. (Lt. Cdr. Tore Holthe) 23rd Destroyer Flotilla

Heinrich Hoffmann's victim was the Norwegian warship *Svenner*, of the Royal Navy's 23rd Destroyer Flotilla, and commanded by Lieutenant Commander Tore Holthe. Her loss had a profound effect on the many who witnessed it, being both unexpected and violent. One remembered *Svenner* 'folding in two, like a penknife'. (Postcard in Author's archives)

Two warships raced to rescue the crew from the water. HMS *Swift* picked up sixty-seven survivors, but thirty-three men had been killed; the *Swift* herself would be sunk by a mine in the same waters eighteen days later. By 0600, with daybreak and now 'under continuous air attack', Hoffmann was leading his little band back to Le Havre, having lost the patrol ship *V-1509* – two dead, twenty-six missing – and fired 20,155 rounds of all calibres in his thirty-five-minute engagement. 'Not a bad rate of exchange,' he must have felt.[11]

This maritime skirmish was potentially significant, though barely rates more than a line in all the D-Day histories, which usually assume the attacks were launched by much smaller E-boats, then based in Cherbourg. Several facts are apparent: Hoffmann didn't know what he was up against and had no opportunity to pick his targets – but because there were so many, he could hardly miss. The British were fortunate that Hoffmann could only deploy three, rather than the original six, torpedo boats in his flotilla, otherwise the damage – and alarm – would have been far greater. The fleet was extraordinarily lucky. The headquarters ship *Largs*, battleships *Warspite* and *Ramillies* and destroyers *Virago* and *Ślązak* (the latter Polish) all reported near misses. Though not a game-changer, their loss, particularly the *Largs*, with a divisional commander on board, might have had a wider impact on Neptune, while the loss of a battleship like the *Ramillies* or *Warspite* would have been a severe dent to Allied morale. The torpedoes passed right through their anchorage and hit the unlucky *Svenner* on the western edge. Her upwards-pointing bow remained visible to all for about thirty minutes.

Had the 5th and 9th E-boat Flotillas – that morning based in Cherbourg; they would appear later in the day – accompanied Hoffmann's dawn sally, the result might well have been carnage. This happened despite the Allied air umbrella, but at that most difficult time – first light. The impotency of the Kriegsmarine in 1944 is represented by the deployment of seven *Vorpostenboote* – basically converted fishing trawlers armed with a few medium-calibre weapons – against the far superior Allied fleet, whose 672 warships in the Seine Bay alone outnumbered Hoffmann with his ten vessels at that precise moment by nearly *seventy-to-one*.[12] In less than two weeks, Hoffmann's remaining vessels in Le Havre would be destroyed in a bombing raid, which also eliminated the E-boats sheltering there.

Shepherding their many charges were flotillas of coastal craft, led by the steam gunboat HMS *Grey Goose*. It was commanded by the future wildlife artist and patron of ornithology Lieutenant Commander Peter Scott (only son of polar explorer Robert Falcon Scott), who had devised the camouflage schemes that decorated many of the Royal Navy's warships on D-Day. Serving on a much smaller Motor Gun Boat with the 1st Coastal Flotilla was the young Sub Lieutenant Douglas Edward Reeman. He remembered the weather as 'mostly bad. It was grey, rough and misty. More like November than early summer. We were loaded down with full tanks, extra ammunition and the steep waves caused the slender hull to lift and plunge so much that I thought I was going to throw up.' At dawn his skipper ordered 'Hoist battle ensigns!' – a tradition Reeman had never witnessed before, and his coxswain appeared on the bridge wearing his best shore-going, gold-braided reefer jacket. 'Might as well do it proper,' the grizzled old mariner told the young officer.

Reeman then sighted

the first labouring formation of landing ships, with ranks of little landing craft tossing about like corks on either beam. They looked so frail, so ugly, and yet everything depended on them and their youthful commanders. They were the slowest vessels afloat and we had to reduce speed to keep station on them. It was getting lighter by the minute, the lines of ships stretching out abeam and ahead like a Roman phalanx on the advance. Someone gave a cheer and we saw the first of the heavy warships sweeping up from astern. The real navy. From our low hull the cruisers looked enormous with their streaming flags and their turrets already swinging towards the land, high-angled and ready to fire. On landing craft soldiers were standing on their tanks to cheer and wave their black berets while the ships surged past. It was infectious and we all waved and shouted into the din.

The reader may detect the hallmark precision in these details that enabled Douglas Reeman to pursue a successful post-war career as a novelist of fine sea-faring tales of the Second World War, and writing as Alexander Kent, the era of sail and shot.[13]

Further west, the bombardment fleet off Juno was led by the six-inch cruiser HMS *Belfast*, flying the flag of Rear Admiral Frederick Dalrymple-Hamilton, whose 10th Cruiser Squadron also included *Ajax*, *Argonaut*, *Emerald*, *Diadem* and *Orion*. Had Winston Churchill had his way, he would have been aboard the *Belfast* to watch the H-Hour bombardment, a distraction narrowly averted by Eisenhower and Ramsay. Thomas Nutter, in the aft control station, remembered *Belfast* 'lay with her starboard side facing the coast: all her six-inch guns were trained on France. Then 'X' turret fired one gun – a signal – after which all hell was let loose. Behind us and firing over us was the monitor HMS *Roberts* flinging its fifteen-inch shells, while hundreds of landing craft, crammed with troops and equipment, drove forward to the coast; it was a wonderful sight.'[14]

Donald Hunter, radio officer on board the Royal Fleet Auxiliary *Empire Pickwick*, recalled being 'between *Belfast* and the shore when she was engaging the coastal batteries, firing broadsides. We were too close for comfort. My ears were battered. It was so bad that I was completely deafened and my ears were bleeding.'[15] Nearby, hurling hot steel at Saint-Aubin and Courseulles, lurked the two Canadian destroyers that sailed with Neptune, HMCSs *Algonquin* and *Sioux* – part of the 26th Destroyer Flotilla. Their presence made Juno – where the 3rd Canadian Division were attacking – an all-Canuck affair, for they were supported by the one Motor Torpedo Boat and two Minesweeping Flotillas, eight boats in each, and all exclusively Canadian outfits.[16] Their charges included thirty Canadian-manned LCIs and a pair of landing ships, HMCS *Prince Henry* and HMCS *Prince David*. Both were former 6,000-ton Canadian National Steamship liners converted in 1943 into assault ships, and each equipped with six landing craft hanging from their davits, the former carrying the 1st Canadian Scottish, the latter the Régiment de la Chaudière.

Douglas Reeman recollected seeing 'the ripple of flashes along the grey horizon', and that he had to force himself

> not to duck as the great shells tore overhead with the sound of tearing canvas. It made speech impossible, and when we shouted to each other, our voices sounded strange, like divers talking under water. And all the while the lines of landing ships sailed on, some breaking away in smaller formations to head for their allotted beaches. It was heart-stopping to see them moving steadily through the smoke and falling spray. Nothing, it seemed, could stop them – the landing vessels, the following flotillas of barges and towed pontoons with grotesque bridges aboard, like giant Meccano sets. There was a single explosion on the far side of the nearest column and tongues of flame made the grey steel glow like burnished copper – another big shell had found its mark.[17]

Aboard HMS *Ajax* – then already well known for her part in the sinking of the *Admiral Graf Spee* in 1939 – was Midshipman Richard Llewellyn, who had left school aged seventeen only the year before. 'Along the French coast our bombers were busy, with fires raging,' Llewellyn noted in his midshipman's journal. '0500 hours. Reached buoy marking end of swept channel, turned to port opposite Gold Beach.' Assigned to *Ajax*'s gun room, Llewellyn recorded, '0530 hours, sighted target and opened fire. We fired 114 six-inch shells at 11,000 yards [6.2 miles] range. Assault craft went in at 0725 hours, smoke and noise, all ships bombarding.'[18]

Their target was the *Marine Küsten-batterie* (naval coastal battery) at Longues-sur-Mer, comprising four 152mm ex-destroyer guns in revolving steel turrets, each encased in a reinforced concrete casemate. In September 1943 the Germans had selected a clifftop position – known appropriately as Le Chaos, midway between Port-en-Bessin and Arromanches-les-Bains – for their guns and an observation bunker perched on the cliff's edge. Oberleutnant Kurt Weil's guns had a range of thirteen miles and were the most modern along the coast: his Kriegsmarine crews practised at firing six shells a minute. This was of huge concern to SHAEF, for Le Chaos could threaten both the Gold and Omaha fleets, as well as the harbour due to be assembled at Arromanches. Gradually they surrounded the area with landmines, built crew shelters, ammunition bunkers, machine-gun Tobruks and anti-aircraft positions, and labelled it on maps as *Widerstandsnest* (Resistance Nest) No. 48. They used compulsory local labour in its construction, compromising the site in two ways: the French workers weakened the concrete with sugar, whilst relaying all of its details to London; thus every aspect of it soon appeared on SHAEF planning maps.

Like the Merville and Azeville batteries, Longues received huge aerial attention before Overlord – and was similarly unharmed, despite the 1,500 tons of high explosive dumped on it between March and June. A further 604 tons of bombs were released in the hours preceding D-Day, again with little noticeable effect. Engaged by *Ajax* from 0530 hours, at 0620 Longues started firing at Allied warships, obliging HMS *Bulolo*, flagship of Force 'G', to shift anchor. *Ajax* and *Argonaut* retaliated and silenced the 180 German gunners at 0845, but later in the morning – after apparently rapid repair work – the battery again opened fire on the Omaha fleet.

Duelling with various Allied warships until well into the afternoon, one of the Skoda rapid-firing guns was eventually destroyed and two were damaged, but the battery had managed to fire a very creditable 115 rounds at the Neptune armada, before its remaining 120 artillerymen surrendered on 7 June to the 2nd Devonshires advancing from Gold Beach. Its significance is twofold. First, it remains in its original condition today, guns as they were found in June 1944, and forms one of the most visual representations of the Atlantic Wall, enhanced by a small visitor centre. Second, the surprisingly intact Le Chaos battery lurks as a monument to the claims of what the British and American 'bomber barons' claimed to be able to do, but failed to achieve.[19]

Near to *Ajax* was Lieutenant Stephen Barney, on the bridge of the brand-new destroyer HMS *Urania*, part of the 25th Destroyer Flotilla, who watched as their four 4.7-inch guns turned to open fire at the French coast. 'I had already been in action in the Saint-Nazaire raid back in 1942, so I sort of knew what to expect,' he related to me. 'We were lying off Gold Beach; it was 0625 hours and through our binoculars we were able to spot the explosions of our own shells and walk them onto the targets. We had to wear ear protectors, since the noise of the guns was really painful, and shout all our orders in the few moments between each salvo. Our cruisers had joined in from further out, and all the destroyers on either side were blazing away. I don't remember much return fire. Each ship was flying a massive battle ensign: it was a thrilling translation into vivid reality of every Nelsonian seafaring story I had ever read.' On the bridge of their sister destroyer, HMS *Undaunted*, Barney spotted its captain, Angus Mackenzie, 'in full Highland rig, playing the bagpipes as the whole thing got under way'.[20]

The American US destroyers off Normandy – affectionately known as the 'tin can fleet' – were all from the sixty-six-strong Gleaves class of vessels, which, unlike their British counterparts, possessed five superior five-inch guns, and fire control radar that allowed them to fire blind through the heavy smoke that shrouded the shore. The Royal Navy equivalents were the eighty-six destroyers of the much smaller Hunt-class vessels, equipped with four-inch weapons, though others, like Brown's S-class *Scourge* and Barney's U-class *Urania*, boasted 4.7-inch guns.

Seaman W. V. 'Bud' Taylor from Chandler, Texas, was a gunner's mate aboard the destroyer USS *Thompson* who knew all about firing guns in anger at the enemy, having engaged the Japanese when they attacked USS *Pennsylvania* on 7 December 1941. 'I was ready for them Germans, having dealt with those Japs at Pearl, when they came at us like a swarm of bees,' Taylor recounted. Normandy found him manning the *Thompson*'s port 40mm off Omaha: 'we'd spot, then we'd fire where them cliffs was; I put down over a thousand rounds. Our guys couldn't get up over them cliffs, so as soon as the Germans showed their heads, we'd shoot. Our guns also hit the pillboxes. We asked the *Texas* to give us a hand with one bunker, and three big old shells came over us, real slow it seemed to me, you could actually see them going *sssshhh*, and when they hit the pillbox there wasn't nothing left of it.'[21]

Don C. Derrah, with the fire direction crew aboard another destroyer, USS *Shubrick*, found himself off Utah Beach undertaking the same duty of gunfire support. '0530 hours: we started lobbing shells on schedule and in our designated areas. Our objectives are small batteries of eighty-eights grouped to one side of the landing area: range to target is seven to nine thousand yards,' he recorded.

> As the shelling rose in intensity, the area became obscured in heavy clouds of smoke. Only ten minutes of this and we slackened fire for observation. We didn't have time to find out the effect, for just then waves of A-20 Havocs and B-26 Marauders gave the beach an unmerciful bombing. As we watched, we wondered how any living thing could escape. The vibrations of the earth actually shook the ship. During the raid, several planes were hit. One, an A-20, was hit and burst into a huge flaming pyre. Only a small piece of the plane ever hit the ground.

Derrah also noted his captain had previously ordered his men 'to shave, shower and dress in clean clothes to reduce the chance of infection if they were wounded'.[22]

The *Shubrick* and the rest of the Anglo-American Force 'U' were directed by Rear Admiral Morton L. Deyo, his flag aboard the cruiser USS *Tuscaloosa*. In addition to seven cruisers, including the Dutch gunboat *Soemba*, he controlled the fourteen-inch guns of Pearl Harbor survivor USS *Nevada* and fifteen-inchers of the monitor HMS *Erebus*, the type named after the ironclad gunboat of the previous century, USS *Monitor*. Woodrow 'Woody' Wilson Derby, another veteran of Pearl Harbor aboard the *Nevada*, remembered being 'at general quarters off Normandy for eighty straight hours – I thought it would never stop. It began with the damnedest noise you ever heard in your life. Hundreds and hundreds of planes. Too dark to see them at first, but you could hear 'em.'[23]

Another witness wrote of the *Nevada* seeming 'to lean back' as her guns hit targets as distant as twenty miles – she fired 337 rounds of fourteen-inch and 2,693 of five-inch – though she would be straddled by counter-battery fire twenty-seven times.[24] Like the rest of the big-gunned warships, her floatplane artillery spotters had been temporarily assigned to HMS *Daedalus*, the 'stone frigate' airbase of Lee-on-Solent, where they learned to fly Spitfires in pairs – one to spot, the other to watch for the Luftwaffe. Ensign Stanley R. Rane, Jr was an airman with the US Naval Reserves. In 2018 I was shown his logbook after a chance encounter with his son who had brought the historic document to *Omaha* beach. It explained how seventeen pilots of the slow floatplanes carried on *Nevada, Texas, Arkansas* and the cruisers *Quincey, Augusta* and *Tuscaloosa* had been formed into Cruiser Scouting Squadron Seven (VCS-7). Their clipped-wing Spitfire Vbs were fitted with auxiliary fuel tanks, enabling missions of up to two hours' duration. Of the 191 sorties flown between D-Day and 26 June, when the squadron was broken up and pilots returned to their ships, Rane's logbook recorded eleven 'operational spotting for the Normandy invasion', flying twice on D-Day, and twice again on both the 7th and the 8th. Six long missions directing gunfire while piloting a single-seat fighter in three days: for these men there was no rest.[25]

Off Omaha, Flight Lieutenant Robert Weighill, piloting an RAF Mustang, was spotting the fall of shot for the six-inch cruiser HMS *Glasgow*: 'I stayed at 1,000 feet and watched five naval vessels turn broadside-on and proceed to belch flame and destruction. By this time, the first boat was almost ashore, the front came down, and I saw the men inside jump into the water and run to the beach. It was a wonderful moment when I reported the first men had actually landed.'[26] Traditionally, all the larger vessels corrected their fire by aerial spotting, but for Overlord, SHAEF's army planners preferred the enhanced accuracy of shore-based Royal Navy Forward Observation Bombardment (FOB) Parties – the US equivalent were the Navy Shore Fire Control Parties. In compromise, both were used, the airmen proving their value when shore parties were killed. Both defenders and invaders competed for the best observation platforms – the dominating spire at Sainte-Marie-du-Mont behind Utah and each of the three church towers along Omaha would be damaged by gunfire as the US Navy removed Wehrmacht spotters from their heights. Inland from Sword, a British FOB team would use the church tower at Ranville for observation.

Rear Admiral Carleton F. Bryant, USN, oversaw the big guns assembled off Omaha, including the battleships *Arkansas* and *Texas* – the two oldest ships present by some margin, launched in 1911 and 1912, respectively. They belonged to another era; there were no toilets or showers on board: men washed from buckets; and latrines consisted of a metal trough with seawater pumped through it. When hot, their guns were hosed down with salt water.[27] Like the larger British warships, it was their firepower that witnesses recalled. In the southern English naval base of Portland, the war correspondent for *Collier's* magazine – then boasting a circulation of 2.5 million, with a readership of many more – had boarded the 7,000-ton attack transport *Dorothea L. Dix*. Ernest Hemingway, larger-than-life adventurer, journalist and First World War hero, who had seemingly already experienced several lifetimes of combat, had made it his business to be present for the invasion. (No doubt he appreciated the irony of sailing to his war in a ship named for the nineteenth-century founder of a chain of American asylums for the mentally ill.)

Before transferring to a smaller LCVP bound for Omaha, Hemingway had previously flown across the English Channel wearing RAF blues adorned with 'War Correspondent' badges, carrying an issue escape kit of a French map printed on silk, money, compass and enough chocolate to last three days if shot down. 'He impressed me', thought his much-decorated pilot, Group Captain Peter Wykeham-Barnes, 'as the sort of man who spends his whole life proving that he is not scared.'[28] Coasting on the reputation and earnings of his bestselling 1940 novel about the Spanish Civil War, *For Whom the Bell Tolls* – probably unread by the average GI – Hemingway spent 6 June coasting in other ways.

He was not a fast writer, but an immensely polished one, and after several days' graft, wrote of D-Day morning:

> Those of our troops who were not wax-gray with seasickness, fighting it off, trying to hold on to themselves before they had to grab for the steel side of the boat, were watching the *Texas* with a look of surprise and happiness. Under the steel helmets they looked like pikemen of the Middle Ages to whose aid in battle had come some strange and unbelievable monster … There would be a flash like a blast furnace from the fourteen-inch guns of the *Texas* that would lick far out from the ship. Then the yellow brown smoke would cloud out and, with smoke rolling, the concussion and report would hit us, jarring the men's helmets. It struck your ear like the punch of a heavy, dry glove. I was glad when we were out of the line of fire of the *Texas* and the *Arkansas*. Other ships were firing over us all day and you were never away from the

sudden, slapping thud of naval gunfire. But the big guns of the *Texas* and *Arkansas*, that sounded as though they were throwing whole railway trains across the sky, were far away as we moved on in.[29]

Hemingway titled his short piece 'Voyage to Victory', and it was as well received by the military as by the general public: his knack of being able to reach the central nervous system of his readership was reflected by US Admiral Samuel Eliot Morison's observation that it was 'the best account yet written by a passenger in an LCVP'.[30]

Although he travelled to the beach in a landing craft, Hemingway did not actually land – none of the three hundred war correspondents were permitted to on the first day – but this was not the impression given by his piece, and a misunderstanding often repeated by D-Day historians.[31] His piece began, memorably, 'No one remembers the date of the Battle

Among those assigned to cover the American landings was the Jewish-Hungarian refugee Endre Friedman (1913–54) (left). Already world famous from his photo-journalism of the Spanish Civil War, as Robert Capa he would record the morning of 6 June on Omaha. So too would the award-winning writer Ernest Hemingway (1899–1961) (right), his War Correspondent's patch visible on his left shoulder. They are seen here with Capa's often un-named driver, Olin L. Tompkins (1917–2007) in France on 30 July 1944. (US Army Signal Corps)

of Shiloh. But the day we took Fox Green beach was the sixth of June, and the wind was blowing hard out of the northwest. As we moved in toward land in the gray early light, the 36-foot coffin-shaped steel boats took solid green sheets of water that fell on the helmeted heads of the troops, packed shoulder to shoulder in the stiff, awkward, uncomfortable, lonely companionship of men going to a battle.'

Whereas most war correspondents took on the role of observers, Hemingway immediately associated himself with the troops: the GIs were 'we', not 'they'. It worked as a piece of writing, though was not strictly accurate, because he was not part of the 'we' that took Fox Green. Semantically, the 'we' might have been referring to America, but the Hemingway-esque implication was there: he was back, fighting another of the wars that had characterised his life. The writer was at the height of his fame, and the 22 July edition of the fortnightly *Collier's* that carried the piece sold the most copies of any in its sixty-nine year history. Nevertheless, Hemingway's picture of the LCVP delivers the goods:

> There were cases of TNT, with rubber-tube life preservers wrapped around them to float them in the surf, stacked forward in the steel well of the LCVP, and there were piles of bazookas and boxes of bazooka rockets encased in waterproof coverings that reminded you of the transparent raincoats college girls wear. All this equipment, too, had the rubber-tube life preservers strapped and tied on, and the men wore these same gray rubber tubes strapped under their armpits ... As the LCVP rose to the crest of a wave, you saw the line of low, silhouetted cruisers and the two big battlewagons lying broadside to the shore. You saw the heat-bright flashes of their guns and the brown smoke that pushed out against the wind and then blew away.[32]

The crew of *LCT-614* noted that because of the narrow channels the minesweepers had cleared, they had to 'chug under the gunfire support ships, where the concussion from the eight-inch guns of USS *Augusta* felt worse than the Luftwaffe's bombs that had fallen around them in Portland'. *Augusta*'s weapons produced 'the most ear-splitting, deafening, horrendous sound I have ever heard,' thought Ensign Victor Hicken.[33] Unknown to him, *Augusta* at that moment was carrying Alan Kirk, commander of the US fleet, and Omar Bradley, the most senior army officer present, who had worked very harmoniously together since Husky in July 1943. Bradley would write later of *Augusta*'s 'curved yachtlike bow and rakish beauty among the snub-nosed LSTs', and was assigned the cabin occupied by President Roosevelt when he met Churchill to sign the August 1941 Atlantic Charter.[34] Bradley's operations room occupied the hangar used by the cruiser's floatplanes: 'The wall had been papered with a Michelin motoring map of France. Next to it hung a terrain study of the assault beaches. Between them a Petty pin-up girl lounged on a far more alluring beach. A long plotting table filled the centre of the room.'[35]

Unaware of *Augusta*'s significance as a headquarters ship, other than as a creator of unpleasant noise, *LCT-614* afterwards rounded the stern of USS *Arkansas*, just as the dreadnought-era battleship loosed a broadside from its twelve-inch guns. 'The blast and noise rattled the little LCT and hurt the men on deck', who thought that 'had they been any closer, the concussion could have easily flipped the little craft over'. They turned and found themselves 'looking straight down the muzzles of the battleship's guns'.[36] On his LCT, Sergeant Hyam Haas from Brooklyn – commanding two half-tracks of the 467th Anti-Aircraft Artillery Battalion and bound for Omaha – noted USS *Texas* letting go: 'I had always wanted to hear what one of those salvos sounded like. The sound wasn't like the distant thunder I had imagined. It was like a very loud rifle shot with plenty of concussion. A sharp crack.'[37] Aboard the eight-inch cruiser USS *Quincy*, one witness thought

> One of the most dramatic places was the upper fire control room. Requests would come in to deliver shots at such and such a place, the coordinates supplied as methodically as ordering groceries. Radio reception was perfect. There would be a tzz-tzz-BOOM signifying the shells were on their way. After an appropriate interval, our man would say 'Flash!' into the microphone, meaning the shells were about to hit. A few seconds later the spotter would report '100 yards over' or something similar, and we would correct. Sometimes he would say: 'Right on the target', and we would feel good.[38]

For Major Robin McGarel-Groves, a Royal Marine gunnery officer serving with the British cruiser HMS *Enterprise*, 6 June 1944 was his twenty-fourth birthday. Assigned to suppress the German battery at Varreville, he noted 'at around 0630 hours, quite near us, the American destroyer USS *Corry* was duelling with a gun emplacement, which soon got her range. She should have been protected by smoke, and we saw her suffer several hits amidships, she went round in a circle and then sank. She soon settled on the bottom and later, a yet-to-be-rescued member of her crew raised the American flag up her main mast, which flew for the rest of the day.'[39] In fact her sister destroyer, USS *Fitch* – who would claim the first shot fired off Utah, at 0535 hours – had also been straddled and only narrowly avoided a similar fate.

Richard Stout, a British war correspondent 'perched on the upper bridge of USS *Quincy*, had a sort of grandstand seat for the whole thing. With binoculars I could see about twenty or thirty miles of cliff and beach. Watching the little American destroyer slowly demolished by shore batteries that had it bracketed was a hard experience. They caught it again and again while our big guns and those of our neighbours tried to silence them.'[40] Fifteen minutes after USS *Corry*'s demise, the destroyer HMS *Wrestler*, an old vessel brought out of retirement to escort convoys, struck a mine off Juno Beach. She managed to limp back to Portsmouth, but was so comprehensively damaged that she would be scrapped within the month. Including the *Svenner*, the invasion had already cost three Allied destroyers before a single soldier had landed.

'We were told that "every grain of sand will be turned over twice before the first waves hit the beach",' Lieutenant Stephen Barney, aboard the destroyer *Urania*, remembered. 'I think it was about 0715 hours when a rocket landing craft appeared alongside. Suddenly she fired, and we could see six hundred or so rockets fly through the air. Each must have been the equivalent of a six-inch shell.' With the big guns of the battle-ships, the eight- and six-inch cannon of the cruisers, and smaller destroyers all hurling their shells at the Germans, the final phase of the bombardment was about to begin.

Barney noted: 'If our guns hadn't done the job, we felt that certainly no one could be alive after those rockets. We had visions of obliterated concrete bunkers and exploded minefields.'[41] He was referring to a few of the long, sleek, keel-less tank landing craft that had been converted for other roles. Those that Barney noticed, which had their front ramps welded shut, were equipped with racks of five-inch, sixty-pound rockets – LCT(R)s. These shallow-draught rocket craft were designed to lay down 'drenching fire' in an intense salvo just prior to the initial assault waves landing, by pointing themselves in the direction of flight, close to the surf. Thirty-six of them accompanied the fleet to Normandy, a handful to each beach.

Sub Lieutenant Bill Golding, RNVR, had served on the light cruiser HMS *Galatea* in the North Atlantic hunting for the *Bismarck*, before being posted to 'dangerous steel boxes', his terminology for landing craft. Commissioned from the ranks, D-Day found Golding in command of *LCT(R)-460* at Gold Beach: 'Crossing the Channel my craft fell behind, forcing me to steam at full speed all night over jet-black waves, frightened not immediately of the mines that we might set off, but of being late, and jeered at.' Golding would later operate the firing mechanism from his armoured bridge and watched the 'devastating effect of the wall of fire and destruction that was unleashed' as his myriad rockets erupted on the German defenders in a giant pyrotechnic display; their damage often proved less impressive than their sight and sound. Golding warned later that 'the heat and blast is not unendurable, though breathing is inadvisable and beards should not be worn'. Later he described 'ships mined, ships blowing up into a Christmas tree of exploding ammunition, ships burning, sinking – and smoke everywhere, slashed by sudden spats of tracer over shell fountains, and broken, drowning men'. (Most

Some thirty-six LCT(R) rocket-equipped landing craft accompanied the fleet to Normandy, a handful to each beach. Sub Lieutenant Bill Golding (later author of *Lord of the Flies*) remembered the 'devastating effect of the wall of fire and destruction that was unleashed'. The rockets appear to have had little effect on the defenders, but were a tremendous boost to the morale of those about to storm ashore. (NARA)

students of a certain age would encounter his dark writings not in terms of D-Day, but of children marooned on an island in *Lord of the Flies*.)[42]

'They were most impressive: firing their missiles over the heads of the troops going in, we were firing over the top of those and HMS *Warspite* was firing over the top of us,' recalled the gunnery officer of destroyer HMS *Scourge*, Stephen Brown. The future High Court judge was watching the rocket craft off Sword. However, his main attention was focused on German bunkers along the seafront at Ouistreham. 'We had just come off an Arctic convoy and found ourselves in the vanguard of D-Day. The bombardment is something I will never forget: at 0630 hours we opened up on our targets in Ouistreham – I recall thinking, "I'm rather glad I am not on the receiving end", but we had tremendous confidence.'[43]

The rocket ships, which released their missiles fifteen minutes before H-Hour at all five beaches, were accompanied by self-propelled artillery in LCTs – British Army 25-pounder 'Sextons' and American 105mm 'Priests' – firing their guns during the final run-in, to add to the 'drenching fire'. Given the sea conditions, it was the noise they generated rather than the damage they caused – mainly rearranging the barbed wire along the promenades – that seems to have been their main impact. Contributing to the artillery fire on Gold Beach during the run-in was Lieutenant Basil Heaton with the 86th (Hertfordshire Yeomanry) Field Regiment, whose troop of four 25-pounder 'Sextons' opened fire at '0650 hours, closing on the shore at 200 yards per minute. We landed at 0805 hours just below the Ver-sur-Mer lighthouse and in front of the Mont Fleury artillery battery, in support of 69th Brigade. I lost my signaller to a sniper's bullet; some small craft had capsized, an armoured car was on fire and, of the armada of landing craft that were unloading, several were burning and some were foundering in the sea.'[44]

Responsible for some of the 'drenching' artillery fire off Omaha were two battalions of self-propelled 105mm guns in LCTs. Jim Weller, with the 62nd Armored Field Artillery, recalled closing in the eastern sector to within 'a thousand yards, firing on targets the navy had selected. We were firing white phosphorus shells and yellow smoke, marking targets for *Texas* and *Arkansas*.'[45] North Carolinian Sergeant John H. Glass, with the 58th Armored Field Artillery, manned another 105mm 'Priest' off Omaha's western beaches. He had already accompanied his gun to North Africa and Sicily; this would be their third amphibious assault together. Billeted before D-Day in the seventeenth-century splendour of Adderbury

House, Oxfordshire, their tracked vehicles had great fun rearranging the park, once landscaped by Lancelot 'Capability' Brown at about the time the United States was founded.

They had departed their marshalling area near Dorchester on 1 June, and – distributed between eighteen landing craft – left Weymouth at 0330 hours on the fifth. The following morning they opened up on shore targets from H−30 (0600) until H−5 (0625). The unit war diary noted, '0630 hours–0730 hours: Heavy casualties among the Forward Observation and Reconnaissance parties landing with leading waves of 116th Infantry. Battalion CO and Recon Officer killed.' Then later, '1030 hours: four LCTs struck mines, another capsized. Eleven guns ashore, one gun and one half-track lost on *LCT-332*.'[46]

It was this craft of the 18th LCT Flotilla that was carrying Glass and his 105mm gun. In May 1992 he recalled stepping off the sinking craft wearing his life preserver, watching the gun plunge with all his possessions beneath the waves. Lieutenant W. Fitzpatrick's LCT crew floated off with him, and all were rescued. Nearly fifty years later, salvage divers located his tracked gun on the seabed off Omaha, raised it with the two tons of ready-to-use ammunition Glass remembered they carried, and the former gunner flew to Normandy to be reunited with the vehicle and remains of his kit, last seen on 6 June 1944. Both gun and Glass's personal effects are on display in the Port-en-Bessin wreck museum, a unique institution that has effectively frozen such moments of time.[47]

These were the final elements of the pre-assault bombardment which had begun with aircraft, followed by the battleships, cruisers, then destroyers, rockets and, finally, light artillery fire. As Sergeant Charles Hurlbut with the US 299th Combat Engineers observed, 'when our craft started toward the beach, all the battleships opened up with their big guns. You never heard noise like that in your life. Prior to that, we had heard the bombers. And as we get closer we can see the fighter planes strafing the beach. Then we pass a rocket ship, a big flat affair loaded with rockets, "*Phshoo! Phshoo! Phshoo!*" We saw the rockets, the naval guns, the planes and thought, "How could anything live through what they're getting? It's going to be a piece of cake – there'll be nothing alive there." We'd been promised way back in England, "There'll be so many craters, all you'll have to do is jump into a crater, and you'll be protected."'[48]

Or, as a soldier in the 1st Hampshires, observing all the bombs, shells, missiles and noise, quipped to his brigadier, 'Fancy having that lot on your breakfast plate, sir!'[49]

21

Boats and Bugles

'All along the fringe of the bay, as far as visibility would permit, I could see smoke, fire and explosions. Inland some areas were completely smudged out by evil clouds of smoke. Underneath it, great flashes of fire would erupt and burst, like bolts of orange lightning. Normandy was like a huge, fire-rimmed boiling cauldron. To seaward, ships of all shapes and sizes lay patiently at anchor. Between them and the beaches, an extraordinary regatta was taking place as hundreds of smaller craft dashed hither and thither.'
Wing Commander Desmond Scott, *Typhoon Pilot* (1982)[1]

IN THE GREAT Neptune armada, after the minesweepers and warships came the assault flotillas. Most soldiers recalled their journey across the waves with varying degrees of discomfort, brought on by the weather or nerves or both. The armies were brought in a variety of vessels, ranging from the largest troopships and LSTs, smaller flat-bottomed craft bearing infantry (LCIs) and tanks (LCTs), right down to the tiny, barely seaworthy LCMs, all of which had to make their own way across the Channel carefully shepherded by Ramsay's grey-hulled fleet. The most diminutive craft, the Landing Craft, Assault (LCAs) and their American equivalents, Landing Craft Vehicle, Personnel (LCVPs) – the Higgins boats – would arrive off Normandy piggybacked on larger assault landing ships.

These tiddlers would convey the fighting men from their mother ships to the surf, but with each small landing craft capable of taking only thirty, less than a battalion could be put ashore from each assault landing ship at any one time. Towards dawn, aboard one Utah-bound LCT, Sub Lieutenant W. B. Carter saw 'the small red lights issued to all troops fixed to the lapels of survivors bobbing about in the water'. Even though against orders, he paused to fish them out of the drink, something accomplished with difficulty, 'for although the tanks were properly secured to the deck, there was barely nine inches between the tanks, and as one slid between them, one could feel one's chest being slightly squeezed as the ship rolled', he recalled. 'It was hardly an auspicious start for the rest of the troops.'[2]

Despite much rehearsing in Scotland and along the south coast, filling a ship's complement of landing craft generally took about an hour – off Omaha, USS *Thomas Jefferson* would unload the 2nd Battalion of the 116th Infantry in a timed sixty-six minutes.[3] Sometimes craft were filled first, then lowered – but with embarrassing results if the mechanism jammed during the descent. Early on 6 June, the 1st Battalion headquarters group of the US 116th Infantry Regiment were left hanging for thirty minutes right under the *Empire Javelin*'s heads (latrines), discharging ordure straight into the Channel. As Major Thomas S. Dallas, XO (executive officer) of the 1st Battalion, noted, 'Streams, colored everything from canary yellow to sienna brown, continued to flush onto the command group, decorating every man aboard. We cursed, we cried and we laughed, but it kept coming. When we started for shore, we were all covered with sh*t.'[4]

Notwithstanding such inconveniences, it then took a minimum of two vomit-inducing hours for ship-to-shore runs, so the major landing ships would spend much of 6 June at anchor discharging their men, retrieving their boats and repeating the process. Thus the Allied land forces who stormed ashore on D-Day did so, trickling in by platoons and companies, rather than as an irresistible phalanx of men and materiel – and making them easier to oppose.

GIs were unhappy at being issued a last-minute special set of overalls, impregnated with chemicals designed to protect against gas attack, as we noted earlier. Landing craft crews were issued with similar garments. The replacement uniforms did not let the skin breathe like regular cotton, 'were hot as hell, itchy and their odor was unbearable', recalled one, 'like rotten eggs'. They made soldiers feel they were 'walking around in a steam bath', which only added to the general nausea brought on by seasickness. Some began to wonder if poison gas might not be more preferable.[5] Chuck Hurlbut with the 299th Combat Engineer Battalion, about to conquer Omaha, recounted, 'They gave us these impregnated coveralls. They were so stiff and unwieldy they could almost stand up by themselves. They had been specially treated with some solution that would withstand gas. You put those on. And on top of that, you had your belt, your gas mask, a bandolier of bullets. And your cartridge belt had a bayonet, a canteen, a first aid packet, and more bullets. Your helmet. And your rifle. And your backpack.'[6]

Anxiety was heightened for those waiting to disembark, with an eye cast always towards the smoking French coastline, lit up with bright flashes, portending nothing good. The loitering at anchor also worried everyone on account of the potential threat from the Luftwaffe. Old hands from Sicily, Salerno and Anzio were particularly nervous, remembering occasions when roving planes had done serious damage to the seaborne invaders. At Gold Beach, Gunner Edwin 'Nobby' Clarke, operating 25-pounders with the 74th Field Regiment, himself a veteran Mediterranean campaigner, recalled his merchant-marine-crewed Liberty ship, whose 'skipper was English, first mate Russian and the remainder multinational. As we waited for landing craft to come alongside, two Messerschmitt 109s flew at us. Three of the crew dashed below deck to get ammunition for the ship's single anti-aircraft gun; they returned in a few seconds each carrying a different calibre shell, none of which fitted the gun. By this time the two Messerschmitts were out of sight.'[7] The air threat was very real: apart from mine-laying, dive-bombing and torpedo runs, in 1943 the Luftwaffe had used their new glider bombs to sink the transport *Rohna* and damage the battleship HMS *Warspite* and cruisers USS *Savannah*, USS *Philadelphia* and HMS *Uganda*, causing severe loss of life. Despite the patrolling air umbrella, on 8 June 1944, more glider bombs launched by the Luftwaffe's KG-200 would account for the destroyer USS *Meredith* and frigate HMS *Lawford*.[8]

As noted in the Introduction, there remains an erroneous impression of American primacy on D-Day, driven by the many newsreels of the era – perhaps understandably so, given their intended target audience. While US dominance would be true later on during the campaign to liberate France, 6 June perhaps represented Britain's last moment of military pre-eminence, before surrendering the whip-hand to the United States. We have seen that eighty per cent of the maritime element deployed on the day of invasion was British, not American. Amongst the landing ships of Admiral Hall's Force 'O', carrying troops to Omaha and the Pointe du Hoc, eight were British-manned – *Empire Javelin* and

Empire Anvil, Ben-my-Chree, Amsterdam, Princess Maud, Prince Charles, Prince Leopold and *Prince Baudouin.* The other seven flew the Stars and Stripes: *Thomas Jefferson, Charles Carroll, Samuel Chase, Henrico, Anne Arundel, Dorothea L. Dix* and *Thurston.*

These last were purpose-built USN attack transports. The former were an array of requisitioned ferries and steamers, converted to an assault landing role and manned by the British Merchant and Royal Navies. In fact, the whole British assault fleet ranged from former liners, like the 10,000-ton HMS *Monowai*, carrying twenty LCAs, to HMS *Ben-my-Chree*, a 3,000-ton Isle of Man ferry, or the 2,000-ton Great Western Railways steamer HMS *St Helier*, both of which carried just six little craft. The landing barges carried on all the larger ships were grouped into flotillas of six to ten boats each, commanded by young reservist officers of the RN, RCN, USN or US Coast Guard.

The transatlantic maritime partnership was perhaps better highlighted during the afternoon of D-Day, when on Sword Beach a flotilla of ten American-manned LCIs landed some of the second wave of the British 3rd Division. Even the splendidly named *Empire*-class assault ships – technically known as Landing Ships, Infantry (Large) and ordered by the British Ministry of War Transport – had been manufactured by the Consolidated Steel Corporation of Wilmington, California. The yard employed twelve thousand folk building over five hundred major wartime vessels, and delivered the *Empires* in early 1944. Each was of about 11,000 tons, carried a crew of 250 with sixteen or eighteen LCAs suspended from their davits, while accommodating 1,500 troops.

They more than proved their value, with all thirteen *Empires* carrying assault-wave troops on D-Day to four of the five beaches; the exception was Juno, where several of the landing ships were converted Canadian steamers, manned by Canadian crews. At H-Hour on Sword Beach, the 537th LCA Flotilla from HMS *Empire Battleaxe* took the 2nd East Yorkshires ashore, *Empire Broadsword* carried the 1st Suffolks, while *Empire Cutlass* landed troops of the 1st South Lancashires – all assault battalions of the 8th Brigade, British 3rd Division. Over at Gold Beach, HMSs *Empire Arquebus, Empire Crossbow* and *Empire Spearhead* landed the 231st Brigade at Le Hamel, with *Empires* Halberd, Lance, Mace and Rapier, putting the 69th Brigade ashore at Ver-sur-Mer (both of the British 50th Division).

The 550th LCA Flotilla from HMS *Empire Anvil* landed troops from the 3rd Battalion of the 16th Infantry, US 1st Division, on the eastern

In 1943 the British ordered thirteen 7,000-ton *Empire*-class assault ships, built in the USA, which could each accommodate 1,500 troops and sixteen landing craft. In this little-known image, a Royal Marine-manned LCA of 536th Flotilla pulls away from the *Empire Cutlass* during rehearsals to land the 1st South Lancashires on Sword beach. (NARA)

edge of Omaha at Colleville, whilst HMS *Empire Javelin*'s 551st Flotilla put the 1st Battalion of the 116th Infantry, 29th Division, onto Omaha's western fringes, at Vierville. Finally, Utah witnessed the eighteen LCAs from HMS *Empire Gauntlet*'s 552nd LCA Flotilla deliver the 8th Infantry of the 4th Division.

Thus far, the fates of those taking part in Operation Neptune had been pretty uniform. Exciting, challenging, dangerous – but a similar range of experiences in the approach to the five beaches. The day began with sailors and soldiers marvelling at the vast array of shipping. Some had glimpsed the armada the previous evening, but many were too seasick to notice – or care. Lieutenant William G. Pepe, with Headquarters Company, US 5th Engineer Special Brigade heading for Omaha, recollected that 'We had absolutely no awareness of the magnitude of this operation until the morning light. We had all made our peace with God and the sudden sight of the fleet infused a massive boost of confidence. Morale soared and adrenalin flowed in rivers throughout our bodies: now, we realised we were no longer alone in our insignificant little ship, but a part of this huge fighting force.'[9]

A jeep driver with No. 5 Beach Group recalled his moment of arrival on 'Queen Red', part of Sword Beach. 'It was 0725 hours and I stood up expecting to see the coast on the horizon – not two hundred yards away. I had no idea we had arrived already. Only then, looking to my right, sorry starboard, did I see the landing craft of all sizes as far as the eye could see, and I realised the fountains of water appearing all around came from the enemy, not spouting whales.'[10] Others were able to watch Neptune remotely: Lieutenant Robert A. Jacobs on the *Liberty Run*, a B-24 of the 389th Bomb Group – the 'Sky Scorpions' from RAF Hethel in Norfolk – recalled: 'As we approached the French coast, the navigator called me over to look at his PRI scope. It clearly showed the vast armada standing just off the coast of Normandy – a thrilling sight even on radar!'[11]

Now the full impact of what was unfolding – and the implications of the minute-by-minute timetable – hit them. Once under way, Neptune would be like some giant industrial machine in Fritz Lang's 1927 film *Metropolis*, whose 'on' button had already been pushed, but for which there was no 'off' button. Colonel Red Reeder of the 12th Infantry thought 'the whole movement looked like a well-rehearsed play'.[12] The steady hum of Allied aircraft overhead – not always visible through the overcast – started the day on an uplifting note. However, as the smaller landing craft were cast off and, in company with the larger LCIs and LCTs, started to make their way over the last few miles of ocean to the sand and shingle, in the fashion of a giant surrealist jigsaw, events would play out in a far from uniform fashion.

The first discordant note was H-Hour. As each individual concentrated on his own few yards of French shoreline, few would have been aware that because of the tide differential and unique geography of the Normandy coast, GIs would be landing sixty minutes ahead of their

Canadian and British comrades-in-arms. The beach reconnaissances had already shown that the seashore gradients were very gentle, gaining on average only one foot of height for every fifty feet of sand. The average distance uncovered between high and low tides was six hundred yards. With a pretty extreme tidal range – the water rising on average twenty feet from low tide, twice a day – the shape of each beach altered dramatically through the day. On 6 June 1944 low water was at 0552 and 1810 hours, with high tide exactly five hours later.[13]

The simple maths was that all along the coast, the tide would rise 240 inches in 300 minutes, four inches every five minutes, a foot every quarter of an hour. This would be lethal for the wounded lying on the shingle, men taking cover, or vehicles fighting for a diminishing water-free patch of sand, but helpful for retracting beached landing craft. Thus, the decision of precisely what time to land, H-Hour, had been the subject of as much debate for Eisenhower as it had been for Rommel and Rundstedt.

The Allied land commanders had advised a high-tide assault, when the killing zones on the beaches would be at their narrowest – something the Desert Fox anticipated, hence his programme of erecting mined beach obstacles, which would be covered by the water at such an hour. Thus invisible, they were designed to rip the landing craft apart. Fearing catastrophe amid the obstructions and surf, Ramsay and his fellow admirals advised a low-water landing – with the obstacles exposed, allowing beach demolition units to clear channels through them for the landing craft. However, this would leave long stretches, averaging a third of a mile, of dangerous beach for the infantry to rush.

The compromise was to attack *after* low tide, with the exposed area narrowing. For Utah and Omaha, this was fixed at 0630 hours. Aboard *LCT-88*, Beachmaster Lieutenant Commander Joseph P. Vaghi noted that his craft 'kissed the sands of Normandy when the tide was almost at its lowest, a half-mile from the dune line of Easy Red sector on Omaha'.[14] However, there was another fly in the ointment. Low water exposed sand bars in the British sector – impossible for landing craft to cross. This necessitated a later H-Hour of 0725 hours on Gold and Sword, when the assault craft would be able to pass over.

The rising tide was to help the landing craft flotillas, which were less likely to get stranded as the waters rose – their job was to shuttle men and equipment ashore, so it was vital they remain seaborne, not beached. However, this was at the cost of many tanks and vehicles potentially drowning, due to faulty waterproofing or unexpected depths in pools and runnels – unlikely to happen with a falling tide. There would be a high price paid by the landing craft, too. Submerged vehicles subsequently became underwater obstacles for following waves of craft, and accounted for much hull damage and fouled anchors among landing fleet. Beaches were easier at low tide with more room to manoeuvre around the debris of earlier waves, when the remaining obstacles were exposed. At high tide, the available sand rapidly became crowded and the waters cluttered with submerged wreckage.

Historical assessments tend to focus on landing vessels sunk, rather than damaged ones still afloat, which consumed valuable resources and slowed timetables. The practical effect of craft mangled by swamped boats and vehicles was that, for example, only nine out of the thirty-six in the American 18th LCT Flotilla at Omaha, which had arrived early on 6 June, were operational by the following morning. This translates as seventy-five per cent non-operational, which was a surprisingly common statistic across all five landing areas, with bent rudders, lost kedge anchors and broken ramps, or ramp winches, being the most common features. This was not damage caused by German guns or mines, but by Allied equipment. All could be repaired locally by the salvage and repair tenders accompanying the fleet, but this took time, and ate into the sustainment schedule. Both *LCT-415* and *LCT-460*, damaged but not destroyed, were recorded as being shipped to Portsmouth on D+9 aboard the LSD (Landing Ship, Dock) HMS *Oceanway*, which had earlier brought LCMs to the area – an example of the huge logistics backup for Neptune.[15]

The next note of discord was how long the naval gunfire support should last. Given that the fleet would open fire simultaneously – in theory at 0550 hours, though earlier in practice – the invasion of occupied France would commence after forty minutes of naval gunfire support in the US sector with their earlier H-Hour, but over double that against the defenders of the British and Canadian beaches.

'This gift of time', wrote Bradley bitterly, 'enabled the warships of the Royal Navy to deliver to Monty's beaches a two-hour daylight bombardment, nearly four times the length of the bombardment at Utah and Omaha.'[16] This weighted the firepower away from Omaha and Utah and towards the Anglo-Canadian sector. It also allowed the latter more sleep – those who could. Captain Donald Gilchrist of No. 4 Commando had dozed in his bunk aboard the *Prinses Astrid*, the converted Belgian cross-Channel ferry. As his batman woke him at 0330 he noticed 'the steel plates juddering as the ship's head rose and fell to plough the sea. "It's me, Sir, McCall. I've brought your tommy-gun, Sir, cleaned and checked – over there, with one filled magazine.'[17] On the *Prince Baudouin*, another Belgian steamer taking the 5th Rangers to their rendezvous with the surf, it was at 0400 that she downed anchor and her loudspeakers sprang into life announcing, 'Attention on deck! Attention on deck! British crews report to their assault boats.' The *Prinses Astrid* reached her anchorage off Sword Beach an hour later, noted Stan Hough, when her master announced, 'Hear ye, hear ye! This is your captain speaking. Crew to action stations, commandos to assault craft! And the best of luck!'[18]

With radio silence broken at 0530 hours – five minutes later in the British sector – the code word 'Floater' flashed through the air to 'A' and 'B' Squadrons, 13th/18th Hussars, off Sword Beach; the Fort Garry Horse and 1st Canadian Hussars off Juno; and the Sherwood Rangers Yeomanry, and 'B' and 'C' Squadrons of the 4th/7th Royal Dragoon Guards, off Gold. This instructed them to launch their DD swimming tanks. Some were launched five thousand yards offshore, but many more were taken much closer in because of the rough seas, and landed later. The American tank battalions – the 70th at Utah and 741st and 743rd at Omaha – were also launched, with mixed results, as Chuck Hurlbut with the 299th Combat Engineers witnessed: 'We passed a craft carrying tanks with the big canvas collar around them. When they hit the water, these canvas things would allow them to float until they could reach land. And this thing started letting them off. The first went "*blooop!*" straight down. Second one: "*blooop!*" Three or four went down like that. And we're right alongside of it. All of a sudden the guys come bobbing up, fighting for breath and air, they're like corks in the water, yelling and screaming. I hope they were rescued. We could not stop: had to go right by them – boy, that hurt to watch.'[19]

Later still, at 0558 hours, seven miles off Gold Beach, the echoes of a bugle could be heard aboard HMS *Empire Lance*, playing reveille. This was to summon the 6th Green Howards of the 69th Infantry Brigade on deck and commence boarding for their voyage to Ver-sur-Mer. Wherever possible, naval veterans of the Mediterranean assault landings were put to good use in Normandy. Lieutenant Alasdair Forbes Ferguson had already landed Canadian troops at Dieppe and the 50th Division in Sicily. This time, in command of the 524th LCA Flotilla aboard the *Empire Arquebus*, his appointment was to lead Brigadier Stanier's 231st Brigade onto Gold Beach at Le Hamel.

The 7,000-ton landing ship HMS *Clan Lamont* heading for Juno was 'crammed full of French-Canadian troops, who spent most of their time on board queuing up to sharpen their commando knives on the grindstone in the galley and playing "Crown and Anchor" on the mess deck, using the invasion money we had been issued'. They were treated to an early breakfast of 'pork chops and a choice of stewed prunes, apricots or fresh fruit. A lot of the men couldn't face it, but one had to be sensible about this – you didn't know when you were going to eat again.'[20] Generally, His Majesty's ships offered little in the way of a cooked meal – though how many might have wanted one in the rough swell is debatable.

At the very least, all British troops were given corned beef sandwiches and tots of rocket-fuel-strength rum that came from great stoneware jars, stowed in each landing craft – a throwback to 'grog' issues of Nelson's day. George Kirkby, coxswain of one of the *Prinses Astrid*'s LCAs, remembered two crewmen being stretchered aboard. They hadn't been wounded, but were legless from having over-indulged on some of the spirit. Many used cigarettes to calm their nerves; Lieutenant Roy Clark, commanding *LCT-770*, packed with 9th Canadian Brigade vehicles, found he had smoked sixty cigarettes on the crossing to stay awake. 'I didn't think I was a heavy smoker, but there was the evidence in my duffle coat pockets: three empty packets of *Capstan Navy-Cut!* It must have been about 0130 hours when I saw the bombing of France over the horizon, which was then about forty miles away, to judge by the flashes in the sky.'[21] Older soldiers showed their experience: the youngsters watched them 'pack cigarettes and matches into Elastoplast tins and seal them carefully with sticky tape. With the same cunning care they stuck pieces of adhesive tape over the muzzles of their weapons.'[22]

'The accommodation for the troops was primitive,' telegraphist Alan Higgins noted of his British LCA bound for Sword. 'Just rows of wooden, ribbed seats, like park benches. The guys were packed like sardines, with all the equipment, weapons and webbing they needed. The stench of vomit was terrible.'[23] Another soldier remembered sitting in his LCA 'on fixed bench seats, one row to port, another to starboard and one along the centre. It was a tight squeeze: thirty or so men with rucksacks, Bren guns, rifles, tommy-guns, bangalore torpedoes, radios, festooned like Christmas trees'.[24] Many GIs wrapped their rifles in waterproof plastic, which can be seen in newsreels and photographs taken on the day. In the Higgins boats, there was no seating; troops stood, crouched or sat on the deck for the ride.

Louisianan John 'J.J.' Witmeyer, a platoon commander with the 12th Infantry destined for Utah, reported of the LCVPs: 'they were made out of quarter-inch plywood, but the navy painted 'em grey so they would look like steel to us. There was a damned ramp at the front, about seven foot high. You couldn't see over it and you couldn't make yourself heard because the flat bottom kept slappin' the waves like thunder. The motor and the waves drowned all conversation.'[25] The British and American landing boats were similar, but not the same: LCAs were heavier, lightly armoured and sat lower in the water, but ran on a pair of silenced engines and had been developed for commando raids; LCVPs could take a small vehicle – which LCAs could not – and were faster. Both could carry weapons: LCVPs often had a pair of stern-mounted 0.50-inch machine guns, the LCA was equipped with a 0.303-inch Lewis gun in its portside armoured shelter – but neither was designed for rough seas.

Whatever the nationality or destination of the infantrymen, the process of leaving their mother ships was generally the same. To do this, they had to perform the hair-raising task of climbing down scrambling nets with all their gear, then leap into craft that were rising and falling at least six feet in the swell, and being flung away from the mother ship, then against it with a ferocious clang. It was an inexact science: those who misjudged their jump were crushed or drowned. At Omaha, Charles Norman Shay, a Native American of the Penobscot Nation in Maine, serving as a combat medic with Company 'F', 16th Infantry, witnessed the danger of just getting into their LCVPs: 'The seas were still very strong, and the craft rose and fell alarmingly beside USS *Henrico* as we went down those net ladders. You had to be very precise when you left them to jump into the Higgins boats. You'd had to time it just so, to avoid injury, and we knew that no one could get us if we fell in the water', he related to me during the 2018 D-Day commemorations. The previous evening Shay had been comforted when a fellow Penobscot warrior named Melvin Neptune sought him out and talked about home, 'knowing I had never been in combat and that all hell was about to break loose on me'.[26]

Another from USS *Henrico* was Earl Chellis, Jr, with the 16th Infantry's Company 'E'. He saw his LCVP 'rocking so bad it was hard to stand up. It was rough going; we were rocking from side to side and bouncing up and down. Men who got seasick were hanging on to each other to keep from falling down. As we were bouncing up and down, our LCVP got stuck on something underwater, about 250 yards from the beach,' Chellis

Before even reaching their beaches, troops of all the invading armies were faced with the perilous task of climbing down ropes into their rocking landing craft, while festooned with heavy equipment and life preservers. Although practised many times, pre-dawn darkness and extreme sea conditions slowed this down, causing injuries and fatalities. The upper image was shot in the perfect light of a daytime rehearsal and shows men leaving the USS *Thomas Jefferson*. On D-Day itself, the troops carried far more equipment. The lower shot belongs to a later campaign, but gives a good idea of the challenge of climbing into a bucking LCVP. (NARA)

recalled. 'The coxswain tried everything to back off; nothing worked. He said he was going to lower the ramp; I jumped off into the water – it was over my head. When I hit the bottom I had to kick up and down, getting air and doing it again, but I was being pushed onto the beach from the tides and waves. Finally, I got a footing and walked out of the water, and fell onto the sand to catch my breath.'[27]

Second Lieutenant Wesley R. Ross, with Company 'B' of the 146th Engineers, was another headed towards Omaha Beach. Ross, from Maupin, Oregon, led a boat team helping the Naval Combat Demolition Units remove obstacles on 'Easy Green' sector. The NCDUs assigned to Omaha included 183 navy and 107 army personnel, who comprised sixteen gap teams, each tasked to clear a lane through the beach obstructions. Some 145 men and eight teams supported the 29th Division, including Ross – the balance worked with the Big Red One. Each gap team was meant to be aided by a Sherman with a dozer blade, in his case from the 743rd Tank Battalion.

They had crossed the Channel by LCT, towing a smaller LCM containing two rubber dinghies. Piled into each of these was about five hundred pounds of explosives, Bangalore torpedoes, mine detectors, gap markers, buoys, and up to one hundred cans of gasoline.[28] At 0330 hours, they had to climb down into their LCM, wearing the 'foul-smelling clothing supposed to protect from chemical and gas attack', carrying rifles, equipment and 'fifty-pound, foot-long sacks stuffed with C2 plastic explosive fitted with hooks and lines for attachment to obstacles. One man had his legs crushed when caught between the landing craft – out of action even before having been a target! We were all were suffering from the greatest case of mass-seasickness ever known to mankind,' Ross recalled.[29]

Captain John R. Armellino commanded Company 'L' of the 16th Infantry, containing many veterans of Tunisia and Sicily. 'My men went over the side of *Empire Anvil* by rope ladders hanging from the ship and into the landing craft, which were rolling and turning in the rough waters. We carried two life preservers per man, one for the soldier and one to float heavy equipment into the beach. On our way to Omaha Beach, one of my landing craft was swamped by the violent seas and sank. To this day, I don't know how many of those men were lost.'[30]

Company 'I' likewise lost two boats swamped, explained Floridian Bill Ryan in 1994. 'Once we departed from the lee side of the *Anvil*, we were like a cork in a bathtub. I was the only one in my boat not to get seasick, no doubt due to my service in the merchant marine before I enlisted in the army. On the way towards the beach we lost two boats to the high waves. The coxswains of the remaining four became disoriented, mainly due to the disappearance of the patrol boat guiding us. The beach was covered in haze and smoke from earlier heavy bombardment, which made the identification of any landmarks completely impossible.'[31]

Tom and Dee Bowles, from Russellville, Alabama, were identical twins serving with Headquarters Company, 2nd Battalion, 18th Infantry. They weren't meant to be serving together but had somehow managed to achieve the proximity they desired before Operation Torch. With the Big Red One they had fought through Tunisia, where both men were awarded Silver Stars; now in the grey morning of 6 June, laden down with heavy pack, field telephone and two rolls of wire, they gingerly made their way down the nets flung over the side of USS *Anne Arundel*. Tom reminisced that his hands were constantly being trodden on by the men above him. 'Feeling kind of nauseated', their journey ashore would take over three hours.[32]

Aboard the *Empire Javelin* was Private Hal Baumgarten with Company 'B' of the 116th Infantry, who had earlier drawn the Star of David on his combat jacket. Eleven miles off the coast, they climbed down into their British-built LCAs. 'Their bilge pumps didn't work. Had we landed in an LCVP Higgins boat, we wouldn't have had that problem. The sides were higher and the water wouldn't have come in. So in order to stay afloat for three hours we had to bail with our helmets: we were wet and freezing when we landed.'[33]

Philadelphian Charles 'Hank' Hangsterfer, a company commander with the 16th Infantry headed for Omaha, had been on board the *Samuel Chase*, a US Coast Guard-crewed vessel, having boarded her on 1 June at Weymouth. Unlike the other American landing ships, he remembered that 'the *Chase* had been designed so that her LCVPs were loaded at deck level, then lowered into the water, thus eliminating climbing down the rope ladders or cargo nets'. He explained, 'here's how it was supposed to go: the Air Force was to bomb the beaches, Navy gunfire was to bombard, and our self-propelled guns were to provide initial artillery support. A special amphibious Engineer Group was to remove the obstacles and mines on the beach, and of course we were hardened, seasoned veterans.'

Looking back on their nonchalance before D-Day, Hangsterfer mused, 'for us no mission was too difficult, no sacrifice too great, it was duty first; nothing in heaven or hell could stop the 1st Infantry Division – we thought all we have to do was to show our Big Red One [patches] and the enemy would run. Besides: it was Easy Red Beach, a good omen.'

Then he paused – 'Was I scared? I was always afraid and even more afraid to let my company know that I was scared. After being in combat for over two years I considered myself a fugitive from the law-of-averages.'[34]

The 3rd Canadian Infantry Division would disembark from a total of 142 LCAs in exactly the same way the majority of Americans left their mother ships. Some of these craft came from the former New Zealand liner *Monawai*, converted into a landing ship with twenty landing craft. Royal Marine Corporal Jim Baker was piloting one of them and observed, 'at first light we dropped twelve craft and started to make our way to shore. I was coxswain in charge of thirty-eight lads of the Régiment de la Chaudière, part of 8 Canadian Brigade. On the way we fished out a Yank from their "Big Red One", who had drifted all the way from Omaha.'[35]

Also depositing Canadian troops ashore on Juno were the former Canadian liners *Prince Henry* and *Prince David*; on the former, attentive sailors made sure that the soldiers had an extra two hard-boiled eggs and a cheese sandwich to take with them. Other Juno-bound troops from the *Clan Lamont* witnessed: 'one of our chaps broke both his ankles in the perilous descent to the landing craft. There was nothing we could do about it. We had to take him to the beach even though he was injured.'[36]

Landing Ship Infantry 'H.M.C.S. Prince Henry (S.S. North Star) of Canadian National Steamship Co.) 7,000 Tons

Apart from the specially commissioned *Empires*, the British and Canadian navies reconstructed passenger liners and ferries as infantry landing ships. Typical of these was the Canadian attack transport HMCS *Prince Henry*. Formerly the steamship *North Star* (inset) and commanded by Captain V. S. Godfrey RCN, she was extensively altered to carry eight craft of the 528th LCA Flotilla, and 550 men. On D-Day, her craft put men ashore on Juno beach. (Author's collection)

Across all five beaches 233 LSTs loitered offshore and unloaded using their Rhino ferries, while 208 LCIs, sixty-four assault flotillas totalling 768 LCTs, and the numerous LCMs, LCVPs and LCAs were obliged to steer their way between the obstacles and dump their cargo as close to the water's edge as possible. 'After the boys had loads of fun whistling to the Wrens on the dockside, later that night they got their comeuppance as *LCI-501* rolled in every imaginable direction,' related Captain Eric Hooper, with the 9th Battalion Durham Light Infantry of the 50th Northumbrian Division. 'I, too, got little sleep during the uncomfortable crossing and at about 0500 hours I made a supreme effort and crawled on deck: the lovely fresh air was worth a million pounds.'

Like many British and Canadian battalions struggling ashore from LCIs, they had been issued cheap rubberised waders, 'which came up to one's chest from one's feet' but tore easily, and lightweight assault jackets 'which felt they were made of lead', in addition to an inflatable life preserver. Hooper and the rest of the 151st Brigade clambered down the LCI's gangplank; he remembered the 'water four-foot deep, and I gasped as the freezing surf swirled around. It was the hardest ten yards I ever had to do, but we all got ashore. Jack Heath serving aboard *LCT-522* of the 20th Flotilla at Juno Beach recollected the waders, too. Watching a nearby LCI unload its men at Courseulles, he recalled 'the first ones down the ramps had bad luck when their trousers filled with water. They were swept out to sea and drowned. We were forced to watch in horror for we could not reach them with our hand lines, though we tried. The following troops realised what was happening and slashed at the water-proofs with their bayonets'.[37] R. G. Watts aboard *LCT-2455*, witnessed the same tragedy. 'The tide was strong and the sea was still very rough. We had attached hawser ropes from wrecked craft to the beach. The soldiers were in a desperate situation carrying full packs on their shoulders. Sadly, we saw too many of them fail to grasp the rope, or slip underfoot. The weight they carried and the force of the sea was just too much for them. They drifted out to sea, while we watched on, helplessly.'[38]

At Gold, Captain Hooper, the Durham Light Infantryman, mused, 'I think we were all mightily thankful to be off *LCI-501* and her terrible motion, though one poor chap was crushed to death, falling between the gangplank and the rocking side of the vessel. First thing I did, even before fighting the Germans, was tear off those blasted waders. One thing was immediately apparent – the water had brought me round like a footballer's magic sponge: my seasickness evaporated instantly.'[39]

PART TWO: INVASION

'*I have also to announce to the House that during the night and the early hours of this morning the first of the series of landings in force upon the European Continent has taken place. I cannot, of course, commit myself to any particular details. Reports are coming in in rapid succession. So far the Commanders who are engaged report that everything is proceeding according to plan. And what a plan! This vast operation is undoubtedly the most complicated and difficult that has ever occurred. It involves tides, wind, waves, visibility, both from the air and the sea standpoint, and the combined employment of land, air and sea forces in the highest degree of intimacy and in contact with conditions which could not and cannot be fully foreseen. The battle that has now begun will grow constantly in scale and in intensity for many weeks to come and I shall not attempt to speculate upon its course. This I may say, however. Complete unity prevails throughout the Allied Armies. There is a brotherhood in arms between us and our friends of the United States. There is complete confidence in the supreme commander, General Eisenhower, and his lieutenants, and also in the commander of the Expeditionary Force, General Montgomery. Nothing that equipment, science or forethought could do has been neglected, and the whole process of opening this great new front will be pursued with the utmost resolution both by the commanders and by the United States and British Governments whom they serve.*'

Winston Churchill, statement to Parliament, 6 June 1944

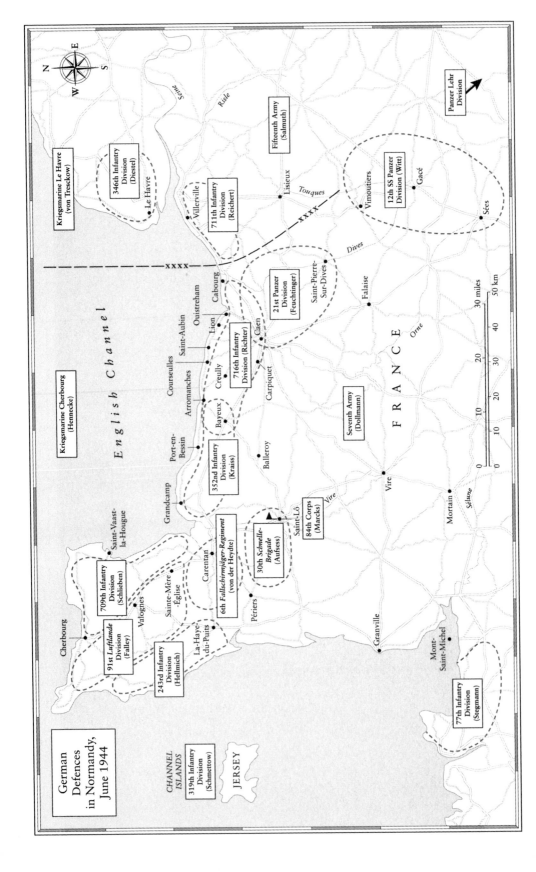

German Defences
in Normandy,
June 1944

N S E W

English Channel

CHANNEL ISLANDS

319th Infantry Division (Schmettow)

JERSEY

Kriegsmarine Cherbourg (Hennecke)

Kriegsmarine Le Havre (von Tresckow)

346th Infantry Division (Diestel)

Le Havre

711th Infantry Division (Reichert)

Villerville

Lisieux

Touques

Fifteenth Army (Salmuth)

12th SS Panzer Division (Witt)

Vimoutiers

Gacé

Sées

Dives

Falaise

21st Panzer Division (Feuchtinger)

Saint-Pierre-Sur-Dives

Cabourg

Ouistreham

Lion

Saint-Aubin

Courseulles

Arromanches

Port-en-Bessin

Grandcamp

Saint-Vaast-la-Hougue

Cherbourg

709th Infantry Division (Schlieben)

91st _Luftlande_ Division (Falley)

243rd Infantry Division (Hellmich)

La-Haye-du-Puits

Sainte-Mère-Église

Valognes

Carentan

6th _Fallschirmjäger-Regiment_ (von der Heydte)

Périers

352nd Infantry Division (Kraiss)

Bayeux

Creully

716th Infantry Division (Richter)

Caen

Carpiquet

Balleroy

Saint-Lô

84th Corps (Marcks)

30th _Schnelle-Brigade_ (Aufsess)

Vire

Vire

Seventh Army (Dollmann)

Orne

F R A N C E

Granville

Mortain

Sélune

Mont-Saint-Michel

77th Infantry Division (Stegmann)

Panzer Lehr Division

Seine

Risle

0   10   20   30   40   50 km
0   10   20   30 miles

Note

P ART TWO ASSEMBLES the jigsaw puzzle of experiences from 6 June by tracking from west to east. This has the advantage of following the chronology. It begins with the airborne drops, then examines each of the beaches in turn, starting with Utah and concluding on Sword.

Picture the five seaborne assault waves as the fingers of an inverted left hand, the thumb pointing towards Utah. The airborne troops were dropped to either side, like shoulders, giving solid protection to the beach attackers who would land a few hours later. In detail, the invasion coast was initially divided into seventeen sectors on Allied planning maps, with code names using the military phonetic alphabet of the day.

They began with 'Able' (west of Omaha) and finished at 'Roger' (on the eastern edge of Sword), with Band 'A', 'B' and 'C' (east of Ouistreham) identified as a reserve beach. With the late addition of the VII Corps attack on the Cherbourg peninsula, seven further sectors – including 'Sugar' to 'Victor' – were added when the invasion was extended to include the eastern Cotentin, and Utah Beach.

Thus, Omaha was assaulted (from west to east) on 'Dog', 'Easy' and 'Fox' sectors; Gold was invaded on 'Item', 'Jig' and 'King' beaches; the Canadians would land on the 'Mike' and 'Nan' portions of Juno; and the British 3rd Division would disembark at 'Queen' and 'Roger'. Each sector was then subdivided into beach areas identified by the colours Green (west), White (centre) and Red (east); hence, for example, Omaha stretched from 'Dog Green' to 'Fox Red' sectors.

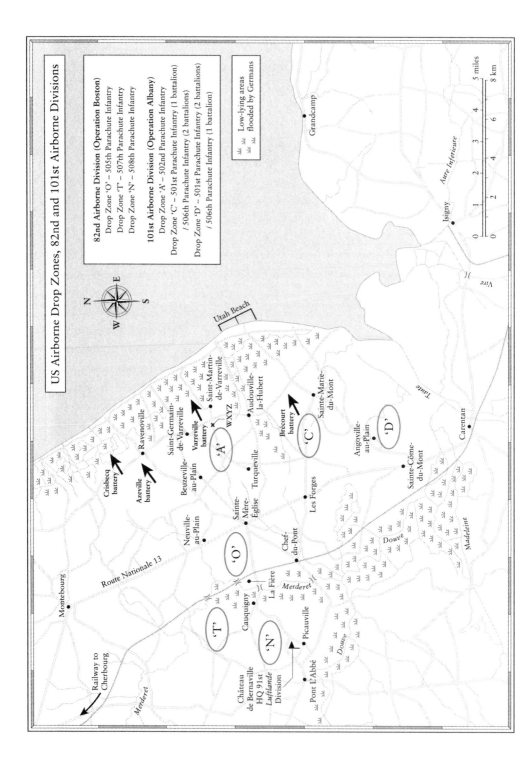

US Airborne Drop Zones, 82nd and 101st Airborne Divisions

82nd Airborne Division (Operation Boston)
Drop Zone 'O' – 505th Parachute Infantry
Drop Zone 'T' – 507th Parachute Infantry
Drop Zone 'N' – 508th Parachute Infantry

101st Airborne Division (Operation Albany)
Drop Zone 'A' – 502nd Parachute Infantry
Drop Zone 'C' – 501st Parachute Infantry (1 battalion)
/ 506th Parachute Infantry (2 battalions)
Drop Zone 'D' – 501st Parachute Infantry (2 battalions)
/ 506th Parachute Infantry (1 battalion)

Low-lying areas
flooded by Germans

22

Night Flyers

'Their faces were darkened with cocoa; sheathed knives were strapped to their ankles; tommy guns to their waists; bandoliers and hand grenades, coils of rope, pick handles, and spades. As they knelt round their padre in prayer, with bent heads and on one knee, the men with their equipment and camouflaged faces looked like some strange creatures from another world.'
Guy Byam, BBC *War Report*, 6 June 1944[1]

Two hours before midnight, their engines coughed, sputtered and came to life. They taxied, and as their four Rolls-Royce Merlins reached full power, the Lancasters left the ground, one by one. Sixteen of them. They climbed to their cruising altitude of 15,000 feet and settled into formation. In addition to their normal crew of nine, each carried three or four extra personnel. This time, the bombers of the famed No. 617 Squadron had no dams to bust, but as Squadron Leader Les Munro, piloting the leading plane, noted, 'I considered this operation to be, in one sense, one of the most important that we carried out.'[2]

This was not in terms of the target or risk from the Germans, but because of the very exacting requirements to which they had to fly and navigate. 'There was absolutely no latitude for deviation from ground speed, compass bearing, rate of turn and timing,' the New Zealander Munro remembered.[3] Flying with him was the squadron commander, Leonard Cheshire, for whom Munro felt 'the greatest respect; I was privileged to have him fly as my second pilot'. Cheshire, then approaching his hundredth mission and soon to be awarded the Victoria Cross, recollected the very long operation, requiring a high degree of precision flying. They had left the comfort of Woodall Spa aerodrome and their mess hall in the nearby Petwood Hotel at around 2200 hours and would not return before seven in the morning; the aircrew were unaware, though may have suspected, that some of the anticipated success of D-Day would depend on their accuracy.[4]

Their mission, Operation Taxable, was so secret that even today, the squadron records are silent about every detail of the flight, apart from the fact that sixteen Lancaster IIIs took off and sixteen later returned.[5] The squadron had been charged with the task of fooling German radar that an invasion fleet was heading towards the Cap d'Antifer, east of Le Havre, a safe distance away from the real armada bound for the Calvados coast. With pinpoint accuracy No. 617 Squadron was ordered to fly in repeated carefully devised patterns at 180mph for five hours, the extra personnel on board each plane dispensing wafer-thin metal strips called 'window', or 'chaff', by the British, and 'düppel' by the Luftwaffe (who had developed the same concept).

Aluminium foil was used, being light enough to fall through the air at a slow rate, and thus remain active for many minutes. The metal reflected radar in the manner of real aircraft, and dropped in repeated patterns and carried forward by the prevailing wind, on radar screens, would resemble a seaborne fleet edging its way towards France with protective air cover.[6] Wireless Operator/Air Gunner Alfred 'Smithy' Smith, DFC, described his 5–6 June sortie as the 'hardest night's work I can remember in all my missions, including the thirty I made after D-Day'. His job was to 'unload bundle after bundle of tin foil down the flare chute, the same as housewives use to cook the Christmas turkey'. He also discharged thousands of leaflets, carried by the wind to French civilians, warning them to 'stay away from transport hubs and communications centres and move to the countryside'.[7]

Below, eighteen launches towing large radar-reflecting balloons – each giving an echo equivalent to a 10,000-ton ship – kept station. They broadcast fake wireless traffic, simulating a major invasion flotilla carrying elements of FUSAG, the 'window' hiding the small size of the actual maritime force. Commencing thirty minutes after midnight, the Dambusters kept up their deception until 0500, in company with two similar operations elsewhere in the skies. Operation Glimmer was flown further east against Boulogne by eight Stirlings of No. 218 Squadron, likewise dispensing window, accompanied by twelve seaborne launches, towing their balloons and broadcasting radio chatter. These launches had earlier put out from HMS *Allenby* (another 'stone frigate', this time Folkestone's Royal Pavilion Hotel). Four years earlier the ferry port had embraced the armada of little ships, ferries, merchantmen and warships bearing a shattered British Expeditionary Force home from Dunkirk. Now, as the Glimmer vessels left on their important mission, their crews glimpsed behind them the long columns of tanks, guns and men, snaking through the streets, impatient to be loaded onto landing craft to (in Churchill's words) 'finish the job'.[8] Operation Big Drum was deployed on the western flank of the real Overlord, with four launches, similarly arrayed with balloons, jamming and broadcasting distracting wireless conversations, all three operations only stopping at dawn within a couple of miles of the French coast.

The challenging weather that delayed D-Day impacted on Taxable, Big Drum and Glimmer. The first two spoofs failed to rouse or distract the Germans, but Glimmer provoked the Luftwaffe into sending their own aircraft to investigate, thus believing a credible threat existed. These ruses were temporary and tactical, as opposed to the strategic deception of Quicksilver, but the needs of the Normandy landings were such that anything capable of diverting German attention at the crucial moment was considered worthwhile – including the use of the RAF's most elite squadron, made world famous a year earlier by their exploits against the Ruhr dams.

Warning leaflets, such as those dropped by Smith, were scattered over French cities thought to be at risk, such as Rennes, Brest, Saint-Malo and Caen. Leutnant Ludwig, with the eighty-strong Luftwaffe signals intelligence unit at Asnières, outside Paris, reported,

> shortly before midnight lively activity of RAF 100th Group commenced obviously for the purpose of neutralising the German radar sets on the Channel coast. The jamming screen moved slowly from East to West, so that it was immediately assumed that the jamming was screening a large shipping formation. The weather reconnaissance for the VIII and IX Bomber Commands and the assembly of the VIII Bomber Command began long before the normal time on 6 June. This striking advancement of the take-off times indicated that something special was under way.[9]

Into the tactical deception category came another, little-known operation – the ominously named Titanic (perhaps the allusion was to the

German ship sinking). There were four Titanic sub-missions planned, using a total of twelve Halifaxes from Nos. 138 and 161 (Special Duties) Squadrons, which normally flew agents and equipment from Tempsford aerodrome, Bedfordshire, into occupied countries. All involved the release of dummy paratroopers, nicknamed 'Ruperts' (a British joke – 'Rupert' was army slang for a dull, upper-crust officer). Manufactured by the Switlik Parachute Company of Trenton, New Jersey, Ruperts were about three feet tall, made of hessian (burlap) and rubber, and filled with sand, which gave them enough weight to descend convincingly on real parachutes. They were designed to explode on contact with the ground, the noise being suggestive of gunfire, not just an airborne drop. Although smaller than the genuine article, the absence of scale as they descended through the skies meant Ruperts could be mistaken for real jumpers. They worked best in areas of dense under-

The dropping of dummy paratroopers played an important part in dislocating Rommel's reserves, such as this highly trained Waffen-SS unit. Operation Titanic provoked the premature deployment of German mobile formations to hunt for non-existent parachute forces away from the beaches. It also played to their fear that 'Nobody knew if suddenly paratroopers might sail down and slaughter us'. The Allies could have made more of this ruse because at minimal cost it diverted two important formations from interfering with the seaborne landings early on D-Day. (Author's collection)

growth, such as marshes and woods, where the notional 'para-dummies' could stay concealed, 'opening fire' from cover, distracting their opponents for longer.

Contrary to their portrayal in *The Longest Day*, the Switlik Ruperts used were not the highly elaborate and lifelike rubber dummies portrayed in the film. Their explosive charge was designed also to destroy them, thus preventing immediate discovery of their deceptive intent. Operation Titanic played to the continuous German fear of a surprise air assault. Even the SS feared this, as tank commander Obersturmführer Hans Siegel of the 12th *Panzer-Regiment* of the *Hitlerjugend* Division explained: 'We were overflown by bomber formations every night. Nobody knew if suddenly paratroopers might sail down and slaughter us.'[10] It was to repel such a menace that Rommel had deployed Generalleutnant Wilhelm Falley's 91st *Luftlande* Division, Major Friedrich von der Heydte's 6th *Fallschirmjäger-Regiment* and other units nearer the coastal areas, strewing barbed wire and embedding wooden stakes on likely drop zones, damming rivers and flooding fields.

Flying out of the secret SOE airfield at Tempsford, the dropping of two hundred Ruperts, simulating an airborne division descant near Yvetot, east of Le Havre, was the task of Titanic I. More would have been dropped east of the River Dives in Titanic II, but this was cancelled; Titanic III saw a further force of fifty phoney parachutists released southwest of Caen, around Maltot – the area that would become the focus of fighting from late June and throughout July, known as Hill 112. Finally, to complement the distraction of a fake airborne division landing to the east of the actual invasion zone, Titanic IV placed another two hundred imitation paratroopers to suggest a second airborne formation landing in the vicinity of Saint-Lô, far to the south of the real drop zones of the US 82nd and 101st Airborne Divisions.[11]

Led by Lieutenant Noel Poole, together with Lieutenant Frederick Fowles, a six-man SAS team – all volunteers – landed at 0011 hours on 6 June with three containers of equipment in Titanic IV. This may have made them the first Allied soldiers in France on D-Day, by a minute or two (over at Pegasus Bridge, John Howard's men would land precisely five minutes later). With a carrier pigeon strapped to his chest, Poole and his squad played thirty minutes of pre-recorded sounds of men shouting and weapons firing. The SAS then had another task after Titanic – to link up with the Resistance and aid them in sabotaging German signal and electrical installations.[12] For minimal cost – four of the SAS team, including Poole, were later captured in July – Operation Titanic yielded impressive results.[13]

Two significant German units were despatched to search for the mannequin paratroops: one with Hans Siegel's comrades of the 12th SS *Hitlerjugend* encountered the Ruperts of Titanic III, while Oberst Ernst Goth of the 352nd Division recalled receiving reports of paratroop landings near Saint-Lô at about 0200 hours, whereupon thousands of men from *Kampfgruppe Meyer* (comprising the 915th *Grenadier-Regiment*, at that moment the sole reserve of the 84th Corps) were lured away from making a potential impact on the landings at Omaha and Gold beaches, to look for the elusive straw men of Titanic IV.[14]

Titanic remained obscure due to its SAS involvement; their files remained closed until 2015, and since then have only been shown to select civilians. The reason is twofold: to maintain the mystique of Britain's most special of special forces, but also to guard the secret of some tactics that might again be used in the future. Its former members still feel particularly bound by a common oath of silence not to reveal details of the past, above even the Official Secrets Act. Titanic reflected a very real uproar in the senior echelons of the 21st Army Group over how to use the SAS, who had honed and proven their skills in the Mediterranean. Initially, Monty's planners wanted to 'drop SAS units thirty-six hours ahead of the main invasion to act as a barrier of shock troops between the fighting front and German reserves'.[15]

Even Titanic had started off as four eight-man teams (thirty-two men) before being scaled back at the SAS's request. The SAS hierarchy were united in their belief that their regiment should operate not tactically on the front line, but strategically deep behind it, and that large drops far in advance of Overlord would place a valuable resource at huge risk for little gain. Lieutenant Colonel Bill Stirling, commanding the 2nd SAS Regiment, felt so strongly that after a series of formal protests, he resigned from the regiment he and his brother David had founded.[16] Then the establishment changed its mind, agreed, and SAS involvement for D-Day itself was limited to Titanic, but later two full squadrons would be dropped in Operations Bulbasket and Houndsworth, cooperating with the Maquis in the disruption of German reserves.

A cost–benefit analysis of all the distracting ruses employed just before Overlord reveals that Titanic was by far the most successful – and, ironically, the cheapest. It removed substantial German units from a place where they might have done damage to the invasion, to rear areas where they could not. The mission might have made an even greater impact had Titanic II been deployed – to simulate a divisional parachute drop south of Caen, something that Morgan's COSSAC had proposed in reality. Though hugely successful, Titanic was undersold and might have contributed far more – possibly in the distraction of a greater part of Feuchtinger's 21st Panzer Division during D-Day, enabling the British 3rd Division to seize Caen, as planned.

Taxable, Glimmer and Big Drum were devised with the aid of the Air Ministry's Telecommunications Research Establishment (TRE) and carried out by aircraft of Air Vice-Marshal Addison's Norfolk-based No. 100 (Bomber Support) Group, responsible for a wide array of jamming and deception ruses to protect the bombers usually striking Germany. In addition to the fifty-six aircraft deployed on Taxable, Glimmer and Titanic, another fifty-nine were deployed on jamming missions to protect Overlord: it would prove to be the busiest night of the war for 100 Group, and a measure of how important electronic protection and airborne deception was to the invasion.[17]

To say that the skies were full of Allied aircraft would be understatement. Some 25,275 sorties were flown in the forty-eight hours between 2100 hours on 5 June and 2100 on 7 June, an average of one every nine seconds. During the twenty-four hours of 6 June itself, the total was 14,674 – one every six seconds. Pilots flew two, sometimes three missions. Lieutenant Russell Chandler, Jr, whom we met earlier flying his 'Gooney Bird' across the Atlantic via Ascension Island, experienced a busy twenty-four hours. On 5 June, 'we were wheels up about 2230 hours, and I dropped twenty-seven paratroopers of the 82nd Airborne into the area just south of Sainte-Mère-Église. We returned the next morning to drop supplies and equipment, and that evening we towed in gliders.'[18] Pierre Clostermann's Free Frenchmen with No. 602 Squadron flying Spitfires 'carried out a sortie at 0355 hours; a second at 0900 hours; one at midday; their fourth at 1730 and a final one at 2035 hours. Everybody was worn out.' As a BIGOT-cleared planner, he was forbidden from flying over enemy-held territory until ten hours into D-Day and only flew the last two.[19]

One source calculated that every cubic yard of airspace between 1,500 and 20,000 feet in a rectangle stretching between Portland, Cherbourg, Calais and Dover had been occupied by an Allied plane during this period.[20] In the preceding days, recognition symbols of five alternating back and white stripes had been applied to the wings and fuselage of Allied aeroplanes – eighteen inches wide on single-engine aircraft, twenty-four for twin-engined planes and gliders; apart from glider tugs, four-engined machines (the heavy bomber fleets) were exempt. This was to avoid the fratricide that had downed many friendly aircraft during the invasion of Sicily a year earlier. The plan was approved by Leigh-Mallory on 17 May, but for fear of the Luftwaffe getting wind of the scheme and imitating the markings, the stripes remained a closely guarded secret until 3 June, when troop carrier units started applying them, with the fighters and bombers waiting for their war paint until the fourth.[21]

Flying Officer Douglas Gordon and his fellow Typhoon pilots with No. 440 Squadron, RCAF, knew something was up after a mission against a French radar station on 30 May. They had flown almost daily for the entire month, usually returning home with battle damage. 'Then, inexplicably the whole squadron was stood down. We were not told what was going on, but we knew something was about to be screwed up when we saw the 'erks' [ground crew] paint black-and-white stripes on our kites [aircraft]. They looked like prison stripes. We thought we were in jail.'[22] The effort virtually robbed Britain of its stock of black and white paint to find the hundreds of thousands of gallons of each required (two and a half gallons of black with three and a half gallons of white were recommended for single-engined craft; three and a half of black and five of white for multi-engined aeroplanes). Personnel struggled through the night with brushes and brooms, as a No. 438 Squadron Typhoon pilot noted: 'Arrived at dispersal this morning to find all aircraft with their invasion markings painted on them. The ground crew completed the job between 1800 hours and 0300 hours.'[23] It was an inexact science: the stripes on the wings of the 357th Fighter Group's P-51s at RAF Leiston, Suffolk, 'were trim', thought Captain Willie Williams, their operations officer, but those on the fuselage 'spoiled the profile, making them look like pregnant turtles'.[24] Allied aircraft would remain so marked until an order to remove them was issued on 6 December.

Accidents were inevitable with such crowded skies. First thing, the Ninth Air Force's 394th Bomb Group, flying out of RAF Boreham, Essex, lost two pairs of B-26 Marauders, which collided in two separate incidents over southern England. Flying above Gillingham, Kent, at 0530 two bombers collided in the overcast, with one crashing into homes in Corporation Road, killing four people. Half an hour later, two more flying on instruments, en route to bomb German positions at Varreville behind Utah Beach, collided over Battle, Sussex. The cause this time was icing due to the poor weather, which would take its toll of other planes before the day was through; only one of the twenty-four aircrew survived.

First Lieutenant Robert J. McCallum in the same group recalled his 6 June:

> D-Day was my fifty-eighth mission. We knew it was the real thing this time, as they woke us at two in the morning for the briefing; showed us messages from Roosevelt and Eisenhower, had the chaplain there to give us all automatic Absolution. I also remember the weather – it was terrible. We took off all right and formed into our groups of six, but at about fifteen hundred feet, entered clouds so thick you couldn't see the plane ten feet to your left. We finally broke through the clouds at twelve thousand and all around us could see other B-26s popping up out of the clouds … We got to the Channel where we had a real close-up view of the thousands of ships all heading toward France. We hit some big guns on the Cherbourg Peninsula, guarding what I later learned was Utah Beach; we made another mission that afternoon to bomb some railroad yards at Vire.[25]

'At a B-26 Marauder Base in England' was the by-line of a report by Donald MacKenzie in the *New York Daily News* on 7 June. He had flown with the B-26s on their early-morning run over France on D-Day, noting their crews 'looked like two-humped camels. The foundation of their massive clothing was a Mae West life jacket. Over that came a bulky parachute and over that the flak suit, which is a smock of iron plates that weighs two-hundred pounds. The whole is topped off with a steel helmet. And none of it seems thick enough when eighty-eight millimetre shells from the ack-ack guns are rocking and bumping the machine.' MacKenzie observed that

> from the moment we arrived at headquarters, we were under strict military law, forbidden all communications with the outside world. We were told D-Day was at hand, briefed for the assault and assigned to our invasion stations. We left our hotels quietly and secretly, carrying only light combat kit and were flown to various airbases …
>
> High above, Allied fighters were milling round in the sky. Long before, a great mass of them had swept over Northwestern France. As H-hour drew near, the sky was black with them …

Our ship was captained and flown by Captain Curt S. Seebaldt of Rochester, Michigan. He said after we landed that he felt profoundly honored to have been among the first United States groups to spearhead the invasion. His co-pilot, a tall youth from Cut Bank, Montana, Lieutenant Carlyle Webb, declared: 'I am no actor, but I believe I have just taken part in the opening scene of the greatest show on earth.' The navigator was Lieutenant Edwin Freeman of El Campo, Texas, who described the mission as the greatest flight he had ever made. The bombardier, Lieutenant Edward Harrison of Tunstall, Virginia, summed up what all the combat crews thought of the sweep: 'It's the first time I've been that close to the enemy.'[26]

Another reporter assigned to accompany B-26s over the invasion zone worked for the *Daily Telegraph*. The rookie – whose twenty-fourth birthday was on 5 June – was given the honour of a place in the base commander's personal Marauder. To the young man's intense frustration, the aircraft developed a technical fault and had to turn back just miles from its target. Repairs were soon made and in the early afternoon he was again over France – and gained a far better impression of the whole operation than he would have done on the earlier mission. 'Away to the west I saw a sight I shall never forget. Hundreds of ships of every kind were moving towards France. From our height they were only distinguishable by the white wash which churned out from their sterns. They looked as if they were strung together by some invisible chain.' His story was more up to date than most and made the newspaper's front page on 7 June. The young man's name was Cornelius Ryan; the sights he witnessed that morning left such an indelible impression that they caused him to begin researching *The Longest Day* ten years later. If anyone was responsible for beginning the whole D-Day commemorative business, it was Ryan.[27]

The airborne troops, mostly in C-47s (Dakotas to the British, Skytrains to the Yanks), some in gliders, started to crowd the skies after midnight. Many of Colonel Roy E. Lindquist's 508th Parachute Infantry had been driven to Folkingham aerodrome by truck and bus from their stately home base of Wollaton Park in Nottingham – where we met them slaying the King's deer. They set up cots in one massive hangar, and ate well, remembered Lieutenant Neal Beaver, a former Michigan National Guardsman who led the Third Battalion's 81mm Mortar Platoon. 'We were so loaded up with ammo, guns, mines, demolition packs and rations that we must have weighed three hundred pounds each.'[28] The deer-slayer Corporal Jack Schlegel – with the Third Battalion of the 508th – recollected, 'We all needed help to get our chutes on, and two air force guys had to push each of us into our C-47. Our plane had two rows of nine. I was the eighteenth, and last, man in our stick [group of parachutists that jumps together from one aircraft] and sat next to the plane's radio man, who lived only three blocks from my house in the Bronx; we chatted all the way over.'[29]

Lieutenant Beaver then recalled, 'When the port engine of our plane wouldn't start we were in a panic. It was the worst feeling of being left behind I've ever experienced. We fell out of that plane like bloated frogs, pulled out our bundles, tripped and waddled across the runway between trios of aircraft roaring by. One bundle chute burst open, we left it behind.'[30] The same feeling of encumbrance pervaded the British 6th Airborne Division, where Major A. R. Clarke recollected the assembly at Broadwell airbase 'of what might have been men, had it not been for the shapelessness of their appearance. Perhaps a better description would have been that of many caravans of heavily laden camels silhouetted against the darkening horizon.'[31]

If Leigh-Mallory had had his way, most of the US airborne troops would not have been deployed at all. We have seen how his lack of Mediterranean experience had denied him first-hand understanding of the benefits of paratroop operations, and how his combative approach rarely led to cooperation. He had a series of run-ins with Bradley throughout April and May, proposing to 'spike the airborne plan for Utah' with its two-division aerial assault – mainly based on fears of the damage to his C-47 troop-carrying fleet. Bradley felt 'the entire Utah assault might be jeopardised by the failure [cancellation] of the air drop'. Leigh-Mallory's objections were based on the casualties sustained over Sicily in July 1943 – at which he was not present. In a series of mishaps, large numbers of C-47s had been destroyed or damaged by friendly fire, many gliders had been released prematurely – landing in the Mediterranean – while other pilots, their formations having been broken by flak, had scattered their human cargo over a wide area.

Afterwards, there had been a move by Lieutenant General Lesley J. McNair, US Army Ground Forces commander, seconded by Eisenhower, to break up the airborne divisions. However, General George C. Marshall,

US Army chief of staff back in Washington DC, was of a different opinion, and persuaded Eisenhower to establish a review board, temporarily withholding judgement on their fate. In December 1943, two airborne formations, the 11th and 17th Divisions, slugged it out near Fort Bragg in North Carolina, delivered by 200 C-47s and 234 Waco gliders.[32] Observing the performance of aircrew, paratroopers and glider infantry very closely, McNair judged the exercise a great success, revised his earlier view and recommended retention and deployment of the 82nd and 101st in Overlord. Meanwhile, an antidote to the problem of scattered drops was found by the creation of US pathfinders, in emulation of their British cousins. These were aircrew with the best available navigators carrying specially equipped paratroops to locate and mark the drop zones. Pilot training had also much improved, so that Leigh-Mallory's aircrew did not generally share their leader's pessimism: they were itching to go.

At the last moment, on 30 May, the air chief marshal again intervened, remembered Bradley: 'abandon the Utah air drop; concentrate the airborne on Caen, estimating fifty percent casualties among the parachute troops, seventy percent among the gliders'.[33] Eisenhower recorded Leigh-Mallory's protest at 'what he termed the futile slaughter of two fine divisions'.[34] Yet the objections were hollow, and the RAF marshal's protests were nothing more than estimates drawn out of the air. He would have saved himself, Bradley and Eisenhower much anguish had he either done his homework, or kept shtum, for the airborne losses would be minimal compared to his wild exaggerations.

However, casualty projections for the whole of Overlord had made sober reading: military hospitals in southern England were preparing to process a minimum of thirty thousand casualties from D-Day alone. On 12 February 1944, 21st Army Group had sent an estimate of British and Canadian D-Day casualties to the War Office. It arrived at the grim conclusion that out of a seaborne landing force of seventy thousand men there would be 9,250 deaths, including three thousand drowned. This figure effectively doubled with the addition of US Army projections, which together with the airborne element, led to expectations of well over twenty thousand killed on D-Day.

These concerns are what made Eisenhower spend the closing hours of 5 June with men of the 101st Airborne Division at Greenham Common and other airfields near Newbury, rather in the manner of Shakespeare's Henry V before Agincourt. As his aide, Harry C. Butcher, recalled, 'We saw hundreds of paratroopers, with blackened and grotesque faces, packing up for the big hop and jump. Ike wandered through them, stepping over packs, guns, and a variety of equipment such as only paratroop people can devise, chinning with this and that one. All were put at ease.'[35] A famous series of photographs show Eisenhower conversing with Wallace C. Strobel from Michigan and Leonard Crawford from Wisconsin. Both survived and would later claim Ike asked them where they hailed from, and got the same answer: 'Oh yes, Michigan/Wisconsin, great fishing there. Been there several times and like it.' To others he simply said, 'Do your duty: be brave.'[36]

Eisenhower also felt he owed it to these men to be with them at this hour of testing: though morally and physically brave, privately he was disappointed never to have faced combat himself. Butcher wrote, 'We

Eisenhower spent the closing hours of 5 June 1944 touring airbases around Greenham Common, chatting to paratroopers of the 101st Airborne Division who would soon be descending into France. Here, the time is around 2030 hours and, with his senior British aide Lieutenant Colonel James Gault of the Scots Guards (1902–77) looking on, Ike discusses fishing – the most relaxing contrast to combat he could imagine. Within five hours, these men from Easy Company, 502nd Parachute Infantry, would be landing in Normandy. (US Army Signal Corps)

concluded the tour with C-47s growling off the runway, carrying the jumpers and their general, Maxwell Taylor, to their uncertain mission – one that Leigh-Mallory went on record against as being too dangerous and costly, and to which Ike also went on record, ordering the deed to be done, as it was necessary to help the foot soldiers get ashore. We returned to camp about 0115 hours, sat around the nickel-plated office caravan in courteous silence, each with his own thoughts.'[37]

A journalist recording the scene later told friends he had seen a hint of a tear in each of the Supreme Commander's eyes. Ironically, one of the first D-Day reports was from Leigh-Mallory with news that only twenty-nine of 1,250 C-47s (costing $138,000 apiece) were missing, with only a few gliders (Wacos were priced at $25,630 each) unaccounted for. These figures would be revised to forty-one aircraft and nine gliders that were shot down or ditched in the Channel. Later that morning Leigh-Mallory wrote Eisenhower a formal letter, stating that it was sometimes difficult to admit that one was wrong, but he had never had a greater pleasure than in doing so on this occasion, and congratulated the Supreme Commander on the wisdom and courage of his decision.

Around the drop zones awaited German soldiers, some of whom were also paratroops. The 6th *Fallschirmjäger-Regiment* were stationed near Carentan. They were an independent formation of fifteen companies, considerably larger than a normal infantry regiment, and led by one of Germany's most experienced parachute officers. This was the Bavarian aristocrat Friedrich, Freiherr (Baron) von der Heydte, who had won a Knight's Cross during the 1941 Crete invasion. Raised from scratch between January and May 1944, the unit was drawn from veterans of the fighting in Russia, Sicily and Italy, with instructors from training schools, and on 19 May they boasted 3,457 well-trained killers, whose average age was seventeen and a half. Rommel was sure no Allied soldier would want to tangle with them. Yet, they had two weaknesses: four calibres of mortars, from German, French, Italian and Soviet armouries, and mobility – the 6th Parachute Regiment had only seventy trucks, of *fifty* different models.[38]

Oberleutnant Martin Pöppel, commander of No. 12 Company in Heydte's regiment, noted in his diary: 'Alarm exercises by day and night increase our combat readiness. The whole terrain has been surveyed for heavy weapons, almost every eventuality has been considered. On 3 June there is a further regrouping as a result of the flooding of some parts of the countryside.' Rommel had ordered this simple expedient throughout the threatened areas, to close off such terrain to paratroop and glider assault. Pöppel continued, 'On 5 June a map exercise is carried out involving all the Third Battalion's officers and platoon leaders, in which the possibilities of an airborne landing by the enemy are played through. We disperse amid laughter, and no one has any idea how near we are to the real situation. In a few hours, all our preparations will be put to the test.'[39]

Heinz Puschmann was in the Signals Section of Heydte's Third Battalion, based in Carentan. For the past few days they had been bombed 'both heavily and regularly' and Heinz was 'pretty sure the Allies would be landing soon somewhere in Normandy'. On 5 June, he recalled, 'The sun went down dark blood-red', and later the night was 'bright, clear and moonlit'.[40] Allied aircraft had been over all that day, dropping bombs, strafing and patrolling: sitting outside their tents, some of the *Fallschirmjäger* sensed something was about to happen – not least because the Alsatian drivers of their motor transport pool had all deserted.[41]

Although part of the Luftwaffe, Heydte's regiment was attached for tactical purposes to General Wilhelm Falley's 91st *Luftlande* (Airborne) Division, an army formation. Grenadiers Ernst Flöter, Paul Golz and Franz Roggenbuck were all young Pomeranians called up in the autumn of 1943 and conscripted into the 1057th Grenadier Regiment of Falley's division. Aged just eighteen by the time they reached Normandy, and at the very beginning of their adult lives, they were not particularly interested in National Socialism, or soldiering – just wanting to get on with their lives. Their motivation was in complete contrast to Heydte's paratroopers, who concluded, 'the combat efficiency of this division was poor'.

Falley's 91st had been formed in January 1944 at Baumholder (in western Germany) for use as the Reich's sole rapid deployment force by air. Heydte's paratroopers were meant to provide its parachute element, who could seize an airfield where Falley's men would be landed. What the Wehrmacht was doing creating an air-portable division in 1944 when the Allies ruled the skies is beyond comprehension. Ernst Flöter, from Stettin (today's Szczecin in Poland), who became a radio operator in the Third Battalion, observed, 'because we were an air landing unit, we had exercises with both big and small gliders. We were all quite pessimistic we could carry out an air landing and be fit to fight.'[42] Paul Golz recalled, 'Our first move was to Saint-Nazaire, but around mid-May we dug in

On 1 May 1944 the 91st *Luftlande* (Airlanding) Division, led by Generalleutnant Wilhelm Falley (1897–1944), arrived in France. Rommel visited them on the seventeenth and before the end of the month they had redeployed by chance onto some of the 82nd Airborne Division's drop zones. Technically subordinate to Falley, and vastly more experienced, was the 6th *Fallschirmjäger* (Parachute) Regiment of Major Friedrich von der Heydte (1907–94) who would prove tough opponents throughout D-Day, north and east of Carentan. (Author's collection)

near Cherbourg.' Most of his short military career involved planting the 'sharpened logs connected with barbed wire' designed to deter an airborne landing.[43]

The 91st's artillery were mountain guns, lighter than conventional weapons, which could be broken down for air transport; it was the Seventh Army's land-based reserve in case of trouble, but had only arrived in France on 1 May. Rommel visited them on the seventeenth, lunching at Falley's HQ, the Château de Bernaville, in the faux Louis XIV splendour of 'a large room with beautifully painted walls which were supposed to look like marble, a promise they did not quite fulfil'.[44] Later Rommel spoke to troops of Falley's and Heydte's units, warning them 'not to expect the enemy during good weather, or during the day.

They would have to be prepared for the enemy to come with clouds and storm, and after midnight.'[45] The advice was almost immediately forgotten, as Grenadier Flöter remembered being told on the night of 5 June, 'No guard duties. The weather's too bad, they won't come tonight.' With that, he enjoyed a watch-free rest in his tent, until the noise of aircraft woke him up.[46]

Among those soldiers of the airborne forces who consider themselves elite, a further distinction is usually made: for the pathfinders consider themselves a cut above even their sky warrior brethren. At about the time the Dambusters were leaving Woodall Spa for their electronic trickery in the Channel, a small fleet of C-47 transports started taking off from RAF North Witham in Lincolnshire at five-minute intervals. They carried two hundred men from the 101st Airborne, whose job was to mark drop zones behind the Normandy beaches, placing lights and radar beacons so that the 13,348 embarked jumpers from the 82nd and 101st could find their drop zones and thence make their way to their various rendezvous. An hour later, around 2300 hours, sixty men of the 22nd Independent Parachute Company, the trailblazing unit for the British 6th Airborne Division, took off from Harwell airfield, Oxfordshire, in six twin-engined Albemarles, bound for the eastern flank of Overlord. This was two-thirds of the company – the remainder were held back as reserves, arriving a few hours later. Flying in the lead plane was the No. 38 Group commander, Air Vice-Marshal Hollinghurst.[47]

The Britons parachuted into France from five hundred feet shortly after midnight, and came under heavy fire almost immediately. 'I saw our CO, Major Francis Lennox-Boyd, riddled with bullets as he floated down into Ranville churchyard,' recalled Sergeant Herb Fussell, whose *nom de guerre* was 'Sergeant Ramage'. Several others broke bones on the grave-stones but Fussell emerged intact to find himself face to face with a German sentry. 'He was about to kill me, but I got him first' was Herb's matter-of-fact explanation for the row of bullet holes stitched into the stonework of Ranville church. The German fired first, but had aimed too high. Fussell's Sten finished him off.[48] The Post Operation Report penned by Captain Bob Midwood of the 22nd pathfinders noted their individual loads were far too heavy; training with similar loads had been done, but not in darkness or landing in fields of growing corn; their issued Holophane lamps were too bulky and sustained many broken bulbs. However, successful landings were made subsequently by most gliders.[49]

The American pathfinder operation was as challenging as the British, and the results equally mixed. The weather, which bedevils any account of D-Day, and cloud cover made it hard for the pilots to navigate, and some of the jumpers ended up far from their targets, while others came under heavy fire. Some Eureka radar homing beacons (which sent signals to airborne-mounted Rebecca receivers) would fail to function, whilst the conditions obscured other drop zones that were marked; nevertheless, a few teams were on their drop zones near Varreville at fifteen minutes after midnight, setting up lights and beacons to guide the main force in.

To transport the two US divisions, Brigadier General Paul Williams' IX Troop Carrier Command (the 50th, 52nd and 53rd Troop Carrier Wings) had assembled 1,116 aircrew, though with only enough trained navigators for forty per cent of the fleet. They would fly 1,207 aircraft, together with some 1,118 Waco gliders (an abbreviation of the Weaver Aircraft Corporation of Ohio, who made them) and 301 British-manufactured Horsas.[50] The American glider could silently transport various loads into battle: thirteen fully equipped infantrymen, a jeep, its trailer loaded with supplies, field guns, medical supplies, ammunition, or five-gallon jerrycans of fuel and water. They would be towed across the Channel on 350-foot nylon tow ropes, which each contained enough nylon to manufacture two thousand pairs of ladies' stockings – to enable the glider war, women had to forego their hose.[51]

Too often the D-Day airborne story is told in terms of the airborne troopers who fell to earth, whereas the men who got them there – the aircrew – are overlooked and often unfairly criticised by the sky warriors who afterwards swore they were dumped anywhere but where they needed to be. A thirty-three-year-old Californian, Lieutenant Colonel Joel L. Crouch from Riverside, commanding officer of the 52nd Troop Carrier Wing, flew the lead C-47 full of 101st pathfinders, with his co-pilot and navigator, out of North Witham. Before the war, Crouch, like many of the early Gooney Bird pilots, had worked for a civilian airline, in his case United, flying passengers between Los Angeles and Seattle. He had witnessed and survived the shambles over Sicily, where aircrew were responsible for some of the errors: fine pilots they may have been, but they were lousy at flying in, and keeping, formation in poor weather or under fire. Crouch helped to iron out these shortcomings, running a Pathfinder School at Cottesmore Airfield, Rutland, to train US paratroopers and aircrew for their perilous job of being 'the spearhead of the spearhead'.[52]

Colonel Charles H. Young, commander and lead pilot of the 439th Troop Carrier Group on 5 June, had taken the earlier poor reputation of C-47 pilots to heart in his final briefing to the aircrew of his eighty-one C-47s before take-off: 'The main thing we're interested in tonight,' he told them, 'even above our own safety – *repeat, even above our own safety* – is to put a closed-up, intact formation over our assigned drop zone at the proper time. So these paratroopers of ours can get on the ground in the best possible fighting condition. Each pilot among you is charged with the direct responsibility of delivering his troops to the assigned DZ. Their work is only beginning when you push down that switch for the green light. Remember that.'[53]

Following their pathfinders, many of the 505th Parachute Infantry were veterans of the Sicilian campaign, including Kansas State College graduate Dean McCandless, communications officer of the regiment's First Battalion. From RAF Spanhoe, Northamptonshire, he was to be flown by his old friends, the 315th Carrier Group, with whom he had gone into battle over Italy. As the 5 June daylight faded, a deep thud reverberated around the airfield: 'As we were loading the plane, one of the guys in our company had a grenade in his pocket go off. It killed him and several others, and damaged the plane. But the ground crew told us, "Go on, go on, we can take care of him" – so we went.'[54] In fact, the Gammon grenade killed three, with another dying of wounds later on, and the C-47 proved a write-off.[55] Yet McCandless and his buddies calmly changed to a spare and took off on schedule. The 82nd's commander, Matthew Ridgway, also at Spanhoe, was planning to land by glider, but at the last minute changed his mind and jumped instead.

Soldiers in Lieutenant Colonel Terence Otway's 9th Parachute Battalion heard a similar sound before they were due to mount their transports and gliders. In the field next to RAF Broadwell, Oxfordshire, a box of hand grenades exploded, killing six soldiers from a neighbouring unit. Otway distracted his men's attention before morale slumped. The 9th Parachute Battalion included nineteen-year-old Private Emil Corteil, in 'A' Company, who jumped into Normandy with a very special companion – his war dog, a German shepherd called Glen. Several hounds were trained to ride in C-47s, jump, and guard prisoners: they were thought to be worth 'six human sentries', sniffing out the opposition, as German troops smelt quite distinctive – on account of their different uniforms, soap, food and tobacco.[56]

To relieve the tension in his unit, Lieutenant Colonel Alastair Pearson ordered a piano brought to RAF Lyneham, Wiltshire, where his 8th Parachute Battalion had assembled in readiness. Sergeant A. G. Reading, already the holder of a Military Medal, recalled, 'As I could play a bit, I was detailed to play a few tunes and we had a sing-song by the waiting planes.' The battalion soon departed on their mission of holding the high ground of Bavent Forest, south-east of Ranville, leaving the piano in the middle of the airfield. On the drop zone, Sergeant Reading received a message from the rear party asked where he had put the piano. It had disappeared; 'they reckoned I had taken it to France and flogged it', he grinned.[57]

'How those fantastic C-47s got off the ground that night is still a mystery to me,' wondered Lieutenant Beaver of the 82nd. 'As I recall, it was a worry to the aircrew, because I can remember much fussing and discussion over the centre of gravity calculator. Someone must have said, "The hell with it – it will probably fly!" I stood in the door with another of our battalion officers all the way to our drop.'[58] The flight plan of both US divisions took them first south-west, turning east over the Channel Islands, approaching the Cotentin peninsula from the west, minimising the amount of time over German-held terrain. Beaver continued, 'We saw the Channel Islands clearly and made landfall well south of our intended route. We were at fifteen to eighteen hundred feet and I could see that the left plane was holding tight and found the same was true of the plane on our right. We had very few cloud problems, just some isolated ground haze. I could see the silver ribbons of the Merderet and the Douve rivers. I had been drilled in the land features and the whole area was just as the sand table had it.'[59]

Colonel Charles H. Young remembered the formations of his 439th Troop Carrier Group: 'Serials of aircraft, made up almost entirely of thirty-six or forty-five C-47s, flew as nine-ship Vs. The leader of each nine-airplane V-flight kept one thousand feet behind the rear of the preceding V-flight. This was a tight formation for night flying, with only one hundred feet between wing tips.'[60] The Skytrains flew towards Portland Bill, a waypoint on the English coast, then as they flew south-west towards the German-occupied Continent, turned off their red and green navigation lights.

In order to carry out their various missions, six compact drop zones (DZs) were identified in the Cotentin peninsula, one for each of the six parachute infantry regiments which formed the two US airborne divisions, with two landing zones (LZs) for their glider regiments.[61] Bradley at the First Army and Collins of VII Corps had identified two tasks for their US airborne formations landing in the Cotentin. One was to protect the Utah landings from a western counter-attack. It was foreseen that the Germans would probably assault from an axis running west–east from La Haye-du-Puits to Carentan, where a good road offered a likely manoeuvre corridor for troops and armour through otherwise difficult terrain.

The same axis could be used to reinforce Cherbourg, so it was vital the area west of Sainte-Mère-Église be occupied and defended. Drop zones were allocated to Matthew Ridgway's experienced paratroops between Sainte-Mère-Église; beyond the Merderet river; and as far west as La Haye-du-Puits, fifteen miles away. These were changed on 27 May with the discovery that Generalleutnant Falley's 91st *Luftlande* Division had deployed onto some of their proposed DZs. There were immediate fears of a leak, but wiser counsel prevailed when it was realised the Germans were professionally picking terrain in exactly the way the 82nd had done.

Ridgway's drop zones were accordingly shifted *eastwards* to overlook the Merderet river crossings – inundated by Rommel to form a mile-wide marsh – and Sainte-Mère-Église. In its final form, starting at 0120 hours, Operation Boston would see 6,420 paratroopers of the 505th, 507th and 508th Parachute Infantry dropping on three DZs west of the *Route Nationale* 13, which connected Carentan with Cherbourg and ran through Sainte-Mère-Église. In addition, some fifty-two C-47-towed Waco gliders from RAF Ramsbury would support the 82nd, making their own night-time assault at 0400 – Operation Detroit.

Later on D-Day, a second glider lift, Operation Elmira, would see a further thirty-six Wacos and 140 Horsas delivering two battalions of glider artillery and howitzers to the 82nd Airborne, beginning at 2100 hours. However, the flooding of the Merderet had been missed in the rush to realign drop zones, because weeds had grown up through the water making the marsh appear as solid ground in air photos. The oversight would cost scores of American lives.

The other airborne task Bradley and Collins identified was in fact a trio of interrelated missions: to seize the causeway roads off Utah, prevent the arrival of German reinforcements from Carentan and capture crossings over the Douve river to link up with troops from Omaha. The less-experienced 101st, under its new commander, Maxwell Taylor, were given this task, considered the easier of the two. The late change in its drop zones also brought the 82nd Airborne closer to the 101st if mutual support was needed. From 0020 hours, Operation Albany planned to deliver the 6,928 men in Taylor's three regiments of the 101st Airborne – the 501st, 502nd and 506th Parachute Infantry – to their drop zones east of the *Route Nationale* 13, between it and Utah Beach.

Likewise, they would be supported by two glider missions: from 0400 hours, in support of the initial parachute drops, fifty-two Wacos towed by C-47s out of RAF Aldermaston would launch into the Cotentin in a mission code-named Chicago. Later on 6 June at 2100 hours, thirty-two more gliders would convey medical, signals and anti-tank equipment to the 101st Airborne in Mission Keokuk. Both divisions would fly in several waves, typically eighteen paratroopers (or three tons) to a plane. The 101st began leaving their airbases first, from 2350 hours, onwards. Flying low to avoid German radar in Brittany and arriving over their target two hours later at a height of 1,500 feet, they planned to jump from seven hundred feet.

One of the 1,118 CG-4A Waco gliders released on D-Day, wearing its invasion stripes in a Cotentin field. Although its payload was small – thirteen troops or a jeep – it could land in most of the many very small fields that defined the Normandy landscape. Nearly 14,000 were produced, including those used by the British, who called them Hadrians. (US Army Signal Corps)

Lieutenant Colonel Mike C. Murphy, a native of Lafayette, Indiana, led Operation Chicago, piloting a Waco glider named *The Fighting Falcon*. As the senior USAAF glider pilot in the European theatre, his job had been to supervise the final training of glider pilots for Overlord. Not originally listed to participate in Overlord, he had talked General Williams of IX Troop Carrier Command into letting him fly. As Murphy led his glider train under tow between German-held Guernsey and Jersey – the same route taken earlier by the paratrooper-laden C-47s – in the next glider behind, surgeon Charles O. Van Gorder noticed below the wing-tip 'blue formation lights of the glider tugs stretching like a ribbon for miles'.

Over the Cotentin, they dropped to six hundred feet and were about halfway across when German gunners opened up on them. The doctor recalled: 'the tracers make lazy arcs in the night sky'; they reminded him of Independence Day fireworks. Murphy felt the *Falcon* taking some hits, which sounded 'like popcorn popping, as the slugs passed through the taut glider fabric'; his No. 2 glider later counted ninety-four bullet holes.[62]

On the ground, Grenadier Ernest Flöter of the 91st *Luftlande* Division – who had been given the night off sentry duty because of the poor weather – was woken up in his tent by 'a horrible noise in the air. American airplanes by hundreds, lots of them, heading eastward.'[63] In Deauville, civilian *résistante* Odette Brefort confided to her diary, 'Oh, what a night! My little head is all shell-shocked. Since midnight it's been impossible to sleep: the humming from planes, anti-aircraft shells, machine-gun noise. I went downstairs because I couldn't sleep and after fifteen minutes it went quiet. Thinking it would be better, I went back to bed. What a mistake! All night, the humming from planes, it was non-stop.'[64]

Renée Olinger, a young girl living in Thury-Harcourt, south-west of Caen, recollected suddenly being 'woken by the noise of a strong bombardment far away; it became louder and louder, and seemed it would never stop. Over Caen the sky was red, and we could hear the different sounds of bombing and shooting getting louder as it got nearer. Slowly we started to realise that it was not like the normal bombardments we were used to and asked ourselves, might it be the Allies landing?'[65]

Fifteen-year-old Pierre Labbé, in Moon-sur-Elle, midway between Omaha Beach and Saint-Lô, remembered the explosions and roar of anti-aircraft cannon in the night sky. 'It woke us. We got out of bed to watch and were not afraid. We knew what it meant: liberation from the yoke of the Germans, with all their rules and regulations. We detested them: we had a curfew from 2000 hours to 0600, which prohibited travel at night. Since 1943 aeroplanes had come twice a week to strafe and once or twice a month to bomb. *Les Boches* made us shield our windows so that aeroplanes could not see us at night. But this evening was different: the planes were continuous and the Germans in our village seemed fearful: running around, not knowing what to do – we enjoyed that, and stayed up till dawn to watch.'[66]

In Villedieu-les-Poêles, south of Saint-Lô, Monique Kraus, a thirteen-year-old Jewish girl in hiding with the local Maquis leader, understood something was about to happen: the BBC had just broadcast '*Les sirenes ont les cheveux decolores*' (Mermaids have dyed hair). 'That night, bombers by the hundreds flew overhead to drop bombs on their targets, and ... rumours abounded. They've landed on the beaches at Granville, some said Cherbourg, some said Le Havre. There was no way of checking because the electricity was out and all means of communication had been cut.'[67]

On the Cotentin's west coast at Barneville, René Baumel recalled being woken at around 0400 by the planes. 'They came from the Cap de Carteret, flying above the water tower of Barneville then up to the left towards the marshes. They were like a swarm in the sky and we could see the cables pulling the gliders. During the day I stood on a little bridge to watch with a friend when an Allied plane flew over us and rocked its wings. When it flew over a second time and did the same thing we understood it wanted to attack the bridge. We scurried away and sure enough, on the third pass it destroyed the crossing.'[68]

Jean Mignon was a fourteen-year-old choirboy serving at mass in Notre-Dame de Saint-Lô church on the morning of 6 June. He was puzzled to see the stained-glass windows opposite him vibrating. He only learned the reason afterwards when the verger told him in the vestry the Allies had landed on the coast. His family fled town that evening: 'Even today I can still hear the noise of the crackling wood as Saint-Lô burned.'[69]

At Carrouges, sixty miles south of the invasion coast, farmer Marcel Rousseau and his parents had been woken by 'dull noises and a distant and continuous rumble that made the windows hum'. It was only in the evening 'listening to the English radio' that their hopes of landings were confirmed. Next morning, however, their optimism was punctured by the sound of tracked vehicles heading north, towards the invasion beaches. 'They drove in groups of ten or twelve, bearing soldiers in full combat gear. Later on which watched Allied planes attack these convoys. After that it was difficult to get news because there was no electricity, radio, newspapers or mail.'[70]

Obergefreiter Rudolf Thiel with the 6th *Fallschirmjäger-Regiment* was on duty and training his binoculars north-west, when he 'saw all kinds of red flares and glaring white light signals. That could only mean one thing to any experienced soldier: "The enemy is attacking!" I reported to Major von der Heydte, who replied "Sound the alarm!" We took our positions and waited for the unknown monster: invasion. It was 0011 hours, German time.'[71]

At 0030, Obergefreiter Günter Prignitz of the *Fallschirmjäger*'s 13th Company in Saint-Georges-de-Bohon, south-west of Carentan, heard his ground observer calling, 'Alarm – Parachutes!' while firing off his machine-gun. On the receiving end, Private Frank Brumbaugh with 'I' Company of the 508th couldn't see much of the ground; 'it was more or less of a blur, but I watched all these tracers and shell bursts in the air around me. A stream of tracers, obviously from a machine-gun, looked like it was coming directly at me. I knew I could not be seen from the ground under my camouflaged chute, but the tracers still came directly at me. I spread my legs widely and grabbed with both hands at my groin as if to protect myself. It was obviously a futile, but normal, gesture, I guess. Those machine-gun bullets traced up the inside of my leg, missed my groin but split my pants, dropping both my cartons of Pall Mall cigarettes onto the soil of France.'[72]

Obergefreiter Prignitz soon reported 'a dead American paratrooper landed on one of our tents; another in a giant tree with a broken leg – our first prisoner'.[73] Grenadier Josef Horn, a signaller with the 191st *Artillerie-Regiment* (91st *Luftlande* Division), had spent the previous few days laying field telephone cables around Sainte-Marie-du-Mont and knew the terrain well. 'On Monday evening 5 June', he recollected, 'I ate supper from 2200 hours but shortly after midnight I heard the sound of low-flying airplanes and saw parachutes coming down. Some were white, others appeared blue, many were camouflaged. Knowing the lie of the land, I was able to evade the Americans, but once in a while I could hear a clicking sound, but I didn't know until much later what it was.'[74]

Horn's boss, Generalleutnant Wilhelm Falley of the 91st *Luftlande*, had just left the Château de Bernaville – visited by Rommel and Admiral

Ruge on 17 May – and clearly heard the roar of aero-engines overhead. He had been intending to drive to Rennes for the scheduled war games, but as the sky lit up with the tracer rounds of his men engaging the passing aircraft, he realised his place was at his headquarters. His companion, Major Joachim Bartuzat, the division's Ib (quartermaster), quickly ordered Obergefreiter Vogt, their driver, to turn back – but as the trio slowed to turn into the grounds, they were caught in a blaze of automatic gunfire from men of the 82nd, led by Lieutenant Malcolm Brannen of the Third Battalion, 508th. Soon after, Feldwebel Alfons Mertens with the 6th *Fallschirmjägers* sent a young runner to report to General Falley. He returned distraught, having found the headquarters 'deserted and destroyed with the general shot dead by the side of the road'.[75] The *Fallschirmjägers* were on their own.

With presence of mind, Brannen – who was dropped exactly where he was supposed to be, squarely in the middle of his drop zone – had scooped up the maps and documents in the wrecked car and read the name written inside the officer's cap – Falley. When daylight arrived, Jack Schlegel came upon the general's 'bullet-riddled car rammed up against a stone wall and two dead officers in the road'; their bodies lay there for about three days until some Germans still in the vicinity ordered a local farmer to bury them. Falley was the first senior officer – of many – to perish in Normandy. Faced with a dearth of so many commanders at a crucial moment, the performance of the Wehrmacht would soon start to unravel in Normandy.[76] Command of the 91st was temporarily assumed by Generalmajor Bernhard Klosterkemper, while a new commander, Generalmajor Eugen König, assigned on 7 June, drove from Germany – but he did not arrive until the afternoon of the tenth.

Although the Germans were fully expecting the assault to include Americans, this never occurred to the French, who had spent the occupation listening to the BBC. Thus they assumed the men falling from the skies were British until they saw the Stars and Stripes neatly sewn on the paratroopers' jump jackets. When told of General Falley's demise, Matthew Ridgway, whose headquarters was then in an apple orchard and consisted of eleven officers and as many men, surrounded by Germans, observed, 'Well in our present situation, killing divisional commanders doesn't strike me as being particularly hilarious right now.' To the north of Falley's former HQ, meanwhile, 'G' Company of the 508th had started to dig in on a small feature labelled on maps as 'Hill 30', where they stayed to repel several German counter-attacks.

Within yards of Falley's headquarters, in nearby Picauville, a testament to the efficacy of the German reaction remains. It is an imposing monument to four C-47s – two from the 435th Troop Carrier Group out of RAF Welford, and two from the 439th flying from Upottery – brought down nearby in the early minutes of D-Day. All eighteen aircrew on board, together with their passengers from the 506th Parachute Infantry, perished. Part of the striking roadside memorial contains a Pratt & Whitney aero-engine discovered by a local family in 1986 at one of the crash sites.

Nineteen-year-old Marguerite Catherine was living on her parents' farm nearby and recalled seeing one of the four C-47s, flames licking the fuselage, flying so low she could make out the pilots. 'Lying on my stomach on my bed facing the window, I saw big, round grey flakes coming down slowly. I understood straight away they were paratroopers. The noise was infernal with the low-flying planes, anti-aircraft fire, flares and our animals breaking their tethers, bellowing and stampeding in panic.'[77]

It was also in Picauville that Captain Ignatius Maternowski from Holyoke, Massachusetts, a Fort Bragg-trained chaplain with the 508th Parachute Infantry, found himself ministering to US airborne wounded and dead. The thirty-two-year-old former Franciscan friar had just met his German opposite number and started to negotiate the location of a common aid station. Although unarmed and prominently wearing his chaplain's insignia and a Red Cross armband, he was returning to American lines when killed by a sniper with a shot to his back, becoming the only US chaplain to be killed on D-Day. It is too easy to dismiss his death as the cowardly work of a fanatical Nazi; it is far more likely that in an area under constant shellfire and drifting smoke from burning farm buildings, the finer points of the chaplain's uniform and lack of a weapon were missed, and that a nervous young grenadier, probably not a sniper, mistook him for an ordinary GI.

Another C-47 was brought down at Beuzeville-au-Plain, north-east of Sainte-Mère-Église; its occupants included First Lieutenant Thomas Meehan III, commanding 'E' Company of the 506th Parachute Infantry and his headquarters group. Their Skytrain had been badly damaged by flak and, attempting to land, hit a bocage hedgerow outside the village and exploded; sixteen paratroopers died with Meehan, alongside five aircrew.

This was unknown to Meehan's successor in command of 'E' Company, Dick Winters, who only knew that his superior had disappeared. Indeed, until 1952 they were posted as missing in action, but then the crash site was found, their remains recovered and buried in a mass grave at Jefferson Barracks, St Louis, Missouri. Minutes before take-off, Meehan had scribbled a note to be forwarded to his wife: 'Dearest Anne, in a few hours, I'm going to take the best company of men in the world into France. We'll give the bastards hell. Strangely, I'm not particularly scared. But in my heart is a terrific longing to hold you in my arms. I love you, Sweetheart – forever. Your Tom.'[78] There is now a memorial to them next to Beuzeville's timeless little Norman church.

23

Across the Water and Into the Trees

'"Gentlemen," the red-tabbed Army officer said dramatically pointing to his watch, "I have to tell you that at this moment, British, Canadian and American paratroopers are dropping into Normandy." It took a few seconds before the full impact of this statement penetrated. Then there were cheers and yells. Pilots got up from their wooden chairs waving their arms about and slapping each other on the back. For them it was a champagne moment and they erupted.'

Briefing to Typhoon pilots of No. 245 Squadron, RAF, 0030 hours, 6 June 1944.[1]

THE GENERAL'S FIELD telephone rang. Erich Marcks limped over to his desk, his artificial leg creaking; Major Hayn, the intelligence officer, remembered that 'as he listened, the general's whole body seemed to stiffen'. In his château overlooking Saint-Lô, his brief birthday celebration over, General Marcks had put off leaving for Rennes. Originally planning to travel in company of Major von der Heydte, the latter had appeared earlier but departed back to his own headquarters. The phone call was not to convey birthday wishes, nor from any units in the Cotentin, but from Generalmajor Richter of the 716th Infantry Division, over in Caen: 'Paratroopers have landed east of the Orne. The area seems to be around Bréville and Ranville, along the northern fringe of the Bavent Forest.' Hayn recalled, 'this struck us like lightning – the corps headquarters soon resembled a disturbed beehive as priority messages were sent in all directions.'² Marcks – who had anticipated such a move in his *kriegsspiel* – immediately telephoned Max Pemsel, chief of staff of Dollmann's Seventh Army, who put the Seventh Army on invasion alert. The time was 0115 hours.

The miscreants were the British 6th Airborne Division, who had deployed by parachute and glider to protect the invasion's eastern flank. We have seen how its commander, Major General Richard 'Windy' Gale, devised Operation Tonga, to insert his men based around two *coup de main* operations, and the cutting of four bridges over the River Dives. These tactical missions overshadowed the importance of the divisional task – the 3rd and 5th Parachute and 6th Air Landing Brigades were to hold the high ground east of the River Dives and Caen, and prevent the Wehrmacht from slamming into the left flank of Overlord before the seaborne assault troops arrived.

In all, some 5,300 British and Canadian troops of Gale's division were to be transported by two RAF groups, Nos. 38 and 46, who – not possessing enough aircraft for a single lift – broke down their tasks into two waves. Tonga was dedicated to the main objectives, with the 6th Airborne's pathfinders deploying at the same time as Howard's glider men. It would involve 264 transport aircraft conveying 4,512 paratroopers and 1,315 containers of equipment to Normandy. Additionally, ninety-eight gliders left southern England, of which seventy-four were released, though only fifty-two reached their correct landing zones. The second operation, 'Mallard', would follow twenty hours later, in the evening of 6 June, enabling RAF pilots to fly two missions. Mallard would deliver heavy equipment, such as Tetrarch light tanks, jeeps, trailers and anti-tank guns, in 216 Horsa and thirty Hamilcar gliders.

The fine details of seizing the Pegasus and Horsa bridges (respectively, over the Caen Canal and Orne river at Bénouville), as well as the gun battery at Merville, had been thrashed out amid conditions of utmost secrecy at Syrencote House, Figheldean, a Georgian pile on the edge of Salisbury Plain. During training, secrecy had demanded that every reference to Normandy be disguised, so on maps and in staff papers, the Orne was code-named 'Prague' and the canal 'Portugal'. Once the operation was under way, to save time encoding locations for radio transmissions, 'Prague' became 'Cricket' and the canal 'Rugger'.

The end result was 181 men of Major John Howard's 'D' Company of the 2nd Oxfordshire and Buckinghamshire Light Infantry, with two platoons borrowed from 'B' Company, thirty Royal Engineers from the 249th (Airborne) Field Company, and medics – and just over 650 men of Lieutenant Colonel Terrence Otway's 9th Parachute Battalion, plus supporting arms – crouched in their gliders and troop carriers on the runways of RAF Tarrant Rushton in Dorset, and Harwell and Broadwell in Oxfordshire.

Four minutes before 2300 hours on 5 June they felt a distinctive lurch forward, as their aircraft started rolling down the concrete strips towards France. If the Ox and Bucks failed at Bénouville, the 7th Parachute Battalion were to drop in Mae West life jackets with dinghies and paddle into battle. Apart from their commanders – themselves mostly in their late twenties – few had seen previous action. Like their US colleagues of the 101st, Normandy was to be the 6th Airborne's first brush with the Wehrmacht.

Hunched over his battered wireless set in a captured pillbox, Corporal Edward Tappenden with his headphones was oblivious to all else. Battling with the static, he was concentrating on sending three words to the outside world. 'Ham and jam; ham and jam; jam and bloody jam,' he repeated endlessly. Tappenden was announcing the success of Operation Deadstick, Howard's mission to capture the two bridges near Bénouville. The force had been carried in six Horsa gliders, twenty-eight men apiece, towed across the Channel by Halifax bombers. With perfect navigation and piloting skill, five of the gliders landed on time and on target within yards of each other – three to Pegasus, two to Horsa. Howard's glider was skilfully placed within a few feet of the canal bridge by Staff Sergeant Jim Wallwork, the London dandy who had volunteered for the Territorials in 1939 to cover himself with 'medals, free beer and adoring females'.

The German guards initially assumed it was one of the bombers then hitting Caen, downed by flak. After a fierce ten-minute gun battle the bridge was captured, the action over by 0035, a full six hours before the beach landings, and within ninety minutes of having left Tarrant Rushton. Len Buckley, with the 7th Parachute Battalion – the backup force – landed after Howard's men and ran over to help them. 'They had obviously had quite a fire-fight,' he reminisced. 'We passed an armoured half-track on fire. Hit by a PIAT, the vehicle was exploding all over the place, as its ammunition cooked off.[3] Some Germans were charging through the field towards us. I stood up to return fire and I took a bullet which glanced off the butt of my Sten, but passed right through my elbow. If it wasn't for the Sten, I would have got it in the chest. I was lucky.'[4]

One of D-Day's first actions was carried out by Major John Howard (1912–99) (left), who commanded 181 men based in 'D' Company of the 2nd Oxfordshire and Buckinghamshire Light Infantry. In Operation Deadstick, men in three of his gliders landed near Bénouville and captured the drawbridge that spanned the Caen Canal (top right). At the same moment, soldiers in two more Horsas seized the nearby swing bridge over the River Orne at Ranville (bottom right). Code-named Rugger and Cricket, they were defended against counter-attacks and afterwards renamed Pegasus and Horsa. (Author's collection)

Responding to several reports coming in from dazed subordinates, at 0200 hours Hauptmann Eberhard Wagemann, duty officer in Saint-Pierre-sur-Dives, had put the 21st Panzer Division on invasion alert (ready to move in less than ninety minutes).[5] Shortly afterwards, patrolling towards Bénouville and Ranville, one of his men, Feldwebel Rainer Hartmetz, a veteran of the *Ostfront*, encountered 'one of our half-tracks with an anti-tank gun, riddled with bullets and smeared with blood, and dead para-troopers hanging by their chutes on trees, telegraph poles and chimneys'.[6] This was the same half-track seen by Len Buckley, and was actually a self-propelled gun, leading a column of four other armoured vehicles from the anti-tank battalion of the 716th Infantry Division, which had been sent to investigate. (To lightly-armed airborne troops, any tracked vehicle clattering around in the dark armed with a large gun was reported as a tank, and often described as such in British memoirs.)

It had been hit by Sergeant Charles 'Wagger' Thornton with his only round of PIAT ammunition, the rest of the ammunition having been lost in the drop.[7] The remaining vehicles, unnerved by their encounter with an unseen enemy, had pulled back. The exploding armoured vehicle had emerged at the crossroads (today a roundabout) outside the Bénouville *mairie*, in front of which lies the commune's war memorial to the fallen of 1914–18. Shells removed the top of the obelisk during the night-time battle, and today, the severed, pockmarked monument stands in tribute to airborne soldiers and, later, commandos who passed that way.

Meanwhile, Howard's sixth glider missed its rendezvous at the swing bridge spanning the Orne river, code-named 'Horsa'. Its occupants became disoriented during the descent, landed by a likely looking structure and captured it, only to find they were miles away from their real objective. As one of the German guards took a bullet, his finger tightened on the trigger and in his death throes he released a round which struck Sergeant Raymond 'Titch' Raynor, whom we met earlier training with John Howard. The wounded Raynor thus gained his reputation of being the only British soldier to be shot on D-Day by a dead German.[8]

During the initial Pegasus Bridge action, platoon commander Den Brotheridge was shot – almost certainly the first British soldier felled by gunfire in Overlord, dying later of his wounds. Undeterred, Howard ordered Corporal Tappenden to send the code words 'Ham and jam', indicating that both bridges had been captured – along with the adjacent café, where the bridge sentries Helmut Römer, Erwin Sauer and Wilhelm Furtner had relaxed between sentry duties. They had seen the first glider and 'at first thought it was a crippled bomber. We wondered whether to take a look at it, or wake our sergeant. Before we knew it, a bunch of about ten wild-looking men were charging at us with guns. We ran.' Römer was soon rounded up, but remembered that many of the guards who were 'Poles and other foreign conscripts' simply melted into the night. The café proprietor, Georges Gondrée, and his family thus became the first French civilians to be liberated, and their establishment – renamed the Pegasus Bridge Café – has acted as a magnet to visitors ever since.[9]

Gondrée provided some light relief when he dug up his vegetable patch and produced ninety bottles of his finest champagne, artfully hidden from the Germans. Howard observed later that 'it was remarkable how many of my men developed injuries which required their presence at the café, then an aid post, in order to be treated with Gondrée's champagne'.[10] More amusement arrived when the local area commander, Major Hans Schmidt, was captured when his Mercedes cabriolet staff car ran into one of Howard's roadblocks. That Schmidt had raced back from an evening of excess with his French girlfriend in Ranville was obvious: the car contained wine, lipstick, food and lingerie. Schmidt demanded to be shot as he had let down his Führer. He was – but only with morphine, to silence his ranting.[11]

The Pegasus Bridge Café is these days presided over by Arlette Gondrée, who is old enough to remember *le bruit du bois casser* (the sound of breaking wood) as the gliders landed, and being offered her first chocolate by one of Howard's camouflaged troopers – who to her seemed like frightening aliens from another planet. This was Lance Corporal Albert Gregory, Royal Army Medical Corps, flying in Howard's third glider. He had treated the first wounded in a hedgerow before moving them to the safety of the café: 'I remember a small French girl, ashen-faced and scared to hell. I reached into my tunic and gave her my bar of chocolate, but still she did not smile.'[12] A Memorial Pegasus museum opened in June 2000 on the appropriately named avenue du Major Howard, and when Pegasus Bridge (which also starred as itself in *The Longest Day*) had to be replaced with a newer model, it was decided to relocate the original structure in the grounds of the museum.

Amongst the twenty BBC war reporters who had learned their trade on Exercise Spartan the previous year and deployed on the eve of D-Day were Guy Byam, waiting to jump with the 6th Airborne, and Chester Wilmot (later the author of the authoritative *The Struggle for Europe*) with its glider-borne contingent. Their vivid despatches, sent back to Broadcasting House on primitive Bakelite discs, were in the best traditions of radio reportage, and transmitted from 6 June onwards after the nine o'clock news in *War Report*. 'I am jumping last but one of my stick. In the crowded fuselage all you see in the pale light of an orange bulb is the man standing next to you,' intoned Guy Byam – destined to die on a bombing raid over Berlin the following February.

> Flak – the word is passed from man to man. The machine starts to rock and jump. We're over the coast now and the run has started – one minute – thirty seconds. Red light – green light, and *out*. And then the ground comes up to meet me. I can't be sure where I am – and overhead hundreds of parachutes and containers are coming down. The whole sky is a

fantastic chimera of lights and flak, one plane gets hit and disintegrates wholesale in the sky, sprinkling a myriad of burning pieces all over.[13]

Meanwhile, the Americans had started to pour out of their aeroplanes over the Cotentin. The vicinity of Sainte-Mère-Église, astride the *Route Nationale* 13, was the objective for many of the 82nd, but few expected – or desired – to land slap in the centre of the garrison town, held by around two hundred men of Oberst Ernst Hermann's 30th *Flak-Regiment*. Corporal Earl McClung hailed from Washington State, where he had been born on the Colville Indian Reservation; he was three-eighths Native American and proud of his ancestry. A 101st Paratrooper with 'E' Company of the 506th Parachute Infantry under Dick Winters, as he glanced up at his twenty-eight-foot camouflaged silken canopy, suspending him by the same number of thin chords, he noticed his sixty-pound kitbag was pulling him towards a town where a fire was burning – Sainte-Mère-Église, a long way from his scheduled drop zone. He came down on a roof near the church. McClung recalled, 'It was pretty hectic for the first few seconds. Two Germans were running toward me. I had jumped with my M1 assembled and in my hands: it was no contest – they were only a few feet away and I took care of those guys. I went on by, headed through the graveyard and out of town, and linked up with the 505th of the 82nd. I fought with them for the next nine days.'[14] A similar experience befell Charles A. 'Gus' Liapes, of Wallingford, Connecticut, with the 506th Parachute Infantry, who came down in a heap in a field. 'Enemy soldiers came charging across with fixed bayonets. I cut and hacked at my harness in a frantic effort to get out of the way. They were almost on top of me when I got my Tommy gun and fired into them.'[15]

With the 91st *Luftlande* Division scattered and leaderless, its operations officer tried to make sense of the situation. As paratroops had been reported in Sainte-Mère-Église, he ordered the 1057th *Grenadier-Regiment* to seize control of the Merderet river crossings – unknown to him, also an objective of the US 82nd Airborne, who had two drop zones beyond. The 1057th's Grenadiers took over the Manoir de la Fière on the east bank, but in their hurry, deployed without artillery or armoured support – which would have swung the battle in their favour immediately.

Encountering them at around 0400 hours, troops of the First Battalion of the 505th Parachute Infantry had struck out towards La Fière bridge, two miles west of town. Although the Merderet was narrow at this point, its banks had been deliberately flooded, creating a mile-wide swamp, over which the small stone bridge threaded its way like a causeway. This inundated region of marsh was where many heavily laden 507th and 508th paratroopers landed – well beyond their drop zones further west. Much equipment was sucked into the mire and an estimated 150 airborne soldiers were drowned by their waterlogged chutes and clothing.

The 82nd Airborne's advance on the bridge was slowed by frequent encounters with roving German troops, and an initial attempt to rush the crossing failed due to alert machine-gunners. It took the day for the 505th just to winkle out their opponents from the Manoir, but American numbers swelled as the eastern embankments overlooking the Merderet became natural assembly points for paratroopers trying to reach their drop zones on the far side.

The bridges at La Fière and further south at Chef-du-Pont rapidly became viciously contested ground. Opposite La Fière, glider troops reached the churchyard at Cauquigny from the west and held off German counter-attacks until ejected in the afternoon by obsolete French tanks, captured in 1940 and operated by the 100th *Panzer-Ersatz- und Ausbildungs-Abteilung* (Tank Replacement and Training Battalion).

This unit's full title reveals it was never meant to be a combat formation but used for driving, formation and gunnery training. Its three companies were led by Major Bardtenschlager, headquartered in the Château de Franquetot – soon to be used by J. Lawton Collins as his command post – in the centre of the Cotentin. Bardtenschlager, a wealthy cavalryman whose family ran a well-known publishing business, commanded thirty-two requisitioned French tanks, mostly Hotchkiss models from the 1930s, but some older Renaults which dated back to 1917. None were remotely capable of intimidating, let alone defeating, the Parachute Infantry, and all would be swiftly disabled whenever encountered in the coming hours.

Three of these thinly armoured, two-man little vehicles moved onto the La Fière bridge and were immediately knocked out by bazooka rounds from the paratroopers defending the eastern bank. Bardtenschlager himself, along with the commander of his No. 1 Company, Oberleutnant Weber, would die later in the day. At Chef-du-Pont, troops led personally by Brigadier General Jim Gavin could make no headway and returned to reinforce La Fière. However, the rearguard Gavin left at Chef-du-Pont, at one stage nearly overwhelmed, was suddenly rescued by the unexpected arrival of a glider carrying an anti-tank gun. They in turn pushed their opponents back and seized the southern bridge. To enable his comrades to cross at Chef-du-Pont, the much-wounded PFC Charles DeGlopper, 325th Glider Infantry, covered them with his Browning Automatic Rifle (BAR), but was killed in the process – an action that would bring recognition of his sacrifice in the form of a Medal of Honor.

La Fière would remain contested for three days, both sides realising the defeat of the paratroopers around Sainte-Mère-Église or the advance on Cherbourg would be enabled by controlling this key location, however insignificant it seemed. In the event, the 82nd finally overwhelmed the grenadiers on 9 June, backed up by Barton's 4th Division and Shermans of the 746th Tank Battalion. Although the *Fallschirmjägers* may have rated their combat efficiency as 'poor', and grenadiers like Ernst Flöter, Paul Golz and Franz Roggenbuck were all ill-trained and 'not interested in fighting', at La Fière the 91st *Luftlande* Division fought like tigers. When GIs were read a G-2 (intelligence) report stating their opponents were second-rate, one suggested 'putting the Germans on the distribution list because they don't seem to realise it'.

The panorama from the high east bank at La Fière is exactly as it was in 1944, without the marsh. From there, the operational importance of the several Merderet crossings for the Wehrmacht and Airborne troops is evident, which was why they were so bitterly contested. For the 82nd Airborne, the fighting in and around La Fière rated as the most intense they experienced in the Second World War, reflected by casualties of 569 killed and wounded amongst the elements of the five battalions directed to the vicinity by Generals Ridgway and Gavin. The road leading down to the bridge 'was continuously dancing with bullet and shrapnel impact as if a giant vibrator was at work', remembered one officer.[16]

Of the ground behind, Jim Gavin recalled, 'The right side of the road was stacked with the poncho-covered bodies of dead troopers. Opposite was the immediate aid station. Wounded troopers were laying on every inch of available space, legs and boots on the road with medics going from patient to patient administering aid, inserting tubes with plasma.'[17] Across the river lies the little twelfth-century chapel at Cauquigny, where the railings around the churchyard are still riddled with holes and shrapnel from the three-day firefight of June 1944. On the east bank, a replica of the Airborne Trooper statue at Fort Bragg ('Iron Mike') was unveiled on 7 June 1997, standing guard over La Fière today.

Taking Sainte-Mère-Église was the task of Lieutenant Colonel Edward Krause's Third Battalion, 505th Parachute Infantry, which they achieved by daybreak, killing or capturing the forty Germans who had remained to slug it out – the rest having fled. However, this vital route centre was to be the objective of several German counter-attacks, and although beaten off, illustrated how fast the Germans could round up scattered troops and initiate tactical actions.

Corporal William F. Falduti of Nutley, New Jersey, recalled their arrival.

> I jumped with my buddy, Peter Black Cloud, a big strapping Indian from North Dakota; we were both 505th and had been all through training and boy, did we raise hell together. When we jumped, the only light we saw was German tracer bullets coming up to meet us. We landed in and around apple trees, and got into a firefight straight-aways. I'll never forget it was apple blossom time. Even now, when I smell the fragrance of apples, I associate it with sharp stench of cordite from discharging weapons. Of the thirty-six in my platoon, only seventeen survived – and my old pal Indian Pete wasn't one of them.[18]

It was mainly the 2nd Platoon, 'F' Company of the 505th, who were sucked into the night-time centre of Sainte-Mère-Église, though some landed in the darkened countryside beyond. Few who landed in the town square stood a chance against the armed and jumpy Germans, who machine-gunned to death those caught in trees or on buildings. Privates Kenneth Russell and John Steele were lucky to survive the encounter when their canopies snagged on a corner of the church steeple. They were part of a stick of fifteen that floated down into the middle of the town. Russell soon cut himself down; Steele decided that the best thing he could do was play dead and took a bullet to the heel. Eventually he was cut down by Gefreiter Rudolf May and Grenadier Rudi Escher, manning a machine-gun in the church tower, taken prisoner and then carried to an aid station – later, he escaped.

Yards away, Private Ernest R. Blanchard was waylaid by the branches of a tree in the town square but immediately hacked at his harness with a knife, dropped to the ground and ran for his life. Only later did he realise in that adrenalin-pumping moment he had cut off the top of his thumb. Eight of the stick died in the square; one was taken prisoner, two died in the Bulge in 1945; just four of the fifteen survived the night and fought through to the end of the war.[19] Through the storytelling of Cornelius Ryan, it is Steele's adventure that the world now recalls, but

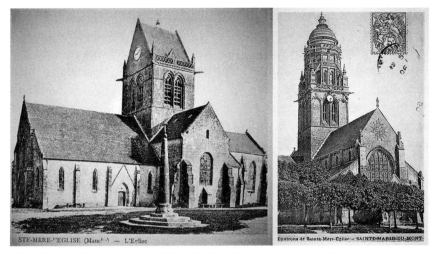

The church of Sainte-Mère-Église (left), where a stick from 'F' Company of the
505th PIR landed. John Steele's parachute caught on the far left pinnacle of the
tower; he was captured by two Germans in the belfry. Kenneth Russell landed on
the left-hand roof and was about to be shot by a German on the ground. However,
the guard was killed by Sergeant John Ray, who had landed in the square; Ray
was gunned down, but, in a final burst of life, felled the German who had shot
him. Ladislav Tlapa landed in a tree to the left and was executed as he struggled
to get free. Ernest Blanchard landed in another tree and was unaware that he had
hacked off his thumb to escape. It was from the distinctive eleventh century
church tower of Saint-Marie-du-Mont (right), the highest in the region, that
Major von der Heydte first saw the invasion fleet off Utah Beach. (Author's
collection)

the equally dramatic escapes of Russell and Blanchard have been
consigned, alas, to the dustbin of history.[20]

Woken up by the low-flying aircraft, eleven-year-old Emil Ozouf stood
on his bedroom windowsill to watch the paratroopers float down. Living
on a farm in Gambosville just outside Sainte-Mère-Église, the following
morning he raced through 'the garden and fields recovering the valuable
silk chutes – there must have been about eighty. We spent a memorable
few days, wandering the countryside, making friends with the Americans,
collecting anything we found. Food, bandages and medicines, military
equipment – even weapons. We took it all home, knowing our parents
could trade them for valuable commodities or make clothes from the
silk. I had a lovely German officer's side hat which my mother used for
ages as an oven glove. My father fixed a handle onto a German helmet

and we used it to feed grain to the hens – very appropriate!'[21] Local families recall that this unexpected bounty from the skies was often the first taste of chocolate, orange juice or coffee in their lives.

John Steele is still in Sainte-Mère-Église today – or at least his effigy hangs from the church (albeit from the wrong pinnacle), for 6 June 1944 gave the anonymous little Norman town a fame it had never achieved in nine hundred years. Many of the town's businesses survive off the D-Day pilgrims who visit each year, and the careful eye will pick out the bullet holes in the church's stone walls. Inside, two modern stained-glass windows depict aspects of the town's liberation, of paratroopers falling to earth. Across the way, the Airborne Forces Museum has grown enormously from its first opening in 1964, and as well as a Waco glider, it now includes one of the actual C-47s from which paratroopers of the 101st Airborne jumped into Normandy.

Near Carentan, and in charge of the *Fallschirmjäger's* 12th Company, Oberleutnant Martin Pöppel – fresh from field training and a map exercise only the day before – received the *Invasionswarnung* (invasion alert):

> All my observation posts are reporting parachute landings. The first wounded prisoners, three Americans, are brought in. The initial inter-rogations don't produce any results, though. The fellows have been well trained and just answer every question by saying, 'I don't know'. The night is stormy and wild. There are single cracks of rifle fire. From time to time the moon lights up the darkness. More prisoners are brought in, great hulking figures. They look as though they could be from Sing-Sing – and our map exercise has suddenly turned into the real thing.[22]

As word spread of the first parachutists, Grenadier Otto Bügener, an eighteen-year-old who could have passed for thirteen, scribbled a hasty note to his parents. He recorded 'intense joy' that the alarm was sounded. 'This is the moment we have awaited for so long,' he wrote, full of confidence they would be victorious. He signed off: 'I am going to rise to the task ahead of me and I will come back to you shortly; we were read the Führer's orders and know that this will be the battle for Germany and for Europe.'[23]

Despite the best efforts of their pathfinders and aircrew, the airborne troopers' principal enemy proved not to be the Germans but the weather:

only ten per cent of the US paratroop force landed on their drop zones. Around thirty per cent were within a mile, and a further twenty per cent within two miles; the British were similarly distributed – though this was nothing like the catastrophe the excitable Leigh-Mallory had predicted. We met Lance Corporal John Ross earlier of the Canadian Parachute Battalion (British 6th Airborne); he and the rest of his 120-strong 'C' Company were flown into action east of Caen by RAF Albemarles, ten to a plane, twelve aircraft in total. 'I would say four of the aeroplanes dropped their men on the drop zone; the rest were badly scattered. The one I was in dropped us right dead on target,' he observed.[24]

Ed Boccafogli from Clifton, New Jersey, fought with 'B' Company, 508th Parachute Infantry of the 82nd Airborne. He reflected, 'I was lucky. I landed within, I'd say, maybe hundreds of yards of where I was supposed to. Others landed five miles away. Many of them were killed, because by the time they tried to work their way back they ran into German units.'[25] Also arriving precisely on his DZ was Captain Frank Lillyman, leading the pathfinders of the 101st Airborne, and possibly the first American to touch French soil; he had been flown to the right spot by Lieutenant Colonel Joel Crouch, the former United Airlines pilot.

Their flight had been uneventful until they made landfall: Crouch ran into a bank of low-lying cloud and disappeared from the rest of the formation. Instead of following their training and flying through, some climbed above, others below, and the force scattered; fire from the ground compounded the issue, with the result that many sticks of pathfinders were dropped away from their DZs. Overall, After Action Reports noted, the excessive weight carried by individuals caused sticks to be strewn over much longer distances.

Meanwhile, the airborne force had already started taking casualties. Waiting for the green light to go, Lieutenant Bob Mathias, a platoon leader with the 508th Parachute Infantry, was about to urge his men out of their C-47. An anti-aircraft shell burst in his face, knocking him over, yet he still raised his right arm and bellowed out 'Follow me!' as he fell into the night. It was 0227 hours – that was the last time his men saw him alive: at daybreak, he was discovered near Sainte-Mère-Église, dead from shrapnel wounds, still wearing his parachute.[26]

In the east near Caen, Private Jan de Vries with the Canadian Parachute Battalion was pulled out of his C-47 by the slipstream, to be met by … silence. The noise and camaraderie of the aircraft faded and disappeared; most paratroopers recalled a sense of being alone as they drifted to earth, which offered a moment of respite.[27] David Rogers of the 101st noticed, 'When my parachute opened, I was directly above the steeple of the church in Sainte-Marie-du-Mont. The moon was full, and there were scattered clouds which made everything on the ground easy to see. It looked just like the picture I had studied so intensely at Upottery.'[28] Another 101st man, Lieutenant Elmer F. Brandenberger with 'B' Company of the 502nd Parachute Infantry, was surprised when the opening shock of his chute 'tore the rifle from my grasp. I can still remember the thought flashing through my mind that it would hit some damned Kraut and bash in his head. I landed in the middle of an open field and, as I lay on my back looking up, I could see chutes blossoming out overhead and machine-gun tracers dancing among them like fireflies.'[29]

Ed Boccafogli fell out of his plane, having 'slipped on vomit. Some guys were throwing up from nerves, and as we pivoted out my feet went out from under me, and I went upside down.' The acutely anxious had been sick in their helmets and when the order came to hook up, adrenalin pumping, had unthinkingly put them back on. Boccafogli had spent 5 June trying to console his friend, baby-faced John Daum of the 508th, that he was not going to die on 6 June: 'Aw, come on. Some of us will, some of us won't, but you ain't gonna be one.' But he was wrong; Daum would die as he'd predicted, and Boccafogli never forgot him.[30]

Once the German gunners started opening up, some – though by no means all – pilots began to twist and weave to avoid the flak, and other aircraft. This threw the jumpers, formed up in line and waiting for their green light, around within their aircraft, tangling static lines and equipment. Canadian paratrooper Bill Lovatt with the British 6th Airborne Division recalled, 'as we approached the DZ the aircraft took violent evasive moves, and I was flung back violently from the doorway to the opposite side of the aircraft in a tangle of arms and legs'.[31] After one such manoeuvre, Louis E. Traux of the 101st recollected, 'I was appalled at the view which greeted me – I was the only one standing. Four men lay in a knotted heap on the floor. One man dived out the door first. I stepped over the top of two men. The closest man to the door crawled out head first. I grabbed the ammo belt of the man I thought was next and gave him a heave out nose first. The next man made it crawling on his own power.'[32] 'Before the light changed from red to green, the plane suddenly lurched,' remembered Sergeant John Feduck in the Canadian Parachute Battalion. 'I couldn't hang on because there was nothing to hang on to, so out I went – there was no getting back in'; at least he was over dry land.[33]

Some C-47s, such as Second Lieutenant Marvin F. Muir's, held level, ploughing on, though mortally hit by ground fire and in flames, buying time for their human cargoes – in Muir's case paratroopers of 'D' Company, 506th Parachute Infantry – to exit before crashing. Muir's Gooney Bird from the 93rd Troop Carrier Squadron spiralled down from 750 feet in a huge ball of flame, killing all five aircrew.[34] After nursing his ship back to Tarrant Rushton, First Lieutenant Richard Randolph counted 326 bullet holes in his airframe, 'some as close as six inches from the gas tanks'; they afterwards renamed their C-47 *Patches*.

Membury-based pilot Don Skrdla, a pre-war rancher from Nebraska, made *three* circuits over the drop zone with his C-47 of the 81st Troop Carrier Squadron, due to heavy equipment bundles that jammed in the doorway. Only on the third pass did his crewmen free the obstructions that allowed his troopers to jump – coolness that brought him a Distinguished Flying Cross, the only one awarded to his squadron. Other aircraft simply carried on through the overcast sky: 'I can't figure out how we went through those clouds without collisions or damage to the planes,' reflected Sergeant Elmer 'Wish' Wisherd, with the 91st Troop Carrier Squadron, ferrying the 101st to their war. 'I could see the other planes around us taking ground fire. We went back up through the clouds; it was quite a layer of clouds. And we came out in formation! How we did it I have no idea. Our pilots were the best, all instrument-rated pilots. There was no talking between planes whatsoever – complete radio silence.'[35]

Captain Richard Todd, the future actor, was then assistant adjutant in the 7th Parachute Battalion. Nicknamed 'Sweeney' Todd after the fictional mass-murderer of old London Town, the opening minutes of 6 June found him sitting with his feet dangling through the exit hole in the base of a converted Stirling bomber. His batman (aide) held on to him as the aeroplane ducked and dived: the dinghy strapped to his leg was reminder enough of the perils of losing his balance. As he observed, 'the buffeting of the strong wind on the aircraft caused quite a lot of people to fall out over the sea: none would have survived, weighed down with all their kit and caboodle. It was ghastly; one of my friends died that way; we lost quite a few over the Channel.'[36] Earlier he had encountered Lieutenant Henry 'Tod' Sweeney of the 2nd Ox and Bucks Light Infantry in the same division. Their introduction went along the lines of: 'Hello, my name's Todd, they call me "Sweeney".' 'How do you do. My name's Sweeney, they call me "Tod".' The latter recalled, 'We were really proud and excited to be making the first foothold in Europe. It was like being selected for the national rugger team, or walking out to open the innings for England at Lord's cricket ground. We glamorised the invasion as a great crusade and all sorts came to see us off; we had never seen so many red tabs [senior officers] in our lives.'[37]

Over the Cotentin two 82nd troopers, Roy O. King and Sergeant William T. Dunfee of the 505th, had the shock of their lives when they noticed C-47s *below* them. 'I was fascinated by the sight of the tracers flying around everywhere when I saw a huge explosion blossom directly below me,' recollected King. 'Somehow I was above the stream of airplanes that had just dropped their troopers and equipment. My immediate concern was that I could be chopped to pieces by the propellers of the oncoming planes.' Dunfee echoed the fear, having known their pilots would be looking down, not up. 'That scared the hell out of me, and I started cussing them. I didn't want to be turned into hamburger by our own air force.'[38] Tom Rice of the 101st Airborne remembered getting shot at from the ground through the heavy fog. 'I had a real hard landing, rolling over on my right arm; I had so much equipment because I weighed 276 pounds. That was all padding – so I didn't get injured at all.'[39] Private William Talbot with the Canadian Parachute Battalion conceded, 'With sixty pounds of equipment strapped to our legs we couldn't run out the aircraft door; we just shuffled towards it and dropped out.'[40]

This was a reminder that in addition to the average paratrooper load – including chute and reserve – of one hundred pounds, many men jumped with heavy kitbags tied to their legs by a long rope, which they were supposed to pay out during their descent. Men watched helplessly as many of these canvas bags fell open or disappeared altogether, scattering heavy weapons, belongings and ammunition into the darkness below. Most units, American, British and Canadian, lost an extraordinary amount of stuff in their night-time drop: up to seventy per cent of support weaponry, ammunition and medical supplies in particular. Much of it remains in the Normandy soil and occasionally surfaces, to the amusement of farmers and tourists.

Dick Winters of the famed 'E' Company, 506th Parachute Infantry, lost his kitbag to the slipstream, 'along with virtually every bit of equipment I was carrying'. Without most of their paraphernalia, Lieutenant Colonel G. F. P. Bradbrooke, commanding the 1st Canadian Parachute

Battalion, mused, 'The hardest part of the job wasn't the fighting – although that was hard enough at times – but getting ourselves organised after we hit the drop zone.'[41]

Vince Occhipinti, with 'F' Company in the same regiment as Winters, noted 'the tremendous noise; I could see tracer bullets coming up after me. Here came a tracer, and another, and another. I could see them coming at me from all directions. What was the most horrifying was that in between each of those tracers was five or six other bullets. Then, suddenly the ground was there, and – *bam* – I hit. I heard a noise not too far from my left, and a large shape suddenly loomed nearby: it said, *Moo*: a cow just stood there, looking at me'.[42]

His buddy was Marion J. Grodowski, whose adventurous life had started in Krakow, Poland. His family later moved to Chicago and Grodowski's D-Day began when 'a .45 pistol that I had holstered on my hip, as well as my canteen, tore away. I looked up and saw a blown panel in my parachute.'[43] Another Screaming Eagle had absolute confidence in his chute: checking it in the plane, Private C. Hillman of Manchester, Connecticut, saw it had been packed by the Pioneer Parachute Company, where his mother worked as an inspector; he knew his luck was in when he read his mother's own initials on the ticket.

In all three airborne formations, paratroopers sustained injuries on landing. Twenty-nine-year-old Benjamin 'Vandy' Vandervoort had been promoted to lieutenant colonel five days before he parachuted into France commanding the Second Battalion, 505th Parachute Infantry. 'I had a little hard luck on the landing and banged up my foot,' the young colonel later played by John Wayne in *The Longest Day* modestly reported later. In fact, his leg was fractured just above the ankle; he merely carried on, tightening up the laces on his boot, and using his rifle as a crutch – until gifted some hand-carved ones by a French civilian.[44]

A 101st Airborne soldier, Eugene Cook from Ohio, remembered jumping 'pretty low. I had a hard landing and didn't know about my broken ankle for a couple of minutes until I got out of my parachute, stood up and fell over. I couldn't go to find anyone from my stick, so was all by myself for a couple of hours.'[45] Cook would fight on for fourteen days with his mangled foot. Lieutenant Russell Chandler, the C-47 pilot, recalled 'a sergeant of the 82nd, who had taken some shrapnel in the leg. By rights, he should have stayed on board and flown back with us. Instead, he told my crew chief, "I'm jumping, it's too dangerous in this thing!" And he did. I guess we all have our own perspective of where the danger lies, and I suppose he did get medical attention as soon as he hit the ground, instead of waiting two hours to go back to England with us.'[46]

American and British doctors scurried around the drop zones and through the night, trying to collect their medical teams, salvage equipment and tend to the injured. Outside Sainte-Mère-Église at around 0235 hours, German medical orderly Fritz Müller, with an artillery battery of the 91st *Luftlande,* found himself walking in and out of curious shadows – the trees above him were filled with parachutes; some were empty, others still bore the dead. Soon he stumbled on a fellow grenadier looting an American corpse, rifling his pockets, looking through family photos in the unfortunate's wallet, wrenching a ring off the man's finger. Müller yelled at him to stop, and the other walked away. Suddenly, Müller recalled, a shot shattered the quiet, and the looter fell dead. Müller froze, realised the American was alive and started to treat him; as he did so, he noticed cigarettes falling around him – other paratroopers trapped in the trees above were showing their gratitude.[47]

Major Johnny Watts, a consultant surgeon who landed with the 195th Airlanding Field Ambulance, set off towards his dressing station on an ancient bicycle left by a French farmer. En route, Watts suffered an attack of hay fever, but when challenged by an alert sentry, he could neither remember the password nor stop sneezing. Neither could he stop the bike. He spluttered 'Friend' as he sailed past and was fortunate not to have been shot.[48] His colleague, Captain David Tibbs of 225th Field Ambulance, recalled recovering 'a dozen men scattered in the corn, mainly with fractured femurs from landing with their heavy kitbags still strapped to one leg'.[49]

Lieutenant Neal Beaver, the 82nd paratrooper who had had to waddle to a replacement aircraft 'like a bloated frog', jumped low: 'As it turns out, the low altitude was a break also, not one man was fired at in the air.' However, the pay-off was that he 'had to leave seven men behind in a French home' when he moved on at 0800. 'All had jump injuries: broken arms, two broken ankles, a wrenched back. It was one hell of a tight jump, even by Fort Bragg training standards.'[50] British Captain Tibbs was struck by the determination of one young officer 'who was hopping along on one leg, with the other trailing loosely behind him, obviously a severe injury', who apologised profusely for being 'such a damned nuisance'. Later, when his aid post was threatened with capture and a jittery medic shouted out 'The Germans are here', Tibbs observed how 'a badly wounded Glaswegian sergeant levered himself up, picked up a Sten gun lying by his side and pointing it at him, growled, "Stop your blathering, ye f**ker, or ye'll be the first to go!"'[51]

Twenty-year-old Robert Elmore had been called up for military service in 1943; a man with strong beliefs, he declared himself a 'devout pacifist' to the War Office, but nevertheless volunteered for the 225th as a surgeon's assistant, where he joined several other conscientious objectors ('conshies' to the soldiers who jeered – until they knew better). He recalled the plan to use Ranville church – where Sergeant Herb Fussell had nearly met his end hours earlier – as their dressing station, but on arrival they found its huge oak doors firmly locked. A blast from a Sten gun had no appreciable impact on the medieval woodwork and its ironmongery, so they moved on to a nearby château; as alert villagers realised what was happening, they whispered 'Bonjour' from their bedroom windows, Elmore recollected.[52]

There were combat injuries, too. In the British sector, Major Hans von Luck, with the 21st Panzer Division, recorded how on 5 June near the Bavent Forest 'The 5th Company of my Second Battalion had gone out on a night exercise, armed with blank cartridges for their rifles – a dangerous situation.'[53] Later on, Feldwebel Rainer Hartmetz, one of his NCOs, met them: 'about forty German soldiers along the road. They were very young – perhaps seventeen – some were wounded and supported by their comrades with a sergeant beside. He addressed us. "They're recruits. We had a night training when they jumped on us. We had only blank cartridges." He had tears in his eyes and started sobbing.'[54] The training ammunition was deemed necessary because of an incident weeks earlier. On one of the Dives bridges, the sentries had been attacked by some of the 774th Infantry Regiment in an unannounced night exercise. They'd thought it was the real thing and shot back with live ammunition, killing two and wounding several more.[55]

Besides injury, death threatened in the crowded skies. As Canadian Corporal Tom O'Connell plunged to earth, his parachute tangled with another: 'they twisted together like a thick rope. I heard the other fellow yell from below, "Take it easy, old man!"' Both hit France with such force that O'Connell lost consciousness. He was out until midday, waking to find the body of his fellow parachutist was none other than that of his padre, Reverend George Alexander Harris.[56] The chaplain, originally from Solihull, England – who had followed his calling to Canada and had been in the army for a year – was thirty-four. He was one of fourteen hundred Canadian chaplains who volunteered to minister to those in uniform. Later a lonely field grave was discovered with his identification discs and Bible on it, but tactfully his mother was told, 'The losses of the unit were so heavy that it is possible we will never know further details.'[57]

The marshy areas flooded beforehand by Rommel also claimed many lives. 'Looking out of the plane it looked like pasture below us, but when I jumped, I landed in water,' recalled Doug Morrison of the Canadian Parachute Battalion. 'The Germans had flooded the area a while back and there was a green algae on the water so it actually looked like pasture from the air.'[58] John M. Marr, a rifle platoon commander in the 507th Parachute Infantry of the 82nd Airborne, dropped into the inundated Merderet river, which looked from the air like a very wet meadow. 'It was armpit deep, in some parts well over the head,' he remembered. 'We were strung out in a long drop; I was the jumpmaster on my plane and the last two of my platoon to get out were immediately captured. I was all alone.'[59] Marr was one of the lucky ones: it is estimated that in the opening hours of D-Day more paratroopers died plummeting into silt and mud than from enemy action.

'I am giving you a grade-A stinker of a job,' Brigadier James Hill had told twenty-nine-year-old Terence Otway. The new CO of the 9th Parachute Battalion, with the British 6th Airborne Division, who had connived at the removal of his predecessor, the patrician Martin Lindsay, was quick of temper, did not warm to people easily and resented those around him with a better station in life. Otway had to put all this aside and ready himself for his mission: to take four German artillery positions at Merville.

There were several more dangerous German batteries east of the Orne that threatened the invasion: six 170mm guns at Houlgate and six 155mm cannon at Berneville, for example. However, the shortage of commandos for the many proposed tasks, coupled with the RAF's bullish insistence that they could neutralise both these sites – as well as Merville – led to their capture being scaled back as two reserve missions (code-named 'Frog' and 'Deer', respectively), should the need arise. Both these sites would be bombed by the RAF and shelled by the Royal Navy – without effect. Curiously, the Merville mission survived as it was the nearest to the 6th Airborne's drop zone, but was the least important of the three.

The site was five miles distant as the crow flies from the dramas at Pegasus Bridge, but hidden by the bulk of the Bavent–Bréville ridge. Otway's opponent was twenty-four-year-old Leutnant Raimund Steiner, promoted as battery commander when his predecessor had been killed in a bombing raid on the position. An Austrian, Steiner was no friend of the regime, his father having died as a result of detention in Sachsenhausen concentration camp in 1940, but as a professional soldier he took pride in doing his duty.[60] Otway was not sure of the calibre of Steiner's guns, which were connected to a fortified observation post on the coast, a mile away. According to the local Maquis and aerial reconnaissance, the weapons – inspected by Rommel and Admiral Ruge twice, on 29 January and 6 March – lurked in huge concrete casemates. The site had been regularly bombed without result, the Allies reasoning that such big structures held long-range weapons, potentially lethal to the invasion fleet. Otway devised a complex plan that required a bombing raid shortly before his men arrived in waves by parachute and glider; if all else failed, the cruiser HMS *Arethusa* was scheduled to open fire on the position at 0530.

The thirty-two C-47s carrying Otway's army flew over the English coast at Worthing, Sussex, thirty-four minutes behind Howard's glider force. Flight Lieutenant Stanley Lee, piloting one of No. 512 Squadron's C-47s, recorded cross-winds 'up to twenty-five knots [39mph] from west to east, which carried the paras further eastwards'. There was little flak, but 'with about 250 aircraft dropping the rest of 3rd Parachute Brigade milling round at different heights, the air turbulence was quite violent at times'. The busy Lee 'did three trips to Normandy and back that day'.[61] Soon everything began to unravel for Otway: the Lancaster raid – one of ten on coastal batteries which began at 2331 hours on 5 June – only managed to hit a herd of cows, not the concrete emplacements, and killed twenty-four of his own advance party.

Of 650 men parachuted into the area, only 160 could be found in preparation for Otway's assault on Steiner's position. Many of the missing had landed in Rommel's flooded fields, inundated by the River Dives, whose brackish waters drowned many a helpless warrior weighed down by his kit. Others, disoriented, were captured, including two who had the misfortune to land in front of Generalleutnant Josef Reichert's 711st Divisional headquarters further east, near Honfleur. The general, playing cards with his staff, was momentarily stunned, and wondered if this was an attack on him, or a drop of personnel to the local Maquis. He reported their presence at 0126 hours to his corps commander in Rouen. As Reichert was stationed *east* of the inter-army boundary, it was Salmuth's Fifteenth Army – already on alert – who received the news. When Salmuth phoned Reichert's headquarters directly to ask 'What the Devil is happening down there?', a firefight with more British paratroopers had broken out. By way of reply, Reichert held the telephone receiver out of the window and Salmuth clearly heard the exchange of automatic fire down the line. Dollmann's Seventh Army, as we have seen, were also alerted at this hour, but by Richter of the 716th Division in Caen, and to a different clash with paratroopers.[62]

The turbulence that affected every aspect of Overlord played havoc with Otway's eight-strong glider force: one returned to England with a severed tow rope; another ditched in the Channel, drowning all on board; five missed the landing zone by miles; and just one landed nearby. A ninth, on a different mission entirely, happened to crash-land on the objective in flames; one of its occupants emerged as a human candle, having been hit by ground fire, which ignited his flamethrower. This alerted the Germans to the imminent attack. The mercurial Otway appears to have suffered a brief crisis of confidence, possibly even a brief, private breakdown, complaining to his batman, Corporal Joe Wilson, that he 'didn't know what to do'. The unperturbable Wilson sometimes felt his job was to act as a Jeeves-like confidant to Otway's frequent outbursts of temper. On this occasion the former valet calmed his master with the hip flask of brandy he had ready for such occasions. When Otway was finally in a position to assault, he did so two hours late, at 0430, with few weapons and a quarter of his original force.[63]

Corporal Edwin Booth, last encountered flinging folding bicycles on parachutes out of aircraft during a pre-invasion exercise, recalled that Otway's advance party, which had preceded the main body, had managed to cut a passage through the barbed wire surrounding Merville. 'As no engineers turned up, we went on through the minefield beyond by feeling our way with bayonets, marking our progress with our heels. All the equipment we needed to destroy the guns was missing, but Colonel Otway had reorganised the parties into small squads to do the various tasks he planned; then as time was short, he ordered "Let's go" – and off we went.' They charged into the position and after fierce fighting with heavy casualties reached the guns, disabling the weapons by removing their breechblocks. 'On the signal to retire', remembered Booth, 'we had to leave the dead and seriously wounded behind; out of the 160 of us, only about sixty-five came out.'[64]

The Germans had lost around twenty-five killed, each side taking about twenty prisoners, whereupon Otway's signals officer, Lieutenant James Loring, pulled a dishevelled carrier pigeon from his jump smock, attached news of their success to a canister on its leg and threw it into the night sky – and watched it head towards Germany. (In fact, it success-fully made a 'home run'.) As the darkness began to fade, Otway's men managed to fire a yellow signal flare, at the very last minute calling off HMS *Arethusa*'s naval gunfire. Instead, Steiner, from his observation post (OP) on the coast, called down fire from other German positions on his own battery, killing many of Otway's wounded left in the open. With the 'streaks of red and gold ranging across the sky', heralding the sunrise of 6 June, a USAAF bombing raid further exacerbated the Allied casual-ties, injuring Otway's brigadier, James Hill, and killing Private Emil Corteil with his German shepherd Glen, among scores of others: the 9th Parachute Battalion would take the heaviest casualties of any British battalion in the 6th Airborne – 423 out of 650 or sixty-five per cent.

Many myths arose about the Merville assault. One is that instead of the four Krupp–Rheinmetall 150mm cannon that Allied intelligence had suggested, possessing all the potency of a six-inch naval gun with a range of thirteen miles, the weapons were found to be of only 75mm calibre, with a range of about six miles, thus bringing into question the entire validity of the mission. This is nonsense; in fact, the Merville casemates contained Czech 100mm wheeled guns, which could throw a thirty-pound shell eight miles, still dangerous to the Allied armada lurking off Sword Beach, six miles away.

Another myth, repeated by writers who parroted Otway's account of the battle, is that the guns were destroyed on capture. Otway was mistaken: on his departure the site was retaken by the Germans, who reinserted the hastily removed breechblocks. Merville artillerymen Hauptwachtmeister (Battery Sergeant Major), Hans Muskotte and Kanonier Hans Staab recalled that the resourceful Steiner (who had controlled the defence from his coastal observation post initially wearing only his pyjamas) brought all of his weapons back into action, despite a later attack by commandos. The German guns stayed in battle-worthy condition, a little pocket of the Wehrmacht surrounded by the Allies, until Steiner successfully evacuated them under the noses of the British on 17 August.[65]

While not wishing to denigrate the bravery of the 9th Parachute Battalion's assault, it is clear that Otway's plan was certainly overcomplicated, proved less successful than Howard's, and neatly illustrated the pitfalls of night-time airborne operations. The military analyst in his comfortable armchair might be left wondering if the unit's original CO, Lieutenant Colonel Martin Lindsay, author of a much simpler scheme, might have pulled off a more successful mission. However, the battalion *had* distracted Merville from firing on the fleet during D-Day. Otway never forgave the RAF for 'losing so many of his men'; nor did he accept that his men had failed to disable Steiner's guns. Obdurate and uncompromising until his death in 2006, Otway refused Steiner's hand when the pair met in the 1990s. When I first visited the Merville site in 1975, the muddy bunkers were occupied by cows. Having been cleaned up by the 10th Field Squadron, Royal Engineers, in 1982, the Merville Battery today is a thriving museum, containing a C-47 and a Czech 100mm cannon of the type Raimund Steiner commanded so resourcefully in 1944.[66]

One of Otway's missing gliders had parted with its glider tug over the Channel, but the pilots had enough height to turn back and land in a cornfield. Before the aircrew could warn their passengers, Otway's men burst out, assuming this was Merville. Adrenalin pumping, they spied an airfield, crept up on the control tower and burst in, temporarily mistaking the RAF blue uniforms for Luftwaffe field grey. WAAF Audrey Hirst, on duty in the control tower at RAF Tangmere, near Chichester, West Sussex, was surprised when the door was suddenly flung wide open and in rushed several soldiers in full battle gear, dripping with hand grenades, waving Sten guns. Stunned into silence by their painted faces, camouflaged tunics and menacing weapons, the duty officer raised his hands in surrender as they demanded – in German – the airfield be surrendered 'in the name of the King'. With her CO a nervous wreck, it was Hirst who took charge of the situation, rounded them up, gave them tea and organised transport back to their base, so they could continue their war elsewhere.

The bulk of the 3rd and 5th Parachute Brigades with four hundred supply containers had landed in France from 0050 onwards; with them, as one of the first British doctors in Normandy, was David Tibbs with the 225th Parachute Field Ambulance. He vividly recalled looking out of his C-47 and 'seeing a white line that was the surf breaking on the Normandy coast'. 'In the split second before my medical section of twenty jumped, a four-engined Stirling suddenly appeared, cutting diagonally across our path. Collision seemed inevitable, but both pilots took evasive action, and everyone was sent sprawling across the floor. Ours – Flying Officer Peter Hakkansson, a Norwegian who gave us immediate confidence – swiftly corrected the plane, the green light came on and I jumped into the darkness.'[67]

Following them, sixty-five Horsa and four Hamilcar gliders transporting the 6th Airborne Division headquarters and an anti-tank battery were shortly to appear. To clear the area, Lieutenant Colonel Peter Luard's 13th Parachute Battalion seized Ranville, earmarked for General Gale's headquarters. On 6 June, his thirty-third birthday, Luard assembled his men, blowing the hunting horn he'd brought along for the purpose. General Gale, headquartered in the Château de Heaume at Le Bas de Ranville, would later ride around inspecting his troops' positions on a white stallion found in a nearby field by his batman. Towed by Stirling bomber across the Channel to Ranville on his twenty-second birthday was glider pilot Staff Sergeant Laurie Weeden, carrying a jeep with its trailer and four soldiers. He squeezed his sixty-seven-foot Horsa onto a field near Ranville and was twice waylaid by helpful Frenchmen – the first confirmed for him where he was on the map; the second gave him two bottles of beer.[68]

Meanwhile, the 521st Parachute Squadron, Royal Engineers, swept the nearby landing zone of 'Rommel's asparagus' wooden poles. John Howard remembered perplexed Italian forced labourers turning up to install the anti-landing staves. When he told them 'their services were no longer required; they had been liberated; they were free', they nodded, thanked him profusely – 'and then the silly sods carried on hammering in their stakes'.[69] With or without the help of the Italians, the clearing work ended minutes before the arrival of the first gliders bearing Gale and his staff, at 0335 hours.

It was only much later in the campaign that the 13th Parachute Battalion learned that one of its soldiers, Private Robert Johns, had enlisted in the army aged fourteen, hoodwinking the recruiter that he was all of the eighteen years he appeared to be. When he jumped into Normandy on D-Day, Bobby Johns was just sixteen, which is the age that appears on his headstone, for he was killed by a sniper on 23 July – after his parents had found out where he was, but before the authorities could haul him back. 'I remember him well,' his platoon commander later recalled. 'He was a very big chap – capable, fearless, and loved being

British airborne forces relied on the large Airspeed AS-51 Horsa glider which could carry between twenty-five and thirty troops (depending on their combat loads), a jeep, a trailer or an anti-tank gun into battle. They brought John Howard's men to their bridges and the 6th Airlanding Brigade and their divisional head-quarters into Normandy. 222 Horsas were also used by the two US airborne divisions. An American Horsa is seen here, the cows giving a sense of its 67-foot length and 88-foot wingspan. (US Army Signal Corps)

a paratrooper. I never suspected that he was underage and it was not until after his death that we were informed that he was just sixteen.'[70]

Throughout Normandy, many paratroopers were taken prisoner in the first hours. Corporal Jack Schlegel, who had come across General Falley's body, was surrounded by men from the latter's division later on 6 June. 'The next day we were loaded onto twenty German trucks with canvas covers; about noon Allied planes strafed our convoy, killing thirty to forty men, many from the 508th,' he remembered. On his fourth escape attempt, from a hospital in Rennes, he would make it back to Allied lines.[71]

For Joseph R. Beyrle of Muskegon, Michigan, 6 June would prove to be the beginning of a very long journey indeed. The sergeant with 'I' Company of Bob Sink's 506th Parachute Infantry recalled jumping onto the church roof at Saint-Côme-du-Mont, and was captured by a dozen German *Fallschirmjäger*. He was sent to various POW camps in Germany and, aided by his proficiency in German (his grandparents had emigrated from Bavaria, so he was bilingual), escaped in January 1945, heading east towards the Russians. He surrendered to a battalion of the 1st Guards Tank Army equipped with Shermans and led by Aleksandra Samusenko, the most senior female tank officer in the Russian forces.

She allowed him to fight with her unit, but he was eventually wounded in the advance to Berlin and evacuated to a Soviet field hospital. There he received a visit from Marshal Zhukov, who learned of Beyrle's story and arranged for his passage to the US embassy in Moscow, where his credentials were confirmed. The paratrooper returned home two years after he had left the United States to find he had been officially listed as killed in action and a memorial mass had been said in his honour. Beyrle remains the only soldier to have fought in US and Soviet forces during the Second World War.[72]

In the British sector, two young members of the 8th Parachute Battalion were setting up homing beacons for the rest of their battalion near Toufreville, when they were surprised by a patrol from the 6th Company of Major Hans von Luck's 125th *Panzergrenadier-Regiment*. They were taken down a farm track and shot in the back of the head, a crime uncovered by a local civilian taking an early-morning stroll before news of the landings had spread.[73] However, British parachute doctor Captain David Tibbs later conceded that his general, Richard Gale, had told them all in a pre-invasion briefing, 'I don't want any bloody nonsense about taking prisoners. You are there to kill Germans!' Tibbs himself went to great lengths to treat German wounded equally to his own.[74]

Combat, particularly between the pumped-up airborne units, was brutal, and would remain so: Manfred Vogt, with the *Fallschirmjäger's* 4th Company, would witness the ill treatment of German casualties whilst hiding in a Cotentin swamp: 'a few Americans gave one of our wounded a good once-over. With fists and the butts of their weapons, they beat the poor guy and kicked him with their boots. When he could no longer move, one of the Americans put his boot on the guy's head and pushed him into the water until he drowned.'[75] Perhaps more typical was the reaction of an American glider pilot, George E. 'Pete' Buckley of the 74th Troop Carrier Squadron, who related finding a German 'lying at a road junction in a pool of blood. He had just been hit by a mortar or shell fragment and was still alive. I felt horrible as I stood there watching him die knowing there was nothing I could do for him. I still had not developed the hate for the enemy – that came to me as the day progressed, when I saw and heard what they did to some of our airborne men. This German, lying in front of me, was a young kid, and sure didn't look like a Nazi Superman.'[76]

Near Carentan, Oberfeldwebel Pelz captured some paratroop officers: 'They were crowded around a map, shining their dim flashlights on it. They were so concerned with reading the map, that they didn't even notice they had been encircled. They hadn't put out a sentry: they were so confident of victory.'[77] This accorded with the recollection of Spencer F. Wurst, a 505th Parachute Infantry staff sergeant with 'F' Company: 'It may seem naïve now, but at no time did we ever dream that we would not be successful in Normandy.'[78] Pelz's *Fallschirmjäger* comrade Feldwebel Eugen Griesser recorded his first prisoners, 'mostly young boys around twenty, big and strong guys. They wore combat uniforms with sewn-on pockets in which they carried half a colonial wares stores: rations in cans, chewing gum, chocolate, reserve ammunition, pictures of naked girls and even explosives.'[79]

Other German reports noted the British carried an escape kit including 'a tiny German phrase book; silk map; an oilskin-wrapped hacksaw; miniature compass; cream-coloured dominoes which turned out to be dehydrated porridge with milk; what looked like gaming dice, which were in fact cubes of tea, milk and sugar; and chocolate in a tin'. They also wondered at the cans of Heinz self-heating soup, which soon became known as *selbstfahrende suppe* (self-propelled soup). These ingenious cans caught the imagination of every serviceman and civilian who encountered them, recalled Henri Biard, a young civilian then living in Trévières who had just finished his *baccalauréat* exams: 'all you had to do was remove a seal from the lid for it to heat up. When I discovered that, my faith in the Allies' final victory soared sky high!'[80]

The German paratroops also observed that their opponents 'were equipped with small metal frogs, a child's toy that clicked when you pressed on it'.[81] The Americans knew these as crickets. Near the Saint-Marcouf battery, Oberleutnant Grieg of the 709th Infantry Division heard frogs croaking loudly in a marshy area where there had never been many frogs. Then Obergefreiter Hermann Nissen and Gefreiter Albrecht Müller brought in an American prisoner, holding 'his ratchet to make a sound like a croaking frog'. Müller called with his captured frog: '*Revit.*' From elsewhere in the swamp came a response: they could use the device to trap the others, and crept towards the answering frogs. 'Soon there were no more frogs croaking and twenty prisoners: a truly fat catch.' '*Rev-it, rev-it,*' grinned Grieg as he locked them in an empty bunker. He soon stopped grinning when he inspected the Americans' escape kits: 'compasses in buttons on a shirt, tiny new testaments and silk neckerchiefs with maps printed on them: the detail was terrific, with every obstacle and machine-gun nest recorded'. His opponents knew more about his own defences than he did.[82]

Demonstrating the epitome of journalistic skill in an era when news was restricted to wireless, papers and newsreels, Chester Wilmot, an irrepressible Australian who had transferred to the BBC earlier in the year, recorded his D-Day glider descent near Caen for the BBC:

With grinding brakes and creaking timbers we jolted, lurched and crashed our way to a landing in Northern France early this morning. The glider in which I travelled came off better than most … All around us we can see silhouettes of other gliders, twisted and wrecked – making grotesque patterns against the sky. Some have buried their noses in the soil; others have lost a wheel or a wing; one has crashed into a house, two have collided with each other. Troops are clambering out almost as casually as they might leave a bus. Some have to slash away the wooden fuselage before they can get out their Jeeps and trailers … A German battery is firing out to sea, and from positions all around us the opposition's ack-ack batteries send up streams of tracer. The airborne forces have gained their first foothold in France by a daring night landing – but all of us know it will be harder to hold the ground than it has been to take it.[83]

Lieutenant Colonel Mike Murphy, meanwhile, was having trouble with his glider, *The Fighting Falcon*. It had been bought for the war effort by the children of Greenville School, Michigan, where the ship was built. In April 1943 they had sold $72,000 in war bonds and stamps, in recognition of which it was decreed that theirs – the *Falcon* – would be the lead glider into Europe. Murphy knew he was taking Brigadier General Don Forrester Pratt, assistant divisional commander of the

101st, into battle with his jeep, but was unaware that the general's staff had installed armour plates on the vehicle for extra protection. Murphy recalled the *Falcon*, overloaded by a thousand pounds, 'handled like a freight train'. Consequently, he hit the ground far above the normal tactical speed of 70mph. When he applied the brakes, nothing happened as the *Falcon* continued to slide downhill on wet grass the full length of the landing zone before crashing into a Normandy bocage hedgerow.

Murphy came to in his mangled cockpit with two broken legs, his co-pilot dead, just as a column of German vehicles halted nearby. Trapped in his seat, the colonel played dead while several Germans nosed around inside for a few minutes, then departed. The surgeon from Murphy's No. 2 glider, Dr Van Gorder, trotted over to treat Murphy, then found General Pratt still in his jeep, seat belt fastened, chin on his chest, with a broken neck; he had died instantly. Buried soon after, his Grave Registration Form No. 1 noted the personal effects found on the body: 'eyeglasses and case, cigarette case, picture case, wallet containing one dollar and 1,500 French francs'.[84]

Within the first hours of D-Day, each side had lost a general. Pratt's superior, Maxwell Taylor, commanding the 101st Airborne, whom Eisenhower had seen off from Greenham Common, meanwhile had landed completely alone, later recording that 'any order he might have given in the following thirty minutes would have been received only by a circle of curious Normandy cows'. His opposite number, Matthew Ridgway of the 82nd Airborne, who had been about to ride into battle by glider, changing his mind to jump at the last moment, made in retrospect a fortunate choice.

Both the RAF and USAAF were widely denounced at the time and afterwards by airborne troops, for their 'incompetence' in widely scattering their passengers. Amongst the most vociferous of critics was Lieutenant Colonel Otway, subsequently author of the British Airborne's official history.[85] On the other hand, glider pilots who generally landed on target, and their tug aircrew usually escaped such harsh judgement. Here, we should remember that British aircrew of the Glider Pilot Regiment were expected to fight as infantry after their feats of flying, whereas their American counterparts were quite logically evacuated back to fly more aircraft: thus, seventy-one of the 196 glider pilots who landed with the British 6th Airborne on D-Day would become casualties – mostly by ground combat rather than from injuries sustained during their crash landings.

Later in the narrative of D-Day, a series of authors pounced on the 'mixed performance' of the airborne forces in Normandy to allege this was solely the fault of the troop carrier pilots, who themselves were rarely interviewed for their side of the story. Some writers went as far as to allege 'near-criminal carelessness' in the way the American pilots released their parachutists, despite the fact that twenty-one aircraft were lost, 196 damaged and ninety US aircrew were killed or wounded over the Cotentin.[86] In fact, careful analysis suggests that paratroopers belonging to the 501st, 502nd or 506th Parachute Infantry were statistically more dispersed than their colleagues in the 82nd Airborne Division, who criticised their aircrew less. Often overlooked, the troop carriers also brought *back* ninety paratroopers for various reasons – some were injured or wounded in flight – with a recorded nine Americans who actually refused to jump; a few who may have similarly hesitated were pushed through the exits by their livid comrades.

The effective remedy against one British paratrooper who faltered and 'braced himself against the frame of the doorway to prevent himself from going through it' was for the corporal behind to swiftly 'chop the defaulter's arms away and use the forward momentum of his own body' to ram him 'into the slipstream beyond'.[87] Most non-jumpers, though, had been wounded in flight. Charles S. Cartwright, piloting a 62nd Troop Carrier Squadron C-47 over the Cotentin, recalled two rounds of flak hitting a paratrooper in his plane, which detonated two of his hand grenades. Attempting to fly the seriously injured man back to England, Cartwright's plane came down near Utah Beach. The five-man crew and wounded paratrooper endured an uncomfortable D-Day, in hiding and under hostile and friendly fire, before making contact with troops advancing from the beach.

Yet the weather, never mind the Germans, should have gone a long way towards exonerating the troop carrier pilots of ineptitude. The 313th Troop Carrier Group reported soon after returning from their first mission over Normandy on 6 June:

Attempted to follow prescribed route, but unable to do so because of weather, which caused group formation to break up completely, aircraft then proceeding individually to DZs. Cloud cover ten-tenths, with base of nine hundred feet, up to eight thousand, which extended to south coast of England ... Ceiling then lifted and visibility improved, and at designated DZs there were scattered five-tenths clouds cover with base of four thousand feet, and visibility ten to twenty miles.[88]

Terrain also made a difference: though the British 6th Airborne were likewise strewn over the Normandy countryside, in their sector there was much less bocage to split up groups and isolate individuals than there was in the Cotentin. Patient examination of the maps drawn up after the war of where each individual American paratrooper stick landed indeed shows the scattering, but prompts as many questions as it answers. The charts were based on the paratroopers' own reports made at least a month after their drop, and often longer. In the intervening period, the men had had to drag themselves out of slimy marshes, zig-zag through the night to rendezvous, avoid German patrols which captured many, and fight a lengthy campaign against a determined enemy.

Despite their efforts, as one pilot later wrote, 'only God and his recording angels know precisely where all the paratroopers landed'.[89] In the words of another, 'the Americans knew what was happening, but few of them knew where they were; the Germans knew where they were, but none of them knew what was happening'.[90] A military psychologist observed that the airborne troopers were actually angry and fearful at finding themselves *alone*, or in small groups, *not* in discovering they were far from their drop zones. After all, the divisions were educated to expect they would end up isolated, behind enemy lines.

Despite the undoubted courage of the C-47 aircrews – as we have witnessed in this mosaic of airborne experiences – complaints like Otway's, and accounts of 101st paratroopers such as Donald Burgett's, with 'A' Company, 506th Parachute Infantry, have dominated post-war accounts:

Another plane came in low and diagonally over the field. The big ship was silhouetted against the lighter sky with long tongues of exhaust flame flashing along either side of the body. Streams of tracers from several machine-guns flashed upward to converge on it ... Then I saw vague, shadowy figures of troops plunging downward. Their chutes were pulling out the pack trays and just starting to unfurl when they hit the ground. Seventeen men hit before their chutes had time to open. They made a sound like large ripe pumpkins being thrown down to burst against the ground. "That dirty son of a bitch pilot," I swore to myself, "he's hedgehopping and killing a bunch of troopers, just to save his own ass. I hope he gets shot down in the Channel and drowns real slow."[91]

Seventy-five years on, we occasionally need to interrogate some of the accounts of those who were there. Having personally witnessed three campaigns in uniform myself – Bosnia, Iraq and Afghanistan – I can understand the confusion of war. Yet, could the otherwise brave and objective Burgett really have heard the evocative sound of 'pumpkins bursting', amid the aero-engines, machine-guns, general noise and terror of battle, as he suggested? By 'pumpkins' Burgett is, of course, implying the heads of *helmeted* paratroopers. A few lines later, Burgett was also recounting of the same moment, 'There was the booming of anti-aircraft guns and mortars all around and the close stitching of German light and heavy machine-guns raking the skies and hedgerows. Small arms fire erupted everywhere and sometimes it broke out hotter than the hinges on hell's gates in one spot. It would rise in ferocity until the fire power became a loud roar'.[92] Without knowing the circumstances, Burgett's understandable fury in the initial oft-quoted passage actually makes little sense, for there were many reasons why that C-47 might have been flying low, other than the aircrew cowardice he was implying.

We have met the 326th Airborne Engineers already, occupying the stately Basildon Park, Berkshire, which had housed convalescent soldiers during the First World War. For D-Day, the battalion had been split between elements of its parent 101st Division. Second Lieutenant Howard Huggett, a North Carolinian with 2nd Platoon, 'C' Company, jumped with the 506th Parachute Infantry.[93] His C-47 was hit by flak soon after crossing the coast, which ignited the six hundred pounds of C-2 explosives on board. 'With the plane on fire, in a dive, the pilot and co-pilot slumped forward and the crew chief unable to determine our position', Huggett gave the order to go, estimating his altitude at 'between 350 and 400 feet'.[94]

It could well have been this C-47 that Burgett recorded. The aircrew, too, were fully aware of the risks to the paratroopers as well as to themselves, as pilot Russell Chandler recalled: 'Once the shroud line was pulled, those guys were on the ground in seconds, with as little time as possible as a target. However, at that altitude and at ninety miles per hour, we were a pretty large target and in range of every type of small arms. I was glad it was still dark, but at that moment we all felt like sitting ducks.'[95]

However, all the sky warriors would concede that the dispersion of their ranks, whether because of German fire, the weather, manoeuvring pilots or unlit drop zones, brought out the best in the survivors. They fought on in small groups; if they lost their leaders, they grew some more. Their years of preparation had made them excessively fit, which gave them the stamina to endure the next few days. Misquoting Carl von Clausewitz, the Prussian general, Brigadier James Hill, commanding the British 3rd Parachute Brigade, had warned during training, 'One must not be daunted if chaos reigns, because it undoubtedly will.' Canadian Corporal Dan Hartigan summed up what many witnessed, that 'the scattering had an operating influence on the whole battle: we lost more than fifty percent of our officers on D-Day, fifteen out of twenty-seven. The fighting in the weeks that followed turned combat from an officer's war to an NCO's war.'[96]

At the end of a very long and confusing night, Major Friedrich von der Heydte of the 6th *Fallschirmjäger-Regiment* made his way by motorcycle to the tiny hamlet of Sainte-Marie-du-Mont. He got the key to the eleventh-century church tower, the tallest in the region, climbed to the top, 'and had a unique picture in front of me that I will never forget', the distinguished post-war professor of international law later wrote. 'The ocean lay before me, deep blue and practically motionless. On the horizon numerous battleships lined up to an almost closed chain. Between the ships and the beach there was a brisk back-and-forth traffic of craft that were transferring American soldiers to the shore. The Americans only met resistance from a single German bunker that was shooting at the landing soldiers.' The tower was an artillery observation post for signaller Josef Horn and his comrades of the 191st Artillery Regiment, but von der Heydte noted that to the last man, the unit had cleared out. 'I needed but a few moments to get a clear impression, and had no reason to stay any longer in this place, upon which American soldiers were marching. The location lay about three miles from the coast and the Americans had already covered half that distance. I returned to my regiment and gave my first combat orders.'[97]

Major von der Heydte had been looking at Utah Beach. At the other end of the invasion front, Captain David Tibbs, the British parachute doctor who had jumped in with the 225th Parachute Field Ambulance, had at first light likewise made his way to high ground – in his case at Bréville, to retrieve several wounded men. Rommel had also paused there exactly a week before, on 30 May. Looking north, both had taken in the double water features of the Orne river and Caen Canal, flowing into the sea at Ouistreham – easy to spot with its distinctive red and white lighthouse. To the west lay Sword Beach. Absent the week before to Rommel, Tibbs now saw 'numerous dots on the sea. The invasion fleet was coming in.'[98]

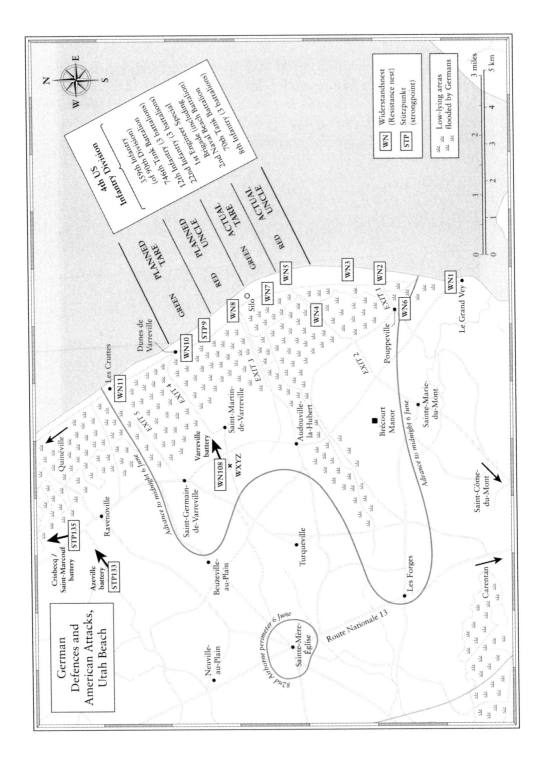

German Defences and
American Attacks,
Utah Beach

**4th US
Infantry Division**

359th Infantry
(of 90th Division)
746th Tank (3 battalions)
12th Infantry (3 battalions)
22nd Infantry Special
1st Engineer (including Battalion)
Brigade (including Battalion)
2nd Naval Beach Battalions)
70th Tank (3 battalions)
8th Infantry

PLANNED
TARE

GREEN

PLANNED
UNCLE

RED

ACTUAL
TARE

GREEN

ACTUAL
UNCLE

RED

| WN | Widerstandsnest (Resistance nest) |
| STP | Stützpunkt (strongpoint) |

Low-lying areas
flooded by Germans

0   1   2   3   4   5 km
0   1   2   3 miles

Les Crutes
Dunes de
Varreville
WN10
STP9
WN8
Silo
WN7
WN5
WN3
WN2
WN1
WN6
EXIT 1
EXIT 2
EXIT 3
WN4
Pouppeville
Le Grand Vey
Saint-Martin-
de-Varreville
Audouville-
la-Hubert
Sainte-Marie-
du-Mont
Saint-Côme-
du-Mont
Brécourt
Manor
Advance to midnight 6 June
WN11
Quinéville
EXIT 5
EXIT 4
Varreville
battery
WN108
WXYZ
Saint-Germain-
de-Varreville
Ravenoville
Advance to midnight 6 June
Crisbecq /
Saint-Marcouf
battery
STP135
Azeville
battery
STP133
Beuzeville-
au-Plain
Turqueville
Les Forges
Carentan
Neuville-
au-Plain
Sainte-Mère-
Église
82nd Airborne perimeter 6 June
Route Nationale 13

24

Utah: Ivy Division

'NAVSITREP 1: To Naval Commander Western Task Force. Force U arrived transport area without incident. Complete surprise achieved. No enemy attack. First wave despatched to beach as scheduled.'

Don P. Moon, commander of Force 'U', 0800 hours

'ALARM! INVASION ALERT!' At a little after 0030 hours, Leutnant Arthur Jahnke had picked up his field telephone. It was Hauptmann Fink, his battalion commander in nearby Beuzeville: 'Enemy paratroops have dropped all around us. Probably you too. Sound the alarm!' Soon Oberstleutnant Günther Keil, his regimental commander, was on the line with the same story – though division headquarters was strangely quiet: Generalleutnant von Schlieben had gone to Rennes for his war games conference. Keil was already in possession of a marked map outlining the Americans' intentions. It had come from a paratrooper unwise enough to have landed right on top of his headquarters in a quarry near Quinéville.[1] Jahnke was in any case wide awake – the constant drone of aircraft flying low overhead had awoken him. They had come often before, but never for so long or in such numbers. He could hear the flak guns engaging them.

As if to confirm Fink's warning, Jahnke heard the crackle of small arms fire, and soon a patrol returned with several wet, disarmed American paratroopers, recovered from the marshes behind. Two of them were injured, and while their wounds were being tended Jahnke managed to find out their unit. He called up Hauptmann Fink: 'Nineteen prisoners of the 2nd Battalion, 506th Parachute Infantry Regiment—' The line went dead. The French Resistance were up to their tricks again, Jahnke thought; on this occasion their timing couldn't be worse, unless …[2]

Always overlooked by historians, the most important point about Utah was recorded after the war by one of its planners back in Washington DC. Deeply involved in Overlord from the start, Major General Thomas Troy Handy was director of operations in the War Plans Division, a job once performed by Eisenhower. Of Utah, Handy would say, 'We all thought Utah was going to be more of a problem than Omaha – the damned terrain, swampy, with causeways on which a crew with one gun could stop tanks from coming through. The performance of the untested 4th Division was remarkable.'[3]

Although Omaha frequently takes the attention in any narrative of D-Day, it was not the most strategically important beach. These were Sword on the eastern flank, because of its proximity to the road hub of Caen, and potential for an early breakout, and almost more significant, Utah in the west, which offered – in conjunction with the two airborne divisions – early access to the port of Cherbourg from the landward side. The landings at Utah were indivisible from the drops of airborne units beyond the coast, designed to overcome the difficult terrain behind the beachhead. We have seen how the employment of the British 6th Airborne Division was almost an afterthought in the plans for Sword; the opposite was true for Utah, where the airborne warriors were seen as the enablers of the seaborne assault – the latter deemed impossible without the presence of the former.

The inland defences of the important transatlantic port – through which hundreds of thousands of migrants to America had passed, including those boarding the *Titanic* in April 1912 – were far weaker than those facing the sea, and its capture was still considered preferable to the untested Mulberries. Brittany also beckoned with good ports such as Brest – indeed US forces had landed on the French Atlantic seaboard during the First World War – but the option was discounted early on by COSSAC because the Breton peninsula was too distant from southern English ports, and much easier than Normandy for the Germans to contain and seal off.

The waters outside Cherbourg were also the unlikely venue for an American Civil War naval engagement in June 1864. Almost exactly eighty years before D-Day, the Confederate blockade runner CSS *Alabama* had been intercepted by the warship USS *Kearsarge*, and after an hour's engagement, fell victim to her guns. Both were of the steam-and-sail era and this represented the first American blood spilled in anger off the Normandy coast, with seventeen of the *Kearsarge's* crew amongst the first recipients of the newly created Medal of Honor.[4]

The eastern Cotentin sands ranged twelve miles from the mouth of the Carentan Canal, north to Quinéville. Only the southern portion was practicable for amphibious attack due to offshore reefs, stronger defensive positions on the coast and inland, and the naval battery of Saint-Vaast-la-Hougue to the north. This boasted four 100mm Skoda cannon – the same weapons Otway found at Merville – plus smaller guns and searchlights, and was a formidable German strongpoint built onto an earlier French fort. The chosen invasion beach stretched from Ravenoville Plage, at the junction of Sugar and Tare sectors, to the Carentan Canal – the end of Victor sector.

The coastline here is like no other part of the Overlord coast, for it is a classic sandy beach. It appears as an uninterrupted stretch of gently shelving shore, topped by low dunes studded with grass. Containing the sand hills, a low sea wall runs for much of the length, almost unchanged since 1944. From directly behind the dunes the Germans had flooded low-lying terrain for at least a mile in width. By controlling all the locks and waterways in the region, they opened flow valves at high tide, closing them at low water, to keep the entire area inundated. Seizing other lock gates at La Barquette, north of Carentan, and controlling the inland flooding of the Douve river was an early US objective.

Beyond this marsh the ground rises to a road running parallel to the coast, from Sainte-Marie-du-Mont (whose church tower Major von der Heydte would climb) via Varreville to Saint-Marcouf and beyond. Seven minor roads running inland, at right angles to the coast and across the flooded areas, were known to the Allies as causeways and the only feasible exits from Utah. Their capture was one mission of the 101st Airborne, to enable the seaborne assault to proceed smoothly. The three most northerly were discounted as being underwater or too close to German positions, but of the remaining four, the capture of the upper pair – Exit 4, leading from the coast to Saint-Martin-de-Varreville, and Exit 3 to Audouville-la-Hubert – were assigned to the 502nd Parachute Infantry, the southern pair – Exit 2 to Sainte-Marie-du-Mont and Exit 1 to Pouppeville – to the 506th.

Along the beach itself were several platoon-sized *Widerstandsnester* (resistance nests), built at roughly one-mile intervals, that comprised machine-guns, mortars and heavier guns – both in the open, and enclosed in concrete – and the occasional tank turret sitting atop a casemate, all surrounded by minefields and barbed wire. Additionally, most villages in the area were home to small groups from the 709th or 91st Divisions. Grouped around Carentan were Heydte's 6th *Fallschirmjäger*, and spread through the centre of the Cotentin in company and platoon positions were Falley's 91st *Luftlande* Division. The 243rd Division held the western Cotentin coast and was expected to immediately support the 91st in counter-attacks.

In the event, it would matter not that the airborne troops were scattered and few attacked the correct objective or in the planned strength. Many parachutists were otherwise occupied, as we have seen, fighting their own personal battles of survival with the Wehrmacht, or with the terrain. The small bands of sky warriors improvised, as they had been taught to do, and attacked the Germans wherever they found them, causing disruption far exceeding their numbers. Collectively, many would never realise how important their presence was in pinning down the reserves who would otherwise have come to the defence of Utah Beach.

On 10 May 1944, and four years to the day since he had invaded France as an unknown general at the head of the 7th Panzer Division, Rommel had driven around the Cotentin, visiting its eastern coast near Sainte-Marie-du-Mont. These were places well known to the surprisingly diminutive field marshal (he stood five feet, six inches), for he had captured Saint-Lô on 17 June 1940, and seized Cherbourg the next day. Now, it was his men who were on the defensive. He'd prowled along the beaches inspecting the positions: here was a problem. Apart from rows of steel anti-landing obstacles in the sands, overlooked by a thin row of bunkers in the dunes, there had been little else to oppose an assault. The terrain was as flat as a pancake and offered little depth for the defender.

He had met twenty-three-year-old Leutnant Arthur Jahnke, from Flensburg, responsible for his platoon of No. 3 Company of the 919th *Grenadier-Regiment*. The bespectacled Jahnke had been awarded the Knight's Cross, fighting in the Ukraine only the previous month. Rommel had congratulated him and asked about the progress of the beach defences – but it was far too slow for the field marshal's liking. He changed tack: 'Show me your hands, *Herr Leutnant*.' Jahnke had taken off his gloves, revealing the scratches he'd received from laying out barbed wire alongside his men. 'Well done, *Herr Leutnant*,' the Desert Fox had said, 'blood on the hands of officers from entrenching is just as valuable as that shed in battle,' and he had moved on.[5]

Although Jahnke had been awarded the Knight's Cross, he had yet to receive it. At the end of the month, in time-honoured tradition, his divisional commander, Generalleutnant Karl-Wilhelm von Schlieben of the 709th, had come down onto the sands, and with a band playing, had hung the *Ritterkreuz* around young Jahnke's neck. His company had been lined up in front of their strongpoint overlooking the coast. The sands where they stood were already known to Allied planners as the future Utah Beach. The date was 30 May – and Jahnke had exactly a week to enjoy wearing his new decoration before he would be marched into captivity.[6]

Along forty miles of the eastern Cotentin coast, from the Carentan Canal to Cherbourg, the defenders were from Schlieben's 709th Division, the formation whose age averaged thirty-six; sometimes their motivation was questionable, but they were well led. Fort W5 at La Madeleine was where Arthur Jahnke lurked with his men, garrisoning a small group of bunkers in the dunes. North and south of Jahnke, a mile distant, were other concrete forts housing an array of anti-tank guns, machine-guns and automatic mortars – Schlieben detailed the weapons at his disposal, including 700 French rifles and mortars, 100 Russian automatic weapons, 300 Czech rifles and 1,200 Belgian and Polish pistols.[7]

His primary problem was that none of his defences possessed depth, for the beachfront fortifications could not hope to contain an assault for very long. They were spread along the littoral acting as outposts, main line of resistance and depth positions all rolled into one, in defiance of all German military doctrine. Ironically, there was more concrete littering the Cotentin than elsewhere along the invasion coast. Many of these were bunkers for ammunition storage or troop accommodation; those coastal units stationed further to the east could make use of seaside villas and their cellars for such purposes, but of these, there were very few on the Cherbourg peninsula, hence a heavier *Organisation Todt* building programme.

Inland, at Azeville, a four-gun battery overlooking the future Utah Beach had been built between May 1943 and February 1944 by over three hundred labourers – mostly captured Russian prisoners. Their efforts resulted in four giant casemates, each one consuming over one thousand cubic yards of concrete, which housed French 105mm cannon with a range of seven miles. Once complete in early 1944, Azeville had been occupied by 173 coastal artillerymen of the 1261st *Küsten-Artillerie-Regiment*, commanded by an artillery officer who had fought in the First World War, Hauptmann Dr Hugo Treiber. With an average age of thirty-four, most were conscripted Germans, but around ten per cent hailed from occupied Austria, Czechoslovakia, Poland and Alsace; incredibly, two were volunteers from neutral Switzerland. On 6 June 1944, Treiber's oldest gunner was fifty-four, the youngest nineteen. The *Atlantikwall* was essentially many such sites replicated up and down the coast, each located where a landing threatened and terrain permitted a useful field of fire – at Azeville the Germans commandeered and destroyed any houses that obstructed their vision.

Six miles inland from Jahnke's position, astride the main north–south *Route Nationale* 13 running to Cherbourg, is the town of Sainte-Mère-Église, first occupied on 18 June 1940 by Rommel's men. The population were used to the comings and goings of the Germans, but in February 1944 the pace had increased. Alexandre Renaud, the town's mayor, charted the changing nature of the Cotentin's defences, watching with the eyes of the soldier he had been at Verdun in 1916. He noted long convoys of wagons heading north, 'the horses driven by French peasants under German escort'. Later an Austrian anti-aircraft unit, the 30th *Flak-Regiment*, set up shop in the vicinity, taking over the school. 'The commander, who was about fifty-eight, and a music critic in civilian life, was more interested in good living than in waging war,' Reynaud recalled.[8]

> Then the requisitioning began. Every day horses and cars were taken. The Germans took, but they paid. Almost every day and every night troops went out on manoeuvres. Sometimes they would cross the town armed to the teeth; their helmets, the wagons, the horses and the cannons were covered with branches. At about the same time, men were being requisitioned every morning. Very few men showed up for work, and the greater part of the labour consisted in eating and drinking.

From 17 April, they were ordered to turn in their radio sets – though not all did – and 'plant tree trucks, which had to be over ten feet high, and strung together with barbed wire. The trunks looked like giant candles and the cows had a good time rubbing up against them.' None of the Frenchmen took seriously the German fears of an invasion in Normandy. 'Everyone thought this was very funny. Most of us were convinced it could never happen,' Reynaud remembered.[9]

Arthur Jahnke's divisional commander, Schlieben, whose men averaged thirty-six years old, was an Eastern Front panzer general who had considered his job in Normandy a demotion. Adding to the insult, he'd soon discovered that the panzer battalion transferred to reinforce his area was the 100th, whom we have just examined, equipped only with light French tanks taken in 1940. Their poor weaponry and thin armour – quite useless on a modern battlefield – were an outrage to him. Schlieben had perhaps greater cause to be heartened by Major Hugo Messerschmidt's military college. Comprising three fully equipped instructional infantry companies, artillery and flak batteries, and an engineer platoon, it was in fact the Seventh Army's combat training facility, located at Le Vicel, east of Cherbourg. Unfortunately, it appeared on headquarters maps as *Sturmbataillon AOK 7* (Assault Battalion, Seventh Army), implying a more warlike function.

Allocated the defence of Cherbourg and the whole of the eastern Cotentin – a forty-mile front – Schlieben understandably worried about the quality and quantity of his manpower and had urgently requested further reinforcements: he was given four battalions of German-officered *Osttruppen* (eastern troops), two of Russians and two of Georgians. These prompted his observation, 'We are asking rather a lot if we expect Russians to fight in France for Germany against Americans.'[10]

Some of Schlieben's *Osttruppen* had come a long way to serve in Normandy. The American troops who captured Yang Kyoung Jong near Utah Beach had enormous difficulty interrogating him, for he appeared to speak no known language – until it was discovered he was Korean. Jong had been conscripted into the Imperial Japanese Army aged eighteen, and captured during the Soviet–Japanese clash at Khalkhin Gol in the summer of 1939 – Soviet Marshal Zhukov's first triumph. In company with thousands of others, Jong was confined to a Siberian gulag until 1942, when released to fight in the Russian Army against the Wehrmacht. Jong was again captured, this time by the Germans in 1943 at Kharkov – and given the option of service in an *Ost-Bataillon* or a German-run gulag, decided on the former. This led one of his US Army captors to ask his officer, 'Captain, just who the hell are we fighting, anyways?'[11]

The ever-observant mayor, Alexandre Reynaud, noted in May 'infantrymen and artillery troops camping in our fields, as well as Georgians and Mongolians with Asiatic features, all commanded by German officers'.[12] Ernst Flöter of the 1057th *Grenadier-Regiment* recollected 'some of the soldiers in our unit were Russians. Most were White Russians from Belarus, conquered by the Russians in 1922, and including parts of Poland annexed in 1939. I remember when the White Russian soldiers marched they always sang beautifully.'[13] Meanwhile, Sergeant Henry Giles with the 291st Combat Engineers recorded in his journal at Vierville, 'Saw my first Germans today. If they are supermen, we've fallen for a lot of propaganda. They look lousy and undersized, scurvy and dirty, with greasy hair, flat mouths and short necks. Their uniforms are rough and shoddy, and they were shuffling along, looking miserable. Suddenly one of the prisoners saw us and grinned, pointed at his chest and yelled, *Russki! Russki!'*[14]

The Allies, the French and even the Germans themselves were surprised at how many Russians they encountered in Normandy, such as these ten Siberians. There were some in every outfit, but also 32 battalions entirely made up of former Soviet troops, recruited from throughout the USSR, who were lightly armed and stationed in France on internal security duties. In the advent of invasion they were expected to perform as proficient combat units. Some fought courageously alongside Poles, Czechs, Georgians, Ukrainians and other waifs and strays from Eastern Europe, though more fled or willingly surrendered at the first opportunity. (NARA)

While comprising around thirty-two infantry battalions in France, others formed artillery batteries and engineer units. The historical record tends to dismiss these foreign volunteers as 'raw', 'untrained', fighting poorly, surrendering easily or possessing little offensive 'spirit'. Yet this is a dangerous generalisation and was sometimes simply not the case: some units fought with great determination, for several of the eastern minority populations were born of generations who had defied Russian and Soviet rule, such as the Georgians, and were, in a sense, 'professional' warriors.

Other non-eastern volunteers in German uniform, such as Italian Fascists, opted to remain true to their political beliefs. They were recruited in various ways: some were fervent anti-Communist volunteers; others were freed prisoners of war; while more found themselves as impressed conscripts after previous service in the Wehrmacht as batmen, cooks or storemen. These 'volunteers' were grouped together by ethnicity, formed into (often understrength) battalions, and poorly armed with the cast-offs from other subdued nations. They possessed few support weapons, and received little further training. Initially they had never been intended for combat, having been designed for internal security duties in the east, or France.

When it came to battle they were an unknown quantity. Some fought well but briefly, though others simply deserted en masse at the first available opportunity. Rarely pro-Nazi, many had been motivated to don *feldgrau* (field grey) to free their corner of the Soviet Union from Communist rule, but as the tide had turned by 1944, so their motivation and cohesion had ebbed. Generalleutnant Richter of the 716th Division – perhaps apocryphally to shield his own defeat – would later report that his 642nd *Ost-Bataillon* simply ran away, leaving only its German officers and NCOs. This battalion had been led by a German CO and adjutant, but at least two company commanders, Leutnants Schumski and Sikorski, were Russian; it had previously been on anti-partisan duty in central Russia.[15] Forrest C. Pogue recorded finding in a German bunker near Isigny

a set of orders written in German and Russian and containing the names of Russian soldiers. The commander had been *Leutnant* Malikow, formerly of Voronezh. He had taken his job seriously, for we noted his Russian–German dictionary and a series of field exercises which, in translation, turned out to be defense practice against landings at Cherbourg and at the mouth of the Orne [i.e. Ouistreham]. The script for the affair indicated that on the fifth or sixth day the Allied forces had been thrown back into the sea.[16]

The 635th *Ost-Bataillon*, with the 709th Division in the Cotentin, were reported as having fought 'with amazing courage despite the poverty of their armament'. Hauptmann Stiller's 795th Georgian Battalion, also under the 709th Division, of four companies, comprising ninety Germans and 833 Georgians, were deployed behind Utah Beach at Turqueville and Beuzeville-au-Plain. They were reckoned to have acquitted themselves well for around forty-eight hours, before combat split them in two, half fighting at Carentan, the remainder withdrawing to Cherbourg, where only 174 surrendered.[17] The 441st Battalion, with the 352nd Division, first posted to Normandy in January 1944, served 'with distinction around Caen', but by 22 June had been reduced to two hundred men and was disbanded, while the 439th Battalion, with Richter's 716th Division, was 'credited with fighting hard in the Carentan area'. Collectively all these battalions would lose 8,400 men by September 1944, and often quickly disappeared from the orders of battle – being disbanded when they ran short of eastern replacements to keep them up to strength.

Apart from these combatant battalions of sometimes exotic easterners, there were other Russians, Ukrainians, Poles and Czechs who were a common sight in France: the *Hilfswilliger*, abbreviated to *Hiwi*. They were non-combatant volunteers, occasionally female, who performed a variety of menial roles, from cooking, repairing equipment and working in the stores to minding horses and mending clothing and boots. Every battalion had a few. Even the panzer divisions and Waffen-SS used them. German troops worried less about the reliability of all these foreign personnel – there were around seventy thousand of them serving in OB West at the time – and more about the language barriers, which produced numerous accidents and delays in the day-to-day running of the occupation forces. By way of example, in the 987th *Grenadier-Regiment* of Generalleutnant Kurt Badinski's 276th Infantry Division, which served in Normandy, the Russian volunteers spoke *thirty-four* different dialects, necessitating the issue of paybooks in *eight* different forms: Russian, Cossack, Armenian, Azerbaijani, Georgian, North Caucasian, Turkestan and Volgar Tartar.[18]

Leutnant Jahnke liked to stroll around his domain of *Widerstandsnest* 5 every few hours, looking for weak spots, thinking of improvements. He paused for a word with Feldwebel Hein at the concrete roadblocks sealing off access to the sea; when he'd first arrived, Jahnke had been shocked to find local fisherman had been allowed to pass through. He'd soon put a stop to that. Beyond lay the only gap in his masonry anti-tank wall, which also did good service protecting the dunes, and the beach with its triple row of obstacles. To the north he could make out his 75mm anti-tank gun in its open concrete emplacement; another hundred yards beyond was a 50mm gun, robbed from an old tank, protected by a pair of machine-guns in little concrete Tobruk shelters. In the vicinity was a 75mm field gun, a wooden-wheeled First World War affair, but still a handy weapon. Behind him was his deadliest weapon, a lethal Pak anti-tank gun, with another 50mm, flamethrowers and machine-guns.

At *Widerstandsnest* 5, Leutnant Arthur Jahnke was equipped with several tracked mines. Resembling miniature First World War tanks, these were essentially electrically-powered, disposable demolition vehicles. Controlling them via a trailing wire, Jahnke was expected to direct them towards Allied armour, then trigger their destruction. All were rendered harmless by the bombardment which severed their command wires. Behind it sits a DUKW and visible on the horizon is Utah's Gooseberry breakwater, comprised of sunken blockships. (US Army Signal Corps)

Jahnke glanced out to sea and saw the silhouette of their French tank turret on top of another concrete Tobruk. It was the pride and joy of Obergefreiter Friedrich, who sat inside the *Panzerstellung*, manning its machine-gun. In the dunes lay their latest toys, delivered the week before – called Goliaths, though that's one thing they weren't. They looked exactly like a miniature First World War tank, with a pathetic speed to match. Jahnke was still learning how to operate them and not sure about their suitability for combat: 'Fancy sending a miniature unmanned vehicle packed with a hundred pounds of explosives into battle! Surely its command wires would be severed before it reached its target! We'll see,' he thought. Spread around Jahnke were concrete personnel and ammunition shelters, but most of their recent efforts had been spent wiring in the minefield that surrounded them on all four sides and digging deep trenches that linked every structure and position.[19]

To give backbone to coastal strongpoints like Jahnke's W5, several major artillery batteries were sited near the inland road, beyond the flooded areas. However, the guns encased in concrete at Saint-Marcouf (three of 210mm calibre; this is where the German garrison had encountered the croaking 'frogs' of the paratroopers), Azeville (Major Hugo Treiber's battery of four 105mm guns that we have already studied) and Saint-Martin-de-Varreville had already been marked for bombing, first by B-26 Marauders, then by the offshore fleet, led by USS *Nevada* and including HMS *Enterprise*, in the minutes before H-Hour. The latter position at Varreville, when approached from behind by the 502nd Parachute Infantry, would be found to have been demolished by bombing and the guns destroyed, but not the other two.[20]

Paratroopers had already caused mayhem throughout the Cotentin, long before the seaborne invasion of the US 4th Infantry Division arrived. Impeding any progress along Exit 4 from Utah, alongside the road between Saint-Martin-de-Varreville and Turqueville, was a group of farm buildings used as a barracks by 150 German artillerymen of the 191st *Artillerie-Regiment* (from Falley's *Luftlande* Division). On American maps it was simply given the designation 'WXYZ'. Its capture, although foreseen as a battalion task, was in the event undertaken by Staff Sergeant Harrison Summers and fifteen men from the 502nd Parachute Infantry – all that could be found from the scattered airborne forces. They would fight for five hours to capture the WXYZ complex.

With tactical surprise and a degree of momentum on the side of the ragtag band, Summers led his team in clearing the structures, room by room, using grenades, Thompson sub-machine-guns and eventually a bazooka: it would take until mid-afternoon before all their opponents were killed or captured, opening the route.[21] Another German position at Brécourt Manor, ancestral home of First World War veteran Colonel Michel de Vallavieille, consisted of four 105mm field howitzers concealed in a wood line, protected by entrenched machine guns. It would be attacked by Lieutenant Dick Winters and eleven others from the 506th Parachute Infantry while it was firing down Exit 2 onto the seaborne invaders at around 0830 hours.

Almost more significant than the disabling of the guns, Winters would also capture a map which detailed every German artillery position on the Cotentin. From it, VII Corps intelligence were able to identify twenty-eight batteries – most of them mobile artillery units – 'comprising 111 guns of medium to heavy calibre' within range of Utah Beach. Winters' Distinguished Service Cross awarded for the action was richly deserved. The young lieutenant, a lifelong teetotaller, would remember the action as much for Vallavieille's celebratory offer of 'hard Norman cider which I thought might slow down my thoughts and reactions, but didn't'.[22] The nature of these last two attacks – squad-sized groups of paratroops from different companies – illustrated the lack of cohesion of the 82nd and 101st at this stage. Yet, despite their scattered drops, their training made up for their lack of numbers – something mirrored by Otway's 9th Parachute Battalion in the east.

Ahead of the main Utah assault, Neptune had already commenced on the extreme western flank. Two little islands off the beach – the Îles Saint-Marcouf – were known to be defended by a German garrison and presented a potential threat. Accordingly, at 0430, LCAs from HMS *Empire Gauntlet* landed detachments of the US 4th and 24th Cavalry Squadrons on the islets, who found the substantial concrete emplacements intact but deserted – this became the first French terrain liberated on D-Day by the maritime forces.

The basic plan was for all three regiments of Barton's 4th Infantry Division – nicknamed 'the Ivy', from the Roman numerals IV, for 4th – to storm ashore sequentially. Short of stature and with a prominent stomach, Barton's Christian names of Raymond and Oscar were consigned to history at West Point in favour of his nickname, Tubby. 'Firm, brisk and energetic, but not sour or stiff', he was rated as a 'disciplinarian who commanded his division with an iron hand', and easily recognised by his 'weathered face with its bushy eyebrows and clipped moustache'. He was the very opposite of his affable assistant divisional commander, Theodore Roosevelt, Jr, as we shall later see.[23]

At H-Hour, Colonel James Van Fleet's 8th Infantry would land first, followed by Hervey Tribolet's 22nd Infantry, then 'Red' Reeder's 12th Regiment.[24] Thirty-two swimming DD tanks of the 70th Tank Battalion would go in on the heels of the 8th Infantry's assault, followed five minutes later by assault gapping teams of demolition experts from the USN's 2nd Naval Beach Battalion, and detachments from two combat engineer battalions – they were to clear lanes for the subsequent landing craft. Another tank battalion, the 746th, would subsequently land, dry-shod, and an additional infantry regiment, the 359th (of the 90th Division), would also disembark before the day was out – over 21,000 men, 1,700 tons of stores and 1,700 vehicles were to be ashore by nightfall.

On the eve of departure, whilst still in Plymouth, Reeder had described their mission to his men using American football terminology: 'Here is the straight dope on the landing. The 8th and 22nd Regiments will land ahead of us and will block to the left and right. The paratroopers are the downfield blockers. We will land and plunge through the hole and head for Cherbourg. The privates stood and yelled.'[25] One of Reeder's chaplains, Lewis Fulmer Koon, a Methodist minister from Virginia, found himself doing such brisk business on their ship in mid-Channel that he led the men of Company 'B' in a multi-faith prayer 'to the God in whom we all believe, whether Protestant, Roman Catholic or Jew, that our mission may be accomplished and that, if possible, we may be brought safely home again'. In those days before ecumenism was common, Koon was eternally grateful to have done so, for their commander, Captain Irving Gray, a Jew, was destined to be killed the next day, one of the regiment's very few fatalities of D-Day.[26] South Carolinian George L. Mabry, Jr, was one of Van Fleet's star officers, lent to division headquarters as staff officer operations. He had spent his time in England perfecting the plans. Late one evening Roosevelt had found him surrounded by files: 'What the hell are you up to, George? Quit worrying. Whatever you plan, the boys are going right in there and'll throw in all they've got. So what d'you want with all this paper?'[27]

Standing in his bunker in the early hours of 6 June and musing over the arrival of the American parachutists, Leutnant Jahnke reassured himself. Of course it couldn't be the invasion. Hadn't Rommel himself stated that a seaborne landing would take place at dawn on a high tide?

He was comforted by the fact the tide would be out at dawn, uncovering all their obstacles and a half-mile killing zone in front of him. Mentally he ran over his defences. His position was four hundred yards long by three hundred deep and stood at the end of the road from Sainte-Marie-du-Mont. He knew every inch of it because his men had built it, all seventy-five of them. He looked through the embrasure of his command bunker with its artillery telescope: still dark, but he could hear the sea. The tide had just turned and was receding. Soon he would be able to look to his left, up the coast, where similar strongpoints, numbered W7 and W8, had been built. To his right, out of sight, lay W2 and W3. Behind him, and themselves dealing with their own paratrooper problems, were his colleagues in W4. It was smaller, just simple dugouts with anti-tank guns protected by logs and sandbags.

Most of the coastal defence positions were like his, Jahnke knew; some had anti-tank ditches and a machine-gun or two more, but as General von Schlieben had briefed them, their purpose was to deter. The combination of these little forts bristling along the coast with the artificial marsh behind would make this stretch of the Cotentin very unattractive to a potential invader – or so Schlieben, a broad-shouldered cavalryman with piercing eyes and a fondness for lobster and champagne, had claimed at the last divisional conference. Jahnke checked on the American prisoners, locked securely into a bunker – and was disconcerted to hear from Gefreiter Hoffmann, the medic who'd treated the injured, that they 'were uneasy, kept asking what time it was, and whether they shouldn't be sent to the rear' – but Jahnke decided to keep them, at least until daybreak. He may have pretended indifference to his men, but the presence of the paratroops – who were probably helping the Resistance and had landed off-course – and the severing of his communications left him uneasy. Although only twenty-three, from his experience of the Russian front, he had that veteran soldier's sense of something being not quite right.[28]

The twelve Utah sub-convoys – the slowest, comprising 293 vessels, travelling at five knots, having been at sea for over thirty-four hours – started to reach their rendezvous areas thirteen miles offshore from 0229 hours, all arriving and taking up their assault stations over the next two hours.[29] They were led by the transport and headquarters ship USS *Bayfield*, carrying Admiral Don P. Moon and General 'Lightning Joe' Collins, VII Corps commander. Although Collins had missed the First

World War, arriving in France just after the Armistice, he had led the 25th Division very ably in the Pacific; Bradley had lauded him as 'independent, heady, capable, and full of vinegar'. The code name for the 25th's headquarters on Guadalcanal was 'Lightning', from which Collins had picked up his much-admired nickname.

As the *Bayfield* anchored, GIs assembled on her decks and those of USS *Barnett* to mount their landing craft for Uncle Red sector. Cables and ropes squeaked through pulleys as the small craft jerked their way down the ships' sides, finally settling into the heaving swell below. Their occupants knew a Higgins boat had about two feet of freeboard in a gentle sea; but this was not a gentle sea. At the same moment, USS *Joseph T. Dickman* and HMS *Empire Gauntlet* disgorged the first invaders heading for Tare Green – the two sectors were left and right respectively on Utah. The first-wave troops in twenty LCVPs were accompanied by eight LCTs – carrying four 70th Tank Battalion DD Shermans each. They chugged towards their line of departure, 3,000 yards offshore, split evenly – ten Higgins boats and four LCTs to each sub-beach. Depositing fourteen landing craft along a stretch of coast might not have seemed a big deal, but the boats would have to pick their way through mines, obstacles yet to be cleared by engineers, and overseen by German gunners: an initial 'suicide wave' of fourteen boats was the most the planners dared risk.

These craft were the very tip of the lance, and each sector followed two guide boats, the 280-ton armed Sub-Chaser *PC-1261* for Uncle Red, her sister *PC-1176* for Tare Green. A second wave of thirty-two LCVPs carrying infantry and engineers would follow on immediately, succeeded by eight LCTs carrying Sherman tanks fitted with dozers – such was the tight schedule of Utah.[30] Similar timetables were planned for Omaha, Gold, Juno and Sword. Britons and Canadians who had fought in the First World War on the Somme and at Passchendaele shook their heads in disbelief at anyone being tied in to such unalterable, lengthy and time-sensitive itineraries.

Nearer to daybreak, the skies were again filled with the throb of aero-engines; Leutnant Jahnke in W5 wondered if they were more troop carriers. This time, though, they were flying higher. Instead of hurrying on to somewhere else, it was still too dark for Jahnke to see that they had their bomb doors open. Then his world became one of high-pitched whistles and deafening blasts that hurled him and his men around. The air was filled with sand, concrete dust, larger chunks of – was that metal part of one of his guns? The reek of high explosive cordite caught in their throats. There was enough of a pause for the smoke to clear and for Jahnke to realise that the landscape around W5 had altered. The moonlight showed him a landscape of rubble and debris; he could hear the moans of wounded men. Then he was conscious of further waves of aircraft and more bombing. During another respite he found he could speak to his friend Leutnant Ritter, further south in W2, who seemed to have escaped much of the bombing. 'They obviously have their eye on you,' Ritter told him.

Jahnke hoped not, and had those of his men still left unscathed dig out the others buried beneath avalanches of sand and stone. While their rescue attempts were ongoing, he waited, nervously, to see what the dawn would bring. Already it had passed 0500, the time of morning nautical twilight, when the sun was still twelve degrees below the horizon: the first streaks of light began to light up the sky. Sunrise was still a way off, but as it grew light, he looked out to the ocean. It was still foam-flecked and restless, with twenty-five minutes till low tide. Visibility further out was impossible, with low banks of thick dawn mist concealing whatever there might have been to see. His position was almost at sea level, so he couldn't observe that far, but hoped against hope that the destruction of W5 – a single glance confirmed it was in ruins – would not herald some kind of seaborne attack.[31]

The assault convoy was huge; Force 'U' had loaded and assembled at nine different ports: Salcombe, Dartmouth, Brixham, Yarmouth, Portland–Weymouth, Poole, Torbay–Torquay and Belfast – the latter hosting the bombardment force, led by USS *Nevada*, in Belfast Lough. With the *Joseph T. Dickman* and *Empire Gauntlet* were a Landing Craft, Headquarters, fifteen 4,000-ton LSTs each towing a Rhino ferry, sixty-nine LCTs, twenty-six little LCMs and twenty-three LCIs (each of the latter carrying 200 troops), plus smaller craft. The vessels following the *Barnett* and *Bayfield* were similar in number, the assault convoys being attended by seven USN destroyers and two French corvettes.

This excluded the battleship, monitor, four cruisers, ten destroyers, two frigates and lone Dutch gunboat of the Force 'U' bombardment flotilla, and close support craft including four Landing Craft, Gun and five Landing Craft, Rocket. The ensemble was attended by twenty-seven large and eighteen smaller minesweepers, while ten US Coast Guard cutters and thirteen PT boats would scurry around the area in close support and to pick up survivors from sunken craft.

They were in addition over a hundred other small vessels, including many specially converted landing craft performing a host of other maintenance, salvage, rescue, supply, lightship, dredging, food preparation and administrative tasks. Other troopships and twenty-five more LSTs were scheduled and ready in southern English ports to follow immediately – in all, 865 vessels, including the 171 smaller LCAs and LCVPs carried on larger ships, would be heading for Utah or were at sea protecting them.

This impressive undertaking was replicated to a greater or lesser extent off the other four beaches, Utah's being by no means the largest. Afterwards, Admiral Alan G. Kirk would record his pride that the performance of 'approximately 125,000 US Naval personnel in the Western Task Force, from flag officers to seamen, was in the highest traditions of the naval service; to command so fine a force in so large an operation was a great privilege. Equally, the performance of British and other allied vessels fulfilled my highest expectations, and the close association in combat with these fine sailors of other nations is a source of great satisfaction.'[32]

Waves of B-26s struck the German coastal positions from 0545 hours; soon visibility became minimal, with smoke, haze and debris all limiting the ability to identify the coastline – though this also protected the fleet. Such obscuration would affect all five beaches and also lead to another problem: shell craters along the shore under the waves. Countless soldiers and vehicles were swallowed up by these sudden dips in the seabed; some would emerge, others not. At 0534, during the final run-in, the 173-foot *PC-1261* was straddled by two shells fired from a shore battery; soon a third hit the engine room amidships, killing thirteen immediately and sinking the craft. About half the crew of sixty-five were eventually rescued, but the primary guidance vessel for Uncle Red was now missing.[33] At the same time, mines accounted for *LCT-593* and *LCT-597*, which sank with their cargoes, including four valuable DD tanks, the latter with no survivors – now only twenty-eight of the thirty-two Shermans were left. The loss of *PC-1261* ordinarily would not have mattered, for each beach – Uncle Red and Tare Green – had two guidance vessels, but the backup craft for the left-hand beach had fouled her propeller and was also absent. This meant, in the smoke and confusion, the assault drifted south with the current. The troops, however, were unaware that they were now aiming for the wrong stretch of beach.

Another glance seawards, thought Leutnant Jahnke. The tide was almost out, his wooden stakes, the hedgehogs, high and dry. Beyond, nothing. The mist thinned. And then he saw them. First, tiny specks that might have been dust in the lenses of his binoculars – had they not been *moving*. And multiplying. Small specks. Different shapes. Some growing in size. *They had arrived* ... here. He felt a kind of relief, as he had known when he had seen the Russians attacking. Fear of the unknown is always worse. 'Let's get this over with,' thought the young officer.[34]

'The low-lying coast of France leapt into the air in a sheet of jagged flame and thunder', noted Captain James R. Arnold, USNR, Utah's senior Beachmaster. He had left the safety and comfort of USS *Bayfield* and joined the run ashore, as the aerial bombardment began. 'Just before we jockeyed into position, a terrific explosion a few hundred yards to starboard rocked our LCI. It was *LCI-707* which had hit a mine, turning her completely over. Then all seemed to cut loose. German shore batteries recovering from the shock of surprise were returning the slugging salvos of the naval fire-support ships, raising great gouts of water as they plumbed for the perfect range.'[35]

More bombers flew overhead. Their vibrations grated through Leutnant Jahnke's whole body. These were B-26s, but Jahnke wasn't plane-spotting. He was riveted by the fleet. A tiny oblong shape turned broadside-on and yellow flashes flickered along its flank. Seconds later he heard – then felt – the shells. A small spotter plane droned overhead; he knew what that meant. Correcting the fall of shot for even bigger guns. There, on the horizon, he could make out a larger warship, now several, and other silhouettes that looked like merchantmen. Smaller shapes were riding the waves towards him. 'Alarm! Enemy ships approaching!'[36]

'My real fear was landing those guys without getting bombed by our own people', recollected Lieutenant Abraham Condiotti, of Brooklyn, New York, coxswain of an LVCP from the attack transport USS *Barnett*. His passengers included the 4th Infantry Division's Brigadier General Roosevelt, and Leonard T. 'Moose' Schroeder, leading Company 'F' of Van Fleet's 8th Infantry. They were in the first boat of the "suicide wave". Earlier, when leaving the little south Devon harbour of Torquay, a bucket-and-spade resort more used to hosting holidaymakers and yachts, Roosevelt had summoned his officers for a final briefing. At the end they 'wished each other well and shook hands', Schroeder receiving an unexpected bear hug from his colonel, with the comment, 'Well, Moose, this is it. Give 'em hell!' Schroeder hadn't expected his boss to use his nick-name and had felt quite emotional.

Roosevelt had strode over and requested, 'Moose, take me in your boat when you go ashore.' Accordingly, 0628 hours, the next morning found both men stepping into the waves. Schroeder, of Baltimore, Maryland, 'waving my .45-caliber pistol as I waded through the waist-high water', was later credited with being the first man ashore on Utah. Condiotti, however, recalled that 'I guess eighty percent of the thirty-two guys on my boat were sick, but more worrying was the fact that the beach was still being shelled and bombed as we arrived. Fortunately at that very second, the firing lifted.'[37]

George Mabry was in Condiotti's craft, too. He recalled that Roosevelt hollered to his aide, 'Stevie, where is my lifebelt?' Came the reproachful response: 'General, I don't know. I've already given you four.' 'Dammit, I don't care how many you've given me, I don't have one now.' Mabry and the aide searched and found one. When Mabry asked whether Roosevelt had a weapon, 'the General patted his shoulder holster and responded, "I've got my pistol, one clip of ammunition and my walking cane. That's all I expect to need."'[38] In the next landing craft with Van Fleet was Princeton graduate and future diplomat Lieutenant John C. Ausland, who recalled, 'The run into the beach was a bizarre experience. Most of us were happy to cower behind the little protection provided by the metal sides of the landing craft, however one officer from regimental headquarters insisted on sitting in a chair above us, where he was exposed to enemy fire. Arms folded, he announced that he did not want to miss a moment of this spectacular show – similar bravado would account for his death a few weeks hence.'[39]

Guy Capobianco, a rifleman with Company 'I' of the 8th Infantry from Roseto, Pennsylvania, remembered Roosevelt addressing the men just before they departed USS *Barnett*. 'It was 0300 hours and he told us frankly it would be a bloody beach. "Some of us will come back, and some of us will not", but reaching Cherbourg meant a ticket home,' Capobianco recounted. 'But of course taking Cherbourg meant nothing of the sort.' Another Capobianco, his brother Nick, was also at Utah. He was a machine-gunner with Company 'H' of Reeder's 12th Infantry. The pair had been deliberately separated. Guy hit the beach first, Nick following about an hour later. Seasickness had taken its toll: 'By the time we got there, I don't think anybody cared what happened,' reported Nick Capobianco. 'The guys just said, "Let's get it over with." I had a life preserver strapped to the business end of my .30-caliber machine-gun and another around my waist. It was more sensible floating my gun to shore than carrying it. I was soaking wet when I landed because I waded through water neck deep. First thing I saw was a decapitated German soldier.'[40]

Leutnant Jahnke could see the tide was fully out now, leaving little runnels of water between the wooden poles and metal hedgehogs. How could the cunning Desert Fox have been so wrong? Rommel had visited this very spot twenty-seven days earlier, when he'd asked the *leutnant* to take off his gloves. A week earlier, Jahnke had stood in the sand to receive his Knight's Cross from General von Schlieben. Now he saw all – the Allies had come at low tide, prepared to take the casualties of the killing zone. Jahnke ordered 'Weapons ready!' The response was pathetic. What was the point of a killing zone if he had nothing left to kill with? He sent a motorcycle despatch rider off to the nearest artillery battery requesting support: 'Defensive fire on areas Ulm and Wien' – the exposed beach to his front, and further out to sea – 'now!' He forgot the paratroopers would probably intercept the messenger. They did. Then Arthur Jahnke took his signal pistol and fired two green flares, waiting for the barrage that would never come.[41]

In the Higgins boat with Roosevelt, Mabry recalled,

as light began to improve, the first casualty I saw was a Navy boat [this was *PC-1261*] which apparently had hit a mine. One sailor was lying on the keel of the boat, holding onto a man who was obviously either critically wounded or dead. That boat had been stationed to mark the lanes for approaching the beach. Soon after, I saw a large transport hit a mine [*LCI-707*]. About this time we passed some of the floating tanks from the 70th Tank Battalion which had worked closely with us in England. They'd been discharged eight or nine hundred yards from the beach. I was trying to pick up landmarks; the bombing apparently knocked them down but we figured there was something wrong.[42]

In fact, the DD tanks should have been launched from five thousand yards, but to save time were launched at three thousand and arrived fifteen minutes after the first troops: according to the US *Official History*, 'they played little part in the assault', though their presence ashore was more than appreciated by the infantry.[43]

'I turned nineteen on 5 June 1944 and prayed to God that I'd make twenty,' reflected Robert H. Gangewere of Wind Gap, Pennsylvania.

We climbed down the cargo net into the assault boat. It was quite an experience, that rope. A lot of guys fell and got hurt. When the ramp went down, we got out into neck-deep water, holding all our stuff up in the air ... I was a bazooka man for 4th Division headquarters. My job was to stop tanks. I had to hold that darned thing over my head. I carried a carbine as well over one shoulder ... With all the stuff we had to carry it took maybe twenty minutes to get to the beach. We'd check on each other as we went up the beach. 'Need any help?' 'Are you OK?' Our ammo carrier got winged, so I took some of his ammo and carried it for him till he could get to the aid station. When I got ashore, I laid down on the dry sand. I had to have a little break.[44]

Helping to supply 'drenching fire' onto Utah, like Jim Weller and John H. Glass at Omaha, were Captain John P. McGirr's eighteen M7 'Priest' howitzers of the 65th Armored Field Artillery. 'It was light then and I recall the beautiful sight of balls of fire streaking across the sky from the *Nevada* – hard to realise the tons of high explosive behind them. I turned back to look. Following the belch of flame, huge clouds of brown cordite smoke veiled the ship,' McGirr recalled. 'The noise was terrific as we neared the beach; but the scene changed quickly from an orderly line of boats knifing through the surf to – well, carnage. Anyone who tells you Utah was a cakewalk is mistaken. One Higgins boat ahead of us completely disintegrated when hit by something from the shore. There were no survivors. I saw another rear up on its end in a bright orange flash. Must have hit a mine.'[45]

'There was stuff blowing up all over the place,' recalled frogman Dennis Shryock, who landed on Utah with a Naval Combat Demolition Unit (NCDU), forerunner to the US Navy's SEALs. He was with one of eight sixteen-man gap assault teams; the NCDU half of the team would handle seaward obstructions, while the larger army engineer force would clear the landward obstacles. Utah's relatively sparse beach obstacles consisted of three rows of steel or wooden posts and concrete pyramids crowned with Teller anti-tank mines, and 'Czech tetrahydra' – a design comprising short lengths of railway track welded or bolted together, sometimes known as a hedgehog. Additionally, several tall steel obstructions on rollers known as Belgian gates (or 'element "C"' on Allied maps) were also placed to block access to roads and tracks. Both the Czech and Belgian devices had come from the frontier defences of those countries and were being recycled by the thrifty Wehrmacht. Several twenty-six-man army demolition teams were to land ten minutes later, directly behind eight LCTs carrying dozer tanks. These navy and army teams were to clear eight gaps fifty yards wide through the beach obstructions for the subsequent waves – the fourth and fifth assaults bringing in the balance of engineers allocated to lane clearing.[46] All these engineers, and the port units that would land later, were grouped into Brigadier General James E. Wharton's 1st Engineer Special Brigade.

Shryock, then a twenty-one-year-old explosives specialist from Springfield, Illinois, was attached to one of thirty-four demolition units sent to England for the invasion. He recalled reaching the peak of fitness, with five-mile swims and hand-to-hand combat training. On 6 June, 'We moved from obstacle to obstacle, lacing each with sixty pounds of explosives, working off data supplied by the French Resistance and aerial photos. We were lucky – on *Utah* our demolition teams suffered only six dead and eleven injured, but nearly all on *Omaha* became casualties – that's where thirty-one of my buddies died and sixty were injured.'[47]

An aerial photograph (left) taken on 6 May 1944 reveals Rommel's anti-invasion obstacles off Utah beach. They include so-called Czech tetrahydra (top right), a simple anti-tank barrier invented to protect their frontier before its absorption into the Reich in 1938–9. Rommel had them transported to Northern France where his troops planted them along the littoral. He also had obsolete tank turrets (bottom right) mounted on concrete bases to beef up his shore defences. (Top right, Author's collection; others, NARA)

His six fellow engineers were killed when the ramp of their LCM dropped onto a mine, but everyone else got ashore safely and immediately began to disable the obstacles. 'I wasn't even thinking about anybody shooting at me until I saw the bullet holes in the sand,' recalled another of Shyrock's buddies in the USN's 2nd Beach Battalion, Henry Hoop. The Pittsburgh native was focused on wrapping his explosives shaped into long sausages around the steel or concrete beach obstacles. He never worried about getting hit, perhaps because he had taken a swig of whiskey on the landing craft, offered by an officer who advised him they all might need one.[48]

Their responsibilities ended at the high-water mark, beyond which army engineers took over. 'I had sixty pounds of explosives on my back, but you had to have a blasting cap to detonate them. As I also carried those, if a bullet had struck, I would have been vaporised,' remembered Jay Rencher. The nineteen-year-old with the 531st Engineer Shore Regiment was also an early arrival on Utah, attached to the 1st Engineer Special Brigade, many of whom served in Torch, Husky and Avalanche. 'We arrived in England the day after Thanksgiving and were quartered in Fowey, Cornwall. Our three-man squad consisted of Otis Hamm of Biloxi, Mississippi, Dan Shellenberg of Youngstown, Ohio, and me. Hamm was the veteran: he'd made all three previous invasions – North Africa, Sicily, Salerno. We worked as a team. One of us had the mine detector that would hum when it found something; Hamm taught us to look for the teeny-tiny detonators, so we needed steady hands,' recalled Rencher, from Snowflake, Arizona.

Neither of his two colleagues made it off the beach (two of the exit roads off Utah were named in their honour, one Hamm, the other Shellenberg), but – incredibly – by 0930 hours the sands had been cleared of all obstacles and work started on demolishing sections of the sea wall and bulldozing paths through the dunes beyond to make exit roads.[49] Colonel Eugene M. Caffey, deputy commander of the 1st Engineer Special Brigade, later observed that what held his attention on 6 June while the air 'was full of scrap iron, was the way the bulldozer drivers went about their work with complete nonchalance. All day long they drove back and forth dragging out drowned artillery and vehicles, shoving off landing craft. They were remarkable people.'[50]

'I saw spurts of water coming up and knew some of us were going to be hit,' recalled Lieutenant Colonel Arthur S. Teague, commanding the Third Battalion, 22nd Infantry. He had joined the outfit as a second lieutenant in 1940 and never left; now he was commanding it. The South Carolinian – rated by his regimental commander as 'the most competent leader in battle I have ever known' – saw a small landing craft hit as they neared Utah. He told his coxswain to ram the shore and the sailor complied. 'We hit the beach and stepped off on dry soil. A couple of boats behind us – about seventy-five yards back – were hit. Many were killed, some were wounded.'[51]

Alongside Roosevelt, Mabry in his LCVP noticed the defences becoming clearer.

Tetrahedrons stood out like bristles on a hog's back. Men began to jump off the left and right corners of the ramp. We'd been trained that once you hit the beach, you run across that thing; never lie down on it and don't crowd up against the seawall. You've got to push on inland. That was drilled into us. I moved forward. Ahead of me a man was carrying ammunition, which he was to drop at the seawall for Company 'H''s mortars. A round came in and hit the top of his head; his rounds detonated also, and this man's body completely disappeared. I felt something hit me on my thigh; it was his thumb. It was the only discernible part of a human being you could see.

The Carolinian backwoodsman, who had grown up running free, hunting and fishing on his family's cotton plantation – and would go on to win the Medal of Honor later in the war – shrugged it off.[52] He had landed alongside Companies 'A' and 'C' of the 237th Engineer Combat Battalion, who, advised by a tank officer on their staff, began gapping lengths in the sea wall to allow the passage of armoured vehicles, removing wire, and mine-clearing paths through sand dunes beyond. For these tasks the two companies had Bangalore torpedoes, mine detectors, explosives, pioneer tools, markers and bulldozers – and heavier plant would soon follow.[53]

At W5, up in his little tank turret Obergefreiter Friedrich was blasting away with his machine-gun. Leutnant Arthur Jahnke watched helplessly as his few remaining weapons were shredded by the offshore fleet. Eyes glued to the artillery rangefinder, he watched the invaders nearing the shoreline. The ramps of their landing barges lowered and men waded into the surf. They were still too distant to engage with effective fire – but in any case, with what? Broken machine-guns and rifles? A blast, a screech of metal and a scream. Poor old Friedrich in his *Panzerstellung* had been hit. The unlikely marksman with glasses as thick as paper-weights had been wounded in the thigh. They pulled him out, wrapped a tourniquet and field dressings round his leg: the loyal *Obergefreiter*; at least he'd live, thought Jahnke. At this stage, the few broken men of W5 could oppose the invaders with not much more than silence.[54]

'The assault boat dropped us off about fifty yards from shore, about 0700 hours,' recalled army engineer Dick Schermerhorn from New York State.

> We didn't know what we faced. Anybody tells you he's not scared, there's something wrong with him. There was a medical officer next to me, and I happened to notice his face was as white as a sheet. When the ramp came down, I jumped in with my mine detector; the water was up to my neck. My buddy who worked with me, Charlie Panisetti, was a short fella, so he just hung on to me … We would take turns working the minefields. One of us swept and the other probed. When you got a reading on the detector, the other guy had to dig with his bayonet to find out what it was.[55]

Kanonier Aloysius Damski was a conscripted Pole serving in a Wehrmacht unit that had helped lay them: 'We had considerable short-ages of minefield equipment. So we planted scraps of metal to confuse the detectors, wired off the areas, and strung up signs reading *Achtung Minen!* Many of the real mines we used were British, captured at Dunkirk, but most of the minefields in our area were false. We had signs to remind ourselves which were genuine. If the writing sloped to the left it was a dummy. To the right meant an anti-personnel field. Upright meant an anti-tank one.'[56]

Scrabbling around on hands and knees, using bayonets like archaeo-logical trowels, was all very well, but time-consuming. Another way of dealing with a minefield was to stick a British-invented explosive-loaded drainpipe known as a Bangalore torpedo along the ground and touch off the detonator. The resultant destruction was usually enough to blow a gap through barbed wire and destroy anti-personnel mines near the surface. At Utah, Schermerhorn continued to sweep his path through the dunes. 'At the top was a wall; every now and again you'd hear the *ping* of a ricochet bullet. General Roosevelt came up and asked, "You finding any mines, men?" I said, "No sir, not at this time." Then he said, "Dammit, I thought there'd be millions of them" and he walked on through the bullets. Didn't touch him. Next time I saw Roosevelt, frogmen were blowing up the obstacles in the water' – this was Dennis Shryock and his comrades. 'The frogmen put up a purple flare when they were about to fire a charge, and you were supposed to hit the deck. This one time, lying prone, I looked up and there was Roosevelt standing there looking around. No fear whatsoever.'[57]

In disbelief, Leutnant Jahnke saw several canvas boats near the surf, then rise up, their tarpaulin sides glistening with water. They became tanks. Fascinated, Jahnke watched tiny figures crab forward, some setting about his obstacles, others rushing forward with the dripping armoured vehicles. Then he remembered his own tanks, the Goliaths. All he had to do was send them forward and they would blow his opponents to pieces. Then a glance confirmed his worst fears. Their command wires had been severed in the shelling and these little tracked mines were worse than useless. The miniature figures in the distance grew in size, becoming men, and the armour trundled nearer. Soon the Shermans were poking their muzzles into his bunkers. Pittsburgh native Staff Sergeant Walter A. Janicki, a bazooka man of the 8th Infantry's 2nd Battalion, recalled missing one of Jahnke's pillboxes with his first shell. 'But I got the sonuvabitch with my second.'[58] Jahnke was again deafened by a blast and buried under debris. He came to, regaining his senses, rearranged his spectacles, and brushed down his uniform. Looking for his men, he became aware of a figure standing over him. 'Take it easy, German!' said a voice. Leutnant Arthur Jahnke, four years a *frontsoldat*, holder of the prized *Ritterkreuz*, was now a prisoner.[59]

Lieutenant W. H. Boies of Gridley, Illinois, with the 22nd Infantry, recalled being 'so heavily loaded we could barely climb into the landing craft'. At the other end of his journey, the position (probably W6, north of Arthur Jahnke) he was tasked to attack was empty. Instead, 'about a dozen Polish men, forced into German uniforms after they were captured, were sitting in front of the pillbox. They were dazed from the naval bombardment, and when their German officers ran off, the Poles all cried *Kamerad!*'[60] Lieutenant Colonel Teague of 22nd Infantry, remembered the Goliaths, noting 'a number of enemy baby tanks which had electrical wiring and were loaded with TNT. Some troops wanted to fire into one, and I told them to stop and posted guards on it.'[61]

While frogmen and engineers were busy with the obstacles and mines, Coxswain Joseph Suozzo, from San Diego, California, was trying to steer

LCT-2310 between the beach obstructions on one engine, flooded and listing to starboard. Suozzo had collected three Shermans from Salcombe, Devon, and was determined to deliver them. Motoring very slowly, his craft was one of the very rare casualties on Utah, being hit ten times in quick succession, wounding two of his crew – but he unloaded his armour. 'The profile of the beach was so flat with no significant features, that we couldn't determine where the gunfire was coming from.'[62]

These were possibly the last shots fired from W5. British Midshipman Kenneth McCaw noticed the jeeps with trailers disembarking from his LCT at Utah 'had the greatest difficulty in getting ashore, because the trailers tend to float away, at right angles to the Jeep, but they all made

Surrounded by a pile of discarded life preservers on the afternoon of D-Day, three GIs lean against a concrete troop shelter. Their collars are turned up and they are wearing gloves – an indication of the poor weather of 6 June. The bunker is attached to a boarded up cottage within Leutnant Arthur Jahnke's W5 strongpoint. Note the painted-on windows, a crude attempt at camouflage. The structure remains there today, with its fake windows, attached to *Café Le Roosevelt.* Inside, scribbled on the walls in faint pencil, are the names of those GIs stationed there in 1944. (US Army Signal Corps)

it. Less fortunate was a DUKW alongside us which hit a mine, and went up in the air, scattering its cargo and pieces of its crew all around us.' On an adjacent craft, a squad of infantrymen 'bought it in front of our eyes as an eighty-eight shell landed smack in the middle of them' – these may have been the six army engineers noted earlier. McCaw wound up his ramp 'in double-quick time and beat a hasty retreat'.[63]

The experience of landing at Utah was uneven; some were barely engaged at all. Sergeant John Beck of the 87th Chemical Mortar Battalion, landing in a later wave, had been given a seasickness pill, 'which made me feel better, and I dozed off only to wake with a start. We had reached the shore. There were about twenty-five yards of beach and then a levee about twenty-five feet high. The crew had brought us right in; we got out into water waist-deep. The cold water helped bring us back to reality.'[64] British signaller Arthur McNeil aboard *LCT-2440* remembered the LCTs of his flotilla forming 'a line abreast for the run in; we were quite proud of the fact that we gave our American friends a dry landing. The water barely touched their axles – the American officer on the bridge thanked us as he departed, remarking "it was quieter than their pre-invasion exercises"' – perhaps a dark reference to the ill-fated Exercise Tiger.[65]

As a piece of primary evidence, the ship's log of *LCT-645* goes some way to suggesting that to those present, Utah on 6 June 1944 seemed every bit as terrible as the world later knew Omaha to have been, and nothing like the 'walkover' the D-Day mythology suggests. Lieutenant Charles Summers, RNVR, commanding its British crew, noted leaving Dartmouth, Devon, the previous morning at 0430 hours, 'loaded with six half-tracks towing anti-tank guns, ten Jeeps and seventy GIs'. A day later, he recorded at 0415 off the French coast: 'a constant stream of aircraft, bombers, fighters, gliders', replaced at 0630 by 'an ear-splitting bombardment with smoke covering the coastline'. Five hours later, having left their line of departure for the beach, 'an LCI coming off the beach about a cable's length on our starboard beam [one tenth of a nautical mile], strikes a mine and sinks. There is no time to pick up any possible survivors.' As they beached with the twenty-fourth wave at 1400, their passengers appeared nervous at disembarking in three foot of water and had to be coaxed ashore, with the result that the tide ebbed and the craft had to wait until 1900 hours, before floating off.

In the meantime the log, written the same day, recorded, 'Utah beach looks a shambles with broken-down tanks, burning and exploding vehicles of all kinds due to enemy mortar and 88mm gunfire, although the beached landing craft appear undamaged. Sub Lieutenant Wyatt and my coxswain examine two other abandoned LCTs: one is full of corpses wrapped in blankets.'[66] Harper Colman, with Company 'H' of the 8th Infantry, echoed this: 'The history books claim this was one of the easier landings. It did not seem good at the time. We went into water more than waist-deep. Our first casualty was just behind me with a serious wound to the stomach. A second man, in front of me, stepped on a land mine. Our squad of six was down to four very early.'[67]

There is another apocryphal tale that surfaces in many memoirs: that landing craft skippers were reluctant to take their passengers close enough to shore, and had to be persuaded to move nearer by drawn .45-calibre pistols. It would perhaps be surprising had this not happened in one or two cases, but occurs in too many recollections to have been true in every case. However, a reluctance to close with the beach often had nothing to do with cowardice, but was born of a concern – for landing craft had their own strict timetable – as to how they were going to *leave*. In all five assaults, as the various kinds of landing craft prepared to beach, they threw a kedge anchor off the stern attached to a steel cable on a drum. Once unloaded, they wound themselves back onto the kedge as the quickest means of retracting their craft off the sand. However, landing craft crews caught on the ebbing tide, such as those on *LCT-645*, were obliged to stay until the waters returned, their crew loitering in the shelter of the sea wall and 'picking among the battle souvenirs of D-Day on the seashore, like holidaymakers looking for crabs and starfish'.[68]

From a warship offshore, the picture for war correspondent Richard Stout was one of seeing 'our shells hit, and saw the earth-clouds go up. Then the detonations shifted further and further back off the beach. The next picture was the busy, animated scene of disembarkation. From our distance it looked like several line of ants to and from a crumb of bread, as small boats going in with men and supplies; empties coming back again. I watched an amphibious craft slowly moving along with a white ruffle of foam then waddle up the beach.'[69] Another eyewitness in the 65th Armored Field Artillery left a series of vivid recollections of those last few minutes aboard his LCT:

Fleeting images: the stomach-churning sound of the ramp going down; the gut-wrenching smell of exhaust as tanks ahead of me started up; putting a pack of Lucky Strikes and my fiancée's photograph under my helmet; cursing the Jeep's designers who had put the gas tank under the driver's seat; waiting for an eternity before it was my turn to exit the landing barge, each vehicle having to wait until the previous one had cleared the ramp; driving down the ramp into the water, only about a foot deep, and finding it got deeper, not shallower; then just as I thought about having to swim for it, the bottom shelving upwards and realising I had made it; the tank ahead of me suddenly exploding, bathed in flames; reading a sign, *Achtung Minen!* with a skull and crossbones, in case I hadn't understood the language – which might as well have said, *Welcome to Hell!*'[70]

Frank Cooney from Troy, New York, observed: 'first that damned beach tried to drown me, then it tried to bury me alive. Because of the shelling, we dug foxholes in the sand with the little spade we carried, like a camping shovel. I didn't expect to survive because the infantry had a high mortality rate.' The private from Company 'A' of the 359th Infantry explained, 'All the time I used to think "This hole could be my grave", so I dug my own grave almost every day. First time it wasn't deep enough and when an eighty-eight landed nearby, half the beach landed on top of me. I nearly suffocated.'[71]

Cooney had landed with the final wave of the day, and was part of the follow-on 90th Division, which illustrates how quickly men were fed ashore at Utah. During the day, twenty-six successive assault flotillas hit the beaches – the initial dozen comprised mostly of LCVPs, the larger LCIs arriving later on. In theory, waves were scheduled at twenty-five-minute intervals, but in practice men, stores and vehicles landed every minute, throughout the day. By 0945, fifteen waves had landed; by late afternoon, the entire 4th Division was ashore. A combination of slightly kinder weather, the coast here offering some protection from the wilder seas, and less concentrated shelling allowed mother ships to empty their GIs at a higher rate than elsewhere.

HMS *Empire Gauntlet* was fully unloaded by 0830 hours, USS *Joseph T. Dickman* and USS *Barnett* by 1245. So speedily did these vessels turn around and re-cross the Channel that by midnight they were already back in Portland harbour embarking their next consignments of GIs with their equipment. Amongst the other troopships unloading at Utah was SS *Sea Porpoise*, on which the American singer-songwriter Woody Guthrie was serving as a volunteer deckhand; he would be aboard her when she was torpedoed off the beach on 5 July, though the attack would not prove fatal to either the ship or its resident folk musician.

Sporadic artillery fire throughout D-Day from the Marcouf and Azeville batteries killed one 4th Division medical officer and several enlisted men on the beach, wounded the regimental surgeon of Red Reeder's 12th Infantry, and peppered the 4th Medical Battalion's ambulances with shrapnel. Navy medics organised two beach aid stations, and collected and loaded casualties onto DUKWs, who took them to waiting LSTs for swift return to hospitals in England; prisoners were moved out the same way. In adherence to the finest traditions of his calling, the regimental chaplain of Van Fleet's 8th Infantry, the Reverend Julian S. Ellenberg, strode the Utah sands ministering to the wounded and dying. The former rector of churches in South Carolina was ashore thirty minutes after H-Hour, and during the day established and maintained an aid station under shellfire, at one stage receiving slight wounds from

On Utah, the 2nd Naval Beach Battalion set up two aid stations to treat the wounded then evacuate them as soon as possible. This rare image shows the process: six medics help a wounded paratrooper aboard an LCVP. He will be taken back to either the sick bay of one of the attack transports, an LST converted to accommodate casualties, or one of four hospital ships. The aim was to get him back to England as soon as possible. (NARA)

splinters himself – actions which would earn him a Silver Star.[72] The battalion surgeon, Marion Adair, recalled setting up their aid station together. His first patient 'was a gunshot wound in the mouth. The next had been blown up by a mine and dies' – one for the chaplain.[73]

One of Ellenberg's fellow chaplains, also doing brisk trade in the Utah first-aid stations that morning, was (in another life) a Capuchin friar known to his Manhattan congregation as Father Bruno. On Utah, he had put away his traditional brown habit and hood, and in his adopted olive drab was addressed as Chaplain Luechinger. Lauded by the GIs, his knowledge of the Bible was matched only by his equally extensive knowledge of every possible profanity, an attribute acquired during his ministry in New York, and deployed with devastating effect on the most sceptical of soldiers.[74]

Another of the fifteen chaplains in the 4th Infantry Division was George W. Knapp, from Lenzburg, Illinois, who walked off the ramp of his landing craft holding 'his Field Altar Communion Set in one hand, a bag with his personal effects in the other and a pack and bedroll on his back'. The twenty-seven-year-old Evangelical and Reformed minister was assigned to 'Red' Reeder as the 12th Infantry's chaplain. As a pastor, he was well used to death in the form of neat caskets and flowers. Utah Beach proved to be a rude awakening, never mind that his chaplain's assistant, Harley, was missing for a week with the chaplain's jeep, trailer, field organ and hymn books – they had been commandeered to evacuate the wounded.[75]

'When the shelling stopped, we looked out from our hole. A guy was going berserk, a sad thing to see. He ran around like a chicken with its head cut off. Right then, I made up my mind that I had to get tough, or else I'd crack,' thought Earl R. Schantzenbach, from Upper Bucks County, Pennsylvania. On the beach, the mortar carrier of Company 'H', with Reeder's 12th Infantry, remembered GIs guarding their first German prisoners: 'First thing we did was to dig "buddy holes", six foot deep, two guys to a hole, one guarding while the other slept. Then we advanced through a gap blasted in the dunes, over a causeway, and on the other side there were dead horses, dead cows, and dead people. It was grue-some,' reported Schantzenbach. 'That's when I toughened up.'[76]

Fear was also witnessed by Second Lieutenant William P. 'Bill' Chapman, of Oakland, California, a young officer in the same Company 'H' of Reeder's 12th Infantry. Immediately on landing, one of his men 'just dropped to the sand and curled into a foetal position'. The officer ordered, 'Let's go! Get up!' but the GI just shivered, insensible through fear. He refused to budge, deaf to the officer's urging, despite more artillery rounds bursting around. Chapman was obliged to leave him behind, shepherding the rest of his men away, lest the contagion spread.

This incident not only tested Chapman but was significant because no small arms fire was being directed at them. Bob Meyer, a Browning Automatic Rifleman (BAR) with Company 'G' of the 22nd Infantry, likewise recalled a private who, 'when bullets were flying everywhere, and we were all keeping as low as possible, suddenly stood up and said the only thing I ever heard from him. It was something like "To hell with this!" We watched him disappear over the little hill behind us as he walked back to the beach.'[77] These GIs had gone through a year's basic training and realistic assault exercises in Devon in the company of their buddies, but still fell to pieces immediately. It underlined the point that no one knew how they would react to their first combat. The 4th Division's officers, most of whom had not seen action before, were especially nervous of failing themselves – and their men – at the first whiff of hostile gunfire. Chapman passed the test on D-Day, but not his man, whom he left 'cowering on the beach for the medics to round up'.[78]

As a twenty-four-year-old officer in the 29th Field Artillery, John Ausland – who had landed in the first wave with Van Fleet – was tasked with guiding three artillery batteries to positions preselected in England from a foam rubber relief map of the beach: 'After crossing the sand dunes that lay just beyond the seawall, I was unable to figure out where I was. When I asked an infantry officer to help me, he laughed and said that the Navy had landed the first wave several thousand yards south of where we were supposed to be.'[79]

25

Wet Feet

'The six-wheel-drive Jimmy lurched forward and down the ramp into the water. The front bumper disappeared into the Channel, and seawater rose over the running boards to the bottom of the doors, spilled onto the floor of the cab, and sloshed around the engine crankcase. It seemed like miles to the beach. Sudden flashes lighting the horizon, and followed moments later, by rumblings, reminded him of an approaching storm. The bursts of light came from American and German artillery that boomed at each other.'
David P. Colley, 'A Foothold in Normandy', 1999[1]

To Brigadier General Roosevelt, it did not matter if they were on the wrong beach. 'We'll start the war from right here!' was his verdict. He knew there could be no pause in the momentum.

Instead of making landfall between Exits 3 and 4, the loss of the left-hand guide vessels, haze from the bombing, and a strong current had pushed Van Fleet's assault flotilla south, to land opposite Exits 1 and 2 at La Madeleine, about a mile south of their intended landing area – as George Mabry had noticed. The long, completely featureless stretch of sand added to the confusion, and the attackers' maps and aerial photographs only detailed where they should have been. The paratroops were expecting the 4th Division to land further north, as were successive waves of tanks, engineers and the follow-on 9th, 79th and 90th Divisions, with all their logistics support.

Colonel Van Fleet, the 8th Infantry's commander, had to decide whether to shift the whole axis of VII Corps to conform to Major General

J. Lawton Collins' plan. It was at this point that Roosevelt, who had arrived on Condiotti's LVCP, and with whom Shryock had conversed, stepped forward.

Despite his run-in with Bradley and Patton in 1943 on Sicily, Roosevelt was one of the US Army's most experienced combat officers from both world wars – in 1918 he had received a Distinguished Service Cross, two Silver Stars and France's *Légion d'honneur* serving with the 1st Infantry Division. In the Mediterranean he had earned a further two Silver Stars. Popular and capable, if at times the bane of senior commanders, Bradley and Collins figured his proven calmness under fire, level head and easy-going nature could make a difference if Utah were to prove a tough fight.

They were keen to use his wisdom, but could not transfer him back to his old Big Red One, from whence he had been removed a year earlier. The solution had been to put him into Barton's 4th Infantry Division in February 1944 as assistant divisional commander. The fifty-six-year-old Roosevelt – the oldest American present on 6 June, afflicted with a heart condition (which he concealed) and arthritis caused by a First World War wound, forcing him to rely on a cane at times – insisted on accompanying the first wave, over Barton's objections. As he later told Lieutenant Ausland, 'finding the 101st Airborne had secured the cause-ways off the beach where we'd landed, I figured it would only cause confusion if we moved the whole assault northwards to the correct beach. So we started the war from where we were.'[2]

Barton subsequently recalled coming ashore:

Ted Roosevelt came up. He had landed with the first wave, had put my troops across the beach, and had a perfect picture of the entire situation, just as he had earlier promised if allowed to go ashore with the first wave. I loved Ted. When I finally agreed to his landing with the first wave, I felt sure he would be killed. When I had bade him goodbye, I never expected to see him alive. You can imagine then the emotion with which I greeted him when he came out to meet me. He was bursting with information.[3]

Lieutenant Colonel Teague of the 22nd Infantry understood they were in the wrong place straight away. A topographical engineer by pre-war profession, Teague, who could look at a plan from every angle for about fifteen minutes then issue precise orders, tried to identify his location on the map. 'Standing with my back to the water, looking inland, a little bit to my right front was the little round windmill or silo standing up which I had observed on aerial photographs and panoramic views of the beach before, which gave me the immediate location of where we were. I tried to get higher on the sand dunes, but someone yelled at me that snipers were firing and for me to come down.'[4] What Teague saw was the concrete grain silo of the farm at Les Dunes de Varreville, still in place today. Its current owner, farmer Raymond Bertot, was also living there in 1944, aged nineteen. 'Up here go many Americans. Many!' he recalled of that happy day – even though the shelling had slain his father's cattle. 'They ride big trucks that make dust. They shout "Hiya. *Comment allez-vous?*" Throw me food, gum and cigarettes. Sad they no came back.'[5]

Teague met Roosevelt at about 0930. 'He called me over and told me we had landed way to the left of where we were supposed to have been and wanted this part of the beach cleared as soon as possible. He wanted

The men of the 4th Infantry Division who landed on Utah soon realised they had not disembarked where they planned. Colonel Teague of the 22nd Infantry orientated himself straightaway, noticing 'to my right front was the little round windmill or silo standing up which I had observed on aerial photographs'. Here his men pause underneath the silo at Les Dunes de Varreville, surrounded by cattle killed in the bombardment. The concrete tower remains in situ today, owned by the family of farmer Raymond Bertot, who remembers his liberators arriving when he was a nineteen-year-old. (US Army Signal Corps)

action from my men as soon as I could.'[6] Roosevelt's decision would prove to be the right call, and needed no intervention from Barton, Collins or Bradley, but was not necessarily an easy one to make in the heat of the moment. It was an excellent example of the enlightened decision-making beginning to be practised by the Allies and known these days as 'Mission Command' – Roosevelt's men had achieved the *intent* of a successful landing, if not in strict adherence to the plan. Such a decision in the 1944 Wehrmacht would have needed to be confirmed in Berlin, with all the implicit time delays and lost opportunities. Roosevelt, however, was able to direct the landing to continue where he was, which brought him a second Distinguished Service Cross.

Having made his decision, Roosevelt signalled the following waves to ignore the divisional plan and conform to his movements. Then he walked along the beach, welcoming his men ashore, refusing to flinch under the hot steel sweeping the sands. If there is a common experience to Utah, it appears to be the sight of Roosevelt's cheery demeanour as GIs crossed the shoreline, exhorting all 'not to pause, but move inland, off the beach'. In this, he was really doing the job of Utah's principal beachmaster, naval Captain (equivalent to an army colonel) James R. Arnold, but with considerably more flair and confidence. He was already a familiar face, known as 'General Teddy' to many of those stumbling ashore.

Colonel Reeder described him as 'about five foot nine, with a wiry frame, a leathery face and fun to be with'.[7] He might have added the sunny countenance – for he had a broad grin, evident in every photograph. From mid-morning, Roosevelt had also observed his men were being 'slaughtered on Red beach where the darn Krauts have them bracketed' – this was the Saint-Marcouf battery firing onto the area of Leutnant Jahnke's now-captured W5. With Captain Arnold, he agreed the temporary expedient of diverting disembarkation to the northern Tare Green sector for three hours, as there was 'no use in landing dead men in the suicide area of Red'.[8] Roosevelt was an inspiration to the entire formation, which made him worth many bayonets, and contributed towards his fame.

Harper Coleman, from Tucson, Arizona, a machine-gunner with Company 'H' of Van Fleet's 8th Infantry, recalled,

> As we came in I saw the craft in front of ours going up with some kind of direct hit; something came through the side of ours, in one side and

out the other, taking a good-sized piece of my backpack with it. When we came ashore, we were greeted by General Roosevelt. How he got there, I do not know, but there he was, waving his cane and giving out instructions, as only he could do. If we were afraid of the Germans, we were more afraid of him, and could not have stopped on the beach even if we had wanted to.[9]

Malcom Williams, with the 12th Infantry, was another greeted by Roosevelt with a cheery 'How do you boys like the beach?'[10] Calvin Grose, a combat medic with the 22nd Infantry, had never been under fire before, but likewise recalled the brigadier general 'walking from soldier to soldier, telling them not to lie there in the sand, but get inland'.[11]

The defenders were in disarray, not only because they were overwhelmed, but due to the absence of much of their command element. Generalleutnant von Schlieben of the 709th Division, having motored to Rennes for the war game, recollected 'being awoken in my hotel at 0530 hours to be told the *kriegsspiel* has been cancelled. Return to your division immediately. From the Rennes *Kommandantur*, Major Messerschmidt of the *Storm-Battalion* brought word the invasion had started at 0100 hours. We left straight away.' Skirting gun battles with paratroopers in the Cotentin and picking up a wounded man on the way, Schlieben did not reach his headquarters at the Château de Chiffrevast, north of Valognes, until after midday. Only then did he discover that his fellow general, Wilhelm Falley, was already dead.[12]

Still managing to inflict damage on the beaches were the gun batteries at Crisbecq – also known as Saint-Marcouf – and nearby Azeville, which would remain unsubdued for several days, despite air and naval attack. The former was commanded by Oberleutnant zur See Walter Ohmsen, with three hundred naval gunners at his disposal. For ground defence he also had a company of Schlieben's 709th, led by Oberleutnant Geissler – whose men had heard the croaking frogs in the nearby marshes and captured twenty US paratroops. Schlieben's artillery commander, Oberst Gerhard Triepel, noted how early on 6 June, the Saint-Marcouf naval battery 'opened fire on a small cruiser and sank it' – this was the USS *Corry*; it most probably sank the *PC-1261* control launch and other landing craft as well.[13] The Marcouf guns had been heavily targeted by aircraft before D-Day and during the early morning – curiously without effect.

On 6 June it was engaged from 0555 hours by fourteen-inch weapons of USS *Nevada* and eight-inchers of the cruisers *Tuscaloosa* and *Quincy*. The reason for the pre-emptive saturation bombing was Saint-Marcouf's three 210mm (8.3-inch) cannon, two of which were housed in ten-foot-thick reinforced concrete casemates. The precision Czech-designed guns had a range of twenty miles, from which they could reach the western edge of Omaha – this put most of the US Western Task Force in acute danger. At Azeville, Hauptmann Dr Hugo Treiber's four 105mm cannon had a more modest range of seven miles, but were still lethal on the sands of Utah. Treiber and his garrison of 170 also managed to escape unscathed, despite all the bombs and shells hurled at their position.

At around 0800, USS *Nevada* knocked out one of Saint-Marcouf's guns and destroyed a second an hour later; yet the resourceful Ohmsen had the first repaired and back in action on 8 June. The third gun was directed not at the ships but from 1100 hours at Jahnke's W5, which Ohmsen knew to have been captured – hence Roosevelt and Captain Arnold's decision to switch unloading from Uncle Red, 'where they were being slaughtered', to Tare Green. Apart from killing and wounding GIs, the Marcouf gun also managed to injure Jahnke, waiting to be evacuated with other POWs: 'A shell fragment tore open his side. His uniform turned red. His American guard crawled out of his foxhole, applied a gauze bandage and tossed him a cigarette.' At this stage Roosevelt strode up, Jahnke staggered to his feet to salute his opponent, but Roosevelt, angered by the shelling, did not return the compliment, instead ordering, 'Get the Germans out of here!'[14] Jahnke and his comrades were quickly bundled onto landing craft for passage to England. The capture of both Marcouf and Azeville on 6 June had been assigned to the 22nd Infantry, which found progress slower than anticipated, with the result that it attacked neither objectives on D-Day. In fact, it would take until the ninth to subdue both positions with formal battalion assaults, aided by tanks.

Another GI whom Roosevelt greeted on the sand was Colonel 'Red' Reeder, at the head of his 12th Infantry. 'I'll stand at the front ramp with Colonel Montelbano [a battalion commander who was killed on D+5] so I can be first out of this thing,' said Reeder to the LCVP sailor who offered him an elevated perch at the back of the craft. He had always understood that a leader needed to be up front. 'That decision saved my life. When the boat grated on the Normandy shore at about

1030 hours, I stepped into waist-high water and ran up the beach while light artillery sprayed the sands with iron. A shell hit the LCVP and killed the young sailor, his coxswain, and the last 12th Infantryman leaving the boat.'[15]

Reeder's lucky escape was a reminder that most injuries on Utah were caused by shells rather than bullets. The aerial and naval bombardment had not subdued the guns inland, despite the impressive tonnages hurled at them. As well as USS *Corry*, the official record shows three LCTs and one LCF (flak barge) succumbing out to sea on 6 June with the minesweeper USS *Tide*, another two LCTs and an LCI on the 7th – by any stretch of the imagination, an incredibly low casualty rate. In several government histories there is confusion as to what sank several of these vessels: often mines were attributed, when clear eyewitness testimony pointed the finger at short batteries. The patient researcher is left with an impression of official reluctance to acknowledge that the bombers and battleships were unable to suppress the intrepid German gunners.

Reeder stormed ashore with his men, having told them, 'I will be up front with you. I'm going to carry a bolt-action 1903 rifle because I want the Germans to think I'm a private. Oh, they'll shoot at you fellows, but they'd much rather hit a non-com or an officer.'[16] He had correctly foreseen that the major problem in Normandy once the GIs had advanced inland would be snipers. Some would be do-or-die Nazis, but many were lost or disorganised Wehrmacht troopers, expecting to fire a few rounds then surrender. Sharpshooters have always made it their business to select high-value targets, so the trick of passing himself off as a humble rifleman was a logical one for Reeder, but it also kept him close to his men. In combat, good leaders and followers need to be able to watch and assess each other, correcting any faults as they go.

Meanwhile, Lieutenant Colonel John C. Welborn's 70th Tank Battalion had landed its armour in the first three waves, Companies 'A' and 'B' swimming ashore, and Lieutenant John L. Ahearn's 'C', equipped with sixteen regular Shermans, four with dozer blades, disembarking from LCTs. 'We dropped our screen and headed for the seawall,' remembered one Company 'B' tank commander. 'Engineers were carrying maybe fifty pounds of TNT on their backs, in half-pound blocks, each the size of a farmer's salt-lick. They made a pyramid of them against the seawall and set it off, blowing out a big hole. One of our dozers was there moving concrete around. We went over chunks of concrete and onto a causeway that went through a flooded swamp.'[17]

Colonel Welborn was an old friend of Roosevelt's, with whom the 70th had served in Sicily when the latter was at the US 1st Division. It was Roosevelt who insisted the battle-hardened 70th be attached to the inexperienced 4th Infantry Division for D-Day, a happy solution which – unusually for an independent tank battalion – would last until the war's end. The 746th Tank Battalion also started to land from 0845 hours, and it is worth observing that these two armour battalions provided the only tank reinforcement available to the 4th Infantry and the 82nd and 101st Airborne Divisions for the first six days in the Cotentin, with the result that tanks were often not available when needed and used sparingly when they were.[18]

Company 'C's Lieutenant Ahearn, a New Yorker from Brooklyn, led the attacks on Arthur Jahnke's pillboxes at W5 and those of W3 beyond, then provided flank support for troops moving down Exit 2. With some of Van Fleet's 8th Infantry, the tank–infantry team then pushed south along the beach, parallel to the sea wall, towards Exit 1 and Pouppeville. On the way Ahearn's tank – named *California Bomb* – was disabled by a mine; he inadvertently stepped on another while trying to rescue a wounded GI he had spotted in another, known minefield. Not long afterwards a medical platoon commander, Lieutenant Eliot L. Richardson, came across the badly injured Ahearn, legs mangled, moaning in agony.

Richardson picked him up and carried him to safety, noting the artillery fire on the causeway had suddenly ceased. This puts Ahearn's rescue at 0830 hours. The silence had been caused by Richard Winters and his band destroying the German 105s at Brécourt Manor. Richardson recalled that although he wore a red cross on his helmet and a Red Cross armband, 'that didn't keep me from getting fired at. They were the most intense experiences of my life. I thought I was going to be killed. It burned into me a disposition to push aside fear and take one thing at a time.' Ahearn was nominated for a Medal of Honor and received a Distinguished Service Cross, Richardson the Bronze Star.[19]

Lieutenant Ausland, who had accompanied Van Fleet ashore, had been looking for firing positions for the three batteries of his 29th Field Artillery Battalion. On telling his CO he could find only two, 'as calmly as if we were on an exercise, the colonel said, "it's alright. We'll only need two. Battery 'B' hit a mine on the way in and the landing craft sank." Before I could think too long about the sixty men on the boat, he told me to get moving and guide the other batteries to their firing positions.'[20]

'The landing barge on which I was riding struck a mine, blowing up the vessel and tossing men and equipment into the sea,' recounted one of his men in Battery 'C', Thomas H. Hawk of Lehighton, Pennsylvania. 'It was only because I had on a Mae West life jacket that I was able to swim to shore. We were about a hundred yards from the beach and the water was quite deep. If it had not been for the life jacket, I could never had gotten to shore because of the heavy pack I was carrying,' Hawk explained. 'Fortunately, only two of our men lost their lives, but when the barge transporting Battery 'B' hit their mine, around seventy-five percent were killed.' Days later, Hawk's duffel bag, lost in the sinking, was washed ashore and found by a British soldier. Inside he found photographs of Hawk's wife with her address on the back and, thinking the artilleryman had drowned, sent her the photos with a gentle note explaining how he had come by them. It took a month for the family to unscramble the mess and discover Hawk was in fact alive.[21]

George Mabry, with Van Fleet's 8th Infantry, had meanwhile moved to the south-west of Uncle Red, towards Exit 1, and tagged onto a squad from Company 'G', following them over the sea wall and through a fence. Their sergeant, a red-headed fellow Mabry recognised, triggered a mine which felled them, but Mabry, unscathed, ran on through the dunes and under rifle fire. He noted: 'I was in a minefield. The wind had blown away the sand and uncovered some of them,' but he continued his one-man advance in short rushes from dune to dune. 'I jumped up and ran directly toward the Germans. Apparently, I startled them.' He shot a soldier about to lob a grenade at him and nine others surrendered. 'After corralling them in a group, I glanced over my shoulder. Through a gap in the dunes a vast panorama lay before me; it was an incredible mass of ships of all sizes that choked the Channel, as far as the eye could see. Now I understood why the Germans had surrendered so readily.'

Moving further inland, Mabry teamed up with other GIs and attacked more pillboxes, one with the aid of a passing 70th Battalion Sherman. Eventually they reached the causeway of Exit 1, and advancing up it at a little bridge just before Pouppeville, they met Germans running towards them whom they realised were being pursued by M1 rifle fire.

I pulled out my square of orange cloth, which identified us as allies, and hoisted it on a stick. A few more rifle bullets cracked around, but then an orange flag waved back and forth from beyond the bridge. An airborne soldier, Lieutenant Luther Knowlton, of the Third Battalion, 501st Parachute Infantry, jumped over a hedgerow and greeted me as if he had not seen an American for years.

He said General Taylor would certainly be glad to see me.[22]

George E. Koskimaki, who had been trying to wrest control of Pouppeville from its German garrison, recalled the elation when the friendly armour 'poked their way through the streets. One paratrooper rushed forth and planted a kiss on the first tank.'[23] It was just before 1100 hours. The link-up between airborne and seaborne invaders had been accomplished.

As Colonel Reeder scrambled up the beach with his 12th Regiment, he had already worked out that the landings were happening too far south. He immediately encountered Roosevelt leaning on his cane by Exit 2 – the only one open to vehicles at that moment – exclaiming, 'Red, the causeway is all clogged up, a procession of jeeps and not a wheel turning.' With northern Exits 3 and 4 not yet open, much of the division had converged on Exit 2. Reeder knew not to hang around. 'It don't matter. We know where to go!' was his practical response – and turning to his regiment yelled, 'We're going through the flooded area.' They followed the white tapes laid by engineers marking safe paths through the dunes to the edge of the marshland. Reeder recalled the church steeple in Saint-Martin-de-Varreville 'looking like a friendly beacon', as they waded through the German-made lake, 'which varied in depth from waist to arm-pit and in a few spots, over our heads. We had the non-swimmers paired with the swimmers, and even so, I was proud of the non-swimmers around me who were holding onto their weapons. The large groups of men in the water made a perfect target', but they splashed across safely.[24]

Second Lieutenant Bill Chapman of Company 'H' recalled his anxiety that gasoline might have been dumped into the marsh, that 'twelve square miles might explode into flames at the touch of a match, turning the watery obstacle into a fiery death trap'.[25] Private Lindley Higgins was a Company 'L' man who also waded into the morass. On the beach he had accidentally inflated his Mae West, but the intense pressure on his chest had caused him to slash the offending life jacket with his bayonet. In the marsh, he rather wished he had kept it. The water soaked all his possessions, including a whole carton of Lucky Strikes he had stowed in his invasion jacket.[26]

Issued as the 'assault vest', this garment was a special Overlord-only design; it had been rushed into production in early 1944 and shipped to England for distribution just before embarkation. Thought to be an ideal way to carry any extra ammunition and equipment, the Brit, Canadian and US assault troops found it heavy, hot and cumbersome to wear. When wet, the quick-release straps were hard to undo, and it was undoubtedly the cause of many drownings as men struggled in the surf with the extra weight. Another remembered of the special tunic, 'It was just the assault wave that had them, but it was a specially made jacket. It had no sleeves, and snap fasteners with a quick release; you could pull it off. It had a lot of pockets, and in the back it had a big pocket for things. We ditched them after the first day; it was just to get on the beach with all of the stuff you have to carry.'[27]

With Company 'K', PFC William Garvin of Epping, New Hampshire, remembered being faced by 'the miles of inundated terrain with deep irrigation trenches every two hundred yards. We had kept our Mae West life-jackets which proved a tremendous aid while floundering across the flooded land, weighed down with our heavy fighting gear. After sloshing and hand-paddling for about one and a half hours, we breathed easier on reaching high ground, and began to see evidence of savage fighting. Torn parachutes hung from trees and shattered buildings indicated where fierce combat had occurred.'[28]

They reached the far side at around 1300 hours, entering the domain of the airborne formations – though they had yet to encounter any friendly paratroops. The unimpeded advance proved that the flooded areas were only a deterrent for wheeled transport and would not stop men. As with any hindrance, the marsh would slow down but not stop the GIs, unless it was covered by fire – but, incredibly, the Germans had fled. The confusion wrought by the paratroops had served its purpose. Once across the marsh, Reeder ordered his men west towards Beuzeville-au-Plain. For the first time, the 4th Division entered hedgerow country, the bocage banks of earth, stones and trees that had grown over the centuries to surround each field. Around this time, they began to encounter small squads of the 502nd Parachute Infantry from the 101st Airborne, and men from the 82nd, constituting the second link-up of the air- and sea-delivered invaders.

Rommel had invested much time in creating his defences at the expense of military training for his troops. The most his obstructions could hope to achieve would be to canalise the Allies into killing areas. However, dynamic leadership from the likes of Roosevelt, Reeder and Mabry – they were all cast from the same mould – saw no impediments and ploughed straight through the obstacle belts, shredding Rommel's plans. The German field marshal might just have kept his troops doing useful military training for all the difference 'Rommel's asparagus' made. Reeder typified the fighting spirit of the US Army, was a fearless, natural-born leader, a great observer of soldiers and full of common sense. A self-confessed 'army brat who had grown up on a series of military outposts across the United States', he had earlier analysed the American experience in the Pacific, writing *Fighting on Guadalcanal*, of which over a million copies were distributed to US servicemen. It was his idea to institute the Bronze Star, officially established by Executive Order on 4 February 1944.

Reeder's troops lionised him: 'mostly he did his colonel-ing at point-blank range, in the forward-most Normandy hedgerow. There was no bravado about it. All good colonels do the same. It's the quickest way to get battle information, and it's good for morale if the leader has the knack of radiating confidence,' wrote one of his friends. One of his GIs, a Browning Automatic Rifleman, Private Walter Mills, of East Lynn, West Virginia, said that 'He took steps that were thirty feet long.'[29] Not surprisingly, fate caught up with Reeder five days into the campaign on 11 June, when an eighty-eight felled him. 'Lightning Joe' Collins pinned the first Distinguished Service Cross awarded in Normandy to his blanket as Reeder was airlifted home; a leg was later amputated, otherwise he would certainly have been commanding an infantry division by the war's end. Instead, Reeder found another role, teaching tactics and athletics at West Point, which is where I met him in 1979 on an exchange visit from Sandhurst. Allegedly retired, he still had a commanding presence; meeting him left one breathless. He had transferred his energy to teaching and writing: he had twenty-five books to his name by that stage – and he was still imparting the wisdom of the bocage to the post-Vietnam generation of young leaders.[30]

Pushing out from Tare Green to the north-west, Colonel Hervey Tribolet's 22nd Infantry had the misfortune to come up against a series of toughly defended locales. As Lieutenant Colonel Teague's Third Battalion was pushing north along the beach, it

ran across a little fortification on the seawall. The Germans were firing down the beach and I could see these shots were hitting in the water. Some skimmed the tops of our heads and some hit small boats. One of our tanks came up and got fired on and hit by small-caliber guns. It was then that we noticed a small steel turret mounted on top of a pillbox behind the wall. Our tank was about twenty-five yards away, but it immediately elevated its guns and opened fire, knocking the turret completely off the little fortification. Here we got quite a few more prisoners.

As his men progressed up the beach from bunker to bunker, 'one of our men with a flame thrower ran about twenty-five Germans out of a pillbox and took two American paratroopers from that same pillbox' – a reminder that several 101st paratroopers had come down in the inundated area and were being held captive, like the ones Arthur Jahnke had taken and those captured by Oberleutnant Grieg at the Saint-Marcouf battery.[31]

However, some positions along the coast and the Crisbecq and Saint-Marcouf batteries remained unsubdued by the paratroopers or the 22nd Infantry. By nightfall, Tribolet's Third Battalion had reached Les Cruttes along the coast, north of Exit 4. The following day the rest of the 22nd Infantry would join up with the airborne forces in Ravenoville, as noted by Donald R. Burgett:

> There were some rumours going around that the beach landings had been repulsed and that we were stranded here to fight it out as best we could. Just before the cold light of dawn, we saw a sight that I will never forget – American infantry coming up the hill through the hedgerows. Glider boots, canvas leggings worn by the infantry and glider men, never looked so good before. There were ten of us from the 101st and a lieutenant and two men from the 82nd, thirteen men left out of the original twenty-two who had entered the town.[32]

One of the 22nd's rising officers was Major John Dowdy, from Telfair County, Georgia, whom we met being defeated by a kippered herring during his rough Atlantic crossing and was executive officer of the Second Battalion. By D+3 he would find himself CO of the First Battalion, his predecessor having fallen, and immediately winning a Distinguished Service Cross for capturing the Quinéville ridge.[33] Dowdy was up against one of Arthur Jahnke's colleagues, Leutnant Meidam, who had moved his 4th Company of the 919th *Grenadier-Regiment* into the nearby Quinéville strongpoint and held out for several days, before being reduced, bunker by bunker, until lack of weapons and food compelled their surrender.

From light casualties on D-Day itself, the dreadful turnover of officer casualties that afflicted the 4th Division – caused by the unforgiving bocage – had begun. Another young leader with Tribolet's 22nd was a platoon commander with Company 'C', Second Lieutenant Preston Niland, from Tonawanda, New York. His three brothers were also in the US forces, two of them in Normandy. Sergeant Frederick 'Fritz' Niland, the baby of the four, was a 101st paratrooper who had dropped into Raffoville, near Carentan, with Company 'H', 501st Parachute Infantry. Robert, an 82nd Airborne trooper, had parachuted into Neuville-au-Plain, with Company 'D', 505th Parachute Infantry. The two middle brothers, Preston and Robert, had enlisted prior to the beginning of the war; the fourth brother, Edward, the oldest Niland, was a B-25 pilot who had been reported missing presumed killed over Burma on 16 May 1944.[34]

The Irish-American Nilands came from a tradition of military service: their grandfather, Michael, had fought with Teddy Roosevelt (later president and father of the brigadier general) and his Rough Riders in the Spanish–American War; an uncle had served in the First World War. Born in 1912–20, the brothers were intelligent and resourceful and would have had a lot to offer America had they all lived: one became a bomber pilot, another an infantry officer, and two, paratrooper sergeants – all military roles requiring aptitude beyond the norm. However, Robert died on D-Day at Neuville manning a machine-gun, covering his platoon's withdrawal towards Sainte-Mère-Église; the following day Preston was killed by a sniper during his battalion's unsuccessful attack on the Saint-Marcouf guns.[35]

When Father Francis L. Sampson, chaplain of the 501st Parachute Infantry, learned that two of Fritz Niland's brothers had fallen in battle, with a third presumed dead in Burma, he initiated the process to send the youngest and last Niland brother home. The order would come through just before Operation Market Garden; Fritz initially refused to comply, stating that 'he was ready to be taken back in handcuffs, as he wanted to stay and fight', and later told his family that it took a Congressional Order to force him out of Europe. There was no drama, no rescue mission. The story, of course with a little help from Steven Spielberg, became the basis for *Saving Private Ryan*, the movie that changed the world's perception of D-Day in 1998, just as *The Longest*

Day had done in 1962. Fritz Niland sounded confusingly German, so Spielberg instead enlisted the surname of the man who had started the whole D-Day industry – Cornelius Ryan.

We have already tracked some of the frantic messages between German headquarters that began in the small hours, reacting to the presence of Allied paratroopers. From these General Erich Marcks concluded the invasion was beginning and persuaded Seventh Army to issue an invasion warning at 0200 hours. Alert and monitoring the command frequencies, Rundstedt's headquarters in Paris actually ordered Panzer Lehr and 12th SS Divisions ready to move at 0400, which would have seen them in the beachhead area on D-Day.

However, because of the Rommel–Geyr acrimony over control of the panzers, all movements of armour were subject to Berlin's approval, which was not forthcoming (for fear that Normandy was a feint) until much later in the day. When, despite Rundstedt's request, Alfred Jodl at OKW refused to release the panzer divisions without higher sanction, Rundstedt became exceptionally bitter at what he perceived as a slight to the Third Reich's senior Field Marshal. When Blumentritt urged his boss to phone Hitler direct, Rundstedt let pride overcome him and refused to beg before 'that Bohemian Corporal'.

With Rommel away, his chief of staff, Hans Speidel, seems to have dithered also, but for different reasons. The evening before had seen him host a dinner party that included the celebrated writer Ernst Jünger (a former stormtrooper who, like Rommel, had been awarded the *Pour le Mérite* during the First World War). After the war, Speidel's reluctance to act was put down to his anti-Nazi sympathies – for Jünger and the others dining at La Roche-Guyon on 5 June were all opponents of the regime.

Yet Speidel was a bureaucrat and a staff officer, not a mover or shaker like Rommel, and his initial sluggishness of response was more likely due to a hangover than to politics. He retired at midnight, to be contacted at 0615 by the Seventh Army's chief-of-staff, Max Pemsel, with reports of a naval bombardment. At about this time, Speidel phoned the news through to Rommel that something was afoot. Awake at this early hour in Herrlingen, near Ulm in south western Germany, the Army Group 'B' commander was preparing his wife's birthday presents when he took the call. Both seem to have concluded the Allies were mounting nothing more than another Dieppe-style raid.

The phone logs at Seventh Army HQ and La Roche-Guyon show that Pemsel called Speidel back at 0910 hours to report actual landings on the Calvados beaches and the two discussed countermeasures for about thirty minutes. Meanwhile, Allied journalists had been summoned to the University of London's Macmillan Hall where at 0933 (0333 hours in New York) Colonel R. Ernest Dupuy, Eisenhower's press officer, rose to announce that the invasion was in progress. Both King George VI and President Roosevelt called their nations to prayer. This was when – through the length and breadth of Britain – churches threw open their doors and shipyard workers in Brooklyn spontaneously knelt down on the decks of partially completed vessels to recite the Lord's Prayer.

In Berlin, Marie 'Missie' Vassiltchikov, an exiled Russian princess working in the German Foreign Ministry, recorded in her diary, 'The long-awaited 'D-Day'! The Allies have landed in Normandy. We had been told so much about the famous *Atlantikwall* and its supposedly impregnable defences; now we shall see!'[36] Another diarist in the capital was the journalist Ursula von Kardorff who noted, 'The invasion began today. Great excitement at the office. Our directive was to write pieces greeting this long-awaited event with positive pleasure. Hurrah! Here it comes at last! Now we'll show them, and throw them all back into the sea! At last final victory approaches! People very much doubt whether the *Atlantikwall* will hold.'[37]

The scepticism of both writers betrays that fact that they were close to the anti-Hitler Stauffenberg conspiracy. The following morning the *Volkischer Beobachter*, the Nazi Party's daily newspaper screamed in red-coloured banner headlines, *Invasion setzte zwischen Cherbourg und Le Havre auf Moskaus Befehl ein. So begann die Schlacht im Western.* ('Invasion begun between Cherbourg and Le Havre on Moscow's orders. So begins the struggle in the West').

Hitler was in far-off Berchtesgaden, and had actually been awake when the first reports started to trickle through, but wasn't told and turned in at around 0300. His military adjutants struggled to make sense of the information coming through SS, Luftwaffe, Kriegsmarine and army channels in France. No one knew if this was the real thing, a raid, or a feint, and given the Führer's tendency towards histrionics, they hesitated to wake him, trading time for a clearer picture. Propaganda Minister Josef Goebbels, also in Berchtesgaden, confided to his diary that the landings came as no surprise. He had received word via one of the Reich's many intelligence services of the BBC broadcasts putting the French

Resistance on standby.[38] In the meantime, Berlin had even reprimanded Rundstedt for issuing preliminary orders to panzer units without prior approval. Hitler was eventually awakened around noon and told the news. He was neither depressed nor flew into a rage, but exuded confidence that his troops would prevail, though it was only at the lunchtime military conference that he agreed to release the two panzer divisions requested by Rundstedt since four that morning.

Rommel, meanwhile, had taken a second phone call from Speidel at 1015. According to his son Manfred, his operations staff officer Hans-Georg von Tempelhof, and Helmuth Lang, the *Generalfeldmarschall* was tending his wife's roses. The colour apparently drained from his face as Speidel relayed the news that a major landing was being attempted. For a second time the Desert Fox had been caught away on leave when Montgomery attacked – the first occasion was Alamein in 1942. Leaving around 1100, Rommel began the long return journey to France with Tempelhof and Lang, but had over five hundred miles to reach La Roche-Guyon.

With Oberfeldwebel Daniel at the wheel, his powerful Horch raced through towns, scattering pedestrians, horn blaring. At 1800 hours they paused briefly in Rheims, where Rommel spoke to Speidel for fifteen minutes before carrying on. Lang noted his boss was quiet and grim-faced. After a little over ten hours on the road, burning rubber, their tyres finally threw up the gravel by the front entrance of the Rochefoucauld château at around 2100 hours. Tired after a long journey with the Army Group 'B' commander 'repeatedly driving his right fist into his left hand', Lang was incredulous to find Speidel calmly listening to opera music. 'Do you believe my listening to Wagner will make any difference to the invasion?' Speidel somewhat frivolously replied when reproached by Tempelhof and Lang.

To the south east of Utah, a great contest developed for Saint-Côme-du-Mont, astride the *Route Nationale* 13. In Périers, Major von der Heydte, ensconced in his HQ at the *Hôtel de Ville*, was aware that controlling the little town would dominate both the main road running north to Cherbourg, and entry to the route centre of Carentan. When reports came in of airborne landings, he despatched one of his three *Fallschirmjäger* battalions to Saint-Côme. A second was sent north across the N.13 to link up with the Georgians in Turqueville, and a third to Sainte-Marie-du-Mont. On his way he absorbed two batteries of the 91st

Luftlande's artillery, one of flak guns and a battalion of the 1058th Grenadiers – a ready-made battlegroup of the kind Heydte had frequently commanded in Russia and Italy.

It was at 0300 hours that the *Flugwachkommando* (Aviation Report Centre) in Caen belatedly sent him a *Fallschirmalarm* (paratrooper alert) – but by then Heydte was already in the thick of his battles. This was the moment when he drove forward, climbed the church tower of Sainte-Marie-du-Mont, and became the first senior German officer to witness the seaborne landings in full swing. Also worthy of note, this resourceful individual was leading a regiment of three battalions, recorded as 3,457 men strong, plus reinforcements, while still a major.[39] The opposing Allied forces would normally have assigned such a responsibility to a colonel or a brigadier general.

It was Heydte's northern battalion with attachments, plus some StuG III assault guns, which he threw against the southern and western edges of Sainte-Mère-Église without success throughout 6 June. Early on the seventh, Heydte's battalion despatched to Sainte-Marie-du-Mont was annihilated by the paratroopers and Barton's 4th Division it had not expected to encounter. The *Fallschirmjägers* sent to Sainte-Mère-Église likewise fell back down the N.13 and slowly Heydte would be forced back into Carentan, which the remnants of his regiment would defend until they abandoned it on the twelfth. Opposing Heydte, by the end of 6 June, were five battalions of the 101st, two artillery battalions, and Company 'D' of M5 Stuarts from the 70th Tank Battalion – the latter landing from the sea – which had collected around the town. On 7 June, as the leading M5 Stuart tank nosed its way out of Saint-Côme heading for the N.13 into Carentan, it was hit by a well-aimed *Fallschirmjäger* anti-tank round. Its commander failed to exit in time and hung dead from his turret for several days. Thus the junction became 'Dead Man's Corner', the name now adopted by the war museum that stands on the same spot.

Initially Rommel despatched the 77th Infantry Division, stationed around Saint-Malo, to block any link-up of the Utah and Omaha forces. On inspecting a VII Corps battle plan recovered near Utah Beach, which suggested Collins' main effort was Cherbourg, Rommel diverted the 77th to the port and brought up the inexperienced 17th *SS-Panzergrenadier* Division to plug the Utah–Omaha gap around Carentan. Whereas the 77th might have succeeded, the SS formation, long on fanaticism but short on combat experience, were pushed back by the combined efforts of the 101st Airborne and US 2nd Armoured Divisions on 13 June.

Heydte's *Fallschirmjäger* fought hard on D-Day but sustained huge casualties. Here one of his battalion commanders, identifiable by his collar patch, awaits interment. The dead were not often photographed in Normandy, but this unique image survives as testimony to the ferocity of the fighting. The fallen of both sides were usually piled high and transported to temporary cemeteries, their details recorded, and quickly buried. (US Army Signal Corps)

A furious Gruppenführer Werner Ostendorff, commanding the 17th SS, refused to accept the limitations of his own division, and had Heydte arrested in an attempt to shift the blame. The latter was fortunate that his *Fallschirmjäger* boss, Eugen Meindl, was in temporary command of the sector, following Erich Marcks' death in an air attack the day before, and able to intervene and halt the nonsense, but it revealed the bad blood that bubbled beneath the surface between the Luftwaffe and the Waffen-SS. For VII Corps this was a turning point, as it removed any further threats to the Utah beachhead, leaving Collins free to concentrate on the capture of Cherbourg.

By the end of D-Day, all the southern strongpoints along the coast, W1 to W10, had fallen. Trying to contain Barton's 4th Division were Heydte's 6th *Fallschirmjäger* Regiment to the south; to the west lay the

1057th *Grenadier-Regiment* (of the 91st *Luftlande* Division), but with paratroopers of the 82nd and 101st all over them. Additionally, Hauptmann Stiller's 795th Georgian Battalion – the divisional reserve of the 91st – was holed up in Turqueville and refusing to give ground. Stiller was later described by his hosts in the château at Beuzeville: 'It was about noon when a soldier with a flat, Asian face handed the captain a paper, then was sent away with a friendly tap on the shoulder. Stiller stood, officer's cap on his head, thinking hard. He poured himself a glass of cider, cried out "To your health!" went toward the door, unarmed, riding crop in hand, half turned and said "Good-bye, Sirs" then disappeared. His body was never found.'[40]

In the north, the 1058th *Grenadier-Regiment* of the 91st Division, with units from the 243rd Division and elements of Hugo Messerschmidt's *Sturmbataillon* – the former Seventh Army Battle School – were endeavouring to block any move towards Cherbourg, the former including the reluctant Grenadiers Ernst Flöter, Paul Golz and Franz Roggenbuck from Pomerania. Throughout the evening of 6 June, they were aided in battling Tribolet's 22nd Infantry by several intact strongpoints along the coast. Some Germans lost heart at the sight of further airborne reinforcements arriving by glider at dusk.

If nothing else, this confirmed the overwhelming material superiority of the Allies, as well as their control of the skies. From about 2100 hours onwards, an initial wave of fifty-four Horsas and twenty-two Wacos with 437 troops, sixty-four vehicles, thirteen anti-tank guns and twenty-four tons of supplies landed; they were followed by another eighty-six Horsas and fourteen Wacos, with still more arriving later. However, for Heydte's enterprising *Fallschirmjägers* – who benefited equally from the timely arrival of a free grocery store of medicines, Hershey bars, Camels and Lucky Strikes, Carnation canned milk and Nescafé coffee powder – captured gliders brought them delights unknown in the Reich, and a boost to their morale.

Providing immediate protection from aerial attack were various anti-aircraft artillery units – and 150 men of Battery 'B' of the 320th Barrage Balloon Battalion, who set up their VLA (Very Low Altitude) inflatables to deter German aircraft. Raised at Camp Tyson, Tennessee, in 1942, the 320th was the only all-black combat unit to take part in the D-Day landings. Their sister Battery, 'A', landed simultaneously at Omaha. A glimpse at any pictures of the beaches will show their handiwork. Each battery deployed up to forty-five of the hydrogen-filled, bullet-shaped gasbags, made of two-ply rubberised cotton and coated with aluminium. They were raised mostly at night, but could be put into the air whenever an air raid sounded in less than a minute.

It would take until 1948 for President Harry S. Truman to issue Executive Order No. 9981, abolishing racial discrimination in the military. Until then, Battery 'B' would remain a segregated unit, alongside

Immediately after the Utah beach area was secured, 150 men of Battery 'B' of the 320th Barrage Balloon Battalion, began to fly their VLA (Very Low Altitude) inflatables to deter German aircraft. The battalion (whose Battery 'A' simultaneously arrived at Omaha) was the only all-black combat unit to land on D-Day landings. (NARA)]

the 582nd Engineer Dump Truck, 385th Quartermaster Truck, and 226th, 227th, 228th and 229th Port Companies which comprised the 1,200 African-American GIs who landed at Utah.[41]

With the infantry forging inland, Utah became a showcase for the engineering skills of the US Army. After obstacle-clearing, they needed to build roads through the sands with steel matting, drain the marshes beyond, and repair bridges and culverts. Until the Mulberry harbour at Omaha was opened or Cherbourg captured, all the logistical needs of VII Corps and its successor formations would arrive through Utah Beach. However, less than half of the road-building equipment anticipated arrived on D-Day: twelve LCTs were scheduled, but only five appeared on the afternoon tide; German shells hit three of the others. Many vehicles – including some of their own – drowned when disembarked into water too deep, and recovering submerged trucks and jeeps was probably the major engineering task on D-Day, as well as keeping the sand clear of wrecked vehicles and landing craft.

All of this, as with every other activity on the beach, was conducted under artillery fire – which accounted for twenty-one killed and ninety-six wounded in the 1st Engineer Special Brigade. However, they had overseen the arrival on D-Day of exactly 21,328 men, 1,742 vehicles and 1,695 tons of materiel.[42] Their memorial lies amid the cluster of commemorative stonework at the main Utah Beach museum site, all the roads in the vicinity being named after the forty-three men, attached or under command, who were killed during the Normandy Campaign. One name is missing – that of their commander on D-Day, Brigadier General James E. Wharton, who went on to become assistant divisional commander of the 9th Infantry Division. On the day he was promoted to lead the 28th Division, 12 August, Wharton was most unlucky to be shot and killed by a sniper while inspecting the forward units of his new command.

The overall casualty count for Utah on D-Day is unclear. The traditional narrative is that the losses were under two hundred – incredibly light. Barton's 4th Infantry Division as a whole noted 197 casualties for the day, including sixty missing from Battery 'B', 29th Field Artillery Battalion. This also encompassed the 118 recorded wounded, twelve of them fatalities, suffered by the 8th and 22nd Infantry Regiments. However, this account has observed deaths amongst US Navy landing craft crews, accompanying warships and obstacle demolition teams – who lost six killed, eleven wounded, to which must be added US Coast Guard and Royal Navy personnel. Several USAAF and RAF aircraft flying over-head were also lost, including troop carriers, bombers and fighters.

Besides Barton's division, elements of the 359th Infantry, the 65th Armored Field Artillery, 87th Chemical Mortar, 899th Tank Destroyer and 70th (who lost three killed, two wounded) and 746th Tank Battalions also made it ashore to Utah on 6 June and took casualties. If the two airborne divisions are included in the Utah totals – not an unreasonable proposition, for they helped open the beach, and some actions, such as the capture of Pouppeville and the 'WXYZ' barracks, were accomplished by a mix of land and airborne forces – then the totals alter radically. The D-Day airborne count was 2,499 casualties, including 238 killed. Finally, what of the VII Corps Exercise Tiger, with its 946 killed and missing, or those seamen who died on 5 June as Neptune began, such as the six on USS *Osprey*? We have seen how some other pre-D-Day deaths were incorporated into the 6 June casualties, so there might be a valid argument to include some of them under the Utah totals, too.

Recording casualties was often secondary to combat operations, with units not filing casualty returns until 8 June; some troops became casualties on D-Day but died only subsequently; while those listed as missing were declared dead only on 7 June 1945, because US soldiers missing in action are officially deceased after a year and a day. Since 2000, Carol Tuckwiller at the National D-Day Memorial Foundation in Bedford, Virginia, has been computing the number of Allied *soldiers* who died on D-day, and has so far identified at least 4,413, a significant increase on the oft-cited figure of around 2,500 killed.[43] One thing, therefore, remains certain: the traditional Utah casualty count is far too low, and may, irrespective of Exercise Tiger, have approached those of Gold, Juno and Sword, with in excess of five hundred killed, if the airborne are included.

With one battalion holding Les Cruttes in the north, the rest of the 22nd Infantry, who had also waded through the marshes, were in posses-sion of Saint-Germain-de-Varreville. In the centre, Reeder's 12th Infantry had gone firm around Beuzeville-au-Plain; nearby, General Barton had set up divisional headquarters at Audouville-la-Hubert. With Van Fleet's 8th Infantry secure in Pouppeville, these five villages represented the perimeter of the 4th Division by the end of D-Day. It was an astonishing penetration of the Atlantic Wall, which at Utah had proven only paper thin. At the handle of the fan was General 'Lightning Joe' Collins aboard USS *Bayfield*, which had been fitted as a headquarters ship as well as an attack transport, giving him excellent communications with all his formations on the ground.

His presence aboard the *Bayfield* served a second purpose: he shared the ship with Rear Admiral Moon. The latter was not an easy character, obsessed with detail and, underneath, was frankly nervy. This may have stemmed from July 1942, when he commanded the US Navy's Destroyer Squadron 8, escorting the Archangel-bound Arctic convoy PQ 17. Due to a misunderstanding of German intentions, the British Admiralty directed the convoy to scatter, which resulted in twenty-four out of thirty-five merchant ships being sunk. Moon was not connected with the decision-making or blamed in any way, but he witnessed the catastrophe, brought on by poor assimilation of information. As a result, he refused to delegate any of his work in planning, training and directing Force 'U', and was observed to be 'burning the candle at both ends'; Collins noted his tendency to 'do too much himself instead of giving responsibilities to his staff'. The impact of the disastrous Exercise Tiger only served for Moon to redouble his punishing work ethic.

Knowing that tired commanders can make poor decisions, Collins may have privately felt he needed to be close to Moon, and indeed this was borne out. As the US *Official History* noted, 'Admiral Moon became greatly concerned over the loss of some vessels in the Task Force. Late in the day [6 June] he considered a recommendation of his staff to suspend landing operations during the night, but General Collins convinced him of the necessity of continuing landing operations as uninterruptedly as possible.'[44] Moon was chosen because he was originally slated to oversee the landings in the south of France; when they were delayed, he was switched to Normandy. The evidence of his stress was revealed starkly when he was reappointed to command the maritime assault in southern France on 15 August – Operation Dragoon. Ten days shy of this second D-Day, Moon retired to his cabin aboard USS *Bayfield*, wrote a note to his wife, wrapped his issue .45-calibre pistol in a towel to minimise the mess, and killed himself.[45]

Offshore, work began immediately to site ten blockships (the 'Corncobs') that would be scuttled to form a breakwater – code-named 'Gooseberry One' – completed by 11 June. It provided a harbour for small vessels, MTBs, launches and minor landing craft, whose crew were quartered above the sea level in the sunken ships. Reflecting the huge logistics resources invested in Utah on D-Day and the days immediately following, by 19 June, some 126,507 men, 49,841 tons of equipment and

As overall Neptune commander Admiral Sir Bertram Ramsay (left) cooperated very harmoniously with his US counterparts, particularly Alan G. Kirk (1888–1963) (bottom right), who led the Western Task Force. They had worked together for the Sicily and Salerno invasions. So too had Rear Admiral John L. Hall (1891–1978), commanding Force 'O' (centre). Rear Admiral Don P. Moon (1894–1944) (top right) commanded Force 'U' from USS *Bayfield*. Nervous by nature and reluctant to delegate, the stress of work resulted in his suicide on 5 August 1944. (NARA)

14,344 vehicles had been landed on the beach.[46] The CO of the US Navy's 2nd Beach Battalion recorded that this figure had increased by 3 July – when he returned to England – to 188,098 men, 119,529 tons of equipment and supplies, and 32,617 vehicles, while 14,802 casualties and 30,805 prisoners of war would be evacuated from the beaches by the latter date.

André Renaud, mayor of Sainte-Mère-Église, recorded the picture as it would have appeared to any arriving GI – or German prisoner going the other way: 'hundreds of ships had run aground or were still floating. All had flat bottoms and stood perfectly upright on the sand. The hull of the cargoes [LSTs] had been opened like closet doors and from them had emerged Jeeps, trucks, tanks and cannon. At high tide the latter closed their trap doors and quickly sped off for England.'[47] On 7 June Utah was widened northwards, into Sugar Red sector, and eventually the small port of Saint-Vaast, eleven miles to the north, was also brought into service.[48]

The D-Day story of the engineers, the navy flotillas and Jahnke's strongpoint at W5 can be found in the Utah Beach Musée du Débarquement, first established in 1962 by Michel de Vallavieille of Brécourt Manor. The site has grown over the years and now includes the command bunker from which Jahnke witnessed the invasion, an original B-26, of the type that pulverised Jahnke's position in the early hours of D-Day, many vehicles and mementos, and a memorial to Andrew Higgins, whose little wooden LCVPs landed many a GI on Utah and nearby Omaha. The nearby Café Roosevelt (named for the brigadier general) is attached to one of Leutnant Jahnke's bunkers. On its interior walls, various GIs stationed there in 1944 left their names and addresses scrawled in pencil.

Before his death in 1960 the former Leutnant Arthur Jahnke also recounted his tale to Paul Carell, a German journalist and former SS propaganda officer writing about the German side of D-Day: Jahnke's defence of W5 therefore represents that of many other positions along Utah Beach, whose histories have dissolved with time, because no one wrote them down. In recent years the German gun batteries – stripped of their weaponry – at Saint-Marcouf and Azeville have also been developed as museums. Azeville remains interesting as its casemates are adorned with the camouflage first applied by the Germans in 1944 in an attempt to disguise their true purpose. The elegant stone-walled cottages and balcony windows painted on concrete don't quite convince, however, but remind the visitor that most bunkers were similarly painted to blend in with their surroundings – ruses quickly revealed by the Maquis, so it was all in vain.

In a short story, written after the war, amid the chaos of shelling and hostile fire, a solitary living figure is depicted crawling around a sector of his D-Day landing beach, amongst the bodies of the fallen, washed by the tide. It was a chaplain searching for his glasses. As the narrator's landing craft nears the beach, he witnesses the frantic search for the spectacles until the man of God, too, is killed. In a neat metaphor that worked on several levels, the writer conveyed the reverend's desperation for the clarity his glasses would provide. The author of 'The Magic Foxhole' had already published several short stories, and landed at Utah ten minutes after H-Hour. In the pack on his back were six unpublished stories that would form the backbone of *The Catcher in the Rye*.

Splashing through the surf, as a member of the 4th Counter Intelligence Corps detachment, J. D. Salinger's proficiency in French and German was soon in use questioning prisoners of war and civilians. Within an hour of landing, he was advancing inland, where he met up with Colonel Red Reeder's 12th Infantry, with whom he would spend the next twenty-

Clearly visible on the sleeve of the middle figure is the insignia of the 4th US Infantry Division. He and his colleague are members of the division's Counter Intelligence Corps, or one of its IPW (Interrogation of Prisoners of War) detachments. They are debriefing one of Heydte's paratroopers, an *Obergefreiter*. This was the role of J. D. Salinger, future author of *The Catcher in the Rye*, who served with the 4th Division, landing on Utah shortly after H-Hour on 6 June. (US Army Signal Corps)

It was the genial Brigadier General Theodore Roosevelt, Jr (1887–1944), Assistant Divisional Commander of the 4th Infantry and son of the 26th US President, who welcomed many soldiers ashore on Utah, urging them to get inland. Understanding they had landed on the wrong beach, he nevertheless instructed those with him to 'start the war from right here!' For his leadership he was recommended for a Distinguished Service Cross, but never knew that on 12 July he had been selected to command the 90th Division, for he succumbed to a heart attack that same night. On 28 September his DSC recommendation was upgraded to a Medal of Honor, as his headstone indicates. It is the most visited of all the 9,387 graves at the Colleville Military Cemetery. (Left, NARA; right, Author's photograph)

six days in combat. Losing very few on D-Day, when their strength was 3,080 men, by 1 July they totalled 1,130.[49]

On 28 September 1944 the Distinguished Service Cross awarded to Brigadier Roosevelt, Jr, for his bold decision-making on D-Day was upgraded to a Medal of Honor, but on 12 July the distinguished old campaigner had died in his sleep of a heart attack. He would never know that Eisenhower had just approved his promotion to major general and command of the 90th Infantry Division. Roosevelt's pall-bearers included

Bradley, Collins and Patton, the latter relenting from his earlier criticism to confide in his diary the former president's son was 'one of the bravest men I've ever known'. In the 1990s, photographs emerged of a grim-faced Patton and other figures at Roosevelt's funeral, snapped by a passing GI. Sidney Gutelewitz had forgotten making the images and developed them only decades later. He saw ten generals lined up in a cemetery behind a slow-moving half-track bearing a flag-draped coffin, and began to capture the ceremony. It included a GI brass band and three-volley salute by rifle-fire with French civilians also throwing earth on the casket. Gutelewitz did not know who was being buried, 'but with so many generals present, it wasn't a PFC'.[50]

Later Roosevelt was reinterred in the American cemetery at Colleville, and in 1955 his younger brother Quentin, killed flying in the First World War, was reburied alongside him: two sons of an American president, one killed fighting in each world war, spelling out the commitment the United States had made in twice fighting for Europe's freedom. It is always a moving moment to stand before the Roosevelt brothers' graves, the lettering on Theodore's picked out in gold, as befits a Medal of Honor winner. It remains the most visited on the cliffs at Colleville.[51]

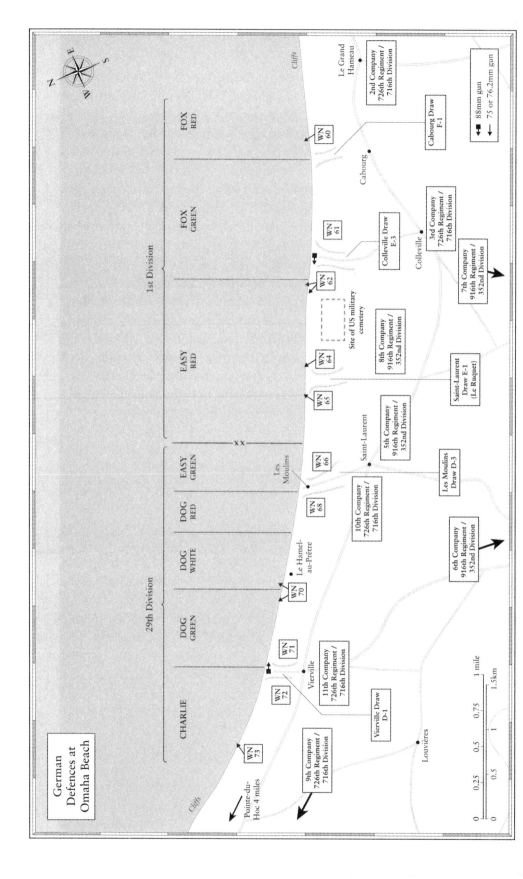

German Defences at Omaha Beach

26

Omaha: Blue and Gray

'I have expressed my deep appreciation of the well-planned and well-executed work performed in so few months. The main defence zone on the coast is strongly fortified and well manned; there are large tactical and operational reserves in the area. Thousands of pieces of artillery, anti-tank guns, rocket projectiles and flame-throwers await the enemy; millions of mines under the water and on land lie in wait for him. In spite of the enemy's great air superiority, we can face coming events with the greatest confidence.'
Generalfeldmarschall Erwin Rommel, 22 May 1944

'STANDING DOWN TONIGHT – we have temporarily ran out of bombs,' read the report of 6 June 1944 submitted by Lieutenant Colonel John B. Kidd, operations officer, 100th Bomb Group, US Eighth Air Force. The B-17 outfit, based at RAF Thorpe Abbotts, Norfolk, flew three missions that day. Kidd's report noted: 'Crew morale bounced up one hundred percent. First take off at 0230 hours. Had a good view of the invasion, the under-cast having broken away. Hundreds of ships unmolested off the coast, maybe indicating shore batteries silenced. Hundreds of gliders going in; no air opposition at all. German radio is something to hear; reporting the invasion a complete flop – a few parachutists who were quickly eliminated. Whom do they think they are kidding?'[1]

Flying in one of those aircraft of the 'Bloody Hundredth', a 351st Bomb Squadron B-17 named *Shack Rat*, was Vincent Fugarazzo of Nutley, New Jersey. From 11,000 feet, the nineteen-year-old radio operator saw a glimpse of the vast invasion armada through a break in the clouds. 'Boy, those poor guys are sure in for it, and here I am safe as can be in an airplane,' thought Fugarazzo.

He was unaware his brother was down below with a Navy Combat Demolition Unit, trying to clear obstacles on Omaha. 'I remember we crossed a headland and the pilot said our guys are landing just along from there. It was *Omaha* beach. It looked like you could walk across the channel to it, there were so many ships,' he recalled thinking. Fugarazzo's safety was illusory: he was shot down in July. 'Flak took out two of our engines and then a German fighter hammered at us, setting the remaining pair on fire ... We flipped end over end until the pilot righted the ship momentarily. He held it level until all of us bailed out. Then it went into a dive, taking him with it. *Shack Rat* did good on D-Day; it's when I always say a prayer for Lieutenant Charles Norby, my pilot.'[2]

Bombing his homeland that early morning was Louis Hervelin, with 346 Squadron RAF, based at RAF Elvington in Yorkshire. Comprised entirely of Free French aircrew, and also known as the *Escadrille Guyenne* – named after a unit raised in 1936, and operating Halifax heavy bombers – it had become operational on 1 June 1944, with its first mission flown early on the sixth. The night before, Hervelin recalled lounging in the officers' mess, reading newspapers covering the liberation of Rome, when the station speakers crackled into life announcing a post-dinner briefing at 2040 hours.

'There, we were told under no circumstances were we to drop any unused munitions into the Channel. But they didn't tell us why. Afterwards into a red bag we emptied our pockets of anything we wanted destroyed if we did not return. Into the white bag we placed everything else we wished sent to our families. We took off at 0055 hours. Two hours and twenty-eight minutes later M for Mike was releasing bombs over the artillery batteries of Grandcamp-Maisy. It was on our way back that we saw the magnificent landing armada. Something we had been expecting, and there it was under our very eyes. It was unforgettable and we all became very misty-eyed and the thought of our beloved *patrie* liberated. We were soon in the air again, that evening taking off at 2120 to bomb the Saint-Lô railway station; it was a busy twenty-four hours.'[3]

Had the US 1st and 29th Divisions landed on Omaha Beach on 6 June 1943, the German defenders wouldn't have had so much as a bucket and spade with which to oppose them. The sands had been bare of obstacles and the heights had been bare of machine-guns. It would have been an open invitation.

Coastal defence was traditionally the realm of the German navy. As a result, the Kriegsmarine had developed long-range, large-calibre guns for engaging warships, designed forts to house them, and trained gunners to operate them. It was the German navy who advised the Turks on their coastal defences at Gallipoli, supplying the Krupp cannon used with devastating effect in 1915. Under Hitler, the Kriegsmarine's efforts were focused solely on protecting ports, concluding the Allies could not sustain an invasion without capturing an operating harbour. After the success of Axis airborne operations in Crete and the establishment of Allied parachute units in 1941–2, German policy shifted by designating selected ports as 'fortress areas', to include landward defences capable of repelling airborne landings. Following the British raid on Saint-Nazaire of 28 March 1942, this had been extended again to include construction of coastal artillery emplacements outside ports, the need seemingly justified by the attack on Dieppe of the same year.

Operation Jubilee of 19 August, which had seen the first mass use of landing craft – sixty LCAs and twelve LCTs – had made the Germans realise they also needed smaller-calibre, shorter-range weapons to destroy barges landing under their noses. This in turn had meant more, and smaller, coastal positions overlooking likely landing beaches, initially only deemed to include areas near ports. The air attacks that had accompanied Jubilee prompted a rethink of fortress construction, and a realisation that open gun positions needed to be upgraded with overhead protection, while extensive offshore minefields needed to be laid.

Such was the state of play when Rundstedt had complained about the *Atlantikwall* in October 1943, prompting Rommel's inspection that December. Along the future invasion coast, only Cherbourg and Le Havre were adequately protected, with most beaches of lower Normandy completely open to attack. Rommel's study of Sicily and Salerno had led him to realise the Allies would not necessarily attack a port. Their landing ships, DUKWs and other craft could circumvent that need for at least a few days. Therefore his attention had turned to the hitherto neglected coastal areas between harbours, where a very thin screen of existing gun emplacements offered little deterrent. Once given control, he had first tried to regularise the chain of command, arranging for the navy to surrender responsibility for the coastal guns, though they still manned them. Rommel had also realised that the navy had neither the resources nor the time to lay offshore minefields, so he compensated by putting his own on the foreshore.

This is the origin of the rows of beach obstacles with mines attached. It was the Desert Fox who had organised the collection of frontier defences from Czechoslovakia and Belgium in January 1944 – the hedge-hogs and gates – with 15,932 of the former and 2,375 of the latter set along the future invasion beaches in the Seventh Army's sector. Most of these devices had mines or obsolete ordnance with proximity fuses attached to them which would damage or destroy landing craft when struck. To supplement these, General Marcks' 84th Corps had also planted 4,634 mine-tipped concrete poles, 4,912 concrete tetrahedrons, 10,939 *Holzpfäle* (wooden stakes) and 4,722 *Hemmbalken* (obstruction beams).

The latter were a simple design of a wooden log rising out of the sand, sloping landwards at forty-five degrees, and kept aloft by two legs, like the bipod of a machine-gun: landing craft were supposed to ride up them at high tide and trigger the mine fixed to their crown. Motivated by the lack of time, Rommel – unwisely in retrospect – had insisted all this work, including tree-felling to obtain the necessary wood, be done by the troops themselves, with varying degrees of expertise, and, as we have seen, at the expense of training. All the beach obstacles along Omaha and ferro-concrete gun positions overlooking the beach, constructed by the *Organisation Todt* and French contractors, thus dated only from January 1944 onwards.[4]

Barely seventeen, André Legallois from Saint-Laurent was one of tens of thousands put to work digging trenches and pouring concrete. 'I worked alongside German soldiers. The ones as young as me were really kind, but their superiors hated us French, and the *Organisation Todt* supervisors were worse,' he recollected. 'Of course I recall the invasion. It killed my father's cows. I went to have a look: you could see the whole bay, but you couldn't see the water for all the ships, and then we understood what was happening.'

Lucien Rigault, then a nineteen-year-old civilian living in the hamlet of La Cambe (which now hosts the German military cemetery), recalled life as a forced labourer, making bunkers behind Omaha Beach. 'We worked really slowly. The Germans were harsh, the food was poor. We had already spent ages building these little forts. We thought we would be making them for the rest of our lives if the Allies didn't come soon.' He married a year after the war and never left La Cambe, ten miles southwest of Omaha Beach. 'I remember 6 June very well. It was the day I stopped working for the Nazis. We saw the planes bombing, heard the firing, and I said to myself, "No point in building anything else now"; then we began seeing American soldiers.' Rigault teared up as he remembered the moment.[5]

Allied intelligence missed the fact that the 352nd Infantry Division of Generalleutnant Dietrich Kraiss, stationed in Le Molay-Littry, west of Bayeux, had deployed some troops and artillery forward to the vicinity of Omaha and Gold beaches in early June. Kraiss, like Wilhelm Falley, was an experienced commander who had served in the First World War and in Russia: both would soon perish under the Normandy sun. His men included Obergrenadier Karl Wegner, called up after his seventeenth birthday in Hanover, given a medical examination and sent for training. He was soon posted to the 352nd in Normandy.

Wegner recalled that much time and energy was wasted giving them compulsory political indoctrination from *Nationalsozialistische Führungsoffiziere* (National Socialist Leadership Officers): 'Once a week during training before the invasion we got a lecture from those guys; it was pretty boring, but you had to go.' Though these things are difficult to measure, analysts have observed that this indoctrination of the western armies may well have contributed in some small way to their effectiveness against the Allies in 1944. Serving in No. 3 Company of Oberstleutnant Ernst Heyna's 914th *Grenadier-Regiment*, Wegner recollected his senior officers: 'Kraiss and Heyna were good leaders. They did their best for us and came up to the front a lot. I still remember General Kraiss: he was very small, with his helmet and MP40.'[6]

Many historians have incorrectly stated the 352nd was a crack unit with a strength of 13,000. In fact, it was formed only in September 1943 from divisions which had been decimated on the Eastern Front and arrived in December; it was, in the affectionate words of one of its own officers, Leutnant Hans Heinze, with No. 5 Company of the 916th *Grenadier-Regiment*, 'a thrown together mob'. The division may have included veterans – although most of its recruits were born between 1924 and 1926 – but was not itself an experienced formation. Its chief of staff, Oberstleutnant Fritz Ziegelmann, noted that 'fifty percent of the 333 officers lacked combat experience; there was a thirty percent shortfall in NCOs, while the 6,800 infantrymen were responsible for defending a thirty-three-mile-long by fifteen-deep divisional front'. It possessed more impounded French bicycles than motor transport – the latter comprising 'civilian trucks driven by lazy Frenchmen. The drivers were volunteers, paid with food and cigarettes.'[7]

Ziegelmann knew the area and its challenges well; his last job was as the Seventh Army's chief quartermaster. Leutnant Heinze reckoned that 'just over ten percent of my regiment, the 916th, had experience of combat, but this number included seventy-five percent of my NCOs.'[8] Lack of ammunition meant that troops had only conducted three live firing exercises and thrown two hand grenades before 6 June. Instead, each soldier had spent his day constructing the *Atlantikwall* – in striking contrast to the peak fitness and training of their Allied adversaries, whose average age across the millions gathered in southern England was twenty-five.[9]

Gefreiter Gotthard Liebich was a seventeen-year-old recruit serving in No. 3 Company of the division's 916th *Grenadier-Regiment*. An apprentice bank clerk living with his widowed mother, brother and sister in eastern Germany, he had just passed his finals when, on his seventeenth birthday in July 1943, he received his call-up papers. 'At the start of 1944 I was posted to the Normandy coast – the first time I had ever seen the sea.' He remembered being taught about the division's crest: 'It was a white horse, the traditional symbol of Hanover, our depot. The horse was leaping over a gate – symbolic of not being able to be stopped or contained.' Liebich was given a rifle with twenty rounds of ammunition. 'I was loaded down like a donkey, ammunition belts around my neck, grenades in my pockets, with a crust of bread and my French dictionary. All our other kit was moved by horse and cart,' he recalled.

'We were billeted in tents in the orchard of a very old manor, Ferme de l'Ormel, owned by Monsieur Leterrier, the mayor of Vierville. It was on the road from Formigny and inland of Vierville, so we had to cycle to get to our positions.' Their tents were made from the *Zeltbahn* (camouflaged cape) each man was issued, which could be joined together to form communal shelters. Liebich remembered the smell of ripening apples in their orchard, mingled with cigarette smoke and combined with the aroma of food from their company *Goulashkanon* (horse-drawn field kitchen), which brought their morning and evening meals. 'I had done very little training; my entire military experience was of helping to construct the fortifications. That was it.'[10]

Oberstleutnant Ziegelmann's report noted the frustrations the 352nd had faced when building their defences. 'During the storms in April, most of the obstacles were torn out and mines detonated. The existing mines, laid two years previously, were no longer reliable. New logs, cut in the Forest of Cerisy, had to be transported nineteen miles by horse-drawn vehicles, because of fuel shortages. And since they had to be logged by hard-to-get circular saws and rammed in position by hand, it took a considerable time, particularly on the rocky shore at Grandcamp.' Ziegelmann concluded, 'In general, we did not achieve Rommel's plans for even one divisional zone of the *Atlantikwall*.'[11] Work speeded up when someone thought of using the pressure hoses of the Bayeux fire brigade – though this came at the price of the firemen noting the layout of every obstacle, bunker and trench, and passing this intelligence to the local Resistance.

Also with the 352nd Division was Heinrich 'Hein' Severloh, assigned to No. 1 Battery of its artillery regiment. A farmer's boy, Severloh was born in Metzingen, in the Lüneburg Heath area of northern Germany. Drafted in July 1942 to a horse-drawn artillery unit in Russia, he had

Soldiers of the German 352nd Division recalled camping near to Omaha Beach in local orchards, joining together their camouflaged *Zeltbahn* capes to form communal tents. Few of the division had attended many live-firing exercises or thrown more than a couple of hand grenades before 6 June. Instead, they had been building up Rommel's defences: 'I had done very little training; my entire military experience was of helping to construct the fortifications,' remembered one. (Author's collection)

suffered frostbite to his toes, but recovered in late 1943 to be posted back to his old unit, which by then was in northern France. On Valentine's Day 1944, he moved into quarters at the Château de l'Epinette, near the small hamlet of Houtteville, about five miles north-west of Bayeux and three and a half miles from the coast. 'Personally, I had a generally good relationship with the French, and believe I was, *despite* my uniform, genuinely well-liked. There was a positive willingness to cooperate on both sides,' he recalled.[12] As Yvonne Lemaire, a farmer's daughter who sold the Germans milk during the occupation, noted, 'At least around Omaha Beach, the Germans treated us correctly. They were not all barbarians.'[13]

Hein Severloh's usual job was driver, batman and bodyguard to the battery commander, Oberleutnant Bernardt Frerking, whose observation post was in a strongpoint overlooking the eastern end of Omaha Beach. Their battalion CO was Major Werner Pluskat, a grizzled veteran of two years on the Russian Front, accompanied everywhere by his German shepherd 'Harras'. Frerking's artillery lurked in camouflaged emplacements inland, and in order not to destroy their beach obstacles, 'practice rounds were fired from a position three hundred metres forward then the guns returned to their positions'. Fire missions were initiated by code word 'Dora', meaning 'fire onto the beach at the low-tide mark'. Frerking's battery completed their last practice shoot on 29 May, but Allied intelligence missed the fact that this additional artillery had been preregistered onto Omaha Beach.

Their bunker on the coast – *Widerstandsnest* (WN) 62 – thought Severloh, 'was the strongest position in the Seine Bay and had a permanent complement of soldiers from the 726th *Grenadier-Regiment*. The observation equipment and communications to our No. 1 Battery were located in our own separate bunker within this position.' Beyond and below, Severloh recalled, 'the entire beach was barricaded with hundreds of large and small steel obstacles, steel "Czech hedgehogs", "Belgian gates", and tree trunks tipped with mines'.[14] Grenadier Severloh's congenial host at the Château de l'Epinette had been an artillery officer in the First World War with a battery of French 105s – the same calibre weapon as Severloh's – and they stayed in touch after the war. 'Many French farmers were still POWs in Germany, and horses were rare on the farms – so German soldiers with their horses were ordered to help with the cultivation of the fields,' Severloh remembered.[15]

The coast assigned to Gerow's V Corps stretched eighteen miles from the mouth of the Vire river to Port-en-Bessin – sectors Able to George. The estuary of the Vire to the west was entirely unsuitable for assault, being full of shallow mudflats. The rest of the frontage was characterised by cliffs and reefs, and offered few desirable landing beaches. The small port of Grandcamp, guarded by strongpoint *Widerstandsnest* 81, was shielded by shoals that limited any direct assault. Out of the eighteen miles allocated, only five – from the headland of the Pointe de la Percée to Sainte-Honorine-des-Pertes, where the cliffs drew back to offer a stretch of beach – were considered viable for a landing. This amounted to a crescent-shaped sandy strip, with an eighteen-foot tide, numerous sandbars and cross-currents.

At low tide the water receded nearly half a mile from a ten-foot mound of stone shingle used as a barrier against the waves. One US officer would note that while the shingle 'afforded some cover from frontal fire, it also presented a good target to weapons sited at the flanks of the beach'.[16] Along the western half of Omaha, a sea wall bearing a road ran beyond the shingle, between the exits to Saint-Laurent and Vierville. This passed collections of elegant beachfront villas, built at sea level at the base of the bluffs. Those grouped around the exit to Saint-Laurent were known as Les Moulins; others stretched along the shoreline towards Vierville, called Le Hamel-au-Prêtre. Before the war, ninety villas had stood in the vicinity, used by the Wehrmacht as rest facilities for the Seventh Army until Rommel's arrival. By 6 June 1944 the Germans had demolished all but seven, along with several hotels, on whose foundations they built bunkers, incorporating the wood and rubble into their positions.

On the eastern side of the beach, behind the shingle bank was a narrow marsh, and running the entire length was a scrub-covered limestone cliff of between one and two hundred feet, that rose at roughly a thirty-degree angle. The marsh and flat area where the villas had once stood at the base of the cliffs were sewn with booby traps, connected by trip wires to mines or grenades, some also incorporated into the barbed-wire entanglements. The only exits from the beach amounted to five narrow draws, resembling dried river beds. The Germans knew that any attempts to land at Omaha would focus on these exits, which is where many of their resistance nests were sited – built in pairs to overlook each side of the draw.

Appreciating the locations of each draw – or valley – is key to understanding both the assault and defence of Omaha on 6 June 1944. From

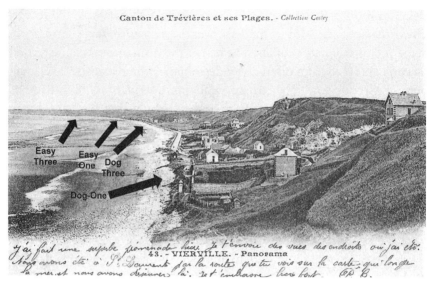

Canton de Trévières et ses Plages. - *Collection Costey*

43. - VIERVILLE. - Panorama

One of the postcards submitted by the British public to help the Overlord planners shows the extent of Omaha beach, looking east. The four principal draws are indicated, with the Vierville exit in the foreground. By 1944 a sea wall ran along the near half of the beach, fronting the road, though the Germans had demolished all but one of the villas. (Author's collection)

west to east, the D-1 draw contained a route leading up to Vierville and was overwatched by WN73, WN72 and WN71. At the bottom, two anti-tank walls, 125 feet long, nine feet high and six feet thick stretched across the road. To open the draw it would be necessary to destroy both of these before any wheels or tracks could leave the beach. The D-3 draw at Les Moulins was also blocked by an anti-tank wall, and defended by WN67 and WN66. The E-1 draw was midway between Saint-Laurent and Colleville, defended by an anti-tank ditch, a wall and overlooked by WN65 and WN64. A small stream – le Ruquet – flowed down this draw, so it was sometimes referred to as the Ruquet valley or draw. Whilst the much-photographed bunker of WN65 remains today, its partner position, WN64, lies under the western edge of the American military cemetery at Colleville. This draw led into the eastern end of Saint-Laurent. E-3 included the most substantial route – up to Colleville – and was flanked by two of the strongest positions, WN62 and WN61.

Finally, there was a fifth draw – only a rough track and far less of a movement corridor – that led up to the hamlet of Cabourg, east of Colleville. Though guarded by WN60, it was never scheduled to be attacked, but when captured, became known as F-1. The defences were not quite continuous, for there were two areas of dead ground that would save many American lives. The most significant comprised an eight-hundred-yard stretch between WN64 and WN62 – midway between Colleville and Saint-Laurent – exactly overlooked by the site of today's US military cemetery, and a shorter stretch below WN60, where GIs would assemble in the lee of the cliffs.

It was terrain totally unlike that of Utah or the other landing areas. The Pointe de la Percée, which contained another defensive position, blocked the line of sight from Omaha to Utah, but three miles further west was a second headland, the Pointe du Hoc, that knifed into the Channel – 'hoc' being Old French for the triangular jib sail of a ship, which it resembled. On Allied maps a spelling error resulted in the feature being referred to as the Pointe du Hoe. On a good day, the breakwater of Port-en-Bessin and some of the artificial harbour at Arromanches can just be seen from the clifftops of the Pointe du Hoc, but in most conditions the much nearer Utah Beach is clearly visible – which is why the Germans had placed a substantial six-gun battery on it, that V Corps determined to attack in the only manner possible: by climbing the cliffs to get at it.[17]

The primary importance of Omaha was in the fact that it lay between Utah and Gold beaches – fourteen miles as the crow flies to the former, sixteen to the latter. Linking up with both would be a critical phase in the success of Overlord. A mile inland, a lateral coastal road ran from Port-en-Bessin west to Grandcamp, threading its way through the little settlements of Sainte-Honorine, Colleville, Saint-Laurent and Vierville-sur-Mer behind Omaha Beach. All were communes of two or three hundred inhabitants, many of whom had been encouraged to move inland. Tracks led up the five draws from the shingle to this lateral route. Farmers and fisherman were still permitted their trade, when they weren't forcibly labouring on the beach defences under German supervision. Henri Biard took his bicycle along this road on the evening of the invasion. 'I had just sat my *baccalauréat* exams and some friends in Vierville invited me round for dinner on 5 June. After the meal and before the 9 p.m. curfew, I returned back through Saint-Laurent. Nothing was happening; the usual Germans; quiet – it was very calm.'

Once he arrived back at Trévières, however, everything changed. 'I sat up having coffee with my father and it was then we saw the first Allied plane fall down in flames not far away. Then we heard the growing roar of many aircraft flying over, the explosions of bombs, and the Germans began to stir, shouting warnings to each other. Then we knew some drama or other was afoot. With my father we stood on the terrace of the town hall and from there realised something was happening on the coast. Incessant artillery and machine guns. Sounds we had not heard before but would soon become common. The town began to be shelled about 9 a.m. and we left to shelter in trenches dug in the countryside. I remembered passing the church at 5.15 p.m. By six, its bell tower had been brought down by a naval shell.'[18]

The only major road in the region was the wide, paved *Route Nationale* 13, flanked by tall poplars, which connected Caen, Bayeux, Isigny and Carentan with Cherbourg. Troops from all the invasion areas hoped to reach this by the end of 6 June. Five miles beyond the V Corps beach lay the meandering Aure river, which flowed into the Vire near the coast; Rommel had ordered it closed to inundate the entire valley from Isigny to Trévières, creating another water barrier up to a mile wide. It was same expedient as applied behind Utah: to deter paratroopers and block exit routes, lessening the attractiveness of this sector of coast for assault. Though the flooding has since disappeared and the draws now contain solid roads, the landscape around Omaha has changed relatively little from 1944.

The hinterland comprised small hedgerow-enclosed apple orchards and fields housing dairy cattle. Unripe cider apples would cause many a stomach upset, while the sight of dead cows, legs raised stiffly in the air, bellies swollen with putrefying gas, and crawling with maggots, became a common sight, and a distressing one for country boys. Occasionally they would encounter beasts in need of milking and could at least put their pre-war skills to practical use.

Eggs and fresh milk would also become an obsession for all GIs, desperate for an alternative to their constipation-inducing C- and K-rations. An officer in the 116th 'Stonewall Brigade' recollected the latter as 'precooked and canned combinations of largely unidentifiable ingredients packaged in a waxed paper carton that, theoretically, could be burned to warm them. The soldier ate the part least offensive to his taste and discarded the rest. The C-ration came in larger cans, required more extensive fire to heat and, in the front line, had usually to be eaten cold.'[19]

Vision was limited due to the summer growth of trees along the bocage hedgerows, which averaged twelve feet in height, roughly two feet in width at the top, with a base of four feet. Often drainage ditches ran along the bottom, forming natural fire trenches. Only where the Germans had trimmed the lower branches for firing lanes could more than two hundred yards of good observation be had: the bocage represented a barrier to men, tanks and vehicles. Fighting in such terrain would put a premium on initiative and aggressive leadership in small units.[20] Curiously, neither side had rehearsed fighting in the dense undergrowth, both armies expecting the major struggle to be on the coast. As a result, the conflict would favour the side that could adapt the quickest.

To occupy the thirty-mile-wide gap between Utah and Gold, and make contact with each beach, Major General Leonard T. Gerow's V Corps needed to land two formations on D-Day: the 29th Infantry Division, which would head west to connect with Collins' VII Corps at Utah, while the 1st Division was to drive east towards Gold, joining up with British XXX Corps.

Gerow therefore divided Omaha in two at its midpoint, with the assistant divisional commander of the 29th, Brigadier General Norman 'Dutch' Cota (who had previously served with the 1st Division), taking responsibility for the two regiments of his formation landing from Dog Green to Easy Green sectors. The Big Red One's Clarence R. Huebner would be in overall charge of the entire Omaha assault, with the 29th's regiments, Rangers and tank battalions subordinate to him. Major General Charles H. Gerhardt was slated to take back his units when he came ashore at 1700 hours on 7 June; in the meantime, his representative during this period would be Cota.

As the Big Red One (the nickname of the 1st Division) was also landing two regiments on Easy Red to Fox Red, shipping shortages and beach congestion would prevent either formation arriving complete on the first day, though the 175th Infantry would be afloat offshore as V Corps reserve if needed. The landing craft and attack transports destined for Utah and Omaha could carry a maximum of four Regimental Combat Teams (RCTs) – an infantry regiment plus all its supporting arms.

Captain Charles H. Kidd, commanding Company 'M', assessed the 116th Infantry as 3,486-strong on D-Day, but the entire 116th Regimental Combat Team, with all its attached 2nd and 5th Ranger battalions, engineers, anti-aircraft, mortars and liaison teams of varying kinds, amounted to 11,076 personnel and 976 vehicles.[21] The follow-on RCTs, the 115th of Virginian Eugene N. Slappey and 175th of Paul R. Goode,

The three US infantry division commanders. Raymond O. Barton (1889–1963), West Point Class of 1912 (left), led the 4th from July 1942 until December 1944. Clarence R. Huebner (1888–1972) was commissioned from the ranks in 1916 and had taken over the Big Red One after its previous commander was sacked by Omar Bradley in August 1943. Charles H. Gerhardt (1895–1976), West Point Class of 1917 (right), led the 29th from July 1943. Each general sports his divisional insignia, as well as his rank, on his helmet. (NARA)

would be smaller, but these were huge organisations to deposit on a defended coast in double-quick time.

Major General 'Gee' Gerow, leading V Corps, had served in the First World War in the Signal Corps; in 1924 he had graduated first from the Infantry School at Fort Benning, Georgia, one place ahead of Omar Bradley. The following year he'd attended the Command and General Staff Course at Fort Leavenworth, where Dwight Eisenhower was his study partner. It was on 17 July 1943 that he turned over his 29th Division to Charles H. Gerhardt to assume command of V Corps, and had been the dominant force behind the plans for the V Corps assault ever since. Gerhardt, West Point class of 1917, was a cavalryman who had seen service in the First World War, but had not previously worked with National Guardsmen. If Gerow was strict with the 29th, Gerhardt's arrival was greeted with consternation when the latter started imposing fines on his men for not wearing helmet chinstraps correctly, or for driving muddy vehicles – a peccadillo which continued once across the Channel – but all acknowledged he raised their standards with excellent training. Gerhardt could be seen riding everywhere in his gleaming jeep (named *Vixen Tor* for a landmark on Dartmoor where the division had trained frequently) while watching training, and challenging men to marksmanship with his .45-calibre pistol.

There would be a huge contrast between the fortunes of the Utah assault force and that of Omaha. In overall terms, the cross-Channel passage of Force 'U' was seriously taxed by the weather and consequent twenty-four-hour postponement; Force 'O' experienced none of this. The Utah landings were protected from the Atlantic weather by the lee of the Cotentin peninsula; the assault on Omaha was hampered by the heavy swell. Rear Admiral Moon's fleet suffered from mines, but was remarkably little bothered by shellfire; Rear Admiral Hall's encountered few mines, but was heavily engaged by shore batteries. Collins' VII Corps met minimal resistance, whereas Gerow's V Corps was effectively stymied with great determination. The story of Utah was the fighting beyond the beach; that of Omaha was exclusively confined to the shoreline.

However, Utah's defenders were largely distracted by the sudden presence of two American airborne formations dropping in their midst. The garrison behind Omaha – larger in strength, and lurking in more and better-prepared defensive positions – would have no such interference. Undoubtedly, the appearance of Allied airborne forces behind the defenders of Omaha would have made all the difference. This had been the original COSSAC plan, and there were additional trained formations (British 1st Airborne Division and the Polish Parachute Brigade) in England, but no additional airlift capacity, spare gliders or tugs, to deploy a fourth airborne formation simultaneously into battle with the existing three.[22] Winston Churchill in 1944 may have complained that 'the destinies of our two great empires are seemingly tied up in some damned things called LSTs', but the same was equally true of air transportation. The availability of more C-47s and trained aircrew would have changed fortunes of the assault on Omaha Beach.

The quickest of overviews indicates just three platoon-sized resistance nests on the coast capable of interfering with the landings at Utah. The same computation for the five miles of Omaha indicates a much greater density: *fourteen* equivalent strongpoints, admittedly some unfinished on 6 June, which is why further postponement of D-Day would have spelled disaster. Patient analysis of the German defences along Omaha reveals that the main reason for their effectiveness was not their weaponry, or number, but that they were all built *at the same time*, with a specific and pressing threat in mind. Whereas strongpoints elsewhere along the coast had been developed ad hoc, over time, being added to when extra weapons became available, those at Omaha had been developed as a single block, after the landings on Sicily and at Salerno had been studied. Weapon ranges and systems were efficiently interlocked and overlapped, providing the maximum possible effect in their zones of fire.

The pair of 88mm bunkers constructed at either end of Omaha are the best example of this, located in WN61 to the east, and WN72 at the western end. These positions were designed to be completely impervious to fire from the sea, with observation only along the shoreline, making the beach their kill zone. With walls seven foot thick to screen them from naval gunfire, their ferro-concrete protection was generally considered proof against the eight-inch guns of an Allied heavy cruiser; only a shot directly through the embrasure would subdue them – as would prove the case on 6 June.

Additionally some of these positions were cunningly set into the cliffs and extremely well concealed. Captain Carroll Smith with the Third Battalion, 116th Infantry, recalled leading a team up the bluffs. Halfway up as they came to a shelf, 'a gun suddenly fired from the left so close that the blast was deafening. After careful examination, the muzzle of what appeared to be an 88mm was discovered protruding from a small niche, so mounted that it could fire only straight up the beach to the west. The amazing thing about this was the excellent camouflage. A whole boat team of thirty men had just crawled fifty yards to the right of this emplacement and didn't see it.'[23]

In hindsight, it is obvious that targets bobbing about on the waves would be difficult to hit, whereas those on the sands presented far easier prey, especially when fixed by physical obstructions and mines. Machine-guns and mortars were similarly sited to act in concert with each other, dispensing at maximum damage. It was left to the plunging shells of field artillery batteries located inland, and bigger coastal gun emplacements, to impose devastation on the flotillas at sea. The latter included the six cannon at Pointe du Hoc, and the Le Chaos four-gun battery at Longues. New research is indicating that two other interrelated positions, WN83 and WN84, eight miles west at Maisy, were overlooked by Allied intelligence at the time – and have been since by historians.

They housed four 100mm and four 155mm weapons, protected by a substantial *Flak* detachment. Importantly, these Maisy batteries would harass the fleets on D-Day and put counter-battery fire onto the Pointe du Hoc, much to the discomfort of Lieutenant Colonel James Earl Rudder's Rangers, though they were too distant to interfere with Omaha.

In fact, mystery currently surrounds both the Pointe du Hoc and Maisy locations, with theories being put forward that the former was a training establishment for coastal gunners, and of less importance than – and possibly even a ruse to distract attention away from – the powerful site at Maisy.[24] While such theories are probably incorrect, the lack of certainty suggests that there is still more to learn about this important corner of the *Atlantikwall*. Nevertheless, whether through ignorance or design, the entire Omaha defences were certainly undersold to the attackers.

We have already met Generalleutnant Dietrich Kraiss and his 352nd Infantry Division, formed in Saint-Lô in November 1943 from new recruits, and leavened by a hard core of Eastern Front veterans. The seven-battalion formation had responded to Rommel's order of March 1944 to take over responsibility for the coast from Carentan to Asnelles (overlooking the future Gold Beach) from the smaller, overstretched 716th Division. This gave the Seventh Army not just more guardians along the coast, but more hands to build its defences.

Allied intelligence and the French Resistance were aware of Kraiss having moved his HQ from Saint-Lô to the eighteenth-century Château du Molay, eight miles rather than twenty behind the coast. They understood, too, that Ernst Heyna's 914th *Grenadier-Regiment* was dispersed around Isigny, while the two battalions of Oberstleutnant Karl Meyer's 915th Regiment was in reserve south-east of Bayeux.

However, SHAEF and V Corps' G-2 intelligence section missed the fact that Oberst Ernst Goth's 916th *Grenadier-Regiment* had taken over responsibility for Omaha and *retained* the local regiment belonging to the 716th Division under his command. Thus, the last SHAEF intelligence estimate of 30 May still put the 352nd in reserve, with only a single battalion of the 716th along the coast. This was not the sort of minor tactical detail to be transmitted by Enigma, thus not a secret for Bletchley Park to unravel.

A seemingly insignificant oversight in failing to understand a realignment of German divisional boundaries meant that waiting for V Corps was not a single unit of perhaps eight hundred men, but almost triple that – a battalion from each division, plus elements of a third, were in position. Some of these, the Americans would be amazed to discover, included the Russians of the 439th *Ost-Bataillon*, belonging to Generalmajor Richter's 716th Division. The S-2 (intelligence officer) of the US Third Battalion, 116th Infantry, recorded finding, 'from interrogation of the few prisoners captured – the accent was on *destroy* [i.e. kill] not *capture* that day – that our beach was held by elements of the 716th Division, as intelligence estimates had stated, but those in Saint-Laurent were from the veteran 352nd Division, which was supposed to be in Saint-Lô'.[25]

Captain Fred Gercke of IPW (Prisoner of War Interrogation) Team 24, with the Big Red One, recorded asking his first German for his documents. 'I could not believe my eyes when I saw he was from the 352nd Division, which was supposed to be about fifty [in reality half that] miles south of us. I checked with several other prisoners and found they were all from the same unit [which had been] emplaced in various field fortifications along the coast for a number of weeks already.'[26]

A story that rapidly gained currency in the months and years after D-Day described how the extra defenders at Omaha were the 352nd Division deploying to the coast for a day of anti-invasion manoeuvres – an extremely unlucky coincidence, no more. Many histories parrot this myth up to the present day. Given that Allied intelligence had an excellent record of accuracy, it was a tale that most wanted to accept, rather than the truth – that Allied intelligence had goofed. Charles H. Kidd, a company commander in the 116th Infantry, recalled his 'excessively sunny' briefing during the crossing from Weymouth on USS *Charles Carroll*. 'The coast line was lightly held, with one battalion occupying the defensive positions on Omaha beach, reserves at least twenty-four hours away and the armour at least three days off.'[27]

In fact, waiting for the 1st and 29th US Divisions were a minimum of eight infantry companies, with two 88mm guns, nine 75mm or 76.2mm artillery pieces, nine 50mm weapons, six tank turret *Panzerstellung*, twenty-eight mortars, fifteen other anti-tank guns, and at least eighty-five machine guns, mostly in protected reinforced concrete positions, connected by deep zig-zag trenches. Also within range were the batteries of field guns controlled by Major Werner Pluskat, Oberleutnant Bernard Frerking and their colleagues.[28] The Desert Fox had been concerned enough to visit the Omaha Beach area on four occasions during 1944: on 29–30 January, 6–7 March and on 18 and 30 May – each time urging more effort in preparing the defences – which very nearly paid off. In light of this, it is all the more astonishing that he left for Germany when he did.

To assemble the jigsaw of experiences of Omaha Beach, it makes sense to divide the terrain into three. First, let us study the western half. Then we will visit the Pointe du Hoc, assaulted by Rangers, and look at their colleagues on the beach itself. Finally, we will conclude by looking at the eastern half, assaulted by the 1st Infantry Division.

The western beach was the responsibility of Major General Charlie Gerhardt's untested 29th Infantry Division. This was a volunteer National Guard outfit recruited in Virginia and Maryland, supplemented by drafted men from other parts of the United States. The 29th was entirely different in character to the 4th, the regular army unit which landed at Utah, or the Big Red One, who both looked down on the Guard as 'weekend warriors'. The formation dated to 1917 and had seen action in the First World War, but drew on an older pedigree. As its men hailed from New Jersey, Virginia and Maryland – both sides of the Mason–Dixon line that delineated the Civil War – it took the nickname 'Blue and Gray' from the blue uniforms of the Union and the grey of the Confederacy. Though diluted with draftees, Gerhardt's three infantry regiments still retained the volunteer ethos of its pre-war soldiers.

Colonel Eugene N. Slappey's 115th comprised companies of the Maryland National Guard, recruited in, for example, Annapolis, Hagerstown and Frederick. Embedded with them as war correspondent was Holbrook 'Hobey' Bradley, a former police reporter for the *Baltimore Sun*, who had shipped to England with the men, and although covering the whole 29th Division, was known for always enquiring, 'Anyone here from Baltimore?'

'As soldiers packed their equipment on transports that would take them to the beaches of Normandy,' Bradley wrote in the *Sun*, 'the dough-boys knew this was the real deal. There was an atmosphere of tense anticipation. They looked seaward toward the distant shore and an enemy they had been waiting to meet.'[29]

Canham's 116th traced its heritage back to the Virginia Militia, with an illustrious history of combat in the French and Indian wars, Revolutionary War, Civil War and the First World War. It traded on its civil war associations with General Thomas J. 'Stonewall' Jackson and the Shenandoah campaign of 1862, becoming known as the 'Stonewall Brigade'. His first Battalion and Company 'B' were headquartered in Lynchburg; 'Able' Company recruited in Bedford, 'D' in Roanoke, 'F' in South Boston, 'H' in Martinsville and 'K' in Charlottesville – where the latter were known as the Monticello Guard, for their proximity to Thomas Jefferson's old estate.

Meanwhile, Paul R. Goode's 175th prided itself in being the seventh-oldest regiment in the United States, first raised in 1774 as the Baltimore Independent Cadets. The 29th's artillery were local Guardsmen, too: the 110th and 224th Field Artillery Battalions were both Maryland and District of Columbia Guard units. The 111th Field Artillery dated back to Civil-War-era units, such as the quixotically named Norfolk Light Artillery Blues and Richmond Howitzers. Each artillery battalion supported an infantry regiment, in this case the 115th, 175th and 116th, respectively. Although the division's 121st Engineer Combat Battalion traced its heritage to the District of Columbia National Guard, its ranks in 1944 were filled with men from Ohio. The 29th Signal Company had long recruited in Norfolk. The medics were also neighbours of the men they would treat. Twenty-nine-year-old Captain Robert Barnes Ware, of Amherst, had just earned his MD from the Medical College of Virginia, when he volunteered for the Guard the same year, eventually serving as battalion surgeon for the First Battalion, 116th Infantry, on D-Day.

What brought them together? Most Guardsmen were teenage buddies in the Depression days, and knew each other from their employers, communities, schools, or local churches (an estimated forty per cent of GIs attended religious services regularly). They were men like Bob Slaughter, who witnessed the *Queen Mary* slicing its escorting cruiser in two. He had joined in 1940 fresh from school. The attraction, as he openly admitted, 'was not entirely patriotic'. The six-foot-five Slaughter was partly attracted by the uniform but mostly by the extra money service would bring, which was hard to come by in his home town of Roanoke, Virginia. Lieutenant Elisha Ray Nance, son of a tobacco farmer from Bedford, a little Blue Ridge town in central Virginia, was another Guardsman who had volunteered in 1933, and enjoyed marching in Fourth of July parades and gathering with friends at the American Legion hall.

Twin brothers Roy and Ray Stevens, also from Bedford, dreamed of one day owning a farm together, and enlisted in 1938. Allen Huddleston joined much later. 'I knew the draft was coming so I thought if I was going to war, I'd rather go with people I knew,' he explained. As many of the older families had lived in these areas since at least the Revolutionary War, and with everyone's roots closely intertwined, these settlements were effectively large families. They regarded service in the Guard, like earlier generations soldiering in the militia or as minutemen, in terms of a civic duty, and there was more than a hint of a social club to local

Guard detachments, scattered throughout the United States – as with volunteer detachments the world over.

The magic may have faded when in February 1941 they were called into federal service, but the regular pay they received was an important compensation: in peacetime the Guard paid $1 per drill (a Monday evening's training) – double what Slaughter was receiving in a saw mill on fifty cents a day – and $15 for two weeks of summer training.[30] On 6 June 1944, Bob Slaughter was soldiering in Company 'D' of the 116th Infantry with many of his buddies from Roanoke. The Stevens brothers and Huddleston were serving in Company 'A', under Nance, alongside two other sets of brothers who also hailed from Bedford, as did their company commander, Captain Taylor Fellers. At the time those in Company 'A' comprised over one per cent of Bedford's entire population.[31]

Local newspapers competed with one another to best record the misty-eyed moment when their young men marched off to war, a forgotten but commonplace experience for Americans during the Civil War and for Britons during the First World War. However, the corollary of enlisting and fighting together is that the same youths might die together, blighting the small communities from whence they came. Whole towns, never mind grieving parents, would never recover from the shock that some of their sons were never coming home. In the case of Bedford, Virginia, twenty-three of her thirty-four boys – who on 5 June 1944 had set sail from Portland, Dorset, aboard HMS *Empire Javelin* – would fail to return.[32]

Clouds prevented most aircraft from identifying their targets ahead of Gerow's V Corps. Of the 448 B-24 Liberators scheduled to release 1,430 tons of munitions onto Omaha's defenders prior to H-Hour, 117 brought their bombs home rather than risk bombing the assault wave. The rest ended up attacking woodland, fields and French dairy herds a couple of miles inland. Post-invasion analysis only identified three positive bomb craters near the beach, one at the rear of WN62, and none inflicting damage. Overseen by Rear Admiral Hall on USS *Ancon*, which reported anchoring at 0251 hours, the bombardment force had concentrated on the big shore emplacements.

USS *Texas* hit the Pointe du Hoc; HMS *Ajax* and the French cruisers *Georges Leygues* and *Montcalm* at various times bombarded Le Chaos at Longues; HMS *Hawkins* concentrated on the Maisy battery; and Hall's destroyers fired at targets all along the V Corps coast. From 0600, drenching fire from the 105mm 'Priests' carried in LCTs followed, supplemented by rocket-firing craft and 75mm guns of the non-swimming Shermans of the 741st and 742nd Tank Battalions. Although this last, more uncertain barrage came from craft moving in the rough waters, they caused some damage, with the defenders first reporting coming under fire at 0604 hours.

It was the western half of Omaha that had been assigned to Charles Canham's 116th Regimental Combat Team. Bob Slaughter recalled that 'Canham didn't look like a soldier, but he sure as hell was one. He was tall and thin, wore wire-rimmed glasses, and had a pencil-thin moustache.'[33] As a sergeant, in 1921 Canham had competed for a place at the United States Military Academy, was selected and graduated with the Class of 1926. Prior to the Second World War, his service had been in the Pacific, where he was assessed as one of the best trainers of men in the army; it was on the strength of this that he had been given command of his regiment in 1942.

Major Carroll B. Smith, of the 116th Infantry's Third Battalion, analysed his experiences of 6 June, and the regiment's rosy-eyed view of what it might achieve on D-Day. He recollected that the First Battalion (Companies 'A' to 'D') would leave the *Empire Javelin* to land on Dog Green, capture Vierville, move west along the coastal highway with the 2nd and 5th Ranger Battalions, clear out positions as far as the Vire estuary, seize Isigny with its bridge over the Vire, nearly fifteen miles distant, and establish contact with Collins' VII Corps.

The Second Battalion, aboard USS *Thomas Jefferson* (Companies 'E' to 'H') was scheduled to land on Dog White and Dog Red, and Easy Green, then push inland to the high ground around Louvières, a more modest mile inland. The Third Battalion (Companies 'I', 'K', 'L' and 'M'), in which Smith was serving as operations officer, would cross the Channel on USS *Charles Carroll*, follow the Second at 0720 hours onto the same beaches, and strike inland to Longueville and La Cambe, ten miles southwest. Smith noted they were 'at full strength, plus a fifteen percent overstrength, which would serve in lieu of replacements until a system could be established on the beachhead; morale was extremely high'.[34]

The 2nd and 5th Ranger Battalions, attached to the regiment, were also to land on Dog Green, although Companies 'D', 'E' and 'F' of the 2nd Rangers would deploy independently. These three companies would transfer into LCAs from the transports *Amsterdam* and *Ben-My-Chree*, scale the cliffs at the Pointe du Hoc, and attack the six-gun battery of 155mm cannon known to be stationed there. Company 'C' of the 2nd Rangers, meanwhile, landing at Dog Green, was to destroy the two 75mm guns in strongpoint WN74, near the radar site on the Pointe de la Percée, both missions scheduled to beach at 0630. The 116th Infantry would be supported by armour (743rd Tank Battalion) and artillery (58th Armored and 111th Field Artillery Battalions).

Following Company 'A' of the 116th, precisely seven minutes later, demolition teams from both the 121st and the 146th Engineer Combat Battalions were to land and blow up obstacles, clearing the way for the subsequent waves. Two companies of swimming tanks (totalling thirty-two) would launch from 6,000 yards out, with a third – sixteen tanks – landing dry-shod. Carefully timetabled, the 58th Armored Field Artillery with their 105mm 'Priests' in five LCTs – we have already encountered John H. Glass escaping as his sank – were to drench the beaches from 0600, and land on Dog White two hours later.

The 111th Field Artillery would land with their twelve 105mm guns mounted in DUKWs shortly afterwards on Easy Green – as would the regiment's own Cannon Company of six 105mm towed howitzers. Following the tight schedule, further units, such as the regiment's Anti-Tank Company and 467th AAA (Anti-Aircraft Artillery) and 81st Chemical Weapons Battalions, would land in sequence. The latter had nothing to do with chemical warfare but was so called because their original 4.2-inch ammunition was for smoke or illumination. The 112th, 121st, 146th and 149th Engineer Combat Battalions would arrive at various stages during the first ninety minutes in support, or to clear obstacles and open exits off the beach.

Initially, Canham's First Battalion had to capture D-1 – the Vierville draw – the most western of the beach exits. Mist and spray, with brush fires caused by the bombardment, contributed to the low visibility that surviving landing craft coxswains complained of, though they missed the fact that a two-knot current was also pushing them eastwards. Two groups of swimming Shermans, Companies 'B' and 'C' of the 743rd Tank Battalion, were scheduled to land with the first wave of four companies ('A', 'E', 'F' and 'G') of the 116th Infantry – just over seven hundred men.

The Naval Demolition Units and army engineers were to follow in the same pattern, now familiar from Utah, succeeded by the third

2 - VIERVILLE-SUR-MER - La plage à marée basse
La mer qui se retire à plus d'un kilomètre, laisse un sable fin et uni

5c

POSTES

Another of the intelligence postcards looking southeast. This one shows the approach to Vierville from Dog Green sector at low tide. While tides had not been a factor in the Mediterranean landings, here the sea receded leaving up to 0.6 miles of sand – lethal to troops storming across it. By 1944 the Germans had built many bunkers set into the cliffs. The Dog One draw is just out of the picture to the right. (Author's collection)

company of Shermans, plus Companies 'B', 'C', 'D' and 'H' from the 116th. The D-1 draw was to be attacked in the west by Ralph Goranson's Company 'C' of the 2nd Rangers, with Taylor Fellers' Company 'A' of the 116th moving in from the east.

The three other 116th companies were to land simultaneously eastwards along the beach and strike inland to seize the upper reaches from behind. In reality, the combination of poor visibility and strong currents pulled the other companies far away to the east. Companies 'F' and 'G' beached near the D-3 draw (Les Moulins), 2,000 yards away, while Company 'E' was three miles off course and fought with the 1st Division. This left just two companies to take D-1.

Captain Taylor Fellers' Company 'A' disembarked from the *Empire Javelin*. Lieutenant Jimmy Green of the 551st LCA Flotilla, skipper of *LCA-910*, was in charge of the first 'flight' of six boats from the *Javelin*. Green remembered Fellers as 'a very serious, thoughtful officer who seemed a lot older than our sailors, in their late teens or early twenties. Taylor Fellers sought me out on the *Javelin* and mentioned his concern that this was his first time in action, the same for his company, and asked for every support.' From the *Javelin*, Fellers and thirty-one men from Company 'A' clambered into Green's craft at 0400 and were lowered away – with considerably more success than his battalion headquarters who, we may recall, were later jammed under the *Javelin*'s heads for thirty unwholesome minutes.

Green launched early, knowing the sea state would slow them down. As they left, his craft was hit in the stern by *LCA-911* and began taking on water. It was too late to change boats so they continued with the hand pump at its maximum. 'We found our escort patrol craft, and set off in the dark, in two columns of three, like Nelson at Trafalgar,' he recounted.[35] They soon passed a group of LCTs wallowing in the heavy seas. 'Fellers told me they were carrying the tanks scheduled to land before us and lead Company 'A' up the beach. We left them in our wake and never saw them again,' Green recollected. 'It was beginning to get light and about time to form line abreast and make our dash for the shore. I turned round to see the bow of *LCA-911* dipping into the sea and disappearing below the waves. It goes against the grain for a sailor to leave his comrades in the sea, but we had no room and our orders were to leave survivors in the sea to be picked up later.'

John J. Barnes from Utica, New York, was a Company 'A' man aboard *LCA-911*, but not a Guardsman. He was a draftee who had shipped out to England in December 1943 and wound up in the 116th. Barnes remembered the sinking: 'It was my fortune to be floating around on our flamethrower which had been wrapped with two life preservers. The boat went down and we all floated to the surface except the radioman who apparently had strapped the radio to his back and got caught in the boat and never did come up.'[36]

Also surviving the sinking was Bedford boy Sergeant Roy Stevens, whose twin brother Ray was elsewhere in the assault, in a different craft. Strong swimmers kept the weaker ones afloat, cutting packs and equipment off each other until *LCA-910* eventually appeared on its return journey, scooped up all but the unfortunate radio man, and took them back to the *Javelin*.[37]

However, on the run-in, Jimmy Green had been watching 'a particularly menacing-looking pillbox at the mouth of the Vierville draw through my binoculars and thought if it was manned we were going to be in trouble'. Green remembered, 'It was dull, grey and overcast; we went flat-out and crunched to a halt some twenty or thirty yards from

A view looking east along Dog Green and Dog White sectors at high tide. This was assaulted by Companies 'A', 'B' and 'D' of the 116th Infantry with very heavy casualties. The obstacles and acres of barbed wire have been removed. The image was taken from the 'particularly menacing looking pillbox at the mouth of the Vierville draw' that one LCA coxswain remembered. 'I thought if it's manned we were going to be in trouble'. (NARA)

the shore. Fellers was gone as soon as the ramp was lowered, before I could wish him luck, his men following in single file, up to their waists in water. In my briefing I was told that the beach would be heavily bombed and there would be craters where the advancing troops could shelter – but the sand was as flat as a pancake with not a crater in sight.' This was a moment Jimmy Green would never forget. 'I can still see them now,' he told me sixty-four years later. 'They were forming an assault line parallel to the shore. That was the last time I saw the men of Company 'A', 116th Infantry Regiment. It reminded me of a scene from the Somme.'[38]

All along the sands, bow ramps dropped and the five assaulting companies threaded their way through the obstacles. They had about five hundred yards of beach to cross before reaching the sea wall. The survivors remembered an eerie silence. The defences appeared untouched, concrete bunkers unmolested by shrapnel damage. Were they empty? All the 116th and 2nd Rangers were a few minutes late, arriving at 0636 hours. Rapid bursts of machine-gun fire soon answered the question. With impressive fire discipline, the defenders waited until the first wave had disembarked and were at their most vulnerable. The Germans were not worried about timetables.

Company 'A', led by Fellers, were met by an impenetrable wall of lead. They had landed exactly where they had intended to be, in the centre of the killing zone defending the most obvious exit from Omaha Beach. This is why of the 180 who set out in Jimmy Green's little flotilla of six boats, ninety-one of the landing party died within minutes from gunshot wounds or drowning. Almost as many were wounded, Bob Slaughter observing: 'the next day, only about fifteen soldiers from Company 'A' were able to continue the fight'.[39] It had taken the German gunners about fifteen minutes to scythe through their ranks. The few survivors cannot remember anyone having the chance to fire their weapon, or hear whatever orders Captain Fellers may have given, their activities focused purely on staying alive.

Exiting his LCA, the second in command, Lieutenant Ray Nance, was the last to reach the sands. He recalled a 'pall of dust and smoke; in the distance I could see the church steeple we were supposed to guide on'. As an officer, he was first out of his landing craft, which probably saved his life: when he looked back he found that nobody had followed him. 'I was off before the German gunners got the range,' Nance observed. 'The rest of the boys back in the boat were mostly killed.' As he waded out of the water onto the beach he met the same continuous fire: 'The bullets were *so* close. The air was full of flying metal which you could hear but not see as it whizzed by, like bugs around your face in the summer.' Weighed down by his water-soaked kit, his rifle disabled by a mortar round, Nance crawled and dodged and ran as best he could, reaching shelter, though wounded by shrapnel in the hand and foot. The survivors fell back to the surf, behind obstacles, or behind the tanks.[40]

'Captain Taylor N. Fellers and Lieutenant Benjamin R. Kearfoot never made it. They had loaded with a section of thirty men in Boat No. 6,' wrote the American combat historian Brigadier General S. L. A. Marshall. 'Exactly what happened to this boat and its human cargo was never to be known. No one saw the craft go down. How each man aboard it met death remains unreported. Half of the drowned bodies were later found along the beach. It is supposed that the others were claimed by the sea.' Marshall's lengthy piece in *The Atlantic* magazine appeared a year after *The Longest Day*, in 1960.

Written in an eye-catching, animated style, it was full of the dramatic carnage of D-Day – sizzling shells, bloodied waters, bullet-ridden sands, mangled bodies, cowardly coxswains, heroic leaders, brave medics, nameless Nazi monsters – and was highly influential and much copied. However – as suggested by this extract – it was highly inaccurate. In fact, the body of Taylor Fellers had soon been found on the beach and buried in Bedford Cemetery, Virginia, as Marshall could have easily discovered.[41]

With the Germans now fully awake at D-1 leading to Vierville, every weapon bloodied and their operators precisely conversant with ranges to various landmarks, at around 0715, a second wave of two companies – 'B' and 'D' of the 116th with the First Battalion's HQ – began to approach the D-1 draw. It was in anticipation of inflicting precisely this carnage that the Germans had named the seaward end of the Vierville draw *der Garten des Teufels* (the Devil's Garden). Still adhering to the timetable – there was no means of altering it – the next companies were thirty minutes behind the first wave, with a third wave twenty minutes behind them. Also disembarking from the *Empire Javelin*, Sergeant Bob Slaughter in Company 'D', who landed on Dog Green just east of the Vierville draw, recalled that 'smoke from the bombardment and the foggy mist obscured our view of the preceding companies, and prevented our coxswain from guiding on the Vierville church steeple'.

The tall, imposing steeple – long a landmark for seafarers – would be brought down at 1400 when it was realised German observers were using it to direct artillery fire. Slaughter continued, 'strong tidal currents diverted us about two hundred yards to the east. No one had set foot where we touched down.' Slaughter's boat got caught on a sandbar, and as the first man leapt off the ramp, 'the craft surged forward and crushed the poor fellow to death. Everyone who followed went off at each side or the rear.'[42]

Slaughter found himself 'struggling in water up to my armpits. A body with its life preserver floated by. The face had already turned a dark purple. All around me, dead men floated in the water, along with live men who acted as if they were dead. I remember helping Private Ernest B. McCanless of Tennessee who was struggling to get closer in. He still had one box of precious .30-calibre machine-gun ammo. He shouted to me, Slaughter, are we going to get through this?' Slaughter ran in a low crouch straight for the sea wall, reaching it with his backpack 'full of holes'.[43]

In another of the Company 'D' boats, an artillery shell or more likely a mine blew off the ramp, killing the CO of the company, Roanokian Captain Walter O. Schilling, and blinding the platoon sergeant. Echoing what had happened thirty minutes earlier to the first assault wave, Company 'D' rapidly became leaderless, losing five of its nine officers and ten sergeants killed, suffering seventy-two casualties in all. Its survivors, too, were soon pinned down.

Meanwhile, Company 'B' landed amid the remnants of Company 'A', not realising until too late the fate which awaited them. In the LCA carrying the company commander, Ettore V. Zappacosta, only one man – PFC Robert L. Sales from Lynchburg, Virginia – survived the landing. His captain shouted 'I'm hit!' before disappearing beneath the water. Sales recollected: 'When we left *Empire Javelin* and boarded the landing craft, Captain Zappacosta, from Yeadon, Pennsylvania, was the first man at the front. I was behind him, being his radio operator. He was very quiet going in. He was not a talkative man anyways, but he was very, very quiet on the trip in. On landing, he was immediately hit in the hip and shoulder.'[44]

In another Company 'B' landing craft was Private Harold Baumgarten, who recalled the boat on his left being hit and blowing up. 'The splintered wood, metal, and body parts were raining down on us from about fifteen feet above. Lieutenant Harold C. Donaldson from Dallas County, Texas, was killed immediately; Clarius L. Riggs, a Pennsylvanian, machine-gunned on the ramp, falling head first into the water. I jumped into the neck-deep waves with my rifle above my head. Some of the fellows were dragged under by their wet combat jackets and heavy equipment; their life preservers didn't help.'[45]

To his right, beaching in Charlie sector where the Rangers had landed, Lieutenant Colonel John A. Metcalfe of Montgomery, Alabama, and part of his First Battalion headquarters arrived, taking heavy casualties until they reached the base of the cliffs. However, there he remained, pinned down by intense fire and unable to influence the battle in any way at all.

Running ashore, Baumgarten with Company 'B' recalled, 'The water was over the head of the average man in my boat. The water was splattered by bullets as I ran through it. A bullet creased the top of my helmet. Robert L. Dittmar from Connecticut was ten feet in front of me to the right, and another of my boat team was behind me on my left. A burst of machine-gun bullets came from above the wall and slightly to our right. I heard a thud from Dittmar's direction, then another to my left: both were down,' the New Yorker said. 'At that moment my rifle, carried at port arms across my chest, was hit and vibrated in my hands; it was struck in front of the trigger guard and stopped the bullet from entering my chest. To my left among the obstacles were two of our amphibious tanks, with their rubber sides down – where were the others? Six 29ers were crouching by the first one which had a dead soldier hanging from the turret, and maybe seven using the other as cover – that one was firing its main gun at the enemy.'[46]

These were the Sherman DDs of the 743rd Tank Battalion, whose officers had taken note of the extremely rough seas – far rougher than anything they had encountered during their preparatory exercises in southern England. They secured agreement for the thirty-two tanks of Companies 'B' and 'C' to be taken all the way to the beaches, with 'A' following them ashore as planned. However, eight tanks of Company 'B' were sunk before reaching shore by direct hits on their LCTs; the remaining eight reached shore safely at Dog Green. Once ashore, however, 'tanks were deprived of their chief tactical advantage: *movement*', noted the After Action Report of the 3rd Armored Group, to which the 743rd belonged.[47] As one tank commander put it, 'We could go straight ahead thirty yards, or straight back twenty yards – that was all.'[48]

As the tide advanced, wrecked vehicles, uncleared obstacles and injured troops sprawled on the sand reduced their manoeuvrability in some cases to zero – hence Hal Baumgarten encountering the stationary armour. They ended up as steel pillboxes slugging it out with the anti-tank guns hiding behind their concrete, but putting down valuable fire on any positions they could see, and receiving equal punishment in exchange. Their machine-gun fire into the marsh beyond the shingle and brush atop the bluffs helped flush out some snipers and trigger anti-personnel mines.

Of the forty-eight 743rd tanks ashore opposite D-1 and further east, Company 'A' lost half their strength, eight; Company 'B' another eight; though 'C' was luckier, only losing one disabled with five men wounded – yet this amounted to the loss of one-third of their armoured vehicles.[49] One of the Company 'A' tank drivers was Corporal William Gast, from

Lancaster, Pennsylvania, who would earn a Silver Star. 'The order was given to go, we started our engines up, they lowered the ramp,' he recalled. 'At first I could feel the tracks spinning, then at last they took hold on the seabed and we went up the beach. I was sealed in and drove with the aid of a small periscope, but with the sea spray, shelling and smoke I could see practically nothing. Our tank radio was so unreliable that I received a kick to my left or right shoulder, by way of telling me which direction to steer,' Gast explained. 'Once on the beach, shells exploded so close you could feel the tank shake. That was the first time I heard machine-gun bullets hitting us while I was inside. They sounded like throwing marbles at a car.'[50]

The surviving Shermans would crawl up the D-1 draw only at about 2200 hours on the evening of 6 June, once the engineers had blasted their way through the obstacles and cleared mines. It is perhaps no accident that the surname Upham appears in *Saving Private Ryan*, for this was also the name borne by the battalion commander of the 743rd. Lieutenant Colonel John S. Upham, West Point Class of 1928, directed operations by radio from an LCT a few hundred yards away, but ended up wading ashore to Easy Green to do the job better. Walking from tank to tank, he personally directed their fire and manoeuvres, though wounded twice in the process. 'It was only after his battalion had seized its objective that he was evacuated for his wounds,' read the citation for his Distinguished Service Cross.[51]

After the war, survivors of Companies 'A', 'B' and 'D', amongst others in the 116th Infantry, alleged that British coxswains had to be persuaded at the point of a Colt .45 to land their soldiers on the beach, an accusation also levelled at American coxswains during the Utah landings and elsewhere on Omaha. We have already observed that landing craft crews had their own timetable, which implied a quick turnaround, but the frequency with which this tale is encountered in all the major histories is troubling, and appears to have become a received wisdom amongst the veteran communities and slapdash historians.

The first instance seems to have originated in S. L. A. Marshall's 1960 piece, where he wrote:

> A great cloud of smoke and dust raised by the mortar and machine-gun fire has almost closed a curtain around Able Company's ordeal. Outside the pall, nothing is to be seen but a line of corpses adrift, a few heads bobbing in the water and the crimson-running tide. But this is enough

for the British coxswains. They raise the cry: 'We can't go in there. We can't see the landmarks. We must pull off.' In the command boat, Captain Ettore V. Zappacosta pulls a Colt .45 and says: 'By God, you'll take this boat straight in.'[52]

Of this particular incident, PFC Robert L. Sales, the only survivor from Zappacosta's craft, was adamant to his dying day that Marshall's version of events was simply untrue: 'I have never told anybody that Captain Zappacosta pulled his gun on that coxswain and told him to take that boat in. It did not happen. The only words from the coxswain were: "I cannot go in any further. I'm going to drop the ramp." There was no argument about it. There were obstacles in the water. He could not do any better. I was the only survivor off that landing craft. Captain Zappacosta never moved out of his position all the way in. He was not the kind of man to pull a gun to the head of a sailor. If we had gone in any further, we would have hit the mines on the obstacle.'[53]

A forensic look at the evidence will help here, for there are several reasons why this confrontation would have been unlikely in a British LCA or Higgins boat. We have already heard how – with its flat bottom continually slapping against the waves and the engine noise – conversation in an LCVP was all but impossible. Although the engines in an LCA were silenced, the noise of the rough seas thumping the hull equally made speech pointless. From their extensive amphibious training in Devon, the 29th and 1st Divisions had learned to distribute their leaders, skills and weapons equally into 'boat teams', so that the loss of any one craft would not be catastrophic.

Commanding officers and their executive officers travelled separately; each landing craft was ordered to carry, in order from bow to stern: one officer in the bow with radio operator and messengers; two Browning Automatic Rifle (BAR) teams of two men each; two bazooka teams; squad of 60mm mortars, flamethrower team; demolition team with prepared charges; medic to the rear.[54] This doctrine was quite specific: the leader, or senior person on board, stood *at the front* and was first to disembark. Thus, a disaffected officer ordering a coxswain in closer would be standing by the ramp, physically some distance away from the sailor in charge of the boat, and out of earshot. With thirty to thirty-five GIs in each boat, plus all their equipment, there was no room to move about, never mind these landing barges 'bucking about like stallions' in the rough water.

Captain Charles R. Cawthon of the 116th 'Stonewall Brigade' recorded of his LCVP heading towards Omaha, 'Talk would have been difficult above the roar of the engine, the wind, slamming of the waves against the ramp, and the labouring of the bilge pump that just managed to keep up with the water washing in over the bow and sides. We simply stood packed together, encased with equipment, inarticulate with the noise.'[55]

Lieutenant Jimmy Green, who took Captain Fellers into Vierville, was particularly troubled by such accusations of cowardice: 'Most of us had taken part in more amphibious operations than our passengers. We knew what we were doing. British landing craft were not like American LCVPs, whose coxswain stood at the wheel towards the stern, surrounded by his passengers. Studying any photographs of Royal Navy LCAs would reveal a sentry-box-shaped object near the ramp on the starboard side. This armour-plated turret was the steering shelter, from where I controlled my LCA by compass, telegraph and voice pipe. I would have been well clear of any Colt-toting mutineer intent on assuming command.'[56]

Having travelled in small landing craft during my military career (which I suspect many authors have not), I can attest to the unlikelihood of making my way towards a coxswain in a heavy swell, never mind waving my pistol and making myself heard in a fast-moving, flat-bottomed boat.

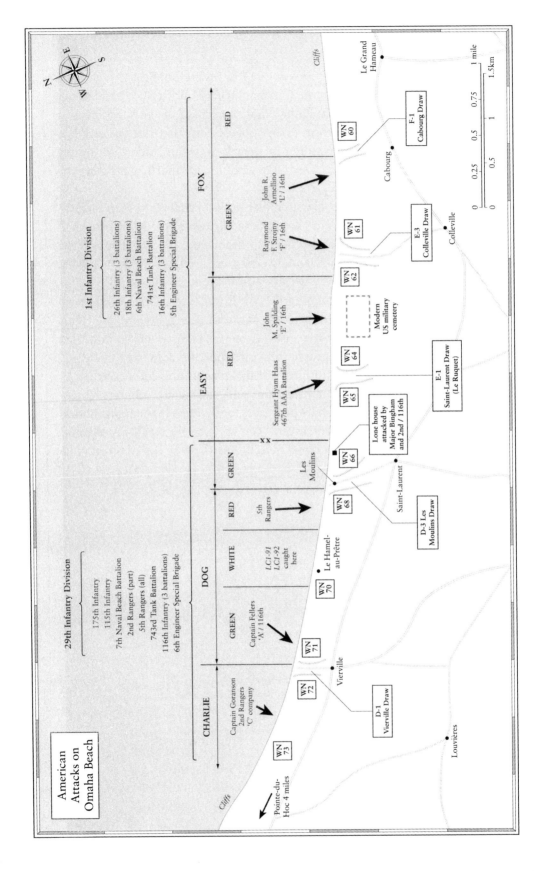

American Attacks on
Omaha Beach

29th Infantry Division

175th Infantry
115th Infantry
7th Naval Beach Battalion
2nd Rangers (part)
5th Rangers (all)
743rd Tank Battalion
116th Infantry (3 battalions)
6th Engineer Special Brigade

1st Infantry Division

26th Infantry (3 battalions)
18th Infantry (3 battalions)
6th Naval Beach Battalion
741st Tank Battalion
16th Infantry (3 battalions)
5th Engineer Special Brigade

CHARLIE

DOG

EASY

FOX

GREEN | WHITE | RED | GREEN

RED

GREEN | RED

Captain Goranson
2nd Rangers
'C' company

Captain Fellers
'A' / 116th

LCI-91
LCI-92
caught
here

5th
Rangers

Les
Moulins

Sergeant Hyam Haas
467th AAA Battalion

John
M. Spalding
'E' / 16th

Raymond
F. Strojny
'F' / 16th

John R.
Armellino
'E' / 16th

xx

WN 73

WN 72

WN 71

WN 70

WN 68

WN 66

WN 65

WN 64

WN 62

WN 61

WN 60

Lone house attacked by
Major Bingham
and 2nd / 116th

Modern
US military
cemetery

Pointe-du-
Hoc 4 miles

Vierville

Le Hamel-
au-Prêtre

Saint-Laurent

Louvières

Cabourg

Colleville

Le Grand
Hameau

D-1
Vierville Draw

D-3 Les
Moulins Draw

E-1
Saint-Laurent Draw
(Le Ruquet)

E-3
Colleville Draw

F-1
Cabourg Draw

Cliffs

Cliffs

0   0.25   0.5   0.75   1 mile

0   0.5   1   1.5km

27

Omaha: Cota Takes Command

'There was disaster everywhere. Anyone who says there wasn't fear that day is nuts. You were told to do it. You went ahead. There was no time to think. If you had, you probably would have jumped back in the Channel and swam back to England.'

Adolf 'Al' Drega, 2nd Rangers[1]

BRIGADIER GENERAL NORMAN 'Dutch' Cota – his nickname came from his childhood days in Chelsea, Massachusetts – was a West Point contemporary of Collins, Gerhardt and Ridgway and had been involved in the planning of Torch and Husky, as well as Overlord. At fifty-one, he and his counterpart in the 4th Division, Theodore Roosevelt, Jr, would be a generation older than most Americans ashore on D-Day. In real life, the craggy, steely-eyed assistant divisional commander of the 29th Division certainly looked more senior than Robert Mitchum, who played him in *The Longest Day*.[2]

On his Command and General Staff Course at Fort Leavenworth, Cota had written a study paper on the Turkish defence of the Gallipoli peninsula against the 1915 British landings; as a result he felt a daylight amphibious assault would not succeed. He was one of the more pessimistic – though capable and eminently practical – commanders on D-Day, and had determined to be present as soon after H-Hour as practicable, to sort out the mess he felt sure would ensue. With commendable foresight, he had warned his officers beforehand, 'The landing craft aren't going in on schedule and people are going to be landed in the wrong place. Some won't be landing at all. The Germans will try, and will have some success, in preventing our gaining a lodgement. But we must improvise, carry on, and *not* lose our heads. Nor must we add to the confusion.'[3]

Company 'C' of the 116th arrived on Dog White between Vierville and Les Moulins, near the breakwaters, towards 0730 hours. They almost lost their commander, Captain Berthier B. Hawks of Emporia, Virginia, who caught and injured his foot in the ramp winch mechanism as he plunged into water over his head; he crawled back on board as the boat retracted and tried again. A neighbouring landing craft hit the beach under such intense fire that men were ordered to jump over the sides rather than the bow ramp be lowered; three GIs refused to leave, huddling on the floor. Another assault vessel flipped over after riding up one of Rommel's wooden obstacles, spilling its contents – men and their equipment, machine-guns, bazookas, flamethrowers, Bangalore torpedoes and explosives – into the water, exactly as the Desert Fox had planned.

Nearby on Dog Green, fourteen more LCAs appeared: these carried Lieutenant Colonel Max Schneider's 5th Ranger Battalion, which, having heard no word from the Pointe du Hoc, had diverted to reinforce Omaha. They landed at the only spot they could find, fortunately away from the withering fire around the draws. Schneider urged his men straight off the beach; only Father Joe Lacy, the Rangers' thirty-nine-year-old over-weight chaplain, remained on the sands, dragging the injured away from the rising tide, administering the last rites to the dying, ignoring the crossfire. Wearing thick glasses and all of five foot six inches, he was known respectfully as Father Ranger – and less reverently as 'that small, fat old Irishman'. To the Rangers, he led a charmed life, being last off his boat, *LCA-1377*, before an artillery shell caught it, but spent the day in 'complete disregard for his own safety, moving about the beach, continually exposed to enemy fire, assisting the wounded, and at the same time inspiring the men to similarly disregard for the enemy fire', as the words of his Distinguished Service Cross citation put it.[4]

Schneider was followed soon after by a single craft containing Colonel Charles Canham, commanding the 116th, and his boss, 'Dutch' Cota. It was certainly an error of judgement to let these two senior officers ride together, for their boat hit a mined obstacle but it didn't explode. The craft also contained the Stonewaller's chief surgeon, Robert Buckley, and his friend the regimental S-4 (supply officer), Major John W. Sours, a Roanoke National Guardsman. Buckley recalled the first few hours:

> Our berths were opposite one other, and first thing we helped each other fix the camouflage nets on our helmets. Then twenty-six of us got into a smaller barge and we soon moved away from our transport … We exited when there was a hundred yards between us and the beach; I threw a glance back and saw 'Big John' Sours following me. After reaching the cover of the seawall, I took in the panorama and noticed two men in the surf needing help. With the soldier next to me, we went to carry them in: one had a leg wound, the other was lying with his head underwater. When I raised it, I recognised my buddy, 'Big John'. He was already dead, killed by a machine-gun round to the head. I helped the soldier with the leg wound across the beach, and back in the water found a helmet floating by. It was his, and had been perforated by a bullet. I moved him as quickly as possible away from the surf and covered him well, as I had to with many others that day.[5]

With several of their fellow passengers wounded or slain, Canham and Cota were lucky to make it ashore alive.

At this stage, around 0740, at the intersection of Dog White and Dog Red – between Le Hamel-au-Prêtre and Les Moulins – two much larger Landing Craft, Infantry appeared, *LCI-91* and *LCI-92*, each determined to land a company's worth of men from their decks via the two ramps that dropped down from either side of the bow. This was seventy minutes after H-Hour, by which time – the timetable said – the assault wave should have overwhelmed the beach defences and engineers opened lanes through the obstacles. Seth Shepherd had been financial news reporter for the *Chicago Daily News* until he joined the US Coast Guard as a combat photographer and was assigned to *LCI-92*. She and her sister ship *LCI-91* were Coast Guard-manned and already veterans of North Africa, Sicily and the Salerno landings, as were many of the crew.

Shepherd remembered sleeping soundly,

> dreaming and hearing nothing until 0340 hours when I was awakened by the clanging of the alarm bell – General Quarters – I sprang out of my bunk and dressed with record speed. Like everyone, I had slept in my clothes except for the outer gas suit and my heavy shoes. I was the last man to scramble up the dark ladder, after grabbing my camera and

8 - VIERVILLE-SUR-MER — Panorama de la plage (côté Est)
Vue splendide sur toute la baie jusqu'aux rochers du Calvados

Les Moulins

DOG RED

DOG WHITE

This intelligence postcard looks down from where *Widerstandsnest* 70 was situated with two 75mm guns. WN68 was further east, looking down onto Dog Red. It was at the intersection of Dogs White and Red that two Landing Craft Infantry, LCIs 91 and 92, were caught in the crossfire of these and other positions and set on fire. The large vessels burned for most of the day, but their smoke also aided the attackers. (Author's collection)

film. In the distance ahead, along the French coast, we could see sharp flashes of brilliant explosions and heavy anti-aircraft fire, and hear the deep rumble of the blasting and firing. As my eyes became more accustomed to the darkness I could make out the dark shapes of landing craft and ships surrounding us. All the while I was conscious of that eerie whistling of the wind through the rigging. It was cold and I pulled up the hood of my gas suit over my steel helmet and tightened my life jacket. I realised that we were in for a tough time as I made out shattered Higgins boats on the beach and men running to take cover. I could see a few houses in the lee of the hill, wrecked and on fire.[6]

Slightly ahead, the first of the pair, *LCI-91*, hit the sand and dropped her foot ramps but as she did so, a teller mine on a pole exploded on the port bow; hastily the ramps were retracted and *LCI-91* pulled away, and re-beached a hundred yards west to continue. As the last Stonewallers left her decks, a shell struck the ship's fuel tanks, enveloping it in flames. The crew abandoned ship, jumping overboard, and as they bobbed up they witnessed their sister craft, *LCI-92*, approach nearby, using the pall of smoke as cover. Seth Shepherd was on the bridge of *LCI-92*, and remembered how his heartbeat raced when he looked over the starboard bow and saw *LCI-91* shrouded in flames and smoke:

> Our Skipper, Lieutenant Robert M. Salmon, of Maplewood, New Jersey, was standing forward in the conn, gripping the handrail as he directed our ship by speaking through the tube to the pilot house. Lambert, the signalman, stood on the starboard side of the conn, with ear phones on. I was on the port side by the signal light with my camera, bracing myself to take a picture … Then a terrifying blast lifted our whole ship upward with a sudden lurch from the bow. A sheet of flame and steel shot out from the forward hold. The ship quivered as if it were pulling apart and the concussion threw the three of us in the conn backward, and down hard. The heat was like the midst of a blast furnace. We were stunned for an instant and our ears were ringing with the deafening vibrations. Seconds later another shattering explosion shook the ship like a toy boat and a rain of shrapnel splattered the shivering vessel. In that first blast from the mine, which set fire to the main fuel tanks and blew out a hole in the starboard side big enough to drive a Higgins boat through, forty-one soldiers in the forward troop compartment were trapped in a fiery furnace, most of them being killed instantly. The first explosion blew two of the soldiers out the hatch and the sheet of flame shot aft through the pilot-house ports. The scene was extreme confusion. The piles of K rations and gear for the soldiers were littered over the well deck. Flames and dense smoke were pouring from the hatch, the ramps were damaged making both impossible to lower. Everywhere were faces blackened from the smoke and fire.[7]

These two big craft burned for hours and defined the catastrophe of the morning for many survivors. To the Germans this seemed like a runaway victory, but the drifting, oily smoke exaggerated the damage they were inflicting on the assault flotilla, and protected some of its passengers. It was seared onto the memory of many, such as Captain John Raaen of the 5th Rangers, pausing for breath at the sea wall. 'We had just arrived by a landing barge that was destroyed after the last man – Father Joe Lacey, our chaplain – exited, killing the British crew. Artillery and mortars continued to search the surf. To the left I saw that big LCI touch down. We watched as men started down the side ramps. *Wham!* An artillery round caught the starboard ramp. Immediately the whole side of the ship burst into flames that spread to her deck – there must have been a flamethrower there. All my life I've been fascinated by munitions, but am scared to death of them. That's why.'[8]

Captain Carroll Smith of the 116th's Third Battalion also saw the vessel hit by the hidden gun emplacement he encountered when climbing the bluffs, almost certainly WN65. 'Later we discovered the burning ship was *LCI-92* carrying the alternate headquarters of the 116th RCT and part of 12lst Engineer Battalion with their demolitions stacked on the forward deck.'[9] Smith crawled back down the bluff to an immobilised 743rd Tank Battalion Sherman, 'got the attention of the crew by pounding on the turret with a rifle butt and directed a dozen tank rounds at the emplacement, but its 75-mm gun made no impression on the concrete whatsoever'. Eventually they 'neutralised it by placing demolition charges around the embrasure and blasting it in. We later discovered the only entrance to this position was through a tunnel over two hundred yards to the rear.'[10] *LCI-92* had been carrying men from the 121st Engineer Combat Battalion, and it was the ignition of their explosives on deck that sealed the fate of the vessel – and many of those on board. Lieutenant Colonel Robert Riis Ploger, West Point Class of 1939, was CO of the engineers, and managed to leap overboard, inflate his life preserver, swim to shore, run up the beach and had just dropped into a shell crater when a bullet hit his left ankle. Just minutes earlier he had been standing on deck surrounded by scores of his men. In addition, he was firmly convinced he had angered the gods when he looked around and found he could not see a single man from his battalion.[11] Other engineers who made the shoreline attempted to work six bulldozers, but lost two straight away to artillery, while the others were prevented from clearing obstacles by GIs sheltering behind them.

The story of many of the landing craft at Omaha was one of trying to find a gap in the obstacles. Where there was space, it was frequently blocked by damaged craft and vehicles. The runnels, bomb craters and sandbars meant that boats sometimes lowered their ramps, found the water too deep for men or vehicles, retracted and tried again. Craft, such as *LCT-149, LCT-195, LCT-305* and *LCT-214*, destined for Dog Red at 0830, spent hours looking for a suitable disembarkation spot, the first only unloading at 1900 hours, the middle pair at 1630, and the last at 1730 – ten and a half, eight and nine hours behind schedule, respectively.[12] According to the log of *LCT-207*, she was carrying 105mm 'Priests' of the 58th Armored Field Artillery Battalion (John H. Glass's unit), which 'commenced shelling beach at 0630 hours. Underway for beach at 0800 hours but unable to approach due to shelling and beach obstacles. Finally proceeded into Dog Red at 1600 hours. Unloaded and retracted at 1638 hours.' After an eight-hour wait to unload, their dramas were far from over. At 1700, they 'Went to assistance of *LCT-27* and removed Army and Navy personnel – *LCT-27* capsized and sank almost immediately with a full load of vehicles.'[13]

For Creed Conwell, a Blue and Gray soldier born and raised in Manhattan, advice given him by the British commandos helped him through the maelstrom on the sands: 'When training with them, the Brits told me "don't stop to help – it might not be the Christian thing to do, but it will keep you alive". They advised me to be a loner and I just went with it,' he explained. 'On that day, I had no friends but me – if a guy fell beside me, I let him,' Conwell said. Having won $300 in a craps game sailing over, his chief remembrance of the morning was 'the gun noise, which was something else. Loud. I mean *real loud*. It was so loud we couldn't hear ourselves scream. There never was a moment when someone wasn't shooting, them at us and we at them.' Wading ashore, the 29er shed his rifle, pack and helmet to stay alive. Conwell soon found another rifle and picked up a helmet bearing a captain's bars before losing it the next day. 'I was a captain for twenty-four hours,' he chuckled.[14]

In spite of the carnage, the 29th were beginning to assemble a critical mass of troops on the beach, and the destruction, flames and fumes were beginning to obscure the true picture of growing American strength beyond the barbed wire. The only way the defending grenadiers could have inflicted certain defeat was by counter-attacking – however, their defences had been designed to avoid this necessity. Now, for the growing legions on the shingle arrived, in the nick of time, firm leadership in the shape of Colonel Canham and General Cota. This is where personal example shone through: we will examine Cota's interaction with the Rangers in the next chapter, but his impact on his own division was just as profound.

He proceeded to walk much of the length of the beach under fire, noting at the point of his landing the scores of men sheltering behind the breakwaters – an inviting target for shells. At one stage he hit the dirt as the shelling got even more intense. Two GIs lying prone near him were desperate for a cigarette. One leaned over and punched the figure lying next to them. 'Hey, buddy, you got a light?' Cota rolled over, his general's star suddenly visible. 'Sorry, sir!' the soldier stuttered. Then 'Cota reached into his jacket, pulled out a Zippo, flicked it and said, "That's OK, son, we're all here for the same reason." Shortly after that he rose and began repeatedly yelling, "You all have to get off the beach, or you're gonna die!" He had to get the dispirited GIs out of the water, and others away from the obstacles, across the sands and off the beach. He urged all to move forward, "Twenty-Nine, let's go!"'[15]

Canham was doing exactly the same: both were demonstrating leadership qualities to an extraordinary degree, being as close to the action as it was possible to be. When Canham saw one of his Company 'C' men shot while cutting through barbed wire, he pulled the cutters out of the dead man's hands and continued the job himself. He had just finished when a bullet drilled though his wrist; he shrugged it off – but the sight of their regimental commander clutching a bloodied handkerchief bawling 'All of you who want to die, stay where you are, and those who want to live, come with me' was a game-changer for the Stonewall Brigade clustered around him. Shunning any protective cover, with gaps in the wire opening, and engineers on hand to deal with the mines beyond, he yelled to his officers, 'Get these men the hell off this goddamned beach and go kill some goddamned Krauts!' – and his men started to flow inexorably towards the base of the bluffs. Company 'C' and some of 'D' of the 116th pushed their way to the heights. Schneider's 5th Rangers were with them (whom we shall follow later). A breakthrough had begun, and it had been brought about by the dynamism of two men, arriving just where and when they were most needed.

At H-Hour, Companies 'F' and 'G' of the Second Battalion, 116th Infantry, landed opposite D-3 at Les Moulins, the junction of Dog Red and Easy Green – their landing barges drawn as much by the current as by easily identifiable landmarks, but this was further east than they had intended. Company 'E' would be pulled further east still and fought with the 1st Division – we will look at them later. Les Moulins was overwatched by positions WN68 and WN66, whose defences comprised a number of concrete bunkers housing 50mm cannon, machine-guns, mortars and revolving tank turrets. The story here started to unfold in a similar way to the Vierville draw. The GIs were initially not fired upon, illustrating the very good fire discipline and training of the defenders – grenadiers from both the 716th and 352nd Divisions. However, once the men were off their boats and vulnerable on the sand, automatic fire from WN68 and WN66 cut into their ranks, the Germans using the same crossfire techniques. The inclination of some was to cower behind the illusionary cover of the beach obstacles, where indirect fire from mortars – whose operators could place rounds with precision into landing craft – and inland artillery batteries took its toll. The defenders had previously registered defensive fire zones with their guns: all that was required was the single code word 'Dora' to unleash fire on the terrain between the sea wall and the sea.

Charles Cawthon, Headquarters Company commander in the 116th's Second Battalion, and his men were offloaded into shoulder-deep surf when their LCVP wedged on a sandbar. Kept afloat by his life preserver, he recalled 'The effect of the alternate lift and fall with the waves was to gain views of the battle [ashore] that were like the stopped frames of a motion picture. From the crests, the beach was visible, and then in the troughs, only the green-black water of the passed wave.' He encountered a surprising silence, 'the wind, like the tide carried the din of invasion inland', and thought the scene 'strangely vacant' of the huge maritime and aerial armada he knew to be present. Floundering in the surf Cawthon couldn't see the warships while the 'P-38s melted into the gloom', all being masked by 'uncertainty and the weather.'

Arriving at around 0730, he could see the first assault wave on the beach resembling 'heaps of refuse, deposited there to burn and smoulder unattended'. Soon, he too, was 'ejected onto the beach, strewn with many dead things, both man and machine … Hundreds of brown life belts were washing to and fro, writhing and twisting like brown sea slugs'. Cawthon tried to rise out of the water but found 'I seemed to be hoisting the English Channel with me', so jettisoned his assault jacket and 'free of its weight, went lumbering up the beach, streaming water at every step'.[16]

It would take up to forty-five minutes for the surviving GIs to work their way to the sea wall, with most of their weapons full of clinging, wet sand. Three-quarters of all radios were destroyed; most engineer equipment was lost in the water; while the Navy Combat Demolition Units and Shore Fire Control Parties, who would direct ship-to-shore bombardment, had perished in the initial bloodletting. Around four hundred yards west of Les Moulins and nine hundred yards east of Vierville, men bunched around fifteen breakwaters (now removed) – they were just rows of rotting wood that jutted into the water, built to prevent beach erosion, but their meagre protection made them lifesavers as scores of men took shelter behind each.

The rough sea challenged the combat capability of the 111th Field Artillery Battalion, supporting the 116th Infantry. It had placed each of its twelve 105mm howitzers in a DUKW, with the intention of making them self-propelled guns when they got ashore on Dog Red from 0820 hours, and put a headquarters element in a thirteenth. These launched from LSTs at 0400, each amphibian containing 'a gun, fourteen men, fifty rounds of 105mm ammunition, filled sandbags for protection and all the essential equipment for set-up and maintenance'. Even during the pre-invasion Exercise Fox, the 111th's officers had become convinced that DUKWs were not practical, and thought them unseaworthy. Now, all but four were swamped within minutes of leaving their LSTs, including the one carrying some of the battalion headquarters. Of sixteen men aboard this last, seven drowned (including the battalion surgeon) and three were wounded by shellfire. 'Their loads made them unmanoeuvrable, few coxswains seeming to know how to handle a craft in high seas.'[17]

Two more DUKWs went down within five hundred yards of the shore, which left two. A shell hit one of them, only five men surviving to swim to the beach; the final DUKW, commanded by Captain Louis A. Shuford, managed to have his gun hoisted aboard a Rhino ferry before his DUKW, too, sank many miles east of his allocated beach. The 111th still contained many pre-war artillerymen who had bestowed on each gun a name: the remaining piece was called 'the Chief', which Shuford turned over to the Big Red One's 7th Field Artillery Battalion, who themselves had lost six of their twelve howitzers.[18] Shuford was awarded a Bronze Star for his sheer tenacity in preserving the only gun left of the battalion.[19] 'Much valuable fire support went to the bottom of the English Channel,' noted one 116th officer, 'the loss of which had a ruinous effect on the efficiency of the battalion as well as on the morale of the troops.'[20]

However, every image of Omaha was unique, some surprisingly so, as Lieutenant Charles Lilly, skipper of *LCT-637*, observed:

My own impression of that morning is so different from what I had expected or anything I have seen written about battle. During the day we waited, orbiting offshore fairly close in, and under sporadic fire from shore. From where we were there was none of the sound or fury that characterize the Hollywood war movie. Everything outside the arena of battle was curiously peaceful: the sky was blue with scattered clouds, just like any normal day. Gulls circled around seemingly undisturbed. Ashore we could see farm houses and cattle grazing – everything seemed to be in order. Yet in front of us, on the beach were explosions, fires, and the crackle of guns. Close inspection with glasses turned up bodies of dead and wounded. Suddenly, to emphasize the point that this was not a normal day, an American destroyer moved in near us, in water so shallow she scraped her keel, to open fire at point blank range, on a spot in the cliffs above the beach. In a neat bit of surgery she chopped out a block of cliff, 88mm cannon, machine-guns, and other assorted debris. We all cheered as though our side had scored in a football game.[21]

Captain Charles Cawthon with the 116th also emphasised the localised nature of the carnage. He remembered that about a thousand yards east of Les Moulins he came across 'a stretch of beach vacant of men and quiet except for the wind, waves and beach birds that were swooping and crying'. He observed 'Omaha Beach was generally of this pattern: violent swirls of death and destruction with areas of quiet in between'. At this place, 'smoky brush fires had swept up the bluffs and screened one of the first penetrations'. Cawthon observed, 'Whatever else was accomplished by the naval cannonade that preceded H-Hour, nothing could have exceeded the value of those brush fires that it had started inadvertently. In fact, they demonstrated that a few smoke shells would have served us better than all the weight of high explosive. They were the salvation of Omaha Beach'.[22]

Whenever the guns of USS *Texas* barked out in fury they were directed by a spotter aircraft. 'Ours was a daring and excitable Englishman,' remembered the warco (war correspondent) of the *Saturday Evening Post*.

We tried desperately to find the enemy batteries causing all this trouble. A destroyer reported receiving word that the Germans were using the church tower at Vierville as an observation post. Our first salvo scored a direct hit, knocking off part of the steeple. Now, in rapid succession, our targets were: a mobile battery near Maisy; German troop concentrations near Formigny; truck convoys centring on Trévières; and armor, converging on a wood near Surrain. "I'm diving down to see if these tanks are friendly", he radioed us. A few seconds later came his last cheerful transmission, "They're definitely not friendly. I'm bailing out. Goodbye!"[23]

Landing on the eastern side of D-3, the Les Moulins draw on Easy Green, was Major Sydney V. Bingham, commanding the Second Battalion (Companies 'E' to 'H') of the 116th Infantry. He gathered as many of his GIs as he could find, but noted that many were in shock. Then Bingham, from Aspen, Colorado, led fifty men in what was essentially a platoon attack on a lone three-storey villa – the only one not demolished by the Germans and well-fortified – aided by his XO, Major Fred McManaway, of Roanoke. By about 0800, they had penetrated the barbed wire, reached the building, and subsequently used it as a base from which to begin to push up the D-3 draw.

Soon, Bingham had made contact with Colonel Paul W. Thompson, commanding the 6th Engineer Special Brigade (ESB) – the umbrella group controlling all the engineer battalions in the 29th's sector. Its sister, the 5th ESB, was likewise working further down the sand with the Big Red One. Thompson immediately perceived that it was riflemen who were needed, not engineers, and had his men down their tools, fix their bayonets and supplement the depleted Second Battalion's ranks. As

The photographer here is standing by the Dog Three (Les Moulins) draw, looking west through the villas that made up Le Hamel-au-Prêtre, towards Vierville. This stretch is where men of Max Schneider's 5th Rangers landed and were told by Brigadier General Cota, striding up and down the shore, pistol in hand, 'Rangers, lead the way'. Off to the right is where Major Sydney Bingham's Second Battalion of the 116th Infantry disembarked. (Author's collection)

Bingham had just been doing, Thompson was soon leading his men in a series of squad assaults, skirmished up D-3, during which he was badly wounded but survived.[24]

Also approaching to the east of Les Moulins, on Easy Green, was Second Lieutenant Wesley R. Ross in an LCM with some of Company 'B', 146th Engineers. He recalled seeing splashes in the water from the mortar, artillery and small arms fire,

> so I quickly lost interest in being an observer, and ducked down behind the steel ramp and sidewalls. This was really fingernail-biting time, as detonation of our explosives by mortar or artillery fire would have been terminal. As we came close in, our stern gunners began hosing down the beach ahead with their .50-caliber machine-guns, which was a morale booster, as we began to notice dead GIs face-down, bobbing and rolling in the surf. There were no visible tankdozers or infantrymen near when we scurried from our craft onto Easy Green, two hundred yards west of our assigned spot. Several of us slid our rubber raft out of the barge containing explosives and Bangalore torpedoes. Running a zig-zag path between the wooden obstacles and steel hedgehogs, I looked eastward into the pre-sunrise sky and saw an artillery round hit the sand sixty feet away. It ricocheted twenty feet into the air, its pointed nose clearly visible against the morning sky before exploding. It split along its length rather than producing multiple high velocity fragments, a faulty round – and much appreciated!

Ross also remembered the capture of the fortified house by Major Bingham, 'Without warning, from ten yards to my rear, our tankdozer fired a 75mm round into the fortified house, two hundred yards to our left front; that silenced the machine-gun that had been giving us so much trouble. We had been so busy, attaching explosives to the wooden obstacles, that until that blast I was unaware that our tankdozer had finally landed, about twenty minutes late.'[25]

Meanwhile, the CO of the 111th Artillery, Lieutenant Colonel Thornton L. Mullins, had landed on Dog Red, west of Les Moulins, at 0730, ahead of his guns. He and his reconnaissance and liaison staff were perturbed to discover 'the beach was quite smooth, had none of the promised bomb or shell craters, neither were any obstacles blown'. With waves running at five to six feet high, an absence of friendly positions and Germans manning the cliffs, the staff agreed immediately their guns should not be brought in, but they had no means of altering the assault.

All of their radios had been destroyed by 'steady 88 and small arms fire on the beach' or soaked in the approach, one radio man stating that 'he had stepped from his LCVP into water over his head and for ten minutes his set had been on the bottom'. They soon found troops of Bingham's Second Battalion, 116th Infantry, whose men 'were beat-up and shocked. Many of them had forgotten they had firearms to use,' observed the 111th Artillery's After Action Report. 'Others who had lost their arms didn't seem to see that there were weapons lying all around, and that it was their duty to pick them up.'[26]

The artillerymen observed how Bingham set to work on his infantrymen, got them cleaning their weapons and, if they were empty-handed, showed them where to pick up arms. Some of them were Company 'H' riflemen, others Bingham's own command group, who had arrived at 0700 hours. Bullets had cut into the latter as soon as their craft beached: his S-3, Captain Sherman V. Burroughs III, of Roanoke, was killed on the ramp; Battalion Surgeon Robert M. DeWitt and five of his medics fell, riddled with shrapnel. Others took cover behind tanks, stationary in about two feet of water, searching for targets on the bluffs.

Perhaps twenty to thirty men did this, including Chaplain Charles D. Reed, but when his tank moved off, the chaplain's leg was caught under a track and mangled. Before he could move, a shell burst, killing all around him, and decapitating Staff Sergeant Arthur Woods. Keeping just ahead of the incoming tide, which drowned the other wounded, Reed crawled ashore, dragging his wounded leg. Bingham later acknowledged how important the tanks had been to his survival: 'they saved the day. They shot the hell out of the Germans, and got the hell shot out of them.'[27]

Major Bingham urged as many men as he could to the cover of the sea wall, harassed by artillery and machine-guns and under incessant sniper fire. Many remembered Captain Charles Cawthon who was issuing an order at about 0900 hours and just in mid-sentence when a piece of shrapnel went through his open mouth, penetrating both cheeks but missing his jawbone. He stoically remained in command, despite his spectacular wound.[28] Lieutenant Ross of the 146th Engineers noted how many of the less seriously wounded did not bother calling for help: 'Minden Ivey, a rugged little Texan, took a bullet through his wrist, resulting in a compound fracture, but he kept on firing his rifle, refusing medical aid in favour of the more seriously wounded. However, he did accept help in reloading his M1 Garand.'[29] The 111th Artillery's CO, Lieutenant Colonel Mullins, behaved similarly to Major Bingham, telling his soldiers, 'To hell with our artillery mission. We've got to be infantrymen now!'

Mullins, a Virginian Guardsman who hailed from Richmond, had spent his entire career with the 111th and was a marksman with a rifle. He organised small groups of his men and pointed out targets to them, although twice wounded: initially on the boat by shrapnel, latterly when 'a sniper had drilled through his hand' – a similar injury to that of Colonel Canham.[30] Mullins led a tank forward, which destroyed a gun emplacement, and was preparing to lead another when, 'looking over the ground, a sniper's bullet hit him in the stomach. He pitched forward on his face and death overtook him sometime within the next twelve hours, hostile fire preventing anyone from reaching him.'[31]

Eventually the rest of the 111th Field Artillery Battalion would join divisional headquarters, camped in a quarry in the Vierville draw, but lost more men and vehicles, hit by shellfire when approaching the beach on Rhino ferries, or drowned by the incoming tide. For his leadership on D-Day, Mullins was posthumously awarded the Distinguished Service Cross, but thirty-two members of his battalion died and nearly a hundred were wounded, or suffered exposure from an overlong dunking in the Channel.

Further east still, between the Les Moulins and Saint-Laurent draws, the Third Battalion of the 116th (Companies 'I', 'K', 'L' and 'M') had also touched down at around 0730 hours, again far to the east of their original objective, but luckily – being between D-3 and E-1 – the heights were not as well defended, and thinly manned. Though they didn't yet know it, the battalion had stumbled on a relative blind spot. Captain Smith, operations officer with the Third, noted arriving about an hour behind the first wave, 'though the bluffs were obscured by the mist and smoke, I was shocked by the fact that the beach seemed to be crawling with men. Obviously something had gone wrong with the assault plans of the first wave. Artillery and mortar fire could be seen landing on the beach and the staccato firing of machine-guns heard.'[32]

He recalled, 'Just as the ramp went down, there was a terrific explosion.' A mine had blown in the bottom; as their craft filled with water, Smith and his CO, Lieutenant Colonel Lawrence Meeks, another Roanoke native, had to swim for it with their men. Most were obliged to shed their equipment and weapons to keep from drowning, crawling ashore almost unarmed. Smith and Meeks, standing at the rear, had escaped injury, but Captain Gaffney, their artillery liaison officer, died on Meeks' shoulder; two other officers were killed, four radio operators were seriously wounded, and three out of four radios destroyed.

Meeks gathered the survivors and urged them across the sand at a lick and into the cover of the shingle bank. Later, in jest, he turned to Smith and blamed the explosion on the 116th's commander, Colonel Canham. In a pre-invasion briefing, Canham had asked Meeks, 'Are your men ready to die?' To which Meeks had responded, 'Hell, no! But we are ready to do our jobs, sir!' Canham's question seemed to Meeks to be altogether too prophetic.[33]

Captain Charles H. Kidd, commanding Company 'M' in Meeks' Third Battalion, recollected,

> Waves were breaking over the top of the craft and the men and equipment were drenched. It was good to hear our naval fire going in, but the personnel soon realised that this operation was not a dry run. Ships were being sunk by artillery, and machine-gun fire beat against the ramps of the LCVPs. It was very misty, which made observation of the beach and picking of landmarks difficult. Immediately it was evident the enemy fortifications had not been neutralised … The well concealed emplacements were hard to locate, and the artillery and tank support was handicapped by the rough sea and poor observation.

Kidd compared how the 116th's First Battalion had suffered a large percentage of casualties, while the Second arrived at the same time 'without much unity, but casualties were comparatively light'. Arriving at 0700 hours, his 'Company "M"' landed on Easy Green, about eight hundred yards east of where it should have landed on Dog Red. 'Small arms fire was heavy, but seemed to be firing on fixed lines.'[34]

He also watched the Third Battalion's alternate headquarters LCVP getting through the obstacles and suffering casualties from machine-gun and mortar fire. One of these was the battalion chaplain, who was struck in the heel as he ran across the open beach. 'That was a long run, across about four hundred yards of flat sand, but most of those wounded on the beach were the ones who paused to rest on the open sand or crouched behind the steel obstacles which caused wicked ricochets and very nasty wounds,' he recalled.[35]

It did not take long for the 116th's Third Battalion – with few casualties – to move off the beach, gap the wire with Bangalore torpedoes and advance up the bluffs. Having reached the top, they were in a position to outflank WN66, controlling the east side of the Les Moulins exit. The defenders of Les Moulins in WN66 and WN68 were busy punishing other waves landing in their vicinity, which included the First Battalion of the 16th Infantry – a Big Red One unit, which truly indicated how mixed up the assault had become. Astride the interdivisional boundary, at 1100 hours, Colonel Taylor, commanding the neighbouring 16th Regimental Combat Team, ordered all available tanks to help the infantry force a passage up the D-3 draw. This failed when two out of three tanks which turned up – a measure of how little intact armour there was along the sand – were knocked out, despite naval gunfire onto the two resistance nests. However, the latter were now having to contend with close-quarter combat and defence of their own perimeters.

Sensing the strength of German opposition from the reports of the first wave, General Gerhardt – still afloat at this stage – immediately took the forthright decision to commit Colonel Eugene Slappey's 115th Infantry, ahead of time. A minimum of three hours was needed to get them assembled on deck, into landing craft and transported twelve miles through the waves, before they could land ashore. By the time they arrived, there was too much congestion and too few gaps off Dog Beach, so they slid eastwards to Easy, touching down from about 1100 hours on Easy Red between the Saint-Laurent and Colleville draws. This was on the turf of the neighbouring 1st Infantry Division.

Beaching in their LCIs at an unscheduled time in a strange place, for which they had no maps and little situational awareness, Slappey's First and Second Battalions refused to pause, and with commendable initiative simply followed the sounds of battle. Landing at high tide, they quickly made it to the base of the cliffs with few casualties and trailed in the wake of their predecessors of the Big Red One up and over the bluffs. Some, like Second Lieutenant William Corbett, a platoon leader with Company 'F', were wounded on the beach, but he was unlucky, for the German gunners were tiring and low on ammunition by then. They had been firing non-stop for four hours without resupply or relief.

Brigadier General Wyman, assistant divisional commander of the 1st Infantry Division, was fortunately on hand to direct Slappey's newly arrived men to re-orientate south-west and attack Saint-Laurent. There were no disputes about prior orders or areas of responsibility. Itching for the fray, Slappey's battalions moved off cross-country, through several minefields, and towards the German-held village. Later, they would be followed by two battalions of the Big Red One's 18th Infantry, forced to land in the vicinity for the same reasons. It was a remarkable tribute to the flexibility of V Corps that the Blue and Gray's reserve regiment was instead used to great effect by the Big Red One.

At around 1730 hours arrived – far too early, but still adhering to *The Timetable* – the first non-American unit to land on Omaha. These were the 180 men of the Royal Air Force's No. 15082 Ground-Controlled Interception (GCI) radar unit who were to set up their equipment on the heights between Vierville and Les Moulins. They were to work in conjunction with the Fighter Direction Tender *FDT-216* off Omaha.[36] Pushed by the current and lack of lanes through the obstacles, they appeared east of D-3, and although the draw was open, emerged from their five LCTs under fire. Totally unprepared for landing on an unsecured beach under fire, Leading Aircraftman John Cubitt recorded discussing the situation with a US liaison officer 'kneeling by a lorry wheel for shelter. Shortly afterward I saw him slide slowly to the ground, his head bleeding on the wheel rim. He was dead. Further down the line a squadron leader was lying with his foot blown off. A flight lieutenant assisting him heard another shell, shielded him by throwing himself on top of the wounded man, and was killed by shrapnel.'[37]

Rapidly losing much of their towed radar array and twenty-six of their thirty-four vehicles, over the next few days they would suffer eleven men killed and thirty-seven wounded, along the way exciting much curiosity, if not hostility, on account of their RAF blue uniforms, not dissimilar to German field grey. Flight Lieutenant Efinberger reported being fired on a number of times – once losing his helmet – by US troops mistaking his unfortunate colour of clothing. This prompted many of the Brits to carry on in olive drabs, eating K-rations and bearing American weapons salvaged from the beaches. It took the RAF hierarchy many days to locate them and haul them back into the British chain of command. 'That was a shame when it happened, I far preferred my unofficial time in the US Army,' remembered one of the squad.[38] In wider terms, their story was typical of the many service organisations whose arrival was not halted, and who contributed to the congestion and clutter of the beachhead for the first forty-eight hours.

The First Battalion, 115th, would push inland to Saint-Laurent, via the E-1 draw, reaching there about dark, but lost its commanding officer,

Lieutenant Colonel Richard C. Blatt, to mortar fire. The 115th's regimental headquarters landed and remained in Easy Red sector under artillery fire until about 1630 when it, too, moved up the E-1 draw towards Saint-Laurent. Although WN66 would fall later in the afternoon, the western strongpoint overlooking Les Moulins remained in German hands until late in the day, as did the village of Saint-Laurent overnight. By going south-west, cross-country, Charles H. Kidd's Company 'M', accompanied by Company 'I' of the 116th, with the battalion's 81mm mortars, managed to reach the northern edge of Saint-Laurent, completely outflanking the troublesome WN66 position. By noon, the entire battalion had followed them. The CO, Lieutenant Colonel Meeks, sent Kidd's Company 'M' to outflank Saint-Laurent from the east, but it was driven out by heavy fire from 20mm flak fired point-blank into their ranks.

Captain Kidd observed that 'more casualties were encountered in this manoeuvre than in crossing the beach'. Nevertheless, by 1800 hours Company 'L' had fought its way into the centre of the village when 'naval fire opened up on the church steeple, firing straight up the D-3 draw over the heads of most of the Third Battalion, but right into the middle of Company 'L'', recorded Kidd.[39] Captain Joseph T. Dawson's Company 'G' had earlier fought their way into the church, intent on seizing the spire as a handy observation post. Just as they had disposed of the four field-grey-clad occupants doing much the same, US destroyers offshore decided the church was in German hands and commenced shelling it.

With more than a little bitterness, Dawson's boss, Major William Washington, XO of the Second Battalion, 16th Infantry, observed, 'I thought it was pathetic that we captured a church steeple in Colleville-sur-Mer that gave us good observation, only to have it shot down by the US Navy.' The culprit was USS *Harding*, which recorded two fire missions against the church at 1655 and 1937 hours, expending 133 rounds of five-inch ammunition.[40] It well illustrates the truism that in the fog of battle, friendly fire casualties are almost always inevitable – but this was the most severe example on Omaha.

In the absence of radio communications, Captain Kidd improvised a white flag and, running up on top of the bluff, 'succeeded in signalling *cease fire* after much wig-wagging but not before Company "L" had received at least a dozen more casualties in addition to those already received in the afternoon. Casualties here had been heavier than on the beach for this battalion.' Kidd reported this friendly fire 'had a demoralising effect upon the troops'.

They tried to attack again under cover of smoke, but were halted by the same heavy fire. A third attempt on Saint-Laurent was made at 2000 hours, this time supported by three 105mm 'Priests' which had made it ashore from the Regimental Cannon Company; the attack failed when they came under fire, knocking out one of the guns.[41] 'It was later discovered the culprits were four Shermans from the 741st Tank Battalion supporting the 115th Infantry who had driven up the E-1 draw in an unsuccessful attempt to enter Saint-Laurent from the east,' Kidd noted.

The D-3 draw was officially recorded as open by 2030 when Captain McGrath of the 116th Service Company was able to walk down from Saint-Laurent to meet some of his vehicles driving up from the beach.[42] 'At 2300 hours, the CO decided to button up for the night.' Captain Smith, operations officer, recorded with some understatement, 'This had been a very demoralising day. In addition to landing wet and miserable on that chilly June morning, seeing all the death and destruction on the beach, getting shot up by our own "friendly" naval and tank fire, the battalion was still far short of its D-Day objectives, which we would reach only on 10 June.'[43]

Towards evening, Daniel Folsom of the 111th Naval Construction Battalion (who had been reluctant to eat the dark meat offered by his landlady because he thought it was the family cat) never forgot the moment his Rhino barge nosed its way towards the western half of Omaha, laden with engineering plant and a bulldozer. 'It was spooky – the water was covered with green algae – but when you got up close, it was soldiers that had drowned, floating face-down.' Attempting to rid his mind of the human suffering he had witnessed – though it never truly left him – Folsom would also recall 'the huge numbers of Man-of-Wars [jellyfish] and dead fish washed up on the shore line amongst the obstacles, stunned by the concussion.'[44]

His first job the next day, using the bulldozer on his Rhino barge, was to 'dig a long trench and lay those deceased kids along the bottom'. At Le Hamel-au-Prêtre he helped bury 456 men while still under fire. Folsom recalled his entire battalion attending a beachhead memorial service for those who had fallen in the assault, conducted at the graveside with a jeep for an altar on 14 June. Today, a small sign commemorates the location of this first temporary cemetery. Among the many Stonewallers whose stories we have encountered, this first cemetery contained the

Virginian surgeon Captain Robert B. Ware, felled on the beach before he could treat a single casualty.[45]

Also enclosed in Normandy sand was Bedford boy Ray Stevens. Standing on the deck of the *Empire Javelin* before mounting their landing craft, Ray had wanted to shake hands with his twin brother Roy, but the latter wouldn't, thinking it bad luck. Instead Roy Stevens had said, 'I'm going to see you when we get to Normandy' – which was the last time they physically met. Roy made it back, but Ray did not.

Private Bedford T. and Staff Sergeant Raymond S. Hoback were another pair of Bedford brothers in Taylor Fellers' Company 'A' who would not return home. Raymond's body was washed out to sea and never recovered, but the mourning Hoback household received a package a few days later. It was sent by a West Virginian soldier, with a note which read, 'While walking on the beach on D-Day plus one, I came upon this Bible, and as most any person would do I picked it up from the sands to keep it from being destroyed.' The Bible had been given to Raymond by his mother and the GI had sent it to the address inscribed inside.[46]

By the evening of D-Day, Colonel Canham's 116th Infantry was scattered along the coastline; the First Battalion was in the vicinity of Vierville with the Regimental Headquarters Company, at the head of the open D-1 draw. The Second and Third Battalions were in the vicinity of Saint-Laurent; Colonel Slappey's 115th Infantry was to the east of the town, having advanced up the E-1 draw, but were denied access to the settlement itself by tenacious defenders who were still blocking the landward end of E-3. Some of the V Corps reserve, the 175th Infantry, remained afloat, on immediate call in case of trouble, though Private E. Barran Tucker of Company 'G' was one of those who landed at around 1220 hours. The native of Spiro, Oklahoma – who would retire as a lieutenant colonel – remembered disembarking under fire, proving the various *Widerstandsnester* were still active, though running low on ammunition. A bullet grazed the side of his helmet, knocking it off his head. 'I didn't have my chin strap on or it probably would have broken my neck; it put a great big dent in,' he recalled. Tucker and the rest of Company 'G' crawled across the beach: 'You couldn't run; if you stood up, they'd kill you.'[47]

The combat historian Forrest C. Pogue was with the 175th aboard *LST-516*, itching to land. He recorded the 175th's GIs flaunting 'gaily decorated field jackets – usually drawings of scantily-clad girls in bust relief. One such girl was quoted as saying "I have big things ahead of me".[48] However, Colonel Paul R. Goode, the 175th's unlucky commander, was destined to be captured along with many of his men by the 17th SS Division in Saint-Lô on 11 June. Also afloat was V Corps' reserve armoured unit, the 747th Tank Battalion. It would land in full strength at Vierville early on 7 June and immediately started developing tank–infantry teams, trying to perfect a methodology appropriate to the bocage. Many officers felt the spirit of mutual cooperation found in armour–infantry groupings was born from the tests hurled at America's citizen-soldiers on Omaha, where everyone had been thrown together, irrespective of branch or arm of service, and had triumphed through mutual assistance.[49]

Two years after D-Day, Captain Kidd of Company 'M' assessed his part in the assault for a study paper at the Infantry Officer School, Fort Benning. While he noted that the 116th Regimental Combat Team included 11,076 personnel, he felt it was their 976 vehicles that most contributed to the confusion. Few of these, he concluded, were necessary in the assault wave, which became a slave to its timetable. Until the engineers had done their job, 'wrecked transport was a menace and a hindrance to our troops', he observed. 'Exploding ammunition and gas tanks caused casualties to our people, unnecessarily damaged many landing barges and blocked cleared areas. Vehicles should be afloat at a safe distance, and be called in only as the beach is cleared. Time, mate-rial, and personnel could have been saved if vehicles were called ashore only as the exits are opened.'[50]

In a similar study, Captain Carroll Smith, also of the Third Battalion, 116th Infantry, decided to note down his regiment's casualties for 6 June. Having landed with a strength of 3,486 (excluding all the attached units), it lost 1,030 including 390 killed, forty-three missing and 597 wounded, or thirty per cent. 'Of this total, over eighty were officers, more than half the officer strength of the regiment.' Observing how they lost seventy-five per cent of its radios, he reflected, 'it seems to me now that more effort should have been exerted towards establishing contact with adjacent units by foot messenger and patrols. However, at the time, after seeing death and destruction on the beaches, each unit got the impression that it was the only one left and its battle became more or less one for survival.'

Charles Cawthon of the 116th's Second Battalion had been staggered to find 'on this day of history, we found three soldiers busily ransacking the poor contents of a cottage. We sent them on, but I am sure it was only a brief interruption to a career of looting'. He observed 'The

Germans lost Omaha Beach for the lack of a single company of riflemen to descend and sweep us up. But, looking down onto our obviously helpless condition, they still stuck to their observation bunkers and gun emplacements'. It was, he thought, 'as costly a day in the regiment's history as Chancellorsville [1863] and the death of Old Stonewall [Jackson] himself'. The factors of the weather, time, tides and the Germans resulted 'in shock, inertia and disorder. The only salvation was the initiative and enterprise of a relative few who rose above the wreckage of the plan.'[51]

Looking back, officers in the 116th Infantry attributed their success

largely to the initiative and aggressiveness of small unit leaders who made the best of a bad situation. Landing in most cases far off their assigned objectives, with large losses of men and equipment in the water, they had to improvise in order to cope with the strange fortifications to their front. Those teams whose leaders were lost became confused and bewildered and made little effort to go further than the protection of the stone shingle. Consequently, casualties were heavier among these units.[52]

The Vierville draw and Dog sector remained under fire for the next couple of days as mobile German artillery continued to shell the area. Corporal Donald E. Myerly of Battery 'B', 110th Field Artillery – a Blue and Gray unit – was driving his truck full of ammunition up D-1 when it was struck on 7 June, killing him instantly. The brief bombardment eventually killed another seventeen of his colleagues, destroyed several trucks and two of the 110th's guns. Other GIs, not yet combat-savvy, strayed away from the paths laboriously marked with white tape by engineers and were killed by mines.

At the base of D-1 – the Vierville draw – the remains of WN72 are very evident today. Two bunkers point east along the beach: the smaller one that is by the sea contained a 50mm weapon; the larger one still houses its 88mm cannon, and is now surmounted by the National Guard monument. This acknowledges where the 29th Division broke through, but also honours all Guardsmen who fought in the European theatre. Looking to the west, there are further bunkers up the hill, which were part of WN73, from where cannon and machine-guns also lashed out at Taylor Fellers' Company 'A', and, later, Companies 'B' and 'D' of the 116th.

Beyond, where the headland curves round, was WN74, housing a further pair of 75mm guns which enfiladed the beach. Driving up D-1, on the high ground to the east, where today there is a small white bungalow, some of the concrete positions of WN71, with embrasures facing towards Vierville, are still visible. The buildings in the area are all post-war structures, but built on the foundations of those demolished in 1944. At the bottom of D-3, the anti-tank ditch – which stood where a roundabout is today – has long disappeared, as has the anti-tank wall, but occupying the space of the former wall is the very informative Musée Omaha 6 Juin 1944 – one of three war museums in the vicinity of Omaha Beach, the others being beyond Vierville and opposite the entrance to the American military cemetery at Colleville. This is where many of the 29ers lie today. As Bob Slaughter of Company 'D' later observed, 'by the time we took Saint-Lô six weeks later, it was said that the 29th was really three divisions: one in the field, another in hospital, and yet a third in the cemetery.'[53]

Holbrook 'Hobey' Bradley, the embedded reporter with the 29th, did not arrive on Omaha until 7 June, being forbidden by his editor from landing earlier, lest he became a casualty. 'The tide was running in, bringing corpses still in their life jackets, or without,' he wrote in his first despatch for the *Baltimore Sun*.

> They were those who'd died trying to make this beach, men with the blue and gray patch of our division, some with the distinctive red one of the First. The Blue–Gray shoulder patch told us this soldier was one of ours. He'd been hit in the left shoulder, the uniform ripped and bloody, a temporary bandage on the jagged tear which seemed to cover a quarter of his torso. The wax-like face, eyes closed, no sign of breathing, will be with me until I die. Those first few hours on the beach must have been living hell. And we saw there had been no discrimination in the way the men fell, for the two bars of captains were among the plain uniforms of the privates.[54]

Before leaving for France, the visiting GIs had left their mark all over England. Prior to Overlord, 150 men of Company 'B', 121st Engineer Combat Battalion, strode into Prideaux Place, Padstow, a beautiful Elizabethan manor on the north Cornish coast. In one of its eighty-one ancient rooms, the name 'Lawrence A. Bekelesky' is inscribed in a cupboard. The Company 'B' men stayed for six months. The north wing of the 1592 mansion remains today exactly as it was when twenty-four-year-old Corporal Bekelesky marched out to board *LST-408*, bound for the Dog Green sector of Omaha Beach. Of the 150 men billeted at Prideaux, thirty-six were killed over 6–8 June. Bekelesky's Company 'B' took fifty per cent casualties and lost seventy-five per cent of its engineering equipment. The Pennsylvanian himself got no further than the beach, where he lies buried today.[55]

28

Rangers, Lead the Way!

'These are the boys of Pointe du Hoc. These are the men who took the cliffs. These are the champions who helped free a continent. These are the heroes who helped end a war.'

President Ronald Reagan, 6 June 1984

'Rangers! Man your craft!' the public address system cracked aboard landing ships, mostly cross-Channel ferries adapted to take a few landing craft. Their chaplain, Father Joe Lacy, had been round the men with some last-minute advice: 'When you land on the beach, I don't want to see anybody kneeling down and praying. If I do, I'm gonna come and boot you up the tail. You leave the praying to me and you do the fighting!' Lacey was as adept a poker player as he was a priest. 'When he came into a poker game, I got out,' remembered one Ranger.[1]

Lieutenant Sidney A. Salomon, a Ranger platoon commander, recalled, 'All conversation came to a halt as if everybody had suddenly become mute. We all were tense. Now a loud smack as the bottom of the landing craft hit the water. We were bobbing objects in the choppy waters of the Channel.'[2]

The first Ranger attack of D-Day was not on the Pointe du Hoc, but a smaller mission led by Captain Ralph E. Goranson's Company 'C', 2nd Rangers, to subdue a strongpoint on the cliffs between the western edge of Omaha and the Pointe. They were to land with Company 'A' of the 116th and help them clear the Vierville draw, advance up it, and attack the WN74 gun emplacement on the Pointe de la Percée from the landward side, before making their way to the Pointe du Hoc. Ranger units were, like British commandos, far smaller than conventional army units – because of their hard training to move fast and operate behind enemy lines. Ranger battalions numbered only 595, comprising six companies of around seventy men each. Their regular infantry counterparts were scaled at nine hundred GIs to a battalion, composed of three 190-man companies and a weapons company of 81mm mortars, .30-inch machine-guns and bazookas. Ranger medical detachments were likewise light-weight, comprising just ten trained medics under a battalion surgeon (each Ranger had a much higher degree of first-aid training and was expected to self-medicate, whereas an army doctor had thirty medics at his disposal). The two Ranger battalions, mostly fighting as separate companies on D-Day, would be pushed to the limit of their endurance and capabilities, sustained principally by their arduous preparations beforehand.

They had disembarked from the 3,000-ton *Prince Charles*, a converted ferry that had carried the very first Rangers to Dieppe two years earlier. Off Normandy, two of her eight LCAs bore Goranson's men to the beach, landing to the right of, and simultaneously with, Taylor Fellers' company. Once ashore, the Rangers, too, were ambushed by machine-gun and mortar fire, which immediately felled many of Goranson's sixty-eight men and destroyed his own craft, *LCA-418*. 'Suddenly there were splashes and white, cascading water, and the sharp *pings* of bullets against the steel hull,' recalled Donald A. Scribner. 'The moment the ramp dropped, we were sprayed with automatic fire.'[3] Unable to raise Taylor Fellers on his left by radio, and under a hail of steel from the east, they veered to the right of the D-1 (Vierville) draw to the partial cover of the cliffs in Charlie sector. His mission already unachievable and his force in shreds, Goranson simply improvised. He led his remaining Rangers along the base of the cliffs about three hundred yards westwards, and, finding a shallow gulley, began to climb using their bayonets and toggle ropes. They reached the top around 0715 hours.

Instead of moving west, they decided to attack the former Villa Gambier – turned into a fortified house, and connected to a network of trenches and dugouts, which Goranson could see to his front. This turned out to be the large strongpoint WN73, armed with a 75mm gun in a concrete casemate and other weapons in protected bunkers, all interlinked by a honeycomb of entrenchments. With all the defenders looking eastwards, focused on the Vierville draw, and assisted by a stray boat team from Company 'B' of the 116th, Goranson's Rangers managed

A westwards-looking post-invasion view of the Vierville draw (Dog One), nick-named *der Garten des Teufels* (the Devil's Garden) by the defenders. This is where the 180-strong Company 'A' of the 116th Infantry, recruited in Bedford, Virginia, and led by Captain Taylor Fellers (1914–44), lost ninety-one killed and around seventy-four more wounded within minutes. Beyond lies WN73, successfully subdued by Captain Ralph Goranson (1919–2012) and the remnants of Company 'C', 2nd Rangers, at a cost of twenty-one dead and eighteen wounded. Monuments and restaurants have altered the landscape today. (Author's collection)

to get into the array of earthworks but had to extinguish the position, bunker by bunker. It was larger than they'd expected, containing a rein-forced Grenadier platoon of the 716th Division. By the time Goranson and his men had subdued all the defenders, it was late afternoon. They later counted sixty-nine German dead, with no prisoners. Lieutenant Salomon 'looked around to see who was still with me. Nine remained from those jammed in my landing craft.'[4] In all, only twenty-nine Rangers were still on their feet, Company 'C' having lost twenty-one dead and eighteen wounded.

Although not a part of their mission, Goranson's decision to re-orien-tate his small group was probably the first glimmer of success anywhere along Omaha. Not that anyone else knew: all the initial American offen-sive activity would be uncoordinated, and undertaken by small ad hoc bands of determined survivors. His attack also directly contributed to the opening of the D-1 draw, and was more effective than any direct attack would have been. The storming of WN73 had also distracted its garrison from directing their considerable firepower at the Vierville draw into defending themselves. Struck by a German potato masher grenade at one stage, in retrospect it is amazing that Goranson, a Swedish-American from Chicago, survived to be awarded the Distinguished Service Cross, as he later counted nine bullet nicks in his clothing and equipment.

Some of his story has since become known the world over, as his character was borrowed and refashioned to become Captain John H. Miller of Addley, Pennsylvania, who in *Saving Private Ryan* also commands Company 'C', 2nd Rangers, with the task of opening the D-1 draw. The strongpoint Miller attacks in the film bears a strong resemblance to the layout of WN73 with its many bunkers and trenches – some still evident today – although the Royal Navy's delivery of the Rangers to their war is absent from the reimagined story.[5]

Goranson's original objective, WN74, lay a mile further to the west, near the Kriegsmarine radar station on the Pointe de la Percée, but its remains are rarely visited these days, being beyond the tourist centre of Vierville. This was a formidable clifftop position housing two 75mm guns and an observation post that looked back to Vierville and along Omaha Beach. Whereas the Pointe du Hoc guns menaced the fleet, those at WN74 endangered the shoreline; as Lieutenant Colonel Rudder told Goranson, 'You have the toughest goddamn job on the whole beach.'

The deep grass today hides the German trenches and old bunkers. These were mangled by naval gunfire; the destroyer HMS *Talybont* recorded shooting one of them into the sea. It was this strongpoint, protected by flak artillery and machine-guns, that Oberstleutnant Fritz Ziegelmann, chief of staff to the 352nd Infantry Division, managed to contact by field telephone between nine and ten during the morning of 6 June. Its commander, a friend of his, reported, 'At the water's edge at low tide near Saint-Laurent and Vierville the enemy is in search of cover behind the coastal zone obstacles. A great many motor vehicles – and among them ten tanks – stand burning on the beach. The obstacle demolition squads have given up their activity. Debarkation from the landing boats has ceased; the boats keep further seawards.'[6] This Sitrep (situation report) accords with the often overlooked order, given at 0830 by the CO of the 7th Naval Beach Battalion – attached to the 6th Engineer Special Brigade – that all landings were suspended on Dog sector for the 116th Regimental Combat Team, so that 'during the next few hours scores of craft, including DUKWs and Rhino ferries were milling around waiting for a chance to come in'.[7]

The assessment given to Ziegelmann was accurate and supplied from a position not yet threatened, with excellent vision of Charlie to Dog Red sectors, the zone specifically attacked by Goranson's Ranger company, Canham's 116th Infantry and armour of the 743rd Tank Battalion. The report concluded: 'The fire of our battle positions and artillery was well placed and has inflicted considerable casualties upon the enemy. A great many wounded and dead lie on the beach.' However, it acknowledged that some communication lines had been severed by naval gunfire or bunkers had fallen: 'Some of our battle positions have ceased firing; they do not answer any longer when rung up on the telephone.'[8]

Cornelius Ryan claimed this report came from Oberst Ernst Goth, commanding the 916th *Infantry-Regiment*, a statement often repeated in histories, but a close reading of the document Ryan was citing reveals that Goth was *with* Ziegelmann, listening to the conversation from a third party. Goth then added to the picture, admitting: 'up till then we had succeeded in frustrating an enemy landing on a wide front. However, casualties on our side were successively rising in number because of the continuous fire of the naval artillery, so that reinforcements had to be asked for. Oberst Goth reported, moreover, that a strong enemy commando operation was in progress against our main battery at Pointe du Hoc.'[9]

'Pointe du Hoc is a knife stood on its edge, pointed into the sea. It looks lethal, a palisade of boulders and mean rocks where Normandy's green softness has reclaimed nothing,' wrote John Vicour in the *New York Times* in May 1984. 'Battlefields: you could walk them from Gettysburg to Waterloo, and go back to your car, thinking of lunch. But not at Pointe du Hoc. The brightest morning roughens there, the wind working like a rasp, still scoring cruel edges on the sheer cliffs.'[10] In 1944 this unknown spot was just another headland, albeit one containing a nasty threat. Just as the airborne drop was indivisible from the Utah landings, so too the suppression of the Pointe du Hoc position was a necessary component of Omaha. Designated by the Germans as WN75, its six 155mm ex-French cannon were each capable of hurling two 95-pound shells per minute at an invasion fleet twelve miles away. It was their range that dictated all the Western Task Force's anchorages, and thus the distance the landing craft would have to shuttle back and forth to their attack transports. The British, faced by shorter-range artillery, would bring their transports closer, with quicker ship-to-shore journeys, shortening the discomfort for all concerned.

The main weapons at the Pointe were huge, wheeled field cannon, each with a barrel length of twenty feet, and the assemblage of each, with shield and trail, weighed in at fourteen tons. The battery had been first established in September 1942 during the aftermath of Dieppe, to defend the fishing harbour of Grandcamp. Then the howitzers had been dug into simple sandbagged gun pits; later they were transferred to circular concrete bases in the open, built in an arrowhead facing north. Two faced towards the future Utah Beach, another pair Omaha, while the remaining two, closest to the cliff edge, had a 180-degree traverse along the entire coast, remembered Grenadier Wilhelm Kirchhoff, one of the garrison.[11] In 1943, the garrison had been suffering from the malaise that Rundstedt observed in his report: the younger and fitter artillerymen were sent to Russia, including its able and popular commander, Oberleutnant Frido Ebeling, and replaced by more elderly reservists or wounded *Ostfront* veterans, and fewer in number. By June 1944 only about 85 gunners remained from the 145 of the previous year.

It was Rommel's arrival that had initiated plans to rehouse the guns in six bombproof reinforced concrete casemates, of which two had been completed by 6 June, with another pair under construction; a protected fire control post on the very edge of the promontory had also been built, commanded by Leutnant Wilhelm Ruhl, and equipped with a telemeter to give accurate fire coordinates to the artillery. In addition, the site was turned into a miniature fortress, with two flak bunkers mounting 37mm anti-aircraft cannon, overseen by Unteroffizieren Helmut Neder and Erwin Thomalla, numerous Tobruk machine-gun-positions and deep, underground personnel shelters. Minefields and barbed wire were also laid around the position, whose eighty-five men comprised the 2nd Battery, 1260th *Heeres Küsten-Artillerie-Regiment* (Army Coastal Artillery Regiment), commanded by Oberleutnant Brotkorb, with the 716th Division supplying a company of 125 grenadiers for close support.[12]

The Pointe had been bombed on 25 April, 13 and 22 May and 4 June, with one gun destroyed in its unprotected position and several casualties. Immediately following the first raid, the garrison commander had hauled his remaining guns to an alternative position in a hedge-screened orchard about a mile away. Some of the protective minefield was also destroyed,

Pointe de
la Percée

This picture records one of the four air raids on the Pointe du Hoc, in this case on 13 May 1944. Seven Douglas A-20 medium bombers can be seen, part of a larger formation. The large splash off the headland indicates that at least one bomb has missed its target. The view also illustrates the Norman terrain of small fields bounded by earthen banks – the bocage. Annotated is the route taken by Colonel Rudder and his Rangers on 6 June. (NARA)

and the five hundred *Organisation Todt* labourers on site were ordered to cease all work due to the air raid hazard. Substitute wooden poles, under camouflage netting, perpetuated the idea that the guns were still in place. This ruse was well known from the American Civil War era, when such decoys were known as 'Quaker guns' (so called since Quakers oppose all violence). This would be a temporary relocation, the guns returning when the building work was complete.

However, all this activity took place under the watchful eyes of men like André Farine, a café owner in nearby Letanville, and Jean Marion in Grandcamp, both near the Pointe. They were part of *Centurie* (Century), the code name for the local intelligence service of the much wider OCM (*Organisation Civile et Militaire*) Resistance movement, created in 1940. Its regional head was Marcel Girard, responsible for

Normandy and Brittany. We have already met two of its members – Guillaume Mercader, intelligence chief for the Vierville–Port-en-Bessin sector, and André Heintz, whose job was to watch the Caen headquarters of the 716th Infantry Division in his street. Comprising forty dedicated operatives and directed from Caen, since 1942 they had been gathering information on every aspect of the *Atlantikwall*.

René Duchez, for example, had applied for a painting job at the *Kommandantur*, and managed to steal a blueprint of the entire Cotentin defences, bunkers, minefields – everything. He'd hidden it behind a mirror, retrieved it later, rolling the map in some wallpaper samples. It was spirited across the Channel to London immediately, part of a paper trail of over three thousand documents sent to SHAEF dealing with the coastal defences.[13] André Farine, in seeking wood for cooking in his café, had discovered both the ruse and the guns in the orchard, and had passed this news back to England, where it reached the ears of the man tasked to destroy them: Lieutenant Colonel James Earl Rudder.

Rudder – Earl to his friends – had been brought up in the tiny central Texan town of Eden, and had graduated from Texas Agricultural and Mechanical ('A&M' – where students and graduates are traditionally 'Aggies') University in 1932, where he entered the ROTC programme. Six foot tall, broad-shouldered, quick of mind and body, an extraordinarily effective trainer and leader of men, Rudder had taken command of the newly raised 2nd Rangers in June 1943 and epitomised everything Bradley desired in his young officers. A year earlier, Colonel Joseph O. Darby had established the first Ranger battalion in emulation of the British commandos, which undertook the latter's courses at Achnacarry. He took three battalions to the Mediterranean theatre, where they rapidly gained a reputation as 'Darby's Rangers'. The remaining two battalions, under Rudder's effervescent supervision, trod a different path, rapidly becoming known as 'Rudder's Rangers'.

On 4 January 1944, the thirty-four-year-old lieutenant colonel had been summoned to First Army headquarters at 29–32 Bryanston Square, London, and given his mission – one of the very first Overlord tasks to be identified and allocated. Rudder would command a Provisional Rangers Group of the 2nd and 5th Rangers. Three companies were to take the guns; Goranson's company would attack WN74 then join them later. The remainder – including the balance of 2nd Rangers and all of Lieutenant Colonel Max Schneider's 5th Battalion – was to reinforce the Pointe du Hoc assault, but *only if* alerted to do so.

If no signal was received, they would land at Dog Green with the 116th Infantry. The rather tenuous nature of these arrangements indicates how little success was expected of the attack on the Pointe. 'When we got a look at it [the mission], Max just whistled once through his teeth. He'd made three landings already, but I was just a country boy coaching football a year and a half before. It would almost knock you out of your boots,' Rudder later recollected of receiving their task at Bradley's headquarters.[14]

Crossing the Atlantic in December 1943, they were billeted and trained around the north Cornish resort of Bude, where they practised cliff climbing – perfected also at Swanage, Dorset, where the geology more closely resembles the Pointe du Hoc. Rudder was one of the most junior officers present at the first 'Thunderclap' Conference at St Paul's School on 7 April, presided over by Montgomery and addressed by Churchill – a mark of his importance in the assault. He recalled taking the assignment back to Bude with Schneider and putting a twenty-four-hour guard on the door. 'Every time the Germans dug another trench or set another minefield, the P-38 reconnaissance planes, skimming over the cliffs, got pictures of it.'[15] Yet Rudder had no means of confirming what the Resistance were indicating about the guns being moved, as aerial photography could offer no clarity.

He decided there was no alternative but to make certain the 155mm guns were disabled wherever they were, and achieve his secondary mission: cutting the coastal road. He shared the news with his executive officer, Captain Cleveland A. Lytle, who would be leading the assault on the Pointe. The latter, to Rudder's surprise, suggested the mission was suicidal and unnecessary. By this time it was 3 June and Lytle, aboard their British assault ship *Ben-my-Chree*, was celebrating his promotion to major with a drink. One led to several, and a very drunken Lytle soon started bad-mouthing the plan, sharing its details and telling his listeners they were heading to their deaths.

Rudder had no option but to relieve Lytle on the spot, hospitalise him ashore under guard and take command of the assault himself – which he had wanted to do in any case, but had been blocked by his seniors as being too valuable to lose. Major General Clarence Huebner of the Big Red One had earlier told him, 'We're not going to risk having you knocked out in the first round.'[16]

The attack on the Pointe du Hoc began at 0504 hours with Operation Flashlamp. This involved 108 RAF Lancasters saturating the area with

635 tons of munitions. For once, the aerial bombing was devastatingly accurate. Only three aircraft failed to return, shot down within minutes by Oberleutnant Helmut Eberspacher in his Focke-Wulf 190 and presumed to have ditched in the Channel; none of the aircrew survived. In his logbook the Luftwaffe ace recorded, 'I noticed above a row of British bombers flying below the moonlit cloud cover. Similar to a shadow theatre, the bombers stood out against the clouds. However they could not see me against the dark earth. Within a few minutes, three British Lancaster bombers went down in flames. Now, it was high time that I landed somewhere, as not to become another casualty of the morning invasion.'[17]

It was only in 2012 that a group of local Frenchmen stumbled on one of the Lancaster crash sites in a marsh outside nearby Carentan. In the confusion of the airborne drop and events of D-Day, Lancaster Z-Zebra, piloted by Wing Commander Jimmy Carter, had lain undiscovered for nearly seventy years until the wreckage was pinpointed by the discovery of an undercarriage wheel and propeller blades sticking out of the earth. Carter, CO of No. 97 Squadron, and his crew had earlier taken off at 0256 hours from RAF Coningsby, Lincolnshire, carried out their mission over the Pointe and were on their way home when bounced by Eberspacher.

One of the archaeologists at the site revealed, 'We've found a couple of torn RAF woollen jumpers, with one still bearing a DFM medal ribbon. Lodged inside the sleeve of one jumper we discovered a single German 7.92mm bullet. There is an officer's forage cap, silk flying glove, a pocket from an RAF tunic with a Waterman pen still clipped inside, and a twisted cigarette case.'[18] The discovery of Carter's seven-man crew – all highly decorated, with four Distinguished Flying Crosses and three Distinguished Flying Medals to their names – is a stark reminder that the suppression of the Pointe du Hoc was a tri-service mission that involved more than 225 Rangers, and that there are many more missing airmen of all nationalities in this small corner of France, whose stories will be uncovered during the years to come.

Although in the safe hands of the American Battlefields Monuments Commission since 1979, the ground at Pointe du Hoc today is highly confusing, littered with huge craters and large lumps of torn concrete. Besides Allied aircraft, the chief culprits were the battleships *Arkansas* and *Texas*, the former firing her twelve-inch guns in anger for the first time in her career on 6 June. By the time the fleet had ceased fire at 0624, the *Texas* had expended 255 fourteen-inch shells, whose impact around the site is still very evident seventy-five years on. While her main guns were hitting the Pointe, the *Texas*'s secondary five-inch batteries were assailing the D-1 draw, just ahead of Taylor Fellers and Company 'A'.

Immediately following her fire mission onto the Pointe, the *Texas*'s main guns also turned to rain steel down on Vierville – these were the 'freight trains' that Ernest Hemingway remembered thundering overhead while ploughing towards the beach in his landing craft. Although directed by Spitfires, the morning mist and smoke cannot have helped the accurate placement of the US Navy's heavy artillery, whereas the tenacity of the German defenders illustrates the solid design and construction of their bunkers. The cost to Rudder when he reached the base of the cliffs was that instead of neat shingle, he found 'bomb holes and muck. The heavy bombers and mediums had plastered the cliff, and the near misses had torn the beach open.'[19]

In considering his various challenges, Rudder had assumed the main issue would be climbing the one-hundred-foot cliffs, nine storeys high, under German fire. He had devised three methods of overcoming this problem. First, his men would take four-foot lengths of lightweight scaling ladders with them. They would also fire grappling irons – small anchors trailing ropes – from hand-held rocket projectors. Finally, he enlisted the help of the London Fire Brigade, borrowing four of their one-hundred-foot extension ladders, each of which were fixed to the hold of a DUKW. Pairs of .303-inch Lewis guns were fixed to the top of the ladders to provide local fire suppression. Combined Operations, then headquartered in 1a Richmond Terrace in central London, thought all three sufficiently innovative and successful to include them in their Secret Bulletin No. 40 of September 1944.[20]

The journey to the cliffs had not been easy. First Sergeant Leonard G. 'Bud' Lomell of Toms River, New Jersey, remembered, 'We were on *Amsterdam*, a Channel steamer. We had private rooms. We went to sleep and, God, before we knew it, we had to be up and on deck at 0400 hours. The weather was bad. We were watching the assault like a bunch of country boys at a fair or something.'[21] Others were aboard the converted Isle of Man ferry *Ben-my-Chree*, an unusual name, meaning 'Woman of My Heart' in Manx, the language spoken on the tiny British-owned island in the middle of the Irish Sea. The 3,000-ton ship had started her military career at Dunkirk and launched her Rangers into craft of the 514th Assault Flotilla comprising ten LCAs and four DUKWs, guided by a British Fairmile motor launch.

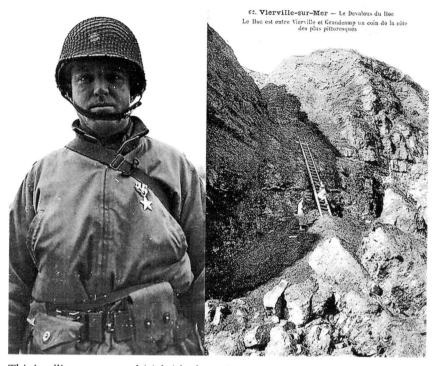

62. Vierville-sur-Mer — Le Devalous du Hoc
Le Hoc est entre Vierville et Grandcamp un coin de la côte
des plus pittoresques

This intelligence postcard (right) had a major impact on plans to storm the Pointe du Hoc. It demonstrated to Colonel James Earl Rudder (1910–70) (left) that earlier in the century holiday-makers had scaled the cliffs by ladder. Rather than a landward attack, Rudder realised it was possible to assault from the sea, which he knew the defenders were not expecting. (left, NARA; right, Author's collection)

Crouched on the triple rows of seating in their LCAs, 'like nervous cattle jammed inside a large phone booth', it soon became a soggy wet ride for all – dangerously so. Soon the seas had overwhelmed *LCA-860*, carrying off Captain Harold K. 'Duke' Slater and twenty others. Four drowned; the remainder were not rescued for several hours and required hospitalisation for exposure. Its demise was followed shortly afterwards by that of *LCA-914*, containing much of their spare ammunition – only one crewman survived. The other supply LCA threw its entire load overboard just to stay afloat. Another landing craft, a Landing Craft, Support, *LCS-91*, holed by gunfire, would go down just off the Pointe. Rudder's numbers were dwindling fast before a shot had been fired. Lomell remembered, 'Waves were breaking over our LCA, and the guys had to take their helmets and bail because the pumps on the boat couldn't take the water out of it.'[22]

The escorting Royal Navy Fairmile launch then made a critical navigational error in the dark, steering the flotilla towards the Pointe de la
Percée, which looked very similar to the Pointe du Hoc at sea level. By
the time Rudder realised the mistake and ordered his craft, *LCA-888*, to
alter course, much crucial time had been lost. Meanwhile the four
DUKWs had joined the LCA flotilla bearing the London Fire Brigade's
hundred-foot extendable Merryweather ladders (which were expected
to be returned in one piece). To now reach their objective, Rudder's
collection of little craft were then obliged to chug parallel to the coast
– the Germans atop alert and by now fully aware of the Americans'
intentions.

They poured fire down into the flotilla as it sailed slowly past, now
head-to-wind, and battling all the while with the heavy swell. The original plan, to land with the same H-Hour as Omaha, and on each side
of the headland, had to be abandoned in the interests of time, and all
made for the shingle rim on the eastern side of the Pointe. During this
run-in, Rudder lost another five casualties when one of his four DUKWs
was hit and went down, and most craft were punctured by sporadic rifle
fire – an illustration of how closely they were hugging the coast. At this
stage, a final B-26 run over the target appeared – in theory scheduled
to drop bombs between 0610 and 0625 hours – to numb the defenders
just as Rudder arrived. On this occasion the air force were late, releasing
their munitions around 0645 which would have decimated Rudder's
ranks – had they been there. Fortune smiled: the navigational error had
kept them from being blown to pieces by their own bombers.

First Sergeant Lomell recollected, 'My whole psyche that day was like
I was in a football game. I remembered my instructions, and we charged
hard and low and fast. That was our secret, and we stayed together. The
2nd Platoon stayed together as a team on D-Day. We got in, and our
ramp went down and all hell broke loose.'[23] The time was 0708: they
were thirty-eight minutes late. Far out to sea the rest of the 2nd and all
of the 5th Rangers waited under Max Schneider. He was impatient for
Rudder to send the signal 'Praise the Lord', meaning he was up the cliffs.
Two signal flares would mean the same thing. If the codeword 'Tilt' was
transmitted or no signal received by 0700 hours, this would indicate
failure and Schneider was to reinforce the attack at Omaha.

No signal came. Schneider waited an extra ten minutes, then with a
heavy heart – assuming Rudder had perished – turned east towards the
big beach. In fact, Rudder had only just begun his ascent and was too

During Rudder's early morning attack, the escorting Royal Navy launch steered the seaborne force toward the Pointe-de-la-Percée, which looked very similar to the Pointe-du-Hoc at sea-level. Rudder corrected the mistake but the error cost valuable time. This post-invasion view of the Pointe-de-la-Percée shows the challenging cliffs from a German position. Along the shore lies the wreckage of the American Mulberry 'A' harbour, wrecked in the storm of 19–21 June. (Author's collection)

busy and under fire to communicate. His radio sets were waterlogged and would only function later when they had been taken apart and dried out. With most of the artillerymen tending to their guns elsewhere, it was German infantrymen who flung automatic fire and grenades down on their foes, mostly from Leutnant Ruhl's observation post to the Rangers' right and the flak emplacement to their left. Not all the defending garrison were present: some had been injured or dispersed in the bombing raid; others had deployed to the interior, fearing a landward attack. In German minds the threat from the seaward side was minimal.

The Rangers' decision to land together in the east undoubtedly saved time, but left the group dangerously bunched: fifteen men went down crossing thirty yards of shingle before they even reached the cliff. Sergeant Lomell picked up the story: 'The boat leader goes off the front straight away. I stepped off the ramp, and was the first one shot. The bullet went through what little fat I had on my right side. It didn't hit any organs, but it spun me around and burned like the dickens. I went down in water over my head with the spare rope, the hand launcher and my sub-machine-gun. Keeping in mind that the idea was to get to the top as fast as we could, I got myself together and went up the cliff.'[24]

Lomell's matter-of-fact account of his injury typifies the Rangers' spirit and well illustrates how their training had toughened them against adversity. Rudder had considered climbing the cliffs his major challenge; in fact it was the sea. Using the four-foot extendable scaling ladders and the grapnels fired from hand-held rocket launchers, his men had reached the top by 0730, though Rudder noted some 'of the rocket-propelled ropes were so heavy from wetting that the grapnels failed to carry to the clifftop'. In fact, only nineteen of the fifty-four grapnels launched made a firm lodging over the clifftop, with the Germans cutting some of their trailing ropes.

More seriously, 'The DUKWs with the ladders foundered and were useless.'[25] The aerial bombing and the bombardment by the *Texas* had dislodged some of the cliff, causing it to cascade into the sea, and with the shingle beach torn open and cratered, none of the four DUKWs could get near the base of the heights, rendering their ladders completely irrelevant. This did not deter the enterprising Staff Sergeant William J. Stivison from extending his ladder ninety feet, climbing up and hosing the Germans with the twin Lewis guns mounted at the top.

Swaying precariously like a metronome, he fired his weapons in the general direction of his foes, who would have caught the odd glimpse of the unfortunate Ranger swinging through forty-five degrees – a surreal if not comic sight. PFC John J. Gilhooly thought Stivison 'looked very much like a circus performer at the time'.[26] Stivison descended when he was more afraid of hitting his own men than the enemy.[27]

Yet the destruction of the cliffs made the Rangers' ascent easier. At this stage Rudder's band was fast shrinking in size, had no supplies or backup, but he had gained two 101st paratroopers. PFCs Raymond Crouch and Leonard Goodgal had bailed out of their stricken C-47 into the Channel, fortunately close to the Calvados coastline. They had swum to the shore, but had no idea of their location; they had walked and waded westwards, following the sound of battle until they arrived where they 'could kill some Germans'.[28]

Rudder had also gained three Brits. Two were the drivers of the ladder-DUKWs, members of the Royal Army Service Corps. Having tried their best with their craft – top-heavy with an extra 6,200 pounds of weight, and hard to control in the choppy waters – unbidden they abandoned their useless vehicles, picked up discarded weapons, scaled the cliffs and joined the Rangers. When ammunition was running low they went back down the cliffs under fire to recover machine-guns from their vehicles. British Private Colin E. Blackmore was wounded in the foot, but after receiving first aid returned to the fight and later rescued a badly wounded Ranger under fire. His colleague, Corporal Joseph J. Wood, similarly fought, salvaged ammunition from the beach, repaired weapons and, as Colonel Rudder's report detailed, 'contributed greatly to the success of the mission and reflected credit to himself and his country'. Both would receive the British Military Medal, the paperwork endorsed in person by Montgomery.[29]

The third Brit was Lieutenant Colonel Thomas 'Big Tom' Hoult Trevor, a commando officer of private fortune who had mentored and advised Rudder during training and had come along as an observer. 'Six foot three with a physique to match', the moustachioed, swashbuckling Trevor had already served with US forces in Tunisia before becoming liaison officer to the Rangers. Adopting the American habit of a steel helmet, rather than his commando green beret which would have attracted unnecessary attention, he was nevertheless shot on the beach, squarely in the forehead. American steel saved his life, for although wounded, the injury was from the metal of the helmet pushed into his skin, rather than the bullet.

'Right here', Rudder later remembered during a return visit to the shingle ten years later, 'was where Trevor, who volunteered to give us a hand, was hit in his helmet and drove him to his knees. I helped him up; the blood was starting to trickle down his forehead, but he was a great big, black-haired son of a gun – one of those staunch Britishers – and he just looked up at the top of the cliffs, "The dirty *****s."' He would stay with Rudder for the entire Ranger mission, shepherding the command group and spotting targets, and found an underground bunker in which to set up the aid station.[30]

Lomell recalled that climbing the slippery, muddy rope was exhausting. 'Next to me was Sergeant Robert Fruhling, our radio man, struggling with his radio set with a big antenna on it. We were approaching the top, and I was running out of strength. Bob yelled, "Help me! I'm losing my strength." I said, "Hold on! I can't help you. I've got all I can do to get myself up." Then I saw Sergeant Leonard Rubin. He was all muscle, a born athlete, a very powerful man. I said, "Len, help Bob! I don't think

During the initial battle for the Pointe, Rudder's men established their aid post and headquarters in a niche just shy of the clifftop. In the centre is a wireless mast. Just visible on the right (see arrow) sits the British commando, Lieutenant Colonel Thomas 'Big Tom' Hoult Trevor, with head bandaged. A sniper had shot him – luckily the bullet only pierced his helmet. The shadows suggest the picture was taken around midday on 6 June, probably by G. K. Hodenfield, a *Stars and Stripes* reporter who accompanied the mission. (NARA)

he's going to be able to make it." He just reached over, grabbed Bob by the back of the neck and swung him over.'[31] At the top, the surviving Rangers broke into six assault teams to attack each gun emplacement, but had to skirmish their way across a moonscape that little resembled the models, maps and photographs with which they had trained.

However, they then discovered the guns were missing. This setback seems to have been taken very much on the chin: led by Sergeant Lomell, they simply moved inland to the coastal road, which they reached at around 0815. Meanwhile, alerted by the small arms fire, other defenders were racing to the scene and started further diminishing the ranks of the Rangers. Lomell remembered he had lost about half of the twenty-two men who had reached the clifftop with him: 'Our orders were to get the guns as quickly as possible. Our secondary mission was to establish a roadblock on the coastal highway to prevent German troops from going east to Omaha beach to help out there.'[32]

Within an hour of landing, Lomell had established a roadblock, and with his colleague Jack E. Kuhn decided to investigate the dirt track opposite. 'It looked like there were some markings on the secondary road. Jack covered me, and I went forward. It was a sunken road with very high hedgerows with trees and bushes and stuff like that. I said, "God, here they are!" The guns were in an orchard, camouflaged in among the trees. Where they protruded out of the foliage they had netting over them. The entire battery, five big coastal guns, were there at the ready. I saw some Germans being talked to, gathering there, putting on their jackets, organising themselves; they were so nonchalant, acting as if there was no enemy about because we were so quiet.'

Lomell continued, 'Staff Sergeant Jack E. Kuhn covered me, and I went to the guns with two thermite grenades. I put one in each of the first two guns' visible moveable gears.' Thermite grenades don't ignite with a huge explosion; instead they weld moving parts – gears, cranks, hinges, breechblocks – together, and are actually more effective at disabling sensitive mechanisms than a conventional munition. 'Through their intense heat, they welded moving parts together and rendered the guns inoperable. That moving, flowing molten metal, wherever it eventually got to, must have done the trick. I don't think I spent ten minutes, all told, destroying those guns. Then I took my Tommy gun, wrapped it in my field jacket and smashed the sights on all five guns.' Unnoticed, they departed. 'We never looked back. We didn't waste a second.'[33]

Rudder's men had achieved their mission and now awaited the friendly faces of their fellow Rangers, the 116th Infantry and other V Corps units, in complete ignorance of what was unfolding on Omaha. The colonel had established his command post beyond the eastern 37mm flak bunker, on the very cliff edge. This offered some cover from fire – though snipers remained active throughout the period – but with an open view of the sea, and the ability to communicate with the navy. This bunker is accessible today, with guard rails added, and the landscape is little changed. Ironically the cliffs were taken at relatively little cost, but holding them became another matter.

At midday, Rudder managed to communicate with USS *Satterlee* lying offshore: 'Located on Pointe du Hoc – mission accomplished – need ammunition and reinforcements – many casualties.' He was more than disappointed to receive the response three hours later that Commander

J. W. Marshall, captain of the destroyer, was directed to send: 'No reinforcements available.' However, the *Satterlee* would remain on station all day in fire support, and recorded expending seventy per cent of her five-inch ammunition – nearly two hundred rounds – by 1723 hours.

Rudder was not to know the reason for the unhelpful message – the chaos of Omaha – but the implication was clear: they were being left high and dry; Rudder's Rangers were expendable. He would have been relieved to know that the initial German garrison had relatively few weapons and little ammunition, not expecting a fire-fight on their doorstep. Reinforcements from the 726th and 914th *Grenadier-Regiments*, based at the nearby Château de Jucoville, were rushed to the scene and more or less bottled up the Rangers on the cliff top. By nightfall on 6 June, one third of the men who had landed were either dead or injured, though many of the wounded continued to fight on: they had no option.

The invaders would remain under shellfire, notably from the Maisy battery, until they were relieved at noon on 8 June. They survived five increasingly desperate counter-attacks to dislodge them, and throughout remained perilously low on food, medical supplies, water and ammunition. Resourcefully, they turned many captured weapons on their former owners. That first evening, twenty Rangers under Lieutenant Charles H. 'Ace' Parker, separated from the 5th Battalion, walked into Rudder's perimeter and helped stem three attacks made during the night. More reinforcements arrived the following day in the shape of twenty-four Rangers, with food, water and ammunition shuttled to the Pointe in two LCVPs, which were able to evacuate fifty-two of the seriously wounded. Rudder was also aware of a mixed armour–infantry relief force trying to punch their way through to him from Vierville. When the link-up came, Rudder could count only thirty per cent of his force able to bear arms, the rest killed, wounded or missing, mostly captured. Some men in the relief column recalled that the hottest fight of the war was battling through to the Pointe, because of the accurate fire brought down on them – by the Rangers. However, the fratricide cost Rudder another four dead and three wounded.

Meanwhile, Rudder's two remaining 2nd Rangers companies, 'A' and 'B', together with Max Schneider's 5th Rangers waiting impatiently aboard three converted ferry boats, the *Prince Charles*, *Prince Baudouin* and *Prince Leopold*, had diverted to Omaha and hit the shore at around 0800 hours. Their fortunes – as with the 116th Infantry – varied according to where they landed. Beaching in the morning mist and smoke depended as much on the vagaries of tide, current and avenues through the obstacles, as on the skills of the various landing craft coxswains.

The two 2nd Rangers companies and a headquarters element landed to the east of the Vierville draw, as ordered, and became caught up in the punishment being meted out to the earlier arrivals of the 116th. One boatload lost twenty out of thirty-four before reaching the sea wall; all of the Rangers' Company 'A' officers were killed or wounded on the sands. Company 'B' were similarly mauled, as were their landing craft. One was so badly hit that it drifted, manned by the dead, amongst the obstacles. This company lost forty-one out of sixty-eight before gaining the slight shelter of the sea wall. The defenders at D-1 and strongpoint WN70, further east, had managed to decimate four companies in the first ninety minutes.

Faced with such casualties, it was up to the non-commissioned officers to rally their shattered men and get them across the beach and into some kind of meaningful assault groups. This is exactly what their tough commando training had been designed to achieve: know your mission; when all else around fails, seize any weapons, become a one-man army and press on. As a result, those who were left penetrated the barbed wire and mines, climbed the bluffs and assaulted resistance nest WN70 from the rear. This position, perched on the edge of the high ground overlooking Le Hamel-au-Prêtre, had caused most of their problems. It consisted of a network of trenches leading to two 75mm guns in bunkers, a flak weapon, four machine-gun posts and a pair of 81mm mortar firing points. However, its defensive wire and minefield had been chewed up by ship-to-shore fire, it had almost run out of ammunition and its garrison of no more than thirty, eroded by casualties, were outnumbered by the survivors of the two Ranger companies bent on revenge.[34] Little quarter was given or expected.

Elsewhere the story was different. The craft containing Schneider's 5th Rangers had observed the destruction at Vierville and their coxswains dutifully managed to beach east of the troublesome strongpoints – on Dog White, and following Company 'C' of the 116th Infantry. This was opposite the demolished villas at Le Hamel-au-Prêtre, and between two strongpoints, WN70 and WN68, something of a blind spot in the defences and less well defended. Consequently, both Company 'C' and the Rangers reached the sea wall with far fewer casualties, the defenders' attention being focused on the draws. These units immediately advanced across the beachfront road, blew four gaps with Bangalore torpedoes in the barbed-wire entanglements to their front and started to worm their way up the bluffs.

It is this moment that became immortalised in the Rangers' iconography. While Schneider was conferring with his XO, Major Richard P. Sullivan, 'Dutch' Cota strode up, pistol in hand, creating order out of chaos. Schneider told the brigadier general of his intention to advance over the bluffs and take the Vierville draw from behind before moving on to Pointe du Hoc, to which Cota assented: 'You men are Rangers, I know you won't let me down,' followed by what would become the Ranger motto – 'Rangers, lead the way!'

The time was around 0830 hours and Captain John Raaen, Jr, of Headquarters Company remembered Cota 'chewing on a big, unlit cigar', coming towards his position. 'When he was about a hundred yards away, I realised he was someone high-ranking and gave him our situation, including the fact that we were about to blow the wire in front so we could move off the beach,' Raaen recalled. With piercing blue eyes and a commanding voice, he looked every inch the major general he had become when I met him. Raaen had graduated from West Point in 1943 as an engineer but immediately volunteered for the Rangers: he earned a Silver Star for his work on D-Day. General Cota's performance on D-Day became the role model for his life: 'When we went through the wire and up the bluffs, General Cota was still with us, right up with the lead platoons, always urging the troops onward.'[35]

The scrub and drifting smoke aided their ascent to the top of the bluffs; they moved in single file because of landmines but once on top, were surprised to discover many empty German trenches. A combination of the barrage and the battle for the draws had sucked the defenders towards the strongpoints, leaving swathes of the heights completely undefended. Rangers, together with those remnants of the First Battalion, 116th Infantry, who had followed Cota, were able to enter the undefended village of Vierville at around 1000 hours, but were unable to move north to the sea, south, or west to the Pointe du Hoc, because they began to tangle with elements of the 352nd Division in a series of meeting engagements. The Rangers remembered some German reinforcements arriving by bicycle, 'as though out for a Sunday-afternoon ride', completely unaware of the GIs until they were mown down. These skirmishes left the men Cota had led there victorious, but robbed them of any further advance.

Enter yet again the big guns of USS *Texas*. At 1233 hours the mighty battlewagon had opened fire on WN71 and WN72, guardians of the entrance to D-1, whose defenders were now running short of ammunition. In response, the Germans began to exit with their hands held aloft. Cota, meanwhile, sensing a change of fortune at D-1, had returned to the beach, and seeing the Vierville exit still blocked by anti-tank walls, found a bulldozer loaded with explosives and an engineer sergeant keen to blow the thick concrete obstruction. Then he turned his back and strode back eastwards, German artillery fire falling around him, restoring order to unit after unit, until he reached the 1st Division's forward headquarters, nearly two miles down the beach – this when most troops were afraid to move a yard because of sniping and shelling.

Despite the hostile fire, 'Dutch' Cota was remembered by many amazed GIs on the beach, fearlessly strolling about, issuing orders, twirling his Colt .45 and seemingly impervious to fire – and later on, walking through Vierville and down the D-1 draw to the beachfront. At the bottom by late afternoon, he found the 121st Combat Engineers busy bulldozing obstacles, stripping out wire and clearing mines. However, the D-1 draw couldn't open until WN73 – under attack by Goranson's Ranger company – had fallen, and also the one further along the coast with its two 75mm guns, WN74. Naval gunfire did the job here, its defenders being shelled into dazed submission at about the same time, 1630 hours.

However, any further attempt on Schneider's part to move his 5th Rangers to the Pointe du Hoc were stymied by the presence of scattered German units. At nightfall, as the surviving armour of Upham's 743rd Tank Battalion trundled up D-1, they were ordered to hunker down for the night with the Rangers, some eight hundred yards west of Vierville. Schneider's force had suffered a fraction of Rudder's losses, at twenty-three killed, eighty-nine wounded and two missing.

Accounts of the D-Day beach landings, particularly at Omaha, tend to be land-centric – for this is where most of the tales of derring-do came from. Yet often overlooked is the fact that the key enablers – who suppressed German fire enough for the Rangers to scale the cliffs, and likewise for the 116th and 16th Infantry to penetrate the defences of Omaha – were the five-inch guns of the fleet destroyers. Accompanied by three Royal Navy Hunts, HMSs *Melbreak, Talybont* and *Tanatside*, nine ships of the US Navy's Destroyer Squadron (DESRON) 18, commanded by Captain Harry Sanders, had been tasked to support the troops on Omaha Beach. USS *Satterlee* and USS *Thompson* did so for the Rangers on the Pointe du Hoc. USS *Carmick* and USS *McCook* performed likewise for the 116th and 115th Regimental Combat Teams on Dog and Easy Green. Supporting the 1st Infantry Division on Easy Red and Fox sectors were USSs *Emmons, Baldwin, Harding* and *Doyle,* while DESRON 18's flagship, USS *Frankford,* cruised the entire landing area. The bigger warships pulled more muscle, but only the destroyers could get in close enough and put their 'bows in the sand' to deal with the troublesome strongpoints at close range.

They had a range of targets in their tightly scripted timetable and probably made the assumption that after the aerial and naval bombardment, followed by the engineers and armour of the first wave, the defences would be overcome. Monitoring the confused and conflicting accounts coming back from the beaches – units who landed away from the draws sustained much less damage and lighter casualties – with visual observation difficult through the smoke and haze, it was not until around 0900 hours that the destroyer skippers realised something had gone very wrong. This had to a degree been anticipated by the *Satterlee, Thompson* and *Talybont* off the Pointe du Hoc, who closed to short ranges to subdue the defenders in support of Rudder, and initially provided his only means of communication.

Having their decks raked by machine-gun fire is not a common occurrence for destroyers, but USS *Satterlee*'s log recorded, '0710 hours: machine-gun fire directed at this ship. Commenced firing at pillbox in vicinity of Pointe du Hoc.'[36] USS *McCook* likewise reported that she knocked one enemy gun off the edge of the cliff, and that another 'flew up in the air'. Had he not been posted away from the ship on gaining his officer's commission, USS *Satterlee*'s company on D-Day would have included Petty Officer Henry Fonda, who had – like James Stewart and others – temporarily put his Hollywood career on hold to fight in the war. Upset at missing D-Day, years later he would get his chance to invade Normandy on celluloid when he played Ted Roosevelt in *The Longest Day*.

The influence of the destroyers is present in many eyewitness accounts. Austin Prosser on board *LCT-1171* had arrived at 0800, but received the beachmaster's order to loiter out to sea because of the build-up of wreckage along the surf. They lay offshore, avoiding the crossfire of German bunkers at either end, while a destroyer 'sailed up and down firing its guns over open sights against the beach emplacements.'[37] It was at 0830 hours when USS *Carmick*, on her captain's initiative, first broke the programmed ceasefire, timetabled after lifting supporting gunfire at H-Hour.

According to her log: 'a group of tanks were seen to be having difficulty making their way along the breakwater road toward Exit D-1 [the Vierville draw]. A silent cooperation was established wherein they fired at a target on the bluff above them and we then fired several salvos at the same spot. They then shifted fire further along the bluff and we used their bursts again as a point of aim.'[38] Following the *Carmick*'s example, Captain Sanders ordered the rest of DESRON 18 to close on the beach in direct support of the men. By 0950 hours, word had reached Admiral Bryant aboard the *Texas*, who sent his own endorsement, in clear over the air for all to hear: 'Get on them, men, get on them. We must knock out those guns. They're raising hell with the men on the beach, and we can't have any more of that. We must stop it.'[39]

Aboard *LCT-544*, US Marine Corporal Bill O'Neill, assigned to land at Fox Green leading to Colleville, noticed a few tanks firing random shots into the bluffs.

Suddenly, like the cavalry in an old western movie, several US Navy destroyers came thundering towards the shore. As near as they probably dared to go in relatively shallow waters, they started to pound the hills and casements with their five-inch guns. There were four behind us, their shells whistling overhead, tearing great chunks of concrete out of the casement walls, which ricocheted high in the air. The noise wasn't deafening, more of a crack than a bang, but the concussion from the blast had ears ringing. They traversed the shoreline, back and forth – an eyeball-to-eyeball street fight with the German forces concealed in the hill.'[40]

However, this intervention came at a cost: one of the destroyers which fired six salvos at the beach came within twenty-five yards of the damaged *LCT-27*. 'The concussion visibly affected the craft, already listing badly to starboard with the bow completely inundated. It turned over and capsized within fifteen hundred yards of the beach with all vehicles aboard.'[41]

Tom Bernard, correspondent for *Yank* magazine aboard USS *Doyle*, wrote of a German battery returning fire on his ship and the neighbouring USS *Emmons* and USS *Harding*:

For a frightening two minutes it pumped shell after shell within bare yards of us. Two screamed between the *Doyle*'s stacks and crashed into the water twenty-five yards off our starboard beam. Others whistled overhead in a nerve-wracking whine. The three destroyers worked slowly along the shore, plastering every grove of trees, every battered emplacement, every visible gulley and hole in the cliffside – everything that might conceivably hide German guns. The *Doyle* drove two men across a field with shells bursting mere yards from their tails.[42]

Second Lieutenant William G. Pepe, with Headquarters Company of the 5th Engineer Special Brigade, recalled the destroyers 'sailing parallel to the beach, heaving shellfire into known enemy positions. At times, they ran so closely to the shoreline it seemed they had to be scraping the bottom with their keels. I have nothing but the greatest admiration and pride for those brave seamen who gave us their support at the most critical phase.'[43]

Fighting with the 1st Division, Bill Ryan, Company 'I' of the 16th Infantry, soon became a casualty. 'When my boat was hit I was knocked unconscious. It was explained to me later that two men from my boat dragged me ashore and placed me up against the face of a small embankment at the foot of the hill. All day long on 6 June I had a front row seat, observing all the organised and disorganised action being played out not only on the beach, but also in the water. After all these years one particular incident has remained with me, I vividly remember a US Navy destroyer coming as close to the beach as he could, turning broadside on, and firing on the various bunkers, gun emplacements and trenches. Those were the positions that were keeping the troops pinned down on the beach and inflicting terrible casualties. This destroyer was later joined by other ships. I firmly believe that the firepower of these small ships turned certain defeat on Omaha Beach into a victory.'[44]

The Pointe du Hoc story was kept alive, but was never centre stage of the D-Day tapestry of events. Earl Rudder returned on the tenth anniversary with his teenaged son and a reporter from *Collier's* magazine – the same title Ernest Hemingway had written for in 1944. He found the site covered with a 'shoulder-high growth of dark-green thorn bushes with stalks of small, tight yellow flowers, that the French call *épines* and the British call gorse. "There wasn't this growth here then, it was just ripped-open dirt,"' he remembered.[45] At the foot of the cliff he found one of the grappling hooks his men had used in 1944.

The battle for the Pointe was also written up at the time by G. K. Hodenfield, a *Stars and Stripes* reporter who accompanied Rudder and stayed with him throughout the battle. Hodenfield worked for Associated Press after the war and on most D-Day anniversaries would pen an article on some aspect of what he had seen. In 1959 under the headline 'Rangers Fire Rockets with Grapnel Hooks to Scale 100 Foot Cliff to Reach Germans; Royal Navy Takes Them to Wrong Beach', he wrote of Sergeant Hayward Robey leading a dozen prisoners back for interrogation when they were caught in a German counter-attack. They were 'crouched in a huge shell hole, with German troops all around them. He told his men to take off, one at a time, and get back to our lines as best they could. The last man to leave, asked Robey what he was going to do about the prisoners. 'Don't you worry about that, I'll handle it,' he replied. When he was alone with the prisoners, Ranger Robey turned his Tommy gun on them and killed them all. Then he made his way back to our command post.'[46] The piece was not designed to provoke outrage; more noteworthy and typical of the era was the anti-British headline, not uncommon, and penned at a time when Anglo-American relations had reached their nadir.

In 1963 the Pointe played host to Eisenhower, who returned to France with Walter Cronkite to make ninety minutes of 'quietly moving television' for CBS. Their programme, *D-Day Plus 20 Years*, aired on 6 June 1964. As the *New York Times* reported, the pair visited

> coastal landing points that twenty years ago were marked by sacrifice and bravery and now are enjoyed by serene bathers. By ship, Jeep and afoot the General and Mr Cronkite revisited the Omaha beach, the forbidding cliffs at Pointe du Hoc that the Rangers climbed and the remnants of the bunkers out of which German officers saw the advancing Allied armada. The personal magnetism of General Eisenhower asserted itself most vividly and it was an effective and novel commemoration of the occasion.[47]

Into the 1970s the site itself remained overgrown, criss-crossed by muddy paths, serviced by a tiny car park and souvenir stand, little visited except by veterans and history buffs (this author included) bent on pilgrimage. In 1979, France gifted the land to America, erecting a tall granite memorial on top of Leutnant Ruhl's former observation post. It represents a

Commando dagger of the kind the Rangers were awarded for completing their gruelling training at Achnacarry in Scotland.

For his sheer tenacity and leadership in overcoming one of the key strongholds of the invasion coast; destroying its guns, even if not where they were thought to be; repelling endless counter-attacks from superior numbers; with a substantial part of his force killed or wounded; without communications and essentially behind German lines for three days with minimal supplies: Rudder, himself wounded, was awarded a Distinguished Service Cross, along with thirteen of his men. When it was awarded on 18 June, a tearful and emotional Earl Rudder called out to his men, 'This does not belong to me. It belongs to you.' The response was unanimous: 'You keep it for us, sir!'[48] For the influence Rudder had had on the wider assault, in retrospect it is surprising this decoration was not upgraded to a Medal of Honor.

Perhaps the answer lies in the differing interpretations of the action. In the official US Army narrative, *Cross-Channel Attack*, the dramas of Rudder's mission were very briefly surveyed in five sentences, which observed that naval gunfire support was of paramount importance:

> Enemy fire, reduced by naval shelling, remained light after the Rangers reached the top of the cliff and began moving inland in groups of three or four across a desert cratered by concentrated aerial and naval bombardment. Patrols found the 155mm gun emplacements deserted. The guns themselves were discovered farther inland in a camouflaged field position. The handful of Rangers who stumbled on them were therefore able to destroy them easily. Thus far the Rangers, despite thirty to forty casualties in the landings, had not had a hard fight.[49]

On the other hand, Cornelius Ryan massively overplayed the 'wild, frenzied scene. Again and again the rockets roared, shooting the ropes and rope ladders with grapnels attached. Shells and 40mm machine-guns [*sic*] raked the cliff top, shaking down great chunks of earth on the Rangers. Men spurted across the narrow, cratered beach, trailing scaling ladders, ropes and hand rockets. Here and there at the cliff top Germans bobbed up, throwing down "potato masher" hand grenades or firing *Schmeissers*.'[50]

Ryan found Rudder to be a very uncooperative eyewitness – he had answered only four of twenty-one enquiries on Ryan's questionnaire with one- or two-word answers. Consequently, the author eschewed any mention of Rudder in *The Longest Day* or his screenplay for the film, which was shot on location.[51] Thus, as S. L. A. Marshall was wont to do, Ryan injected his own storytelling into the history and concluded, in the manner of a Greek tragedy, that the mission 'had been a heroic and futile effort – to silence guns which were not there. The battered bunkers atop the Pointe du Hoc were empty – the guns had never been mounted.' This latter statement, as we have seen, is nonsense – Rudder knew the guns, temporarily relocated, might not be there.

However, any reading of the facts has to refute both the *Cross-Channel Attack* and *Longest Day* interpretations, because the cannon, wherever they might have been, were useable, supported by trained artillerymen and well stocked with ammunition, and thus posed a serious threat to the invasion – as the frantic German defence of the area well illustrates. A cold, hard reassessment of the threat from German batteries might conclude that the four brand-new 152mm naval guns in the fully finished Le Chaos battery at Longues-sur-Mer were more dangerous to the fleet than the much older cannon of the incomplete Pointe du Hoc fortress. A Ranger assault on them might have been more logical, given that they, too, were in a very similar dominant, clifftop position. However, this presupposes confirmed intelligence of the German weaponry, unavailable before 6 June. As it was, Le Chaos was suppressed by naval gunfire support alone, as could have been the guns – wherever they were – from the Pointe; but here we are moving into the uncertain realms of speculation and hindsight.

Perhaps the true reason for lack of further recognition at the time lay in the Rangers themselves. They were a brand new outfit. Their founder, Colonel William O. Darby, was serving in the distant Italian campaign, where he would be killed in 1945. Rudder and his men had no one well-placed to lobby on their behalf, and after the war their units disbanded. Rudder's exploits were overlooked in favour of others who served with more established formations, better connected within the US military hierarchy. There was also a bit of James Earl Rudder in the fictional Ranger Captain John H. Miller in *Saving Private Ryan* – both pre-war teachers and football coaches in small-town America. After graduating as an 'Aggie', Rudder had worked first at Brady High School, then Tarleton Agricultural College, which looked set to be the pattern of his life – but the war intervened. Rudder's military service gave him a renewed sense of direction and of his own leadership qualities. He was promoted to command the 109th Infantry – a Pennsylvanian National Guard regiment of the 28th Division commanded by 'Dutch' Cota, also elevated for his service on D-Day.

They saw gruelling service in the Battle of the Bulge, after which Rudder returned home in 1945 to become a very big man in Texas. In due course Colonel Rudder became the greatly revered Major General Rudder, in charge of the state's National Guard, and a highly respected president of Texas A&M University, his alma mater, for over twenty years.[52] Rudder's old university has retained close links with Normandy: in 2004 I joined them on an archaeological and engineering survey of the Pointe du Hoc, which discovered amongst other things that the Germans had sited their battery on the least geologically suitable part of the limestone coast, whose cliffs are now eroding fast into the Channel. One day, the bunkers, representing several years' handiwork of the *Organisation Todt* will join them.

29

Omaha: Big Red One

'In civilian life you get dressed, eat breakfast, go to work, have lunch, work some more, go home, have dinner then relax and read, watch TV, listen to the radio, and finally go to bed. On D-Day, I put on underwear, wool trousers, shirt, combat boots, field jacket, raincoat, along with two canteens of water, my pistol belt with pistol and ammo clips, and also a first aid packet. Plus, a musette bag with cans of C-Rations, K-Rations, D-Rations, two changes of socks and underwear, cigarettes and candy bars, chewing gum, map case with maps, various types of documents, gas mask and steel helmet. After a breakfast of scrambled eggs, bacon and coffee, around 0400 hours I started my day. First I checked with the Battalion CO, and then I rode to work in a landing craft for a day on the beach, waded through a swamp, dodged enemy fire, climbed a hill, found a safe place to work and sleep. Then I rested in a foxhole behind a hedgerow trying to go to sleep. No one was there to ask if I'd had a good day. If they had, my reply would have been yes – I was alive.'

Captain 'Hank' Hangsterfer, 16th Infantry[1]

IT WAS Harras, his German shepherd, who woke him first. Surfacing from a deep sleep, Major Werner Pluskat dimly heard his field telephone jangling. He fumbled for the receiver, wondering why his artillery commander should be calling him in the small hours. There were no pleasantries, he recalled, just a curt order: 'Alert your men and get down to the coast right away – paratroopers reported in the [Cotentin] peninsula. This could be the invasion.' About three miles inland from his coastal bunker, Pluskat was billeted in the comfortable sixteenth-century Ferme de la Marguerie in the hamlet of Étréham, with the commander of his 2nd Battery, Hauptmann Ludz Wilkening, and Leutnant Fritz Theen, his gunnery officer. Together with Harras, they drove to his observation post on the cliffs at Sainte-Honorine-des-Pertes, to the east of, but overlooking, Omaha Beach.

Pluskat stayed for a while, scanning the coast, and at 0335 hours was about to leave when he first spotted the arriving Allied fleet. The dramatic moment is described at the midpoint of Cornelius Ryan's *The Longest Day*, and echoed in the 1962 movie, with Hans Christian Blech memorably playing the thirty-two-year-old Pluskat, frantically screaming that the invasion fleet was heading 'Right for me!'

Although someone certainly saw the maritime threat around then, it may *not* have been the CO of the First Battalion of the 352nd *Artillerie-Regiment*. This is why the story of D-Day has become a fascinating, never-ending saga. New evidence suggests that Pluskat may have misled Ryan and had actually been absent from his command post at this crucial time. It is now thought that he was succumbing to the same temptations as Generalleutnant Feuchtinger of the 21st Panzer Division and Major Hans Schmidt, commanding the troops at Bénouville – and no doubt many other Wehrmacht officers – on this most inclement of June nights.[2] Gefreiter Heinrich 'Hein' Severloh would later recount that his boss, Oberleutnant Frerking 'hadn't been able to reach the Major at his quarters at Étréham, at battalion HQ or his command post: Pluskat was simply not there', whereupon Severloh joked that 'he's probably taking the girls of the *Front-Theatre* back to Paris right now'.[3] The role of German officers' French girlfriends in winning D-Day needs further examination.

Be that as it may, *someone* saw the new arrivals offshore, and ever since 0335 the defenders had been waiting for the assault. Crouching in his concrete shelter, Severloh first heard the 'dull drone of aircraft motors coming from the sea. The noise got louder and louder, and the roar rose to a hellish thunder as a powerful, ghostly fleet of bombers came directly at us in the grey, cloudy sky.'[4] Expecting bombs, Severloh, his fellow artillerymen and grenadiers cowered as the aircraft passed overhead and only then did their bomb loads come 'howling, whistling and crashing down. The bombs fell like heavy rain, and the first hit barely fifty yards behind our strongpoint', he recalled. 'Everything started to shake, even our small, dug-in observation post vibrated from the detonations, and earth and chunks of the limestone cliff fell around close to us – but the bombers had missed.'[5]

In a neighbouring position, Gefreiter Franz Gockel 'hid under the big wooden platform on which my machine-gun was mounted. The only thing I could do was pray,' he recollected. 'I said the short prayers I had said with my family while sheltering from air raids, getting myself into a trance.' As he looked out to sea, Gockel noticed 'black shadows looming on the horizon. First, we thought they were German motor boats, but the shadows grew, and pretty soon, they were so numerous that we could no longer hold on to our hope. We could make out the outline of smaller and larger boats in increasing numbers. Huge warships were lining up as if assembling for a parade. All of a sudden assault craft and special landing boats were rushing towards the beach.'[6]

Major General 'Gee' Gerow's V Corps was split equally in effort along Omaha Beach. The first wave it would hurl at the German-occupied coast comprised 34,142 men and 3,306 vehicles sailing mainly from Weymouth, Portland and Poole. While they had consolidated the beach-head, a follow-on wave of 25,117 men with 4,429 vehicles, putting out of Plymouth, Falmouth and Fowey, intended to land from the early afternoon.[7] Half of these numbers would be directed at the eastern sector of Omaha, running from Easy Red to Fox Red, and assaulted by methodical timetable.

The formation known as (and that continues to be called) the Big Red One was named after its distinctive shoulder badge, displayed prominently on every asset, flag, building and person associated with the formation. On uniforms, it – like the Blue and Gray insignia – was worn on the upper left shoulder. Although its individual regiments dated back to Civil War days, the 1st Infantry Division itself traced its heritage to the American Expeditionary Force deployed to France in 1917. Colonel George A. Taylor's 16th Infantry was raised in 1861, and in the words of its Latin motto, *Semper paratus* (Always ready), had seen continuous service thereafter – Colonel George A. Smith's 18th Infantry likewise. Colonel John 'Jeff' Seitz's 26th had been formed by an Act of Congress in 1901.

Many of the division's units, such as the 5th, 7th, 32nd and 33rd Field Artillery Battalions, were likewise pre-war military professionals. The latter would boast that 'on 8 November 1942 at 0832 hours, Battery 'B' fired the first American artillery rounds in the European Theater' – the first of a recorded 175,000 rounds the battalion would fire during 422 days of combat in the Second World War.[8] It contained Brigadier General Roosevelt's son, Quentin Roosevelt II (named after his uncle, an Air Corps pilot killed during the First World War). Both father and son had served together in the Big Red One in Tunisia and Sicily, both winning Silver Stars in separate engagements, and the pair would be in the spearhead on 6 June – Ted, as we have seen, on Utah, Quentin as a captain on Easy Red. Quentin's mother Eleanor was probably the only individual with a husband and son landing in the first wave on D-Day.

Collectively, the 1st Division possessed the lion's share of combat experience outside the Pacific, with the three battle streamers of Algeria–French Morocco, Tunisia and Sicily already to its name. A high proportion of its officers were thus not only career professionals, but hardened on the battlefields of the Mediterranean. A steady rock of the Big Red One was Brigadier General Clift Andrus, commanding its artillery. The son of a career officer, Andrus had once studied at Cornell University, was a graduate of Leavenworth and the War College, had also known battle in North Africa and Sicily – and would one day command the division.

Like many in the 1st Division, Colonel George Arthur Taylor, from Flat Rock, Illinois, was the product of the US Military Academy, West Point – in his case, Class of 1922. He understood amphibious operations better than most, had led his 16th Regiment well in the Sicilian campaign, and feared the neatness and tight schedule arranged for Omaha. Aboard USS *Samuel Chase* on 5 June, he had warned the warcos Don Whitehead, Robert Capa and Jack Thompson, 'The first six hours will be the toughest. This is the period during which we will be the weakest. But we've got to open the door.'[9] Taylor and Colonel George Smith had led their regiments through the Mediterranean; Seitz had not, but arrived with Pacific experience under his belt, notably as a battalion commander in Hawaii during 7 December 1941.

Like 'Dutch' Cota and Charles Canham in the Blue and Gray Division, Taylor was a soldier's soldier who operated on instinct and gut feeling, far different in temperament to his boss, Clarence R. Huebner, known as a stickler for drill and detail. Huebner may have shared the roots of small-town Kansas life with Eisenhower but had joined the army as a private in 1909. He possessed no fancy college education, having earned himself a battlefield commission. He was self-made through and through, and serious, and had taken command over from the popular and irreverent duo of Allen and Roosevelt in August 1943, but was still viewed with a degree of suspicion by some of the division.

Although Huebner's prior service shouted 'Big Red One', having worked his way up from private to colonel within the 1st Division – including First World War service, where he earned a Distinguished Service Cross – Huebner was fully aware that Overlord would be his first test in modern war. Before taking over the 1st, his previous appointments had been desk jobs in Washington DC, overseeing military training.[10] His assistant divisional commander, Brigadier General Willard G. Wyman, was cast from the same mould, being the consummate staff officer. He had been Deputy Chief of Staff Allied Forces Headquarters (AFHQ) in the Mediterranean before being parachuted in to replace Ted Roosevelt. Thus Andrus, Taylor and Smith had difficult paths to tread, having 'sand in their shoes' as successful commanders in the Mediterranean – Seitz, too, in the Pacific – in receipt of the widespread trust of their men, something their divisional commander and his deputy had yet to earn. However, as Huebner was not due to land until evening, when his formation was completely ashore, the weight of command would fall on the shoulders of Colonel George Taylor.

It is worth observing that collectively the 1st Infantry Division regarded themselves – and were seen as – the US Army's premier field formation. Its officers tended to write more official reports, climb higher in the US military hierarchy and leave voluminous memoirs, unlike their contemporaries of the 29th, who have not deployed as a division since the Second World War.[11] In more modern operations, the Big Red One still traces its traditions of leadership and combat skills back to the experience of Normandy.

Thus in terms of influence and sheer volume of paper, the Big Red One overshadows the Blue and Gray, but on Omaha Beach on 6 June 1944 they were equal. Whatever cocky pretensions to glory the 1st Infantry Division may have had were cut down to size. At the end of the day the origins of the two formations mattered not: both were full of draftees and both rose to overcome their challenges equally well. Whereas National Guardsmen had volunteered before the draft, and knew each other, those conscripted came from every state and were strangers to one another.

The story of draftee Hyam Haas, who had risen to the rank of sergeant in the 467th Anti-Aircraft Artillery Battalion, is not untypical. A poor Jewish kid from Brooklyn, New York, he had 'barely made it through the depression, when food was sometimes scarce. The only workouts I got was walking to wherever I had to go, as I didn't have the fare for subways, trolleys, or buses'. For many like Haas, military service was a welcome release. The army sent him 'travelling to places I never heard of, never dreaming I'd ever get to the land of the movies, California. Moreover I was hiking my way to the best physical shape I had ever been. I spent nearly five years in the Army: some of it was pure fun. So when I was inducted and got over my missing my widowed mother and my sisters, in spite of the regimentation, I began enjoying the relative freedom from the rigors of depression living.'[12]

This echoed the experience of many in the First World War, whose generation of soldiers had frequently emerged from nineteenth-century urban and agrarian squalor to enjoy three square meals a day for the first time in their lives, decent footwear, warm clothing and their own bed under a dry roof. It is often forgotten that mass conscription frequently benefited those who had least to lose, and set them up for a better life – if they survived. Haas found that he thrived. His buddies in Battery 'A' came from 'Louisiana, mostly from New Orleans, or the mid-west – Denver, Colorado, and different areas of Kansas: it seemed to me they were all farmers. Here was I, a city kid just recently able to tolerate Army life, giving orders to big husky farm boys who could probably turn me inside out if they so desired.'[13]

Many of those afloat, such as Frederick E. Boyer of Baker County, Oregon, were similarly sucked into war by the draft, taking their lives in unexpected directions. Boyer grew up on the family ranch, homesteaded by his grandfather in 1882, eking out a meagre living through the Great Depression, attending school by horse, buggy and sleigh. He had entered the navy after graduating from Oregon State College in 1943, assigned as ensign to USS *Dorothea L. Dix*, where on D-Day he would find himself in charge of several landing craft.[14] Brooklyn and Oregon to Normandy were just two of the strange voyages of self-discovery a whole generation of young Americans were making.

With the 29th busy capturing and opening the D-1 and D-3 draws, two more – E-1 leading to the eastern side of Saint-Laurent, and the prominent exit of E-3 which led uphill to Colleville – were assigned as 1st Division tasks. During the course of the day a fifth draw – the much smaller defended track winding up from the beach to Cabourg – would be captured and dubbed F-1. As we have seen, they were policed by

Widerstandsnester, but not all these had been completed. Unlike the 29th Division's half of the beach, the Big Red One's eastern sector had shingle mound instead of a sea wall, no seaside villas – or their remains – and no roadway running parallel to the surf. Anti-tank walls and ditches, however, blocked all the exits, guarded by the inevitable pillboxes. As with the bunkers on the Pointe du Hoc, the *Atlantikwall* here was evolving on a daily basis. At the back of Eisenhower's mind, when weighing up whether to postpone D-Day again, had been the knowledge that every week would see more mines laid, more obstacles and yards of barbed wire erected, and more concrete bunkers completed.

Sitting in those bunkers were Oberst Walter Korfes' 726th *Grenadier-Regiment*. His First Battalion, headquartered in Maisons (south of Port-en-Bessin), covered Sainte-Honorine-des-Pertes and Colleville, the eastern end of Omaha. The Third Battalion, based in Jucoville (north of La Cambe), had companies stationed in Grandcamp, Vierville and

Facing east, the photograph on this intelligence postcard illustrates the different nature of the beach looking towards the E-3 (Colleville) draw. There was no sea wall or road here, just a small mound of shingle thrown up over the years by the restless English Channel. The beach huts had been removed, replaced by a marshy area, strewn with barbed wire and mines. The Germans on the heights had a clear field of fire. Beyond lie the cliffs of Fox sector, where many sheltered. Just out of the picture, to the right, is the present-day American cemetery. (Author's collection)

Saint-Laurent – the western half. Since mid-morning they had been helping to defend the Pointe du Hoc. The headquarters of his Russians – the 439th *Ost-Bataillon* – who also manned some coastal strongpoints, was located in Les Veys (west of Isigny).[15] Having survived the initial aerial bombing, along the coast the defenders picked themselves up, amazed their positions were still intact. Few had been injured and their weapons remained undamaged.

However, the grenadiers barely had time to come to their senses before another bombardment started, this time from the sea rather than the air. 'Rockets and shells of the heaviest calibres thumped down continuously on our positions. The ground of the entire length of high coastal bluffs trembled under the head-on attack, and the very air vibrated,' recollected Hein Severloh. 'The sky was darkened by dense smoke and clouds of dirt. In between were the flashes of thundering explosions, and it seemed as though the whole world would sink down in a howling and crashing inferno of bursting shells. On the slope of our position, dry grass and gorse bushes began to burn.' Yet this second attack, too, did little damage: the Germans had built well. Almost worse was the aftermath, observed Severloh: 'thick, yellow, choking dust filled the air. It smelled like the remains of a fire and tasted bitter.'[16]

For soldiers unused to such a cannonade, this was a living hell, though many had experienced this on the Russian Front or under Allied bombs in their cities. It was enough to overawe Severloh's NCO, Wachtmeister Fack, whom he found cowering at the entrance to his observation bunker, Luger pistol cast aside, face contorted with fear and eyes wild. 'Then', he remembered, 'it was almost completely quiet, with not a single shot being fired. We had strict orders to wait until our foes were in knee-deep water.' They had been expecting 'Tommies' to invade, but could clearly read in large white letters 'U.S.' on the sides of the vessels. So it was the Americans. Severloh and his buddies watched the GIs jumping 'into the cold, chest-to-shoulder-high water. Many went under for a moment and, half-swimming, half wading, they began to move slowly toward the beach in front of our strongpoint.'[17]

As elsewhere, among the first ashore on the eastern sector of Omaha were the Navy Combat Demolition Units, comprising the army and navy obstacle-clearing engineers. Ensign Lawrence S. Karnowski, a civil engineering graduate of the University of Kansas, was leading Naval Combat Demolition Unit 45 onto Easy Red. Before departing Portland in an LCT, all the NCDU officers were briefed aboard USS *Ancon* by Rear Admiral

Hall that 'the pre-invasion naval bombardment would clear the beaches and overlooking bluffs. Not a living soul would be left upon the beach.' They were sceptical. In the event, Karnowski led his team ashore just after 0630 hours, midway between the Saint-Laurent and Colleville draws, to the west of Severloh's position. They began placing satchel charges on obstacles, successfully blowing a hundred-yard line of obstructions at 0650. The technique was to place all the charges then blow them simultaneously. As soon as the first detonation occurred German machine-guns and mortars opened up from the bluffs, and they started to take casualties.[18]

'It took about five minutes for the Americans to reach shallow water; I moved the safety lock of my machine-gun to the off position,' reminisced Severloh.

> I could see the water spouts where my machine-gun bursts were hitting, and when the little fountains got close to the GIs, they threw themselves down. They all lay in the shallow water; many tried to get to the most forward beach obstacles to find some cover behind them. I fired some more at the many dark forms in the water. Oberleutnant Frerking appeared next to me and observed the Americans. 'Poor swine,' he said softly to himself and picked up the handset of the field telephone to send the coordinates and firing orders for our artillery.[19]

Undeterred, Karnowski's men managed a second detonation at 0700 hours; army engineers triggered two more at 0710, which cleared almost the entire fifty-yard gap from the surf to the dunes. Earlier, another team had been under the impression that H-Hour was 0620 and had landed all alone – this hardly compromised the element of surprise, as the bombardment had awoken Severloh and all his colleagues in a fifty-mile radius. As the leading engineers struggled through the water, a shell hit their landing craft and detonated the explosives, killing most left on board.

A tension now arose (also encountered in the western sectors of Omaha): the infantry stumbling ashore were huddling among the obstacles, using them for cover, denying the engineers the chance to wire and destroy the obstructions. No amount of urging could move them; there was no beachmaster present yet, and thus the assault gapping effort failed in many places. Some engineers thereupon gave up their task, fixed their bayonets and took up firing positions with the infantry on the shingle. Where in a few cases obstacles were prepared for destruction, the Germans seemed to be precisely aware of the activity, for the 'fusillade from the shore cut away fuses as rapidly as the engineers could rig them. One burst of fragments carried away a fuse-man's carefully set mechanism – and all of his fingers.' Most surviving NCDUs collapsed under cover of the shingle bank, 'soaking wet, unable to move, and suffering from cramps. It was cold and there was no sun.'[20]

Unlike most other teams, Karnowski managed to open a passage and landing craft bearing the 16th Infantry started to beach. However, while sheltering in the dunes, his team took further casualties from mortar and artillery fire; Karnowski would be awarded a Navy Cross for his work, although just six of his thirteen-man NCDU-45 remained unwounded.[21] Closely following the NCDUs were army engineer battalions, to which Beachmaster units and Underwater Demolition Teams were attached. With one of them in Company 'C' of the 299th Combat Engineer Battalion was Robert N. 'Lefty' Lowenstein, a former railroad worker from Tonawanda, New York State. 'Our battalion had eight assault teams,' he remembered. 'We were to cut pathways through the obstacles, the tetrahedrons, the hedgehogs, the Belgian gates, the poles, that were all along the beach.' Incredibly, Lowenstein survived unscathed, though he was hit 'twice in the helmet, my gas mask was shot through, and my canteen also'.[22]

Landing at 0630 hours with the DD Shermans of the 741st Tank Battalion would be four companies from Colonel Taylor's 16th Infantry along with the obstacle clearers and other engineers, and supported by artillery. The assault vessels carrying Taylor's riflemen neatly reflected the make-up of the maritime component. His First Battalion would launch from the Coast Guard-manned attack transport *Samuel Chase*, the Second Battalion from the US Navy's *Henrico*, while the Third Battalion would disembark from the Royal Navy's *Empire Anvil*.

At H-Hour the Second Battalion would throw its Companies 'E' and 'F' against the centre sectors of Easy Red, to seize the E-1 draw. At the same moment, the Third Battalion was to despatch its Companies 'I' and 'L' at Fox Green, and take the E-3 exit. Thirty minutes later, the next wave would see Company 'G' leave the *Henrico* and Company 'K' the *Anvil*, to hit the same pair of beaches with the anti-aircraft half-tracks of the 397th AAA Battalion. After a lapse of only ten minutes, the third programmed wave of Taylor's Companies 'H' and 'M' would land in the same area, where eight gaps through the obstacles should by then have been cleared by the engineers.

Subsequent waves would deposit more troops, tanks, the 81st Chemical Mortar Battalion, anti-aircraft and field artillery battalions, as well as the 6th Naval Beach Battalion. These would all comprise the 16th Regimental Combat Team. Taylor planned for his Second Battalion (Companies 'E' to 'H') to land and seize Colleville. The Third Battalion (Companies 'I', 'K', 'L' and 'M') was to swing round to the east, securing Sainte-Honorine-des-Pertes. Meanwhile, the First Battalion (Companies 'A' through 'D') would advance through Colleville and take Formigny, to the south-west. They would be followed by the three battalions of Smith's 18th Infantry – carried by the attack transports *Anne Arundel*, *Dorothea L. Dix* and *Thurston* – scheduled to begin landing from 0930 hours. The 18th were to eventually forge eastwards to link up with the British 50th Division advancing from Gold Beach. Seitz's 26th Infantry Regiment would act as a reserve, prepared to beach on V Corps' orders in the afternoon, and deploy wherever Gerow or Huebner thought best.

Armour accompanied the first-wave GIs. We have seen how the 743rd Tank Battalion decided to go all the way by LCT instead of swimming, to support the 29th Division on the western sands of Omaha. At 0530 hours, the same decision had to be made by their sister 741st Battalion, waiting 6,000 yards offshore, and preparing to swim ashore in support of the Big Red One. Knowing the scheduled launch could be overridden at the discretion of the tankers or the naval commander, the sight of four-foot-high waves – with the occasional six-foot breaker whipped up by eighteen-knot winds – caused Captain James Thornton, Jr, commanding Company 'B', to discuss the matter earnestly with his counterpart from Company 'C', Captain Charles Young, by radio. They knew the rubber-ised canvas of their DD rigging only provided three feet of freeboard above the sea. The pair concluded that although the waters were much rougher than any they had known during training, the need for armour on the beach justified the risk, and they decided to go.

It was a tragic error: within minutes the air-filled rubber struts were snapping and canvas screens buckling, as the waves overwhelmed tank after tank. The fully-laden Shermans plunged straight to the seabed. Company 'B' lost all but five – two somehow managing to swim ashore. Later, Ensign R. L. Harkey, skipper of *LCT-602*, would record, 'I am not proud of the fact nor will I ever cease regretting that I did not take the tanks all the way to the beach.'[23] Ironically, Staff Sergeant Turner G.

Sheppard, commanding one of the surviving pair which arrived on Fox Green, thought it 'was the smoothest landing the crew had ever managed'. To his left, he could see the other surviving DD Sherman commanded by Sergeant George R. Geddes on the sand; both reckoned they survived because they had sailed small boats in peacetime.[24] The two intrepid Company 'B' sergeants would receive battlefield commissions as a result of their actions on D-Day. However, every single one of Company 'C's sixteen tanks sank like stones between 5,000 and 1,000 yards from the surf, losing on average one crew member per tank.

All the swimming tanks had been told to aim for the prominent steeple of Colleville church. Recent analysis by divers of the sunken tanks suggests they did exactly that. However, they had set out in line abreast and converged on their landmark like the spread of a fan: this caused them to broach – meeting the full fury of the waves sideways on, parallel to the shore. Those of Company 'C' were also head-to-wind and battling against the current – conditions challenging enough for a sailboat, never mind 'thirty tons of metal in a canvas bucket'. The two Company 'B' survivors, using their seamanship, had managed to steer direct for the surf and remain at right angles to the coast.

Accusations of stupidity or ignorance levelled at the two company commanders thus appear to be misplaced, for it was the orders handed to them – to head for the spire – that directly caused the sinkings.[25] Having rehearsed underwater escapes, the majority of the crews bobbed up to the surface, or waited in the small orange dinghies issued to each DD tank, to be scooped up by rescue launches and taken back to southern England. The other lucky survivors were three Company 'B' tanks which failed to launch: a wave had sunk Second Lieutenant Patrick J. O'Shaughnessy's DD shortly after it exited, and lashed the landing craft so severely that the remaining three collided on deck, tearing their screens.

As the first crew scrambled back on board, Staff Sergeant Paul W. Ragan, the next senior tankman, demanded the skipper take the three remaining Shermans – the other two commanded by Sergeants Maddock and Kenneth V. Williams – to the beach. 'When we drove off *LCT-600*, I couldn't see much in front of me except smoke, but there was a clear spot in it, and through this I could see a pillbox. We fired at least forty rounds of 75mm at it,' Ragan recalled. This meant there were precisely three tanks on Easy Red for the first half hour of the assault, and two on Fox.[26]

Apart from three Shermans sunk with their LCT by shelling, all of Captain Cecil Dallas Thomas's non-swimming Company 'A' reached shore with the second wave at 0700 hours, astride the boundary between Easy Red and Fox Green. They had blazed away from their LCTs in the remote hope of hitting something – but from a pitching, rolling craft this was unlikely. Once ashore, with the command radio ruined by seawater, Thomas, a Virginia Polytechnic graduate from Rockingham County, had to move from tank to tank, directing fire and moving vehicles into cover. In doing so, both his technical sergeants and radio operator were wounded. Thus, instead of the planned forty-eight tanks on Easy Red and Fox Green that morning, only eighteen were present, driving up and down the beach, hemmed in by the rising tide and the target of every German gun.

Some escaped destruction by seeking cover in the drifting smoke and keeping mobile. However, they made the landings easier for successive waves by drawing fire onto themselves – not a traditional use of armour. We have already acknowledged the often undervalued contribution of naval gunfire support from the destroyers, but this began only between 0830 and 0900. In the timetable, warships had been ordered not to fire until communication was established with Navy Shore Fire Control Parties – many of whom were dead. This meant that on some areas of Easy Red and Fox Green, the only supporting fire for over two hours came from the few tanks on the shingle.[27]

Infantry companies 'E' and 'F' of Taylor's RCT should have landed midway between the Saint-Laurent and Colleville draws, in a long line abreast, and were to open E-1. Behind them would follow Company 'G', then 'H', in further waves. As it was, the morning murk, sea spray, haze from burning brush on the clifftops (set alight by the rocket craft), wind and waves combined to push all but one of their boats east, towards the strongly defended E-3 exit to Colleville. A single boatload of thirty-two men actually grounded as planned, but slightly late, at 0645 hours, the rest of Companies 'E' and 'F' ending up in a huddle either side of the Colleville draw, under the noses of Hein Severloh and his colleagues in WN62. The 16th Infantry men on target were led by Second Lieutenant John M. Spalding of Owensboro, Kentucky, who would soon recognise their fortune in landing between the two draws. Spalding had noted on the run-in 'several yellow rubber boats with personnel from the DD tanks which had foundered' but exited their landing craft into water over their heads.[28]

They were puzzled to see not a single craft anywhere to the west, and eventually realised they were the extreme front right of their division. All reached the shoreline intact, but Spalding's boat team could not race across the beach – instead tottering as fast as they could, their burdens doubled by the seawater in their clothes and equipment. Even so, occasional bursts of machine-gun fire raked the shingle, with random heavier shelling. Spalding later realised that to have got twenty out of thirty-two men across the beach was a good result. They had arrived at a weak point in the German defences, about halfway between the powerful WN62 to their left, which dominated the Colleville exit, and WN64 to their right, which overlooked the Saint-Laurent valley. Both these positions had much of their weaponry oriented to defend the exits, and at the moment Spalding landed that was where the defenders' attention was focused also.

Spalding recounted in 1945, 'To our left, we passed a pillbox from which machine-gun fire was mowing down Company 'F' people a few hundred yards to our left. There was nothing we could do to help them' – this was certainly WN62. Rather than make for the right-hand Saint-Laurent draw as planned, it seemed to him and his sergeant, Philip Streczyk of East Brunswick, New Jersey, a more sensible course to forge directly ahead where they perceived little apparent opposition. Soon they had blown gaps in the concertina wire, followed a well-trodden path through a minefield at the foot of the bluffs, and were climbing the heights. At the top, they rushed a machine-gun nest, capturing its occupant. Fortune smiled as Streczyk, of Polish extraction, discovered their first prisoner was a fellow Pole, albeit in field grey, who was happy to divulge what he knew of the defensive layout.

Spalding soon found some of his own regiment's Company 'G' had followed his path up the bluffs, though the unit, under their commander, Captain Joseph T. Dawson, peeled off left towards Colleville, further east. They would fight their own war; Dawson immediately overcame another machine-gun post with an extremely accurate grenade throw. Meanwhile, Spalding and Streczyk had led their motley crew westwards along the cliffs, mopping up positions as they went, and eventually attacked and overcame WN64 at around 1000 hours. During their advance, Spalding's band killed forty Germans and captured a further twenty besides their Pole.[29] Corporal Samuel M. Fuller, the Hollywood-screenwriter-turned-soldier whom we met roaming *Henrico* with Robert Capa in Weymouth, was soon ordered to relay news of Lieutenant Spalding's success to the

16th Infantry's commander, Colonel Taylor. Dashing across the beach, here and there, in full view of the Germans, he eventually tracked down his colonel by following the butts of the Havana cigars Taylor enjoyed chewing. Taylor was pleased with the news – and impressed with the corporal's ingenuity: he presented Fuller with a box of the same Havana cigars for his arduous trek under fire and, later, a Silver Star.[30]

Opposite WN64, later waves of Canham's Company 'M' had already landed west of the E-1 draw from around 0700 hours, and were protected from the worst of its fire by the shingle bank. However, without heavy weapons or tank support they were unable to make any impression on either WN64 or WN65 guarding its entrance. They slid to their right in an attempt to outflank the E-1 draw, and were instead drawn towards the fight for the D-3 (Les Moulins) draw. The beachmaster for this sector, Easy Red, was the twenty-three-year-old Lieutenant Commander Joseph Vaghi, Jr, who landed from *LCI-88* at 0735 hours with his men of the 6th Naval Beach Battalion.

'We were 333 men and forty officers, attached to the 5th Engineer Special Brigade, 16th Regimental Combat Team,' he recollected. Their CO, Commander Eugene C. Carusi, 'was thirty-eight or so, over six feet, slim, with light grey eyes and prematurely gray hair'. A Naval Academy graduate, Carusi had become a lawyer; now he was back in uniform. 'He dubbed us Carusi's 400 Thieves.' On landing, Vaghi raced off his craft 'as if I was running with a football under my arm. Using the obstacles as shelter, I moved forward over the tidal flat under full exposure to machine-gun fire until I finally reached the dune line.' Vaghi recalled an apocryphal panorama of soot and flame, where 'the stench of expended gunpowder filled the air. Purple smoke drifted from the base of the beach obstacles as our Underwater Demolition Teams went about their business with the obstacles.'[31]

His colleague Manuel R. Perez soon realised everything had gone wrong.

Nobody seemed to be where they should have been according to plan, and that included us. All up and down the beach tanks were sitting in the surf line knocked out, impotent and burning. Heavy smoke and mist covered everything; visual signals were absolutely no good – and worst of all, equipment of every conceivable sort was piling up in huge hills at the waterline. The time schedule, as well as the schedule of priority objectives, had jumped the track, the great ships lying offshore were pumping men and munitions toward the beaches with which they had no communication, and if ever disaster threatened the whole gigantic undertaking, it was at that moment.[32]

Vaghi somehow survived a nearby explosion which killed one of his men, and set his clothes alight – and a jeep full of gasoline and hand grenades. 'They called us the traffic cops of the invasion,' he recalled, 'though most of my traffic got blown up before it went anyplace.' He was one of the few meant to stay on the beach: 'My job was to get everyone else off the shingle. If your helmet had a white rainbow on it you were a Beach Battalion or Engineer Brigade guy and could stay. Everyone else was meant to go. Of course that never happened. That day we had a hundred professions. One minute I was driving a stranded bulldozer out of the sea, the next I was seeing my men struck by bullets and having one die in my arms.'[33]

Perez recalled another beachmaster, Lieutenant Vince Perrin, having to 'use his arms in semaphore code to direct an LCT with two tanks aboard, to the edge of the beach. The LCT finally made it.' Even as this was going on, Perez noticed a nearby LCVP with eight men of Navy Demolition Team-11 aboard. 'Even as I looked, an eighty-eight shell burst in the air above them, detonating a load of Primacord they were carrying. That stuff has a bullet sensitivity of zero! The LCVP seemed to rise bodily out of the water, burst apart in a great mushroom of red-orange flame, and the next moment there were hardly even fragments visible to mark the spot. I learned later only one man survived.'[34]

Bernard Friedenberg was a medic in Headquarters Company, First Battalion of the 16th Infantry. When he volunteered for the army, the son of Atlantic City, New Jersey, was rejected by the infantry because of poor eyesight, but being Jewish was determined to fight. 'Give me a weapon and take me where the Germans are. They want to kill Jews. I'm a Jew,' he'd thought; 'I want to be able to fight back.' He had crossed to France aboard USS *Samuel Chase*, climbed down a rope cargo net and threw himself into a landing craft as it bobbed and crashed into the side of the ship. He worked his way to the front, observing that 'machine-gun fire often caught the last bunch of men disembarking, so I made it a point to get off the craft quickly'. Immediately, Friedenberg was pulled down by the heavy load of medical supplies he was carrying.[35]

On the beach I raced from one wounded soldier to the next, administering morphine, sulphur powder, and talking to them. I lied; I'd say anything to put them at ease, keep their blood pressure down. I would claim their wound was not so bad even if it was. I'd reassure them: 'You're lucky, pal. You've got a million-dollar wound.' I'm still haunted by this one kid who had a sucking hole in his chest and as he breathed, air would come out the hole. I tried to seal it with adhesive tape but there was so much blood the tape wouldn't stick. Looked like a high school kid. Died under my hands. I never got over that.

Friedenberg would receive the first of two Silver Stars for carrying five wounded men on his back, one at a time, out of an Omaha minefield. 'I also treated this badly wounded German; first thing that went through my head was, "Screw him" but I just couldn't, so I sprinkled sulphur powder on his wounds and dressed them. He kept kissing my hand and thanking me, took out his wallet; showed me pictures of his sons. He spoke English and he said, "My boys will thank you; my wife will thank you."'[36]

Serving in the US Coast Guard, James Carrie was on his fourth invasion aboard the *Samuel Chase* and responsible for getting many of the 16th Infantry ashore. 'We knew this was going to be the *Big One*. We'd been through three'. Then 'just a kid' of twenty-three, he recalled of the morning, 'The soldiers were all huddled together. There was a lot of nervous tension. You could feel it. You knew somebody was going to get it that day'. His vessel, named after a signatory to the Declaration of Independence, carried thirty-three Higgins boats [LCVPs] to Normandy. 'Only nine returned, and they came carrying dead and wounded. The others were lost to the tides and damage from the German guns and mines. When they started bringing back the dead and the wounded, there were so many we were stacking the dead up five high', Carrie remembered.[37]

At around 0900, Sergeant Hyam Haas, the poor Brooklyn kid thriving on army life, disembarked from *LCT-244* just east of the E-1 draw with his section of two anti-aircraft half-tracks. These were Battery 'A' vehicles, one mounting four .50-calibre machine-guns, the other a 37mm auto-cannon with two machine-guns in an armoured turret. He remembered during the final run-in seeing the body of a GI floating by. 'We could clearly hear the distinctive sound of German machine-guns – they had such a high rate of fire they sounded like a *burrrrp* and that's how they got the name burp guns. Our LCT found a clear spot through the obstacles and made for shore and soon the ramp was down and we started our motors.'

The water was far deeper than Haas had expected, but they had thoroughly waterproofed the vehicle. 'I found myself in the cab, in sea that went up to my chin, and held my weapon and that of the driver aloft out of the waves.' From the shoreline he noticed 'a bunker that looked to me to be built into the hills. At the same time I also spotted an American officer with a moustache and wearing shiny cavalry boots running towards me pointing at that bunker. Captain Napier, standing nearby said, "Go get it!"'[38] The moustachioed officer may well have been Colonel Charles Canham, commanding the 116th Infantry, whose men had been pinned down in the area, and who had been striding around trying to energise the move off the beach.

'I took up position behind the rangefinder and in an instant we opened fire,' recalled Haas. 'The first three shots from our 37mm autocannon missed; I made an adjustment and the next fifteen shots went right into the gun port of the bunker. I heard the .50 Brownings firing also. No doubt it was dead.' This concrete blockhouse was part of WN65, and Sergeant Haas's actions resulted in twenty Germans stumbling out of the position in surrender. The fall of shot places Haas and his vehicles to the east of E-1 draw, in the dead centre of Easy Red sector. To his right he saw 'LCIs afire with exploding ammunition' – this was Seth Shepherd's *LCI-92*, with *LCI-91* beyond, which had been struck hours earlier and would burn for the rest of the day. However, Haas had destroyed only a part of WN65, which comprised a second 50mm gun, a 37mm, two mortar posts and several machine-guns, each in a concrete bunker, and all connected by a honeycomb of zig-zag trenches, the ensemble surrounded by wire and mines. Nevertheless, his two half-tracks had taken out a significant portion of the position and the morale of its survivors must have begun to dip at this point.

The guys on the shingle needed a break. Manuel R. Perez with Carusi's '400 Thieves' naval beach battalion had found himself tending a casualty

leaning up against a disabled tank that was broadside to the enemy fire. His eyes were glassy. Both his legs were broken, and he held his guts in his two hands. He was dazed – I didn't know whether he could feel the pain yet or not. His mouth hung open in a hideous grin. I crawled over to him, broke open a morphine syrette and jabbed it in his right leg. There was no need to cut his clothing; it was ripped off him. He was completely inert, giving no sign of life save for an occasional moving shadow in the depths of his shocked eyes.[39]

On top of all this chaos was the self-made problem of the timetable. Nobody offshore had a clear enough picture of the situation onshore to tinker with the scheduled waves – so more troops and many soft-skinned vehicles unloaded onto the beaches, providing a plethora of targets for the defenders. Inland artillery batteries had long since joined in, barely needing to correct their fire, safe in the knowledge that every round would damage something. Motivated as much by their inability to blow obstacles – which would send red-hot lumps of steel careering around their own troops and vehicles, as the German guns were doing – the demolition teams resorted to removing mines from the stakes, ramps, hedgehogs and Belgian gates by hand.

Once stripped of their mines, the navy discovered the obstacles were not as lethal as supposed. One of the keys to later waves of the 18th Infantry being able to cross the beach at the junction of Easy Red and Fox Green, with relatively light losses, were the performances of *LCT-30* and *LCI-544*. Skippered by two young USNR lieutenants, Sidney W. Brinker and E. B. Koehler, at about 1030 hours, both craft steamed at full speed through the obstacles, guns blazing at WN62, the defenders of the Colleville draw. Hastily unloading her passengers, *LCI-554* managed to escape, but after disembarking her GIs, *LCT-30* was riddled by shellfire and peppered with holes, which knocked out all power and flooded the engine room. This forced her abandonment – but the intrepid captains had demonstrated that demined beach obstacles could be breached by ramming, under cover of destroyers peppering the shore positions with five-inch gunfire.[40]

At this time Colonel George Smith's 18th Infantry had begun to arrive. They had been due at 0930, but had been directed to wait offshore for thirty minutes. With most of Taylor's 16th Infantry focused on the fighting around E-3 (the Colleville draw), Brigadier General Wyman, the Big Red One's assistant divisional commander, directed Smith to take over Taylor's former task of opening E-1. It took time for Smith to collect his regiment, as their craft became dispersed, having to land where they could. Although they reached the shore with relatively few casualties, twenty-eight of the craft bearing them were destroyed by underwater obstacles.

Landing to the east of the E-1 draw was Dean Weissert of Eustis, Nebraska, a linesman with the Communications Platoon in Headquarters Company, First Battalion, 18th Infantry. Weissert remembered their 'vile run-in', the coxswain opening out the engine and the jar of grounding as they hit the sands. 'We took off running, and got into water about chest deep; it didn't take us long to get to the beach, and we made it across the sands with everything in our pack soaked.'⁴¹ Private Carlton Barretter, from Albany, New York, and with the same unit as Weissert – found himself under fire in neck-deep water, but this did not deter him from time after time rescuing floundering comrades and saving them from drowning. These efforts would bring him one of four Medals of Honor awarded on D-Day.

Beyond the beach lay wire which had already been breached and the marsh at the foot of the bluffs, as Weissert recollected: 'We came up to a little swamp. Green, slimy looking water, and we had to cross it. And I thought, well, maybe this isn't very deep. But the water just crept up on me, shoulder deep, so as I was still wearing a couple of life preservers, I inflated them, and crossed the water bobbing up and down, as I didn't want to swallow any of that green, slimy muck.'⁴²

Landing with Company 'E' in the Second Battalion of the 18th was Ernie Leh, the corporal who remembered the soldier being shot days earlier in Dorchester. Aboard his LCI he had been terribly seasick. 'I threw up in my helmet. All through the night I lay in misery below deck, hardly caring whether I lived or died', he recalled. Stepping into four feet of rough, icy water, Leh witnessed how close all of the Big Red One were to extinction. By the time he was making his way up the bluffs, he felt the call of nature. 'I had to relieve myself. I stopped and went behind a rock about five or six feet high. Others passed me and went on ahead. I remember seeing a major and some enlisted men pass by. Just as they got over the next rise, a shell exploded right in their midst, getting all of them. That would have been me had I not stopped.'⁴³

At around 1020 hours, Leh's unit – the Second Battalion of the 18th – supported by the fire of a lone 741st Tank Battalion Sherman, started to force the E-1 draw. Initially they stalled, but summoned by radio, DESRON 18's destroyers then sailed within a mile of the sands, and sometimes nearer – perilously close for an ocean-going vessel – and were

This well-known image captures the 'vile run-in' to Omaha that many remembered, soldiers jammed like sardines in their puny Higgins boat. A sailor wearing a life vest (front right) peers out cautiously. An officer (front left), sporting the badge of the Big Red One on his left sleeve, stands to observe their progress. His men are crouching to avoid incoming fire, clutching their weapons wrapped in waterproof plastic, their helmets drenched in spray. The smoking cliffs of Omaha are a smudge in the distance, perhaps another forty minute voyage in this LCVP. (NARA)

able to pump endless rounds of five-inch shells accurately into the other concrete positions. The ship's log of USS *Frankford* noted at 1036 hours firing on one of the pillboxes at E-1: 'Commenced firing using direct fire, range about twelve hundred yards [two-thirds of a mile]. On the fifth salvo a direct hit was obtained, a large cloud of green smoke was noted and the battery ceased firing. Our troops then advanced and a number of Germans were seen to surrender.'[44] Captain 'Hank' Hangsterfer with the First Battalion of the 16th witnessed the moment: 'From our vantage point on the ridge we could see ... countless dead and wounded, wrecked landing craft, blown up tanks, hostile fire of all types. A US destroyer came very close to shore and was firing directly at a pillbox;

after a few salvos it was knocked out.'[45] By 1130 hours the entire defence of E-1 had collapsed.

There were other German positions in depth further up the E-1 draw who could see what was happening. One of them rapidly relayed the penetration to Oberst Walter Korfes, commanding the 726th *Grenadier-Regiment*. He received the message at 1140 hours in the Château de Sully (now a fine hotel), and warned his counterpart Oberst Ernst Goth in his HQ in Formigny – that their front was now porous and in danger of disintegration. This was in complete contrast to the optimistic picture painted only two hours earlier – recorded by Oberstleutnant Fritz Ziegelmann, chief of staff to the 352nd, from the commander of WN74 – that the landings had ceased and the beach was littered with burning American equipment.

However, with most German troops tied to their bunkers, if any counter-attack was to be made, it would have to be with whatever reserves Generalleutnant Dietrich Kraiss of the 352nd Division – also covering this sector – could muster. Two hours in battle can make all the difference, and on 6 June in Normandy the earlier mist and low cloud had been replaced by midday with bright sunlight – good flying weather for the Allied tactical air forces, and spotter planes of the big guns floating offshore. Generalleutnant Wilhelm Richter, based in Caen – the other general covering the invasion coast – was completely overwhelmed, with his troops behind Gold, Juno and Sword under seaborne attack and no reserves readily available.

Dietrich Kraiss had many challenges that morning, but his most important was interpreting the battle picture. Initially, at 0310, he had ordered his infantry reserves – the divisional Fusilier battalion, and the two battalions of 915th *Grenadier-Regiment*, deployed as *Kampfgruppe Meyer* (so named after Oberstleutnant Karl Meyer, its commander) – from their location south-east of Bayeux to contain the parachute landings on his western flank. By 0550 hours, Kraiss was aware of the far greater threat assembling off the coast. He halted the *Kampfgruppe*, which then remained immobile for two hours until at 0735 hours Kraiss ordered Meyer's Second Battalion of the 916th back east, to seal the American penetrations first reported to him between Sainte-Honorine and Colleville. This battalion – comprising bicycle troops with heavy equipment borne on commandeered French trucks – took the better part of the morning to reach their destination, harried by Allied fighters and pedalling furiously over scores of miles of Norman roads.

Sixteen-year-old Grenadier Wilhelm Gerstner, who had just been drafted into the 352nd Division, recollected of his bicycle journey: 'It was terrifying; we were always scanning the skies for *Jabos* [Allied *Jagdbombers* – fighter-bombers]. We were on and off our saddles all morning cowering in ditches while they flew past. It was uncomfortable. I had no water; my bicycle had no brakes – there was a lack of rubber. In the night some partisans had spread tacks across the roads and there were many punctures – but I was fine because I rode on tyres full of stuffing because there were no inner tubes available. Several of us whose bicycles buckled or twisted in these manoeuvres got a lift on the French *camions* carrying our heavy guns and ammunition. Then you would ride clinging to the front right mudguard facing rearwards and shout a warning to the driver if you saw anything in the sky. We had to travel slowly because a higher speed meant dust, which we soon learned would attract aircraft like flies.'[46]

These cycle-men would arrive at midday to meet elements of the 16th and 18th Infantry Regiments occupying Vierville, Saint-Laurent and Colleville. Though the GIs were tired, they outnumbered the cyclists and had better weaponry, endless ammunition, and air and maritime support. The commitment of the main reserve at the right time in the right place is a signature in many famous battlefield victories. Influenced by the early reports of American defeat at Vierville, Kraiss made a major error in despatching the remaining two battalions of *Kampfgruppe Meyer* to the area of Gold Beach, where the 69th Brigade of the British 50th Northumbrian Division was steaming towards Bayeux.

To Meyer's not-insignificant force was added some of the bicycle-borne 30th *Schnelle-Brigade* under Oberstleutnant Freiherr von und zu Aufsess. Based in Coutances, we will meet more of this unit behind Gold beach. Collectively, these grenadiers would be overwhelmed by a combination of aerial attack and finding themselves up against far superior numbers. Meyer himself, Rittmeister Gerth (the Fusilier battalion commander) and Hauptmann Lochner, leading the division's assault gun detachment, were all reported killed or missing by 2300 hours.[47] This is where the fog of war worked against Kraiss – his poor picture of the battlefield caused him to throw a handy reserve in a direction where it could make no impact.

However, the timely arrival of two grenadier battalions at Vierville, Saint-Laurent or Colleville could have swung the battle for Omaha Beach back in the Germans' favour. Throughout the day the Allied fleet, guided by its spotter planes, harried every road move they could see, and Kraiss's troops – whether infantry, assault guns and mobile artillery, or trucks bringing ammunition and food up to the forward troops – were pursued to the point of extinction. At no stage on D-Day were any of the Omaha troops aware of anything more than hasty, local counter-attacks by platoons or sections.

Moving through E-1 in the afternoon and mopping up the few depth positions remaining was Walter D. Ehlers, who had just been promoted to sergeant and transferred to Company 'L' of the 18th Infantry, so that he and his older brother Roland, a sergeant with Company 'K', would not be fighting in the same outfit. From Junction City, Kansas, Ehlers was leading a twelve-man squad with plenty of experience of playing music but none of shooting at Germans. 'One was a banjo player, another was a violist and a third played the ukulele,' he recalled. Although he had seen action in North Africa and Sicily, Ehlers' men had no battle experience: 'My guys wanted to dig in instead of advancing up the beach, but I told them that was a sure-fire way to die, so they followed me up a path.'

The route they took was that initially taken by Spalding and Company 'G', but by the time Sergeant Ehlers arrived, on either side were the bodies of soldiers blown apart by mines. 'We made it through the mine-field to the heights without a single casualty, eventually got into some trenches and took out a pillbox from behind. You didn't dare run up in front because they'd mow you down.' All the while he had no idea his brother had been killed when a mortar shell hit his landing craft – 'I didn't learn this until 14 July.'[48]

Three days later, Ehlers and his men would be surprised by a German patrol, which, while covering their withdrawal to safety, he almost single-handedly destroyed. For this and his leadership from D-Day onwards, Sergeant Ehlers would receive a Medal of Honor. After the ceremony in November 1944 in front of the press, General Clarence R. Huebner put his arm around him, and explained, 'I'm making you a second lieutenant.' Ehlers' natural modesty came to the fore: 'Well, sir, I don't think I qualify,' was his response. 'You do,' said the general. 'I wasn't going to argue with him,' recounted the humble Ehlers in 1998. 'That was General Huebner, himself a Kansas country boy – like General Eisenhower – and me.'[49]

To fully open the E-1 draw, specialists from the 37th and 149th Combat Engineer Battalions had arrived from 1030 and, working under fire, started to clear mines to the front, while two bulldozers filled in its anti-tank ditch, and other men blasted gaps through the wall, or put down steel matting for easier passage off the sand. However, shells, mortars and bullets didn't discriminate between units or ranks. The 37th Engineers lost twenty-four men on D-Day, including their CO, but by 1500 hours, the E-1 draw was open, easing the overcrowding on the beach where units had been arriving faster than they could be moved inland. This would be the only exit open to the Big Red One until the Germans had been forced out of Colleville on 7 June, opening up E-3.

Hyam Haas with the rest of his unit later drove through a gap in a stretch of anti-tank wall the Germans had constructed. He recalled that 'many of our GIs had taken cover by this wall and they died in groups or just been blown apart'.[50] Shortly afterwards Haas and his buddies were obliged to leave their open-topped vehicles and shelter under them for a while, as mortar fire rained down, and next he recollected a landing craft violently exploding that 'sent a large amount of burning oil over our heads putting the bluffs ahead of us on fire. It seemed to me that everything was on fire and that it wouldn't be long before we would all be dead.'

Soon, Battery 'A' and Haas received word to drive up E-1 and ride to the top of the western bluffs. 'On the way up the road we paused in front of the pillbox we had knocked out. Two wounded German soldiers were lying on the parapet: one of them was vomiting blood. As we waited to go on, Sergeant Baynaird M. McNeil – later to receive a battlefield commission – ran over to me and shouted "Hey that's your bunker."'[51] It was indeed, and remains in situ today exactly as it was on 6 June, complete with its 50mm gun, still pointing east in enfilade along the beach. The facade is peppered with strike marks from Sergeant Haas's two half-tracks, with an equal number of chips around the doorway on the opposite side. In the afternoon, Brigadier General Wyman took it over as his command post, and would have seen the remaining armour and vehicles of the 741st Tank Battalion drive up E-1 at around 1700 hours, followed two hours later by the arrival of his boss, General Huebner, who took over WN65 for his advanced HQ, renaming it 'Danger Forward'.

The capture of the E-1 exit, the first draw opened on D-Day, was undoubtedly a team effort, achieved by Spalding's capture of WN64, and the destruction of WN65 by Sergeant Haas, navy destroyers, some of the 18th Infantry and a single 741st Tank Battalion Sherman. Some

This is the WN65 bunker (left) with its 50mm gun (top right), attacked by Sergeant Hyam Haas of the 467th AAA (Anti-Aircraft Artillery) Battalion. His M15 half-track (bottom right) mounted a 37mm autocannon with two .50-inch machine-guns. The suppression of this pillbox was a major factor in the surrender of the defenders at E-1, and the opening of the Le Ruquet draw. (top right, Author's collection; others, NARA)

five-inch rounds from the attack transport *Henrico* – which fired more than 380 rounds of ammunition from her pair of five-inch guns and nearly nine thousand rounds from her 40mm – may also have assisted.

This reflects the true nature of combat on Omaha: most progress was made by small groups from different outfits, thrown together by fate, rather than by formed units. Nevertheless, at E-1, Spalding – a future member of the Kentucky House of Representatives – had been a major contributor, acting without any orders or direction. The route his group took was through what is now the American military cemetery to WH64, today invisible amongst the trees. Their endeavours resulted in the award of a Distinguished Service Cross for Spalding and Streczyk, along with three other members of his ad hoc team. A similar honour was accorded to Captain Joseph Dawson, who had acted similarly to Spalding, but turned left at the clifftops, when Spalding veered right.[52]

Their blockhouse – sometimes named Le Ruquet after the nearby meandering stream – remains one of the most photographed relics of D-Day, and fifty years later the 467th AAA Battalion adopted the structure and placed a plaque above its gun to commemorate their activities

The concrete structure in the middle right of this famous image is the rear of Sergeant Haas's WN65 bunker. It is 7 June and already another formation is pouring ashore at the E-1 draw. These troops are from the 2nd (Indianhead) Infantry Division. The second man in the file, looking at the camera, is Private Vincent M. Killen from Pennsylvania. He would die in battle on 22 June. (US Army Signal Corps)

in the area. WN65 also formed the backdrop of one of the better-known images of Omaha Beach (pictured), in which a column of the 2nd Infantry Division climb the heights in front of it. They are identifiable by their distinctive Indianhead badge worn on the left shoulder. The follow-on division was pictured arriving on 7 June, and the second man in the file has just turned to look at the camera. This was Private Vincent M. Killen from Pennsylvania, destined to die in action with the 38th Infantry fifteen days later: a reminder that D-Day was the beginning of a long liberation campaign.[53]

30

Omaha: E-3 – the Colleville Draw

'It was an endless day. I expected to die any minute. As soon as the ramp on our boat went down, one of the three lieutenants aboard was killed. We stepped over his body into water that was up to our necks. We had to keep our rifles dry, so we walked with them raised above our heads. I'd just gotten out of the water when I saw a ring of guys laying around, about a dozen of them, all from my assault boat, every one of them dead. The shell had hit that close. If I had been with them, I would have been killed.'
Daniel L. Curatola, Third Battalion, 16th Infantry[1]

THE DEFENDERS OVERLOOKING the Colleville draw were waiting. Their fire discipline was excellent. Colonel Taylor's men grew closer. Then Oberleutnant Frerking heard the slow *rat-tat-tat* of Gefreiter Gockel's old machine-gun, and the grenadiers around him opening fire; their two mortars coughed. As Gefreiter Severloh unleashed his MG-42 fire at the invaders in the shallows, Frerking bellowed, 'Aiming point Dora, fire!'[2]

As with all the units landing on Omaha, those who arrived near the E-3 draw leading to Colleville had expected to be landing a mile further west, in the vicinity of E-1. Instead, disembarking from the *Henrico* at 0415 hours, the 16th Infantry's Company 'E' (whose lone boat containing Lieutenant Spalding had been on target) landed either side of the Colleville draw. On their left were other LCVPs with Company 'F'. Joining them, and way off course, were men from Company 'E', 116th Regiment – a 29th Division unit – whose four LCAs beached near WN61. The same drift applied to Companies 'I' and 'L', originally scheduled for E-3 – they were carried even further eastwards and ended up under the cliffs of Fox Red sector, on the far left-hand edge. The latter would prise open the final draw, F-1.

Unfortunately for Companies 'E' and 'F' beaching in front of the E-3 draw, they were setting foot in another 'Devil's Garden', dominated by two of the strongest of the fourteen strongpoints overlooking Omaha. WN62 and WN61 were each manned by twenty to thirty men from the 3rd Company of the 716th *Grenadier-Regiment*. Alongside them were artillery observation posts for the gunners of the 352nd Division. Despite Rommel's urging, WN62 had not been completed by 6 June, though the 88mm bunker opposite at WN61 had been finished on 25 April.

The latter, encased in thick concrete, swept the entire beach in concert with another in WN72 at Vierville; these were unusual in being near the beachfront, but heavily protected by aprons of barbed wire, booby traps and mines. Most other positions were up on the heights. Two 75mm guns in WN62 also enfiladed the beach westwards, as did a single 75mm at WN60, with a tank turret-mounted machine-gun. Everywhere were numerous mortar pits and machine-guns housed in Tobruks. (The concrete positions are all still evident to the trained eye today, searching among the brambles.) Collectively, these *Widerstandsnester* dominated the shoreline with carefully preregistered fire zones, which paid dividends straight away.

Approaching the E-3 draw, Lieutenant William G. Pepe, 5th Engineer Special Brigade, remembered thinking, 'So here I am, Mines and Booby Traps Officer in Headquarters Company, with a bunch of other civilians in olive drab, playing at soldiering. An IQ of 110 had sent me to Officer Candidate School for ninety days – which is why we young officers were the "ninety day wonders". I was now entitled to make life and death decisions.' Pepe 'bobbed around' in his staging area, while the twelve boats of his wave assembled. 'In such extremely tight quarters, we were soon wearing each other's breakfast,' Pepe recollected. 'On coming ashore I immediately ditched my carbine when I saw a discarded .45-caliber Thompson – I never thought what had happened to its owner.'[3] With an air of bitterness shared by all the attackers, Pepe observed, 'We searched for bomb craters, vital for our survival; the Air Corps had promised us one hundred tons of bombs for every five hundred square yards of beach; sure enough, we found the craters two days later – three miles inland.'[4]

As the assault wave landing craft slowed to negotiate the obstacles, one gun put two rounds into an LCVP carrying naval demolition personnel, killing and wounding fifteen men; only four men got to shore. The incoming tide also played its part in forcing engineers away from their work on the obstructions, and they were obliged to seek the shelter of the cliffs at Fox Red, on the far eastern end of the beach. Engineer tankdozers were of little help, their strength reduced to a single machine: of sixteen Shermans equipped with bulldozer blades, only six got ashore, and five of them were soon picked off mostly by WN62 – leaving a single tank available for fire support for over a mile of the 16th Infantry's front.

Other fire support which might have come from the division's artillery battalions, or the Regimental Cannon Company, was not forthcoming. The latter's six 105mm howitzers sank aboard their DUKWs; the gunners who made it ashore fought as riflemen. The story for Lieutenant Colonel George W. Gibb's 7th Field Artillery Battalion echoes that of the 111th Artillery supporting the Blue and Gray Division: they lost six of their twelve DUKW-borne guns, had been given the 111th's last howitzer – 'the Chief' – but did not in any case beach until after 1400 hours because of the congestion and shelling. The 7th's guns would be the only artillery on Omaha to get ashore and into action – at 1615 – on D-Day. The 62nd Armored Field Artillery with their 105mm tracked 'Priests' were delayed until near nightfall for similar reasons.

The men from Taylor's Second Battalion – Companies 'E' and 'F' and some of the 116th Regimental Combat Team – ran straight into the same kind of disaster that befell Company 'A' at the Vierville draw. Not every German position was encased in concrete, however, and that of Gefreiter Franz Gockel was a dugout halfway down the bluffs, protected by logs and sandbags. He had a First World War-era water-cooled Polish machine-gun sitting on a tripod mounted on a wooden platform – under which he had sheltered during the bombardment earlier. This was in every sense an echo of his own father's experience of the Western Front of 1916–18 – and a reminder of the vast array of captured weaponry the Wehrmacht used in Normandy. Ironically, Gockel was operating a Polish copy of the US Army's M1917 machine-gun, being used on the beach against him.

WN62 was mostly complete, with their underground troop bunker finished in May. On the forward slope were two huge casemates, each facing west and housing a wheeled 75mm gun, but these lacked armoured shutters and doors.[5] Twenty-two-year-old Henri Leroutier was a local

Frenchman forced to help build the defences, when he should have been working on the family farm at Saint-Laurent. 'I worked on a big bunker at Colleville-sur-Mer, with about thirty others,' he reminisced. 'We were supervised by only two Germans, which allowed us to sabotage the work by hiding or slowing things down as much as we could. For example, we let the wagons that we used for carrying the sand and gravel roll down to the bottom of the cliff. We couldn't do it too often or they would come down hard on us.' He remembered the naval bombardment of 6 June – 'from about 0600 hours artillery shells fell continuously in our fields. We went up to the attic and saw the sea full of boats, the aeroplanes dropping bombs, then hurried down to a prepared shelter trench to protect ourselves.'[6]

Gefreiters Heinrich 'Hein' Severloh (352nd Division) and Franz Gockel (716th Division) manned different bunkers within the WN62 complex. Their *Widerstandsnest* – cleverly sited on a spur overlooking the Coleville draw and the beach – was the strongest of all on Omaha. It stymied all attempts to open the E-3 exit until 1530 hours, by which time it had run out of ammunition and was outflanked by Company 'G' of the 16th Infantry. Both men were fortunate to escape alive; most did not. The site now houses the 1st US Infantry Division's memorial. (Author's collection)

Given time, no doubt Gockel would have had his own concrete bunker, too, but for the moment, with his weapon oiled and ready, ranges worked out to every landmark in front of him, the young grenadier was prepared for his first battle. A hundred yards away uphill, still within the perimeter of WN62, was the observation post of Oberleutnant Frerking and Gefreiter Severloh, with No. 1 Battery of the 352nd Division's artillery regiment. Cramped and accommodating a maximum of three, it had been hardened against shelling only in the spring. Alongside Severloh with his MG-42, Frerking held the field telephone close to his mouth: 'Aiming point Dora, charge two, impact fuse, entire battery baseline direction, plus twenty, forty-eight-hundred-fifty. Wait for my order to fire.'

With no cover apart from a slight mound of shingle, from which bullets ricocheted alarmingly in all directions, the 16th's ranks were soon depleted. Company 'E' would lose its commander, Captain Edward F. Wozenski, and 104 men before the morning was through. To Captain William A. Friedman from Manhattan, the 16th's regimental S-1 (staff officer in charge of personnel), approaching the E-3 draw at 0810 hours bore a horrific similarity to newsreels he had seen of the assault on Tarawa the previous November. In front of him were 'landing craft on their sides, turned the wrong way. It was surreal. I joined that great pile of men on the shale. We were immobilised. I did not know what to do or where to go. I remember looking at the sea, there were bodies and equipment just rolling in the surf.'[7] Their two assault companies were well and truly pinned down.

Shortly afterwards, Daniel L. Curatola had stepped off the *Empire Anvil* with the rest of the Third Battalion's headquarters company: 'I didn't expect to live. All through Africa and Sicily, all the battles, guys dying around me, my friends, I thought sooner or later the law of averages was going to get me. What kept me going? Inside me, I had fear. But we were told we had to follow our orders. No matter whether your best friend or your brother gets killed, you've got to do your job. If you stopped when a guy was wounded, an officer would yell: "Take cover, don't worry about that guy!"'[8]

Gefreiter Gockel's water-cooled machine-gun was a heavy, cumbersome beast which put out a steady six hundred rounds a minute. Crouched behind it, traversing left and right on the tripod, the eighteen-year-old knew the trick was to go easy on the trigger – just five- or ten-round bursts. As long as he had enough water for the gun and

250-round canvas belts of ammunition, he could keep firing for a long time. However, soon after Gockel had begun, sand from nearby explosions jammed his gun. He paused, opened the gun and found the problem was dirt between the cartridges. 'I laid some stick grenades on the sandbags and had my pistol ready for self-defence while I removed the ammunition belt, cleaned everything quickly and started shooting again, but my hands had been trembling,' he recollected.[9]

Yards uphill to his right, Hein Severloh had an altogether more modern machine-gun, an MG-42 – this was the *burrrrp* gun that Sergeant Hyam Haas recollected. With its very high rate of fire, the drawback was that an MG-42 went through fifty-round belts like a knife through butter, and the barrel would overheat quickly, causing it to jam. When this happened, Severloh used one of two rifles in his bunker until it cooled down. Gockel, Severloh and their buddies opened fire at five hundred yards, the range narrowing to 150 as the tide drew in. Meanwhile, Obergefreiter Siegfried Kuska's 50mm anti-tank gun facing east into the E-3 draw accounted for at least three Shermans. The position's two 50mm mortars, each fired from inside a little concrete Tobruk bunker, in the hands of their expert two-man crews, were placing mortar bombs inside landing craft and on the sands at up to five hundred yards range.[10]

In the face of such concentrated fire, the previous battle experience of the Big Red One was vital. The extreme confusion they faced would have shredded more inexperienced units. 'We had to keep moving,' mused Curatola. 'Thank God, I had seen dead men before, in Africa and Sicily. But some of the younger troops who hadn't seen action just went out of their minds. You'd see them screaming and running the wrong way.'[11] Captain Bill Friedman, the regimental S-1 [personnel officer] and a professional soldier with combat experience in North Africa, still had to control his own nerves. 'At one point I was lying down and shouting in the ear of the Regimental S-4 [quartermaster], Major Leonard C. Godfray. My mouth was next to his ear; it was so noisy that he could not hear me otherwise. While I was trying to make myself understood above the din, a bullet struck him dead. It had hit him in the centre of his helmet. Our faces were inches away when it happened. It could have been me.'[12]

But what did being a veteran mean? Joe Argenzio – the sixteen-year-old who had lied about his age to enlist and had been dubbed 'Baby Face' as he walked up the gangway onto the *Empire Anvil* in Weymouth harbour – recalled, 'a lieutenant gave me a carbine and some .30-cal ammo; that's all I knew. As we approached the beach, I said to one fellow on my right, "Thank God I'm with you veterans." He replied, "Kid, the minute the ramp drops, you're going to be a veteran."[13]

Captain John G. Wilhelm Finke, commanding Company 'F', was one of the first officers ashore opposite the E-3 draw. The thirty-two-year-old, who had won a Distinguished Service Cross in Sicily, explained that once ashore, 'we had difficulty getting the men to move. There was a great deal of enemy fire and they would take cover behind these obstacles, which were about the size of a ten- or twelve-foot telephone pole with a Teller mine [a flat, plate-sized anti-tank ordnance, one foot in diameter] on the top of it. The whole area was just full of these obstacles. People would just try to take cover behind one of these poles. Any port in a storm. Well, it didn't provide any cover so you just had to force them to move no matter how you did it. It so happened that I had sprained my ankle in the marshalling area and had to go ashore carrying a cane instead of a rifle. I used it to very good effect to just whack people until they moved' (an interesting image amid the confusion of Omaha).

The setback was immediately obvious enough for patrol craft *PC-552*, anchored offshore and monitoring proceedings, to radio back to USS *Samuel Chase* at 0641 hours, ominously: 'Entire first wave foundered'. By 0830, the 7th Naval Beach Battalion's beachmaster had ordered a temporary suspension of landings, and at 0945, for want of anything else to report, V Corps signalled to Bradley aboard USS *Augusta* the understatement of the morning: 'Obstacles mined, progress slow, DD tanks for Fox Green swamped.' Although the Big Red One had come through North Africa and Sicily, it had suffered considerable casualties. Consequently when they landed in Normandy their ranks included draftees, new to combat. However, it was noticeable how many officers and NCOs had survived the Mediterranean, and it was their leadership – if they survived – that provided the glue for unit cohesion during the first few hours.

'Everybody had a heck of a large load to carry so that the men were worn out when they got across the sand,' recalled Captain Finke. 'We landed in an area that was right in the mouth of the beach exit, where all weapons were sited to fire. Of the four officers that were killed on the beach from my company, I think three of them died right at the water's edge. Once you get involved in something like this, you're thinking about what you have to do, and more or less forget about your own personal danger, because you don't have time to think about it. The more you have to do, the better off you are in a situation like that. My company had lost all of its officers by the time I was wounded around noon.'[14]

Roger Hutchinson, with Company 'C' of the 299th Combat Engineers, distracted his buddies from their nerves and nausea by passing around a two-dollar bill for everyone in *LCA-15* to autograph. It worked, as the entire boatload added their thirty signatures to the paper – but for a third of them, it would be the last time they would ever sign their name.[15] A fellow engineer with Company 'C', Chuck Hurlbut – who had laughed at the name of their ship, the *Princess Maud*, in Weymouth harbour – remembered they were supposed to land on Easy Red, but their craft was pushed by the strong current to the next sector, Fox Green, just to the east of the Colleville draw.

'Everything was nice and quiet,' he recalled, 'then all of a sudden, *brrrrr, ping, ping, ping* – we could hear the bullets hitting the ramp. To my knowledge, we all got off OK. First thing I did was to take my rifle and aim it at a pillbox. *Pow!* I still don't know why I did that. It was an impulse. That was the only shot I fired all day. I started pulling the rope of our raft full of explosives. All of a sudden I felt it get heavier. I looked around, and there's three bodies inside, face down; I kept pulling, and all of a sudden, *boom!* A mortar round blew all our explosives. I was knocked head over heels, and blacked out. When I came to, I was on my hands and knees, spitting blood with the worst headache you can imagine. It took me a few moments to realise what happened. I pulled my rope in, and all I got was a big piece of tattered rubber. That was the raft. The three guys, gone.'[16]

Hurlbut's buddy, Tom E. Legacy from Niagara Falls, had come up to him before disembarkation. 'We'd been through a lot together. He opened his jacket. And he had on the ugliest, gaudiest, most outlandish necktie I ever saw in my life. We laughed about what we were going to do when we hit Paris. Later in the landing craft, amid the vomit and the spray, he flashed the necktie again, and I gave him a thumbs-up.' Subsequently, when sheltering in the lee of the cliffs east of E-3, 'about sixty yards away a guy wanders along the beach, staggering, floundering like he's blind drunk. His backpack is tattered; his clothes are in shreds. One arm is dangling. He turns and half his head is blown away. And something told me I know that guy,' recounted Hurlbut, 'something about his stature, his walk. And he turned toward me and looked at me, and through all that gore and all that tattered clothing, I saw *the tie*. I wanted to cry out to him; I couldn't. I didn't have any voice. I was frozen. He just staggered away.'[17]

Just west of the Colleville draw, beaching his LCT on Easy Red, skipper Bill O'Neill remembered their sister craft *LCT-540* withdrawing, her bow damaged so the ramp couldn't be raised. Off to starboard, another of their flotilla, *LCT-305*, was under heavy shellfire, unloading some 741st Tank Battalion Shermans which raced off, firing. Beyond her, *LCT-25* was about to disembark half-tracks of the 197th Anti-Aircraft Artillery Battalion, but the first was hit as it raced down the ramp, bursting into flames. 'Instantaneously the rest of the craft and its contents blew up in a violent burst of exploding ammunition and fire'.

O'Neill recalled LCVPs quickly unloading and withdrawing. 'One alongside us, with wood chips flying as bullets hit her hull, gunned out in reverse, zig-zagging wildly, its coxswain not bothering to wait for his deck hand to raise the ramp.' O'Neill's *LCT-544* contained eight jeeps and a large Cat tractor towing steel tracks to lay on the sand. 'The bow ramp was dropped with a splash, and without a moment's hesitation the Cat with its blade elevated roared off, attracting every machine-gunner in range. Bullets showered on the blade from every direction.'[18]

One of the luckiest landing craft – which demonstrates well the random nature of the carnage – was *LCT-199*, which disembarked her load of half-tracks at 0845 hours on Easy Red. She withdrew and took in a second cargo of eighteen jeeps and three hundred GIs to the same destination at 1330.[19] In the same 18th Flotilla, *LCT-305* was as unlucky as *LCT-199* was fortunate. As she approached Fox Green at 0900, her bridge was raked by crossfire from WN60 and WN61, wounding her skipper. Her crew pulled out and tried again five hundred yards west, but were directed away; again they retracted and tried beaching twice more. Afterwards, they transferred their wounded skipper to USS *Ancon*, obtained a replacement, but on their fifth attempt to land, *LCT-305* detonated a mine, which 'completely demolished the crew's quarters', so they withdrew rapidly. After six hours offshore, on their *sixth* beaching attempt at 1500, they at last disembarked all their anti-aircraft half-tracks, but hit an underwater obstacle retracting. Then they were struck by several shells, which killed one man and wounded the new skipper alongside seven others. *LCT-305*'s luck had run out, and she began to sink by the stern.[20]

The 299th Engineer Charles Hurlbut came across 'one guy laying and moaning in the water, just being washed with the waves. I look at him.

Jesus Christ, it's one of my pals, Joe Nokovic of Buffalo, New York. If I leave him he's gonna drown. I'm a little guy, and he was pretty big. I knew I could never lift him so I got my hands under his armpits, planted my feet in the sand and pulled with my arms. It was torturous, but we made progress, very slowly, to the dune line but I was exhausted. I was able finally to attract a medic; he took one look and gave him morphine. But I'd made the dunes in one piece, sat there and looked at all the chaos. Guys floating in the surf. The wounded screaming. Out in the water ships burning, smoking. I was numb. You thought you were tough, brave and gung-ho. This was not the way it was supposed to be.'[21]

All morning, GIs dragged their wounded to the waterline where landing craft could shuttle them back to the medical facilities of troop-ships offshore. Beaching at around 0730 hours, skipper Bill O'Neill's *LCT-544* survived almost four hours on Easy Red, taking on wounded all the time. 'The living quarters were soon filled, then the inside spaces, then every available free spot on the deck,' he recalled.

> There was no end to the supply of blood-stained casualties. At 1130 hours the last few injured were rushed aboard, ramp raised, and using the engines and winch we slowly backed off into deep water, reaching the troopship anchorage, twelve miles out, in less than two hours. We let the larger ship's trained medics take over, then cleansed our craft of all the discarded bandages, morphine capsules, bits of tissue and clothing. Crew bunks, mattresses, and blankets were soaked with blood. Everything was thrown overboard; the fire pump rigged, the ramp lowered, and the decks were flushed with seawater pushing everything into the sea, attempting to wash away the misery we had just witnessed.[22]

*

However, small bands of survivors were hitting back. Several men from Company 'E' of the 116th had gapped the concertina wire east of E-3 with Bangalores and pushed halfway up the bluffs. From there they took out one of WN61's mortar pits with rifle grenades. Looking down, they witnessed a one-man frontal assault by Technical Sergeant Raymond F. Strojny, of Company 'F'. This was John Finke's company, but he was elsewhere on the sands. In the absence of his officers, Strojny first ordered his men into better cover. Then the resourceful twenty-six-year-old from Massachusetts, who had already won a Silver Star in Sicily, picked up a bazooka from a wounded soldier nearby; it had been pierced by shrapnel and should not have been fired. Tucking the weapon under his arms, with six bazooka rounds, he crawled through WN61's protective minefield; the bodies of several GIs lay about as he wormed his way to the closest bunker.

Strojny's first shots merely antagonised his opponents, who in return peppered the lone GI with machine-gun and sniper fire. One round pierced his helmet, grazed his skull and exited, but nothing more. With more bazooka rounds he destroyed the pillbox, actions that would bring him a Distinguished Service Cross, but, more importantly, two key parts of WN61 had been destroyed. Finally, its 88mm gun, which had engaged three 741st Shermans in quick succession, fell victim to a fourth – Staff Sergeant Turner Shepherd's DD tank – which had swum ashore onto Fox Green after 0630. The Sherman managed to put several shots through the embrasure, killing the gun crew and damaging the weapon. WN61 was all but silenced. The operations log of the 352nd Division recorded baldly at 0720: 'Landing of forces on beaches in front of WNs.60, 61 and 62, and further to the west. Between WN61 and WN62 American strength is one company on the beach, under fire from our own artillery. The 88mm in WN61 has been knocked out by a direct hit.'[23]

Across the way, the two west-facing 75mm guns of WN62 were doing brisk trade along Easy Red. However, one of the surviving 741st DD Shermans, commanded by Sergeant Geddes, had silenced the upper emplacement early in the morning, killing or wounding the gun crew of Gefreiters Lehrmann, Kriefteworth and Hans Selbach and Kanonier Emil Drews, all friends of Franz Gockel. The Sherman's gunner was Jack Borman, whose tank later bogged down in the shingle mound before the entrance to the Colleville draw. This would act as an effective barrier to many tracked and wheeled vehicles until it could be bulldozed aside by engineers. 'As we were immobilised, the crew then decided it would be better to remain completely impassive,' Borman explained. 'So the tank remained motionless and no one – from either one side or the other – took any serious notice of us. Only as darkness fell did we finally risk leaving the tank.'[24]

At 0725 hours, the duty officer of the 352nd Division noted in their log, 'One company is attacking in front of WN60 and WN62. Four further boats have landed in front of WN61. One boat has been shot in flames by the 50mm gun [from WN62]. The Americans have penetrated WN62 and at the same time, WN61 is being attacked from the beach in front and the rear [Strojny and the 116th detachment]. Five minutes later the same source recorded "352nd *Artillerie-Regiment* had no connection to its observation post near Colleville [WN62]".[25]

At this point, Severloh remembered, two of his frightened colleagues 'were sitting in a foxhole quite near me to the east. They kept loading their rifles, which they poked up over the wall of the trench and, without being able to see any target at all from their cover, simply fired.' To his front, 'Wounded moved around on the bloody, watery slime, mostly creeping, trying to get to the upper beach and find some cover behind the shingle embankment; one by one they would occasionally run in a crouch.'[26]

Down on the sands, hard on the heels of 'E' and 'F' came Company 'H', containing machine-gunner Valentine Miele – the Jersey City veteran of the Sicilian campaign. He recalled floating his tripod ashore, attached to a life preserver but having to ditch a box of ammunition just to stay afloat himself. His assistant gunner carried the actual gun tied to another life jacket. They lost men to drowning and bullets as the company waded ashore and reached the shingle mound. Then 'some guy came running up and said "a machine-gun up there is cutting the hell out of Company G". So my sergeant says, "Miele, get on the gun." I set the gun up, and he says, "See if you can spot him." All of a sudden I saw him, about two hundred yards away, and I'd say maybe thirty or forty feet higher than me. He wasn't firing at me. He was firing down across. So when he opened up again, I picked him up, I got about ten rounds in there, and that sonofagun never fired any more.'[27]

An advance element of the 16th's regimental headquarters had landed at 0720 hours, but was unable to function because all their communication equipment was either lost or destroyed by enemy action and key personnel killed, including the regimental executive officer, Lieutenant Colonel John 'Huey' Mathews. Leaving USS *Charles Carroll*, and steered in by coxswain Ricardo Feliciano, Colonel Taylor himself stepped ashore from *LVCP-71* with the main body at 0820 on Easy Red, just to the right of the Colleville draw, and, in the words of the 16th's After Action Report, 'was immediately subjected to enemy artillery, machine-gun and small arms fire'.[28] As Taylor later observed, 'It was a helpless feeling wading while shot at.' Private Warren Rulien, a member of the I&R (Intelligence and Reconnaissance) Platoon, remembered that his colonel had 'laid down on his stomach and started crawling towards shore', then overheard Taylor bellow to one of his staff, 'If we're going to die, let's die up there,

Numerous eyewitnesses from the 29th Division recalled its Assistant Divisional Commander, Brigadier General Norman Cota (1893–1971) (left) and Colonel Charles Canham of the 116th Infantry (1901–63) (right, wearing spectacles), striding along the shingle of Dog and Easy sectors, urging men to grab their weapons and equipment and move inland. The 16th Infantry's Colonel George Taylor (1899–1969) (centre, receiving medal) was responsible for rousing his men in a similar fashion around the E-3 draw. Taylor's rallying cry has since become famous: 'Two kinds of people are staying on this beach: the dead and those who are going to die – now let's get the hell out of here!' (both US Army Signal Corps)

pointing at the bluffs.'[29] Immediately Taylor noticed groups of his men, bunched up on the beach, cowering behind anything that seemed to offer shelter, as he had done, momentarily. Very much in the manner of 'Dutch' Cota and Charles Canham – and at about the same time – Taylor realised that he, personally, needed to instigate change by personal example.

The bland words of the regimental After Action Report, that 'Reorganisation was instigated immediately by the Regimental Commander and the beaches were rapidly cleaned of personnel through the one gap available on Easy Red', do not do Taylor justice.[30] Under fire, Taylor rose to his feet and would remain upright for much of the rest of the day, striding purposefully through the shot and shell, rallying his men. His regimental surgeon, Major Charles E. Tegtmeyer, never forgot Taylor's example: 'He passed us walking erect, followed by his staff and yelled for me to bring my group along.' Picking up Taylor's cue, Tegtmeyer exclaimed to the medics around him, 'I'll be damned if I go back into that water even if Hitler himself should order me.'[31]

The magic spread: in full view of the defenders, Lieutenant Colonel Robert N. Skaggs of the 741st Tank Battalion stood on the beach, swinging his life jacket in the air to beckon his men, and ordered them check the weapons of every abandoned tank and get those that could be operated back in action. Somehow, German snipers were looking the other way. Three of Skaggs' tank crewmen later recalled the breakdown of the remaining two members of their crew. 'Coming in, Sergeant Holcombe was so shocked and would not give any order except, "Abandon tank!" The loader couldn't load the gun so the bow gunner had to get in the turret to load the gun and command.'[32]

This was the context of Taylor's oft-quoted words which have since become US Army shorthand for the leadership on Omaha Beach that morning: 'Two kinds of people are staying on this beach: the dead and those who are going to die – now let's get the hell out of here!' It is a tribute to Taylor's effectiveness that many claimed this order was directed at them. In reality, Taylor was everywhere with the same message, but word of his actions was also spreading among his men.[33] Skaggs' tankers were galvanised into action: 'The tank was almost drowned out, we had to drain the water and dry the motor. We pushed up a bank of dirt to shield the infantry, shared our blankets with the wounded, and loaned them the tank's machine-guns, to keep the snipers down while we were working.'[34]

Taylor's encouragement was sorely needed; as Tegtmeyer recollected, 'at the water's edge, floating face downward with arched backs, were innumerable human forms eddying to and fro with each incoming wave, the water about them a muddy pink in color. Floating equipment of all types like flotsam and jetsam, rolled in the surf mingled with the bodies. Units of infantry and amphibious engineers were inextricably mixed together, officers without men and men without their officers, lay perplexed awaiting orders.'

Spurred on by his commander's example, the surgeon soon established an aid post through which a succession of his friends passed.

Major Dave McGovern, our Air-liaison Officer, had been hit and before I could ask him about his injury, he pointed upward to the planes flying overhead and said, 'Look at them, you guys should be damn thankful

This picture of Easy Red during the late afternoon of 6 June captures the chaos of the landings. The first barrage balloons are up. In the foreground and centre lie dead soldiers covered with blankets, tangles of German barbed wire, and a stranded LCVP from the attack transport USS *Thurston*. The GI (right) standing by the DUKW wears the insignia of the 1st Infantry Division. (NARA)

they're there.' I agreed readily enough and he continued, 'You guys said this would be rough, but God, I didn't think it would be this rough. You guys can have my pay-and-a-half anytime.' I admitted it had been rough, a hell of a lot rougher than Africa and Sicily, in fact rougher than anything I ever want to go through again. I examined his wound; it was a jagged shell fragment just to the left of the heart, and the fifth and sixth ribs were broken. I asked Dave if he wanted to be evacuated and he replied, 'No', he didn't want morphine either, but he was having a helluva time getting a decent breath. Captain John Finke came in with a compound fracture of the right arm and a wound of the right leg, both wounds were already dressed, but he needed morphine.[35]

Captain Friedman, Taylor's S-1, found his commander's actions the spur he needed. First, he understood that he could not do anything to change his fate. Such an acceptance that he was probably going to die steadied his nerves and he could think calmly. Next – like Taylor – he needed to inspire those around him. Friedman came across three soldiers lying prone, rigid with fear as the bullets whipped all around them. Standing tall, he drew his pistol to urge them on. 'I wanted them to go forward to attack, but one of them shouted at me, "Captain, are you out of your f**king mind?"' Prodded, cajoled, threatened by pistols, whipped by canes or simply shamed by example, men began to move laterally to the bluffs, through gaps already blown in the wire – or blew some more.

Friedman remembered, 'Once we got to the base of the bluffs we were relatively safe. We were quite well protected from view and from the enemy's fire. I don't think they expected anyone to get off the beach, because once we'd started moving up the hill and clearing their positions, it became just a matter of time. The positions really did not have any depth to them.'[36]

We last met Chaplain John G. Burkhalter – former Miami Baptist minister turned chaplain with the Big Red One – in southern England with his jeep, trailer, portable organ and song books. He was one of many who would write home – in his case to his wife Mabel – recalling how his colonel had 'stood on the beach where thousands of men were pinned down by enemy fire, and in a quiet drawl said, "Gentlemen, we are being killed here on the beaches; let's move inland and be killed there."'

As far as Burkhalter was concerned, this was the pivotal moment when everything changed.

> In from the beach were high hills which we had to climb. We crawled most of the way up. As we filed by those awful scenes going up the hill and moving inland, I prayed hard for those suffering men, scattered here and there and seemingly everywhere … We filed over the hill as shells were falling on the beach back of us, meaning death for others who were still coming in. Before going over the top of the hill we crouched for a while close to the ground just below the top. While lying there I did most of my praying. The shells were falling all around and how I knew that God alone was able to keep them away from us. I shall never forget those moments. I am sure that during that time I was drawn very close to God.[37]

First Lieutenant Quentin Murdock in regimental headquarters was another inspired by his colonel. The Idaho farmboy had returned from the Mediterranean with a Silver Star – and malaria. He was incensed as military doctors instructed him to sit out the invasion. 'The 16th's surgeon and I argued back and forth about it. He finally relented and gave me some quinine. I guess he thought I was crazy.' This was a surprisingly frequent occurrence within the Big Red One and 2nd Armored Divisions from their service in the mosquito-ridden wastelands of North Africa and Sicily. Triggered by bites from European bugs, the illness reappeared and caused twenty per cent of US Army non-battle casualties in the Normandy campaign.

Of the journey to the shore Murdock remembered, 'One minute you'd be up on top of the waves and you could see all the ships firing. The next minute you'd be way down in a valley of water.' He crawled ashore with the second wave, and lay on the sands 'for a bit, maybe twenty minutes, trying to get my mind together again'. He explained: 'There was so much enemy fire and you couldn't do anything. It was demoralising how bad it was. Then Taylor came along; was hitting everybody on their rears to get over the hill. It shook us out of the daze we were in and got us going.'[38]

Also moving about the men, getting them to collect their weapons and move through the gaps, was Brigadier General Wyman. He had arrived about 0800 hours, immediately sized up the situation, and sent a signal to the effect, 'Halt all vehicles, send only infantry reinforcements.' This was extremely timely and resulted in the 18th Infantry arriving on Easy Red in time to assault the E-1 Saint-Laurent draw. Wyman's deployment of his reserve was done at the appropriate moment and in the correct spot. Unlike Generalleutnant Dietrich Kraiss, he had made the right decision, but his contribution tends to get squeezed out of the standard histories, in favour of the more charismatic combat leadership of Taylor.

One of the assault wave soldiers with the 16th Infantry was T-5 (Technician, Fifth Grade) and radio man John J. 'Joe' Pinder, of Headquarters Company. He was a very gutsy, determined one-year combat veteran from the Mediterranean – and a pre-war professional baseball player. Pinder hailed from McKees Rocks, Pennsylvania, but the family moved around the state to wherever work could be found. Described in 1941 as 'the stocky, square-set little Pennsylvanian with the blinding fast ball', he had entered military service in 1942. For Pinder, 6 June was a special day – he shared a birthday with one-legged General Erich Marcks, and Frau Lucie Rommel, and had just turned thirty-two.

During the run-in Pinder's craft was hit and began to sink, but made it to the beach. He was clipped by two bullets as he reached the sand, but three times returned to find more radio equipment and code books. This time a burst of machine-gun fire caught him as he struggled to the shingle. It was his last journey: he dumped his equipment with the rest, set up his radios, but soon passed out from loss of blood, dying later that morning. Maybe Pinder's activities didn't stand out in the collective memory in the way Taylor's did – but soldiers remembered, and a year later Pinder would be awarded a posthumous Medal of Honor.

By about 0900, irrespective of the urgings of Taylor, Canham and Cota, perhaps five hundred GIs in small groups, often undirected, had made multiple penetrations all along the front. In the absence of officers and NCOs, life's natural leaders had bubbled to the surface – reflected by the 235 Medals of Honor, Distinguished Service Crosses or Navy Crosses awarded on D-Day.[39] Independently they reached the heights and were beginning to mop up some of the defenders' positions. However, it would take hours for this news to filter back to the senior commanders nervously waiting offshore.

Landing with the last wave of the 16th Infantry was Captain 'Hank' Hangsterfer, HQ Company commander with the First Battalion. He noted,

> as we got in view of the shore, some of the landing craft from the first wave were returning to the transports. They waved to us; we waved back just like you would do on a pleasure boat ride. As we approached the beach I could see the water obstacles still in place. It appeared to be high tide so it was perilous trying to land. When the ramp was lowered the troops ran off in a hurry, but not before we were raked with machine-gun fire which hit a few men. There were so many troops on the beach it was difficult to find a space to take cover from the enemy small arms fire.
>
> On the beach I saw Bob Capa, the combat photographer, taking pictures of the carnage. He was behind one of the self-propelled guns [DD tanks] which had been knocked out.

The two had previously met in Sicily and knew one another slightly. 'There was one path through the barbed wire which led to what appeared to be a swamp. However, it was over waist deep so the troops had to hold their rifles overhead. On the hill up the ridge was evidence of the price that was paid. Dead bodies either shot or blown up by personnel mines. It's hard to express the feeling I had when I saw the dead soldiers I knew, ones I'd seen in training.'[40]

'The coast of Normandy was still miles away when the first unmistakable popping reached our listening ears. We ducked down in the puky water in the bottom of the barge and ceased to watch the approaching coastline,' wrote the man responsible for some of the defining, grainy, fuzzy images of D-Day – breathing movement, drama and also fear. He was Endre Friedmann, a Jew forced to flee his native Hungary, later Berlin and ultimately his beloved France. His life seemed to be a tale of staying one step ahead of Fascism, but staying close enough to turn and photograph it. Reinventing himself as Robert Capa in 1930s Paris – his sought-after American citizenship would be bestowed in 1946 – he had risen to fame photographing a soldier at the moment of death during the Spanish Civil War. Capa's images began to be published around the world, and by 1944, in his thirtieth year, he was a regular freelancer for *Life* and *Collier's*. Present for many of the iconic moments of the Second World War, including the invasion of Sicily, it would be unthinkable for him to miss D-Day – and so it proved. Aboard the *Samuel Chase*, he had chewed over with Colonel Taylor – whom he also knew from Sicily – with whom he should land. Taylor offered him space in his own boat, but as Capa later explained, 'I was a gambler. I decided to go in with Company 'E' in the first wave.'[41]

'There was too much going on to be afraid,' remembered Gefreiter Franz Gockel of being in WN62. He knew every inch of the beach, and every obstacle because he had spent the previous few months putting them there, never believing he would one day be spraying the area with fire. His position overlooked their anti-tank ditch and 'tangle-foot' barbed wire entanglements, which resembled 'exposed tree roots', pegged out at ankle-level and designed to trap advancing infantry. He was also equipped with two automatic flamethrowers which at the flick of a switch could project fire onto anything – or anyone – attempting to cross. The controls were in Gockel's dugout. Through the morning, he watched the tide coming in, drowning the wounded and pushing the survivors closer towards him. He recollected after the smaller craft, a bigger landing boat came in as the waters rose [*LCI-554* ramming its way through the obstacles at around 1000 hours] from which scores of men exited down ramps on both sides.

'One comrade who was about fifty yards forward of me crawled back to my dugout. *Achtung*, Franz! They're much closer. Now we really have to defend ourselves.' His buddy fed the canvas belts into the gun, while Gockel quartered the weapon back and forth, but shortly afterwards this 'there was a massive splitting noise and the gun was torn from my hands; it was shot to pieces. The water-cooled barrel had been split open by a piece of shrapnel, and it is still hard for me to imagine how I survived the blast without a wound. At the same moment a grenade hit one of the flamethrowers near to me. It exploded, leaving only a few wires where it had once been.'[42]

This may have been the handiwork of Staff Sergeant Walter Skiba's tank from Company 'A' of the 741st, which, 'from our defiladed position behind the shingle, fired on several machine-gun nests from which fire was visible, then picked up a log emplacement and fired several rounds of 75mm at it, before a shell landed quite close, and Skiba was killed almost immediately'.[43]

'My beautiful France looked sordid and uninviting, and a German machine-gun, spitting bullets around the barge, fully spoiled my return,' wrote Capa of landing with the 16th Infantry. 'I paused for a moment on the gangplank to take my first real picture of the invasion. The boatswain, who was in an understandable hurry to get the hell out of there, mistook my picture-taking attitude for explicable hesitation, and helped me make up my mind with a well-aimed kick in the rear.' Capa had been covering war since he had first gone to Spain in 1936, and was certainly no coward, but this was not the invasion he had expected, observing:

> The bullets tore holes in the water around me, and I made for the nearest steel obstacle. A soldier got there at the same time, and for a few minutes we shared its cover. He took the waterproofing off his rifle and began to shoot without much aiming at the smoke-hidden beach. The sound of his rifle gave him enough courage to move forward and he left the obstacle to me. It was a foot larger now, and I felt safe enough to take pictures of the other guys hiding just like I was.[44]

Leaving his now useless machine-gun, Gockel and his wounded comrade crawled through their zig-zag trenches uphill, but as they did Gockel felt a violent blow to his left hand: the Americans were close at hand. 'When I looked, my mitt was covered in blood and three of my fingers were dangling from their tendons. But for me it was a million-dollar shot – it meant I could leave the battlefield.'[45] As he hurried away he

dropped some of his possessions, but with several other wounded grenadiers commandeered a horse and cart and headed into Bayeux, where
their wounds were patched up. Incredibly, the Big Red One's Joint Assault
Signal Company (JASCO) lineman, Patrick J. Hughes, later picked up a
pocket-sized German Bible and kept it as a souvenir of his service in
Normandy. Inside the cover was written one name – Franz Gockel.[46]

'I finished my pictures and the sea was cold in my trousers,' wrote
Capa. 'Reluctantly, I tried to move away from my steel pole, but the
bullets chased me back every time. Now the Germans played on all their
instruments, and I could not find any holes between the shells and the
bullets that blocked the last twenty-five yards to the beach,' explained
the photographer in his 1947 autobiography, *Slightly Out of Focus*.
Reaching the sand, he threw himself flat and his lips touched the earth
of France. 'I had no desire to kiss it. I didn't dare to take my eyes off
the finder of my Contax and frantically shot frame after frame. Half a
minute later, my camera jammed – my roll was finished. I reached in
my bag for a new roll, and my wet, shaking hands ruined the roll before
I could insert it in my camera. The empty camera trembled in my hands.'

Then Capa with remarkable honesty relates what many soldiers –
grizzled old veterans and greenhorns alike – must have been feeling that
morning on Omaha. He writes of 'a new kind of fear shaking my body
from toe to hair, and twisting my face. An LCI braved the fire and medics
with red crosses painted on their helmets poured from it. I just stood
up and ran toward the boat. I stepped into the sea between two bodies
and the water reached to my neck. I held my camera high above my
head, and suddenly I knew that I was running away.'[47]

Hein Severloh in his artillery observation post had also been hit –
physically. He recollected, 'There was a bright, loud report directly in
front of me. Something flew at me from the muzzle of my machine-gun,
and it was as though I had been hit in the face with a whip under my
right eye. I noticed the front sight was missing from my gun.' By now
he had fired over ten thousand rounds from his MG-42, and was obliged
to switch to tracer, used for night firing. This allowed him to correct his
aim, but gave his position away at the same time: soon afterwards a shell
landed directly in front of his post, then a second tore his gun away,
with a third and fourth arriving in very quick succession.

Robert Capa knew he was doing what none of the troops on Omaha
could do that morning – simply leave when he felt like it. He boarded
the LCI, which, he explained, 'was listing, and we slowly pulled away

from the beach to try and reach the mother ship before we sank. I went down to the engine room, dried my hands, and put fresh films in both cameras. I got up on deck again in time to take one last picture of the smoke-covered beach.' Further away from danger, his sense of profession reasserted itself and he

> took some shots of the crew giving transfusions on the open deck. An invasion barge came alongside and took us off the sinking boat. The transfer of the badly wounded on the heavy seas was a difficult business. I took no more pictures. I was busy lifting stretchers. The barge brought us to the USS *Chase*, the last wave of the 16th Infantry was just being lowered, but the decks were already full with returning wounded and dead. This was my last chance to return to the beach. I did not go.[48]

Oberleutnant Frerking had been directing fire from his inland battery until it ran out of ammunition. Incredibly, only two weeks earlier half their ammunition stocks had been moved back to a more secure arsenal. When he requested more from his battalion commander, Major Werner Pluskat – who had much earlier spotted the invasion fleet from his command bunker – Frerking was initially told it was on its way. Later he was informed that no shells would arrive: an Allied fighter had pounced on the truck and destroyed it.

Soon, Frerking and Severloh realised that they had been outflanked and a strong force of American troops – Company 'G' of the 16th – were attacking from the west (today's car park and Visitor Center for the US cemetery). It was time to leave. Frerking ordered the last rounds from his battery down on their own position. Outside, his colleague Leutnant Grass, a former NCO who had been using rifle grenades with great effect throughout the day, Platoon Leader Feldwebel Pieh and radio men Herbert Schulz and Kurt Wernecke queued up to make their escape. Bullets whipped past. 'You go next, Hein – take care,' Frerking said to Severloh. 'He addressed me with the familiar "du" for the first time. We didn't have time to say much more.'[49] Severloh ducked and dived his way to safety. He looked back. Frerking, Grass and Pieh had not followed. It was 1530 hours; WN62, the strongest resistance nest behind Omaha, had fallen.

Safely back on USS *Samuel Chase*, Robert Capa fell asleep, exhausted. He arrived back in England and sent his film up to London. 'Seven days later', he recorded, 'I learned that the pictures I had taken on *Easy Red* were the best of the invasion. But the excited darkroom assistant, while drying the negatives, had turned on too much heat and the emulsions had melted and run down before the eyes of the London office. Out of the hundred and six pictures in all, only eight were salvaged. The captions under the heat-blurred pictures read that Capa's hands were badly shaking.'[50] This was the 19 June edition of *Life*, one of its most famous. In fact eleven were salvaged and ever since, no news feature of D-Day is complete without one of Capa's 'magnificent eleven' images.

And yet ... and yet ... Capa's narrative and photographs have excited the imagination down to the present day; given the quality of the 'magnificent eleven', made more dramatic by their rescue, the world has wondered what the rest might have contained. Robert Capa was certainly there on Easy Red – if not quite in the *first* wave with Company 'E': there are too many troops and tanks already ashore in his images to have been at the tip of the spear, and in his own text, he wrote of 'The first empty barge, which had already unloaded its troops on the beach, passed us on the way back to the *Chase* and the Negro boatswain gave us a happy grin and the V sign. It was now light enough to start taking pictures, and I brought my first Contax camera out of its waterproof oilskin.'[51]

He probably arrived with Taylor's headquarters group around 0820 to 0830 hours. Had he landed opposite the Colleville draw with Company 'E', Capa might not have survived. Fortunately, he landed further west, where there was less incoming fire, in the area overlooked by the American cemetery today. Close examination of his images shows four tanks and many troops of the earlier waves ahead of him, milling about on the beach, some standing. When pointing his camera seaward, his images of men clustered around the beach obstacles, often interpreted as using them for cover, are in fact of engineers with the 5th Engineer Special Brigade, wiring them up for demolition. Capa seems to have spent between thirty minutes to an hour on Easy Red – not long, but brave for anyone without a weapon – where he saw and waved to Captain Hangsterfer, before boarding *LCI-94*. This vessel also contained a US Coast Guard photographer, David T. Ruley, and the latter's film recorded the return of *LCI-94* to the *Samuel Chase* and the transfer of casualties, and contains glimpses of Capa helping with the wounded. Yet their LCI, though damaged, was *not* listing or sinking.

However, another vessel nearby *was*, which, holed by numerous shells and listing badly, limped back to the *Chase* and would later capsize. This was *LCI-85*, and it seemed that Capa borrowed the drama and fate of the latter vessel for his own narrative. This false note has triggered much research which now suggests that Capa suffered a real breakdown on Easy Red, as he started to recount, and that the extremely traumatic morning resulted in him being able to take no more than the few images developed.[52]

Sometime afterwards he also wrote privately to friends in the USA of 'saltwater contaminating his film', so he *knew* that not all the images would survive. The world-famous story of the incompetent or overexcited darkroom assistant was an ingenious camouflage to mask his sudden breakdown. After eight years of covering war at close quarters, it is not unreasonable to observe that Robert Capa may indeed have been suffering from PTSD, though he would very soon return to Normandy and produce many more fine pictures of the campaign. However, the camouflage was unnecessary: the surviving images delivered the goods and none of this lessens the man, or his photographs – in fact, it makes him more human. One's respect for the photographer braving fire on Omaha beach, armed only with a camera knows no bounds, but is a lesson for historians in accepting received wisdoms at face value.[53]

General Bradley, aboard the *Augusta*, had been biting his nails all morning, first at the lack of news, then because the reports were growing worse. For the first few hours offshore, he had as little to go on as Gerow and Huebner on board USS *Ancon*, but as early as 0913 hours, the First Army commander had already pessimistically signalled Ramsay and SHAEF, 'Opposition Omaha considerable. If required, can US forces be accepted through Jig and King [sectors of Gold Beach, sixteen miles to the east]? Most immediate. Pass to GOC 21st AG [Montgomery].' It is illustrative of the mass of paper flying around that morning that Bradley's missive was not read until the afternoon, by which time the crisis had passed – but such a move would surely have been interpreted in terms of a Gallipolian disaster. Even sending the signal would have involved much eating of humble pie on Bradley's part, with issues of national pride at stake – made worse by Montgomery's own inclination to gloat over American mishaps whenever given the opportunity.

Information famine is an affliction that bedevils every military head-quarters in war, and the usual solution is to go see for yourself. Bradley despatched his twenty-seven-year-old aide, Major Chester 'Chet' B. Hansen, along with Kirk's gunnery officer, to cruise along the shore and report what they could see. They returned at the end of an hour with depressing news. Along Fox, in the Big Red One's sector, few channels had been opened through the obstacles, causing craft to divert to Easy Red, where more gaps had been blown, but this in turn was leading to congestion as the tide crept in.

At noon, V Corps was forced to admit, 'Situation critical at all four exits.' The time lag between achievement and reporting was abysmally slow. If by 0900 maybe five hundred men had landed safely in every sector of the beach, negotiated their way through the minefields, climbed the bluffs and in small groups were moving inland, by midday this figure had climbed to something like five thousand, with much of the 18th and 115th Infantry Regiments ashore and forging onwards.

However, V Corps were not in a position to confirm these first flickers of success until 1309 hours, when they informed Bradley, 'Troops formerly pinned down on Easy Red, Easy Green, Fox Red, advancing up heights behind beaches.'[54] Bradley recorded these moments in his 1951 memoir *A Soldier's Story*, though many of the words were actually Hansen's. The stocky, pink-cheeked and baby-faced former journalist had kept a meticulous diary and ghost-wrote much of the book for his general.[55] The seemingly strong German dam at Omaha had been breached, and with the Americans pouring through, in the words of another historian, 'nothing short of a panzer division could plug that hole now'.[56]

Originally there had been no plan to capture the little track that led towards Cabourg, five hundred yards east of E-3. It was more of a notch in the cliffs with a gentle scramble up to the top, rather than the broad winding valleys, sloping gently uphill, that characterised the rest of the draws. It worried the Germans sufficiently to site the last of the resistance nests overlooking Omaha, WN60, at its head, comprising several concrete gun emplacements. On the beach below, most of Company 'L', 16th Regiment, had landed half an hour late, at 0700, never intending to attack this feature. They had been pushed east, away from E-3, where they'd intended to land. Likewise Company 'I', some of whom had drifted off course as far as Port-en-Bessin – as much a navigational error as the fault of the current – and would return to land in the vicinity of F-1, but at 0800, one and a half hours behind schedule.

At this stage the destroyers offshore had realised the very tenuous hold Taylor's regiment had on the coast of France, and USS *Doyle* had started to close with fire support. Company 'L's commander, Captain John R. Armellino, remembered, 'straightaway one of my landing craft was swamped by the violent seas and sank. To this day, I don't know how many of those men were lost.' Closing fast, his men, too, encountered the eerie 'silence on the way to the beach. You could hear a pin drop. We didn't know what to expect when we landed. We soon found out. About a quarter-mile from the beach, all hell broke loose.'[57]

With the incoming tide, the waters had closed to three hundred yards, and most German attention in the two positions that could see Fox sector, WN60 and WN62, was focused away to the west, on the Colleville draw. Thus, Company 'L' made it across the sands in a matter of a few minutes, though losing twenty-seven men to machine-gun fire. 'I lost many of those young soldiers who joined my company right before the invasion in England,' reported Armellino. 'They had no fear, and failed to hit the ground after every few yards, instead running directly for cover. The more seasoned men hit the ground very often, and as a result avoided being hit by enemy fire.' However, Armellino himself became one of those casualties, injured by a mortar bomb.[58]

One of a sequence of images taken at the foot of the cliffs on Fox Red sector during the morning. It shows seven dead GIs washed ashore, probably from the 16th Infantry. The thin line of darker shingle suggests the tide is just on the ebb, implying the time is about 1130 hours. The fact that the fallen are covered with clothing, life preservers and, in one case, a cardboard box, suggests they have been badly disfigured by gunfire rather than drowned. (US Army Signal Corps)

Company 'L' Sergeant Mike McKinney – 'the lucky Irishman from Brooklyn' and pre-war soldier seasoned in the Mediterranean whom we have met already – recalled, 'we just sort of flopped down. Caught our breath. I'm looking around to see who's with us, see what kind of help we've got. Who made it to the shore? Do we have the satchel charges? Do we have the flamethrower? We had the flamethrower. We had the satchel charges and the Bangalores. And we had a few guys from the 116th Infantry; these strangers showed up and said, "We don't know where to go," so I said, "Stay with us." I knew they were supposed to be down the beach a little further, but I didn't know what they were supposed to do. So we made riflemen out of them, and put them along the water-line and had them start shooting at a pillbox, to close up the apertures.'[59]

By this time, two of the 741st's Shermans had arrived and were led by Lieutenant Jimmie W. Monteith on foot through a minefield, to fire positions that would best help suppress the German strongpoint. Needing to destroy the troublesome WN60 before they could do anything else, the unplanned assault by Company 'L' up what would become known as the F-1 draw evolved, despite their captain's wounding. Monteith led one of the assault sections through the wire and minefields, while other sections crept up the draw using ground which offered a covered approach from the strongpoint. Sergeant Hugh Martin recalled that Monteith 'paid no attention to the shells and machine-gun fire when he went to the wire and afterwards led us through the minefields'.

They outflanked it, entered the outlying trenches, and mopped up with grenades and satchel charges. By 0900 hours, Company 'L' was able to signal Third Battalion headquarters that WN60 had been captured and they were pushing on to the high ground east of the Colleville draw. Reinforcing success, a heavy machine-gun section from Company 'M' and another section from Company 'K' had also joined them, but at around ten a counter-attack infiltrated the Company 'L' advance, during which Monteith was killed. Armellino would recommend him for a Distinguished Service Cross; Bradley and Bedell Smith concurred. However, Eisenhower took one look at the citation and mused, 'Looks like a Medal of Honor to me. This man was good.' Thus Monteith became the fourth and last recipient of the supreme honour, awarded for actions on D-Day itself.[60]

Control of the high ground east of the E-3 draw was key to its eventual capture, thus the peripheral action of the Cabourg draw would prove central to the opening of what became the key exit off the beach.

Another image taken at the foot of the cliffs at Fox Red sector during the morning of 6 June. Protected from fire, several wounded GIs have gathered to await medical evacuation. The two on the right wear the badge of the 29th Division on their left sleeves. They are from Easy Company of the 116th Infantry, who were swept miles east from the rest of their formation. The others are with the 16th Infantry of the Big Red One. (US Army Signal Corps)

Although three Company 'L' men were captured and spent the night in Cabourg, the next morning PFC Lawrence Mielender would return with fifty-two prisoners.[61] This was the first substantial penetration of the Omaha defences in the eastern sector, and happened at about the same time Captain Goranson's Ranger company beyond Vierville in the west were also making their way up a shallow gully – and penetrating the maze of WN73.

Towards the end of the day, Chuck Hurlbut, the Company 'C' 299th Engineer, was clearing obstacles at the eastern end between the E-3 and F-1 draws. 'I had lost my rifle; the thought in my mind was – army discipline: "I'm going to catch hell."' He started looking for one. 'There were hundreds of them, laying all over. I picked one that looked pretty good. Later, up on the bluffs our officers told us, "We've taken a pretty bad beating. We'll talk about it in the morning. Tonight just try to dig in up here. Stay close." So we went and dug a foxhole and lay down, but you couldn't sleep, because the infantry and tanks was still moving up. Down on the beach, they were still unloading stuff. You were so excited and revved up that you couldn't sleep,' explained Hurlbut. 'You learned an awful lot in those hours, realised that, hey, this is not a game. A lot of the craziness, the gung-ho attitude disappeared. It hit you that so many of your buddies were no longer with you.'[62]

Captain James Milnor Roberts, aide to General Gerow, crossed the Channel on the attack transport *Charles Carroll* before transferring to an LCVP. Approaching Easy Red at 1700 hours, he remembered his craft being hit with artillery fire about a hundred yards out. 'It was like a summer thunderstorm; a few drops at first, then everything all at once. Only this was lead. Fragments were knocking us around; several people were hit, including the skipper who was killed. It is very difficult to dig a hole in a steel deck, but there isn't much cover on a Higgins boat. I recall mass confusion and fear; frankly I was in a panic,' Roberts admitted later. He disembarked in chest-deep water and climbed the bluffs to Saint-Laurent under shell and sniper fire; at the top he looked back: 'It was just fantastic; vessels of all kinds as far as you could see.'

Roberts set up V Corps HQ just north of Saint-Laurent, ready for Gerow's arrival at around 2100 hours. The general's priorities were communications and the possibility of an armoured counter-attack. There was no contact with either flanking formation – the British 50th Division at Gold, or VII Corps at Utah – if the Germans counter-attacked in the night, V Corps would be on its own. As darkness fell, Roberts broke out his K-rations and ate his first meal of the day. 'Around midnight when things seemed to be fairly quiet, I remember thinking – Man, what a day this has been. If every day is going to be as bad as this, I'll never survive the war.'[63]

Landing with the reserve regiment, Colonel Jeff Seitz's 26th Infantry, was Major Donald E. Rivette of Dearborn, Michigan, XO of its anti-tank company. He had been one of the first soldiers in the 502nd Parachute Infantry, but had broken his leg during training and wound up with the 26th instead. Rivette spent his D-Day waiting to land. Early in the morning, he remembered,

the clam doors of our LST opened and three DUKWs carrying 105mm howitzers slid into the stormy seas. They hadn't gone fifty yards when each floundered and sank. No more disembarked for over an hour, waiting for the sea to subside. By about 0930 hours when it had calmed a bit, several more were launched: these seemed to stay afloat. At 1000 we saw a destroyer charging past us, firing several shells at the cliffs, but our LST was five miles out and too far away to make out what was happening.[64]

It must have been mid-morning when Rivette observed a German fighter shot down. Two Focke-Wulf 190s flown by Oberstleutnant Josef 'Pips' Priller and his wingman, Feldwebel Heinz Wodarczyk, had earlier made a low pass over Omaha from the direction of Gold Beach and, despite the torrent of anti-aircraft artillery thrown against them, had survived. Priller, already a renowned ace, who would eventually chalk up 101 victories in 1,307 combat missions, was based in Lille. Considered the leading Luftwaffe 'expert' on the Channel Front, he had just sent some of his pilots to Biarritz for a week's leave and had ordered others to move inland on 5 June, to Reims and Nancy; their ground echelons were still on the road on 6 June.

Priller's sortie is well known through being recounted in *The Longest Day*, though other Luftwaffe flyers in Fw 190s were active over the beachhead area – but failed to return – at least one hundred missions being recorded during the day. Rivette remembered the moment the German aircraft crashed: 'every soldier and sailor seemed to stand up and cheer as in a football stadium'. As the day wore on, he recounted how 'First Division Headquarters warned us around midday we had troops ashore but they had not broken out, so our landing was pushed back. Initially it was 1300, afterwards 1600 hours, then postponed. In fact some of the 26th did land on the sixth; but I had to wait till dawn on 7 June, landing just opposite the large draw on Easy Red.'[65]

Once ashore, Rivette noted

tanks and other vehicles stuck in the sand or destroyed by mines or gunfire. Other debris including hedgehogs, barbed wire, wrecked landing craft and all sorts of equipment littered the beach. I saw eight or ten wounded enemy prisoners, waiting for attention in the battalion aid station: they had an oriental look about them; it turned out they were recruited from somewhere in Russia. The Graves Registration units had been busy throughout the night and bodies were piled in neat rows like cordwood: it looked like we had lost half the assault wave.[66]

By the end of the day, the casualties suffered by Taylor's 16th Infantry were broadly similar to those of Canham 116th's, the After Action Report noting thirty-six officers and 935, killed, wounded and missing.[67] This formed the bulk of the Big Red One's losses for D-Day, estimated at 1,036; 29th Division losses at 743; and V Corps', including the Rangers, at 441. The 741st Tank Battalion's operations log noted 'laagering in a field two miles from the water and watching a canopy of red tracers slice the air overhead to drive off Luftwaffe raiders'. Their first tank status report, submitted to V Corps at 2315 hours on 6 June, indicated that it had precisely three battle-ready Shermans, two damaged but repairable, and forty-eight reckoned lost. 'Working through the night, salvage and repair operations would succeed in getting the damaged armour operational, so that on the morning of 7 June the battalion could field a provisional platoon of five tanks ready for action.'[68]

Hyam Haas, whose anti-aircraft half-tracks had silenced the WN65 bunker, remembered afterwards driving up

> to the top of the bluffs and soon the sounds of battle began to recede from our area and we began to breathe a little freer. We were off the beach and the sun came out and warmed us. We were soaking wet most of the day and now we began to dry. At that position we sort of recuperated from the trauma of the landings. We had lots of ground coffee and we kept a pot on our stove – we even gave passing generals coffee. We stayed on the top of the bluff, a sort of plateau, where an airfield was built.[69]

Indeed, many GIs would recall the buzz of aircraft taking off and landing as they landed on Omaha after D-Day. The airfield was a 3,400-foot-long by 120-foot-wide strip of bulldozed earth, opened for aircraft within forty-eight hours. Soon it was handling P-38s and C-47s, flying casualties back to England. Long since returned to nature, the airstrip overlooked the beach and was on the heights immediately west of WN65 and east of the Les Moulins draw.

Today, Omaha is much as it once was; the obstacles are long gone, as are the mines and barbed wire. Much of the shingle mound was bulldozed aside by engineers to facilitate access off the sands, and the holiday villas have been rebuilt. Rommel's *Atlantikwall* proved more difficult to remove, so nearly all of it remains in situ, enabling the keen historian to interpret every battlefield action. A counterpart to the Blue and Gray memorial on top of the WN72 bunker at Vierville is the Big Red One's memorial obelisk atop the WN62 strongpoint dominating the Colleville draw. It overlooks the beach Easy Red and Fox Green sectors where the 16th, 18th and 26th Infantry Regiments landed, and commemorates by name those in the 1st Infantry Division killed in the Normandy battles from 6 June to 24 July, when the breakout began. Similar pillars track the division's progress all the way to Cheb, on the Czech-German frontier.

The polished granite obelisk, like a sundial, lies at the heart of WN62, once occupied by Gefreiters Hein Severloh and Franz Gockel and Oberleutnant Bernhard Frerking. Their mortar pits, gun emplacements and the observation post from which Frerking and Severloh fought the invasion are still present, as are the zig-zag trenches – now shallow depressions in the ground – through which Severloh and Gockel made their escape, and Frerking did not. A walk onto the forward slope brings the visitor to the 5th Engineer Special Brigade Memorial, mounted on top of the upper 75mm gun emplacement, knocked out by Sergeant Geddes' DD tank.

The shallow scars in the concrete of this and the lower 75mm bunker illustrate how difficult these structures were to defeat. A commemorative stone acknowledging the service of the counterpart 6th Engineer Special Brigade, whose commander, Colonel Paul W. Thompson, was wounded during the day, sits in the Vierville draw. Both brigades were huge organisations, formed especially for D-Day, and each comprised around a dozen battalions of engineers and quartermaster, medical, ordnance, port and naval beach staff. The fairly intact strongpoints of WN61 and WN60, beyond to the east, also repay a visit, though they sit on private land.

To the west lies the Colleville American military cemetery, where the first fallen warriors arrived in November 1948. They came from temporary burial sites established throughout Normandy, where the dead of all nationalities had been laid to rest together, in carefully recorded plots. Two were within the confines of Omaha Beach, one at Utah, and a further pair at Sainte-Mère-Église. Once American service personnel were removed to Colleville, some of these other sites would be taken over by the Germans as permanent graveyards for their own war dead. At La Cambe, for example – originally known as the 29th Division's cemetery – 4,534 Americans were buried alongside 8,574 Germans. Now La Cambe has become the principal site for the commemoration of 21,222 soldiers, mostly from the Seventh Army, including Hein Severloh's boss, Oberleutnant Bernard Frerking. Orglandes and Marigny are two further examples of German burial sites that were originally US Army graveyards. Among the former's 10,152 graves is that of Generalleutnant Wilhelm Falley. The Marigny site, near Saint-Lô, commemorates 11,172 soldiers, including the one-legged General Erich Marcks who celebrated his last birthday on 6 June 1944.

The village of La Cambe, home to fewer than seven hundred souls in June 1944, rapidly became known as 'Little America'. Besides the cemetery, four field hospitals, two airfields, a petrol depot and an assembly workshop for GMC trucks were established in the vicinity, the latter employing 150 locals. Similar Allied infrastructure existed all over Normandy in 1944–5, employing tens of thousands of French men and women. At La Cambe, 6×6 'Jimmy' trucks were assembled from parts shipped over in wooden crates and processed through Omaha Beach. At peak efficiency they turned out up to sixty 6×6 trucks a day; a similar depot at Isigny producing as many as one hundred jeeps in the same timeframe, which were also parked at La Cambe, causing an American war correspondent to label the area 'Mini Detroit'. Pierre Darondel remembered the moment some GIs came to his farm at La Cambe and offered their jeep in exchange for a bottle of Calvados. Darondel refused the deal, pointing out the hundreds of jeeps parked behind his house.[70]

The task of honouring the dead was mammoth: by the end of the war, the Army Graves Registration Service and the Burial and Registration Command had identified 206,577 American personnel killed in Europe, of whom 76,360 lay in twenty-four temporary cemeteries in France, sixteen of them within the duchy of Normandy. In 1947, families were offered repatriation of their loved ones and within a year 34,874 of America's fallen had returned home. From 1948 onwards, the remainder who served in northern France were concentrated at Colleville – and a second site on the Normandy–Brittany border at Saint-James, and today 9,387 Americans, including three servicewomen, are interred in the 172-acre Colleville plot under the Normandy sun. One of the women was 27-year-old American Red Cross volunteer Elizabeth A. Richardson from Indiana, who died in an air crash. We have met her already, handing out doughnuts and coffee from her Clubmobile in southern England.

A further 1,557 individuals, who were never recovered or could not be identified, have their names inscribed on the walls of a semi-circular garden on the east side. This is why Captain Taylor N. Fellers is buried in Bedford cemetery, Virginia, Private Bedford T. Hoback has a grave at

Colleville, but his brother Staff Sergeant Raymond S. Hoback is commemorated on the wall of the missing.

Eighty miles to the west, in a further twenty-eight acres of French earth, the less well-known Saint-James American cemetery contains the remains of 4,410 US servicemen who lost their lives fighting in the later breakout battles, including ninety-five headstones of unidentified GIs, and the names of 498 of the missing – a small rosette device helpfully marking those since recovered and identified. Its lookout tower gives a panorama of their battlefields and Mont-Saint-Michel. It also marks the point where American forces exited the hedgerow country of Normandy and entered the plains of Brittany during the offensive around Avranches. Saint-James also contains a famous 29er – Pennsylvanian Staff Sergeant Sherwood H. Hallman, who landed on D-Day with Company 'F' of the 175th Infantry and was awarded a Medal of Honor for his bravery on 13 September, only to be killed by a sniper the following day.

Under the soil of Normandy still lie the sons of every nation in scattered, yet-to-be-discovered graves. In June 2004, Fallschirmjäger Alfred Gartner, killed on a summer's day in the Cotentin, was found by a farmer in a bocage hedgerow, identified by tunic buttons, a rusting pistol and his aluminium dog tags.[71] In May 2009, five German soldiers including an officer killed on D-Day were discovered with their helmets, scraps of camouflage clothing and tunic buttons in a shallow grave overlooking Caen.[72] Meanwhile, the detective work of identifying the 'unknowns' resting in the cemeteries – these days using DNA testing – continues. In 2016 the occupant of grave X-91 at Colleville was determined to be Motor Machinist's Mate John E. Anderson, of Willmar, Minnesota, who died on 6 June when his craft, *LCT-30*, was struck while pulling off Omaha Beach.[73] In 2017 it was the turn of 'Unknown X-9352' to be identified as Ludwig Julius Wilhelm 'Louie' Pieper and laid to rest alongside his twin brother Julius Heinrich Otto 'Henry' Pieper at Colleville. The nineteen-year-old twins from Esmond, South Dakota, were radio operators aboard *LST-523* when she hit a mine on her way to Utah Beach. While Louie's body was soon found and laid to rest, the remains of Julius were only recovered in 1961 by French salvage divers.[74]

Often forgotten was the arrival of the Corncobs – the twenty-two blockships sunk from 7 June to form the Gooseberry 2 breakwater a few hundred yards out to sea. They – with the component parts of Mulberry 'A' – would start to arrive off Omaha at 0600 hours on D+1. However, three Phoenix concrete caissons were lost in transit; additionally, one of the Whale floating roadways was found adrift, with no sign of its thirty crew, other than blood. They were presumed to have been massacred by a passing E-boat.[75] Long before Mulberry 'A' was in operation, the logistical pressure would begin to mount because of the unexpectedly high D-Day losses and slow process of unloading LSTs onto smaller LCTs, DUKWs and Rhino ferries, which shuttled their contents ashore.

The US Navy had had concerns that were their LSTs to land at high water on the uneven sands off Omaha, at low tide the beached craft might experience undue stress on their keels, causing them to break their backs. The undulating seabed was caused by the four-knot current that constantly shifted the sands, but this movement ceased with the Corncobs. With the breakwaters partially complete from 7 June, at low tide engineers with bulldozers flattened the beach, removing craters, runnels and sandbars.[76]

On 8 June, the first LST beached with great success, and the many familiar photographs of rows of LSTs offloading onto the Omaha sands date to this later period – earlier they would have been at anchor offshore. Thereafter beaching became standard practice, removing the need for most Rhinos and increasing by a factor of ten the speed with which LSTs could be unloaded. This development also spread to Utah and the other Allied landing beaches at the same time. Over one hundred LSTs would beach on Omaha in the next ten days until Mulberry 'A' began operating on 16 June, three days ahead of schedule. Collectively, they – together with smaller LCTs and DUKWs shuttling cargo from Liberty ships and coasters further out to sea – disgorged just shy of fifty thousand tons of military equipment, an average of 5,337 tons per day.

However, beaching LSTs at Omaha still cost valuable time: they had to wait for the tide to recede, unload, then linger until high water, and be pulled off the beach before sailing – a process which took approximately twelve hours, excluding the Channel passage. The value of Mulberry 'A' was proven with the first vessel to be unloaded on 16 June. *LST-342* discharged seventy-eight Sherman tanks and trucks in thirty-eight minutes, then immediately turned about and made for southern England. Over the next three days, 26,101 tons – or 8,700 tons per day – would arrive onto Omaha through Mulberry 'A'. On 17 June, eleven LSTs took an average of fifty-six minutes each to offload their complete cargoes. By 18 June, some 205,762 personnel, 74,563 tons of supplies and 29,242 vehicles had been unloaded at Omaha – including those processed through Mulberry 'A', which had operated for three days.

It was deemed so successful, against expectations, that talks were afoot to winterise it.[77] However, these impressive statistics would be its legacy, for on 19 June the Great Gale hit, devastating Mulberry 'A'. Although salvage experts assessed it could be put back into operation, Admiral Kirk – who had never fully embraced the concept – decided to abandon it. His decision was influenced by the fact that there was almost no American input into what was essentially a British idea, and his understanding that Cherbourg would soon fall. It never resumed its function, and any components salvageable were transferred to Mulberry 'B'. In retrospect, Kirk made an extremely rash decision, for Cherbourg would not fall to Collins' VII Corps for another ten days – 29 June – by which time its harbour facilities had been so comprehensively destroyed that the first Liberty ship could not dock for over three months – until 8 October. The US Mulberry has been all but forgotten: halfway down the gulley in front of the American cemetery at Colleville a bronze plaque commemorates Mulberry 'A', but of the huge undertaking, only a small concrete portion remains as part of the small pier at Vierville.[78]

On 8 June the Big Red One would link up with the British 50th Division, at Port-en-Bessin, as planned. Mike McKinney remembered the moment: 'They told me to scout ahead and make sure there's no Germans between us and the British. So I took this combat patrol out and I saw the British up ahead. They had a half-track with them. This guy is sitting there, and we start to approach him, and he says, "Oh, hi, Yank. Cup of tea?" I got a kick out of that. Here we're in the war, he's sitting with a pot of tea, he had a tin can and he's got a fire going. I said, "Sure, a cup of tea."'[79]

When he had time to pause for breath after D-Day, Captain Joseph T. Dawson, the commander of Company 'G' who had followed Lieutenant Spalding up the bluffs, penned a letter to his parents in Corpus Christi, Texas, on 16 June. He wrote 'from an Apple Orchard, Normandy':

My Dearest Family, you must forgive me for not writing a detailed letter to you before now because there were certain things that occurred to prevent me from gathering my thoughts long enough to inscribe them. One never realises the utter loneliness of separation until one has had the privilege of living and being a part of the finest group of men on the face of the earth. What I'm trying to say is that justice can never be properly accorded to the magnificent fortitude and heroism of the fine American soldier and man. He is without peer, and these past few days have implanted in the hearts of all, a realisation of the true greatness of these men. I say this because I've had an honor, never to be equalled, of being part of a group that will ever stand as a symbol of greatness to all who witnessed, or know how they measured up to, the supreme test without faltering or wavering. I cannot say more for my heart forbears it, but God is my witness that the men of my company lived, fought, and died in true glory. I am with the bravest, finest, grandest bunch of men that God ever breathed life into.[80]

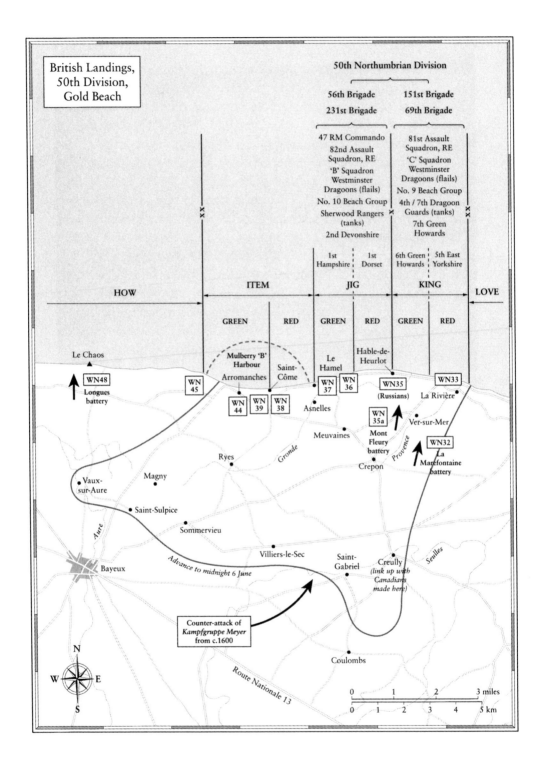

31

Gold: Men of the Double-T

'We had dug a trench in the garden, just big enough to shelter me and my seven children. When the bombing started we were in the house, but it grew so bad that we soon took refuge in our trench, which was fortunate because the windows and roof of our home were soon smashed. During a lull one of my children seized the opportunity to climb onto the garden wall to see what was happening. Suddenly he shouted excitedly, "Mummy, Mummy! Look – the sea – it's black with boats!"'

Madame d'Anselm, resident of Asnelles, Gold Beach[1]

THE ENTIRE GOLD Beach sector stretched ten miles across from Port-en-Bessin, via Arromanches to La Rivière, but any landing along most of the shoreline would be impossible until where the cliffs abruptly end at Le Hamel. Beyond, as far as the Orne river and Caen, lies a completely different geology: wide sand or shingle beaches and a deep coastal plain. The three stretches invaded by the Anglo-Canadians would be across this terrain. All along this part of the coast many seaside villages had grown up, connected by a narrow-gauge railway. They were often fronted by a sea wall and dotted with smart villas from the late nineteenth and early twentieth centuries.

This stretch of the future invasion littoral had been a popular destination for middle-class Parisians, the French capital being a mere three hours away by train. To this end, the region encompassing Gold, Juno and Sword Beaches was promoted by railway companies in the nineteenth century as the *Côte de Nacre* (Pearl Coast), beyond, from Merville to

Deauville, the *Côte Fleurie* (Flowered Coast). This had brought tens of thousands of holidaymakers every year, from Britain as well as Paris. The wealthier watched horseracing, gambled in casinos or dined in sumptuous restaurants. The less affluent lodged in boarding houses and hotels, paddled in the sea and built sandcastles – hence the widespread availability of guidebooks, picture postcards and holiday snaps that had helped the COSSAC and SHAEF staff formulate their plans.

The coastline that continues eastwards from Omaha is dominated by high limestone cliffs. Officially, the next few miles still belonged to the US First Army, as far as Port-en-Bessin, sixteen miles away, where the Anglo-Canadian sector began. There the cliffs retreat and a small harbour had developed over the centuries, connected by road to Bayeux six miles to the south. The stone jetties offered passage through the reefs that foot the cliffs on either side, and were prized by mariners for the calm water they offered. It had become a favourite in the late nineteenth century with the impressionist Georges Seurat, who painted its colourful fishing fleet. In 1944, the little town was occupied by the 1st Company of the 726th Grenadier Regiment, who established three strongpoints in the area: WN56 defended access to the port with two 47mm guns, while the heights to the west and east were controlled by the concrete emplacements of WN58 and WN57. Its harbour was too small to host an invasion flotilla or even a portion of it – a few landing craft was the limit.

Yet it was important to seize for two reasons. The fishing village of 1,500 represented the inter-army boundary between Bradley's First and Dempsey's Second Armies, and would be an important basis for liaison between the two, with Bradley, Montgomery and Dempsey intending to establish headquarters in the vicinity. Second, the Allies had determined that part of their ingenious submarine fuel pipeline apparatus – dubbed PLUTO (Pipe-Line Under The Ocean) – would come ashore at Port-en-Bessin, where petrol and oil storage depots were to be sustained from tankers offshore, using buoyed pipelines. Its capture from the landward side was assigned to 47 Royal Marine Commando, who would land at Asnelles on Gold Beach and march eight miles west to seize their important prize.

The cliffs continue for another six miles east of Port-en-Bessin, until another slight geological cleft in the limestone heights occurs at Arromanches-les-Bains. Over the centuries a very small fishing village also developed here; later the commune sold itself as a health resort – a sort of downmarket rival to Ouistreham, Cabourg and Deauville further along the coast – hence the 'les-Bains' suffix. However, as Arromanches did not possess a casino or cinema, unlike its competitors, and with the First World War knocking the stuffing out of the health business, the village settled back into comfortable obscurity. The Second World War was not generally kind to France, but by a quirk of fate, Arromanches is about the only place that can claim to have benefited, for this would be the site chosen for the second Mulberry harbour – inevitably christened 'Port Winston' – whose remarkably durable remains are still evident seventy-five years later.

The specific areas identified by COSSAC and SHAEF suitable for the landing craft of Force 'G' were Jig sector at Le Hamel, on the edge of Asnelles, and, two and a half miles east, King sector at La Rivière, near the town of Ver-sur-Mer. Immediately beyond lay Juno Beach, realm of the 3rd Canadian Division. Today, the region's increased population and advent of holiday homes has meant the formerly separate settlements of Le Hamel and Asnelles have merged into a single entity, likewise La Rivière and Ver. However, these two coastal villages were – and remain – separated by low-lying marsh; for this reason the Germans considered the future Gold as a poor landing area. Inland, between Le Hamel/Asnelles and La Rivière/Ver, are the little towns of Meuvaines and Crépon, both significant because they sat on the road network that controlled access to Jig and King. Although the 50th Division was throwing two brigade groups – the equivalent of a US Regimental Combat Team of around 10,000 – at Gold, the geography dictated that the operation would not result in a single simultaneous assault along one long stretch of beach. Rather, this would be two separate landings, each brigade fighting its own battle on a mile-wide front, with no chance to support the other.

Generalleutnant Dietrich Kraiss had gambled by placing the better troops of the 1st Company, 916th *Grenadier-Regiment*, in the strong western positions, putting the 3rd Company of his Russians – Hauptmann Richardt Roth's 441st *Ost-Bataillon* – in the weak, central defences, clustered around the strongpoint at Hable de Heurlot, and the same battalion's 4th Company, stiffened by the 7th Company of the 736th *Grenadier-Regiment*, manning the more robust eastern bunkers.[2] This messy solution – men from three different units spread along the front – reflected the fact that Gold Beach was on the inter-divisional boundary between Kraiss's 352nd and Richter's 716th Divisions. The German-officered battalion of Russians had arrived in France at the beginning of the year for internal security duties, and was only lightly armed. Soon deployed on coastal defence, they remained poorly equipped with only half the normal allocation of machine-guns and mortars; however, Kraiss had assessed the probability of a landing here as low. Behind these coastal defenders were four-gun batteries in the vicinity of Crépon, Creully, La Marefontaine, Ryes and Mount-Fleury, as well as mobile units of horse-drawn artillery.

Kanonier Aloysius Damski found himself behind Gold Beach in the artillery regiment of the 716th Division.

> I was a Pole. I was impressed into the German Army in February 1943 and after training sent to Normandy, to a mixed unit of Poles, Czechs and Russians, under the command of German NCOs and officers. Most of the older men had no faith in Hitler and believed that Germany could never win the war ... My job was fire control, coordinating the fire of three batteries positioned between Arromanches and Asnelles. Our batteries were equipped with old-fashioned horse-drawn artillery. They were ordinary field guns on hard rubber tires, not emplaced in concrete but in open field positions, with about four hundred shells each. For the year before the invasion I was billeted with an old French lady who was very sympathetic and kind because I was Polish. Occasionally we used to go into Bayeux and meet French girls, but most of our spare time was spent drinking. I used to listen to the BBC on the radio – the *leutnant* in charge of our battery listened too, but he would always vigorously deny the claims made by the British, saying they were 'rubbish' – but it didn't stop him listening.[3]

In every case, the protective concrete bunkers of the stationary batteries were incomplete, or the cannon were sited in field positions, with no overhead cover and minimal local defence. Gefreiter Friedrich Wurster was an artillerymen stationed at La Marefontaine, known as WN32, which comprised the 7th Battery of Generalleutnant Richter's artillery regiment. He had served two tours in Russia, being wounded on each occasion, and was languishing in Normandy as 'a semi-invalid, aged twenty-one'.[4] Wurster felt safer than his brother in the Luftwaffe or the civilians being bombed back in the Fatherland.

He and his father – stationed in Norway – both believed the propaganda that the *Atlantikwall* was impregnable. The son of a farmer, Wurster could not wait to return to the land again. This was why he enjoyed rural France, surrounded by farms and cattle. Known as *Batterie Vera*, his position comprised four 100mm Czech guns, formerly horse-drawn of First World War vintage, and exactly the same type installed at Merville, where their 1st Battery was established, and with whom they spoke often by field telephone.

Although there were eleven *Widerstandsnester* in the Gold sector, few were concrete strongpoints of the kind encountered at Omaha. The most significant was WN39 on the clifftops midway between Saint-Côme and Arromanches, which housed a Würzburg radar station and two 75mm field guns in concrete casemates which faced eastwards, supplemented by WN38, with two 50mm weapons in bunkers. These positions overlooked an old *préventorium* (sanatorium) at Le Hamel, numbered WN37. Easily the strongest position defending Gold, and protected on the landward side by minefields, an anti-tank ditch and machine guns, this was a series of stout buildings constructed for Parisian children who had succumbed to tuberculosis and were brought to the coast for fresh air and sun. Within the partially demolished hospital complex lurked a strong concrete bunker with a 75mm gun, sited to fire east in enfilade along the beach, along with other pillboxes containing a 50mm anti-tank weapon and machine guns, including one in an old tank turret. A 50mm cannon and machine-guns at the eastern end of Le Hamel were known as WN36.

Between Asnelles and Ver, with marshes to their rear, was the six-bunker complex of WN35 at Hable de Heurlot, manned by Russian troops under German officers and NCOs. It was equipped with machine-guns and small anti-tank weapons. On the eastern edge of Gold, the WN33 blockhouses at La Rivière housed the lethal threat of an 88mm facing west and two 50mm cannon. As elsewhere, some bunkers were still under construction, and further delays to the invasion date would have seen more obstacles on the Gold beaches and the coastline bristling with further deadly weapons. Collectively, these positions also possessed about twenty standard 50mm infantry mortars, which would cause many casualties throughout the day.[5]

The defenders' dilemma here was similar as for those at Utah Beach: they were thinly dispersed along a strip of coast in positions that had no depth and were too far apart to offer mutual fire support. Penetration of just one position would result in the rest being rolled up from the flanks or to the rear – which would be made easier by the lateral road that ran parallel to the coast behind the shoreline. Thus these little forts could only hope to delay any penetration for a few hours at most, until the swift arrival of reinforcements. Overall, four infantry companies defended the Gold sector with eighteen machine guns, five 75mm field howitzers and seven 50mm anti-tank cannon. The density of defending troops and weaponry was less than half of that encountered on Omaha. There were the usual obstacles on the beaches, miles of barbed wire and numerous minefields – real and fake: these were defences designed principally to deter, for on their own, they could not block.[6]

Generalleutnant Kraiss's immediate reserves were bicycle troops. They were a common sight in Wehrmacht units, but far less so to the Allies, as Fred Archer, a paratrooper captured on D-Day, related: 'As we were being escorted to the rear, a long line of Boche cyclists hove into view. They were led by a very fat, bespectacled NCO, and the rest looked very young. On their shoddy grey-green uniforms none bore the ribbons or medals we expected to see on seasoned stormtroopers. As they clattered along the *pavé*, making quite a noise, they looked – how can I put it? – ridiculous. I can still see them now, their helmets bobbing up and down, but cycling in military unison,' recalled Archer.

'All their jackbooted legs seemed to hit the pedals at the same time. We could imagine the fat man drilling them, like a ski instructor – "Nein, bend ze knees, Heinrich!" We realised they were a unit, for behind their saddles, each bore racks bearing stick grenades or ammunition boxes, and each had a rifle or machine-gun strapped to the frame. As we passed, they looked at us with the same degree of curiosity as we must have looked at them. This was our first sight of a Jerry bicycle squad riding to certain death, while we paratroopers, with dirty faces and torn tunics, must have frightened the life out of them.'[7]

The British Army had scrapped cyclist battalions at the end of the First World War, and they had not been part of Canadian or US forces within memory, so the sight of a squad of German military cyclists somewhere near Caen on D-Day came as something of a shock to the Tommies passing it. In fact, most German Army reconnaissance units from 1939 onwards had used detachments of cyclists, particularly in cavalry regiments, and in successive campaigns they became a common sight in infantry divisions, pedalling into France, the Balkans and Russia. Within every regiment there would be a cyclist company, so that by 1944 the designation of a cyclist company or battalion – which to the Allies was a laughable concept – was an established tradition of the Wehrmacht. Alongside horses, they helped overcome the lack of vehicles and shortage of fuel, and everyone knew how to ride a bike.

Allied intelligence failed to detect the forward move of 352nd Division, led by Generalleutnant Dietrich Kraiss (1889–1944) (left) from Saint-Lô to behind Omaha and Gold beaches. Better trained and equipped than other formations along the invasion front, it nevertheless compared poorly with its Allied counterparts. With many troops and most artillery batteries assigned to static positions, the mobility of its reserves was entirely reliant on bicycles. After several false starts, the cyclists were already exhausted by the time they encountered their opponents. (Author's collection)

The Wehrmacht attempted standardisation, with models strong enough to carry a fully equipped soldier with his weapons and ammunition: in 1943, the Reich manufactured 1.3 million bicycles, mostly for its armed forces, but many were seized from occupied countries – especially the Netherlands. It was a cheap and plausible way to give the Wehrmacht mobility when on static occupation duty, but the notion soon fell apart when confronted with the superior mechanisation of the Allies, and their dominance of the skies. Bicycles were not cross-country tools of war.

Both the Fifteenth and Seventh Armies boasted bicycle units in every infantry regiment. There was also, attached to Erich Marks' 84th Corps, an independent outfit, designed as a sort of fire brigade, to rush to one trouble spot or another in the Cotentin. Led since February 1943 by a cavalry officer, Oberstleutnant Hugo, Freiherr von und zu Aufsess, the 30th *Schnelle-Brigade* was stationed in the vicinity of Coutances. It possessed no armour or artillery; its few motor vehicles towed a small number of light anti-tank guns. Most of the formation was bicycle-mounted and expected, in formation, to pedal into battle. The *Schnelle-Brigade* was a grouping of several 'reconnaissance training battalions', designed to combine schooling and security roles. Their manpower had a regular turn-over as trained men were posted and new recruits inducted. Noticed by a bright young staff officer in Berlin, they were appended to the Seventh Army's order of battle as a combat unit, which probably seemed like a good idea at the time.[8]

While some of the 352nd Division's mobile reserves relied on cycling to the invasion, it has to be said that the Wehrmacht was not alone in their obsession with spoked wheels and handlebars. Most of the 70,000-plus folding bicycles made for Allied airborne forces by the Birmingham Small Arms (BSA) company were in fact issued to the D-Day Anglo-Canadian assault wave troops, including commandos, in an effort to improve their mobility once ashore. Each assault battalion on Gold, Juno and Sword was issued a company's worth of bicycles in order to pursue retreating Germans. An extra burden, none were used once ashore.

However, as John Shanahan, a Cork man who had crossed the border to enlist in the 2nd Royal Ulster Rifles (8th Brigade), and who landed on Sword Beach with the British 3rd Division, recalled, 'Lots of us were given these fold-up bikes; personally I couldn't see the point of them. Perhaps it was some sort of trick by the brass – to make us believe we could just stroll on up the beach and bike over to Caen, as though it were a Sunday afternoon.' Shanahan observed, 'Coming down the gangplank from the landing craft, I stumbled and my bike tried to drown me. Once we got away from the beach, I couldn't wait to get rid of it. We just dumped them in a great pile. Such a waste, but it was obvious we wouldn't be cycling anywhere. I believe they disappeared in the night, and presumably the French thought they were a gift!'[9]

The attackers, led by Major General Douglas Graham, would have a busy D-Day, being allotted the four tasks of linking up with the Canadians on their left, and with the Americans to the right, capturing the city and route centre of Bayeux, and generally reaching or dominating the Caen–Carentan *Route Nationale* 13 highway, six miles inland. With a total strength of 18,381, the 50th Northumbrian Division was theoretically manned by Territorial Army soldiers – the British equivalent to the National Guard – recruited from the industrial towns of north-east England. However, all three battalions in its 231st Brigade hailed from southern England. Brigadier Pepper's 56th Independent

Brigade was a new formation, formed from three regular army battalions – the 2nd South Wales Borderers, 2nd Glosters and 2nd Essex. It had been formed only in February 1944 and was attached to the 50th Division from 1 March, completely untested and a stranger to itself. The divisional Machine Gun Battalion were the 2nd Cheshires from the West Midlands, and of the three Royal Artillery field regiments (a British artillery battalion is confusingly called a regiment), the 90th was a London-recruited unit. All the division's artillery regiments comprised three eight-gun batteries, each equipped with towed 25-pounder guns.

Thus the 50th Division was far from being Northumbrian, as its title implied. Although Douglas Graham's soldiers may have worn the 'double-T' badge, signifying the formation's origins around the Tyne and Tees rivers of north-east England, fewer than half his men came from those parts or had ever visited them, and many were in any case conscripts from all over the British Isles. A good example of the vagaries of conscription can be found with Nathan Lerner, a Jewish lad from Hackney in east London, who served in the 1st Dorsets, a regiment associated with south-west England, in a division whose roots lay in the north-east. Some came from much further afield. Due to the chronic shortage of junior infantry officers – lieutenants and captains – Canadian officers were encouraged to volunteer to be loaned to British infantry battalions under the Canloan scheme. This highly successful innovation resulted in 673 Canuck officers transferring to the British Army. The 50th Division gratefully accepted seventy of these enthusiastic young men. However, their service came at a huge cost: 128 were killed, with 337 wounded – a casualty rate of sixty-nine per cent.

Even though the 50th Division had an impressive war record from the Mediterranean, they had experienced such significant casualties that, as Sergeant Max Hearst noted, 'There were only about ninety originals left from the 5th East Yorkshires on their return from the Mediterranean in November 1943, a battalion that had served at Dunkirk, El Alamein and in Sicily.'[10] Another Dunkirk veteran in the 50th Division, Bill Cheall, with the 6th Green Howards in the 69th Brigade, reckoned there were 'two hundred or so' newcomers in his battalion of nine hundred as they set sail for France.[11]

What constituted a veteran (i.e. combat-hardened) division was a moot point. Around fifty per cent of the 50th Division were reckoned to be newcomers to battle, whereas for its 231st Brigade, Gold Beach would be their third amphibious assault. Under command of the dashing Roy Urquhart, it had already landed first in Sicily, then in southern Italy. When he was promoted to lead the 1st Airborne Division, destined to drop into Arnhem, Monty had brought in the one-eyed former Welsh Guardsman Sir Alexander Stanier. As the latter recalled, 'Monty came down to inspect my 183 Brigade. He asked me a lot of searching questions to which I felt I'd given many wrong answers. He was a bully and at the end of the day I was thoroughly gloomy. To my great surprise I received a telegram the next day offering me command of 231 Brigade. It was part of the Northumbrian Division but contained no Geordies at all, and was entirely made up of south coast regiments, who had just come back from a long stint in the Middle East and were pretty tired and battle-weary. Nevertheless, as soon as they knew what they would be doing, morale bucked up enormously and I am sure it helped that each battalion had a new CO at this time, though none of them had experience of landings.'[12]

When General Graham gathered his divisional officers in a cinema at the beginning of 1944, he had told them that Monty 'had been in grave doubt as to whether they or 51st Division should be one of the initial assault formations for the Second Front. In the end Monty had tossed a coin for it.'[13] Graham was 'delighted to say that 50th had won and would have the great honour of leading the invasion of Europe'. Whereupon – in the words of Major Peter Martin of the 2nd Cheshires (Vickers Machine-Gun Battalion for the division) – 'there was a colossal *boo* from all around the cinema'.[14] Elsewhere in the 50th, the response was equally muted, as a private in the 6th Durham Light Infantry remembered: 'We weren't happy about being used as the attacking troops on D-Day but there was nothing we could do about it.'[15] Another warrior mused, 'Why does it have to be us? They brought us all the way back for the landing. Haven't we done our share?'[16]

A signaller who joined the 50th Division in January 1944 found 'their pet hates were Montgomery and the 51st Highland Division; they reckoned the 51st took the credit for all the 50th's exploits'. Private Stanley Dwyer also noted the nicknames of the two divisions: the Highlanders called the 50th, whose badge was 'TT', the 'Town Titivators'; whereas the 51st were known by their rivals as the 'Highway Decorators' for plastering their HD divisional sign everywhere possible. Dwyer concluded, 'It was a surprise to me about Montgomery, but they [the 50th] were adamant that he was a rotter.'[17]

Brigadier Stanier's brigade would land two battalions abreast on the western sector, Jig. The 1st Hampshires and 1st Dorsets would lead; the 2nd Devons were to follow. Their task was to strike out west for Arromanches and link up with the Blue and Gray Division coming from Omaha. Each of these infantry battalions had a notional strength of 845 all ranks and ninety vehicles, giving infantry brigades, with a headquarters element, manpower of around 2,600 riflemen. However, for D-Day, Stanier commanded the much larger 231st Brigade Group, which included No. 10 Beach Group – based on the 6th Border Regiment (an infantry battalion), Royal Navy and RAF commandos, and including over a dozen company-sized attachments.

At Stanier's additional disposal were also two artillery battalions (regiments in Anglo-Canadian parlance), and one of tanks; assault engineer companies; a light anti-aircraft battery; two anti-tank batteries; as well as his brigade signals company; RASC (truck) company; REME field workshop (for vehicles); ordnance company (for repairing weapons); and RAMC field ambulance. The anti-tank batteries came from the Northumberland Hussars, the 50th Division's anti-tank regiment, equipped with towed cannon and American-made M10 'Wolverine' tank destroyers. These were turreted, tracked vehicles mounting a three-inch (76.2mm) gun on a Sherman hull – at a distance they resembled tanks; other M10s would accompany the 69th Brigade, and the thirty-two which landed would be extremely effective in supporting infantry companies during the day.[18] Stanier's 231st Brigade Group in effect amounted to a miniature army of nearly ten thousand.[19]

Stanier's armoured support comprised the Sherwood Rangers Yeomanry, a Nottinghamshire tank battalion, who would send in two squadrons of swimming tanks, the third arriving dry-shod later by LCT. The yeomanry originated in the Napoleonic era as volunteer cavalry – every county raised a regiment, but they were never used in action until the 1899–1901 Boer War, then the First World War. By D-Day all the yeomanries had lost their horses in favour of tanks or artillery pieces. Also attached was 47 Royal Marine Commando, who would land on the 231st's western flank with the specific task of striding out to capture Port-en-Bessin. The Neptune timetable noted that following Stanier into Asnelles would be Brigadier Ernest C. Pepper's 56th Independent Brigade, programmed to land from 1000 hours. They were temporarily attached to the division on account of General Graham's multitude of tasks, and had the particular mission of seizing Bayeux.

Along Gold's eastern half, King sector was the landing beach chosen for Brigadier Fergus Y. C. Knox's 69th Brigade. They would also attack on a two-battalion front, with the 6th Green Howards and 5th East Yorkshires leading, and the 7th Green Howards in reserve. The Howards' curious name dates from the eighteenth century, when infantry regiments were named after their colonel. In 1744, the British Army found itself with two units led by a Colonel Howard. Thus they were instead identified by their uniform facings, and Howard's Buffs and the Green Howards emerged, the latter recruiting from the large English county of Yorkshire.

Knox's brigade were supported by Sherman tanks of the 4th/7th Royal Dragoon Guards, a regular army cavalry unit that had surrendered its horses in favour of Sherman tanks. With him was No. 9 Beach Group, a similarly huge organisation built around the 2nd Hertfordshire Regiment, another infantry battalion. Once established ashore, a further wave would bring in Brigadier Ronald H. Senior's 151st (Durham Light Infantry) Brigade from 1000 hours.

The two armoured regiments of the Sherwood Rangers and the 4th/7th Dragoons would be joined by a third tank battalion, the 24th Lancers. Each fielded sixty-one Sherman tanks bearing 75mm or 76.2mm (seventeen-pounder) guns. Alongside them rode the 147th (Essex Yeomanry) Field Regiment, equipped with three batteries, each of eight 25-pounder 'Sexton' self-propelled guns.[20] Conveniently these were constructed on Sherman hulls, bringing a commonality of spare parts and far easier maintenance. Together these four units, with the 12th King's Royal Rifle Corps (a motorised infantry battalion), formed Brigadier Bernard Cracroft's 8th Armoured Brigade. However, modern warfare dictated decentralised deployments and these units tended to operate with a squadron of nineteen tanks and battery of eight guns supporting an infantry battalion, sometimes troops of four tanks and four guns working closely with infantry companies.[21] Montgomery's wildly optimistic plan aspired to see the 8th Armoured Brigade in the vicinity of Villers-Bocage – twenty-five miles to the south – by the end of D-Day. Its eventual capture by the 50th Division – by which time the town would be in total ruins – was not to materialise for two months, on 4 August.[22]

We have seen how the Northumbrian Division was substituted relatively late for the inexperienced 49th Division, who had spent much of their war garrisoning Iceland. Yet analysis suggests that only half of the 50th Division were Mediterranean combat veterans, with some of them

– as with the Big Red One – suffering from malaria. Thus Montgomery's switching of units here seems to have made little sense and caused huge resentment within both formations. The 49th Division would give a good account of themselves when they landed from 10 June onwards – certainly suggesting the switch had been unnecessary. In the 50th Division the resentment was expressed by a recorded one thousand AWOL (absent without leave) cases whilst the formation was assembling in the New Forest in May 1944.[23] Mostly these were soldiers simply wishing to see their families before going overseas again, and they voluntarily returned after a few days in time for the invasion. Given that the 50th had fought in France in 1940, left for the Middle East in March 1941, and had remained in the Mediterranean theatre as part of the Eighth Army until November 1943, this was entirely understandable – if not understood by Montgomery. An extreme example of this overseas longevity was the 1st Hampshires of the 231st Brigade. Since 1920 they had been 'policing the empire' in Turkey, India and Egypt before becoming part of the Malta Brigade in 1941. Their arrival 'home' in late 1943 was the first time this regular army battalion had set foot on English soil in *twenty-three years*.

With General Graham watching from his headquarters vessel HMS *Bulolo*, at 0500 hours the landing ships at anchor eight miles off the coast started to disgorge their passengers into smaller craft. Shortly afterwards, the air reverberated with the naval bombardment, as elsewhere. This and the previous aerial bombardments had left the defenders shaken but not silenced, with most munitions missing their intended targets. Thus the Allied infantry, engineers and armour were pretty much 'naked' when they landed – as on Omaha – and would have to spend valuable time contesting the shore – a task they had been assured would have been completed by the heavy bombers and the fleet. The attackers were aided by the generally poor visibility, exacerbated by much smoke drifting in the wind down from Omaha Beach, already under attack for an hour. Although the assault format was similar to that on the two American beaches, the timetable was different: the Anglo-Canadians took their cue from the arrangements at Sword Beach, where H-Hour was scheduled for 0725, in order for landing craft to negotiate a tricky sandbar on the rising tide.

The English Channel played havoc with the plan. During the crossing, five LCTs, a Rhino ferry and three Rhino tugs foundered in addition to a Landing Craft, Personnel (LCP) and seven little LCAs carrying spigot mortars to fire onto the beaches. While the 50th Division was launching closer to shore and the waves were not as rough, several landing craft still sank before reaching the shore. The loss of some of the Royal Engineers' specialised armour would inhibit their ability to clear lanes on the beaches. This was a major divergence in Anglo-Canadian tactics: much of the work of obstacle clearing and suppression of bunkers was done by engineers *inside* armoured vehicles. The few that landed more than proved their value: it was two specialist tanks that – separately – would destroy the bunkers, one at Le Hamel, the other at La Rivière, which were causing the main hold-ups on Gold. These so-called 'funnies' and the weaker German defences would contribute to the overwhelming of the guardians of Asnelles and Ver-sur-Mer. However, for the assault wave, their first hour was as tough as on Omaha.

Four teams, each of an officer and ten ratings, of Royal Navy frogmen from Landing Craft, Obstacle Clearance Units (LCOCU) landed in the first wave to open up channels through the rows of beach obstructions, two for Jig and the remaining pair to King. Clad in wetsuits with diving apparatus and bearing explosives, they were to destroy obstructions between the ten-foot- and four-foot-six marks. Royal Marine Sergeant Peter Jones recalled swimming into a maze of steel pylons, gates and hedgehogs, and finding twelve major obstacles in the thirty-yard gap he had to blow, some of them fourteen feet long.[24] By the end of the day, 2,500 obstacles had been cleared by the frogmen at the remarkably low cost of only Acting Leading Seaman Allister Austin being killed and several other divers wounded.[25] Above the four-foot-six mark, two 145-man field companies of Royal Engineers took over the task up to and over dry land. Five officers and 140 men of the 73rd Field Company dealt with the wood, concrete and metal barriers on Jig, while the 280th Company did the same on King. However, both LCOCUs and field companies were challenged by the weather and hostile fire, which caused casualties and pushed the surf up the sands faster than anticipated. On Jig, two LCTs carrying the 73rd Engineers were hit and at least one engineer vehicle drowned, but still the engineers managed to open at least one passage on each sector of Gold within the first hour.

With them came the armoured engineer vehicles of the 82nd Assault Squadron, bound for Jig, with the 81st Squadron heading for King. These comprised armoured bulldozers, Crocodiles, Petards, Bobbin and bridge-laying tanks – the exact mix had been worked out beforehand to match the terrain they would assault. Battened down and waterproofed in, just driving the Churchill AVREs was hazardous enough, as R. J. Mellen recalled: 'We bottomed out in about six feet of water which meant my only way of seeing, via the periscope, was blocked by seawater.' He was coaxed ashore by his commander, head out of the turret, when 'suddenly my periscope began to clear and I could see a sandy beach dotted with gun emplacements and tank traps. There was a babble of shouts from the crew. We had arrived.'[26]

However, the 82nd's squadron commander, Major H. G. A. Elphinstone, was killed and the combined firepower of the three 75mm guns at WN39 and WN37 knocked out at least six of his tanks and one LCT, with mines accounting for another three armoured vehicles. The wind and current also pushed some of the 82nd Engineer Squadron eastwards, so they landed dispersed along a front of over a mile. Their comrades of the 81st Squadron landing at King were fortunate to land in a more compact group, and better able to offer one another mutual support.[27] They were accompanied on Jig by Crabs (Sherman flail mine-clearing tanks) of 'B' Squadron, Westminster Dragoons, and by 'C' Squadron at King. All the armour would work with the dismounted engineers to tow obstructions out of the way, clear minefields, cross ditches and suppress pillboxes. Other armour for Jig appeared in the shape of Royal Marines-manned Centaur tanks fitted with a 95mm gun, but of the ten that should have arrived, the angry sea and even angrier Germans together sank five.

The waves in the 50th Division's sector were judged too rough and their supporting DD tanks were not launched two miles out as planned, but within a few hundred yards of the shore. Each beach – Jig and King – was allocated two squadrons of swimming tanks to accompany the initial infantry assault, but even so, the Sherwood Rangers Yeomanry lost eight heading for Jig in support of the 231st Brigade, including that of Lieutenant Stuart Hills. Seven hundred yards offshore, Hills watched

> two of the flails brewing up just to my front, and I could not help wondering what had caused them to catch fire, and whether our tanks would meet the same fate. Sure enough the shots soon came. Without more ado I gave my driver the order to *go*, and down the ramp we went. As soon as we hit the water I knew something was very wrong. The screen was very flimsy in the rough sea and water poured in everywhere. Soon I was giving the order to bail out. Corporal Footitt pressed the

button on our rubber dinghy which inflated automatically. I scrambled inside the turret to get my map case, but we were going down so fast I didn't have time to retrieve it. I followed Troopers Reddish and Storey over the side and a few seconds later our tank disappeared into the murky depths.[28]

From the destroyer HMS *Jervis*, its highly experienced captain – a veteran of both Malta and Arctic convoys – Lieutenant Commander Roger Hill, noticed 'the flotillas of landing craft coming in, and as we watched, they formed in line abreast and rushed for the surf line of the beach; at 0730 hours the swimming tanks went out from their landing craft; then suddenly we saw them on the beach, like little models – moving forward, stopping, firing, and moving forward again.'[29] LCTs carried Roly-Poly cylinders of matting which the armoured crews were meant to lay from their craft to the shore and over the sand.

Lieutenant Alastair Morrison, commanding the 4th Troop of 'A' Squadron, 4th/7th Dragoon Guards, recalled that just before setting sail from England a Royal Engineers motor barge came alongside his LCT

> with an officer, fifteen Sappers and a vast five-ton coil of beach matting. As the Sappers feverously worked away installing this contraption, cutting out hunks of the landing craft just behind the ramp and welding on the mat, the officer collected all the tank crews together. 'This', he said, 'is the Roly-Poly beach mat. As soon as you hit the beach, two men are to run forward and unroll the mat up the beach.' And with that rather terse instruction, he left. Our tank crews were sceptical and that night my troopers set about the mat. After a brief resistance it disappeared overboard with a huge splash to cheers from the soldiers.[30]

As the 50th Division After Action Report observed, those Roly-Polys taken to France were generally a waste of time, the vicious surf wrenching them away from those detailed to unwind them.

As elsewhere, self-propelled guns in landing craft would contribute to the drenching fire of warships and rocket craft during the final run-in. In the case of Gold, this was provided by the tracked 25-pounder 'Sextons' of the 86th (Hertfordshire Yeomanry) and 90th (City of London) Field Regiments; the towed 25-pounders of the division's 74th and 124th Northumbrian Field Regiments would not land till later.[31] There is little evidence of the drenching fire – launched from small craft bobbing about in fierce waves – having any effect on the defenders. In addition, the 'Sextons' of the 147th Field Regiment (of the 8th Armoured Brigade) should have put fire down on Jig, but their guiding patrol boat broke down. Without professional help in their navigation, the 147th's gunners instead tagged along with the 90th Field Regiment, augmenting their fires onto La Rivière. This meant that the landing-craft-borne artillery did not engage the defences at Le Hamel at all. Not that offshore fire would have made a difference: the thickness of the concrete encasing the WN37 bunker rendered its 75mm gun proofed against everything but a very localised attack.

The infantry assault on Jig sector did not go to plan. Lieutenant Geoffrey Picot, a young officer with the 1st Hampshire, explained that 'nearly everything went wrong for the Hampshires'.[32] Tim Dudley-Ward, in the Assault Pioneer Platoon of Support Company, later wrote home:

> I don't know if you want to hear anything of my short stay in France? To begin with, they nearly drowned us by landing too far out. We were wearing waders up to our armpits and as we dashed off the boat, water just surged over us. As a result the damn things got full of water and together with the equipment and a strong tide we had a rough time for a couple of minutes. I just cut everything loose and swam for it. When the tide went out, we salvaged our guns and got cracking on cleaning them up.[33]

Both 'A' and 'C' Companies were soon pinned down on the beach by fire from pillboxes unscathed from the bombardments. Most of their radios had been immersed in the surf or damaged on the beach, so contact with the offshore fleet was broken, meaning no shelling could be directed onto the offending German positions.

Lieutenant Alan Norman of 'A' Company was aware that many of the veterans in his platoon were taking Mepecrine for the malaria they had contracted in Sicily, while seasickness had made one of his men 'so ill we had to carry his equipment, I carried his Bangalore torpedo and we dragged him up the beach by his epaulettes'.[34] It was at this stage, RN frogman Sergeant Jones recalled, that an infantry landing craft struck a mine. Like a slow-motion cartoon, 'the men, standing to attention, shot up into the air as though lifted by a water spout ... at the top of the spout, bodies and parts of bodies spread like drops of water'.[35] Trooper Joe Minogue observed from his Westminster Dragoons flail tank:

The scene on the beach is etched so deeply in my mind that I can hear it, feel it, smell it in fine focus, so many years after the events of that summer day. It was a sobering sight as the Hampshires left their craft. German machine-guns must have been firing along fixed lines, for men were dropping while still in the shallow water, to be dragged forward by their mates and left on the sand, while their comrades ran on in a purposeful steady jog-trot, which betrayed no sign of panic.[36]

The Hampshires' CO, the punchy David Nelson-Smith who insisted on landing with the first wave, was soon injured, and Majors Martin and Baines, his second in command and 'A' Company commander, were killed almost immediately. Instead, David Warren, commanding 'C' Company, took over, recollecting, 'We landed a good two or three hundred yards east from where we should have been.' His craft hit a sandbank, 'we went into four or five feet of water and everyone was carrying a lot of equipment and ammunition, so quite a few of the shorter men drowned'. Warren then encountered the twice-wounded Nelson-Smith, who shouted to him, 'You'll have to take over, I can't go on', as he was stretchered away.[37] 'B' Company Commander Antony Mott recalled disembarking into an LCA from HMS *Empire Crossbow* and thought the battalion's challenges were exacerbated by the weight of the kit, ammunition and extra equipment his men had to carry. 'Wading through the surf, my watch stopped at 0748 hours, my map case had floated away, my binoculars were misty and for all I knew my Sten would not work. I heard a bang and a steel helmet flew up in the air.'[38]

Seeing the Germans 'on top of the sea wall chucking hand grenades over the top onto our men below just like Mediaeval siege warfare', Warren reorganised the companies, abandoned the attack on strongpoint WN37, and instead moved his men left in an assault on the less formidable WN36 at the eastern edge of the beach. Major Dick Gosling, commanding the artillery observer parties, had landed with Nelson-Smith and initially thought Jig beach pleasantly quiet, until the little fountains of sand at his feet and 'swarm of angry bees overhead' alerted him to the fact that he was under machine-gun fire for the first time in his military career. He was soon wounded, and while waiting medical evacuation translated a letter he found addressed to a German soldier from a French girl named Madeleine, arranging to meet him on the evening of 6 June – an assignation Gosling felt pleased to have interrupted.[39] The fury of WN37's defence persuaded the beachmaster for

Jig, Lieutenant Commander Brian Whinney, RN, to suspend landings in his sector and order landing craft east to King, also stopping the clearance of obstacles because 'with the heavy surf and enemy fire it was too great a risk for the personnel concerned'.[40]

On the Hampshires' left, along the eastern end of Jig, and preceded by flail tanks, the 1st Dorsets stormed – or rather dragged themselves – ashore. Frank Wiltshire disembarked from HMS *Empire Spearhead* into an LCA then jumped into about seven feet of water, having to jettison his mortar baseplate, which weighed over fifty pounds, in preference to drowning. Of six weapons in the Dorsets' three-inch Mortar Platoon, five were lost in the landing and Wiltshire recalled, 'Eventually we managed to assemble one mortar out of six. I got it in a firing position but the barrel was full of sand and water because someone had trailed it along the beach. After seeing my friends killed and injured around me, I thought it would be my turn at any moment.'[41] They swiftly lost 'A' Company's commander, its CSM and a platoon leader, but finding the position of WN36 already destroyed, the Dorsets moved inland, whereupon the Hampshires used the penetration to outflank Le Hamel and attack it from behind.[42] This took much of the day, for at 1425 hours, Sir Alexander Stanier of 231st Brigade was informed that 'stiff fighting for Le Hamel continued, with a squadron of the Sherwood Rangers pinned down, while a company of Hampshires were working round to the rear'.[43]

Meanwhile, some forward elements of the follow-on 56th Brigade had started to land two hours ahead of the main body, and immediately became entangled in the battle for Le Hamel. Les 'Titch' Holden, with the Mortar Platoon of the 2nd Essex, had been about to drive his waterproofed jeep ashore when 'The ship next to us received a direct hit from Le Hamel. It went up in smoke and flames. A sailor from a deck above crashed down, dead, behind my Jeep.' Then they hit a mine. As fast as he could, Holden drove down the ramp. 'Water came up to my armpits. My passengers stood up to avoid the angry sea. We were making good progress, but it was short-lived. A massive wave, funnelling its way between the ships, broke over the Jeep washing my team-mates overboard. The wave receded, carrying the Jeep and me out to sea, ignominiously behind the landing craft.' Having lost all their kit and equipment, on the beach Holden soon learned 'when someone said "Down!" you went down, no matter what lay ahead. Dead and wounded lay everywhere. Le Hamel gunfire raked the beach; bullets that did not find their target sent sprays of sand into the air.'[44]

To subdue the main Le Hamel bunker, the 1st Hampshires enlisted the help of the sole surviving Churchill AVRE of the 82nd Assault Squadron, 'armed with a 290mm Petard mortar looking like a short length of wicked looking drainpipe' that fired a forty-pound projectile. Lance Sergeant Bert Scaife directed his tank up to the rear of the WN37 bunker at Le Hamel and his gunner 'dropped a petard through the back door which completely shattered the interior, and as a result many prisoners were taken'. Five Sherwood Rangers tanks supported the action with their 75mm guns and Major David Warren, whose 'C' Company had remained behind to mop up Le Hamel, found the defenders who emerged 'were Poles, Czechs or Russians and a few Germans, and though they gave us a pretty rough time, they caved in pretty quickly'.[45] Soon after, Scaife loosed off another petard at a different part of the sanatorium complex causing trouble. 'It hit just above the front door and the building collapsed like a pack of cards, spilling the defenders with their machine-guns, anti-tank weapons and an avalanche of bricks into the courtyard.'[46] It is a tribute to the fortress-building expertise of the Wehrmacht as well as the determination of the defenders that Le Hamel fell only at 1700 hours.[47]

Lieutenant Pat Blamey, RNVR, commanding an LCT, recalled the Germans he saw 'were completely shattered by the bombardment. They appeared to be Mongolians.'[48] Amongst the three-man Forward Observation Bombardment (FOB) party for HMS *Belfast* was Able Seaman Ronald Seaborne, who had landed further east, intending to direct the fire of his cruiser. Between La Rivière and Crépon they were confronted by three men in German uniform. Seaborne expected to be frogmarched to a Wehrmacht POW camp, but instead 'they raised their hands and by a mixture of French, German and English, I learned that they were Russians'. Later they took another eight prisoners including five more Russians, and 'three who hotly denied being Russian – they were Lithuanians who hated the Russians just as much they did the Germans'.[49]

The Oxford-educated Dr Chris W. Bartley was serving with an RAMC detachment aboard an LST 'as a sort of seaborne field ambulance attached to 231st Brigade' and remembered his surprise 'that among the early casualties and more seriously wounded were a number of foreigners, some clearly of Mongolian origin. They had hunted, scared expressions, and were unbelievably grateful for their lives being spared, their injuries being attended to and for the comfort of a single cigarette.'[50]

The reserve battalion, the 2nd Devons, began landing from HMS *Glenroy*'s LCAs at 0705. In the words of their CO, Lieutenant Colonel Cosmo Nevill, 'We expected to see a nice clear beach. A very different picture greeted us. The beach was covered with swarms of troops lying flat on their faces, ostrich-like, trying to make as small a target of themselves as possible. All was not well.'[51] One of 'B' Company's landing craft surged over Major Howard, the company commander, who had just disembarked with his sergeant major – crushing but not killing the pair. Initially, the Devons could not penetrate the concertina wire because their Bangalore torpedo fuses were too wet to ignite, and they had few working radios due to their dunking in seawater. Nevill tried to keep his battalion east of the troublesome Le Hamel and started to move inland to Ryes, but shortly afterwards, the commander of 'C' Company was killed and that of 'D' Company wounded. Within half an hour of landing, Lieutenant Colonel Nevill had lost three of his majors, and several other officers and senior NCOs besides.[52]

Brigadier Stanier, mindful that during rehearsals Monty had chided him for being 'too far back', brought his 231st Brigade headquarters ashore at 0830 hours from the frigate HMS *Nith*, from where he had been monitoring the landing. They left to the cheers of the frigate's crew, but struck a sandbank then drifted onto a mine which ripped a hole in their craft's side, destroying every vehicle except a single jeep.[53] This was driven by his interpreter, Lieutenant Charles Hargrove, son of an English journalist and French mother. He had just graduated from Cambridge and was destined to become – in the words of Général de Gaulle – 'Monsieur Hargrove *du Times*', covering French affairs for the British newspaper, eventually settling in Paris. 'As soon as I was on the beach', recollected Hargrove of D-Day, 'the brigadier told me I was his driver for the day having the only serviceable jeep – although I had only received my driving licence the week before – and he later admitted that being driven around by me was more alarming than our assault landing.'[54]

In the brigadier's wake followed Major Peter Johnson with the 200th Field Ambulance, Royal Army Medical Corps, intent on setting up a much needed dressing station on the beach: 'Nowhere to set up my show. Dotted everywhere were sodden bundles of Hampshires, Devons and Dorsets that had led the infantry spearhead. Tanks still burning, LCTs blown up by mines, houses afire, craters, smells, *Achtung Minen!* signs with skulls and crossbones. And so many, many wounded and nowhere to put them.' He set up on a road verge, three feet wide, bordered by traffic on one side and a minefield on the other.[55]

Two hours behind schedule – as much because of the sea state as the Germans – the main body of the 56th Brigade, with the self-propelled 'Sextons' of the 147th (Essex Yeomanry) Field Regiment, started to land on Jig from about noon. They were brought in by Canadian LCIs of the 264th RCN flotilla, which included three US Navy craft. Gunner Charles Wilson with the Essex Yeomanry remembered, 'We hit two mines. They didn't stop us, although our ramp was damaged and an officer standing on it killed. The first man off was a sergeant in full kit. He disappeared like a stone in six feet of water. The beach was strewn with wreckage, a blazing tank, bundles of blankets and kit, bodies and bits of bodies. One bloke near me was blown in half by a shell and his lower part collapsed in a bloody heap in the sand.'[56] Another gunner in the same regiment, Frank Topping, recalled that 'we had not travelled many yards from the beach when an anti-tank gun opened up on one side and we received an armour-piercing shell in the engine. We all bailed out and lay with the infantry at the side of the road. After hitting two other tanks, it was knocked out by one of our own guns firing over open sights.'[57]

With 56th Brigade, Lieutenant Nick Somerville, the twenty-year-old intelligence officer of the 2nd South Wales Borderers, was waiting offshore to be called in when the beach was free. He had been brought up on his father's tales of landing at Gallipoli in 1915. The younger Somerville recalled his men singing hymns, while his landing craft 'wallowed like a snorting hippo making for the beach. We grounded with a judder, the ramp went down and Major Martin, 'D' Company commander, bellowed, "24th of Foot, follow me!" – and promptly disappeared with his bicycle in about ten feet of water. All our tension and nerves evaporated as everyone roared with laughter at the major's misfortune. The rest of us were more circumspect and clung to a lifeline that two sailors then connected to the shore, but still found ourselves up to our necks in the cold, choppy surf, clutching our bicycles and holding weapons above our heads.'[58]

The 2nd Glosters – last in France in May 1940 – landed 'at 1158 hours', noted their war diary. 'As we moved in we began to see evidence of the fighting for the beaches. There were wrecked landing craft, drowned vehicles, the odd disabled tank, floating pieces of equipment, but not on the scale, I think, most of us had expected'. The writer was reflecting the experiences of the more senior members of the battalion who had come out from Dunkirk exactly four years earlier amid precisely the same detritus. They moved up from the beach to Mont-Fleury, observing 'German bodies flung into the trees from the bombardment' – the first sight of death for the youngsters. That the unit had scores to settle was very evident, as the same document blandly recorded, 'Seventeen Germans were flushed out by 'C' Company, and as they ran away down the road, they were pursued and shot by Sergeant Davies.'[59]

The fortunes of the 231st Brigade had turned by mid-afternoon with tanks of the Sherwood Rangers Yeomanry signalling at 1425 that they had captured the two 75mm guns in WN39 on the western cliffs at Saint-Côme. One of the offending field pieces taken was found to have fired some 124 rounds at Jig beach and had undoubtedly caused some of the chaos usually attributed to Le Hamel alone. Afterwards, it was assessed that the naval bombardment had scored over a hundred near misses on the concrete casemates, but only one direct hit, which had not been lethal. With these suppressed, shortly after, Lieutenant Colonel Nevill's 2nd Devons advanced inland to tackle the village of Ryes, reported to Generalleutnant Kraiss as being captured at 1638. Three hours later, 'D' Company of the Hampshires also recorded moving up to seize the radar station just beyond the 75mm bunkers on the clifftops at Saint-Côme, where they took forty prisoners.

Later the Hampshire men cleared Arromanches, which they managed with no casualties at all, the town being declared clear of Germans at 2100 hours and 'full of French people. Flowers came out with Tricolours and Union Jacks.'[60] This was no mean feat, as the town possessed four separate *Widerstandsnester*; they included WN44, another large 105mm bunker covering the town from the eastern heights, complemented by WN45 on the western heights with a 47mm cannon, but the garrison had lost the will to resist or had simply melted away. However, the day had cost the Hampshires 182 casualties, including sixty-four killed; the 1st Dorsets recorded losses of 128, including fourteen officers, and the 2nd Devons reported another eighty killed, wounded or missing.[61]

The 1st Dorsets' chaplain, the Reverend Robert Watt, recorded being out on a burial patrol, looking for his dead, when surrounded by several dozen Germans. Before he could raise his hands in defeat, their officer surrendered the group to *him*. Watt recalled later having to conduct one of his first field burials, but being so tired himself, he slipped and fell into the grave.[62] The brigade's armoured support had suffered, too: Major

Peter Selerie, one of the Sherwood Rangers squadron commanders, noted that by the end of the day only five of his squadron's nineteen original tanks were still mobile. With the 231st Brigade firm in a series of villages protecting the division's western flank, Brigadier Stanier's interpreter, Lieutenant Hargrove, recollected, 'On our first night we camped in the grounds of the château at Saint-Côme-de-Fresné. I went to the big house for water, but the elderly spinster had barricaded herself inside "terrified of being raped by the rough British soldiers".'[63]

Behind him, 56th Brigade had thrust through Jig beach, heading for Bayeux. At about midday, as Nick Somerville of the South Wales Borderers was pedalling inland, his column of men was fired at by a German gun from the high ground at Meuvaines. As Somerville glanced back, he saw a solid shot remove the head of the cyclist behind him. This position had been held by some of the 441st *Ost-Bataillon*, but as Generalleutnant Richter asserted, 'they ran as soon as they could and we could not stop them'. This is not altogether true, as some defended Le Hamel and La Rivière with great spirit, and Richter may have been trying to cover up his own lacklustre performance. Be that as it may, the defences on the important Meuvaines ridge had crumbled by 1300 hours, because at that hour Major General Graham set up his tactical divisional HQ in the village.

Meanwhile, with too few exits off Jig beach and the high tide diminishing the real estate, serious congestion developed with men and vehicles queuing to move inland. By this stage, German artillery and mortar fire was sporadic, otherwise hundreds could have been felled within minutes. Lieutenant Colonel R. W. Craddock of the 2nd South Wales Borderers grew so impatient that he ordered his men across what he assessed as a dummy minefield. They crossed with no casualties and thereafter regarded '*Achtung Minen!*' signs with 'cautious scepticism', but their pace increased accordingly. By 2130, the 2nd Essex had reached Saint-Sulpice, less than a mile north-east of Bayeux; the South Wales Borderers took Vaux-sur-Aure, the same distance north, at midnight; while the 2nd Glosters entered Magny – between the two former villages, at a similar hour, cohabiting with Brigadier Pepper and 56th Brigade headquarters, whose formation now ringed the north of the city. For some units, though nerve-wracking and tiring, D-Day had been far gentler than they had had any right to expect. The 2nd South Wales Borderers, for example, lost an astonishing four men killed and twenty wounded from a battalion of over nine hundred.[64]

Also landing with 231st Brigade, but having their own personal war to fight, was 47 Royal Marine Commando. At 420 men, they were – like all such units – half the strength of an infantry battalion, yet expected to match its fighting power, through their fitness, training and initiative. Lieutenant Colonel Cecil F. Phillips had studied his objective, Port-en-Bessin, and decided to attack it from the landward side, where the defences were weaker, his task being code-named Operation Aubery. He possessed five troops of sixty-three men, a mortar and machine-gun troop, as well as transport and headquarters elements, and confidently expected to land on Jig at 0925, arriving at Port-en-Bessin around 1300 hours.

The weather and German obstacles took their toll, sinking five of the fourteen LCAs from HMS *Prinses Josephine Charlotte* and SS *Victoria*, and drowning or wounding seventy-six men before they even reached the shore, along with much equipment. Only one landing craft ever made it back to either mother ship. Ted Battley with 'B' Troop recalled, 'The whole beach was covered with stranded landing craft and wrecked vehicles. Our coxswain headed for a gap, but the craft hit a spike and we got stuck there. We could not lower the ramp so we went over the side.'[65] Another bemoaned, 'Years I'd been practising for this, and minutes short of the objective, the f**king boat sinks.' None of Corporal Gordon Tye's group of LCAs reached the shore: 'They all got shelled or holed. We were fired on all day long. Sniper fire and mortars. I've got to give them their due, the Germans were very good mortar men. They could put their bombs on a sixpence.'[66]

Marine Frank Wright remembered catching 'glimpses of the shore as the boat's stern lifted on the swell. Black-looking tanks crawled along the yellow sand like squat stag beetles. One was standing still and burning with a hot transparent red flame. Figures were scurrying to and fro.'[67] Augmenting their stocks with as many captured German weapons as they could find, Major P. M. 'Paddy' Donnell temporarily took charge until Colonel Phillips, who had got separated amidst the foundering LCAs, appeared at 1400.

They set off at a brisk pace into a curious countryside, mused Ted Battley. One moment a farmer was seen ploughing a field with his two horses as though the invasion was a figment of someone's imagination, almost a scene from the nearby Bayeux Tapestry. The next, the commandos were diving into cover as convoys of German trucks drove past. Their trek, he thought, was less of a march and more like a cautious rural walk at times.[68] Despite their best efforts, continuous skirmishes and road blocks delayed the arrival of 47 Commando until 2230 hours, too late to launch an attack on their objective of Port-en-Bessin. They would attack the following day and eventually capture the town, and two flak ships moored in the little harbour, after a bitter battle lasting thirty-six hours, by which time they had suffered 136 casualties – one third of their strength.

On the dot of H-Hour, under the gaze of the La Rivière strongpoint WN33 on King Beach, 69th Brigade's assaulting companies landed. As in the west, these men from the 6th Green Howards and 5th East Yorks arrived before the DD Shermans of the 4th/7th Dragoon Guards. It was only on board their landing craft that Sherman crewman Trooper Austin Baker was told where they were going: 'It turned out to be a little place between Caen and Arromanches called La Rivière. Major Barker read out messages from Eisenhower and Montgomery and told us that he personally thought we should all be very honoured to be in on this affair. I think most of us felt that we could have stood the disgrace of being left out of it.' As they approached King Red, he saw 'a navy motorboat drifting past with a dead sailor lying across the foredeck. I'd never seen anybody dead before; the sea was still rough and I saw several lorries overturn in the breakers.'[69]

Aware of the sea state, while conning his Sherman-laden LCT towards King, Lieutenant Jim Ruffell had decided 'There was no doubt in my mind that to launch these crack troops [the DD tanks] would have had even worse results than the Charge of the Light Brigade at Balaclava' – an action that would save many lives.[70] Ever grateful was Lieutenant Robert Ford, by then the intelligence officer, whose tank we have already encountered sinking with the rest of his crew during the Smash rehearsal in Studland Bay. The Shermans were taken to within five to seven hundred yards of the shore, then released. Even so, the 4th/7th still lost five tanks to the surf during their final approach. Major Jo Gullet, an Australian officer serving with the 6th Green Howards, remembered them: 'Some tanks had been fitted with giant kapok lifebelts and propellers. They floated in the water, and rolling and heaving, clumsily joined us, heading for the shore.'[71]

Brigadier Knox, aboard the frigate HMS *Kingsmill*, noted how 'land-marks on the coast soon became obliterated by vast clouds of dust and smoke rising from the coastal belt. The terrific pounding from cruisers, destroyers and smaller supporting craft as well as from aircraft, rose to a crescendo immediately before H-Hour, and very little enemy battery fire was directed at the larger ships now lying off shore'.[72] With the swimming tanks launched late on both Gold beaches, the assault troops, LCOCU frogmen and engineers attached to both brigades were thus without armoured support for the first half hour, excepting the Royal Engineers' AVREs and flails of the Westminster Dragoons.[73]

Sub-Lieutenant Dick Boustred aboard *LCT-884* remembered the eighty-eight gun at La-Rivière as a 'nasty little German pillbox away to our left which was doing a fair bit of damage. An LCM passing our stern received a direct hit on his port quarter, reared up, and went down like a stone. The next one must have been carrying petrol, and went up in a sheet of flame'.[74] Captain Roger Bell of 'C' Squadron, Westminster Dragoons, landed from *LCT-930* at H-Hour with a selection of engineer armoured vehicles that comprised the most easterly breaching team for King. These included an AVRE pushing a Roly-Poly mat; an AVRE Bobbin scheduled to lay another mat up the beach; two Sherman flails; an AVRE with a bundle of logs (fascine) for filling gaps; and an armoured D7 bulldozer – and these armoured breaching teams would be replicated up and down Gold, and on Juno and Sword.

Captain Bell and the engineers landed in conjunction with the 5th East Yorks, who managed to cross their beach, despite murderous fire from WN33, which had been missed by the pre-invasion bombardment. The La Rivière bunker was supported by a 50mm anti-tank cannon and machine guns, under Oberleutnant Hans-Gerhard Lilloch, which directed fearsome punishment onto the landing craft bearing the East Yorks and their men wading ashore. Both 'C' and 'D' Company commanders were hit, three other officers killed and eighty-five other ranks killed or wounded. However, lack of numbers and fewer German weapons made a difference, and the attackers were able to reach the sand and breach the barbed wire and minefield beyond to attack the four-gun battery of Mont-Fleury, 1,000 yards inland.

Code-named WN35a, it contained four powerful ex-Russian 122mm guns, but only one of its four concrete casemates had been completed and the aerial bombing and fleet gunfire from the cruisers *Belfast* and *Orion* had made a difference here: the demoralised battery commander shot himself as he saw the 'Tommies' approaching his position; thirty others chose the less drastic option of surrender. We will revisit Mont-Fleury with the 6th Green Howards in a moment, but suicide or surrender was the last thing on the mind of Hauptmann Gustav-Adolf Lutz on the coast, who urged his men to ever-swifter activity along the sea wall and within the WN33 strongpoint. They and a neighbouring 50mm below the Mont-Fleury lighthouse succeeded in pinning down engineers of the 280th Field Company and 5th East Yorkshires' 'C' and 'D' Companies – but only briefly.[75]

On landing, Captain Bell's Sherman flail had halted momentarily on the sand, when a neighbouring Churchill AVRE took a direct hit from the 'nasty German pillbox' and exploded, raining bodies and tank parts in a wide radius. When a second loud clang sounded against their own hull, Bell and his crew feared the worst – that they, too, had suffered a mortal blow. Bell was relieved to report to his fellow crew members that it was in fact the Churchill's flaming engine that had struck their rear deck – but it was an indication of the violence of the eruption. The ferocious blast was caused by the large amount of demolition charges the tank was carrying, which also wiped out a company HQ nearby, killing or wounding its major, his second in command and three platoon leaders. A second AVRE was soon in flames, but one of Bell's crew had spotted the muzzle flash of the offender. 'Eighty-eight; pillbox; eleven o'clock; armour-piercing; engage!' Bell hastily ordered, for the 75mm main weapon of their mine-clearing tank could still function if the rotating flails were not in action. In a superb piece of shooting, they managed to put two rounds through the tiny embrasure and moved on, unaware they had destroyed the troublesome gun.

Their tank had soon flailed through a minefield, and as Bell pulled the pin on a green smoke grenade to indicate a cleared passage, it fell out of his hands into the turret floor. He scrabbled around to retrieve it, but emerged stained all over a vivid emerald green, and remained so for the next few days, but his bunker-busting exploit had just earned him a Military Cross.[76] With the third squadron of the 4th/7th Dragoon Guards ashore, by around 1100 hours the defence completely collapsed as the last forty-two Germans with the 7th Company of the 736th *Grenadier-Regiment* raised their hands – though Hauptmann Roth's Russians from the 441st *Ost-Bataillon* had for the most part already decamped.

Major Gullet had witnessed the non-swimming 4th/7th Shermans wading ashore, completely waterproofed.

They rolled straight down the ramps onto the seabed. We could see little of them but their breathing snorkels and the bubbles of their exhausts. As the water shallowed, turrets appeared, then the bereted heads of their commanders opening their hatches; next the dripping gun and finally the body of the tank. Once ashore, commanders blew off their waterproofing which had been lined with a cordtex detonating fuse. This went off with a sharp crack, and the tanks swung their guns to make sure the traversing mechanism was clear, like a spaniel shaking its ears after leaving water.[77]

Meanwhile, Robin Hastings' 6th Green Howards had landed west of the La Rivière bunker, catching some of its venom as they made their way inland. The Stowe- and Oxford-educated Hastings was something of a rising star, who had already won a Military Cross and two mentions in despatches when he took over his battalion aged just twenty-six. He would go on to be awarded two DSOs and an OBE by the war's end.[78] As they beached, Hastings recalled, 'There was no danger of being trampled in the rush. No one moved: all stared at the sea which came right up into the craft. The only thing was for me to test the depth of the water for all to see. Very gradually I sat down, like a Brighton paddler, and dangled my feet over the edge. The water came up to my knees. Confidently, I rose to my feet and set off up the beach.'[79]

Major Henry 'Jo' Gullet had earlier watched the swimming tanks. The son of an Australian cabinet minister, and a former *Melbourne Herald* journalist, Gullet had already won an MC fighting the Japanese in New Guinea. Now it was the Germans' turn. He had volunteered for the assault wave, landing with Hastings' battalion, and recalled that he did not even get his feet wet: 'The pillboxes had fallen and our leading companies were mustering up the prisoners, a motley collection, mostly Russians. Some were big and blond, but there were many Mongol types also, nasty-looking men. We found out afterwards they had no idea where they were, but had been conned and bullied into manning the defences.'

Gullet took out his intelligence photographs to orient himself and was pleased to find they tallied exactly with the terrain before him. 'There was the white house with the circular drive, and beyond, on the little ridge, were the tall trees that hid a German field battery, our first objective.'[80] These were the 122mm guns of the Mont-Fleury battery whose commander had just shot himself, above the house that Gullet had noticed in his aerial photographs, which the 6th Green Howards had taken to calling 'Lavatory-pan Villa' – because on the aerial images, its white circular drive seemed to resemble a toilet bowl.[81]

It was to this battery that the Green Howards' 'D' Company made their way, led by Major Ronnie Lofthouse, with his very able company sergeant major, Stan Hollis. During the retreat to Dunkirk in 1940, the latter had come across a street in Lille where civilians lay slaughtered by German soldiers; ever since, he had sworn revenge. Serving with the Eighth Army in North Africa and Sicily, he had counted ninety personal kills and had been recommended for, but did not receive, a Distinguished Conduct Medal for his leadership during the battle for Primosole Bridge, south of Catania, during the Sicilian campaign. His CO described him as 'a straightforward Yorkshireman keen on horse-racing, personally dedicated to winning the war'.[82] In the run ashore, Hollis squeezed off several magazines of Lewis-gun ammunition at a menacing-looking bunker on the shore. Bracing himself to land, he gripped the gun's hot barrel, giving himself 'a stupid, self-inflicted wound'.

One of his colleagues, Sergeant 'Ruffy' Hill in the 16th Platoon was killed straight away when he leapt ashore only to have his landing craft literally run over him. On landing, Hollis was somewhat abashed to find his 'bunker' was in fact a deserted shelter for passengers waiting for the little narrow-gauge train that formerly ran holidaymakers along the shore. Amidst the smoke, hostile fire and battle noise Hollis recalled noticing a line of birds quietly sitting on some barbed wire a few feet away. 'Private Mullaly followed my gaze and observed, "No bloody wonder, Sergeant-Major. There's no bloody room for them in the air."'[83]

About level with 'Lavatory-pan Villa', as Lofthouse and Hollis started to inspect one of Mont-Fleury's bunkers, they came under machine-gun fire from some lurking grenadiers whom their own forward companies had overlooked. Seeing them about to shoot the Green Howards from behind, Hollis didn't hesitate, and fired his Sten, charged the position, emptied his weapon through the firing slit, lay on top of the pillbox and posted a grenade into the embrasure as well. Several dazed and wounded Germans emerged, but Hollis was already on his way down a trench to a second pillbox that he had seen. The one-man army was too much for this other blockhouse, which promptly surrendered. Hollis took over twenty-five prisoners and saved 'D' Company from extinction by flanking fire. The WN35a battery as a whole was firmly in the battalion's hands by 0945 hours. Charles Hill of 'D' Company remembered the gunners emerging, 'crying, and all had their family photographs spread out.'[84]

With his two assault brigades, the 231st and 69th, ashore, though not as far inland as he had planned, at about 1000 hours Major General Graham aboard HMS *Bulolo* decided to unleash his two reserve brigades, the 56th and 151st. It would take each two hours to plough through the surf, although both already had advance parties ashore. An hour later he left himself, to join his tactical HQ (TAC) which had set up ashore at ten, and, as we have seen, he re-established it at Meuvaines at 1300. We have followed the progress of Brigadier Pepper's 56th Brigade, but at the same time Senior's 151st Brigade, which comprised the 6th, 8th and 9th Durham Light Infantry battalions – units that had been with the division ever since 1940 – also arrived. In another example of the Allied nature of the assault along all five beaches, they were brought to King Beach in seven US Navy LCIs.[85] The original plan was for all the follow-on formations to be shuttled ashore by LCA from their larger transports. However, aspirations to tranship them into smaller craft for the final run to shore was abandoned due to the very high losses of landing vessels – thirty-four LCTs and fifty-two LCAs. Much of the coastal fighting had ceased, but men continued to be lost to sporadic shell and mortar fire, including two officers in 151st Brigade HQ.[86] This also affected the 69th Brigade, who were pressing on ahead.

Due to officer losses in the 6th Green Howards, Company Sergeant Major Hollis was given Sixteen Platoon to lead as they progressed towards nearby Crépon at about 1300 hours. In his haste to move inland, Lieutenant Colonel Hastings bypassed the village with his battalion to attack another battery beyond at La Marefontaine, leaving Major Lofthouse and 'D' Company to mop up the settlement. Scouting ahead, the intrepid Hollis spied several field guns in an orchard attached to Le Pavilion farm. The artillerymen spotted him at the same moment and laid down a furious machine-gun barrage, which pinned down many of his men. Hollis engaged the guns with a PIAT, the clumsy-looking British equivalent of a bazooka, but when one of the artillery pieces lowered its barrel to engage him, Hollis realised it was time to withdraw, ordering his Bren gunners to do likewise.

He was soon debriefing Lofthouse on the German presence, but realised his own machine-gunners had yet to emerge. Consequently he went back to the orchard, Bren gun at the hip, exposing himself to fire but enabling the others to escape. Duty done, at 1500 'D' Company decided to move on and leave the guns to a more numerous contingent of the 5th East Yorks. By the evening, Hollis had increased his tally of Germans to 102, but more importantly, Major Lofthouse, Lieutenant Colonel Hastings and Brigadier Knox had nominated Hollis for a Victoria Cross, the only one to be awarded for actions on D-Day.[87]

During the 50th Northumbrian Division's landings at Gold Beach, Company Sergeant Major Stanley Hollis (1912–72) (left) became the only soldier to win a Victoria Cross on D-Day. It was awarded for two actions in the advance of 6th Green Howards of the 69th Brigade, who assaulted King Beach at Ver-sur-Mer. Further west, the attack of 231st Brigade on Jig Beach at Asnelles was held up by WN37 – a powerful German position in this old sanatorium complex (right), which pinned down the 1st Hampshires and only fell at 1700 hours after prolonged attack. (Author's collection)

The position at La Marefontaine, marked on German maps as WN32 and containing Gefreiter Friedrich Wurster with his four 100mm cannon, surrendered without a fight. Their commander at his observation post on the shore had been overwhelmed earlier. Wurster and the entire battery heard his last message: 'They're coming right into the post. *Lebt whol, Kameraden* [Farewell, comrades]', then the line had fallen silent. Each gun in their position fired no more than twenty-five rounds, the rest having been used in an earlier exercise and not replaced: proper ammunition storage bunkers had yet to be built.

The appearance of three companies of Green Howards, the shelling by HMS *Belfast* – which fired 224 rounds of six-inch shells at it – and the arrival of armour, including a pair of flame-throwing Crocodile tanks, combined to sap their will to fight on. Their treatment by the Green Howards 'with old fashioned courtesy and honour' made a deep impression on Wurster and his comrades, who expected to be shot or, at the very least, roughed up. Their resolve simply melted away when faced with the sheer firepower of the Allies, coupled with the speed of their advance.[88]

However, Generalleutnant Kraiss had been painfully aware for much of the day of the growing gap in the Meuvaines area of his front, and had directed *Kampfgruppe Meyer* – less one battalion sent to Colleville – there to plug the hole. Meyer's battlegroup of over two thousand comprised the bicycle battalions of General Marcks' 84th Corps reserve, whom we met being ordered westwards to Carentan to contain the US parachute landings, then redirected east. A proportion of Meyer's troops and equipment were conveyed on commandeered French trucks, some of which began to be attacked from the air – when the skies cleared from about 1100 hours – while others started to break down. Pairs of Spitfires circling overhead were also directing naval gunfire onto them, which prompted some of their French drivers to desert. All these factors combined to delay Meyer's progress, so that they only started trickling into Villiers-le-Sec, south of Meuvaines, from around 1600 hours, accompanied by 30th *Schnelle-Brigade* – more bicyclists – and the 352nd Division's ten StuG 75mm tracked assault guns.

They got no further north, immediately colliding with the 5th East Yorks and 4th/7th Dragoon Guards in a meeting engagement. However, Meyer's men did manage to capture Brigadier Senior at 1645, when 151st Brigade's war diary recorded his sudden disappearance. Senior had been travelling to visit his forward units in his jeep when it was ambushed, his driver and signaller shot and the commander wounded and hauled away. Further consternation was caused when it was realised he had in his possession a series of marked maps and all the signal codes for the next fourteen days. Within two hours Senior had escaped and made his way back to safety, and in the succeeding maelstrom the Germans were unable to make use of his documents.[89]

However, the 5th East Yorks lost their CO wounded at 1500 during a two-hour slog to capture Saint-Gabriel, south of Villiers-le-Sec. They reported their prisoners were from the *Fusilier-Bataillon* of the 352nd Division, and 915th *Grenadier-Regiment*. Under air attack, and harried by the fleet, never mind Allied ground troops, very few grenadiers appear to have survived this brief encounter. It was reported to the 352nd Division at 1730 hours in terms of a complete annihilation, in which all the senior German officers were killed, wounded or captured, valuable documents and maps captured, and the survivors pushed south across the River Seulles.[90]

The units of 69th Brigade halted and dug in for the night, a mile short of *Route Nationale* 13, though the engagement carried on until 2300, by which time the 4th/7th Dragoon Guards had lost four tanks, but had secured Brécy.[91] Most importantly in Creully, a mile to the east, at 1800 hours they had made contact with 'A' Company of the Royal Winnipeg Rifles, part of the 7th Canadian Infantry Brigade, fulfilling one of General Graham's original directives.

Gold and Juno Beaches had linked up, meaning the eastern flank of 69th Brigade was secure. Major Henry 'Jo' Gullet witnessed Creully's liberation. 'Everyone who could walk or be carried was in the streets. They were wildly excited. Bands played – discordantly and in keen competition. The people sang and cried and cheered and danced. They gave us wine and flowers and kisses. On the steps of the town hall stood the mayor, helmeted and bemedalled in his 1918 glory, a grizzled, square-built man, the tears pouring down his face, his right hand stiffly saluting.'[92]

The engagement with *Kampfgruppe Meyer* was significant because it amounted to the only organised German counter-attack behind Omaha or Gold Beaches. Its failure can be attributed to the premature use of the corps reserve. Had Generals Marcks or Kraiss a better intelligence picture of the Allied dispositions during the morning, and a little more patience, these battalions would not have had to cycle forty miles hither and thither before attacking their foes. We have examined the possible impact of three fresh battalions attacking the Americans much earlier behind Omaha. The same applies, were those units to have hit the 50th Division sooner in the day, while the latter were still establishing their beachhead and preoccupied with the defenders of Le Hamel and La Rivière.

This was the real reason for General Graham not entering Bayeux on 6 June – which sloppy history has labelled as a failure. It was nothing of the sort: Graham was being prudent and his formation was already dominating – if not actually occupying – all the terrain he had been allocated. By nightfall, the 50th Division had not quite reached all their ambitious objectives, due to the delays imposed by the opposition and the weather. Yet they had delivered in style, with every significant German position in their sector overwhelmed, and a major city on the verge of capture. At Gold Beach, the *Atlantikwall* had not been merely penetrated, it had been irreparably torn asunder.

Some troops were tantalisingly close to Bayeux, as Stanley Cox, a tank gunner with 'A' Squadron of the Sherwood Rangers, recalled: 'We reached the outskirts at nightfall on D-Day. All day long we had seen the cathedral's spires getting closer. How would we wriggle past the Jerries to get in there? we kept asking ourselves. However, the general didn't want us fighting though a German-occupied city in the dark, so we left entering until first light. Instead we pulled back to an apple orchard for the night and watched the whole beachhead lit up with shell and bullet tracers – a firework display unmatched by anything else I ever saw. At 0400 hours on 7 June our tank commanded by Lieutenant Mike Howden was sent into Bayeux on reconnaissance, but the Germans had scarpered, and the people were running about going nuts. We were the first liberators of the place.'[93]

Later in the day, the 2nd Glosters of 56th Brigade followed them, noting, 'Civilians waving, rushing out with food, all deliriously happy. As we went down the hill the crowds became dense. The houses were already draped with flags. Imagine a long column of dusty, grimy British soldiers moving through masses of excited people, being offered jugs of beer, glasses of Calvados, flowers and kisses. At that moment each man found himself in the unaccustomed role of a conquering hero.'[94] The battalion had been preceded by at least a few of their men scouting ahead, for Private Harry Pinnegar, with 'B' Company, always swore blind that 'my platoon was in Bayeux Cathedral at seven minutes to midnight on D-Day'. They therefore beat the Sherwood Rangers into the city, and – with the Germans having left – could reasonably claim to have just fulfilled Graham's mission of taking Bayeux on the sixth. Pinnegar was always put out that his experience was at variance with the official record of Bayeux having fallen on D+1.[95] He would fight on without injury, but four days later, Stan Cox's Sherman was hit by a shell at Tilly-sur-Seulles, 'which started a fire. The other four crew got away, but as I jumped off, I was hit by shrapnel. They pulled me clear not a moment too soon: minutes later our tank blew up.'[96]

By midnight some 24,970 British soldiers had landed on the various Gold sectors, at a cost of 413 killed, wounded and missing. As with the casualty totals for Utah Beach, this is almost certainly too low, and does not include 47 Royal Marine Commando, the 8th Armoured Brigade, the two beach groups or losses suffered by the naval personnel shuttling troops and equipment to and fro. Whatever the true figure, it was a fraction of what the planners had expected. The material losses in terms of landing craft – eighty-nine written off through shelling, mines or the waves – and their cargoes were almost more serious. They created many dangerous underwater obstacles which made the beaches hazardous for weeks to come.

From the first telling of the D-Day story to the most recent, brevity has been the enemy of accuracy. While many accounts linger over the carnage of Omaha, in 1951 Gold Beach was portrayed thus: 'the commander of the British 50th Division had been advancing against very slight opposition'.[97] An oral history of 1993 related how 'British troops assaulting Gold Beach in the centre of the invasion front had little difficulty piercing defences and fighting their way inland'.[98] In 1994, a wide-ranging account read: 'At Gold, the Atlantic Wall held up the British 50th Division for about an hour.'[99] Another, of 2008, described how 'the Fiftieth (Northumbrian) Infantry Division landed without encountering strong resistance in its zone, adjacent to the villages of Asnelles and Ver-sur-Mer'.[100] In 2011 it was the turn of a collection of first-hand accounts to announce that the 'British 50th Division came ashore east of Arromanches on a beach called Gold. They were able to land without much trouble even though tidal conditions prevented the timely clearing of beach obstacles.'[101] Even the official British military history of 1962 unhelpfully suggested that, 'apart from the hold-up at Le Hamel, the leading brigades of 50th Division were making good progress'.[102]

Although some authors went on to qualify the resistance at Le Hamel, all overlooked the defence of La Rivière, *Kampfgruppe Meyer*'s counter-attack, also ignoring the awful sea conditions and the threats from many small groups of Germans, bypassed, surrounded, but not yet ready to surrender and still dangerous. Somehow the 50th Division's low butcher's bill has been translated in some minds to a lack of hard fighting, as if the measure of achievement on D-Day lay in the casualties suffered, rather than ground gained. Dwelling on the losses is to overlook the skill and professionalism of the formation. Their sheer determination and hard fighting was demonstrated by the award of a Victoria Cross to Stanley Hollis. Success was achieved not because there were poor defences or few defenders in the area. General Graham's men prevailed because they had been properly trained, were excessively well equipped and strongly supported from the sea and in the air. The poor recounting of the battle for Gold is not national prejudice at work, merely a slide towards sloppy history-telling, which this account has tried to arrest.

A keen eye will soon locate the sites of Gold Beach's various D-Day dramas. Apart from the enormous 75mm blockhouse on the seafront at Asnelles, now surrounded by a car park, and the odd Tobruk bunker, the whole Le Hamel *préventorium* site was levelled after the war, and modern housing makes the former WN37 difficult to trace. To the east, at La Rivière, the WN33 bunker – minus its gun – still lurks on the seafront at Ver-sur-Mer, bearing its battle scars from Captain Bell's tank. Close examination of the lifeguard's tower will reveal its erection on top of the former 50mm gun emplacement, while today's sea wall was the structure built by the defenders, intent on keeping out Allied tanks rather than the waves of the English Channel. One of the car park spaces is permanently occupied by the smashed remnants of a machine-gun nest. Inland from the traffic lights of the Ver-sur-Mer crossroads sits a 'Sexton', restored and placed in memory of the gunners who landed and fought in the vicinity. Nearby, the Musée America–Gold Beach tells the story of 69th Brigade in the landings and development of nearby airstrips. The 'America' part of the museum focuses not on the war, but on a Fokker triplane called *America*, the first mail-carrying flight from the United States to Europe, which ditched into the sea off Ver-sur-Mer in June 1927.

'Lavatory-pan Villa' remains, though now difficult to pick out, submerged in a modern housing estate. At the top of the hill, the four Mont-Fleury casemates still lurk in the fields – one now converted into a bijou apartment – and a mile beyond lie the other set that was once the La Marefontaine battery. Below them on the beach is Sergeant Major Hollis's train shelter that he thought was a pillbox. The stonework, still splattered by bullet holes, was adopted by the Green Howards in 2006 but the local council misunderstood its significance and carefully restored it, covering over the 1944 scars of battle. It is now named the 'Hollis VC Hut'. Crépon, the scene of the second half of Hollis's VC-winning exploits, was untouched by the war and is an excellent example of those delightfully sleepy, ancient villages which dot the Normandy countryside.

Passing its twelfth-century church dedicated to Saint Médard et Saint Gildard – used as a German OP and sniper post, and by a Royal Navy Forward Officer Bombardment (FOB) team – a statue to the Green Howards sits at a prominent junction. It was unveiled by the King of Norway in 1996 – the King was colonel of the regiment that guarded him when in exile during the Second World War – and depicts a seated British Tommy, rifle in hand. It is modelled on the regiment's favourite son, Stan Hollis. Beyond is *Ferme de la Rançonnière*, a German headquarters in 1944. The thirteenth-century farm was built for security, its medieval gateway and battlements allowing local peasants and their livestock to shelter within from the usual enemy: English pirates. Such architecture was replicated in every village and used to deadly effect by the Germans, who sheltered behind their thick stone walls and poked machine guns through the slits once designed for crossbows. The establishment is now a splendid hotel, one I often use as a base for exploring the region.

No trip to the Gold sectors would be complete without a visit to Arromanches-les-Bains. The concrete base of the radar station and bunkers of the WN38 and WN39 strongpoints overlooking Jig Beach are evident on the clifftops where today's viewing platform and car park have been built. Often ignored is the nearby obelisk to an earlier battle of Arromanches – a rare French victory over the Royal Navy of 8 September 1811, and a reminder that the Franco-German difficulties of 1939–45 are a mere speck compared to far older Anglo-French tensions. Descending into the little town from the east, a Sherman tank comes into view, painted in the colours of Général Philippe Leclerc de Hauteclocque's 2nd French Armoured Division, which would land on Utah Beach from 31 July 1944. It sits on top of a massive bunker, once

ARROMANCHES - Monument commémoratif du Centenaire du Combat Naval 7 et 8 septembre 1811 — LL

The small village of Arromanches where the British constructed their artificial harbour, and the site of an earlier Anglo-French naval battle. The camera is looking west, from the clifftops where the Germans built a coastal radar station. Other guns in the vicinity looked east, covering the future Gold Beach. It has since become one of the centres of D-Day commemorations and houses the region's first war museum, opened on 6 June 1954. (Author's collection) known as WN44, which housed a 105mm gun, and was abandoned without a fight at 2100 hours on D-Day.

Now, cruise ships at Cherbourg pour their passengers into coaches and convey them to Arromanches. Other busloads of schoolchildren, students, soldiers and veterans alight here throughout the year, for there is plenty to view in this Waterloo-on-Sea. Amidst the ice-cream parlours and souvenir shops, an 88mm gun guards the car park, along with assorted military vehicles, field guns and landing craft. And then, of course, there is the wartime harbour, lurking a short way out to sea. It is well explained via models, films and displays in the *Musée du Débarquement*, the first Normandy war museum to open on D-Day's tenth anniversary, 6 June 1954. In every respect, being almost in the geographical centre of the invasion front, this is an excellent place for an introduction to the Normandy campaign.

Yet these day-trippers only scratch the surface of Operation Overlord; sometimes not even that. The town has developed as a symbol of what the June 1944 invasion – *le débarquement* – was all about. Some visitors might be forgiven for thinking that landing craft deposited troops at Arromanches itself on D-Day, or that a pitched battle took place there, though neither is true. I enjoy my visits to get a feel for the logistical effort behind the campaign, but the area – notwithstanding its excellent museums – has instead become a sort of clumsy shorthand for the whole liberation story.

Gold Beach was chosen partly to enable the development of the British Mulberry harbour, which in the long term showed its true value. Up to the end of August, Mulberry 'B' would unload forty per cent of all British supplies. By the end of October, twenty-five per cent of all Allied supplies, twenty per cent of personnel and fifteen per cent of vehicles would pass through the artificial port, the size of Dover. The two Mulberries were designed to handle twelve thousand tons of stores per day, Mulberry 'B' averaging between six and ten thousand tons each day, depending on the bottlenecks ashore.[103]

Bayeux beckons as much as Arromanches, chiefly for the cathedral – liberated ahead of the rest of the city on 6 June, according to Harry Pinnegar – and the tapestry, a 230-foot embroidery hidden from the Germans during the war, depicting an earlier cross-Channel invasion, that of William, Duke of Normandy, against England in October 1066. He took with him Roger de Montgomerie, later 1st Earl of Shrewsbury, whose distant descendant, General Bernard Law Montgomery, oversaw the D-Day landings in 1944. The fascinating symmetry of the 1066 and 1944 invasions is emphasised on the Bayeux Memorial facing the Commonwealth War Graves cemetery on the south-western edge of the ring road. It commemorates 1,808 men – including 270 Canadians – who died in Normandy and have no known grave. The Latin inscription along its frieze reads: '*Nos a Gulielmo Victi Victoris Patriam Liberavimus*' – 'We, once conquered by William, have now set free his native land.'

In another cemetery lies Nathan Lerner, the Jewish boy from east London in the 1st Dorsets. Back in 1936 at Cable Street in London he had fought against Oswald Mosley's British Union of Fascists. Eight years later on 28 June he was killed in action. The simple inscription on his Commonwealth War Graves Commission headstone says it all: 'Fell fighting Fascism from Cable Street to Normandy'.[104]

On 7 June, 231st Brigade moved beyond Arromanches and Stanier's 2nd Devons seized the four-gun battery on the clifftops at Longues-sur-Mer, considerably battered the day before by the fleet. The brigadier himself came to inspect the site and its haul of prisoners. Keen to know what it was like to be at the receiving end of the Allied assault, he asked if any of them spoke English. One man put his hand up and volunteered, '*Herr* General, it vas like being in a cocktail shaker.' 'My man, what do you know of cocktail shakers?' asked Brigadier Sir Alexander Stanier in amusement. The other bowed and clicked his heels and with ruffled pride answered, 'I vas barman in London at your Savoy Hotel before all this var business began.'[105]

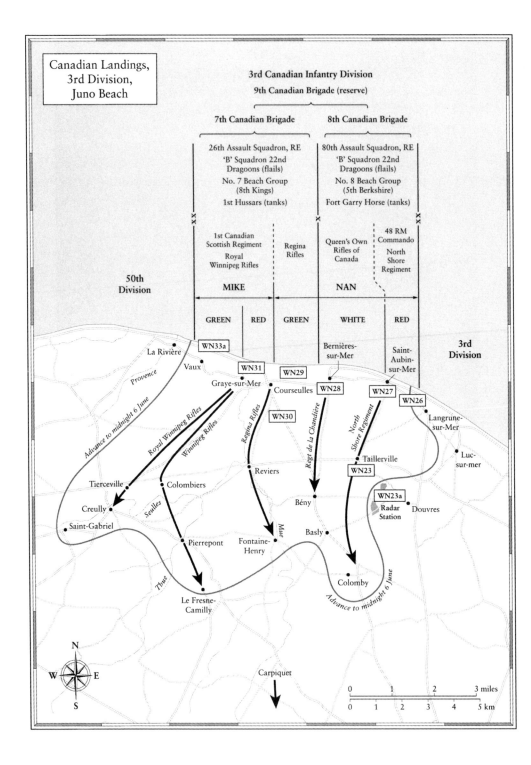

Canadian Landings, 3rd Division, Juno Beach

3rd Canadian Infantry Division

9th Canadian Brigade (reserve)

7th Canadian Brigade

8th Canadian Brigade

26th Assault Squadron, RE
'B' Squadron 22nd Dragoons (flails)
No. 7 Beach Group (8th Kings)
1st Hussars (tanks)

80th Assault Squadron, RE
'B' Squadron 22nd Dragoons (flails)
No. 8 Beach Group (5th Berkshire)
Fort Garry Horse (tanks)

1st Canadian Scottish Regiment
Royal Winnipeg Rifles

Regina Rifles

Queen's Own Rifles of Canada

48 RM Commando
North Shore Regiment

50th Division

MIKE

NAN

3rd Division

GREEN | RED | GREEN | WHITE | RED

La Rivière

WN33a

Vaux

WN31

Graye-sur-Mer

WN29

Courseulles

Bernières-sur-Mer

Saint-Aubin-sur-Mer

WN28

WN27

WN26

Provence

WN30

Langrune-sur-Mer

Royal Winnipeg Rifles

Winnipeg Rifles

Regina Rifles

Reviers

Regt de la Chaudière

North Shore Regiment

Luc-sur-mer

Advance to midnight 6 June

Tierceville

Colombiers

Taillerville

WN23

Creully

Seulles

Mue

Bény

WN23a
Radar Station

Douvres

Saint-Gabriel

Pierrepont

Fontaine-Henry

Basly

Le Fresne-Camilly

Thue

Colomby

Advance to midnight 6 June

N
W E
S

Carpiquet

0   1   2   3 miles
0   1   2   3   4   5 km

32

Juno: Maple Leaf at War

'I remember a bulldozer to the right of us on the beach. It was pushing landing craft out when their ramps had got stuck in the sand. Suddenly it hit a mine and went spinning up into the air.'
Landing craft coxswain at Courseulles, Juno Beach[1]

As AT OMAHA and Gold, but not Utah, the Canadian Major General Rod Keller would be hurling two brigade groups at the Normandy coast, deploying the maximum combat power that his shipping would allow. The central focus of his attack would be Courseulles, astride the River Seulles. This was an important location, less because of its small harbour and more because it controlled access across the river, which in German hands would impede any link-up with the British 50th Division to the west.

Its port was man-made, the Seulles snaking round to the west, but was tidal and unusable for some of each day. The little harbour was one reason for the narrow-gauge railway that ran along the coast from Ouistreham – goods unloaded at Courseulles could be sent around the region at speed. From the sea, the town's appearance was different to that of Asnelles and Ver to the west or Bernières and Saint-Aubin to the east: Courseulles was a working fishing port, not a tourist centre, and possessed no promenade, beach wall or smart seafront housing. This necessitated the *Organisation Todt* building their bunkers on the beach itself, where they were very obvious to an attacker.

The Germans understood the importance of the small fishing town equally well, and were concerned that the gap in the offshore reefs opposite the river mouth seemed to beg for Allied attention. Securing the western flank of Courseulles – also marking the extreme western boundary of Juno – on a slight ridge inland and overlooking Mike Green sector (which was not assaulted), lay strongpoint WN33a. Anchored between the settlements of Vaux and Graye-sur-Mer, this was the head-quarters of the 1st Company of the 441st *Ost-Bataillon*, and hosted a 75mm gun. Some of the 7th Company of the 736th *Grenadier-Regiment* also lodged here, but much of this unit's attention was directed west-wards, for they were also responsible for the defences at La Rivière that did so much to hold up the 69th Brigade of the 50th Division.

It is perhaps worth emphasising that the Germans would have had no comprehension of the separate beach landings; on 6 June the defenders were simply aware of attacks all along the coast. While we look back with hindsight at the beaches codenamed Omaha to Sword, this know-ledge was of course denied to the Germans – and indeed to the wider world at the time. To Generals Marcks, Kraiss and Richter in their various headquarters, the realisation of the separate divisions, and therefore defined beaches with operational boundaries, only came when they started capturing maps and taking and interrogating prisoners. Of course, such knowledge would have helped the Germans immeasurably. For they merely needed to surround each individual beachhead, aware that in the first few hours they were all acutely vulnerable and each fighting their own battles for survival.

Across the meandering Seulles river was *Stützpunktke-Courseulles*, collectively the strongest position on the invasion coast after those at Omaha. Commanded by Hauptmann Grote of the 6th Company, 736th *Grenadier-Regiment*, it comprised three resistance nests, one either side of the river and a third to the south. WN31, commanded by Grote on the western bank, was fronted by a minefield, overwatched by three 50mm guns in various emplacements and a 75mm field gun in a thick concrete casemate in enfilade facing west, plus machine-guns and mortars. On the opposite (eastern) bank lay WN29, led by his second in command, Oberleutnant Herbert Hallbaur, sporting both an impres-sive anti-tank wall to the front and a ditch to the rear, an 88mm in a reinforced concrete blockhouse facing east, and – five hundred yards away – two 75mm cannon, one German, the other French, in eastwards-facing bunkers, one 50mm (which remains on the harbour wall to this day, its gun shield pierced by tank fire), a 37mm in a Renault tank turret, and several machine-guns. As we have seen, these employed a wide range of different ammunition, much of it from French and Russian stocks. The 88mm – decidedly German – would, until silenced, also cause trouble further down the coast for the attackers on Nan White at Bernières. The WN30 depth position inland consisted of machine-guns and mortars in field positions.

With Courseulles the object of an H-Hour assault by the 7th Canadian Brigade, a mile to the east, the 8th Canuck Brigade would launch themselves at the two seaside settlements of Bernières and, a further mile beyond, Saint-Aubin. Bernières was one of the oldest settlements on the *Côte de Nacre*, with Roman origins and its twelfth-century Romanesque church built on land belonging to Bishop Odo, William the Conqueror's half-brother. Its street plan had evolved in the days of oxen and carts, and had not progressed much since, offering a potential bottleneck to any invader, and a gift to the defenders. A more modern twelve-foot sea wall lined some of the beachfront at Saint-Aubin, on top of which ran a road, overlooked by many brick-and-mortar houses, shops, hotels and restaurants. These had all closed and their occupants evacuated.

Commanding the 5th Company of the 736th *Grenadier-Regiment*, Hauptmann Rudolf Grüter at Bernières – Nan White sector to the Canadians, WN28 to the Germans – had a wide frontage to cover. He was protected to the front by minefields and to the rear by an anti-vehicle ditch south of the railway line. Scheduled for assault by the Queen's Own Rifles of Canada, the defences were in reality a reinforced platoon-sized location of several concrete positions housing single 75mm and 50mm guns, a tank turret, six machine-guns and three mortars, placed to dominate the exits from the beach. Grüter's second in command, Oberleutnant Gustav Pflocksch, oversaw WN27, the defences at the western end of Saint-Aubin, where the Germans had demolished most of the buildings to create fields of fire for a 50mm and several machine-guns. This was Nan Red, attacked by the North Shore (New Brunswick) Regiment.

Immediately after the invasion, a special observer team assessed the Saint-Aubin defences in terms that applied equally to many of the other Juno and Gold positions:

Several houses had all windows and openings to seaward bricked up. Some had sandbags beneath first floor windows to provide cover for snipers. Elaborate and very strong reinforced concrete portions housing the main weapons and command posts were constructed, with walls and roofs estimated to be three-to-five-foot thick. Shelters with eight-inch concrete slabs covered with masonry and earth were provided, with exceptional command of the beach. In general the defences consisted of a series of earthen strongpoints from which machine-guns could be sited, linked by an intricate and extensive system of communication trenches. Numerous mortar positions existed consisting of concrete chambers with magazines attached built flush with the land [Tobruks]. All defences were blended in with the general character of the locality. Wire was used extensively along the seawall and around areas marked as *Mines*.[2]

At Saint-Aubin, all these defensive works have long been swept away in the name of tourism, save for one prominent bunker built into the sea wall, which still houses its 50mm anti-tank gun, the muzzle damaged on D-Day.

Langrune, a smaller seaside village, and virtually a continuation of Saint-Aubin, likewise had a twenty-foot-high sea wall and in appearance and architecture was not dissimilar to Saint-Aubin. Its WN26 strongpoint consisted of half a dozen machine-gun nests, two mortars and a 50mm gun emplacement, mostly set in the coastal wall and surrounded by mines and wire. With a concrete anti-tank wall, ten feet high and four feet deep, barring access from the eastern edge of the beach, its arcs of fire were integrated with those of Saint-Aubin to the west and Luc-sur-Mer in the east. WN26's defenders were based on the 9th Company of the 736th *Grenadier-Regiment*, led by Hauptmann Kurt Mickish and his second in command, Oberleutnant Herbert Wlost, who were also responsible for WN24 and WN25 at Luc-sur-Mer. Langrune stood on the boundary between Juno and Sword and was not attacked from the sea, but assaulted by 48 Commando coming from the west. The larger plan was for 41 Commando to land on Sword, proceed west and link up with their 48 Commando brethren, thus closing the gap between the two beaches.

These six strongpoints in the four towns comprising Juno Beach were manned by little more than four companies (about a battalion's worth) of men with five field guns, nine anti-tank cannon, seven mortars and around forty machine-guns – but this amounted to well under half the density of Omaha's defences – and nothing like enough to face six well-trained infantry and two tank battalions. Most German crew-served weapons were sited to create a killing zone along the shore. Once inland, attackers would have an easier time because these positions were sited too far apart to support one another. Preregistered artillery zones offshore were code-named 'Köln' – all an observer had to do was correct the fall of shot by degrees or metres.

Yet of all this weaponry, it was the relentless arrival of 81mm and 50mm mortar bombs throughout the day that would cause the most casualties. The instance of sudden death or injury, launched from an unknown position, also dented morale, and until the hinterland was cleared would continue to act as a nuisance factor. To the uninitiated – especially landing craft crews and beach group personnel – mortar fire was often misreported as artillery, leading to the initial and erroneous assumption that the Germans had deployed more field guns than was actually the case. All these positions were fronted by the usual rows of beach obstacles, often armed; other coastal weapons included a few electrically operated static flamethrowers – of the type Franz Gockel had at Omaha – none of which came into action on the day. An occasional log shelter also held a miniature Goliath tank, of the kind we first encountered at Utah. None would be deployed on account of the severing of their command wires, or demise of their operators.

The object of the 3rd Canadian Division, Juno Beach, extended immediately east of Ver-sur-Mer for six miles via the port of Courseulles to Saint-Aubin. Following on from Jig and King, allotted to 50th Division, Juno encompassed Love, Mike and Nan sectors. Love would not be assaulted but was reserved for the later offloading of equipment and stores. Mike, subdivided into Green and Red – west of the River Seulles – would be attacked by the 7th Canadian Infantry Brigade. Everything east of the Seulles, including Nan Green, White and Red, as far as Bernières and Saint-Aubin, was scheduled for invasion by the 8th Canadian Brigade. Additionally, 48 Royal Marine Commando would land at Saint-Aubin for their sally to Langrune-sur-Mer.

The 3rd Canadian Division's forty-four-year-old Major General Rod Keller was actually English-born, from Gloucestershire; he migrated with his family when young and had been commissioned into the Princess Patricia's Canadian Light Infantry at the end of the First World War. Attending the British Staff College at Camberley, he took command of his regiment in 1941. Keller had been promoted very quickly to lead the 1st Infantry Brigade a few months later, and within a year had taken over the 3rd Canadian Division. This was too rapid in the eyes of some, who expressed doubts about his suitability for such an important command.[3] However, the Canadian Army General Staff was fishing from a very small pond for its senior personnel and Keller was popular with his troops, who appreciated his legendary bluntness.

His 3rd Division traced its roots back to the formation that had fought in the First World War, had been disbanded afterwards, then to be re-formed in 1940. With the 1st Canadian Infantry Division fighting in Italy and the 2nd badly mauled at Dieppe and still recovering its strength and confidence, the 3rd was the obvious choice as an assault division for Overlord. After its performance in Exercise Spartan, Keller was informed of their role on 3 July 1943. They had thus spent a year in preparation, concluding with Exercise Fabius III in May. Keller's objectives were to reach the line of the Caen–Bayeux *Route National*, code-named 'Oak' – via two preliminary phase lines, 'Yew' and 'Elm' – capture Carpiquet airfield to the west of Caen, and link up with the British 3rd and 50th Divisions. It was Keller who had ensured that his division was the most motorised of all to land on D-Day; all his field regiments of artillery were fully self-propelled using American 105mm 'Priests', and most of his anti-tank units employed the US-designed, -tracked and -turreted M10, rather than towed weapons.

His formation would land in two brigade groups. Courseulles was Brigadier Harry Wickwire Foster's 7th Brigade Group's territory. Foster had already fought in the Pacific under the Americans and would go on to command two Canadian divisions. Somewhat the opposite to his divisional commander, Foster was bullish and self-confident, loathed paperwork and directed in a hands-off manner – much appreciated by his officers. His group attacked with two battalions up, the Royal Winnipeg Rifles tackling the western Mike Red and Green beaches, with the Regina Rifles – who hailed from Saskatchewan – to the east of the Seulles, on Nan Green. The Canadian Scottish – his third infantry battalion, recruited in Victoria, British Columbia – would follow behind the Winnipegs, the whole attack being supported by artillery field regiments, and engineer companies. The two attacking battalions would be supported by tanks of the Ontario-based 1st Hussars, a unit of Brigadier Robert A. Wyman's 2nd Canadian Armoured Brigade; Wyman had joined Keller with the experience of handling the 1st Armoured Brigade in Sicily.

To their left, in the east, Brigadier Kenneth G. Blackader's 8th Brigade Group would storm ashore on Nan White and Red – Bernières and Saint-Aubin. Older than Keller and Foster, Blackader had been wounded and won a Military Cross during the First World War, and by 1938 was commanding the Black Watch of Canada. He oversaw the assault from the frigate HMS *Waveney*, outfitted as a headquarters ship, from which he had led the pre-invasion exercises in April and May. In reserve, Keller had Brigadier Douglas G. Cunningham's 9th Brigade to deploy where he thought best. Extraordinarily bright, and whose memory and meticulous attention to detail were legendary, Cunningham was a reservist and prominent barrister in Kingston, Ontario, who would eventually become commandant of the Royal Military College before returning to his legal practice.

In addition to his fifteen-thousand-strong division, Keller had been loaned from the British 26th and 80th Assault Squadrons, Royal Engineers, equipped with their Churchill AVREs; eleven Sherman flail tanks from 'B' Squadron, 22nd Dragoons, and nine of 'A' Squadron, the Westminster Dragoons; Centaur tanks with 95mm guns from the 2nd Royal Marine Armoured Support Regiment; the armoured cars of 'C' Squadron, the Inns of Court Regiment; as well as having 48 Royal Marine Commando under command. The Canadians also had the services of No. 7 Beach Group, built around the 8th King's Regiment for Mike sector, and No. 8, including the 5th Royal Berkshires, for Nan sector. Bizarrely, the latter had no connection with the rolling acres of the Thames valley, recruiting instead in north-east London and known as the Hackney Pals battalion. Both these beach groups were similar in size and organisation to those employed on Gold and Sword. Collectively, these units amounted to a further nine thousand Britons under Canadian command.

Force 'J' had received their orders to set sail within fifteen minutes of Eisenhower's decision to 'Go', made at Southwick House. 'Church services held on practically all craft,' noted one war diary; 'More ships than a leopard with measles,' noted another. Weighing anchor late on 5 June, and preceded by sixteen RCN minesweepers led by HMCS *Caraquet*, the armada followed a channel marked to port and starboard by small illuminated buoys dropped by the sweepers. It had already been decided – due to some of the Calvados reefs offshore – to make H-Hour later on Juno, with split timings. Landing in the west on Mike and Nan Green sectors, 7th Canadian Brigade would disembark at 0735 hours. In the East, 8th Brigade would assault Nan White and Red ten minutes later at 0745. During the night, however, the atrocious weather had slowed down the Force 'J' assault convoys and some had strayed off course. The conditions prompted Commodore Oliver and Major General Keller aboard their headquarters vessel HMS *Hilary* to delay H-Hour for the two brigades by a further ten minutes, to 0745 and 0755 hours, respectively. As the Royal Winnipeg Rifles set off from their mother ships for their 'six miles of hell' to shore, Private Hamilton noted 'Rifleman [Andrew G.] Mutch, who was, as we all were, very, very seasick. He was lying on the gunwale and about two miles offshore, a large wave washed him off, and he went down. We never saw him again.'⁴

A larger-than-life Briton was one of the first figures many Canadians would have met on Juno. As chief beachmaster, Captain Colin Maud, RN, was perhaps the most prominent of his ilk. A veteran of Dunkirk, Narvik, the hunt for the *Bismarck,* and Malta and Arctic convoys, he 'was fearless to the point of scorn of hostile shellfire', a necessary characteristic for any beachmaster, who had to operate not just on D-Day, but for weeks afterwards. Described as 'one of the most popular officers in the British Navy', Maud is another character handed down to posterity by director Darryl F. Zanuck's movie version of *The Longest Day*, where he was played by the British actor Kenneth More. Maud was the real deal: an eccentric naval officer, once encountered, never forgotten. With his heavy black beard, looking not unlike a pirate, he strode around Juno Beach, his commanding presence emphasised by his German Shepherd called 'Winnie' (translated into a bulldog for the movie) held on a tight leash, and shillelagh – a blackthorn stick. Maud, an advisor on Zanuck's film, lent More the same stick he had carried on D-Day. The 'props' and bluster concealed an inner calm: Maud had earlier in the war been rescued from the waves after the torpedoing of his destroyer.

Leaving their moorings in the Solent the previous evening, the first Canadians touched Norman sand at 0749 hours. They arrived with the LCOCUs, with whom Royal Marine Sergeant Keith Briggs served. He recalled swimming out 'with wires, ropes and hawsers to attach to obstacles so the armoured bulldozer drivers at the other end could clear a gap. Whilst we were working in the water it was mostly snipers who were our biggest problem. They were in the houses above us, sniping all the time. We didn't let them frighten us and carried on and did our job.'⁵

When the rising water temporarily obliged them to abandon this work, Briggs and his colleagues attached lifelines from the shore to landing craft, allowing troops wading through the surf to cling to a rope rather than be washed away. Right across Juno, all were delayed by the appalling weather, some witnesses recording even brief rain squalls. Those awake and on deck marvelled at the sight of the midget submarine *X-20*, at sea since 2 June, which had surfaced at 0400 hours and was guiding Force 'J' to its anchorage, with her eighteen-foot-high navigation mast showing a bright light to seaward; she flew additional large flags after dawn.

As the German defenders woke up to the threat offshore, the future novelist Douglas Reeman noted,

> Tall waterspouts shot towards the sky and then drifted down again very slowly. Lines of red and green tracer ripped across the water and were answered immediately by the destroyers and gunboats. There was a sigh as one of the smaller landing craft came to a dead stop with smoke pouring from her box-like hull as she began to heel over. The soldiers were swarming up and away from the sea, and I saw a motor launch speeding towards her to take them off before they were flung into the water. Weighted down with their weapons and ammunition, steel helmets and heavy boots, they would not stand much of a chance. Another of them was hit, vivid blobs of tracer licking out from the shore in straight, lethal lines.[6]

In the west, 'B' and 'D' Companies of the Royal Winnipeg Rifles left their landing ships, *Canterbury* and *Laird's Isle*, aboard LCAs which took them to Mike Green sector at Courseulles, under heavy fire for much of their final approach. Well ahead of their DD tanks, their war diary noted, 'The bombardment having failed to kill a single German, or silence one weapon, these companies had to storm their positions "cold" and did so without hesitation.'[7] A Royal Navy report later concluded that of 106 itemised German positions targeted by the fleet, only fourteen per cent were disabled by naval gunfire.

'The first Tommies jumped into the sea, which was quite shallow', noted the teenaged Grenadier Hans Weiner of the first few minutes from his position at WN31. 'The bullets hit them and their boats to good effect and I was a little surprised to see them falling – I don't know why. Never having been in a battle before, it did shake me to be hurting those men, although they were enemies. Even then in my naivety, I thought that I was only hurting them. There was so much fire going at them I was surprised to see any survive. Tanks began shooting at us and we were forced to get down. Part of our blockhouse collapsed and we thought

Men of the Royal Winnipeg Rifles of the 7th Canadian Brigade are seen heading to Mike Red beach at Courseulles in the opening hour of the assault. Their mother ship is often claimed to be HMCS *Prince David*, but careful research reveals she is the converted liner HMS *Llangibby Castle*, which carried 1,500 men to Juno, but lost ten of her fourteen LCAs in the process. As with many units, the 'Pegs' found themselves split between several landing ships, including the SS *Canterbury* and HMS *Laird's Isle*. (NARA)

we would be buried alive. Then we ran out of ammunition so it seemed the sensible thing to surrender.'[8]

Captain Phil Gower of 'B' Company kept up a relentless pressure on the defenders, urging his men forward all the while; some recalled him taking off his helmet and waving it to show there was nothing to fear.

Clearing the beach obstructions, the 6th Field Company, Royal Canadian Engineers, as well as the Winnipegs suffered very heavy casualties. The engineers started the day with one hundred men, but would number just twenty-six by nightfall. One Winnipeg casualty was Corporal Walter J. Klos, nicknamed 'Bull' due to his huge physique, who though wounded in the legs and stomach still managed to crawl his way into a machine-gun nest and despatch two of his opponents before he succumbed. He was found inert, his hands still gripping the throat of one of his victims. Another was Sergeant Cosy, who with fifteen men charged another casemate and subdued it with grenades and machine-gun fire, but Cosy had been hit in the lungs and died on the spot. The bunker, recognisable by its extreme tilt, the foundations having eroded with time, is today known as Cosy's Pillbox.

However, such bravery left Captain Gower with just twenty-six out of the 119 men with whom he had started. Many of his soldiers were old sweats, and though they had volunteered four years earlier, this was their first taste of battle. The sight of old friends felled in the initial seconds of their first combat was acutely traumatic. As they took the brunt of the fire, on their left, 'D' Company under Major Lockie R. Fulton cleared paths through the minefields and headed inland for Graye-sur-Mer, followed by 'A' and 'C' Companies and battalion headquarters.

By this time Lieutenant 'Red' Goff's troop of Shermans from 'A' Squadron of the 1st Hussars had launched from LCTs of the 4th Flotilla, swam ashore and started taking on the pillboxes. Earlier in the landing craft, the Winnipegs had exchanged banter – one faux British accent shouted, 'I say, old chaps, anyone for tennis?' in the moments before landing.[9] As one of the Hussar tanks was hit and its crew shot and machine-gunned as they bailed out, the message was immediately clear. This was no tennis match. Later the Winnpegs' CO, Lieutenant Colonel John M. Meldram, praised the Hussars' 'gallantry, skill and cool daring in coming to the assistance of the battalion time and again, without thought of their own safety or state of fatigue'.[10]

Offshore, from the safety of his MGB, Douglas Reeman watched the armour land:

I found I could hardly breathe as the ramp crashed down and after the merest hesitation the leading tank rumbled onto the sand. Then there were others, huddled together, or so it seemed, as fire raked the beach and some of the running khaki figures fell down and stayed down. All along the beach the vehicles were rolling ashore. Some were hit, or crawled like blinded beasts with a track shot away. Like many of the little warships, we held station on the army's flank, firing at anything which moved, until our minds were blank to everything else and our guns jammed from overheating. It was like a great tidal wave. Nothing could stop it as the army with infantry and sappers, stretcher-bearers and mine-detectors charged after the tanks … there was no recognition of time. It just went on and on, as if the vast panorama of battle was too great to ignore.[11]

For the assault, Brigadier Foster's third battalion, the Canadian Scottish Regiment – or 'Can Scots' – was split. Major D. G. Crofton's 'C' Company landed in LCAs from SS *Ulster Monarch* and under command of the Winnipegs. Their task was to destroy the 75mm gun at WN33a, west of Courseulles. Finding the fleet had managed this first, Lieutenant Roger Schjelderup's platoon moved on, overwhelming three machine-gun nests in succession, taking fifteen prisoners. One of them was persuaded to lead them through his protective minefield, which opened the way for the rest of 'C' Company to follow, advancing in tactical formations through fields of tall, ripening wheat. It took some time to persuade the Germans in the vicinity – in fact mostly Russians from the 441st *Ost-Bataillon* – to surrender at the Château Vaux and Graye-sur-Mer, which both fell at a similar hour. The rest of the Can Scots arrived at 0830 hours with bicycles – many of them were photographed struggling ashore with their unwieldy iron steeds, issued to enable them to dash inland. By the end of the day only nineteen out of forty-five in Schjelderup's platoon were still on their feet, the officer himself being wounded. A natural leader from a family of Norwegian immigrants, whose father had fought for Canada in the First World War, Schjelderup would soon return to battle, having earned a Military Cross for his exploits on D-Day. He would go on to win a DSO and a second MC and retire as a full colonel.

Each of the assault battalions relied on the intimate support of a regiment (a battalion in US terminology) of Royal Canadian Artillery, usually equipped with twenty-four 105mm M7 'Priest' self-propelled guns. These had blazed away from their landing craft during the approach and once landed would aid the infantry's advance, as directed by the Forward Observation Officers (FOOs). Unfortunately supporting fire was not always available, due to heavy casualties in the ranks of their eyes – the FOOs and FOBs, their naval observation opposite numbers. When the 12th RCA landed west of the River Seulles at 0830 hours, the timetable had slipped so much because of the weather that there was nowhere for them to go but line up on the beach and train their guns inland. However, this prevented their sister 13th RCA from landing at all, the latter circling uselessly in LCTs until the beach cleared sufficiently for them to land at 1500.

Major Mike Morrison with 'A' Company, 8th King's Regiment, landed on Mike sector, as part of No. 7 Beach Group. He recalled: 'The sea was very rough with troughs so deep that our assault craft appeared to be the only one around – and there were hundreds. A craft to my left was blown sky high, but we manoeuvred through the gap it created. I was first off and disappeared in nine feet of water. No one followed me.'[12] This beach group included Royal Canadian Navy Volunteer Reservists who had trained as commandos; one of these was W. K. 'Bill' Newell, who served in 'W' Commando, the only Canadian beach commando unit, comprising three troops of three officers and twenty-five men each.

He landed on Mike Red and recalled,

we were set up to organise and control the flow of vehicles, men and supplies onto and through *Juno* beach on D-Day. The water was cluttered with the debris of combat from German bombing, strafing and shelling, but wreckage of landing craft and armoured vehicles were impediments to be avoided until conditions permitted their salvage. There were German prisoners gathered on the beach and many of them had soiled field dressings on their wounds. I spent much of my time guiding in tank and assault landing craft, unloading Shermans and Churchills, retrieving bodies floating in on high tides and generally doing what had to be done to help keep the operation moving. The first day I found a vacant enemy bunker in the sand dunes behind the beach which was close enough for me to use for short naps during any lapse in the traffic. I was taken aback to find twelve German army blankets for a bed and a large picture pinned on the sand bags of Betty Grable taking a bath; I had stumbled into a luxury suite.[13]

With seven succumbing to the waves, twelve 1st Hussars' tanks managed to swim ashore after the Winnipegs. As soon as the major weapons had been silenced, 'A' Squadron were able to trundle up and down the sands engaging machine-gun nests, allowing the 'Pegs' to disengage and push inland. There were delays while assault engineers forced exits through the dunes but by 0920 hours the Hussars with the Winnipegs were on their way towards Graye-sur-Mer. The engineers were from the British 26th Assault Squadron, which had arrived between eight and eight-thirty. Split into two troops, they included ten AVREs, two BARVs (Beach Armoured Recovery Vehicles) and four D7 armoured bulldozers. Accompanying them were nine flail tanks of the 22nd Dragoons, whose

1st Troop leader, Lieutenant Ian C. Hammerton, had been amused to find his Canadian colleagues trimming their hair to Mohican style before they left Lymington.[14]

The assault engineers' commander, Major Tony Younger, was particularly aware of the exit from Mike Red sector being blocked by a large water-filled crater, twenty yards long and three yards deep. With much dirt and weeds floating on the surface giving it the appearance of solid ground, the leading Churchill AVRE, call sign 'One Charlie', mistakenly drove into it. All six crew members escaped but afterwards came under mortar fire, which killed four and wounded the remaining pair. The vehicle's own fascine was pushed forward of the tank and an assault bridge placed over it, effectively spanning the crater. By 1000 hours vehicles were driving over 'One Charlie' and the crater was further filled with rubble. The assault bridge was later replaced with another structure, named 'Pont AVRE', and crossed over time by King George VI, Winston Churchill and Général de Gaulle. It was only in 1976 that 'One Charlie' was remembered, recovered, restored and repainted, and it now stands close to where it disappeared from view in 1944. Of the many pieces of restored hardware scattered across Normandy today, 'One Charlie' is one of the few genuine D-Day relics.

Another D-Day 'relic' who had an enduring presence afterwards was Lieutenant James M. Doohan of the 13th RCA. After a breathless and nerve-wracking D-Day, at around midnight the Command Post Officer of the 22nd Battery had been too slow with a password when challenged by a highly strung sentry armed with a Bren gun. Of the six bullets that hit Doohan, one struck a cigarette case, rather than entering his chest, but four rounds passed into a leg and one severed a finger. Evacuated to England, Doohan's war, for which he had trained since 1940, had lasted precisely twenty-four hours. He was just one example of the multitude of casualties from 'friendly fire', an affliction that continues to dog modern warfare. Doohan would later find fame as Montgomery 'Scotty' Scott, Captain Kirk's dour engineering officer, highly protective of his vessel's engines, aboard the starship *Enterprise*. In the alternate 1960s universe of television's *Star Trek*, the careful eye will detect that Scotty's right hand – missing the finger – was invariably concealed on screen.

However, the trials of the 13th RCA or 26th Assault Squadron were as nothing compared to the British Inns of Court Regiment, a Territorial Army unit of reservists recruited from the professional classes of central London. Their thirty armoured and scout cars from 'C' Squadron, plus

Leaning at a surreal angle as the sea erodes its foundations, the pillbox (left) subdued by Sergeant Cosy of the Winnipegs remains in the sand dunes west of Courseulles. From 1500 hours on D-Day, the vicinity also saw the deployment of the 13th Field Regiment, Royal Canadian Artillery, with their 105mm self-propelled 'Priests'. The Command Post Officer of 22nd Battery was wounded by a nervous sentry the same night. That officer was Lieutenant James Montgomery Doohan (right), who lost a finger in the mishap. He later found fame as Scotty, the engineering officer aboard the starship *Enterprise*. (Author's collection)

a headquarters group in twelve half-tracks, started to beach early on 6 June as their chaplain, Reverend John de Boulay Lance, remembered: 'I was asked by the Colonel to land with "C" Squadron. The Royal Army Chaplain's Department thought otherwise and ordered me to stay in England. Rather than find myself at the centre of a row I told some fibs and went,' recorded the future Archdeacon of Wells. 'Our craft struck two mines, which caused some minor casualties and one scout car damaged. The vehicle, parked just over the explosion, was mine and I was sitting on top of it. It did not harm me, but the suspension was ruined. There was nothing for it, and I watched thousands of pounds' worth of armoured vehicle being tipped into the sea.' The task of Lance's beefed-up squadron was to dash ahead of the Canadians, circle round Caen and destroy bridges over the Orne or, failing that, the structures spanning the River Odon instead – hare-brained in the extreme and excessively dangerous.

Their good fortune was that they failed to even make it out of the Juno beachhead, for the Inns of Court would most certainly have been annihilated by the 12th SS or 21st Panzer Divisions racing towards the invasion. The Reverend Lance grabbed his 'communion vessels, medical box, bed roll and scrambled ashore. But the landing ramp was damaged and two of the half-tracks could not make the sea at that depth. Meanwhile the water was rising and in the end the only thing to do was to wait for the tide to reach its height and recede again. This meant a frustrating wait of some six hours, with all hope lost of an early start.'[15] Before the day was out his unit would lose two half-tracks, three armoured and three scout cars, some to friendly fire – from an American P-47 which mistook their vehicles out ahead for a German reconnaissance – but the padre would win a Military Cross by the war's end. They were followed by Brigadier Foster, who had watched the initial assault from the frigate HMS *Lawford*, and with his main headquarters party was taken ashore in motor launches – wading through the surf at 0930, establishing themselves, as planned, at 1215 hours in Graye.

Further east, the Regina Rifles landed at Nan Green on the left bank of the Seulles. Known as the 'Johns' because of the number of 'Farmer Johns' in their ranks, they were delayed by the weather, with 'A' Company disembarking from the SS *Isle of Thanet* and ashore only at 0805 hours, the others later still. LCTs brought the armour of Major Frank Simpson's 80th Assault Squadron, Royal Engineers, to the beach at the same time. Major Gordon Baird recorded that 'Courseulles had been divided into twelve blocks, each was to be cleared by a designated company. Careful study of enlarged air photos made the ground itself easily recognisable. Every foot of the town was known before we entered.'[16]

Sergeant Léo Gariépy, commanding one of the DD tanks, remembered 'Standing on the command deck at the back of my turret, trying to steer and navigate, was the longest journey of my life. I noticed that many of the tanks had sunk and the crews were desperately trying to board bright-yellow salvage dinghies. The struts which kept the rubberized skirt around the tank were groaning and I had visions of them giving out at any moment. On the beach, I gave orders to deflate the canvas skirt and what happened next will always remain vivid in my memory. The German machine-gunners were absolutely stupefied to see a tank emerging from the sea. Some of them ran away, some just stood up and stared, unable to believe their eyes. We mowed them down. The element of surprise was a total success.'[17]

This was probably the first beach where the Sherman swimming tanks delivered as they had been designed to: the Reginas arrived to discover fourteen out of nineteen 'B' Squadron DD tanks of the 1st Hussars had managed to swim ashore and were setting about the gun emplacements. Both found that they were overwhelmed quicker by tank–infantry teams. The bunkers containing the 88mm, 75mm and 50mm guns fell in succession to direct hits, though not before one of the German 75s had expended two hundred rounds at them, judging by the number of shell cases counted later. In return, one Sherman loosed off twenty-five rounds from its main gun before being stranded by the incoming tide. With the most dangerous weapons out of action, 'A' Company followed by the rest of the battalion pushed into the town, mopping up the east bank of the Seulles as they went.

In one of the bunkers opposing the Reginas, Heinrich Siebel assumed he was safe in his thick concrete emplacement housing the 88mm cannon. 'We shot and shot, especially at the strange tanks that came up the beach', he recollected. 'It was hard for us to see much because of the smoke, but I believe we destroyed two before our gun received a direct hit. There was a flash and a great bang and I was blown backwards onto the concrete floor and knew nothing else for a time. When I woke up I found two of our men dead and I tried to get out through the rear exit, pulling one of my wounded friends with me, but debris made this difficult.'[18]

When swimming ashore, the mount of 'B' Squadron's commander, Major Stuart 'Stu' Duncan, was flooded by an immense wave, which collapsed its protective canvas siding, forcing the crew to bail out two hundred yards short of safety. Trooper Larry G. Allen watched it happen. He recalled initially of his own tank, 'shells began to fall around us, sending up miniature geysers of water. After what seemed to be hours I felt our tracks touch land.' Then he looked to port and saw 'the Commanding Officer was swimming merrily along on our left flank when his tank was seen to stagger, as a giant wave broke over the top. This acted like a hole in the dyke, the force of the water coming over the top caused the canvas to be forced down and in a very short time the tank was lost. The crew were seen throwing anything that would float overboard.' Although Duncan and three of his crew swam to shore, Trooper Roswell Toffelmire drowned.[19] In 1971 their tank, named *Bold*, was recovered from the sea and set up by the harbour as a memorial.

The Reginas were almost the only unit on D-Day whose task immediately on landing was to clear a built-up area. Lieutenant Bill D. Grayson

of the Reginas' 'A' Company dashed towards one of the defended buildings as a German threw a stick grenade at him. Grayson picked it up
and threw it back, then – armed only with a Colt automatic pistol –
followed a communications trench to an underground shelter, where he
took thirty-five prisoners. He subsequently repeated this action several
times in clearing Courseulles; perhaps unsurprisingly, a Military Cross
later went to Grayson for his coolness under fire.[20]

The rest of the battalion left the comfort of the landing ships *Llangibby
Castle* and *Mecklenburg* for the perilous journey ashore in which 'D'
Company lost two LCAs to obstacles and mines hidden by the surf. This
caused heavy casualties, including their commander, Major Jack Love
– only two of the thirty-six men in his LCA reached the beach. 'B' and
'C' Companies recorded house-to-house combat as they cleared the town,
but found Germans were returning by tunnels and trenches to reoccupy
their positions, necessitating going over the same ground again. The
narrow streets of Courseulles were especially challenging for the
Shermans and Centaurs, and several tank commanders, heads out of
their protective hatches, succumbed to snipers.

On the southern edge of town, when Sergeant Léo Gariépy saw a
marksman fire at another tank, his vehicle charged up to the building
and blasted the second-floor window on the right. He held his fire as a
civilian woman emerged, a baby in her arms, then dismounted and leapt
up the indoor stairs. Inside, Gariépy confronted a Frenchwoman, clutching
a rifle, whose German boyfriend had been killed earlier. Mindful of the
deaths of other tank commanders, he cut her down in an angry blast
from his Sten gun.[21] Meanwhile, the Reginas' 'D' Company simply reorganised under the command of its remaining officer, Lieutenant Hector
L. Jones, cleared a part of Courseulles, and set out as scheduled to Reviers,
two miles away, where they arrived at 1100 hours. Battalion headquarters
followed at 1500, and two hours later the unit moved south, taking
Fontaine-Henry and Le Fresne-Camilly by eight that evening, where they
dug in for the night. Both commanders of the two Royal Engineers assault
squadrons would win a DSO that morning through dismounting from
the safety of their tanks and directing the subjugation of individual houses,
strongpoints and bunkers, ungumming the congestion that reigned on
each beach, and dealing with the rising tide – all on top of a plan that
hourly threatened to unravel with the much delayed timetable.

By the evening, 'B' Squadron of the 1st Hussars had reached Pierrepont,
a mile south-east of Creully. Much earlier, however, they had lost five

tanks to a single 88mm gun – possibly belonging to the 21st Panzer Division, which had deployed some of its anti-tank battalion to the area. As Sergeant Gariépy recalled, 'I saw Lieutenant McLeod's tank burst high in flame. The troop corporal's tank suffered the same fate, and several others.' Spotting the barrel of the perpetrator, Gariépy gave evasive orders to his driver, while telling his gunner to engage. 'He fired two rounds, the second scoring a direct hit. I moved up to the gun emplacement and shot all the crew of fourteen cowering in the trench.'[22] By then, 'B' Squadron was down to four tanks, out of nineteen.

Also in Pierrepont that first evening were the Canadian Scottish, hourly expecting a counter-attack which never materialised; they had suffered eighty-seven casualties, but had taken about two hundred prisoners. Laagering nearby, the 1st Hussars later noted, 'In view of the losses in DD tanks due to the unsuitable weather, we ended D-Day with a considerably smaller number of tanks than was desirable for our first night in Europe, but by nightfall Harry Foster's 7th Brigade was firmly astride the line running through Fontaine-Henri, Pierrepont and St Gabriel.'[23] Foster later noted, 'The outstanding features of the day were the admirable spirit of the men, and the excellent fire support of the artillery. No request for support went unanswered and many infantry professed to understand for the first time that the gunner's role was something more than to block traffic.'[24]

Brigadier Blackader's 8th Brigade Group assault in the east was of necessity far more spread out. The Toronto-based Queen's Own Rifles of Canada would launch themselves at Bernières, while on their left, the North Shore (New Brunswick) Regiment were to simultaneously tackle Saint-Aubin, each supported by a squadron from the 10th Armoured Regiment – better known as the Fort Garry Horse tank regiment, which recruited in Winnipeg, Manitoba. Reverend Raymond Hickey, chaplain to the North Shores, remembered of their cross-Channel journey, 'Into the night we sailed as silently as thieves bent on their journey under the cover of darkness. Not a light showed in all that vast expanse of boats, but here and there, by the reflection of the water, you could make out the indistinct form of a boat, like a giant whale sleeping. Only the dull throbbing of the engines broke the silence.'

Hickey, aboard HMS *Brigadier*, a 2,000-ton former Channel ferry carrying six LCAs and 180 men from the North Shores, then vividly described the next morning, a common experience for all of the 3rd Canadian Division:

> The engines had stopped and the boat was still. We rushed up to the deck and there about ten miles away was the coast of France, about to awaken to a tragic day. Overhead our planes droned past and in a few minutes the coast lit up with the well-known flares of bombing. Then, with a terrific crash, heavy guns on the destroyers behind us opened up and the air was filled with the whistling of shells speeding on their way to destruction and death. Breathless we stood and watched – and there before us broke the scarlet dawn! No sun came up; the clouds hung low and dark; the waves rose cold and unfriendly-like, and along the coast our bursting bombs and shells threw up a crimson curtain.[25]

The Queen's Own Rifles were to put 'A' Company down west of Bernières and 'B' Company to the east, hoping to avoid the worst of the defences and envelop the town. After reveille at 0315 hours, Company Sergeant Major Charlie Martin of 'A' Company caught the moment of leaving the safety of their mother ship, HMS *Monowai*, the converted New Zealand liner: 'All that remained within sight was our own fleet of ten assault craft, moving abreast in the early-morning silence in a gradually extending line facing the shore, 'A' Company boats on the right and 'B' on the left.' However, instead of depositing the two assault companies either side of Bernières, the wind pushed them in front of the coastal settlement, looking into the muzzles of its defenders.

Waiting for them in WN28 was Grenadier Christian Hubbe, who had slept as usual in his bunker, but was woken before the naval bombardment started 'by our Sergeant-Major who yelled that an enemy fleet was off shore and we must get to our battle stations at once. I will never forget the first sight of that invasion fleet. We were amazed and frightened and wondered how we could possibly repel such an armada. Then our *Leutnant* came to remind us of our drills and not to fire until the enemy was in the water and at their most vulnerable. At last the noise seemed to lessen and our Sergeant told us to Stand-to as the enemy were about to land, so we jumped to our weapons, trembling with fear. Then we could see the enemy landing craft coming in and the warships still firing. We forced ourselves to get ready'[26]

'A' Company immediately encountered heavy machine-gun and mortar fire, but managed to scramble off the beach and began clearing

Bernières. 'B' Company were less fortunate, landing directly in front of a blockhouse which cut down sixty-five Riflemen within minutes. CSM Martin remembered:

> the moment the ramp came down, heavy machine-gun fire broke out from somewhere back of the seawall. Mortars were dropping all over the beach. The men rose, starboard line turning right, port turning left. I said to Jack, across from me, and to everyone: *Move! Fast!* 'Don't stop for anything. Go! Go! Go!' We raced down the ramp. None of us really grasped at that point – spread across such a large beach front – just how thin on the ground we were. Each of the ten boatloads had become an independent fighting unit. Bert Shepard, Bill Bettridge and I were running at top speed and firing from the hip.[27]

Being on the extreme right flank of the 8th Brigade attack, Martin's company was also within range of the eastwards-facing 88mm at Courseulles, which set about his men with lethal shrapnel bursts. Lieutenant P. C. Rea's platoon was almost wiped out: the officer was wounded twice, Lance Sergeant J. M. Simpson killed, and two-thirds of the men killed or wounded. Sergeant C. W. Smith counted their survivors – ten out of nearly fifty – and led them off the beach towards the railway station.[28] CSM Martin and his mates, meanwhile, had spotted a small gap in the sea wall, defended by a lone machine-gunner. 'We knew from our training that you cannot be on the move and fire accurately at the same time. If you stop you become a target. Bill Bettridge did stop for a split second. He took his aim and that seemed to be the bullet that took the gunner out, although Bert Shepard and I were firing too. We got to the wall and over it, then raced across the railway line.'[29]

'We saw the five pillboxes on top of the seawall,' recalled Rifleman Doug Hester, with 'B' Company. 'These were our first objective. About five hundred yards out, they had us in their sights and began shooting. The Royal Marines lowered the door. The three in front of me were hit and killed. By luck I jumped out between bursts into their rising blood. Cold and soaking wet, I caught up to Gibby. The first burst went through his back pack. He turned his head grinning at me and said, "That was close, Dougie." The next burst killed him.'[30] Scrambling over the wall, Hester lobbed a grenade into a pillbox, prompting its three occupants to rush out, weapons in hand. One took aim with his Luger pistol but, as Hester later observed, 'the Luger was no match for a Lee Enfield'.

Hester took some of the soldier's possessions as keepsakes, including an inscribed prayer book. Later he mused, 'We were the ones who carried bibles and prayer books. We were the good guys. Weren't we? They were the bad guys. What's he doing with a prayer book?' In 1950, Hester returned the volume to the German's family and was astonished to receive a reply from his mother: 'We lost five children. Ernst was our last, the war took all that we possessed including five children. In this letter you find a photo of my son. Take this as a souvenir of a German comrade, whom you saw only dead, but who was, in the depth of his heart, never your foe.'[31]

Amidst the death and destruction there were some surreal moments. Rifleman Les Wagar with 'C' Company of the Queen's Own Rifles watched a flight of Spitfires patrolling low overhead just as the drenching fire from the rocket ships erupted. The last aircraft collided with a rocket, exploded and fell into the water just offshore. The CO, Major Nickson, was trying to pick things out with his binoculars when he suddenly blurted out, 'My God! There's a Frenchman in a boat out there pulling the pilot out of the water.'[32] Very many recollected the Spitfire's demise, including Lieutenant Peter Rea, who pointed out, 'I had the advantage of standing up, unlike my men who had to stay under cover and were very sick.'[33] Major C. R. Wampach, Royal Engineers, recalled some Canadian sappers attacking a German blockhouse, when a hundred yards away they spotted a group of civilians standing together in a huddle. Their work completed with the pillbox and its occupants, the sappers advanced cautiously to the group. Though the soldiers were greeted with joy and delight when the locals found they could speak French, to the question 'what the hell they were doing there?', the Canadians could only shake their heads in wonder at the answer from the French group – they were waiting for a bus.[34]

The hardiness – or foolhardiness – of the Norman citizenry was further demonstrated in the war diary of the Queen's Own Rifles, which observed '0940 hours. Battalion HQ arrives. At this time it is noted that a café just one hundred yards off the beach is opened up and selling wine to all and sundry.'[35] John Powell, son of a village blacksmith, enlisted in the regular army in 1939. After surviving Dunkirk as part of Montgomery's 3rd Division, he was posted to the 5th Royal Berkshires in 1942 when they became No. 8 Beach Group. 'The training was nothing but a long, hard, boring slog; it was excitement about the second front that kept me going; I thought it would be sweet revenge for what I'd seen in 1940, but I was too busy at Bernières on D-Day to think about it much. My war was a mixture of extremely long periods of mind-numbing boredom mixed with very brief moments of being scared sh*tless.'[36]

On the Bernières beachfront, Lieutenant Herbert, Lance Corporal Tessier and Riflemen Chicoski rushed the main bunker, firing through the embrasures, then posted grenades through the gun slits and silenced it. The rest broke through the beach defences and moved into the town. By 0845 hours, 'A' Company had secured the road through the village to its south-western point, 'B' Company following suit, and by nine Bernières had fallen. Their supporting armour was delayed, not unreasonably because of the last-minute decision to take 'B' and 'C' Squadrons of the Fort Garry Horse DD tanks to within a thousand or so yards of the beach – mirroring what had happened at Gold. Blasting away at the bunkers from the shoreline, with an anxious eye on the rising tide, Major J. A. Meindl's 'B' Squadron remained on the beach until 0930 hours, when the assault engineers cleared a gap in the sea wall, allowing the Shermans through.

Lieutenant Ian. C. Hammerton commanded the Sherman flail troop that landed with them. 'Driver advance!' he ordered: 'As we pass down the LCT ramp my tank's rotor jib strikes a tetrahedron, exploding a shell attached to it. But now we are moving onto a wide sandy beach and I can see the second flail already beating up to the wall. The AVRE tries petarding the sea wall for some time without success.' Hammerton's tank climbed a narrow concrete slipway leading to a gap in the sea wall and destroyed the Belgian gate obstruction at the top, but when he backed off to let an AVRE tow away the wreckage, 'it tips over on its side, one track off the ramp. Another AVRE goes up the narrow ramp, pushes the wreckage and sets off a mine, which halts it on top of the wall.' Hammerton towed away the damaged tank, which allowed a flail to exit ahead of him. Just as he was carefully lining up his Sherman to ascend the slipway, 'Collinge, my driver says "Sir, the water's coming in up to my knees." Then the engine dies and we are flooded. "Bail out!" I yell.'[37]

It was a battle many vehicles lost on the narrow D-Day beaches, where the incoming tide drowned hundreds of valuable vehicles, including Hammerton's mine-clearing tank. Later on in the day he would catch up with his remaining flails, and command the troop again, but his tank on the beach was a write-off. 'C' and 'D' Companies of the Queen's Own Rifles followed their colleagues, but suffered casualties in a different way, striking mined obstacles on the run in. However, Bernières and the inland villages of Anguerny and Anisy – seven miles inland, their D-Day objectives and where they dug in later on – came at a cost of 143 killed, wounded or captured.[38] While 'B' Squadron's leader, Major Meindl, was badly wounded, the rest of his tanks patrolled in a circuit between Fontaine-Henry and Anguerny. It was at about 1500 hours from high ground near Thaon that in the mid-afternoon haze they spotted the 3rd Canadian Division's ultimate objective – Carpiquet airfield, six miles distant. Tantalisingly close, it would not fall into their hands for another thirty-three days.[39]

While the Queen's Own Rifles were busy with their war in Bernières, Lieutenant Colonel Don Buell's North Shore (New Brunswick) Regiment were assaulting Nan Red at Saint-Aubin, landing in LCAs from HMS *Brigadier* and SS *Clan Lamont* at 0810 hours. They had been preceded by a rather eccentric naval bombardment, which Lieutenant J. G. Pelly aboard the destroyer HMS *Eglington* wrote about to his parents soon afterwards:

> we were so close one could plainly see people opening windows or cycling, and it was with sadistic delight that we knocked things down. Finding hardly any opposition, and thus probably few gunsights, the Captain chose his own targets and we were so close that we couldn't miss. Down came a tower, the top of the gasworks went for six; any German who ran out of a house up the street had four-inch shells overtaking him. In fact we had the time of our lives -- all pointing out targets and shooting up anything that took or didn't take our fancy – like the green house the Captain thought to be an eyesore.[40]

The *Eglington* should have been engaging the shoreline bunkers, but was probably aware that her puny four-inch shells would not destroy them. All they could hope to achieve was to distract or harass the defenders while the infantry fought it out with them. Reverend Hickey with the North Shores noted that

> the sea was rough. Soon the area was dotted with our little boats bobbing up and down like sea gulls on a choppy sea. We lined up in position and started slowly over the ten miles to shore. The last three miles were to be covered with a burst of speed. Joel Murray from Cross Point and

I landed together in the water but we could reach bottom and made shore. A young lad next to me fell, a bullet got him. I dragged him ashore, and there in that awful turmoil I knelt for a second that seemed an eternity and anointed him – the first of the long, long list I anointed in action.[41]

'Tracer bullets seemed to fill the air as we came in', recollected Lieutenant Richardson of No. 4 Platoon. 'In our boat morale was never higher and the platoon was merrily singing "Roll Me Over, Lay Me Down" as we approached the shore. The Germans held fire until we were fairly close in. Our first casualty was when an armour-piercing bullet came through the LCA and struck Private White a stunning blow on the forehead.'[42] Lieutenant John 'Bones' McCann recalled, 'We found the guns and emplacement, which were to have been put out of business by the air force, intact and very much in use. Also, Jerry had a beautiful underground system of communicating with his pillboxes. Things weren't going as planned, and unless we captured those heavy guns Jerry was potting landing craft with, things were going to get worse.'[43]

McCann was describing the 50mm gun still in place on the Saint-Aubin seafront today, which is where 'B' Company landed. To attack it the North Shores had a mad dash of three hundred feet to reach the cover of the high beach wall, where many of the battalion sheltered – a gap that constantly narrowed as the tide came in. Hickey, the North Shores' chaplain, remembered the wide, open beach between the water's edge and the cement wall: 'If you could make the wall you were safe, for a time at least, from the enemy fire; but ah, so many of our fine young men didn't make it. The beach was sprayed from all angles by the enemy machine-guns and now their mortars and heavy guns began hitting us.'[44]

All the New Brunswickers remember the open beach littered with the dead or dying. Hickey's job was to retrieve them,

so with our stretcher bearers and first aid men, Doc Patterson and I crawled back again across that fifty yards of hell. By the little disc around their neck I knew their religion. If Catholic, I gave them Extreme Unction with one unction on the forehead, but whether Catholic or Protestant, I would tell the man he was dying and be sorry for his sins, and often I was rewarded by the dying man opening his eyes and nodding to me knowingly. It was a hard job to get the wounded on the stretchers and

East-facing intelligence postcard of Nan Red beach at Saint-Aubin (top), with its high sea wall, assaulted by the Reverend Raymond Hickey and the North Shore Regiment. They were told to orientate themselves using the distinctive 'witch's hat' roofline (see arrow). The pointed roof is visible in the below image, having survived the naval bombardment. An endless tangle of barbed wire hangs down from the sea wall. Below it a DD tank of 'C' Squadron, the Fort Garry Horse, lies where it was knocked out. The P-47 plane belonged to 2nd Lieutenant John A. Weese of the 386th Fighter Squadron, shot down on 10 June. It crashed into the sea; the pilot died and his aircraft was dragged ashore. (NARA)

carry them to the shelter of the wall. I will never forget the courage of the stretcher bearers and first aid men that morning.

At one stage Hickey went over the sea wall to rescue more wounded and mused how on earth he survived. 'I like to think that a German sniper had me in his telescopic sight, but when he saw by my collar and red cross arm band that I was a chaplain, he stayed his finger – well, I like to think it.'[45]

Three swimming Shermans of the Fort Garry Horse had to be abandoned when their LCT sank beneath them, trapping them in the wreck, and a fourth disappeared beneath the waves. The remaining fifteen of 'C' Squadron started waddling to the beach following the infantry of the North Shores, putting effective fire onto the defenders. However, the armour could find no quick exit from the beach and waited for the Royal Engineers' AVREs to provide some – the latter, however, were late. Therefore the squadron's commander, Major William Bray, pointed his own tank at the minefield and ordered the squadron to follow him. They lost three more Shermans to mines, but forged into the town. Soon Saint-Aubin was under Canadian control except for the 50mm strongpoint, which only fell after four hours of bitter fighting. Its forty-eight surviving defenders were lucky the North Shores accepted their dirty-white rags of surrender.

On the western edge of town, 'A' Company managed to break through and after two hours of combat and twenty-five casualties, had linked up with the Queen's Own Rifles on their right, allowing the war diary to boast, 'At 1115 hours, four hours and five minutes after landing, the area was cleared. Thus one of the Atlantic Wall's bastions which had taken four years to build, was completely reduced. Forty-eight prisoners of war were taken and it is estimated the same number were killed.'[46]

As soon as he landed with the British 62nd Anti-Tank Regiment, driving an M10 Tank Destroyer, Gunner Roland Johnston was presented with the ugly side of war. Attached to the North Shores, he never forgot that, 'When we got to the beach we drove straight off and had to run right over a lot of casualties to get up the beach. You had to put it out of your mind. Just forget about it. There was only one way up and a lot of the infantry were still in the water. They were pinned down and took cover behind every tank that went up the beach.'[47]

Of 48 Commando landing with the Canucks on the eastern flank, Royal Marine Dennis Smith recollected that their plan 'was to land on the beach just to the right of the church spire in Saint-Aubin, towards Bernières'.[48] This was to have been *after* the 8th Canadian Brigade, whose task was to secure the beach, using the North Shore riflemen assisted by the armour of the Fort Garry Horse. With the violent weather delaying both the infantry and the tanks, the current instead dumped much of 48 Commando in front of the unsubdued, strongest German positions. Nearly half their landing craft were disabled or destroyed by Rommel's obstacles – implying that even more obstructions and better-trained defenders might well have defeated the landing.

Some of those who waded into the violent surf with their heavy packs perished. The unit's war diary recorded that 'A', 'B', 'X' and HQ Troops

> were able to wade ashore in about three feet of water, but 'Y' and 'Z' Troops could only get ashore by swimming. Many officers and men attempted to swim ashore from these craft and a high proportion of these were lost through drowning, owing to the strong current. Some got to land. The commander of 'Y' Troop, Major Derek de Stacpoole [son of an Anglo-Irish Duke] just made the beach although wounded before he left his LCI. His craft had been damaged by an obstacle and being unable to land, personnel were shuttled ashore by LCT. Captain Frederick Lennard, a strong swimmer was drowned. TSM [Troop Sergeant Major] Trewers was carried far to the east and landed under the guns of the strongpoint at Langrune.[49]

What the war diary tactfully overlooked was that disembarkation was painfully slow from de Stacpoole's damaged LCI. With casualties mounting from incoming fire, the LCI commander lost his nerve and set sail for England with fifty commandos still on board. An incandescent Stacpoole argued vigorously. Muttering 'That's absurd', along with fruitier epithets, the twenty-five-year-old already-wounded officer promptly dived overboard, rather than miss his appointment fighting the Germans. Twenty minutes later, hard on 48's heels, two more LCIs brought Brigadier Leicester with his 4th Special Service Brigade headquarters to Saint-Aubin – welcome reinforcements, but adding to the cluttered beach. This was a graphic illustration of the chaotic experiences of the other Canadian assault battalions caught in near gale-force seas off Juno, as well as those on Gold and Omaha.

Due to the foresight of their CO, Lieutenant Colonel James Moulton, 48 Commando's casualties were lower than they might have been.[50] He had trained his men to fire two-inch mortar smoke from the bows of their LCAs during the approach to the beach. The smoke hid those exiting the damaged craft onto the beach. Commanding HQ Troop, Captain Daniel Flunder noted, 'The surf was incredible, with beached and half-sunken landing craft wallowing about in it.'[51] Depleted in numbers and soaking wet, they found the beach a chaotic and confusing environment, having to rush the sea wall with the New Brunswickers. The commandos thus landed in the middle of the battle for the shore.

Sergeant Clive 'Joe' Stringer from Brownhills in the English Midlands remembered his CO gathering all the survivors together – roughly fifty per cent of 48 Commando were missing at that stage – reallocating tasks and calling 'Forty-eight, this way!': 'It was really chaotic and this is where Colonel Moulton really shone.' Three troops were down to half strength, while 'Y' and 'Z' had only some forty-five (out of 130) between them, Headquarters had lost twenty men and Support Troop had a single three-inch mortar and one Bren gun. As Stringer listened to the commander of 'B' Troop issue his orders in one of the seafront houses, 'Captain James Perry stepped outside to take a last look and was hit and killed by a sniper's bullet.'[52]

On the beach Captain Daniel Flunder watched with slow-motion horror as one of the newly arrived Fort Garry's Shermans, hatches down, trundled along the sand: 'I was sickened to see it run over two of our wounded and was heading for our good padre [chaplain], John Armstrong, who had been badly wounded in the thigh.' Flunder sprinted down the beach shouting, 'They're my men! They're my men!' He reached the tank and hammered on its turret with his stout ash walking stick, the surf having robbed him of all his other weapons and equipment. 'When this failed, I stuck a Hawkins anti-tank grenade in the sprocket, pulled the pin and blew the track off – that stopped it.'[53] Reverend Hickey, the North Shores' chaplain, also recollected the moment: 'The noise was deafening; you couldn't even hear our huge tanks that had already landed and were crunching their way through the sand; some men, unable to hear them, were run over and crushed to death.'[54]

Once through the beachfront houses, the commandos dumped their heavy packs in the small orchard of a house and fought their way through Saint-Aubin, garden by garden. Overwhelming Saint-Aubin cost them three hours of fierce fighting – a job they had thought would be accomplished prior to their arrival. Marine Dennis Smith remembered 'two young girls looking at him in bewilderment from the window of their house, before being pulled away by their mother'. They would attack the WN26 strongpoint at Langrune, which would not fall until the following morning, but on the way there Smith encountered his first French casualty, a youth lying dead in the road, next to his bicycle.[55] The attrition of leaders was great: of the twenty-five officers of 48 Commando, photographed at their camp in Southampton before D-Day, nine would perish.

Reverend Hickey observed that 'like a hospital patient you lost all idea of time in action. Time meant nothing. We were told after that we had been on the beach for two hours.' Eventually he recalled leaving the beach and 'following a little path that led through an apple orchard, we reached the one cobble stone street of Saint-Aubin'.

There Hickey met his first French casualties:

> A man ran across the street, he wanted help; we followed him into his house and there on the floor lay his young wife badly wounded. Doc Patterson stopped the bleeding with a first aid dressing, and she tried to bless herself when I told her I was a priest and would give her Absolution and Extreme Unction. Their children, three little girls of about four, six and eight, looked on terrified, maybe as much because of us as their mother. I spoke to them, but it only seemed to terrify them all the more.

In a gesture replicating the interaction of Lance Corporal Albert Gregory with Arlette Gondrée at the Pegasus Bridge Café, Hickey then remembered he had 'three chocolate bars in my pocket, part of my day's rations. I gave them to the little girls. Oh the power of a chocolate bar! The terror vanished from six brown eyes, and even as terror reigned, the three little girls attempted a smile as I patted their curly heads.'[56]

Not all the civilians had been evacuated: Jeannine Mahia, then a young girl living in Langrune, was woken up by the shelling. As she told me in 2008, her family hurried down to their basement shelter, she noticed with astonishment that the sea was 'so black with ships that it was as though a sprawling city had secretly arrived in the night and been built just off our beach. At first I did not trust my eyes. We could not see any ocean between the separate boats: it was a solid mass. Their masts stuck up like the trees and towers of a town. It was overwhelming for us. Only the day before we had looked out and noticed the Germans kicking a ball about on the sand, like children, and then the water was empty.

How all those vessels suddenly got there without anyone knowing was a complete mystery to us.'[57]

By 0945 hours, the entire North Shore Regiment was ashore, had met up with the Fort Garry's Shermans and were advancing towards Tailleville. The latter noticed maybe one hundred Germans withdrawing from Saint-Aubin towards the village, whose château here housed not only the local Gestapo detachment, but the military headquarters of two neighbouring units – Hauptmann Deptolla's Second Battalion and Hauptmann Johann Grzeski's 8th Company, both of the 736th *Grenadier-Regiment*. 'It was a real bird shoot. We caught them in the open, with all the guns. The exhilaration after all the years of training, the tremendous feeling of lift. It was like the first time you had gone deer hunting', noted one of the Fort Garry Horse.[58] However, Tailleville château would prove an altogether more difficult fight. With several underground bunkers, a communications centre and tunnels connecting Tobruks with machine-guns, mortars and a 50mm cannon, the Germans had designated this position, a mile from the sea, as WN23. It represented the beginnings of Rommel's planned second defensive line, inland from the coastal strongpoints.

A strong stone wall ringed the perimeter into which many loopholes had been drilled (they are still there today), and at least one tree, used as an observation and sniper post, remained in 2014, bearing metal staples hammered into the trunk allowing access to the upper branches. 'C' Company's Major Ralph H. Daughney's report of this engagement read, 'At 1015 hours we started our advance towards Tailleville with a troop of tanks. Progress was slow on the account of mortars and machine-gun fire, as well as sniping, coming from the direction of the Château. It was not until 1730 that this was finally taken and 1900 hours before the entire complex had been searched and some seventy prisoners being taken.'[59] The German defence was ferocious, their last message to General Richter in Caen was entered at 1548 hours: 'Hand to hand fighting inside command post. Hemmed into a closely confined area, but still holding out. Heil Hitler.'

Reverend Hickey observed that

the place was an old château hidden in a clump of trees; it looked as silent as an abandoned farmhouse, but, when we got in range, every tree spoke with a tongue of fire. Quickly we dug in with the small shovels we carried on our backs. How you can dig when you're digging for your life! Foot by foot our men advanced through the network of trenches and barbed wire around the chateau. The Germans took their last stand inside the building and fought on till our tanks came up and blasted the side out of the place. Finally, about twenty Germans, with their hands in the air, ran out to surrender. The rest of their garrison lay around the yard or in the chateau, dead. They were the first German prisoners I had seen. They stood trembling with their hands up, you could see they thought we were going to shoot them. And now, when I recollect, I almost think shooting would have been more merciful than the awful barrage of words and tongue lashing they got from Captain McElwain.[60]

The North Shores continued to search the bunkers and tunnels at Tailleville, and reported capturing more prisoners at 2300 hours, including 'two wounded monocled officers'. In *The Scarlet Dawn*, Hickey's 1949 account of his war, the chaplain recorded that Tailleville

> was a maze of trenches and underground passages. One trench ran right to the beach. We knocked down the door of one underground passage and out trotted a dozen horses, three or four cows and a flock of hens, cackling their indignation. The Germans must have intended to make a stand there. What we were most afraid of now were booby traps. You might innocently open a door and step right into the next world; or press the starter of a newly acquired German car and go sailing through the air with it.[61]

The hard-won battle for Tailleville was unexpected and in some ways more difficult than the much anticipated and planned capture of Saint-Aubin, despite the loss of one officer, Major J. A. MacNaughton, thirteen men killed, and several wounded (one was Alphonse Noël, commemorated by a plaque in the village today). Before the end, the North Shores had brought up portable flame-throwers to winkle out the last of the die-hards. By ten that evening the North Shores had gone firm anchored around Tailleville but had suffered 125 casualties during the day.[62]

A mile away lay another of this inner belt of fortifications. The Luftwaffe radar station outside Douvres, labelled WN23a, originally had had little in the way of protection. Under Rommel's initiative in 1944 the twenty-acre site had been upgraded to include thirty concrete structures, its main command bunker extending five storeys underground.

Led by Oberleutnant Kurt Egle of No. 8 Company, 53rd *Luftnachrichten* (Luftwaffe Signals) Regiment, some 238 personnel, including electricians, engineers and thirty-six air controllers, were stationed here, with their own diesel generators powering several devices, multiple cannon, machine guns and minefields. Although it was bombarded by naval gunfire and its radars inoperative, the Canadians observed many troops entering its perimeter and decided to bypass it on 6 June. The decision was wise. The Douvres garrison would prove too strong to subdue until 41 Royal Marine Commando overwhelmed the site eleven days later, on 17 June, with tank and engineer support.[63]

The 8th Brigade reserve battalion, Lieutenant Colonel J. B. Mathieu's Régiment de la Chaudière, was split between four transports, the *Lady of Man, Monowai, Clan Lamont* and, appropriately, a Canadian vessel, HMCS *Prince David*. They would not begin to arrive until after 0830 hours, following the Queen's Own Rifles into Bernières. Landing on the rising tide, several of their LCAs struck mines and obstacles ensuring many Chauds had to swim ashore. The coxswain of one of these was Jim Baker, a Royal Marine from Blackpool, assigned to the *Monowai*'s 445th LCA Flotilla.

> We were packed with thirty-eight lads of the Chauds, with two other RM crew members … We lost ten of our twelve LCAs to enemy gunfire and mines, which left just two of us in that final assault to the beach. When we got to within a thousand yards of the shore, I looked across at my pal, 'Hooky' Walker – coxswain of the other LCA – who gave me a thumbs-up and a broad grin to say 'we've made it; we're there', but I froze. I could see three Teller mines strapped to an obstacle just under his bow. It vapourised him, the boat, the troops, everything – all gone in a split second. The blast blew our boat up in the air to about twenty feet and we came down amongst the beach defences of Bernières. That was how we landed … Once up the beach, we came under more fire from the church; this time it was snipers. By this point we were climbing over bodies, already victims of sniper fire and mortars. Using these and whatever we could find for cover, we reached the church and the sergeant climbed the tower. In the mood everyone was in, there was no mercy shown to the sniper he found.

Wounded by a mortar bomb shortly afterwards, Baker would be awarded the Distinguished Service Medal for his exploits.[64] Leaving the 7,000-ton

Clan Lamont, Lance Corporal Reg Clarke's LCA of the 558th Royal Marine Assault Flotilla found navigation difficult in the

> black acrid smoke and sea spray. There was a terrific jarring, grating sound underneath, as though the whole bottom of the craft was being torn out. We all lurched forward with the impact. I gripped my rifle. The stench of spilled diesel oil and cordite stung my nose and made my eyes water. Two explosions occurred about fifty yards to our left. Water spurted up and showered down onto our craft in an absolute deluge. We surged back a bit from the beach then moved forward again, dug in and held, 'bottomed'. *Crash!* Down went the armoured ramp and we had our first view of the beach.

They had landed at Nan Green, on the western edge of Bernières, instead of Nan Red, three miles east, opposite Saint-Aubin. Reinforcing the confusion, Clarke was confronted with

> An assault craft, broadside onto the beach, lay on its side next to us. It was shattered; not a single Canadian soldier or the crew had made it. It was a bloody mess – two bodies were actually hanging from the side, where they had been blown by the force of the explosion. The clothing on the lower parts of their bodies, badly mutilated, was missing and large streaks of red ran down the side of the assault craft to the sea, where their life blood had drained away. A nasty wire fence just in front of the concrete wall was decorated with the sprawled bodies of about twenty Canadians [men of the North Shores]; one was headless, God only knows what had hit him. A beachmaster was standing right out on the open beach at the water's edge bellowing his instructions to the incoming assault through a megaphone held to his mouth. He was a very brave man ignoring his dangerous surroundings.[65]

The Chauds reorganised behind the sea wall while the Queen's Own Rifles finished clearing the town. By 1030 hours the former had formed a battle group with 'A' Squadron of the Fort Garry Horse and 105mm 'Priests' of the 14th RCA, but immediately encountered trouble just south of Bernières. Three of the 'Priests' were destroyed by a concealed 88mm gun on high ground, and accurate machine-gun fire prevented the Chauds from closing to deal with the menace. Lieutenant W. Moisan led his men forward but was struck by a bullet which ignited a

The value of the postcards given up by the British public is demonstrated in this pair of images. Canadian troops due to land on Nan White beach at Bernières were briefed to orientate themselves by looking out for the distinctive seafront villa shown above. Men of the 9th Canadian Brigade are shown landing opposite this house in the below photograph, taken by official Canadian war photographer Gilbert Milne at around midday. The distinctive curved concrete sea wall has been breached by engineers, an assault bridge laid across the gap, and troops have advanced to the AVRE parked in front of the villa. (Author's postcard/US National Archives)

phosphorous grenade he was carrying. He continued despite his smouldering battledress, but eventually had to be evacuated for severe burns. He received some consolation in the form of a Military Cross, but it took a section of Queen's Own Rifles, riding on a tank, to outflank and destroy the position – a demonstration of ad hoc tactics which would rapidly become the norm.

The battalion then moved on to Bény-sur-Mer, Basly and Colomby-sur-Thaon in the afternoon, where 'B' Company under Major L'Espérance captured six 105mm cannons and fifty-four prisoners. The Chaud's Carrier Platoon led by Captain Michel Gauvin took four vehicles and twenty POWs, including a colonel and fourteen- and fifteen-year-old German youngsters manning anti-aircraft guns. They, like the rest of the 3rd Canadian and British 50th and 3rd Divisions, halted and dug in at nightfall, when General Sir Miles Dempsey of the Second Army ordered all under his command to pause for the night and consolidate their hard-won gains.

By 1000 hours, General Keller had landed and was trying to assess where to land his reserve, the 9th Canadian Brigade, already an hour behind schedule. However, because neither Courseulles nor Saint-Aubin were fully cleared of their defenders, Keller chose – as if he had a choice – to funnel the entire formation through Bernières. Unfortunately for him this was the town least suited to having a fully motorised brigade group descend on it. Additionally, the 9th Brigade started to land as the tide approached its highest extent, robbing the formation of any room to deploy on the sands. Therefore, it took the 9th an inordinately long time to land, process through Bernières and be in a position to contribute to the battle. It was their mission to seize Carpiquet airfield, but through no fault of their own, the brigade moved off too late to achieve this in daylight. In any case, advance elements of the 21st, and later the 12th SS, Panzer Divisions had already started to block their way, correctly guessing the airbase as a likely objective of the invaders. Keller was recorded as becoming first frustrated, then angry at the realisation that his left flank had stalled in front of Tailleville and was hemmed in by the radar station at Douvres. His centre, too, was sluggish, constrained by the bottleneck of Bernières, which threatened to unbalance his whole front. Fortunately the Germans in the area had been overwhelmed, but throughout the afternoon of 6 June, this seemed anything but the case to Keller.

The decision of all Canadian commanders to dig-in and consolidate before nightfall was wise, although the division has been criticised since for failing to meet its D-Day objectives. In the afternoon there was a general fear of a major counter-attack by the armour of the 21st Panzer Division. It was averted when some clusters of German armoured vehicles were broken up by naval gunfire, and a major tank thrust was destroyed in the Sword sector, as we shall see. However, the latter stages of D-Day saw most units searching for good defensive positions from which to repel the hourly-awaited armoured assault. This was not timidity or poor handling, but in accordance with Anglo-Canadian doctrinal thinking of the time – move forward in controlled bounds, dig in at the first sign of trouble, and let the artillery provide a protective umbrella of fire. It meant that when the Germans counter-attacked on 7 June, their foes were well balanced, prepared and properly entrenched. A further advance on D-Day would have left Keller's Canadians overextended, strung out and very probably destroyed in the ensuing fighting.

Though loath to admit it, the Canadians had been much haunted by memories of Dieppe. In a single day they had completely slain that ghost. In August 1942, the 2nd Canadian Division had lost 907 killed, 586 wounded and 1,946 captured. Less than two years later their army had undergone a revolution in their professionalism and preparation for modern combat. Canada's achievement during 6 June was immense, penetrating deeper than any other assault formation. Their casualties reflected this: 574 men of the 3rd Canadian Division were wounded and 340 were killed. However, securing Juno Beach had allowed 21,400 troops and their equipment to come ashore on D-Day.

At 1600 hours, the Régiment de la Chaudière had started to dig-in along the eastern flank, all the while glancing into the threatening countryside beyond, that – according to the plan – should have been occupied by members of the British 3rd Division. But where were they?

The day had gone so well for the Canadians that the leading elements of 153rd Brigade of the 51st Highland Division were able to start disembarking in the afternoon. Troops of the 5th Black Watch recalled one of their pipers playing 'Bonnie Dundee' as they descended into the cold and still-rough waters. Despite their manifest success, Canada was poorly served for many years in D-Day commemorations. Ignored in both *The Longest Day* and *Saving Private Ryan*, many accounts of the invasion fold Juno into Gold and Sword as the 'British beaches', overlooking the significant contribution from north of the 45th and 49th parallels.

However, that changed with the campaigning of Garth Webb, who had landed in 1944 with the 'Priest'-equipped 14th Royal Canadian Artillery, his unit experiencing significant casualties. Following the fiftieth anniversary celebrations, Webb – from Burlington, Ontario – and several colleagues began a grass-roots movement to remind future generations that fifteen thousand Canadians landed across Normandy on D-Day, of whom 359 (including paratroopers, maritime and air personnel) died, with a further 5,020 perishing in the subsequent two-and-a-half-month-long campaign.[66]

Although a fraction of the five thousand casualties that Allied planners had anticipated at Juno on D-Day alone, these numbers represented a considerable national sacrifice. The result of their considerable lobbying and fund-raising labours was the $10 million Juno Beach Centre. It is located on the western bank of the Seulles at Courseulles, appropriately in the midst of the former WN31 strongpoint. Designed to resemble a maple leaf from the air, this arresting museum opened on the fifty-ninth anniversary of D-Day and, with its excellent archive and multiple displays, has ensured that Canada now has an equal voice when it comes to understanding the battle for Normandy.

Apart from 'One Charlie' at Courseulles and the 50mm gun emplacement intact with its gun at Saint-Aubin, there is one other landmark on Juno that draws visitors. This is a large, timber-framed house that appeared in the background of many black-and-white photos and news-reels of the landings on Nan White. It is owned today by Hervé Hoffer, whose grandparents were evicted from it by the Germans in 1942; Hoffer, who works in Caen, is proud of the fact that 'the Queen's Own Rifles were in this house twenty minutes after the landings started; this was the first house liberated by the Canadians on D-Day'.

It is now known as *La Maison des Canadiens* – Canada House. A plaque on the front reminds the visitor: 'Within sight of this house over one hundred men of The Queen's Own Rifles were killed or wounded in the first few minutes of the landings.' Inside are many relics left by veterans, including an inscription in Hoffer's guestbook. 'Ernie Kells, Queen's Own Rifles – one of five soldiers who arrived at this house on D-Day, now eighty-four years old. Sorry about throwing grenades into your cellar.' Every June, Hoffer lights a paraffin lantern which he hangs on his balcony. At sunset on the sixth, he carries the flickering light down to the beach and holds it aloft, whilst wading into the Channel up to his waist, 'to symbolise the Canadians who came that day from

3. - BERNIERES-sur-MER (Calvados). — La Plage · Le Jeu de boules

Apart from providing a good impression of Nan White Beach at Bernières with its sea wall, this intelligence postcard (top) shows Frenchmen enjoying a game of *pétanque* in front of another distinctive, half-timbered villa. It appears in the background of the lower image of prisoners captured on D-Day being marched to landing craft for evacuation to England. They are guarded by the 5th Royal Berkshires of No. 8 Beach Group. The villa is now known as *La Maison des Canadiens* – Canada House – where a moving act of commemoration takes place every 6 June. (Author's collection)

the sea, to give us back our freedom'. Veterans applaud, bystanders sob, and bagpipers play; it is always intensely moving.[67]

Canadian casualties suggest how doggedly the Germans resisted along Juno Beach, but worse lay in store for them with the deployment of the 12th SS Panzer Division. On 6 June itself, its reconnaissance elements were busy scouting the ground for the rest of their formation, as Obersturmführer (Lieutenant) Peter Hansmann recollected: 'At 0230 hours my NCO in charge, Hannes Rasmussen, was shaking me by the shoulders, shouting "Herr Obersturmführer, the invasion has started. This is not an exercise. The commander is on the phone and waiting for you."' Hansmann was ordered to survey the coast around Bayeux and Courseulles with two armoured cars, and raced north via Lisieux and Caen in the early hours at speeds of up to 60mph. He first went to a vantage point a mile south of Magny-en-Bessin, overlooking Gold Beach. 'To the east stretched an endless dark-gray mass, the sea. Looking through my binoculars I recognised the individual outlines of ships. At irregular intervals flashes of ship's artillery were coming from various spots. Fast boats with high, white, foamy bow waves were spitting out brown clumps of men on the beach.'

At 0745, Hansmann radioed back that he was looking at 'more than four hundred ships with a wall of tethered balloons along the whole coastal strip of twenty miles, as far as the mouth of the Orne'. He then drove east to Creully on the Gold–Juno border, noting the 'bright, wavy lines of fast landing craft constantly racing towards the beach. Hundreds of these boats were sitting in the shallow water, unloading.' Vehicles drove into the sea and waded ashore. Tanks were already rolling along the coastal road. Their short silhouettes gave them away as Shermans. Tearing himself away from the unfolding spectacle, Hansmann sent his last report before speeding back at 1100 hours. 'Heavy fighting taking place along the coastal road at Courseulles-Saint-Aubin-Luc-Lion.' He reflected, 'I wanted to shout at all the generals right up to Adolf Hitler, "Over here, quickly, before it's too late! Whoever can still fight, come here! The fastest, most powerful divisions, send them here! The Luftwaffe – where is it? The Kriegsmarine – where is it? It must get here!"'[68]

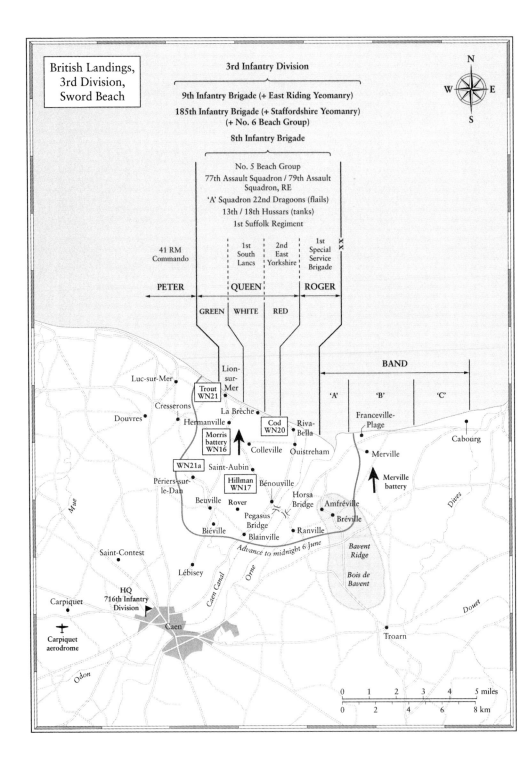

British Landings,
3rd Division,
Sword Beach

3rd Infantry Division

9th Infantry Brigade (+ East Riding Yeomanry)

185th Infantry Brigade (+ Staffordshire Yeomanry)
(+ No. 6 Beach Group)

8th Infantry Brigade

No. 5 Beach Group
77th Assault Squadron / 79th Assault
Squadron, RE
'A' Squadron 22nd Dragoons (flails)
13th / 18th Hussars (tanks)
1st Suffolk Regiment

41 RM
Commando

1st
South
Lancs

2nd
East
Yorkshire

1st
Special
Service
Brigade

PETER   QUEEN   ROGER

GREEN   WHITE   RED

BAND

'A'   'B'   'C'

Luc-sur-Mer
Cresserons
Douvres
Hermanville
Lion-sur-Mer
Trout WN21
La Brèche
Morris battery WN16
Cod WN20
Riva-Bella
Colleville
Ouistreham
Franceville-Plage
Cabourg
Merville
Merville battery
WN21a
Saint-Aubin
Périers-sur-le-Dan
Hillman WN17
Bénouville
Horsa Bridge
Amfréville
Bréville
Beuville
Rover
Pegasus Bridge
Ranville
Biéville
Blainville
Advance to midnight 6 June
Bavent Ridge
Saint-Contest
Lébisey
Bois de Bavent
Caen Canal
Orne
Dives
Douet
Mue
HQ
716th Infantry
Division
Carpiquet
Caen
Troarn
Carpiquet
aerodrome
Odon

0   1   2   3   4   5 miles
0   2   4   6   8 km

33

Iron Division at Sword

'No, you can't stop and have a cup of tea on my beach. Or dig in. Now, get cracking, don't loiter. Through the wire, over there. Go inland. The Germans will get you if you stay here. If they don't, I will. Now move inland. Knock off a few Germans and then have a cup of tea.'

Instructions by beachmaster Lieutenant Commander Edward Gueritz, as recalled by his bodyguard, Able Seaman Ken Oakley[1]

THE FINAL BEACH, Sword, stretched five miles from the eastern edge of Saint-Aubin via Luc-sur-Mer, Lion-sur-Mer and La Brèche d'Hermanville to Ouistreham. This landing area lay opposite the city of Caen, which had long been assessed as key to a successful invasion of Normandy. While the initial Overlord objective was to seize the trans-atlantic port of Cherbourg within fourteen days, the French road and rail network dictated that German reserves from the Pas-de-Calais or Paris would rush to the area through the choke point of Caen, including those heading towards the American sector.

General Miles Dempsey later recalled, 'It would be my job to make sure that they [the Germans] didn't move across, that they were kept fully occupied fighting us in the Caen sector. Monty also stressed that whatever happened, my left flank had to be kept absolutely secure. The Eastern wall along the Orne must be held otherwise the entire bridgehead could be rolled up from that flank.'[2] The Wehrmacht had long assessed the city as a vital hub for counter-attacks, were an invasion to hit the Calvados region.

Meanwhile, their opponents always envisaged using Caen as a springboard – or pivot – to break out. Montgomery had long set his sights on the Caen–Falaise plain to the south as ideal to assemble his mobile forces and strike east towards the German frontier. Denying Caen to the Germans would create a major bottleneck for Rommel's military operations and would be the first place where his panzers met the Allied beachhead. For this reason, taking Caen straight away had consistently been the primary British objective throughout COSSAC and SHAEF planning. Afterwards, both the British and Americans envisaged an attritional phase while the former absorbed a series of vicious German punches designed to let them keep or dominate the city.

The nearest stretch of coast to Caen lay eight miles north, identified as Sword Beach. It encompassed four sectors, each just over a mile wide: Oboe, Peter, Queen and Roger. Of these, Queen had been assessed as the most suitable for assault, on account of the adjacent gap in the offshore rocks, as the local name La Brèche ('the Breach') implied. The availability of good exits off the sand and a helpful inland road network that led directly to Caen – via Colleville-sur-Orne, Biéville and Lébisey – also drew planners to this sector.[3] To the west the presence of the reefs and lack of useful interior routes made Oboe and Peter at the coastal resorts of Luc-sur-Mer and Lion-sur-Mer far less attractive options. Behind both lay the small towns of Douvres and Hermanville, whose narrow roads between stone-walled mansions would act as natural bottlenecks, putting a brake on any swift march on Caen.

In the east, Roger sector was astride the seaside town of Ouistreham Riva-Bella, with a wider beach, but whose very strong defences acted as a deterrent to a frontal assault. Initially the landings were to have been made on a two-brigade front, on Queen and Peter, but in February 1944 this was scaled back to just the 8th Brigade in the van.[4] This was partly due to the shortage of small landing craft – more boats were needed to put in an assault wave; subsequent waves could be brought in by LCI and other craft shuttling from large landing ships.

The main drawback was Queen's narrow frontage of 1,500 yards at La Brèche d'Hermanville, limiting the landings to a single brigade group. Here the sea receded out to an average distance of four hundred yards, but at high tide would leave as little as thirty yards on which troops and vehicles could deploy. The frontage – further subdivided into White and Red sectors – presented another problem: Caen, their objective, lay eight miles distant, over three ridges the Germans were bound to contest, and had rehearsed defending.

While General Frederick Morgan and COSSAC had concluded that it would take the invading forces from Juno and Sword two days to fight their way into Caen, Montgomery had ordered General Sir John Crocker's I Corps to achieve this in one – on D-Day. In the earlier COSSAC schemes, the attack on Caen was to be supported by divisional airborne drops to the south of both Juno and Sword beaches, none of which migrated to Montgomery's eventual plan. Air Chief Marshall Leigh-Mallory's intransigent opposition to the whole notion of airborne operations, and lack of sufficient aerial lift, appear to have been the reasons – deploying three Allied airborne divisions had stretched USAAF and RAF air transport resources to the limit.

However, it seemed to several in the 21st Army Group that once the highly ambitious prize of Caen (code-named 'Poland' on all pre-invasion preparatory maps) had been allocated to John Crocker as a D-Day objective, remarkably little was done to assist him in achieving this aim. Crocker instructed Major General Tom Rennie's 3rd Infantry Division to 'capture or effectively mask' Caen. This ambiguous wording perhaps betrays the confusion of Montgomery's aspirations. To 'mask' a city is medieval military terminology meaning to cloak or surround it, neutralising its defenders, which was not what the 21st Army Group commander had in mind.[5] He needed possession of the town and the commander of the 185th Brigade of the 3rd Division later recorded that for D-Day he had also been instructed to 'establish fortified roadblocks on the other [i.e. southern] side of the ancient city'.[6]

Although the offshore reefs ended before the entrance of the Caen Canal at Ouistreham, the beaches immediately beyond, to the east, stretched seawards into soft mudflats – deposits washed from the mouth of the River Orne. These extended out about 2,000 yards at low tide, double the width of Omaha at low water. Any landing there might be hampered by Allied troops and armour bogging down whilst labouring through the soft sand – under the gaze of German gunners, and it was closer to the heavy batteries around Le Havre. These were not impossible constraints, but would consume huge logistical and engineering resources.

For this reason the five-mile coastline between Franceville-Plage (the coastal resort in front of Merville), via Cabourg, to the mouth of the River Dives at Houlgate was not exactly ignored, but assigned as the reserve beach, split into three equal stretches – Band 'A', 'B' and 'C'.[7] It appeared on larger staff planning maps and is identified as the sixth landing area on the preserved wall map at Admiral Ramsay's former headquarters in Southwick Park. The beachfront of Band was similar to the coast from Luc-sur-Mer to Ouistreham, with developed holiday villas, hotels, a seafront esplanade onto which the Germans had built a series of resistance nests, and the shore studded with the usual obstacles and mines.

No detailed landing plans for this sector appear to have been made, which nonetheless offered access routes inland to the high ground of the Bois de Bavent, overlooking Caen to the east. A landing here might have yielded significant results, as the Bavent ridge was already the focus of the 6th Airborne Division's parachute drop. Just as the Gold and Juno assault plans involved two brigade groups landing and initially fighting their own separate battles until the beachheads merged later in the day, if John Crocker and Tom Rennie had put two brigades onto Queen and Band at H-Hour, they might have had sufficient combat power ashore early enough to have seized Caen on D-Day, as planned.

The drawback was that the two brigades would have been separated by the significant double obstacle of the Caen canal and Orne river. Whereas the waters offered a physical backstop against any German penetration of Overlord's eastern flank, Band and any associated divisions beyond would have had no such luxury. COSSAC and SHAEF seem to have concluded that fears about Band's vulnerability outweighed any contribution using the extra beach could have made to the capture and sustainment of Caen. Just as lack of aircraft prevented the use of more airborne units, the shortage of landing craft probably scuppered any thought of a second H-Hour assault on Band, for it is impossible to believe that the very able Second Army commander, General Sir Miles Dempsey, had not considered in depth the drawbacks of Queen and the possibilities offered by Band.

The upshot was that on 6 June, the 3rd Infantry Division would have to land its 8th Brigade Group (1st South Lancashires, 2nd East Yorkshires and 1st Suffolks) alone. Their task was to open up the beachhead. Within a couple of hours, the 185th Brigade (1st Royal Norfolks, 2nd Royal Warwicks and 2nd King's Shropshire Light Infantry) were to land on the exact same beach and pass through their predecessors. Their objective was to forge eight miles due south and seize Caen, with a population of 60,000. It was with astonishing understatement that one 3rd Division history recorded: 'It seems surprising that General Montgomery had ordered Dempsey and then down the line, via Croker and Rennie to Brigadier K. P. Smith, to capture the large, well-defended city of Caen with one infantry brigade.'[8]

This was hardly a credible proposition unless the defenders were caught seriously off guard and the attackers rushed forward boldly with none of the hesitation that had marked the near failure at Anzio earlier in the year. Indeed, Anzio was the elephant in the room for much of the planning of Overlord. Air Chief Marshal Sir Arthur Tedder noted after Montgomery's first presentation at St Paul's School of 7 April 1944, 'Montgomery, Dempsey and [J. Lawton] Collins seemed to have clearly learnt the Anzio lesson – failure to risk an aggressive action while the enemy still off his balance from surprise.'[9] Capturing such a prize with three battalions might have been an incredible coup, but holding it would have been another matter altogether. Here British operational thinking seems to have been seriously in error, for a German counter-attack would surely have surrounded or ejected any slender hold on Caen. Neither side would have welcomed costly urban warfare, but the Germans certainly had institutional experience on their side from Russian cities such as Stalingrad.

The 3rd Division's reserve formation – the 9th Brigade, comprising the 1st King's Own Scottish Borderers, 2nd Lincolnshires and 2nd Royal Ulster Rifles – would land when circumstances permitted. This was assumed to be around midday, when they would also disembark on Queen. The brigade's mission was to advance south-west to Carpiquet airfield, in conjunction with the Canadians, and assist in reducing Caen.[10]

Also elbowing their way across the narrow landing strip would be a fourth brigade – Brigadier 'Shimi' Lovat's 1st Special Service Brigade, of which No. 4 Commando, with three additional French Troops, were due to arrive on the beach an hour after the assault troops. The specific task of the French – the only ground troops from that nation to land on D-Day – was to turn left and clear Ouistreham of opposition. On the opposite flank, 41 Royal Marine Commando planned to land on the western edge of Sword, turn right and link up at Luc-sur-Mer with 48 Commando coming from Juno, whose fortunes we have explored already. The latter two units, with 46 Commando, also landing on Juno, and 47 Commando, assaulting Port-en-Bessin from Gold, comprised Brigadier B. W. 'Jumbo' Leicester's 4th Special Service Brigade.

Each infantry brigade would be supported by tank battalions: the 13th/18th Hussars would land mostly with DD Shermans in support of

Brigadier Edward E. E. 'Copper' Cass's 8th Brigade. The Staffordshire Yeomanry, experienced veterans of the Western Desert, would land 'dry' and assist the 185th Brigade, led by Brigadier K. Pearce Smith. They were to be followed by the East Riding Yeomanry, accompanying Brigadier James C. Cunningham's 9th Brigade in the race for Carpiquet, who were to link-up with Canadian forces to their right.[11] Comprising the 27th Armoured Brigade, these three armoured units each possessed sixty Sherman tanks, of which fewer than one in four was a 'Firefly', mounting a seventeen-pounder gun capable of drilling satisfactory holes in most panzers.

Major General Rennie's 3rd Division, comprising well-trained regulars – though none with combat experience after 1940 – had been languishing in Britain since Dunkirk, when the 'Iron Division' had been commanded by Montgomery. In the summer of 1942, it had expected to be part of the Dieppe raid, but their role was usurped by the 2nd Canadian Division. The following year this happened again: its then commander, Major General William Ramsden, had taken his formation to train in Scotland in the expectation that they would be invading Sicily in July 1943.

However, the Canadians had been keen to engage in battle and Churchill had happily indulged them. The 1st Canuck Division had been despatched to Operation Husky, leaving the 3rd British Division nursing a dip in morale and fearful the war might be concluded before they could play their part. Now they had a front-row seat and were more than keen to demonstrate their soldierly qualities under the gaze of their former general, now commanding the 21st Army Group. Rennie could also rely on the huge manpower of two beach groups. No. 5 was built around the 5th King's Regiment, No. 6 utilised the 1st Buckinghamshire Battalion of the Ox and Bucks Light Infantry, both Territorial units that had spent most of the war to date in Britain, although the Buckinghamshires ('Bucks') had fought in France during the 1940 campaign.

When the 1st Bucks were nominated as No. 6 Beach Group in 1943, remembered eighteen-year-old Bill Adams, 'this was greeted with mixed emotions as we had envisaged ourselves splashing through the surf, wielding bloodied bayonets. Our battalion had been the rearguard in 1940, holding up the Germans at Hazebrouck to allow the Dunkirk evacuation. Seventy were killed, most taken prisoner; only ten officers and two hundred men had escaped. I wasn't with them then, but there was definitely a feeling of retribution in the air. We bucked up when our CO told us: "From now on, we'll have a seat in the front row of the stalls.'"[12] Also with the 1st Bucks was Robert Gardiner, who was posted into the battalion just before D-Day. Born on 13 December 1926, he was just seventeen when he landed on Sword Beach, undoubtedly making him one of the youngest present.[13] They would start to land twenty-five minutes after H-Hour.

It is easy to assume that all British soldiers were highly motivated to invade France and take on the Germans, but Gunner James Sims, who would later undertake paratroop training, understood that 'why we fight' had to be spelled out to him and his mates. This was done 'in propaganda films and lectures which were designed to clarify what we were fighting for. Getting the English worked up to defend democracy was an uphill task, as the average soldier appeared to have only three basic interests, football, beer and crumpet.'[14] Or as the *Spectator* more primly suggested in that invasion year, 'the British soldier is fighting not for any ideal – although he hates his enemy and the ways of the enemy – but because he knows that Germany must be utterly defeated before he can get home to his family, his football, his beer and his fireside'.[15]

Not for nothing was the regimental motto of the Staffordshire Yeomanry, who would be part of the 3rd Division story, '*Pro Aris et Focis*' – 'For Our Hearths and Homes'. On his final leave before D-Day, Corporal Bob Littlar of the 2nd King's Shropshire Light Infantry, with the 185th Brigade, was taken by his father, a First World War veteran, to the top of a hill in Herefordshire. 'The view was absolutely brilliant. He said to me, "This is what it's all about, this is why we are fighting this war, and if you see a view like this, you know it's worth it." I couldn't have agreed more. That's what you want in life – a beautiful view like that, not a jackboot stomping on your neck.'[16]

The coastline of Sword was very similar to much of Juno and some of Gold: pretty flat and featureless, continuously lined with seaside villas with only the occasional church spire or water tower to help with navigation. Due to the lack of significant landmarks, annotated panoramic photographs, taken by low-flying aircraft and submarines, were supplied to all assault units with key beachfront houses identified by shape or silhouette. Just as the frontage on Queen was very tight, so were the timings. For example, after landing at 0725 hours, two companies (of roughly one hundred men each) from the 2nd East Yorks and another pair from the 1st South Lancs were allotted a mere half hour in which to suppress all the seafront strongpoints. Simultaneously, assault engineers would be creating eight gaps – four each on Red and White sectors – through the obstacles, thick barbed-wire entanglements and mines, and laying white tape to mark them.

This would be under fire and in competition with a fast-rising tide, in the similarly tight window of *thirty* minutes. After this, other waves were scheduled to arrive in a timetable that was impossible to suspend or reverse. In all, twenty-two different waves were programmed to land in the initial six hours (H+360). It is easy with hindsight to label these plans as hopelessly optimistic, but it was thought the massive air and sea bombardment would deliver a more suppressive effect than it actually did. The official narrative of the aerial preparation for Sword and Juno concluded: 'all the evidence available goes to show that the great bulk of the 2,944 tons of bombs missed the beaches, chokepoints and headquarters altogether'.[17] The chief cause was low cloud, which caused fears of the mass slaughter of French civilians or friendly troops.

Rear Admiral A. G. Talbot, commanding Force 'S' from HMS *Largs*, had eighteen flotillas of Royal Navy and Royal Marine landing craft under his command. All were marked with a broad green identification band around their bridges, funnels or bows, and additionally sported the divisional badge of a red equilateral triangle surrounded by three black triangles, which Montgomery had designed for his formation in 1939. Talbot had earlier warned his staff that up to fifty per cent of Force 'S' might perish in the landings. 'We had been warned that we stood little chance of coming back and I think we all felt the wings of the Angel of Death over us,' recalled Commander J. C. Turnbull, chief electrical officer on Talbot's staff.[18]

Protecting them fell to Rear Admiral Patterson's battleships *Warspite* and *Ramillies*, the monitor *Roberts* – mounting a total of eighteen fifteen-inch guns – one Polish (the *Dragon*) and four Royal Navy six-inch cruisers, and fourteen destroyers, two of which were Norwegian and one Polish. All would respond to directed fire from Spitfires or FOB parties when ashore. *Largs* could also direct fighters, several squadrons of which would be roving, permanently on call. Others equipped with auxiliary 'slipper' fuel tanks could be tasked from southern England, and take less than an hour to scramble and fly to the eastern beach areas, with a loitering time of up to forty-five minutes.

The battleships and the *Roberts* would use their heavy guns to suppress coastal batteries east of the Orne, particularly around Le Havre, while the others targeted positions west of the Orne immediately overlooking the two Queen beaches. Additional 'drenching fire' came from the rocket craft – the LCT(R)s, carrying a thousand rockets apiece; Centaur tanks from the 5th Independent Royal Marine Armoured Support Battery; and Royal Artillery 105mm 'Priests' firing from their landing craft, as Lieutenant Sidney Rosenbaum of the 33rd Field Regiment explained: 'At 0655 hours we opened fire at eleven thousand yards. The rate of fire was three rounds per minute for each of the division's seventy-two guns – four tons of high explosive every minute.'[19]

For the assault, the British artillery battalions had opted to use American-made 105mm-equipped M7 'Priests', instead of 'Sextons' mounting British 25-pounders. The 105mm had a longer range and a more lethal high explosive charge, albeit with a less intense rate of fire – three rounds per minute, versus five of the 25-pounder. These guns would discharge over two hundred tons during the thirty-five minutes of their shoot. Before the landing craft arrived, the destroyers anchored off Sword would collectively fire 1,636 rounds, the lowest of any of the supporting maritime forces, but this reflects the limited front they were covering.

In this sense some officers felt that D-Day, with its strict timetable and reliance on a massive pre-assault bombardment, was not unlike a battle of 1916–17. One recalled the horror of 'being locked into the [artillery] timetables of meticulously planned large battles. These invariably left the junior commanders no scope for exploitation. If you found a gap in the enemy defences, adherence to the artillery programme, which rarely could be altered, effectively stopped any personal initiative.' For him, the preparations were like aspects of 'a Kafka-like nightmare ballet. The irony was that this support was planned and given with the best of intentions. The Somme had also cast its shadows on our artillery and armoured commanders. Both genuinely believed that in their hands they had the panacea which would protect us, the infantry, from the terrible slaughter of 1916. Instead they put us in a straitjacket.'[20]

The drawback of the narrowness of the beach was compounded by the rising tide, which would leave precious little room for all the vehicles and equipment due to be landed. Worse still, there were more heavy weapons sited behind Sword, protecting Ouistreham and its access to Caen, while its beach defences were no less dense than on Gold or Juno. Ouistreham (thinly disguised as 'Oslo' on pre-invasion maps) was the key to Caen. Although there was a small fishing harbour at Ouistreham – its name derives from the 'hamlet where oysters were brought ashore and sold' – far more important were its wide lock gates which controlled access to the nineteenth-century canal. The waterway to the city had allowed Caen to develop as a substantial inland port, whereby goods were imported and exported. Earlier, the Orne river had enabled Caen's growth as an international port. A creamy-yellow limestone quarried locally and known as Caen Stone featured in many Norman-era castles and cathedrals constructed in England after 1066, including the Tower of London.

Deployed west of the Dives river with the Seventh Army since May 1942 was Generalleutnant Wilhelm Richter's 716th Infantry Division, with a strength of under eight thousand men.[21] To most military minds, such a formation would be regarded merely as a large brigade. It possessed only six battalions of regular infantry, mostly located in bunkers, but was reinforced by three further battalions of German-officered *Osttruppen* – Ukrainian and Russian volunteers.[22] The 736th *Grenadier-Regiment* of Oberst Ludwig Krug also relied on a number of *Italienisches Freiwillige* (volunteer Italians), mostly employed as drivers and mechanics, but also former experienced *Bersaglieri* who had volunteered to keep fighting in German uniform after Italy's surrender in September 1943. Several of the division's machine-guns dated from the First World War, its transport consisted of bicycles, while its three horse-drawn artillery battalions comprised seized Soviet, Czech and French guns of 100mm and 155mm calibre.[23]

The fifty-two-year-old Generalleutnant Richter commanded from a series of bunkers in a quarry at La Folie-Couvrechef, on the outskirts of Caen. The site is now filled in and occupied by *Le Mémorial* – Caen's war museum. Richter's chief of staff, Major Karl Bachus, flagged up their deficiencies in a risk assessment of March 1944, when he noted their twenty-one-mile-frontage – which included the future Sword, Juno, Gold and Omaha beaches. German military doctrine suggested that divisions should defend a front of no more than about six miles. Bachus also noted the minimal depth of their coastal positions; absence of aerial support and the total lack of coordination with naval gunners who manned some of the artillery positions within their sector.[24]

Richter's men were thus spread thinly over a wide area; some, like Grenadiers Wilhelm Furtner, Erwin Sauer and Helmut Römer, with the rest of their *Zug* (platoon), had the tedious job of guarding crossroads, railways, important buildings and bridges – in their case the crossing over the Caen Canal at Bénouville. In between shifts Römer, Sauer, Furtner and their comrades amused themselves in the local café, sitting at the table nearest the door so they could watch the bridge, sipping ersatz coffee made from roast barley or acorns, sugar beet and chicory, the real stuff having long since disappeared.[25]

Most of Richter's artillery were in fixed positions; thirty-three-year-old Hans Holub, a pre-war bookbinder from Vienna, served in one of these at Colleville-sur-Orne just outside the little Calvados port of Ouistreham. When he joined No. 2 Battery in April 1944, work had just begun to encase its four Czech 100mm field guns in reinforced concrete emplacements to protect them from the increasing aerial attacks that afflicted everyone. Air raids slowed down the work, with the result that only three bunkers were complete by 6 June.[26]

Holub, who had been wounded by a bullet when fighting in the Ukraine, observed a cow tethered in the battery position on his arrival, which changed daily. He found most of his fellow gunners were Poles who were running a thriving black market, taking home cheese and butchered meat on leave, selling it at a vast profit, and reinvesting the proceeds with local Norman farmers. Holub also noted streaks of rust on some of the gunners' equipment and thought they neglected their work – the guns had a range of six miles, and the battery, being within a mile of the coast, would be a major threat to an Allied landing force, were one to land on their doorstep.[27]

Oberleutnant Karl Heyde, on the staff of their parent artillery regiment, recorded,

> Many of our officers had been severely wounded previously. *Oberleutnant* Rudi Schaaf had been shot through the legs; Major Grünewald and Major Hof had both suffered during the winter battles [i.e. Russia], *Oberleutnant* Thiemet had severe injuries to his lungs, and *Hauptmann* Engels had been hit by shellfire at Verdun in the First World War. Some became unpleasant, or socially inept, due to their earlier harsh war experiences. I will not deny that some did get drunk at times.[28]

Richter's mobility came from old French armour that had been adapted to the division's needs: Rudolf Schaaf commanded No. 10 Battery of its 1716th *Artillerie-Regiment*, operating four 155mm howitzers mounted on old tank hulls, supplied courtesy of the French Army in 1940. Schaaf found his posting to France convivial, with plenty to eat and drink, and good weather – a drastic alternative to life in Russia, where he had been twice wounded in the leg, and thus walked with a pronounced limp. 'The soldiers did as little work as possible,' he recalled, 'we were too busy putting up wire and planting Rommel's asparagus to have much time for training.'[29]

On hearing his parents had been bombed out of their Cologne apartment in 1942, the future writer Heinrich Böll, then stationed in France, had likewise reflected on the contrast between his comfortable occupation duties and the terror of living in Germany: 'It's really a fantastically strange war. We soldiers are sitting here almost at peace, brown and healthy, and you are starving at home and experiencing the war in the most terrible way, in the basement.'[30]

Along the length of Sword, some 911 beach obstacles of all kinds had been installed, arranged in the usual rows, mostly with some kind of explosive device attached.[31] There were many resistance nests along the coast. WN25 and WN24 covered Luc-sur-Mer (on maps code-named 'Vienna'), with two 50mm cannon, several 81mm mortars and machine guns housed in purpose-built concrete casemates. Lion-sur-Mer was protected to seaward by WN21, code-named 'Trout' by the Allies. It comprised several positions perched on top of a twenty-foot cliff – for this reason it would not be frontally assaulted but taken from the eastern flank. Like those in Saint-Aubin, the remaining houses within its perimeter had sandbagged windows and strengthened basements, and were interconnected by trenches to the front and rear. Amongst its concrete bunkers were many troop shelters, two observation posts for an inland battery (WN16), a 75mm gun, two 50mm, a 37mm and a heavy mortar.

WN20 at La Brèche was the command post of Hauptmann Heinrich Kuhtz's 10th Company of 736th *Grenadier-Regiment*. Code-named 'Cod' by the attackers, the position comprised several reinforced emplacements set into seafront houses, and mounted a westwards-facing 75mm gun, three 50mm, an 81mm mortar, tank turrets and multiple machine guns in Tobruks. This was not only a major position, but sat at the junction of Queen White and Queen Red – the centre of the 3rd Division's front. Its destruction was actually entrusted to the 2nd East Yorks. Failure to suppress it might tie down either or both assault battalions – as would prove the case – and threaten to snuff out the entire Sword landings. Out to sea, four defensive fire zones had been identified by German artillery firing from a couple of miles inland, code-named 'Goslar', 'Freiburg', 'Füssen' and 'Engers'. One single word to the gunners would be enough to bring down a deadly rain of shells onto these predetermined areas.

WN18 was on the beach at Riva-Bella, in front of Ouistreham, where the Germans had replaced the art nouveau casino with an anti-tank wall

6 — LION-SUR-MER — Enfants sur la Plage   L L

Position of
WN21 TROUT

The seafront of Lion-sur-Mer was not directly assaulted for two reasons: the offshore reef that prevented access to all but the smallest of assault craft, and the WN21 strongpoint – code named 'Trout' by the British. Looking west, this intelligence postcard (top) depicts the defenders' field of fire across the sand at low tide, necessitating that 'Trout' be attacked from the landward side. The immediate post invasion image (below) shows WN21 in more detail, with at least four bunkers or embrasures visible. Today even the bunkers themselves have been demolished, leaving no trace of this strong defensive position. (Author's collection) and two casemates housing 75mm and 50mm cannon and two machine guns, directed by a 55-foot, four-storey concrete fire control tower, which still stands today.[32] The whole of Ouistreham-Riva-Bella was very strongly fortified indeed. With no naturally commanding terrain, the Germans demolished around eighty per cent of the coastal buildings, keeping only those they wished to put to military use. Over thirty bunkers of various kinds housed six 155mm guns, a 75mm, three 50mm, several 20mm anti-aircraft guns, besides a large catalogue of mortars and machine-guns. They also erected several dummy positions, with telegraph poles resembling gun barrels poking out through camouflage netting. *Stützpunkt-08-Riva-Bella* was exactly that: a strongpoint. Across the water on the east bank on the Orne river lay WN8, mounting two 50mm, a 47mm, several mortars and machine-guns. It commanded the approaches to Ouistreham harbour, the canal lock gates and lighthouse. Its steel observation dome resting atop a substantial concrete bunker on the eastern jetty remains in situ today – one of the very few to have escaped the post-war scrap dealers. The key to all these positions was that their arcs of fire had been carefully calculated to interlock in every direction.

The British code-named German positions on the coast with names of fish – 'Trout', 'Cod' and 'Sole', for example – whilst those inland were named after vehicle manufacturers. Directly behind 'Cod' was a depth position, WN17, which lay a mile inland near *Hohe-61* (Height 61 metres), the first of three gentle ridges between the coast and Caen. A sixty-acre site, six hundred by four hundred yards, outside Colleville-sur-Orne, it comprised twenty underground concrete bunkers interlinked by seven-foot-deep trenches. Known to the Allies as 'Hillman', it was capable of all-round defence, was protected by machine guns in Tobruks, sported a 75mm and two 47mm anti-tank weapons, and was ringed by two belts of barbed wire. All approaches were sown with anti-tank and anti-personnel mines. Two bunkers were topped by Krupp steel observation cupolas, which projected two or three feet above ground and were equipped with periscopes and machine guns.

The position was commanded by Oberst Ludwig Krug, responsible for all of the forward defences from Bénouville to Juno Beach. Born in 1894, he led the 736th *Grenadier-Regiment* of Richter's 716th Division, and was a highly professional and meticulous officer who had spent his life in the army. From a long line of soldiers, Krug enlisted just before the First World War and had seen action throughout 1914–18, France in 1940 and Russia in 1941–2, and was thoroughly used to combat.[33] Krug's bunkers were brand new and the position not quite complete, with steel doors and shutters yet to be installed. In the words of the attacking British battalion's war diary, 'The whole position was very well equipped with modern instruments, telephones and every comfort possible in the circumstances. It was in fact very much stronger and better guarded and equipped than had been supposed prior to the operation. It was not known that there were any of the concrete shelters.'[34] Krug's headquarters complex was cleverly sited, extremely well-protected and largely over-looked. A final air photo sortie by the USAAF on 3 June missed the position; being covered in crops, it was invisible from the air. Estimated to be garrisoned by a platoon of around fifty men, it turned out to be Krug's regional headquarters, with a strength of nearer three times that.

'Hillman' served two functions: it was Krug's command post, but a second headquarters bunker also controlled a nearby artillery position. This was WN16, code-named 'Morris'. It contained the four Czech 100mm field guns encased in concrete bunkers, surrounded by wire and machine-guns, that Leutnant Hans Holub had noticed were streaked with rust, suggesting they were not well maintained. Raimund Steiner had been stationed there before moving to command identical weapons at Merville. Located on the northern outskirts of Colleville, 'Morris' constituted a major threat to Queen sector, which it overlooked. The cheese and butch-ered meat business that preoccupied its Polish gunners was hidden from Oberst Krug, who was quite clear about his task. Linked to Richter's headquarters in Caen by a buried telephone cable, Krug was to obstruct the Allies from reaching Caen for as long as possible, whatever the cost.

Had the invasion been further delayed, Rommel would have had time to build a second line of defences in depth. Many more 'Hillmans' would have made the invasion an infinitely more challenging proposition. Rommel knew time was short; in February, Rundstedt's chief of staff, Gunther Blumentritt, recalled, 'Rommel expressed the hope that the Allies would give him time up to May and ended these reflections with the words: *Then they can come*. He meant that by then he would have strengthened his coastal defences sufficiently.'[35] But there was never going to be enough time or resources, and both probably knew it.

Repeating the formula adopted on the other beaches, frogmen, DD tanks and assault engineers with specialised armour started to hit the Queen White and Queen Red from H-Hour, 0725 hours. They were guided in by another miniature submarine, *X-23*, commanded by Lieutenant

George Honour, accompanied by Sub Lieutenant Jim Booth and two colleagues. They had surfaced after waiting on the seabed 7,000 yards offshore since the evening of 3 June. As soon as the convoys passed, Operation Gambit ended for *X-23* and her sister *X-20* off Juno, and they made their way to HMS *Largs* for a debrief and short rest, followed by a tow home after an exhausting mission which had involved remaining submerged for around sixty hours.

SHAEF's planners had warned Major General Rennie to expect eighty per cent casualties in his two assault battalions, a fact which had under-standably not been communicated to the units themselves. Neither had the secret contents of a 14 April 1944 letter from Montgomery to Bradley concluding that the former 'would risk even the total loss of the [two] armoured brigade groups. The delay they would cause to the Germans before they could be destroyed would be quite enough to give us time to get our main bodies ashore and organised for strong offensive action.' In other words, the assault waves were completely expendable in Montgomery's eyes.[36] In ignorance of their commander's sheer ruthless-ness, there was unrestrained optimism as the 1st South Lancs disem-barked from two Empire-class landing ships, *Cutlass* and *Battleaxe*, in their LCAs at 0600 to make their way to Queen White.

Enticed by a poster 'showing a marine, rifle held out front, charging up a beach', young William R. 'Bill' Jones had volunteered in 1942. Itching to take part in the war, he knew the Royal Marines 'accepted seventeen-year-olds whereas you had to be eighteen for the army'. Having trained as a commando, Jones soon heard that 'the crews of minor landing craft were to be Marines rather than naval sailors, on the grounds that if the craft became disabled, the crew would grab their rifles and storm ashore with the troops', which suited him. Early morning on 6 June found Jones with the 537th LCA Flotilla on the *Empire Battleaxe*, ordered to take a section of LCOCU Royal Marine divers with their cargo of explosives, detonators and buoys to Queen White.

Just before D-Day, he and his crew had been warned that LCA crews were to be volunteer-only, because of the expected high casualties, but no one felt like backing out after their months of arduous training. The dangers were very apparent, for

> Suddenly, without warning, all hell was let loose. There was a blinding flash of orange and white light as the LCT in front of us seemed to be lifted out of the water, throwing vehicles and other equipment like

children's toys into the air, before they cascaded back down into the water. Just as our minds and bodies were recovering from the detonation, another cataclysmic explosion came from our rear. The rescue launch disappeared skywards to rain down as a million disembowelled parts.

Jones was in the second wave of LCAs with a line of swimming tanks between him and the first wave. 'The tanks sat very low in the water and were not easy to see. The most prominent feature on our part of the coast was a stark line of three-storey boarding houses at a seaside resort of La Brèche. The rough seas, and other landing craft charging in to the beach, made our task of putting divers down to clear obstacles almost impossible.'[37] Nevertheless his divers slipped overboard around four hundred yards short of the beach, carrying most of their explosives, and began working on the obstacles, unnoticed by the Germans in all the confusion. As elsewhere, they would prepare a row of obstructions to be blown, and detonate them only when the vicinity was clear of friendly forces: this usually provoked a German response.

Many of the assault wave were their own worst enemies as commanders had loaded everything they could think of into landing craft – far more than on training exercises. The result was vessels taking more than they were designed to carry – particularly in terms of vehicles. We have already seen the fatal results this produced on the crossing, but it meant that whole convoys were slowed, travelling at the pace of the slowest boats in the unkindest of seas. While the smaller craft were going in, LCTs carrying the division's three artillery units – the 7th, 33rd and 76th Field Regiments, each unit equipped with twenty-four 'Priest' self-propelled guns – engaged the shoreline with their 105mm guns, firing thirty-three-pound shells. Bombardier John Foster recalled the 20mm Oerlikon anti-aircraft gun on his LCT 'received a direct hit. One minute it was firing away. The next minute a gaping hole and the handrail hanging over the ship. Of the eighteen LCTs which put our three artillery regiments ashore, fourteen became total wrecks, five from obstacles, three from mines and six from enemy fire.'[38]

Lieutenant Colonel M. A. Philp, commanding the 185th Brigade Signals Company aboard the Captain-class frigate HMS *Dacres*, observed gunnery of a very different kind as he passed the battleships *Warspite* and *Ramillies* to port. Shelling shore batteries at Le Havre, he saw how they emitted 'a slow leisurely great tongue of flame licking from their gun barrels, huge mushrooms of smoke formed at the leading end of the flame, the sound of a heavy dull boom reaching us some seconds later. To the west a landing craft exploded with one enormous flash of flame. When it cleared away there was nothing to see – quite terrifying – one moment on the sea, the next moment it had gone.'[39]

Also heading for Queen White was 'A' Squadron of swimming tanks belonging to the 13th/18th Hussars; the 77th Assault Squadron of AVREs and bulldozers and the 629th Field Squadron – both Royal Engineers; 'A' Squadron of the 22nd Dragoons with flail tanks; the Royal Marine Centaur tanks; and the 'poor bloody infantry' of the 1st South Lancs. As the latter set about their task of subduing the defenders, the engineers had to clear four gaps through the mines and obstacles – all these personnel and tasks were replicated on Queen Red. The 13th/18th Hussars were scheduled to launch 'A' and 'B' Squadrons with DD tanks at 7,000 yards.

Surveying the sea from the bridge of the Hunt-class destroyer HMS *Goathland*, however, Brigadier Erroll Prior-Palmer, commanding the 27th Armoured Brigade, altered this to 5,000 because of the waves. At 0630 hours, he announced over the air to his waiting tank crews, 'Floater, five thousand.' Prior-Palmer's forthright decision emerged after a discussion with Captain Eric Bush, RN, the veteran of Gallipoli – a handy example of how prior experience often comes to the rescue. Observing the scene from his destroyer, HMS *Scourge*, Lieutenant Stephen Brown saw that 'the sea between us and the shore was filled with craft carrying tanks and men, all passing our starboard beam. We were instructed to go and lay down a smokescreen and give covering fire for them. We watched the action on the beaches through binoculars and the rangefinder: our troops had very good support from the flail tanks and others which threw flame into the German gun-posts.'[40]

Major Hendrie Bruce of the 7th Field Regiment, Royal Artillery, witnessed the 'LCTs swing round with their bows down-wind and lower their ramps. This allowed those extraordinary little amphibious tanks with high, inflated bulwarks, to crawl down into the water and set off for the shore, looking like a lot of rubber dinghies. We were content to cruise along in their wake, scanning the coastline with our special-issue RN binoculars.'[41] Tank commander Lance Corporal Patrick Hennessey recalled his battle with the angry ocean, and was especially worried about his driver, the only one who remained physically within the Sherman, eleven feet below the canvas, and the one with the least chance of survival should the tank founder. 'We were buffeted about unmercifully, plunging into the troughs and somehow wallowing up again to the crests. It was a struggle to keep the tank on course, but gradually the shoreline became more distinct and before long we could see the line of houses which were our targets. Seasickness was now forgotten.'

With a top speed of around four knots per hour it would take over an hour of hard work for them to reach the beach, arriving with or following – rather than preceding – the infantry. Marine Corporal Bill Jones had noted how the DD tanks were difficult to see, as they sat so low in the water, and indeed three were rammed and sunk by their own LCTs, helplessly being pushed landwards by the storm surge. Hennessey remembered that as he approached 'we felt the tracks meet the shelving sand of the shore, and slowly we began to rise out of the water'. With the driver continuing to manoeuvre, the remaining four crew members 'took post to deflate the screen, one man standing to each strut. When the base of the screen was clear of the water, the struts were broken, the air released and the screen collapsed. We leapt into the tank and were ready for action.'[42] Major Derrick B. Wormald, commanding 'A' Squadron, watched as an LCT bearing assault engineers landed its armour onto Queen White, a few yards to port. 'The turret of a Churchill AVRE was struck and the contents thereof spun into the air after a violent explosion.'[43]

Due to Brigadier Prior-Palmer's intervention, Sword was perhaps the most successful application of DD tanks on 6 June. However, even here, of the two squadrons' worth – forty Shermans – scheduled to launch, thirty-four entered the water, three sank en route, and nine were swamped on the sand by the incoming tide while engaging the defenders. Those swamped were either blocked from moving forward by obstacles or reluctant to advance into suspected minefields, and waiting for a path to be cleared and marked. Just eighteen made it beyond the beach. A forty-five per cent survival rate among the DD tanks may have exceeded the planners' wildest hopes, but was devastating for their crews. Though most were rescued, training for four years to spend an hour in action before being sunk, losing all their possessions, was hardly the blaze of glory of which these regular army cavalrymen had dreamt.

This happened to Hennessey's tank, whilst they were stationary on the sand shooting at German positions:

Suddenly, one particularly large wave broke over the stern of the tank and swamped the engine which spluttered to a halt. Now, with power gone, we could not move, even if we wanted to. We kept our guns going for as long as possible, but the water in the tank was getting deeper and we were becoming flooded. At last, we had to give up. We took out the Browning machine-guns and several cases of belted ammunition, inflated the rubber dinghy and, using the map boards as paddles, began to make our way to the beach.

Hennessey's fate illustrates both the aggressiveness of the incoming tide and the speed with which it surged ashore. 'We had not gone far when a burst of machine-gun fire hit us. Gallagher [his co-driver] received a bullet in the ankle, the dinghy collapsed and turned over, and we were all tumbled into the sea, losing our guns and ammunition. The water was quite deep and flecked with bullets all around us. We got clear of the water and collapsed onto the sand, soaking wet, cold and shivering.'[44]

Both the assault engineer squadrons (the 77th on Queen White, 79th on Queen Red) were part of the 5th Assault Regiment, commanded by thirty-nine-year-old Lieutenant Colonel Arthur D. B. Cocks, Royal Engineers. His formation had double the number of flails and AVREs than for Gold or Juno, the logic being that stronger engineer support would lead to a speedier opening of the beach exits. A regular soldier born in India, he would become the first British officer to die on Sword, as Lieutenant Lambton Burn, RNVR, skipper of Cocks' craft, *LCT-947*, carrying two Sherman Crabs (mine-clearing flail tanks) and four Churchill AVREs, recorded:

> Shells are bursting all round. They are not friendly shorts from bombard-ment warships, but vicious stabs from an enemy who has held his fire until the final two hundred yards. An LCT to port goes up in flames. There is a sudden jerk as our bows hit the beach. Down goes the ramp, and there is a roar of acceleration as the first Crab, named *Stornoway*, disembarks. Colonel Cocks leans from the turret of his AVRE, called *Plough*, and motions the other tank-commanders to follow. But enemy fire is now concentrated on us. There are bursts on both sides and then two direct hits on our bows followed by a third like a whip cracking over the tank hold.

Not unlike the failed cannonade before the Somme in 1916, nothing could better illustrate the sheer inadequacy of the Allied aerial and naval bombardment, which just seems to have warned the coastal defenders to be on their guard. Burn continued: 'The First Lieutenant is flung sideways against a bulkhead and lies stunned. The next Crab, *Dunbar*, stops in her tracks slews sideways blocks the door. Another and greater explosion as the Bangalore torpedoes on board [the AVRE called] *Barbarian* explode with a flash of red. Colonel Cocks is killed as he stands, and there is a scream from within his tank.'[45]

This was witnessed from the neighbouring LCT by telegraphist Alan Higgins, who had already been torpedoed once escorting a Russian convoy. 'While Able Seaman Harry Gee, a Yorkshireman, in our foc's'le was blazing away with his 20mm Oerlikon, an LCT shot alongside us and onto the beach with its cargo of tanks ablaze and ammunition exploding,' he recalled.[46] Unable to discharge any more armour, Lieutenant Burn steered his badly damaged craft back to England, where the dead were buried and survivors transferred to another LCT.

The two assault squadrons of Cocks' regiment would suffer 117 casualties on D-Day, while the 22nd Dragoons operating the Crabs lost 42 men – mostly Armoured Corps personnel inside tanks – and fifteen out of its twenty-six flail tanks. One of the flail tank commanders on Queen White, Sergeant Andrews, 'had already bailed out three times in France in 1940, fought in the Spanish Civil War and had caught it straight away on returning for his revenge. I was extremely sorry to lose him,' remembered William Carruthers, leading 3rd Troop of the 77th Assault Squadron.[47]

Irishman Lieutenant Redmond 'Reddy' Cunningham was commanding 1st Troop of the 79th Assault Squadron. Born in Waterford on Christmas Day in 1916 and one of thirteen children, he had yearned for escape from the closed society that characterised the Irish Free State, and noting with distaste the swastika flag that flew outside the German embassy in Dublin, Cunningham had quietly slid over the border to enlist in Belfast – an act illegal in his home country, although thousands did likewise during what was termed 'the Emergency'. Already a bon viveur with an eye for a good horse, Cunningham's pre-war training as an architectural draughtsman had secured him an immediate commission in the Royal Engineers. Landing on Queen Red, his companion AVRE was destroyed by shellfire, killing all the crew, leaving him with a double task. However, he went on to clear all the anti-tank obstacles in his sector, for which he won a Military Cross, the only Irishman to gain this distinction on D-Day.[48]

Hard on their heels were other dismounted engineers, intending to clear the beach above the high-water mark: on Queen White this was the 629th Field Squadron, whose commander, Major C. H. Giddings, observed the 'landmarks we had been taught to observe from air photos, loomed through the smoke, but a bit damaged, of course. Fountains of spray, bullets whipped up the water, the noise pressed our eardrums, the smell of explosives and smoke filled our noses – and our eyes took at a glance all the debris, human and material, lying everywhere.'[49] One of his men, Sergeant A. J. Lane, recorded how 'When I dropped off the ramp, my Bren gun took me down like a stone leaving me with several feet of water above my head.' Lane kept a cool head, shed his weapon, and managed to scramble ashore but observed: 'Many were wounded whilst in the water and were unable to move away from the advancing tide. The whole area was under fire with casualties high and rising.'[50]

The tight timetable, never mind the weather and the Germans, proved too much for the sappers: none of the eight lanes planned across Queen White and Queen Red were opened in the planned thirty minutes, and after sixty minutes just one was cleared for use. It took seventy-five minutes for the first tracked vehicles to exit – no mean feat in itself – and four hours for the first wheeled vehicles. Part of the reason was the aftermath of the bad weather, which had caused a storm surge. The Channel rose far higher onto the beaches than had been anticipated – in places an extra four feet – and this was the difference between life and death for those wounded and unable to move.

Of the infantrymen heading for Queen White, the 1st South Lancs' adjutant, Captain Arthur Rouse, recollected: 'The boat crews had been ordered to go in at four knots and hit the beach hard. Out of the haze the obstacles loomed up. We had studied them on air photographs and knew exactly what to expect, but somehow we never realised the vertical height of them, and as we weaved in between the iron rails, ramps and pickets with Teller mines on top, we seemed to be groping through a grotesque petrified forest.'[51] Lieutenant Eddie Jones, commanding 8 Platoon, observed how the holiday resort of La Brèche looked 'astonishingly like Blackpool [a north-west English coastal resort], except that instead of the promenade there was a low sea wall, but the gently shelving golden sands were there and a line of seaside villas. The sands were covered with tripods, with mines on top. These towered above us as we made our way between them and were much taller than the photographs had led us to believe.'[52]

Swooping low above them, cloud and smoke permitting, was Flying Officer Douglas Gordon and seventeen other Hawker Typhoon pilots of

This aerial view of Sword Beach, taken during the first few moments, shows how the 3rd Division's assault was confined to the fifteen-hundred-yard stretch of coast centred on Queen White sector. Twenty-five LCTs can be seen milling around – it is too early for the LCIs to arrive. Smoke from two explosions behind Queen Red and numerous fires can be seen. The coastal area under attack is La Brèche; Lion-sur-Mer lies to the right, and Hermanville is just visible under the port wing of the B-26 wearing its invasion stripes. Observation posts at 'Cod' and 'Trout' are spotting for the artillery position at 'Morris'. (NARA)

No. 440 (City of Ottawa) Squadron, Royal Canadian Air Force. Gordon had earlier noted the 'prison invasion stripes' painted on their aircraft. Flying the first of two missions that day, his logbook noted, 'Bombed beach at Lebreche [sic]. Direct support to 3rd British Army [division] on beaches. Flak hot.' Gordon recollected, 'Our job was to dive-bomb some German pillboxes. Did we do anything good? I don't know. All we did was get in and get out. They shot at us.'[53]

Also heading for Queen White, Able Seaman Ken Oakley, with 'F' Royal Navy Beach Commando and bodyguard to beachmasters Lieutenant John Bruick, RNVR, and Lieutenant Commander Teddy Gueritz, had been cheerfully briefed by Lieutenant Colonel D. H. V. Board, commanding

No. 5 Beach Group, 'Do not worry if you do not survive the assault, because we have plenty of backup troops who will just go in over you.' Oakley's D-Day started with reveille at 0330 hours, when he noted

> sighting the Plough formation of stars ahead of us. It was a little too rough for some of the soldiers on board our landing craft and there was much sickness. The sea was one mass of landing craft of all kinds, shapes and sizes. Finally, we got within sight of the stakes – the dreaded stakes, with shells and mines on – which protected the beaches. Our coxswain did a marvellous job. We headed straight for this stake, and at just the last second he missed it; he got it just right; steered us between, and got us through.[54]

One officer in the Beach Group sprinted across the shore, 'dropped down under the lee of a sandbank beside another soldier. "Well, that wasn't too bad after all," he commented, without looking at him. He got no reply, and looking sideways, saw that the man's head had been blown almost off his shoulders.[55] On each stretch of coast, order and discipline was maintained by a principal beachmaster and several subordinates. We have met several of them already. Their job was to guide the flow of men, equipment and vehicles off their patch as quickly as possible, simultaneously supervising the removal of casualties and prisoners of war. They and their small teams of military policemen, medics and signallers (using visual and wireless) had to keep the shingle as clear of clutter as possible, ensuring the strips of sand did not turn into car parks. The beachmaster teams were the ones who summoned landing craft in, told others to wait, and were generally considered to hold a rank 'just above God' on their beach. One of their unforeseen challenges was the diminishing beach space caused by the unusually high tide. When under fire, those on the many stationary vehicles dismounted and started to dig shell scrapes in the sand to protect themselves from shrapnel, which clogged the beach further.

Eighteen men from various arms and services, principally naval officers, fulfilled this unique role across the five beaches; on Sword, this was Gueritz, assisted by Bruick. Within minutes of landing on 6 June, the former had to take over from his badly wounded superior, Commander Rowley Nicholl, whilst his army opposite number, Colonel Board, accompanied by his batman, had just been sniped and killed. Gueritz deployed with a blackthorn walking stick – but no other weapon – further distinguishing himself with a blue-painted helmet and red scarf. Marine Warwick Nield-Siddal of 41 Commando remembered him: 'The most calm man I've ever met in my life. Came along swinging a cane while shells and mortars were landing, and people falling, and he was walking through it, in his blue uniform and gold braid. "Come off the beach. Others have got to land. Come off the beach," he told us.'[56]

Part of Gueritz's job was to create an orderly beach as soon as possible. His organisation included military policemen, as Royal Marine despatch rider Raymond 'Mitch' Mitchell of 41 Commando observed. 'Early in the afternoon I came across an MP, resplendent in white belt, anklets and gauntlet gloves, directing traffic at a road junction.' Mitchell was amazed to find, in a few hours, the chaos of the beach he had landed on transformed. 'The shore was neatly lined with tank landing craft, nosed onto the sand, disgorging vehicles of all descriptions. Royal Engineers were hard at work with bulldozers, clearing mines, laying white tape to mark cleared areas, towing obstacles and abandoned vehicles out of the way, and constructing roadways of Somerfield tracking across the soft ground.'[57] In the dangerous environment of his landing beach, Gueritz lasted nineteen days before shelling inflicted on him a serious head wound. Having just put on his helmet, he 'didn't duck quickly enough', he recalled, as a shell splinter punched a hole through it.[58]

All the LCAs arrived at Queen White on time at 0725, but found the sand still dominated by Hauptmann Kuhtz's WN20 strongpoint at La Brèche, code-named 'Cod', whose various weapons started to inflict many casualties. Later waves, including 'B' Company and battalion headquarters, were pushed by the current to arrive directly under its guns – this would cost them dear, with both 'A' and 'B' Company commanders, Majors John F. 'Spook' Harwood and Robert H. Harrison, killed. Responsibility had come to these men early: they were aged twenty-eight and twenty-six, respectively. Private Malcolm 'Lofty' Petfield had volunteered for the South Lancs at seventeen because in the recruiting office 'there was a large framed picture on the wall and I liked the badge'. He recorded of his H-Hour assault, 'When we landed I was that frightened that I just kept running forward. Where to, it didn't matter, I just followed the lads in front.'[59]

The South Lancs CO, Lieutenant Colonel Richard P. H. Burbury, a regular officer seconded from the Duke of Cornwall's Light Infantry, arrived with a regimental flag attached to a staff around which he intended the battalion to rally – as in days of old. Nearby was the battalion signals officer, Lieutenant Eric Ashcroft, who described their brisk canter along the shore. 'About two-thirds to high-water mark, I was knocked sideways when an 88mm splinter struck my right arm as I was moving across the beach. I just kept moving until the party got clear and took stock of our position some two hundred yards inland.' Ashcroft paused beneath a bank with a barbed-wire entanglement ahead, and applied a field dressing to his wound. 'Colonel Burbury was about two feet away from me and the next thing I knew he rolled to his side, shot in the chest.'

Rouse, the adjutant, remembered that Burbury 'turned to me with his map in his hand and said, "Where are we, Arthur?" Immediately after, and before I could answer, he was shot. His jaw went into spasms and he dropped down. I turned to the second in command who had followed us up the beach, and told him, "You're in command now."'[60] Alas, Burbury's flag was too quixotic a gesture for modern war and had attracted the fatal attention of a sniper. The battalion medical officer was wounded at his side. Ashcroft brought up his son, Michael, on tales of the South Lancashires' heroism and bravery on D-Day, which made such an impact that the boy, later the businessman and politician Lord Ashcroft, became the world's foremost collector of Victoria Crosses and other awards for military bravery.[61]

Throughout the morning, continuous attacks by men from the South Lancs and East Yorks, supported by engineers, Shermans from the 13th/18th Hussars, and Vickers machine-guns from the 2nd Middlesex chipped away at 'Cod' – trench by trench.[62] When 'B' Company's Major Harrison was killed in front of 'Cod', Lieutenant Robert C. Bell-Walker took command, immediately charging its far right-hand machine-gun bunker. 'We saw Bob B-W deal with it in a classic battle school fashion. He crept round behind it, lobbed a grenade through a gun port then gave it a burst of Sten gun fire, but was immediately hit and killed by another machine-gun nest on his left,' remembered the adjutant, Captain Rouse.[63] However, Bell-Walker had eliminated a troublesome pillbox on the western edge of 'Cod', enabling the South Lancs to enter the position and begin to roll it up.

The fanatical officers and NCOs of the 3rd Battalion, 736th *Grenadier-Regiment*, appear to have been responsible for rousing their men, many of them non-Germans, warning that they had no alternative to a vigorous defence – victory or death. Only fifteen of them would survive. Major Maximilian de L'Orme of the Royal Engineers, descended from a famous French medieval architect and commanding the 263rd Field Company, remembered the situation on Queen beach in front of 'Cod' when he arrived: 'It was an absolute inferno, burning tanks, broken down vehicles, and very many dead and wounded lying about in a narrow strip between the sea and the wire at the back of the beach. There were shells, mortars and the occasional bomb falling, and a considerable amount of small arms fire. We were now nearly one and a half hours late, the tide was almost high. Our task of clearing beach obstacles was obviously hopeless,' thought L'Orme.[64]

In fact, 'Cod' would not fall until 1030 hours, by which time the timetable for getting off Queen White was 150 minutes behind schedule. The South Lancs headed for Hermanville, where battalion headquarters was installed, while 'A' Company attacked WN21, aka strongpoint 'Trout', in Lion-sur-Mer, but without success. Their D-Day would cost the battalion 126 killed, wounded and missing, including their CO and ten other officers.

Crossing in *LCT-589* and landing at H+195 (1040 hours), Major Steven Sykes, a former artist serving with No. 5 Beach Group as its Camouflage Officer, recalled 'Cod' as:

> roughly the size of a football pitch. It lay along the top of a fringe of sandhills overlooking the beach to the north, and was bounded to the south by a road running parallel to the coast. There was a large block-house on the western and seaward corner, sited to fire westwards across the open beach, soon converted into a Casualty Receiving Station [it is still there today]. There were other large concrete pill boxes, a medium gun in an open pit, sited to fire all round the area, and also many underground dugouts, some quite large and containing stores. In the south-western corner was an elaborate pill box disguised to look like a house, and all were connected by deep, narrow trenches. We had a wonderful view of the warships, lying not very far out. These were good old-fashioned heavy battleships, ideal for this kind of support, and their heavy guns could reach targets far inland.[65]

With Sykes in No. 5 Beach Group was Major Basil Spence, later a modernist architect best-known for the rebuilding of Coventry Cathedral, destroyed by the Luftwaffe in 1940. Both had served together in North Africa and fifteen years after D-Day, Sykes again found himself working with Spence, creating an important mosaic in Spence's finished church.

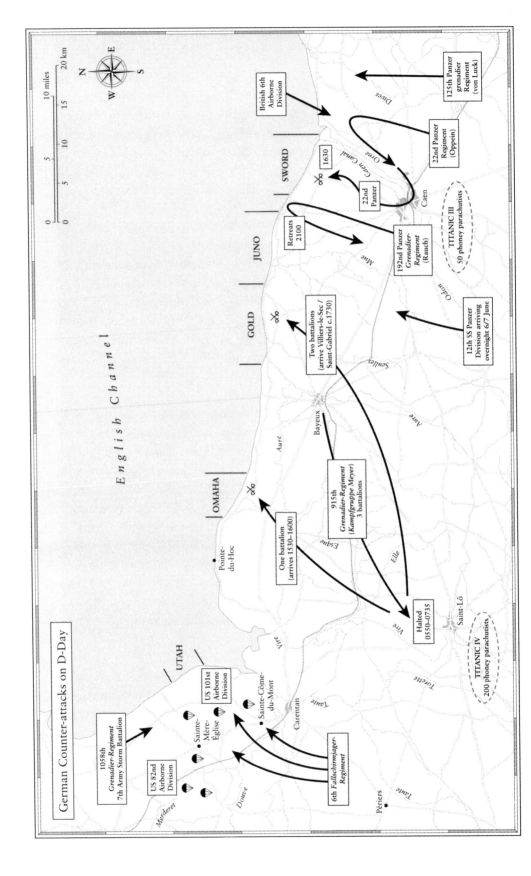

German Counter-attacks on D-Day

English Channel

UTAH

OMAHA

GOLD

JUNO

SWORD

1058th *Grenadier-Regiment* 7th Army Storm Battalion

US 82nd Airborne Division

Sainte-Mère-Église

US 101st Airborne Division

Sainte-Côme-du-Mont

6th *Fallschirmjäger-Regiment*

Carentan

Périers

Pointe-du-Hoc

One battalion (arrives 1530–1600)

915th *Grenadier-Regiment* (*Kampfgruppe Meyer*) 3 battalions

Bayeux

Halted 0550–0735

Saint-Lô

TITANIC IV 200 phoney parachutists

Two battalions (arrive Villiers-le-Sec / Saint-Gabriel c.1730)

12th SS Panzer Division arriving overnight 6/7 June

192nd Panzer *Grenadier-Regiment* (Rauch)

TITANIC III 50 phoney parachutists

Caen

22nd Panzer

1630

192nd Panzer

22nd Panzer Regiment (Oppeln)

125th Panzer grenadier Regiment (von Luck)

Retreats 2100

British 6th Airborne Division

Mderet

Douve

Vire

Taute

Taute

Tortette

Vire

Elle

Esque

Aure

Aure

Seulles

Mue

Odon

Orne

Caen Canal

Dives

N E S W

10 miles
20 km

34

Yeomen of England

'I see you stand like greyhounds in the slips,
Straining upon the start. The game's afoot:
Follow your spirit, and upon this charge
Cry "God for Harry, England, and Saint George!"'

William Shakespeare, *Henry V*, Act III, Scene One,
recited over the PA system to his troops while on their
landing craft by Major C. K. 'Banger' King, 'A' Company,
2nd East Yorks

B OUND FOR QUEEN Red, Lieutenant Colonel Frank Hutchinson's
2nd East Yorks had left the *Empire Battleaxe* and HMS *Glenearn*
in their little LCAs. Lieutenant Hugh T. Bone wrote home that it was
a 'very dull morning, with the land obscured by mist and smoke'.[1]
Others reported repeated rain squalls throughout the morning: the
weather was frequently worse than historians have suggested. All were
aghast to find the defenders very much alive and inflicting severe
punishment on their attackers. Extreme fear played inevitably on the
behaviour of some of the attackers, as Sergeant Arthur Thompson of
16 Platoon, 'D' Company, recollected of one young East Yorkshireman:
'The ramp dropped, but he stood there, petrified, so nobody could
move. Everybody was shouting "Get on the bloody road" and eventually I just pushed him into the waves, so we could exit. By this time
the beach was getting covered with dead and wounded, and that's when
you started to say your prayers.'[2] Perhaps to soothe his own nerves as
much as those of his men, 'A' Company's Major C. K. 'Banger' King

read extracts from *Henry V* over the ship's tannoy to his waiting troops aboard their craft.

A snapshot of the attrition on the beach for the East Yorks can be seen in the thirty men that rode ashore in 10 Platoon's LCA, commanded by Lieutenant Reginald Rutherford. Six were killed and fourteen wounded before exiting Queen, giving a loss rate of sixty-six per cent.[3] Racing up Queen Red towards a gap in the wire to the left of 'Cod', Lionel Roebuck in 13 Platoon of 'C' Company noted, 'wrecked boats lay broadside on, dead comrades floated face down in the tide, others lay in grotesque positions on the beach. Exploding shells fell as we raced towards a gap in the defences. It was being made wider by stalwart engineers who swept the sands with their mine detectors, then laid out tapes to mark a safe track.'[4] Roebuck's ability to bypass 'Cod' indicates that the strongpoint was by then focused on self-defence, allowing other companies of the East Yorks and South Lancs to continue inland to their other tasks.

HERMANVILLE-sur-MER (Calvados) — La Brèche   *Cliché Lesage*

This is La Brèche, in the middle of strongpoint WN20 'Cod' and at the junction of Queens White and Green. The beach can be seen, though the tide is not fully out. Here and to the right, the 1st South Lancashires came ashore at H-Hour, losing their commanding officer straight away. The signals officer, Lieutenant Ashcroft, paused beneath a barbed wire entanglement. 'Colonel Burbury was about two feet away from me and the next thing I knew he rolled to his side, shot in the chest,' he recalled. The location is little changed today, with many of the same houses still in situ. (Author's collection)

However, the delays in front of 'Cod' presented a huge challenge for Brigadier Cass and the 8th Brigade. Due to the fact that the entire division was disembarking on a single beach, the brigade's supporting tanks and artillery – when the defenders had been sufficiently suppressed to enable them to land – were obliged to wait on the fast-diminishing sand while the engineers opened exits. This was why Corporal Hennessey had to lurk at the water's edge while the Channel slowly engulfed his tank. Overall, ninety-two armoured vehicles of all kinds had landed on Sword at around H-Hour, of which over fifty per cent were put out of action, either by mines, gunfire or the tide, including twenty-two Shermans and fifteen flails.

The attrition of landing craft was just as great. By 1150 hours, when the landing ship HMS *Prinses Astrid* up-anchored, having put all her men ashore on Sword, Able Seaman Stan Hough noted she had lost four of her eight landing craft. 'That was not all,' he concluded. 'Out of our little convoy of six ships that set sail last night, over half of our LCAs are missing.' He calculated: '*Maid of Orleans* has lost one out of six; *Empire Broadsword*, eleven out of eighteen; *Empire Battleaxe* eight out of sixteen; *Empire Cutlass* eight out of eighteen, and *Glenearn*, eighteen out of twenty-four' – a total of fifty craft lost out of ninety that had started the day.[5] Twenty-nine LCTs had also been written off, from shelling, mines and the damage caused to hulls by obstacles.

The area behind Queen had been flooded, and beyond the marshes lay WN14, the strongpoint code-named 'Sole', a company headquarters position, but protected by little in the way of fixed defences apart from barbed wire. With armoured support, the East Yorks overran this by 1000, yielding eighty eager prisoners. They then pressed on to attack another inland strongpoint, WN12, known as 'Daimler'. Protected by minefields, it was a substantial artillery position with four 155mm howitzers housed in concrete bunkers, a pair of 20mm flak guns, a mortar and six machine guns. During the preparations to seize 'Daimler' using tanks from the 13th/18th and 'A' and 'C' Companies, Colonel Hutchinson, who had survived Dunkirk in 1940 – where he had been on the 13th Brigade staff of a certain Brigadier Miles Dempsey – was caught by mortar fire and evacuated. The attrition of colonels was becoming very great.

Hutchinson's men attacked successfully in mid-afternoon, but suffered several casualties, Lieutenant Robert Neave of the 13th/18th recording, 'We deposited a smokescreen to the western side of the objective and a troop attacked with all guns blazing. Almost before we started we saw little dejected figures in grey uniforms appearing from the complex. Rather like Singapore, *Daimler* collapsed like a pack of cards almost at once, since it was being fired on from every side, against which it had no real defence.'[6] For some, the war was as brief as that recorded by Private Harold A. Rowland of the East Yorks, whose diary noted: '4 June: Church service on board; 5 June: Cleaned all weapons. Received maps; 6 June: D-Day: Left boat at 0605 hours. LCA hit beach at 0720 hours. Captured beach. Became a casualty; 7 June: On board LCT converted to hospital ship; 8 June: Docked at Tilbury. Arrived Romford hospital.'[7]

By the end of the day they had reached Saint-Aubin-d'Arquenay, a small village midway between Colleville-sur-Orne and Bénouville, but had suffered 206 casualties – including Rowland – during the day, sixty-five of them killed.[8] It was a costly day for the East Yorkshire Regiment, for their sister 5th Battalion had landed on Gold Beach and suffered eighty-five casualties.

Brigadier Cass's reserve battalion, the 1st Suffolks, had arrived on craft from the landing ships *Empire Battleaxe* and *Empire Broadsword*. As with every assault battalion, around ten per cent were held back and placed on an LCI to land later as first-line reinforcements. They were known as LOB (Left Out of Battle), which caused much resentment, though was a practical solution to finding immediate reserves. 'A' Company's radio operator, Frank Varley, had watched HMS *Warspite* firing broadsides – 'the flames appeared half a mile long and the firepower was awesome'. His comrades in 'C' Company, meanwhile, had amused themselves by shaving a victory 'V' into the hair on top of their heads.

In 'B' Company, Private Stanley Gardner recalled queuing up at 0330 hours 'for a breakfast of porridge, two hard boiled eggs, four rounds of white bread and butter and jam and a mug of tea. We gave our rifles the once over, filled the magazines and made sure our ammunition and grenades were ready for use. Slowly the winches began to turn and we slid down the ship's side into the stormy sea.' As he splashed ashore through the freezing water, Gardner felt a huge explosion behind him – he turned to see his LCA had just been torn apart by a shell. Moments later, exactly the same happened to the landing craft of his CO, Lieutenant Colonel Dick Goodwin. Captain Geff Ryley of 'A' Company, a schoolmaster in civilian life, was the first man off his boat – and promptly disappeared. Like a cartoon character, only his helmet showed above the water. Laughter lessened the tension as his men hauled him back on board and the vessel went in closer.[9]

Ashore at 0830, the Suffolks heard over their brigade radio net that 'Rugger' (Pegasus Bridge) and 'Cricket' (the Orne river crossing) were confirmed as captured. Elated by the good news that their left flank was secure for the time being, they advanced through the carnage inflicted by 'Cod' to their assigned task of clearing Colleville, south of La Brèche. Though many Germans were known to be billeted there, they had all fled, and the mayor, Monsieur Lenauld, was soon divulging all he knew about his former guests and their defences over a glass or two of Calvados.

Using his *mairie* as a headquarters, the battalion steeled themselves to take WN16, code-named 'Morris', containing the artillerymen who were more keen on butchering than gunnery. Gardner noted that as he and the rest of 'B' Company approached 'Morris', 'to my surprise, white flags began to appear. Out they came, by ones and twos – mostly Poles – a woebegone, bomb-happy [shell-shocked] crowd.' The garrison of sixty-seven had suffered severe air raids on 1 and 2 June, as well as an early-morning pounding from the six-inch guns of the Polish cruiser *Dragon*, and gave up at 1130 without firing a shot. The Poles were in any case only reluctantly wearing Wehrmacht field grey. As 'B' Company roamed 'Morris' looking for souvenirs, Gardner watched his colleagues looting French food and wine from its cookhouse, playing with German banknotes from a payroll they had liberated, and sporting Luger pistols tucked into their belts.[10]

However, for the rest of the battalion a more formidable challenge lay ahead – half a mile away uphill set in ripening fields of corn lay Oberst Ludwig Krug and 'Hillman'. Lieutenant Colonel Goodwin was not aware of the strength of its defences, and probably was lulled into a false sense of security by the early surrender of 'Morris' without having to fight. With a troop of 13th/18th Hussars tanks, and engineers to hand-clear a path through the mines, he sent in Ryley's 'A' Company, covered by Major Charlie Boycott's 'C' Company to take the position. An account written afterwards bitterly noted that 'Captain Llewellyn, the FOB officer, and his entire party were killed in their LCA, depriving us of our naval support – the cruiser *Dragon* and destroyer, *Kelvin*. Six B-17s were allotted to drop 228 one-hundred-pound bombs on *Hillman*, but not a single one was dropped because of heavy cloud. No flails were allocated to deal with the minefield, either.'[11]

It was not a successful day for the naval FOB parties on Sword – two out of the three groups that landed became casualties or had their wireless link severed in combat. At 1310 hours and under cover of smoke, 'A' Company's assault broke through the barbed-wire perimeter, but was pinned down amid the mines by machine-gun fire. Ryley, the company commander, his leading platoon and section leaders were all killed, and there were no means available to suppress the accurate and interlocking fire of the defenders. Oberst Krug's steel cupolas proved impervious even to seventeen-pounder armour-piercing shells from Sherman Fireflies of the Hussars.

At this point, the leading pair of companies of 1st Norfolks – a battalion from the second-wave 185th Brigade, who had been waiting in Colleville with the 2nd Warwicks behind them – were ordered by Brigadier K. P. Smith to bypass 'Hillman'. They were to press on to their intermediate objective of 'Rover', a farm complex a mile south suspected of housing Germans – soon renamed 'Norfolk House' – before moving to Caen. Moving to the east, however, their right flank was spotted and caught by Oberst Krug's machine guns. The leading companies soon suffered forty casualties, including Captain A. M. Kelly of 'A' Company, and both companies of the Norfolks were pinned down for two and a half hours, their radio sets hit and contact with battalion headquarters lost. Private Geoffrey Duncan with 'B' Company remembered 'several lads from the Suffolks lying dead in various places. One had been shot down in the middle of the road and a tank had run over him. We detoured out of the village and into the cornfields.' Duncan soon developed what he called the 'Normandy crouch', musing, 'I took cover behind earth and clumps of grass that would not have concealed a rabbit. I even tried to squeeze my frame into a rut made by a cartwheel. Self-preservation is a very strong instinct, believe me.'[12]

Private W. Evans remembered the Norfolks' advance: 'We had covered two or three miles and we were doing well until we came to a cornfield. Then Jerry machine-guns in a small pillbox opened up. The lads were soon being cut to pieces as the guns, with their tremendous rate of fire, scythed through three-foot-high golden corn.'[13] 'We had a hell of a baptism,' observed stretcher-bearer Lance Corporal Ernie Seaman with 'B' Company. 'I was detailed to go with 8 Platoon across cornfields. All you could do was lay low; it was suicide to lift your head. We had so many wounded and killed, I was the only stretcher-bearer left. With one of the riflemen to help me, I bandaged and carried them down to an old track where RAMC ambulances picked them up. At midnight, a padre joined us and we buried the dead.'[14]

While Seaman's D-Day medical work would win him a Military Medal, the official campaign and regimental histories omitted to mention that the Norfolks' casualties appear to have been caused in part by the 'friendly' tanks that were supposed to be supporting them. Sergeant Jack Cutting thought 'It was terrible; our company commander held up aircraft recognition triangles to try and make them stop firing, but he was shot down and badly wounded. I think we lost more men to our own fire than we did to the Germans.'[15] Friendly fire incidents are a hallmark of most battles, though rarely recorded; but as at the eastern end of Omaha Beach, careful examination of the records reveals it was a surprisingly common occurrence, as here.

Thus the 3rd Division's 'rapid advance' on Caen had quickly stalled, with two battalions pinned down by a single strongpoint. At this precise moment, with only six infantry battalions ashore, the stalemate opposite 'Hillman' meant that one-third of the 3rd Division's riflemen were being tied down by Oberst Krug, along with perhaps ten per cent of General Rennie's available armour, engineers and artillery. Krug was unaware of this achievement, but he more than adequately demonstrated how a determined opponent can quickly erode an attacker's combat power. More significantly, the German colonel had just shredded the whole 21st Army Group plan to reach Caen that evening.

At this early stage, with the main route into Caen blocked by 'Hillman', General Rennie – who had come ashore at 1030 – appears to have already given up on the idea of taking the city on D-Day, for he met Colonel Goodwin and Brigadier Cass after the first failed attempt and warned them, 'You must capture the strongpoint before dark and be dug in before the expected armoured counter-attack.' In making the not unreasonable assumption that the 21st Panzer Division would soon try to interfere with the landings, Rennie had already – perhaps unconsciously – slipped from an aggressive frame of mind onto the defensive.

The general himself was obliged to battle to get ashore in the first place. On the bridge of HMS *Largs*, he was heard to argue with Admiral Talbot that he should go in as soon as the assault wave had landed. Talbot was unmoved, mindful of the narrow shave they had experienced earlier, from the torpedoes which struck the *Svenner*. 'Rennie insisted that he should embark in a landing craft forthwith, while Talbot stated firmly that he was in command and the General would land at his discretion,' recollected one of the admiral's staff officers.[16] Talbot was correct in standing his ground, but this was a debate the pair should have had over the months beforehand.

After Colonel Goodwin had requested two flail tanks from his brigadier to tackle 'Hillman', and arranged a fire plan with two batteries (sixteen guns) of 25-pounders, he assembled 'C' Squadron of the Hussars and 'A' Squadron of the newly-landed Staffordshire Yeomanry to make another attempt on the irksome strongpoint. His signals officer, Lieutenant Alan Sperling, remembered how impressed he was by the 'utter coolness of Goodwin's planning and orders while under continuous fire, bullets whistling very close'.[17] Yet more trouble lay in store. Only one flail tank arrived, the FOO (Forward Observation Officer) for the guns lost his tank to a mine, and the Staffordshire Yeomanry were called away to deal with the 21st Panzer Division.

Straight away the second attack yielded results and it was immediately apparent that 'Hillman' should have been the object of an all-arms battalion assault, not the limited company-sized affair of earlier. Covered by tank fire, artillery, mortars and smoke, Royal Engineers crawled into the minefield and eventually realised they were dealing with obsolete British Mark III landmines, stock captured at Dunkirk. Following the flail, three Shermans rumbled through the gap and the Suffolks started to mop up the position. Intense machine-gun fire still held them back until Private Jim 'Tich' Hunter of 8 Platoon decided to charge the main bunker, jumping into the trench network, all the while firing his Bren gun from the hip. His mates started to thrust grenades and smoke bombs down the ventilation shafts of each position, and although a bullet grazed the top of Hunter's head, the defenders had started to surrender.

By 2100, fifty of them had been collected and were being interrogated. At that moment the adjutant, Captain Hugh Merriam, was interviewing a group of German prisoners when he was interrupted by shouts and the sound of hundreds of aircraft coming in from the sea. Suddenly, the sky was full of transports towing gliders – this was Operation Mallard to reinforce the 6th Airborne Division nearby. The Suffolks and their prisoners alike stared open-mouthed as 256 heavy Horas and Hamilcars – some carrying Tetrarch light tanks – landed in the neighbourhood. Surrounded by their dead and wounded, it was a well-timed morale boost for the battalion. For their opponents such technology and resources were a confirmation that they had already lost the war. Yet Mallard was not without loss. The airborne armada was watched by Midshipman John Lund aboard *LCT-354*: 'I never realised how frail the airborne bridge was', he reminisced, 'until a large Stirling bomber came hurtling into the sea less than two hundred yards away from us. When it hit the sea it seemed to burst into flame and vanish without a trace of survivors. No wreckage, nothing. As though it had never existed.'[18] Lewis Goodwin aboard HMS *Largs* remembered the moment, too. 'There must have been at least three hundred aircraft with the same number of gliders. Flak could be seen bursting all around the gliders as they circled to land. One Stirling, having released its glider, with its engines on fire, was heading straight for us as we lay broadside onto the beach. It crashed in flames no more than a hundred yards away.'[19]

Supply containers floated down at the same time, those in No. 5 Beach Group noting, 'The parachutes were in many colours indicating their load and they looked lovely in the evening sun. The aircraft turned to the west after the drop and seemed to fly quite slowly and low, right over the section of coast still held by the Germans at Luc-sur-Mer. I saw at least one hit and set on fire as it pulled away over the sea.'[20] An artillery officer thought it 'an impressive demonstration of power precision and planning which lifted our morale'.[21] The action at 'Hillman' was deemed to be over by 2200 hours, when the Suffolks dug in beyond the position, stray shells continuing to cause casualties, but for Major Boycott and the other surviving Suffolks, their stumble before 'Hillman' – for which, in a sense, they had been training since Dunkirk – was a very rude awakening, and an experience that would haunt them long after the war.

With two companies delayed by 'Hillman', the rest of the Norfolks swung further east to reach 'Rover'. Once there, they were ordered to dig in when the threat of a panzer attack in the afternoon materialised. It lay only a mile beyond 'Hillman', but four miles distant from Caen – visible in the distance. The Norfolks' D-Day had cost them fifty casualties, including twenty killed, mostly at 'Hillman'. Meanwhile, Major Sir Delaval Cotter, 6th Baronet, descendant of an ancient Anglo-Irish family that traced its roots back to a Viking king of Dublin, and on D-Day commanding 'C' Squadron of the 13th/18th, suffered the ultimate indignity of his Sherman falling into the German officers' latrine at 'Hillman', breaking a track. 'Defeated by German sh*t' was the phrase that sprang to his mind as darkness fell.

His squadron remained in situ to protect the Suffolks, who had suffered thirty-five casualties, mostly attacking 'Hillman', and a remarkably light toll compared to the other pair of battalions in 8th Brigade. The supporting units lost a further fifteen men in the fight for the position.[22] At 2000 hours, the war diary of the 13th/18th noted twenty-four casualties, and eighty-three personnel missing (many would be reunited on 7 June), and that 'A' Squadron was down to six tanks out of twenty; 'B' Squadron possessed ten, 'C' Squadron thirteen and Regimental Headquarters three. This amounted to thirty-one Shermans disabled, though many would be repairable by the workshops now coming ashore.[23]

Some historians have criticised the Suffolks for their delay in subduing 'Hillman', WN17, and the divisional and brigade commanders for being too formulaic, but under the circumstances – once the first attack had failed – it is difficult to see what else could have been done, for there was no means of bypassing the position.[24] Simply put, no one had expected such a vicious defence of an underrated but formidable obstacle. Later on in Normandy, troops and their commanders were to display far more dash and vigour. Objectives such as 'Hillman' would be routinely drenched with high explosives and automatically seen as a battalion-sized task, with plenty of air support available. However, these were the early minutes of a long and viciously fought campaign, and neither the Suffolks nor the British Army as a whole were acclimatised to its demands.

Meanwhile, Colonel Goodwin nominated the wounded Private Hunter for an immediate Military Medal, puzzled that his battalion's most troublesome soldier had proved one of its saviours. Hunter was a 'tearaway Londoner, kicked out of the Norfolks before the invasion and his officers were tearing their hair out about what to do with him'. On hearing how Hunter had galvanised the second attack which had begun to stall, Brigadier Cass upgraded Goodwin's recommendation to a Distinguished Conduct Medal. The concrete position he helped subdue, opened as a memorial in 1989, is now labelled 'Bunker Hunter'.[25]

The Suffolks were unaware that they had not fully cleansed 'Hillman' of its garrison. Within some of the underground rooms still lurked Oberst Krug and many of his men. Through his periscope, he had watched the slow reduction of his strongpoint, staying in touch with his divisional commander, Generalleutnant Richter in Caen, via his buried telephone cable. As night fell, he phoned Richter with the news: 'The enemy are on top of my bunker. I have no further means of resisting them. What should I do?' Krug's call was not defeatist in tone, for he had been in similar situations in the trenches of the First World War and on the Eastern Front. He knew the solution was to sit tight and wait for reinforcements.

Oberst Ludwig Krug (1894–1972) (centre) put up a remarkably robust defence all day from his headquarters at WN17 (right), code-named 'Hillman' by the allies. Its many deep bunkers had a commanding view in every direction, and blocked the main route to Caen. His tenacity took Lieutenant Colonel Dick Goodwin of the 1st Suffolks by surprise, and the first British attack failed. A second succeeded, but Krug had held up 3rd Division's advance all day. After consulting his divisional commander in Caen, Generalleutnant Wilhelm Richter (1892–1971) (left), by phone, Krug surrendered early on 7 June, unaware that he had completely shredded Montgomery's plan to seize Caen. (Left and right, Author's collection; centre, courtesy Krug family)

This is what he was asking Richter: how long before you counter-attack through to my position? Instead, Richter – never a first-rate commander, and who had been shocked into indecision as his division was destroyed in front of his eyes – replied, 'I can give you no more orders. You must make your own decision now. Goodbye.' Krug was devastated to be let down, but standing next to Richter in Caen was Standartenführer Kurt 'Panzer' Meyer of the 12th SS Panzer Division. A fervent Nazi, he was disgusted with this weak army general and vowed vengeance in the morning. 'Little fish,' Meyer said to those present. 'Tomorrow morning we will throw them back into the sea.'[26]

The 'Hillman' drama finally ended early on 7 June, when at 0645, much to the Suffolks' astonishment, Oberst Krug, immaculately turned out with highly polished boots, emerged from his underground head-quarters, with his batman, two junior officers and seventy other ranks. He was the first senior officer to fall into Allied hands on D-Day and, once it was assessed he was no Nazi but simply an experienced officer doing his job, was treated with great respect for the sheer profession-alism of his defence over nearly twenty-four hours. For his resolute leadership at 'Hillman', Krug was accorded the unusual honour of promotion from Oberst to Generalmajor on 1 July 1944, whilst in British captivity.[27]

What of Brigadier Smith's dash to Caen? The plan had been for his three infantry battalions to assemble by 1100 at Hermanville, link up with tanks of the Staffordshire Yeomanry and self-propelled 'Priests' of the 7th Field Regiment, then surge forward to Caen via Colleville and Lébisey, with the 2nd King's Shropshire Light Infantry (KSLI) clinging to their hulls. The 1st Norfolks and 2nd Warwicks would mop up on their flanks, following on foot. It was a plan – not his – that had been handed down via Generals Dempsey, Crocker and Rennie, and devised by 21st Army Group planners. It seemed to have been dreamt up without reference to weather, terrain or the Germans, and at least one historian has drawn attention to the fact that once Montgomery had put his master plan in place, he showed remarkably little interest in the details of making it work.[28] However, it couldn't work.

Captain Robin Dunn – later a prominent High Court judge and Lord Justice of Appeal – then with the 7th Field Regiment, Royal Artillery, observed that Brigadier Smith, even on Exercise Fabius in May, did not believe in Rennie's plan for the 'dash to Caen'. The presence of the 21st Panzer Division became a fixation in Smith's mind and he was anxious that the formation would cut him off from the beaches. 'There was wooded country on the left and "K. P." wished to infiltrate his infantry through the woods beside the river and approach the objective [Caen] along the divisional left flank. During our final rehearsal he attempted this manoeuvre, which involved keeping one battalion on our original thrust line and passing the other two round their left flank in a wide turning movement.' Lacking confidence in the divisional plan, Smith fought his own war, and the battalions lost contact with one another and their commander, and ground to a halt. Dunn was at 185th Brigade headquarters when Rennie arrived and warned, 'You won't let this happen on the day, will you, K. P.?' Dunn thought it would have been better for Smith to have been sacked on the spot.[29]

Lieutenant Commander Maxwell O. W. Miller, RN, was in charge of 'I' Squadron of landing craft, which put the 185th Brigade on Sword Beach, and included flotillas of LCTs carrying the Staffordshire Yeomanry and American-crewed LCIs. He remembered that,

In the vanguard were twelve Infantry Landing Craft, carrying between them three battalions of infantry who were to advance from the beaches on the tanks that would follow them ashore from the twelve LCTs. Bringing up the rear of the convoy were no less than twenty-four landing craft full of vehicles plus, of course, the baggage we had thrown off the tanks. I hoisted 'Prepare to beach', and the next moment we were in among the mines and struggling to find a patch of bare sand on which to land. My own craft, luckily, escaped and, after dodging a few sunken tanks, we ground our way through the wreck of an assault craft onto the sand.

As his passengers disembarked, to his great surprise Miller

passed half-a-dozen soldiers lying on the deck, kicking and struggling. I could not make out what was happening for a moment, and then I suddenly realised that the men had been wounded. I must admit that it gave me the shock of my life. It was the first time that morning that I realised that we were being fired at. I had been so interested in what I was doing that it had never occurred to me that the shells were meant for us and that they were lethal. I was rather sorry I had woken up, and nipped up the bridge ladders for my tin hat quicker than a dose of salts through a cormorant.[30]

Unencumbered by quantities of vehicles, the three infantry battalions – 1st Norfolks, 2nd KSLI and 2nd Warwicks – were quickly ashore. Sword Beach was awash with eccentrics, besides 'Banger' King of the East Yorks. Major Humphrey M. Wilson, second in command of the 1st Norfolks, had spent many years in India and was fluent in Urdu. As one of his company commanders recalled, 'Wilson was regaling the French in Urdu and when he saw me, he turned round and said, "Eric, these bloody fools can't even speak their own language."'[31] Private David Davies in 14 Platoon of the Norfolks 'was stood up on the steps of the boat telling the lads what I could see. I was bloody terrified, but the adrenaline had started to kick in and we were all ready to go. The noise was incredible, like a demented woman screaming. Time seemed to stand still, but at the same time everything happened so quickly. It was hard to get your bearings. We must only have been twenty yards from the beach but it seemed like miles.'[32]

Not having experienced war since 1940, with many officers and men totally inexperienced, the 1st Norfolks found their advance into the unknown, through villages and down leafy lanes dominated by snipers, extremely nerve-wracking. Regimental Sergeant Major Brooks of the battalion recalled: 'one of my sergeant-majors trod on an anti-tank mine, and it lifted him clean up and flung him into a hedge; he was completely unharmed – he was lucky. We took our first prisoners. They looked a sorry lot and were dirty and untidy. I learned later that they were mostly Poles and Czechs, whose officers and NCOs were Germans.'[33]

Although the beach fighting had largely died down, much artillery was still ranging out to sea. On board one of Commander Miller's LCIs, Captain Harry C. Illing of the Warwicks' 'A' Company recorded the 'spouts of water shooting up as bombs and shells fell into the sea. One of our three LCIs was hit offshore three times by shellfire, had both its ramps shot away by mortar fire, and another hit a mine as it grounded.' Their assembly area off the beach, in and around a walled cemetery on the southern outskirts of Hermanville, came under sniper and machine-gun fire from Cresserons – on their right flank – which is where they started taking casualties. As Illing observed, 'the war did not seem really quite what we expected'.[34]

One of Illing's platoon commanders, Lieutenant Kingston 'Tiny' Adams, recollected that 'it was misty and we could just make out the houses behind the beach which were getting heavily bombed. All the men were packed below deck and it was pretty grim for them. There was a lot of seasickness and they did not get much sleep. I had all my men to worry about, so this took my mind off what was about to happen – but the privates only had their own concerns to dwell on; it was harder for them.' Adams had joined his battalion on leaving Shrewsbury School with my father in 1940, and had spent his war years training for D-Day. He recalled that year being interviewed by Montgomery on applying to become an officer in the Royal Warwicks, the general's old regiment. Shrewsbury had also educated Montgomery's predecessor at the 21st Army Group, Bernard Paget, and General Sir Miles Dempsey of the Second Army. Tiny Adams would be injured at Lébisey Wood the following morning, his combat during the Second World War amounting to little over a day.[35] Once ashore, one of his soldiers reminisced of the battalion, 'They were all local Birmingham lads, and in between the shells falling and the general noise of war, you could hear a heated argument going on about the merits of [Aston] Villa and Birmingham City football clubs in a couple of slit trenches behind you, and it seemed then as if you weren't so far from home.'[36]

The narrowness of the beach, the delay imposed by 'Cod', clearing sufficient lanes through the beach obstacles, and the tiny real estate on which to park a growing number of vehicles then combined to great congestion of staggering proportions. Some vehicles, including those of the engineers and anti-aircraft units, had to stay close to the sand, while Sherman tanks, self-propelled guns, artillery tractors towing their weapons and Bren gun carriers all queued up to exit the beach and deploy to where they were needed. Although the 185th Brigade Group began landing at 1000, the strong onshore wind pushed the incoming tide further up the beach than expected. At high tide the depth of useable beach available was down to just ten yards – *thirty feet*. The Staffordshire Yeomanry, arriving alongside the 105mm 'Priests' of the 7th Field Regiment at 1030 hours, recorded 'a terrible jam on the beach where no organisation appeared to be operating and no marked exits were to be seen. The majority of our tanks remained stationary for one hour and even after leaving the beach, vehicles remained head-to-tail for long periods on the only available routes.'[37] This was also the tragic consequence of landing with a single brigade at a time.

Some of the advance elements of Rennie's reserve formation, the 9th Brigade Group, had started to land as early as 1000, but the main body did not arrive until 1300 hours, when Brigadier Jim Cunningham stepped ashore. As he did so, in his mind he was already visualising the initial moves of the 2nd Lincolns, 1st King's Own Scottish Borderers (KOSB), 2nd Royal Ulster Rifles and East Riding Yeomanry. First to Cresserons – firming up the division's right flank, and making contact with the Canadians – then striking towards Carpiquet. To his amazement, Cunningham found 'not only Tom Rennie but John Crocker, in their red hats. I said I had never before been beaten into battle by my divisional and corps commanders and we had a good laugh about it.' The latter pair had come to the conclusion that the 3rd Division's most important task lay not in seizing Caen, but in shoring up the eastern flank, which seemed to be under pressure. Since mid-morning, the Royal Engineers' 17th Field Company had been furiously assembling rafts and Bailey bridges as alternative crossings over the canal and the Orne, should the bridges be destroyed – though they remained intact.

Cunningham was told that his mission of seizing Carpiquet on the right flank had been cancelled, and he was now to move to the left flank and shore up the 6th Airborne Division at 'Rugger' (Pegasus Bridge).

He initially put up a token protest, but was warned that a panzer attack was expected, most likely against the lightly equipped airborne forces. As he went towards his armoured command vehicle to relay the necessary orders, accompanied by his anti-tank staff advisor and intelligence staff,

> at that moment a stick of six mortar bombs landed on us, killing six and wounded six more. I was unable to convey the new instructions to my staff. Colonel Dennis Orr, my second-in-command, had gone over to Pegasus Bridge to report on the situation. When I was wounded, he was not present to take over and it was a very long time before he got back. The result was a long hiatus when the Brigade should have been moving and nothing happened. In short, if a number two is considered worthwhile, do not use him on some other job instead.[38]

Just as Rennie had earlier abandoned the idea of Caen – if only subconsciously – by insisting 2nd Suffolks seize 'Hillman' only 'by nightfall', not earlier, he and Crocker reinforced that decision by abandoning the march on Carpiquet. Though disappointing in view of the later bloodshed to seize the airfield, it was the correct decision, for 'Panzer' Meyer's advance elements of the 12th SS Panzer Division, with armoured vehicles, were already in possession. They would almost certainly have bested Cunningham's brigade, whose East Riding Yeomanry armoured support had yet to land when he was ordered to change tack. The wounding of 9th Brigade's Brigadier Jim Cunningham also removed the anomaly that 9th Canadian Brigade was commanded by Brigadier Ben Cunningham.

Due to the long delay waiting for orders, (the British) Cunningham's 9th Brigade contributed little to the march on Caen, or defence of Pegasus Bridge. The 2nd Royal Ulster Rifles dug in near Périers-sur-le-Dan; the KOSB eventually moved across to the left flank as Rennie had intended, overnighting on the high ground overlooking Saint-Aubin-d'Arquenay and Bénouville; while the Lincolns were left at Cresserons on the right flank. Cunningham's 9th Brigade had been needlessly scattered across the divisional front. Meanwhile, their armoured support in the shape of the sixty Shermans of the East Riding Yeomanry – in every way a mirror of their Staffordshire brethren, just a different county 'set' – were only allowed by beachmasters to land after the congestion had cleared, at 1400 hours. This was woefully late, not their fault, and the price paid for an inflexible timetable.

Future novelist David Holbrook, commanding a troop of the East Ridings, had arrived by LST and was waiting to transfer to a Rhino ferry. He recalled:

Two shells straddled our ship and with cracking pillars of sea, spoke to us closely of death and the enemy. This was the new thing that showed it was not an exercise. Everything else we had done so much before that it was automatic and uninteresting, but the violence of the battle onshore, and the new factor of calculated death directed at you, produced a dryness of the mouth. We bellowed ashore through the breakers onto a beach cleared by those who had left their derelicts behind them and their dead mourned by white beachmarker flags. The windsocks showing the gaps they had made spoke their message – get on and inland, through our achievement.[39]

As they did so, a flight of Junkers 88s managed to penetrate the anti-aircraft defences and make a low-level bombing run, aiming at landing craft off Sword and Juno. An eyewitness aboard one vessel reported seeing at least one Ju 88 'flying so low along that it raised plumes of spray from its propellers just yards above the sea'. Despite numerous assertions that 'there were just two Luftwaffe aircraft over the landing beaches on 6 June – "Pips" Priller and his wingman, Heinz Wodarczyk' – there were other missions, the erroneous assumption entirely due to the publicity Cornelius Ryan gave to Priller's mission. The Ju 88s were witnessed by many, also the raid by nineteen ground-attack Focke-Wulf 190s equipped with rockets which flew missions in the late afternoon, claiming two direct hits on landing craft off Saint-Aubin at around 5.40 p.m.. *Luftflotte* 3 recorded they flew 139 strike sorties over and around the invasion area on 6 June, twenty-four reconnaissance missions and thirty-five night-fighter sorties, claimed nineteen aircraft shot down, losing two.[40] In contrast, on D-Day, the Allies admitted 127 of their own aircraft lost to all causes.

Rifleman Richard R. Harris, with 'B' Company of the Suffolks, noted the aircrafts' arrival as preparations were being made for the second attack on 'Hillman'. 'For the first and only time [as far as he was aware] that day, the Luftwaffe decided to intervene in the shape of four Ju-88s which, to our great joy, were pounced on by a hoard of Spitfires and all were destroyed.'[41] Private J. Garner, driver of a Bren Gun Carrier with the 1st South Lancs, landing in a later wave with the Carrier Platoon of Support Company, also remembered them.

Out of the clouds to the east came thundering at least seven Ju-88s. In a flash every anti-aircraft and machine-gun, probably rifles too, was directed at them. Most of them were hit and one, a mass of flames, ploughed into the beach very near us. My carrier lifted and rocked violently as the Junkers' bomb load went off. Dirt, sand and other debris rained down on us. Green, red and white flares were shooting from the wreckage and ammunition was going off like Chinese crackers at a funeral.[42]

This was the same raid recalled by Sapper Eric Saywell, with the 205th Works Section, Royal Engineers, who saw 'around 1600 hours a squadron of twin-engined bombers zoomed low across the fields, and as they unloaded and the string of explosions came nearer, I screwed up in my slit trench, face down with helmet on the back of my head. At least one was brought down, cartwheeling onto the beach nearby.'[43] The numbers of planes in these descriptions vary, and there seems to have been at least two attacks by Junkers, for the 22nd Dragoons noted in their war diary: '0900 hours. Eight Junkers bombed us, causing casualties in 13th/18th HQ. Also sniping from Hermanville church tower which we ranged our guns on and eventually blasted out.'[44] Even though little damage was caused, these few Luftwaffe attacks certainly slowed down disembarkation, which prolonged the congestion.

On 6 June Generalfeldmarschall Hugo Sperrle's *Luftflotte* 3, covering France and the Low Countries, could only field 891 aircraft of all types, of which 497 (or fifty-six per cent) were operational.[45] Once powerful, it was represented by only a few fighter squadrons, widely scattered to avoid being bombed. Most Luftwaffe fighters had been pulled back for the air defence of German airspace. As Allied aircraft would manage to block the Luftwaffe from even reaching the *Invasionsfront*, in desperation Sperrle threw in everything he had, including trainers. Among them were long-obsolete Junkers 87 Stuka dive bombers. On 6 June, P-51 pilot Bud Fortier recalled spotting 'about twenty heading north towards the beachheads at treetop level. We could hardly believe our luck. Ju-87s were old and slow, with a crew of two: the pilot and a rear gunner who had one machine-gun, hardly a match for the Mustang with its four .50-inch calibres. The 357th Squadron was also in the area and eager to get in on the turkey shoot. Our biggest problem was avoiding collisions with other P-51s scrambling to get at the Stukas. None reached the beachhead.'[46] None should have been flying – the Luftwaffe records indicate these were from a non-combatant pilot-training squadron near Chartres, about a hundred miles' direct flight from the assault area.

Of the nine shot down, one was an aircraft that had served in the Spanish Civil War, and two were experimental versions, designed for aircraft carriers. This pointless gesture cost the Luftwaffe eighteen valuable aircrew. All were instructors, like twenty-three-year-old Feldwebel Josef Weiszenbrunner, an Iron Cross-decorated experienced flight commander on Fw 190s. With no spare fighters on his airbase, he chose to head towards certain death in an old Stuka.[47]

The Luftwaffe had no hope of winning even local or temporary air superiority over the Normandy beachhead – but it could still have fought a more effective campaign than it did. The failure of the Luftwaffe to contest the skies would have grave consequences. Yet in March 1946, Generalleutnant Friedrich Dihm, special artillery advisor on Rommel's staff, would write in captivity of his belief that 'had it not been for Allied air power, it would have been possible, in my opinion, to prevent a successful invasion during the first few days after the initial assault. These were the most critical days for the Allies.'[48]

The Staffordshire Yeomanry's cap badge was originally a Stafford Knot, surmounted by a crown – a century earlier they had been known as the Queen's Own Royal Regiment. When James A. Eadie took over as its commanding officer, he had suggested they add a background of a red triangle, similar to the logo of Bass breweries, of which he was a director, and where many of the regiment had worked before the war. As perhaps the first-ever 'commercial sponsorship' of an established military unit, this neatly illustrates the close relationship between part-time reservist officers and their men, many of whom doubled as employers in peacetime. Neville Patterson, who served with them on D-Day, reflected on three of his fellow yeomanry crewmen buried in a Normandy cemetery: 'There was Topper – trooper extraordinaire, bank clerk and self-appointed toff, whose real function was to fire the gun. Then there was Ginger – driver, but also womaniser par excellence whose modest ambition was to remain alive long enough to confer his favours on the local talent. And Jim – the wireless operator, whose war had interrupted the reading of Greats at Oxford, the only one capable of reading a map and compass accurately.'[49]

The regiment's unusually strong bond had seen them through heavy losses incurred during the Western Desert campaign. As such, they were used to engagements at long ranges against opponents they could see. They had not trained for duels at a few hundred yards with near-invisible opponents, which would become the norm from D-Day onwards. As a Territorial Army tank battalion, its ranks all knew each other socially and the officers hunted together. Familiarity with landscape from horseback easily translated into proficient tank commanders, able to anticipate terrain from the turret, and spy out covered hull-down lairs from which to watch, as well as ambush positions which threatened them. Both would be needed in the coming hours.

While the yeomanry tanks waited immobile, through no fault of their own, Brigadier Smith and the 2nd KSLI's Lieutenant Colonel Jack Maurice met near Hermanville at 1115 hours to decide on a course of action. Both were riding bicycles, which is highly illustrative of the traffic chaos. Should the infantry start on their own, or wait for their tanks? In the background, a sense of occasion had been introduced by the town's chief fireman greeting his liberators, bearing champagne and wearing his formal polished brass helmet. Mindful of General Crocker's I Corps order that 'The task of the assaulting divisions is to break through the coastal defences and advance some ten miles on D-Day. Great speed and boldness will be required to achieve this', the upshot was that the Shropshiremen would march to Lébisey, with two rifle companies leading astride the main axis, 'X' to the left, 'W' on the right, followed by 'Z' and 'Y'. They set off at 1230.[50] Valuable time had already been lost.

General Crocker had gone on to order:

> As soon as the beach defences have been penetrated, not a moment must be lost in beginning the advance inland. Armour should be used boldly from the start. Such action will forestall the Germans' reaction, confuse him, magnify his fears, and enable ground to be made quickly. All available artillery must be ready to support the advance. If opposition is met which cannot be overcome by these strong advance guards, simple plans embodying the full resources of artillery and armour must be employed to dislodge the opponent quickly and certainly.[51]

Starting at El Alamein in 1942, Montgomery had found that large quantities of artillery was his solution to all battlefield problems, and these orders might just as well have been written by him. In their language, it is evident these orders were written by Crocker and his staff as much for Montgomery to approve as for his subordinates to enact. The invasion would be the pinnacle of everyone's military career, and Montgomery controlled access to it. Ambitious officers either played it the general's way, or not at all.

Halfway to Caen, the KSLI were held up by snipers in the church tower at Beuville, and a passing M10 tank destroyer was enlisted to remove them. Its shell caught the bells, which 'rang out like the Hunchback of Notre Dame'. Corporal Bob Littlar remembered, 'A corporal came up and told me who had been hit by snipers. Most of them were other NCOs. We got our jack knives out and removed the stripes from our uniforms and put them in our pockets. We rubbed some dirt onto our uniforms where the stripes had been.'[52]

This would soon prove a divisive issue during the campaign, with some British commanders content to let this happen, while others considered this a test of discipline and insisted rank be worn. Perhaps sensing the disquiet due to snipers, Colonel Maurice of the KSLI was seen 'walking unconcernedly at the centre of the road, playing as usual with the chinstrap of his helmet. Everyone followed his example in moving steadily forward under fire.'[53] In searching for the inspiring British equivalent of Colonels Canham and Taylor or Brigadier General Cota on Omaha Beach, it becomes apparent that the British Army ticks in a different way. Calm indifference to danger was the method many officers chose to motivate their men, and Maurice's behaviour was a good example of its tactical effectiveness.

At about 1600 hours, the reconnaissance troop of the Staffordshire Yeomanry had caught up with the KSLI and deployed round Beuville and neighbouring Biéville, where the latter captured a soldier of the 21st Panzer Division, which caused great consternation. This appeared to un-nerve Brigadier Smith who, like Rennie, started thinking only in terms of defence, rather than a bold strike to Caen. Mopping up on their left were the 1st Norfolks and, to their right, the Shropshires' 'W' Company had advanced onto the high ground around Périers-sur-le-Dan, where a large German gun position was sited. This was WN21a, the Second Battery of the 155th *Artillerie-Regiment*, which featured four 122mm ex-Russian guns in field emplacements surrounded by wire. As with 'Morris', many of the artillerymen were Polish and it was a captured Pole in field grey who showed the KSLI the way through the protective wire entanglement. With help from 'C' Squadron of the Staffordshire Yeomanry, the guns were silenced, but it cost the company thirty casualties.

Importantly, this allowed the armour, including tank destroyers, to ascend to the Périers ridge and deploy in overwatch against any threat to the beachhead. Meanwhile, Major Peter Steel's 'Y' Company of the KSLI had pushed on as far as they could, reaching Lébisey Wood, a mile north of Caen, by nightfall. However, the constant engagements along the way and the stalemate at 'Hillman' meant that the 192nd *Panzergrenadier-Regiment* had beaten them to it. Lébisey was less of a wood than cornfields with high-standing crops, surrounded by hedges and copses – difficult going for the infantry with almost no visibility. The settlement of Lébisey was described by Brigadier Smith as a 'long straggly village with narrow, heavily wooded lanes, and commanding view of the whole area. It was a formidable obstacle not revealed in the air photographs.'[54] When Major Steel was killed at nightfall, the KSLI withdrew, being too far ahead for the rest of 185th Brigade to support, and the D-Day objective of seizing Caen was finally recognised for the gamble it was.

The KSLI moved back to stronger positions around Biéville and Beuville at 2315 hours, the day having cost them 113 casualties, mostly in and around Lébisey. The 2nd Warwicks, to the left of the KSLI, and who might have helped at Lébisey, had instead been ordered by Brigadier Smith to bypass 'Hillman' beyond the Norfolks and make their way towards Caen via Bénouville and Blainville-sur-Orne. They skirted around the troublesome strongpoint far to the east where the ground falls away to the Caen Canal, and followed some of the route taken earlier by the commandos. The Warwicks then left their 'D' Company in Bénouville, assisting the 6th Airborne Division, while the remainder advanced along the western bank of the canal, and dug in at Blainville, two miles short of Caen. Their losses on D-Day would be light – four killed and thirty-five wounded – but on the following day they would get drawn into the fight for Lébisey Wood and suffer disproportionately, with the catastrophic loss of their CO, nine other officers and 144 other ranks.

The KSLI's departure from Lébisey was in miniature the way the battle would have played out, even had Brigadier K. P. Smith achieved the 'speed and boldness' required, and arrived there with all of his 185th Brigade. They would have had to contend with the 21st Panzer Division and other forces, who knew the terrain, had rehearsed fighting across it and had already staked out their claims. With many other calls on the 3rd Division's resources, Smith's men would have been on their own, at the end of a long piece of elastic stretching back to Sword Beach, and run the risk of being cut off, surrounded or having all three battalions ejected by the Germans. They had few support weapons ashore with which to protect themselves, and most of Brigadier Prior-Palmer's armour had been switched to guarding the flanks of the beachhead.

However, Captain Robin Dunn with the 7th Field Regiment, Royal Artillery, thought this was an 'incredible' use of armour. 'The country east of the Orne was wooded and unsuitable for tanks.' Dunn assessed the failure to reach Caen lay not just with Brigadier Smith's fear of panzers. General Rennie seems to have shared this, and in switching armour to the flanks, Dunn assessed that Rennie had effectively sabotaged all hope of reaching Caen. 'The plan now lay in ruins. 9th Brigade and the East Riding Yeomanry hardly fired a shot all day and took no part in the advance towards Caen.' Dunn echoed what many commentators have noted throughout military history. 'You can do with a platoon on D-Day, what you cannot do with a battalion on D+1 or a division on D+3'.[55]

'Speed and boldness' were all very well, but the simple truth was also that the 3rd Division had simply too few troops on the ground for the several missions it was attempting. In addition to reaching Caen, it had to consolidate the beachhead and link up right and left with the airborne and Canadian divisions. Meanwhile the Germans heavily reinforced Lébisey – the gateway to Caen – overnight. They would remain there for the next six weeks.

Brigadier Smith's 1984 autobiography was written in self-justification and defence of the decisions he took on D-Day. However, he had already demonstrated a lack of faith in the plan during Exercise Fabius, and appears not to have been wholeheartedly behind it on D-Day. However, if the 185th Brigade was 'sticky' in reaching Caen, it was because Rennie, Crocker and Dempsey had become infected with Montgomery's overconfidence in his 'master plan'. None paused before the invasion to reassess its viability and give Smith enough combat power. In many ways, thought one historian, 'Montgomery's greatest error was not his failure to take Caen, but his prediction of its capture in the initial assault.'[56]

'Hillman' has been restored in recent years and is now one of the best-preserved positions along the Calvados coast. Positions like 'Hillman' in Normandy, together with the obstacles and gun positions, were not designed to block or halt the Allies – but to delay. Their purpose was to buy time, while the invasion location was identified, confirmed and reinforcements sent. Today's holiday resort developers are reconstructing the Normandy coastline with as much energy – and concrete – as their *Organisation Todt* predecessors, but only now are the French authorities beginning to list the Reich's bunkers as historic landmarks, ensuring the few that are left will be saved for posterity.

There is no better place from which to understand the *Atlantikwall* than to stand atop Ludwig Krug's position at 'Hillman' and gaze at the nearby coast. Then look inland; the outskirts of Caen are also just within sight from this prominent spot. Here, in a single glance, the whole story of the eastern sector of the Allied assault unfolds, for the coast would witness the landing of the British 3rd Division on D-Day, whose objective, Caen, proved just beyond their grasp.

There was now a protective ring of armour and artillery around Sword, including Sherman tanks, 105mm 'Priests', M10 tank destroyers (in British service, armed with a seventeen-pounder and known as an 'Achilles') and towed six-pounder anti-tank guns to meet an expected counter-attack by panzers. Colonel Jim Eadie had anticipated that they might pounce and make for the ridges of high ground at Biéville and Périers. He determined to occupy them first.[57] He was accompanied by the KSLI's own six-pounders and M10s from the 41st Battery of the 20th Anti-Tank Regiment, who were able to select some good concealed reverse slope positions. Eadie knew all about clinging to ridges and using high ground to his advantage, from his experiences at Mersa Matruh and El Alamein, for which he had been awarded a DSO. He was correct in his homework, accurately predicting his opponents' precise moves. Unfortunately for the 21st Panzer, tasked with defending the vicinity of Caen, the River Orne flowed through the city into the sea. This imposed a physical barrier that would channel Generalleutnant Feuchtinger's two armoured infantry regiments to either side, meaning they could not support one another.

When the Allies war-gamed the likely reaction of the 21st Panzer during the equivalent of one of Erich Marcks' *kriegsspielen*, they concluded one threat would be an attack from Lébisey heading towards the western flank of Sword, which is precisely what happened. Wisely, Oberstleutnant Josef Rauch, the experienced commander of its 192nd *Panzergrenadier-Regiment*, had exercised his men over the same terrain on which they would fight from 6 June onwards. Another dangerous avenue was identified astride the River Mue, which flows from near the

Carpiquet aerodrome west of Caen into the Channel at Courseulles, in the Canadian sector – and was exactly the route some of its units attempted to take, together with the 12th SS, on 7–8 June.[58]

The 21st Panzer Division had been ready to move since 0200 hours, when alerted by its duty officer, Hauptmann Eberhard Wagemann, at the formation's headquarters in Saint-Pierre-sur-Dives. After the war, Generalleutnant Feuchtinger, his divisional commander, deliberately misled many historians with his memoirs, debriefings and commentaries on British Army staff rides with his claim that 'I waited for instructions, then on my own initiative placed a battalion of my *panzergrenadiers* under the local 736th *Grenadier-Regiment*, with orders to recover the Bénouville bridges.'

However, Feuchtinger had no idea what was happening: he was still carousing in distant Paris. 'Ever since the first reports concerning enemy landings were received, the Divisional Commander had been in constant telephone communication with Seventh Army,' Feuchtinger would later claim.[59] Yet his subordinate Hans von Luck recorded that Feuchtinger returned 'at daybreak', which on 6 June was at 0558.[60] The general's mistruths pepper the various campaign narratives he wrote after the war, and he glossed over the fact that on New Year's Day 1945, when Nazi Party officials arrived to investigate why he had been absent from his command post on 5–6 June, they *again* found him absent without leave. Court-martialled, he would be reduced to the rank of private.

Oberst Hans von Luck, leading the 125th *Panzergrenadier-Regiment*, remembered of his boss that he 'was an artilleryman, with no combat experience, and none of panzers'.[61] Feuchtinger was an opportunist Nazi, who had helped organise the pre-war Nuremberg Rallies, the *Parteitage*, and owed his position more to political zeal than military competence. The division had originally been stationed in Rennes, but in April 1944, Rommel had been successful in lobbying for it to be moved closer to the coast. Feuchtinger's headquarters at Saint-Pierre-sur-Dives, south-east of Caen, would enable his units to reach the Calvados coast, Dieppe or the Somme equally fast.

Messages decoded at Bletchley Park had confirmed the 21st Panzer's worrying move nearer to Caen on 14 May, the day before Montgomery's second briefing at St Paul's School. Yet German dispositions on any particular date before 6 June need to be taken as a blurred snapshot at best, for Rommel had been in the process of shuffling many units, trying to persuade Berlin to move reserves closer to the coast, and narrowing the frontages of those on the littoral. From the positioning of his mobile units, it is obvious that the Desert Fox was hedging his bets by making sure that several threatened areas – Brittany, Normandy and the Somme estuary – were covered.

The 21st Panzer Division had been one of Rommel's most trusted Afrika Korps units – which James Eadie had previously met in battle – and because of this, it was greatly feared. SHAEF planners and intelligence estimates vastly overrated its firepower, assessing it possessed '240 Panthers, Mk. IVs and Tigers, as well as forty assault guns', unaware that in truth it had been disbanded and reformed with 112 Panzer Mark IVs and some obsolete French armour, and some of its armoured infantry were conveyed in commandeered trucks, rather than armoured half-tracks.[62] Ultra may have provided insights into formations, but not necessarily their precise order of battle. Likewise, Montgomery's 21st Army Group seemed unaware that the 21st Panzer possessed no Tiger tanks at all. All of these sixty-ton heavy tanks in the west were grouped exclusively into *Schwere Panzer-Abteilungen* (heavy tank battalions) of about forty-five Tigers each, which were switched around the battlefield, usually attached to a corps, as required. Only three such battalions would ever find their way to Normandy.[63]

Typical of the old hands with the 21st Panzer was Oberfeldwebel Ernst Röhling, a thirty-one-year-old pre-war career soldier from Wiesbaden, who had earlier seen service in France and Russia before his posting to No. 8 Company of Hans von Luck's 125th *Panzergrenadier-Regiment*. Röhling was destined to be wounded on D-Day leading his platoon against British paratroopers from the 6th Airborne Division. Feuchtinger's other armoured infantry regiment was Josef Rauch's 192nd, which included Unteroffizier Hermann Schiller, a veteran of almost continuous service from 1941 to 1943 in Russia, where he had been wounded twice and decorated by the Romanians. In July 1943 he had been rested by being transferred to the newly formed No. 3 Company of the 192nd *Panzergrenadiers*, with whom he would serve in Normandy and be wounded a third time.[64]

The teeth of the 21st Panzer Division were its two tank battalions of Panzer IVs, of about fifty tanks each, in the 22nd Panzer Regiment, led by the personable Hermann von Oppeln-Bronikowski, a former gold medal winner in dressage at the 1936 Olympics. Oppeln was a holder of the Knight's Cross, 'having three times survived the destruction of his own tank by enemy fire', as Admiral Ruge recalled. When Rommel dropped in on Oppeln's unit at Falaise on 11 May 1944, the latter had 'arrived *after* us, having apparently celebrated the previous evening, and uttered without much emotion the single word – "Catastrophe"'. Arriving drunk after a visiting general would have been enough to finish most careers, but Rommel had 'noticed at once that Oppeln was an excellent soldier, refrained from making any angry remarks, and learned all he wanted to know. The unit made a good impression.'[65]

Oppeln was supported by a first-class selection of officers and NCOs, including Hauptmann Anton Herr, commanding No. 5 Company. A professional soldier, Herr was candid about his fears: 'I was terrified to suffocate in my tank and burn alive.'[66] Another of Oppeln's tankers in No. 4 Company, wireless operator Werner Kortenhaus from Solingen, near Cologne, recalled, 'we assumed we would be able to push back a sea landing. Indeed, we took it for granted. We young panzer men were enthusiastic at the thought we were perhaps going to be in action.'[67]

The division's artillery regiment and anti-tank battalion consisted entirely of self-propelled guns. Rather than utilising regular German equipment, one of its officers, Major Alfred Becker, in his civilian life an engineer with a PhD in metallurgy, had cleverly married field and anti-tank guns with French tank hulls captured in 1940, the work undertaken in steelworks in Paris and Caen. The artillerymen were led by officers like twenty-five-year-old Leutnant Hermann Dauscher, who had started the war as a *Kanonier* (private). Two years later, as an experienced soldier in Russia, Dauscher had been commissioned in the field and posted to Crimea. But his various wounds from the east took their toll, and 1944 saw him in Normandy with No. 9 Battery of the division's 155th *Panzer-Artillerie-Regiment* operating four old French 155mm guns, expertly attached to armoured hulls by Dr Becker.[68]

Some of this artillery was already stationed north of Caen before 6 June in static or semi-permanent positions. It was men like Luck, Röhling and Schiller, Dauscher, Becker and Oppeln who kept the 21st Panzer together, as Feuchtinger had no aptitude, or interest, in command. Feuchtinger was a charlatan who commanded by keeping competent leaders close. Many of his subordinates were highly decorated – another was Günter Halm, who had won a Knight's Cross aged eighteen in North Africa: he was Rauch's *Ordonnanzoffizier*, or ADC. Feuchtinger liked to surround himself with such accomplished soldiers, and was quick to promote or decorate others, as a way of deflecting attention from his own shortcomings as a commander.

It was Hans von Luck's 125th *Panzergrenadier-Regiment* that had started to clash with elements of the 6th Airborne Division during the morning of D-Day. They were stationed on the eastern side of the Orne river and knew the terrain well. Luck's units – his men were equipped with armoured half-tracks, trucks and bicycles and some self-propelled artillery, but not tanks – were committed piecemeal, as they arrived, enabling the airborne troops to fight them off, though with dwindling numbers and ammunition. The rest of the 21st Panzer wasted valuable time concentrating behind Luck's men, securing the eastern bank of the canal, just as Montgomery and Dempsey had feared. Having manoeuvred a substantial portion of the formation – less Rauch's 192nd *Panzergrenadier-Regiment* – into place to pummel the 6th Airborne in and around Bénouville, Ranville and on the Bavent ridge, new orders were suddenly issued.

When the first deployments had been ordered, the panzermen were aware only of the airborne drops. By 1000 hours the full extent of the threat from Sword and Juno beaches was evident, and the priority

The weakest German commander in Normandy, Generalleutnant Edgar Feuchtinger (1894–1960) (left) of 21st Panzer Division, often left the running of his formation to abler subordinates. He spent the night of 5–6 June with his mistress in Paris. Oberst Hans von Luck (1911–97) (centre), of the 125th *Panzergrenadier-Regiment*, was about to crush the British airborne forces east of the Orne when Feuchtinger ordered him to break off the engagement. The talented Hermann von Oppeln-Bronikowski (1899–1966) (right), commanding the division's tanks, tried to exploit the gap between Sword and Juno, until ordered back by Feuchtinger, who was unnerved by the arrival of scores of gliders. (Author's collection)

changed to destroying the beachhead. The timing was rotten. The armoured troops were about ready to attack the 6th Airborne Division and might well have succeeded: panzers against paratroops with few support weapons were bound to have created mayhem.

Although Rundstedt in Paris was soon persuaded this was *an* invasion, he was uncertain that it was *the* invasion. However, caution dictated that he request release of the panzer divisions from OKW, and as we have seen, sent a signal to this effect at 0445. It was denied. At ten, Marcks at the 84th Corps made a similar request of Dollmann at Seventh Army headquarters, and was again turned down. Dollmann was at the very least unaccustomed to modern war, and was more nervous of incurring the wrath of Berlin than prevailing in Normandy, so did not press his case. Although Berlin finally permitted the 12th SS Division to *move* to the invasion coast, permission had to be sought for its *use*. Marcks cleverly interpreted this as permission to deploy the 21st Panzer also, and at 1030 halted their moves east of the canal. Soon he had made his appreciation and demanded a full-scale panzer attack against Sword by as many units as possible. He immediately ordered the division to re-cross the Orne, skirt the northern edge of Caen and drive to the sea. With 'Rugger' and 'Cricket' in British hands, the assembled panzers had to turn around and drive south to the only other available crossings, in Caen.

Meanwhile, Rundstedt had sent OKW another signal at 1415 warning that 'no time should be lost in throwing the enemy out. It may be too late tomorrow for what, added to the advantage of cloudy weather, is possible today.' The bar on using the panzers was finally lifted fifteen minutes later. The first time local Wehrmacht commanders were permitted a free hand in the use of armour was at 1430 hours.[69] The move of the 21st Panzer took nearly five hours to complete, with the bottleneck of the crossings, harried by air attack, and inconvenienced by the fifteen- and six-inch shells of the Royal Navy. Every man and vehicle had to queue to race over the few remaining bridges in Caen, whose streets were now filling with rubble – and refugees.

Losses in men and machines began to mount before a shot had been fired at their foes, when eight rocket-firing Typhoons struck the column, disabling six tanks. It was 1620 before they were in position to attack. Led by Major Wilhelm von Gottberg, both battalions of Oppeln's panzers, totalling around ninety tanks, plus armoured infantry and engineers in half-tracks, would attack on the right flank, from Lébisey. Simultaneously, two further battalions of Rauch's *Panzergrenadiers* were to advance from

Saint-Contest further west. Most had been in combat before, and the formation had rehearsed just such an attack. They would move to the ridge at Périers-sur-le-Dan which overlooked the landings, and destroy what they could see.

Marcks correctly judged the attack's operational significance. Driving a wedge between the British and Canadians could enable him to attack both their flanks. He knew that the 12th SS Panzer Division would be arriving on 7 June, with others, such as the Panzer Lehr Division, not far behind. If his men could reach the coast – linking up with those still holding out in Langrune and 'Trout' – then they would have made a dangerous salient into the Anglo-Canadian beachhead. Oberst Krug, at this stage still holding on in 'Hillman', was warned as well that the panzers were on their way. With Feuchtinger already present, Marcks arrived in his staff car at the western end of Lébisey and hastily conferred with Oppeln, making a dramatic and entirely correct observation: 'Oppeln, the future of Germany may very well rest on your shoulders. If you don't succeed in driving the English into the sea, then we've lost the war.' It must have been a proud moment, full of adrenaline, as the columns of tanks and half-tracks moved off. Reminding him perhaps of the early advances into Russia, and standing erect in his staff car, Marcks accompanied the panzers and half-tracks for the first leg of their advance.[70]

This is where timing was everything, for Jim Eadie's Staffordshire Yeomanry, the 41st Anti-Tank Battery and KSLI had beaten Oppeln to possession of the Périers ridge. 'A' Squadron Shermans in Biéville and Beuville were the first to engage *Kampfgruppe Oppeln*'s armour, followed by 'C' and 'B' Squadrons on the ridge itself. Oppeln's First Battalion, on his right, suffered six Panzer IVs shot to pieces in the opening minutes, then as his Second Battalion came into view, another nine on the left went up in flames. Sliding left – westwards – the panzers continued to search for a gap in the British defences, but eventually gave up and started trundling towards whatever scrap of cover the landscape offered.

The 21st Panzer Division's history noted that 'the fire of the English from their outstandingly well-sited defensive positions was murderous'.[71] A Canadian military analyst described their advance as lapping along the Périers ridge 'like a long ocean swell rolling down a beach, and like a wave it broke as it went'.[72] Trooper Bernard Cuttiford, who had served with the 13th/18th Hussars before transferring to 'C' Squadron of the Staffordshire Yeomanry, remembered, 'the CO ordered battle positions west of Biéville. The panzers advanced fast and were engaged as soon as they reached the western end. Two troops of 'A' Squadron caught them at a range of about six hundred yards.'[73]

Sergeant Billings, commanding a yeomanry Firefly, 'knocked out at least one enemy tank before being hit himself. The tank caught fire and the crew bailed out. But after seeing it was not serious, Billings and his crew extinguished the flames, remounted and carried on', while Sergeant Joyce of 'A' Squadron accounted for four others. He allowed his opponents 'to come well into the open and fired at the last tank scoring a direct hit with the first shot. He then traversed down the line, knocking out two with three shots and finished off the fourth.'[74]

The road down which some of the panzers clattered 'ran straight and true. Fields of green corn and maize stretched endlessly on either side. Lush and simmering in the early summer,' mused yeoman Neville Patterson. He thought the advancing German tanks resembled

toy ducks in some macabre fairground attraction. Down they went, nosing and probing their way out of the shelter of the grey, dusty village [Beuville]. Their route was stalked by selective death which spat from our superbly sited guns. Hissing steam and resonant, ringing echoes as each one exploded, armour-piercing shells destroying the men inside and igniting petrol and ammunition. A few luckier crewmen escaped to scramble into ditches under a hail of machine-gun fire, their mounts rendered harmless and marked only by a large pall of smoke.[75]

This was the yeomanry regiment with whom I spent a considerable period of my reservist service. Its exploits on D-Day were still the subject of admiration and discussion fifty years later, when I was serving alongside later generations of the same families who had fought on D-Day.

By nightfall, Oppeln's 22nd Panzer Regiment reported losses of fourteen Panzer IVs, with fifteen others damaged. German morale slumped, while some of the British, expecting a lengthy and heavy engagement with an ocean of panzers representing the successors of the Afrika Korps, were left scratching their heads, musing, 'Was that it?'

Meanwhile Josef Rauch's *Kampfgruppe*, which departed from Saint-Contest, slightly further west than Lébisey – both villages now swallowed up as drab suburbs of Caen – had far greater success. His First Battalion managed to discover and enter the unoccupied space between the British and Canadians, and follow it to the sea at Lion-sur-Mer. His job was made easier with attention focused on Oppeln's panzer attack to their right; within an hour they had linked up with some of the defenders on the coast. Aware of the disaster that had befallen Oppeln's armour, Rauch was pondering his next move when at 2100 hours came the great aerial armada of Operation Mallard's transports and gliders that so overawed the Suffolks and their prisoners at 'Hillman'.

Fearing an Allied airdrop into the rear of the division, the incompetent Feuchtinger ordered Rauch to withdraw from the coast and Oppeln to abandon his position at Périers, throwing away his one opportunity to destroy the landings – and abandoning those defending their bunkers to an uncertain fate. Feuchtinger certainly proved his unfitness to command – though he was subsequently kept in place as a party loyalist; but Rauch had the presence of mind to drop a company of infantry off at the Douvres radar station, which, as we have seen, enabled them to hold out for another eleven days.

There were two German counter-attacks launched on D-Day: that of *Kampfgruppe Meyer* against the 50th Division at Gold Beach, and – at

It was the 84th Army Corps of General Erich Marcks (1891–1944) (left) that experienced the full impact of the invasion. A bright and respected commander, he nevertheless wrongly committed both his principal reserves on D-Day. In the west he was hoodwinked into directing his bicycle troops against phoney parachute drops before – too late – sending them back to Omaha and Gold. In the east he switched 21st Panzer from probable success against the 6th Airborne to certain failure when meeting British tanks inland from Sword. As the weather improved, his armoured attack (right) also began to be eroded by air attack. (Left, Author's collection; right, NARA)

almost the exact same hour – the assault of the 21st Panzer Division. Of the two, the latter was far more serious, with its sizeable number of armoured vehicles. Both failed for the same reason. In each case, the units had been committed against the paratroopers landing on either flank, then recalled as the threat against the beaches materialised. In the first attack, it was General Marcks who first committed his principal reserve formation of cyclists prematurely. By the time he had realised his error and recalled Meyer, he was too late and the *Kampfgruppe* was thrown against a ready and waiting opponent.

With the 21st Panzer, Marcks pulled the division away from a possible victory on the Orne, and committed it too late against the 3rd Division at Périers. 'The long wait from the early morning, in addition to the diversion via Colombelles [Caen], had consumed a total of fourteen hours, and given the English time to build a strong defence,' noted Werner Kortenhaus, then serving with the 21st Panzer Division and later its historian. 'Our one and only chance on D-Day was thrown away. Never again would there be such an opportunity.'[76] On both occasions, Erich Marcks – often hailed as a wise head amongst the German generals in Normandy – had got it disastrously wrong.

35

Green Berets and *le Général*

'At around 0830 hours I heard the sound of bagpipes. I looked over my shoulder and there was the piper walking up the beach in his kilt and beret. I couldn't believe my eyes. He was playing as if he was on Horse Guard's Parade. It was fantastic. I thought it was an indication of how in control we were at that moment. We all felt ten feet tall after hearing that.'

Able Seaman Ken Oakley, beachmaster's
bodyguard[1]

'INVADED MY own country on D-Day,' Commando Léon Gautier, who settled in Ouistreham after the war, told me in 2014, when I met the last of Kieffer's men. 'I trained to become a commando at Achnacarry, which was hell. We had to run seven miles in one hour and did lots of close combat; one guy was injured by a hand grenade.'[2]

The Kieffer unit – whom we met at the beginning of this volume – was part of Brigadier 'Shimi' Lovat's 1st Special Service Brigade, formed in October 1943 for operations in Italy.[3] Initially an experimental grouping, its success at Termoli on 3 October prompted COSSAC to recommend it as a permanent formation under Shimi Lovat, formerly CO of No. 4 Commando. Commissioned from Sandhurst in 1930, Lovat was clearly a charismatic character, as Commando Signaller Colin Hughes observed: 'I was at Dunkirk with the 1st/7th Royal Warwicks. My parents were killed in a bombing raid; I thought, "I want to get back at the bastards." First opportunity I got, I joined Combined Operations and served under Lord Lovat. As far as I'm concerned he was the most inspiring man I ever met in my life. I'd follow him anywhere; I followed him on D-Day with No. 4 Commando.'[4]

Galway native Patrick D. Gillen was another who admired Lovat. He had illegally slipped over the border of his Irish homeland to serve, in his case in the 4th Royal Norfolks. As often with adventurers, life was too quiet and he had volunteered for more hazardous duties, finding himself, aged nineteen, in HQ Troop of No. 6 Commando on D-Day. In 1985, Gillen used exactly the same phrase as Hughes in his interview with me. 'He was a Pied Piper to me: I'd follow him anywhere'.[5] Also in awe of Lovat was Reuters correspondent Doon Campbell. Medically ineligible to join the British forces, being born with only a stump of a left arm, he had chosen instead to report from the front line and at the age of twenty-four was attached to Lovat's brigade just before D-Day. 'A real leader, tall, slim, with charismatic presence. A man of action, he led from the front, where his men could see him. Without any sugges-tion of softness, he had exceptional sensitivity. What other commando chieftain would reminisce on the eve of D-Day about willow wrens nesting beside his tent?'[6]

Lovat had taken No. 4 Commando to Dieppe in 1942, and was one of the few to successfully complete his mission and return. One of his officers, Major Pat Porteous, had won a Victoria Cross during the action. Porteous had been severely wounded, but on recovering insisted on accompanying his old unit to Ouistreham on D-Day.[7] For Overlord, Lovat had under command Nos. 3, 4, 6 and 45 (RM) Commandos, to land on Queen Red. As at Gold and Juno, all the commandos had planned to land after Sword had been cleared of Germans, enabling them to push inland immediately.

At Southwick House in late May, Lovat had attended a briefing by Montgomery. In a quiet moment, Major General Francis 'Freddie' de Guingand, Monty's long-suffering chief of staff and known as the power behind the throne, had drawn Lovat aside. Their relationship was easy-going and one of equals – and it helped that they had been educated at the same school, Ampleforth, Britain's leading Roman Catholic academy, and later worked together in Combined Operations HQ. Lovat was aware his brigade would be attacking Ouistreham, and de Guingand had further news for him: 'If they can land and move off *Sword*, you will have swim-ming tanks in the assault. But intelligence says Rommel has thickened up the underwater obstacles; frogmen will go in early, but there'll be no chance to clear them all up in time.' However, warned the general, 'The

The Art Nouveau Casino at Ouistreham, the main target for Philippe Kieffer's Frenchmen of No. 4 Commando. This was the establishment whose impending demise was lauded by Guy, Comte de Montlaur, who exclaimed 'It will be a pleasure. I have lost many fortunes in that place.' Its dominating position on the Riva-Bella seafront overlooking the beach is clear from this intelligence postcard. By June 1944, the Germans had demolished all above the front steps, leaving the basement level as a series of very well-fortified bunkers. It bore no resemblance to the Casino bunker depicted in *The Longest Day*. (Author's collection)

Ouistreham end of *Sword* looks like a hot potato; the town is strongly garrisoned – so *please* knock out the battery in the Casino at Riva-Bella in double-quick time'[8]

When later briefing his men, one of his commandos reacted, 'It will be a pleasure. I have lost many fortunes in that place.'[9] The unlucky gambler was Guy, Comte de Montlaur, then a sergeant in Philippe Kieffer's Free French unit attached to No. 4 Commando. Kieffer's 177 men of the 1st *Bataillon de Fusiliers Marins Commandos* would be the only Frenchmen to storm the Normandy shores on 6 June. As de Guingand had warned, Ouistreham was known to be strongly defended – too much for the slim ranks of No. 4 Commando. In compromise, Lovat added two French troops from No. 10 Inter-Allied Commando, who comprised volunteers from German-occupied Europe including Belgium, the Netherlands, Norway, Denmark, Poland and Yugoslavia. The French were the most numerous, organised into two troops commanded by Capitaines Kieffer and Alex Lofi. For Overlord, they were transferred, with the French-manned Gun Troop, into Lieutenant Colonel Robert Dawson's No. 4 Commando. As the senior Frenchman, Kieffer was promoted to *Commandant* (major), Capitaine Guy Vourch taking his place as troop commander.

Opposing them was Wilhelm Richter's 716th Division and the six-battalion 711th Infantry Division of Generalleutnant Josef Reichert. The latter's formation held the extreme left flank of Salmuth's Fifteenth Army and was tasked with defending the Calvados coast, eastwards from the Dives river. Reichert noted that 'At about the turn of the year 1943–44 the threat of an invasion became more acute. The troops became aware of it on account of the inspection tours by Field Marshal Rommel, who had been given extraordinary powers and brought new life into the work of construction of the so-called *Atlantikwall*, progressing, it is true, steadily, but nevertheless slowly.'[10] Reichert assessed that the few weapons of his division 'rendered the defence of a coastal sector of twenty-eight miles completely illusory', which required 'almost the entire infantry employed in strong points on the coast, handling either artillery or heavy infantry weapons'.[11]

Although his front would not be directly assaulted on 6 June, British airborne troops and commandos would soon be scattered widely through his domain. Reichert's was the first formation to react to D-Day, not least because two paratroopers landed on top of his command post at Vauville, inland of Deauville, a little after midnight, and his division would be sucked into the fighting around Sword Beach from the first moments.[12] On Reichert's divisional staff was Oberschütze Albert Brieden, a thirty-two-year-old car mechanic who had worked for Daimler-Benz in Westphalia before the war. He had joined the 711th Division back in 1941, and was employed as a driver. He wrote home regularly about his comfortable life on occupation duty, observing how he was one of the very few in the primarily horse-drawn formation familiar with motor vehicles.

Thirty-year-old Wilhelm Lichtenberg from Laurenburg, near Koblenz, had completed his compulsory military service before the war, was recalled to the colours in 1939 and fought his way to the streets of Warsaw, after which he was medically downgraded from all further combat. Like Brieden, Unteroffizier Lichtenberg nevertheless was sent to the 711th in 1941, in his case posted to No. 10 Company of its 731st *Grenadier-Regiment*. Both might have known Obergefreiter Anton

Fillmann from Recklinghausen, a rifleman in one of the 711th's six battalions. Poor Anton had a recurring stomach complaint which kept him out of uniform, but even he was conscripted in late 1943. Being medically downgraded after training – which saved him from the Eastern Front – he found himself posted to No. 2 Company of Oberst Maier's 744th *Grenadier-Regiment* and stationed at La Motte, outside Villers-sur-Mer on the Calvados coast. Fillmann and his comrades had stockpiled some good German beer and were looking forward to Tuesday, 6 June, because it would be Fillmann's thirty-sixth birthday.[13] They would never get to drink it.

After discussion with Lovat, Lieutenant Colonel Robert Dawson, a French-speaker, general Francophile and CO of No. 4 Commando, had wisely and sensitively offered Kieffer's men the honour of landing first. He used the alluring words *'Messieurs les Français – Tirez les premiers'* (French gentlemen, you may fire first) – a reworking of the well-known invitation first uttered by a French noblemen before the Battle of Fontenoy (1745), who had appealed to his opponents, 'My English sirs – you may shoot first!' Hubert Faure, whom we met earlier escaping occupied France, observed, 'It was a very gallant gesture and we loved him for it.'[14] No. 4 Commando's broader objective was to destroy the German positions in Ouistreham; Kieffer's men would make landfall on Queen Red, some bearing bicycles, where Eight Troop were to clear the dunes, then with One Troop, supported by Gun Troop, seize the WN10 casino complex on the western edge of town. The rest of Dawson's commando would clear the main part of town, including the fire control tower, WN8, beyond the casino. The remainder of Lovat's 1st Special Service Brigade, landing forty-five minutes afterwards, would bypass the port, moving cross-country to reach out to the 6th Airborne Division and help hold the bridges spanning the River Orne and the Caen Canal.

We met several of Kieffer's men at the start, but absent from that roll call was René Rossey, just seventeen when he landed in France for the first time in his life, and too young to have been able to respond to de Gaulle's 18 June 1940 broadcast. He had been brought up by his French father and Italian mother in Tunis, and, lying about his age, enlisted at the Free French recruiting bureau in August 1943 after the Allied conquest. 'I soon left for England and was welcomed at a French camp in Camberley,' Rossey recalled to me in 2004. 'There I met the magnetic Capitaine Kieffer, who invited me to join his unit. I first had to undertake commando training at Wrexham, after which I was integrated into Nine Troop, armed with Vickers 'K'-guns [a lightweight machine-gun, popular with Special Forces], of the 1st *Bataillon de Fusiliers Marins Commandos* (1er BFMC).[15] We wore *bérets verts* and in April 1944 were absorbed into No. 4 Commando, and started training with the craft that would take us to Normandy. I remember they were the LCIs *523* and *527*, skippered by Jack Berry and Charles Craven.'[16]

On 5 June 1944, they left Warsash in Hampshire and began crossing the Channel at 2230 hours, Kieffer's One Troop on *LCI-523*, Eight Troop aboard *LCI-527*, while the rest of No. 4 Commando were distributed amongst HMS *Prinses Astrid* and the *Maid of Orleans*. Hubert Faure's voice still shook with emotion as he remembered the march to their boats: 'at the sight of our green berets, and the word "France" embroidered on our shoulder flashes, everybody applauded us. It was very moving.'[17]

Lovat addressed them that night in French: '*Vous allez rentrer chez vous. Vous serez les premiers militaires français en uniforme à casser la gueule des salauds en France même. A chacun son Boche. Vous allez nous montrer ce que vous savez faire. Demain matin on les aura.*' ('You are returning home. You will be the first in French military uniform to break the jaws of the swine in France. To each his Boche. You will show us what you can do. Tomorrow morning, we'll have them.')[18] 'At six in the morning, we could see France,' remembered Léon Gautier. 'Seeing my country after four years away was very emotional; it was a great honour to be first ashore.'[19] 'The first thing I did that day was kiss the sand of France,' recollected François Andriot, who would settle in England after the war.[20]

Kieffer himself recorded landing from their LCI: 'at that moment, the land and the sea seemed to be raised by a roar of thunder. Mortar bombs, whistling shells, annoying yelps of machine-guns, everything seemed to be focused on us. In a flash, the gangplanks were thrown down. The first group of *bérets verts* rushed onto the beach, but a few seconds before the rush of the second group, a 75-mm shell removed the gangplanks of the landing craft in a tearing of wood and metal.'[21] Quartier-Maître (Corporal) Maurice Chauvet recollected, 'our landing craft hit the sand and its ramps were pushed down. Four sailors were wounded on the bridge and machine-gun bullets whistled by on all sides, coming from our left. Kieffer's craft next to ours had its ramps blown away by a shell. The water came up to our belts, but after thirty or so yards we reached dry sand, all the time under machine-gun fire. I noticed Kieffer wounded in the thigh.' Chauvet remembered in the streets seeing a Frenchman emerge from his house in pyjamas, stunned to see that the troops were his compatriots. 'Once we affirmed we were here to stay, and not just for a raid, the locals relaxed.'[22]

From his LCA Captain Donald Gilchrist, adjutant of No. 4 Commando, remembered:

> there came the searing sound of sand scraping the bottom. The naval lieutenant worked the lever. Cog teeth chattered on oiled chains. The ramp yawned open. As the tidal wave of green berets surged ashore, they swept all with them – the wounded, the dying, the half-crazed. Further out to sea, wisps of smoke from the funnels of steaming ships mixed with the orange and red flashes as salvo after salvo of shells was projected towards the land in a sensational pyrotechnical display.[23]

However, as they were landing after the two assault battalions, No. 4 Commando had not expected to fight their way off the beach. Lovat was particularly critical in his memoirs of the 3rd Division, observing that his men had to waste time – and suffer casualties – securing Queen Red in the wake of the 2nd East Yorks, who were largely pinned down on the sand. Bill Bidmead – a twenty-year-old former soldier in the King's Royal Rifle Corps who had volunteered for 'hazardous duties' and joined 'A' Troop – recalled, 'My landing craft was hit and reared up almost vertically and I was jammed between my seat and the boat under a pile of men. The ramp was kicked open and the first Commando practically ripped in half by a burst of machine-gun fire. Still trapped, I feared I would drown as the craft began to fall back and sink. A comrade, seeing my plight, dashed back and freed me. As I waded ashore, I saw men drowning in shallow water. Wounded, their ninety-pound rusk-sacks weighed them down.'[24] Their war diary noted their arrival at 0820 hours: 'Mortar bombs were falling in and around the LCAs and as the Commando landed. There were forty casualties, including the CO, Lieutenant Colonel R. W. P. Dawson, who was wounded in the leg, and subsequently a second time in the head.'[25]

Mindful of their mission, the commandos refused to be drawn into the battle for 'Cod' and simply blew the barbed wire surrounding the beach with Bangalore torpedoes, rushed through the resultant gaps and raced off to their objective. Corporal Alf Ackroyd with 'B' Company of the East Yorks, remembered the difference between the commandos and themselves:

> When the Commandos landed behind us we were still pinned down on the beach. They come out [from their landing craft] in a rugby scrum and stormed over the wire and got through. Where these Commandos had gone was about fifteen yards at the most to the right of where I was. In fact after they'd gone, my mate Jack said "well, I am going to try it". I said "well, keep your behind down", and he jumped up, got about two paces, and he was shot through his behind.'[26]

As the Commandos receded into the distance, heading east, the Yorks and Lancs soldiers turned their attention back to 'Cod'.

Kieffer's men never forgot the first few moments of fighting on their own land. Léon Gautier told me about their load: 'we were carrying four days of food and ammunition. We planned to dump these packs, weighing perhaps eighty pounds, at a site chosen from an aerial photograph. We were never more relieved than when we got to the chosen place.' He remembered seeing Capitaine Robert Lion, their medical officer, shot through the heart by a sniper at 1000 hours on the beach, while administering morphine to his friend, the wounded Lance Corporal Paul Rollin, and Father René du Narois, their chaplain, 'tall, burly, bald, saintly, with round innocent eyes', giving him the Last Rites.[27] Guy Hattu, one of the 'three Guys' we met at the start, was injured at the same time. When all the officers of Guy Vourch's troop had been wounded, it was the gambling count, Sergeant Guy de Montlaur, who took over command.

The adjutant, Captain Gilchrist, noted the temporary obstacle of a German-occupied house and the timely arrival of a Royal Engineers AVRE Churchill tank, equipped with a Petard mortar to deal with it. 'The tank sallied forth, halted and turned slowly. Its tracks squealed on the surface. The crew operated a mechanism to throw a huge object like a large oil drum, a sort of aerial depth charge. The canister hurtled through the air, turning and revolving, to strike the front of the house. There was a big explosion. The building caved in, the roof dizzily canting and spilling vermillion tiles, as if a landslide of scree on the Cairngorms.' This was the petard round which caused so much discomfort to the defenders of Gold, Juno and Sword.[28] These tanks were from Irishman 'Reddy' Cunningham's troop of the 79th Assault Squadron, on their way to the eastern end of Ouistreham, with a mission to seize the all-important locks gates and their various mechanisms.

The first position assaulted by Capitaine Alex Lofi's troop proved too strong to subdue, and having taken casualties, they wisely left it to join Vourch preparing to attack the rear of the casino. There they found a hornet's nest of machine-guns, mortars and anti-tank weapons. Gilchrist remembered that 'from nowhere a Frenchman appeared, dressed in civilian clothes and wearing a black beret. He and Kieffer forgot the war and embraced.' An old friend, this was the 'splendidly moustachioed' Marcel Lefèvre, a local *résistant*, who briefed Kieffer on the layout of the defences, showed them where the German field telephone lines were buried, and had already 'cut the electric cables to the gun battery and casino, both of which were electrically controlled, also putting out of action the position's automatic flame-throwers'.[29]

There were many such spontaneous acts of bravery by individual French men and women along the coast that morning. Back at Hermanville, soldiers lying prone, taking cover from a sniper, watched the door opposite open and a young French girl calmly get on her bicycle and pedal away. How could they compete with that? Other women put on Red Cross armbands, braved the fire and arrived at British aid posts enquiring what they could do to help.

Unable to make an impression on the defenders, Kieffer retraced his steps to flag down a 13th/18th Hussars DD tank that had managed to exit a gap on Queen Red. At 0925, he recalled, 'the tank went into an adjacent courtyard and commenced firing under my direction. The first two shells went straight into the Casino. At that moment I was once more lightly wounded in the arm by a rifle bullet. By hand signals, I directed the tank to fire into all the German positions and the fire from their machine-guns was stopped.'[30] The fighting gradually died down and thirty minutes later the surviving defenders were marching into captivity. 'Lanternier brought back the first eleven prisoners of whom three or four were Poles. While they were being brought back, one of them threw a grenade which slightly wounded two of my men. At once we fired and killed three of them.'[31]

No. 4 Commando found the defences across Ouistreham very challenging and noted, 'Heavy casualties were inflicted on the Germans who put up a very stiff resistance from their strong fortifications and cunningly camouflaged blockhouses, with excellent fields of fire. The concrete emplacements had withstood severe naval bombardment exceedingly well, and although outnumbered, the Germans were in excellent defensive positions, which had successfully withstood a terrific pounding from the sea and air.' One of the outstanding features, they thought, 'was the careful sighting [sic] of their positions, and from the Commandos' view point, the difficulty of pinpointing enemy fire during the mopping up stages, so well had the emplacements been prepared. But at least one point of Hitler's Western Wall had proved vulnerable under determined enough attack.'[32]

The rest of No. 4 Commando had experienced an equally tough fight for Ouistreham, but had silenced their foes at roughly the same time as Kieffer. Retrieving their rucksacks, they then fought their way to Amfréville, on the Bavent ridgeline, but Kieffer's detachment alone had lost eight dead, including their doctor, Captain Lion, and fifty-five wounded.

Ninety minutes after H-Hour and half an hour behind No. 4 Commando, Lovat himself set foot in France, with No. 6 Commando leading, followed by the Royal Marines of No. 45, then No. 3 Commando accompanying his brigade HQ. Lovat intended his formation to rally on Queen Red to the sound of bagpipes – hence his insistence on Bill Millin's presence with his instrument – and move cross-country to Pegasus Bridge and Bénouville. This would relieve the pressure on the 6th Airborne Division, which had already landed behind German lines and needed to link up with the seaborne invaders. By the time the rest of the brigade arrived, there was relatively little opposition – apart from snipers – on the beach itself, though much shelling from inland batteries. They formed up to Millin's rendition of 'Blue Bonnets Over the Border', the headquarters war diary noted: 'the beaches seemed curiously deserted as the troops waded ashore and streamed up the sand. The gaunt and gutted buildings among a maze of tangled wire and shell craters made up a kind of Martian landscape.'[33] There is a famous image of Lovat and Millin descending from *LCI-519* on Queen Red. The kilt-wearing Millin explained to me years later that (wearing, as is traditional, nothing underneath his kilt) the coldness of the water took his breath away and played havoc with his anatomy, while his garment floated around him 'like a tartan jellyfish', and he gamely carried on piping.[34]

The popular images of D-Day are overwhelmingly American. This was down to the unenlightened suspicion maintained by the War Office (and continued to this day by their successors at the Ministry of Defence) of photographers and journalists. Ironically, the publicity-hungry Montgomery did not intervene to correct this. While there were nearly three hundred civilian journalists and photographers roaming the US sector and its transports on D-Day (Hemingway and Capa to mention two), very few accredited war correspondents – given officer status and uniforms – were allowed into the British area. The Canadians thoughtfully fixed movie cameras inside their assault-wave LCAs, triggered by the lowering of the bow ramp. The resultant footage, shot from behind, of helmeted men scrambling out of their rocking craft, gripping weapons and ladders, is staple coverage for every D-Day documentary and news item.

The very British solution was to limit coverage to the BBC's war reporting organisation, and assemble the 5th Army Film and Photographic Unit (APFU), comprised of conscripted pre-war photographers and journalists. Just fifteen APFU soldiers deployed to the British sector, of whom eight landed on Sword. This minimal allocation of men and resources to recording the United Kingdom's effort on D-Day amounted to a lamentable disservice to posterity. Many researchers are struck, when investigating Britain's air, land and maritime achievements on 6 June 1944, how pathetically few photographs and feet of film exist. Two of the APFU were wounded on D-Day and two killed shortly afterwards, but one of the survivors was Sergeant George Laws, who landed with No. 4 Commando and took the Lovat–Millin image. Armed with three rolls of black-and-white film, totalling thirty-six exposures, Laws took his own Zeiss Super Ikonta camera and carried an issue Voigtlander clockwork movie camera: 'I took several shots of the other assault craft on the way, and as we neared the beach, everybody was ordered to crouch down during the final run-in. On landing I found my cine camera, carefully wrapped in plastic, had been switched on and about a third of my 100-foot roll of film had been wasted. I wound up the clockwork and chased after the commandos to their assembly area.'[35]

One of those with pencil, rather than camera, in hand and accompanying Laws was Reuters correspondent Doon Campbell, the first journalist to set foot on the Normandy beaches, landing with the commandos. 'A smudge, brown on black in the far distance marked our landing area. The craft zig-zagged the last mile or two, and at 0906 we rammed Sword Beach. The ramp thrown down from the landing-craft was steep and slippery, and I fell chest-deep into the sea lapping the mined beaches,' he wrote later of his arrival on Queen Red. 'My pack, sodden and waterlogged, strapped tight round my shoulders, seemed made for easy drowning. But a lunge forward, helped by a heave from a large corporal already in the water, gave me a first toehold. Ahead lay the beach: a sandy cemetery of the unburied dead. Bodies, some only half-dead, lay scattered about, with arms or legs severed, their blood clotting the sand.' While the commandos 'surged ahead until swallowed up in the brooding woods', Campbell edged along the protective shelter of a stone wall, crossed a potholed road into a field and stumbled into a ditch about two hundred yards from the beach, struggling all the while to ease himself out of his commando pack harness.

> When it was finally detached, I opened it almost furtively, and found my portable typewriter undamaged. I got a sheet of paper in and started pecking at the keyboard, but it was hopeless; every time I tried to type, a mortar exploded a few yards away or hit the lip of the ditch and a shower of dirt clogged the keys. So I tore a page from a school exercise book and scribbled a few lines from "A ditch 200 yards inside Normandy" ... I wriggled and crawled back to the beach, flinging myself flat every few yards. A naval officer, operating a shuttle between Normandy and the English coast, agreed to take my grimy bits of paper and try to get them back to Reuters. I gave him five pounds, and never saw him again ... It never reached Reuters.[36]

As No. 4 Commando's war diary noted, the troops then had 'a strenuous and back-breaking nine miles march under constant sniping and mortar fire to cross the Caen Canal and the River Orne'.[37] Sergeant Laws observed, 'We were moving inland to support 6th Airborne when a German plane, flying very low, strafed us and bullets splattered along the road – no time to take cover. Later when a mortar and shellfire caught us, I dived into a ditch and broke the spring on my camera's motor. It was an anti-climax to all my training.' Thereafter, Laws was forced to concentrate on still photography.[38]

Preceded by No. 6 Commando, Lovat pushed diagonally inland, moving south-east and cross-country in avoidance of any likely German positions, but found it heavy going through the German-flooded marsh areas, as the headquarters war diary observed:

> The country beyond the road was marshy and intersected by deep ditches up to six feet deep with a thick mud bottom which made progress

The kilted young Bill Millin (1922–2010) is seen here in the foreground clutching his bagpipes, and about to descend the ramp of *LCI-519* towards Sword Beach. In the background (see arrow) and inset is his charismatic brigade commander, Lord Lovat (1911–95), who had ordered Millin to accompany him, in defiance of War Office regulations. In the water, the piper remembered his kilt floating around him 'like a tartan jellyfish'. (Author's collection)

> extremely slow for such heavily laden men, who sank into the mud and found great difficulty in climbing out of the ditches. Scaling ladders were used effectively as hand rails across the ditches, but the area was also being mortared and it was about twenty-five minutes before the leading troops reached the pre-arranged forming up point.[39]

Campbell recalled Lovat 'in a loose pullover and open-necked shirt, he might have been out for a stroll in the Highlands, but for the green beret and rifle slung over his shoulders'.[40] The brigadier's men pressed on to Pegasus Bridge, obstinately defended by Howard's company of the Ox and Bucks, and men of Geoffrey Pine-Coffin's 7th Parachute Battalion. At this stage the historical records diverge. Traditionally the commandos ran across Pegasus Bridge, Millin still piping. Others remember them scuttling across, and some eyewitnesses mention the furious pedalling of bicycle-borne commandos. Millin was certainly playing as he approached the bridge, and told me that he then 'folded his pipes under his arm and scampered over the structure' and resumed playing the other side, all while sniper's bullets pinged on its metal framework. This makes more sense, but was not quite the 'striding out in step' that Lovat would later claim, or which was portrayed in *The Longest Day*. Most rushed across in small groups, and twelve were killed by sniper fire, mostly head shots. Thereafter they discarded their green berets and adopted helmets, going on to establish defensive positions around Ranville, east of the Orne.[41]

Sergeant Henry Cosgrove of 45 (Royal Marine) Commando remembered his arrival at 'Rugger' (Pegasus Bridge), slightly later, at 1430. Their mission was to move beyond to destroy the Merville battery if Terence Otway's men had failed to suppress it, or support them if they had. 'There were snipers about and they were firing at us now and again, but the brigadier – Lord Lovat – he must have thought he was on his estate. He marched along with a bloody bagpiper playing alongside him. We went over the bridge and then the problems really started. We started to lose a lot of men, so we moved to a higher piece of ground [the Bavent ridge] and dug in. I didn't know where the hell I was, other than I was digging a hole as fast as I could.' The casualties included Cosgrove's CO, Lieutenant Colonel N. C. Reis.[42] As an example of the pressure on the airborne perimeter, at around 1300 a small formation of Germans wearing captured airborne smocks and red berets with self-propelled guns had advanced to within five hundred yards of 'Cricket', the swing bridge over the River Orne, before being driven back.

The commandos and airborne troops were supported by the 76th (Highland) Field Regiment of self-propelled 105mm 'Priests', attached to the 3rd Division. Captain Tony Turnbull remembered that they fired their guns during the run-in, then when the infantry went ashore, 'our LCTs with their guns wheeled out to sea again, returning to land an hour later. When we did land we had been instructed to send one person off the LCT to walk ashore to ensure there were no bomb or shell craters into which our precious guns would disappear. The "volunteer" undressed and waded ashore and reported all was well.'

Turnbull thought the 'situation on the beach was pretty chaotic with damaged craft in and on the water, and the occasional bursts of machine-gun and artillery fire, but my guns were lucky. We spent about five hours firing from the beach, which was becoming narrower as the tide came in, but we were the only guns that could support the British 6th Airborne Division at Pegasus Bridge at that time. We eventually left the beach in the afternoon when sufficient paths had been cleared through the mine-fields.'[43]

No.3 Commando under the legendary Peter Young, who had joined the Territorial Army six years earlier whilst studying at Oxford – and was another early commando officer who shone in battle, later destined to become a distinguished military historian – suffered around twenty wounded from shells hitting their landing craft. He brought with him the unit's administration officer, who had first seen action at the Battle of Mons in 1914. Young's predecessor was John Durnford-Slater ('J.D.S.') who had raised the first commando. On D-Day, as second in command of the Commando Group, in charge of both brigades, 'J.D.S.' accompanied Lovat.

He required his commando padres to be able to help with medical and intelligence work and shortly before D-Day had told them how 'the attitude of the padre in battle quickly spread to the men. They must be the friends and advisors of the soldiers and not to try and alter their ways in terms of gambling, drinking and chasing the girls. The most important thing was sincerity. One good church parade a month was enough, with a short, topical sermon, preferably stressing the activities of Saint Paul, whom I always regarded as the patron saint of the Commandos.'[44]

After a frustrating time waiting for the congestion to clear on Queen Red, Young at the head of No. 3 advanced inland, passing through 45 (Royal Marine) Commando in Colleville and moving as far as Saint-Aubin-d'Arquenay. Private Tom Duncan, formerly a Gordon Highlander before serving under Young in No. 3, who would be wounded by a hand grenade that evening, recalled the mortar bombs raining down 'like flocks of partridges'.[45] He and his mates finally – as planned – linked up with the airborne and glider troops. Doon Campbell of Reuters remembered the landing zone as a 'Disney fantasy scene' where 'hundreds of pancaked gliders, some intact, some nose-up, some in ditches, some half-hidden by walls into which they had crashed, together forming a crazy pattern covering several acres'.[46]

Crossing Pegasus Bridge, Young – whose original orders bade him take Cabourg on the coast – was redirected to Le Bas de Ranville, eventually joining No. 4 in the vicinity of Amfréville.[47] No. 6 Commando, meanwhile, had passed through the village of Saint-Aubin-d'Arquenay, on their way to Bénouville, several times under mortar fire, the day costing them thirty-five casualties.[48] The Marines of 45 Commando took a different route via Colleville, successfully avoiding the fight for 'Hillman'.

In the west, 41 (Royal Marine) Commando had landed as planned on Queen White and peeled off to the right to destroy 'Trout'. They suffered heavy casualties at the hands of the 'Trout' defenders, but also artillery positions in the vicinity, which were effectively directed against the attackers. Despite the later arrival of some of 9th Brigade, with resistance focused on two areas called 'the Château' and 'the Strongpoint', Lion would remain unsubdued at the end of D-Day, by which time 41 Commando had suffered 133 casualties. Amongst them were eight officers, including the second in command.[49] Of far more immediate concern was the gap, nearly six miles wide, from 'Trout' to Langrune, which 48 (Royal Marine) Commando were in the process of capturing – though it, too, would not fall until the next day.

The commandos and airborne forces would remain on the Bavent ridge, doing the vital job of shoring up Overlord's eastern flank, but it was a curious and wasteful role for both elite formations. More numerous and better-equipped regular infantry units would have been far better employed there. Lovat would be wounded on 12 June, ironically by a British shell falling short, which also injured Hugh Kindersley, commanding the 6th Airlanding Brigade. Shimi's place was taken by Derek Mills-Roberts ('Mills-Bomb' to those encountering him in a combative mood), formerly of No. 6 Commando.

Their men and those of the 4th Special Service Brigade – the titles about to be changed to 'Commando' brigades (the French understandably upset at being liberated by a British 'SS' formation) fought on, suffering a forty per cent attrition rate. Of the 146 commando officers and 2,252 other ranks who had landed on D-Day, by the time their advance to the River Seine started on 17 August, some seventy-seven officers and 890 other ranks had become casualties.[50] They would eventually return to England on 8–9 September, landing at Southampton and Gosport, and left behind them a fitting memorial stele in the village square at Amfréville.

With such erosion of their numbers, a brigade of the 51st (Highland) Division was soon sent to reinforce this vital piece of high ground. The airborne troops – or what was left of them – would similarly remain in situ on the ridge until 17 August, when they, too, advanced to the River Seine. By the time they embarked for England at the beginning of September, Major General Richard Gale's airborne formation had suffered 4,457 casualties, of whom 2,709 were wounded and 821 killed, with 927 missing. Many of these now lie in Ranville cemetery, unofficially the final resting place of those who fought wearing the hallmark red beret. Many of their commando colleagues, who had trained so hard to earn their green berets at Achnacarry, lie alongside them.

The British Army as a whole would be badly mauled in the campaign that started on D-Day, and it was infantrymen who would bear 63.7 per cent of the total casualties, despite comprising only fifteen per cent of the force. This is a shocking statistic that exceeded even the most pessimistic calculations of the War Office – by a heady seventeen per cent – and would cause two divisions, including the 50th Northumbrian, to be broken up to provide replacements.[51] British generals had been warned before invading France that they would soon run out of manpower – the Second Army's commander, Miles Dempsey, being aware that by the end of the year, using SHAEF's projected loss rates, he would be 60,000 casualty replacements short – of which at least two-thirds would be trained infantrymen.[52] In fact, losses would exceed their worst fears. In the six-week period following 6 June 1944, Monty's 21st Army Group suffered 11,910 fatalities – an average daily toll of 270, which far outstripped the 146 per day of El Alamein.[53]

Even before D-Day, soldiers in military prisons had been given a chance to clear their names by taking part in the invasion. One was Private John Vernon Bain, who, having deserted his battalion in Tunisia, was released after six months' incarceration in Egypt to invade France. Bain – whom we met earlier crossing on a troopship – recorded the moment of his release from the clink: 'The only reason you're being let out of here is because they want all the poor buggers they can get hold of to start the Second Front. They're letting you out tomorrow and they're going to send you home. And then they're going to get you killed. That's what you're being let out for. To be killed. You understand that?'[54]

The Bavent ridge – encompassing Amfréville in the north, Bréville in the centre and the much fought-over Château Saint-Côme and Le Mesnil to the south – overlooks Sword Beach and Ouistreham, as Rommel had noted on 30 May, and Captain David Tibbs of the 225th Parachute Field Ambulance recorded early on 6 June. Today, the port not only houses the former fire control tower – now the excellent Le Grand Bunker museum – but also another museum dedicated to No. 4 Commando, opposite the rebuilt casino. The cross-Channel ferry service from Portsmouth that arrives twice a day is a good way to follow the route – in considerably more comfort – of Admiral Bertram Ramsay's Neptune armada. The sight of its vessels leaving and entering the port also offers a useful yardstick when trying to imagine the D-Day flotillas off the coast.

Due to it being continuously shelled by the unsubdued batteries east of the Orne, Sword would become the first beach to close on 12 July (or D+34 in the parlance of the day), by which time Beachmaster Teddy Gueritz and his companions had overseen the landing of 46,644 men, 7,677 vehicles and 59,228 tons of stores. The Anglo-Canadian beaches as a whole, excluding the facilities of the Mulberry 'B' harbour, would disgorge the impressive total of 286,586 personnel, 120,729 tons of supplies and 50,400 vehicles by 19 June, when the storm hit.[55] Standing by the crossroads in Bréville-les-Monts, where the Desert Fox's staff car once lingered, there is no better place than to conclude a tour of the invasion area and understand the true cost of 'the Longest Day'.

The exploits of Kieffer's commandos were subsequently made famous – but not by France. It was Darryl F. Zanuck's movie version of *The Longest Day* in 1962 that brought them to the attention of their own compatriots and the wider world. In it, all the component nationalities in the D-Day story (except, curiously, the Canadians) had a fairly equal presence on screen – the Americans, British and Germans, but also the French underground and Kieffer's men. While Kieffer himself was one of the movie's historical consultants, his persona was played in the film by Christian Marquand, a well-known face of the time, with Georges Rivière acting the part of Guy de Montlaur, as the French commandos attacked the Ouistreham casino.

All of Zanuck's main cast of forty-two – which included John Wayne, Henry Fonda and Richard Todd – were well-known actors, this being the only way to sustain a narrative with scores of characters. Uniquely, Zanuck also had the characters speak in their own national languages, which encouraged German and francophone audiences to like it more.[56]

The film, with a huge cast and over two thousand military extras, won two Academy Awards and was a massive hit around the world. Thus, the minuscule land contribution by France on D-Day received disproportionate attention. No one minded, except the one man who should have been most impressed: Charles de Gaulle.

After the war, commemoration of the Normandy invasion sites and significant anniversaries of D-Day reflected Charles de Gaulle's post-war ambitions for France on the world stage. The French leader was bitter about American intervention which halted the Franco-British occupation of Suez in 1956. He had visions of an independent role for France in world affairs, closer to the Soviet Union, which he always referred to as Russia, and for whom he thought Communism was a passing fad. Despite receiving billions of dollars of Marshall Aid, de Gaulle spent the 1950s and 1960s steering France away from dependency on American arms and money, promoting the alternative power base of France alone, and subsequently the European Economic Community (now the European Union).

This policy affected Britain, too, who felt bitterly excluded by de Gaulle's refusal to allow the United Kingdom entry to the EEC twice – in 1963 and 1967, and something only achieved after his death in 1970. For the twenty-five years of de Gaulle's 'reign' (whether in or out of office, he was France's unofficial 'king' in this period) the Frenchman's pronouncements on the war and those of his contemporaries were highly critical of the United States. They made frequent attempts to hijack memories of the Normandy campaign for explicitly French nationalist purposes. Relations were so strained that in 1966, in pursuit of his international 'middle way', de Gaulle announced the withdrawal of France from participation in NATO affairs, and requested that US forces leave French bases by 1967 – triggered over dissatisfaction with American activity in Vietnam, formerly French Indo-China. This prompted Dean Rusk, then US Secretary of State, to ask de Gaulle whether the removal of US military personnel included the exhumation of American war dead buried in French soil.

Even when de Gaulle was out of office, Communist politicians saw the commemorations in terms of glorifying left-leaning maquisard heroes and denigrating the behaviour of the Allies to the French people. *Libération* was 'out', *résistance* was 'in'. The destruction of Caen, Saint-Lô and Lisieux (among others) was alluded to – demolition that began on the morning of 6 June, and left a very conservative minimum estimate of 13,000 civilians killed by Allied bombs and shells.[57] All of this antipathy peaked on 6 June 1964, when de Gaulle actually refused to attend the twentieth-anniversary celebrations in the American military cemetery at Colleville.

His representative, Jean Sainteny, Minister of Veterans Affairs, hit completely the wrong note when claiming, 'It is thanks to the French Resistance that the landings were successful', an assertion that puzzled even *résistants* themselves. The minister then reproached the Allies for not having sufficiently armed the Maquis. Two months later, de Gaulle further fuelled the fire by then attending the ceremonies along the Riviera coast on 15 August 1964, where large numbers of Free French forces had landed twenty years earlier. His message was clear – he saw 1944–5 through the lens of French military power and influence, and on D-Day he had been powerless.

Churchill and de Gaulle enjoyed a fractious relationship – one of hostility interspersed with admiration, or the other way about. 'He thinks he is Joan of Arc, but I can't get my bloody bishops to burn him,' Churchill once said of de Gaulle, who reciprocated with the observation, 'When I am right, I get angry. Churchill gets angry when he is wrong. We are angry at each other much of the time.' The truth was that they possessed remarkably similar, dogmatic characteristics, de Gaulle probably being the more egotistical of the two, if that were possible. Yet neither were consistent in their loathing – and admiration – of each other.

On 4 June 1944, *le Général* arrived at RAF Northolt, London, having been summoned by Churchill, who had despatched his private plane to Algiers, luring him with a note explaining that 'very great military events are about to take place'. De Gaulle had been kept completely in the dark about Overlord, and assumed he was being invited to view the plans, or participate in some command capacity. Neither he nor any of his staff had been invited to either of the 'Thunderclap' Conferences – in retrospect an astonishing and wounding omission. At the very least, de Gaulle expected to become a bystander to plans long set in motion. Tempers soon frayed when the Frenchman discovered Roosevelt was still refusing to recognise his right to power in France, whereupon he demanded that French currency notes printed by the Allies and already distributed to every invader – to pay for goods and services in France – be withdrawn. 'Go and wage war with your false money,' he declared, further threatening to remove Free French liaison officers and interpreters from all the assault-wave units.

An immediate post-war view of the American military cemetery at Colleville, overlooking Omaha beach. The grave-markers have yet to be made permanent and the Corncob blockships of the temporary Gooseberry breakwater will soon be removed by salvage divers. Although it was not yet traditional for an American president to attend D-Day commemoration events, Charles de Gaulle refused to attend the twentieth anniversary services here, at the very nadir of Franco-US relations. (Getty Images)

De Gaulle also declined to broadcast an eve-of-invasion message to the French following a pre-agreed script, after Eisenhower had spoken, and demanded to be flown back to Algiers 'in chains if necessary'. In the event, de Gaulle made a generous radio speech demanding of 'the sons of France, whoever they may be, wherever they may be', that their 'simple and sacred duty is to fight the enemy with every means in their power', and gave heartfelt thanks to the British for their effort in the liberation of France. He was mollified, also through Eisenhower's efforts, with a last-minute agreement that the Allies would cooperate with local civic authorities, rather than imposing their own. However, de Gaulle was essentially at the mercy of the Anglo-Saxon politicians until he could build his own power base, as France was liberated town by town.[58]

Churchill observed of his counterpart in August 1944, 'I have never forgotten, and can never forget, that de Gaulle stood forth as the first eminent Frenchman to face the common foe in what seemed to be the hour of ruin of his country and possibly, of ours.'[59] On 10 November 1944, Churchill would fly to Paris, where the pair were greeted by thousands of cheering Parisians. According to Foreign Secretary Anthony Eden, 'not for one moment did Winston stop crying; he could have filled buckets by the time he received the Freedom of Paris'.[60] At the following official banquet, de Gaulle observed publicly, 'It is true that we would not have seen the liberation if our old and gallant ally, England – and all the British dominions under precisely the impulsion and inspiration of those we are honouring today – had not deployed the extraordinary determination to win, and that magnificent courage, which saved the freedom of the world. There is no French man or woman who is not touched to the depths of their hearts and souls by this.'[61]

Even in November 1958, the Frenchman was moved to bestow on Churchill the *Croix de la Libération*. In the ceremony, a clearly emotional de Gaulle remarked, 'I want Sir Winston to know this. Today's ceremony means that France remembers what she owes him. I want him to know this: the man who has just had the honour of bestowing this distinction upon him, values and admires him more than ever.'[62] Later, on Churchill's death in January 1965, de Gaulle penned an impossibly magnanimous note of condolence to Her Majesty the Queen, 'In the great drama he was the greatest of all.'[63]

The Frenchman enjoyed a worse relationship with Roosevelt, who had initially recognised Pétain, then backed Giraud, before being forced to acknowledge de Gaulle in 1944. American policy was to govern France via an Allied Military Government for Occupied Territories (AMGOT), as in Sicily and Italy, until democratic elections would determine a new government. De Gaulle, though, already saw *himself* as leading the only legitimate alternative to the deeply collaborationist and anti-Semitic Vichy. His own views resonated widely within France by the time of the invasion, where the predictions of the sole voice, consistently exhorting resistance since 1940, seemed to be justified in 1944. Ironically, though everyone had heard of de Gaulle in the invasion year, no one had met him, much less knew what he looked like. To a much younger generation of *résistants*, such as schoolboy Jean Jammes with the Maquis in Épernon, he was a hero, the conscience of France.[64]

Thus the various post-war D-Day commemorations only served to remind de Gaulle of his relative powerlessness at this sensitive time, when he risked all to defy his allies. Hence, in 1964, his petulant refusal to even appear in Normandy, preferring instead to associate himself with the anniversary of the first reappearance of French military power in Europe – on the Riviera.

The Kieffer Commandos were caught in the middle of this, when de Gaulle in 1964 removed them from a list of those to receive Liberation Day honours, on the grounds that they had been under British command. The international thaw only began twenty years later with President Ronald Reagan's participation in the 6 June 1984 commemorations and a memorable speech he made on the Pointe du Hoc (at which I was present).

It continued with François Hollande's timely and astute offer, made on 6 June 2014, to award the *Légion d'Honneur* in the rank of chevalier to 'all surviving veterans of the Normandy landings, and of the wider campaigns to liberate France in 1944', regardless of nationality. This was triggered by Jacques Chirac's 1999 award of the same medal – instituted by Napoleon in 1802 – to surviving veterans of the 1914–18 Western Front, then numbering 350. Five years later, in 2004, it was the turn of the surviving thirty-three Kieffer Commandos – although their commander had died in 1962 – to receive the privilege denied them for decades by de Gaulle.

The master of ceremonies was Admiral Jean-Louis Battet – chief of the French Navy – who, when asked why it had taken sixty years for France to honour its commandos, suggested diplomatically that 'the day should be one of celebration, not argument'. However, as Léon Gautier then observed, 'Tens of thousands of Frenchmen did what we did; the difference, really, is that we did it on 6 June 1944. They give the *Légion d'Honneur* to people who do their job well. That's what we did. This is all very nice and touching, but they rather took their time.'[65]

'*Ils ont débarqué* [they have landed], people started whispering to one another': Pierre Wilson in distant Roubaix picked up rumours straight away of paratroops and assaults, soon confirmed by the BBC. 'I became conscious of an atmosphere of contained excitement in the streets. People were smiling and winking knowingly at each other on seeing the Germans rushing around.'[66] As the first defenders were being overwhelmed, and some Normans began to celebrate their liberation, the midday calm in Le Pontet, a suburb of Avignon in southern France, was shattered. Eyewitnesses recollected that a little after midday on 6 June 1944, several dark grey Citroën Traction Avants suddenly burst into the main street and screeched to a halt. Five men in dark tailored suits, wearing fedoras with brims turned low, rushed into houses. Neighbours stopped in their tracks, picked up playing children and hauled them inside. Moise Benyacar and his wife, not quick enough, were dragged away – along with their screaming three-and-a-half-month-old son and three other women.

Some of fifteen arrested on D-Day, they were taken first to a local Wehrmacht barracks, and eventually to the transit camp of Drancy, just north of Paris, for the crime of being Jewish. Benyacar would survive, but the trail of Benyacar's wife and son goes cold after one word – Auschwitz. It was only fifty years later that another survivor discovered the five fedora'd men who rounded them up 'spoke French with the accent of Marseilles' and identified their leader as Charles Palmieri, a local notorious gangster. The Gestapo, bristling with hoodlums and shady characters, each expert in the language of manipulation and violence, had found natural allies in the neighbourhood's criminal underworld. French muscle had been employed to do the Gestapo's dirty work for them.[67]

Likewise, liberation could not come soon enough for the oppressed elsewhere in Europe. In the Netherlands, Anneliese Marie Frank was looking forward to celebrating her fifteenth birthday on the twelfth, but of 6 June she wrote in her diary, '"This is D-Day," the BBC announced at twelve. This is the day. The invasion has begun. Is this really the beginning of the long-awaited liberation? The liberation we've all talked so much about, which still seems too good, too much of a fairy tale ever to come true? Will this year, 1944, bring us victory? We don't know yet. But where there's hope, there's life. It fills us with fresh courage and makes us strong again.' She had fifty-nine days of freedom left before the machinery of the Holocaust discovered her hiding place and sucked her into oblivion.[68]

The sixth of June 1944 may have been a day of rejoicing for much of the free world, but a petulant and rather selfish ex-commando named Evelyn Waugh, recently returned from his adventures with Yugoslav partisans, was struggling to finish the manuscript of *Brideshead Revisited*. He grumbled to his diary, 'Heard the Second Front had opened. Worked through until four o'clock and finished the last chapter – dialogue poor – and took it to the post. My only fear is lest the invasion upsets my typist in St Leonards or the post.'[69]

One statistic that doesn't often appear in connection with D-Day is 36,525: 'Readers might guess that the number represents the tally of soldiers who landed at *Omaha* beach or the number of ships and aircraft used in the cross-Channel operation or the number of German defenders or the number of casualties or any number of other things associated with Operation *Overlord*,' wrote Douglas Brinkley in *Time* magazine. 'But 36,525 is simply the number of days in a century, and of all the days in the twentieth century, none were more consequential than 6 June, 1944.'[70]

Brinkley precisely echoed veteran war reporter Andy Rooney's thoughts, when the latter observed

> We all have days of our lives that stand out from the blur of days that have gone by, and the day I came ashore on Utah Beach, four days after the initial invasion, is one of mine. As we approached the French coast, there were small clouds of smoke and sudden eruptions as German artillery blindly lobbed shells over the hills behind the beach. They were hoping to hit US troops or some of the massive amount of equipment piled up on the shore. Row on row of dead American soldiers were laid out on the beach just above the high-tide mark where it turned into weedy clumps of grass. They were covered with olive-drab blankets, just their feet sticking out at the bottom, their GI boots sticking out. I remember their boots – all the same on boys all so different.[71]

Postscript: Fortitude and the Spies

'In wartime, truth is so precious that she should always be attended by a bodyguard of lies.'

Winston S. Churchill

THIS ACCOUNT HAS addressed the military aspects of Overlord. Yet, with the passage of time and declassification of documents, it has become increasingly apparent that there was an additional reason for the triumph of Overlord from D-Day onwards. In parallel to the uniformed activities we have examined, both sides used spies in attempts to lever the maximum advantage against their foes. Earlier narratives, including for example *Defeat in the West, The Struggle for Europe* and *The Longest Day*, and all the major memoirs, from Eisenhower and Churchill to Bradley and Montgomery, were unaware or unable to reveal that alongside the more tangible facets of Operation Fortitude, a network of double agents were highly successful in inducing Hitler to order a series of mistaken moves based on false intelligence. Several relevant aspects of the espionage war are analysed here, and although in every case the results were not obvious until well after D-Day, their success meant that the Normandy landings would not be defeated.

Dressed 'in richly embroidered brocade, shoes with turned up toes, a fez with a tassel, and an immense scimitar', Elyesa Bazna was the valet of the British ambassador to Turkey. By day, he guarded his master's door, but at night the thirty-nine-year-old Kosovar Muslim rifled his master's safe. As adept a cameraman as he was a locksmith, Bazna photographed Sir Hughe Knatchbull-Hugessen's most sensitive documents and sold the negatives to the local SD agent in Ankara for large sums (alas for him, partly paid in forged Sterling notes).[1] The German embassy code-named him 'Cicero', after the Roman orator, for his 'astonishing eloquence'. Not that Bazna was a gifted communicator – but his documents spoke volumes about British strategic thinking.

He copied diplomatic notes of the Roosevelt–Stalin–Churchill Tehran Conference and it was through him the Germans first learned of the code name 'Overlord'. Following a telegram to Churchill on 13 December 1943, reporting that the Turks were demanding 'impossible amounts of armaments' before they allowed Britain the use of Turkish airbases or would enter the war on the Allied side, Eden replied, 'To sum up. Our object is to get Turkey into the war as early as possible, and in any case to maintain a threat to the Germans from the eastern end of the Mediterranean, until *Overlord* is launched.'[2]

The document also carried the BIGOT security classification, prompting the Germans to look for further documents of this type. However, this memo revealed no operational details, and Cicero's information fell victim to the Reich's aforementioned 'stove-piping' of intelligence – it was not widely circulated. Even within Ribbentrop's Foreign Office, due to the volume and clarity of Cicero's documentation, opinion was divided as to whether he was a double agent – though in all probability he was not.[3] Intelligence from other Axis-leaning powers was important, too: on 30 May 1944, Finnish codebreakers decoded a US diplomatic message indicating that Ira Hirschmann (an influential Washington businessman and War Labor Board executive) would be in Europe with Overlord on 6 June. However, Finland was neither a willing ally of the Axis powers nor a permanent belligerent, and although their intelligence service realised this might have been referring to the Allied invasion, they did not pass it on.[4]

Other formal Axis partners, though enthusiastic, proved to be a liability. In November 1943, the Japanese ambassador Lieutenant General Hiroshi Oshima was given a four-day conducted tour of the Atlantic Wall fortifications; on his return to Berlin, he wrote a twenty-page report of his visit, detailing the location of every German division, as well as its manpower and weaponry. He noted obstacles, armament of turrets on bunkers, and available mobile forces. On 27 May 1944,

Hitler discussed with him the belief that Allied 'diversionary attacks' would take place in Norway, Denmark, south-west France and the Mediterranean coast, with a major diversionary assault against Normandy or Brittany. Once consolidated, it would be followed by the main attack in the Calais area.[5]

Three days after D-Day, he confirmed to Tokyo (copied to his opposite numbers in Istanbul, Sofia, Madrid and Lisbon), 'because one separate Army Group is stationed on the southeast coast of Britain, it is expected that plans will be made for this to land in the Calais and Dunkirk areas'. He would also communicate FUSAG's demise, reporting on 25 October 1944 that it had been disbanded, due to the success of the other formations already on the Continent.[6] Oshima meticulously wrote detailed reports on all he saw and heard, which he transmitted to Tokyo using the Japanese 'Purple' diplomatic code. Alas for him, this had been broken by American cryptanalysts in 1940; consequently, much of the intelligence gained by Eisenhower on the Atlantic Wall defences came from Oshima's reports rather than from Enigma decodes at Bletchley Park; they also confirmed that Hitler was taken in by the notion that Normandy would be a diversionary assault.

By 1944 most German spies had been turned by the British – we will come to them shortly – but there was one not controlled by the Allies: Paul Fidrmuc alias 'Ostro', a former Austrian military officer living in Portugal. Able to speak six languages besides his native German – English, Italian, French, Danish, Spanish and Portuguese – he was a natural candidate for espionage. In 1940, Fidrmuc, a member of the Nazi Party, moved to neutral Portugal, garnering US and British intelligence for the Nazis, through a fabricated network of non-existent subagents – for which he was paid a good deal of money.

The British were very aware of his activities and astutely fed him fake information in the hope of discrediting him, though in February 1944 it was noted he had recently been awarded the Iron Cross. His file overview at the UK National Archives reads, 'a freelance *Abwehr* agent in Lisbon, whose prolific reporting was based on gossip, speculation and press reports. Most of it was inaccurate; however, in the run-up to *Overlord* his reports were sufficiently close to the truth, that he was for a time considered as a candidate for elimination'.[7] It is rare to find in official archives such a blatant reminder that this was total war, not a time for the normal niceties of liberal democracies, and occasionally such extreme measures were required.

In fact, Ostro survived the war and was debriefed afterwards because his information was occasionally very accurate. According to information he'd received from 'a staffer of Field Marshal Montgomery' – almost certainly non-existent – the Allies had massed 'twenty thousand soldiers for an invasion in early June on the *Manche* (i.e. Cherbourg) peninsula'. Isigny and Carentan were mentioned as areas for attention – but as well as the Channel Islands. Maybe the result of guesswork and speculation, and without knowing it was the intelligence coup of the century, Ostro sent this report marked 'urgent' to Berlin on 1 June 1944, where it was added to a huge pile of others from many sources – and there it sat.[8]

If the conceptual component of Operation Fortitude comprised the Quicksilver I and II notion of Patton's FUSAG and associated phoney radio transmissions, its physical expression was the Quicksilver III fake landing craft fleet and other bogus military equipment strewn across south-east England, and Quicksilver IV bombing of the Pas-de-Calais defences. However, dominating Fortitude was the moral – human – dimension of key German agents in Britain leaking information to Berlin. This was Operation Bodyguard, yet another aspect of the Fortitude plan, and devised by the London Controlling Section (LCS), a secret department established in 1941 to coordinate Allied strategic military deception, answering directly to the War Cabinet.

The LCS realised it could not conceal the build-up of forces in southern England, and chose instead to use German agents – who were in fact working for the British – to mask the *target* of the invasion. Bodyguard was approved on Christmas Day 1943, being agreed in outline a month earlier at the Tehran Conference. Its script – generally that Normandy was a diversionary landing, with the main effort arriving across the Pas-de-Calais forty-five days later – would be carefully fed to the Germans over time. Amongst the members of the LCS was the prolific, bestselling author Dennis Wheatley. Though initially only an RAF flight lieutenant (later wing commander), he used his fame to disarm sceptical high-ranking officers, while his fertile imagination and writing skills crafted many a plausible scenario to 'leak' to Berlin.

The LCS worked closely with 'R' Force at the 21st Army Group, and General Thorne in Edinburgh, who was also in charge of Fortitude North. Both required notice of every fake military location or movement – and, of course, genuine ones – to be disclosed to the Germans, so the necessary imitation tanks, guns, aircraft or landing craft could be readied in case of Luftwaffe overflight, and scripted military radio transmissions prepared for the benefit of Wehrmacht listeners. Nothing could be left to chance, and BIGOT-cleared officer despatch riders were daily travelling between headquarters – the operation was so sensitive that even encoded radio transmissions were forbidden – to ensure there were no lapses in the deception story.

The principal misinformation would come from three double agents code-named 'Brutus', 'Tricycle' and 'Garbo'. All were controlled by Colonel J. C. Masterman's highly secretive 'Twenty Committee', named after the Roman numerals XX, also signifying a double-cross, which met 226 times during the war and acted as the clearing house to review all the true and the false information passed to the *Abwehr*. 'Brutus' was a diminutive Polish officer called Roman Czerniawski, alias Walenty, Hubert or Armand, who had successfully run the *Interallié* Resistance network in France, was arrested by the *Abwehr* in Montmartre, but persuaded his interrogator, Feldwebel Hugo Bleicher, to send him to England as a German agent in 1942.

Despite the seeming naivety of Czerniawski's approach, Bleicher, his identity concealed by the moniker 'Colonel Heinrich', was one of the most effective *Abwehr* agents operating in France against the Resistance and hoped to bask in the reflected glory of his man in London. However, once across the Channel, Czerniawski immediately offered his services to the British – technically making him a triple agent – who code-named him Brutus, unsure as to whether he might switch sides yet again, and stab them in the back. Yet '*Brutus* has proved one of the most outstandingly successful double agents', one of his MI6 handlers wrote in documents declassified only in 2018.[9]

'Tricycle', so named because of the three spy networks he supposedly ran, was the wealthy Serbian lawyer Dušan Popov, a pre-war student in Germany and from 1940 an agent of the *Abwehr*, who code-named him 'Duško'. Popov moved freely around Nazi-occupied Europe and, when later recruited by MI6, between London and neutral Portugal under the guise of an import–export businessman.[10] Brutus compiled fake reports on Polish, Free French and American airborne units, while in February 1944 Tricycle hand-delivered a list of FUSAG units to his German contact in Lisbon. Both continued to submit data concocted by Allied counterintelligence that contained enough truth to make them believable, slowly creating the picture of Patton's army group forming in south-east England throughout the spring of 1944, alongside Montgomery's in the south and west.[11]

The extent and detail of these regular reports fooled both the SD and *Abwehr*, but there is evidence that Oberst von Roenne of the German Army's Foreign Armies West was more sceptical, suspecting that FUSAG was not what the double agents said it was. However, Roenne, with much of the *Abwehr*'s senior hierarchy, was disillusioned with the war, wanted peace with the western Allies, and thus had his own reasons to support the exaggerated estimates of Allied strength.[12] Other UK-based double agents, such as 'Tate' (the Danish-born Wulf Schmidt) and 'Treasure' (the Russian-French Nathalie Sergueiew) also supported the Fortitude ruse, the former reporting fake railway movements of FUSAG units towards the coast, and the latter claiming to have a boyfriend in the notional US Fourteenth Army.

'Bronx' (Peruvian Elvira Chaudoir) further confused the Germans with Operation Ironside, which hinted that a two-division landing might take place in the Bordeaux region – in order to fix the 11th Panzer Division stationed there.[13] In New York, another double agent, 'Albert van Loop' (in reality the Dutchman Walter Koehler), allowed the FBI to feed the *Abwehr* information in his name about the fake FUSAG divisions that were embarking on America's east coast, bound for the British Isles.[14]

The final piece of the espionage jigsaw lay with 'Garbo'. Known to the *Abwehr* as 'Alaric Arabel', the British recognised the sheer creativity of the Spanish fantasist and double agent Juan Pujol García by code-naming him after 'the best actor in the world', Greta Garbo. Perhaps the most inventive and influential of wartime double agents, Garbo had been recruited by the Germans in 1940 when posing as a fanatically pro-Nazi Spanish government official and was instructed to move to Britain to spy. Instead he relocated to Lisbon, sending in fake reports gleaned from newsreels, reference books and magazines in the Lisbon Public Library.[15] MI6 – for whom he had wanted to work all along – became aware of his misinformation campaign, recruited him and moved García and his family to London in 1942, in spite of considerable opposition from Mrs García.[16]

With British help, Garbo concocted a network of twenty-seven fictional agents who fed him titbits of information about Allied shipping and troop movements which he reported to his *Abwehr* control in

Madrid, who relayed them to Berlin. His messages were a blend of facts of limited military value, fiction, and valuable military intelligence artificially delayed. Between January 1944 and D-Day the 'Garbo network' bombarded their German paymasters with over five hundred radio messages (four transmissions a day), but Garbo's key transmission was sent after, not before, D-Day.[17]

On 8 June, Brutus would assess that the future boundary between Montgomery and Patton 'will be roughly along the Seine' – hinting at a Pas-de-Calais assault.[18] The same day, Garbo began to transmit information on those units already identified by the Germans as being in Normandy, pointing out that many FUSAG units had not participated in the invasion, and therefore the 'first' landing should be considered a diversion.

> After personal consultation on 8 June in London with my agents, Jonny, Dick and Dorick, I am of the opinion, in view of the strong troop concentration in southeast and eastern England, which are not taking part in present operations, that these operations are a diversionary manoeuvre designed to draw off enemy reserves in order to make an attack at another place. In view of the continued air attacks on the concentration area mentioned, which is a strategically favourable position for this, it may very probably take place in the Pas-de-Calais, particularly since in such an attack the proximity of air bases will facilitate the operation by providing continued strong air support.[19]

This was a high-risk stratagem, but Garbo had already established his credentials. However, no one in the Allied team realised that his transmissions were being shown to Hitler *personally*. This last message was forwarded to Hitler's Berchtesgaden headquarters at 1030 hours on 9 June. Oberst Friedrich-Adolf Krummacher, the senior *Abwehr Verbindungsoffizier* (*Abwehr* liaison officer, now working for Schellenberg) on the Führer's staff, had underlined in red the words 'diversionary manoeuvre designed to draw off enemy reserves in order to make a decisive attack in another place' and added the marginalia 'confirms the view already held by us that a further attack is expected in another place (Belgium?)', while Jodl had underlined the words 'in southeast and eastern England' in his signature green ink.[20]

This signal – found at Berchtesgaden after the war, and marked by Jodl as having been shown to Hitler – has been wildly described as the 'message that changed the war'. Although some able historians conclude the battle for Normandy was already lost, Garbo's signal would certainly have had an effect on the campaign. On 8 June, under pressure from Rundstedt and Rommel, OKW had released the 116th and 1st SS Panzer and two infantry divisions from the Fifteenth Army and directed them to Normandy. However, at 0730 hours on 10 June this was counter-manded, when Generalfeldmarschall Keitel ordered, 'As a consequence of certain information, a state of alarm has been declared for the Fifteenth Army in Belgium and North France.' The same day's intelligence summary parroted Garbo's message: 'The fact that not one of the forma-tions still standing by in the southeast and east of England has been identified in the present operation, strengthens the supposition that the strong Anglo-American forces which are still available, are being held back for further plans.'[21]

On 11 June, the FUSAG threat was still being devoured whole, as Garbo was informed, 'The reports received in the last week have been confirmed almost without exception, and are to be described as especially valuable. The main line of investigation in the future is to be the enemy group of forces in the south eastern and eastern England.' A month later, on 8 July – still under the sway of Garbo – Hitler would order that reserves behind the Fifteenth Army's front were to remain 'until such time as it can be ascertained whether the American Army Group [FUSAG] is going to undertake another landing operation, or whether its forces will follow Montgomery's Army Group into the present beach-head'.[22] Of course, no attack would ever come in the Calais area, and some of the success of keeping the Fifteenth Army there can be attributed to one man: Garbo.

How to measure the success of Fortitude – or indeed whether it was successful? In the fixing of Salmuth's Fifteenth Army at Calais, instead of it immediately decamping and streaming straight to the aid of Dollmann's Seventh Army in Normandy, the deception campaign, with all its subsidiary aspects, notably Quicksilver and Bodyguard, would appear to have been a victorious formula. Indeed, as a direct consequence of Garbo's signal received at Berchtesgaden on 9 June, Theodor Wisch's 1st SS Panzer Division was switched from moving to Normandy, to an assembly area west of Bruges in Belgium, a decision admittedly reversed within the week. Graf von Schwerin's 116th Panzer was retained on the Seine, between the two armies, where it would remain until late July;

and Kurt Chill's 85th Infantry Division, stationed north of the Somme, had its orders to move to Normandy cancelled.[23] On the same day, 9 June, when Dollmann's Seventh Army asked Army Group 'B' for reinforcements, Rommel's response was to refuse, claiming expectation of a 'big landing higher up the coast in the course of the next few days'.[24] However, this is not the whole story.

Do we attach too much importance to Garbo and his colleagues? The traditional narrative of Normandy was that the Fifteenth Army had to be prevented at all costs from moving swiftly to the invasion front. But had it arrived earlier and en masse, would it have made a difference? Even if it had been ordered to march west, this would have been beyond the Fifteenth's ability for at least four reasons. First, the majority of infantry divisions within Salmuth's Army were 'static' formations. Second, they were mostly not battle-hardened, comprising some surprisingly young and old soldiers, many convalescing from wounds received in Russia. Third, as with the Seventh Army's static units, those designed to lurk in concrete emplacements for purely defensive purposes lacked vehicular transport, much support weaponry and possessed a bewildering mixture of hardware seized from conquered nations. And finally, of Salmuth's formations, the 17th and 18th Luftwaffe Field Divisions were still coping with the notion of air force personnel being rerolled as infantry, were half the size of their army counterparts, but had more motor transport and better anti-aircraft guns.

The ribbons and decorations on Obergefreiter Otto Schmidt's tunic showed him to be a much-decorated veteran of the Russian Front; his black wound badge was a reminder of the shell splinters he had received in Crimea – he would receive more in Normandy. Schmidt remembered his relief at being posted to the 85th Division in March 1944 on the Channel coast, near the old battlefield of Crécy. His battery commander had a fixation about it, and kept reminding them that they would see off the Allies, as the English had beaten the French there in the summer of 1346. Yet Schmidt was far more worried about a comb-out and transfer back to the Eastern Front than an appearance of the English on his doorstep. Their day-to-day concerns were the increasingly frequent attacks by Allied aircraft, and looking after their horses. 'Without our loyal friends [the horses], we in the 7th Battery were powerless to do anything,' Schmidt argued. He thought his 185th *Artillerie-Regiment* was 'hopelessly understrength and ill-prepared for the invasion; Russia was an equal man-to-man struggle, but in the West, we were up against endless machines: we had no machinery and no transportability, so we couldn't win.'[25]

Even those allegedly mobile infantry formations sent to Normandy fielded only 10,000 or fewer men. Each had earlier been labelled 'static' but given a few vehicles, this somehow transformed them into 'fully mobile' units. Ordered to Normandy on 6 June, Generalmajor Diestel's 346th Division in the vicinity of Le Havre had, in the words of his report to Rommel, 'one regiment completely mobile; the other had one horse-drawn battalion, the men rode bicycles, and the artillery regiment was horse-drawn'.[26] Its total strength was 9,534. The 326th Infantry at Le Touquet was designated as an 'improvised mobile division' and, using confiscated French vehicles, despatched westwards, crossing the Seine on 22 July. The 331st Infantry had only just returned from Russia and was reorganising at Boulogne when the invasion began; they belatedly started their journey to Normandy on 28 July. The newly formed 84th and 85th Infantry Divisions, raised in February 1944, had just been 'declared operational, having reached their reduced establishment strength of eight thousand men each' (according to an Ultra intercept of 17 May).[27] None of these Fifteenth Army formations would have made much difference to the battle in Normandy, whenever they arrived.

Once the campaign was under way, all German deployments – whose intentions had often been plotted by Ultra – were harassed continuously and very effectively from the air. This brake on movement was compounded by the effectiveness of the Resistance's *Tortue* (sabotage of roads) and *Vert* (damage to railways) plans. Together these all served to slow down – but did not prevent – German arrivals in Normandy, who also trickled into the battle space, rather than arriving as concentrated units. The 1st SS and 116th Panzer Divisions stationed with the Fifteenth Army certainly worried the Allies, and the former was very potent, battle-hardened and fully mobile. However, Gerhard, Graf von Schwerin's 116th, the *Windhunds*, was a different matter. They had been formed only in March 1944 by merging two formations, the 179th Reserve Panzer with the 16th *Panzergrenadier* Division, decimated at Stalingrad. It was not ready for battle on D-Day, possessing 13,621 personnel, 252 half-tracks and 86 Panzer IVs (half its allocation of tanks), had only twenty-nine operational guns in its artillery regiment, no flak detachment, and was desperately short of trucks.[28]

Its Panther tank battalion was still training in Germany; when ordered into battle, it had to borrow those of another panzer division. With impaired mobility and harassment from the air, if ordered to Normandy on D-Day, they would probably have arrived in separate groups – as indeed they did when they eventually arrived in July. If we accept Rommel's dictum that the fight would be won or lost on the beaches, it seems unlikely that these poorly-equipped panzer and infantry divisions, dribbling into the western battle space of Normandy any earlier than they actually arrived, would have made much difference against the crushing preponderance of air and materiel superiority the Allies had assembled.

Furthermore, it will be recalled that the earlier Allied air forces' Transportation Plan – apart from pulverising the French railroad system – had destroyed the thirty-six significant bridges over the Seine between Paris and Rouen before 6 June. As a result, all reinforcements from beyond Normandy to the east would have to arrive ponderously, usually on foot, by road and ferry. Finally, the Fifteenth Army was critically short of fuel: the Transportation Plan had also contributed towards difficulties in the distribution of *benzin*, Keitel complaining on 1 May about delays in the repairs of railways; on the tenth, he was asking OKW if he could use POWs to repair railway damage.[29] On 2 May, the 12th SS Panzer Division communicated a lack of fuel for training – so even those formations with vehicles were beginning to be constrained from using them. It was on 8 May that OB West with great foresight informed Berlin, 'The enemy is already effectively hampering our supply and troop movements, and in the event of active operations, would hamper the latter in particular.'[30]

Thus, although most of Salmuth's divisions were only tardily sucked into the Normandy campaign, this was not – or not only – because Fortitude induced them to linger around Calais, but also because they couldn't actually move anywhere very fast.

It should also be remembered that there was another purpose entirely for the defence of Calais, to which Hitler had referred in his *Führerbefehl* No. 51 of 3 November 1943: the protection of his V-weapon sites, which would begin their deadly trade of hurling buzz bombs at London a week after D-Day, on 13 June.

This, however, overlooks the evidence of OKW's deployment of other German divisions towards the invasion. Careful analysis of the mobile infantry divisions based in southern France with Blaskowitz's Army Group 'G' reveals that four were sent to Normandy. These travelled over longer distances, when fuel was in short supply, and were despatched *before* the (much nearer) mobile formations in Salmuth's Fifteenth Army. They were the 276th Infantry Division, despatched from Biarritz on 14 June; the Narbonne-based 277th, sent on 23 June; the 271st, which departed Montpelier on 30 June; and the 272nd Infantry Division at Perpignan, which started out on 2 July. Thus it seems that OKW were hedging their bets, in feeding divisions to Normandy from southern France, also others from Brittany, ahead of those from the Pas-de-Calais. This also emphasised the success of Fortitude North, which not only fixed German units in Norway fearing an invasion there, but prevented their redeployment to France.[31]

While the double agents reinforced the Quicksilver aspects of Fortitude, what no one could anticipate was whether and how much Brutus, Tricycle and Garbo – and the others – would be believed. The results were surprising. Operation Fortitude, and its Bodyguard subcomponents, are normally lauded as a triumph of Allied planning. And yet, despite the many pointers from methodical signals analysis, and penetration of the French Resistance, the Reich's internecine war between its own intelligence agencies masked any significant achievements it might have made.

What is astonishing is the often overlooked admission in one official British record that 'the OKW *Lagebericht* – daily intelligence summary – provides no single example of the wireless deception programme having brought any item in the *Fortitude* story to the knowledge of the Germans in the first instance'.[32] So the vast Quicksilver II operation – which included signaller John Emery from HMS *Largs* and Corporal Les Phillips transmitting their scripted phoney signals that supported the notion of FUSAG – was not even noticed, except when double agents brought it to their attention.[33]

Even more surprisingly, neither have any OKW, Luftwaffe or other German documents come to light indicating the extensive presence of Quicksilver III's imitation landing craft erected by Lieutenant Colonel White of the Royal Engineers and his colleagues, that Ray Marshall remembered seeing in the Thames estuary – or the other military weaponry in south-east England created by Arthur Merchant and 'R' Force, the Shepperton Film Studios, the 603rd Camouflage Engineers and 406th Engineer Combat Company. Thus this aspect, too, of Fortitude's fake invasion preparations seems to have been completely missed by the Germans, though much written about in the extensive literature on D-Day.[34]

Overall, it seems that Fortitude was a qualified success, mostly (and surprisingly) in terms of the contribution of Masterman's agents – rather than the more well-known aspects of FUSAG and Quicksilver. As one of the LCS members later crowed, 'every phase in the story can be directly attributed to the three double-cross agents, *Garbo, Brutus* and *Tricycle*'.[35] The Führer's inclination previously had been to accept Normandy as the *Schwerpunkt*, despite his asides to the Japanese. This is not to say that FUSAG and Quicksilver should have been abandoned: they were, after all, the insurance policy against any doubts about the veracity of Garbo and the others – and vice versa.

The London Controlling Section was fortunate, and could not have known in advance that in the ivory tower that was Hitler's headquarters at the Berghof in Berchtesgaden – the lair of the mad mountain king, surrounded by the Bavarian Alps and far from the military bustle of Berlin or the *Wolfsschanze* (Wolf's Lair) HQ in East Prussia – Hitler's whim would induce him to believe Garbo over the SD and Wehrmacht's patiently assembled mass of military intelligence.

Garbo's credibility remained sufficiently high for a surprise signal from Berlin, dated 29 July 1944: 'With great happiness and satisfaction I am able to advise you today that the Führer has conceded the Iron Cross to you for your extraordinary merits.' It seemed only right under the circumstances to reciprocate, and in a secret ceremony in December, Garbo was made a Member of the British Empire (MBE) by King George VI, who also awarded Brutus and Tricycle each an Order of the British Empire (OBE).

In May 1984, the author Nigel West identified and tracked down the elusive Juan Pujol García, then living undercover in Venezuela. In recognition of his specific contribution to Fortitude and Overlord, he was immediately flown to London 'to attend a private audience with HRH The Duke of Edinburgh at Buckingham Palace', went on to see some old comrades at the Special Forces Club, and on 6 June 1984 was escorted to Normandy to tour the invasion beaches.[36] 'Connoisseurs of double cross', wrote Sir John Masterman in 1945, 'have always regarded the *Garbo* case as the most highly developed example of their art' – an unintended pun, for Garbo, the supreme example of the double-cross, had indeed been awarded two crosses.[37]

It is easy to assume that the Normandy landings have always been celebrated with the dignity, pomp and circumstance we have come to expect from recent commemorations. However, this was not so until 1984, when President Ronald Reagan decided to make the fortieth anniversary of D-Day the highlight of a three-nation tour. He would deliver a speech using the lessons of 6 June 1944 to remind the free world of the contemporary threat from Soviet Russia. To his direction, a new White House speechwriter, Peggy Noonan, crafted a stirring address that emphasised the deeds of James Rudder and his Rangers in overcoming adversity on the Pointe du Hoc.

Noonan also suggested that the key moment of Reagan's visit be moved from the traditional setting of the Colleville military cemetery to the Pointe. Appropriately, on 5 June 1984 present-day Rangers re-enacted the famous climb – accompanied by Herman Stein, formerly of Company 'F', who insisted, at sixty-three, on doing again what he had

It was Ronald Reagan who first instituted the tradition of US Presidential attendance in Normandy for key D-Day anniversaries. In 1984, on the shrewd advice of speechwriter Peggy Noonan, the main focus of commemoration moved from the cemetery at Colleville, symbolising sacrifice, to the Pointe-du-Hoc, representing achievement – in this case, of Rudder and his Rangers. It was an occasion at which the author was present. Here the Reagans are pictured viewing the Channel from the German observation post, on top of which sits the Rangers' memorial. Since the Reagans' visit, D-Day celebrations have evolved into unofficial world summit meetings, first with German and latterly Russian presence. (Getty Images)

accomplished once before, aged twenty-three. On reaching the top, Stein was movingly given a bear hug by his old company commander, Captain Otto Mansy; the drama of their endeavour coincided perfectly with the dramatic backdrop of the landscape and coastline.

That Reagan's visit was a personal pilgrimage, not just politics, was evidenced by one of those invited to join him, Kathryn Morgan Ryan, widow of Cornelius, who had died of cancer ten years earlier. Her Irish-American husband, author of *The Longest Day*, had been part of John F. Kennedy's campaign team in the 1960 election campaign, and had remained close to his Democrat administration. Thus, although no political friend of the Republican Reagan, Kathryn Ryan's presence underlined Reagan's personal fascination with the Second World War, respect for its veterans, and his belief that he should do all in his power to prevent World War Three. Others present included another widow, Margaret Rudder, in addition to sixty-two of her late husband's surviving Rangers.

Reagan was the first president to attend a D-Day anniversary in person; it has since become a tradition, but none of his predecessors had made the journey. Eisenhower in office turned his invitation down, perhaps understandably due to the slower nature of air transport and more primitive means of communication in those Cold War days. Instead, he issued a tenth-anniversary statement that echoed contemporary East–West tensions, talking of 'the spirit of that wartime union, if some of the peoples who were our comrades-in-arms have been kept apart from us, that is cause for profound regret, but not for despair'.

Lyndon B. Johnson at the twentieth anniversary addressed the 1964 Normandy delegation led by Omar Bradley: 'Your country remembers and will never forget, the resolve born on that D-Day. When this nation has stood for two thousand years, we shall not have forgotten the lands where our sons lie buried, nor the cause for which our sons died. Where we have commitments to the cause of freedom, we shall honour them – today, tomorrow and always.' The shadow of Vietnam then pushed the Second World War into the background in the minds of a generation drafted once again to fight an overseas war, though one whose cause was more opaque.

Reagan's bold departure from the norm would also represent the first major occasion, since before Vietnam had torn America apart, when the nation could acknowledge its Second World War veterans and celebrate their achievements. More recently, Barack Obama at the sixty-fifth anniversary in 2009 was able to cite his grandfather, a US Army supply sergeant stationed in southern England, crossing the Channel six weeks after D-Day. Reagan's 1984 message would echo a piece written by Thomas L. Wolf in the *Smithsonian* magazine, 'D-Day – the first time when the free world hurled its might, its treasure and the lives of its young men and women against the most powerful fortress ever erected: *Festung Europa*'.[38]

Also incorporated in Reagan's fortieth-anniversary address was a moving appeal by a later generation; Lisa Zanatta Henn had written movingly to the President months before of her desire to travel to Normandy to see where her father, Private Peter Zanatta of the 37th Combat Engineer Battalion, had fought on Omaha Beach. For their household, 6 June anniversaries were like Father's Day, Independence Day, Memorial Day and Veterans Day all rolled into one. The double tribute, to the Rangers and Private Everyman, represented by Zanatta, became one of the defining moments of Reagan's first presidency and was reckoned to have helped his re-election that November, as well as rekindling the flame of recognition in Normandy.

As the 40th President was making his famous address at the Pointe, surrounded by hundreds of veterans – an occasion I witnessed – far away in West Palm Beach, Florida, forty years to the day since he had scaled the cliffs, Robert Fruhling, the radio man who had climbed that day with Sergeant Bud Lomell, ended the mental battle he had been fighting ever since. He took his own life – a reminder that some scars from D-Day never healed. Twenty years on in 2004, President Ronald Reagan would himself join the Great Muster Beyond, sixty years to the day after those veterans he had lauded set sail for their 1944 rendezvous with the Normandy coast. He could have no finer epitaph than his closing words on the Pointe, given in 1984: 'We will always remember. We will always be proud. We will always be prepared, so we may always be free.'

Before leaving the world-changing events of 6 June 1944, we owe ourselves a moment of contemplation. Did the Allies make the right call in selecting Normandy in June 1944? Was there any other choice? Could the Germans have won? The London detective Sherlock Holmes (who first appeared in print in the year of Bernard Montgomery's birth – 1887) was fond of declaring that a challenging case was a 'three-pipe problem', demanding a lengthy period of contemplation before the solution was clear. He would settle before his fire and think hard about the facts as he knew them. 'I beg that you won't speak to me for fifty minutes', he would say to his companion Dr Watson. 'It is a capital mistake to theorise before you have all the evidence. It biases the judgment.' Pipe or no pipe, the reader will have taken more than Holmes' allotted fifty minutes to ponder these important questions.

Although several German commanders – not just Erich Marcks – wargamed a theoretical Allied invasion, they could not know the scale of resources available to Eisenhower. They had little awareness as to the extent of training the invaders had received. Neither did they anticipate the inventiveness of their opponents. German thinking revolved around capturing ports; Churchill's two 'synthetic harbours' liberated COSSAC and SHAEF from this constraint, allowing a greater range of options.

The greatest gift of Normandy came in the form of operational surprise. Given that some of England's south-eastern coast is visible with the naked eye from France, a distance of eighteen nautical miles, it is impossible to conceive of any major assault against the Fifteenth Army around Calais being made with secrecy.

In German minds, the events of Dunkirk and the Battle of Britain in 1940 had driven home the advantages of Allied air power operating from bases close to France, ten to fifteen minutes' flying time away. By 1944 this had morphed into a terrible destructive capacity, and for this reason, many German commanders assumed the Allies would play to this advantage and mount landings under the tightest – and closest – umbrella of airpower. Thus the Calais area beckoned. To OB West the option of Normandy, being further away, required more flying time and fuel, and would require greater numbers of aeroplanes to maintain continuous air cover over an invasion. Fortitude and the spies played to these German assessments.

In fact, distance mattered not to Leigh-Mallory, who had enough aircraft, aircrew and fuel at his disposal. Dependent on the location of their airbases, Allied fighters and other fast aircraft took around 30–40 minutes to reach Normandy in 1944. US troop transports flying from further inland deposited airborne troops in Normandy after an average of three hours, less for the British.

Examining other locations, the Allies correctly feared a landing in Brittany would be too easily contained. An assault around the Somme, as Rommel feared, offered little in the way of good beaches. Apart from Calais, the other German anxiety was the major port of Antwerp (Anvers to the French), forty miles inland along the River Scheldt. However, this involved the Allied risk of a lengthy sea crossing, whilst both river banks were well-guarded, as was the former island of Walcheren at its head. (This would play out as a costly battle in October–November 1944.) While the Somme, Calais and Antwerp offered quicker routes to the Third Reich, they also offered faster avenues for German reinforcement. The other alternatives of Norway, Southern France, Italy and the Balkans amounted to no more than Allied subterfuge or Churchillian whim. Generals Paget and Morgan had earlier come to the same conclusions, confirmed by SHAEF.

Time-wise, Overlord had to be mounted in the summer of 1944. Time was of the essence. Mindful of the Japanese, Roosevelt was impatient. Stalin needed appeasing, and his armies were already making stupendous headway in eastern Europe. Every day's delay meant the *Atlantikwall* grew stronger, and – as Chapter 16 has demonstrated – the Germans were beginning to unravel the secret of the objective.

Could the Reich have prevailed? Both the German Seventh and Fifteenth Armies were far weaker and less mobile than the Allies had imagined. Bletchley Park gave little insight into the fact that the defenders were old, often unfit and frequently non-German, and therefore of limited motivation. The panzer divisions had far fewer tanks, less transport and more limited fuel than expected. The vast array of captured weaponry and equipment proved a logistical nightmare. Air cover was negligible. Their transportation routes were shattered.

The land forces were shackled by a convoluted chain of command, with the headquarters of each Army, each Army group, OB West, Panzer Group West, OKW and Hitler all possessing a veto over proposed tactical moves. Despite a profusion of liaison officers, none worked in concert with the Kriegsmarine or Luftwaffe. This resulted in a glacial speed of reaction. The only leader with the energy and authority to sidestep this tendency – Rommel – was away in Germany when he was needed most in France. Yet, even with the Army Group 'B' commander at the helm, it is difficult to foresee any other result. The Desert Fox was hampered as he had been two years earlier at Alamein, by dwindling resources and a lack of air power.

Yet, there was one factor that might have spelled disaster for the Allies, over which they had no control: the weather. High winds scattered the airborne forces, and at least ten per cent of the seaborne fatalities on 6 June were due to drowning. Another point on the Beaufort scale might have been enough to literally sink the assault, while a delay to 19 June – with its tempest – would have been catastrophic. The choice of times and dates was dictated by the necessity for a full moon and low water, though a decision to land at high water (which in practice most units ended up doing) might have yielded some different dates.

The airborne operations were successful and achieved their objectives, additionally distracting German reserves away from the beaches at a crucial time. The Commandos and Rangers also proved their worth. It was German tactical professionalism, rather than any American mistakes, that held up the 1st and 29th Divisions at Omaha. The same cannot be said of Sword beach, where an over-ambitious plan, and the timidity of a brigade commander – possibly the divisional commander also – led to a disappointing result, even if the only major German counter-attack of the day was halted in its tracks. The late morning change of plan for 9th Infantry Brigade and wounding of its brigadier also meant that those on Sword failed to link-up with the Canadians on their right – a potentially fatal gap which fortunately the Wehrmacht did not exploit. On Utah, Gold and Juno, the assaulting troops delivered in style, overcoming the weather and the Germans (which was worse is a moot point). The Canadians slew the ghost of Dieppe and deserve more praise than they have usually received. The seaborne assaults, including the slender hold at Omaha, created an adequate beachhead from which to launch a victorious campaign.

None of this would have been possible without Eisenhower's team. COSSAC under Morgan had produced the blueprint for attack, inherited by SHAEF. Air power was vital but poorly managed in an arena containing many prima donnas. Montgomery – probably a better trainer of Allied troops than he was a subsequent battle captain – superbly prepared the armies for battle. Bertram Ramsay got them across the Channel and sustained them. The unsung admiral, whose contribution to victory was of Nelsonian proportions, deserves far more recognition than history has accorded him. However, managing all of this was the Supreme Commander, supported by Tedder and Bedell Smith, who rose to the challenges with aplomb.

No other destination would have delivered quite the same shock and surprise that stunned virtually every significant German headquarters into inactivity. The time this bought the Allies was exploited to the maximum. Assessing all this evidence during the course of his three pipes, Mr Sherlock Holmes, from the comfort of his armchair at 221B Baker Street, would have arrived at the same conclusion. Eisenhower made the correct call. D-Day in Normandy was launched at the right time and in the right place.

Acknowledgements

I N 1763, MR Edward Gibbon was released from service as an officer in the South Hampshire militia. He thought the experience made him 'an Englishman and a soldier'. The following year he journeyed to Rome, where on 15 October 1764 he 'sat musing amidst the ruins of the Capitol, whereupon the idea of writing the decline and fall of the city first entered my mind'.[1] Gibbon was so emboldened by the many insights into military organisation and tactics offered from his militia days that he was moved to observe, 'the Captain of the Hampshire Grenadiers has not been useless to the historian of the Roman Empire'.[2]

My own lengthy adventures with the armed forces of Britain and America in the Balkans, Iraq and Afghanistan have led me to agree with the author of *The History of the Decline and Fall of the Roman Empire* – that the soldier is unusually well-placed to make sense of history. And, just as Gibbon did, the professional historian in me shouts that it is impossible to understand past events – much less analyse and write about them – without walking the ground where they took place.

I must thank those with whom I served for their soldierly insights, and the levelling experience of bonding with strangers around a camp fire, punctuated by the odd whiff of grapeshot. The genesis of *Sand and Steel*, however, lay in the years before I donned uniform. *After the Battle* magazine (www.afterthebattle.com) is a quarterly publication – still going strong today – that matches black and white wartime photographs to contemporary locations as a way of narrating history. I read its very first edition, published on the twenty-ninth anniversary of D-Day in 1973, and was immediately struck by then then-and-now format, these days much imitated. Thus I tip my hat to its editor, Winston Ramsey, who is too modest to admit that he has been responsible for a step-change in the writing of military history. *After the Battle* directly encouraged a group of D-Day veterans and military vehicle-owners to visit Normandy and in the summer of 1975 I joined them on the landing beaches.

Since then, I have returned to that corner of France every single year for some defence-related reason. This is often to guide military staff from the UK and other NATO countries around the battlefields to explore their own heritage, along with issues of leadership, logistics and morale – 'what happens if the wheel suddenly comes off?' Military history does not purport to offer clear templates for action, but always provides the reassurance that in the past someone else managed to find their way out of a similar mess. I therefore owe a huge debt to those thousands who have accompanied me on over five hundred battlefield tours and staff rides around the world, and who have shared their own insights of combat, or asked me pertinent questions that set me thinking.

Second World War tank and submarine aces were the creatures of German propaganda. As a concept, this particular elevation of individuals to celebrity status was fundamentally flawed – for it overlooked the invaluable services of the rest of the military team, who serviced and operated the panzers and the U-boats, making the activities of the various aces possible in the first place. I first met Hauptmann Otto Carius, winner of the Knight's Cross with Oakleaves, at the Royal Military College of Science, Shrivenham, in 2004, where I was then lecturing. He told me of his embarrassment that his gunner, Unteroffizier Kramer, never gained the recognition he as an officer had been accorded, 'even though it was Kramer who was responsible for our more than 150 Russian tank "kills", including the unique feat of shooting down a Soviet aircraft attacking us, destroyed with the tank's main gun.'[3] Later, I twice had the pleasure of meeting Herr Günter Halm in 2016 and 2017, who had been awarded the Knight's Cross personally by Rommel. His anti-tank gun had destroyed fifteen British tanks at the First Battle of El Alamein in July 1942, but as he modestly admitted, 'there were six of us in the gun crew, but they chose me, aged nineteen, because I was the youngest.'[4]

As in the First World War, the Allied air forces of the Second World War recognised the idea of the fighter ace – who required five victories over his opponents to qualify for the title – but this also tended to overlook the substantial support of the ground crews, who spent many hours preparing each aircraft for their pilots. With more than five books under my belt, I qualify as a military history 'ace'. Yet none of my literary ramblings, and certainly not *Sand and Steel*, would have been possible without the 'ground crew', who have fed me ideas, sustained my morale, dragged me out of writer's block, checked my facts, and offered much needed help, advice and fine claret, cognac or calvados when needed. I have dedicated this book to two of the more significant who have been guiding lights for the last twenty-five years.

Writing a book is not unlike fighting a battle; resources are assessed and marshalled, intelligence reviewed, commanders, troops and weapons chosen, terrain surveyed, and the campaign launched to a methodical plan – that is immediately shredded when the Clausewitzian fog of new facts and interpretations appear. To keep me focused on the road to victory, my 'ground crew' formed a team who – alongside my publishers and agent (who were as much forward air controllers as ground crew) – should take pride in the knowledge that they are every bit as responsible as the author for the appearance of this volume.

Trevor Dolby and Nigel Wilcockson at Penguin Random House, and Tim Bent and Jonathan Kroberger at Oxford University Press, have acted as my generals, commanding the battlefield, directing my efforts, encouraging or chiding me as necessary, with Alison Rae and Rowan Borchers marshalling my facts and sentences, occasionally calling down air strikes to destroy recalcitrant paragraphs or irrelevant chapters. That this is the fourth book I have written with Penguin Random House and the third for OUP is testament to the faith they have in their humble scribe. My agent, Patrick Walsh of PEW Literary, with his unrivalled knowledge of the terrain, has been my adjutant, assisted by John Ash, chivvying me along, and suggesting attacks to the left or right flank. All of these figures themselves have important battalions behind them, largely unknown to me – to all I say a hearty thank you and salute you all.

Edward Gibbon is a good model for historians. Unusually for the eighteenth century, he sought primary sources whenever he could, advising that he had 'always endeavoured to draw from the fountainhead; that my curiosity, as well as a sense of duty, has always urged me to study the originals; and that, if they have sometimes eluded my search, I have carefully marked the secondary evidence, on whose faith a passage or a fact were reduced to depend.'[5] For *Sand and Steel*, my fresh look at D-Day draws heavily on my own interviews with the veterans of the

Second World War, and has been sustained logistically by the impressive archival resources of several institutions, which in my notional army comprise the Royal Corps of Archives and Libraries, identified more fully in my notes. They have been always ready to point the weary soldier in the right direction, introducing me to fresh 'voices' and suggesting new lines of attack.

I have leaned on seven principal sources in the UK alone. The Imperial War Museum, London (www.iwm.org.uk), has an unrivalled set of memoirs in its Department of Documents, oral interviews in its Sound Archive, as well as its Montgomery papers. Burrowing deep into its vaults, I found the National Army Museum (www.nam.ac.uk) newly refurbished and splendidly sited next to the Royal Hospital in Chelsea under its dynamic new director, Justin Maciejewski, which has much in the way of photographs, diaries and other ephemera on Normandy. As part of King's College, London, the Liddell Hart Centre for Military Archives (www.kcl.ac.uk/archives) has an impressive and scholarly collection of memoirs relating to many British military figures.

More documents and a fascinating range of interviews are to be found at Wetherby, near Leeds in northern England, at the Second World War Experience Centre (www.war-experience.org). Dealing specifically with the Normandy landings, the D-Day Story Museum (www.theddaystory.com) on the southern English coast at Portsmouth, from where much of the invasion flotilla sailed, has become an important repository for artefacts and documents relating to 1944. In Cambridge, the Churchill Archives Centre at Churchill College (www.chu.cam.ac.uk/archives) has since its inception in 1973 been the only place to visit when attempting to grapple with Sir Winston's domination of Second World War history. I have also leant heavily on unit war diaries and other official documents to be found in south-west London at the Public Record Office at Kew, these days known as the National Archives (www.nationalarchives.gov.uk).

Across the Channel, there are around thirty-five war museums (the number changes as some private ventures close and others open) dealing with different aspects of the Normandy occupation, invasion or campaign. I have visited them all over the years, and without exception, each has extended the hand of friendship and allowed me access to their exhibits and archives. However, I would especially like to acknowledge the help afforded to me by the following (in geographical order, from west to east): the Musée du Debarquement Utah Beach (www.utah-beach.com) at Sainte-Marie-du-Mont; the Airborne Museum in Sainte-Mère-Église (www.airborne-museum.org); Dead Man's Corner D-Day Experience Museum at Saint-Côme-du-Mont, Carentan (www.dday-experience.com); and the Normandy Institute in Generalleutnant Wilhelm Falley's old headquarters at the Château de Bernaville (www.normandyinstitute.org).

Apart from several excellent D-Day museums in the vicinity, the official Omaha Beach visitor centre, opened in 2007 (www.abmc.gov/cemeteries-memorials/europe/normandy-american-cemetery), provides a moving overview of the early morning fight on the sand below, its staff ever willing to help with my enquiries and open their archives. It is run by the American Battlefields Monuments Commission, who also administer the Pointe du Hoc, and which has always been most helpful with insights and advice. So too have the Commonwealth War Graves Commission (www.cwgc.org) and its German equivalent, the *Volksbund Deutsche Kriegsgräberfürsorge*, often abbreviated to the VDK (www.volksbund.de), who were always instantly able to identify and locate their charges, and often able to illuminate for me the backgrounds of those in their care who gave their lives for their country.

In is impossible to visit Arromanches without a visit to the region's oldest war museum, first opened on the tenth anniversary of D-Day, *La Musée du Debarquement* (www.arromanches-museum.com), and its newest at Courseulles, the Juno Beach Centre (www.junobeach.org). Two centres in Ouistreham tell very well the stories of 6 June 1944: the tiny No. 4 Commando museum opposite the Casino relates the Allied battle for the seaside resort, while *Le Grand Bunker* vividly displays the German defence. If in the vicinity, Arlette Gondrée will not forgive you for failing to visit her Pegasus Bridge Café at Bénouville; perhaps you might persuade her to relate her memories of liberation by John Howard's men on the eve of D-Day. Across the Caen Canal is the British Airborne Museum (www.musee.memorial-pegasus.com) which opened in 2000, and beyond is the *Site et Musée de la Batterie de Merville* (www.batterie-merville.com)

Inland lies the important *Le Mémorial de Montormel*, overlooking the Falaise Pocket (www.memorial-montormel.org), which holds important memoirs. But the largest and most scholarly of all is *Le Mémorial de Caen*, appropriately built on the site of Generalleutnant Wilhelm Richter's headquarters, and which incorporates some of his bunkers (www.normandy.memorial-caen.com). It is like an iceberg in that the visitor sees only a fraction of its exhibits and archives; their important holdings of memoirs from the French civilian population relating to occupation, invasion and liberation are unrivalled elsewhere in the world. In Freiburg, Germany, the staff of the *Militärarchiv* have been most helpful in tracking down files and photographs, answering queries and suggesting material (www.bundesarchiv.de).

In the United States, seven sites have been kind and generous to the itinerant Brit attempting to sniff out new voices or dramas relating to D-Day. It goes without saying that one's first port of call should be to the impressive National World War II Museum in New Orleans, Louisiana (www.nationalww2museum.org). Founded in 2000, and still growing in size with impressive speed and scholarship, it was originally based on the efforts of the late Professor Stephen E. Ambrose to research and tell the story of Operation Overlord. Its oral history program is supreme and they have been kind enough to invite me to guide battlefield tours for them around Europe. The National D-Day Memorial at Bedford, Virginia (www.dday.org), has a smaller scope, but its archives dig deep into what D-Day meant for America and the state of Virginia.

A previously largely untapped resource has been the Cornelius Ryan Collection of World War II Papers at Ohio University Libraries in Athens (www. library.ohio.edu). There is much there for the patient researcher, as Ryan used only the merest fraction of material he had assembled for *The Longest Day*. Likewise, the US Army Quartermaster Museum has proven to possess a wealth of memoirs and artefacts (www.qmmuseum. lee.army.mil). The US Army's Heritage and Education Center at Carlisle, Pennsylvania (www.ahec.armywarcollege.edu) and Command and General Staff College at Fort Leavenworth, Kansas, both have extensive documents contemporarily recorded by those who were there; originally my visits were in person, though much is available on line these days.

Finally, at College Park, Maryland, the impressive resources of the US National Archives (www.archives.com) have always been available to shed light on American activities during the training for, and fighting on, 6 June 1944. Most of these I visited in person, while others were 'raided' by good friends on my behalf, such as Roger Cirillo, or James Holland. On a personal level, through the kind help of Robin Sink McClelland, daughter of Lieutenant General Robert Sink – wartime commander of the indefatigable 506th Parachute Infantry Regiment (who turned down promotion to remain with his regiment, such that it was referred to as the 'Five-Oh-Sink') – I came to know many of the veterans of her father's regiment, mostly alas, through their posthumous memoirs. Their war, as many others, can be followed from their billets and training area in England, through drop zones in Normandy, to Hitler's Eagles Nest in Berchtesgaden.

In addition, many American, Canadian, British, French, German and Irish newspapers and magazines contained fascinating interviews and articles, particularly in special anniversary editions. To all these centres of excellence, and others I have used – as noted in the text – I owe an enormous debt of gratitude. Without the help and guidance of their directors, journalists, librarians, archivists, curators and other staff, this book would have been a very lame beast.

To conduct my own campaigns in Normandy, the staff of the Hotel de la Marine in Arromanches (www.hotel-de-la-marine.fr) and La Ferme de la Rançonnière in Crépon (www.ranconniere.fr) have welcomed me back year after year, plying me with mussels and other fine seafood, while putting up with my travelling circus of computers, printers and combat mobile library. As always, there has been the guiding star of my late friend, colleague and mentor, Professor Richard Holmes, CBE, with whom I strolled across many a European battlefield while guiding the UK Defence Academy's annual staff ride. The maestro died far too young, but always urged me to write about Normandy. His colleague and co-mentor, Professor Chris Bellamy, has likewise indulged my fascination for all things Norman – no doubt because the origin of his own surname, Bel-Ami, is clearly Norman French.

A project like this required such focus and dedication that I realised I had to find a suitable command post from which to tackle *Sand and Steel* to the exclusion of all else, laying minefields and wire around my perimeter. My thanks go to my long-suffering friend and former sergeant, Barton Simpson, for the generous loan of his home in Croatia, where easy access to the fleshpots of Trieste and Venice, and views of the Adriatic both calmed and inspired: I elevate a flute of chilled prosecco in salute to you. Also to Richard and Gina Goldsbrough, who have likewise been far too generous in housing the wandering author in both Portugal and Hampshire. A glass of the finest Rioja is likewise raised in your direction. This is the reason why many of my endnotes on this occasion find an origin in my new-fangled Kindle or the World Inter-network (in the phraseology of Timur Vermes), rather than the traditional fireside comfort of my fifteen-thousand volume, dust-shrouded but orderly, library.

Then there is the 1st Division of Fellow Footsoldiers – my loyal friends and academic colleagues, many of them writers also – who have always been there to pitch in with ideas and provide hospitality, port and help at the drop of a hat. Their standard-bearer and commanding officer – whose name should really precede even the first paragraph of these acknowledgements – is James Holland, cricketer, film-maker and historian extraordinaire (www.griffonmerlin.com), and driving force behind the annual Chalke Valley History Festival (www.cvhf.org.ok). While our friendship far transcends merely diving into the past, he has been most generous in allowing me access to his own extensive archives and library, while his sage thoughts frequently provided a much-needed beacon when in the dark. Lieutenant Colonel John Starling, a colleague at the UK Defence Academy, has always been willing to discuss the finer points of his 'babies' – the contents of the small arms collection.

Other fellow footsoldiers, to whom I am deeply indebted, include Dr Duncan Anderson, Julian and Liz Bailey, Colonel Paul Beaver, Colonel David Benest, Professor Brian Bond, Professor Jeremy Black, Colin Blackwell, Dr Philip Blood, Dr Anna-Maria Brudenell, Air Commodore Adrian Burns, Air Chief Marshal Sir Brian Burridge, Keggie Carew, Colonel John Cargill, Colonel Roger Cirillo, Professor Rob Citino, Professor Laura Cleary, Cath and Jim Convery, Professor Paul Cornish, Seb Cox, Rachel Daniels, Major General John Drewienkiewicz, Si and Gilly Edwards, Russell Emm, Sandra Fairthorne, Professor Ann Fitz-Gerald, Dr Christina Goultier, Brigadier Charles Grant, John Fuller, Helen Haislmaier, Dr David Hall, Lieutenant Colonel Tom and Marina Hamilton-Baillie, Anne Harbour, Colonel Peter Herrly, Major General Graham Hollands, John Jammes, Colonel Nick Jenkins, the late Sir John Keegan, Brigadier John Keeling, Oberst Christian Krug von Einem, Guy Leaning and the BOCs, David and Lucy Leigh, Jason and Sarah Light, Colonel Matt Limb, Tim and Lisa Loughton, Toby Macleod, Lieutenant General H. R. McMaster, Pippa Markham, Major General Mungo Melvin, Tom and Oonagh Moulton, Al Murray, Tim Newark, Dr Helen Peck, Caroline Pilkington, Stephen Prince, General Klaus Reinhardt, Brigadier Alan Richmond, Professor Andrew Roberts, Elisabeth Countess de Rocquigny, Cristina de Santiago, Dr Chris Scott, Brigadier Jamie Scott-Bowden, Colonel James Scott-Clarke, Colonel James Senior, the late Bill Shand-Kydd, General Sir Richard Shirreff, Mike St Maur Sheil, Brigadier John Smales, Professor Sir Hew Strachan, Sir Desmond Swayne, Brigadier Jim Tanner, Mike Taylor, John A. Thomas, Jonathan Thompson, Dr David Turns, Dr Angeliki Vasilopoulou, Annabel Venning, Brigadier Miles Wade, the late General Sir Christopher Wallace, David and Carla Walsh,

Guy Walters, Dr Bryan Watters, Angela Weir, Dr Harry Woodroof, Major General David T. Zabecki and Professor Peter Zioupos. Julian Whippy and Clive Harris of Battle Honours (www.battle-honours.eu), and Mike Peters, Chairman of the International Guild of Battlefield Guides (www. gbg-international.com) have also been incredibly supportive, as have my professional colleagues in the Battlefields Trust (www.battlefieldstrust. com), British Commission for Military History (www.bcmh.org.uk), Royal Geographical Society (www.rgs.org), Royal Historical Society (www. royalhistsoc.org), Royal United Services Institute (www.rusi.org), and Society for Military History (www.smh-hq.org). Likewise, two websites in particular – the BBC's The People's War (www.bbc.co.uk/history/ ww2peopleswar) and Combined Operations (www.combinedops.com), which incorporates the old Landing Craft Association – have been a treasure trove of valuable information; to them both I am most grateful. Nataliya Kreminska has been such a bedrock of support that by the time *Sand and Steel* was completed, she had become Nataliya Caddick-Adams.

When Gibbon finished *Decline and Fall*, he was moved to record, 'It was on the day, or rather the night, of 27 June 1787, between the hours of eleven and twelve, that I wrote the last lines of the last page in a summer-house in my garden. I will not dissemble the first emotions of joy on the recovery of my freedom, and perhaps the establishment of my fame. But my pride was soon humbled, and a sober melancholy was spread over my mind by the idea that I had taken my everlasting leave of an old and agreeable companion.'[6] It is an emotion I completely understand.

I have spent the last year of my life totally immersed in the minutiae of Operation Overlord, but in some ways this book has been over forty years in gestation, since I first strode the landing beaches in 1975. Through their words, recorded voices and photographs, in every archive across the world, I have enjoyed meeting those of whatever nationality who contributed in some way to D-Day. I am humbled by what they achieved, and already miss them – ever present – metaphorically tapping my shoulder, reminding me to pursue this question, and not to forget that story. This is my salute to their generation. I hope I have done them proud.

Notes

Introduction

1 D-day is a post-1940 standard abbreviation for the first day of *any* military operation, just as H-hour specifies the start time of the undertaking.

2 The phrase was Rommel's, referring to the impact of a future Allied invasion of France. Cornelius Ryan's *The Longest Day* (Simon & Schuster, 1959) was the first bestselling book about the dramatic hours of 6 June 1944, later a well-received Hollywood movie of 1962. The book appeared less than fifteen years after the events it narrated, and was based entirely on exhaustive first-hand interviews. It remains an invaluable primary source.

3 Judith A. Bellafaire, *The Army Nurse Corps in World War II* (US Army Center of Military History, 2000); *WAAC-WAC 1942–1944, European Theatre of Operations* (US Army Historical Section, ETO, 1945).

4 Jack Heath, courtesy of BBC, *The People's War*, 2005.

5 Robin Neillands, *The Battle of Normandy* (Cassell, 2002), p. 407.

6 US Navy: USS *Thomas Jefferson*; USS *Charles Carroll*; USS *Samuel Chase*; USS *Henrico*; USS *Anne Arundel*; USS *Dorotheal. Dix*; USS *Thurston*; Royal Navy: HMS *Empire Javelin*; HMS *Empire Anvil*; SS *Ben-My-chree*; SS *Princess Maud*; SS *Princess Leopold*; SS *Prince Baudouin*; SS *Prince Charles*

1. France and America

1 'Moi qui vous parle en connaissance de cause et vous dis que rien n'est perdu pour la France. Les mêmes moyens qui nous ont vaincus peuvent faire venir un jour la victoire. Car la France n'est pas seule! Elle a un vaste Empire derrière elle. Cette guerre n'est pas limitée au territoire malheureux de notre pays. Cette guerre n'est pas tranchée par la bataille de France. Cette guerre est une guerre mondiale.

Quoi qu'il arrive, la flamme de la résistance française ne doit pas s'éteindre et ne s'éteindra pas.'

2   The third of his major speeches since taking office on 10 May. The first was 'Blood, toil, tears, and sweat' of 13 May, followed by 'We shall fight on the beaches' on 4 June, after Dunkirk.

3   He was never *brigadier*, a French rank equivalent to corporal.

4   Peter Caddick-Adams, 'Anglo-French Co-operation during the Battle of France', in Brian Bond and Mike Taylor (eds), *The Battle for France and Flanders: Sixty Years On* (Leo Cooper, 2001), pp. 35–51.

5   Courtesy of *L'Alliance Française de Londres*.

6   'How de Gaulle Speech Changed Fate of France', BBC *Newsnight*, 18 June 2010.

7   Simon Berthon, *Allies at War* (Carroll & Graf, 2001), p. 46.

8   'How de Gaulle Speech Changed Fate of France', op. cit.

9   Ibid.

10 Jean Jammes, interview, Olney, Buckinghamshire, 2016.

11 Guy Hattu, *Journal d'un Commando Français* (Librarie Bleue, 1994).

12 Donald Gilchrist, *Don't Cry For Me* (Robert Hale, 1982), p. 44.

13 In June 2014, I had the privilege of meeting most of the remaining Kieffer Commandos: François Andriot, Louis Bégot, Paul Chouteau, Hubert Faure, Léon Gautier, Jean Masson, Yves Meudal, Jean Morel and René Rossey.

14 Ed Stourton, interview, Chalke Valley History Festival, 2018.

15 Lord Moran, *Winston Churchill: The Struggle for Survival 1940–1965* (Constable, 1966), p. 88.

16 Author's research; serving until the war's end, Flagg would be slightly wounded in action on 11 November 1944.

17 It would remain part of the US Army until 1947.

18 The US Army grew to 5,400,888 in December 1943, and a year later 4,933,682 Americans were serving abroad in eighty divisions; these were supported by three divisions in reserve. In 1945 the US Army reached a total of ninety-one divisions, but three of these had to be broken up for reinforcements. The remaining eighty-eight were maintained at full combat strength despite the fact that by the end of the Ardennes campaign in January 1945, forty-seven regiments in nineteen divisions had suffered between 100 and 200 per cent battle casualties. The original, over-ambitious plan to create an army of 114 divisions was never realised.

19 *Instructions for American Servicemen in Britain 1942*, reproduced in book form by the Bodleian Library, Oxford (2004), pp. 10–11; 23–4.

20 Minnesota Military Museum correspondence, June 2017; Henke later earned a Silver Star in Tunisia, survived the war, returned as an honoured guest to Belfast in 1992, and died in 1998.

21 In fact the 34th Division were not destined to fight in Normandy, but shipped out to the Mediterranean in November 1942 for Operation Torch. Thereafter, they fought at Salerno, Monte Cassino and Anzio, ending their war in May 1945 in northern Italy.

22 *Instructions*, op. cit., pp. 22–3.

23 Philip D. Caine, *Spitfires, Thunderbolts and Warm Beer: An American Fighter Pilot Over Europe* (Brassey's, 1995), pp. 17–27.

24 Winston S. Churchill, *The Second World War, Vol. 3: The Grand Alliance* (Cassell, 1950), pp. 538–40.

25 Charles 'Chuck' Hurlbut, Company 'C', 299th Combat Engineer Battalion, interview courtesy of Aaron Elson.

2. Atlantikwall

1 Oberfeldwebel Karl Daniel died aged twenty-nine whilst driving Rommel on 18 July 1944, and is buried at Champigny-Saint-André German military cemetery, block 10, grave 665.

2 Rommel appointed Helmuth Lang as *Ordonnanzoffizier* (ADC) to keep a historical record, intending to write a book about his Second World War exploits after the war; he had already published a bestselling memoir of the First World War, *Infanterie greift an: Erlebnis und Erfahrung* (*Infantry Attacks: Experience and Expertise*) in 1937. Many of Lang's notes made their way into *The Rommel Papers* (ed. B. H. Liddell Hart, Fritz Bayerlein and Manfred Rommel, 1953); Lang did not write any memoirs, but assisted every biographer of Rommel. Friedrich Ruge wrote *Rommel in Normandy*, based on Army Group 'B''s *Kriegstagebuch* (war diary, or KTB), published by Macdonald & Jane's (1979); on occasion, Ruge also used his own staff car.

3 Burkhart Müller-Hillebrand, *Das Heer 1933–1945, Entwicklung des organisatorischen Aufbaues, Vol. 3: Der Zweifrontenkrieg* (Mittler, 1969), citing the *Oberkommando der Wehrmacht* (OKW) war diary, gives the recorded ration strength in the west on 1 March 1944 as: *Heer*: 806,927; SS and Police: 85,230; Kriegsmarine: 96,084; Luftwaffe: 337,140; *Wehrmachtsgefolge* (Armed Forces Auxiliaries): 145,611; Foreign volunteers, mainly Eastern troops: 61,439; German allies: 13,631; Total: 1,546,062. On the other hand, Horst Boog, Gerhard Krebs and Detlef Vogel, in *Germany and the Second World War, Vol. 7: The Strategic Air War in Europe and the War in the West and East Asia 1943–1944/5* (Oxford University Press, 2006), pp. 476–7, cites different figures for the same date: *Heer*: 865,180; SS and Police: 102,610; Kriegsmarine: 102,180; Luftwaffe: 326,350; *Wehrmachtsgefolge*: 157,210; *Sonstige* (others): 91,110; Total: 1,644,640, plus 114,921 horses; of the latter, 103,475 were issued to the *Heer* and 4,139 to the Luftwaffe. Another source, Richard Hargreaves in *The Germans in Normandy* (Pen & Sword, 2006), tries to break down the actual OB West (Rundstedt) figures as follows: Divisional and brigade units: 348,888; Non-divisional combat units: 58,047; *Fallschirmjäger*: 39,476; Waffen-SS: 75,587; *Ersatzheer* (training) units: 74,746; *Osttruppen*: 39,000; *Hiwis*: 28,000; Total OB West: 663,744.

4 ETHINT B-283, Gen. Günther Blumentritt, 'Evaluation of German Command and Troops in OB West' (1946).

5 As argued by, for example, Max Hastings, *Overlord* (Michael Joseph, 1984), p. 64.

6 *Macbeth*, Act 5, scene 2; ETHINT B-283, Blumentritt, 'Evaluation', op. cit.

7   Günther Blumentritt, *Von Rundstedt: The Soldier and the Man* (Odhams, 1952), pp. 177–85, 197.

8   H. R. Trevor-Roper (ed.), *Hitler's War Directives* (Sidgwick & Jackson, 1964), Directive No. 51.

9   Ibid.

10 Ibid.

11 Blumentritt, *Von Rundstedt*, op. cit., p. 203. While Blumentritt's observations ring true, we must remember that many analyses written for the US Army by senior German officers in the first few years after the war, and other published memoirs such as Blumentritt's, corresponded to guidance circulated unofficially by Genobst. Franz Halder, former Chief of the *Oberkommando des Heeres* (Army General Staff) from 1938 to 1942. Halder, who had been imprisoned at Dachau concentration camp after the 20 July 1944 assassination attempt, directed that post-war military papers should be written to downplay the Wehrmacht's mistakes, and exaggerate Hitler's interference. For testifying against senior Nazis at Nuremberg, and helping the US Army's European Theatre Historical Interrogations (ETHINT) of senior German officers (to which I frequently refer), Halder would be awarded the US Meritorious Civilian Service Award in 1961. Critics believe these German authors wrote a self-serving view of the war; certainly some of their earlier manuscripts were written from memory without access to official records, but many studies are still regarded as objective and reliable.

12 Throughout the war the three Lindemann cannon engaged in pointless exchanges with British guns, and by 1944 had expended some 2,226 shells at Dover.

13 These included huge quantities of captured Czech, Polish, French and Russian artillery systems, some of which dated back to 1914.

14 B. H. Liddell Hart (ed.), *The Rommel Papers* (Collins, 1953), p. 457.

15 Paul Carell (pseudonym for SS-Lt-Col Paul Karl Schmidt), *Invasion – They're Coming!* (George Harrap, 1962; first pub. as *Sie Kommen!* by Gerhard Stalling Ullstein, 1960), p. 21.

16 The indirect value of Operation Chastise, the famous dam-busting raid of 16–17 May 1943. Shortage of motor vehicles and fuel also made *Organisation Todt* (OT) officials reluctant to undertake projects away from major railheads, an issue which the future Transportation Plan would further exacerbate.

17 Gilles Perrault, *Le Secret du Jour J* (Librairie Arthème Fayard, 1964), p. 154.

18 Heinz Guderian, *Panzer Leader* (Michael Joseph, 1952), p. 331.

19 ETHINT B-284, Gen. Warlimont, 'OB West, 6 Jun–24 July 1944' (1946).

20 Perrault, *Le Secret*, op. cit., p. 154.

21 Blumentritt, *Von Rundstedt*, op. cit., p. 195.

22 Rommel was not associated with the final defeat in Tunisia, having left North Africa beforehand.

23 SD – *Sicherheitsdienst*, the Security Service of the SS. Horst Boog, Gerhard Krebs and Detlef Vogel, *Germany and the Second World War, Vol. 7*, op cit., p. 581.

24 One of France's oldest families, whose nobility stretched back fifty generations; their château is open to public view.

25 Blumentritt, *Von Rundstedt*, op. cit., p. 204.

26 On 1 March 1944, the Seventh Army had 197,946 men and 33,739 horses; on the same date, the Fifteenth Army possessed 312,604 men and 33,162 equines; by 1 June 1944 this had risen to 43,000 horses for the Seventh Army, and again to 48,000 on 20 June.

27 Cited in Marc Hansen, 'The German Commanders on D-Day', in John Buckley (ed.), *The Normandy Campaign 1944: Sixty Years On* (Routledge, 2006), p. 38.

28 ETHINT B-403, Genlt Reichert, '711th Inf. Division, 1 Apr 1943–24 Jul 1944' (1947).

29 His full name was Leo Dietrich Franz, Freiherr (Baron) Geyr von Schweppenburg; historians often refer to him by part of his surname, Geyr.

30 Guderian, *Panzer Leader*, op. cit., p. 329.

31 Geyr von Schweppenburg, 'Invasion Without Laurels, Part 2', *Australian Army Journal*, No. 8 (1950), p. 25.

32 Guderian, *Panzer Leader*, op. cit., pp. 332–3.

33 Marc Milner, *Stopping the Panzers* (University Press of Kansas, 2014), Kindle, p. 1768.

34 Blumentritt, *Von Rundstedt*, op. cit., pp. 208–9.

35 Liddell Hart (ed.), *The Rommel Papers*, op. cit., p. 467.

36 Schweppenburg, 'Invasion Without Laurels', op. cit., p. 25.

37 Ibid.

38 Johannes Börner, interview, 4 April 2014, courtesy of James Holland, http://www.griffonmerlin.com.

39 Ian Gooderson, 'Allied Fighter bombers versus German Armour in NW Europe 1944–1945: Myths and Realities', *Journal of Strategic Studies*, Vol. 14/2 (1991), pp. 210–31.

40 NARA FMS B-845, Genlt Karl-Wilhelm von Schlieben, 'The 709th Infantry Division' (1946).

41 Vince Milano & Bruce Conner, *Normandiefront. D-Day to St Lô* (History Press, 2011), Kindle, p. 399.

42 Panzer IV and Panther, plus Independent Tank Battalions of Tiger and King Tiger; reconnaissance tanks included Lynx variant of Pz II or Pz III; assault guns were StuG III or StuG IV; anti-tank and artillery mounted weapons included *Jagdpanther, Jagdpanzer IV, Hummel, Wespe, Hornisse* and *Marders*, plus all the captured French tank hulls.

43 Max Hastings, *Overlord: D-Day and The Battle for Normandy* (Michael Joseph, 1984), p.24.

44 John Keegan, *Six Armies in Normandy* (Jonathan Cape, 1982), p. 60.

45 Blumentritt, *Von Rundstedt*, op. cit., pp. 207–8.

46 Ruge, *Rommel in Normandy*, op. cit., p. 165.

47 Blumentritt, *Von Rundstedt*, op. cit., pp. 207–8.

48 Ibid., p. 158.

49 William F. Buckingham, *D-Day: The First 72 Hours* (History Press, 2004), Kindle, pp. 552–61.

50 According to Aggregate Industries, the Channel Tunnel used 2.3 million tonnes of sand, cement and aggregates, equating to 1.3 million cubic metres of concrete; see https://www.aggregate.com/news-and-resources/case-studies/channel-tunnel.

51 Buckingham, *D-Day*, op. cit., p. 552.

52 Edward R. Flint, *Development of British Civil Affairs during the Battle of Normandy, Jun-Aug 1944* (PhD Thesis, Cranfield University, UK Defence Academy, 2008) p. 215; Caen had a population of 70,000, though its arrondissement totalled 177,000. Bayeux totalled 7,000, and its arrondissement 54,000.

53 Blumentritt, *Von Rundstedt*, op. cit., p. 207; it should be noted, however, that the author's intention was to cast Rundstedt in a favourable light.

54 Obstlt. Fritz Ziegelmann, 352nd Infantry Division Normandy (NARA Foreign Military Studies, ETHINT B-021, 1946).

55 Flint, *Civil Affairs*, op. cit., p. 215.

56 Carell, *Invasion*, op. cit., p. 27; ten grams of sugar (three cubes) could rob 100 kg of cement of its binding cohesiveness.

57 Blumentritt, *Von Rundstedt*, op. cit., p. 206.

58 Gen. Leo Freiherr Geyr von Schweppenburg, 'Panzer Tactics in Normandy' (NARA ETHINT-13, 1947).

59 John F. Hale and Edwin R. Turner, *The Yanks Are Coming* (Midas, 1983), p. 162.

60 Richard L. DiNardo, *Mechanized Juggernaut or Military Anachronism? Horses and the German Army of World War II* (Praeger, 1991), Kindle, pp. 1212, 1283.

61 Ibid., p. 1241.

62 Dr Reinhardt Schwartz, interview, Normandy, 1994.

63 R. L. DiNardo and Austin Bay, 'Horse-drawn Transport in the German Army', *Journal of Contemporary History*, Vol. 23/1 (1988), pp. 129–42.

64 Romanian oil wells were heavily bombed in Operation Tidal Wave (aka 'Soapsuds') and after; this source of supply was finally terminated when Romania changed sides on 23 August 1944.

65 DiNardo, *Mechanized Juggernaut*, op. cit., p. 1203.

66 Adam Tooze, *The Wages of Destruction: The Making and Breaking of the Nazi Economy* (Viking, 2007).

67 Milano and Conner, *Normandiefront*, op. cit., p. 606.

68 Robert Kershaw, *D-Day: Piercing the Atlantic Wall* (Ian Allen, 1993), p. 36.

69 Ibid., p. 38.

70 Rémy and Marguerite Cassigneul, interview, Tailleville, May 2014.

71 Volker Griesser, *The Lions of Carentan* (Casemate, 2011), p. 83.

72 Heinrich Böll, *Briefe aus dem Krieg* (Deutscher Taschenbuch Verlag, 2003), letter, 1943.

73 Michael Strong, *Steiner's War: The Merville Battery* (self-published, 2013), pp. 12–13, 17.

74 Dollmann was so dangerously out of date that he would order the Panzer Lehr and 12th SS forward in daylight and in radio silence on 6 June, which contributed to the disorganisation of both and the loss of many vehicles.

75 Wilhelm Falley (91st *Luftlande*) was killed by US paratroopers in the early hours of 6 June outside his HQ when setting off for Rennes; Marcks died from aerial attack on 12 June; Heinz Hellmich (243rd Division) was killed on 17 June; the following day, Rudolf Stegmann (77th Division) was struck in the head by 20mm

cannon fire from a strafing Allied plane; while Dietrich Kraiss (352nd Division) died of wounds on 6 August.

76   Horst family archives.

77   Michael Ginns, 'The 319th Infantry Division in the Channel Islands', *Channel Islands Occupation Review*, No. 19 (1991).

78   Blumentritt, *Von Rundstedt*, op. cit., p. 202.

79   The Allies had deceived the Germans into thinking that amongst the Allied divisions waiting to invade were the fictional 2nd British, and 9th and 21st US Airborne Divisions. These were in addition to the real British 1st and 6th, and US 13th, 17th, 82nd and 101st Airborne Divisions, plus the Polish Parachute Brigade – ten airborne formations allegedly just waiting to descend from the skies into German-occupied France.

80   Ruge, *Rommel in Normandy*, op. cit., pp. 166–7.

81   ETHINT B-597, Gen. Wolfgang Pickert, 'III Flak Corps Normandy, May–14 Sept 1944' (1947).

82   ETHINT B-283, Blumentritt, 'Evaluation', op. cit.

83   Ibid.

84   Blumentritt, *Von Rundstedt*, op. cit., p. 179.

85   7th Army *Kriegstagebuch*, Report of *Sonderstab Oemichen*, 13.5.44.

86   Maj. Friedrich Hayn, *Die Invasion: Von Cotentin bis Falaise* (Kurt Vowinckel, 1954), p. 16.

87   At the last moment, when the initial reports of paratroop landings arrived, Dollmann's chief of staff, Max Pemsel, cancelled the war games and insisted those who had set off return to their posts.

3. Heading Over There

1   The Canadian Active Service Force was mobilised on 1 September 1939 in anticipation of the declaration of war. The 1st Canadian Infantry Brigade was raised in Ontario and embarked for the UK on 17 December, arriving at Greenock on 25 December; 2nd Canadian Brigade was raised in western Canada, and embarked from Halifax on 22 December 1939; 3rd Canadian Brigade was raised in Quebec, moving to Halifax and embarking on 8 December, arriving on 17 December; all moved on to Aldershot on arrival.

2   Canadian conscripts were eventually sent to war in Europe, but not until November 1944.

3   Tony Foster, *Meeting of Generals* (Methuen Ontario, 1986), p. 289.

4   Another 511 RCN personnel crewed Royal Navy vessels; Mark Zuehlke, *Juno Beach: Canada's D-Day Victory* (Douglas & McIntyre, 2004), Kindle, p. 742.

5   David Ian Hall, 'Creating the 2nd Tactical Air Force: Inter-service and Anglo-Canadian Co-operation in the Second World War', *Canadian Military Journal* (Winter 2002–3), p. 41.

6   Rev. R. M. Hickey, *The Scarlet Dawn* (Tribune Publishers, 1950), p. 112.

7   Given to the British under Lend-Lease in exchange for permanent US bases in Newfoundland and the Caribbean.

8   Barney Danson, *Not Bad for a Sergeant* (Dundurn, 2002), chapter 2.

9   David Reynolds, *Rich Relations: The American Occupation of Britain 1942–1945* (HarperCollins, 1995), p. 339.

10   Stephen Dyson, *Tank Twins* (Leo Cooper, 1994), p. 25.

11   Murrow was so pro-British and proficient in advancing the Allied cause over the airwaves that Churchill offered to make him joint director-general of the BBC, in charge of programming, in 1943. He declined, but was later awarded an honorary KBE (Knight Commander of the British Empire) for his friendship and services.

12   Michael Burleigh, *Mortal Combat* (HarperCollins, 2010), p. 506.

13   *Instructions*, op. cit., pp. 7, 17.

14   27 July 1942, at http://www.greenshouse.com/Seaton_Diary_files/Getting_there.htm.

15   Philip Ardery, telephone interview; see his memoir, *Bomber Pilot: A Memoir of World War II* (University Press of Kentucky, 1978). Ardery died in May 2012 at his home in Louisville, Kentucky.

16   Cy Cyford, interview, Baltimore, 1984; he died in August 2008.

17   Lt Russell Chandler, Jr, interview courtesy of A. Russell Chandler III (*Aviation History*, July 2004).

18   Capt. Curt Vogel, memoir courtesy of www.458bg.com. Vogel flew thirty missions out of England, his last to Berlin the day before D-Day. He also served in Korea from 1951 to 1952, then pursued a successful legal career before dying in January 2007 in his native Missouri.

19   Mavis Boswell, interview, Truro, 1985.

20   David J. Pike, *Airborne in Nottingham: The Impact of an Elite American Parachute Regiment on an English City in World War II* (self-published, 1991), p. 20–1.

21   R. S. Raymond, *A Yank at Bomber Command* (David & Charles, 1977), p. x.

22   Allan Nevins, *A Brief history of the United States* (Clarendon Press, 1942); Louis MacNeice, *Meet the US Army* (Board of Education/Ministry of Information, HMSO, 1943).

23   Winifred Pine, interview, 2004, courtesy of BBC, WW2 People's War, http://www.bbc.co.uk/history/ww2peopleswar/.

24   Norman Longmate, *The GIs: The Americans in Britain 1942–1945* (Hutchinson, 1975), p. 301.

25   Birdie Schmidt, 'Reminiscences About the ARC Aeroclub at Wendling, Gleaned from Reports Made to ARC English Headquarters', 2017, courtesy of 392nd Bomb Group Memorial Association, www.b24.net.

26   *The Times*, 4 August 1942.

27   Forrest C. Pogue, *Pogue's War: Diaries of a WWII Combat Historian* (University Press of Kentucky, 2001), p. 12.

28   Ibid.

4. The Commandos

1   *Instructions*, op. cit., pp. 24–5.

2   Pogue, *Pogue's War*, op. cit., p. 7.

3 William B. Dowling, interview, 2017, courtesy of 392nd Bomb Group Memorial Association, www.b24.net.

4 *Instructions*, op. cit.

5 Pike, *Airborne in Nottingham*, op. cit., p. 11.

6 Cited in Hale and Turner, *The Yanks Are Coming*, op cit., pp. 78–9.

7 Robert S. Arbib, Jr, *Here We Are Together: The Notebook of an American Soldier in Britain* (Longman's Green, 1946). Arbib later became a noted ornithologist and died in July 1987.

8 Bernard Sender, interview, 2017, courtesy of 392nd Bomb Group Memorial Association, www.b24.net.

9 The Eighth Air Force peaked in 1944 at over 200,000 personnel, whilst the Ninth amounted to 185,000.

10 Steven Karoly, 'Report of Activities of the 25th Naval Construction Regiment' (1998) @ http://www.seabeecook.com/history/25th_ncr/

11 Bill Coughlan, letter, *Guardian*, 4 January 2017.

12 Desperate women began to stain their legs with household items like gravy browning, coffee and cocoa powder to give the appearance of stockings, then drew a 'seam' down the backs of their legs with an eyebrow or eyeliner pencil, enlisting help to get it straight.

13 Davis, *Frozen Rainbows*, op. cit., p. 47.

14 Margaret Seeley, interview, cited in Roderick Bailey, *Forgotten Voices of D-Day* (Ebury Press, 2009).

15 Mavis Boswell, interview, op. cit.

16 Davis, *Frozen Rainbows*, op. cit., p. 73.

17 Brian Selman, interview, Southampton, 2004.

18 Pogue, *Pogue's War*, op. cit., p. 33.

19 *Instructions*, op. cit., pp. 5–7.

20 Juliet Gardiner, *Over Here: The GIs in Wartime Britain* (Collins & Brown, 1992), p. 56.

21 *Instructions*, op. cit., p. 18.

22 British Army pay was only double that of 1914. Hansard, HC vol. 357, cols 1884–5 (27 February 1940); Hansard, HL vol. 133, cols 597–608 (18 October 1944). Average civilian earnings were £6/week; http://ww2today.com/16th-april-1942-wartime-taxes-rise-again-in-the-uk.

23 US rates of pay, http://www.cbi-history.com/part_xii_wwii_pay.html; Longmate in *The GIs*, op. cit., pp. 378–9, provides a useful comparison chart of US and UK military wages.

24 Isaac A. Coleman, interview, 1984, cited in Lynn L. Sims, *'They Have Seen the Elephant': Veterans' Remembrances from World War II for the Fortieth Anniversary of VE-Day* (Logistics Center, Fort Lee, Virginia, 1985).

25 There was a not dissimilar impact on the urban working class males of Britain who likewise were seen to benefit from their military service during 1914–18.

26 *Current Affairs* (ABCA Publication No. 26), 19 September 1942.

27 Bill Cheall, *Fighting Through from Dunkirk to Hamburg: A Green Howards Wartime Memoir* (Pen & Sword, 2011), Kindle, p. 90.

28 George Richardson and George Self, interview, Normandy, 1994.

29   Reynolds, *Rich Relations*, op. cit., p. 267.

30   Pike, *Airborne in Nottingham*, op. cit., p. 15.

31   Ibid, pp. 266–7.

32   Capt. Robert K. Morgan and his crew actually flew twenty-nine combat missions with the 324th Bomb Squadron, but only twenty-five in the *Memphis Belle*, during which time they shot down eight German aircraft. The story was remade as a feature film in 1990.

33   James A. McDowell, Park Tudor School Words of War Oral History Collection, Indiana State Library, 2011.

34   Anthony Powell, *A Dance to the Music of Time, Vol. 9: The Military Philosophers* (Heinemann, 1968), p. 114.

35   Pogue, *Pogue's War*, op. cit., p. 15; Davis, *Frozen Rainbows*, op. cit., p. 101.

36   Paul Wagner, *The Youngest Crew* (Lagumo Press, 1997).

37   Marthe Watts, *The Men in My Life* (Christopher Johnson, 1960), p. 234; see also Julia Laite, 'Sex, War and Syndication: Organized Prostitution and the Second World War', in *Common Prostitutes and Ordinary Citizens: Commercial Sex in London, 1885–1960* (Springer, 2017), pp. 149–70.

38   Martin W. Bowman, *We Were Eagles: The Eighth Air Force at War, Vol. 2: Dec 1943–May 1944* (Amberley, 2014), pp. 38–9.

39   Dyson, *Tank Twins*, op. cit., p. 21.

40   James A. McDowell, interview, op. cit.

41   Owen Bowcott, 'Top Brass Feared Worst as GIs and Good-time Girls Enjoyed Blackout', *Guardian*, 1 November 2005; Neil Tweedie, 'How Our Piccadilly Commandos Had the GIs Surrounded', *Daily Telegraph*, 1 November 2005.

42   Caine, *Spitfires, Thunderbirds and Warm Beer*, op. cit., p. 134.

43   Joan Wyndham, *Love Lessons: A Wartime Diary* (Heinemann, 1985); obituary, *Daily Telegraph*, 14 April 2007.

44   Amongst more conservative Britons, there was resentment in the way Americans threw their money around indiscriminately, but this was probably 'old' money resenting the new. It is also tempting to assert – though hard to prove – a concern that American 'culture' was somehow undermining or eroding 'British values' – whatever they were (there were old 'American values', too). Subliminally by 1944–5 the GIs, with their high wages, dashing uniforms and confident and flirtatious nature, may have come to represent in some minds the gradual domi-nance of the US in the Anglo-American alliance, but this may simply be the wisdom of hindsight.

45   Dougie Alford, interview, Truro, 1985.

46   Pogue, *Pogue's War*, op. cit., p. 16.

47   Derek James, 'Voices of America', *Let's Talk*, 19 July 2013.

48   Roy Bainton, *The Long Patrol* (Mainstream, 2003), Kindle, pp. 3445, 3593, 3608.

49   Pike, *Airborne in Nottingham*, op. cit., p. 10.

50   James, 'Voices of America', op. cit.

51   Gerald Astor, *The Mighty Eighth: The Air War in Europe as Told by the Men Who Fought It* (Random House: New York, 1997), pp. 122–6; see also Bowman, *We Were Eagles, Vol. 2*, op. cit., p. 7.

52 Harry H. Crosby, *A Wing and a Prayer: The 'Bloody 100th' Bomb Group of the US Eighth Air Force in Action over Europe in World War II* (HarperCollins, 1993).

5. Warm Hearts

1 Mildred A. MacGregor, *World War II Front Line Nurse* (University of Michigan Press, 2008), p. 23.

2 Norman 'Bud' Fortier, *An Ace of the Eighth* (Presidio, 2003), p. 44.

3 John Robert 'Bob' Slaughter, *Omaha Beach and Beyond: The Long March of Sgt. Bob Slaughter* (Zenith, 2007), pp. 47–50.

4 Fortier, *An Ace of the Eighth*, op. cit., p. 46.

5 MacGregor, *World War II Front Line Nurse*, op. cit., p. 32.

6 Harry P. Carroll, interview, cited in Sims, *'They Have Seen the Elephant'*, op. cit.

7 Dr Hal Baumgarten, telephone interview, June 1999; Hal died on Christmas Day 2016, aged ninety-one.

8 Stephen J. Ochs, *A Cause Greater Than Self* (Texas A&M University Press, 2012), p. 42.

9 'God Was on the Beach on D-Day: Chaplain Burkhalter Tells Power of Prayers', *Miami Daily News*, 6 August 1944.

10 One of the US Army's famous chaplains, Burkhalter landed on Omaha Beach on D-Day, later serving in Korea; he died in 1992 and is buried in Arlington cemetery.

11 Don R. Marsh, *The Sergeant's Diary: Unknown Destination* (courtesy of The Marsh Family Trust), at: http://3ad.com/history/wwll/memoirs.pages/marsh.pages/crossing.channel.htm.

12 Carl Dannemann, 'Troopships That Took a GI to War and Back Again', courtesy of Ocean Liner Museum/South Street Seaport Museum, New York.

13 Donald R. Burgett, *Currahee! A Screaming Eagle at Normandy* (Random House, 1967), p. 52.

14 Belton Y. Cooper, *Death Traps: The Survival of an American Armored Division in World War II* (Presidio, 1998), pp. 3–6.

15 Hobart Winebrenner and Michael McCoy, *Bootprints: An Infantryman's Walk Through World War II* (Camp Comamajo Press, 2005), pp. 6–11.

16 Charles Hurlbut, interview, op. cit.

17 Marsh, *The Sergeant's Diary*, op. cit.

18 MSgts Lincoln Couch and N. H. Gorges (eds), 'History of the 756 Railway Shop Battalion' (typewritten 82-page manuscript, n.d., but *c*.1945), pp. 17–20.

19 Charles Hurlbut, interview, op. cit.

20 Guy Charland, interview, 2003, courtesy of Colin and Chad Charland and Aaron Elson.

21 Daniel Folsom, interview, 2005, Park Tudor School Words of War Oral History Collection, Indiana State Library.

22 Davis, *Frozen Rainbows*, op. cit., pp. 32–47; having kindly agreed to an interview, Davis died in May 2015 before we could meet.

23   James H. Madison, 'Wearing Lipstick to War: An American Woman in World War II England and France', *Prologue*, Vol. 39/3 (Fall 2007).

24   Ruth Haskins, interview, 2004, courtesy of BBC, WW2 People's War, op. cit.

25   Bernard Peters, interview, Truro, 1985.

26   *A Welcome to Britain*, at https://www.youtube.com/watch?v=SyYSBBE1DFw.

27   *Know Your Ally: Britain*, at https://www.youtube.com/watch?v=jrH77D3fiuk.

28   Stanley Jones, interview, Trowbridge, 1994.

29   Patricia Barnard, interview, 2004, courtesy of BBC, WW2 People's War, op. cit.

30   Pogue, *Pogue's War*, op. cit., p. 21.

31   Omar N. Bradley, *A Soldier's Story of the Allied Campaigns from Tunis to the Elbe* (Eyre & Spottiswoode, 1951), p. 174. Eisenhower donated an American flag to Clifton College in 1953 as a thank you for the important role it played, which is flown every year on Independence Day, 4 July.

32   Clifton College soon reverted back to being a distinguished school; Norton Fitzwarren today is an HQ of the Royal Marines and the manor is its officers' mess; Breamore House is open to the public and enormously proud of its wartime associations.

33   Evelyn Waugh, *Brideshead Revisited: The Sacred and Profane Memories of Captain Charles Ryder* (Chapman & Hall, 1945).

34   Guy Charland, interview, op. cit.

35   Dale Gillespie, interview, Park Tudor School Words of War Oral History Collection, Indiana State Library; Gillespie died in January 2011.

36   Slaughter, *Omaha Beach and Beyond*, op. cit., pp. 51–2.

37   Burgett, *Currahee!*, op. cit., pp. 53–4.

38   Pogue, *Pogue's War*, op. cit., p. 25.

39   Daniel Folsom, interview, op. cit.

40   Slaughter, *Omaha Beach and Beyond*, op. cit., p. 52.

41   Arthur Whalen, interview, 2005, Park Tudor School Words of War Oral History Collection, Indiana State Library.

42   George Forty, *Frontline Dorset: A County at War 1939–45* (Dorset Books, 1994), p. 79.

43   Handwritten diary of HM King George VI, Wednesday, 24 May 1944, Royal Archives, Windsor; by kind permission of Her Majesty Queen Elizabeth II.

44   Parnham, Littlecote and Wilton are all open to the public. In many ways the stereotypical English country mansion, and now a National Trust house open to the public, Basildon Park was the setting for *Pride and Prejudice* (2005) and many scenes from *Downton Abbey* (2010–15).

45   'Top Secret D-Day Plans Found Hidden Under Hotel's Floorboards', *Daily Telegraph*, 9 February 2015.

46   Couch and Gorges (eds), 'History of the 756 Railway Shop Battalion', op. cit.

47   US Army Hospital at Kingston Lacy, National Trust Archives.

48   Jean Treasure, *The 228th American Hospital at Haydon Park near Sherborne, Dorset* (self-published, 2004). There were several different kinds of hospitals: field (400-bed) and evacuation (400–750 beds); both were tented and fully mobile, being designed to follow the troops into battle. More permanent were station hospitals

(250–750 beds), general (1,000-bed) and convalescent (2,000–3,000 beds): these fixed establishments were the ones more often found in the grounds of country estates. They used large numbers of Quonset huts (the US equivalent of the prefabricated Nissen hut, a twenty-by-forty-foot half-cylinder tin shed erected on a concrete floor), which had flushing toilets, clean water and were heated by coal-burning stoves. Such hutted hospital complexes resulted in vast military villages springing up around England's country houses. Siegfried Sassoon's Georgian mansion in Wiltshire, Heytesbury House, was not untypical, accommodating the headquarters of the US XIX Corps, 7th Armored Group and 3253rd Signal Service Co. in the house and stables, whilst the 14th Field Hospital was scattered over its two-hundred-acre parkland. All of this infrastructure is now long gone, but the careful eye will detect initials and dates from the war years carved into the bark of the older trees, while the decaying concrete bases and remains of cinder pathways are to be found in the undergrowth of many a country estate.

49   Pike, *Airborne in Nottingham*, op. cit., p. 16; LeFebvre served in HQ Company, 2nd Battalion, 508th Parachute Infantry, and died in 2010.

6. A Question of Colour

1   Reynolds, *Rich Relations*, op. cit., pp. 206–8.
2   Lt Helen Pavlovsky Ramsay, USNR, interview, US Navy Oral History program.
3   Author's archive.
4   Valentine M. Miele, 16th Infantry, interview, 2014, courtesy of Aaron Elson.
5   Bradley, *A Soldier's Story*, op. cit., p. 279.
6   Stuart Preston obituary, *Daily Telegraph*, 1 March 2005.
7   Henry Buckton, *Friendly Invasion: Memories of Operation Bolero* (Phillimore, 2006), Kindle, p. 3542.
8   Reynolds, *Rich Relations*, op. cit., pp. 418–22.
9   The majority of Canadian brides were British, the rest French, Belgian or Dutch. The record also shows that well over a thousand Poles, then stationed in Scotland, had taken local brides by 1943.
10   David P. Colley, *The Road to Victory: The Untold Story of Race and World War II's Red Ball Express* (Brassey's, 2000), p. 71.
11   Leon Hutchinson, interview, 2003, Park Tudor School Words of War Oral History Collection, Indiana State Library.
12   Mary Pat Kelly, *Proudly We Served: The Men of the USS Mason* (Naval Institute Press, 1995).
13   Sir James Grigg (1890–1964) was Permanent Under-Secretary of State at the War Office (i.e. a civil servant) who was promoted by Churchill to become Secretary of State for War (a political positon) in February 1942 – an unprecedented and unparalleled move in modern times; see also Thomas E. Hachey, 'Jim Crow with a British Accent: Attitudes of London Government Officials Toward American Negro Soldiers in England During World War II', *Journal of African American History*, Vol. 59/1 (1974).

14   Patricia Barnard, interview, op. cit.

15   Cited in Reynolds, *Rich Relations*, op. cit., p. 342.

16   Patrick Sawer, 'Revealed: How Britons Welcomed Black Soldiers During WWII, and Fought Alongside Them Against Racist GIs', *Daily Telegraph*, 6 December 2015.

17   Ralph Ellison, 'In a Strange Country', in *Flying Home and Other Stories*, ed. John F. Callahan (Random House, 1996); in 1953, Ellison would win the US National Book Award for Fiction for his major novel *The Invisible Man* (1952); see also Daniel G. Williams, '"If we only had some of what they have": Ralph Ellison in Wales', *Comparative American Studies: An International Journal*, 4/1 (2006).

18   Joseph O. Curtiss, interview, 1983; cited in Reynolds, *Rich Relations*, op. cit., p. 24.

19   Cited in Robin Neillands and Roderick De Normann, *D-Day 1944: Voices from Normandy* (Weidenfeld & Nicolson, 1993), p. 6; and author's interview with 82nd Airborne Division veterans, 1994; see also Adam G. R. Berry, *And Suddenly They Were Gone: An Oral and Pictorial History of the 82nd Airborne Division in England, February–November 1944* (Overlord Publishing, 2017), and *My Clear Conscience: The Memoirs of Cpl. George Shenkle, Easy Company, 508th Parachute Infantry Regiment, 82nd Airborne Division* (CreateSpace, 2014).

20   Forty, *Frontline Dorset*, op. cit., p. 88.

21   *Yank*, 21 April 1944; see also 'Citizen Soldiers, Jim Crow and Black Segregation', at http://worldwar2history.info/Army/Jim-Crow.html.

22   Neville Paddy, interview, Truro, 1984.

23   Pike, *Airborne in Nottingham*, op. cit., p. 27.

24   Slaughter, *Omaha Beach and Beyond*, op. cit., p. 85.

25   Tim Parr, interview, Launceston, 1994.

26   Ann Willmott (née Rowan), interview courtesy of BBC, WW2 People's War, op. cit.

27   The Crown in Kingsclere is still in business today.

28   James Hudson, interview, Washington DC, 1984.

29   Reynolds, *Rich Relations*, op. cit., p. 121.

30   *Pittsburgh Courier*, 13 December 1941 and 31 January 1942.

31   Mike Pryce, 'Naked Officers and Injured GI's – War-time Britain Has Many Memories for Marjorie', *Worcester News*, 12 January 2009.

32   Nevil Shute, *The Chequer Board* (Heinemann, 1947).

33   Reynolds discusses this case at length in *Rich Relations*, op. cit., pp. 234–7.

34   Gen. Dwight D. Eisenhower, *Crusade in Europe* (Doubleday, 1948), Kindle, p. 4406.

35   *A Welcome to Britain*, op. cit.

36   *Twelve O'Clock High* marked a departure from the optimistic, morale-boosting genre of wartime films and a move towards a grittier realism that dealt with the realities of daylight precision bombing in 1943 without fighter escort, prior to the arrival of the long-range P-51 Mustang. It was directed by Darryl F. Zanuck, who will feature again in our story as producer of the 1962 story of D-Day, *The Longest Day*.

37   Hale and Turner, *The Yanks Are Coming*, op. cit., p. 158.

38   Buckton, *Friendly Invasion*, op. cit., p. 1730.

39   Ibid., p. 1688.

40   Now Margaret Meen-Parker; see her article, 'When They Arrived, I Was Nine', 2017, courtesy of 392nd Bomb Group Memorial Association, www.b24.net.

41   *War Horse*, of the 577th Bomb Squadron, was lost on her seventeenth mission over the North Sea on 4 January 1944 after bombing Kiel. Her crew of ten all perished. Her markings were described as a 'helmeted horse's head snorting steam from nostrils'; painted on her starboard nose was 'Marcy', named for Margaret Meen.

42   Meen-Parker, 'When They Arrived', op. cit.

7. Committees and Code Words

1   Andrew Roberts, in *Masters and Commanders: How Four Titans Won the War in the West, 1941–1945* (Harper, 2009), explores the workings of the Combined Chiefs during the war.

2   By April 1942, the Combined Chiefs had agreed to nine operations: Imperator, a major raid scheduled for the summer of 1942; Jubilee, against Dieppe; Wetbob, to capture and hold the Cherbourg peninsula in 1942; Sledgehammer, an assault on Le Havre in 1942; Roundup, a full-scale invasion of France in 1943; Lethal, a small-scale assault to seize and hold the Brest peninsula in 1943; Hadrian, to capture and hold the Cherbourg peninsula in 1943; Cruickshank, against the Low Countries in 1943; and Torch, an opposed invasion of north-west Africa in November 1942. Of these, only Jubilee and Torch were executed.

3   Eisenhower was promoted to brigadier general on 29 September 1941, acting major general on 27 March 1942, acting lieutenant general on 7 July the same year, and acting general on 11 February 1943. His substantive rank remained major general until 30 August 1943.

4   Previously known as Operation Gymnast, Torch involved three landings at Algiers, Oran and Casablanca. All were ineffectively opposed.

5   Churchill's chosen name of 'Symbol' suggested a conference with a hidden agenda, whereas Husky referred to the coming trial of strength on Sicily between the big, strong (husky) Allied armies and their Axis counterparts (who may have looked husky, but weren't).

6   Operation Sickle suggested the harvesting of Germany by the USAAF's tool with its sharp, unforgiving curved blade; whereas Trident also reflected the Anglo-US–Soviet direction of the war; Quadrant – held in Quebec – acknowledged the Canadian contribution, thus implying its strategic direction was a four-way affair.

7   David Reynolds, *In Command of History* (Allen Lane, 2004), p. 318.

8   Eisenhower, *Crusade in Europe*, op. cit., p. 4303.

9   Lt Gen. Sir Frederick Morgan, *Overture to Overlord* (Hodder & Stoughton, 1950).

10 Ex-Wren Ginger Thomas, interview courtesy of BBC, WW2 People's War, op. cit.

11 *History of COSSAC 1943–1944* (Historical Sub-Section, SHAEF, May 1944).

12 Ginger Thomas, interview, op. cit.

13 *History of COSSAC 1943–1944*, op. cit., p. 27; Rankin was a unsubtle reference to the Montanan legislator Jeannette Rankin (1880–1973), the first US Congresswoman, and only representative to oppose American involvement in both world wars; the code name was ironic, for it was felt the troublemaker couldn't have opposed Operation Rankin, which would have been a non-belligerent occupation of an already-collapsed Germany.

14 Julian Paget, *The Crusading General: The Life of General Sir Bernard Paget* (Pen & Sword, 2008), pp. 57–77.

15 Ginger Thomas, interview, op. cit.

16 Richard Collier, *D-Day: June 6 1944: The Normandy Landings* (Cassell, 1992), p. 105.

17 Hughes-Hallett (1901–72) had observed the Norwegian campaign, planned and executed the August 1942 Dieppe raid, and would go on to prepare Force 'J', bound for Juno Beach.

18 Ginger Thomas, interview, op. cit.

19 By D+24 the British and Americans had each built ten airstrips within the beachhead, and by D+90 there were an astonishing eighty-nine temporary airfields in use, underlining the importance of air power. The runways were paved with steel mesh tracking (SMT) and perforated steel plate (PSP), which can still be seen today fencing the farms of Normandy.

20 The attackers lost 3,670 killed, wounded and taken prisoner, over half the force, and 106 RAF planes were destroyed. The Germans lost 500 men and 46 aircraft.

21 The National Archives (TNA): CAB 80/71, Memoranda (O) Nos. 331–400.

22 *History of COSSAC 1943–1944*, op. cit., p. 32.

23 See the excellent Combined Operations website, https://www.combinedops.com, section on Mulberry harbours.

24 Winston S. Churchill, *The Second World War, Vol. 6: Triumph and Tragedy* (Cassell, 1953), p. 8.

25 Mick Crossley, interview, cited in Frank and Joan Shaw, *We Remember D-Day* (Ebury Press, 1994), pp. 11–16.

26 *Picture Post*, 6 May 1944.

27 The fifty-nine Corncob vessels were sunk as follows: Utah Beach (Gooseberry 1), ten vessels; Omaha Beach (Gooseberry 2), fourteen ships; Gold Beach (Gooseberry 3), fifteen ships; Juno Beach (Gooseberry 4), eleven vessels; Sword Beach (Gooseberry 5), nine ships.

28 The Corncob warships included the old British battleship HMS *Centurion*, cruiser HMS *Durban*, Dutch cruiser *Sumatra* and French battleship *Courbet*. The upper decks of the Corncobs were used as facilities for first aid, repairs, fuelling and accommodation. See Brig. Sir Bruce White, Notes on Mulberry Harbours, 9 January 1981, Imperial War Museum; and Guy Hartcup, *Code Name Mulberry: The Planning, Building and Operation of the Normandy Harbours* (Pen & Sword, 2006).

29 Winston S. Churchill, *The Second World War, Vol. 5: Closing the Ring* (Cassell, 1951), p. 226; David Reynolds develops this point at length in chapter 24 of *In Command of History*, op. cit.

30 *History of COSSAC 1943–1944*, op. cit., p. 28.

31 Reynolds, *In Command of History*, op. cit., p. 376.

32 *History of COSSAC 1943–1944*, op. cit.

33 Reynolds, *In Command of History*, op. cit., p. 381.

34 Ibid., pp. 384–7.

35 George C. Marshall was clearly the front runner for the supreme command, but it became apparent that he was the key link in Washington DC and that Roosevelt had come to rely on him. Thus Marshall nominated Eisenhower, his star pupil, who had already been Mediterranean supremo and had previously authored draft invasion plans of France.

36 Field Marshal Lord Alanbrooke, *War Diaries 1939–1945*, eds. Alex Danchev and Dan Todman (Weidenfeld & Nicolson, 2001), pp. 546–7.

37 Desmond Scott, *Typhoon Pilot* (Leo Cooper, 1982), p. 103.

38 George Chambers and William Brown, interviews, 1988, Imperial War Museum Sound Archive, ref. 10415.

39 Reynolds, *Rich Relations*, op. cit., p. 345.

40 Montgomery to Brooke, letter, 4 April 1943, Imperial War Museum, BLM 49/25.

41 Alexander to Brooke, letter, 3 April 1943, Liddell Hart Military Archive, King's College, London, 14/63.

42 Tom Bigland, interview, Shrewsbury, 1984; also Maj. Tom Bigland, *Bigland's War: War Letters of Tom Bigland, 1941–45* (self-published, 1990), p. 62.

43 Norman Kirby, *1100 Miles with Monty: Security and Intelligence at Tac HQ* (Alan Sutton, 1989), p. 32.

44 Alistair Horne and David Montgomery, *Monty 1944–1945* (Macmillan, 1994), p. 106.

45 Rommel the spaniel was killed in a traffic accident in the Netherlands on 18 December 1944.

46 Goronwy Rees, *A Bundle of Sensations: Sketches in Autobiography* (Chatto & Windus, 1960).

47 Alanbrooke, *War Diaries 1939–1945*, op. cit., entry for 30 November 1943, p. 486.

48 Ibid., entry for 11 December 1943, p. 496.

49 Ibid., entry for 21 September 1943, p. 454.

50 Carlo D'Este, *Bitter Victory: The Battle for Sicily, 1943* (Dutton, 1998), p. 106.

51 Field Marshal Montgomery of Alamein, *Memoirs* (Collins, 1958), Kindle, pp. 3874–86.

52 Churchill, *Second World War, Vol. 5*, op. cit., p. 393.

53 Eisenhower, *Crusade in Europe*, op. cit., pp. 4320–9.

54 Ibid., Appendix C, Memo dated 8 August 1943.

55 Unlike the United States, post-war British governments have failed to take Churchill's good advice to heart; the UK's recent military code words are hardly inspirational and disgracefully blander than bland, as witnessed by, for example, Operations Corporate (Falklands, 1982), Granby (Kuwait, 1991), Palliser and Barras (Sierra Leone, 2000), Telic (Iraq, 2003), Fingal and Herrick (Afghanistan, 2002), Ellamy (Libya, 2011) and Shader (Syria, 2014).

56 Bradley, *A Soldier's Story*, op. cit., p. 222.

57   Henry J. Cordes, 'D-Day: Was Omaha Beach Named in Honor of Local Man's War Efforts?', *Omaha World-Herald*, 9 November 2008.

8. Soapsuds and Tidal Waves

1   Still a military airbase today, US records referred to De Koog airfield, spelt by the Dutch De Kooy.

2   Col. Hal Radesky, interview, 1987, courtesy of Strategic Air Command. This fine old soldier died in May 2014, aged ninety-five.

3   Marshal of the RAF Sir Arthur Harris, *Bomber Offensive* (Collins, 1947), p.70.

4   This was Operation Margin, an attack on the MAN U-boat diesel engine factory on 17 April 1942; seven of the twelve Lancasters were shot down with the loss of forty-nine crewmen – thirty-seven killed and twelve taken prisoner. Many aircraft were damaged, Sqn Ldr Nettleton nursing his crippled Lancaster aircraft home, for which he would be awarded the Victoria Cross. Post-war analysis indicated the damage inflicted on the enemy was tiny.

5   Ken Delve, *D-Day: The Air Battle* (Arms & Armour Press, 1994), p. 28.

6   Martin W. Bowman, *We Were Eagles, Vol. 1: The Eighth Air Force at War, July 1942 to November 1943* (Amberley, 2014).

7   Caine, *Spitfires, Thunderbolts and Warm Beer*, op. cit., pp. 176–7.

8   Best described in Martin Middlebrook, *The Schweinfurt–Regensburg Mission: The American Raids on 17 August 1943* (Allen Lane, 1983).

9   Pierre Clostermann, *The Big Show* (Chatto & Windus, 1951), p. 94.

10   Ibid., p. 98.

11   David Ian Hall, 'Creating the 2nd Tactical Air Force: Inter-Service and Anglo-Canadian Co-operation in the Second World War', *Canadian Military Journal* (Winter 2002–2003), p. 44.

12   Air Marshal Sir Denis Crowley-Milling, 'Air Preparations', in *Overlord 1944: Symposium of the Normandy Landings* (RAF Historical Society, 1995), p. 28.

13   Scott, *Typhoon Pilot*, op. cit., pp. 97–8.

14   Cy Cyford, interview, op. cit.

15   Bill Youngkin, 'Carlos B. Pegues, WWII Veteran', *The Eagle* (Bryan, Texas), 9 May 2016.

16   Delve, *D-Day: The Air Battle*, op. cit., pp. 24–8.

17   Caine, *Spitfires, Thunderbolts and Warm Beer*, op. cit., p. 169.

18   Ibid.

19   William B. Dowling, interview, 2017, courtesy of 392nd Bomb Group Memorial Association, www.b24.net.

20   Bernard Sender, interview, 2017, courtesy of 392nd Bomb Group Memorial Association, www.b24.net.

21   Steven J. Zaloga, *Operation Pointblank 1944: Defeating the Luftwaffe* (Osprey, 2011), pp. 22, 41 and 49.

22   Horne and Montgomery, *Monty 1944–1945*, op. cit., p. 93.

23   Intelligence Analysis Division, European Branch, *Status of Air Prerequisites for Operation Overlord with Estimate of Situation* (Staff Study, 29 March 1944); cited

in Eduard Mark, *Aerial Interdiction, Air Power and the Land Battle in Three American Wars* (Center for Air Force History, 1994), pp. 216–17.

24   Crowley-Milling, 'Air Preparations', in *Overlord 1944*, op. cit., p. 29.

25   Birdie Schmidt, 'Reminiscences about the ARC Aeroclub at Wendling, Gleaned from Reports Made to ARC English Headquarters', 2017, courtesy of 392nd Bomb Group Memorial Association, www.b24.net.

26   Ibid.

9. COSSACs, Spartans and Chiefs

1   Admiral Sir Bertram H. Ramsay (eds. Robert W. Love & John Major), *The Year of D-Day* (University of Hull Press, 1994), p. 18.

2   D. K. R. Crosswell, *Beetle: The Life of General Walter Bedell Smith* (University Press of Kentucky, 2010).

3   Forrest C. Pogue, *US Army in World War II, ETO: The Supreme Command* (Office of the Chief of Military History, Department of the Army, 1954), p. 61.

4   Crosswell, *Beetle*, op. cit., p. 569.

5   Bradley, *A Soldier's Story*, op. cit., p. 226.

6   Peter Caddick-Adams, 'General Sir Miles Christopher Dempsey (1896–1969) – Not a Popular Leader', *RUSI Journal*, Vol. 150/5 (October 2005).

7   Maj. Johnny Langdon, interview, Army Junior Division (AJD) Study Day, Staff College, 3 November 2000.

8   Griffiss was named for Lt Col Townsend Griffiss, a high-flying officer killed during a diplomatic mission on 15 February 1942 and one of the first US officers to die in Europe.

9   Edna Hodgson, interview, BBC, WW2 People's War, op. cit.

10   Montgomery of Alamein, *Memoirs*, op. cit.

11   Eisenhower, *Crusade in Europe*, op. cit., pp. 270–1.

12   Bradley, *A Soldier's Story*, op. cit., p. 236.

13   Churchill, *Second World War, Vol. 5*, op. cit., p. 431.

14   Alanbrooke, *War Diaries 1939–1945*, op. cit., p. 558.

15   Craig L. Symonds, *Neptune: The Allied Invasion of Europe and the D-Day Landings* (Oxford, 2014), pp. 179–80.

16   Robert Woollcombe, *Lion Rampant* (Black and White Publishing, 2014), Kindle, p. 349.

17   Known as STANTA, an abbreviation of Stanford Training Area, the British Army retains 30,000 acres in the area today as a training ground.

18   Reg Warner, 1st/7th Middlesex, interview, Battersea, 1994.

19   In his military life, the author has exercised around both Imber and Stanta training areas and was often struck by the tragedy of both sets of communities that are no more.

20   'GHQ Exercise Spartan, March 1943', [typewritten] Report No. 94 by Maj. C. P. Stacey, Historical Officer, Canadian Military HQ, 12 May 1943 [15 pp. plus appendices], Canadian military archives.

21   Ibid.

22 'Deception in Exercise Spartan' [typewritten report], 11th Corps District, Home Forces, 2–12 March 1943, Imperial War Museum.

23 Alanbrooke, *War Diaries 1939–1945*, op. cit., p. 388, entry for 7 March 1943.

24 John Nelson Rickard, 'The Test of Command: McNaughton and Exercise Spartan, 4–12 March 1943', *Canadian Military History*, Vol. 8/3 (1999).

25 Crowley-Milling, 'Air Preparations', in *Overlord 1944*, op. cit., p. 27.

26 Ibid.; see also Delve, *D-Day: The Air Battle*, op. cit., pp. 15–21.

27 See obituary, *Daily Telegraph*, 18 March 2006.

28 Capt. John Ross, interview, Alberta, 2004.

29 Brig. Peter Young, *Storm from the Sea* (William Kimber, 1958), pp. 140–1.

30 Alan Whiting, interview, cited in Peter Liddle (ed.), *D-Day: By Those Who Were There* (Pen & Sword, 1994), Kindle, pp. 592–601.

31 Max Arthur, *The Navy: 1939 to the Present Day* (Hodder & Stoughton, 1997), p. 473.

32 The National Archives (TNA): Letter, Mountbatten, Combined Operations HQ to War Office, 1 May 1942.

33 Derek Oakley, 'The Origin of the Green Beret', *Globe and Laurel* (Sept.–Oct. 2002), p. 346.

34 The National Archives (TNA): 'Berets, Green – Introduction of', 13 October 1942.

35 Donald Gilchrist, *Don't Cry For Me*, op. cit., p. 49.

36 Robert Luther 'Bob' Sales, 29th Division, interview, cited in Neillands and De Normann, *D-Day 1944*, op. cit., p. 35; Sales died aged eighty-nine in February 2015.

37 Tom Duncan, 3 Commando, interview, Aberdeen, 1980; Duncan died in 2012.

38 'Lord Lovat: Obituary', *Independent*, 20 March 1995.

39 Ibid.

40 Bill Millin, interviews, 1975; 1979; 1984; 1994; 2004. See obituaries, *Scotsman*, 11 March 2016, and *Daily Telegraph*, 19 March 2016.

10. Rhinos, Camels and Roundabouts

1 David Holbrook, *Flesh Wounds* (Methuen, 1966), p. 101.

2 Alistair Cooke, *American Journey: Life on the Home Front in the Second World War* (Allen Lane, 2006), pp. 92–3.

3 Arthur Herman, *Freedom's Forge: How American Business Produced Victory in World War II* (Random House, 2012), pp. 204–6; see also Douglas Brinkley, 'The Man Who Won the War for Us', *American Heritage*, Vol. 51/3 (2000).

4 Landing craft total from http://naval-history.net/WW2CampaignsNormandy. htm.

5 Peter Prior, interview, cited in Liddle (ed.), *D-Day: By Those Who Were There*, op. cit., Kindle p. 391 and obituary, *Daily Telegraph*, 30 May 2011.

6 William Tomko, interview courtesy of *Press of Atlantic City*, 6 June 2014; he died in 2017.

7 Pete Fantacone, interview, June 2014, courtesy of oral history programme of the US Naval Institute.

8   John Sharples, interview, Portsmouth, 1994.

9   Ibid. Sharples and *LST-405* did, in fact, beach on Gold Beach in the late afternoon of D-Day.

10   Holbrook, *Flesh Wounds*, op. cit., p. 124.

11   Wally MacKenzie, interview, 2009, courtesy of Stockport NVA (Normandy Veterans Association).

12   Arno J. Christiansen, interview, Imperial War Museum, Dept. of Documents, Ref. 13208.

13   'HMLBK-6: A Normandy Veteran', at combinedops.com.

14   Col. H. S. Gillies, MC, DL, Typescript memoir, 1987, Imperial War Museum.

15   The 2nd Glosters suffered 678 casualties defending Cassel in 1940, 472 of them POWs; Maj. F. D. Goode, 2nd Glosters, Unpublished memoir, Soldiers of Gloucestershire Museum, Custom House, Gloucester Docks.

16   Peter Brown, interview 2004, courtesy of BBC The People's War.

17   Ibid.

18   J. P. Kellett and J. Davies, *A History of the RAF Servicing Commandos* (Airlife, 1989).

19   Courtesy of Jill Kidder and Geoff Slee, via combinedops.com.

20   David McKenna, 'On the Trail of Britain's WWII Explosive Beauty Spots', BBC *News*, 1 July 2013.

21   Midshipman Troy A. Shoulders, *The US Navy in Operation Overlord under the Command of Rear Admiral Alan G. Kirk* (USNA Report, Annapolis, 1994), pp. 134–5.

22   Alan Moorhead, *Eclipse* (Hamish Hamilton, 1945), p. 93.

23   Freddie Robertson and Jed Luckhurst, interviews, 2001, courtesy of combinedops.com.

24   John Emery, interview 2005, courtesy of BBC The People's War.

25   Steven J. Zaloga, *D-Day Fortifications in Normandy* (Osprey, 2005), pp. 9, 20, 27, 29.

26   Michael Dolski, Sam Edwards and John Buckley (eds), *D-Day in History and Memory* (University of North Texas Press, 2014), p. 198.

27   Zaloga, *D-Day Fortifications*, op. cit., p. 34.

28   Shoulders, *The US Navy in Operation Overlord*, op. cit., p. 147.

29   US National Archives: US Assault Training Center ETO, 'Conference on Landing Assaults, 24 May–23 June 1943', N-6138-B.

30   Richard T. Bass, *Spirits of the Sand: The History of the US Army Assault Training Centre, Woolacombe* (Short Run Press, 1991).

31   Roy Burton, 1st Grenadier Guards (Motor Battalion, Guards Armoured Division), interview, Stafford, 1994.

32   Courtesy of Assault Training Center website, Veteran's Tales, at http://www.assaulttrainingcenterfriends.co.uk/veterans-tales.html.

33   Ibid.

34   Ibid.

35   Charles Hurlbut, interview, op. cit.

36   Peggie Walsh, 'D-Day Reflections from a Soldier', *Huffington Post*, 6 December 2017, text by Colonel Charles M. Hangsterfer.

37 D. Zane Schlemmer, interview, D-Day Overlord (French) archive.

38 Sub-Lt Peter Miles, RNVR, interview, Lechlade, 2002.

39 The National Archives (TNA): WO 222/97, 120304, 'Secret – Notes on the Use of Benzedrine in War Operations', Appendix 'E'.

40 Len Bennett, interview, cited in Sean Longden, *To the Victor the Spoils* (Arris, 2004), p. 123.

41 Historical Officer, Canadian Military Headquarters, Report No. 104, 'Position and Roles of Canadian Forces in the United Kingdom', 13 October 1943, para. 7.

42 https://www.youtube.com/watch?v=dL3NdZJcOOk.

43 The 21st Army Group commander was a notorious 'hirer and firer' throughout his career; Ramsden joined another ex-corps commander, Herbert Lumsden, who on arriving back in London announced, 'I've just been sacked because there isn't room in the desert for two cads – Montgomery and me.'

44 Bradley, *A Soldier's Story*, op. cit., p. 81.

45 Ibid, pp. 154–6.

46 Maj. R. J. Rogers, 'Leadership Study of the 1st Infantry Division during WWII: Terry De La Mesa Allen and Clarence Ralph Huebner' MA thesis, US Army Command and General Staff College, 1965; see also Steven Flaig, 'Clarence R. Huebner: Story of Achievement' (MSc thesis, University of North Texas, 2006).

47 Bradley, *A Soldier's Story*, op. cit., pp. 236–7.

48 Pogue, *Pogue's War*, op. cit., p. 24.

49 Bradley, *A Soldier's Story*, op. cit., pp. 227–8.

50 'The Secret Beach Where Britain Rehearsed D-Day', *Scotsman*, 29 May 2004.

51 Eddie Williams, interview, 2004, courtesy of BBC, WW2 People's War, op. cit.

52 Edwin 'Nobby' Clarke, interview courtesy of BBC, WW2 People's War, op. cit.

53 Maj. Gen. Derrick Bruce Wormald, DSO, MC, 'Recollections of the Operations Undertaken by "A" Squadron of the 13th/18th Royal Hussars (QMO) During the 1944–45 Campaign in Europe' (courtesy of Mark Hickman, The Pegasus Archive).

54 Recollections of Private Douglas Edwin Patrick Wileman and Lt Julius Arthur Sheffield Neave, both 13th/18th Hussars, 2004, Imperial War Museum Sound Archive, ref. 27183 and Documents, ref. 7872.

55 *Oxfordshire and Buckinghamshire Light Infantry Chronicle*, Vol. 3: July 1942–May 1944, pp. 282–92.

56 Capt. Douglas G. Aitken, RAMC, Typescript memoirs, Imperial War Museum Dept. of Documents, ref. 12085.

57 War Office figures calculated on an average Liberty ship's capacity of 9,650 tons.

58 Rear Admiral Teddy Gueritz, interview, Portsmouth, 1994; Adm. Gueritz died in January 2009.

59 Lord Chief Justice Sir Robin Dunn, interview, London, 1994; Sir Robin Dunn, *Sword and Wig: Memoirs of a Lord Justice* (Quiller Press, 1993), p.54; see also obituary, *Daily Telegraph*, 31 March 2014.

60 Albert Walker, interview 2003, courtesy of BBC The People's War.

61 Steven Sykes, *Deceivers Ever: Memoirs of a Camouflage Officer* (Spellmount, 1990), pp. 119–20.

62 Maj. J. B. Higham and E. A. Knighton, *Movements* (War Office/HMSO, 1955), chapter 8, section 5.

63 William Smith, letters, 1984 and 1990, East Lothian at War, http://www.eastlothianatwar.co.uk/ELAW/D-Day_Rehearsals.html.

64 The DUKW's initials stood for D = Designed (in 1942); U = Utility; K = All-wheel drive; W = Dual-tandem rear axles; a total of 20,000 were manufactured in the USA.

65 Douglas Day, interview, cited in Frank and Joan Shaw, *We Remember D-Day*, op. cit., pp. 193–4.

66 With No. 5 Beach Group, formed round the 5th King's Regt, they constituted No. 101 Beach Sub-Area.

67 Bill Adams, 1st Bucks Battalion, interview, Aylesbury, 1995.

68 Norman Smith, 48th Division and 22nd Field Dressing Station, interview Aylesbury, 1994.

11. Ducks and Eagles

1   Lt Cdr Maxwell O. W. Miller, RN, courtesy of combinedops.com.

2   *United States Naval Administration in World War II, Vol. V: The Invasion of Normandy, Operation Neptune* (Director of Naval History, 1948), pp. 361–2; one of these two Shermans was salvaged and stands at Slapton Sands as a memorial to the dead of the later Exercise Tiger.

3   Slaughter, *Omaha Beach and Beyond*, op. cit., p. 80.

4   Valentine M. Miele, 16th Infantry, interview, 2014, courtesy of Aaron Elson.

5   Roland G. Ruppenthal, *US Army in World War II, ETO: Logistical Support of the Armies, Vol. 1: May 1941–September 1944*, chapter 8, pp. 328–54.

6   Bradley, *A Soldier's Story*, op. cit., p. 278.

7   One of these was later salvaged and forms the memorial to US troops lost at Slapton Sands.

8   Lt Col. S. L. A. Marshall, '110th FA Bn on D-Day', p. 2, courtesy of the Maryland Military Historical Society. These interviews date to September 1944, when the 29th Division were in reserve. Marshall's efforts resulted in some of the most valuable D-Day historiography, for shortly after, the GIs were ordered back to the front, and many interviewees were killed in action during the final assault to liberate Brest, or in later fighting.

9   Arnold Hague Convoy Database. The *George Washington* carried 6,326 troops, the *Britannic* 5,574, the *Franconia* 4,571 and the *Capetown* Castle 5,350.

10 William S. Boice (ed.), *History of the Twenty-Second United States Infantry in World War II* (22nd Infantry, 1959).

11 Richard M. Good, interview, 1984, cited in Sims, '*They Have Seen The Elephant*', op. cit.

12 Theodore A. Wilson (ed.), *D-Day 1944* (University Press of Kansas, 1994), p. 224.

13 Gary Guimarra, unpublished paper. I am indebted to Maj. Gen. Graham Hollands for this reference.

14 Harry Cooper, interview courtesy of the *Los Angeles Times*, 5 June 1994.

15 Milton E. Chadwick, interview, Ohio, 1994. He was a lifelong Anglophile, and I was sad to receive news of Chadwick's death in July 2008.

16 Jack Schlegel, later chief of police in Shandaken, New York, interview. Schlegel died very shortly after this June 2014 interview, conducted in Normandy during a 70th Anniversary Reunion visit, when he stood with President Obama and 82nd Airborne colleagues at the US Omaha Beach cemetery. In June 1994, I watched this inspiring veteran, then aged seventy-one, undertake a parachute jump into his old Normandy drop zone.

17 Caddick-Adams, *Monty and Rommel*, op. cit., p. 18. Fred Patheiger died in 1989, Bobbie Jack Rommel in 2009; Aaron L. Rommel was killed in action, 15 April 1945.

18 Sampson jumped into Normandy on D-Day, and again into Arnhem, and served in the Battle of the Bulge, where he was captured and imprisoned for four months. He saw action later in Korea and was Chief of US Army Chaplains from 1967–71, when he retired from a thirty-year career as both soldier and chaplain. He wrote the wonderfully titled *Look Out Below: A Story of the Airborne by a Paratrooper Padre* (Catholic University of America Press, 1958) and died in 1996; see William J. Hourihan, PhD, *A Paratrooper Chaplain: The Life and Times of Chaplain (MG) Francis L. Sampson* (Army Chaplain's Branch, 2010).

19 Capt. F. O. Miksche, *Paratroops: The History, Organization, and Tactical Use of Airborne Forces* (Faber & Faber, 1943), p. 64.

20 Papers of Lt Col Ferdinand Otto Miksche (1904–1992), Liddell Hart Centre for Military Archives, King's College, London. I am indebted to my friend and colleague Professor Chris Bellamy for this reference.

21 John Howard, interview, Browning Barracks, Aldershot, 1995.

22 David Wood, interview, cited in Bailey, *Forgotten Voices*, op. cit.

23 SSgt Jim Wallwork, interview, Pegasus Bridge, 2004. Jim died in January 2013; see his many obituaries, e.g. *Independent*, 30 January 2013, and *Daily Telegraph*, 19 March 2013. He emigrated to Canada after the war and his moving obituary in the *Vancouver Sun* concluded: 'James Harley (Jim) Wallwork October 21, 1919–January 24, 2013; Jim glided peacefully on the last cast-off of his 93 years, January 24th 2013, White Rock, B.C.

24 Ibid.

25 Ibid.

26 Raymond 'Tich' Raynor, interview, Bletchley Park, 2006; the nickname Tich was due to his being the youngest in his family.

27 Edwin Booth, interview, 2000, courtesy of www.warlinks.com.

28 Ibid.

29 Stuart Tootal, *The Manner of Men: 9 Para's Heroic Mission on D-Day* (John Murray, 2013), Kindle, p. 1536.

30 Sgt Les Daniels, interview courtesy of pegasusarchive.org.

31 Lt Col. Stuart Tootal relates this at length in chapter 5 of his excellent *The Manner of Men*, op. cit.; Neil Barber also deals with this in *The Day the Devils Dropped In: The 9th Parachute Battalion in Normandy, D-Day to D+6: Merville Battery to the Chateau St Côme* (Pen & Sword, 2002). Martin Lindsay went on to write *So*

Few Got Through (Collins, 1946), an acclaimed account of his service with the 51st Highland Division, and died in 1981; see obituary, *The Times*, 7 May 1981. This author has interviewed friends and members of the Lindsay family and soldiers of 9 Para. Whereas Lindsay is easy to admire, Otway is a challenging figure, difficult to warm to, whose behaviour continues to perplex this author, as it did, seemingly, to many of his own battalion. Terence Otway died in 2006; see obituary, *Daily Telegraph*, 25 July 2006.

32 This was Maj. Allen Parry; see Tootal, *The Manner of Men*, op. cit., p. 1654.

33 Lt Gen. Sir Napier Crookenden and Air Marshal Sir Denis Crowley-Milling, 'Planning the Operation', in *Overlord 1944*, op. cit., p. 34. Crookenden died in 2002; see obituary, *Daily Telegraph*, 2 November 2002.

34 Brig. James Hill, interview, cited in Liddle (ed.), *D-Day*, op. cit., pp. 588–9.

35 Lt Russell Chandler, Jr, interview courtesy of A. Russell Chandler III (*Aviation History*, July 2004).

36 Barkston Heath, Cottesmore, Folkingham, Fulbeck, Saltby and Spanhoe for the 82nd, whilst the 101st took off from Exeter, Greenham Common, Merryfield, Membury and Upottery.

37 Lt Russell Chandler, Jr, interview, op. cit.

38 Dyson, *Tank Twins*, op. cit., pp. 20–1.

39 Author's archive.

40 Zuehlke, *Juno Beach*, op. cit., p. 836.

41 Arthur Hill, interview, 2004, courtesy of Landing Craft Association, via Sub-Lt Peter Miles, RNVR.

42 Zuehlke, *Juno Beach*, op. cit., p. 847.

43 Ramsay, *The Year of D-Day*, op. cit., pp. 54–5.

44 The National Archives (TNA): WO 194/2317, 'Exercise Trousers, 3rd Canadian Infantry Division'.

45 Symonds, *Neptune*, op. cit., p. 210.

46 Laurie Burn, interview, 1994, via 13th/18th Hussars Old Comrades' Association.

47 Patrick Hennessey, *Young Man in a Tank* (self-published, 1984).

48 Ramsay, *The Year of D-Day*, op. cit., p. 25. Ramsay's diary entry here is for 12 February, but there was only one such exercise viewed from Fort Henry by this set of VIPs (Churchill, King George VI, Monty, Leigh-Mallory, Dempsey, Hobart, Vian, etc.), which was held on 4 April. The transposition of dates is confusing.

49 Gen. Sir Robert Ford, interview, 1990, during 4th/7th Dragoon Guards battlefield tour to Normandy; see also obituary, *Daily Telegraph*, 26 November 2015.

50 In 2012, Fort Henry, specially built by Canadian Royal Engineers in 1943 for VIPs to watch landing exercises, was handed over to the care of the National Trust, due to its historical significance.

51 Memoirs of Peter Mitchell, courtesy of David Mitchell, http://www.davidmitchell. co.uk/David_Mitchell/The_Essex_Yeomanry.html.

52 Paul Lund and Harry Ludlam, *The War of the Landing Craft* (Foulsham, 1976), p. 146.

53 Willie Williamson, interview, 1994, courtesy of West Midlands Normandy Veterans Association (NVA).

54   Harry Yeide, *Steel Victory: The Heroic Story of America's Independent Tank Battalions at War in Europe* (Presidio, 2003), p. 30.

55   It was Basil Liddell Hart, the well-known writer, military theorist and correspondent of *The Times*, who first drew Churchill's attention to Hobart's talents; later on Hobart was also sponsored and protected by Brooke.

56   Cited in Keith Grint, 'Technologies', in *Leadership, Management and Command* (Palgrave Macmillan, 2008).

57   Each AVRE was equipped with a turret-mounted 290mm-calibre Petard mortar, which was loaded from the outside and designed to lob a forty-pound charge at concrete bunkers from a range of about eighty yards.

58   Tony Younger, *Blowing Our Bridges: A Memoir from Dunkirk to Korea via Normandy* (Pen & Sword, 2004); see obituary, *Daily Telegraph*, 26 July 2010.

59   Letter, OR 2, HQ 21st Army Group, Brig. Otway Herbert to War Office, 16 February 1944.

60   Adrian R. Lewis, *Omaha Beach: A Flawed Victory* (University of North Carolina Press, 2001), p. 30.

61   Harry Yeide, *Weapons of the Tankers: American Armor in World War II* (Zenith Publishing, 2006), p. 79.

62   Tim Kilvert-Jones, *Omaha Beach: V Corps' Battle for the Normandy Beachhead* (Leo Cooper, 1999), p. 76.

63   Bradley, *A Soldier's Story*, op. cit., pp. 214–15.

64   I am indebted to Maj. Gen. Scott-Bowden's son, Brigadier Jamie, with whom I explored Normandy in 2008, for making available interview transcripts and articles by his father; see also obituary, *Independent*, 15 April 2014.

12. Bigots and Tigers

1   Entry for 14 May 1944, *Among You Taking Notes: The Wartime Diary of Naomi Mitchison* (Gollancz, 1985).

2   The Thistlethwaite family still own everything in the region today, except Southwick House.

3   Ramsay, *The Year of D-Day*, op. cit., pp. 13–14.

4   Wren Kay Martin, interview, Frank and Joan Shaw Collection, D-Day Museum, Portsmouth.

5   The Admiralty never got round to returning Southwick House to the Thistlethwaite family and compulsorily purchased the mansion in 1950 – and it remains Ministry of Defence property at the time of writing.

6   SHAEF original copy No. 78, Dwight D. Eisenhower Presidential Library, Abilene, Kansas.

7   Bradley, *A Soldier's Story*, op. cit., p. 224.

8   US National Archives: Ref. N-11474.2, 'Operation Overlord, Administrative Order No. 7', South Western Zone (HQ Southern Base Section, SOS ETOUSA, US Army, 10 April 1944), declassified 31 December 1945.

9   Pogue, *Pogue's War*, op. cit., p. 30.

10   Stephen E. Ambrose, *D-Day* (Simon & Schuster, 1994), p. 125.

11 Bradley, *A Soldier's Story*, op. cit., p. 223.

12 George M. Elsey, *An Unplanned Life: A Memoir* (University of Missouri Press, 2005), p. 52; see obituary, *New York Times*, 8 January 2016.

13 Wren Ginger Thomas, interview, op. cit.

14 Ramsay, *The Year of D-Day*, op. cit., p. 78, entry for 29 May 1944.

15 Wren Jean Irvine, interview cited in Martin Bowman, *Remembering D-Day* (Collins, 2004), p. 28.

16 Ramsay, *The Year of D-Day*, op. cit., p. 78, entry for 29 May 1944.

17 *The Commercial Motor*, 3 November 1944, p. 248.

18 It was in the Western Desert when commanding the Eighth Army that Monty first devised the idea of Tactical (TAC), Main and Rear headquarters, enabling a higher formation, when necessary, to stay close to the battle, without loss of communication. His three trailers, now on display at the Imperial War Museum, Duxford, comprised an office, a bedroom and a map room.

19 Bradley, *A Soldier's Story*, op. cit., pp. 253–4. The disparity in the overall totals of destroyers rests on the differing definitions of a destroyer by the USN and RN; some American destroyers and destroyer escorts were classified as frigates by the RN.

20 The eight maritime forces were the RN, USN, RCN, French, Polish, Dutch, Norwegian and Greek navies; seventy-five years later, the total of warships available for Overlord was more than the total surface fleet of the world's principal navies. Ships totals from the D-Day Heritage Ships Association; for comprehensive list, see Warren Tute, John Costello and Terry Hughes, *D-Day* (Sidgwick & Jackson, 1974), p. 256.

21 Sub-Lt Peter Miles, RNVR, interview, Lechlade, 2002, courtesy of the Landing Craft Association.

22 Lewis, *Omaha Beach*, op. cit., p. 37.

23 *The Defense of Gallipoli: A General Staff Study Prepared pursuant to instructions from Maj. Gen. Hugh A. Drum, Department Commander* by G. S. Patton, Lt Col, General Staff. HQ Hawaiian Dept., Fort Shafter, 31 August 1936: 'The Problem: To examine the methods used in defense against landing operations as illustrated by the Turkish defense of Gallipoli.'

24 Ramsay, *The Year of D-Day*, op. cit., p. 24.

25 Maj. Stephen C. McGeorge, 'Seeing the Battlefield: Brig. Gen. Norman D. Cota's "Bastard Brigade" at Omaha Beach', in *Studies in Battle Command* (Combat Studies Institute, Fort Leavenworth, 2000).

26 Walsh, 'D-Day Reflections from a Soldier', op. cit.

27 B. S. Barnes, *The Sign of the Double 'T'* (self-published/Sentinel Press, 1999), p. 61.

28 Interview, Brig. Sir Alexander Stanier, Bt., Shropshire, 1984; see his *Sammy's Wars. Recollections of War in Northern France and Other Occasions* (Welsh Guards, 1998), pp. 38–9; also obituary *Daily Telegraph*, 11 January 1995.

29 Ramsay, *The Year of D-Day*, op. cit., pp. 60–1.

30 Lt Eugene E. Eckstam, MC, USNR (Ret.), 'The Tragedy of Exercise Tiger', *Navy Medicine*, Vol. 85/3 (May–June 1994), pp. 5–7.

31 Ibid.

32 Max Arthur, *The Navy: 1939 to the Present Day* (Hodder & Stoughton, 1997), pp. 476–7.

33 David Kenyon Webster, *Parachute Infantry: An American Paratrooper's Memoir of D-Day and the Fall of the Third Reich* (Bantam, 1994).

34 Forty, *Frontline Dorset*, op. cit., pp. 80–1.

35 Daniel Folsom, interview, op. cit.

36 Pete Nevill, interview, 2005, courtesy of Imperial Museum Sound Archive, ref. 27499.

37 Bradley, *A Soldier's Story*, op. cit., pp. 247–8.

38 Mark Townsend, 'Did Allies Kill GIs in D-Day Training Horror? Scores of US Soldiers Died in a Mock Invasion of a Devon Beach and Their Corpses Were Secretly Buried', *Guardian*, 16 May 2004.

39 *United States Naval Administration in World War II: Vol. V*, op. cit., p. 370.

40 Eckstam, 'The Tragedy of Exercise Tiger', op. cit.

13. Thunderclaps and Fabius

1   Churchill was here referring to Eisenhower's position overseeing Operation Torch and the subsequent campaign in Tunisia of November 1942–May 1943.

2   Bradley, *A Soldier's Story*, op. cit., p. 239.

3   John Green, interview cited in Liddle (ed.), *D-Day*, op. cit., pp. 352–9.

4   Horne and Montgomery, *Monty 1944–1945*, op. cit., p. 90.

5   Alanbrooke, *War Diaries 1939–1945*, op. cit., p. 538.

6   Gen. Sir John Kennedy, *The Business of War* (Hutchinson, 1957), pp. 326–7.

7   Ramsay, *The Year of D-Day*, op. cit., pp. 52–3.

8   Bradley, *A Soldier's Story*, op. cit., pp. 239–41.

9   Prof. Richard Holmes, interview, UK Defence Academy, Shrivenham, 2001.

10 Ramsay, *The Year of D-Day*, op. cit., pp. 52–3; naval split: Churchill, *Second World War, Vol. 5*, op. cit.

11 All figures: author's calculations from list on ships in Tute, Costello and Hughes, *D-Day*, op. cit., p. 256.

12 Goronwy Rees, interview recorded for Thames Television, *The World at War*, 1973, Imperial War Museum.

13 Eisenhower, *Crusade in Europe*, op. cit., p. 269.

14 Harry C. Butcher, *My Three Years with Eisenhower* (Simon & Schuster, 1946).

15 Sir John Wheeler Bennett, *King George VI: His Life and Times* (Macmillan, 1958), pp. 599–600.

16 Kennedy, *The Business of War*, op. cit., p. 328. The final conference was interpreted convincingly in the 2004 made-for-television movie *Ike – Countdown to D-Day*, in which actor Tom Selleck re-enacted some of Eisenhower's most difficult decisions and personality clashes during the ninety days before the invasion.

17 Lord Ismay, *The Memoirs of Gen. The Lord Ismay* (Heinemann, 1960), p. 352.

18 Alanbrooke, *War Diaries 1939–1945*, op. cit., p. 547, entry for 17 May 1944.

19 Bernard Montgomery, *The Memoirs of Field-Marshal Montgomery* (Collins, 1958), p. 221.

20   Ibid.

21   Christopher D. Yung, *Gators of Neptune: Naval Amphibious Planning for the Normandy Invasion* (Naval Institute Press, 2006), p. 153. The name 'Fabius' came from the Roman commander who exhausted Hannibal with well-prepared and -executed skirmishes, and was regarded as the model for George Washington's strategy against the British.

22   Slaughter, *Omaha Beach and Beyond*, op. cit., p. 87.

23   Lt George (Jimmy) Green, 551st Landing Craft Assault (LCA) Flotilla and HMS *Empire Javelin*, interview, Help for Heroes battlefield tour Normandy, 2008.

24   *United States Naval Administration in World War II: Vol. V*, op. cit., p. 366.

25   Sgt Vincent 'Mike' McKinney, 16th Infantry Regiment, interview, 1999, courtesy of Aaron Elson.

26   Stanier, *Sammy's Wars*, op. cit., pp. 39–40.

27   Stanley Ernest Hodge, MM, interview, 43rd Division reunion, 2005; Hodge later transferred to the 4th Dorsets of the 43rd Wessex Division.

28   Ken Watts, interview, 2004, courtesy of BBC, WW2 People's War, op. cit.

29   Ian C. Hammerton, *Achtung! Minen! The Making of a Flail Troop Commander* (self-published, 1991), p. 62. I accompanied Ian Hammerton on several battlefield tours across Europe, beginning in 1999, and was sad to learn of his death in January 2017.

30   John Lanes, interview via Sherwood Rangers Yeomanry Old Comrades Association, 1994.

31   The APFU film and photographic footage of the exercise is in the Imperial War Museum.

32   Bracklesham Bay is littered with the wrecks of RAF and Luftwaffe aircraft from the Battle of Britain, a pair of swimming tanks from the Fabius exercises, and landing craft that sank during Operation Neptune.

33   Zuehlke, *Juno Beach*, op. cit., p. 857.

34   Doris Hayball, interview via Australian War Memorial, Canberra, 1994.

35   HMS *Glenearn* was a converted eighteen-knot cargo vessel of 10,000 tons that acted as mother ship to the two flotillas (twenty-four) of smaller landing craft (LCAs) she carried.

36   Richard Harris, 1st Suffolks, interview courtesy of Littlehampton Fort Restoration Project, http://www.littlehamptonfort.co.uk/wp-content/uploads/2014/04/Exercise-Fabius.pdf.

37   Peter Cruden, No. 6 Commando, interview courtesy of Littlehampton Fort Restoration Project, op. cit.

38   Lord Lovat, interview via Colin Hughes, 7th R. Warwicks & No. 4 Commando, 1994.

39   Ramsay, *The Year of D-Day*, op. cit., p. 63.

40   Dempsey and his staff would return on 6 June 1948 to present two fine stained-glass windows commemorating their moment of peace before the storm.

41   Royal Army Chaplain's Department (RAChD) archives, Amport House, Andover, Hampshire.

42   Alanbrooke, *War Diaries 1939–1945*, op. cit.; Stan Proctor, *A Quiet Little Boy Goes to War* (self-published, 1996).

43   Nigel F. Evans, 'British Artillery in World War 2', 2014, http://nigelef.tripod.com/recruitrain.htm.

44   Ben Kite, *Stout Hearts: The British and Canadians in Normandy 1944* (Helion, 2014), p. 152.

45   Norman Smith, interview, op. cit.

46   Pogue, *Pogue's War*, op. cit., p. 22.

47   John McGregor, *The Spirit of Angus* (Phillimore, 1998), p. 112.

48   Eric Patience, interview, 1994, Romford, Essex.

49   Lund and Ludlam, *The War of the Landing Craft*, op. cit., p. 146.

50   Lord Lovat, *March Past* (Weidenfeld & Nicholson, 1978).

51   Maj. F. D. Goode, unpublished memoir, op. cit.

14. My Headmaster Was a Spy

1   Bradley, *A Soldier's Story*, op. cit., p. 247. Many of these 'hards' still exist around southern England's minor ports – great ramps assembled from smaller concrete non-slip 'chocolate bars', which aided vehicular and personnel access direct onto landing craft and LSTs.

2   Arthur Berry, interview 2004, courtesy BBC The People's War.

3   First World War battlefield on Gallipoli.

4   Abbreviation of *Stammlager*, a German prisoner-of-war camp.

5   Jack Swaab, *Field of Fire: Diary of a Gunner Officer* (Sutton, 2006), Kindle, pp. 2744–94.

6   Capt. Douglas G. Aitken, RAMC, Typescript memoirs, Imperial War Museum Dept. of Documents, ref. 12085.

7   Ralph Frederick Cheshire, interview, 2004, courtesy of BBC, WW2 People's War, op. cit.

8   Jim Sullivan, interview, Portsmouth, 1994.

9   Charles Hanaway, interview, 2001, courtesy of warlinks.com.

10   Moorhead, *Eclipse*, op. cit., pp. 89–90.

11   Charles Hanaway, interview, op. cit.

12   Robert Woollcombe, *Lion Rampant: The Memoirs of an Infantry Officer from D-Day to the Rhineland* (Black and White Publishing, 2014), Kindle p. 149.

13   Cited in George E. Koskimaki, *D-Day with the Screaming Eagles* (Vantage Press, 1970), p. 1. Lt Dick Winters wrote up his early experiences on 22 June 1944, while recovering from a wound in a Normandy aid station. Koskimaki was the first US veteran of D-Day this author met, when aged thirteen in 1974; the wonderful Koskimaki, author of three books about his beloved 101st, died in February 2016.

14   George Rosie, interview, 2013, courtesy of the 506th Airborne Infantry Regiment Association.

15   Eric Broadhead, interview, Frank and Joan Shaw Collection, D-Day Museum, Portsmouth.

16   Valentine M. Miele, interview, op. cit. The USS *Samuel Chase* was a purpose-built 9,000-ton landing ship, which participated in five major US amphibious assaults:

Torch, Husky, Avalanche, Overlord and Anvil; she carried thirty-three Higgins boats (LCVPs).

17 Dr Hal Baumgarten, telephone interview, June 2011.

18 Alex Hankin, Wessex Film and Sound Archive, 22 September 1999/Hampshire Record Office: W/C35/5/18, courtesy of Alresford Museum Photograph Gallery and Iris Crowfoot.

19 Henry 'Jo' Gullet, *Not As a Duty Only: An Infantryman's War* (Melbourne University Press, 1976), p. 132.

20 Pogue, *Pogue's War*, op. cit., p. 39.

21 Koskimaki, *D-Day with the Screaming Eagles*, op. cit., p. 5.

22 SSgt Jim Wallwork, interview, op. cit.

23 Lt Peter Prior, interview cited in Liddle (ed.), *D-Day*, op. cit., pp. 403–19.

24 Mary E. Harrison, interview cited in Shaw and Shaw, *We Remember D-Day*, op. cit., pp. 162–4. Harrison also wrote a poem about the potency of her creations. She had modelled Cologne for an RAF thousand-bomber raid; when comparing the photographs before and after, she was stricken with guilt. 'My Hands' begins, 'Do you know what it is like to have death in your hands?' It was published in the *Voice of War Anthology* (Michael Joseph, 1995).

25 Elsie Horton, interview, 2004, courtesy of BBC, WW2 People's War, op. cit.

26 Andrew Holborn, *The D-Day Landing on Gold Beach* (Bloomsbury Academic, 2015), p. 113.

27 Tim Parr, interview, op. cit.

28 Mollie Panter-Downes, *London War Notes 1939–1945*, ed. William Shawn (Farrar, Straus & Giroux, 1971), p. 322.

29 Brian Selman, interview, op. cit.

30 Joan Dale, interview, 2004, courtesy of BBC, WW2 People's War, op. cit.

31 Symonds, *Neptune*, op. cit., p. 221.

32 Gullet, *Not As a Duty Only*, op. cit., p. 132.

33 Shaw and Shaw, *We Remember D-Day*, op. cit., p. 77.

34 Gerald Reybold, interview, 1994, cited in Forty, *D-Day Dorset*, op. cit., p. 107.

35 Brian Selman, interview, op. cit.

36 Peter and Keith Ashton, *Hampshire and the United States* (self-published, 1986), p. 45.

37 The *Princess Maude* had also lifted troops off the Dunkirk beaches in 1940; Hurlbut, interview, op. cit.

38 Pogue, *Pogue's War*, op. cit., p. 40.

39 Lionel Thomas, interview, NFU (National Farmers' Union) Conference, 1992.

40 Pogue, *Pogue's War*, op. cit., pp. 36–7.

41 Tute, Costello and Hughes, *D-Day*, op. cit., p. 111.

42 John Colville, *Footprints in Time: Memories* (Collins, 1976), p. 160. Colville as a pilot in the 2nd TAF was on leave from his job as Churchill's private secretary, hence knowing the Overlord secret. Because of this, he was not allowed to fly over France until after D-Day.

43 James Kyle, *Typhoon Tale* (self-published, 1989), pp. 152–3; John Leete, *The New Forest at War* (Sutton, 2004), p. 64.

44   Val Gilbert, 'D-Day Crosswords Are Still a Few Clues Short of a Solution', *Daily Telegraph*, 3 May 2004.

45   Andrew Rawson (ed.), *Eyes Only: The Top Secret Correspondence Between Marshall and Eisenhower* (The History Press, 2012), Kindle, pp. 2749–62.

46   Bradley, *A Soldier's Story*, op. cit., pp. 223–4.

47   Rawson (ed.), *Eyes Only*, op. cit., pp. 1899–2001.

48   Horne and Montgomery, *Monty 1944–1945*, op. cit., p. 99.

49   Goronwy Rees, interview cited in Bailey, *Forgotten Voices*, op. cit.

50   Tute, Costello and Hughes, *D-Day*, op. cit., p. 85.

51   Corey Charlton, 'Top Secret Documents Unearthed by Officer's Son Reveal the Names of Second World War D-Day Operations Were Changed Almost Three Weeks Before Invasion', *Daily Mail*, 26 December 2014.

52   Alexander Baron, *From the City, From the Plough* (Jonathan Cape, 1948), pp. 7–8.

53   Norman Brooks, interview, courtesy of BBC, WW2 People's War, op. cit.

54   Symonds, *Neptune*, op. cit., pp. 231–2.

15. Big Week, Berlin and Nuremberg

1   Vincent Orange, 'Arthur Tedder and the Transportation Plan', Buckley (ed.), *The Normandy Campaign 1944*, op. cit., pp. 147–8.

2   This was C. K. M. Douglas, senior forecaster, Dunstable Central Forecasting Office (Meteorological Office); see Brian Audric, *The Meteorological Office Dunstable and the IDA Unit in World War II* (Occasional Papers on Meteorological History, No. 2, September 2000).

3   Maj. Jon M. Sutterfield, 'How Logistics Made Big Week Big', *Air Force Journal of Logistics*, Vol. 24/2.

4   Cited in Collier, *D-Day*, op. cit., p. 41.

5   Elmer Bendiner, *The Fall of Fortresses: A Personal Account* (Putnam's, 1980), p. 139.

6   Maj. Timothy A. Veeder, *An Evaluation of the Aerial Interdiction Campaign Known as 'The Transportation Plan' for the D-Day Invasion, Early January 1944–Late June 1944* (Research Paper, US Air Command & Staff College, 1997), p. 6.

7   Morgan, *Overture to Overlord*, op. cit., p. 102.

8   Richard G. Davis, 'Gen. Carl Spaatz and D-Day', *Air Power Journal* (Winter 1997).

9   Carl F. Spaatz papers, Box I: Official, April 1944, Library of Congress.

10   Wesley Frank Craven and Maj. James Lea Cate, *The Army Air Forces in World War II, Vol. 2: Europe: Torch to Pointblank, August 1942 to December 1943* (Chicago University Press, 1949), p. 735.

11   Richard G. Davis, 'Pointblank vs Overlord: Strategic Bombing and the Normandy Invasion', *Air Power History*, Vol. 41/2 (Summer 1994), pp. 4–13.

12   Henry Probert, *Bomber Harris: His Life and Times* (Greenhill, 2001), pp. 300–3.

13   Cited in Delve, *D-Day: The Air Battle*, op. cit., p. 44.

14   Vern L. Moncur (1916–1985) Manuscript Collection, File MS 221, Family History Center, Brigham Young University–Idaho.

15 Ibid.

16 Fortier, *An Ace of the Eighth*, op. cit., p. 127.

17 The tower in the Humboldthain Park was one of several designed to defend Berlin and is the only one surviving; its lower two floors are open to the public for ninety-minute tours by the Berlin Underground Association.

18 Gerda Drews, interview, 2014, courtesy of Elinor Florence's Wartime Wednesdays.

19 Ursula von Kardorff, *Diary of a Nightmare: Berlin 1942–1945* (Rupert Hart-Davis, 1965), pp. 91–2.

20 Christabel Bielenberg, *The Past Is Myself* (Chatto & Windus, 1968), p. 127.

21 James Hudson, *There and Back Again: A Navigator's Story* (Tucann Books, 2001), pp. 143–50.

22 Zaloga, *Operation Pointblank 1944*, op. cit., pp. 84–9.

23 Arthur William Doubleday, RAAF, interview, Australian War Memorial.

24 Wg Cdr F. Lord and Flt Lt P. Fox, 'The Nuremberg Raid', *South African Military History Journal*, Vol. 4/3 (June 1978).

25 Ibid.

26 The best account is Martin Middlebrook, *The Nuremberg Raid: 3–31 March 1944* (Allen Lane, 1973).

27 Peter Gray, 'Caen – the Martyred City', in Buckley (ed.), *The Normandy Campaign 1944*, op. cit., p. 162; Delve, *D-Day: The Air Battle*, op. cit., states 63,609 tons (p. 55), whereas Veeder, *An Evaluation of the Aerial Interdiction Campaign*, op. cit., states totals of 29,019 sorties, with 75,433 tons of bombs dropped.

28 Air Chief Marshal Sir Arthur Harris, *Bomber Offensive* (Collins, 1947), pp. 203–4.

29 Ibid., p. 266.

30 Wireless Operator/Air Gunner Bertie 'Butch' Lewis, interview, op. cit.

31 Hampden 4,000 pounds, Wellington 4,500 pounds.

32 Clostermann, *The Big Show*, op. cit., p. 148.

33 Alanbrooke, *War Diaries, 1939–1945*, op. cit., p. 543, entries for 2 and 3 May 1944.

34 Cited in Veeder, *An Evaluation of the Aerial Interdiction Campaign*, op. cit., p. 30.

35 Clostermann, *The Big Show*, op. cit., p. 147.

36 Directive by the Supreme Commander to USSTAF and Bomber Command for Support of Overlord during the preparatory period, 17 April 1944, cited in Veeder, *An Evaluation of the Aerial Interdiction Campaign*, op. cit., pp. 14–15.

37 Crookenden and Crowley-Milling, 'Planning the Operation', *Overlord 1944*, op. cit., p. 35.

38 Ibid., p. 33.

39 Scott, *Typhoon Pilot*, op. cit., p. 101.

40 Figures calculated from naval-history.net.

41 Wilbur R. Richardson, interview, Planes of Fame Air Museum, Chino, California, 1984, where Richardson worked as a ground volunteer each Saturday.

42 Fortier, *An Ace of the Eighth*, op. cit., pp. 190–2.

43 Franklin L. Betz, interview courtesy of 329th Bomb Group Archives.

44 Fortier, *An Ace of the Eighth*, op. cit., pp. 190–2.

16. Fortitude, FUSAG and France

1   Sun Tzu, *The Art of War* (Oxford University Press, 1963), p. 66.

2   Jane Fawcett (née Hughes), interviews, Bletchley, September 1997 and June 2004. I was most sad to read of the death of this sparkling, formidable and seemingly indestructible lady; see obituary, *Daily Telegraph*, 25 May 2016.

3   Ibid.

4   Richard Townshend Bickers, *Air War Normandy* (Leo Cooper, 1994), p. 43.

5   Ralph Bennett, *Ultra in the West: The Normandy Campaign 1944–45* (Hutchinson, 1979), p. 15.

6   Ibid., p. 58.

7   The Public Record Office (PRO) is now The National Archives (TNA), located at Kew in Surrey; Bletchley Park has been open to the public since 1993.

8   T. L. Cubbage, 'The Success of Operation Fortitude: Hesketh's History of Strategic Deception', *Intelligence and National Security*, Vol. 2/3 (1987), pp. 327–46.

9   Anthony Cave Brown, *Bodyguard of Lies* (HarperCollins, 1975).

10 David Kahn, *Hitler's Spies: German Military Intelligence in WWII* (Macmillan, 1978), p. 493.

11 Michael Howard, *Intelligence in the Second World War, Vol. 5: Strategic Deception* (HMSO, 1990), pp. 115, 168; Bennett, *Ultra in the West*, op. cit., p. 53; this was Enigma signal KV 5792.

12 Of the real forty-five divisions, twenty-three were British and Canadian, twenty American divisions, one Free French and one Polish.

13 Roger Hesketh, *Fortitude: The D-Day Deception Plan* (Overlook, 2000), p. 244.

14 Sir John Masterman, *The Double-Cross System in the War of 1939 to 1945* (Yale University Press, 1972), p. 156.

15 Hein Severloh, *WN 62: A German Soldier's Memories of the Defense of Omaha Beach*, trans. Robert R. Wolf (HEK Creativ Verlag, 2015), p. 84.

16 Juliet Gardiner, *D-Day: Those Who Were There* (Collins & Brown, 1994), p. 121.

17 Maj. Ernest S. Tavares, Jr, USAF, *Operation Fortitude: The Closed Loop D-Day Deception Plan* (Research Report for the Air Command & Staff College, Maxwell AFB, 2001), p. 29.

18 Gardiner, *D-Day*, op. cit., pp. 76–7.

19 Ibid., p. 76.

20 Ray Marshall, interview, 2004, courtesy of the Royal Artillery Firepower Museum Archives.

21 Expanded from the force used in the Western Desert and commanded by Lt Col David Strangeways, 'R' Force fielded scout cars; vehicles equipped with loud speakers to broadcast the sounds of tanks; Royal Engineers camouflage units; and No. 5 Wireless Group which could simulate the radio traffic of an army corps.

22 Gardiner, *D-Day*, op. cit., p. 74.

23 John Emery, interview, op. cit.

24 M. E. Clifton James, *I Was Monty's Double* (Rider & Co./Popular Book Club, 1957).

25 ETHINT P-038, Genlt Praun, 'German Radio Intelligence' (1950), Ref. A56970.

26 The National Archives (TNA): ADM 1–27186, 'Review of Security of Naval Codes and Cyphers, Sept 1939–May 1945' (Naval Signals Division, Nov. 1945), pp. 84–5; see also Peter Matthews, *SIGINT: The Secret History of Signals Intelligence 191–-45* (History Press, 2013).

27 R. A. Ratcliff, *Delusions of Intelligence: Enigma, Ultra, and the End of Secure Ciphers* (Cambridge University Press), p. 46.

28 ETHINT B-675, Obst. Staubwasser, 'Army Group B Intelligence Estimate, 1 Jun 1944' (1947).

29 ETHINT P-038, Praun, 'German Radio Intelligence', op. cit.

30 Walter Schellenberg, *The Schellenberg Memoirs: Memoirs of Hitler's Spymaster* (André Deutsch, 1956), p. 418.

31 F. P. Pickering, 'Notes on Field Interrogation of Various German Army and Air Force SIGINT Personnel, Berchtesgaden, 18–20 May, 1945' (NARA RG 457, Entry P-4/Box 1/NR 7419/TICOM IF-5 Declassified 18 Jan. 2012), and 'Notes on Interrogation of Obstlt. Friedrich' (NARA/TICOM 1–13, 16 June 1945, Declassified 18 Jan. 2012).

32 Robert Gerwarth, *Hitler's Hangman: The Life of Heydrich* (Yale University Press, 2011).

33 Horst Boog, 'A Luftwaffe View of the Intelligence War', *Intelligence and National Security*, Vol. 5/2 (April 1990).

34 Schellenberg, *Schellenberg Memoirs*, op. cit., p. 418.

35 Kenneth J. Campbell, 'Walter Schellenberg: SD Chief', *American Intelligence Journal*, Vol. 25/2 (Winter 2007–8), pp. 88–94; Reinhard R. Doerries (ed.), *Hitler's Last Chief of Foreign Intelligence: Allied Interrogations of Walter Schellenberg* (Frank Cass, 2003).

36 Thaddeus Holt, *The Deceivers: Allied Military Deception in the Second World War* (Weidenfeld & Nicolson, 2004), pp. 218, 270.

37 Kenneth J. Campbell, 'Gen. Erich Fellgiebel: Master of Communications Intelligence', *National Intelligence Journal*, Vol. 1/1 (2009), pp. 43–63.

38 Boog, 'A Luftwaffe View of the Intelligence War', op. cit.

39 Ibid.

40 Ben Macintyre, *Operation Mincemeat* (Bloomsbury, 2010), Kindle, pp. 4201–46. Roenne was married to the extraordinarily well-connected Ursula von Bülow, of the very old aristocratic family that had produced generations of writers, scholars, statesmen and generals. There is circumstantial evidence that Roenne possibly suspected he was submitting inflated Allied data and false locations, but that his strong Christian ethics were guiding him to subvert Hitler's regime; he was another who perished in the aftermath of the Stauffenberg Plot; see also David Johnson, *Righteous Deception: German Officers Against Hitler* (Praeger, 2001).

41 My thanks to 'German Intelligence on Operation Overlord', Christos Military and Intelligence Corner (22 June 2012), courtesy of chris.intelblog@yahoo.com.

42 Much of avenue Foch was occupied by German headquarters: the *Kommandantur* was at No. 72; SD Signals occupied No. 78; other SD departments were at Nos. 60, 77 and 83.

43   Olivier Wieviorka, *The French Resistance* (Harvard University Press, 2016), p. 435.

44   David Pryce-Jones, *Paris in the Third Reich* (Collins, 1981).

45   Philip W. Blood, *Hitler's Bandit Hunters: The SS and the Nazi Occupation of Europe* (Potomac Books, 2006).

46   'Der Militärbefehlshaber in Frankreich, 1a Nr.558/44 g.Kdos v.12.2.44. Betr.: Banden-und Sabotagebekämfung' (BA-MA Freiburg, RW 35/551); Peter Lieb, *Konventioneller Krieg oder Weltanschauungskrieg? Kriegführung und Partisanenbekämpfung in Frankreich 1943–44* (Oldenbourg, 2007).

47   'Geheime Kommandosache [Secret Commando Operation], 12 February 1944' (BA-MA Freiburg, RW35/551).

48   Gaël Eismann, *Hôtel Majestic: Ordre et sécurité en France occupée, 1940–1944* (Editions Tallandier, 2010), pp. 431–7.

49   Allan Mitchell, *Nazi Paris: The History of an Occupation, 1940–1944* (Berghahn, 2008), p. 159.

50   This was Enigma signal KV 7502. Perrault, *Le Secret du Jour J*, op. cit., pp. 184–5; Bennett, *Ultra in the West*, op. cit., p. 51.

51   F. H. Hinsley et al., *British Intelligence in the Second World War*, Vol. 3, Part 2 (HMSO, 1988), p. 54.

52   Aurélie Luneau, *Radio Londres, 1940–1944: Les voix de la liberté* (Librairie Académique Perrin, 2005). The significance of the Verlaine poem was first identified in an SD/*Abwehr* report of 14 October 1943, filed after the interrogation of two captured *résistants*.

53   Ralph-Georg Reuth, *Rommel: The End of a Legend* (Haus, 2006), p. 174.

54   *Les Français parlent aux Français* broadcast nightly to France between 6 September 1940 and 22 November 1944. Although Buckmaster later claimed credit for the idea, the concept of inserting messages to Resistance groups in BBC broadcasts can be traced to Georges Bégué, the first SOE agent to land on French soil.

55   Hubert Verneret, *Que faisiez-vous au temps chaud?: Journal de guerre d'un adolescent* (Éditions Desvignes, 1972), English edn, *Teenage Resistance Fighter* (Casemate, 2017), p. 24.

56   Franck Bauer, interview, Paris, June 1994. I was sad to read of Bauer's death whilst writing this book; the last BBC wartime announcer, he died aged ninety-nine in April 2018.

57   Marie-Josèphe Bonnet (ed.), *Les Voix de la Normande combattante – Été 1944* (Éditions Ouest-France, 2010).

58   Richard Collier, *Ten Thousand Eyes* (Collins, 1958), p. 256.

59   André Heintz, interview, Caen, June 1994.

60   Paddy Ashdown, *The Cruel Victory: The French Resistance, D-Day and the Battle for the Vercors 1944* (Collins, 2014), p. 172.

61   The immediate results were fifty-two locomotives were destroyed on 6 June and railway lines in south-eastern France cut in more than five hundred places, isolating Normandy from 7 June (1965 report, Counter-insurgency Information Analysis Center). Likewise, the telephone network in the invasion area was put out of order. From around 20 June most French railways were rendered inoperable, though the Marseilles–Lyon line through the Rhône Valley was kept open

despite the efforts of the Resistance. While German reserves did reach the *Normandiefront*, they did so with significant delays. The overall French assessment was that the Resistance delayed up to twelve divisions for eight to fifteen days.

62 Jean Dacier, *Ceux du Maquis* (Arthaud, 1945), p. 79, cited in Ashdown, *The Cruel Victory*, op. cit., p. 172.

63 Collier, *Ten Thousand Eyes*, op. cit., p. 257.

64 Caroline Bannock and James Meikle, 'D-Day: Memories from the Frontline', *Guardian*, 5 June 2014.

65 Jean-Louis Crémieux-Brilhac, interview, Paris, June 1994.

66 This misquotes Verlaine slightly, for in the original the poet wrote '*Blessant mon coeur*' (Wound my heart). The story of the BBC coded messages is taught to all French schoolchildren today.

67 Carell, *Invasion*, op. cit., pp. 27–9; Ryan, *The Longest Day*, op. cit., pp. 31–6.

68 Perrault, *Le Secret du Jour J*, op. cit., pp. 155–60.

69 Kahn, *Hitler's Spies*, op. cit., pp. 510–11.

70 Maurice Buckmaster, *They Fought Alone: The True Story of SOE's Agents in Wartime France* (Odhams, 1958), cited in Edward Stourton, *Auntie's War: The BBC During the 2nd World War* (Doubleday, 2017), p. 356

71 ETHINT-1, 'Interrogation of Gen. Warlimont by Maj. Ken Hechler' (19–20 July 1945). Warlimont was referring to the transfer of the 91st *Luftlande* Division, several armoured battalions and anti-tank battalions to the Cotentin peninsula and for the assembly by OKW of the Panzer Lehr Division. In ETHINT B-675, 'Oberst Staubwasser's Army Group B Intelligence Estimate, 1 Jun 1944', it is claimed the German High Command were convinced that Normandy would be the site of Allied landings in April or May 1944; both NARA, Maryland. See also The National Archives (TNA): TICOM report I-143, 'Interrogation of Genobst. Jodl' (27 September 1945), p. 3.

72 The National Archives (TNA): TICOM report I-143, 'Interrogation of Genobst. Jodl' (27 September 1945), p. 3.

73 Not to be confused with Asnières-sur-Mer behind Juno Beach.

74 The National Archives (TNA): TICOM report I-109, 'Translation of a Report by Lt. Ludwig' (24 September 1945), pp. 15–18.

75 Ibid.

76 Ibid.

77 Ibid., p. 18.

78 Kahn, *Hitler's Spies*, op. cit., p. 499.

79 E. R. Hooton, *Eagle in Flames: The Fall of the Luftwaffe* (Weidenfeld & Nicolson, 1997), p. 284. This was the P-47 flown by 2nd Lt William E. Roach of 358th Squadron (355th Fighter Group, 8th Air Force). Roach, on his third mission of 7 November 1943, became disoriented in poor weather, spotted an airfield, landed, taxied after a vehicle and shut down; only then did he realise the people surrounding the plane wore the wrong uniforms; the US Signal Corps photo #204141 shows its recapture by the US 809th TD Battalion at Göttingen /Bad Worlshofen on 8 April 1945.

80   Chester Wilmot, *The Struggle for Europe* (Collins, 1952), p. 246; Perrault, *Le Secret du Jour J*, op. cit., pp. 184–5.

81   Ibid., p. 150.

82   The National Archives (TNA): Enigma signal KV 3242, dated 8 May 1944, from Luftflotte 3, Ref. HW (Intercepted German Cipher Messages) 11/2781; Bennett, *Ultra in the West*, op. cit., p. 51.

83   The National Archives (TNA): Enigma signal KV 3763, dated 8 May, Ref. HW (Intercepted German Cipher Messages) 11/2784; Bennett, *Ultra in the West*, op. cit., pp. 50–1.

84   Severloh, *WN 62*, op. cit., p. 23.

17. The Giants

1   Dyson, *Tank Twins*, op. cit., p. 18.

2   Woollcombe, *Lion Rampant*, op. cit., p. 107.

3   Lovat, *March Past*, op. cit.

4   Montgomery, *Memoirs*, op. cit., pp. 209–10.

5   Colonel Red Reeder, *Born at Reveille: Memoirs of a Son of West Point* (Duell, Sloan & Pearce, 1965), Kindle, p. 4307.

6   Moorhead, *Eclipse*, op. cit., pp. 83–4.

7   https://www.youtube.com/watch?v=cHi7LvjVxZg.

8   I was given a copy of Ike's inspiring Sandhurst speech when I graduated from there, thirty-five years later, in 1979; it has travelled well across the years: '*You young men have this war to win. It is small unit leadership that is going to win the ground battle, and that battle must be won before that enemy of ours is finally crushed. You must know every single one of your men. It is not enough that you are the best soldier in that unit, that you are the strongest, the toughest, the most durable, and the best equipped technically. You must be their leader, their father, their mentor, even if you are half their age. You must understand their problems. You must keep them out of trouble. If they get in trouble, you must be the one to go to their rescue. Then you will be doing your duty and you will be worthy of the traditions of this great school and of your great country. To each one of you I wish Godspeed and Good Luck.*'

9   *Life, 60th Anniversary D-Day Commemorative Issue* (LIFE, 2004).

10   Harold Akridge, interview courtesy of National D-Day Museum, New Orleans.

11   Walsh, 'D-Day Reflections from a Soldier', op. cit.

12   Lewis Goodwin, interview, Portsmouth, 1994.

13   Ramsay, *The Year of D-Day*, op. cit., p. 80.

14   Churchill dealt with the issue of his going to Normandy at length in *The Second World War, Vol. 5*, op. cit., pp. 546–51.

15   Courtesy of Nicholas de Rothschild, whose home, Exbury House, was then HMS *Mastodon*.

16   Lund and Ludlam, *The War of the Landing Craft*, op. cit., p. 148.

17   Norman Green, interview cited in Shaw and Shaw, *We Remember D-Day*, op. cit., p. 44.

18 Lt Harold B. Sherwood Jr, USNR, interview, Washington DC, 1984.

19 Patton immediately confided to his own diary that for his blatant mistruth 'the lightning did not strike me'; Horne and Montgomery, *Monty 1944–45*, op. cit., p. 106.

20 Trevor Hart-Dyke, *Normandy to Arnhem: A Story of the Infantry* (4/Yorks Volunteers, 1966), p. 1.

21 Cited in Hastings, *Overlord*, op. cit., p. 47.

22 Forty, *D-Day Dorset*, op. cit., p. 85.

23 Tim Saunders, *Commandos and Rangers: D-Day Operations* (Pen & Sword, 2010), Kindle, p. 3042.

24 Tracy Craggs, 'An "Unspectacular" War? Reconstructing the History of the 2nd Battalion East Yorkshire Regiment during the Second World War' (PhD thesis, University of Sheffield, 2007), pp. 51–2.

25 Thomas G. Finigan, interview, 1993, Imperial War Museum Sound Archive, ref. 12989.

26 William Douglas Home, *Sins of Commission* (Michael Russell, 1985), p. 40.

27 The National Archives (TNA): ADM 1/29985: '2nd Bn Essex Regiment Sea Loading Accident'.

28 Donald S. Vaughan, 79th Armoured Division, interview cited in Jon E. Lewis (ed.), *D-Day as They Saw It: The Story of the Battle by Those Who Were There* (Robinson Publishing, 2004), p. 96.

29 Edward Wallace, interview cited in Bailey, *Forgotten Voices*, op. cit.

30 Vernon Church, interview, 2004, courtesy of BBC, WW2 People's War, op. cit.

31 Maj. Ellis 'Dixie' Dean, '13th Battalion The Parachute Regiment: Luard's Own' (unpublished memoir), courtesy of pegasusarchive.org.

32 William Cockburn, interview, 2004, courtesy of BBC, WW2 People's War, op. cit.

33 Charles R. Cawthon, *Other Clay. A Remembrance of the World War II Infantry* (University of Nebraska Press, 2004), p.33

34 2nd Lt Wesley R. Ross, 'Essayons – Journey With the Combat Engineers in World War II' (unpublished), pp. 19, 32, 35, courtesy of 6th Corps Combat Engineers Association.

35 Interviews by Frank Whelan, *The Morning Call*, 29 May 1994 and 6 June 2004.

36 Stephen E. Ambrose, *D-Day*, op. cit., p. 140.

37 Ramsay, *The Year of D-Day*, op. cit., p. 63. This resulted in the sinking of *MTB-708* on 5 May.

38 Marcus Cunliffe, *History of the Royal Warwickshire Regiment 1919–1955* (William Clowes, 1956), p. 121.

39 J. L. Moulton, *Haste to the Battle: A Marine Commando at War* (Cassell, 1963), p. 56.

40 Baron, *From the City, From the Plough*, op. cit., p. 77.

41 Mike McKinney, interview, op. cit.

42 Harry Cooper, interview, op. cit. USS *Henrico*, in company with the USS *Samuel Chase* and HMS *Empire Anvil*, six LCI(L)s, six LSTs, and ninety-seven smaller craft formed Assault Group 'O-1'.

43   Capa transferred to the USS *Samuel Chase* for his passage across the Channel. Fuller's *The Big Red One* was released in 1980; Capa related his view of D-Day in his autobiography, *Slightly Out of Focus* (Henry Holt, 1947).

44   Geoff Ziezulewicz, '1st Infantry Division Led Assault on D-Day: Youngest "Big Red One" GI at Normandy Remembers Pivotal Day', *Stars and Stripes*, 28 August 2006. Argenzio was born on 8 June 1927 and died in 2010; thus he may have been the youngest soldier of any nation fighting on D-Day.

45   *LCI(Large) 35* first proceeded to Penarth, south Wales, and was originally assigned to Force 'U', before being switched to Force 'S' in Newhaven; Stanley Galik archives, courtesy of galik.com website.

46   Kenneth P. Baxter, MC, memoir, Warren Tute Collection, D-Day Museum, Portsmouth and National Army Museum.

47   Sub-Lt (later Capt.) Michael Hugh Hutton, RN, interview, Portsmouth, 1994. Captain Hutton died in 2003.

48   Swaab, *Field of Fire*, op. cit., p. 2892.

49   Memoirs of Peter Mitchell, courtesy of David Mitchell, op. cit.

50   Moorhead, *Eclipse*, op. cit., pp. 88–9.

51   Lewis E. Johnston of Air Mobility Command Museum, Delaware, interview, 2013.

52   David Irving, *The Trail of the Fox* (Weidenfeld & Nicolson, 1977), pp. 356–8. The letter was a central feature of the 2014 ITV drama-documentary *If I Don't Come Home: D-Day Letters*; see obituary, *Daily Telegraph*, 3 March 2009.

53   Moorhead, *Eclipse*, op. cit., pp. 85, 90.

54   'HMS *Glenearn*', combinedops.com.

55   Craggs, 'An "Unspectacular" War?', op. cit., p. 117.

56   Lt George (Jimmy) Green, 551st Landing Craft Assault (LCA) Flotilla and SS *Empire Javelin,* interview, Help for Heroes Bicycle Battlefield Tour of Normandy, 2008; he died in 2011.

57   Charles Shaeff, interview courtesy of *Los Angeles Times*, 5 June 2014, National D-Day Memorial, Bedford, Virginia, and VMI interview, February 2005; Shaeff died in March 2017.

58   Obituary for John 'Frank' Dulligan, died 2 October 1985, Shrewsbury, Massachusetts, courtesy of Dulligan family; his letter was cited by Ryan, *The Longest Day*, op. cit., p. 71.

59   'Biography of Hyam Haas', courtesy of Justin Army Oral History Center.

60   Memoirs of Peter Mitchell, courtesy of David Mitchell, op. cit.

61   Alan Johnson, interview courtesy of the Stockport and District NVA (Normandy Veterans Association).

62   'Biography of Hyam Haas', op. cit.

63   Alan Wellington, interview, 2006, via Age Concern, Shrewsbury. SS *City of Canterbury* delivered GIs to Omaha on D+1.

64   Dennis Chaffer, interview, Kirklees, West Yorkshire, 1994.

65   Harold Addie, interview courtesy of the Stockport and District NVA (Normandy Veterans Association).

66   Dick Boustred, interview cited in Shaw and Shaw, *We Remember D-Day*, op. cit., p. 115.

67   James Douglas, interview, Falkirk, 1994. Based at RAF Tangmere, 126 (Canadian) Wing was part of No. 83 in Coningham's 2nd TAF. Douglas eventually helped establish the airstrip at Bény-sur-Mer, operational on 16 June, ten days after he had landed.

68   Harry Farrar, interview, 2004, courtesy of BBC, WW2 People's War, op. cit.

69   Virginia Fraser, 'Lord Lovat: He Was a Giant Among Giants on D-Day', *Daily Telegraph*, 6 June 2014.

18. Weathermen

1   Moorhead, *Eclipse*, op. cit., p. 85.

2   Ryan, *The Longest Day*, op. cit., pp. 62–3.

3   James R. Fleming, 'Sverre Petterssen and the Contentious (and Momentous) Weather Forecasts for D-Day', *Endeavour*, Vol. 28/2 (June 2004).

4   Lawrence Hogben, interview, France, June 1994, and obituary, *Daily Telegraph*, 4 March 2015.

5   Stagg (1900–75) was knighted in 1954 and published his own account in *Forecast for Overlord* (Ian Allan, 1971).

6   Charles R. Cawthon, *Other Clay. A Remembrance of the World War II Infantry* (University Press of Colorado, 1990), p. 45.

7   Ramsay, *The Year of D-Day*, op. cit., pp. 78–80.

8   Jim Booth, interview, June 1994, via Peter Shand-Kydd, X-Craft Association. Specifically designed to attack the battleship *Tirpitz* lurking in her Norwegian fjords, X-Craft were offered to the USN to help direct their D-Day flotillas, who nevertheless declined them. Their use as navigation beacons off Juno and Sword on D-Day, Operation Gambit, was considered a huge triumph and more than justified their development.

9   David Keys, 'Concrete Traces Reveal Eisenhower's D-Day HQ: Historians Have Found the Site of the Allies' Wartime Command Post in a Hampshire Wood', *Independent*, 13 May 1994.

10   Churchill, *Second World War, Vol. 5*, op. cit., pp. 518–21.

11   Alanbrooke, *War Diaries, 1939–1945*, op. cit., p. 515.

12   Lawrence Hogben, interview, op. cit.

13   Audric, *The Meteorological Office Dunstable*, op. cit.

14   Sverre Petterssen, *Weathering the Storm: Sverre Petterssen, the D-Day Forecast and the Rise of Modern Meteorology*, ed. J. R. Fleming (American Meteorological Society, 2001).

15   Bradley, *A Soldier's Story*, op. cit., p. 253.

16   John Cox, *Storm Watchers: The Turbulent History of Weather Prediction from Franklin's Kite to El Niño* (Wiley, 2002).

17   Ramsay, *The Year of D-Day*, op. cit., p. 82.

18   Eisenhower, *Crusade in Europe*, op. cit., p. 274.

19   Dr Irving P. Krick, *The Role of Caltech Meteorology in the D-Day Forecast* (American Meteorological Society, 1984).

20   Neillands and De Normann, *D-Day 1944*, op. cit., p. 58.

21   Ramsay, *The Year of D-Day*, op. cit., p. 82.

22   John Winton, *Freedom's Battle, Vol. 1: The War at Sea 1939–45* (Hutchinson, 1967), p. 408.

23   Leslie Hasker, interview, June 2005, courtesy of BBC, WW2 People's War, op. cit.

24   Eisenhower, *Crusade in Europe*, op. cit., pp. 274–7.

25   Joe McCabe, 'How Blacksod Lighthouse Changed the Course of the Second World War', *Irish Independent*, 1 June 2014.

26   Lawrence Hogben, interview, op. cit.

27   Alan G. Kirk, 'Report of Commander, Western Task Force', 15 September 1944 (NARA), p. 18.

28   Deutsche Wetter Dienst (DWD) Meteorological Library, Offenbach, 4 June 2014.

29   Prof. Werner Schwerdtfeger, 'The Last Two Years of Z W G, Parts 1 and 2', *Weather: Journal of the Royal Meteorological Society*, Vols. 41/4 and 5 (April and May 1986).

30   Robert Kershaw explores this mismatch in *D-Day: Piercing the Atlantic Wall*, op. cit., pp. 88–9.

31   Correspondence, *London Review of Books*, Vol. 16, Nos. 12–17 (23 June–8 September 1994).

32   Tempelhof (1907–85) was a *Kriegsakademie* graduate who had also served with 21 Panzer Division and had an English wife.

33   Hayn, *Die Invasion*, op. cit., p. 16.

34   Gen. Eberhard Wagemann, interview, Hamburg, June 1984. Wagemann (1918–2010) served with 22 Panzer Division in Normandy and later rose to major general in the *Bundeswehr* and was commandant of its *Führungsakademie*, 1974–7, where he used the example of Feuchtinger's absence as an illustration of 'catastrophic command'.

35   Hans von Luck, *Panzer Commander* (Praeger, 1989), Kindle, p. 136.

36   Ramsay, *The Year of D-Day*, op. cit., p. 83.

37   Lawrence Hogben, interview, op. cit. He left the room before the decision was made.

38   Eisenhower, *Crusade in Europe*, op. cit., p. 275. No one actually recorded those present or the text of Ike's actual words to confirm Overlord, although 'OK, let's go' seems to be the consensus. The various eyewitness accounts state between eleven and fourteen were present at the final Southwick 5 June conference, but even the time was variously recorded as 4, 4.15 and 4.30 a.m. See Tim Rives, '"OK, We'll Go": Just What Did Ike Say When He Launched the D-day Invasion 70 Years Ago?', *Prologue*, Spring 2014.

39   Alanbrooke, *War Diaries 1939–1945*, op. cit., p. 554.

40   Ramsay, *The Year of D-Day*, op. cit., p. 83.

41   Martin Gilbert, *Road to Victory: Winston S. Churchill*, Vol. 7 (Heinemann, 1986), p. 794.

42   Charles R. Cawthon, *Other Clay*, op cit., p. 46.

43   Cited in Rives, '"OK, We'll Go"', op. cit.

44   John Ross, *Forecast for D-Day: And the Weatherman Behind Ike's Greatest Gamble* (Lyons Press, 2014).

45   Lawrence Hogben, interview, op. cit.

46 Zoe Jackson, Stephen Grey, Thomas Adcock, Paul Taylor and Jean-Raymond Bidlot, 'The Waves at the Mulberry Harbours', *Journal of Ocean Engineering and Maritime Energy*, Vol. 3/1 (2017), pp. 185–92.

47 Wilmot, *Struggle for Europe*, op. cit., p. 246.

48 Jim Booth, interview, op. cit.

19. The Great Armada

1   David Holbrook, *Flesh Wounds* (Methuen, 1966), pp. 118–19.

2   Courtesy of Norfolk and Suffolk Aviation Museum, Bungay, www.aviation-museum.net. Varner's thirty-first and last mission was on 10 August 1944, when *Call Me Later* bombed a railroad bridge at Joigny; afterwards, the crew returned to America aboard RMS *Aquitania* with 5,000 German prisoners and 2,000 US wounded.

3   Ibid.

4   Ibid.

5   Lt Russell Chandler, Jr, interview, op. cit.

6   SSgt Arthur Een, memoir cited in Lew Johnston, 'Troop Carrier D-Day Flights', https://amcmuseum.org/history/troop-carrier-d-day-flights/.

7   Thorne 'Douglas Gordon (Part 1): Bail Out or Glide for England', *Canadian Legion Magazine*, op cit.

8   Personal log book, Flight Lt Tony Cooper, No. 64 Sqn, RAF Museum Archives, Hendon.

9   Clostermann, *The Big Show*, op. cit., p. 161.

10 Clarence E. 'Bud' Anderson, *To Fly and Fight: Memoirs of a Triple Ace* (Pacifica Military History, 2001).

11 Richard P. Hallion, *The US Army Air Forces in World War II: D-Day 1944: Air Power Over the Normandy Beaches and Beyond* (Air Force History & Museums Program, 1994), p. 8.

12 Vogel, memoir, op. cit.

13 Hudson, *There and Back Again*, op. cit., p. 176. James Hudson died in 2013.

14 Jim Frolking flew fifty-two combat missions with the 479th Fighter Group: fifty in the P-38 and two in P-51s. He was shot down by flak on 7 October 1944, over the Netherlands; the Dutch underground rescued him and advancing Canadian troops liberated him a few weeks later. 'Normandy to the Netherlands: A Fighter Pilot's View', talk to Lakewood Historical Society, Ohio, 2018.

15 Richard Payne, interview, Portsmouth, June 1994.

16 Brenda McBryde, interview, September 1997, via Col. John Watts, MC.

17 John Grant, interview, Portsmouth, June 2004.

18 'D-Day, 70 Years On: "We Watched an American Destroyer Slowly Demolished by Shore Batteries"', *Observer*, 1 June 2014.

19 Garry Johnson and Christopher Dunphie, *Brightly Shone the Dawn: Some Experiences of the Invasion of Normandy* (Frederick Warne, 1980), p. 56.

20 Max Hastings, *Bomber Command* (Michael Joseph, 1979), Appendix A, p. 354.

21 Lt Russell Chandler, Jr, interview, op. cit.

22 James L. Bass, *Fait Accompli: A Historical Account of the 457th Bomb Group* (JLB Publications, 1995).

23 Frank L. Betz and Kenneth H. Cassens (eds), *379th Bombardment Group (H) Anthology, Nov. 1942–July 1945* (Turner Publishing, 2000).

24 Charles H. Freudenthal, *A History of the 489th Bomb Group* (American Spirit Graphics, 1989).

25 Henry Tarcza, interview courtesy of 95th Bomb Group Memorials Foundation.

26 Birdie Schmidt, *Reminiscences about the ARC Aeroclub at Wendling*, op. cit.

27 Zdeněk Hurt, *Czechs in the RAF* (Red Kite Books, 2004).

28 The ten minesweepers were HMSs *Albury, Halcyon, Kellett, Lydd, Pangbourne, Ross, Salamander, Saltash, Speedwell* and *Sutton*, mostly members of the 4th Minesweeping Flotilla; the eleven requisitioned steamers at Dunkirk and D-Day were *Biarritz, Brigadier, Canterbury, Dinard, Lady of Mann, Maid of Orleans, Royal Ulsterman, Prague, St Julien, Princess Maude* and *Ben-my-Chree* (author's research).

29 Author's research.

30 Knight Commander of the Bath (KCB) 1940; Knight Commander of the British Empire (KBE) 1944. He would have undoubtedly become Viscount Ramsay in the New Year's Honours List of 1946, had he not been tragically killed in an air crash at Toussus-le-Noble, France, on 2 January 1945.

31 'British West European Force' (BWEF) was soon changed to the more pleasing 'British Liberation Army' (BLA).

32 Author's archive.

33 Ludovic Kennedy, *On My Way to the Club* (Collins, 1989).

34 Lund and Ludlam, *War of the Landing Craft*, op. cit., pp. 167–9.

35 Author's archive.

36 Sir Alexander Stanier, Bt, interview, Shropshire, 1984.

37 Tom Bigland, interview, Shrewsbury, 1984.

38 David Verghese, 'Operation Neptune: The Minesweeping Operations, 5–6 June 1944', Minewarfare and Clearance Diving Officers' Association (MCDOA), http://www.mcdoa.org.uk/operation_neptune_minesweeping.htm.

39 Historical Section, Commander US Naval Forces Europe (OMNAVEU), *Administrative History of US Naval Forces in Europe, 1940–1946, Vol. 5: The Invasion of Normandy: Operation Neptune* (London, 1946), pp. 301–37.

40 Ramsay, *The Year of D-Day*, op. cit., entry for 24 March 1944, p. 48.

41 Austin Prosser, interview, Lechlade, 2002, via Sub-Lt Peter Miles, RNVR, Landing Craft Association.

42 Charles Lilly, 'Landing in Normandy', undated memoir courtesy of ww2lct.org.

43 Stan Hough, interview, 2004, courtesy of BBC, WW2 People's War, op. cit.

44 *LCT-2428* lies in Bracklesham Bay, her cargo of tanks and bulldozers littering the seabed, providing much interest to local diving clubs.

45 Moorhead, *Eclipse*, op. cit., pp. 93–5.

46 Bill Millin, interviews, op. cit.

47 Capt. Eric W. Bush (1899–1985) archive, Liddell Hart Centre for Military Archives, King's College London.

48 Courtesy of www.wpepe.com/dday.

49 Field Marshal the Lord Bramall, interview, Chalke Valley History Festival, July 2016.

50 Charles H. Freudenthal, *History of the 489th Bomb Group*, (self-published, 1989).

51 Edward Francis Wightman, diary, courtesy of Lynette Foster, née Wightman.

52 Bill O'Neill, 'D-Day as Seen from US *LCT-544*', 1994, memoir courtesy of ww2lct. org.

53 Vernon Scannell, in his autobiographical novel *Argument of Kings* (Robson, 1987), p. 145.

54 Bob Heath, interview, Orpington, 1994.

55 Joseph Alexander, memoir courtesy of ww2lct.org.

56 Thomas Carter, *Beachhead Normandy: An LCT's Odyssey* (Potomac Books, 2012), p. 78.

57 Other sources state these were *LCT(A)-2404* and *LCT(A)-2301*.

58 Ross, 'Essayons', op. cit., p. 41.

59 Stan Blacker, interview, 2002, via Sub-Lt Peter Miles, RNVR, Landing Craft Association, Lechlade.

60 Eric Brown, interview, 2002, via Sub-Lt Peter Miles, RNVR, Landing Craft Association, Lechlade.

61 Tony Lowndes, interview, 2002, via Sub-Lt Peter Miles, RNVR, Landing Craft Association, Lechlade.

62 Neillands and De Normann, *D-Day 1944*, op. cit., pp. 120–2.

63 Rev. Canon Mike Crooks, RN, interview courtesy of Portsmouth D-Day Story Museum Archives.

64 Sir John Ford, KCMG, MC, Newcastle, Staffordshire, 1999.

65 Rt Hon. Sir Stephen Brown, GBE, PC, interview aboard MV *Minerva*, Normandy, 6 June 2014.

66 Ryan, *The Longest Day*, op. cit., p. 99.

67 Symonds, *Neptune*, op. cit., p. 249.

68 Some sources give 121 RCN ships in Neptune; see Fraser McKee, 'Ships of the Royal Canadian Navy Present off Juno Beach on 6–7 June 1944', www.nautica-pedia.ca, and 'Canadian Participation on D-Day and in the Battle of Normandy', www.forces.gc.ca.

69 'D-Day: Canadian Troops Land in Normandy as Part of the Largest Invasion in History', courtesy of cbc.ca.

70 Alan Johnson, interview, 2002, via Sub-Lt Peter Miles, RNVR, Landing Craft Association, Lechlade.

71 Leslie Hasker, interview, op. cit.

72 Vice Admiral Sir Louis Le Bailly, interview, London, 1992.

73 Ronald Martin, interview, Imperial War Museum Sound Archive.

74 John Dennett, interview, 1994, courtesy of Wirral and Chester Branch of the NVA.

75 Gilchrist, *Don't Cry for Me*, op. cit., pp. 50–1.

76 Lund and Ludlam, *War of the Landing Craft*, op. cit., p. 168.

77 R. G. Watts, interview, 2003, courtesy of BBC, WW2 People's War.

78   Edward Francis Wightman, diary, op. cit.

79   Buster Brown, interview, op. cit.

80   Kennedy, *On My Way to the Club*, op. cit.

81   Ibid.

82   Peter Walker, interview, Portsmouth, June 1994.

83   *Historia*, No. 69 (1969); *39–45 Magazine*, No. 96 (1994).

84   Tadeusz Lesisz, interview, Bolton, 1985; see also obituary, *Independent*, 12 October 2009.

85   Franciszek Rumiński and Jan Stępek, interviews via Martin Stępek, courtesy of www. kresy-siberia.org.

20. Shells, Rockets and Flies

1   Carell, *Invasion*, op. cit., pp. 30–2.

2   Ibid.

3   Ibid., p. 39.

4   Ibid., pp. 80–1.

5   Rt Hon. Sir Stephen Brown, interview, op. cit.

6   Stan Hough, interview, op. cit.

7   Philip Webber, interview, Dewsbury, 1994.

8   Edward Francis Wightman, diary, op. cit.

9   Patrick Delaforce, *Monty's Ironsides* (Bounty Books, 1999), p. 30.

10   Alfred Lane, memoir courtesy of Royal Engineers Museum, Gillingham, Kent.

11   After Action Report, '15. Vorpostenflottille/2. Sicherungs-Division (Boulogne), 6. Juni, 1944', NARA.

12   In Kirk's Western Area: 324 warships (including 151 RN, 166 USN, 6 French, 1 Dutch); in Vian's Eastern sector, 348 naval vessels (306 RN, 30 USN, 3 French, 3 Polish, 3 Norwegian, 2 Greek and 1 Dutch).

13   Douglas Reeman, *D-Day 6th June 1944: A Personal Reminiscence* (Arrow, 1984), pp. 1–7. Reeman died in 2017, his obituary recording his possession of 'a chair from HMS *Victory* and a Nelsonian cannon, its muzzle trained permanently towards France'.

14   Thomas Nutter, interview, 2004, courtesy of BBC, WW2 People's War, op. cit.

15   Don Hunter, interview, HMS *Belfast*, Queen's Jubilee Pageant, June 2012.

16   29th Motor Torpedo Boat Flotilla and 31st and 32nd Minesweeping Flotillas.

17   Reeman, *D-Day 6th June 1944*, op cit., pp. 8–9.

18   Richard Llewellyn, interview, 1994, courtesy of Wirral and Chester Branch of the NVA.

19   Zaloga, *D-Day Fortifications*, op. cit., p. 38.

20   Stephen Barney, interview, aboard MV *Minerva*, Normandy, 6 June 2014.

21   Bud Taylor, interview, USS *Pennsylvania* Reunion, San Diego, California, 1998. Bud died in 2015.

22   Donald C. Derrah, personal war diary, USS *Shubrick* (DD-639), courtesy of ussshubrick.com; Thomas B. Allen, 'The Gallant Destroyers of D-Day', *Navy History Magazine*, Vol. 18/3 (June 2004).

23   Woodrow 'Woody' Derby, interview, USS *Nevada* Reunion, Burlingame, California, 1998.

24   Ryan, *The Longest Day*, op. cit., p. 186; Symonds, *Neptune*, op. cit., p. 265.

25   Logbook courtesy of Stanley R. Rane, Jr.

26   Air Commodore R. H. G. Weighill, CBE, DFC, interview, RAF Halton, 1984.

27   Symonds, *Neptune*, op. cit., p. 263.

28   Obituary, Air Marshal Sir Peter Wykeham, *Independent*, 28 February 1995.

29   Ernest Hemingway, 'Voyage to Victory', *Collier's*, 22 July 1944.

30   Samuel Eliot Morison, *History of US Naval Operations in World War II, Vol. XI: The Invasion of France and Germany 1944–1945* (Oxford University Press, 1957), p. 138.

31   Photographer Robert Capa memorably bent these rules, disembarked, took some pictures and then re-embarked. By contrast, BBC reporters, having trained extensively in their War Reporting Units after Exercise Spartan, were integrated into the assault units and allowed ashore, as were military photographers.

32   Hemingway, 'Voyage to Victory', op. cit.

33   Carter, *Beachhead Normandy*, op. cit., pp. 79–80.

34   Bradley, *A Soldier's Story*, op. cit., p. 252.

35   Ibid., p. 253. George Petty was one of the pioneer artists of the American pin-up, known for his paintings of skimpily clad women that appeared in *Esquire* magazine from 1933 until 1956.

36   Carter, *Beachhead Normandy*, op. cit., pp. 79–80.

37   'Biography of Hyam Haas', op. cit.

38   'D-Day, 70 Years On', op. cit.

39   Interview, Brigadier Robin McGarel-Groves, Hampshire, 1994; he died in 2014.

40   'D-Day, 70 Years On', op. cit.

41   Stephen Barney, interview, op. cit.

42   John Carey, *William Golding: The Man Who Wrote Lord of the Flies* (Faber & Faber, 2009), pp. 100–5; Peter Green, 'The Stranger from Within: William Golding: The Man Who Wrote *Lord of the Flies*', *New Republic*, 1 September 2010.

43   Rt Hon. Sir Stephen Brown, interview, op. cit.

44   Basil Heaton, interview, Shrewsbury, 1984; 'D-Day, 6 June 1944', memoir, Flintshire Record Office; see also obituary, *Daily Telegraph*, 29 May 2012.

45   James Matthew Weller, interview, National World War II Museum Oral History Program, New Orleans. Weller died in June 2017.

46   Fran Baker (ed.), *Hot Steel: The Story of the 58th Armored Field Artillery Battalion* (Delphi Books, 2014); 'After Action Report, 58th Field Artillery Battalion, 6 June 1944', NARA. The 58th lost nine officers and thirty-two enlisted men killed and wounded on D-Day, along with five M-7s, five half-tracks, four jeeps, three 6×6 trucks and two L-4 spotter planes.

47   John H. Glass, interview, 1992, courtesy of Musée des Épaves Sous-Marines du Débarquement, Port-en-Bessin.

48   Charles Hurlbut, interview, op. cit.

49   Sir Alexander Stanier, interview, op. cit.

21. Boats and Bugles

1   Scott, *Typhoon Pilot*, op. cit., pp. 110–11.

2   Sub-Lt W. B. Carter, *D-Day Landings* (Silent Books, 1993), p. 9.

3   *Omaha Beachhead* (War Dept., US Army Historical Division, Washington DC, September 1945), p. 38.

4   Maj. Thomas S. Dallas, Bn Executive, 'After Action Report, 1st Bn Command Group, 116th Infantry Regt, 29th Infantry Division, 19 June 1944', courtesy of www.dday-overlord.com.

5   Symonds, *Neptune*, op. cit., p. 229.

6   Charles Hurlbut, interview, op. cit.

7   Edwin 'Nobby Clarke', interview, 2004, courtesy of BBC, WW2 People's War, op. cit.

8   Samuel Eliot Morison, *History of United States Naval Operations in WWII, Vol. XI: The Invasion of France and Germany* (Little, Brown, 1957), pp. 170–1. With both the sinking of the *Corry* and the *Meredith* the official USN position was that a sea mine was the culprit, though in each case, all the documentary evidence pointed to shore batteries (for USS *Corry*) and a glider bomb (for USS *Meredith*).

9   Courtesy of www.wpepe.com/dday.

10   Unnamed jeep driver, 5th Bn, Kings Regiment, No. 5 Beach Group, interview, 1994, via Sub-Lt Peter Miles, RNVR, Landing Craft Association.

11   Lt Robert A. Jacobs, interview courtesy of 389th Bomb Group Memorial Exhibition, Hethel, Norwich.

12   Reeder, *Born at Reveille*, op. cit., p. 4564.

13   Calculations taken from Port-en-Bessin, in the centre of the invasion coast.

14   Joseph P. Vaghi, 'D-Day, Easy Red Beach, Normandy', April 1994, memoir courtesy of www.6thbeachbattalion.org.

15   Robert D. Blegen, 'LCT(5) Flotilla 18 at Omaha Beach, D-Day, June 6, 1944', memoir, ww2lct.org/history/stories/flot_18_at_omaha.htm.

16   Omar Bradley and Clay Blair, *A General's Life: An Autobiography by General of the Army Omar N. Bradley* (Simon & Schuster, 1983), p. 252.

17   Gilchrist, *Don't Cry for Me*, op. cit., p. 46.

18   Stan Hough, interview, op. cit.

19   Charles Hurlbut, interview, op. cit.

20   Reg Clark, interview 2003, courtesy of BBC The People's War.

21   The Imperial War Museum holds the duffle coat that was worn by Lt Gerald Roy Clark, RNVR, commander of *LCT-770*.

22   Gilchrist, *Don't Cry for Me*, op. cit., p. 49.

23   Alan Higgins, interview, 1994, via Sub-Lt Peter Miles, RNVR, Landing Craft Association.

24   Gilchrist, *Don't Cry For Me*, op. cit., p. 49.

25   John 'J.J.' Witmeyer, interview courtesy of National World War II Museum Oral History Program, New Orleans. Witmeyer died in September 2014.

26   Charles Norman Shay, interview, Omaha Beach, Saint-Laurent-sur-Mer, 5 June 2018.

27   Earl Chellis, Jr, interview, 2000, courtesy of Laurent Lefebvre at www.american-dday.org.

28   Alfred M. Beck, Abe Bortz, Charles W. Lynch, Lida Mayo and Ralph F. Weld, *United States Army in World War II: The Corps of Engineers: The War Against Germany* (Center of Military History, US Army, 1985), p. 320.

29   Ross, 'Essayons', op. cit., pp. 37–43.

30   John R. Armellino, interview, 2000, courtesy of John N. Armellino and Laurent Lefebvre at www.americandday.org.

31   Bill Ryan, interview, April 1994, courtesy of Wirral and Chester Branch of the NVA. Ryan died in 2015.

32   James Holland, *Twenty-One: Coming of Age in World War II* (Harper, 2006), p. 42.

33   Dr Hal Baumgarten, interview, op. cit.

34   Walsh, 'D-Day Reflections from a Soldier', op. cit.

35   James Baker, DSM, interview, 1994, courtesy of Wirral and Chester Branch of the NVA. Jim died in 2016.

36   Reg Cole, interview, op. cit.

37   Jack Heath, courtesy of BBC, WW2 People's War, 2005.

38   R. G. Watts, interview, 2003, op cit.

39   Eric Neville Hooper, interview, Imperial War Museum Sound Archive, ref. 11208/ reel 11.

22. Night Flyers

1   Broadcast on 8 June 1944. *War Report: A Record of Despatches Broadcast by the BBC's War Correspondents with the Allied Expeditionary Force, 6 June 1944–5 May 1945* (Oxford University Press, 1946), p. 60; my thanks to BBC Radio 4 stalwart Ed Stourton for reminding me of *War Report*.

2   Kevin Wilson, *Men of Air: The Doomed Youth of Bomber Command* (Hachette, 2008), p. 362.

3   Ibid.

4   Stephanie Nield, 'Our Founder's Role in D-Day's Secret Mission', Leonard Cheshire Foundation, 6 June 2014.

5   The National Archives (TNA): AIR/27/2128.

6   Laurie Brettingham, *Even When the Sparrows Were Walking: The Origin and Effect of No. 100 Bomber Support Group RAF, 1943–45* (Gopher Publishers, 2001), pp. 43–52.

7   The translated text read, 'Urgent Message from the Supreme Command of the Allied Expeditionary Force to the inhabitants of this town. So that the common enemy is defeated, the Allied air forces will attack all transport hubs and all the ways and means of communications vital to the enemy. If you are reading this leaflet you are in or near a centre essential to the enemy for the movement of troops and their equipment. The vital objective which you are near to is going to be incessantly attacked. You quickly leave with your family, for a few days, the danger zone where you are. Do not clutter the roads. Spread out into the coun-

tryside, as far as possible. LEAVE THE AREA! YOU DO NOT HAVE A MINUTE TO LOSE!'

8   An allusion to Churchill's radio broadcast of 9 February 1941, addressed to the United States, which concluded: 'Give Us The Tools: And We Will Finish The Job'.

9   The National Archives (TNA): TICOM report I-109, 'Translation of a Report by Lt Ludwig' (24 September 1945), p. 18.

10   Kershaw, *D-Day,* op. cit., p. 90.

11   This was at Marigny, site of the start of Operation Cobra in late July.

12   'D-Day Airborne Deceptions: The Tempsford Squadrons' Involvement', *Tempsford Veterans and Relatives Association Newsletter* (Summer 2011).

13   My thanks to Lt. Col. Alan Miller for alerting me to Poole. The officer (awarded an MC) and his SAS team spent 42 days behind German lines, being captured when they tried to cross through the front. See his obituary, *Daily Telegraph*, 7 July 2015.

14   Meyer was CO of *915. Grenadier-Regt*, part of Dietrich Kraiss' 352nd Infantry Division.

15   Ben Macintyre, *SAS: Rogue Heroes* (Viking, 2016), p. 215.

16   Ibid.

17   Ibid. See also AVM Jack Furner, '100 Group – Confound and …', *RAF Historical Society Journal*, No. 28 (2003), pp.24–32, and Martin Streetly, '100 Group – Fighter Operations', *RAF Historical Society Journal*, No. 28 (2003), pp. 33–42.

18   Lt Russell Chandler, Jr, interview, op. cit.

19   Clostermann, *The Big Show*, op. cit., p. 161.

20   By contrast, 195,255 sorties had been flown in the preceding two months (1 April–5 June 1944), or an average of one every 30 seconds for the entire 65-day period; see Delve, *D-Day: The Air Battle*, op. cit., p. 81.

21   In fact, the concept had been laid down earlier, before Leigh-Mallory's approval, in SHAEF Operational Memorandum No. 23, 'Distinctive Marking – Aircraft', issued on 18 April 1944; orders were issued to No. 11 Group RAF and IX Fighter Command USAAF in 'Joint Air Plan and Executive Orders for Operation Neptune', issued at Uxbridge, 25 May 1944.

22   Stephen J. Thorne, 'Douglas Gordon (Part 1): Bail Out or Glide for England', *Canadian Legion Magazine*, 26 December 2018.

23   Delve, *D-Day: The Air Battle*, op. cit., p. 80.

24   Lew Johnston, 'Troop Carrier D-Day Flights: Fighter Cover', op. cit.

25   Courtesy of http://www.b26.com.

26   Donald MacKenzie, 'At a B-26 Marauder Base in England', *New York Daily News*, 7 June 1944.

27   *Daily Telegraph*, 7 June 1944; Dominic Phelan, *Cornelius Ryan: D-Day Reporter* (self-published, 2014), Kindle, pp. 19–20.

28   Neal Beaver, interview, February 2013, via Lewis Johnston of the Air Mobility Command Museum, Dover AFB, Delaware.

29   Jack Schlegel, interview, op. cit.

30   Beaver, interview, op. cit.

31   Philip Warner, *The D-Day Landings* (William Kimber, 1980), pp. 33–4.

32   This was the Knollwood Maneuver (designed to capture Knollwood airbase, near Fort Bragg), which began on 7 December 1943 and involved over 10,000 participants.

33   Bradley, *A Soldier's Story*, op. cit., pp. 234–6.

34   Eisenhower, *Crusade in Europe*, op. cit., pp. 270–1.

35   Harry C. Butcher, *Three Years with Eisenhower: The Personal Diary of Capt. H. C. Butcher, Naval Aide to General Eisenhower, 1942–45* (Heinemann, 1946).

36   Wallace C. Strobel and Leonard Crawford, interviews, June 2018, Band of Brothers Aldbourne to Berchtesgaden battlefield tour.

37   Butcher, *Three Years with Eisenhower*, op. cit.

38   Volker Griesser, *The Lions of Carentan* (Casemate, 2015), p. 82.

39   Martin Pöppel, *Heaven and Hell: The War Diary of a German Paratrooper* (Spellmount, 1988), pp. 172–4.

40   Holland, *Twenty-One*, op. cit., pp. 311–12.

41   Griesser, *Lions of Carentan*, op. cit., p. 83.

42   Ernst W. Flöter with Lynne Breen, *I'll See You Again, Lady Liberty: The True Story of a German Prisoner of War in America* (WingSpan Press, 2014), p. 23.

43   Paul Golz, interview, June 2016, courtesy of Liesl Bradner.

44   The Château de Bernaville now houses the Normandy Institute, whose mission is to 'engage leaders and educators in shaping the future creating strategic alliances, advancing understanding of history, and applying this knowledge to complex global issues'.

45   Ruge, *Rommel in Normandy*, op. cit., pp. 162–3.

46   Jay Wertz, *D-Day: The Campaign Across France* (Casemate/Monroe, 2012).

47   The National Archives (TNA): WO 171/1249.

48   Sgt Herb Fussell, interview, Ranville, Normandy, October 2008. Because of their language skills, several Pathfinders were of Jewish or Continental origin and were given pseudonyms; due to a likelihood of being cut off, alone, behind enemy lines, many other Pathfinders were also given fake identities also, hence Fussell/'Ramage'.

49   'Post Op. Report by Capt. Mildwood on Pathfinder Troops Drop onto DZ "K", Normandy' (dated Oct. 1944), courtesy of paradata.org.uk.

50   WACO eventually made 14,000 of their CG-4A gliders, which were known to the British as the Hadrian.

51   Maj. Leon B. Spencer, 'They Flew into Battle on Silent Wings: World War II Glider Pilots of the US Army Air Force', p. 2

52   Tony Reichhardt, 'The Pilot Who Led the D-Day Invasion', *Smithsonian Air and Space Magazine*, 6 June 2014.

53   Lew Johnston, 'Troop Carrier D-Day Flights: The Heart of the Matter', Air Mobility Command Museum, 6 June 2001, op. cit.

54   Mark Alexander and John Sparry, *Jump Commander: In Combat with the 505th and 508th Parachute Infantry Regiments, 82nd Airborne Division, in WWII* (Casemate, 2010), p. 274.

55   Privates Robert L. Leaky and Pete Vah and Corporal Kenneth A. Vaught died instantly, Private Eddie O. Meelberg later that night.

56   Corteil and Glen died together on 6 June and were buried together in Ranville War Cemetery.

57   Tute, Costello and Hughes, *D-Day*, op. cit., p. 149.

58   Neal Beaver, interview, op. cit.

59   Ibid.

60   Col. C. H. Young, *Into the Valley: The Untold Story of USAAF Troop Carrier in World War II, from North Africa through Europe* (PrintComm, 1995).

61   Thirty-nine square kilometres.

62   Maj. Leon B. Spencer, USAFR (ret.), 'Normandy D-Day CG-4A Glider Crash Claims Life of General Don F. Pratt', *Silent Wings* (National WWII Glider Pilot Association, June 1997); courtesy of worldwar2gliderpilots.blogspot.com.

63   Flöter and Breen, *I'll See You Again*, op. cit., p. 27; Wertz, *D-Day*, op. cit., pp. 82–3.

64   Lynda Laird, photo exhibition: '*Dans le noir*', words by Odette Brefort, Deauville, 21 October 2017.

65   Renée Olinger, interview, Thury-Harcourt, June 1994.

66   Pierre Labbé, interview, Normandy, February 2014.

67   'They Came Out of the Sea!', *Press Democrat*, 22 May 1994.

68   René Baumel, interview, Normandy, June 2013.

69   Jean Mignon, interview, Normandy, June 2013.

70   Marcel Rousseau, interview, Normandy, June 2013.

71   Griesser, *Lions of Carentan*, op. cit., p. 88.

72   Kevin M. Hymel, 'Dropping into Normandy: First-Hand Accounts of the D-Day Airborne Invasion', *Warfare History Network*, 6 June 2018.

73   Griesser, *Lions of Carentan*, op. cit., p. 89.

74   Wertz, *D-Day*, op. cit., p. 137.

75   Ibid., pp. 89–90.

76   Schlegel took Falley's personal swastika flag as a souvenir, hid it before he was taken prisoner, retrieved it after the war and later gave it to the Airborne Museum in Sainte-Mère-Église. The current owners of the Château de Bernaville have recently discovered an aerial photo showing Falley's crashed staff car. Falley is buried in the German military cemetery, Orglandes, block D, row 10, grave 207.

77   Marguerite Catherine, interview, Picauville, June 2013.

78   Dalton Einhorn, *From Toccoa to the Eagle's Nest: Discoveries in the Bootsteps of the Band of Brothers* (Booksurge Publishing, 2009).

23. Across the Water and Into the Trees

1   John Golley, *The Day of the Typhoon: Flying with the RAF Tankbusters in Normandy* (Patrick Stephens, 1986), pp. 16–17.

2   Hayn, *Die Invasion*, op. cit., pp. 16–20.

3   Projector Infantry Anti-Tank, the British bazooka.

4   Len Buckley, interview, Bayeux, June 2014.

5   Gen. Eberhard Wagemann, interview, op. cit.

6   Neillands and De Normann, *D-Day 1944*, op. cit., p. 101.

7   Charles 'Wagger' Thornton, interview, 1993, Imperial War Museum Sound Archive, ref. 11559.

8   Raymond 'Tich' Raynor, interview, Bletchley Park, 2006.

9   Helmut Römer, interview, Dusseldorf, 1995, and numerous interviews with Arlette Gondrée, Pegasus Bridge Café.

10 John Howard, interview, Browning Barracks, Aldershot, 1995.

11 Stephen E. Ambrose, *Pegasus Bridge* (Simon & Schuster, 1997), pp. 122–4.

12 *Stourbridge News*, 29 May 1997.

13 Broadcast on 8 June 1944. *War Report*, op. cit., p. 63.

14 Marcus Brotherton, 'In Honor of Earl McClung (1923–2013)', 27 November 2013, courtesy of www.marcusbrotherton.com.

15 Ibid.

16 Col. Keith Nightingale, 'The Taking of La Fière Bridge', *Small Wars Journal* (28 May 2012).

17 Ibid.

18 William Falduti, 'The Invasions of Normandy and Holland', Nutley Historical Society (New Jersey), 29 May 2009.

19 Company 'F', 2nd Platoon Mortar Squad: Lt Cadish, KIA 6 June; Sgt John Ray, DOW 7 June; Sgt Edward White, KIA 6 June; Cpl Vernon Francisco, KIA 3 January 1945; PFC Charles Blankenship, KIA 6 June; PFC Clifford Maughan, taken prisoner; PFC Penrose Shearer, KIA 6 June; PFC Alfred Van Holsbeck, KIA 8 June; PFC Ernest Blanchard, survived; Pvt. H. T. Bryant, KIA 6 June; Pvt. Phillip Lynch, KIA 13 January 1945; Pvt. Kenneth Russell, survived; Pvt. John Steele, survived; Pvt. Ladishaw Tlapa, KIA 6 June; Pvt. Steven Epps, survived.

20 See Ryan, *The Longest Day*, op. cit., pp. 133–6.

21 Emile Ozouf, interview, Sainte-Mère-Église, June 2014.

22 Pöppel, *Heaven and Hell*, op. cit., p. 174.

23 Otto Bügener would be killed on 27 June 1944 and is buried with 555 other Germans in the Saint-Manvieu Commonwealth War Cemetery, Cheux, in plot 17.B.2.

24 John Ross, interview, op. cit.

25 Aaron Elson, *A Mile in Their Shoes: Conversations with Veterans of World War II*, 'The Last Hurrah': interview with Ed Boccafogli, Clifton, New Jersey, 19 February 1994, courtesy of www.tankbooks.com.

26 Mathias was allegedly the first American officer to fall on D-Day; Stephen E. Ambrose, 'The Kids Who Changed the World', *Newsweek*, Vol. 132/2 (13 July 1998).

27 Bernd Horn & Michel Wyczynski, 'A Most Irrevocable Step: Canadian Paratroopers on D-Day: The First 24 Hours, 5–6 June 1944', *Canadian Military History*, Vol.13/3 (2004).

28 Hymel, 'Dropping into Normandy', op. cit.

29 Major Brandenberger as he became, later won a Silver Star and served in Korea.

30 Elson, *A Mile in Their Shoes*, op. cit.

31 David Owen, *Portrait of a Parachutist*, unpublished manuscript, 1st Canadian Parachute Battalion Archives.

32 Hymel, 'Dropping into Normandy', op. cit.

33 John Feduck, interview, 19 December 2001, courtesy of Oral History Project, 1st Canadian Parachute Battalion Archives.

34 Muir's sacrifice brought him a posthumous Distinguished Service Cross. He lies buried at Colleville-sur-Mer cemetery, plot C, row 12, grave 5.

35 Elmer Wisherd, interview courtesy of www.witnesstowar.org.

36 Richard 'Sweeney' Todd, interview, Pegasus Bridge, July 2005. Seventeen years after D-Day he played the character of Maj. John Howard in *The Longest Day*. Todd died in 2009.

37 Henry John 'Tod' Sweeney, interview during Normandy battlefield tour, June 1995. Col. Tod Sweeney MC died in June 2001.

38 Hymel, 'Dropping into Normandy', op. cit.

39 Justin Covington, 'D-Day Army Paratrooper Tom Rice Recalls Dropping into Normandy', circa.com, 6 June 2018.

40 Horn and Wyczynski, 'A Most Irrevocable Step', op. cit.

41 Lt Col. G. F. P. Bradbrooke, letter, 1st Canadian Parachute Battalion Archives.

42 Bill Brown and Terry Poyser, *Fighting Fox Company: The Battling Flank of the Band of Brothers* (Casemate, 2014).

43 Sgt Marion Grodowski, winner of *four* Bronze Stars, died in January 2012, aged ninety-one.

44 Vandervoort would win two Distinguished Service Crosses and be played by John Wayne in *The Longest Day*. He died in 1990.

45 Wertz, *D-Day*, op. cit., p. 90.

46 Lt Russell Chandler, Jr, interview, op. cit.

47 David Howarth, *Dawn of D-Day* (Collins, 1959), Kindle, pp. 1514–44.

48 Col. John Watts, MC, interview, Warminster, September 1997. He wrote *Surgeon at War* (Allen & Unwin, 1955) and died in 2010.

49 David Tibbs, MC, interview, Oxford, January 2014; sadly, I was unable to interview him again, for he died in August 2017 whilst I was writing this book. See also Capt. David Tibbs, *Parachute Doctor*, ed. Neil Barber (Sabrestorm, 2012), pp. 45, 49, 50.

50 Beaver, interview, op. cit.

51 David Tibbs, MC, interview, op. cit.

52 Prof. Robert Elmore, interview, Kellogg College, Oxford, 1994. Prof. Elmore died in 2016.

53 Luck, *Panzer Commander*, op. cit., p. 3222.

54 Neillands and De Normann, *D-Day 1944*, op. cit., p. 101.

55 Carell, *Invasion*, op. cit., p. 38.

56 Michael Hanlon, 'Paratroopers Landed at Night', *Toronto Star*, 6 June 1994.

57 'Remembering Two Canadian Chaplains Who Fell on D-Day', 6 June 2014, courtesy of The Mad Padre blog. Rev. Harris is buried at Ranville War Cemetery, plot VA, row C, grave 6.

58 Doug Morrison, interview with Bernd Horn, February 2002.

59 Wertz, *D-Day*, op. cit., p. 84.

60 Strong, *Steiner's War*, op. cit.

61   Ibid., pp. 44–6.

62   ETHINT FMS B-403, Joseph Reichert, 'The 711th Infantry Division and the Airborne Invasion'; Col. C. P. Stacey, *Official History of the Canadian Army in the 2nd World War, Vol. 3: The Victory Campaign: Operations in NW Europe, 1944–45* (Queen's Printer, 1966), p. 121.

63   Strong, *Steiner's War*, op. cit., pp. 85–7; Tootal, *The Manner of Men*, op. cit.

64   Edwin Booth, interview, 2000, courtesy of www.warlinks.com.

65   Strong, *Steiner's War*, op. cit.

66   Barber, *The Day the Devils Dropped In*, op. cit.

67   David Tibbs, MC, interview, op. cit.

68   Laurie Weeden, interview, Normandy, 6 June 2014.

69   John Howard, interview, op. cit.

70   David Reynolds, 'The Runaway Boy Hero of D-Day: At 14, He Lied His Way into the Army. At Just 16 He Parachuted into France … With His Frantic Family Hot on His Tail', *Daily Mail*, 17 May 2014.

71   Jack Schlegel, interview, op. cit.

72   His son, Joseph Beyrle, Jr, served with the 101st in Vietnam and was later US ambassador to Russia (2008–12). Beyrle, Sr, died whilst visiting the old 101st camp at Toccoa, Georgia, in 2004 and is buried in Arlington National Cemetery.

73   They were Privates Arthur Platt and Tom Billingham; no one was ever charged with their murder.

74   David Tibbs, interview, op. cit.; Tibbs, *Parachute Doctor*, op. cit., p. 46.

75   Griesser, *Lions of Carentan*, op. cit., p. 96.

76   George E. 'Pete' Buckley, memoir cited in Johnston, 'Troop Carrier D-Day Flights', op. cit.

77   Griesser, *The Lions of Carentan*, op cit., p.91.

78   Spencer Wurst, *Descending From the Clouds* (Casemate, 2004), p. 205 and see interview at http://jumpwith.pathfindergroupuk.com. A North African veteran, SSgt Spencer Wurst was commissioned in 1945, retiring as colonel; he died in 2015 and was buried in Arlington cemetery.

79   Griesser, *The Lions of Carentan*, op cit., p.91.

80   Henri Biard, interview, Normandy, June 2013.

81   Griesser, *Lions of Carentan*, op. cit., p. 91.

82   Carell, *Invasion*, op. cit., pp. 47–51.

83   Broadcast on 8 June 1944. *War Report*, op. cit., pp. 66–7.

84   Spencer, 'Glider Crash Claims Life of General Don F. Pratt', op. cit.

85   *By Air to Battle: The Official Account of the British Airborne Divisions* (His Majesty's Stationery Office, 1945).

86   Hastings, *Overlord*, op. cit., p. 74; statistics from Steven J. Zaloga, *Utah Beach* (Osprey, 2004), p. 64.

87   Tootal, *The Manner of Men*, op. cit., Kindle p. 2821.

88   Col. James J. Roberts, Jr, CO, Fulbeck AFB (Lincolnshire) After Action Report, 313th Troop Carrier Group, 52nd Troop Carrier Wing, IX Troop Carrier Command, Ninth Air Force.

89 Martin Wolfe, *Green Light! A Troop Carrier Squadron's War from Normandy to the Rhine* (Center for Air Force History, 1993), pp. 116–17.

90 Howarth, *Dawn of D-Day*, op. cit., p. 86.

91 Donald R. Burgett, *Currahee! A Paratrooper's Account of the Invasion* (Presidio, 1967), pp. 87–8.

92 Ibid.

93 Huggett's jump jacket is an exhibit at the Dead Man's Corner D-Day Experience Museum, Saint-Côme-du-Mont, Carentan.

94 Neillands and De Normann, *D-Day 1944*, op. cit., p. 102. Huggett was lucky, for the rest of his battalion left Swansea aboard the troopship USS *Susan B. Anthony*, which struck a mine off Omaha Beach on 7 June; the ship hit the bottom, allowing all 2,689 personnel aboard to be rescued.

95 Russell Chandler, Jr, interview, op. cit.

96 Dan Hartigan, interview with Bernd Horn, 30 October 2000.

97 The 'single German bunker' was Arthur Jahnke's W5 (now the Musée du Debarquement Utah Beach); Griesser, *Lions of Carentan*, op. cit., p. 93.

98 David Tibbs, interview, op. cit.; Tibbs, *Parachute Doctor*, op. cit., p. 46.

24. Utah: Ivy Division

1 NARA FMSB-844: Obstlt Günther Keil, 'Commitment of the 1058th Infantry Regiment' (1946).

2 Jahnke, recollections, *Utah Musée du Débarquement*; Carell, *Invasion*, op. cit., pp. 41–5, 57–67, 71–5.

3 Gerald Astor, *June 6, 1944: The Voices of D-Day* (St Martin's Press, 1994), p. 279.

4 Then called the Navy Medal of Valor.

5 All Overlord historians incorrectly report Rommel's visit to Jahnke as 11 May, the earliest being Paul Carell in *Invasion*, op. cit., p. 42.

6 Jahnke survived the war, dying in 1960. A press photograph, dated 30 May 1944, exists of Schlieben and the newly decorated Jahnke marching past the 3rd Company on what will become Utah Beach. Rommel inspected Jahnke's HQ in WN.104 (often wrongly named WN.5), on La Madeleine beach. This is now the Utah Beach Museum. Rommel then stopped by at the 709th Infantry Division's headquarters in the Château de Chiffrevast, a huge castle north of Valognes.

7 NARA FMS B-845, op. cit.

8 Alexandre Renaud, *Sainte Mère Église: First American Bridgehead in France* (Julliard, 1984), pp. 14–21.

9 Ibid., p. 23.

10 Schlieben formerly commanded the 18th Panzer Division. His reinforcements were the 635th, 649th, 795th and 797th *Ost* Battalions; see ETHINT B-845, Genlt. Karl Wilhelm von Schlieben, '709th Inf. Division & the Defense of Cherbourg' (1948).

11 Jong was mercifully not expected to fight for the US Army, but conveyed first to Britain as a POW, then to America, where he later took citizenship and died in Illinois in 1992.

12 Reynaud, *Sainte Mère Église*, op. cit., p. 28.

13 As the 1057th Grenadiers did not have an *Ost-Bataillon*, these were either individuals, or units attached to the neighbouring 709th Division.

14 Janice Holt Giles (ed.), *The GI Journal of Sgt Giles* (Houghton Mifflin, 1965), p. 34.

15 ETHINT B-621, Genlt. Wilhelm Richter, '716th Inf. Division Normandy'.

16 Pogue, *Pogue's War*, op. cit., pp. 85–6.

17 Combined Services Detailed Interrogation Centre (CSDIC) POW interrogation report SAR. 455, 'Information obtained from PW DZ/3095(M) Oberleutnant Lomtatidse, CO 4th Coy, 795th Georgian Bn' (29 June 1944).

18 Milton Shulman, *Defeat in the West* (Secker & Warburg 1947), pp. 131–2.

19 Jahnke, *Utah Musée du Débarquement*; Carell, *Invasion*, op. cit., pp. 41–5.

20 *Utah Beach and Beyond* (Historical Division, US War Department, 1948), p. 18.

21 Ibid., p. 18.

22 Stephen E. Ambrose, *Band of Brothers, E Company, 506th Regiment, 101st Airborne: From Normandy to Hitler's Eagle's Nest* (Touchstone/Simon & Schuster, 1992), p. 87.

23 Colonel Russell Potter 'Red' Reeder, *Born at Reveille: The Memoirs of an American Soldier* (Duell, Sloan and Pearce, 1966).

24 Despite being a popular officer within his Regiment, Hervey Tribolet would be relieved of command on 11 June for his slow progress and was replaced by Col. Robert Foster.

25 Reeder, *Born at Reveille*, op. cit., p. 4541.

26 Ryan, *The Longest Day*, op. cit., p. 94; and author's research.

27 Howarth, *Dawn of D-Day*, op. cit., p. 1719.

28 Jahnke, *Utah Musée du Débarquement*; Carell, *Invasion*, op. cit., pp. 41–5, 57–67, 71–5.

29 This comprised 11 LSTs (ten towing Rhinos), 2 Landing Craft, Hospital, 168 LCT 'types', 84 minor craft with 28 escorts.

30 *Utah Beach and Beyond*, op. cit., p. 44.

31 Jahnke, *Utah Musée du Débarquement*; Carell, *Invasion*, op. cit., pp. 41–5, 57–67, 71–5.

32 Alan G. Kirk, 'Report of Commander, Western Task Force', 15 September 1944 (NARA), p. 18.

33 Courtesy of Halsey Vail Barrett, Jr. His father was navigator aboard *PC-1261* and died in August 2008.

34 Jahnke, *Utah Musée du Débarquement*; Carell, *Invasion*, op. cit., pp. 41–5, 57–67, 71–5.

35 Tute, Costello and Hughes, *D-Day*, op. cit., p. 177.

36 Jahnke, *Utah Musée du Débarquement*; Carell, *Invasion*, op. cit., pp. 41–5, 57–67, 71–5.

37 '"J'ai Débarqué le Premier en Normandie" – le Colonel Schroeder à Utah Beach', *VSD Magazine*, No. 874 (2 June 1994).

38 Howarth, *Dawn of D-Day*, op. cit., p. 1761.

39 John C. Ausland, 'A Soldier Remembers Utah Beach', *International Herald Tribune*, 6 June 1984.

40   Interview by David Venditta, *The Morning Call* (Allentown, Pennsylvania), 2 June 1994.

41   Jahnke, *Utah Musée du Débarquement*; Carell, *Invasion*, op. cit., pp. 41–5, 57–67, 71–5.

42   Howarth, *Dawn of D-Day*, op. cit., p. 1812.

43   *Utah Beach and Beyond*, op. cit., p. 44.

44   Interview by David Venditta, *The Morning Call*, 5 June 2012.

45   John P. McGirr, interview, 1984; see also 65th Armored Field Artillery Association (ed.), *The Thunderbolt Battalion, 1941–45: Rounds Complete* (Fidelity Press, Philadelphia, 1947).

46   Beck et al., *The Corps of Engineers*, op. cit., p. 333.

47   Kevin Dougherty, 'Veteran Frogman Was Among First to Hit Normandy Beaches', *Stars and Stripes*, 6 June 2008.

48   Interview by Brian Albrecht, *The Plain Dealer* (Cleveland, Ohio), 6 June 2009.

49   Rob Morris, 'A Combat Engineer on D-Day', courtesy of Warfare History Network, 22 June 2016.

50   Joseph Balkoski, *Utah Beach: The Amphibious Landing and Airborne Operations on D-Day* (Stackpole, 2005), p. 238.

51   Dr William Boice, *History of the Twenty-Second United States Infantry* (22nd Infantry, 1959).

52   Howarth, *Dawn of D-Day*, op. cit., p. 1871.

53   Beck et al., *The Corps of Engineers*, op. cit., p. 334. A shell-splattered part of Utah's sea wall now sits as an exhibit outside the main entrance to the National World War II Museum in New Orleans.

54   Jahnke, *Utah Musée du Débarquement*; Carell, *Invasion*, op. cit., pp. 41–5, 57–67, 71–5.

55   Interview by David Venditta, *The Morning Call*, 5 June 2013.

56   Russell Miller, *Nothing Less Than Victory: An Oral History of D Day* (William Morrow & Co., 1993).

57   Venditta, *The Morning Call*, 5 June 2013, op. cit.

58   Dewitt Gilpin, 'D+365', *Yank Magazine*, 4 August 1945.

59   Jahnke, *Utah Musée du Débarquement*; Carell, *Invasion*, op. cit., pp. 41–5, 57–67, 71–5.

60   Astor, *June 6, 1944*, op. cit., p. 267.

61   Boice, *History of the Twenty-Second United States Infantry*, op. cit.

62   Joseph Michael Suozzo, interview, San Diego, 1984, via Sub-Lt Peter Miles, RNVR, Landing Craft Association. They were towed back to Portsmouth, Suozzo winning a Silver Star for his coolness under fire; he died in 2008.

63   Lund and Ludlam, *War of the Landing Craft*, op. cit., pp. 178–9.

64   Astor, *June 6, 1944*, op. cit., p. 271.

65   Neillands and De Normann, *D-Day 1944*, op. cit., p. 122.

66   Ship's log, *LCT-645*, courtesy of Charles Summers.

67   Astor, *June 6, 1944*, op. cit., p. 270.

68   Lund and Ludlam, *War of the Landing Craft*, op. cit., p. 181.

69   'D-Day, 70 Years On', op. cit.

70 65th Armored Field Artillery Association (ed.), *Rounds Complete*, op. cit.

71 Frank Cooney, interview, 2002, Park Tudor School Words of War Oral History Collection, Indiana State Library

72 *Stars and Stripes*, 6 July 1944.

73 Astor, *June 6, 1944*, op. cit., p. 275.

74 Howarth, *Dawn of D-Day*, op. cit., p. 1999.

75 Rev. George W. Knapp, *A Chaplain's Diary* (Deeds Publishing, 2011), Kindle, pp. 681–707.

76 Interview by David Venditta, *The Morning Call*, 24 March 2003.

77 Astor, *June 6, 1944*, op. cit., p. 273.

78 Craig S. Chapman, *Battle Hardened: An Infantry Officer's Harrowing Journey from D-Day to V-E Day* (Regnery, 2017), Kindle, p. 783.

79 Ausland, 'A Soldier Remembers', op. cit.

25. Wet Feet

1 David P. Colley, *The Road To Victory: The Untold Story of Race and World War II's Red Ball Express* (Brassey's, 1999), pp. 2–3.

2 Ausland, 'A Soldier Remembers', op. cit.

3 'Maj. Gen. Raymond O. Barton', courtesy of Charles A. Lewis.

4 Boice, *History of the Twenty-Second United States Infantry*, op. cit.

5 Raymond Bertot, interview, Varreville, 2004.

6 Boice, *History of the Twenty-Second United States Infantry*, op. cit.

7 Reeder, *Born at Reveille*, op. cit., p. 4209.

8 Tute, Costello and Hughes, *D-Day*, op. cit., p. 182.

9 John C. McManus, *The American at D-Day: The American Experience at the Normandy Invasion* (Forge Books, 2004).

10 Astor, *June 6, 1944*, op. cit., p. 276.

11 Neillands and De Normann, *D-Day 1944*, op. cit., p. 131.

12 NARA FMS B-845, op. cit.

13 NARA FMS B-260, Genmaj. Gerhard Triepel, '6 June: Cotentin Coast Artillery' (1946).

14 Jahnke, *Utah Musée du Débarquement*; Carell, *Invasion*, op. cit., p. 74.

15 Reeder, *Born at Reveille*, op. cit., p. 4596.

16 Ibid., p. 4552.

17 Marvin Jansen, *Strike Swiftly: The 70th Tank Battalion from North Africa to Normandy to Germany* (Presidio, 1997), pp. 135–40.

18 Lt Col Maynard D. Pederson et al., *Armor in Operation Neptune* (Research Report, Armored School Fort Knox, 1948–9), p. 72.

19 Tim Wells, 'Elliot L. Richardson Remembers D-Day', *D.C. Bar*, 26 May 2017. Richardson later became Richard Nixon's attorney general, and received the Presidential Medal of Freedom in 1998.

20 Ausland, 'A Soldier Remembers', op. cit.

21 Interview by David Venditta, *The Morning Call*, 6 June 1985.

22 Howarth, *Dawn of D-Day*, op. cit., pp. 1881–921.

23 Koskimaki, *D-Day with the Screaming Eagles*, op. cit., p. 165.

24 Reeder, *Born at Reveille*, op. cit., p. 4622.

25 Chapman, *Battle Hardened*, op. cit., p. 822.

26 Hastings, *Overlord*, op. cit., p. 86.

27 Sgt Vincent 'Mike' McKinney, interview, op. cit.

28 Neillands and De Normann, *D-Day 1944*, op. cit., pp. 135–6.

29 Ibid., pp. 135–6

30 I was very proud to have met Reeder, who died in 1998.

31 Boice, *History of the Twenty-Second United States Infantry*, op. cit.

32 Burgett, *Currahee!*, op. cit., p. 112.

33 Lt Col John Dowdy would be killed in action on 16 September 1944, by then holder of the Distinguished Service Cross, two Silver Stars and a Bronze Star.

34 In fact, Edward Niland was captured after bailing out and lived until 1984; memoir courtesy of Pete (Preston) Niland, 'Niland Brothers: The Story Behind Saving Private Ryan', 10 January 2011.

35 Robert Niland is buried at Colleville, plot F, row 15, grave 11, next to his brother Preston, at grave 12.

36 Princess Marie 'Missie' Vassiltchikov, *The Berlin Diaries 1940–1945* (Chatto & Windus 1985), p. 178.

37 Ursula von Kardorff, *Diary of a Nightmare: Berlin 1942–1945* (Rupert Hart-Davis, 1965), p. 112.

38 Peter Longerich, *Goebbels* (The Bodley Head, 2015), Kindle p.12347. The source was the *Forschungsamt* ('Research Office' of the Air Ministry), established by Hermann Göring in 1933, and numbering 6,000 by 1944. It monitored and decoded internal and external communications, but cooperated little with other Nazi organisations, including Göring's own Luftwaffe.

39 Friedrich von der Heydte was a cousin of Claus von Stauffenberg. After the latter had tried and failed to assassinate Hitler on 20 July, von der Heydte was in danger of being summoned to Berlin for questioning. However, his name was misspelled on the arrest warrant and – apparently – an unfortunate major by the name of 'von der Heide' was instead arrested on the Eastern Front, and spent the rest of the war behind bars.

40 Renaud, *Sainte Mère Église*, op. cit., pp. 65–6.

41 Linda Hervieux's excellent *Forgotten: The Untold Story of D-Day's Black Heroes, at Home and at War* (Harper, 2015) deals with this hitherto unknown aspect of the US Army on D-Day.

42 Beck et al., *The Corps of Engineers*, op. cit., p. 337.

43 Carl Bialik, 'The Challenge of Counting D-Day's Dead', ABC News, 6 June 1014.

44 *Utah Beach and Beyond*, op. cit., p. 56.

45 Symonds, *Neptune*, op. cit., pp. 203–5, 355–6.

46 Guy Hartcup, *Code Name Mulberry: The Planning, Building and Operation of the Normandy Harbours* (David & Charles, 1977).

47 Renaud, *Sainte Mère Église*, op. cit., p. 99.

48 Commander John F. Curtin, USNR, '2nd Beach Battalion After Action Report', 25 July 1944.

49 Kenneth Slawenski, 'Holden Caulfield's Goddam War', *Vanity Fair*, February 2011.

50 'How a Soldier Shot a Famous General's Funeral in Normandy after D-Day, *Los Angeles Times*, 8 May 2014.

51 Brig. Gen. Roosevelt remains only one of thirty-five men to earn all three top valour awards: Medal of Honor, Distinguished Service Cross (or Navy Cross) and Silver Star. Roosevelt's son, Quentin, was also present on 6 June 1944, landing on Omaha with the 1st Infantry Division and later earning himself a Silver Star.

26. Omaha: Blue and Gray

1 HQ 100th Bombardment Group (H), Office of the Operations Officer, APO #634, 7 June 1944, 'Report of the Operations Officer, Missions of June 6, 1944' (Pennsylvania State University Special Collections Library, Eighth Air Force Archive).

2 Albert J. Parisi, 'Recalling a World in Flames', *New York Times*, 5 June 1994.

3 Colonel Louis Hervelin, interview, Yorkshire Air Museum, 2004.

4 Zaloga, *D-Day Fortifications*, op. cit., pp. 5–16.

5 André Legallois, interview, La Cambe, June 2004; Lucien and Germaine Rigault, interview, La Cambe, 6 June 2014. Lucien Rigault died in November 2014, followed by his wife Germaine in September 2015.

6 Karl Wegner, interview, June 1993, by Vince Milano; courtesy of *Der Erste Zug*.

7 ETHINT B-021, Obstlt. Fritz Ziegelmann, '352nd Infantry Division in Normandy' (1946).

8 Milano and Conner, *Normandiefront*, op. cit., p. 487.

9 By 25 July, the 352nd Infantry Division would have suffered 8,583 casualties, or 67 per cent of its 6 June strength of 13,228 men.

10 Gotthard Liebich, interview, Omaha Beach, June 2004. He was captured on 7 June and sent to England. In 1948 he married an English girl, stayed in touch with the Leterrier family, took British citizenship and settled in St Albans.

11 ETHINT B-021, Ziegelmann, '352nd Infantry Division', op. cit.

12 Severloh, *WN 62*, op. cit., pp. 47–51.

13 *Daily Telegraph*, 30 May 2004.

14 Severloh, *WN 62*, op. cit., pp. 47–51.

15 Ibid., pp. 25–47.

16 Maj. Carrol B. Smith, '116th Infantry, Omaha Beach, 6–10 June 1944' (Advanced Officers' Course, Infantry School, Ft Benning, Georgia, 1946–7), pp. 11–12. Today, the wide-open sands of Omaha Beach can be confusing because the shingle bank mentioned in contemporary accounts was afterwards bulldozed away, and not a trace remains, except at the western and eastern extremities.

17 Ibid., pp. 6–7.

18 Henri Biard, interview, Normandy, June 2013.

19 Cawthon, *Other Clay*, op cit., pp. 69–70.

20 Smith, '116th Infantry, Omaha Beach', op. cit., p. 12.

21 Capt. Charles H. Kidd, 'The Operation of Company "M", 116th Infantry in the Landing on Omaha Beach' (Advanced Officers' Course, Infantry School, Ft Benning, Georgia, 1946–7), pp. 36–40.

22   The US 17th Airborne Division did not arrive in England until 26 August 1944 and would first see action in the Battle of the Bulge.

23   Smith, '116th Infantry, Omaha Beach', op. cit., p. 19.

24   See Gary Sterne, *The Cover-Up at Omaha Beach: D-Day, the US Rangers and the Untold Story of Maisy Battery* (Pen & Sword, 2013). Both the Pointe du Hoc and Maisy sites have been developed as museums, Maisy most recently by the Briton who bought the site in 2004, opening it to the public in 2006.

25   Smith, '116th Infantry, Omaha Beach', op. cit., p. 23.

26   Joseph Balkoski, *Omaha Beach* (Stackpole, 2004), pp. 264–5.

27   Kidd, 'Operation of Company "M"', op. cit., p. 16.

28   Ibid, p. 20.

29   Obituary, *Baltimore Sun*, 13 July 2010.

30   Slaughter, *Omaha Beach and Beyond*, op. cit., p. 20. One of the founders of the National D-Day Memorial in Bedford, Virginia, Bob Slaughter died in 2012.

31   Ray Nance was the last of the Bedford Boys to die, in 2009; see obituary, *New York Times*, 22 April 2009.

32   See: Alex Kershaw, *The Bedford Boys* (Da Capo, 2003). Nineteen Company 'A' Bedford boys were killed on D-Day, with four more in the ensuing Normandy campaign.

33   Slaughter, *Omaha Beach and Beyond*, op. cit., p. 113.

34   Smith, '116th Infantry, Omaha Beach', op. cit., p. 10.

35   George (Jimmy) Green, interview, op. cit.

36   John Joseph Barnes, interview, 6 November 2001, courtesy of New York State Military Museum.

37   George (Jimmy) Green, interview, op. cit.

38   Ibid.

39   Slaughter, *Omaha Beach and Beyond*, op. cit., p. 116.

40   Nance interview with *USA Today* of 6 June 1994 cited in *LA Times* article, 'Ray Nance dies at 94; D-day survivor was last of Bedford Boys', Dennis McLennan, 6 May 2009.

41   S. L. A. Marshall, 'First Wave at Omaha Beach', *The Atlantic* (November 1960). The piece contained numerous inaccuracies: Marshall spoke of seven LCAs, not six, and omitted to name any British LCA crewmen, other than explicitly stating they were frightened and behaved in a cowardly fashion.

42   Slaughter, *Omaha Beach and Beyond*, op. cit., pp. 105–11.

43   Ibid.

44   Robert L. Sales, interview, 1999, courtesy of National D-Day Memorial, Bedford, Virginia. Bob died in 2015.

45   Dr Hal Baumgarten, interview, op. cit.

46   Ibid.

47   '3rd Armored Group, 6 June 1944, After Action Report' (NARA).

48   Yeide, *Steel Victory*, op. cit., p. 52.

49   S3 Journal, 743rd Tank Battalion, 6 June 1944 (NARA).

50   'D-Day: The View from a Tank on Omaha Beach', *Agence France-Presse*, 23 May 2014.

51 Upham retired as a lieutenant general commanding the US Second Army and died in 1993.

52 Marshall, 'First Wave at Omaha Beach', op. cit.

53 Robert L. Sales, interview, op. cit.

54 Smith, '116th Infantry, Omaha Beach', op. cit., p. 16.

55 Cawthon, *Other Clay*, op cit., p. 51

56 George (Jimmy) Green, interview, op. cit.

27. Omaha: Cota Takes Command

1 Interview by Cynthia Simison, 'World War II – Fifty Years Later', in *The Republican* (Springfield, Massachusetts), 6 June 1994. Drega died in 1996.

2 Roosevelt was born in 1887, Cota in 1893.

3 Kilvert-Jones, *Omaha Beach*, op. cit., pp. 75–6.

4 Donald R. McClarey, *The American Catholic*, 6 June 2009.

5 Robert Buckley, memoir, January 1945, courtesy of Clive Tirlemont, Mémoire & Data.

6 Seth Shepherd, 'The Story of the LCI(L)-92 in the Invasion of Normandy on June 6, 1944', in Commander Arch A. Mercy and Lee Grove (eds.), *Sea, Surf and Hell: The US Coast Guard in World War II* (Prentice Hall, 1945). Shepherd died in 2006.

7 Ibid.

8 Maj. Gen. John C. Raaen, Jr, lecture, USAEUR (US Army Europe), 1979.

9 Smith, '116th Infantry, Omaha Beach', op. cit., p. 20.

10 Ibid.

11 Maj. Gen. Robert Riis Ploger, interview, Washington DC, June 1984. A decorated Vietnam veteran, Gen. Ploger died in 2002, having never recovered from the death of his son during the 9/11 attacks.

12 'LCT-149, After Action Report, 26 June 1944' (NARA).

13 'LCT-207, After Action Report, 25 June 1944' (NARA).

14 Interview by Dave Bergmeier, *Abilene* (Kansas) *Reflector-Chronicle*, 7 June 2009. Conwell died in 2016.

15 Maj. Gen. John Raaen, *Intact: A First-Hand Account of D-Day* (Reedy Press, 2012), p. 49.

16 Cawthon, *Other Clay*, op cit., pp. 53–7.

17 '111th Field Artillery Battalion on D-Day', After Action Report (NARA), pp. 1–2.

18 'The Citizen Soldiers of the 111th Field Artillery', courtesy of Tom Ligon, Jr, http://www.tomligon.com/Toms/Dad/FA111.pdf.

19 '111th Field Artillery Battalion on D-Day', op. cit., pp. 1–2.

20 Smith, '116th Infantry, Omaha Beach', op. cit., p. 36.

21 Charles Lilly, 'Landing in Normandy', undated memoir, courtesy of ww2lct.org.

22 Cawthon, *Other Clay*, op cit., pp. 58–60.

23 *Saturday Evening Post*, 10 June 1944.

24 Col. Paul W. Thompson, 'D-Day on Omaha Beach', *The Infantry Journal*, Vol. 66 (June 1945), p. 40.

25 Ross, 'Essayons', op. cit., pp. 47–8.

26   '111th Field Artillery Battalion on D-Day', op. cit., p. 3.

27   Pederson et al., *Armor in Operation Neptune*, op. cit., p. 98.

28   Cawthon refuted this in *Other Clay*, stating that he received two separate wounds to opposite sides of his face, at different times, which gave the appearance of a bullet passing through. See *Other Clay*, pp. 58–9.

29   Ross, 'Essayons', op. cit., pp. 43–4.

30   'The Citizen Soldiers of the 111th Field Artillery', op. cit.

31   '111th Field Artillery Battalion on D-Day', op. cit., pp. 3–4.

32   Ibid., p. 17.

33   For his gallantry and leadership on 6 June, Meeks was awarded a Silver Star. He kept the boots he wore on D-Day and in 1998 they were donated by his son to the D-Day Memorial, Bedford, Virginia.

34   Kidd, 'Operation of Company "M"', op. cit., p. 19.

35   Ibid., p. 18.

36   The National Archives (TNA): CAB 106/1055.

37   LAC John Cubitt, 'Memories of D-Day', 1984, courtesy of www.therafatomaha-beach.com.

38   Ibid.

39   Kidd, 'Operation of Company "M"', op. cit., pp. 21–2; Smith, '116th Infantry, Omaha Beach', op. cit., p. 22.

40   Balkoski, *Omaha Beach*, op. cit., pp. 284–8.

41   Kidd, 'Operation of Company "M"', op. cit., pp. 21–2.

42   Stephen Badsey and Tim Bean, *Battle Zone Normandy: Omaha Beach* (Sutton, 2004), p. 156.

43   Smith, '116th Infantry, Omaha Beach', op. cit., p. 22.

44   Daniel Folsom, interview, op. cit.

45   Dr Robert Barnes Ware is buried at Colleville, plot G, row 17, grave 8.

46   Both Hoback brothers are commemorated at Colleville, Bedford at plot G, row 10, grave 28, Raymond on the Memorial to the Missing.

47   Barran Tucker, interview, US Department of Veterans Affairs, 30 May 2014.

48   Pogue, *Pogue's War*, op. cit., p. 57.

49   Pederson et al., *Armor in Operation Neptune*, op. cit., p. 121.

50   Kidd, 'Operation of Company "M"', op. cit., pp. 36–40.

51   Cawthon, *Other Clay*, op cit., pp. 57–63.

52   Smith, '116th Infantry, Omaha Beach', op. cit., p. 36.

53   Slaughter, *Omaha Beach and Beyond*, op. cit., p. 118.

54   Obituary, *Baltimore Sun*, 13 July 2010; also see Holbrook Bradley, *War Correspondent: From D-Day to the Elbe* (iUniverse, 2007).

55   Lawrence A. Bekelesky is buried at Colleville, plot B, row 5, grave 44.

28. Rangers, Lead the Way!

1   Thomas M. Hatfield, *Rudder: From Leader to Legend* (Texas A&M University Press, 2011), p. 117.

2   Douglas Brinkley, *The Boys of Pointe du Hoc* (William Morrow, 2005), pp. 66–8.

3   Ibid., p. 72.

4   Ibid., p. 74.

5   Goranson died at Libertyville, Illinois, in 2012.

6   NARA FMS B-432: Obstlt. Fritz Ziegelmann, 'The Invasion: 352nd Infantry Division'.

7   *Omaha Beachhead, 6 June–13 June 1944* (American Forces in Action Series, Historical Division, War Department, 1945), p. 79.

8   NARA FMS B-432: Ziegelmann, 'The Invasion', op. cit. He talks of being at 'Pillbox 67', but this cannot be right because WN67 was beyond the Pointe du Hoc, near Grandcamp, and had no line of sight to Omaha; Ziegelmann also spoke of Pillbox 76 being attacked by enemy commandos (Rangers), 'but after being repelled with casualties withdrew toward Gruchy', which is near WN74.

9   NARA FMS B-432: Ziegelmann, 'The Invasion', op. cit.

10 Cited in Brinkley, *The Boys of Pointe du Hoc*, op. cit., p. 136.

11 Helmut Konrad von Keusgen, *Pointe du Hoc: Rätsel um einen deutschen Stützpunkt* (Hek Creativ, 2006), p. 82.

12 Steven J. Zaloga, *Rangers Lead the Way: Pointe-du-Hoc D-Day 1944* (Osprey, 2009), pp. 10–30.

13 André Heintz, interview, op. cit.

14 W. C. Heinz, 'I Took My Son to Omaha Beach', *Collier's*, 11 June 1954.

15 Ibid.

16 Ibid.

17 'Lost Lancaster Crew Identified after 68 Years by Wireless Operator's Wedding Ring', *Daily Telegraph*, 1 October 2012.

18 Ibid.

19 Heinz, 'I Took My Son to Omaha Beach', op. cit.

20 COHQ (Combined Operations HQ), 'Mechanical Aids for Scaling Cliffs', Bulletin X/40 (September 1944).

21 Leonard Lomell, interview, WW2 Ranger Battalions National Reunion, New Orleans, August 2001; he died in 2011.

22 Ibid.

23 Ibid.

24 Ibid.

25 Heinz, 'I Took My Son to Omaha Beach', op. cit.

26 Ronald L. Lane, *Rudder's Rangers* (Ranger Associates, 1979), p. 91.

27 Hatfield, *Rudder: From Leader to Legend*, op. cit., p. 129.

28 Ibid., p. 127.

29 My thanks to my colleague Frank Baldwin for this reference; their citations are at The National Archives (TNA): WO/373/50.

30 Heinz, 'I Took My Son to Omaha Beach', op. cit.; obituary, Lt Colonel Thomas H. Trevor, *Daily Telegraph*, 26 November 2011.

31 Leonard Lomell, interview, op. cit.

32 Ibid.

33 Ibid. Jack Kuhn ended up as chief of police in Altoona, Pennsylvania, and died in 2002.

34   Each German strongpoint at Omaha was afterwards mapped in detail; see *From Report on German Fortifications* (Office of Chief of Engineers, US Army, 1944).

35   Raaen, lecture, op. cit.

36   William B. Kirkland, Jr, *Destroyers at Normandy: Naval Gunfire Support at Omaha Beach* (Naval Historical Foundation, Washington DC, 1994), pp. 28–30.

37   Austin Prosser, interview, op. cit.

38   Kirkland, *Destroyers at Normandy*, op. cit., p. 33.

39   Kilvert-Jones, *Omaha Beach*, op. cit., p. 127.

40   O'Neill, 'D-Day as Seen from US *LCT-544*', op. cit.

41   Blegen, 'LCT(5) Flotilla 18 at Omaha Beach', op. cit.

42   Tom Bernard, '64 Hours of Battle', *Yank*, 18 June 1944.

43   Courtesy of www.wpepe.com/dday.

44   Bill Ryan, interview, op. cit.

45   Heinz, 'I Took My Son to Omaha Beach', op. cit.

46   *Gettysburg Times*, 5 June 1959.

47   'Omaha Beach, As It Was and Is; Eisenhower Conducts Tour for CBS Show', *New York Times*, 6 June 1964.

48   Hatfield, *Rudder: From Leader to Legend*, op. cit., p. 157.

49   Gordon A. Harrison, *Cross-Channel Attack* (US Army Center of Military History, 1951), p. 322.

50   Ryan, *The Longest Day*, op. cit., p. 210.

51   Hatfield, *Rudder: From Leader to Legend*, op. cit., p. 166.

52   Lane, *Rudder's Rangers*, op. cit.

29. Omaha: Big Red One

1   Walsh, 'D-Day Reflections from a Soldier', op. cit.

2   Pluskat's bunker was at WN59; see Ryan, *The Longest Day*, op. cit., pp. 116–19, 173–4. Pluskat survived the war and died in June 2002. New evidence suggests Pluskat may have hoodwinked Ryan for *The Longest Day*, and was actually absent from his post. 'At 0300 hours on 6 June 1944 a blacked-out armada was seen on the horizon from WN.62 and three white and three red flares were fired off inviting the recognition signal of the day. WN.60 also fired off its recognition flares. The armada did not reply ... Machine-gunner Gefreiter Hein Severloh suggested to his artillery officer, Oblt Frerking at WN.62, that Maj. Pluskat should be informed. A short while later Frerking emerged from his bunker and told Severloh that Pluskat could not be found at his HQ, nor at his forward command post, nor at his quarters. It was common knowledge that Pluskat had spent a lot of time in the company of four ladies of the Front-Theatre in recent days, though he knew that the invasion was imminent.' See: Helmut, Freiherr von Keusgen, *Stützpunkt WN.62* (HEK Verlag, Garbsen, 2004), p. 52.

3   Severloh, *WN 62*, op. cit., p. 52.

4   Ibid., pp. 53–4.

5   Ibid.

6   Franz Gockel, interview at WN62, 6 June 2004.

7   Badsey and Bean, *Battle Zone Normandy: Omaha Beach*, op. cit., p. 24.

8   Surpassed only by firing 435,165 rounds during 738 days of combat in Vietnam.

9   John C. McManus, 'The Man Who Took Omaha Beach', *Politico Magazine*, 5 June 2014.

10 Steven Flaig, 'Clarence R. Huebner: An American Military Story of Achievement' (Master's thesis, University of North Texas, 2006).

11 Although I have served with many individually mobilised 29th Infantry Division soldiers in the Balkans, Iraq and Afghanistan.

12 'Biography of Hyam Haas', op. cit.

13 Ibid.

14 Obituary, Frederick E. Boyer, *Baker City Herald*, 7 March 2018.

15 Obst Walter Korfes: Château de Sully; I Battalion: Maisons; 1.Kompanie: Port-en-Bessin; 2.Kp: Sainte-Honorine; 3.Kp: Colleville; 4.Kp: Longues; II Battalion: Saint-Croix; 5.Kp: north of Creully; 6.Kp: Bazenville; 7.Kp: Saint-Croix; 8.Kp: north of Creully: III Battalion: Château du Jucoville; 9.Kp: Château de Gruchy, Englesqueville; 10.Kp: Saint-Laurent; 11.Kp: Manoir de Than, Vierville; 12.Kp: Grandcamp: 439 *Ost-Bataillon*: Les Veys.

16 Severloh, *WN 62*, op. cit., pp. 53–4.

17 Ibid., p. 56.

18 'Opening Omaha Beach: Ensign Karnowski and NCDU-45', 6 June 2014, courtesy of Dr Frank Blazich, Jr, historian, US Navy Seabee Museum.

19 Severloh, *WN 62*, op. cit., p. 58.

20 Beck et al., *The Corps of Engineers*, op. cit., pp. 323–5.

21 'Opening Omaha Beach', op. cit.

22 Obituary, Robert N. Lowenstein, courtesy of 299th Combat Engineers Association.

23 John C. McManus, *The Dead and Those About to Die: D-Day: The Big Red One at Omaha Beach* (NAL/Penguin, 2014), p. 69.

24 Pederson et al., *Armor in Operation Neptune*, op. cit., pp. 79–80.

25 BBC, *Journeys to the Bottom of the Sea – D-Day: The Untold Story*, aired 20 May 2002.

26 Pederson et al., *Armor in Operation Neptune*, op. cit., pp. 80–90.

27 Ibid., pp. 95–8.

28 Spalding interview cited in Pogue, *Pogue's War*, op. cit., pp. 64–75.

29 Ibid.

30 McManus, *The Dead and Those About to Die*, op. cit., pp. 182–3.

31 Joseph P. Vaghi, 'Easy Red Beach, Normandy', memoir courtesy of 6th Naval Beach Battalion Association; obituary, *Washington Post*, 8 September 2012.

32 Manuel Perez, 'Carusi's Thieves', courtesy of 6th Naval Beach Battalion Association. Perez died in 2003.

33 Vaghi, 'Easy Red Beach, Normandy', op. cit.

34 Perez, 'Carusi's Thieves', op. cit.

35 Edward Colimore, 'A Medic's Memory of D-Day: Unimaginable Carnage', *Philadelphia Inquirer*, 6 June 2016. Friedenberg died in 2018.

36 Ibid.

37 Interview by Cynthia Simison, 'World War II – Fifty Years Later', in *The Republican* (Springfield, Massachusetts), 6 June 1994.

38 'Biography of Hyam Haas', op. cit.
39 Perez, 'Carusi's Thieves', op. cit.
40 Blegen, 'LCT(5) Flotilla 18 at Omaha Beach', op. cit.; 'Report of Damage to Landing Craft due to Enemy Action, by Commander, LCT Flotilla 18' (11 July 1944).
41 Dean Weissert, interview, 2005, Library of Congress Veteran's History Project.
42 Ibid.
43 Interviews by Frank Whelan, *The Morning Call*, 29 May 1994 and 6 June 2004.
44 'After Action Report, USS *Frankford*', 6 June 1944 (NARA).
45 Walsh, 'D-Day Reflections from a Soldier', op. cit.
46 Wilhelm Gerstner, interview, Normandy, June 2013.
47 The Anti-Tank Battalion of 352nd Division (HQ at Vouilly) comprised a company of fourteen or fifteen Marder 75mm self-propelled guns (based at the Ferme Buhours de Bricqueville); a company of ten StuG 75mm assault guns (Château de Colombières); and a company of nine Opel-mounted 37mm flak guns (HQ Pont l'Abbé).
48 Obituary, *New York Times*, 21 February 2014.
49 Col. S. B. Mason, *Danger Forward: The Story of the First Division in World War II* (Society of the First Division, 1947).
50 'Biography of Hyam Haas', op. cit.
51 Ibid.
52 Pogue, *Pogue's War*, op. cit., pp. 64–75.
53 Killen is buried at Colleville cemetery, plot J, row 15, grave 23.

30. Omaha: E-3 – the Colleville draw

1   Interview by David Venditta, *The Morning Call*, 25 May 2009.
2   Carell, *Invasion*, op. cit., p. 84; Franz Gockel, interview, op. cit.
3   Courtesy of www.wpepe.com/dday. Pepe died in April 2017, requesting the 'few handfuls of costly Omaha sand' he had brought home on a return trip 'be added to my ashes and spread out over the ocean, when I will once again join my Band of Brothers'.
4   Ibid.
5   Franz Gockel, interview, op. cit.
6   Henri Leroutier, interview, Trevières, November 2013.
7   Kilvert-Jones, *Omaha Beach*, op. cit., p. 149. Friedman would win a Silver Star for his actions on D-Day; he died in 2002 and is buried in Arlington National Cemetery.
8   Venditta, *The Morning Call*, op cit.
9   Franz Gockel, interview, op. cit.
10 Carell, *Invasion*, op. cit., p. 84; Franz Gockel, interview, op. cit.
11 Venditta, *The Morning Call*, op cit.
12 Kilvert-Jones, *Omaha Beach*, op. cit., p. 152.
13 Ziezulewicz, '1st Infantry Division Led Assault on D-Day', op. cit.
14 John Finke, interview, 1972, Thames Television, *World at War* archives. Finke died in 1996 and is buried at Arlington National Cemetery.

15 The two-dollar bill is now a prized exhibit at the National D-Day Memorial in Bedford, Virginia.

16 Charles Hurlbut, interview, op. cit.

17 Ibid.

18 O'Neill, 'D-Day as Seen from US *LCT-544*', op. cit.

19 '*LCT-199*, After Action Report', 26 June 1944 (NARA); this report was endorsed on 7 August with Admiral Hall's recommendation of a Silver Star for the skipper.

20 '*LCT-305*, After Action Report', 13 June 1944; 'Damage Report', Commander 18th LCT Flotilla, 11 July 1944 (both NARA).

21 Charles Hurlbut, interview, op. cit.

22 O'Neill, 'D-Day as Seen from US *LCT-544*', op. cit.

23 'Auszug aus dem Fernsprech-Meldebuch (1a) der 352. I.D (Extracts from Telephone Diary of 352nd Division (Coastal Defence Section Bayeux))', cited in David C. Isby (ed.), *The German Army at D-Day* (Greenhill, 2004), p. 210.

24 Severloh, *WN 62*, op. cit., pp. 115–16.

25 'Extracts from Telephone Diary of 352nd Division', op. cit., p. 211.

26 Ibid., pp. 63–6.

27 Valentine M. Miele, interview, op. cit. Miele died in June 2017.

28 Major Carl W. Plitt, Regimental S-3, '16th Infantry: Summary of Regimental Situation on D-Day, 6 June 1944' (NARA/ Box 5919).

29 McManus, *The Dead and Those About to Die*, op. cit., p. 179.

30 Plitt, '16th Infantry: Summary of Regimental Situation', op. cit.

31 *Personal Wartime Memoir of Maj. Charles E. Tegtmeyer, Medical Corps, Regimental Surgeon, 16th Infantry* (US Army Medical Department, Office of Medical History, 1960). Tegtmeyer received a Distinguished Service Cross for his actions on 6 June.

32 Yeide, *Steel Victory*, op. cit., pp. 51–2.

33 McManus, *The Dead and Those About to Die*, op. cit., pp. 180–1.

34 Yeide, *Steel Victory*, op. cit., pp. 51–2.

35 *Personal Wartime Memoir of Maj. Charles E. Tegtmeyer*, pp. 4, 9.

36 Kilvert-Jones, *Omaha Beach*, op. cit., pp. 154–5.

37 'God Was on the Beach on D-Day', op. cit.

38 Interview, *Daily Gazette* (Utah) and Associated Press, 12 July 2014.

39 Details of the medal recipients are contained in Phil Nordyke's *American Heroes of World War II: Normandy June 6, 1944* (Historic Ventures, 2014).

40 Walsh, 'D-Day Reflections from a Soldier', op. cit.

41 Robert Capa, *Slightly Out of Focus* (Henry Holt, 1947), Kindle, p. 1649.

42 Franz Gockel, interview, op. cit.

43 Interview with Corporal Steven Hoffer, cited in Balkoski, *Omaha Beach*, op. cit., p. 254.

44 Capa, *Slightly Out of Focus*, op. cit., p. 1684.

45 Franz Gockel, interview, op. cit.

46 Franz Gockel's boots and Bible are now exhibits at the National World War II Museum, New Orleans.

47 Capa, *Slightly Out of Focus*, op. cit., pp. 1729–39.

48   Ibid, p. 1739.
49   Severloh, *WN 62*, op. cit., pp. 70–2.
50   Capa, *Slightly Out of Focus*, op. cit., p. 1770.
51   Ibid., p. 1674.
52   Madalena Araujo, 'Robert Capa's "Lost" D-Day Photos May Never Have Been Shot at All, says His Former Editor', CNN, 12 November 2014.
53   I am enormously grateful to internationally renowned photo-critic A. D. Coleman and his www.nearbycafe.com website for alerting me to the alternative history of Robert Capa on D-Day, reconstructed in thirty-seven forensic articles spanning four years.
54   Bradley, *A Soldier's Story*, op. cit., pp. 270–2.
55   At his death in 2012, Chet Hansen was probably the last to have had a ringside view of the SHAEF commanders before, during and after the invasion; see obituary, *New York Times*, 25 October 2012.
56   Balkoski, *Omaha Beach*, op. cit., p. 262.
57   John L. Armellino, memoir courtesy of Laurent Lefebvre, Omaha Beach Memorial.
58   Ibid.
59   Mike McKinney, interview, op. cit.
60   Monteith is another name that crops up in *Saving Private Ryan*.
61   'Company "L" After Action Report' (NARA).
62   Charles Hurlbut, interview, op. cit.
63   Maj. Gen. J. Milnor Roberts, ADC to Gen. Gerow, memoir, 2004, American Veterans Center, Arlington, Virginia.
64   Donald E. Rivette, 'Notes on 6 June, 1944', courtesy of Richard Rivette, *The Mountain Enterprise* (California), 6 June 2008.
65   Ibid.
66   Ibid.
67   Plitt, '16th Infantry: Summary of Regimental Situation', op. cit.
68   Yeide, *Steel Victory*, op. cit., p. 53.
69   'Biography of Hyam Haas', op. cit.
70   Pierre Darondel, interview, La Cambe, June 2013.
71   'German Soldier Buried 60 Years After Dying in Battle', *Daily Telegraph*, 7 June 2004.
72   'Remains of Five Nazi Soldiers Killed on D-Day Are Discovered in France', *Daily Mail*, 20 May 2009.
73   'Willmar Sailor's Remains Return Home 72 Years After His D-Day Death', *Star Tribune*, 28 April 2016.
74   'Twin Brothers Reunited 74 years After WWII Death at Normandy, *Associated Press*, 19 June 2018.
75   Rear Admiral Edward Ellsberg, *The Far Shore: An American at D-Day* (Dodd, Mead, 1960), p. 300.
76   Beck et al., *The Corps of Engineers*, op. cit., pp. 340–4; Major Brett Peters, 'Mulberry-American: The Artificial Harbour at Omaha' (MA thesis, US Army Command & General Staff College, 2011), pp. 42–3.
77   Peters, 'Mulberry-American', op. cit., pp. 44–50.

78   Ibid., pp. 54–8.

79   Mike McKinney, interview, op. cit.

80   Cole C. Kingseed (ed.), *From Omaha Beach to Dawson's Ridge: The Combat Journal of Captain Joe Dawson* (Naval Institute Press, 2005), pp. 155–6.

31. Gold: Men of the Double-T

1   Tute, Costello and Hughes, *D-Day*, op. cit., p. 199.

2   As at Omaha, the 736th Grenadier Regiment was part of Richter's 716th Infantry Division, but under command of Dietrich Kraiss and the 352nd Division; on 29 May 1944, the 441st *Ost-Bataillon* was located as follows – HQ: Crépon; 1st Company: Vaux; 2nd Company: Reviers; 3rd Company: Meuvaines; 4th Company: Ver-sur-Mer.

3   Russell Miller, *Nothing Less Than Victory: An Oral History of D-Day* (Michael Joseph, 1993).

4   Howarth, *Dawn of D-Day*, op. cit., p. 174.

5   The National Archives (TNA): WO 291/246, '[British] Army Operational Research Group (AORG): Opposition encountered on British beaches in Normandy on D-Day' (1945).

6   Ibid.

7   Fred Archer, interview, Brighton, 2014. He was captured on D-Day with the 9th Parachute Bn; the Maquis later helped him to escape from a hospital in Paris.

8   Some sources claim this unit comprised five battalions (*Schnelle-Abteilungen* 505, 507, 513, 517, 518). Obstlt Hugo von und zu Aufsess died in action on 18 July 1944, and his unit was disbanded on 5 September.

9   John Shanahan, interview, Manchester, June 1994.

10   Max Hearst, interview, 1991, cited in B. S. Barnes, *The Sign of the Double 'T': The 50th Northumbrian Division July 1943–December 1944* (Sentinel Press, 1999), p. 62.

11   Cheall, *Fighting Through from Dunkirk to Hamburg*, op. cit., p. 96.

12   Sir Alexander Stanier, interview, op. cit.; see his *Sammy's Wars*, op. cit., pp. 37–8; also obituary *Daily Telegraph*, 11 January 1995.

13   Initially the inexperienced 49th (West Riding) Division had been slated to lead the assault on Gold Beach.

14   Peter Martin, interview cited in Bailey, *Forgotten Voices*, op. cit.

15   Private George Worthington, interview, 1991, cited in Barnes, *The Sign*, op. cit., p. 62.

16   Private J. Foster, interview, 1995, cited in ibid.

17   Stanley Dwyer, interview cited in ibid., p. 65.

18   The Northumberland Hussars (a former horsed yeomanry regiment) were given two extra anti-tank batteries for D-Day: Stanier's 231st Brigade would land with the 234th and 288th Batteries; Knox's 69th Brigade was to be supported by the 99th Battery, while the 198th Battery would land after the first assault.

19   No. 10 Beach Group Comprised: RN Beach Commando Unit Q & RN 7th Beach Signal Section; 6th Borderers; 25th and 31st Field Dressing Stations, 30th, 41st

and 42nd Field Sanitary Units, 24th and 30th Field Transfusion Units, RAMC; 12th Ordnance Beach Depot, RAOC; 73rd, 112th, 120th, 173rd and 243rd Pioneer Companies; 25th Beach Recovery Section, REME; 5th Detail Issue Depot, 356th and 705th General Transport Companies and 244th Petrol Depot, RASC; 90th Field Company, 51st Mechanised Equipment Section, 23rd and 1,035th Port Operating Companies and 23rd Stores Section, Royal Engineers; 240th Provost Company, Corps of Military Police; 108th RAF Beach Flight and 55th Balloon Squadron, RAF.

20   In British and Canadian armoured formations, a squadron equated to a company and a troop to a platoon; regiments comprised three squadrons, each of four troops of four Shermans (total sixteen), plus three in Sqn HQ; regimental HQ possessed another four, with a large Recon Troop of eleven Start M5 tanks.

21   Wheeled and tracked Royal Artillery regiments comprised three eight-gun batteries, each of two four-gun troops; most operated the 25-pounder field gun.

22   The National Archives (TNA): ADM 179/1558, 'Force G Operations Order'.

23   The National Archives (TNA): CAB 106/1060, 'Brigadier Hargest Reports, 6 June–10 July'.

24   Ryan, *The Longest Day*, op. cit., p. 216.

25   Ten LCOCU personnel were decorated for 'gallantry, skill, determination and undaunted devotion to duty during the initial landings on the coast of Normandy', winning three DSCs, an MC and six DCMs.

26   Warner, *The D-Day Landings*, op. cit., pp. 121–2.

27   The National Archives (TNA): ADM 179/505, 'Report of Eastern Task Force G'.

28   Neillands and De Normann, *D-Day 1944*, op. cit., p. 163.

29   Roger Hill, *Destroyer Captain* (Collins, 1975); and see obituary, *Daily Telegraph*, 22 May 2001.

30   Johnson and Dunphie, *Brightly Shone the Dawn*, op. cit., p. 72.

31   The National Archives (TNA): WO 171/517, '50th Infantry Division, 6 June 1944'.

32   Geoffrey Picot, *Accidental Warrior: In the Front Line from Normandy till Victory* (Penguin, 1994), pp. 43–4.

33   Letter of 23 June 1944, courtesy of his daughter Susan Dudley-Ward.

34   Andrew Holborn, *The D-Day Landing on Gold Beach, 6 June 1944* (Bloomsbury, 2017), Kindle, pp. 3385–400.

35   Ryan, *The Longest Day*, op. cit., p. 217.

36   Neillands and De Normann, *D-Day 1944*, op. cit., p. 164.

37   Gardiner, *D-Day*, op. cit., pp. 156–7.

38   Major A. R. C. Mott, memoir, Imperial War Museum, Documents ref. 8217.

39   Hastings, *Overlord*, op. cit., p. 106.

40   Ambrose, *D-Day*, op. cit., p. 523.

41   Holborn, *The D-Day Landing on Gold Beach*, op. cit., Kindle, p. 3426.

42   The National Archives (TNA): WO 171/1285, '1st Dorsets War Diary, June 1944'.

43   WO 171/517: 'HQ 50th Division War Diary June 1944', op. cit.

44   Les Holden, memoir cited in Holborn, *The D-Day Landing on Gold Beach*, op. cit., p. 3871.

45   Gardiner, *D-Day*, op. cit., p. 157.

46 WO 171/517: 'HQ 50th Division War Diary June 1944', op. cit.

47 The National Archives (TNA): WO 171/1305, '1st Hampshires War Diary, June 1944'.

48 Ambrose, *D-Day*, op. cit., p. 521.

49 Ibid., pp. 523–6.

50 Dr Christopher Bartley, interview, Oxford, 1994.

51 Lt Col. C. A. R. Nevill, 'We Landed on D-Day', memoir courtesy of Devon and Dorsets Museum, The Keep, Dorchester; see his obituary, *Daily Telegraph*, 12 October 2002.

52 The National Archives (TNA): WO 171/1278, '2nd Devons War Diary, June 1944'.

53 The National Archives (TNA): WO 171/714, 'HQ 231 Brigade War Diary, June 1944'.

54 Charles Hargrove, interview, Paris, June 1994.

55 Holborn, *The D-Day Landing on Gold Beach*, op. cit., p. 3741; memoir courtesy of the Johnson family.

56 Hastings, *Overlord*, op. cit., p. 107.

57 Neillands and De Normann, *D-Day 1944*, op. cit., p. 166.

58 Brigadier Sir Nick Somerville, interview, Hampshire, June 1984.

59 The National Archives (TNA): WO 171/1298, '2nd Glosters War Diary, June 1944'.

60 TNA: WO 171/1305, '1st Hampshires War Diary', op. cit.

61 WO 171/517: 'HQ 50th Division War Diary June 1944', op. cit.

62 Memoir courtesy of Rev. Robert Watt's son, Tom Watt.

63 Charles Hargrove, interview, op. cit.

64 The National Archives (TNA): WO 171/1380, '2nd South Wales Borderers War Diary, June 1944'.

65 Holborn, *The D-Day Landing on Gold Beach*, op. cit., p. 3769.

66 Gardiner, *D-Day*, op. cit., p. 158.

67 Warner, *The D-Day Landings*, op. cit., pp. 232–3.

68 Holborn, *The D-Day Landing on Gold Beach*, op. cit., p. 4368.

69 Edward Austin Baker, interview, 2008, Imperial War Museum Sound Archive, ref. 31328.

70 Kershaw, *D-Day*, op. cit., p. 261.

71 Gullet, *Not As a Duty Only*, op. cit., p. 136.

72 The National Archives (TNA): WO 171/651, 'HQ 69 Brigade War Diary, 6 June 1944'.

73 Lt Gen. Sir B. G. Horrocks (Intro.), *A Short History of 8th Armoured Brigade* (8 Armd Bde, 1945), ch. 4.

74 Boustred, interview cited in Shaw and Shaw, *We Remember D-Day*, op. cit., p. 115.

75 The National Archives (TNA): WO 171/1398, '5th East Yorks War Diary, June 1944'.

76 The National Archives (TNA): WO 373/48/78, Roger Francis Bell, Citation for award.

77 Gullet, *Not As a Duty Only*, op. cit., p. 136.

78 In the pecking order of gallantry and service medals, the Victoria Cross (VC) rates above all others, followed by Distinguished Service Order (DSO), Order or

Member of the British Empire (OBE/MBE), Military Cross (MC) and mention in despatches.

79   Lt Col. R. H. W. S. Hastings (1917–90), interview, Alresford, 1980; see his auto-biography, *An Undergraduate's War* (Bellhouse Publishing, 1997).

80   Gullet, *Not As a Duty Only*, op. cit., pp. 136–7.

81   The National Archives (TNA): WO 171/1302, '6th Green Howards War Diary, June 1944'.

82   Hastings, *Overlord*, op. cit., p. 110.

83   'Recollections of Sergeant Major Hollis, VC', Camberley Staff College Battlefield Tour Notes, 1960–70, JSCSC Library, Watchfield, UK.

84   Holborn, *The D-Day Landing on Gold Beach*, op. cit., p. 3633.

85   LCIs *499, 500, 501, 502, 506, 508* and *511.*

86   The National Archives (TNA): WO 171/670, 'HQ 151 Infantry Brigade War Diary, June 1944'.

87   Lofthouse would receive an MC for his leadership of 'D' Company; The National Archives (TNA): WO 373/48 0308.

88   Howarth, *Dawn of D-Day*, op. cit., pp. 189–91.

89   TNA: WO 171/670, 'HQ 151 Infantry Brigade War Diary, June 1944', op. cit.

90   TNA: WO 171/1398, '5th East Yorks War Diary, June 1944', op. cit.

91   Major L. F. Ellis, *Victory in the West, Vol. 1: The Battle of Normandy* (HMSO, 1962), pp. 210–11.

92   Gullet, *Not As a Duty Only*, op. cit., pp. 138–9.

93   Stan Cox, Sherwood Rangers, interview June 1995.

94   TNA: WO 171/1298, '2nd Glosters War Diary, June 1944', op. cit.

95   William Harry Pinnegar, interview, 1999, Imperial War Museum Sound Archive, ref. 18827.

96   Stan Cox, interview, op. cit.

97   Harrison, *Cross-Channel Attack*, op. cit., p. 332.

98   Russell A. Miller, *Nothing Less Than Victory: An Oral History of D-Day* (Michael Joseph, 1993), p. 335.

99   Ambrose, *D-Day*, op. cit., p. 566.

100 Olivier Wieviorka, *Normandy* (Harvard University Press, 2008), p. 197.

101 Jay Wertz, *World War II Firsthand: D-Day* (Weider History, 2011), p. 144.

102 Ellis, *Victory in the West, Vol. 1*, op. cit., p. 178.

103 Alan Harris, 'The Mulberry Harbours', *Royal Engineers Journal*, Vol. 108 (April 1994).

104 My thanks to Andrew Holborn, author of *The D-Day Landing on Gold Beach*, for drawing this to my attention.

105 Sir Alexander Stanier, interview, op. cit.; see his *Sammy's Wars*, op. cit.

32. Juno: Maple Leaf at War

1   'D-Day and the Gooseberry, 6th June 1944', 25 May 2004, courtesy of BBC, WW2 People's War.

2   The National Archives (TNA): DEFE 2/433, 'Report of Special Observer Party Investigating the Effect of Fire Support, 22 June 1944'.

3 Keller (1900–54) was known to have a drinking problem and viewed as shell-shy, jumpy and highly strung. His British superiors (Crocker of I Corps and Dempsey at the Second Army) thought him unfit to command, but issues of national pride were also at stake, and even his own offer to go was rejected. He was wounded on 8 August and left the theatre, dying exactly a decade later on a tenth-anniversary D-Day pilgrimage to Normandy.

4 I am most grateful to Major Tim Saunders for the use of this and other extracts from his excellent *Battleground Europe: Juno Beach* (Pen & Sword, 2003). This is Kindle p. 887. Mutch's body was later washed ashore and was buried in the nearby Canadian war cemetery at Beny-sur-Mer.

5 Keith May Briggs, interview, Imperial War Museum Sound Archive, ref. 16696.

6 Reeman, *D-Day 6th June 1944*, op. cit., p. 8.

7 'Royal Winnipeg Rifles War Diary June 1944', RG24-C-3, Vol. 15233, courtesy of Laurier Military History Archive.

8 Saunders, *Juno Beach*, op cit., Kindle p.1419.

9 Major Lockhart Ross Fulton, interview, Imperial War Museum Sound Archive, ref. 34424.

10 'Royal Winnipeg Rifles War Diary June 1944', op. cit.

11 Reeman, *D-Day 6th June 1944*, op. cit., pp. 8–9.

12 Neillands and De Normann, *D-Day*, op. cit., p. 184.

13 Bill Newell, memoir, courtesy of the Memory Project, Historica Canada.

14 Hammerton, *Achtung! Minen!*, op. cit., p. 64.

15 Memoir courtesy of the Tank Museum, Bovington, Dorset.

16 'Regina Rifles Regiment War Diary June 1944', RG-24-C-3, Vols. 15198–9, courtesy of Laurier Military History Archive.

17 Saunders, *Juno Beach*, op cit., Kindle. p. 1253.

18 Ibid., Kindle. p. 1298.

19 Memoir courtesy of the 1st Hussars Museum, London, Ontario.

20 'Regina Rifles Regiment War Diary 6 June 1944', op. cit.

21 Memoir and personal interview, Léo Gariépy, Mont Ormel Museum, 1994.

22 Ibid.

23 '6th Canadian Armoured Regiment (1st Hussars) War Diary June 1944', RG-24-C-3, Vol. 14213, courtesy of Laurier Military History Archive.

24 Marc Milner, *Stopping the Panzers* (University Press of Kansas, 2014), Kindle, p. 3520.

25 Hickey, *The Scarlet Dawn*, op. cit.

26 Saunders, *Juno Beach*, op. cit., Kindle. p. 896.

27 Charles C. Martin, *Battle Diary* (Dundurn Press, 1994); also documentary *Battle Diary: A Day in the Life of Charlie Martin*, dir. Martyn Burke, CBC, and courtesy of Queen's Own Rifles of Canada Regimental Museum and Archives, Toronto.

28 Memoir courtesy of Queen's Own Rifles of Canada Regimental Museum and Archives, Toronto.

29 Ibid.

30 Memoir courtesy of Juno Beach Museum.

31 Doug Hester, memoir, courtesy of Queen's Own Rifles of Canada Regimental Museum and Archives, Toronto.

32 Neillands and De Normann, *D-Day*, op. cit., pp. 194–5.

33 Ibid., p. 197.

34 Memoir, 2004, courtesy of BBC, WW2 People's War.

35 'Queen's Own Rifles of Canada War Diary June 1944', RG-24-C-3, Vols. 15168–9, courtesy of Laurier Military History Archive.

36 John Powell, 4th and 5th Royal Berkshires, interview, Normandy 2004.

37 Hammerton, *Achtung! Minen!*, op. cit., pp. 72–3.

38 'Queen's Own Rifles of Canada War Diary June 1944', op. cit.

39 Carpiquet was liberated, appropriately enough, by the 8th Canadian Brigade on 9 July.

40 Lieutenant J. G. Pelly, RNVR, memoir, private papers, Imperial War Museum, Documents ref. 833; as part of Force 'S', the *Eglington* was supposed to be bombarding the tiny settlement of Luc-sur-Mer, but seems to have been hitting next-door Langrune.

41 Hickey, *The Scarlet Dawn*, op. cit.

42 Saunders, *Juno Beach*, op. cit., Kindle. p. 1122.

43 Memoir courtesy of New Brunswick Military History Museum, Oromocto.

44 Hickey, *The Scarlet Dawn*, op. cit.

45 Ibid.

46 'North Shore (New Brunswick) Regiment War Diary June 1944', RG-24-C-3, Vols. 15127–8, courtesy of Laurier Military History Archive.

47 Saunders, *Juno Beach*, op. cit., Kindle. p. 1195.

48 Dennis Smith, memoir courtesy of 48 Royal Marine Commando Association.

49 The National Archive (TNA): ADM 202/111, 'War Diary, 48 RM Commando, June 1944'.

50 Later Maj. Gen. James Louis Moulton, CB, DSO, OBE, and author of *Haste to the Battle: A Marine Commando at War* (Cassell, 1963).

51 Major Daniel Flunder, MC, memoir courtesy of Commando Veterans Archive.

52 John Clive 'Joe' Stringer, MM, interview, Imperial War Museum Sound Archive, ref. 20485.

53 Flunder, op. cit.

54 Hickey, *The Scarlet Dawn*, op. cit.

55 Smith memoir, op. cit.

56 Hickey, *The Scarlet Dawn*, op. cit.

57 Jeannine Mahia, interviewed during Help for Heroes Bicycle Battlefield Tour of Normandy, 2008.

58 Saunders, *Juno Beach*, op cit., Kindle, p. 1971.

59 The National Archives (TNA): ADM 199/1647, 'Account of 6 June 1944'. Major Daughney would win a DSO for his leadership at Tailleville on 6 June but was killed on 10 August.

60 Hickey, *The Scarlet Dawn*, op. cit.

61 Ibid.

62 'North Shore (New Brunswick) Regiment War Diary June 1944', op. cit.

63 Kurt Egle later received the Knight's Cross for his leadership at the radar station.

64 Jim Baker, memoir courtesy of d-dayrevisited.co.uk.

65 Reg Clarke, interview 2003, courtesy of BBC The People's War.

66 Ian McCulloch, 'The RCAMC and the beaches of Normandy', *Canadian Medical Association Journal 1994*, Vol. 150/11, pp. 1866–1971.

67 Hervé Hoffer, interview, Bernières-sur-Mer, 6 June 2012.

68 Hubert Meyer, *History of the 12th SS Hitler Youth Division*, Vol. One (Fedorowicz, 1994), pp. 99–108.

33. Iron Division at Sword

1 Ken Oakley, memoir courtesy of Rick Smallman, Port Macquarie, NSW, Australia. Oakley died in 2007.

2 Carlo D'Este, *Decision in Normandy* (Collins, 1983), p. 74.

3 Colleville-sur-Orne (now Colleville-Montgomery) should not be confused with Colleville-sur-Mer, behind Omaha Beach.

4 D'Este, *Decision in Normandy*, op. cit., p. 1856.

5 Wilmot, *Struggle for Europe*, op. cit., p. 271.

6 Kenneth Pearce Smith, *Adventures of an Ancient Warrior* (self-published, 1984), p. 103.

7 This Cabourg should not be confused with the tiny hamlet that gave its name to the Cabourg draw at the eastern end of Omaha.

8 Patrick Delaforce, *Monty's Ironsides: From the Normandy Beaches to Bremen with the 3rd Division* (Sutton, 1995), p. 40.

9 Cited in D'Este, *Decision in Normandy*, op. cit., p. 78.

10 After disembarking at 1 p.m., the 9th Brigade Group was redirected from its original task by Gen. Rennie to instead support the 6th Airborne Division.

11 Brigadier J. C. Cunningham, MC, memoir, Imperial War Museum, Dept of Documents, ref. 10909.

12 Bill Adams, interview, op. cit.

13 Robert Gardiner, interview, Aylesbury, 1994.

14 James Sims, *Arnhem Spearhead: A Private Soldier's Story* (Seeley Service, 1978), p. 41; and 'British Paratrooper at Arnhem: An Interview with James Sims', Warfare History Network, 16 May 2017 at http://warfarehistorynetwork.com/daily/wwii/british-paratrooper-at-arnhem-an-interview-with-james-sims/.

15 'Captain, B.L.A.', 'What the Soldier Thinks', *Spectator* (24 November 1944).

16 Bob Littlar, 2nd KSLI, interview, Shrewsbury, 1994.

17 The National Archives (TNA): CAB 44/244, 'Overlord: D-Day 6 June 1944, Book Two', pp. 205–6.

18 Warner, *The D-Day Landings*, op. cit., p. 92.

19 Sidney Rosenbaum, memoir, Imperial War Museum, Dept of Documents, ref. 4242.

20 Sydney Jary, *18 Platoon* (self-published, 1987), p. 19.

21 By 11 July, the 716th Infantry Division listed 6,261 casualties of its 6 June strength of 7,771, exactly 80 per cent.

22 *Ost-Bataillone* 439, 441 and 642.

23 Weapons issued to the 716th Division included 6,215 rifles, 318 mortars, 485 machine pistols, 1,212 pistols, 16 MG08, 352 MG34, 11 French MG, 22 anti-tank guns, 40 light and heavy artillery pieces, and 5 heavy mortars.

24 ETHINT B-621, Generalleutnant Wilhelm Richter, '716th Inf. Division Normandy, 1943–28 Jun 1944' (1947).

25 Helmut Römer, interview, Dusseldorf, 1995, and numerous interviews with Arlette Gondrée, Pegasus Bridge Café. Römer was *not* sixteen, as some historians claim, but eighteen (neither was he the first German to be killed, as others have suggested). He was one of the first captured and sent to England. As a POW he was taught English at Cambridge University before being sent to Canada; he returned to Germany in 1947, better fed and educated than most of his contemporaries.

26 Holub family and members of Morris Battery (WN16), interview during staff ride, Ouistreham, June 1994. Holub survived to become a well-known German photographer.

27 Ibid.

28 Strong, *Steiner's War*, op. cit., pp. 12–13, 17.

29 ETHINT B-621, Richter, '716th Inf. Division', op. cit.; see also Hastings, *Overlord*, op. cit., pp. 65–6.

30 Böll, *Briefe aus dem Krieg*, op. cit., letter, May 1942.

31 See: The National Archives (TNA): DEFE 2/490, 21 Army Group RE 1944 on Queen sector; aerial photos of the defences can be found at WO 205/1108, 21st Army Group.

32 The tower – today's Le Grand Bunker museum, did not fall on D-Day, but was captured by Royal Engineers on 9 June, whereupon its garrison of fifty surrendered.

33 The Krug family have become good friends of mine, and both Ludwig's son and grandson became soldiers, likewise reaching the rank of colonel. Krug died in 1972.

34 The National Archives (TNA): WO171/1381, 'War Diary, 1st Suffolks, June 1944'.

35 Blumentritt, *Von Rundstedt*, op. cit., p. 208.

36 Cited in D'Este, *Decision in Normandy*, op. cit., p. 81.

37 Bob Jones, *Bill's Brilliant Military Career* (self-published, 2004), courtesy of combinedops.com.

38 Delaforce, *Monty's Ironsides*, op. cit., p. 22.

39 Lt. Col. M. A. Philp, memoir, Dept. of Documents ref. 7188, Imperial War Museum, London.

40 Rt Hon. Sir Stephen Brown, interview, op. cit.

41 Robin McNish, *Iron Division: History of 3rd Division 1809–1989* (3rd Armoured Division, 1990), pp. 98–9.

42 Patrick Hennessey, *Young Man in a Tank* (self-published, 1984).

43 Major Derrick B. Wormald, *Recollections*, op. cit.

44 Hennessey, *Young Man*, op. cit.

45 'Arthur Denis Bradford Cocks 1904–1944', courtesy of the Frimley and Camberley 1939–1945 War Memorial.

46   Alan Higgins, interview, op. cit.; and see James Al-Mudallal, 'The Arctic Convoy Veteran who Survived Sinking, Air Strikes and Seasickness', 20 June 2013, courtesy of www.walesonline.co.uk.

47   William Carruthers, MC, memoir courtesy of Royal Engineers Museum, Gillingham, Kent.

48   Obituary, Maj. Redmond Cunningham, *Daily Telegraph*, 11 August 2000.

49   Major C. H. Giddings, '629 Field Sqn in the Assault on Queen Sector Red and White Beaches', pp. 7–8, with the Brigadier E. E. E. Cass collection of papers, Imperial War Museum, Dept of Documents, ref. 1471.

50   Delaforce, *Monty's Ironsides*, op. cit., p. 25.

51   Maj. Arthur Rouse, interview, 1994, Imperial War Museum Oral History Collection, ref. 14255.

52   Andrew Stewart, *Caen Controversy: The Battle for Sword Beach 1944* (Helion, 2014), Kindle, p. 2427.

53   Stephen J. Thorne, 'Douglas Gordon (Part 1): Bail out or glide for England', *Canadian Legion Magazine*, op cit.

54   Ken Oakley, memoir, op. cit.

55   Sykes, *Deceivers Ever*, op. cit., p. 136.

56   Warwick Nield-Siddal, interview, 1999, Imperial War Museum Oral History Collection, ref. 19672.

57   Raymond Mitchell, memoir courtesy of Frank and Joan Shaw Collection, D-Day Story Museum, Portsmouth.

58   Rear Admiral Teddy Gueritz, interview, op. cit.

59   Malcolm Petfield, memoir courtesy of the Wartime Memories Project and his son, Dave Petfield, who also remembered, 'When I took him to Sword Beach at 7.25 on 6 June 1989, forty-five years after he had landed, he walked away from me, and for the first time in my life I saw my father actually shed tears. This was a shock for me because he was not normally the emotional type.'

60   Maj. Arthur Rouse, interview, op. cit.

61   Michael Ashcroft, 'If the Sniper's Bullet Had Been Just Two Feet to One Side, My Father's Life Would Have Been Over', *Daily Telegraph*, 31 May 2014.

62   The 2nd Middlesex were the divisional machine-gun battalion, equipped with twelve Vickers .303-inch machine-guns and eight 4.2-inch mortars.

63   McNish, *Iron Division*, op. cit., p. 100.

64   Major-General R. P. Pakenham-Walsh, *History of the Corps of Royal Engineers*, Vol. VIII (Institution of Royal Engineers, 1958), p. 347.

65   Sykes, *Deceivers Ever*, op. cit., pp. 136–155.

34. Yeomen of England

1   H. T. Bone, memoir, Imperial War Museum, Dept of Documents, ref. 1464.

2   Arthur Thompson, interview, 1993, Imperial War Museum Sound Archive, ref.13370.

3   Craggs, 'An "Unspectacular" War?', op. cit., Appendix 'C', pp. 261–2.

4   Lionel Arthur Roebuck, interview, 1993, Imperial War Museum Sound Archive, ref. 13584.

5   Stan Hough, diary courtesy of BBC, WW2 People's War, 2003.

6   Warner, *The D-Day Landings*, op. cit., p. 157.

7   Craggs, 'An "Unspectacular" War?', op. cit., p. 17.

8   This Saint-Aubin should not be confused with the much larger town behind Juno Beach.

9   Frank Varley and Stanley Gardner memoirs courtesy of Friends of the Suffolk Regiment via Museum of the Suffolk Regiment, Bury St Edmunds.

10 Stanley Gardner, memoir, op. cit.

11 Lt Col. Eric T. Lummis, *1st Suffolks in Normandy* (Suffolk Regimental Museum, 2009).

12 Steve Snelling, 'Royal Norfolks' Battle in the Cornfields of Hell', *Eastern Daily Press*, 1 June 2014.

13 Private W. Evans memoir courtesy of Stacia Briggs and the Norwich War Memorial Trust.

14 Ernie Seaman memoir courtesy of ibid.

15 Snelling, 'Royal Norfolks' Battle in the Cornfields of Hell', op. cit.

16 McNish, *Iron Division*, op. cit., p. 101.

17 Dick Goodwin and Alan Sperling memoirs courtesy of Friends of the Suffolk Regiment via Museum of the Suffolk Regiment, Bury St Edmunds.

18 Lund and Ludlam, *War of the Landing Craft*, op. cit., p. 168.

19 Lewis Goodwin, interview, Portsmouth, 1994.

20 Sykes, *Deceivers Ever*, op. cit., p. 147.

21 Dunn, *Sword and Wig*, op. cit., p. 61.

22 Major Sir Delaval Cotter, 6th Bt, memoir courtesy of Friends of the Suffolk Regiment via Museum of the Suffolk Regiment, Bury St Edmunds.

23 The National Archives (TNA): WO 171/845, '13th/18th Hussars War Diary for June 1944'.

24 For example, Wilmot, *Struggle for Europe*, op. cit., p. 310, and David Belchem, *Victory in Normandy* (Chatto & Windus, 1981), pp. 109–10.

25 Dick Goodwin memoir, op. cit.

26 ETHINT B-621, Generalleutnant Wilhelm Richter, '716th Inf. Division Normandy, 1943–28 Jun 1944' (1947).

27 Eric Lummis, 'D-Day, 6 June 1944: The Truth About 3 British Division', *Army Quarterly and Defence Journal*, Vol. 199/4 (1989), pp. 393–407, and 'Caen and D-Day', *Journal of Army Historical Research*, Vol. 74/297 (1996), pp. 39–49; and see Robin Dunn, 'A Disastrous Change of Plan: Why Caen Was Not Captured on D-Day', *Royal Artillery Journal* (1995), pp. 33–5.

28 D'Este, *Decision in Normandy*, op. cit., p. 127.

29 As it was, Brigadier K. P. Smith was removed on 2 July 1944, in the face of stinging criticism of his drive and energy on D-Day. See Sir Robin Horace Walford Dunn, MC, PC, memoir, Imperial War Museum, Dept of Documents, ref. 2848, and his autobiography, *Sword and Wig*, op. cit.

30 Cdr Max Miller, memoir courtesy of his son, Robin Miller, via Peter Miles, RNVR, Landing Craft Association.

31 Major H. M. Wilson, *History of the 1st Battalion Royal Norfolk Regiment during the World War 1939–45* (Jarrold, 1947).

32 Interview, *Eastern Daily Press*, 8 October 2012.

33 'Meet the British Tommy', BBC interview with RSM Brooks, 1st Norfolks, 2 October 1944.

34 The National Archives (TNA): WO 171/1387, '2nd Royal Warwicks War Diary for June 1944'.

35 Lt Col Kingston Adams, interview, Malvern, 1991; interview, *Warwick Courier*, June 2004.

36 Private Geoff Peters, memoir courtesy of Royal Regiment of Fusiliers (Royal Warwicks) Museum, Warwick.

37 The National Archives (TNA): WO 171/863, 'Staffordshire Yeomanry War Diary for June 1944'.

38 Brigadier J. C. Cunningham, MC, memoir, op. cit.

39 David Holbrook, memoir cited in Warner, *The D-Day Landings* William Kimber, 1980); and see Holbrook's autobiographical novel of D-Day, *Flesh Wounds*, op. cit. David Holbrook was a Cambridge-educated, left-leaning student whose comfortable university life was interrupted by the war in 1942. He was called up for military service and commissioned as an officer with the East Riding Yeomanry. His 1966 novel *Flesh Wounds*, also his first work, recounted the military life of Holbrook's very thinly disguised self, Paul Grimmer, through his officer training, service as a tank commander in France, wounding on D+14 and return to Blighty.

40 Kurt Mehner (ed.), *Die geheimen Tagesberichte der deutschen Wehrmachtführung im Zweiten Weltkrieg 1939–1945, Band 10: Berichtzeit 1.3.1944–31.8.1944* (Biblio Verlag Osnabruck, 1986); and see E. R. Hooton, *Eagle in Flames: The Fall of the Luftwaffe* (Brockhampton Press, 1997), pp. 283–5, 290.

41 Warner, *The D-Day Landings*, op. cit., p. 185.

42 Ibid., p. 180.

43 Eric Saywell, memoir courtesy of Frank and Joan Shaw Collection, D-Day Story Museum, Portsmouth.

44 Ibid.

45 The 891 (497 operational) comprised: day fighters 315 (220), night fighters 90 (46), bombers 402 (200), transport 64 (31); by contrast there were 4,120 Luftwaffe aircraft on the Eastern Front at this time.

46 Fortier, *An Ace of the Eighth*, op. cit., pp. 195–6.

47 Another eleven Ju 87s would suffer a similar fate on 8 June. Weiszenbrunner family, interview, 1994.

48 ETHINT B-259, Genlt Friedrich Dihm, 'Rommel, 1944' (1945).

49 Neville Patterson, typescript interview, via Newbury Normandy Veterans Association (NVA).

50 The National Archives (TNA): WO 171/1325, '2nd KSLI War Diary for June 1944'; WO 171/258, 'I Corps Operational Order No. 1, 5 May 1944'.

51 Ibid.

52 Bob Littlar, interview, op. cit.
53 Peter Duckers, *The King's Shropshire Light Infantry: 1881–1968* (Tempus, 2004), p. 230.
54 Delaforce, *Monty's Ironsides*, op. cit., p. 44.
55 Dunn, *Sword and Wig*, op. cit., pp. 62 and 64.
56 Alistair Horne, 'In Defence of Montgomery', *Military History Quarterly*, Vol. 8/1 (1995), p. 61.
57 D'Este, *Decision in Normandy*, op. cit., p. 128.
58 Milner, *Stopping the Panzers*, op. cit., Kindle, p. 2328.
59 ETHINT FMS A-871, Feuchtinger, '21st Pz Division in Combat'; B-441, '21st Pz Division, 1942–3 Jul 1944' (1947). The 726th was commanded by Oberst Ludwig Krug at 'Hillman'; the battalion he received belonged to the 192nd *Panzergrenadier* Regt.
60 Luck, *Panzer Commander*, op. cit., Kindle, p. 3249.
61 Ibid., p. 132.
62 '21st Army Group Intelligence Assessment, 28 May 1944', WO 205/532, The National Archives (TNA).
63 The Wehrmacht's 503rd, and the 101st and 102nd of the Waffen-SS.
64 Interviews with Röhling and Schiller families, Normandy, 1994. Röhling was wounded and awarded an Iron Cross on D-Day, ending up surrendering to the US Army in Prague in 1945.
65 Ruge, *Rommel in Normandy*, op. cit., p. 158.
66 Herr reckoned he owed his survival to his father-in-law, the Seventh Army's commander, Friedrich Dollmann. When Cherbourg fell on 29 June, the general died of heart failure and Herr was withdrawn from the front to attend his funeral. 'For thirty years I was mistaken that my father-in-law had died because of his heart, but I have since learned Hitler threatened him with a military court over the fall of Cherbourg, and he took the course of suicide instead.' Herr would return to his unit afterwards. Michaela Wiegel, 'Gezeichnete Erde hinter den Landungssträanden', *Frankfurter Allgemeine*, 4 June 2004.
67 Interview with Werner Kortenhaus, *CBC TV News Special*, 6 June 1994; see also Werner Kortenhaus, *Combat History of the 21st Panzer Division 1943–45* (Helion, 2014).
68 Dauscher family, interview, Normandy, 1944. He would see action on D-Day against paratroopers, but was wounded by machine-gun fire and captured on 8 July during Operation Charnwood. He was taken POW and sent to the USA.
69 The National Archives (TNA): CAB 146/377, 'Commander-in-Chief West's War Diary, 6 June 1944' (copies at the IWM and TNA).
70 Marcks did not survive the war, but Oppeln did, later coaching the Canadian Equestrian Team and dying in 1966.
71 Kortenhaus, *Combat History*, op. cit.
72 Milner, *Stopping the Panzers*, op. cit., Kindle, p. 2244.
73 The author served with Bernard Cuttiford's son and grandson, and two of James Eadie's grandsons.
74 Maj. D. F. Underhill, *Staffordshire Yeomanry: An Account of the Operations of the Regiment during World War II* (Staffordshire Libraries, 1994), p. 26.

75 Neville Patterson, memoir courtesy of Frank and Joan Shaw Collection, D-Day Story Museum, Portsmouth.

76 Kortenhaus, *Combat History*, op. cit.

35. *Green Berets and* le Général

1 Ken Oakley, interview for BBC News, 3 June 2004.

2 Léon Gautier, interview, Normandy, June 2014.

3 At this stage it comprised No. 3 (Army) Commando, 40 (Royal Marine) Commando and the Special Raiding Squadron, and successfully seized Termoli on 3 October 1943, after sailing from Bari.

4 Colin Hughes, 7th R. Warwicks and No. 4 Commando, interview, Aylesbury, 1994.

5 Interview with Pat Gillen, Dublin, 1985.

6 Doon Campbell, *Magic Mistress: A 30-year Affair to Reuters* (Tagman Press, 2000), pp. 59–60.

7 Col. Pat Porteous, interview, Dieppe, August 1992; obituary, *Daily Telegraph*, 11 October 2000.

8 Lovat, *March Past,* op. cit.

9 Ryan, *The Longest Day*, op. cit., p. 69.

10 ETHINT B-403, Genmaj. Joseph Reichert, '711th Inf. Division on the Invasion front, 6 Jun–24 Jul 44' (1946).

11 Ibid.

12 This was portrayed in the film *The Longest Day.*

13 Lichtenberg, Fillmann and Brieden families, interviews, 1998. Sadly, Anton Fillmann did not live long after his birthday and died in action on 19 June 1944; Albert Brieden did survive, due to a medical condition which put him in hospital for the last months of the war.

14 Hubert Faure, interview, Normandy, June 2014.

15 An offshoot of the Commando Basic Training Centre at Achnacarry, Scotland.

16 René Rossey, interview (in French), Normandy, 2004. After seventy-eight days in Normandy, No. 4 Commando was brought back to England to recover. On 1 November they embarked for Operation Infatuate, to attack Walcheren and open up the Scheldt estuary for ships to unload at Antwerp. Rossey, the youngest of Philippe Kieffer's 177 Free French commandos, died on 19 May 2016, aged eighty-nine.

17 Hubert Faure, interview, op. cit.

18 Lovat, *March Past,* op. cit.

19 Léon Gautier, interview, op. cit.

20 François Andriot, interview, Kent, 2014.

21 Philippe Kieffer, *Béret Vert* (Éditions France-Empire, 1948).

22 Maurice Chauvet obituary, *Daily Telegraph*, 7 June 2010.

23 Gilchrist, *Don't Cry For Me*, op. cit., p. 51.

24 Papers of W. H. Bidmead, Dept. of Documents, Ref. 25971, Imperial War Museum, London.

25   The National Archives (TNA): WO 218/66, 'No. 4 Commando War Diary for June 1944'.

26   Craggs, 'An "Unspectacular" War?', op. cit., p. 125.

27   Léon Gautier, interview, op. cit.

28   Gilchrist, *Don't Cry For Me*, op. cit., pp. 51–4.

29   Ibid., pp. 54–5.

30   Kieffer, *Béret Vert*, op. cit.

31   Ibid.

32   TNA: WO 218/66, 'No. 4 Commando War Diary', op. cit.

33   The National Archives (TNA): WO 218/59, 'Headquarters 1st Special Service Force War Diary for June 1944'.

34   Bill Millin, interviews, op. cit. Also see obituaries, *Scotsman*, 11 March 2016; *Daily Telegraph*, 19 March 2016.

35   George Laws, interview made with Angus Beaton, SE London, December 2001.

36   Campbell, *Magic Mistress*, op. cit., p. 64.

37   TNA: WO 218/66, 'No. 4 Commando War Diary', op. cit.

38   George Laws, interview, op. cit.

39   TNA: WO 218/59, 'Headquarters 1st Special Service Force War Diary', op. cit.

40   Campbell, *Magic Mistress*, op. cit., p. 68.

41   Bill Millin, interviews, op. cit.

42   Sgt Henry Frank Cosgrove, interview, 1988, Imperial War Museum Sound Archive, ref. 10177.

43   Tony Turnbull, memoir, 2005, courtesy of BBC, WW2 People's War.

44   John Durnford-Slater, *Commando*, op. cit., p. 155.

45   Tom Duncan, 3 Commando, interview, Aberdeen, 1980, op. cit.

46   Campbell, *Magic Mistress*, op. cit., p. 67.

47   The National Archives (TNA): WO 218/65, 'No. 3 Commando War Diary for June 1944'.

48   The National Archives (TNA): WO 218/68, 'No. 6 Commando War Diary for June 1944'.

49   The National Archives (TNA): ADM 202/103, 'No. 41 Royal Marine Commando War Diary for June 1944'.

50   TNA: WO 218/59, 'Headquarters 1st Special Service Force War Diary', op. cit.

51   Kite, *Stout Hearts*, op. cit., p. 78; Hart, *Montgomery and 'Colossal Cracks'*, op. cit., pp. 50–61.

52   Rostron, *Military Life and Times*, op. cit., p. 88.

53   Cited in Allport, *Browned Off and Bloody-Minded*, op. cit., p. 184.

54   John Vernon Bain, interview, Shrewsbury, 1978. Bain later pursued a successful literary career as the poet Vernon Scannell; see *Argument of Kings* (Robson Books, 1987), pp. 105–6.

55   Hartcup, *Code Name Mulberry*, op. cit.

56   Richard Oulahan, Jr, 'How Filming *The Longest Day* Produced the Longest Headache', *Life*, 12 October 1962, pp. 113–20.

57   Dolski, Edwards and Buckley (eds.), *D-Day in History and Memory*, op. cit., pp. 159–80.

58   Terry Reardon, 'Lion of Britain, Cross of Lorraine: Churchill and de Gaulle', *Finest Hour*, No. 138 (Spring 2008).

59   Winston S. Churchill, *The Dawn of Liberation* (Cassell, 1945), p. 206.

60   Harold Nicolson, *Diaries and Letters 1939–1945* (Collins, 1967), p. 412.

61   Ibid.

62   François Kersaudy, *Churchill and de Gaulle* (HarperCollins, 1981), p. 424.

63   Ibid., p. 413.

64   Jean Jammes, interview, Olney, Buckinghamshire, 2016.

65   John Henley, 'Honours for Elite Snubbed by de Gaulle', *Guardian*, 7 June 2004; and personal interviews.

66   Pierre Wilson, interview, May 2004, courtesy of BBC, WW2 People's War, op. cit.

67   Isaac Levendel and Bernard Weisz, *Hunting Down the Jews: Vichy, the Nazis and Mafia Collaborators in Provence 1942–1944* (Enigma Books, 2012). Palmieri later admitted arresting fifteen Jews in Le Pontet on 6 June 1944, and was executed in Marseilles in August 1946.

68   Quote courtesy of The Anne Frank Trust UK.

69   Philip Eade, *Evelyn Waugh: A Life Revisited* (Weidenfeld & Nicolson, 2016).

70   Douglas Brinkley, 'Remembering the Battle that Won the War: 70 Years Later', *Time*, 20 May 2014.

71   Andy Rooney, 'The 60th Anniversary of D-Day', 3 June 2004, courtesy of CBS *60 Minutes* commentary.

Postscript: Fortitude and the Spies

1   Mark Simmons, *Agent Cicero: Hitler's Most Successful Spy* (History Press, 2014).

2   Elyesa Bazna, *I Was Cicero* (André Deutsch, 1962).

3   By early 1944, British intelligence was aware there was a spy in their Ankara embassy, but did not know who it was; Cicero left his employment shortly afterwards, unmasked. Theories abound that Cicero was an Allied 'plant', or that he was working for Turkish intelligence (as he did post-war); see Christopher Baxter, 'Forgeries and Spies: The Foreign Office and the "Cicero" Case', *Intelligence and National Security*, Vol. 23/6 (December 2008), pp. 807–26; Richard Wires, *The Cicero Spy Affair: German Access to British Secrets in World War II* (Praeger, 1999); Robin Denniston, *Churchill's Secret War: Diplomatic Decrypts, the Foreign Office and Turkey 1942–44* (Sutton, 1997).

4   Bengt Beckman and C. G. McKay, *Swedish Signal Intelligence 1900–1945* (Routledge, 2014), p. 208.

5   Originals at NARA, Maryland, ref. RG 457 SRDJ, Nos. 59973–5; see also Ben Fischer, 'The Japanese Ambassador Who Knew Too Much', *Center for the Study of Intelligence Bulletin*, No. 9 (Spring 1999), pp. 6–9; Carl Boyd, 'Significance of MAGIC and the Japanese Ambassador to Berlin (V): News of Hitler's Defense Preparations for Allied Invasion of Western Europe', *Intelligence and National Security*, Vol. 4/3 (July 1989), pp. 461–81, and *Hitler's Japanese Confidant: General Hiroshi Ōshima and Magic Intelligence, 1941–1945* (University Press of Kansas, 1993).

6   Masterman, *The Double-Cross System*, op. cit., pp. 155–8.

7   The National Archives (TNA): KV 2/197 – see particularly Folder One of three; see also John P. Campbell, 'Some Pieces of the *Ostro* Puzzle', *Intelligence and National Security*, Vol. 11/2 (April 1996), pp. 245–63.

8   TNA: KV 2/197, op. cit.

9   Cubbage, 'The Success of Operation Fortitude', op. cit.

10 Russell Miller, *Codename Tricycle: The True Story of the Second World War's Most Extraordinary Double Agent* (Secker & Warburg, 2004); Larry Loftis, *Into the Lion's Mouth: The True Story of Dusko Popov, World War II Spy, Patriot, and the Real-Life Inspiration for James Bond* (Berkley, 2016).

11 Christopher Andrew, *The Defence of the Realm: The Authorized History of MI5* (Allen Lane, 2009).

12 Ben Macintyre, *Double Cross: The True Story of the D-Day Spies* (Bloomsbury, 2012); Masterman, *The Double-Cross System*, op. cit.

13 The National Archives (TNA): Enigma signal KV 2/2098.

14 Walter Koehler had come clean to US consular officials about the true nature of his role when applying for a visa in Madrid; J. Edgar Hoover approved his recruitment by the FBI and managed the flow of information back to Berlin, which Koehler never saw. In the 1970s the espionage writer Ladislas Farago uncovered the truth that Koehler was a *triple agent*, all along working for the *Abwehr*. Fortunately, Fortitude was not damaged because Koehler never saw what had been sent by the FBI on his behalf. See David Alan Johnson, 'Walter Koehler and J. Edgar Hoover', Warfare History Network, August 2016.

15 Howard, *Strategic Deception*, op. cit., pp. 16–18.

16 Juan Pujol García and Nigel West, *Operation Garbo: The Personal Story of the Most Successful Double Agent of World War II* (Weidenfeld & Nicolson, 1985); Tomás Harris, *Garbo: The Spy Who Saved D-Day* (National Archives, 2000).

17 'Agent Garbo', MI5 (Security Service) website, https://www.mi5.gov.uk/agent-garbo, accessed July 2018; Stephan Talty, *Agent Garbo: The Brilliant, Eccentric Secret Agent Who Tricked Hitler and Saved D-Day* (Houghton Mifflin, 2012).

18 Hesketh, *Fortitude*, op. cit., p. 200.

19 Cited in Maj. T. L. Cubbage, '"Fortitude: A History of Strategic Deception in North Western Europe, April, 1943 to May, 1945 by Roger Fleetwood Hesketh, printed but unpublished (On His Majesty's Secret Service) February 1949": A Review Essay' (http://www.tomcubbage.com/history/Hesketh-Fortitude-Report.pdf), pp. 11–13; see also Klaus-Jürgen Müller, 'A German Perspective on Allied Deception Operations in the Second World War', *Intelligence and National Security*, Vol. 2/3 (1987), pp. 301–26.

20 Maj. T. L. Cubbage, '"Fortitude"', op. cit., p. 15.

21 Craig Bickell, 'Operation Fortitude South: An Analysis of Its Influence upon German Dispositions and Conduct of Operations in 1944', *War and Society*, Vol. 18/1 (2000), pp. 91–121.

22 Ellis, *Victory in the West, Vol. 1*, op. cit., p. 322.

23 Michael Reynolds, *Steel Inferno: 1st SS Panzer Corps in Normandy* (Spellmount, 1997), p. 83. As argued earlier, the location of the 116th Panzer had nothing to

do with the alleged anti-Nazi sentiments of its commander; Bennett, *Ultra in the West*, op. cit., pp. 82–3.

24 Masterman, *The Double-Cross System*, op. cit., p. 163.

25 Otto Schmidt, interview, Aachen, April 1985.

26 Ruge, *Rommel in Normandy*, op. cit., p. 104.

27 The National Archives (TNA): Enigma signals KVs 1171, 3185, 4371 and 6160; ibid., p. 59.

28 Heinz Gunther Guderian, *From Normandy to the Ruhr: With the 116th Panzer Division in World War II* (Aberjona Press, 2001).

29 The National Archives (TNA): Enigma signal KV 5314; ibid., p. 64.

30 The National Archives (TNA): Enigma signal KV 3766, dated 8 May, ref. HW (Intercepted German Cipher Messages) 1/2784.

31 My thanks to Richard C. Anderson, Jr (author of *Cracking Hitler's Atlantic Wall: The 1st Assault Brigade Royal Engineers on D-Day* (Stackpole, 2009)) for these observations.

32 Sir Ronald Wingate, *Historical Record of Deception in War against Germany and Italy*, Vol. II (The National Archives: Communications and Intelligence Records/ Directorate of Forward Plans, DEFE 28/49), pp. 407–8.

33 Mary Kathryn Barbier, *D-Day Deception: Operation Fortitude and the Normandy Invasion* (Praeger, 2007), pp. 188–9.

34 Wingate, *Historical Record*, op. cit., p. 408.

35 Ibid.

36 Pujol García and West, *Operation Garbo*, op. cit., p. 118.

37 Masterman, *The Double-Cross System*, op. cit., p. 114.

38 Brinkley, *The Boys of Pointe du Hoc*, op. cit., p. 148.

Acknowledgements

1 John Murray (ed.), *The Autobiography of Edward Gibbon*, (John Murray, 1896), p. 302.

2 Ibid., p. 190.

3 Otto Carius, interview, RMCS Shrivenham, 2004. In later life a pharmacist, Carius died in January 2015.

4 Günter Halm, interviews, Chalke Valley History Festival, July 2016 and 2017. The charming Günter died shortly after our last meeting, in September 2017.

5 Gibbon, *Decline and Fall*, Preface to Decline and Fall, Volume 2.

6 Murray (ed.), *Autobiography*, op. cit., pp. 333–4.

Bibliography

Published Memoirs – Allied

Adkins, Andrew Z., *You Can't Get Much Closer Than This* (Casemate, 2005)

Alanbrooke, Lord (eds Alex Danchev & Dan Todman), *War Diaries* (Weidenfeld, 2001)

Annan, Noel, *Changing Enemies. The Defeat & Regeneration of Germany* (Collins, 1995)

Astley, Joan Bright, *The Inner Circle: A View of War at the Top* (Hutchinson, 1971)

Baret, Joël G. (ed.), *I Wouldn't Want to Do It Again* (Helion, 2011)

Bashow, David L. (ed.), *All the Fine Young Eagles* (Stoddart, 1996)

Bastable, Jonathan (ed.), *Voices From D-Day* (David & Charles, 2004)

Belchem, Maj. Gen. David, *All in a Day's March* (Collins, 1978)

Bellamy, Bill, *Troop Leader: A Tank Commander's Story* (History Press, 2005)

Bigland, Lt Col. T. S., *Bigland's War: War Letters of Tom Bigland, 1941–45* (Self-pub., 1990)

Blackburn, George G., *The Guns of Normandy* (McClelland & Stewart, 1995)

Blythe, Ronald (ed.), *Private Words: Letters & Diaries from the Second World War* (Viking, 1991)

Bolloré, Gwenn-Aël, *J'ai débarqué le 6 juin, Commando de la France libre* (Le Cherche Midi, 2004)

Boothby, Lord, *My Yesterday, Your Tomorrow* (Hutchinson, 1962)

Boscawen, Robert, *Armoured Guardsman* (Pen & Sword, 2001)

Botsford, Gardner, *A Life of Privilege, Mostly* (St Martin's Press, 2003)

Bowman, Martin W. (ed.), *Remembering D-Day* (HarperCollins, 1994)

Bracken, Patrick P. J., *2500 Dangerous Days. A Gunner's Travels 1939–46* (Merlin, 1988)

Bradley, Gen. Omar N., *A Soldier's Story* (Henry Holt, 1951); & Clay Blair, *A General's Life* (Simon & Schuster, 1983)

Brinkley, Douglas & Ronald J. Drez (eds), *Voices of Valor. D-Day* (Bulfinch Press, 2004)

Burgett, Donald R., *Currahee! A Paratrooper's Account of the Invasion* (Presidio, 1967)

Butcher, Capt. Harry C., *My Three Years with Eisenhower* (Simon & Schuster, 1946)

Cadogan, Sir Alex (ed. David Dilkes), *Diaries, 1938–1945* (Cassell, 1971)

Caine, Philip D., *Spitfires, Thunderbolts & Warm Beer* (Brassey's, 1995)

Capa, Robert (aka Endre Friedmann), *Slightly out of Focus* (Henry Holt, 1947)

Carrington, Charles, *Soldier at Bomber Command* (Leo Cooper, 1987)

Carrington, Lord, *Reflect on Things Past. Memoirs of Lord Carrington* (Collins, 1988)

Carter, Sub-Lt W.B., RNVR, *D-Day Landings* (Silent Books, 1993)

Cheal, Bill, *Fighting Through from Dunkirk to Hamburg* (Pen & Sword, 2011)

Christopherson, Stanley (ed. James Holland), *An Englishman at War* (Bantam Press, 2015)

Churchill, Winston S., *Second World War, Vol. VI: Triumph & Tragedy* (Cassell, 1954)

Close, Bill, *Tank Commander* (Pen & Sword, 2013)

Close, Roy, *In Action with the SAS: From Dunkirk to Berlin* (Pen & Sword, 2005)

Closterman, Pierre, *The Big Show. Experiences of a French Fighter Pilot* (Chatto, 1951)

Collins, Gen. J. Lawton, *Lightning Joe: An Autobiography* (Louisiana State Univ., 1970); *Conversations with Gen. J. Lawton Collins* (ed. Maj. Gary Wade, CSI Report, 1983)

Colville, John, *Footprints in Time: Memories* (Collins, 1976)

Comer, John, *Combat Crew: The Story of 25 Missions over North West Europe* (Pen & Sword, 1988)

Cooke, Alistair, *Alistair Cooke's American Journey: On the Home Front* (Allen Lane, 2006)

Cooper, Duff (ed. John Julius Norwich), *The Duff Cooper Diaries* (Weidenfeld & Nicolson, 2005)

Corlett, Maj. Gen. Charles H., *Cowboy Pete: The Autobiography* (Sleeping Fox, 1974)

Courtney, Richard D., *Normandy to the Bulge* (Southern Illinois Univ. Press, 1997)

Crosby, Harry H., *A Wing & a Prayer: The 'Bloody 100th' Bomb Group* (HarperCollins, 1993)

Crosthwaite, Ivor, *A Charmed. Life: Grenadier Guards 1936–46* (TWM Publishing, 1996)

Dalzel-Job, Patrick, *Arctic Snow to Dust of Normandy* (Pen & Sword, 1991)

Danson, Barney, *Not Bad For a Sergeant* (Dundurn, 2002)

Davis, M. Bedford, *Frozen Rainbows. A Combat Medical Officer* (Meadowlark, 2003)

Deam, Sgt. Donald L., *General Toothpick …. WW II Memoirs* (CreateSpace, 2014)

Deedes, W. F., *Dear Bill: W.F. Deedes Reports* (Macmillan, 1997)

Ditcham, A. G. F., *A Home on the Rolling Main, Memoirs 1940–46* (Seaforth Publishing, 2013)

Douglas Home, William, *Half Term Report. An Autobiography* (Longmans, Green, 1954); *Sins of Commission* (Michael Russell, 1985)

Drez, Ronald (ed.), *Voices of D-Day by Those Who Were There* (Louisiana State Univ., 1994)

Dube, Gilbert H. & Alan Dube (eds.), *A Navy Soldier on Omaha Beach* (Lulu.com, 2005)

Duboscq, Genevieve, *My Longest Night. A French Girl's Memories of D-Day* (Secker, 1984)

Dunn, Sir Robin, *Sword & Wig. Memoirs of a Lord Justice* (Quiller, 1993)

Durnford-Slater, Brig. John, *Commando: Memoirs of a Fighting Commando* (William Kimber, 1953)

Dyson, Stephen, *Tank Twins. East End Brothers in Arms 1943–45* (Pen & Sword, 1994)

Edwards, Denis, *The Devil's Own Luck. Pegasus Bridge to the Baltic* (Pen & Sword, 1999)

Eisenhower, Gen. Dwight D., *Crusade in Europe* (Doubleday, 1948); 'What is Leadership?', *Reader's Digest* (June 1965); *Papers* (ed. Stephen E. Ambrose): *The War Years, Vols. I-V* (JHU Press, 1970)

Embry, ACM Sir Basil, *Mission Completed.* (Methuen, 1957)

Fendick, Reginald F., *A Canloan Officer* (Self-published, 2000)

Forfar, John, *From Omaha to the Scheldt. Story of 47 RM Commando* (Tuckwell Press, 2001); *Gold to Omaha: Battle for Port-en-Bessin, 6–8 June 1944* (Les Gens du Phare, 2009)

Fortier, Norman J., *An Ace of the Eighth: A Fighter Pilot's Air War* (Presidio, 2003)

Forty, George (ed.), *Jake Wardrop's Diary: A Tank Regiment Sergeant's Story* (Amberley, 2009)

Frankland, Noble, *History at War* (Giles de la Mare, 1998)

Franklin, Robert 'Doc Joe', *Medic!* (Univ. of Nebraska Press, 2006)

Fraser, Gen. Sir David, *Wars & Shadows* (Allen Lane, 2002)

Gale, Gen. Sir Richard, *Call To Arms* (Hutchinson, 1968)

Gavin, Gen. James, *On to Berlin: Battles of an Airborne Commander 1943–46* (Viking, 1978)

Gellhorn, Martha, *The Face of War* (Rupert Hart-Davis, 1967)

Gethyn-Jones, Canon Eric, *A Territorial Army Chaplain in Peace & War* (Gooday, 1988)

Gordon, Harold J., *One Man's War: A Memoir of World War II* (Apex Press, 1999)

Gordon, Ralph J., *Infantrymen: Company C, 18th Infantry, 1st Division* (CreateSpace, 2012)

Grady, Stephen, *Gardens of Stone: My Boyhood in the French Resistance* (Hodder, 2013)

Greenwood, Sgt. Trevor (ed. S.V. Partington), *D-Day to Victory* (Simon & Schuster, 2012)

Guarnere, William, Edward Heffron, & Robyn Post, *Brothers in Battle* (Berkley, 2007)

Guehenno, Jean, *Diary of the Dark Years, 1940–1944* (Éditions Gallimard, 1947)

Guiet, Jean Claude, *Dead on Time: Memoir of an SOE & OSS Agent* (History Press, 2016)

de Guingand, Maj. Gen. Sir Francis, *Operation Victory* (Hodder & Stoughton, 1947); *Generals at War* (Hodder & Stoughton, 1964)

Gullett, Henry ('Jo'), *Not as a Duty Only* (Melbourne Univ., 1976)

Hammerton, Ian C., *Achtung Minen! A Flail Tank Troop Commander* (Book Guild, 1991)

Hanford, William B., *A Dangerous Assignment* (Stackpole, 2008)

Harrison, A. Cleveland, *Unsung Valour. A GI's Story* (Univ. of Mississippi, 2000)

Harvey, Oliver (ed. John Harvey), *The War Diaries of Oliver Harvey 1941–45* (Collins, 1978)

Haward, Jeff (ed. Neil Barber), *Fighting Hitler from Dunkirk to D-Day* (Pen & Sword, 2015)

Hayward, Greg, *D-Day to VE-Day with the 2nd Tactical Air Force* (AuthorHouse, 2009)

Hennessey, Patrick, *Young Man in a Tank* (Self-published, 1984)

Henry, Jacques (ed.), *La Normandie en Flammes* (Éditions C. Corlet, 1984)

Hickey, Rev. Raymond M., *The Scarlet Dawn* (Tribune, 1949); *D-Day Memories* (Keystone, 1980)

Hicks, Mike, *Difficult Days: A Rifleman's Wartime Memoir 1939–1946* (Indepenpress, 2014)

Hills, Stuart, *By Tank into Normandy* (Orion, 2002)

Holbrook, David, *Flesh Wounds* (Methuen, 1966); autobiographical novel

Hopkins, Harry L., *White House Papers of Harry L. Hopkins, 1942–45* (Eyre & Spottiswoode, 1949)

Houston, Robert J., *D-Day to Bastogne: A Paratrooper Recalls* (Exposition Press, 1980)

Howard, Maj. John & Penny Bates, *Pegasus Diaries* (Pen & Sword, 2006)

Howarth, T. E. B. (ed.), *Monty at Close Quarters: Recollections* (Leo Cooper, 1985)

Huot, Paul, *J'avais 20 ans en 1943* (Sauve Terre/Atlantica, 2000)

Instone, Frank A., *Deputy Provost Marshal – I Slew My Dragon* (Pallaton, 1977)

Irgang, Frank, *Etched in Purple: One Soldier's War in Europe* (Caxton Press, 1949)

Ismay, Lord, *Memoirs of Lord Ismay* (Heinemann, 1960)

Jary, Sydney, *18 Platoon* (Self-published, 1987)

Johnson, Group Capt. J. E. 'Johnnie', *Wing Leader* (Chatto & Windus, 1956)

Jones, Mel (ed.), *Fifty Years On: Memoirs of the 2nd WW* (Thamesdown Community Arts, 1990)

Kennedy, Maj. Gen. Sir John, *The Business of War* (Hutchinson, 1957)

Kennedy, Ludovic, *On My Way to the Club* (Collins, 1989)

Kennedy, Paul A. *Battlefield Surgeon* (Univ. Press of Kentucky, 2016)

Kieffer, Philippe, *Béret vert* (France-Empire, 1952)

Kirby, Norman, *1100 Miles with Monty: Security & Intelligence at TAC HQ* (Sutton, 1989)

Kitching, Maj. Gen. George, *Mud & Green Fields: Memoirs* (Battleline Books, 1986)

Koskimaki, George E., *D-Day with the Screaming Eagles* (Vantage, 1970)

Kotlowitz, Robert, *Before Their Time: A Memoir* (Knopf, 1997)

Kyle, James, *Typhoon Tale* (George Mann, 1989)

Langehough, Philip A., *When Hearts Were Brave Again* (Information International, 2005)

Lefebvre, Laurent (ed.), *They Were on Omaha: 213 Eyewitnesses* (D-Day Editions, 2003)

Lewis, Jon E. (ed.), *Voices From D-Day* (Constable & Robinson, 1994)

Liddle, Peter (ed.), *D-Day: By Those Who Were There* (Pen & Sword, 1994)

Lindsay, Sir Martin, *So Few Got Through* (Collins, 1946)

Lovat, Lord, *March Past* (Weidenfeld & Nicolson, 1978)

MacLellan, Roger, *Wave an arm, 'Follow me!': A Canloan Platoon Commander* (Lancelot Pr., 1993)

Mallaby, Sir George, *From My Level: Unwritten Minutes* (Hutchinson, 1965)

Marks, Leo, *Between Silk & Cyanide: A Codemaker's Story 1941–45* (HarperCollins, 1998)

Marshall, Gen. George C. (ed. Larry I. Bland), *Papers of George Catlett Marshall: Aggressive & Determined Leadership, Jun 1, 1943- Dec 31, 1944. Vol. IV* (JHU Press, 1996)

Martin, Charlie, *Battle Diary: From D-Day & Normandy to the Zuider Zee* (Dundurn, 1994)

McAlpine, Kenneth, *We Died with our Boots Clean* (History Press, 2009)

McLennan, Alex, *Signals Home: 1944–46* (Quay Books/ Mark Allen, 1995)

Mercer, John, *Mike Target* (Book Guild, 1990)

Messiter, Ian, *My Life & Other Games* (Fourth Estate, 1990)

Mitchell, Raymond, *Commando Despatch Rider 1944–45* (Pen & Sword, 2001)

Mitchison, Naomi (ed. Dorothy Sheridan), *Among You Taking Notes* (Gollancz, 1985)

Montgomery, FM (later The Viscount) Bernard, '21st Army Group in the Campaign in NW Europe 1944-45', *RUSI Journal*, Vol. XC, Nov 1945); *Normandy to the Baltic* (BAOR/21st Army Group, 1946); *Memoirs of FM Montgomery* (Collins, 1958)

Morgan, Lt Gen. Frederick E., *Overture to Overlord* (Hodder & Stoughton, 1950)

Moulton, J. L., *Haste to the Battle: A Marine Commando at War* (Cassell, 1963)

Newman, Bernard, *American Journey* (Robert Hale, 1943)

Nicholas, H. G. (ed.), *Washington Despatches 1941–45* (Weidenfeld & Nicholson, 1981)

Nicolson, Harold, (ed. Nigel Nicolson), *Diaries & Letters 1939–45* (Collins, 1967)

Obermayer, Herman J., *Soldiering for Freedom* (Texas A&M Univ. Press, 2005)

Palmer, Bennett J., *The Hunter & the Hunted: 2 Years in a Rifle Company* (Palmer, 2002)

Pearce, Donald, *Journal of a War: North-West Europe, 1944–1945* (Macmillan, 1965)

Picot, Geoffrey, *Accidental Warrior. From Normandy till Victory* (Book Guild, 1993)

Pogue, Forrest C., *Pogue's War: Diaries* (Univ. Press of Kentucky, 2001)

Powdrill, E. A., *In the Face of the Enemy: A Battery Sergeant Major in Action* (Pen and Sword, 2009)

Pyman, Gen. Sir Harold, *Call to Arms: Memoirs* (Leo Cooper, 1971)

Ramsay, Adm. Sir Bertram (eds. Robert W. Love & John Major), *Year of D-Day* (Univ. of Hull, 1994)

Rawson, Andrew (ed.), *Eyes Only. Marshall & Eisenhower's Correspondence* (Spellmount, 2012)

Rees, Goronwy, *A Bundle of Sensations* (Chatto & Windus, 1972)

Renaud, Alexandre, *Sainte Mère Église June 6 1944* (Julliard, 1984)

Renault, Gilbert (aka Col. Rémy), *Trente ans après – 6 Juin 1944/6 Juin 1974* (Librairie Académique Perrin, 1974)

Richardson, Gen. Sir Charles, *Flashback. A Soldier's Story* (William Kimber, 1985)

Ridgway, Gen. Matthew B., & Harold H. Martin, *Soldier* (Harper, 1956)

Riols, Noreen, *Secret Ministry of Ag. & Fish: Churchill's School for Spies* (Macmillan, 2013)

Roberts, Maj. Gen. G. P. B., *From the Desert to the Baltic* (William Kimber, 1987)

Roberts, James Alan, *The Canadian Summer* (Univ. of Toronto, 1981)

Rogers, Duncan & Sarah Williams (eds.), *On the Bloody Road to Berlin* (Helion, 2005)

Salinger, Margaret A., *Dream Catcher: A Memoir of J.D. Salinger* (Pocket Books, 2000)

Scannell, Vernon (pseud. for John Bain), *The Tiger & the Rose* (Hamish Hamilton, 1971); *An Argument of Kings* (Robson Books, 1987)

Schaffer, Mollie Weinstein, *Mollie's War: The Letters of a WW II WAC* (McFarland, 2010)

Schott, Richard L., *The Jumping Doc in World War II* (Outskirts Press, 2015)

Scott, Desmond, *Typhoon Pilot* (Leo Cooper, 1982)

Scott, Hugh A., *The Blue & White Devils: A Personal Memoir* (Battery Press, 1984)

Scott, Jack L., *Combat Engineer* (American Literary Press, 1999)

Skinner, Leslie F., *The Man Who Worked on Sundays: War Diary of Revd. Leslie Skinner* (1991)

Slaughter, John Robert, *Omaha Beach & Beyond: Sgt Bob Slaughter* (Zenith, 2007)

Slessor, Sir John, *The Central Blue: Recollections & Reflections* (Cassell, 1956)

Smith, Brig. Kenneth Pearce, *Adventures of an Ancient Warrior* (Self-published, 1984)

Smith, Norman, *Tank Soldier* (Book Guild Publishing, 1989)

Smith, Thomas W., *Infantry Rifleman: WW II Reflections* (CreateSpace, 2012)

Stagg, J. M., *Forecast for Overlord* (Ian Allan, 1971)

Stanier, Brig. Sir Alexander, Bt., *Sammy's Wars* (Welsh Guards, 1998)

Stevens, Charles N., *An Innocent at Polebrook: An 8th Air Force Bombardier* (1ˢᵗ Books, 2003)

Stillwell, Paul (ed.), *Normandy: Accounts from the Sea Services* (USNI Press, 1994)

Summersby, Capt. Kay, *Eisenhower Was My Boss* (Prentice Hall, 1948)

Swaab, Jack, *Field of Fire: Diary of a Gunner Officer* (Sutton, 2005)

Sylvan, Maj. William C., & Capt. Francis G. Smith, *Normandy to Victory. The War Diary of Gen. Courtney H. Hodges & First US Army* (Univ. Press of Kentucky, 2008)

Tarrant, Chris (ed.), *Dad's War: Father, Soldier, Hero* (Virgin Books, 2014)

Taylor, Brig. George, *Infantry Colonel* (Self-published, 1990)

Taylor, Gen. Maxwell D., *Swords & Plowshares* (W. W. Norton, 1972)

Tedder, Arthur, *With Prejudice: War Memoirs of Lord Tedder* (Cassell, 1966)

Tibbs, David (ed. Neil Barber), *Parachute Doctor: Memoirs of Capt. David Tibbs* (Sabrestorm, 2012)

Turnbull, Fred, *The Invasion Diaries* (Veterans Publications, Canada, 2008)

Valenti, Isadore, *Combat Medic* (Word Association Publishers, 1998)

Verity, Hugh, *We Landed by Moonlight: Secret RAF Landings in France* (Ian Allan, 1978)

Vian, Adm. Sir Philip, *Action This Day. A War Memoir* (Frederick Muller, 1960)

Watkins, Leonard, *A Sapper's War* (Minerva, 1996)

Watts, Lt Col. J. C., *Surgeon at War* (Allen & Unwin, 1955)

Webster, David Kenyon, *Parachute Infantry* (Louisiana State Univ. Press, 1994)

Webster, George, *The Savage Sky: Life and Death in a Bomber Over Germany* (Stackpole 2007)

Wedemeyer, Gen. Albert C., *Wedemeyer Reports* (Henry Holt, 1958); 'Footnotes to D-Day', *American Legion Magazine*, Vol. 106/6 (June 1979)

West, Kenneth J., *An' It's Called a Tam-o'-Shanter* (Merlin Books, 1985)

Whidden, Guy, *Between the Lines & Beyond: A 101st Airborne Paratrooper* (Thomas Pubs., 2009)

Whitehouse, Stanley & George B. Bennett, *Fear is the Foe* (Robert Hale, 1995)

Wilson, Andrew, *Flame Thrower* (William Kimber, 1984)

Winebrenner, Hobert, & Michael McCoy, *Bootprints* (Camp Comamajo Press 2005)

Wingfield, R. M., *The Only Way Out* (Hutchinson Universal Book Club, 1956)

Winterbotham, F. W., *The Ultra Spy: An Autobiography* (Macmillan, 1989)

Winters, Maj. Dick & Cole C. Kingseed, *Beyond the Band of Brothers* (Berkley, 2006)

Womack, J. A., (ed. Celia Wolfe), *Summon Up the Blood* (Leo Cooper, 1997)

Womer, Jack & Steven C. DeVito, *Fighting with the Filthy Thirteen* (Casemate, 2012)

Woods, Imogene (ed.), *The Ordinary Infantrymen: Heroes Then, Heroes Again* (I. Woods, 2003)

Woollcombe, Robert, *Lion Rampant* (Black & White, 2014)

Young, Derek (ed.), *Scottish Voices from the Second World War* (Tempus, 2006)

Young, Brig. Peter, *Storm from the Sea* (Greenhill, 1989)

Younger, Tony, *Blowing our Bridges: From Dunkirk to Korea via Normandy* (Pen & Sword, 2004)

Published Memoirs – German

Assmann, Adm. Kurt, 'Normandy 1944', *MR*, Vol. XXXIV (Feb 1955)

Balck, Gen. Hermann (transl. & ed. by Maj Gen David T. Zabecki), *Order in Chaos: Memoirs of General of Panzer Troops Hermann Balck* (Univ. Press of Kentucky, 2015)

Bielenberg, Christabel, *The Past Is Myself* (Chatto & Windus, 1968)

Choltitz, Gen. Dietrich von, *Soldat unter Soldaten* (Europa-Verlag, 1951); French title, *De Sebastopol à Paris* (J'ai Lu, 1964)

Donitz, Admiral Karl, *Memoirs. Ten Years & Twenty Days* (Weidenfeld & Nicolson, 1959)

Fischer, Wolfgang, *Luftwaffe Fighter Pilot* (Grub Street, 2010)

Galland, Gen. Adolf, *The First & the Last* (Methuen, 1955)

Gersdorff, Gen. Rudolf Christoph, Freiherr von, *Soldat im Untergang* (Ullstein, 1982)

Gockel, Franz, *La Porte de L'enfer: Omaha Beach, 6 Juin 1944* (Ronald Hirlé, 2004)

Grossjohann, Georg, *Five Years, Four Fronts* (Aegis, 1999)

Guderian, Gen. Heinz, *Panzer Leader* (Michael Joseph, 1952)

Günther, Helmut, *Eyes of the Division: Reconnaissance Bn of 17th SS Division* (Fedorowicz, 2012)

Hayn, Maj. Friedrich, *Die Invasion: Von Cotentin bis Falaise* (Kurt Vowinckel, 1954)

Heilmann, Willi, *Alert in the West: A Luftwaffe Airman* (William Kimber, 1955)

Henning, Otto, *Panzer Leader: Memoirs of an Armoured Car Commander* (Frontline, 2013)

Heusinger, Adolf, *Befehl in Widerstreit* (Wunderlich Verlag, 1950)

Horner, Helmut, *A German Odyssey: The Journal of a German Prisoner of War* (Fulcrum, 1991)

Jahnke, Karl Heinz, *Hitler letztes Aufgebot. Deutsche Jugend im sechsten Kriegsjahr* (Klartext, 1993)

Kardorff, Ursula von, *Diary of a Nightmare. Berlin 1942–1945* (Rupert Hart-Davis, 1965)

Keitel, FM Wilhelm (ed. Walter Görlitz), *Memoirs* (William Kimber, 1965)

Kindler, Werner, *Obedient unto Death. A PanzerGrenadier of the SS-LAH* (Frontline, 2014)

Klapdor, Ewald, *Die Entscheidung: Invasion 1944* (Siek, 1984)

Klemperer, Victor, *To the Bitter End: Diaries of Victor Klemperer, 1942–1945* (Weidenfeld & Nicolson, 1999); originally published as *Tagebücher, 1933–1945* (Aufbau, 1955)

Knoke, Heinz, *I Flew for the Fuhrer. Story of a German Airman* (Evans Brothers, 1953)

Luck, Hans von, *Panzer Commander: Memoirs of Col Hans von Luck* (Cassell, 1989)

Pöppel, Martin, *Heaven & Hell: War Diary of a German Paratrooper* (Spellmount, 1988)

Ritgen, Helmut, *Western Front, 1944: Memoirs of a Panzer Lehr Officer* (Fedorowicz, 1996)

Rommel, FM Erwin (ed. Basil Liddell Hart), *The Rommel Papers* (Collins, 1953)

Ruge, Adm. Friedrich, 'The Invasion of Normandy', Chapter IX in *Decisive Battles of World War II: The German View* (André Deutsch, 1965); *Rommel in Normandy* (Macdonald & Jane's, 1979)

Schramm, Maj. Percy Ernst (ed.), *Kriegstagebuch des Oberkommando der Wehrmacht (Wehrmachtführungsstab), BAND IV/7: 1. Jan 1944–31. Dez 1944* (Bernard & Graefe, 1982)

Schweppenburg, Gen. Leo, Geyr von *The Critical Years* (Allan Wingate, 1952); 'Reflections on the Invasion', 2 articles in *MR*, Part 1: Vol. XL/2 (Feb 1961); Part 2: Vol. XL/3 (March 1961)

Severloh, Hein, *WN 62: Memories of the Defence of Omaha Beach* (Hek Creativ, 2011)

Speer, Albert, *Inside the Third Reich* (Macmillan, 1970)

Speidel, Gen. Hans, *We Defended Normandy* (Herbert Jenkins, 1952)

Steinhoff, Johannes et al (eds.), *Voices from the Third Reich* (Regnery Gateway, 1989)

Strong, Michael (ed.), *Steiner's War. The Merville Battery* (Self-published, 2013)

von Studnitz, Hans-Georg, *While Berlin Burns: Diary 1943–45* (Prentice-Hall, 1964)

Vassiltchikov, Marie 'Missie', *Berlin Diaries 1940–1945* (Chatto & Windus, 1985)

Warlimont, Gen. Walter, *Inside Hitler's Headquarters* (Weidenfeld & Nicolson, 1964)

Westphal, Gen. Siegfried, *The German Army in the West* (Cassell, 1951)

Wolff-Mönckeberg, Mathilde (ed. Ruth Evans), *On the Other Side* (Peter Owen, 1979)

D-Day Campaign

Ambrose, Stephen E., *Pegasus Bridge: June 6, 1944* (Simon & Schuster, 1985); *D-Day, June 6, 1944: Climactic Battle of World War II* (Simon & Schuster, 1994)

Badsey, Stephen, 'Terrain as a Factor in the Battle of Normandy 1944', chapter in Peter Doyle & Matthew R. Bennett (eds), *Fields of Battle. Terrain in History* (Kluwer, 2002)

Bailey, Roderick, *Forgotten Voices of D-Day* (Ebury Press, 2009)

Balkoski, Joseph, *Omaha Beach: D-Day, June 6, 1944* (Stackpole, 2004); *Utah Beach: Landing & Airborne Operations on D-Day* (Stackpole, 2005)

Barber, Neil, *Pegasus & Orne Bridges: Capture, Defence & Relief* (Pen & Sword, 2009)

Baxter, Colin F., *The Normandy Campaign, 1944: Bibliography* (Greenwood, 1992)

Beevor, Antony, *D-Day. The Battle for Normandy* (Viking, 2009)

Blakeley, Maj. H. W., 'Artillery in Normandy', *Field Artillery Journal* Vol. 39/2 (March-April 1949)

Blandford, Edmund, *Two Sides of the Beach: Invasion & Defense of Europe* (Airlife, 1999)

Blumenson, Martin, *Duel for France, 1944* (Houghton Mifflin, 1963); 'Politics & the Military in the Liberation of Paris', *Parameters* (Summer 1998)

Buckingham, William F., *D-Day: The First 72 Hours* (Tempus, 2004)

Buckley, John, *British Armour in the Normandy Campaign 1944* (Routledge, 2004); (ed.), *The Normandy Campaign 1944: 60 Years On* (Routledge, 2006)

Buffetaut, Yves (ed.), *Le Mur d'Atlantique* (Batailles #1 (2004)

Chandler, David, & J. Lawton Collins, *D-Day Encyclopaedia* (Simon & Schuster, 1994)

Copp, Terry, '21st Army Group in Normandy: Towards a New Balance Sheet', *Canadian Military History*, Vol. 16/1 (2007)

D'Este, Col. Carlo, *Decision in Normandy* (HarperCollins, 1983)

Doherty, Richard, *Normandy 1944: The Road to Victory* (Spellmount, 2004)

Dolski, Michael et al, *D-Day in History & Memory* (Univ. of North Texas, 2014)

Dunphie, Christopher, *The Pendulum of Battle* (Pen & Sword, 2004)

Ellis, Maj. L. F., *Victory in the West, Vol. 1: The Battle of Normandy* (HMSO, 1962)

Ford, Ken, & Steven Zaloga, *Overlord. The D-Day Landings* (Osprey, 2009)

Ganz, A. Harding, 'Questionable Objective? Brittany Ports 1944', *JMH*, Vol. 59/1 (1995)

Gardiner, Juliet, *D-Day. Those Who Were There* (Collins & Brown, 1994)

Harrison Gordon A., *Cross-Channel Attack* (US Army CMH, 1951)

Hart, Russell A., *Clash of Arms: How the Allies Won* (Lynne Rienner, 2001)

Hastings, Max, *Overlord. D-Day & the Battle for Normandy* (Michael Joseph, 1984)

Holman, Gordon, *Stand By to Beach!* (Hodder & Stoughton, 1945)

Jackson, Gen. W. G. F., *Overlord: Normandy 1944* (Davis-Poynter, 1978)

Jefferson, Alan, *Assault on the Guns of Merville* (John Murray, 1987)

Keegan, John, *Six Armies in Normandy: from D-Day to the Liberation of Paris* (Cape, 1982)

Kemp, Anthony, *The Normandy Landings & Liberation of Europe* (Thames & Hudson, 1994)

Kershaw, Robert, *D-Day: Piercing the Atlantic Wall* (Ian Allan, 1993)

Keusgen, Helmut Konrad von, *Omaha: Die Tragödie des 6. Juni 1944* (Hek Creativ, 2014)

Kite, Ben, *Stout Hearts. The British & Canadians in Normandy 1944* (Helion, 2014)

Leclerc, Benoit, *L'été '44: Édition Spéciale* (La Manche Libre, 2014)

Lewis, Adrian R., *Omaha Beach: Flawed. Victory* (Univ. of North Carolina Press, 2001)

Marshall, Gen. G. C. (intro.), *Omaha Beachhead, 6–13 June 1944* (US Army CMH, 1945)

Marshall, S. L. A., *Night Drop: American Airborne Invasion of Normandy* (Macmillan, 1962)

Mayo, Jonathan, *D-Day: Minute by Minute* (Short Books, 2014)

McAndrew, Bill, *Normandy 1944: The Canadian Summer* (Vanwell, 1996)

McManus, John C., *Americans at Normandy: from the Beaches to Falaise* (Forge, 2004); *The Americans at D-Day: The American Experience at Normandy* (Forge, 2005); *The Dead & Those About to Die. The Big Red One at Omaha Beach* (NAL, 2014)

Miller, Russell, *Nothing Less Than Victory: Oral History of D-Day* (Michael Joseph, 1993)

Milner, Marc, 'The Guns of Bretteville & 13th Field Regt, RCA, 7–10 June 1944', *Canadian Military History*, Vol. 16/4 (2007); *Stopping the Panzers* (Univ. of Kansas, 2014)

Morgan, Mike, *D-Day Hero: CSM Stanley Hollis VC* (Sutton, 2004)

Neillands, Robin, *The Battle of Normandy 1944* (Cassell, 2002); & Roderick De Normann, *D-Day 1944: Voices from Normandy* (Weidenfeld, 1993)

Nekrassoff, Philippe & Eric Brissard, *Magneville. Ce Jour Là ... 6 Juin 1944* (Self-published, 2000)

Norman, Albert, *Operation Overlord: Design & Reality* (Greenwood, 1970)

Parry, Dan, *D-Day. The Dramatic Story of the World's Greatest Invasion* (BBC Books, 2004)

Patard, Frédéric, *Normandy: The Beating Heart of History* (La Presse de la Manche, 2014)

Powers, Stephen, 'Battle of Normandy: Lingering Controversy', *JMH*, Vol. 56/3 (July 1992)

Prados, John, *Normandy Crucible: The Decisive Battle* (Signet, 2011)

Ramsey, Winston G. (ed.), *D-Day Then & Now*, 2 Volumes (After the Battle, 1995)

Ruppenthal, Maj. Roland G., *Utah Beach to Cherbourg* (US Army CMH, 1947)

Ryan, Cornelius, *The Longest Day* (Victor Gollancz, 1960); 'The Longest Day Revisited', *Reader's Digest*, Vol. 104/626 (June 1974)

Shannon, Kevin & Stephen L. Wright, *Operation Tonga: The Glider Assault* (Fonthill, 2014); original title: *One Night in June* (Airlife, 1994)

Simpson, Keith, 'A Close-Run Thing? D-Day: German Perspective' *RUSI Journal*, Vol. 139/3 (1994)

Sterne, Gary, *Cover-Up at Omaha Beach: D-Day, the Untold Story of Maisy Battery* (Skyhorse, 2014)

Stewart, Andrew, *Caen Controversy: The Battle for Sword Beach 1944* (Helion, 2014)

Turner, John Frayn, *Invasion '44. The Full Story of D-Day* (Harrap, 1959)

Tute, Warren, John Costello & Terry Hughes, *D-Day* (Sidgwick & Jackson, 1974)

Wegmüller, Hans, *Die Abwehr der Invasion* (Verlag Rombach, 1986)

Wieviorka, Olivier, *Normandy: The Landings to the Liberation of Paris* (Harvard, 2008)

Wilkins, Thomas S., 'Analysing Coalition Warfare from an Intra-Allied Politics Perspective: The Normandy Campaign', *JSS*, Vol. 29/6 (2006)

Williams, Clifford, 'Supreme Headquarters for D-Day', *After the Battle* Magazine, No. 84 (1994)

Wilmot, H. P., *June 1944* (Blandford Press, 1984)

Wilson, Col. John, 'Beaches, Bocage & Breakout', *British Army Review*, No. 106 (1994)

Wilson, Theodore A. (ed.) *D-Day 1944* (Univ. Press of Kansas, 1994)

Winter, Paul, *D-Day Documents* (Bloomsbury, 2014)

Zaloga, Stephen J., *D-Day Fortifications in Normandy* (Osprey, 2005)

Zuehlke, Mark, *Breakout from Juno* (Douglas & McIntyre, 2013)

Civil Affairs, Logistics, Media, Medical and Weather

Anon, *Administrative History of the Operations of 21st Army Group* (21AG, November 1945)

Anon, *BBC Year Book 1945* (BBC Books, 1945)

Benamou, Jean-Pierre, *10 Million Tons for Victory* (OREP, 2003)

Brian, Denis, *The Faces of Hemingway* (Grafton Books, 1998)

Burke, Carolyn, *Lee Miller: On Both Sides of the Camera* (Bloomsbury, 2005)

Carey, John (ed.), *The Faber Book of Reportage* (Faber & Faber, 1967)

Coakley, Robert W. & Richard M. Leighton, *Global Logistics & Strategy* (US Army CMH, 1968)

Colley, David P., *Road to Victory. Race & WW II's Red. Ball Express* (Brassey's, 1999)

Collier, Richard, *The Warcos: War Correspondents of World War II* (Weidenfeld, 1989)

Cosmas, Graham & Albert E. Cowdrey, *Medical Service in the ETO* (US Army CMH, 1992)

Creveld, Martin van, *Supplying War. Logistics from Wallenstein to Patton* (CUP, 1977)

Crew, Francis A. E., *Army Medical Services, Campaigns, Vol. 4: NW Europe* (HMSO, 1962)

Donnison, Frank S. V., *Civil Affairs & Military Government: NW Europe* (HMSO, 1961)

Dorman, Angelia Hardy, *Reflections on the Human Legacy of War: Martha Gellhorn in Europe 1943–1945*, essay at http://home.nwi.net/~dorman/angie/gell2.htm

Flint, Edward R., *Development of British Civil Affairs during the Battle of Normandy, Jun–Aug 1944* (MSc Thesis, Cranfield Univ., UK Defence Academy, 2008)

Franklin, William M. (ed.), *British Casualties & Medical Statistics* (HMSO, 1972)

Gay, Timothy M., *Assignment to Hell* (NAL Calibre, 2012)

Gropman, Alan L. (ed.), *The Big 'L': American Logistics in WWII* (NDU Press, 1997)

Hall, H. Duncan, *UK in the 2nd World War: North American Supply* (HMSO, 1955); *UK in the 2nd World War: Studies of Overseas Supply* (HMSO, 1956)

Harrison, Mark, *Medicine & Victory: British Military Medicine in WW II* (OUP, 2004)

Hart, Russell A., 'Feeding Mars: The Role of Logistics in Normandy', *War in History*, Vol. 3/4 (1996)

Hawkins, Desmond (comp.), *War Report, Dispatches from D-Day to VE-Day* (BBC, 1985)

Hench, John B., *Books as Weapons* (Cornell Univ. Press, 2010)

Kershaw, Alex, *Blood & Champagne. Life & Times of Robert Capa* (Macmillan, 2002)

Kiley, Anne (ed.), *Writing the War: Chronicles of a WWII Correspondent* (Prometheus, 2015)

King, Cecil Harmsworth, *With Malice Toward None: A War Diary* (Sidgwick & Jackson, 1970)

Knightley, Phillip, *The First Casualty* (André Deutsch, 1975)

Laffin, John, *Combat Surgeons* (J.M. Dent, 1970)

Miall, Leonard (ed.), *Richard Dimbleby – Broadcaster* (BBC Books, 1966)

Mitgang, Herbert, *Newsmen in Khaki: A WW II Soldier-Correspondent* (Taylor, 2004)

Montgomery, FM Bernard (Foreword), *BBC War Report, 6 June 1944–5 May 1945* (OUP, 1946)

Moynihan, Michael, *War Correspondent* (Leo Cooper, 1994)

Musketeer, 'Campaign in NW Europe: Administration', *RUSI Journal*, Vol. 103 (1958)

Nicholas, H. G. (ed.), *Washington Despatches, 1941 to 1945: Weekly Political Reports from the British Embassy* (Univ. of Chicago Press, 1981)

Ohler, Norman, *Blitzed: Drugs in Nazi Germany* (Allen Lane, 2016)

Penrose, Antony & David E. Scherman, *Lee Miller's War: 1944–45* (Thames & Hudson, 2005)

Ravenhill, Brig. C., 'The Influence of Logistics in NW Europe', *RUSI Journal*, Vol. 91/564 (1946)

Ross, John, *Forecast for D-Day, & Weatherman behind Ike's Greatest Gamble* (Globe Pequot, 2014)

Royle, Trevor, *War Report. The War Correspondent's View of Battle* (Mainstream, 1987)

Ruppenthal, Roland, *US Army in World War II: The ETO, Logistical Support of the Armies, 2 vols.,* (US Army CMH, 1953–59)

Snelling, Stephen, *Commando Medic: Doc Harden, VC* (Spellmount, 2012)

Stursberg, Peter, *Sound of War: Memoirs of a CBC Correspondent* (Univ. of Toronto Press, 1993)

Sündermann, Helmut, *Tagesparolen, Deutsche Presseweisungen 1939–1945, Hitlers Propaganda und Kriegsführung* (Druffel, 1973)

Taylor, Eric, *Wartime Nurse: 100 Years from the Crimea to Korea 1854–1954* (Hale, 2001)

Thomson, Harry C. & Lida Mayo, *Ordnance Dept.: Procurement & Supply* (US Army CMH, 1960)

Tyrer, Nicola, *Sisters in Arms. Army Nurses Tell Their Story* (Weidenfeld & Nicolson, 2008)

Vaughan-Thomas, Wynford (intro.), *Great Front Pages: D-Day to Victory* (Collins, 1984)

Waddell, Steve R., *The Communications Zone (COMZ): American Logistics in France, 1944* (PhD Thesis, Texas A&M Univ., 1992); *US Army Logistics: Normandy Campaign* (Greenwood, 1994)

Whiting, Charles, *Papa Goes to War: Ernest Hemingway in Europe 1944–45* (Crowood, 1990)

German Armed Forces/Third Reich

Bartov, Omer, *Hitler's Army: Soldiers, Nazis, & War in the Third Reich* (OUP, 1992)

Boog, Horst, Gerhard Krebs & Detlef Vogel, *Germany & the 2nd World War, Vol. VII: The Strategic Air War in Europe & the War in the West & East Asia, 1943–1944/5* (OUP, 2006)

Carell, Paul (pseud. for SS-Lt-Col Paul Karl Schmidt), *Invasion – They're Coming!* (George Harrap, 1962; first pub. as *Sie Kommen!* (Gerhard Stalling Ullstein, 1960)

Chazette, Alain & Alain Destouches, '1944: Le Mur de L'Atlantique en Normandie', *39–45 Magazine* #11 (Mai-Juin 1986)

Evans, Richard J., *The Third Reich at War* (Allen Lane, 2008)

Fritz, Stephen G., *Frontsoldaten: German Soldier in WW II* (Univ. of Kentucky, 1995)

Graves, Donald E., *Blood & Steel. Wehrmacht Archive: Normandy 1944* (Frontline, 2013)

Griesser, Volker, *The Lions of Carentan. Fallschirmjäger Regt. 6, 1943–45* (Casemate, 2015)

Hargreaves, Richard, *The Germans in Normandy* (Pen & Sword, 2006)

Heber, Thorsten, *Der Atlantikwall 1940–1945: Die Befestigungen der Küsten West- und Nordeuropas im Spannungsfeld Nationalsozialistischer Kriegführung und Ideologie* (Dissertation, Heinrich Heine Univ., Düsseldorf, 2003)

Hunter, Wilson, *Where Have All the Nazis Gone? A Study of German Memoirs from the 2nd World War* (BA Thesis, Vanderbilt Univ., 2007)

Isby, David C., (ed.), *Fighting the Invasion: at D-Day* (Greenhill, 2004)

Kater, Michael H., *Hitler Youth* (Harvard Univ. Press, 2004)

Klapdor, Ewald, *Die Entscheidung: Invasion 1944* (Siek, 1984)

Koch, H. W., *Hitler Youth. Origins & Development 1922–45* (Barnes & Noble, 1975)

Kortenhaus, Werner, *Combat History of 21st Panzer Division, 1943–45* (Helion, 2014)

Kuhn, Volkmar, *German Paratroops in World War II* (Ian Allan, 1978)

Latzel, Klaus, *Deutsche Soldaten, nationalsozialistischer Krieg?* (Ferdinand Schöningh, 1998)

Lefèvre, Eric, *Panzers in Normandy Then & Now* (After the Battle, 1983)

Lieb, Peter, *Konventioneller Krieg oder Weltanschauungskrieg? Kriegführung & Partisanenbekämpfung in Frankreich 1943–44* (Oldenbourg, 2007)

Lucas, James & Matthew Cooper, *Panzer Grenadiers* (Macdonald & Jane's, 1977)

Maclean, Maj. French L., *German Corps Commanders in WW2* (Monograph, US Army CGSC, 1988)

Mason, C., *Falling from Grace: German Airborne in WW2* (MA Thesis, USMCU, Quantico, 2002)

Messerschmidt, Manfred, *Die Wehrmacht im NS-Staat* (R V Decker, 1969)

Meyer, Hubert, *12th SS: History of the HitlerJugend Pz Division, Vol. 1* (Fedorowicz, 1994)

Milano, Vince & Bruce Conner, *Normandiefront. D-Day to St Lô* (History Press, 2011)

Mitcham, Samuel W., *Rommel's Last Battle* (Stein & Day, 1983)

Müller, Rolf-Dieter & Hans-Erich Volkmann (eds), *Die Wehrmacht: Mythos und Realität* (Oldenbourg, 1999)

Nafziger, George, *German Order of Battle in WWII, Vol. I, Panzer Divisions* (Stackpole, 1999); *Vol. II, Infantry Divisions* (Greenhill, 2000)

Neitzel, Sönke & Harald Welzer, *Soldaten: On Fighting, Killing & Dying* (Knopf, 2012)

Ose, Dieter, *Entscheidung im Westen 1944* (Deutsche Verlags-Anstalt, 1982)

Perrigault, Jean-Claude, *21st Panzer Division* (Heimdal, 2003)

Rolf, Rudi & Peter Saal, *Fortress Europe* (Airlife, 1988)

Seidler, Franz, *Die Organisation Todt* (Bernard & Graefe, 1987)

Sonnenberger, Lt Col. Martin, *The Philosophy of Auftragstaktik: Understanding Initiative in the German Army 1806–1955* (MA Thesis, US Army CGSC, 2013)

Stargardt, Nicholas, *The German War: A Nation Under Arms, 1939–45* (Bodley Head, 2015)

Stober, Hans, *Die Sturmflut und das Ende. Die Geschichte der 17. SS-PanzerGrenadier Division, Band I: Die Invasion* (Munin Verlag, 1976)

Thomas, Nigel, *German Army 1939–45 (5): Western Front 1943–45* (Osprey, 2000); *Hitler's Russian & Cossack Allies 1941–45* (Osprey, 2015)

Tooze, Adam, *Wages of Destruction. Making & Breaking of the Nazi Economy* (Allen Lane, 2006)

Tsouras, Peter, *Disaster at D-Day, The Germans Defeat the Allies* (Greenhill, 1994)

Wette, Wolfram, *The Wehrmacht. History, Myth, Reality* (Harvard Univ. Press, 2006)

Wilhelmsmeyer, Helmut, 'From Invasion to Breakout', *British Army Review*, Nos. 74 & 75 (1983)

Wood, James A., 'Captive Historians, Captivated, Audience: German Military History Program, 1945-1961', *JMH*, Vol. 69/1 (January 2005); (ed.): *Army of the West. Army Group 'B'* (Stackpole, 2007)

Zetterling, Niklas, *Normandy 1944: German Military Organisation, Combat Power & Organisational Effectiveness* (Fedorowicz, 2000)

Index

Peter Caddick-Adams is a writer and broadcaster who specialises in military history, defence and security issues. He previously lectured in Military and Security Studies at the UK Defence Academy for twenty years, and in Air Power for the Royal Air Force. A Fellow of the Royal Historical Society and the Royal Geographical Society, he also spent thirty-five years as an officer in the UK Regular and Reserve Forces, and has extensive experience of various war zones, including the Balkans, Iraq and Afghanistan. He was educated at Shrewsbury School, Sandhurst and Wolverhampton University, where he gained first class honours in War Studies; he received his PhD from Cranfield University. His previous works include *Monty and Rommel: Parallel Lives* (2011), *Monte Cassino: Ten Armies in Hell* (2012), and *Snow and Steel: Battle of the Bulge 1944–45* (2014).